W9-AQP-454

TOLEDO
NEW COMMERCE LIBRARY
OHIO

THE HISTORIANS'
HISTORY
OF THE WORLD

PRESCOTT

D 20
W74
v. 10

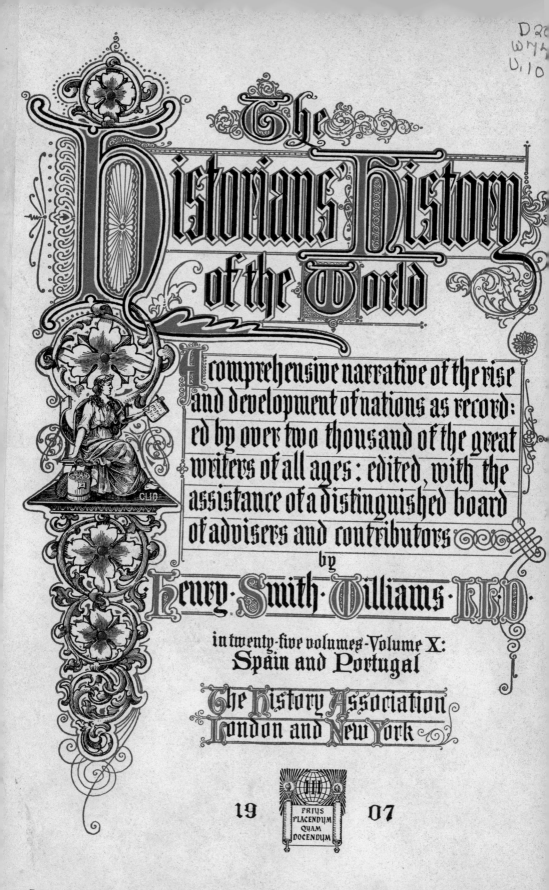

The Historians' History of the World

A comprehensive narrative of the rise and development of nations as record: ed by over two thousand of the great writers of all ages : edited, with the assistance of a distinguished board of advisers and contributors

by

Henry Smith Williams LL.D.

in twenty-five volumes · Volume X:
Spain and Portugal

The History Association
London and New York

19   07

PRIUS
PLACENDUM
QUAM
DOCENDUM

TITLE-PAGE DESIGNED AND ENGRAVED
BY TIFFANY & CO NEW YORK

COPYRIGHT, 1904, 1907
By HENRY SMITH WILLIAMS

—————

ALL RIGHTS RESERVED

Contributors, and Editorial Revisers

Prof. Adolf Erman, University of Berlin.

Prof. Joseph Halévy, College of France.

Prof. Thomas K. Cheyne, Oxford University.

Prof. Andrew C. McLaughlin, University of Michigan.

Prof. David H. Müller, University of Vienna.

Prof. Alfred Rambaud, University of Paris.

Capt. F. Brinkley, Tokio.

Prof. Eduard Meyer, University of Berlin.

Dr. James T. Shotwell, Columbia University.

Prof. Theodor Nöldeke, University of Strasburg.

Prof. Albert B. Hart, Harvard University.

Dr. Paul Brönnle, Royal Asiatic Society.

Dr. James Gairdner, C.B., London.

Prof. Ulrich von Wilamowitz Möllendorff, University of Berlin.

Prof. H. Marczali, University of Budapest.

Dr. G. W. Botsford, Columbia University.

Prof. Julius Wellhausen, University of Göttingen.

Prof. Franz R. von Krones, University of Graz.

Prof. Wilhelm Soltau, Zabern University.

Prof. R. W. Rogers, Drew Theological Seminary.

Prof. A. Vambéry, University of Budapest.

Prof. Otto Hirschfeld, University of Berlin.

Dr. Frederick Robertson Jones, Bryn Mawr College.

Baron Bernardo di San Severino Quaranta, London.

Dr. John P. Peters, New York.

Prof. Adolph Harnack, University of Berlin.

Dr. S. Rappoport, School of Oriental Languages, Paris.

Prof. Hermann Diels, University of Berlin.

Prof. C. W. C. Oman, Oxford University.

Prof. W. L. Fleming, University of West Virginia.

Prof. I. Goldziher, University of Vienna.

Prof. R. Koser, University of Berlin.

1035

PART XV

THE HISTORY OF SPAIN AND PORTUGAL

BASED CHIEFLY UPON THE FOLLOWING AUTHORITIES

LOPEZ DE AYALA, BAKHUYZEN VAN DEN BRINK, H. BAUMGARTEN, F. DE
FONSECA BENEVIDES, G. BERGENROTH, ANDRES BERNALDEZ, ULICK R.
BURKE, E. CASTELAR, NUÑEZ DE CASTRO, PINHEIRO CHAGAS, J. A.
CONDE, W. COXE, R. DOZY, S. A. DUNHAM, FLOREZ Y LAFUENTE,
V. DE LA FUENTE, L. P. GACHARD, DAMIÃO DE GOEZ, A. HER-
CULANO, A. DE HERRERA, N. ROSSEEUW ST. HILAIRE, M. A.
S. HUME, H. C. LEA, DIOGO DE LEMOS, JUAN A. LLORENTE, R. H. MAJOR,
JUAN DE MARIANA, W. F. P. NAPIER, JOÃO P. OLIVEIRA-MARTINS,
J. ORTIZ Y SANZ, W. H. PRESCOTT, P. DE SANDOVAL, M. SURIANO,
A. DE VERTOT, GERONIMO ZURITA

WITH ADDITIONAL CITATIONS FROM

PEDRO DE ABARCA, GIULIO ALBERONI, CRÓNICA GENERAL DE ALFONSO X,
ANNALES COMPLUTENSES, ANNALES TOLEDANOS, BARONIUS, IBN BASSAM,
M. BAUDIER, A. BAUMGARTNER, E. BÉGIN, A. BUCHOT, J. DE BURGOS,
M. M. BUSK, CESARE CANTÙ, L. G. DE CARBAJAL, F. S. CASADO,
BARTOLOMÉ DE LAS CASAS, BERMUDEZ DE CASTRO, PEDRO
CEVALLOS, F. A. DE CHÂTEAUBRIAND, V. CHERBULIEZ, N. DE
LA CLÈDE, DIEGO DE CLEMENCIN, CABRERA DE CORDOBA,
FELIX DAHN, F. DENIS, JOHN DUNLOP, EL-LAGI, ANTONIO ENNES, E. GARIBAY,
MANUEL DE GODOY, A. GOMEZ, H. GRAETZ, F. PEREZ DE GUZMAN, GUS-
TAVE HUBBARD, VICTOR A. HUBER, MODESTO LAFUENTE, P. VAN
LIMBORCH, WILLIAM LITHGOW, FERNÃO LOPES, J. M. ORTO Y
LARA, LUCIO MARINEO, M. DE MARLIANI, J. F. DE MASDEU, J. M.
MAS-LA TRIE, LUIS DE MENEZES, CHARLES DE MOÜY, W.
MÜLLER, JAMES C. MURPHY, CHR. G. NEUDECKE, ISIDORUS PACENSIS, AMÉ-
DÉE PICHOT, RUY DE PINA, ANTONIO DE PIRALA, HERNANDO DEL
PULGAR, G. T. RAYNAL, H. REYNALD, W. H. RULE, SEBASTIANUS
SALMANTICENSIS, HEINRICH SCHURTZ, MONACHUS SILENSIS, E.
SILVERCRUYS, ROBERT SOUTHEY, H. MORSE STEPHENS, W. C.
SYDNEY, JEAN B. R. DE TESSÉ, RODERICUS XIMENES TOLE-
TANUS, J. M. DE TORENO, OVIEDO Y VALDES, A. VARILLAS,
H. E. WATTS, N. W. WRAXALL, WULSA, ZANETORNATO

COPYRIGHT, 1904

BY HENRY SMITH WILLIAMS

——————

All rights reserved

CONTENTS

VOLUME X

SPAIN

CHAPTER I

CHAPTER II

CHAPTER III

CONTENTS

CONTENTS

CHAPTER IX

CHAPTER X

CHAPTER XI

CHAPTER XII

CHAPTER XIII

CONTENTS

CHAPTER XIV

BOOK II. THE HISTORY OF PORTUGAL FROM THE EARLIEST TIMES TO THE PRESENT

CHAPTER I

CHAPTER II

CHAPTER III

BOOK I

THE HISTORY OF SPAIN FROM THE EARLIEST TIMES TO THE PRESENT DAY

CHAPTER I

LAND AND PEOPLE; AND GOTHIC SWAY

[TO 711 A.D.]

FEW histories afford lessons of greater value than those of Spain and Portugal. They teem with proofs that independence and liberty are not less important to the wealth and political power of a country than to its happiness; that neither natural advantages nor the character of the inhabitants, neither increase of territory nor external peace and domestic tranquillity can in any measure counterbalance the destructive effects of a foreign yoke, or of a despotic government.

The Spanish peninsula, considered as a whole, combines most of the advantages of an insular, with those of a continental, position. Almost entirely surrounded by the sea, Spain is an island with regard to trade and fisheries; whilst the neck of land that connects her with France at once furnishes in the Pyrenees a mountainous barrier against that country, and preserves her from entire dependence upon winds and waves in her external relations.

In the climate, the genial warmth of the south of Europe is tempered by sea-breezes, in nearly every direction, and the fertile soil yields equally the necessaries and the luxuries of life — corn, fruit, wine, fine merino wool, and olive oil. The mountains abound in mineral treasures, and afforded in early times one of the principal supplies of gold and silver. The natives of this favoured land are brave, sober, hardy, and enterprising. Yet notwithstanding all these sources of prosperity, Spain, which in the sixteenth century startled Europe with the first fears of universal monarchy, was long the most enslaved, oppressed, ignorant, and indigent, of civilised countries.[b]

In the earliest stage of its history we find Spain occupied by a comparatively homogeneous people — the Iberians, who are related as to language; but this is probably only the result of a long, already complete development and does not at all represent the original state of the country. Unfortunately, prehistoric investigation in Spain is too far behind to offer much towards a solution of even the most pressing problems. We may assume primarily that the Pyrenean peninsula, like northern Africa, southern Europe, and western Asia, was originally settled by that short-headed, dark-haired, and light-skinned race for whom the name of Armenoids, or, from a philological standpoint, of Alarodians, has been suggested.

But the people who afterwards were called Iberian are probably nothing else than a mixture of this ancient population with the long-headed, blond race of Cro-Magnon, which came from the north and appears in France and northern Africa. For that reason alone they might be supposed to have been in Spain, situated as it is between the two, even if certain remains of their culture did not make this supposition almost a certainty. The large number of blonds which, contrary to general opinion, are found in Spain and Portugal may in the main go back to this earliest invasion of northern hordes, which was followed by two more in the course of history. Possibly the new race forced its language upon the original inhabitants and perhaps the traditions of the Iberians, which tell of the immigration of their forefathers from Gaul, refer to the invasion of this blond population. The Sicanians and Siculians in southern Italy, likewise inhabitants of territories neighbouring northern Africa, are also supposed to be related to the Iberians.[c]

Whence the Iberians came has always been, and must remain, a matter of dispute. That they, like the Celts, were a branch of the great Indo-European family, and had spread along the south of Europe from the slopes of the Caucasus, was long held as an article of faith by scholars whose opinions were worthy of respect ; but more recent investigations tend somewhat to shake belief in this theory. That they were a dolichocephalic (long-headed) race of short stature and very dark complexion, with plentiful curly black hair, is certain, and they probably inhabited the whole of Spain in the neolithic age, either as successors of a still earlier race — of which it is possible that the Basques, who still form a separate people in the north of Spain and southwest of France, may be the survivors — or as the primitive inhabitants dating from the prehistoric times when Africa and Europe, and possibly also America, were joined by land. In any case, what is known of their physique seems to negative the supposition that they were of Indo-European or Aryan origin ; and to find their counterpart at the present time, it is only necessary to seek the Kabyle (Kabail) tribes of the Atlas, the original inhabitants of the African coast opposite Spain, who were driven back into the mountains by successive waves of invasion. Not alone in physique do these tribes resemble what the early Iberian must have been, but in the more unchanging peculiarities of character and institutions the likeness is easily traceable to the Spaniard of to-day. The organisation of the Iberians, like that of the Atlas peoples, was clannish and tribal, and their chief characteristic was their indomitable local independence.

From the earliest dawn of history the centre of Spanish life, the unit of government, the birthplace of tradition, and the focus of patriotism have been the town. A Spaniard's *pueblo* means infinitely more to him than his town means to an Englishman or a Frenchman. No master race has succeeded in welding the Kabyles, Tuaregs (Tuariks), and Berbers into a state, as the Romans did with the mixed Iberians and Celts; and in Spain, to the present day, with its numberless paper constitutions and its feverish political experiments, the pueblo keeps its practical independence of a centralised government, which has federated pueblos into provinces, but has never absorbed or entirely destroyed the primitive germ of local administration. The village granary (*posito*) still stands in the Spanish village, as its counterpart does in the Atlas regions ; the town pasture and communal tillage land continue on both sides of the straits to testify to the close relationship of the early Iberians with the Afro-Semitic races, which included the Egyptian or Copt, the Kabyle, the Tuareg, and the Berber. The language of the Iberians has been lost, but enough of it remains on coins of the later Celtiberian period to prove that it had a common root with the Egyptian and the Saharan tongues, which extend from Senegal to Nubia on the hither side of the negro zone. With all this evidence before us we may be forgiven for doubting the correctness of the theory which ascribes a Caucasian origin to the primitive Iberian people. Long before the dawn of recorded history, while mankind was hardly emerging from the neolithic stage, a vast incursion of Celts had come from the north and poured over the western Pyrenees into Spain.*d*

THE CELTS AND CELTIBERIANS

The second invasion from the north, that of the Celts, falls in the first period of recognised history, so that we know little of how it came about or the conditions preceding it, and can only enumerate the results. It cannot even be determined if the march of the Celts upon Spain was contemporaneous with the violent incursion of Celtism into upper Italy and southern Germany, which in its further advance carried single troops as far as Asia Minor and Greece; at any rate it is probable.

The Celts introduced a new culture into the land south of the Pyrenees, which lay off from the main track, since they represent the period which as the advanced iron age followed the age of bronze. Before them agriculture was yet in its beginning; the pure-blooded Iberians for a long time afterwards held to the rough conditions of the preceding era, lived from the products of their goat-herds, on the acorns from the mountains and from the scanty grain they raised by their primitive methods of agriculture. The Celts, indeed, like most conquering nations, considered agriculture unworthy a free man, but compelled their dependents to cultivate their territory regularly and to deliver up a part of its products.

The Celtic flood inundated only a portion of the peninsula. One tribe — later called the Celtics — settled in the region about the middle Guadiana, the centre of which is the present Badajoz. The Artebrians inhabited the northwestern coast without mixing much with the native population. On the other hand a large mixed race, afterwards called the Celtiberians, grew up in what is to-day Old Castile, and brought into subjection the neighbouring Iberian tribes who were more cultured and less warlike than the dwellers in the mountains. The domination of the Celts over the whole Pyrenean peninsula is not to be thought of: not even among the Celtic tribes themselves was there unity. The genuine mountain peoples, such as the Lusitanians in the west, the Asturians, Cantabrians and Vasconians in the north, preserved complete independence. Southern Spain, where under a milder sky a certain culture had developed at an early date, was also preserved from Celtic encroachment and saw indeed more welcome strangers at its coasts — the Phœnicians, whose commercial spirit found here a glorious field for its activity. Even before their arrival the inhabitants of the country may have fashioned ornaments from the precious metal which was so abundant in their land, without valuing this treasure particularly, or expending much toil in procuring it; now for the first time, when the marvels of a foreign culture were offered them in exchange for these things, did they turn their attention to the hidden treasures of their land. But the

Phœnicians were hardly the first to visit the western shores of the Mediterranean as traders and pirates; the very fact that tribes of Iberian descent had pushed as far as lower Italy points to the existence of intercourse by ships. In the same way Etruscan commerce must have touched Spain. The *nurhags* — those curious solid towers, which are especially frequent on the coasts of Sardinia and which must once have served as places of refuge for the people when in danger — are dumb but intelligible witnesses to the fact that the Mediterranean must have been peopled with pirates even in prehistoric times. Egypt, the only country in the world whose inhabitants at that time already kept historical records, often saw robber hordes appear on its coasts. But we know no further particulars of these ancient conditions.[c]

THE PHŒNICIAN INVASIONS

The Phœnicians, as already observed, were among the first who, attracted by the never-failing instinct of gain, directed their course to a country which promised the highest advantages to their commerce. The precise period of their entering into relations with the inhabitants is unknown. For some time their settlements, of which Gades, now Cadiz, was the first and most powerful, were confined to the coasts of Bætica, whence they supplied the natives with the traffic of Asia Minor and the shores of the Mediterranean, in exchange for the more valuable productions of the peninsula, such as gold, silver, and iron.[1] Previously to their arrival, the use of these metals was, it is said, unknown to the Celts and Iberians. At first, for the convenience of their trade and their worship the Phœnicians obtained permission to build magazines and temples: these soon expanded into villages, and the villages into fortified towns. Besides Cadiz, Malaga, Cordova, and other places of minor note were monuments of their successful enterprise, and proofs of their intention to fix their permanent abode in a country on which nature had lavished her choicest gifts. In time they penetrated into the interior, and arrived in the heart of the mountainous districts of the north, probably to superintend the operations of the mines which they had prevailed on the natives to open. Coins, medals, and ruins, attesting their continued location, have been found in most provinces of Spain, and even at Pamplona in Navarre. Almost everywhere have they left traces of their existence, not only in medallic and lapidary inscriptions, but in the religion, language, and manners of the people.

It is possible, however, that the residence of this people in Spain may have been confounded with that of the Carthaginians. The similarity in language, manners, and superstitions might naturally have diminished the distinction between the two nations, and in time destroyed it. The uncertainty which hangs over this period, and the apparent incongruity of the few dates handed down to us, with the transactions which accompany them, confirm the suspicion. The whole period, indeed, from the first settlement of the Tyrians to the wars between the rival republics of Rome and Carthage, is too conjectural to deserve the name of historical, though some few facts are seen to glimmer through the profound darkness which surrounds them.

[1 Aristotle shows more credulity than philosophy when he makes the Phœnicians acquire at Tarifa (then Tartessus) a quantity of silver so prodigious that the ships could not carry it; and says that their anchors and commonest implements were of the same metal. The exaggeration only proves, perhaps, the abundance of silver in the country.]

THE GREEK COLONIES ; THE CARTHAGINIAN CONQUEST

The successful example of the Phœnicians stimulated the Greeks to pursue the same advantages. The Rhodians arrived on the coast of Catalonia, and founded a town, which they called Rhodia (Rosas) from the name of their island. They were followed by the Phocians, who dispossessed their countrymen of Rosas, and extended their settlements along the shores of Catalonia and Valencia. Other expeditions departed from the numerous ports of Greece, towards the same destination, but at intervals considerably distant from one another, and gave names to new establishments, some of which may be still recognised, notwithstanding the changes that time has made. It does not appear that either the Phœnicians or the Greeks aimed at domination; the towns which they founded, and continued to inhabit, were but so many commercial depots — populous indeed, but filled with peaceable citizens, whose lucrative occupations afforded them neither time nor inclination for hostilities. Not so with the Carthaginians, who joined all the avarice of merchants to all the ambition of conquerors.

The African republic had long watched with jealousy the progressive prosperity of the Tyrians, and waited for an opportunity of supplanting them. That opportunity at length arrived (480 B.C.). The avarice of these merchants had caused them to adopt measures which the high-spirited natives considered as oppressive. A dispute arose : both parties recurred to arms ; and, after a short struggle, the lords of the deep were forced to give way before their martial enemies. Several of the Phœnician settlements fell into the hands of the victors, who appeared bent on rescuing their soil from these all-grasping strangers. Seeing Cadiz itself threatened, the latter implored the assistance of the Carthaginians, who had already a settlement on the little island of Iviza. The invitation was eagerly accepted ; perhaps, as has been asserted, the Carthaginians had fomented the misunderstanding, and urged it to an open quarrel. However this be, they landed a considerable force on the Bætican coast ; and, after a few struggles, the details of which we should vainly attempt to ascertain, they triumphed over both Phœnicians and natives, and seized on the prize they had so long coveted. Thenceforth Cadiz served as a stronghold whither they could retreat whenever danger pressed too heavily, and as an arsenal where fetters might be manufactured for the rest of Spain.

The progress of the Carthaginian arms, we are told, was irresistible ; it was not, however, rapid, if any reliance is to be placed on the dates of ancient writers : the provinces of Andalusia, Granada, Murcia, Valencia, and Catalonia did not acknowledge the supremacy of the republic until, with some other provinces, they were overrun, rather than subdued, by Hamilcar, father of the great Hannibal (235 B.C.), and most of the warlike nations in the interior, especially in the mountainous districts, never afterwards bent their necks to the yoke, though the veteran armies of Africa were brought against them.

Eight years were spent by the Carthaginian general in extending and consolidating his new conquests. He had need of all his valour — and few captains had ever more — to quell the perpetual incursions of tribes glorying in their independence, and strangers to fear. For this purpose he built several fortresses (the important city of Barcelona is said to have been among the number), in which he distributed a portion of his troops to overawe the surrounding country ; while, with another portion, he moved from place to place, as occasion required his presence. Probably his severity alienated the minds of the people from the domination he laboured to establish.   He was checked in the career of his conquests by the Edetani and Saguntines, who openly revolted, and made vigorous preparations for their defence.   He fell upon them, but neither the number of his forces nor his own bravery could succeed against men to whom the hope of freedom and of revenge gave irresistible might.   Two-thirds of his army perished, and himself among the number.   His son Hannibal being too young to succeed him, the administration of the Carthaginian provinces and the conduct of the war devolved, by a decree of the senate, on his son-in-law Hasdrubal, who adopted towards the natives a line of conciliation; he could be cruel when he chose; but as there is reason to believe that he aimed at an independent sovereignty, he wished to secure their support in the event of a struggle with Carthage. Punic loyalty, like Punic faith, could subsist no longer than a regard to self-advantage would permit.

The city of Cartagena, which Hasdrubal founded on the modern gulf of that name, and which he furnished with an admirable harbour, was the most glorious monument of his administration.   The success of his arms, the nature of his designs, roused the fears both of the Greek colonies on the coast of Catalonia and Valencia, and of several independent nations in the interior.   They resolved to call in a third power, which had long regarded with jealousy the growing prosperity of Carthage.   Rome eagerly embraced the cause of the discontented states (227 B.C.), probably, indeed, she had secretly fomented that discontent.   She sent a deputation to Carthage, which obtained from the senate two important concessions: that the Carthaginians should not push their conquests beyond the Ebro; that they should not disturb the Saguntines and other Greek colonies.   Though Hasdrubal promised to observe them, he silently collected troops, resolved to make a final effort for the entire subjugation of Spain before Rome could succour the confederates.   In three years, his formidable preparations being completed, he threw off the mask, and marched against Saguntum.   On his way, however, he was assassinated by the slave of a man whose master, a native prince, he had put to death.[1]   The attachment of this slave to his master's memory could be equalled only by the unshaken firmness with which he supported the incredible torments inflicted on him by the fierce Hannibal.

This famous Carthaginian was in his twenty-fifth year.   He was more to be dreaded than all his predecessors united.   To military talents and personal valour, perhaps unexampled in any age, he joined astonishing coolness of judgment and inflexibility of purpose.   While Hasdrubal was actuated only by selfish considerations, Hannibal recognised, as the great principle of his actions, revenge — revenge against the bitter enemy of his country, and still more against the destroyers of his kindred.   There is a moral grandeur in this all-engrossing purpose of Hannibal, which, notwithstanding its fell malignity, unaccountably rivets our admiration.

The young hero lost no time in extending his conquests, and amassing resources for the grand approaching struggle with the Romans.   Having subdued some warlike tribes of modern Castile and Leon, and brought into full activity some rich silver mines at the foot of the Pyrenees, he marched at the head of 150,000 men against Saguntum, which he invested in due form.   In vain did the Roman deputies whom the senate despatched for the purpose intimate to him that an attack on the ally of the republic would be

---

[1] Polybius*e* says that he was murdered one night in his tent by a certain Gaul, in revenge of some private injury.   The variation in the account is exceedingly slight.

regarded as a declaration of war against the republic herself. He had vowed the destruction of the city. Yet, though he pressed the siege with the utmost vigour, such was the valour of the defenders that neither his mighty genius for war nor his formidable forces could reduce the place in less than nine months: it would not even then have fallen, had not famine proved a deadlier enemy than the sword. The citizens resolved that the last act of this fearful tragedy should be a suitable consummation of the preceding horrors. Having amassed all their valuable effects, and everything combustible, into one pile, and placed their wives and children around it, they issued from the gates, and plunged into the midst of the surprised enemy. The slaughter was prodigious on both sides ; but, in the end, numbers and strength prevailed against weakness and desperation ; the Saguntines were cut off almost to a man. No sooner was their fate known in the city than their wives, who were in expectation of the result, set fire to the pile, and cast both themselves and children into the devouring element. The city in flames soon discovered the catastrophe to the Carthaginians, who immediately entered, and put what few stragglers they could find — chiefly the aged of both sexes — to the sword.[1] Some, however, had previously secured their safety by flight. Thus perished one of the most flourishing cities of Spain, and one which will be forever memorable in the annals of mankind (219 B.C.). Its destruction hastened, if it did not occasion, the Second Punic War, as described in the history of Rome.

Hannibal mustered his forces for the invasion of Italy. The exploits of the Carthaginian hero beyond the bounds of the peninsula have been treated of in the history of Rome. While he is spreading destruction around him, and the towers of " the eternal city " themselves are tottering, our task must be to cast a hurried glance at the transactions which, after the invasion of Scipio, happened in the country he had left behind. The Carthaginian yoke is allowed on all hands to have been intolerable. The avidity with which the local governors sought pretexts for seizing on the substance of the natives ; the rigour with which some of the captive tribes were made to labour in the mines ; the exactions of a mercenary and haughty soldiery ; the insolence of success on the one hand, and the smart of wrongs endured on the other — prepared the way to the commotions which shook all Spain to its centre, and ultimately ended in the destruction of its oppressors.*g*

THE ROMANS IN SPAIN

The Romans, either alarmed by the progress of Hannibal, or becoming aware of the value of such allies as the Spaniards, now sent larger armies to their assistance, headed by their ablest generals. Spain was the theatre of the first exploits of Publius Cornelius Scipio, afterwards surnamed Africanus from his victories over the Carthaginians in Africa. In Spain, Scipio gained the hearts of the natives by his great and good qualities, not the least of these being his self-command — one instance of which has ever since been a favourite theme with painters, poets, and moralists. The charms of a beautiful captive had touched his young heart, and the laws of the age made her in every respect his slave. He respected her undefended loveliness, and restored her, in unsullied purity, to her betrothed bridegroom.

[1] For an interesting account of this siege, the reader is referred to Livy.*f* It is improbable, however, that the destruction was so universal as is affirmed. Polybius*e* says it was stormed and plundered ; but he makes no mention of the conflagration or the self-immolation.

In cordial co-operation with the Spaniards, Scipio finally expelled the Carthaginians from Spain in 206 B.C.

The object of the Romans, in assisting the Spaniards against Carthaginian oppression, had not been the emancipation of their gallant allies. They immediately proceeded to reduce the peninsula to the condition of a Roman province, governed by their prætors. This was not easily or speedily accomplished. The natives resisted their new, as they had done their former invaders. Numantia, besieged by a second Scipio, emulated the heroism of Saguntum.[b] In vain did the inhabitants send deputations to the consul; he coolly replied that he was content to await the inevitable effects of famine. But their impatience could not await the slow effects of such a death; some took poison; some fell on their swords; some set fire to their houses and perished in the devouring flames. Thus perished all; not a living creature survived (133 B.C.).[g] The Cantabrians, who inhabited the northwestern part of the peninsula, were not even nominally subdued during the continuance of the Roman Republic. The other portions, Celtiberia in the north, Bætica in the south, and Lusitania in the west, were conquered after a long struggle, and constituted the Roman province, but remained the scenes of constantly recurring warfare. The natives revolted against the extortion and tyranny usually practised by the Roman governors of subject states; and the leaders of republican factions, when defeated everywhere else, often found in Spain abundant means of making head against the masters of the world.

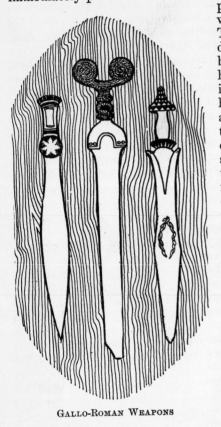

GALLO-ROMAN WEAPONS

The most remarkable of the native insurrections was that organised in Lusitania by Viriathus. This extraordinary man was bred a shepherd; he turned robber, became the captain of a band of outlaws, and raising a standard to which all the disaffected flocked, he defeated several Roman armies. He was vanquished by treachery, the consul Servilius having bribed three of his followers to assassinate him in his sleep. After his murder, the rebellion, as the haughty conquerors termed every insurrection for self-defence, was speedily quelled. Spain was soon afterwards the theatre of the last struggle of the horrible civil wars with which Marius and Sulla desolated the Roman world. When Sulla had finally triumphed at Rome, Sertorius, a leader of the defeated party, fled to Spain, and there long bade defiance to the dictator's power. He was at length vanquished by Cneius Pompeius Magnus, familiarly called Pompey the Great, and, like Viriathus, was murdered by his own treacherous partisans. Pompey, during his command in Spain, merited the good-will of the nation, which subsequently espoused his cause in his contest with Julius Cæsar. After Pompey's death his party still held out in Spain. But Cæsar repaired thither in person; his military skill prevailed, and the province was shortly pacified.[b] As long as Rome treated the provincials merely as a conquered people the provincials remained unsubdued ; but as soon as wiser and more friendly counsels generally prevailed, the Roman Spaniard grasped the hand that was extended to him, and became one of the proudest and most loyal citizens of the empire. Left to themselves, the tribes were ever divided, factious, disturbed. United under Lusitanian Viriathus or even under Roman Sertorius, they long successfully withstood the power of the republic. United under Julius and Augustus Cæsar, they became the most Roman of the provincials of Rome.

A great susceptibility to personal influence has ever been a striking characteristic of the Spanish people. Under the sympathetic Hasdrubal they accepted the dominion of Carthage ; under the fiery Hannibal they fought, the hardiest and most loyal of his soldiers, in the Punic armies in Italy. In the early days after Saguntum, when Roman Scipio came, not as a destroyer but as a deliverer, and displayed his greater qualities of clemency and justice, the Spaniards would have compelled him to be their king. But Scipio was not always clement. The successors of Sempronius Gracchus were not always just. They were not even judicious. "For great men," says the Spanish proverb, "great deeds are reserved." And the coming of one of the greatest men the world has ever seen was the beginning of the end of the dark days of early Spanish history. Cæsar, indeed, marched sternly through the country at the head of his legions ; nor did he stay his hand until he had reached far off Corunna, where he chastised and astonished the wild tribes of Brigantium or Finisterre ; but his policy in the more settled districts was ever genial and pacific. Four times did Cæsar visit the peninsula ; and the fourth time — his legions well filled with loyal and admiring Spaniards — he fought, "not for glory but for existence," on the bloody field of Munda. And with the final triumph of the great Julius begins the peace and prosperity of Roman Spain.[j]

A GALLO-ROMAN

Disturbances, however, again broke out, and it was only under Cæsar's successor, Augustus, that it was finally and completely subjugated, even the Cantabrians being then at last subdued. Once reduced to submission, Spain appears to have slumbered for ages in the tranquillity of servitude, under the despotic sway of the Roman emperors. It was esteemed one of the most valuable and flourishing provinces of the empire, containing, as we learn from Pliny,[h] not less than 360 cities. During her subjection to a thraldom, shared with all the then known world, Spain boasts of having given birth to the celebrated Roman poets Lucan and Martial, to the philosopher Seneca, and to two of the very few good Roman emperors, Trajan and Hadrian, as well as to many other men of distinguished character, though of somewhat inferior note.[b]

ROMAN ADMINISTRATION

It must not be supposed that the authority of the Roman officers extended at first over all the cities of the peninsula. Some cities were governed even in the last resort by their own laws; some depended immediately on the metropolis of the Roman world; some were free, and left to their ancient laws and tribunals. They were colonial, municipal, Roman, allied, tributary; and others there were which enjoyed the right of Latium. Thus the province of Tarragona contained 179 cities, of which 12 were colonial, 13 Roman, 18 enjoying the Latin law, 1 ally, and 135 tributary. Bætica had 185 cities; *viz.*, 9 colonial, 18 municipal, 29 of the Latin law, 6 free, 3 allied, 120 tributary. Lusitania had 45; 5 colonial, 1 municipal, 3 Latin, 36 tributary.

A GALLO-ROMAN WOMAN

The colonies were peopled by the citizens of Rome, chiefly by soldiers. The inhabitants of these establishments forfeited not the slightest of their privileges by their location in the provinces. The municipal cities were those which were admitted to the honour of Roman citizenship; which were in like manner exempted from the jurisdiction of the provincial governors; and the inhabitants of which could aspire to the highest dignities even in "the eternal city." The right of Latium was less valuable : in the cities possessing it, the magistrates only were recognised as Roman citizens. The free cities (*immunes*) were such as the conquerors left in the undisturbed possession of their native laws and tribunals, and were not taxed towards the support of the rest of the empire. This privilege was conferred with reluctance, or rather extorted by necessity, and was always regarded with jealousy; to six Spanish cities only was it granted. The allied cities (*confœderatœ*) were still fewer in number, and were at first really independent, as the word implies. The tributary cities (*stipendiariœ*) occupied the lowest grade in the scale of civic society, and were those which chiefly supported the cumbrous frame of Roman government.

But the distinctions between these various classes were not long maintained. By Otho many Spaniards were admitted to the rights of citizenship; by Vespasian, such of the cities as had not the privilege already were presented with the right of Latium; and by Antoninus every remaining barrier was removed, all his subjects throughout his vast empire being declared citizens of Rome : from this moment the civil constitution of that empire was of necessity uniform. The cities which obeyed the constitution of Rome were governed in a manner similar to those of Italy. Each had its municipal council or curia, the members of which (*decuriones*) were chosen from the principal inhabitants of the provinces. Their office, however, appears to have been unenviable, because it was in all probability gratuitous and because they were responsible for the payment of customs. Nothing need be said on its laws, as they are the same as those which governed Rome under the republic and the empire.

The military state of Spain under the Romans is a subject little understood. That a considerable number of troops for foreign wars was furnished by this important province is attested by numerous inscriptions; but, except in cases of difficulty and danger, the Roman troops in the peninsula seldom exceeded three legions — a force so inconsiderable that either the natives must have lost all desire to recover their ancient independence, or they must have become completely reconciled to the domination of their proud masters. The policy, indeed, which admitted them not only to the honour of citizenship, but to the highest dignities, civil, military, and even religious, must have been admirably adapted to insure not merely the obedience but the attachment of the conquered.

So long as the empire continued prosperous, Spain, notwithstanding the evils it was made to endure, could not but participate to a certain extent in the general prosperity. The arts of life, the most elegant no less than the useful, were taught to flourish: that architecture had reached a high degree of perfection is evident from the numerous remains of antiquity which time has spared; that agriculture was cultivated with equal success, is no less apparent from the testimony of that most excellent of judges, the naturalist Pliny. The riches of the soil, in corn, in oil, and in fruits, were almost inexhaustible; and the sheep were held even in higher estimation in those days than in the present. The vine was cultivated with so much success that the juice of the grape produced in the environs of Tarragona was pronounced equal to the best wines of Italy. These productions, with those of the mines, and the demand for native manufactures, gave rise to an extensive commerce; more extensive, indeed, than that which had existed under the Carthaginians. There was this important difference between the two conquering nations: while the African, with the characteristic selfishness of a trader, engrossed every advantage to himself, the noble-minded Roman admitted others to a free participation in those advantages.

INTRODUCTION OF CHRISTIANITY

If tradition as an authority had not long ceased to be recognised on this side the Pyrenees, the historian would have little difficulty in fixing the period of the introduction of the Christian faith into Spain. Its uninterrupted voice has named St. James the Elder as the first herald of the Gospel to the idolatrous people of that country. That the apostle traversed the peninsula, from Lusitania and Galicia to the heart of Aragon; that while at Saragossa he was honoured by a visit from the Virgin, and that by her express command he erected on the spot a church in her honour; that after his martyrdom at Jerusalem his body was brought by his disciples from Syria to Iria Flavia (now El Padron), in Galicia, and thence transferred to Compostella, to be venerated by the faithful as long as the world shall endure, no orthodox Spaniard ever doubted. With equal assurance of faith it is believed that St. Paul, in person, continued the work of his martyred fellow-disciple, and sowed the seeds of the new doctrine in Catalonia, Aragon, Valencia, and, above all, in Andalusia. Certain it is that Spain can adduce her martyrs as early as the second century — perhaps even in the first.

It was during the reign of the fierce Diocletian that the fires of persecution blazed with the greatest fury throughout the peninsula. It must not, however, be concealed that the crown of martyrdom was sometimes pursued with an eagerness that evidenced rather the intemperance of a mistaken zeal, than the soberness of a rational principle. The fury of persecution cooled after the death of Diocletian. During the civil wars which ravaged the empire under Maximian and Constantius Chlorus, the Christians began to breathe : Constantine followed ; and, after his conversion, the church had peace from without ; but within, the partisans of Athanasius and Arius clouded the horizon of her tranquillity.

Of the three national councils held during the first four centuries, the first is that of Illiberis or Eliberis, a town once seated near modern Granada. It may also be termed the most interesting, as it was probably held before the conversion of Constantine, and, therefore, some years anterior to that of Nicæa : if so, it is the most ancient council, not merely of Spain, but of the Christian world, the acts of which have descended to us. That of Cæsar-Augusta (Saragossa, 380 A.D.), which was also national, consisted of only twelve bishops, and was convened for the sole purpose of condemning the heresy of Priscillian. The third, which was the first council of Toledo (400 A.D.), was attended by nineteen bishops, with a corresponding number of inferior ecclesiastics. Its first act was to admit the canons of Nicæa ; especially those which relate to the ordination of priests ; but it is chiefly remarkable for its symbol of faith, in which that great Catholic doctrine, the procession of the Holy Ghost from the Father and the Son [filioque], is expressly asserted ; a doctrine, as is well known, not formally received by the universal church before the fourth Lateran council in 1215. Its twenty canons relate to holy orders, to the chastity of virgins devoted to God, and to the continency of ecclesiastics and their widows. From these councils it does not appear that the Spanish church had yet received the dignity of primates, archbishops, or metropolitans. The bishops seem to have been equal in power, and independent of one another, the only superiority admitted arising from priority of consecration ; neither is there any reason for concluding that appeals were of necessity carried to Rome, though the superior veneration attached to that see, and the superior characters of those who filled it, rendered such appeals by no means uncommon. The bishops and the clergy were elected by the people. Baptism was administered by the bishop or the presbyter, or, in their absence, by the deacon. In cases of urgent necessity, it could also be administered by a layman, provided he had not contracted a second marriage.

Ceremonial penance was a public satisfaction given to the church where the crime was more than usually scandalous; the penitent, in this case, occupied a place separated from the rest during a period proportioned to the heinousness of the offence. A penance of one year was inflicted on the player of dice, because the heathen deities were necessarily invoked in this ancient game ; of two years on the subdeacon who married a third time, and on the ecclesiastic who wore a crown in imitation of the pagan priests ; of three years on him who lent his apparel for the use of pagan processions; on the deacon who confessed a mortal sin before ordination, and on the parents who broke the betrothals of their children ; of five years on him who married his daughter-in-law or sister-in-law, on the widow who sinned and married her accomplice ; on backbiters, in however trivial an affair, of husbands or wives guilty of adultery, on single women guilty with different men, on deacons proved guilty of any capital crime previous to ordination ; and on housewives who by stripes occasioned, involuntarily, the death of their slaves (if voluntarily, the penance was seven years) ; of ten years on the apostate or heretic on returning to the faith, on the Christian whom curiosity led to the heathen sacrifices, on all prostitutes, and on all consecrated virgins who broke their vow ; of the whole life on the widow of a bishop, presbyter, or deacon, who remarried, on those who frequently violated their conjugal fidelity, and on the gentile priests who, after conversion and baptism, sacrificed to idols. Besides these regulations, the bishop had power to suspend from all intercourse with the faithful the man who sat at the table of a Jew, him who distributed satirical or libellous compositions, and him whose scandals deserved public censure.

There was one means by which the offenders just mentioned could obtain their restoration to the privileges of communion, even before the expiration of the time of penance decreed by the canons. This was, by soliciting peace from the confessors; that is, from such as had sustained persecutions and torments for the faith of Christ. The confessor gave his peace to the penitent in an instrument which he called *literæ confessoriæ* or *pacificæ*. This the penitent presented to the bishop, who immediately absolved him; and in token of his readmission to the rights of communion, gave him another instrument, *literæ communicatoriæ*, which secured him access to the sacramental table in whatever church he appeared. This superstitious custom was founded on the opinion that, from the abundance of their merits, the confessors could well afford a portion to such penitents as had none of their own. What a fruitful train of abuses indulgences occasioned at a much subsequent period, and how repugnant they appeared to the common sense and common justice of mankind, is well known.

On the matrimony and continency of the Spanish clergy, there has been much acrimonious disputation: one party contending that strict celibacy was obligatory on them from the apostolic times; the other, that marriage was permitted to them, under certain restrictions, no less than to laymen. One of the most singular characteristics of

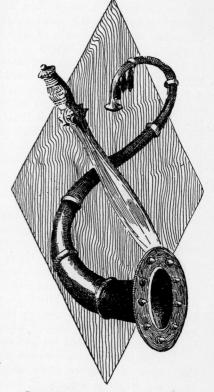

GALLO-ROMAN SWORD AND HORN

the early councils of Spain is the permission granted to bishops and other ecclesiastics to follow any honourable branch of commerce, but in their own districts.

Persons consecrated to God were acknowledged and protected by the early church; but monasteries were not introduced into Spain during the first four centuries. The women who took, in the hands of the bishop and before the altar, the vows of virginity; and the men who, in the same manner, subjected themselves to the obligations of continence and religious contemplation, passed their lives sometimes in their own houses, but generally in communities of two or three in the abodes of aged ecclesiastics. The former assumed the veil from their first profession, as a public sign of their calling. But lest war should be sworn before the strength of the enemy was known, the council of Saragossa decreed that no woman should utter the irrevocable vow, or assume the veil, before the age of forty years, though previous to that period chastity was strongly recommended, and its observance consecrated. Some of the provisions, especially of the first council, will appear unreasonably severe. We must, however, take into consideration the prevalence of idolatry at the beginning of the fourth century, and the anxiety of the fathers of Illiberis to preserve their flocks from the infection of paganism. The canons which regard the remarriage of the widows of ecclesiastics are sufficiently absurd. The sixty-seventh, which prohibited Christian women from keeping long-haired slaves, requires explanation. These slaves were males, generally of Gaul or Germany, and their ostensible business was to dress the hair of the rich ladies; their real one—such was the depravation of manners produced by paganism—was to gratify the licentious desires of their mistresses. But the gradual decline of heathenism, no less than the increasing influence of Christianity, purified the female mind.

Like the other Christian provinces of the empire, Spain had its heresies. Omitting that of Arius—which, during the reign of Constantine and his sons, so much distracted the Christian world, and against which Osius, the bishop of Cordova, signalised himself with a zeal only inferior to that of Athanasius himself—the most remarkable was the heresy of the Priscillianists. One Mark, an Egyptian heretic, having sown the seeds of gnosticism in Gaul, passed into Spain, where the fluency of his speech, no less than the nature of his doctrine, procured him some disciples, among whom Priscillian was the most eminent. This Spaniard was rich, eloquent, subtle, enterprising, and consequently well adapted both to extend and to multiply the errors of Mark, of which he soon became the acknowledged head. He taught that marriage was an unnatural and tyrannical restraint; that pleasure was one of the great privileges of our nature; that to live according to the impulses of nature was the part no less of virtue than of wisdom. He held the Manichæan doctrine of the two great principles; and, with Sabellius, confounded the persons of the Trinity. To all this he joined the Chaldean superstition of starry influences, and the metaphysical subtleties of the Egyptians and Greeks. A multitude of women soon embraced the sensual system of this arch-heretic; their example constrained the other sex: even the clergy were at length infected by the pleasing errors; and, to crown all, two bishops of Bætica openly professed themselves the followers of Priscillian. The orthodox party beheld with alarm the progress of this detestable heresy. Finally the vindictive fury of his enemies prevailed, even more than the justice of their cause. Priscillian and his partisans were beheaded (384 A.D.).

So long as Maximus lived, the numerous adherents of Priscillian were pursued with unrelenting severity by Idatius; but soon after the death of that emperor, this turbulent prelate, whose cruelties had long revolted his episcopal brethren, was banished, and the heat of persecution began to abate. Yet Priscillianism was not extirpated; notwithstanding its renewed condemnation by the first council of Toledo, it continued to distract the church of Spain long after the accession of the Gothic dynasty.

BARBARIAN INVASIONS

From the accession of Honorius the Roman Empire existed only by sufferance. The fierce hordes of northern Europe now prepared to inundate the fertile provinces of the south, and the more powerful local governors to secure themselves an independent sovereignty. Spain was soon agitated by the spirit which spontaneously burst forth from Britain to Thrace. While Constantine, who had assumed the purple, raised England and the Gauls against the feeble successor of the Cæsars, his son Constans passed the Pyrenees to gain over the natives of the peninsula. The youth found or made adherents, and was for a time successful; but in the sequel he was compelled to return to Gaul for reinforcements. The appearance of another candidate for empire (Jovinus) distracted the attention and weakened the efforts of the kindred adventurers; and ultimately all these became successively the victims of imperial vengeance, chiefly by means of the warlike tribes whom the minister of Honorius had marched from the shores of the Baltic, to crush the new insurrections. But the policy of that minister was, if not perfidious, at least short-sighted.

The barbarians whom he had thus introduced into the heart, and to whom he thus betrayed the weakness of the empire, from allies soon became masters. They looked with longing eyes on the rich plains of southern France and of Spain. At length, finding the Pyrenean barrier but negligently guarded, the Suevi, under their king Hermeric, the Alans under Atace, and the Vandals or Silingi, under Gunderic, burst through it, and poured the tide of destruction over the peninsula (409 A.D.). The ravages of these barbarians, we are told, were dreadful. Towns pillaged and burned, the country laid waste, the inhabitants massacred without distinction of age and sex, were but the beginning of evils. Famine and pestilence made awful havoc; the wild beasts, finding nothing to subsist on in their usual haunts, made war on the human species; and the latter consumed the very corpses of the dead. Nay, mothers are said to have killed their children to feed on their flesh.[1] The conquerors at length ceased from their wantonness of desolation. They found that to turn the country into a wilderness was not the best policy in men who designed it for a permanent abode. They divided it by lot: Bætica fell to the Vandals, Lusitania to the Alans, and Galicia, with a great portion of Leon and Castile, to the Suevi.

The Goths Arrive (411 A.D.)

A fourth people, more formidable than the rest combined, came to trouble the new settlers in their possessions. These were the Goths under Atawulf, (Ataulphus) whom Honorius had the address to remove from Italy, by ceding to them the fertile provinces of southern Gaul, and the peninsula. Having established the seat of his kingdom at Narbonne, where he married his imperial captive Placidia, he passed the Pyrenees, made a triumphant entry into Barcelona, and from thence undertook several expeditions against the Vandals. A conspiracy was formed against his life; and the sword of a dwarf pierced his body, as he was conspicuously watching the evolutions of his cavalry, in the courtyard of his palace at Barcelona.

Sigeric succeeded, whose ruffianly conduct instantly drew on him the detestation of the Goths. Scarcely had he put to death the six surviving children of Atawulf, and compelled the widowed Placidia to adorn his triumph by walking barefoot through the streets of Barcelona, than another conspiracy deprived him of his throne and his life. The election of the Goths now fell on Wallia, a chief every way worthy of their choice (415). His first expedition, however, against the Roman possessions in Africa was disastrous. A violent

[1 " *Matres quoque necatis vel actis per se natorum suorum sint pastæ corporibus*," according to old Idatius,[i] but this statement always accompanies stories of famine.]

tempest destroyed his fleet, and forced him to relinquish his design. The news of this disaster soon reached Gaul, and brought Constantius, the general of Honorius, at the head of a numerous army, towards the Pyrenees. Wallia collected the remnant of his troops, and hastened to receive him. Fortunately for the Gothic king, love rather than ambition occasioned the hostile approach of Constantius. That general was more anxious to gain possession of Placidia, whose hand had been promised him by the emperor, than to effect the destruction of the king. No sooner did the two armies encamp in sight of each other, than he proposed peace on conditions too advantageous to be rejected. Wallia had only to surrender the royal widow, and promise to march against the Suevi and the other nations who held possession of the peninsula, to secure not merely the neutrality but the favour of the Romans. Placidia was restored, and peace made with the Romans.

Hostilities were now vigorously commenced against the kindred barbarians. The Vandals were expelled from their habitations, and forced to seek an asylum among the Suevi of Galicia. The Alans of Lusitania were almost entirely cut off, with their king Atace: the remnant incorporated with the Vandals, and their name forever disappeared from the peninsula. The Suevi would doubtless have shared the fate of one or other of these people, had they not hastened to acknowledge themselves tributaries of Rome; they were left in undisputed possession of the country they inhabited. The pride of Honorius caused him to regard these signal successes as for his own benefit. The victor was rewarded with a portion of Languedoc and Gascony, from Toulouse to the ocean. That city he made the seat of his kingdom, where he died, two years after his glorious triumphs. From this time to the reign of Euric, the Goths remained chiefly in their new possessions, and were seldom in Spain. Though they considered themselves the rightful lords of the country, the real sovereignty rested with the Suevi and Vandals.

Under the reign of Theodoric I, Wallia's successor, the Vandals made war on the Suevi. The latter retreated to the fastnesses of the Asturias. The Vandals forsook Galicia, and fought their way to their former settlements in Bætica, whence Wallia had expelled them. To that province they communicated their name — Vandalusia; which was subsequently changed into Andalusia.[1] There they maintained themselves, in opposition to the imperial generals. The ports of Andalusia and Granada presented them with facilities for pushing their successes on the deep. They constructed a fleet; infested the Balearic Isles; pillaged the coast of Valencia; sacked the city of Cartagena; laid waste the shores of Mauretania; and returned to Seville, where the last act of their king, Gunderic, was to despoil the opulent church of St. Vincent.[2] A new and higher career was now opened before them. The offer made them by Boniface, the African prefect, of two-thirds of that country, if they would assist him against his enemies, they joyfully accepted. Before embarking, however, they inflicted a terrible blow on their enemies, the Suevi, whom they overthrew near Merida — whom they precipitated, with their king, into the waters of the Guadiana. They then tranquilly returned to the sea coast; and, to the number of eighty thousand, passed over to Africa, in March, 429, eighteen years after their arrival in Spain.

[1 The etymology of this name has been disputed, some claiming with Casiri k and Gibbon l that it comes from the Arabic Hondalusia, " the region of the West "; but Condé,m Hume,d Burke,j and the general majority prefer the Vandalusian theory.]

2 Of course the death of Gunderic was the work of the offended saint. He was struck dead on the threshold, says one account; he died after securing the plunder, says another. Both agree that he was carried away by the devil. Idatius i says: " Gundericus Rex Vandalorum, capta Hispali, cum impie elatus manus in ecclesiam civitatis ipsius extendisset, mox Dei judicio dæmone correptus, interiit."

PROGRESS OF THE GOTHIC CONQUEST

The retreat of these restless barbarians did not insure tranquillity to Spain. The Suevi, under their new king, Hermeric, issued from their dark mountains, and bore down on the peaceable inhabitants of Galicia. But it was reserved for his son Richilan, to whom, in 438, he resigned his sceptre, to raise the fame of the nation to the highest pitch. He routed the Romans on the banks of the Venil, and seized on Merida and Seville.

In the meantime, Theodoric was no less occupied in humbling the Roman power in southern Gaul. While meditating hostilities against the triumphant Suevi, he was summoned to encounter the renowned Attila, king of the Huns. His well-known valour placed him at the head of the right wing of the Franks, Romans, and Goths, who combined to arrest the progress of the tremendous torrent. His death on the plains of Châlons (451) where the pride of the barbaric king was humbled, endeared him still more to his subjects, who gratefully elevated his son Torismond to the vacant throne. But the reign of the new king was brief, and his end tragic. In one year, by the hands of his two brothers, he was deprived of empire and of life, in his capital of Toulouse; and Theodoric II, the elder of the fratricides, was elected in his place.[1] The reign of this prince was diversified by alternate success and disaster. He first turned his arms against the Suevi, whom he vanquished, and made their king, Richiarius, prisoner; but being recalled to France, the army which he left in the peninsula was routed by the natives of Leon, who were indignant at the excess it committed. The whole country was now in the most miserable condition. Goths and Romans and Suevi traversed it in every direction, and everywhere left melancholy vestiges of their barbarous fury. Another fierce tribe, the Herulians, landed on the coast of Catalonia, and zealously prosecuted the same work of desolation. Then the Suevi split into two parties, which pursued each other with the most vindictive feelings, but which were always ready to combine when the natives were to be plundered, or when Goths and Romans were to be opposed.

The Spaniard was the prey of all: his labour was doomed to support the innumerable swarms which spread from the Pyrenees to the rock of Calpe, and which, like so many locusts, destroyed wherever they settled. The scourge was more than galling — it was intolerable. Native bands were at length formed in most parts of the peninsula, not merely to take vengeance on the rapacious invaders — for in that case they would have been a blessing to their country — but to plunder all who came in their way. Many of these horrors would have been averted, had Theodoric been at liberty to return in person to Spain, and finish its subjugation; but his wars with the Romans, the Burgundians, and the Franks found him for some years employment enough. At length he was assassinated, it is said, by his brother Euric, in his capital of Toulouse. One of the first acts of Euric was to despatch an army to humble the pride of the Suevi. His arms were eminently successful. The Suevi sued for and obtained peace, and were allowed to remain in undisturbed possession of Galicia, with a portion of modern Leon and Portugal, and to retain their kingly form of government. So completely were they become the vassals of the victors that during a whole century they remained

---

[1] Jordanes *y* extends the reign of Torismond to more than three years; the authority of the bishop Idatius *i*, who was a contemporary, is to be preferred. From the same prelate the death of the king appears not to have been wholly unprovoked: he had probably meditated as much towards his brothers, who seem to have acted from self-defence. "*Thorismo rex Gothorum spirans hostilia in Theodorico et Frederico patribus jugulatur,*" are the meagre words of Idiatus. Of this catastrophe Jordanes *y* gives a different account.

in quiet subjection.   We hear no more of them until the time of Leuvigild, who dealt the last blow to their national existence, and, as we shall hereafter see, incorporated them with his Gothic subjects.

The Romans were less fortunate ; their domination in the country was ended forever by the fall of Tarragona.   They continued, indeed, to hold a few unimportant places on the coast; not because they had valour to defend them, but because Euric had no naval force to assail them from the sea.   The conqueror, though master of all Spain, disdained to be confined within limits which his ambition deemed much too narrow.   Rome was now tottering to her fall ; and he resolved to pluck some of the most fertile provinces of Gaul from her feeble grasp.   Odoacer the Mercenary, king of Italy, renounced in his favour all the Roman provinces beyond the Alps, as far as the Rhine and the ocean : and thenceforward the Goths regarded Gaul and Spain as their lawful inheritance.   The victor established the seat of his empire at Arles, where he passed in tranquillity the remainder of his days.   He died in that capital, (484 A.D.) after engaging his subjects to elect for their king his son Alaric. Euric was the founder of the Gothic kingdom of Spain.   The extinction of the Roman sway, and the subjection of the Suevi, rendered him absolute lord of the country.   The six kings, his predecessors, were rulers in Gaul, not of Spain ; however they might regard its provinces as rightfully their own, they could obtain possession only by force of arms.   Their conquests, however, had been partial and temporary ; before Euric, the peninsula was overrun, not subdued.   He was also the first legislator of his nation.   The laws which he collected and committed to writing served as the foundation of the famous Gothic code, known by the name of the *Forum Judicum*, or *Fuero Juzgo*.   He was a great prince ; but the fratricide which is believed to have opened him the way to the crown, and the cruelty with which he persecuted the orthodox (like his predecessors, he was an Arian), are dreadful stains on his memory.

But Alaric was unable to tread in the steps of so great a prince as his father.   In vain did his father-in-law Theodoric, who had just founded the kingdom of the Ostrogoths in Italy, interpose in his behalf : the fierce Clovis marched towards Poitiers, where Alaric then lay, resolved, as he said, to expel the heretical Arians from the soil of Gaul.[1]   The Visigoths, after a sharp conflict, were routed with great loss, and their king was left dead on the field.   Clovis pursued his successes, and soon reduced the greater part of their possessions in the south of France, and entered victorious into their capital of Toulouse.[2]   Alaric left a son ; but as he was too young to be intrusted with the government, his bastard brother, Gesalric (Gensaleic) had the address to procure the elective crown.   But the king of the Ostrogoths invested Gaul, overthrew the Franks, who were pressing the siege of Carcassonne, and forced Gesalric to seek for safety in Barcelona.   The humbled Clovis was glad to sue for peace from the formidable Theodoric, who united the two kingdoms of the Ostrogoths and Visigoths under his own sceptre.   To Theudes, one of his ablest generals, he intrusted the administration of the country and the guardianship of his grandson.   Theodoric resigned the sceptre of Spain to his grandson, on that prince's arriving at a suitable age.   Theudes now retired into private life.

[1 This has been called a " fifth century crusade " and " the first religious war of Europe."]
[2 The single combat between Alaric and Clovis, the miraculous fall of the walls of Angoulême, and other circumstances related by Gregory of Tours *n* render his authority in these wars of little weight in any case, unless supported by other testimony, as that of Procopius *o* and St. Isidore.*p* Burke *j* calls this battle " the foundation of the Frankish Kingdom of France and the origin of the Gothic Kingdom of Spain."]

Amalaric was the first Gothic king who established his court in Spain, in the city of Seville. To Athalaric, the successor of Theodoric, he ceded that portion of France which lies between the Rhone and the Alps, and received in return his father's treasures, which Theodoric had removed from Carcassonne to Ravenna : in the rest of Gothic Gaul, with all Spain, he was solemnly confirmed by Athalaric. To secure his possessions in Gaul against the formidable Franks, Amalaric demanded and obtained the hand of Clotilda, the sister of the royal sons of Clovis. But the union was unfortunate. The king was a violent partisan of Arius ; the queen as obstinate a professor of orthodoxy : at first each attempted to convert the other ; but finding their efforts ineffectual, the one was filled with rage, the other with contempt. Childebert marched against his brother-in-law ; the result was fatal to Amalaric, who fell by the swords of the Franks, whether on the field of battle, as Procopius⁰ asserts, or afterwards as he was seeking sanctuary in a church, must forever remain undecided. The battle in question appears to have been fought, not in Gothic Gaul, but in Catalonia. Childebert returned to France with his sister and the immense treasures which he had seized in the Arian churches.

With Amalaric ended the royal line of the mighty Alaric. Theudes was unanimously elected to the vacant throne (531). He appears to have been engaged in hostilities for some years with the vindictive or ambitious sons of Clovis. Gothic Gaul he was compelled to abandon to its fate, but he vigorously defended his peninsular dominions, which were invaded and laid waste by Childebert and Clotaire. Elated with his successes, the victorious Theudes passed the straits of Gibraltar, and laid siege to Ceuta, then in possession of the imperial troops. The place was invested with vigour ; and this recent conquest of Belisarius would soon have passed to the Visigoths or the Vandals, but for the pious scruples of the king. Though an Arian, he revered the Sabbath ; on which he not only refrained from hostile operations, but with his soldiers was occupied in public worship. Less strict than their foe, the besieged issued from the walls, fell on the Goths at the hour of prayer, and committed on them a carnage so horrible that the king had some difficulty to escape. He did not long survive this disaster. An assassin contrived to penetrate into the recesses of his palace, and with a poniard to deprive him of life. Before he expired, he is said to have ordered that the murderer should not be punished, as in his death he recognised the hand of heaven, which thus chastised him for a similar crime he had himself committed many years before. He left behind him the character of a just, a valiant, and an able ruler, who secured to his kingdom the blessings of internal peace by avoiding all invidious preference of his own religious sect, and treating the orthodox with as much favour as his Arian brethren.

Of the next two princes who successively swayed the Gothic sceptre, very little is known. The former, Theudisela, who had been the general of Theudes, and had acquired considerable fame in the war with the Franks, was a monster of licentiousness. This second Sardanapalus had scarcely reigned eighteen months before his destruction was effected by his enraged nobles. He was supping with them one evening in his palace at Seville, when the lights were suddenly extinguished, and a dozen swords entered his body. He was succeeded by Agila, whose reign was one continued series of commotions. Many cities refused to recognise his election. He marched to chastise them, but was vanquished and ultimately slain by his own soldiers after being defeated by Atanagild, a Gothic noble (554).

Scarcely had Atanagild obtained the throne, the great object of his wishes, when he discovered how fatally his ambition had blinded him. The troops of Justinian, his imperial ally, had no intention of leaving the country. From their fortresses in the Carthaginian province they defied his power to expel them. Nor were his successors more fortunate ; the unwelcome intruders remained until they were insensibly incorporated with Gothic inhabitants. This prince is more famous from the misfortunes of his two daughters than from his own deeds. The one he married to Sigebert king of Metz, the other to Chilperic king of Soissons. The latter, Galeswintha, Galsvinda, or

TOLEDO

Gosvinda, was murdered by order of her husband — no doubt at the instigation of his mistress, Fredegund. In Spain the memory of her sister Brunehild, is held in the highest reverence : in France, it is branded with infamy. The persecutions which after her husband's death she sustained from the unprincipled Fredegund, and the ferocious Chilperic, and her tragical end, many years afterwards, by the command of Clotaire, are events which belong to the history of France rather than that of Spain. Into the question of her guilt or innocence no inquiry need be instituted here : there are authorities enough to be consulted on both sides ; and in both abundant reason may be found to lament the influence of national prejudice, which can blind the wise and exasperate the good.[1]

During the reign of Atanagild, the Suevi, who had abandoned paganism for the errors of Arius, in the time of their king Rechiarius, about a century before, were converted to the orthodox faith. Though subject to the Goths,

[1] See Mariana,q and above all, Masdeu,r who base their defence on the praises bestowed on the princess by her contemporaries, as Gregory of Tours,n and on the silence of contemporary writers as to the crimes reported to have been committed by her. Both charity and chivalry would induce us to take part with the Spanish historians in favour of a lady, did they not attempt to conceal her real frailties (of crimes she was probably guiltless), and raise a weak, in some respects an imprudent woman into a saint. That she was undeserving the severe censures of Baronius s is more than probable ; but we must agree with Montesquieu t that the queen, daughter, sister, and mother of so many kings would never have been permitted to sustain the torments she did, had she not forfeited, in some way or other, the favour of a whole nation.

they had still preserved, as before observed, their kingly form of government. Theodomir, their present monarch, and his court solemnly abjured Arianism, were rebaptised, and admitted into the bosom of the church. After a peaceful, just, and useful reign of near fourteen years, and an interregnum of five months, occasioned by want of unanimity among the electors, the party of Narbonne in Gothic Gaul succeeded in raising Liuva [Leuva or Leova] to the throne. He contented himself with Gothic Gaul; and, in the second year of his reign, he confided to his brother Leuvigild (Leovigild) the sovereignty of Spain. Of Liuva no more is known except that he died in three years from his election, leaving his brother sole ruler of the kingdom.

LEUVIGILD AND ERMENIGILD

The reign of Leuvigild is more interesting than that of his predecessors. His arms were triumphant in every direction. The soldiers of the empire were again compelled to take refuge in their fortresses on the coast; and the fierce inhabitants of Biscay, Alava, and even Cantabria, to surrender at discretion. But the most painful, if not the most formidable of his enemies, he found in his eldest son Ermenigild. Yet few sons had ever more reason for filial gratitude. By an affectionate father, on his marriage with the princess Ingunda, daughter of the famous Brunehild and of Sigebert (which was celebrated in Toledo in 582) he had been associated in the royal dignity, and in every other respect treated with the utmost liberality. But Ingunda was orthodox, and Gosvinda, the second wife of Leuvigild, a professor of the Arian sect. The two queens could not long agree: the two husbands, finding that their palace was scandalised by disgraceful scenes, agreed to have separate courts: while the elder remained at Toledo, the younger established his court at Seville, which in splendour was little inferior to that of Leuvigild.

Ermenigild had not long been established in his new palace before he abjured Arianism, and embraced the Catholic religion. His conversion was chiefly the work of his consort, who had acquired great ascendency over him. Leuvigild declared that the crown of the Goths should never adorn the brow of an apostate. It is difficult to say which of the two first drew the sword in this unnatural warfare; but there is probability for throwing the guilt on the son. When no hope of resistance remained the rebel betook himself to a church, whence he implored pardon from his justly incensed father. The king promised to spare his life, if he would leave the sanctuary. By the persuasion of his brother Recared, who appears to have acted throughout in a manner highly creditable both as son and brother, he came out; and, with all the outward signs of repentance, threw himself at the feet of the king. The latter raised him, kissed him, and wept. For some time the father struggled with the king. At length he ordered that the rebel should be despoiled of the royal ornaments, and exiled to Valencia, thenceforward to live as a private individual.

Had all ended here, the justice of Leuvigild would have been approved by posterity, and the rebel would never have been lauded for virtues which he did not possess. But Ermenigild had scarcely arrived at his place of exile, when he again pursued his guilty plots against his country and king. He again connected himself with the Greeks, the most faithless and most formidable enemies to the repose of Spain; instigated the natives to rebellion; and, at the head of this combined force, made an irruption into Estremadura.

The indignation of Leuvigild may well be conceived. Having collected a veteran body of troops, he opened another melancholy campaign against the arch-rebel; he was delivered — or he fell — into their hands, and thrown into the dungeons of a prison in Tarragona. Leuvigild despatched several confidential messengers to the prince, promising, it is said, not only pardon but a restoration to royal favour, if he would return to the Arian faith. With a constancy which certainly does him honour, Ermenigild alike disregarded promises and threats, and declared his unalterable resolution of living and dying in the Catholic communion. Then it was that Leuvigild, in a fit of ungovernable fury, gave orders for the execution of the youth. The order was but too promptly obeyed: the ministers of vengeance hastened to the dungeon, and a hatchet cleft the head of the prince of the Goths.

That the crimes of Ermenigild deserved death, no one can attempt to deny; but nature shudders when a parent, in however just a cause, becomes the executioner of his child: no excuse can shield Leuvigild from the execration of posterity. But neither will historic truth permit the victim to be called a martyr. But what are we to think of St. Ermenigild[1] — what of the daring impiety which could invest a weak and wicked youth with attributes little less than divine? By the breviary of the Spanish church, and one or two ancient chroniclers, we are told that the dungeon of the saint, on the night of his execution, was illuminated with celestial light; that angels hovered over the corpse, and celebrated his martyrdom with holy songs! Then as to the miracles wrought by his intercession — omitting all mention of those which are said to have occurred during the darkness of the Middle Ages — a darkness in Spain "that might be felt" — what are we to say of Morales,[u] a writer who, so late as the close of the sixteenth century, gravely tells us that in his behalf a signal miracle has been performed through the instrumentality of this precious saint?[2] Even the judicious Masdeu,[r] at the close of the eighteenth century, could not, or perhaps dared not, divest himself of the pitiful prejudices of his country's faith.

After the news of Ermenigild's death, the brothers of Ingunda armed in the cause of their widowed sister. At the same time the Suevi showed a disposition to be restless, and prepared to descend from the mountains of Galicia, on the plains of central Spain. Nothing could exceed the promptitude with which Leuvigild met these threatening disasters. While he himself marched to subdue his rebellious vassals, whose nationality he had long resolved to destroy, he despatched his son Recared into Gaul to oppose the Franks. Both expeditions were eminently successful. All Galicia submitted, and a final period was put to the domination of the Suevi, 177 years after their arrival in Spain. In the latter expedition, Recared, after various successes, expelled the invaders from Gothic Gaul. The great Leuvigild was now undisputed master of the peninsula, with the exception of some maritime fortresses still held by the Greeks. Unfortunately, however, for his fame, he stained the lustre of a splendid reign by persecuting the orthodox

---

[1] Ermenigild was not canonised until the pontificate of Sixtus V, towards the close of the sixteenth century. One of his bones is preserved as a holy relic in the church of Saragossa. As he
[2] Morales,[u] fell, he says, into the water at Port St. Martin, enveloped in his cloak. As he could not swim, he called on God and "his glorious saint" for his soul's salvation, being hopeless of bodily safety. He had sunk twice, when a sailor from an adjoining vessel stretched out a pole on which he laid hold, and was thereby extricated from death. On measuring the pole afterwards, he found it so short that it could not reach the water! No doubt the saint had lengthened it, and when its service was done, permitted it to regain its natural dimension. He assures us that he could enumerate many mercies vouchsafed to him "through the intercession of this holy prince." In honour of his patron this author has a poem in Latin hexameters, equal in extent to a book of the Æneid.

or Catholic party. He is the first of the Visigoth kings[1] represented on ancient coins, with the royal diadem on his brow. But his riches were not wholly expended in idle pomp. The city of Recopolis, which he founded in Celtiberia, in honour of his son Recared, was a monument of his patriotism. Such, also, were the improvements which he introduced into the national legislation.

Leuvigild died in 586. A year before his death, he associated his son in his royal dignity. His greatest glory, in a Spaniard's eye, is his suspected conversion to the Catholic faith a few days before his death. If the alleged change were less disputable, we should hear no more of his defects; they would be carefully covered by the veil of orthodoxy.

RECARED I AND CATHOLICISM

On the death of his father, Recared I was unanimously acknowledged sole king of the Goths. In about a year after his accession, this prince conceived the hardy project of reclaiming his subjects from heresy. Time and patience, as well as a prudent dexterity, were indispensable towards the success of his project. By inviting his Catholic and Arian prelates to dispute in his presence, and by assuming the appearance of perfect impartiality between them, he laid the foundation of the change he meditated.

His next was a bolder step, though in perfect accordance with his new policy: he restored to the Catholic churches the treasures of which they had been deprived by his predecessors, and secured to the more indigent ones a considerable augmentation of revenue. When he saw his preparations sufficiently matured, he assembled his nobles and clergy at Toledo (May 8th, 587), to discuss his proposal. Having prevailed on the assembly to pass three consecutive days in fasting and prayer, he opened the business of the meeting in an elaborate speech. He submitted that, if unity of religion could be restored, an end would be put to the troubles which had so long agitated the kingdom. Lastly, he caused an instrument to be read, containing his abjuration of Arianism, and the confession of his belief in the co-equality of the Three Persons, and in the authority of the Catholic and apostolic church; and entreated all who were present to follow his example. When he and his queen had solemnly signed the act of confession, most of the prelates and nobles in the assembly hastened to do the same. The Catholic faith was thus declared the religion of the state. Spaniard, Sueve, and Goth were thus joined in one communion; and a canon was drawn up at the suggestion of St. Leander and the king, and with the full concurrence of the several members present, that henceforth no person should be admitted to the Lord's Supper who should not previously recite the symbol of belief, as sanctioned by the council of Constantinople.

Scarcely had the Gothic monarch effected the conversion of his subjects, when he was called to defend those of southern Gaul against Gontram, king of the Franks (589). Near Carcassonne they were utterly routed, and their camp seized by the general of Recared, nine thousand of their number being left dead on the field. Not less signal was his success over the Basques, who, with their characteristic restlessness, had long harassed the neighbouring provinces. The imperialists, too, he humbled, and compelled them to seek refuge in their fortresses. The rest of this monarch's reign was a continual

[1 Yet Burke*j* says, " If Recared is called the first of the Catholics, Leuvigild may fairly be styled the last of the Visigoths in Spain."]

effort to promote the happiness of his people: his administration was beyond example prosperous; and he enjoyed to an unrivalled extent their confidence and affection. It has been truly said of him that there arose no war in which he was not victorious; no rebellion which he did not crush; no conspiracy which he did not discover. In his last illness this king was devout enough, according to St. Isidore,ᵖ the contemporary bishop of Seville, to make a public confession of his sins, in conformity with the practice of the primitive church. He died in 601.

PETTY MONARCHS (601-672 A.D.)

Of the eleven succeeding sovereigns little is known, and that little is not very interesting. In general their reigns were brief, and their actions unimportant; so that we have the less reason to regret the scantiness of our historic materials. Liuva II, the eldest son and successor of Recared, ere two years were passed, was assassinated by the same Witteric whom his father's clemency had pardoned. Witteric had little reason to congratulate himself on his success. In his wars he was uniformly unfortunate; and in his family he was not more to be envied. In the seventh year of his reign he was murdered at his own table, and his body buried without honour.

Gundemar, the next king (610), was more fortunate in his warlike enterprises. He triumphed over the Basques and the imperialists. He had one advantage — an advantage not always enjoyed by the Visigoth monarchs of Spain — that of dying a natural death. Sisibut (Sisebert) was much superior. His successes over both the Basques and the imperialists were more signal: they were also more solid, since he reduced and retained several fortresses belonging to the latter; those which lay near the straits of Gibraltar were lost to them forever. But he deserves greater praise for his humanity than for his valour or skill in war. He wept over the wounds of his prisoners; and, with his own money, often redeemed such as were taken by his soldiers. Whenever a town was sacked, he ordered it to be proclaimed that the enemies who, even when the contest was hopeless, should reach his quarters and claim his protection, should escape with both life and liberty. Such an expedient is indicative enough both of his own admirable clemency and of the blood-thirsty disposition of his Goths, who were accustomed indiscriminately to massacre every living thing that fell in their way.

Strange that this prince, who was thus indulgent to his very enemies, should so rigorously have persecuted his Jewish subjects! He published an edict which left them no alternative but baptism or scourges and utter destitution. Eighty thousand of the poor wretches submitted to the rite; a great number escaped into France; such as remained and were obstinate in their faith were treated with great cruelty. At length, however, the church wisely desisted from this execrable policy. It was accordingly ordained by the fourth council of Toledo that the holy sacraments should no longer be administered to such as were unwilling to receive them. In other respects Sisibut was a wise and patriotic monarch. The construction of a fleet for the purpose not only of the country's defence, but of making his subjects acquainted with maritime affairs, was, in a Gothic king, a magnificent thought. He is also believed to have surrounded the city of Evora with fortifications. He died in 621. His son, Recared II, reigned only three months. Suintila, the next in succession, is represented as a strange compound of great and vicious qualities; at least his life exhibited, at two different periods, a strange contrast with itself. On the one side he had the glory of effecting what his predecessors had attempted in vain — he reduced all the fortresses held by the imperialists, and forever ended their influence in the peninsula: he was thus the first Gothic monarch of all Spain. With equal success he quelled the commotions of the Basques. His triumphs changed him: the hours which he had formerly devoted to the happiness of his people were now passed in sensuality. He became cruel. What still more exasperated the Goths, so tenacious of their original equality, and so jealous of their sovereign's prerogatives, was his conferring on his son Recared the title of king, and thereby laying the foundation of hereditary monarchy. Seeing the universal dissatisfaction inspired by this once popular ruler, one Sisenando, a noble Goth, planned his deposition. The Goths deposed their king, and proclaimed Sisenando the successor (631). The fourth council of Toledo (assembled in 633), after passing some canons for the better discipline of the church, entered fully into his views by excommunicating Suintila, the wife, children, and brother of that monarch.

On the death of this monarch the choice of the Goths fell on Chintella (Chintila), who, in conformity with the regulation just mentioned, convoked the prelates at Toledo to confirm his election. These fathers issued another decree, that in future no one should be nominated as king who was not of noble blood and of Gothic descent; all candidates, too, were subjected to excommunication who should endeavour to attain their end by unlawful means. In another council (the sixth of Toledo), held about eighteen months afterwards, the third canon obliged all future kings to swear, not only that they would not suffer the exercise of any other religion than the Catholic, but that they would rigorously enforce the laws against all dissidents, especially "that accursed people," the Jews. Tulga, who was elected in 640, was also a model of the peaceful virtues. The aged and inflexible Cindasuinto (Chindaswind), who ascended the throne in 642, associated with him in the royal dignity his son Recesuinto (Receswind), and on his death in 653 that prince remained in secure possession of the crown. The piety of this monarch made him the favourite of the church; the readiness with which he sanctioned a law that the wealth acquired by future kings should be transmitted, not to their children or heirs, but to their successors, rendered him no less that of the nation.

THE REIGN OF WAMBA

After the death of Recesuinto in 672, the eyes of the Gothic electors were turned on Wamba, whose wisdom and virtues were well known to the whole nation. But this excellent man, who had filled some of the most honourable posts in the monarchy, and had found little happiness in greatness, was little inclined to accept the proffered dignity. He alleged his advanced age, and his consequent incapacity to undertake duties requiring such labour and activity. Prayers and tears were vainly employed to move him. At length, one of the dukes of the palace placed a poniard at his breast, and bade him choose between the sepulchre and a throne. Such a choice was no longer difficult, and Wamba reigned.

If Wamba, as there is reason to believe, had been induced to refuse the crown chiefly from an apprehension of popular levity, his prudent foresight was verified by the event. The Basques revolted, and their example was instantly followed by the inhabitants of Gothic Gaul. The evil was increased by the bigotry of the king; he issued a decree, banishing all Jews who refused to be baptised: these exasperated exiles flocked to Nîmes, whose count, Hilderic, had drawn many nobles and prelates into the rebellion. The cause of the monarch appeared hopeless, when Duke Paul, a Greek by nation, and consequently wily and unprincipled, who had been despatched at the head of an army to suppress the commotion beyond the Pyrenees, prevailed on his troops to join the malcontents, and on several important fortresses to open their gates to him. Even Barcelona and Narbonne were detached from their fidelity to the king.

In the meantime the artful Greek had prevailed on the Goths of Gaul to proclaim him king. The prudent Wamba, after the successful issue of the Cantabrian war, marched towards Catalonia. On the confines of that province, he divided his forces into three considerable bodies; of which, while one was conveyed by sea, the other two proceeded towards the Pyrenees by two different routes. Barcelona submitted almost without resistance; Gerona offered none; two of his generals speedily reduced the fortress of Clausina, on the site of the modern Clusas, and made Hilderic and Ranosind prisoners. The victorious king now marched on Narbonne, in the hope of ending the war by the reduction of that capital, and the seizure of the rebel. But Paul, whose self-confidence seemed to have greatly abated, had precipitately retired to Nîmes, leaving the defence of Narbonne to Duke Wittimer. He surrendered, and, with his companions, was publicly scourged as a rebel.

A SPANISH FLAGELLANT

The reduction of Narbonne was followed by that of other strong places in the neighbourhood. No time was now lost in marching against Nîmes, where Paul was entrenched with his bravest troops. The assault was delivered with fury, and was as furiously repelled. Eventually the walls were surmounted: the struggle on the summit was terrible, but short; it was renewed in the streets, but the sword of the Goths still pursued its destructive career. Wamba now entered triumphantly into Nîmes, by the pardoned inhabitants of which he was received with unfeigned gratitude. By his command Paul, with the other leading rebels, was dragged, by the hair of the head, from the vaults of the amphitheatre. The judges of the tribunal voted for the death of the most guilty; but the merciful monarch satisfied himself with condemning them to wear shaven crowns, and to a religious confinement within the walls of Toledo. Having pacified the whole of Gothic Gaul; having deposed some governors, and created others; having repaired the towns which had been injured, and banished the Jews, Wamba returned to his capital.

After those glorious exploits, Wamba applied his undivided cares to the interests of his subjects. By cultivating the arts of peace, by bettering the temporal condition of the people, by encouraging the clergy to greater diligence, by strengthening the walls of Toledo, and by causing justice to be administered with mercy, he secured the confidence of his kingdom.   The bases of his character seem to have been incorruptible integrity, an ardent zeal for his country's good, and a rare union of moderation with firmness. He was also unrivalled for prudence ; he provided for everything.   Foreseeing the enterprises to which the fanatic ambition of the Saracens would inevitably impel them, he prepared a fleet for the defence of the coast.   He had soon to congratulate himself on his prophetic caution.   About the year 677, a fleet of 170 barques, filled with these barbarians, passed the straits of Gibraltar, and attempted to land : they were assailed, dispersed, or taken by the ships of the king, whose vigour long kept the Mussulmans in awe. Though masters of nearly all northern Africa, from the Nile to the Atlantic Ocean, they wisely respected for many years the territories of the Goths. Had Wamba been succeeded by monarchs of equal prudence and activity, the scourge of Saracenic domination, the greatest, perhaps, that ever afflicted any people, would probably have been forever averted from Spain.

But neither the virtues nor the abilities of Wamba, it is said, could exempt him from the fate common to so many of the Visigothic kings — from domestic treason.   If that fate, however, be common in kind, it differs widely in manner, in the present instance.   On Sunday, October 14th, 680, the king fell into a state of insensibility, and seemed to be deprived of life. As no doubt appeared to be entertained by his servants that he was dying, in conformity with the custom of his times, his head was hastily shaven, and he was enveloped in a penitential habit ; in other words, he was transformed from a layman into a member of the monastic profession.   Though he recovered in about twenty-four hours, his doom was everlastingly sealed : though his profession had been involuntary, and even forced on him while in a lifeless state, the obligation was not the less imperative.   Disqualified thus strangely from enjoying the honours and from participating in the duties of public life, he retired to the monastery of Pampliega, near Burgos, where he passed the remainder of his days.

Such are the facts of this strange occurrence.   The only difficulty is to determine whether the suspension of the vital powers in Wamba was a natural or a previously contrived event.   Two chroniclers of the ninth century (Sebastian[v] of Salamanca, and the anonymous monk of Albelda [w]) assert that the indisposition or trance of Wamba, and his consequent tonsure, were the work of Ervigius, a nephew of King Cindasuinto, who had long aspired to the throne.   He administered, say they, a draught to the monarch, which he considered potent enough to destroy reason, if not life itself ; and in the lethargy which followed the monastic penitence was imposed, whether by his contrivance, or through the piety of the royal attendants, is doubtful. But what reliance is to be placed on the testimony of these chroniclers, who wrote so long after the event ?   Not a hint is given of this treason in the work of the contemporary prelate St. Julian,[x] nor in the acts of the twelfth council of Toledo, assembled after the retirement of Wamba, nor in the epitome of Isidore of Badajoz,[z] who wrote about seventy years after the time ; in short, there is no contemporary authority whatever for fixing so deep a stain on the character of Ervigius.   On the contrary, the three instruments which he produced on his accession were acknowledged to be authentic : the first, which was signed by the great officers of the palace, stated the fact of the tonsure and habit being imposed ; the second, which was signed by Wamba himself, contained his renunciation of the crown in favour of

Ervigius; and the third was an injunction addressed by that monarch to the metropolitan of Toledo to proceed with the coronation of his appointed successor.

On the other hand, it may be contended with some appearance of reason that the silence of St. Julian and of the fathers of the council is sufficiently explicable: neither would wish to draw on themselves the vengeance of the reigning king by giving utterance to their suspicions. And as to the three instruments so carefully adduced, does not that very care imply an apprehension on the part of him who took it that his proceedings would be narrowly watched, his motives, perhaps, called in question? Would innocence, which, like charity, never judges harshly, or suspects, have taken such pains to furnish evidence so connected and elaborate? Undue anxiety has often shot beyond its mark. Then the subsequent conduct of Ervigius, which, as we shall soon see, is censurable for something worse than imprudence, must naturally confirm the suspicions of such as incline to the opinion of his guilt. On such a subject, however, where certainty can never be expected, the wise will hesitate to decide, and the good to condemn.[1]

ERVIGIUS AND ERGICA

Having summoned a council at Toledo, the twelfth held in that city (680), Ervigius had little difficulty in persuading the fathers to acknowledge the authenticity of the three instruments he produced; and, consequently, his claim to the Visigothic crown. They even showed a blind devotion to his will in other respects, not very honourable to their characters, nor respectful to the memory of an excellent prince. But, with all his wily contrivances, Ervigius had the mortification to see the bulk of the people still attached to their late sovereign. To make that sovereign appear tyrannical, and to attach to his interests all who now justly suffered for their participation in the rebellion of Paul, he summoned the thirteenth council of Toledo, and requested the assembled prelates to reverse the salutary measures of his predecessor. Accordingly, the first canon restored to their ranks, possessions, and rights, all who had ever taken arms against Wamba. Even yet Ervigius was apprehensive. He sent for Ergica, the nephew[2] of Wamba; and offered that prince the hand of his daughter, with the succession to the throne, on the condition that the latter would swear to protect his family when he should be no more. The proposal was eagerly accepted; the marriage was solemnised; and, on the death of Ervigius, the crown of the Goths fell on the brows of the son-in-law.

Gratitude is not always the virtue of princes. Scarcely was Ergica in possession of the envied dignity, than he showed his hostility to the memory of his benefactor. Resolving to use the same weapons as had been employed by that king, he convoked the fifteenth council of Toledo to aid his views of vengeance; he represented to the fathers the oath which he had taken to protect the family of Ervigius, and how difficult it was to be observed amidst the general complaints of his people against the rapacity of that family. The supple ecclesiastics, who had long lost sight of the independence of

[1 Among modern historians few feel any doubt of the guilt of Ervigius or Erwig. Among those who believe he administered the sleeping draught may be named Mariana,*q* Ferreras,*aa* Hume,*d* and Burke.*j* But the caution expressed above by Dunham*g* and by Masdeu*r* should modify the certainty of opinion.]

[2 Dunham*g* says the "brother," but he is generally called the nephew.]

their vocation, and were become the mere ministers of the monarch (in fact, the bishops were, *ex officio*, ministers of the crown, in a state which has been truly called theocratic), immediately declared that an unjust oath was not binding; and that the king might punish or reward any of his subjects, the relatives of Ervigius among the rest, as justice or equity dictated. In consequence of this decree, Ergica is said to have punished with severity the enemies of Wamba and his house — in other words, the partisans of Ervigius; and even to have repudiated his wife, thus dissolving the only remaining bond which connected him with the rival family.

In the sixth year of his reign Ergica was afflicted with a rebellion, which spread into Gothic Gaul. He had also engagements with the Franks — probably connected with the conspiracy of Sisebert; but in none did he obtain any advantage. A more formidable conspiracy was discovered the following year. Notwithstanding the severity of the penal laws against their nation, many Jews, though outwardly Christians, were retained in the peninsula by the attractions of a lucrative commerce; but their souls groaned within them under the oppressions they were made to endure; and they were naturally eager to engage in any undertaking which promised them toleration and revenge. On the present occasion they were said to have secretly conspired with their brethren of Africa; perhaps, too, with the Saracens, on whose arms they had long prayed for success. To avert the threatened explosion, the king convened the seventeenth council of Toledo, which decreed severe penalties against the guilty. The eighth canon (*de Judæorum damnatione*) not only reduced to perpetual slavery all the baptised Jews — and Spain had long suffered no other — who relapsed, or who conspired against the state, but ordered that, at seven years of age, their children should be taken from them, and educated under the direction of approved Christians.[1] In 698 this king associated with him his son Witiza, and caused that prince to be recognised as his successor. Witiza, to whom Galicia was confided, established his court at Tuy; and thenceforth, to the death of Ergica, the coins of the kingdom bore two royal heads, with the motto *Concordia Regni*. The father died at Toledo in 702, leaving behind him a doubtful reputation.[2]

WITIZA (702-709 A.D.)

Of Witiza we know little that is certain, but much that is apocryphal. Over his character, his actions, and even his death, there rests a cloud of uncertainty which will probably never be removed. It is, however, agreed that in the beginning of his reign he evinced many great qualities; that he redressed many grievances inflicted by his father; that he restored their possessions and liberty to many who had been unjustly deprived of both; and that he remitted the heavy arrears of taxes due at his accession — nay, that, to prevent the possibility of their being collected, he caused the books in which the names of the defaulters were contained to be publicly burned. On the other hand, we are told that he was addicted to the greatest luxury; that he took many concubines, with whom he lived openly, in defiance

---

[1 The unending torments the Jews endured in Spain are described in detail in the work of Amador de los Rios.*bb*]

[2 Some writers, among whom are the respectable names of Florez *cc* and Cardinal Lorenzana,*dd* fix the death of Ergica in 700. Mariana *q* and Masdeu,*r* with better reason, give 701. The difference wholly rests on the interpretation of the Roman numerals in the Visigothic chronicle of Wulsa,*ee* No. 34.]

of church remonstrances; that in the indulgence of his brutal appetite he spared neither the high nor the low, neither wife nor maiden; and that, to stifle complaint, he published an edict by which he allowed all his subjects, ecclesiastics no less than laymen, as many concubines as they could obtain.

All this, however startling and improbable, may possibly be true. Though not a word of it is to be found in the continuator of Joannis Biclarensis,*ff* nor in the contemporary historian Isidorus Pacensis,*z* the brevity of those writers, who do no more than chronicle, in the most meagre terms, a few of the more striking facts, may perhaps account for the omission. The vices too of Witiza are mentioned by the monk of Moissiac,*hh* who wrote about one hundred years after the destruction of Spain, and are alluded to by Sebastian of Salamanca,*v* who finished his chronicle towards the close of the ninth century.*g*

The history of Witiza's reputation is a model of the gentle art of blackening a character, especially in the interests of a religious cause, which can command the progressive aid of generations. Paquis *gg* tells the story briefly, noting that "the further the historians are from the time of Witiza, the more detailed become their recitals, and the more severe their reprobation." A century after his death the foreign and anonymous writer of the *Chronicle of Moissiac* *hh* says that he was addicted to extreme luxury. Nearly a century more, and the Spanish Sebastian of Salamanca *v* broke out more strongly: "Witiza plunged into odious debauches, lived in a cloud of women and concubines, and finally to escape the censures of the priests dissolved the assemblies of the bishops and braved the canons of the church; he even ordered the bishops and priests to marry. His impieties caused the ruin of the Goths."

Another chronicler *w* of the same time omits mention of the orgies and the attack on the church, but accuses Witiza of killing the father of the great Pelayo and of pursuing the famous hero himself. Two centuries more, and the monk of Silos *ii* adds that Witiza put out the eyes of a prince of whom he was jealous. Yet again two centuries, and Lucas Tudensis *jj* discovers that, in addition to previously recorded crimes, Witiza, fearing rebellion, disarmed every subject and tore down the walls of every city but three; and that he chased from Toledo the bishop Julian to place there his own son Oppas, besides mutilating the son of King Cindasuinto. In fact, there was no Bishop Julian at that time; Oppas was not Witiza's son; and the son of Cindasuinto, of whom Witiza was said to be jealous, must have been over eighty years old at the time, even imagining him to have been the son.

About this time Roderic Ximenes,*kk* finding the old chronicles praising Witiza as virtuous and the later condemning him as vicious, combined the two by representing Witiza's character as undergoing sudden degeneration from its high beginnings. This patchwork mantle was long worn by Witiza in the later histories of Morales,*u* Mariana,*q* Ferreras,*aa* and Aschbach.*ll* More recent authorities have, however, inclined to discard the evil side of Witza's reputation as a mere fiction of later writers who hated him because he spared the Jews and resisted the church in some things.

As a picturesque example of how closely allied to fiction is the development of supposed history, the story of Witiza is of value. There is much uncertainty as to his end. There seems to have been a rebellion, and the power seems to have been divided with Roderic, who was called the son of King Cindasuinto, but was more probably a descendant. The story was told that Roderic finally, with the aid of Greek allies, captured Witiza and put out his eyes; but of this the contemporary Isidorus Pacensis[z] says no word. We can only be sure that Roderic reigned supreme in 709. So fabulous is the fame of this Roderic, "the last of the Goths," that some historians have been tempted to deny that he ever existed at all. Dahn[mm] calls him an historical phantom; and even less credence is given to the famous romance of the lovely Florinda, to whose virtues he showed no mercy, and whose father in revenge called in the Arabs from Africa to the rich conquest lying at their very feet. This romance, though so little credible, is so closely allied with the Moslem conquest of Spain, that it may well be briefly told, especially as there is nothing impossible or improbable in the main incidents, once the story is rid of its miraculous fairy-story accretions, such as the enchanted tower of Hercules, where Roderic found inscriptions prophesying the coming Arab storm.[a]

THE FABLE OF RODERIC AND FLORINDA (709–711 A.D.)

Among the ladies of King Roderic's court, say the later chronicles of Spain, there was one of uncommon beauty, named Florinda or La Cava, the daughter or wife of one Doyllar or Don Illan, or Don Julian. She had the misfortune to please the king; but as her virtue was equal to her loveliness, she indignantly rejected his overtures. But kings, and least of all Gothic kings, were not to be repulsed with impunity; and Roderic accomplished by force what he could not do by persuasion. The lady dissimulated her deadly hatred until she had an opportunity of communicating her dishonour to her father, then absent against the Moors.

All on fire at the indignity done his child and house, the count resolved on a revenge with which the whole earth should ring. He entered into a compact with the misbelievers, engaging to put them in possession of the whole country, if they would wash away his dishonour in the blood of the foul ravisher. He wrapped his purpose in great secrecy until he had rescued his daughter from the clutches of the king: he himself fetched her from the court of Toledo, and behaved to Roderic with so much courtesy that no one could suspect he knew of his wrong, much less that he was about so fatally to avenge it. On his return to Ceuta, the seat of his government, he found the Moors prepared for the expedition: he openly joined them, accompanied the infidel general to Gibraltar, and thus commenced the famous struggle which was to end in the subjugation of a great nation.

The whole story of Florinda is evidently a romance — probably of Arabic invention — similar to the many thousand others which formed the amusement of the people in the Middle Ages. It is first mentioned by the monk of Silos,[ii] who wrote about four hundred years after the Mohammedan invasion. No doubt, however, can be entertained that Count Julian was among the most influential and active of the conspirators who called the Arabs into Spain.

The chivalric *Romance of Don Roderic*[nn] — about as good an authority as the monk of Silos on such a subject — gives us a minute account of the amour, its progress, and termination. From the whole conversation, as given by this anonymous novelist, Roderic might be justified in believing that the scruples of La Cava were not insuperable[1] — that, in fact, she was willing in heart, but coy through maiden bashfulness. Even at last, when she might have so easily alarmed the palace, she was silent through fear of

[1 Burke[j] notes that in Arabic La Caba or La Cava would suggest a woman of evil life.]

her cries reaching the ears of the queen. Count Julian's daughter is made a model of virtue by Southey, and Roderic himself is represented as scarcely inferior.

VISIGOTHIC CIVILISATION

The government of the Visigoths was, in appearance, an absolute monarchy; yet the power of the chief was so restrained in its exercise by the controlling influence of the prelates, that it might, with equal propriety, be termed a theocracy. In the infancy of their office, the Gothic kings were no less controlled by their nobles; they were, in fact, but *primi inter pares;* they had no royal descent, no hereditary honours, nor, indeed, much transmitted wealth, with which to captivate or influence their rude companions. Every fierce chieftain considered himself as good as his king, and might become one himself. His titles were high-sounding: "Your Glory" was the most usual; though the epithets of Pious, Conquering, etc., were often added. Recared was the first of the Visigothic kings distinguished by the name of Flavius. Whether he assumed it after the imperial family of that name, or from its reputed Gothic signification, is unknown; but it continued to adorn the titles of his successors. His father was also the first who surrounded the throne with regal state, and whose effigy bore the impress of a crowned head. The successors of that monarch improved on his magnificence: robes of purple, thrones of silver, sceptres and crowns of gold, distinguished them still more from the time of Cindasuinto.

Soon after the establishment of the Visigothic monarchy at Toledo, the power of the crown seems to have been bounded by two restrictions only: (1) The king could not condemn without legal trial, but he had power to soften the rigour of severe justice or entirely absolve the delinquents brought before his tribunals; (2) the second restriction related to the decrees of king, which were received as binding during his life; but which had no force in perpetuity, unless sanctioned at the same time by the signatures of the bishops and barons in council assembled. In other respects he was unshackled. He could make war or peace at pleasure; he could issue proclamations which had the force of law, subject to the restriction just mentioned; he commanded in the field, and presided in the court of justice. The jurisdiction of the king was not confined to affairs purely temporal. He could issue general regulations relating to the maintenance of discipline, or the interests of religion. He could preside in tribunals of appeal, even in affairs purely ecclesiastical. The king nominated to all vacant bishoprics, and even translated from one see to another; but this prerogative was very gradually acquired. The fourth and last ecclesiastical prerogative of the king was that of convoking national councils, and of confirming them by his authority. He was thus, in the widest sense, in a degree unknown among other Catholic nations, the protector of the church. In consequence, the bishops became courtiers, and generally submissive to the royal will; and even the fathers of the Toledan councils were swayed by fear, or by the hope of gaining favour.

In other respects the king was invested by the laws with much outward reverence. Whoever conspired against his life was punished with death; or if the capital penalty was remitted, the delinquent was blinded, shaven, and doomed to perpetual confinement. He who even affronted the king was, if rich, mulcted in half his possessions; if poor, he remained at the monarch's disposal. Whoever defamed the character of a dead king, was punished with fifty stripes. Yet, with all this studied respect, no monarchs were ever so unfortunate as those of the Visigoths—none whose empire, liberty, or even life, was so insecure. From Atawulf to Roderic, the greater number were assassinated or deposed.

We cannot fail to be struck with the national pride of the Goths : they alone were styled *nobiles*, while the rest of the community were *viliores*. Under the latter humiliating term were included not merely *servi* and *liberti*, or slaves or freedmen, but even the *ingenui*, or free-born, whatever might be their wealth or consideration ; and, to preserve the privileged caste uncontaminated, marriages were rigorously forbidden between the victors and the vanquished, until Recesuinto abolished the prohibition. Not only was the slave who presumed to marry a free woman put to death, but the free woman, who either married or sinned with a slave, was burned at the stake with him. Again, the relative importance of the three classes, nobles, freemen, and slaves, was carefully graduated by the laws. For the same crime a greater punishment was awarded to the second than the first, and to the third than the second. If from the civil we pass to the military state of the country, we shall find that the Goths were one vast nation of soldiers, the words soldier and man being considered almost as synonymous. The obligation of service was imperative on all freemen ; nor were the sons of the king admitted to his table until they had made their essay in arms. Slaves were also admitted to join the levies, since every owner was required to take with him to the field one-tenth of the number he possessed. All Goths capable of bearing arms, whether lay or clerical, were subject to military duty ; and heavy were the penalties with which he was visited who absented or hid himself to escape the conscription.

Matrimony, the last of the sacraments mentioned in the Visigothic canons, was considered of unrivalled importance among a people so tenacious of their privileges, and so jealous of the purity of their blood. As before observed, marriages between the victors and the vanquished were rigorously prohibited, until Recesuinto repealed the obnoxious law. The damsel could not give her hand to anyone, unless he were not merely approved, but selected for her, by her parents ; or, if an orphan, by her natural guardians ; and, if she married contrary to their wishes, she not only forfeited all right to her share of her future prosperity, but both she and her husband became slaves—the slaves of the man for whom her relatives had intended her. The dowry was given by the bridegroom, not by the guardians of the bride, and was carefully preserved by them. The impediments to matrimony were numerous. (1) The male was always to have the advantage of years over the female. (2) He or she who had been betrothed to anyone could not marry another before the expiration of two years ; if this prohibition was disregarded, slavery was the doom of both. (3) He who forced a woman could not marry her. (4) If a Christian married a Hebrew, both were banished to different places. (5) The monastic orders, public or devotional penitents, virgins veiled and vowed, were naturally excluded from this sacrament; so also were kindred to the sixth degree.

A married couple could at any time separate by mutual agreement ; but they could not return to each other, much less remarry. It was only in case of adultery, or when the husband committed the most abominable of sins, or when he wished his wife to commit adultery, that the *vinculum matrimonii* was declared forever dissolved, and she was at liberty to marry another man. Adultery was reputed so enormous a crime among the Visigoths, that the person who committed it became the slave of the injured partner. If a

H. W.—VOL. X. D

husband caught his wife *in flagrante delicto*, he could, with perfect impunity, destroy both her and her paramour — a permission of which a modern Spaniard would not be slow to avail himself. When the actual guilt was not witnessed, every means, not excepting tortures, were used to arrive at its knowledge.

HARDSHIPS OF THE JEWS

Under the Goths, Spain was no more exempt from heresies than she had been under the Romans. The first is that of Nestorius, respecting the mysterious union of the divine and human natures in Christ; but it was speedily repressed. The Manichæans and Priscillianists were not more successful; both Arians and Catholics united in banishing them : extirpation was reserved for later times. After the accession of Recared, when the Catholic religion became the only one in Spain, severe penalties were decreed against all who presumed to differ from the established faith. In the reign of Chintella, and in a council held at Toledo (the sixth), a decree was made that thenceforth none but Catholics should be allowed to remain in the country ; and all succeeding kings were to swear that the Jews, the only misbelievers remaining, should not be tolerated.

By a subsequent law this odious intolerance was more clearly and fatally defined. Under the penalty of confiscation of property and perpetual banishment, it prohibited all men, of whatever condition, whether natives or resident foreigners, ever to call in question, either in public or private, the holy Catholic and apostolic faith, the evangelic institutions, the definitions of the fathers, the decrees of the church, whether ancient or recent, the sacraments, or anything whatever which that church held as holy. After these decrees the poor Jews could expect little mercy ; they had never, indeed, enjoyed much security since the Roman domination. Sisibut, Sisenando, Chintella, Cindasuinto, Recesuinto, Wamba, and Ervigius were the most eager rivals in the race of persecution. They decreed that the Jews should be baptised ; that such as were baptised should not be allowed to have Christian servants ; that they should observe Easter Sunday according to the Christian rite ; that they should respect the matrimonial impediments already noticed ; that they should eat whatever Christians ate, however solemnly forbidden in their own law ; that they should neither read nor receive into their houses any book contrary to the Christian religion ; that they should not be admissible to any civil offices ; that their evidence should not be received in a court of justice, unless ample testimony were borne to their moral habits ; that when travelling they should make their confession of faith, and exhibit an episcopal passport at every town they entered ; that they should spend every Sunday in company with Christians, who should then witness their devotions ; and that they should always be present whenever the catechism was repeated or expounded.

But as, in spite of all these tyrannical measures, the sincerity, if not the conduct of the forced converts, was naturally suspicious, two successive confessions of faith, expressed in the most awful terms, were framed for them. In these confessions they were compelled to swear, in the most solemn and public manner, by the great Incommunicable Name and Attributes, that they utterly abhorred, and from their souls forever renounced, all the rites, ceremonies, customs, and solemnities they had previously respected and observed ; that they would thenceforward live in the most holy faith of Christ, their Creator and Redeemer ; that they would observe all the rites of God's church, and shun even the most distant form of intercourse with Jews. This oppressed nation was, in the sequel, righteously revenged. Who can blame the readiness with which they received the Mohammedans, and the zeal with which they endeavoured to overthrow the most accursed government that ever existed in Europe.*g*

BURKE'S ESTIMATE OF GOTHIC RULE

Spain, with its fertile soil, its varied climate, its noble rivers, its extensive seaboard, its inexhaustible mines, and its hardy and frugal population, was the richest inheritance of the Gothic race. Yet, after three centuries of undisputed enjoyment, their rule was overthrown at once and forever by a handful of marauders from Africa. The Goth had neglected all his opportunities, despised all his advantages, heeded no warnings. He had been weighed in the balance and found wanting; and his kingdom was taken from him — for he had shown himself unfit for power.

Of all the various systems of government that have been attempted on this earth, theocracy, or more properly hierocracy, is undoubtedly one of the very worst. And in all circumstances and conditions where the priest and the confessor usurp the authority that properly belongs to the magistrate and to the man, disaster is the inevitable result. From the death of Recared to the death of Roderic, the government of Spain was a theocracy, tempered by revolution. At the opening of the eighth century, Spain had no industry, no commerce, no arms. Not even letters had survived. For the Catholic church discouraged, if it did not actually prohibit, the study of polite literature. Virgil and Homer, Tacitus and Livy, were pagans and atheists, and their works were unprofitable and impious. The study of natural science or of medicine, the development of manufactures or of industry, the cultivation of the arts — these were equally unedifying to the devout Catholic. That sublime manifestation of "poetry in stone," so strangely called Gothic architecture, is not only not Visigothic, but it was unknown in Spain for over four hundred years after the destruction of the Goths. And although the great province is still covered with the glorious remains of Roman constructive art, there is scarcely found trace or fragment of the rude architecture of the Visigoths to tell of their dominion in the peninsula.

When Atawulf first crossed the Pyrenees at the head of the Visigoths, Latin was already the language of the Roman diocese. When Roderic threw away his crown on the banks of the Guadalete, Latin was still the language of the Visigothic kingdom. The Goth had been absorbed by the Roman. But a nation without a national language is doomed; a state without a state language is dead. Latin was the mother-tongue of the Romish church of Spain; but the Visigothic state was speechless. The kingdom, like Wamba, had been shorn and habited by the ecclesiastical power, and the kingdom, like the king, disappeared at the touch of the aggressor.*j*

CHAPTER II. THE TIME OF MOSLEM DOMINATION

"They come! they come!   I see the groaning land
    White with the turbans of each Arab horde:
Swart Zara joins her misbelieving band,
    Allah and Mahomet their battle word,
The choice they yield, the *Koran* or the sword.
    See how the Christians rush to arms amain!
In yonder shout the voice of conflict roar'd;
    The shadowy hosts are closing on the plain.
Now God and Saint Jago strike for the good cause of Spain!

"By heaven, the Moors prevail! the Christians yield!
    Their coward leader gives for flight the sign!
Their sceptred craven mounts to quit the field —
    ' Is not yon steed Orelia ? ' — ' Yes, 'tis mine !
But never was she turn'd from battle line.'
    Lo! where the recreant spurs o'er stock and stone ! —
' Curses pursue the slave, and wrath divine !
    Rivers engulf him ! ' — ' Hush ! ' in shuddering tone
The prelate said; ' Rash prince, yon vision'd form 's thine own.'

"Just then a torrent cross'd the flier's course ;
    The dangerous ford the kingly likeness tried,
But the deep eddies whelm'd both man and horse,
    Swept like benighted peasant down the tide."
            —SCOTT, *The Vision of Don Roderic.*

THE young Arab power was at the door of Spain before the degenerate Goths were half awake to their danger. They had hardly shaken off their slumbers before they were prisoners or fugitives from the house they had ruled for almost exactly three centuries. Roderic and his sixty thousand men fought madly for three days at Xeres near the junction of the Guadalete and Guadalquivir, but when the brave king himself lost courage and fled — if indeed he fled — the whole race took panic with him. The end of Roderic is lost in a tangle of fable and tradition. Scott has embalmed the legend as quoted above, and Southey in his poem, *The Last of the Goths,* has built him a splendid mausoleum ; but all that history can say is that his crown and sceptre were found on the bank of the stream and that his kingdom was as completely disembodied as its empty emblems. And now, as Hume[b] says, "The purely Gothic element in Spain was withered up as if by fire."

The story of the Moslem conquest has been already told in the fifth chapter of the history of the Arabs, in the eighth volume of this work. To that the reader is referred for the details of the invasion. The original Spanish people who had been regarded by the Goths as an inferior race unworthy of marriage, though the restriction was withdrawn shortly before the Moslems came, and the Jews, treated by the Goths as a cursed pest whom it was a virtue to torment — both welcomed the new-comers. They were rewarded with a gentleness of tolerance and a growth of intellectuality and commerce that lead one to question if the Arab domina-tion of Europe would have been indeed the horror it is usually imagined ; and if the repulse Charles Martel gave the Saracens at Tours in 732 were really the benefit to civ-ilisation that we are wont to imagine it.

The chapter on Arab civili-sation in the eighth volume argues that the Arabians gave to Spain a glory and a culture of the most brilliant type, ex-tending from the restoration of Greek letters to the awak-ening of modern science and commerce of the most splendid sort. When at length they were cast out of Spain, the reaction against them was it-self the effort of an intolerant, tyrannous, and blood-thirsty religious system, which even

A Mohammedan Chief

in its triumph at the time of Ferdinand and Isabella distinguished itself by the greatest blot on human civilisation, the Inquisition, and by cruelties that spread zealously round the world to the enslavement and torture, often the annihilation of remote and innocent races.

It would be so easy to adduce evidence that the Christian powers have done more harm to civilisation than the Moslem, that perhaps it would be wiser to omit bigoted self-gratulations on the failure of Arab ambitions in Europe, and be content with an impartial and non-dogmatic recital of a con-flict in which Europeans and Africans fought with a common greed of power and masked primeval instincts under the names of religion and patriotism. The aims of both were checked as much by internal dissensions and treach-eries as by any united opposition, and in neither Christian nor Arab politics is there much food for pride in humanity. Leaving the reader to find in the previously mentioned history of the Arabs the account of Moslem rule, misrule, and feud in the regions they conquered, we may turn to the equally sordid and selfish, and at times equally lofty and heroic story of the Chris-tians, who found refuge in rocky fastnesses and there grew slowly and pain-fully to a new life and a large hope.

They had much to complain of from Arab cruelty to those who would not accept the alternatives of "*Koran*" or tribute," but war was especially brutal in the Middle Age, and the Christians did not fail to revenge their mal-treated women and children on the non-combatants of the other side. The pity one instinctively feels at the sufferings of the Christians is somewhat stifled on realising that the same sufferings had been or would speedily be visited on the Mohammedans or on other Christians at the first opportunity. The examples of clemency which are now the commonplaces, the demands of warfare, were at that time so rare and amazing that they might almost be said to be always due to the eccentricity of the conqueror. But to take up the story of the Christian *Reconquista:*

Roderic was miscalled "the last of the Goths," for there were two Gothic rulers to succeed him. In the southeast Theodomir made peace with the Arabs; reigned as a vassal; and was succeeded in 743 by the Gothic Atana-gild, whose realm was absorbed by Abd ar-Rahman in 755. In the northwest was Pelayo, who made a great name on small capital.[a]

THE ASTURIAS AND LEON UNDER PELAYO (718 A.D.)

The more zealous or more independent Christians, who, after the triumphs of Tarik and Musa, were dissatisfied with the submission of Theodomir, gradually forsook their habitations in the south to seek a more secure asylum amidst the northern mountains of their country. They knew that in the same hills the sacred fire of liberty had been preserved, in defiance of Cartha-ginian, or Roman, or Goth; and they felt that to them was now confided the duty of reviving its expiring embers.

At first, indeed, the number which resorted to these solitudes was few, and actuated by the mere hope of individual safety: but as the Mohammedan excesses became more frequent and intolerable; as neither prompt submis-sion, nor the solemnity of treaties could guarantee the unhappy natives from plunder,[1] persecution, and destruction; and, consequently, as the number of refugees increased, the possibility of a combined defence on a larger scale, and even of laying the foundation of an infant state, was eagerly indulged. The care of the sacred relics, which, on the reduction of Toledo, were care-fully conveyed to these mountain fastnesses, the presence not only of prelates, but of nobles descended from the blood of the Goths, and the necessity of self-preservation, united these refugees in an indissoluble bond. But they could do nothing without a head: they proceeded to elect one; and their unanimous suffrages fell on Pelayo, said by Sebastian of Salamanca[f] to be the son of Favila, duke of Cantabria, belonging to the royal house of Cin-dasuinto.[3]

[1 Compare what the Arab historian Al Lagi[j] said of Alfonso the Catholic: "The terrible Alfonso, the manslayer, son of the sword, killed tens of thousands of Moslems. He burned houses and dwellings, and no treaty could be made with him." Christian historians equal this. The archbishop Rodrigo[c] draws a worse view of the desolation of Spain than even Isidore[d]: "Children are dashed on the ground, young men beheaded; their fathers fall in battle; the old men massacred, the women reserved for greater misfortune." He tells us that "every cathedral in Spain was burned or destroyed"; that "the national substance, etc., was plundered, except what the bishops could save in the Asturias"; that "the cities which were too strong to be stormed immediately, were deluded into a surrender"; that "oaths and treaties were uniformly broken by the Arabs," etc. Both he and Isidore may exaggerate, but the exaggeration only proves the fact.

3 The monk of Albelda[e] calls Pelayo the son of Bermudo, and nephew of king Roderic. His origin is wrapped in much obscurity. [Burke[g] says "Pelayo, no doubt, was but a robber chief-tain, a petty mountain prince, and the legends of his royal descent are of later date and of obvi-ously spurious manufacture; but Pelayo needs no tinsel to adorn his crown. He was th[e] founder of the Spanish monarchy. The Arabs called him "Belay."]

At the time this unequivocal demonstration of defiance was made by the Christians, Al-Haur, the Mohammedan governor, was in Gaul; but one of his generals, Al-Khaman, accompanied, as we are informed, by the renegade archbishop Oppas, and obedient to his orders, assembled a considerable force, and hastened into the Asturias, to crush the rising insurrection. Arriving at the foot of the Asturian mountains without obstacle, the Arabian general did not hesitate to plunge into the defiles : passing along the valley of Cangas de Onis he came to the foot of Mount Auseva, near the river Sella. On the heights of Covadonga, and in the cavern of St. Mary, the small but resolute band of Pelayo was concealed, waiting for the attack. Loath to run the risk of one where the advantage of position was so much in favour of the Christians, Al-Khaman is said to have despatched Oppas to Pelayo, representing to that prince the inutility of resistance, and the advantage of instant submission. The refusal of the Asturian, who well knew his position, and what stout hearts he commanded, was followed by the ascent of the Arabs up the steep acclivity. But to their consternation huge rocks and stones came thundering down on their dense ranks, by which they were precipitated into the narrow valley below. The destruction did not end here : it met those who attempted to ascend the opposite acclivity. Thousands were crushed beneath the vast fragments ; and the rest would speedily have shared the same fate, had they not precipitately fled by the way they had advanced. The confusion attending this retrograde movement was turned to good account by the Christians, who now issued from their hiding-places, and inflicted a terrific loss on the fugitives. The extent of that loss we should vainly attempt to estimate ; but that it was great may be learned from the very admission of the vanquished.[h]

The brilliance of Pelayo's success naturally inspired the old chroniclers to a belief in divine interposition, and the account of this battle by Sebastian of Salamanca is too vivid an example of history, as it was written by the churchmen, to be omitted.[a]

SEBASTIAN'S ACCOUNT OF THE BATTLE OF COVADONGA (718 A.D.)

And when Pelayo knew the approach of the Arabs, he betook himself to a cave, which is called the cave of Santa Maria, and immediately posted his army around it. And Oppas, the bishop, approaching him, thus said : "Brother, thou art not ignorant how, when all Spain was under the rule of the Goths, and when all her armies were joined together, she was unable to cope with the Ismailites : how much less will be thy power to defend thyself here in such a strait ? Now listen to my advice: relinquish all thoughts of resistance ; that, being in peace with the Arabs, thou mayst enjoy much prosperity, and preserve whatever thou didst or dost possess." And Pelayo replied, " I will neither have the Arabs for friends, nor will I submit to their dominion. Thou dost not perceive that the church of God is like unto the moon ; now it decreases, and now it regains its former magnitude. And we trust in God's mercy that from this very hill which thou beholdest, salvation may arise for Spain, and the Gothic army be renewed ; so that in us may be fulfilled the saying of the prophet, ' I will visit their iniquities with a rod, and their sins with stripes ; but my pity will I not withdraw from them.' Wherefore, though we have undergone a righteous judgment, we yet believe that there will descend grace from on high for the restoration of our church, our nation, and kingdom. We fear not ; we utterly despise this multitude of pagans."

Then the wicked bishop returned to the enemy, and said: "Hasten and fight; for by the sword only shall ye have peace with this man." Immediately they handle their weapons, and begin the battle: the engines are raised, the missiles fitted to the sling; the swords shine, the spears glitter, and the arrows are sent forth. But the weapons of the Lord were not wanting; for as the stones were shot from the slings and engines, and reached the temple of Holy Mary, ever a virgin, they were miraculously driven back on those who sent them, and killed a multitude of the Chaldeans. And as the Lord doth not number the spears, but giveth the victory to whom he pleaseth, so when the faithful left the cave to join in the battle, the Chaldeans forthwith fled, being divided into two bodies. And Bishop Oppas was soon taken, and Al-Khaman slain; in the same place were also slain 124,000 of the Chaldeans. Sixty-three thousand who remained alive ascended the top of Mount Auseva, and hastily descended by a precipice, which is usually called Amosa, to the territory of the Liebanians. But neither did these escape the Lord's vengeance; for when they reached the banks of the Deva, near a heritage called Casegadia, that part of the hill which overhung the river suddenly gave way,— manifestly through God's judgment,— forced the sixty-three thousand Chaldeans into the river, and covered them all. So that, even at this day, when the channel is swollen by the winter torrents, and the banks are overflown, vestiges of arms and human bones are clearly to be seen. Do not esteem this a vain or false miracle, but remember that He who thus covered the Arabs, the persecutors of God's church, with such a vast mountain heap, is the same who plunged the Egyptians into the Red Sea while pursuing Israel. *f*

Sebastian further adds that 375,000 Moors took refuge in France from the divine vengeance. His generosity with his numerals equals his liberality with miracles, but is more confusing. The result of the battle, however, was most definite. Al-Khaman and his colleague Suleiman were both killed. *a*

Oppas, too, is said to have been taken prisoner, and justly put to death for his treachery. This was splendid success; but it was almost equalled by the defeat of Manuza. This chief, who was then governor of a northern city, hearing of the disastrous defeat of his countrymen, and apprehensive that the enemy would soon be upon him, ordered his troops to retreat; but he was overtaken, defeated, and slain by the Asturian hero. These memorable events fixed the destiny of the infant kingdom; they were the first of a succession of triumphs which, though sometimes tardy, and often neutralised by accident, ended in the final expulsion of the invaders from the peninsula. The Asturias were now left in the undisturbed possession of the Christians, nor were the Mohammedans for some years in any disposition to assail their formidable neighbours.

The remainder of Pelayo's reign is unknown: it was probably passed in peace. He died in 737, and was buried in the church of St. Eulalia, at Cangas de Onis. Of Favila, the son and successor of Pelayo, nothing is known beyond his brief reign and tragical death. In 739, he was killed by a boar while hunting near the church of the Holy Cross, which he had founded.

ALFONSO THE CATHOLIC (739–757 A.D.)

Alfonso I, surnamed the Catholic, a son-in-law of Pelayo, descended, we are told, from Leuvigild, was the next prince on whom the suffrages of the Asturians fell: not that Favila left no children; but they were doubtless of tender age, and therefore unfitted for bearing so heavy a burden as the duties of monarchy in times so critical.[1] Besides, among these rude mountaineers, hereditary right seems to have been as much unknown as among their Gothic fathers; the crown, however, was always confined to the same family, and the election was generally sure to fall on the next prince in succession, provided he was not disqualified for the dignity either by age, or impotence of body or of mind.

Though no record remains of Alfonso's battles with the Arabs, it is certain that he must have been victor in several; for he made ample additions to his territories. Lugo, Orense, and Tuy, in Galicia; Braga, Oporto, Viseu, and Chaves, in Lusitania; Leon, Astorga, Simancas, Zamora, Salamanca, and Ledesma, in the kingdom of Leon; Avila, Sepulveda, Segovia, Osma, Corunna del Conde, Lara, and Saldaña, in Castile — these, and many other places of less note, were reduced by him. It appears, however, that he acted with cruelty towards the Mohammedan inhabitants, whom he exterminated to make rcom for his Christian colonists.[2] Biscay, too, and Navarre, obeyed Alfonso; so that his kingdom extended from the western shores of Galicia into Aragon, and from the Cantabrian Sea to the southern boundary of the Tierra de Campos; that is, over about one-fourth of all Spain. To account for the rapidity and extent of these conquests — conquests, however, which for the most part were frequently lost and regained in succeeding wars, — the reader has only to remember the civil dissensions of Mohammedan Spain some years prior to the accession of the caliph Abd ar-Rahman.

But Alfonso was not merely a conqueror: the colonies which he established, the towns which he founded or restored, the churches which he built or repaired, are justly adduced as signal monuments of his patriotism and religious zeal. Hence the appellation of "Catholic" — an appellation which continues at the present day. His end happened in 757.[h]

In the chronicle of Alfonso the reign of the first Alfonso is treated with great reverence and his death thus described :

"In the nineteenth year of the reign of Alfonso the Catholic, of the era 791, of the Incarnation of our Lord 753, of the empire of Constantine 15, and of the Alarabes since Muhammed was their king, 132, it befel that King Alfonso, having populated such places as he saw he could maintain, and laboured ever to serve God as far as in him lay, and to maintain his kingdom in peace and justice, fell sick and died, and rendered his soul to God, and at the hour of his death voices were heard in the air singing, 'The righteous perisheth and no man layeth it to heart, and merciful men are taken away, none considering that the righteous is taken away from the evil to come. He shall enter into peace.'[3] And King Alfonso was buried with great pomp in the town of Cangas with his wife Doña Hermesinda, in the church of Santa Maria of that town."[k]

---

[1] Mariana[i] says, that Alfonso inherited in virtue of Pelayo's will. This is one of the assertions so common in this writer, without the shadow of a foundation. Equally unfounded is the assertion that he inherited in right of his wife, Hermesinda, though that circumstance would doubtless have some weight with the electors. His best claim was, that "in tempore Egicani et Witizani regum, princeps militiæ fuit," according to Sebastian.[f]

[2] "Dunham,[h] quoting Sebastian of Salamanca,[f] omnes Arabes occupatores civitatum interficiens, says placidly, 'Such an extermination of the Mohammedan inhabitants to make room for his Christian colonists was a just retribution on the heads of the followers of a sanguinary faith.' A strange nineteenth century Christian gloss! If such things can be written in 1832, it is hardly surprising that the retributive justice practised in the mountains should have been somewhat one-sided in 750." — BURKE.[g]

[3] Isaiah lvii, 1-2. In a note upon this Dunham[h] says, "Not a single historian of Spain, from Bishop Sebastian[f] to Masdeu[l] and Ortiz,[m] has ventured to express his disbelief in this miracle."]

ALFONSO THE CHASTE AND BERNARDO DEL CARPIO

Fruela I (757–768) Alfonso's son, made Oviedo his capital. To strengthen his position, endangered by the civil distractions of his reign, he obtained his recognition as king of the Asturias and Oviedo from the caliph of Cordova in exchange for an annual tribute. He was very pious, but killed his own brother, and his difficulties were ended only by his assassination. Four usurpers, Aurelio, Silo, Mauregato, and Bermudo I, followed one another on his throne and continued to pay the tribute to Cordova, coupled, the legend says, with the yearly present of one hundred virgins. Alfonso II, called the Chaste, is credited with putting an end to this humiliating relation to Cordova. He was the son of Fruela I and began his reign in 791 by vigorously repulsing a Moorish invasion. He added to the kingdom on the southern frontier, but his relations with Charlemagne constitute the chief interest of his reign. He is said to have offered to make the Frankish monarch his heir, in return for the latter's assistance against the Moors, and Louis le Débonnaire, Charlemagne's son, twice led an army into Spain, which conquered the "Spanish Mark." But Alfonso's promise to Charlemagne was disapproved by the nobles; whereupon (so the Spanish writers affirm), a quarrel ensued between the Franks and the Spaniards of Oviedo. With this quarrel they connect the great battle of Roncesvalles, where Charlemagne's forces under his nephew Roland were defeated and Roland was slain. But this battle is assigned by Arab writers to 778 A.D., thirteen years before the accession of Alfonso.[a]

Of the legendary slaughter, of the heroism of Roland, of the valour of Bernardo del Carpio, of the hundred and one stories which have been embroidered upon the simple happening of this mountain ambuscade, no account can be given here; but at least one important fact comes out of the legend, namely, that Spaniards of all sorts and races, though divided enough to be constantly fighting among themselves, had now, for the first time in their history, the early promptings of the nationality of soil, as apart from that of faith or tribal connection, sufficiently strong to permit of a coalition against a foreigner as such. This feeling was again demonstrated a few years later (797), when Alfonso II, encouraged by his successful raids against the Moors in the south, bethought him to beg the aid of Charlemagne to establish himself in his new conquest, even as tributary of the Frankish emperor. But this the Spanish-Gothic nobles would not endure, and incontinently locked up their king in a monastery until he promised that no foreigner should ever be allowed to interfere in struggles on the soil of Spain.[b]

Alfonso the Chaste was succeeded in 842 by Ramiro I, son of King Bermudo. His election was disputed but he put down this as other rebellions. He repelled the Norse invaders, who then ravaged the Moslem coast. His alleged victories over the Saracens are not recorded by Arab historians. In 850 his son Ordoño I succeeded him. He won a battle at Clavijo — the great victory at the same place credited to his father being pure legend. He unintentionally aided the Moslems by defeating the Arab rebel Musa, but also drove off the hungry Norse pirates and was a famous builder of cities and castles. When he died in 866 he left the whole region from Salamanca to the Bay of Biscay to his eldest son.

Alfonso III, who was then only eighteen and was driven from the throne for a time, showed his native vigour by re-establishing himself against his enemies, though his pacificatory schemes to end the rebellions of Navarre ended in the eventual loss of that realm to Spain.[a]

ALFONSO THE GREAT

But Alfonso's victories over the Mohammedans almost atoned for his imprudent policy with regard to Navarre — if, indeed, that policy was not the compulsory result of circumstances. He removed the boundary of his dominions from the Douro to the Guadiana, and the territories thus acquired were possessed by his successors above a century, until the time of the great Almansor. From 870 to 901, his contests with the enemy — whether with the wickedness of the kings of Cordova or their rebellious vassals, who aimed at independence — were one continued series of successes. His last exploit at this period was the destruction, in the battle of Zamora, of a formidable army, led by the rebel Kalib of Toledo, whose ally, Abul-Kassim, fell on the field.

But this great prince, if glorious in his contests with the natural enemy, was unable to contend with his rebellious barons, headed by his still more rebellious son Garcia. At the prospect of a civil war, the king no longer wished to uphold his rights. Having convoked an assembly at Bordes, in the Asturias, in 910, he solemnly renounced the crown in favour of Don Garcia, who passed at once from a prison to a throne. To his second son, Ordoño, he granted the government of Galicia; and another, Fruela, he confirmed in that of Oviedo. These concessions were, doubtless, extorted from him — a

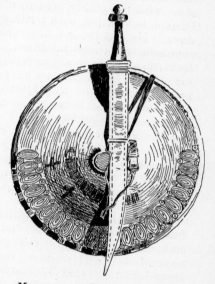

MOHAMMEDAN SWORD AND SHIELD

fact that does not speak much for the firmness of his domestic administration; he appears, like many other princes of his country, to have been great chiefly in the field of battle.

Alfonso did not long survive his abdication. Having paid a visit to the shrine of Santiago in Galicia, on his return to Astorga he solicited permission and adequate forces from his son to make a final irruption into the Mohammedan territories. Both were granted; and in laying waste the possessions of the enemy, he had the consolation of reflecting that he had done great service to the church, and left another signal remembrance of his valour before his departure. He died at Zamora, at the close of the year 910; leaving behind him the reputation of one of the most valiant, magnanimous, and pious sovereigns that Spain ever produced.

ALFONSO'S SUCCESSORS

Of Garcia, the successor of Alfonso III, little more is known than that he transferred the seat of sovereignty from Oviedo to Leon; made a successful irruption into the territories of the misbelievers; and died in 914. The nobles and bishops of the kingdom — henceforth called the kingdom of Leon — having met, according to custom, for the purpose of nominating a successor, placed the royal crown on the head of Ordoño, brother of the deceased Garcia. Ordoño II, under the reigns both of his father and brother, had distinguished himself against the Mohammedans; and he resolved that no one should say his head was weakened by a crown. In 917 he advanced towards the Guadiana, stormed the town of Alhange, which is above Merida, put the garrison to the sword, made the women and children captives, and gained abundant spoil. With the wealth thus acquired he founded the magnificent cathedral of Leon. In a subsequent expedition he ruined Talavera, and defeated a Mohammedan army near its walls. Indignant at these disasters, Abd ar-Rahman III assembled a powerful army, not only from all parts of Mohammedan Spain, but from Africa; but this immense host was also defeated, under the walls of San Pedro de Gormaz. In a subsequent battle, however, which appears to have been fought the same year in Galicia, victory declared for neither party. Nearly three years afterwards (in 921), Ordoño was entirely defeated in the battle of Val-de-Junquera, whither he had advanced to aid the king of Navarre. He took his revenge for this disaster by an irruption into Andalusia, which he laid waste from the Navas de Tolosa to within a day's journey of Cordova. Soon after his return to Leon, the king committed a rigorous but treacherous act of justice. Four counts of Castile, whom he suspected of disaffection, were put to death. Ordoño died in 923, immediately after his third marriage with a princess of Navarre.

Fruela II, brother of Ordoño, was elected in preference to the children of the deceased king. Alfonso IV, who succeeded in 925, in preference to the sons of Fruela II, is represented as a prince more addicted to piety than to ambition. In the sixth year of his reign, he renounced the vanities of the world, resigned the sceptre into the hands of his brother Ramiro, and retired into the monastery of Sahagun. The following year, however, he forsook his cell, and, with a considerable force, hastened to Leon to reclaim the throne. His brother compelled him to surrender, and again consigned him to his monastery, with three princes (the sons of Fruela II) his counsellors. In accordance with the laws of the Visigoths, the punishment of death was commuted to all four by the loss of their eyes. Alfonso survived his misfortune about two years and a half.

Ramiro II, who ascended the throne in 930, is chiefly distinguished for his wars with the misbelievers. He gained a considerable advantage over Abd ar-Rahman III at Simancas. Like most of his predecessors, Ramiro had also to struggle with internal discord. The dependent count of Castile, Fernan Gonsalez, and one Diego Nuñez, a count also in the same province, for reasons with which history (however communicative romance may be) does not acquaint us, revolted against him. The king marched against them, seized their persons, and confined them in two separate fortresses. His displeasure was not of long duration: he suffered the counts to resume their offices on their taking the usual oaths of obedience; and he even married his eldest son, Ordoño, to Urraca, daughter of Fernan Gonsalez. To that son, on the vigil of the Epiphany, in the year 950, he resigned the crown: his growing illness convinced him that he had not long to live; he therefore assumed the penitential garb, and passed his few remaining days in religious retirement.

Ordoño III had scarcely ascended the throne before he was troubled by the ambitious projects of his younger brother, Don Sancho. That prince, wishing to share the sweets of power, modestly requested that the government of one or two provinces might be confided to him; and on the refusal of the king, he persuaded Garcia of Navarre and the count of Castile to espouse his interests. That Fernan Gonsalez, the father-in-law of the rightful sovereign, whose forfeited life had been spared by the generosity of that sovereign's father, should thus conspire against Ordoño, proves the infamy of his character; neither gratitude nor oaths had any influence over this unprincipled governor. But on this occasion treason and perjury met with deserved failure: Sancho and the count, at the head of the Castilians and Navarrese, in vain invaded the territories of Leon; they found Ordoño so well prepared to receive them that they retreated without risking a single battle. Incensed at this conduct of his vassal, the king repudiated his wife Urraca, and immediately married Elvira, a lady connected with the chief families of Leon. Fernan Gonsalez was now compelled to bow the knee before him. With equal success he triumphed over the Galicians, who rebelled. He died in 955.

Sancho I, surnamed from his corpulency the Fat, now arrived at the summit of his ambition. But by the retributive justice of heaven he was doomed to bear, and in a still heavier degree, the burden of anxiety which he had laid on his brother and predecessor. Aided by the restless count of Castile, whose daughter, the divorced Urraca, he had married, Ordoño, son of Alfonso IV, aspired to the throne. Despairing of success by open arms, the two rebels artfully seduced the troops of Sancho from their allegiance, and persuaded them to join the intruder. This unexpected event deprived the king of the means of resistance, compelled him to flee secretly for his life, and raised Ordoño IV to a precarious dignity. The exiled Sancho sought the aid of his maternal uncle, the king of Navarre. But instead of an army to regain his rightful possessions, he received the consoling admonition that he ought to submit with patience to the dispensations of heaven; and that if he could not regain his kingdom, he might at least rid himself of his excessive corpulency, with which he appears to have been seriously inconvenienced. As no Christian leech could be found skilful enough to effect the change, and as the physicians of Cordova were renowned over all Europe, he wrote to Abd ar-Rahman III for permission to visit that capital. It was readily granted: Sancho was courteously received and magnificently entertained by the caliph; by the juice of certain herbs in a short time he was effectually rid of his cumbrous mass of flesh, and restored to his former lightness and agility.[1]

But this was not the only advantage which Sancho derived from his residence in the court of the caliph. He so won the favour of Abd ar-Rahman and the Moslem chiefs that they wished to restore him. At the head of his new allies the king returned to Leon, and was everywhere received with open arms. The tyranny of the intruder had rendered him obnoxious; his cowardice made him contemptible to the people. In utter hopelessness of aid from any of his former subjects, he retired into the Mohammedan territories, where he ended his days in misery. The restored king did not long survive his good fortune. In an expedition against Gonsalo Sanchez, count of Galicia, who aspired to render that government independent of Leon, he was poisoned under the mask of hospitality by that perfidious rebel, after a troubled reign of twelve years.

As Ramiro III was only five years of age on the death of his father, his education fell to the care of his aunt, Doña Elvira, abbess of the convent of San Salvador, who also appears to have been regent of the kingdom. His

[1] *Ipsi Agareni herbam attulerunt, et crassitudinem ejus abstulerunt à ventre ejus, et ad pristinam levitatis astutiam reductus*, etc. — SAMPIRO.[n] It is a pity the Mohammedan doctors did not leave the prescription behind them.

minority offers little that is interesting, if we except a predatory irruption of the Normans, in 968. As Ramiro grew in years, the qualities which he exhibited augured anything but good to his people. He became so odious to the nation that the counts of Castile, Leon, and Galicia threw off their allegiance to him, and proclaimed in Compostella Prince Bermudo, grandson of Fruela II. Ramiro immediately assembled an army, and marched against his rival, whom he encountered near Monterroso in Galicia, in 982. The contest, though long and bloody, was indecisive ; so that both kings, afraid of renewing it, retired to their respective courts — Ramiro to Leon, and Bermudo to Santiago. The calamities arising from this civil strife were increased by the hostile inroads of Almansor, the celebrated hajib of Hisham II, who now began a career of unrivalled military splendour, and who was destined to prove the most formidable enemy the Christians had experienced since the time of Tarik and Musa. Fortunately, however, for the distracted state, Ramiro did not long survive his return to Leon : his death again consolidated the regal power.

In the reign of this prince (in 970) died the famous Fernan Gonsalez, count of Castile, whose fruitless efforts after independence have been already noticed. His fame arises not so much from the real as from the romantic exploits with which the fertility of fiction has invested him.

As mention has been frequently made of the counts of Castile, and as that government is about to form a conspicuous portion of Spanish history, the subject may be properly introduced here.

ORIGIN OF CASTILE

Ancient Cantabria, which the writers of the eighth century usually termed Bardulia, and which, at this period, stretched from the Biscayan Sea to the Douro, towards the close of the same century began to be called Castella — doubtless from the numerous forts erected for the defence of the country by Alfonso I. As the boundaries were gradually removed towards the south, by the victories of the Christians, the same denomination was applied to the new as well as to the former conquests, and the whole continued subject to the same governor, who had subordinate governors dependent on him. Of the first governors or counts, from the period of its conquest by that prince in 760 to the reign of Ordoño I (a full century), not even the names are mentioned in the old chroniclers ; the first we meet with is that of Count Rodrigo, who is known to have possessed the dignity at least six years, viz., from 860 to 866.

Bermudo II, who, on the death of Ramiro, in 982, was acknowledged king of Leon, had little reason to congratulate himself on his elevation, since his reign was one of the most disastrous in the national annals — distracted alike by domestic rebellion and foreign invasion. The fierce Almansor laid waste the greater part of his kingdom, entered his very capital, and forced him to seek refuge in the heart of the Asturias. He died in 999.

Alfonso V was only five years of age on the death of his father ; and the government was consequently entrusted to a regent. That regency is eventful, from the defeat of Almansor in 1001 — a defeat which not only occasioned the death of that hero, but which was the forerunner of the fall of Cordova. In the dissensions which followed among the candidates for the throne of Hisham, the Christian princes of Spain embraced different sides, as their interests or inclinations dictated. In 1010, Alfonso was imprudent enough to confer the hand of his sister on Muhammed, king of Toledo — a prince who was subsequently raised to the throne of Cordova, but was soon deposed and put to death by Hisham. As the king of Leon grew in years, he endeavoured to repair the disasters which had been occasioned by the hostile inroads of the Arabs: he rebuilt and repeopled his capital, whither the seat of government was again transferred from Oviedo. His good intentions, however, were not a little thwarted by the rebellion of Count Sancho Garces of Castile. In 1021, Don Sancho died: his son, Don Garcia, a mere child, succeeded him. With Don Garcia ended the counts of Castile — which was thenceforth to be governed by kings, and to remain more than two centuries dissevered from Leon. Alfonso carried his arms into Portugal, and laid siege to Viseu, then held by the Mohammedans. He was mortally wounded by an arrow from the ramparts.

SANCHO EL MAYOR

Like his father, Bermudo III, though already married to the infanta of Castile, was at a tender age on his accession. Of this circumstance advantage was unworthily taken by Sancho el Mayor, king of Navarre, who, not satisfied with assuming the sovereignty of Castile in right of his queen, Doña Muña Elvira, the elder sister of the queen of Leon, and daughter of Don Garcia, the last count of Castile, made a hostile irruption into the states of his brother-in-law. Having passed the Pisuerga, the western boundary of Castile, he conquered as much of Leon as lay between that river and the Cea. Peace was, however, made on the condition that the king of Leon should confer the hand of his sister, Doña Sancha, on Don Ferdinand, one of King Sancho's sons. But this peace appears to have been subsequently broken, doubtless through the ambition of the enterprising Navarrese; for, according to the Complutensian *p* and Toledan *q* annals, that king in 1034 possessed Astorga, and indeed most of the country as far as Galicia. Yet what need of conquest? As Bermudo continued childless, the wily monarch might safely cherish the hope that the crown of Leon would devolve on the brows of his son in right of the infanta, his daughter-in-law.

On the death of Sancho, in 1035, his ample states were thus divided: to Garcia he left the kingdom of Navarre, the lordship of Biscay (which had been hitherto annexed to Castile), and a part of Rioja; to Ferdinand he bequeathed the new kingdom of Castile, and the conquests he had made between the Pisuerga and the Cea; to Ramiro fell the states of Aragon, which had hitherto continued a stateship as much dependent on Navarre as Castile on Leon; to another son, Gonsalo, he left Ribagorza, with some forts in Aragon. This policy could not fail to be followed by fatal results. While Ramiro made war on his brother of Navarre, Ferdinand I was summoned to the defence of the conquests which he held beyond the Pisuerga, and which Bermudo resolved again to incorporate with the kingdom of Leon. Aided by some auxiliary troops under his brother Garcia, he encountered Bermudo on the banks of the Carrion. The battle, which was fought in 1037, was sanguinary and long-continued; until the king of Leon impatiently spurred his horse into the midst of the hostile squadrons, and fell mortally wounded by the thrust of a lance.

With Bermudo III ended the male line of the house of Leon. This prince deserved a better fate than that of falling by hostile hands at the premature age of nineteen. The zeal with which he rebuilt churches and monasteries; the valour which he exhibited against the Mohammedans of Portugal, from whom he took several fortresses; the firmness with which, even at that early age, he enforced the administration of justice; and his affability of disposition, rendered him deservedly dear to his people.[h]

THE HISTORY OF CASTILE (1037-1109 A.D.)

After this fateful battle on the Carrion, in which Bermudo fell, Ferdinand, who had taken Bermudo's sister to wife, seized upon the whole of Leon and its dependencies and united them with the rest of his dominions to form the kingdom of Castile.

His solemn coronation at Leon ushered in a new epoch in the history of Christian Spain. To pacify the Leonese, who were profoundly aggrieved at the loss of their supremacy, he caused an assembly of the estates to be held at Coyanza, and there confirmed all the civil and ecclesiastical privileges and liberties which had come down to them from earlier times, and added others. At the same time he augmented the defensive armaments of his dominions, with the twofold object of repressing rebellion and making war upon the Saracens.

His elder brother, Garcia, cast envious glances at the flourishing neighbour country, which rose steadily to greater heights of prosperity and power under Ferdinand's wise governance. He was mortified that his hereditary kingdom of Navarre should be ousted from the dominant position it had taken under his great father. He therefore laid snares in his brother's way and embarrassed his dominion by perpetual intrigues till at length a fratricidal war broke out between them. The hatred he bore his brother led Garcia to conclude an alliance with the emir of Saragossa and Tudela. But the battle of Atapuerca (1054), not far from Burgos, decided the struggle in Ferdinand's favour; Garcia was slain by a lance-thrust, the Navarrese were routed, and most of their Moorish auxiliaries killed or taken prisoners. Ferdinand then added the district on the right bank of the Ebro to his own dominions, and left the rest of the kingdom to the late king's son, Sancho III.

Having thus tranquillised his own kingdom and assured its safety, he endeavoured to extend it southwards by making war upon the infidels. He destroyed the fortresses in the northern provinces of what is now the kingdom of Portugal, crossed the Douro, and took Lamego, Viseu, and other fortified towns, under whose walls Christian and Moslem had so often measured their strength in days gone by. These successes inflamed the Castilians with martial ardour and religious enthusiasm and made them eager for fresh ventures. Having first secured the consent of his knights and nobles in an assembly of the estates, the king conquered a chain of fortified towns on the eastern frontier of Castile which had long served the enemy as a *point d'appui*, and then pressed forward into the heart of the Moorish provinces. He laid the country waste, and spread terror as far as Andalusia. The aged ruler of Seville purchased peace with rich gifts, among which were the relics of St. Isidore, which Ferdinand buried with great pomp at Leon in the church he had built and dedicated to the saint.

Ferdinand crowned his glorious career by the conquest of the great fortified city of Coimbra, which for six months had offered a stubborn resistance. The soul of the monarch overflowed with martial ardour and religious devo-

THE ALHAMBRA

[1064–1072 A.D.]

tion. In time of peace he was to be seen devoutly kneeling at the altar and joining in the chants of the priests. War was likewise a religious act in his eyes. With the sword he desired to maintain the honour of God among the infidels and win a heavenly crown for himself. Returning stricken with disease from one of his campaigns, the pious king had himself carried into the church of St. Isidore, where he laid aside the insignia of royalty, and, wrapped in the garment of a penitent, passed away in the arms of the priests, in 1065.

At an assembly of the estates, held a few years before, he had made arrangements for the succession and for the partition of his dominions. According to these, Castile passed to Sancho II, his first-born son; Leon and Asturias to Alfonso, his favourite; Galicia and the newly conquered districts as far the Douro to Garcia, the youngest. The cities of Zamora and Toro he assigned to his two daughters, Urraca and Elvira, and conferred on them the patronage of all abbeys in the kingdom. We know from the romance of *The Cid* — who in the reigns of Ferdinand and his sons performed those prodigies of valour which later generations celebrated in song — that shortly after his father's death Sancho made war upon his brothers with the intention of seizing their dominions for himself.[1] After several battles Alfonso and Garcia were stripped of their possessions and compelled to flee to Toledo and Seville. All the country from the range of the Pyrenees to the shores of the west Atlantic Ocean, which Ferdinand had acquired partly by inheritance and partly by conquest, thus fell under the sway of his son Sancho. Only the rocky stronghold of Zamora still owned allegiance to the princess Urraca, and afforded a safe refuge to the adherents of the fugitive king Alfonso and other malcontents.

Sancho resolved to conquer this city too, for fear it should become a centre and bulwark of rebellion; but was treacherously

KNIGHT OF THE ORDER OF ST. IAGO

murdered under its walls by the lance of a traitor knight, Vellido Dolfo by name. His army speedily dispersed; only a band of brave Castilians loyally kept guard over the king's body and bore it to the abbey of San Salvador at Oña, where it was solemnly committed to the earth. On receiving the tidings of his brother's murder, Alfonso fled secretly from Toledo, where he had been hospitably entertained, and took possession of Sancho's kingdom. Garcia, the younger brother, also came in haste, hoping to regain Galicia, the share his father had bequeathed him. But Alfonso, who was no less ambitious and unjust than the murdered Sancho, had his brother perfidiously seized on his arrival, and kept him in captivity, loaded with fetters, for the rest of his life.

[1 Previously to this he waged "the war of the Three Sanchos," so called from the fact that he, Sancho of Castile, attacked his cousin Sancho of Navarre, who called in the aid of Sancho of Aragon; and together the latter Sanchos defeated the Castilian, in 1068.]

Alfonso VI was now master of the whole of his father's kingdom of Castile, Leon, and Galicia; and when his royal cousin of Navarre, a few years later, fell a victim to conspirators, he joined the king of Aragon in the conquest and partition of the bereaved kingdom; and after its brief hour of glory it was long before Navarre was again counted among independent states.

Henceforward history follows the fortunes of the two kingdoms of Castile and Aragon, which rose upon its ruins. Side by side with them Catalonia flourished in the east, blest with culture and prosperity, but exercising no particular influence on the course of events; and towards the end of the century some knightly adventurers laid the foundation of the kingdom of Portugal in the west, the northern part of which Alfonso conferred first on his son-in-law, Raymond of Burgundy, and then on Count Henry, the husband of his natural daughter Theresa, as a fief of the kingdom of Castile.

All these kingdoms turned their arms against the disunited Mohammedan world in the centre and south of the peninsula. When once he had gained secure possession of his kingdom, Alfonso, guided by the judicious advice of his sister Urraca, who always retained great influence over the brother she loved so dearly, endeavoured by the excellence of his administration and legislation to efface the stains that had defiled his path to the throne. He took counsel with honourable and capable men on affairs of state, he delivered the communes from the oppressions of royal officers and judges, abolished the burdensome turnpike toll which had been levied on all pilgrims who visited the famous shrine of Santiago de Compostella and had given occasion for many exactions and abuses, and by the disuse of the Gothic liturgy established in Christian Spain the Roman and hierarchical system of church government, which had been striving to extend its sway over all the countries of Europe ever since the time of Gregory VI. By the zeal of the Benedictines of Sahagun and the French clergy whom he appointed to many important preferments in the Pyrenean peninsula, the Spanish church was soon brought at all points under the supremacy of Rome.

He then availed himself of dissensions which had arisen amongst Moslem rulers to carry his arms into the heart of the Moorish states. After the conquest of Toledo he was able to cherish the proud hope of extending Christian rule over the whole peninsula. The arrival of the Almoravids, however, put an end to his triumphant progress. After a long reign which succeeding generations have ever borne in mind as a period of glory, justice, and general prosperity, Alfonso VI died in 1109 of a broken heart at the defeat of Ucles and the loss of his only son. His daughter Urraca, queen of Leon and Castile, who governed the country during her son's minority, espoused Alfonso I, king of Aragon, as her second husband. But instead of strengthening the unity and power of Christian Spain, this alliance led to furious civil wars which served to strengthen and prolong Moslem dominion.

ORIGIN AND EARLIEST HISTORY OF THE KINGDOM OF ARAGON

On the right bank of the river Noguera, which takes rise in the Pic de la Maladetta, the loftiest summit of the Pyrenees, and flows southward along the frontier between the districts now known as Catalonia and Aragon, to mingle its waters with the Segre, had lain from time immemorial the county of Ribagorza. The owners of this land, men of strong arm and devout faith, strove with all their might to check the warlike enterprise of the Moslem, who possessed a sure centre and stronghold in the governorship of Saragossa.

Their family possessions were broken up by repeated partitions, but various members of the ancient stock were scattered over the whole country north of the Ebro and formed fresh alliances and made fresh acquisitions by marriage and inheritance. Thus the line of the counts of Aragon, who ruled the town of Jaca and the province of Sobrarbe, early entered into matrimonial alliances with the family of the counts of Ribagorza. The royal house of Navarre was also connected by marriage with both families, and, on the extinction of the male line in both at the end of the tenth century and the beginning of the eleventh, King Sancho, who was in a position to enforce the claims of kinship with the sword, took possession of Aragon, Sobrarbe, and Ribagorza, and on his death bequeathed the province of Aragon, as has already been stated, to his natural son Ramiro (1035).

The latter assumed the title of "king of Aragon," and endeavoured by fraud and force to gain a fitting extension to the territory of his kingdom. An attempt which he made to wrest Navarre from his elder brother Garcia was frustrated, but, on the other hand, after Gonsalo, the other brother, had been assassinated, he succeeded in gaining possession of his territories of Sobrarbe and Ribagorza, whether by popular election or otherwise cannot be certain. Ramiro also took the field against the Saracens, but the power and personal abilities of the emirs of Saragossa (Mundhir ben Yahya and the Banu Hud) prevented him from gaining any brilliant successes. At the same time he continued to give proof of his piety by founding abbeys and giving gifts to the church in the spirit of the counts before him. The abbey of San Juan de la Peña was the most favoured sanctuary of all, and was richly endowed with lands and revenues, privileges and liberties by the king and the nobles of Aragon. The donation which the king had sent to Pope Alexander II when he introduced the Roman liturgy into Aragon was declared by Gregory VII to be a tribute due to the apostolic see.

Ramiro fell in battle against the Saracens at the siege of Grados (1063), and his son Sancho Ramirez, a young prince full of energy, courage, and adventurous spirit, ascended the throne. He promptly turned his arms against the Moors. Having first wrested from them all the possessions they held in the mountainous districts of Aragon, Sobrarbe, and Ribagorza, he came down upon the fertile plains watered by the Cinca, Gallego, and other tributaries of the Ebro, and after a fierce engagement in which his ally, Count Ermengol of Urgel, lost his life (1065), took the important city of Barbastro which, though lost again a short time after, finally passed into the power of the Aragonese, and provided them with a favourably situated base for subsequent conquests. Soon afterwards King Sancho III of Navarre, the son of Garcia, was murdered at Peñalen by a band of conspirators headed by his ambitious brother Raymond and his sister Ermesenda (1076). As his children were not of age and the Navarrese refused to acknowledge the fratricide as their sovereign, the two kings Alfonso VI of Castile and Sancho Ramirez of Aragon marched into the neighbour kingdom, put Raymond to flight and divided the country between them; the country as far as the Ebro being united to Aragon, and Rioja, with Najera and Calahorra and the Basque provinces of Alava, Guipuzcoa, and Biscay falling to the share of Alfonso VI of Castile and Leon.

Sancho then undertook a war of revenge against the emir Ahmed Muktadir of Saragossa, who had given shelter to the fugitive regicide Raymond.

Having first seized some favourably situated places on the Ebro he advanced upon the city of Huesca, which, with the surrounding district, lay like a broad wedge driven into Aragonese territory, fortified with many strongholds and severing the north of his dominions from the south.   In a war which lasted for several years and which was marked with every accompaniment of horror, the brave king succeeded in subjugating a large part of this district and making a safe road to the very walls of Huesca by a succession of skilfully planned fortifications.   But he was not destined to witness the fall of the city ; he received his death-wound in the siege from the enemy's arrows (1094).   His valiant son Pedro carried on with vigour and energy the work which his father had begun and urgently enjoined on him with his dying breath.

The Moslems strained every nerve to save the bulwark of their dominion in northern Spain.   The emir Ahmed Mostain led a great confederate army, which numbered not only Almoravids but Christian auxiliaries in its ranks, into the field against Aragon.   But Pedro's victory at Alcoraz decided the fate of Huesca.   In the very year (1096) in which western Christendom was making ready to drive the infidels out of Jerusalem, Huesca and all the country north of the Ebro fell into the hands of the Christians of Spain. Henceforward the fall of Saragossa could only be a question of time, a question which would have been decided earlier than it was if a civil war had not broken out between Alfonso I of Aragon (Alfonso VII of Leon) who succeeded Pedro in 1104, and his wife Queen Urraca of Castile.[o]

Before taking up the story of the war of Urraca and Alfonso, we may consider the exploits of the most famous warrior in Spanish history, the Cid, whose fame was so overgrown with romance that it became the fashion to deny that such a man ever existed in reality.   But the critical historian who has robbed us of so many traditions has restored to us the Cid.   His deeds are so typical of the period that they may claim some liberality of space, for in the words of H. E. Watts,[r] "The history of mediæval Spain without the Cid would be something more barren than the Iliad without Achilles.[a]

BURKE'S ESTIMATE OF THE CID

The three favourites of mediæval Spanish romance, says the Señor Lafuente,[cc] Bernardo del Carpio, Fernan Gonzalez, and the Cid, have this at least in common, that they were all at war with their lawful sovereigns, and fought their battles independently of the crown.   Hence their popularity in Spain.   The Castilians of the Middle Ages were so devoted to their independence, so proud of their *fueros*, such admirers of personal prowess, that they were disposed to welcome with national admiration those heroes who sprang from the people, who defied and were ill-treated by their kings.

The Cid is the only knight-errant that has survived the polished satire of Cervantes.   For his fame was neither literary nor aristocratic ; but like the early Spanish proverbs, in which it is said he took so great a delight, it was embedded deep in the hearts of the people.   And although the memory of his religious indifference may not have added to his popularity in the sixteenth century in Spain, it is a part of his character which must be taken into account in gauging the public opinion of earlier days.   From the close of the eighth century to the close of the fifteenth, the Spanish people, Castilians and Aragonese, were if anything less bigoted than the rest of Europe. The influence of their neighbours the Moors, and of their Arab toleration

[*ca.* 1050–1099 A.D.]

could not be without its effect upon a people naturally free, independent, and self-reliant ; and the Cid, who was certainly troubled with no religious scruples in the course of his varied career, and who, according to a popular legend affronted and threatened the pope on his throne in St. Peter's, on account of some fancied slight, could never have been the hero of a nation of bigots.

To judge the Cid, even as we now know him, according to any code of modern ethics, is supremely unreasonable. To be sure that, even now, we know him as he was is supremely presumptuous. But that Ruy Diaz was a great man, and a great leader of men, a knight who would have shocked modern poets, and a free lance who would have laughed at modern heroes, we can have no manner of doubt. That he satisfied his contemporaries and himself ; that he slew Moors and Christians as occasion required, with equal vigour and absolute impartiality ; that he bearded the king of Leon in his Christian council, and that he cozened the king of Saragossa at the head of his Moslem army ; that he rode the best horse and brandished the best blade in Spain ; that his armies never wanted for valiant soldiers, nor his coffers for goldpieces ; that he lived "my lord the challenger," the terror of every foe, and that he died rich and respected in the noble city that had fallen to his knightly spear — of all this at least we are certain ; and, if the tale is displeasing to our nineteenth century refinement, we must be content to believe that it satisfied the aspirations of mediæval Spain.*g*

THE HISTORICAL CID

The real existence of the Cid and the most important events in his life have been proved by a sufficient, although not by a large number of documents, which, being amplified by Middle Age chroniclers, have formed the basis of later tradition. It is more or less in this traditionary form that the Cid appears, in Spanish history.

Mariana[i] related the chief events of his life as popular tradition has collected them from history and fable, and contented himself with adding, "Some persons hold a large part of this account to be fabulous ; I also relate many more statements than I believe, because I do not dare to pass over in silence what others assert, nor would I like to assert as certain that which I doubt for reasons which compel me to do so and which others have stated."

Prudencio de Sandoval[u] questioned many single items and declared whole episodes to be unhistorical. He was followed by Ferreras.[v] When finally, in 1792, the Augustine Manuel Risco,[w] supported by the *Gesta Roderici Campidocti* which he had discovered, tried to rescue some part of the old traditions, the Jesuit, Juan Francisco de Masdeu, doubted not only the genuineness of this document but the very existence of the Cid. The English historian Dunham[h] was even more firmly sceptical. Robert Southey,[x] who published an English translation of the *Chronicle of the Cid*, tried hard to steer between history and story and rescue as much as possible of the latter.

Victor Aimé Huber[y] has the credit of being the first to distinguish between the historical and mythical elements with great critical ability. The material used by Huber was not materially enriched until the Dutch orientalist R. Dozy[z] discovered in the library at Gotha, in 1844, an Arabic account of the Cid and his most celebrated deed of arms, the conquest of Valencia. This was found in the third volume of a history of literature (*Zakira*) written by the Moorish author Ibn Bassam,[aa] in the year 503 of the

Hegira, according to his statement (1109 A.D.), that is, only ten years after the death of the Cid. It is thus the oldest, the only really contemporary account of the celebrated Spanish hero that we possess, and is of great historical value even though written by an enemy. The Dutch scholar was not satisfied merely to publish the text with a French translation, but also enumerated the known sources in order to distinguish between the historical and the more or less legendary traits of the same and to get as historically accurate a picture as possible of the Cid. At the same time he put entirely too much confidence in the Arabic account, placing himself in fact on the side of the Moors. Hence in order to get a correct idea of the Cid's character one should not follow Dozy blindly, but should rather consider as to how far the Arab historian deserves credence on his own account.

THE CID
(From an old engraving of an alleged portrait)

The date of the Cid's birth is not known. However, it cannot be far from the middle of the eleventh century, certainly not more than ten to twenty years before the battle on the Carrion river (1037), in which Ferdinand I of Castile conquered the allied kings of Leon and Navarre, and Bermudo III, king of Leon, met his death. With this king, who left no descendants, the Visigothic dynasty came to an end, that dynasty which since Pelayo for three hundred years had carried on the struggles of Christian Spain against the superior force of the Moors, under the most variable circumstances, but ever with increasing success. The birth, as well as the youth and first warlike deeds of Rodrigo Diaz de Bivar, later called the Cid,[1] fall in that brilliant period when the kingdom of Spain first acquired a greater power by the union of Castile and Leon and attained a certain moral supremacy over Moorish Spain. In a battle led by the eldest son of the king Sancho, against Sancho of Navarre, the Cid conquered a knight of Navarre in single combat and thus received the surname Campeador, *i.e.*, "Challenger." With the death of Ferdinand I, however (1065), the scarcely established union fell asunder. In his will he divided his kingdom among his five children.

[1 It is a curious fact that this warrior is known to the Spaniards by his Arab name of *Cid* or *Saïd*, that is, lord or leader, while to the Arabs he is known by his Spanish name of *Campeador* or "Challenger."]

Scarcely three years after his father's death Sancho was in open fight with his brother Alfonso at Llantado and won a temporary, though not a decisive victory. On this occasion Rodrigo de Bivar was promoted to be "banner-bearer," *i.e.*, "chief commander" of Sancho's troops. The brothers kept the peace for only three years. Eventually Sancho was assassinated. Since there was no suitable pretendant to the throne, the crown of Castile was finally offered to Alfonso, but only on condition that he take a solemn oath to the effect that he was not a party to Sancho's death. Rodrigo Diaz de Bivar and eleven other knights administered this oath. The king at the same time was seized with a violent dislike towards the Campeador. Policy, however, advised him not to indulge this for the present, but to try to attach this powerful and influential Castilian to himself by showing him favour. He even gave him his cousin Ximena in marriage (the 19th of July, 1074).

Alfonso sent him to the court of Mutamid, the king of Seville, to collect the tribute due him. At the very time of his arrival Mutamid was threatened by an attack from Abdallah, king of Granada, in whose army were several Christian nobles, among them Count Garcia Ordoñez, a prince of royal blood. The Campeador attacked them with his own people, and the Sevillians defeated them and took Garcia Ordoñez and other Castilian knights captive, although he freed them again after three days. That was enough for his enemies, especially Garcia Ordoñez, to malign him before Alfonso, after his return, saying that he kept a part of their presents for himself. The earlier dislike of the king was revived, and when Rodrigo, in 1081, on his own initiative and without permission undertook an attack on the Moors, the king seized the occasion to banish him. Thus the hero, with whose help the king might have been able to break completely the power of the Moors, was banished from Christian Spain and compelled to lead the life of a warrior chieftain or *condottiere* and even to seek service with the Moors themselves.

Just at this time (October, 1081) the emir Muktadir of Saragossa died, leaving two sons, one of whom, Mutamin, received Saragossa, the other, Mondzir, had Denia, Tortosa, and Lerida. They at once began to dispute each other's possessions. Mondzir allied himself with King Sancho Ramirez of Aragon and Count Berengar of Barcelona. Mutamin won over the Campeador to his cause and found him his surest support. Rodrigo conducted expeditions of incredible boldness and became the terror of the princes allied against Mutamin. The latter besieged the fortress Almenara in overwhelming numbers and reduced it to such straits that Rodrigo himself advised treating for peace, in order to save the garrison, but when Mutamin insisted on holding out he repulsed the enemy in spite of superior force and even took the count of Barcelona captive. His entry into Saragossa was like a triumph, and the emir loaded him with honours and presents. Nevertheless the valiant Castilian would not be bound. As soon as an opportunity offered he tried again to approach King Alfonso. Not until the latter, in his pride and anger, had again repulsed him, did he continue to use his talents of generalship and his personal bravery in the service of Mutamin. He ravaged a large part of Aragon in an expedition lasting five days, and his attacks were executed so swiftly that his followers were usually up and away before the alarm could even be sounded for a repulse. He next attacked Mondzir's possessions and plundered large tracts of territory with the same rapidity. When Sancho of Aragon came to assist his ally, Rodrigo defeated his troops, took sixteen nobles and two thousand soldiers captive and returned again to Saragossa with enormous booty. After Mutamin's death (1085) he continued to serve his son Mostain; but no details have been preserved of his further warlike deeds until 1088. In that year he concluded a contract with Mostain, the object of which was the conquest of Valencia.

In the complicated intrigues for the ownership of the city, the Campeador would seem, according to the account of Dozy,[z] at first to have played a double, not to say a many-sided part. He made a secret compact with Mostain, promising to help him get the city but reserving all booty for himself ; but when Kadir made him rich presents he excused himself to Mostain by saying that an attack on Valencia could not be made without declaring war on Alfonso, and Mostain himself hesitated before such a step. At the same time he sent word to King Alfonso that he still regarded himself as his vassal and that all his expeditions were carried out only for the purpose of weakening the power of the Moors and of supporting an army at their expense, which would later bring the whole land into subjection to the king. So the latter let him keep his troops, with which he occasionally undertook his favourite raids of conquest and plunder. When reproached for them he declared that he did it only to earn his living. In 1089 he went to Castile to have a personal interview with the king. The latter received him graciously, gave him several castles and drew up a document, deeding all the fortresses and lands he should conquer from the Moors to him and his heirs forever. Thereupon the Cid returned to the neighbourhood of Valencia to join his army, which numbered seven thousand picked men.

But the Cid had another mischance with Alfonso. When the latter asked him to take part in an expedition against the castle of Aledo, near Larca, the Cid, through no fault of his own, arrived too late, and the king, although he suffered no injury thereby, allowed himself to be influenced by spiteful insinuations, deprived the brave warrior of his favour, took away the document he had given him the year before, confiscated all his estates, and imprisoned his wife and children. All attempts of the offended Cid to prove his innocence were repulsed ; the only concession which the king made was to give back his wife and children. Again was the Cid obliged to fight his own way as an independent leader, with his own means, and to support his army by plunder. His bravery and ability met with unusual success. Kadir of Valencia paid him annually 120,000 dinares, the lord of Alborracin 10,000, the one of Alpuente the same, the lords of Murviedro and of Segorbe 6,000 each, of Jerica 4,000, of Almenara 3,000. The most important deed of arms in the next period was a brilliant victory over Berengar of Barcelona, who had attacked him unexpectedly but was defeated and himself taken captive with five thousand soldiers. The Cid demanded a high ransom, but set the prisoners free before it could all be paid.

For the sake of Alfonso he broke off the siege of Liria, which had been progressing favourably, but an interview with the suspicious monarch led only to new discord. The latter felt offended on account of a mere trifle and wanted to take the Cid prisoner. When he escaped, the king, in revenge, himself undertook an expedition against Valencia, which to a certain extent was already in the power of the Cid. Rodrigo was deeply offended ; with the speed of lightning he hurled himself on the counties of Najera and Calahorra, whose governor was his most implacable and powerful enemy, Count Garcia Ordoñez, the most important man next to the king. He committed such depredations with fire and sword in his provinces that Alfonso was obliged to abandon the siege of Valencia to protect his own land from Rodrigo's plundering raids. This tragic self-destruction of Spanish force was fortunately brought to an end again by the dissension and strife among the Moors.

[1094–1101 A.D.]

While thus the inhabitants, split up into various parties, were fighting among themselves, some expecting help from one quarter, others from another, the Cid by a sudden attack surrounded the city, cut off all provisions and forced it to surrender on June 15th, 1094, because of most terrible famine. He was at first very lenient towards the conquered, promised them a just administration, and warned his own people to be merciful. Roderigo made Ibn Jahhaf draw up an inventory of all his possessions and swear that he had concealed nothing. Ibn Jahhaf took the oath and declared himself ready to die if anyone found anything not on the list. The oath was a false one. The deceit was soon discovered and then the Cid acted with all the severity of the times. He caused the treacherous and perfidious royal murderer to be burned (May or June, 1095), and with him a number of his friends and associates ; he also wanted to condemn his wife and children to death by burning, but the Christians intervened and obtained their pardon.

Hated as Ibn Jahhaf had been before, he now became a martyr in the eyes of the Moors. Consequently in their accounts the Cid is charged with perfidy and cruelty. Now for the first time was the Cid fully and completely master of this rich and powerful city, the conquest of which was in some respects more important than that of Toledo by Alfonso. In the eyes of the Castilians it was a deed having few parallels, the highest and best which their much-feared warrior-hero achieved in a life so rich in battles. Olocau and Serra, two fortified places of great strategic importance, now fell into his hands and he thought with all seriousness of driving the Moors out of the whole of remaining Spain. An Arab of that time claims to have heard him say : "A Rodrigo lost this peninsula ; another Rodrigo will win it back." The Moors themselves saw these thoughts threateningly embodied in him, and Christian kings had to sue for his friendship.

In 1094 he allied himself with King Pedro of Aragon in order to force the power of the Almoravids further toward the south. At Beira, near Candia, where a Moorish fleet could support the attack of the land army, the Christians were hard pressed ; only the heroism, personal bravery and tact of the Cid revived their sinking confidence and led them to victory, so that the superior force of the enemy was completely defeated and an immeasurable booty fell into their hands. After a short rest in Valencia he marched against Murviedro. Finally on St. John's day, June 24th, 1098, he entered the city, celebrated the new victory with a *Te Deum*, and commanded the laying of the foundation for a St. John's church in commemoration of the event. That he did not pursue selfish ends may be gathered from the testimony of the Mohammedans themselves, who state that his real end was to drive them out of Spain. But for the continuous struggle he carried on for this purpose, especially for the tedious sieges, he had to furnish his own means entirely. Even when disease and weakness did not permit him to carry a sword himself, he did not give up his great plan. But his followers were not so successful as he. They met with Ibn Aisha's army, which had just won a brilliant victory at Cuenca over Alvar Fañez who commanded the royal army of Castile. Even the brave warriors of the Cid, who felt the need of their old leader, succumbed to the victorious might of the Moslems, and only a few of them returned to Valencia.

According to the Arab accounts the Cid died in 1099 from rage and grief at this defeat. For two years after the death of the unconquered warrior his widow Ximena succeeded in holding the city against the repeated attacks of the Almoravids. But in October, 1101, having decided to abandon it, the Christians set it afire in order to spoil the Mohammedan joy of victory.

Mazdali and his army found only smoking ruins when they entered on May 5th, 1102. The body of the Cid was brought by his faithful wife herself and buried in the cloister of San Pedro de Cardeña at Burgos, where she had numberless masses said for the deceased. She outlived him only five years and was likewise buried at Burgos. His son [?] Diego Rodriguez fell in the battle of Consuegra. Of his two daughters one, Christina, married the infante Ramiro of Navarre, the other, Elvira, Raymond IV (Raymond Berengar III) of Barcelona. Through her the Cid became the ancestor of the later royal dynasty of Spain.

One hundred and thirty-six years passed before Valencia was reconquered for Christian Spain by James I of Aragon after a difficult and tedious siege (1238). The heroic life of the Cid, however, did not remain unfruitful during this interval.*bb*

CHRISTIAN SPAIN IN THE TWELFTH CENTURY

The war between Alfonso of Aragon and his wife Queen Urraca of Castile lasted many years and was accompanied by conspiracies and partisan warfare among the nobles, by scandals in the royal palace, by the papal annulment of the marriage, by plunder of the treasures of the church, by the spoliation and impoverishment of the people. Even the queen's death in 1126 did not immediately put an end to the war, for the two Alfonsos (her husband, and the son of her first marriage, Alfonso Raymond) now turned their arms against each other. Finally the clergy negotiated a peace. The two kingdoms were separated, a compromise being effected with regard to the disputed districts. Castile with Leon and Galicia formed the territory of Alfonso VII (or VIII,[1] since his stepfather is also counted amongst the Castilian kings); Aragon and Navarre were left to king Alfonso I (1126).

The Aragonese now once more turned his arms against the Moslem; the proud name of Batallador, "the fighter," which his compatriots bestowed on him, may serve as evidence of the strength and energy with which he pushed on the struggle. [He also assumed the title of emperor.] It has been mentioned that by the conquest of Huesca, his predecessor Pedro had confirmed and consolidated the kingdom of Aragon. Ten years after his death, Tudela on the Ebro was won, and formed an important base for further conquest; but it was only when Alfonso, supported by the knights from the southern kingdom, had conquered the Saracens in several sharp encounters

[1 Burke *g* explains the inconsistent enumerations of the kings of this period as follows:

The curious confusion arising from a twofold or threefold system of numeration of the Alfonsos of Castile and Leon in the twelfth and thirteenth centuries seems to call for some special notice. Dunham[h], Romey[g], and other foreign historians and chronologists, among whom the count de Mas-Latrie[i] must ever be spoken of with the greatest respect, call Alfonso *el Batallador*, of Aragon, Alfonso VII of Leon and Castile, as in right of his wife Urraca; and thus call Alfonso *el Imperador* number VIII; and keep Alfonso III of Castile out of the Leonese or *Junto* numeration altogether. Thus and in other ways confusion has been introduced, and by imperfect explanation still worse confounded.

The following, it is to be hoped, is plain:

Alfonso VI of Leon was the first of the name to reign in Castile; and, as in the course of the next hundred and fifty years the two kingdoms were sometimes under the same king, though not formally united, and sometimes each with a king of its own, the plan has been generally adopted by modern Spanish writers of numbering the Alfonsos of Leon and of Castile consecutively, without regard to the kingdoms over which they reigned, taking no account of the Alfonsos of Aragon. Thus Alfonso *el Sabio* was Alfonso IV of Castile, and Alfonso IX of Leon, but Alfonso X of the consecutive Alfonsos, by which title he is always known. And it is by this numeration that the late king of Spain was Alfonso XII, and his present majesty is Alfonso XIII.]

[1118–1150 A.D.]

and finally, after a siege of seven months, had compelled the surrender of the city of Saragossa, 1118, the bulwark of the Arab rule in the northeast, that the kingdom of Aragon was able to proceed with its political development. Saragossa, so long the seat of a Mohammedan emir, became Alfonso's capital. The principal mosque served henceforth for the worship of the Saviour. The knights and nobles who had stood bravely by the side of the king, as well as the soldiers who had gathered to his banner from beyond the Pyrenees, were richly rewarded.

The Moslems were deeply affected by the loss of Saragossa, the result of their own want of unity; that they might not be entirely driven from the territory of the Ebro they nerved themselves to a general resistance. There was a series of sanguinary conflicts on the Segre and Ebro, and then under their brave commander Yahya ben Gania they won by stratagem the battle of Fraga, July, 1134, with which Alfonso ended his heroic life. His efforts had undermined his strength, and grief at this severe defeat did the rest. He sank on a bed of sickness from which he never rose again.[1]

The existence of the kingdom was endangered by his death. As he was childless he had designated the Christian orders of the knights of the Holy Sepulchre, who had taken the most active share in the struggles against the Saracens and who possessed lands and castles in all parts of the peninsula, as his heirs. But this disposition was not carried into effect.

In the "royal city" of Jaca, the Aragonese elected a brother of the dead man for their king. This was Ramiro II (1134–1137), who had lived in a cloister from his youth; and thus the warrior was replaced by a monk. On the other hand the Navarrese raised to the throne Garcia IV, a scion of their old princely house, and declared their independence of Aragon. Indeed, the priest-king was a feeble substitute for "the fighter"; still he secured the continued existence of Aragon. Immediately after his accession Ramiro espoused Inez, sister of the duke of Aquitaine and Poitou; she bore him a daughter, Petronilla, who at the age of two years was betrothed, on the advice of the grandees, to Raymond Berengar IV [or V] of Barcelona, or Catalonia, and when Ramiro soon after returned to the cloister the count received the regency of Aragon till the age of the bride should make the nuptials possible. The result of this marriage was the lasting union of Aragon and Catalonia[2] under Alfonso II, the son of Raymond and Petronilla.o

Want of space forbids us to give the details of the history of Raymond Berengar's dominions. The district had been conquered by the Moslems in the eighth century, but part of it was recovered for Christianity by the Franks and formed into a province under the name of the Spanish Mark. The various counts soon asserted their independence, and those of Barcelona increasing in power and importance gradually absorbed the dominions of the rest and became masters of the whole of Catalonia.a

FOUNDATION OF THE SPANISH ORDERS OF KNIGHTHOOD

Raymond sought to fulfil the testamentary dispositions of Alfonso by founding a special order of knighthood, modelled on the pattern of the Temple, "for the defence of the Western church and to oppose the Moors

[1] His ambitious assumption of the title of "emperor of Spain" was scarcely justified by his uncertain conquests from the Almoravids and was made ridiculous by his failure to subdue his Christian neighbours in Leon and Castile.g]

[2] Burke g says, "The union of Catalonia with Aragon by the marriage of Queen Petronilla with Raymond Berengar of Barcelona in 1150, was the foundation of the greatness of Spain."]

in Spain," and he bestowed on it large possessions with castles and revenues. As a special Aragonese branch of the order of the Temple, it was under the grand-master of Jerusalem. The large profits which the brethren of the order might hope to derive from the spoils of the Arabs in case of a victory were a powerful incentive to enterprises and expeditions of conquest.

Before this, Raymond IV, Raymond's father, a valiant warrior in the service of Christ, had himself joined the order of the Temple and had granted it extensive lands and rights. With the help of these, and supported by the Catalan knighthood and the Pisans, he had fought against the infidel with courage and success, and in a hotly contested struggle had taken from them many towns and citadels. He had also extended his territory in the north of the Pyrenees and had acquired the countship of Carcassonne, Besalu, Cerdagne, etc. Raymond V was not only the heir to these possessions which he united to Aragon; he continued the war of conquest against the Saracens, now single-handed, now in alliance with his brother-in-law, Alfonso VII (VIII) of Castile, who, like his predecessor, assumed the title of "emperor of Spain" and claimed the suzerainty over the other Christian kingdoms.

The Christians soon again succeeded in winning the upper hand of the Moslems. It was not only that religious enthusiasm, the chivalrous fighting spirit of the time and the prospect of knightly lands and spoil continually attracted fresh combatants to the standard ; but dissensions and disorganisations amongst the disciples of Mohammed facilitated the progress of their arms. One party of the Moors called in the aid of the Castilian king. Alfonso VII did not hesitate to profit by the disorder amongst the Mohammedans. While the Portuguese king conquered Lisbon with the help of the crusaders, the Castilian "emperor," in conjunction with Raymond of Barcelona, Count William of Montpellier, and the Christian chivalry of all the Spanish kingdoms, marched to the coast towns of Almeria, the headquarters of the Mohammedan pirates, invested it on the land side whilst the fleet of the Genoese and Pisans blockaded the harbour, and after a long siege compelled it to surrender. The garrison were put to the sword, and incalculable spoil was carried off. Raymond Berengar fought with like success against the Moslems on the Ebro, where, again supported by the Genoese and Pisans, he took the important city of Tortosa, and then added the whole territory on the river to his kingdom (1148).

Alfonso VII lived to see the hardly won town of Almeria again wrested from Castile. On his return from a military expedition he died in the pass of Muradal, a prince endowed with strength, intelligence, and the love of justice, full of zeal for the Christian faith and generous to churches and cloisters. With him the series of "emperors of Spain" comes to an end (1157).

With the death of Alfonso VII of Castile, and that of Raymond of Aragon and Catalonia, which followed five years later, the Christian kingdoms of the Spanish peninsula again entered on evil times. Whilst the Mohammedan world, united and strengthened under the rule of the Almohades, acquired fresh power in the south and southeast, and won back much of its ancient possessions, in the north the vigour of the attack and resistance was broken by divisions and civil contentions.

Although the kingdom of Aragon and Catalonia passed undivided to the young King Alfonso II, and his suzerainty extended over a great part of Languedoc and the country of Provence which was governed by a relative of the royal family, on the other hand, under the sons and successors of Alfonso VII the Castilian kingdom was dismembered ; for Leon with Galicia and Asturias, and Navarre with the Basque provinces seceded from it and started an independent political existence under their own princes, without paying any further attention to the feudal superiority of Castile. The results of these partitions were intestine disputes and family quarrels which stood the Moslem in good stead.

The divisions and weakness of Spanish Christendom would have gained a still greater ascendency, had not the clergy admonished the knighthood to the struggle against the infidels as a religious duty and kept alive their zeal for the faith. They encouraged the formation of the Spanish orders of knighthood to which the preservation of the Christian kingdoms and the final overthrow of the Mohammedans was principally owing. Besides the order of Calatrava which Raymond, abbot of the monastery of St. Mary at Fitero, founded in 1158 on the model of the Templars and according to the Cistercian rule, another brotherhood of the faith had come into existence in the year 1156. This was subsequently called the order of Alcantara, after its chief fortress. In Galicia the priesthood enrolled a number of warlike robber knights in the order of St. James of Compostella (1175), for the protection of the church of the tomb of St. James (St. Iago) in that city, and laid on them as their most sacred duty the obligation of escorting pilgrims thither.

It was principally the courage and religious enthusiasm of these armed brotherhoods that prevented the Moslem from again bearing the banner of Islam across the Ebro and Douro in the second half of the twelfth century, when Castile was distracted by internal strife, due to the enmity and jealousy of the two princely houses of Lara and Castro, when the Christian kings of the various states turned their arms against each other, when in Catalonia the confusion mounted to such a height that two archbishops of Tarragona were murdered and Portugal and Leon lay under ban and interdict on account of a marriage between near relatives, and anarchy and the right of the strong hand ruled unchecked.

Since the days of the great Almansor no prince had warred against Christian Spain with so much success as the Almohad, Abdul-Mumin, "the commander of the faithful." But when, against the advice of his officers, he risked a battle at Santarem, he suffered a defeat in which he lost his life. But his son Yakub Almansor, a prince whose virtues and great qualities were not inferior to those of his contemporary Saladin, soon avenged his father's death. The Third Crusade increased fanaticism even in the Pyrenean peninsula. Undisciplined hosts of pilgrims landed in the west and south, marking their path by robbery and devastation, and Christian and Saracen were spurred to fresh encounters. Roused by a devastating raid of the archbishop of Toledo against Seville, and by a written challenge of the Castilian king Alfonso "the noble," Yakub Almansor took the field with his whole army. The Christian host, especially the numerous knights of the fraternities, both those of the country and foreign Templars and knights of St. John, opposed him at Alarcon and suffered a complete defeat (1195). The flower of the Christian chivalry were left on the battle-field. Almost all New Castile, as far as the fortress of Toledo, fell into the hands of the infidels ; the mountains and citadels of Guadarrama and the want of provisions alone prevented the Moslems from again penetrating to the mountain districts of Asturia. Moreover the Castilians were at war with the Leonese and it was not until the marriage of Berengaria, the daughter of the Castilian king, with the king of Leon that a reconciliation was effected (1197). But, for this, king and kingdom were laid under an interdict, because the marriage was against the church's law on account of the relationship of the parties, until Berengaria agreed to a divorce and returned to Castile. Her children, however, were considered as legitimate. At the same time Sancho of Navarre concluded an alliance with the Moorish party of the Almohads, in the hope of obtaining the supremacy over the Christian kingdoms by their assistance.

Under these circumstances it seemed as though the Spanish Christians must succumb. Fortunately for them, Yakub Almansor died four years after the battle of Alarcon. It was not till the new emir Muhammed al-Nasir had succeeded in mastering his enemies, after several bloody battles, that he again undertook a " holy war " against the Christians. But in the meantime the northern kingdoms had revived and the zealous efforts of pope and clergy had succeeded in temporarily adjusting intestine feuds.

OVERTHROW OF THE MOSLEMS

Consequently when, after an interval of fourteen years, Muhammed renewed the struggle and took the field with vast hosts from Africa and Andalusia, he met with a powerful resistance (1211). It was not merely that the whole Spanish chivalry, headed by the members of the orders of every description, thronged to the standards of the kings of Aragon and Castile ; many *ultramontanes* from the provinces of southern France and other districts were to be found there, who, fired by itinerant preachers, had travelled across the Pyrenees to earn a heavenly reward and earthly possessions as soldiers of God. By an ordinance of the pope, the assistance of heaven had been invoked throughout Christendom by fasts and processions. The religious excitement which at that time had gained possession of all minds, furthered the enterprise. Never before had such great hosts of warriors encountered one another in the peninsula.

In numbers, orders, and military discipline the Moslems were superior to the Christians ; like the crusaders in the Holy Land, the Christian warriors in Spain, especially the free companies who had flocked thither from abroad, sullied the cause of faith by savage crimes and robbery and persecutions of the Jews in and about Toledo ; and when the Saracens, having wasted their best strength during eight months before the mountain fortresses of Salvatierra, saw themselves compelled to agree to deliver up to the king of Castile the beleaguered city of Calatrava with the treasures collected there, in return for a free passage, the majority of the ultramontanes withdrew in anger, because the Spanish princes would not allow the retreating enemy to be waylaid in defiance of the promise given. Fanaticism had hardened their hearts and stifled the sentiments of honour and humanity. But in spite of the defection of the foreign soldiers, the Spanish Christians won a glorious victory in the battle of Las Navas de Tolosa, in the Sierra Morena, when the rule of the Africans in Spain received its death-blow (1212), as described in the history of the Arabs. More than a hundred thousand corpses, amongst them that of Muhammed's first-born, strewed the battle-field, and for long after the 16th of July was celebrated in Toledo by a great thanksgiving festival, called " the triumph of the cross." The spoil was enormous, but the brilliant victory was stained by cruelty and rapine at the capture of the surrounding cities.o

CHAPTER III

THE HISTORY OF CASTILE TO THE DEATH OF PEDRO THE CRUEL

[1214-1369 A.D.]

ALFONSO III of Castile did not long survive the glorious triumph over the Moslems at Navas de Tolosa. After two hostile irruptions into the territories of the enemy, he died in 1214, and was succeeded by his only surviving son, Henry [Enrique] I. As the new king, however, was only in his eleventh year, the regency was entrusted to his sister Berengaria [or Berenguela], the most excellent princess of her age. But neither her wisdom, her virtues, nor the near relation she held to the infante could avail her with the fierce nobles of Castile. The house of Lara, whose unprincipled ambition had on a former occasion been productive of such evils to the state, again became the scourge of the country. She resigned the custody of the royal ward to Count Alvaro Nuñez de Lara, the chief of that turbulent family.

No sooner was Don Alvaro in possession of the regency than he exhibited the true features of his character — haughtiness, rapacity, tyranny, and revenge. Those whom he knew to be obnoxious to his party he imprisoned or confiscated their possessions. His exactions, which fell on all orders of the state, were too intolerable to be long borne : remonstrances were addressed to him by the clergy ; but as they produced no effect, and as he had laid violent hands, not only on the substance alike of rich and poor, but on the temporalities of the church, he was solemnly excommunicated by the dean of Toledo. Even this ordinarily terrific weapon was powerless with one who disregarded both justice and religion.

He continued his iniquitous career, running from place to place with the young king, destroying the habitations and confiscating the substance of such as dared to censure his measures. But an accident, as unexpected as its consequences were fortunate for Spain, deranged all his views. Towards the end of May, 1217, while Henry was playing with his young companions in the courtyard of the episcopal palace of Palencia, a tile from the roof of the tower fell on his head, and inflicted a wound of which he died on the 6th of June following. Knowing how fatally this event must affect his interests, Don Alvaro, with the intention of concealing it as long as he could, conveyed the royal corpse as the living prince to the fortress of Tariego ; but the intelligence soon reached the queen, who, on this critical occasion, displayed a prudence and promptitude justly entitled to admiration. By the laws of Castile she was now heiress to the crown; but she resolved to transfer her rights to her son Ferdinand, heir to the crown of Leon, and thereby to lay the foundation for the union of the two kingdoms. Knowing that the young prince and his father, her former husband, were then at Toro, she despatched two of her knights with an earnest request that King Alfonso would allow her to see her son. The request was immediately granted, and Ferdinand was conducted to Antillo, where he was met by his impatient mother, and received with acclamation by the people. The states swore allegiance to her as their lawful sovereign. Immediately afterwards a stage was erected at the entrance of the city; and there, on the 31st day of August, 1217, — near three months from the death of Henry, — the queen, in presence of her barons, prelates, and people, solemnly resigned the sovereignty into the hands of her son, who was immediately proclaimed king of Castile.

COUNT ALVARO NUÑEZ DE LARA
(From an effigy)

But Ferdinand III was not yet in peaceable possession of the crown: he had to reduce the towns which held for Don Alvaro, and, what was still worse, to withstand his father the king of Leon, who now invaded the kingdom. Aided by the party of that restless traitor, Alfonso aspired to the sovereignty. The Castilian nobles were not slow in combining for the defence of their king: they hastened to Burgos in such numbers, and were animated by such a spirit, that Alfonso, despairing of success, or perhaps touched by the more honourable feelings of nature and justice, desisted from his enterprise.

Tranquillity being thus restored, the kings of Leon and Castile prepared to commence an exterminating war against the Mohammedans. The crusade was published by the archbishop Rodrigo, the celebrated historian; and the same indulgences were granted to those who assumed the cross in Spain, as to those who visited the Holy Land. Though partial irruptions, generally attended with success, were made into the territories of the Moors from various parts, — from Aragon, Castile, Leon, and Portugal, — it was not until 1225 that the career of conquest commenced, which ended in the annihilation both of the African power and of all the petty kingdoms which arose on its ruins. In that and the two following years Murcia was invaded, Alhamha taken, and Jaen besieged, by Ferdinand; Valencia invaded by King James of Aragon; Badajoz taken by Alfonso, and Elvas by the king of Portugal. The king of Castile was present before Jaen, which his armies had invested two whole years, when intelligence reached him of his father's death (in 1230), after a successful irruption into Estremadura.

The inestimable advantage which this event was calculated to procure for Christian Spain—the consolidation of two kingdoms often hostile to each other—was near being lost. In his last will, Alfonso named his two daughters—for the kingdom had long ceased to be elective—joint heiresses of his states. Fortunately for Spain, the majority of the Leonnese took a sounder view of their interests than Alfonso. Nobles, clergy, and people were too numerous in favour of the king of Castile, to leave those princesses the remotest chance of success. No sooner did that prince hear how powerful a party supported his just pretensions, than he hastened from Andalusia into Leon. As he advanced, accompanied by his mother Berengaria,—a princess to whose wisdom he was indebted for most of his successes,—Avila, Medina del Campo, Tordesillas, and Toro opened their gates to him. Directing his course towards Leon, Villalon, Mayorga, and Mansilla imitated the example of the other towns. As he approached the capital, he was met by the bishops and clergy, the nobles, and the people of the greater portion of the kingdom, who escorted him in triumph to the cathedral, where he received their homage.[b]

FERDINAND (III) EL SANTO

Thus the kingdoms of Leon and Castile were forever united. The king afterwards visited the towns of his new kingdom, administering justice and receiving on all sides the homage of the different towns, and the most promising demonstrations of affection from his new subjects.

Ferdinand, having recommenced his campaign in Andalusia, conquered the town of Ubeda (1234); and in the same year the Christians took possession of the western suburb of Cordova, defending themselves there with daring courage. As soon as this news reached the king, who was at Benavente, he set out and bore down upon Cordova, which the king of Seville dared not succour, and the siege becoming every day more rigorous, this large town, formerly chief seat of the Mussulman monarchy, was compelled to capitulate (1236), the inhabitants being allowed to depart freely with such of their goods as they could carry.

This conquest filled Christian Spain with joy, not only from its importance but as being the herald of more glorious victories. The cross was raised upon the highest pinnacle of the mosque, which was converted into a Christian church. The pious monarch caused the bells of the church of Compostella, which were being used as lamps, and which had been brought thither by Almansor on the shoulders of captive Christians more than two centuries and a half previously, to be carried back to the church of the Apostle by captive Mussulmans.[c]

BURKE'S ESTIMATE OF QUEEN BERENGARIA

Ferdinand's mother, Berengaria [who died in 1246], was one of those rare beings who seem to have been born to do right, and to have done it. From her earliest youth she was a leading figure, a happy and noble influence in one of the most contemptible and detestable societies of mediæval Christendom. Married of her own free will to a stranger and an enemy, that she might bring peace to two kingdoms, she was ever a true and loyal wife; unwedded by ecclesiastical tyranny in the very flower of her young womanhood, she was ever a faithful daughter of the church; inheriting a crown when she had proved her own capacity for royal dominion, she bestowed it on a strange and absent son, with no thought but for the good of her country and of Christendom ; and, finally, as queen-mother and ever-faithful counsellor, she accepted all the difficulties of government, while the glory of royalty was reserved for the king whom she had created. Berengaria was ever present in the right place and at the proper time, and her name is associated only with what is good, and worthy, and noble, in an age of violence, and wrong, and robbery — when good faith was well-nigh unknown, when bad men were all-powerful, when murder was but an incident in family life, and treason the chief feature in politics.[d]

QUEEN BERENGARIA, SPAIN

(From an effigy)

FERDINAND'S CONQUESTS

In the following campaigns the king took possession of the kingdom of Cordova, of all the passes of Sierra Morena on the side of Estremadura, and finally of Jaen (1246) which was ceded after a siege of more than a year by its lord, Muhammed al-Akhmar, who in the first place was king of Arjona, of which he was a native, and afterwards of Granada when he acknowledged himself the vassal of Ferdinand.

This enterprise being so successfully terminated, Ferdinand resolved to employ the great military resources now at his disposal in the conquest of the town and kingdom of Seville, the richest and most powerful of the remaining Mussulman possessions, but almost entirely dependent on its own strength. The Christians were well aware that Seville could expect but little assistance from Africa, and therefore undertook the enterprise with celerity. Immediately on the fall of Jaen, Ferdinand set out for Seville with his whole army, accompanied by the king of Granada and his troops, as vassal of Castile. He laid waste to the territory of Carmona, and took possession of Alcala de Guadaira, which he made into his arsenal ; he also commanded the country surrounding the capital and Xeres to be devastated.

The following year (1247) commenced the celebrated siege of Seville, in which a fleet, which had been constructed in Santander and Biscay, took part commanded by the admiral Boniface, penetrating by San Lucar on the Guadalquivir. The Moors could receive provisions and relief solely from Nieblo and Algarve by means of a bridge of boats uniting the fortress with Triana. This was destroyed by the admiral, who got ready two of the strongest ships of his fleet and awaited a violent sea wind, when, with all the sails of both ships set, he weighed anchor at the moment the full tide was strongest, and let the ships be hurled against the bridge of boats, which was broken by the force of the shock, thus well-nigh destroying the only hope of the besieged. From that day a scarcity of food was experienced in the thickly populated town, but the stores laid in were sufficiently abundant to enable the town to hold out for another six months.

Eventually, driven by hunger, the besieged proposed terms, which were rejected, King Ferdinand desiring that all the Moors should leave the town, taking with them only such of their property as they could carry. Three hundred thousand of them left Seville, and on the evacuation of the town Don Ferdinand entered with his army and took up his residence in the palace of the Moorish kings. There he devoted himself to organising his new court, summoning settlers to the country, and granting them licenses and privileges. After settling matters in Seville, Ferdinand marched with his army to the maritime towns of the kingdom, taking possession of Xeres (1250), Medina Sidonia, Cadiz, Puerto de Santa Maria, and other places. Master of the maritime towns, and unable to make war on the Mohammedans of Granada, his vassals, he resolved to cross to Africa and overthrow the empire of the Almohads, leaving instructions to the admiral Boniface to assemble a large fleet in the ports of northern Spain. Such were the plans of this great monarch, in spite of his suffering from dropsy, which disease was slowly sapping his vitality, and of which he finally died in 1252, his death being most exemplary.

St. Ferdinand is without doubt the greatest hero of the Spanish nation ; to his military genius, manifested in many great expeditions which he brought to a successful termination, he united two qualities rarely combined — a prudent policy and an acute sense of justice, which caused him to be loved and respected by all the kings of Spain and even by his enemies. It was through the fame of his rectitude that Murcia submitted to him without warfare, and that from an enemy the king of Granada became his loyal and submissive vassal. He respected the rights of the rich, but would not suffer their violence, knowing when to punish and when to pardon. When it was proposed in the cortes to impose taxes on the people, he would merely say: "Take heed of what you do, for I fear the curses of an old woman more than the united power of the Moors." His enlightened policy is clearly manifested in that he never acceded to the instances of his cousin, St. Louis of France, that he would accompany him to Palestine. "There is no lack of Moors in my own country," was his answer.

He had a great aversion to making war upon a Christian prince, which he was never known to do during the whole of a long reign. His qualities as a governor were superior to the century in which he lived ; he commanded a collection to be made of the ancient laws and customs, he gave a great impetus to national literature, commanding all public documents, formerly published in Latin, to be published in the vulgar tongue ; and finally, during his reign, the custom of summoning the deputies of the principal towns to the cortes was firmly established. He faithfully fulfilled his promises to the vanquished Moors, and was careful to see that the priests laboured to convert them. In this he showed greater zeal than in extending his kingdom.c

That he was a just, a pious, an able, and a paternal ruler, as well as a valiant soldier, is undoubted ; but his justice sometimes degenerated into revenge ; and his persecution of heretics — especially at Palencia, where, with his own royal hands, he condescended to set fire to the fagots on which they perished — proves either that his disposition was naturally cruel, or that the very demon of bigotry had smothered within him the best feelings of humanity. It was probably to this latter circumstance, more than to his prayers, his fasts, and his frequent use of the discipline, that, in 1671, he was canonised by Clement X.b

ALFONSO THE LEARNED (EL SABIO) AND HIS SUCCESSORS

When Ferdinand the Saint died, after a long and glorious reign, he was succeeded by his eldest son, Alfonso X, surnamed the Learned,[1] a prince who concerned himself less with the enlargement of his kingdom than the cultivation of science, and who, in emulation of the old court of the caliphate of Cordova, valued culture and learning more highly than military renown. Although the contentions with the Moors did not quite cease and Castile not only asserted her supremacy over Granada, but also fitted out a fleet to carry out the crossing into Africa which had been already meditated by Ferdinand, yet the mind of Alfonso preferred to dwell on intellectual matters, on observations of the heavens, and researches into the historical past of his native country. A prince of various knowledge, and penetrated with the love of study, he encouraged art and science with much generosity, shared the tasks of the learned, and sought to accomplish works during his life-time which might win greater glory in the eyes of posterity than feats of war and arms.

Alfonso X enlarged the University of Salamanca by the establishment of new professorships and by increasing its privileges, so that it could vie with the institutions of Paris and Bologna; he established observatories and caused a band of fifty astronomers, some of whom he sent for from a great distance to prepare the "Alfonsine Tables," a solid foundation for the astronomy of a future day, even though he himself diverted astronomical observations to astrological superstition. Under his supervision learned historians drew up the *Universal Chronicle,*[e] compiled from ancient sources and dealing with the period from the most ancient times to the date of his accession. He also encouraged the cultivation of the national language by introducing the Castilian mother-tongue into the administration of justice and the state, instead of the Latin which had hitherto been used, and he had the Bible translated into the language of the people; and that he might do away with the vast crowd of special *fueros* (privileges), laws and judicial usages, he drew up a scientific code of law (*Las Siete Partidas*), grounded on the principles of Roman jurisprudence, which was to apply to the whole kingdom, and superseded not only local laws, but also the free Old Gothic law. Only three Castilian towns preserved their ancient *fueros*.

But however distinguished King Alfonso might be as teacher and poet, as historical and astronomical author, his reign was nevertheless full of calamity and disorder. The revenues of his kingdom were not sufficient for the vast expenditure required for the generous support of learned men and scientific institutions, as well as for the maintenance of a brilliant court. And when he allowed his pride and vanity to lure him, as son of the Hohenstaufen princess Beatrice, into assuming the crown of the Holy Roman Empire and purchasing the votes of the covetous princes at a heavy price, he found himself in want of money. He contracted debts at high interest, he laid new taxes on the people, and when all this did not suffice, he debased the coinage and thus brought about a dislocation of trade and commerce which placed the nation at the mercy of money-lenders and Jews; and when, after having made use of the latter as his instruments, he persecuted and had them tortured until they ransomed themselves by new sacrifices, still no improvement was effected in the situation. But the greatest misfortune to the kingdom came from a dispute about the right to the succession.

[[1] Usually, but improperly termed, " the Wise " and also " the Astronomer." [b]]

Alfonso's eldest son, Ferdinand de la Cerda, died before his father in a campaign against the Moors, who had attacked and defeated the governor of Algeciras in his fortified camp and conquered and slain the archbishop Sancho of Toledo, a brother of King Pedro III of Aragon, who marched against them (1275). A decree solemnly promulgated by the king in accordance with ancient Spanish law declared the second son Sancho heir to the throne, regardless of the fact that the dead man had left two sons, Ferdinand and Alfonso. But his widow, Blanche, daughter of St. Louis of France, now came forward in defence of her sons' rights and her claims were powerfully supported both by her brother Philip III and by her stepmother Iolanthe, a sister of Peter III of Aragon. Thereupon a war ensued, which outlasted Alfonso's reign and threw Castile into the greatest disorder and party strife. The king of France, with whom his sister sought refuge and help, took up the cause of his two nephews, now living in Aragon, and for several years conducted a destructive war against Alfonso on the borders of Navarre and Castile. The attempted intervention of the pope had no effect. The situation grew still worse when the king, having quarrelled with his son Sancho, wished to proceed to a partition. This plan was opposed by the members of the royal house and by a great part of the nobles. At an assembly at Valladolid Sancho was declared heir to the throne and regent, and invested with the government of the kingdom in his father's stead (1282). Forsaken by his family and the estates, Alfonso called in the aid of Abu Yusuf of Morocco, while Sancho, disinherited and laid under a ban by his father in his turn, entered into an alliance with the emir of Granada. Thus, through the schism in the royal house, the power of the Moors in southern Spain was once more strengthened. At the same time the unhappy party wars in Castile itself led to the demoralisation of the people and the increase of the power of the nobles.*f*

Burke gives the following picturesque, if perhaps somewhat overdrawn estimate of Alfonso: " For nigh on five centuries all that was learned and all that was refined in Spain was found among the Arabs of Andalus. But on the taking of Seville by St. Ferdinand, the centre of gravity was completely changed. In the thirteenth century, Spain was passing through a great social and intellectual revolution, and the first man of intellectual Spain was Alfonso of Castile. If his royal highness, the heir apparent to the crown of England, were a senior wrangler, and a double first-class man at the English universities; if he were called upon to fill the post of Astronomer Royal of England, in default of any other man in the kingdom worthy even to be compared with him in that department of science ; if he had written a more brilliant history than Macaulay, and a finer poem than Tennyson ; if he were fit to teach Wagner music, and Cayley mathematics ; and if in the intervals of his studies he had found time to codify the entire laws of England into a digest which might endure for six hundred years to come : then, and only then, would the practical pre-eminence of his intellectual attainments, in modern England, represent the practical pre-eminence of the *sabiduria* of Alfonso X, in mediæval Spain. No Spaniard but Isidore of Seville, and no sovereign of any age or nation, not even Alfred the Great, so much surpassed all his contemporaries in learning as the king of Leon and Castile ; and the *Siete Partidas* is a work which as great a scholar as Isidore, and as great a statesman as Alfred, might well have been proud to own. But learning, or even lawgiving is not wisdom, and many a wiser and better king than Alfonso has performed his most elaborate calculations on his ten fingers, and signed his name with the pommel of his sword."*d*

This was still more apparent when, after Alfonso's death, Sancho IV succeeded to the kingly power (1284). The families of Lara and Haro, with their vast wealth and the great number of their vassals, had attained such overwhelming power that the king was quite subordinate to them. Only their mutual jealousies and conflicting desire for rule made it possible for him to still preserve some power and authority over them; but if he favoured one party he had the other for his bitterest enemy.

At an assembly of the estates (1288) Lopez de Haro, the head of this family, whose daughter Don Juan, Sancho's brother and enemy, had married, became so excited that he not only flung insults at the king, but even threatened him with his sword. Enraged at this arrogance Sancho's followers slew the insolent noble before his eyes. The renewal of the civil war was the consequence, for the son and brother of the victim fled to Aragon and joined the party of La Cerda for the overthrow of Sancho. Don Juan in his hatred for his brother so far forgot himself as to join Abu Yakub, and marched at the head of a Moorish army against the fortress of Tarifa, which was defended by the brave Alfonso Perez de Guzman. In vain, however, did he seek to compel the commander to surrender by threatening to murder the latter's son, whom he had taken prisoner; with the heroic spirit of a Brutus, Guzman himself threw down a sword from the wall, and Don Juan, furious at his contempt, was inhuman enough, as it is said, to stab the son before his father's eyes (1294). Sancho hurried to the rescue and saved the beleaguered town. Not long after, the king died (1295), and such a storm broke from all sides against the Castilian kingdom that its dissolution or dismemberment seemed almost unavoidable.

As Sancho's son Ferdinand IV, whom he had appointed his successor, was still under age, and the marriage of his mother Maria de Molina was regarded as illegal, not only did the two infantes, Don Juan and Alfonso's brother Henry, hitherto kept in captivity at Naples, lay claim, the former to the crown and the latter to the regency, but Alfonso de la Cerda came back across the Pyrenees from his sojourn at the French court and, supported by James II, the king of Aragon, and the powerful nobles of the families of Lara and Haro, also appeared as a pretender. At the same time the kings of Portugal and Granada sought to take advantage of the discordant condition, and the pope refused to grant a recognition of legitimacy.

But the prudence and governing talents of Maria de Molina, to whom the king had entrusted the regency, met all these difficulties with skill and success. She managed to divide the infantes by conceding to the elder of them, the feeble Henry, a share in the government; by a double marriage she attached the powerful king Diniz of Portugal to the royal house of Castile; to the Aragonese, the protector of the prince de la Cerda, she offered so successful and so obstinate a resistance that the union or *hermandad* of the estates of his kingdom compelled him to make peace with Castile; she prevailed on the pope to declare her marriage lawful and the king's birth legitimate, and she won over the estates by lowering the taxes. It is true that fresh troubles afterwards broke out when Ferdinand IV began to reign in his own name (1305); at last, however, by the Treaty of Campillo, the long dispute about the succession was adjusted, and Ferdinand remained in possession of the throne while the princes Ferdinand and Alfonso de la Cerda were indemnified with revenues and feudal lordships. The latter indeed preferred to live as a refugee in Germany, rather than give up the kingly title, but his son, the founder of the ducal house of Medina Sidonia, submitted to the stipulations of Campillo. But Castile had been too long distracted by civil strife, and men's minds were too much demoralised for peace and tranquillity to return at once without further disturbance. Neither was Ferdinand IV exactly the man to rally the different parties round his throne. His cruelty and the violence of his disposition called forth enmity and hatred and increased the discontent and variance. Jealousy and dissension amongst the grandees were the chief cause why a campaign entered upon in conjunction with the Aragonese king against the emir Mulei Nazar of Granada had no success. On this occasion Ferdinand laid before the pope a complaint against his uncle Don Juan, the soul of all hostile intrigues, charging him with having an understanding with the infidels, and he procured a judical inquiry, the issue of which he did not, however, live to see. *f*

The story of Ferdinand's death may be told in the following translation from the old Spanish historian Mariana:

Mariana's Account of the Divine Judgment on Ferdinand IV

By order of King Ferdinand IV of Castile, two brothers, Pedro and Juan Carvajales, were arrested, being accused of the murder of a nobleman of the house of Benavides, who was killed in Palencia when leaving the royal palace. The identity of the murderer was not ascertained, and many were ill-treated upon suspicion, in particular these two knights, who, after their defence was heard, were condemned for this crime against the king, without a proper trial, although they had not confessed their guilt, a dangerous course to pursue in such cases.

They were condemned to be thrown down from a steep rock near by, none being able to appease the king, who was intractable when enraged, and knew not how to restrain his anger. The courtiers, being well aware of this, took advantage of it to maliciously inform against and ruin those who stood in their way. At the moment of execution, the knights proclaimed aloud that their death was an injustice and a great wrong, calling upon God as witness before heaven and earth; they declared that since the king turned a deaf ear to their defence and protestations, they appealed to the divine tribunal, and summoned him to appear before it within thirty days. By a remarkable coincidence these words, at first looked upon as vain, came to be regarded in a very different light.

Heedless of the incident, the king set out for Alcaudete, where his army was encamped; there he fell seriously ill, and was compelled to return to Jaen, notwithstanding that the Moors were negotiating to deliver up the town. His condition grew daily worse, and his suffering increased so greatly that he was unable to treat with them personally. Rejoiced, however, at the news brought him, that the town was taken, he mentally planned new conquests, but on Thursday, the 7th day of September, having retired to rest after dining, he was shortly afterwards found dead. He died in the flower of his age, being twenty-four years and nine months old, at a time when his affairs were prospering. He reigned seventeen years four months and nineteen days, and was the fourth of the name. It was believed that his death was caused by excess in eating and drinking; others declared that it was the judgment of God, as, marvellous to relate, it occurred precisely thirty days after he was summoned [1] to appear, and therefore he is known as Don Fernando *el Emplazado*, that is, "the summoned."*g*

[1 The reader may remember that the Templar Jacques de Molay, when burned alive, similarly summoned Philip the Fair of France and the pope to meet him before the Judgment Seat, and that they died soon after.]

ALFONSO XI (1312–1350 A.D.)

Over Ferdinand's grave, party passion once more lifted its bloody stand-ard. As the heir to the throne, Alfonso XI, was only two years old at his father's death, Don Juan advanced claims to the government of the kingdom, but found himself thus brought into collision with Ferdinand's brother, Don Pedro, and the royal ladies. The kingdom was soon again divided into two hostile camps, which carried on a savage war with one another. Order and discipline were at an end, the royal authority disappeared, the possessions of the crown were alienated, commons, corporations, and powerful nobles seized what they wanted and freed themselves from all authority ; the young king's mother, Constanza, and his grandmother, Maria, had entrusted his education to the archbishop of Avila, who had to hide his pupil in his cathedral to preserve him from being kidnapped.

To restore some measure of order recourse was at length had to a division of the governing power. Each was to rule where he had the greatest following, Juan in the north and west, Pedro in the south and east. At the same time the pope interfered to effect a reconciliation (1315). The rulers of the kingdom now undertook a campaign against Ismail, who had snatched the lordship of Granada from his uncle, Mulei Nazar, the ally of Castile, a Moorish commander who had been summoned from Fez to the aid of his co-religionists, and defeated Juan and Pedro in a battle at the river Venil, in which they lost their lives (1319).

And now whilst the Saracens were profiting by their victory to make raids and conquests in the kingdom of Castile, four infantes laid claim to the regency and again filled the kingdom with civil wars and party rage. In vain did the states endeavour to bring about a settlement, in vain did the queen-mother Maria and the pope labour to effect a reconciliation; the strife continued for years, almost uninterruptedly ; even when, at fifteen years old, the king was declared of age and took the reins of government into his own hand, the confusion was not ended. Alfonso XI had grown up amidst vio-lence and party intrigues, and exhibited a harsh and savage temper. He enticed his cousin, Don Juan the younger, who had followed in his father's footsteps, to the court at Toledo, had him murdered at a banquet, and seized from his family the patrimony of Biscay; he repudiated his betrothed, Con-stanza, daughter of the infante Juan Emmanuel (a nephew of Alfonso X), that he might marry a Portuguese princess, which so enraged the injured father that he again set up the standard of revolt (1328), and supported by the Castilian grandees and the king of Aragon, conducted a long war against Alfonso.

Civilisation and morals declined, and vice and crime throve to such an extent as to bring the Castilian people everywhere into contempt. From the court itself all sentiment of honour and justice had disappeared. The king neglected his Portuguese wife in the most insulting manner, and treated his mistress, Leonora de Guzman, as queen. Garcilasso de la Vega, Alfonso's favourite, made himself notorious by perfidy, trickery, and murder till he and his son were slain by the indignant nobles ; Osorio and the Jew Joseph, who, as the king's all-powerful advisers and high officials, had acquired for themselves great wealth, but had also roused the hatred of the people by their covetousness and extortions, were at last delivered to their enemies by Alfonso himself, when the one was surreptitiously murdered and the other hunted from the country with disgrace and ignominy ; their wealth went to feed the royal coffers. Under such circumstances the Saracens could have easily made new conquests, had not Granada too been distracted at the same time by internal wars. The king concluded a truce with Castile, by which Alfonso gained time for the complete overthrow of his domestic enemies.

After having won over the Basques to his side by confirming their rights and liberties in an assembly of that bold mountain people under the famous oak of Guernica, he conquered one hostile town after the other, divided his enemies by making separate treaties with each, and aided by the diligent mediation of Pope Benedict XII compelled them, one by one, to make homage and submission. Alfonso de Haro and other faithless barons made atonement with their lives. Even the king of Portugal overcame his indignation at the insults offered to his daughter, and the machinations of the royal quasi-wife Leonora de Guzman, and, on Alfonso's promising to atone for the injury and treat his wife as her position rightfully demanded, he made his peace with him (1339). Immediately afterwards a new Saracen army from Africa landed on the Spanish coast under Abul-Hakam, and in conjunction with the emir of Granada began a holy war with the siege of Tarifa (1340). But the battle of Salado struck the death-blow of the Mohammedan power in Spain, and enriched the Christian victors with unlimited booty. The pope too, who had forwarded the undertaking by briefs and exhortations to a crusade, received magnificent tokens of the victory as a reward.

This great campaign ended with the conquest of Algeciras and covered Alfonso's name with glory and honour, both in the estimation of his contemporaries and of posterity; to defray its cost the estate of Burgos, after the example of the Moors, granted the Alcabala tax, a twentieth on all movable and real property, whenever it was sold or bartered, an impost most injurious to trade and commerce which though first intended to last only during the war was afterwards continued for the future. Six years later (1350), at the siege of Gibraltar, King Alfonso was carried off by the plague, which, coming from Asia, now spread itself like a destroying angel over the whole of Europe./

MARIANA'S ACCOUNT OF PEDRO THE CRUEL

In Castile, grave disturbances, storms, events, cruel and bloody wars, deceit, treachery, exiles, and innumerable deaths, followed one on the other; many great lords met with a violent end, numerous were the civil wars, no care was taken of matters either sacred or profane; none knew whether to attribute these disorders to the new king or to the nobles. By common opinion they were laid to the king's charge, so much so that he earned from the people the nickname of "the cruel." Some trustworthy authors attribute the majority of these disorders to the intemperance of the nobles, who, heedless of right, followed their inclinations and inordinate avarice and ambition in all things good or evil, so that the king was compelled to punish their excesses.

Upon the death of Don Alfonso, Don Pedro, his son by his lawful wife, was there and then proclaimed king in the camp, as was just, though he was only fifteen years and seven months old and was absent in Seville, where he had remained with his mother. In years he was unfitted for such grave cares, in natural disposition he showed capacity for great things. He had a pale complexion, handsome countenance, and majestic air; his hair was fair, and his stature commanding. He showed signs of great courage, wisdom, and other qualities. In mind and body he was undaunted by difficulty and fatigue. Falconry and hawking were his chief pleasures. He was upright in the administration of justice. To these virtues he joined vices equally great, which were already visible and increased with age. He despised others, spoke insolently, listened haughtily, and granted an audience with difficulty, not only to strangers but also to members of his own household. These bad qualities were visible from his early childhood ; avarice, dissoluteness, and harshness were added to them in the course of time.

These failings, to which he was naturally addicted, increased under the tuition of Don Juan Alfonso de Albuquerque, the tutor given him by his father when a little child to train him in good habits. This may be suspected from the fact that, after he was king, this man was admitted to his intimacy, and in all things was given great authority, to the envy and discontent of the nobles, who declared that he endeavoured to increase his wealth at the expense of the public good — the worst possible of all plagues.[g]

LEONORA DE GUZMAN
(Thrown into prison by order of Pedro the Cruel)

Thus the historian Mariana.[g] The figure of Pedro I stands in history and romance for that of a monster of cruelty, though it must be borne in mind that Pedro Lopez de Ayala,[h] the chronicler who has left us an account of his reign, was the friend and supporter of his rebellious brother Henry of Trastamara. Pedro was the only son of Maria of Portugal, queen of Alfonso XI, but Alfonso's mistress, Leonora de Guzman, had several sons of whom Henry (Enrique) was the eldest. His father had settled on him the great domain and title of Trastamara, and he is generally known as Henry of Trastamara.[a]

On the accession of Pedro, Leonora de Guzman, dreading his resentment, or rather that of the queen-mother, retired to the city of Medina Sidonia, which formed her appanage. Through the perfidious persuasions, however, of a Lara and an Albuquerque, who governed the mind of Pedro, and who pledged their knightly faith that she had nothing to fear, she proceeded to Seville to do homage to the new sovereign. No sooner did she reach that city, than she was arrested and placed under a guard in the Alcazar. The eldest of her sons, who was permitted to visit her there, would have shared the same fate, had he not precipitately retreated from the capital. From Seville she was soon transferred to Carmona ; and if her life was spared a few months, it was not owing to the forbearance, but to the indisposition of the king, which was at one time so dangerous as to render his recovery hopeless. Unfortunately for Spain, he did recover; and one of his first objects, early in 1351, was to draw her from Carmona, and make her accompany him to Talavera, where she was consigned to a still closer confinement. Her doom was soon sealed: in a few days she was put to death by the express order of the queen; no doubt, with the concurrence of the king.

This murder was quickly followed by another. Having despatched one of his creatures to Burgos, to levy, by his own authority alone, a tax which, to be legal, required the sanction of the states, the people resisted, and slew his collector. Accompanied by his unscrupulous adviser, Don Juan de Albuquerque, he hastened to that capital, to inflict summary vengeance on the inhabitants. They naturally took up arms; and being joined by Garcilasso de la Vega, the *adelantado* of Castile, sent a messenger to the king, disclaiming all wish to oppose his authority, but beseeching him not to allow Albuquerque, whose violent character they well knew, to attend him. The request was disregarded; the count arrived, and the doom of Garcilasso was sealed.

No sooner did Pedro perceive him, than the command was given; "Ballasteros,[1] seize Garcilasso!" The adelantado begged for a confessor; but no attention would have been paid to the request, had not a priest accidentally appeared in sight. Both having retired for a few minutes into a corner, Albuquerque, who bore great enmity to the prisoner, desired the king to order what was to be done, and the ballasteros were immediately told to kill Garcilasso. On receiving the order, the men, who could not conceive it was seriously given, hesitated to fulfil it: one of them, approaching the king, said, "Sir king, what are we to do with Garcilasso?" "Kill him!" was the reply.

The man returned, and with a mace struck the adelantado on the head, while another associate despatched him. The bleeding body was thrown into the street; where, after lying for some time to be trodden under foot by some bulls which were passing, it was removed outside the walls of the city, to be there buried. The same fate would have befallen the child Nuño de Lara, who by his father's death was become the hereditary lord of Biscay, had not his governess, apprised of the intention, removed to a fortress in the heart of the Biscayan Mountains. The child, however, soon died; and Pedro, by imprisoning the female heirs, obtained what he so much coveted — the rich domains of that house.

Pedro proceeded to Ciudad Rodrigo, to confer on the interests of the two kingdoms with his grandfather, the sovereign of Portugal. Well had it been for him had he followed the advice of that monarch, who urged on him the necessity of living on a good understanding with his illegitimate brothers, and of forgiving the natural indignation they had shown at the death of their mother. But both brothers soon left him and revolted. Some of the confederates were reduced and put to death; but the princes themselves eluded his pursuit, — Don Tello by fleeing into Aragon. While besieging the places which had thrown off his authority, he became enamoured of Doña Maria de Padilla, who was attached to the service of his favourite's lady, Doña Isabella de Albuquerque. Through the persuasion of this unprincipled minister, the uncle of the young lady, Don Juan de Henestrosa, did not hesitate to sacrifice the honour of his house by consigning her to the arms of the royal gallant. The connection thus formed, which continued unto the death of Doña Maria, brought the greatest disasters on the country.

[1] A sort of men-at-arms, whose usual weapon was a short club, or mace.

Some months previous to this connection, Pedro, in compliance with the request of the cortes of Valladolid, had agreed that an embassy should be sent to the French king, soliciting for wife a princess of the royal house of that nation.   The choice fell on Blanche de Bourbon, a princess of excellent qualities, who, early in 1353, arrived at Valladolid.   But the king, infatuated by his mistress, who had just been brought to bed of a daughter, was in no disposition to conclude the marriage ; and it was not without difficulty that his minister Albuquerque, who was already jealous of the favours accorded to the relations of Maria de Padilla, and for that reason the more eager for its solemnisation, prevailed on him to meet the princess at Valladolid.   Leaving Padilla and his heart at Montalvan, he reluctantly proceeded towards that city.   On his way he accepted the submissions of his brothers Henry and Tello, whom, on an occasion like the one approaching, he could not decently punish for their rebellion.   Monday, June 3rd, 1353, the ceremony took place with due splendour.[b]   The contemporary chronicler Ayala gives so intimate a view of the king and his household that we may quote part of the sequel in his words.

AYALA'S ACCOUNT OF THE KING'S HONEYMOON

On the Wednesday after his marriage the king dined in his palace.   And he dined alone that day, with no companions whatever.   And while the king was at table there came to him Queen Doña Maria, his mother, and Queen Doña Leonora, his aunt, in tears.   Then the king rose from the table and spoke with them aside, and as both he and they afterwards reported they said to him :

" My lord, it is made known to us that you are minded to go from hence and rejoin Doña Maria de Padilla, and we beg you in mercy to desist.   For if you do this thing you make but little of your honour in thus forsaking your wife immediately after your marriage, when all the best and highest in your kingdom are assembled here.   And further, the king of France will have good cause of complaint against you, who has newly allied himself to you by this marriage, and has sent you this niece of his whose hand you asked of him; and he sent her hither with great pomp and retinue, as was but just.   Further, my lord, it will cause grave scandal in your kingdom, should you thus go hence, for all the highest in your kingdom have come hither at your command, and it will not be for your good service thus to depart without word or speech with them."

The king made answer that he marvelled greatly that they should believe that he would thus leave Valladolid and his wife, and bade them not believe it.   And the queens replied that they had been most certainly informed that he was minded to seek Doña Maria de Padilla at once.   And the king assured them that he would not do so, and had no thought of it, and bade them never believe it.   Upon this the queens withdrew, knowing full well that the king would set out at once, but powerless to prevent it.   An hour after the king called for his mules, saying that he would visit Queen Doña Maria, his mother.   And as soon as the mules were brought he left Valladolid, and went and slept that day at a place called Pajares.   The next day he went to the village of Montalvan where Doña Maria de Padilla was, for though he had left her in the castle of Montalvan, he had already sent her word to come to Montalvan.   But many others who were to accompany him arrived the next day.

Great clamour and excitement arose in the town of Valladolid, when it was known that the king had departed thence and had rejoined Doña Maria de Padilla. Then Don Juan Alfonso de Albuquerque and other knights visited the queens Doña Maria the king's mother and Queen Blanche his wife, and Doña Leonora, queen of Aragon, the king's aunt, and found them very sad. And all those who remained there were anxious and dismayed thinking that this day's work would bring war and evil on Castile, as indeed it did. They held their council, saying that it was ill-done of the king thus to desert his wife, and they were sore grieved at it. And they resolved that the master of Calatrava, Don Juan Nuñez de Prado, and Don Juan Alfonso should follow the king, and many other gentlemen with them, and that they should do their utmost to induce the king to return to his wife, Queen Blanche, and to amend his ways.

When Don Pedro heard that Don Juan Alfonso de Albuquerque and the master of Calatrava, Don Juan Nuñez, had turned back, not daring to seek him, and that the master had gone to his own land, and Don Juan Alfonso to the castles which he had on the frontiers of Portugal, he immediately resolved to return to Valladolid in order to meet Queen Doña Maria his mother, and his wife Queen Blanche, to avoid a scandal in the kingdom. This was the counsel given him by the gentlemen who were with him. And thus the king came to Valladolid, and remained there with his wife Queen Blanche for two days. But he could not be prevailed upon to remain there longer and he left Valladolid and went to Mojados a village close by. And the next day he went to Oviende, and remained there for some days ; and he never saw his wife Queen Blanche again.

The next year he ordered Juan Ferrandez de Henestrosa his chamberlain, and uncle of Doña Maria de Padilla, to go to Arevalo where his wife Queen Blanche of Bourbon then was, and bring her to Toledo, and place her in the Alcazar of the said city. And so it was published that all might be aware of it. The knights of Toledo heard of it, and it was great grief to many that such a lady as this should be a prisoner and that Toledo should be chosen for her prison. And Juan Ferrandez de Henestrosa as the king commanded, brought Queen Blanche to Toledo. And when Queen Blanche of Bourbon entered Toledo, she said it was her will to go and pray in the church of Sancta Maria. And she went thither, and as soon as she reached it she refused to leave the church, fearing imprisonment or death. This she did by the advice of the bishop and of those who had come with her. Then Juan Ferrandez de Henestrosa, who had brought Queen Blanche to Toledo, when he saw that she would not leave the church, begged her graciously to accompany him to the Alcazar which belonged to the king and her, for she would find good apartments there ; but she would not do so. And the king replied that he would come himself to Toledo and take such measures in this matter as best befitted his service.

After Juan Ferrandez de Henestrosa left Toledo, Queen Blanche held converse with many great ladies of that city, who dwelt there and came every day to visit her. And she told them how she went in fear of her life, and that she had heard that the king was minded to come to Toledo, and have her seized and put to death ; and therefore she begged and prayed for some protection. And all this business of Queen Blanche, she being very young, for she was not then more than eighteen, was managed by a lady who was her governess, holding this office by the appointment of Queen Doña Maria, the king's mother, who had bestowed it on her. The ladies of Toledo, when they heard these things every day from Queen Blanche and her governess,

Doña Leonora de Saldaña, were filled with pity for the queen, and they spoke to their husbands and kinsmen, saying that they would be the meanest men on earth if such a queen as this, their lady and the wife of their lord the king, should die such a death in the city where they were ; but since they had power, let them prevent it. For the queen thought and feared that Juan Ferrandez de Henestrosa would return with the king's order to seize and imprison her in the Alcazar, where she was certain she would be put to death. And she thought that this was not the true will of the king, but that he had been persuaded to it by certain of his counsellors, kinsmen of Doña Maria de Padilla, and that the time would come when the king her lord and husband would hold that they who had saved her from such a death had done him good service, and would understand that they had not done wrongfully, but in his interest.

The knights of Toledo, by the many representations made to them, with tears for the imprisonment and death of so noble a lady as Queen Blanche, who was a creature without blame and of so high lineage, and because the highest and best in the kingdom were ill contented with the kinsmen of Doña Maria de Padilla, were for the most part moved to defend the queen to the utmost of their power, and to hazard their lives and possessions for her. And when the knights and squires and true men of the city heard that Juan Ferrandez de Henestrosa was coming to Toledo, although he was with the king, and that he was about to seize the queen and imprison her, as they were given to understand, they took Queen Blanche from the church of Sancta Maria where she abode, and placed her in the Alcazar of the said city, on Thursday at the hour of tierce, on the eve of the feast of St. Mary in August, of that year. And with her all her ladies and damsels, and many other ladies of the city. And they gave the towers of the Alcazar and of the city into the keeping of the knights and loyal citizens of that city, for their defence ; for all came to this work right willingly. And on the day that this was done they seized all their kinsmen who would not take part in it.[h]

PEDRO'S FALSE MARRIAGE

In the meanwhile Pedro wavered in his fidelity to his mistress long enough to be infatuated with Doña Juana de Castro. Not being able to win her to his desires, he proposed marriage ; and the bishops of Avila and Salamanca stooped first to substantiate his pretence that he had not really married Blanche of Bourbon and then to marry him to Juana de Castro. When he had tired of her person, the king told her that his marriage with Blanche was a true marriage, and the other only a ruse to overcome her scruples. A son was born of this outrageous deception.[a]

When news of this base transaction reached the brother of Juana, Ferdinand Perez de Castro, who was one of the most powerful lords of Galicia, he instantly joined the league of the discontented. A civil war now commenced, which, during some months, raged with more animosity than success to either party. On its commencement, the king, persuaded that the fortress of Arevalo was not a secure prison for the unfortunate Blanche, ordered her, as we have seen, to be conveyed to Toledo and lodged in the Alcazar of that city. She was immediately rescued from the power of her jailer, who returned to acquaint his employer with the event. Furious at the intelligence, Pedro ordered the commanders of Santiago, first to depose their grand-master, his brother Fadrique, then to march on Toledo, and force the princess from her sanctuary. But she was no longer there ; the whole city had taken her part, and honourably placed her, under a strong guard, in the palace of their kings. These defenders of oppressed innocence were now joined by the heads of the league, whose party daily acquired strength.

Neither the sudden, perhaps suspicious, death of Albuquerque, nor the deposition of Don Fadrique, depressed their zeal. To show that a redress of grievances, and not individual ambition, was their object, they despatched messengers to the king, with the assurance of their attachment to his person, and proposed that, if he would dismiss his mistress with her kinsmen, and return to his queen, they would instantly lay down their arms. Pedro was resolved to do neither ; but, as it suited his views to protract the negotiation, he nominated commissioners to treat with those of the league, which was now strengthened by the accession of the queen-mother. To bring about an amicable adjustment between her son and his barons, she invited both to Toro, where she then abode — an invitation which both accepted. But Pedro now found that he was the prisoner of the leaguers, who changed the officers of his household, substituted others from their own body, and closely watched his motions at the time they were treating him with the highest outward respect. To escape from his situation, he had recourse to his usual arts — to bribing some heads of the league, and, above all, to dissimulation, in both cases with success. The king soon contrived to escape, and threw himself into the fortress of Segovia.

After his escape (1355), Pedro assembled his states at Burgos, and, by artfully representing himself as thwarted in all his proceedings for the good of his people by his mother, his brothers, and the other rebels, whose only aim was to tyrannise over the nation, he procured supplies for carrying on the war. These supplies, however, were granted on the condition of his living with Queen Blanche — a condition which he readily promised to fulfil, without the slightest intention of so doing. After an unsuccessful assault on Toro, he returned to Toledo, the peculiar object of his hatred. Contrary to all reasonable expectation, he forced an entrance, and expelled the troops of his brother Henry. This success would, however, have been unattainable, had not most of the inhabitants believed in the sincerity of his declaration to the pontifical representative. The unfortunate Blanche was transferred — not to his palace, to enjoy her rights as queen, but to the fortress of Siguenza ; the bishop of that see was also consigned to a prison ; and some of the most obnoxious individuals of the league were beheaded or hung.

The legate, Bertrand, no longer withheld the thunders of the church : Pedro, Maria de Padilla, and even Juana de Castro, were excommunicated, and the kingdom subjected to an interdict. But these thunders passed harmless over the head of the royal delinquent, who lost no time in marching against Toro, where his mother and many of the leaguers still remained. His first attempt on that place was repulsed with loss ; but, after a siege of some months, he prevailed on the inhabitants, by lavishing extraordinary promises of clemency, to open their gates to him. How well he performed his promise appeared the very day of his entrance, when he caused some barbarous executions to be made in his mother's sight.[1] The queen fainted at the spectacle ; and, on recovering her senses, requested permission to retire into Portugal, which was granted. About the same time many Castilian barons fled into Aragon.

[1 It is said that she stood to her ankles in the blood of the slaughtered noblemen.]

During the next few years Pedro waged a desultory war against the king of Aragon, both by sea and land ; but the result was decisive to neither of the belligerents. In this war many of the disaffected barons fought in the ranks of the latter — a policy for the condemnation of which no words are sufficiently strong, and which greatly detracts from the commiseration that must be felt at the fate of some who afterwards fell into his hands. It cannot be denied that the Castilian king had many provocations to vengeance : his nobles rebelled for the slightest causes — often without any cause at all ; nor is he known to have put to death any of his subjects, whom he did not conceive, at one time or other, either openly or secretly to have aimed at subverting his authority. But the barbarity of his executions ; the duplicity with which he planned the destruction of such as submitted under the assurance of pardon ; his perfidious disregard of promises, or even oaths, when the openly pardoned objects of his hatred were fully in his power — not even excepting his nearest connections — stamp him at once as a ruthless barbarian, and a bloody tyrant.

The execution of his brother Fadrique, grand-master of Santiago, in 1358, is, perhaps, more characteristic of him than any other of his actions. On some suspicion — whether founded or not in justice must remain unknown — that the grand-master maintained an understanding with the king of Aragon, Fadrique was recalled from the Valencian frontier to Seville, where Pedro then was. He found the king apparently in the best of humours, and his reception was very friendly.[b]

The account of the horrible and cold-blooded deed which followed may be quoted from the contemporary Ayala.

AYALA'S ACCOUNT OF THE MURDER OF FADRIQUE

The king Don Pedro being in Seville in his Alcazar, on Tuesday the 29th day of May of this year, there came thither Don Fadrique his brother, master of Santiago, who had just recovered the town and fortress of Jumilla which is in the kingdom of Murcia. In the truce of a year established by the cardinal Don Guillen between Castile and Aragon, this town was claimed for Aragon by a nobleman called Don Pero Maza, who said it belonged thereto and not to the dominion of the king of Castile, and that it was not included in the truce. But in this war that town was first for Castile, and as soon as the master Don Fadrique heard of it, he went thither and besieged and recovered it, to do the king service. For the master Don Fadrique was eager to serve the king and do him pleasure. And when the master had recovered the said town and castle of Jumilla, he went to the king, from whom letters came every day requesting his presence.

The master arrived in Seville on the said Tuesday in the morning, at the hour of tierce, and coming immediately to pay his duty to the king, he found him playing draughts in the Alcazar. And as soon as he came in the master kissed his hand, and the many knights who came with him likewise. The king received him with a show of good-will, asking him from whence he came that day, and if he had good lodgings. The master replied that he had set out that day from Cantillana, which is five leagues from Seville, and for his lodgings he knew not of them yet, but was full sure they would be good. The king bade him go and look to his lodging and then return to him ; and the king said this because many companies had come into the Alcazar with the master.

Then the master left the king and went to see Doña Maria de Padilla and the king's daughters, who were in another part of the Alcazar called the Caracol. Doña Maria de Padilla knew all that was planned against the master and at the sight of him she assumed a countenance so mournful that all might read it; for this lady had a very good heart, and sound judgment, and liked not the deeds of the king, and the death decreed against the master lay heavy on her.

After the master had visited Doña Maria and his nieces the king's daughters, he went down to the courtyard of the Alcazar, where he had left his mules, intending to seek his lodgings and bestow his companies. But when he reached the courtyard of the Alcazar he found that his beasts were gone, for the king's porters had given orders for everyone to leave the courtyard, and they turned out all the beasts and closed the gates; for so they had been commanded, that there might not be many there. When the master could not find his mules he was at a loss whether he should return to the king or what he should do; and one of his knights, whose name was Suer Gutierrez de Navales, an Austrian, perceived that some mischief was afoot, for he saw a stir in the Alcazar, and he said to the master, "My lord, the postern of the courtyard stands open; go out and you shall not lack mules." This he repeated many times, for he thought that if the master got outside the Alcazar he might perchance escape, and there they must needs slay many of his followers ere they could take him.

In the meanwhile there came to the master two knights who were brothers, and their names were Ferrand Sanchez de Tovar, and Juan Ferrandez de Tovar, and they knew nothing of this business. By the king's orders they said to the master, "My lord, the king calls for you"; and the master turned back to go to the king, in dread, for he now suspected evil. As he passed the doors of the palace and of the different apartments the number of his followers grew less and less, for those who guarded the doors had ordered the porters not to let them pass.

When the master came to the place where the king was, none was allowed to enter save only the master Don Fadrique, and the master of Calatrava, Don Diego Garcia (who that day accompanied Don Fadrique, the master of Santiago, and knew nothing of all this), and two other knights. The king was in a hall called "del Fierro" with the door closed. And when the masters of Santiago and Calatrava came to the door of the hall where the king was, it was not opened to them, and they stood at the door. And Pedro Lopez de Padilla, the king's ballestero mayor, was outside with the masters, and thereupon a wicket opened in the hall where the king was, and the king said to Pedro Lopez de Padilla:

"Pedro Lopez, seize the master;" and he replied, "Which of them?" and the king said, "The master of Santiago." Then Pedro Lopez de Padilla laid hold of the master Don Fadrique, and said, "I arrest you," and the master stood silent full of dread, and the king said to some ballesteros who stood by, "Ballesteros, kill the master of Santiago."

But even so the ballesteros durst not do it. Then one of the king's bedchamber, a man named Rui Gonzalez de Atienza who was in the secret, cried aloud to the ballesteros:

"Traitors! what are you about? Did you not hear the king command you to kill the master?"

Then the ballesteros, seeing that it was indeed the king's order, raised their maces to strike the master Don Fadrique. When the master of Santiago saw this, he disengaged himself from the grasp of Pedro Lopez de

Padilla, and jumped into the courtyard.   He seized his sword but could not draw it, for it was slung round his neck under the tabard which he wore, and when he would have drawn it the hilt caught in the strap and he could not get it free.   The ballesteros pursued him to wound him with their maces but they could not succeed, for he eluded them and fled from side to side, in the courtyard.

Then Nuño Ferrandez de Roa, who pursued him more closely than the rest, came up with him and dealt him a blow on the head with his mace, so that he fell to the ground, and thereupon all the other macemen came up and wounded him.   As soon as the king saw the master lying on the ground, he went through the Alcazar thinking to find some of his followers and put them to death, and he found none ; for some had not entered the palace when the master returned in answer to the king's summons, because the doors were well guarded, and some had fled and concealed themselves.   But the king found a squire named Sancho Ruiz de Villegas, who was surnamed Sancho Portin, and he was the master's chief equerry.   The king found him in the part of the palace called the Caracol, where Doña Maria de Padilla dwelt with the king's daughters, where he had taken refuge when he heard the noise of the master's murder.   The king entered the room, and Sancho Ruiz had taken Doña Beatrice, the king's daughter, in his arms, thinking to escape death through her.   But when the king saw it, he caused his daughter Doña Beatrice to be torn from his arms, and stabbed him with the dagger which he wore in his belt.

The king returned to where the master lay, and found that he was not yet dead, and the king took a dagger from his belt and gave it to a groom of the chambers, to kill him with.   When it was done the king sat down to eat in the place where the master lay dead, a hall called the Azulejos, which is in the Alcazar.   Then the king sent for his cousin, the infante Don Juan, (of Aragon) and told him in secret that he was going from thence to Biscay at once, and that he should come with him, for it was his intention to put Don Tello to death and give Biscay to Don Juan.   For the infante Don Juan was married to Doña Isabella, sister of the wife of Don Tello, and both were daughters of Don Juan Nuñez de Lara, lord of Biscay, and of Doña Maria his wife.   And the infante kissed the king's hands, thinking that he would act according to his word.   That day, after the death of the master Don Fadrique, the king took the adelantadoship of the frontier from his cousin the infante Don Juan, saying that he would make him lord of Biscay, and bestowed it upon Enriquez, who was alguacil mayor of Seville ; and he gave that office to Garci Gutierrez Tello, an honourable gentleman dwelling in Seville.

That same day on which the master of Santiago died the king sent orders to Cordova for Pero Cabrera, a gentleman who dwelt there, to be put to death, as well as a *zurat* whose name was Ferrando Alfonso de Gabete.   And he sent to kill Don Lope Sanchez de Bendaña, chief commander of Castile, and they killed him in Villarejo, a place belonging to the order of Santiago, the property of the commander.   In Salamanca they killed Alfonso Jufre Tenorio; and Alfonso Perez Fermosino in Toro.   In the castle of Mora they slew Gonzalo Melendez de Toledo, who had been held a prisoner there.   And the king ordered all these to be put to death, saying that they were concerned in the rebellion when some in the kingdom took up the causes of Queen Blanche, as has already been related.   And although he had indeed pardoned them it appeared that his wrath against them was not dead.[h]

OTHER ROYAL MURDERS

The king and the prince of Aragon departed for Biscay; but, on reaching Aguilar, they found that Don Tello had been apprised of his intended doom, and had fled. Pedro followed him to Bermeo, where he learned that the fugitive had just embarked for Bayonne. In his blind fury he embarked in the first vessel he found in the harbour, and ordered a pursuit; but the sea began to rise so high that he soon abandoned it, and returned to the port. The infante Juan now requested the fulfilment of the royal promise; but he who had made it had now changed his mind. With his usual duplicity, however, he amused his cousin, saying that he could do nothing without the states of the province; that he would speedily convoke them, and procure the recognition of the new feudatory. He did convoke them; but it was to persuade them to confer their sovereignty on himself alone.

The disappointed claimant now left Pedro in disgust; but was speedily recalled to Bilbao, where the king repaired, by the promise that his ambition should be gratified. The infante hastened to that town, and proceeded to the house occupied by the court. As he approached the royal apartments, some of the tyrant's creatures, as if in jest, deprived him of his poniard — the only weapon which he had about him, and, at the same moment he was struck on the head by a mace; another blow brought him lifeless to the ground. His corpse was thrown from the window of the apartment occupied by the king into the street; but was afterwards conveyed to Burgos, and cast into the river.

To revenge the murder of these victims, the two brothers, Henry and Tello, who had returned to Aragon, made frequent irruptions into Castile. In a battle fought in 1359, they triumphed over Henestrosa, whom they left dead on the field; and, in subsequent invasions, they obtained no small portion of plunder.[1] But none of these things moved the king, who persevered in his course of barbarities as if his throne rested on a rock of adamant. It is impossible to specify all his individual acts of murder; such only can be represented here as are either more than usually characteristic of him, or as exercised some influence on following events: in revenge for the aid afforded to his revolted subjects by the infante of Aragon, he put to death Leonora, the dowager queen of that country, who had long resided in Castile, and who was also his own aunt. But his famous, or rather infamous compact with the Portuguese king, Pedro, is most indicative of the man. Knowing how much that sovereign longed to extirpate all who had been concerned in the murder of Iñes de Castro,[2] and of whom a few had sought refuge in Castile; and no less eager on his own part to take vengeance on three or four of his own obnoxious subjects, who had implored the protection of the Portuguese, he proposed to surrender the Portuguese in exchange for the Castilian refugees. The kindred soul of the Lusitanian felt a savage joy at the proposal; in 1360, the men were exchanged and put to death.

That he cared as little for the king of France as for the pope — both were distant enemies — Spain had a melancholy proof, in 1361, in the tragical

---

[1] While Pedro was at Najera, for the purpose of protecting his frontiers against these irruptions, a priest of San Domingo de la Calzada is said to have waited on him, and foretold, that, unless he kept on his guard, he would be assassinated by his brother Henry. "Who has advised you to tell me this?" asked the king. "No one," replied the priest, "except San Domingo." Pedro regarded this as some "weak invention of the enemy," and caused the priest to be burned alive. This anecdote, true or false, is extracted from the chronicle of the contemporary Lopez de Ayala.[h]

[2] The fate of this lady, which has so frequently occupied the tragic muse of the peninsula, must be looked for in the history of Portugal.

death of that unhappy queen, Blanche de Bourbon. His orders for her removal by poison were first given to the governor of Xeres, to whom the custody of her person had for some time been intrusted; but that governor, whose name (Iñigo Ortiz de Zuniga) ought to be revered by posterity, refused to become the executioner of his queen. It is somewhat surprising that his life was not the penalty of his disobedience — a doom which he doubtless expected. A less scrupulous agent for this bloody business was found in one of the king's ballasteros, Juan Perez de Robledo, who hastened to the fortress, superseded the noble Iñigo Ortiz in the command, and perpetrated the deed — whether by poison or by steel is unknown. The same violence befell Isabella de Lara, widow of the infante Don Juan, whom the tyrant had murdered at Bilbao.

The death of Blanche was followed by the natural one of the king's mistress, Maria de Padilla. Whether through the example of the Portuguese sovereign, who had shortly before proclaimed his secret marriage with Iñes de Castro, or whether because the Castilian had in like manner actually married Maria, certain it is, that, in 1362 — immediately after the murder of the king of Granada by his own hand — Pedro convoked the cortes at Seville, and declared that Maria de Padilla had been his lawful wife, and that for this reason alone he had refused to live with Blanche de Bourbon: he therefore required that his son Alfonso should be declared his legitimate successor. Three of the king's creatures were brought forward, who swore on the holy Gospels that they had been present at the nuptials; and the cortes, though far from convinced of the fact, affected to receive it as such, declared Maria the queen and Alfonso the heir of the kingdom; and, after him, the daughters of their monarch by that favourite. If such a marriage were really contracted, Blanche was deceived as well as Juana de Castro; but, from want of sufficient evidence, history can place the French princess only in the rank of Castilian queens. The man who had imposed on the credulity of Doña Juana, who had broken his faith whenever it suited his views, whose character was as much distinguished for duplicity as for violence — must produce some better voucher than his word, or his oath, or those of his creatures, before he will obtain credit with posterity.

THE WAR WITH HENRY OF TRASTAMARA

It was to defend himself against the probable vengeance of France, and the present hostility of Aragon, that, in 1363, Pedro sought the alliance of Edward III of England and the heroic Black Prince. The danger was the more to be apprehended, when the king of Navarre joined his brother of Aragon. For some time, the advantage lay on the side of the Castilian; who, early in 1364, reduced several towns in Valencia, and invested the capital of that province; the siege of which, however, he was soon compelled to raise. But these temporary successes were more than counterbalanced by the activity of Henry; who, in 1365, prevailed on Bertrand du Guesclin, the count de la Marche, and other French chiefs, to aid him in his projected dethronement of the Castilian tyrant.

The French king, Charles V, anxious to avenge the cruel insult done to his royal house, espoused the cause of Henry, and commanded his disbanded soldiers to serve in the expedition destined against Castile. To meet it, Pedro, in 1366, assembled his troops at Burgos. He had not long to wait: under some noted leaders, the French soon entered Catalonia; they were favourably received by their ally the king of Aragon, and reached Calahorra unmolested, the gates of which were speedily opened to them. There Henry was solemnly proclaimed king of Castile.

The inactivity of Pedro on the invasion of his kingdom was such as to leave it a doubtful point with posterity whether he was a coward, or whether he knew too well the disaffection of his people to hazard a battle with the enemy. In opposition to the urgent remonstrances of the inhabitants, he precipitately left Burgos for Seville, without venturing his sword with his aspiring brother. Henry hastened to the abandoned city, where he was joyfully received by many deputies of the towns, and crowned in the monastery of Huelgas. With the money he found in the Alcazar, and the presents made him by the Jewish inhabitants, he was able to gratify his followers; their chiefs he rewarded more nobly: thus, to Du Guesclin he gave the lordship of Molina and Trastamara; and to the Englishman Hugh de Calverley, who, with the former, had the chief command of the auxiliaries, the city and lordship of Carrion; on his brother Tello he conferred the sovereignty of Biscay; on Sancho, another brother, that of Albuquerque and Ledesma. He now lost no time in pursuing the fugitive Pedro. Presenting himself before Toledo, he summoned that important place to surrender; which, after some deliberation, obeyed the summons. There he was joined by deputies from Avila, Segovia, Madrid, Cuenza, Ciudad Real, with the submission of those towns. He was now master of the whole of New Castile.

A SPANISH KING OF THE FIFTEENTH CENTURY

The rapidity of these successes convinced the guilty Pedro that his own subjects alone would form but a poor rampart against the assaults of his brother. To procure the aid of Portugal, he sent his daughter Beatrice, now the heiress of his states (his son Alfonso was no more), into that country, with a great treasure as her marriage portion, for the infante Don Ferdinand, to whom she had been promised. He was himself soon obliged to follow her: an insurrection of the Sevillians, who openly declared for Henry, inspiring the detested tyrant with a just dread of his life, he fled into the territories of his uncle and ally. But here new mortifications awaited him: the Portuguese returned both his daughter and his treasures, on the pretext that, the states of Castile having acknowledged Henry, the latter had no wish to plunge the two kingdoms into war; all that he could obtain was permission to pass through the Portuguese territory — he durst not venture into Estremadura — into Galicia. No sooner was he arrived at Monterey, than the archbishop of Santiago, Ferdinand de Castro, and other Galician lords, joined him, and advised him to try the fortune of arms; especially as Zamora, Soria, Logroño, and other cities still held for him: but, though they offered to aid him with two thousand foot and five hundred horse, either through cowardice or distrust he rejected the proposal, and set out for Santiago, with the resolution of proceeding thence to Corunna, and embarking for Bayonne, to join his ally the prince of Wales.

Pedro reached the city of Santiago about the middle of June. While there, he resolved on the murder of Don Suero the archbishop — a resolution almost too extraordinary to be explained, yet sufficiently characteristic of the man; who, whenever blood was to be shed, or plunder to be procured, little troubled himself about reasons for his conduct. But his most powerful motive for this atrocious deed was his desire to obtain the towns and fortresses of Don Suero. The fortresses of the murdered prelate were immediately occupied. The assassin, leaving them, as well as the support of his interests, to the care of Ferdinand de Castro, proceeded with his daughter to Corunna, where, with a fleet of twenty-two sail, he embarked for Bayonne. Thus, in three short months, without a single battle on either side, was this cowardly tyrant deprived of a powerful kingdom. It may, however, be doubted whether the majority of the people cared much for either prince; on them the fantastic cruelties of Pedro fell harmless: indeed, there is room for believing that, whatever were his cruelties towards his obnoxious and usually rebellious barons, he caused justice to be impartially administered, and wished no unnecessary imposts to be laid on the great towns.

The exiled king was well received by the English hero, who undertook to restore him to his throne. The treaty into which the two princes had entered rendered the aid of Edward almost imperative: besides, it was his interest to oppose the close ally of France; and his own personal ambition was not a little gratified by the offer of the lordship of Biscay, with 56,000 florins of gold for his own use, and 550,000 for the support of his army. To insure the punctual performance of the other conditions, Pedro delivered his daughters as hostages into the hands of the Black Prince. The enterprise was sanctioned by the English monarch, and the necessary preparations were immediately commenced.

In the meantime Henry had been joyfully received at Seville, and acknowledged by the whole of Andalusia. Seeing himself thus master of the kingdom, except Galicia, he marched to reduce it. He closely invested Ferdinand de Castro in the city of Lugo. From Lugo the king proceeded to Burgoo, where he convened his states and obtained the necessary supplies for the defence of the kingdom. He renewed his alliance with the king of Aragon; and, in an interview with the sovereign of Navarre, on the confines of the two monarchies, he prevailed on the latter, for a gift of 60,000 pistoles, and by the promise of two fortresses, to refuse a passage to the prince of Wales. No sooner, however, was the king of Navarre returned to Pamplona, than he received messengers from the dethroned Pedro, who offered to put him in possession of Alava and Guipuzcoa, with the two important places of Logroño and Vittoria, if he would suffer the English prince to march through his territories unmolested. Charles had no difficulty in accepting the latter proposition, as he had accepted the former.

The preparations of the English prince being completed early in the spring of 1367, he passed the Pyrenees at Roncesvalles, and descended into the plains of Navarre. In his combined army of English, Normans, and Gascons, were some of the flower of English chivalry. Instead of opposing his passage, Charles secretly desired Oliver de Manny, one of Edward's generals, to seize him (the king of Navarre) while hunting in a certain place, and make him prisoner: by this contrivance he hoped to excuse his inactivity to Henry. Oliver did as directed, and the English prince pursued his march towards the Castilian frontiers. He was joined by Sir Hugh de Calverley, who preferred the loss of the new lordship of Carrion to violating a vassal's faith by bearing arms against his natural chief. Henry also advanced; but so well was he acquainted with the valour of his renowned antagonist, that he was undetermined whether he should do more than hover round the flanks of the invaders, cut off their supplies, and force them, by famine, to return.   In a council of war, however, which he assembled to hear the opinion of his officers as to the plan of the campaign, his Castilian chiefs so justly convinced him that, if he refused the battle, several towns would immediately declare for Pedro, that he resolved to risk all.   No wonder that he should; for if, as Froissart *i* informs us, his army was near seventy thousand strong, he might well have little fear as to the result. One of his detachments had the advantage over a foraging party of the allies.   On the 2nd of April, the two hostile armies met, west of Logroño, a few miles south of the Ebro.

BATTLE OF NAJERA OR NAVARRETE (1367 A.D.)

The Castilians immediately occupied the vicinity of Najera: the allies encamped at Navarrete.   To spare the effusion of Christian blood, Edward sent a letter, by a herald, to the camp of Henry, explaining the causes which had armed the English monarch in defence of an ally and a relation; but offering, at the same time, to mediate between the two parties.   His letter, which was addressed, "To the noble and powerful Prince Henry, count of Trastamara," not to the king of Castile, was courteously received by Henry.   In his reply, he dwelt on the cruelties and oppressions of Pedro's government, whose expulsion he represented as the act of an indignant nation, and expressed his resolution to maintain both that nation's rights and his own by the sword.

The battle which decided the fate of the two kings commenced the following morning, April 3rd, 1367.   The war-cry of "Guienne and St. George!" on the one side, and of "Castile and Santiago!" on the other, were soon drowned by the clash of arms, the shouts of the victors, and the groans of the dying.   The struggle was for a short time desperate: but who could contend with the victor of Crécy and Poitiers?   A fierce charge on the left wing of Henry, by the prince in person, so terrified Don Tello, who commanded a body of cavalry, that he fled from the field; perhaps he was as treacherous as he was cowardly.   Henry fought nobly; so also did his antagonist, who, like his celebrated counterpart, Richard III of England, was as brave as he was cruel.   But after the flight of Don Tello, the infantry of Castile began to give way; and, after some desperate efforts by Henry to support the contest, resistance was abandoned.   The number of slain, on the part of the vanquished, was eight thousand.   Many thousands were made prisoners — all but a handful, who accompanied the defeated count into Aragon, whence he escaped into France.   Success so splendid is seldom to be found in the annals of history: it at once restored Pedro to the Castilian throne.   But the heroic victor met with little gratitude from his faithless ally: as on a former occasion, the states of Biscay were secretly advised not to accept him for their ruler; and it was not without difficulty that he could obtain from Pedro an oath that the money due to his troops should be paid at two instalments — the first in four, the second in twelve months.   But what most disgusted the humane conqueror was the eagerness which the restored king showed to shed the blood of the prisoners. *b*

The Spanish historian Ayala has drawn a picture of the Englishman's protest against Spanish ruthlessness.

AYALA'S ACCOUNT OF THE QUARREL BETWEEN EDWARD AND PEDRO

You must know that so soon as the battle was won, from that day onwards there was little harmony between Don Pedro and the prince, and the reason thereof was as follows. In the first place, upon the day of the battle, a gentleman named Iñigo Lopez de Orozco was taken prisoner by a gentleman of Gascony, whereupon Don Pedro rode upon horseback, and slew the said Iñigo Lopez; and the gentleman whose prisoner he was complained to the prince that, this man being his prisoner, Don Pedro came up and killed him; and he complained not only for the loss of his prisoner, but also because he held himself greatly dishonoured by the death of this gentleman who had surrendered to him, and was in his power.

The prince said to Don Pedro that it was not well done of him, for he knew full well that one of the chief articles of those agreed, sworn, and signed between them, was that the king should not put to death any gentleman of Castile, nor any person of note, while the prince was there, until he had been justly judged, save those whom he had previously sentenced, among whom this Iñigo Lopez was not included. And that it appeared from this that the king did not intend to fulfil his engagements towards him, and he presumed that his fidelity on all points would be the same as in this matter. The king excused himself as best he might, but neither he nor the prince was well pleased that day. The day after the battle Don Pedro asked the prince that all the knights and squires of note, natives of Castile, who were taken prisoners in the battle, should be delivered to him, and that a reasonable price should be set upon them, and he would pay it to those who held them prisoners. And that the prince should be security for such payments to the knights and men-at-arms who held them prisoners; and the king, Don Pedro, would pledge himself to the prince for the sum to which they amounted. And the king said that, if these knights were delivered to him, he would deal and speak with them in such a way that they should remain on his side; but if their ransom should be procured by other means, or they should escape from the imprisonment in which their captors held them, they would always remain his enemies and be active in his dis-service. Don Pedro insisted strongly on this point, on Sunday, the day after the battle, which was fought on the Saturday before Lazarus Sunday, the 3rd of April. The prince of Wales said to Don Pedro that, saving his royal majesty, his request was beyond reason, for these lords, knights, and men-at-arms, who were there in the king's service and his own, had laboured for honour, and if they had taken any prisoners they were theirs. And the knights who held them were of such sort that for all the wealth of the world, though it were a thousand times the worth of their prisoners, they would never deliver them to him, for they would think his purpose was to kill them. And he bade the king urge the point no more, for it was a thing to which he never could agree; however, if there were any among the captive knights against whom he had passed sentence before the battle, he would order them to be delivered to him.

The king said to the prince that if things were to fall out thus, his kingdom was now more surely lost than ever, for these prisoners were those by whose fault he had lost his kingdom, and if they were to escape thus, and not be delivered to him, that he might come to terms with them and win them to his cause, he held that the prince's help was of small account, and that he had expended his treasure in vain. Then the prince was angry at the words the king, Don Pedro, had spoken to him, and thus made answer:

[1367-1368 A.D.]

" Sir kinsman, methinks you are now more like to recover your kingdom than when it was yours indeed, and you governed it so ill that you were fain to lose it. And I would counsel you to cease these executions and seek some means whereby you may recover the good will of the lords, knights, and noblemen, and the towns and cities of your kingdom ; but if, on the contrary, you govern yourself as you did formerly, you are in sore peril of losing your kingdom and life, and of being brought to such a pass that neither the king of England, my lord and father, nor myself, will avail to help you, though we were so minded."

Such was the discourse held between Don Pedro and the prince that day, Sunday, after the battle, when they lay in that camp.[h]

A NEW REVOLT ; THE END OF PEDRO THE CRUEL

Pedro's cruelty soon raised new discontent of which Henry was ready to take advantage, while the English prince was too disgusted[1] to support further with his bravery the odious tyranny of the Spanish Nero.[a]

Towards the close of the year (1367), Henry entered Spain by Roussillon, at the head of a very small force, not exceeding four hundred lances. At first the king of Aragon attempted to arrest his progress through that kingdom, but with little zeal ; the soldiers sent to oppose him connived at his passage into Navarre. Having passed the Ebro at Azagra, and set foot on the Castilian territory, he drew a cross on the sand, and by it swore that he would not desist from his undertaking while life remained. The neighbouring inhabitants of Calahorra readily received him within their walls. He was joined by many of the Castilian barons with considerable reinforcements, and by the archbishop of Toledo. Leon was besieged and taken ; the Asturias submitted ; Illescas, Buytrago, and Madrid opened their gates after a short struggle ; and Toledo, which promised a more obstinate resistance, was invested. It is useful to observe that the resistance of these places was the work of the citizens who were generally attached to Pedro ; while the barons and hidalgos were generally for Henry. This circumstance gives great weight to the suspicion that, while Pedro ruled the privileged orders with an iron sceptre, he favoured the independence of the people.

The success of the invader roused Pedro to something like activity in defence of his tottering crown. His ally, the king of Granada, was persuaded to arm in his behalf ; and to join him with six thousand horse and thirty thousand foot. His own troops did not much exceed seven thousand, but the united force was formidable. Cordova was immediately assailed by the two kings ; but the defence was so vigorous, and the loss on the part of the besiegers so severe, that the enterprise was soon abandoned. The troops of Muhammed V returned to Granada ; and though they afterwards took the field, they did so, not so much to aid their ally, as to derive some advantage for themselves from the confusion of the times. The operations of the war were now very desultory, though destructive to the kingdom. In the north, Vittoria, Salvatierra, Logroño, and some other places which held for Pedro, submitted to the king of Navarre in preference to Henry — so great

[1] He did not escape without being the victim of an attempt at poisoning which ruined his health. He returned, as Burke [d] says, " with the loss of his soldiers, of his money, and of his health, befooled and cheated in one of the worst causes in which English blood and English treasure had been squandered on the continent of Europe." Burke, who also calls Pedro " one of the greatest blackguards that ever sat upon a throne," notes that to the last it was two Englishmen who defended him.]

was their repugnance to that champion of feudal tyranny. Toledo manfully resisted his assaults. To relieve that important city, which had now been invested nearly twelve months, Pedro left Seville in March, 1369, and passed by Calatrava towards Montiel, with the intention of waiting for some reinforcements advancing from Murcia, before he ventured an action with his rival.

At this time, Bertrand du Guesclin arrived from France with an aid of six hundred lances. Henry now put his little army in motion; was joined by the grand-master of Santiago; and, arriving at Montiel with incredible despatch, he fell on the outposts of his rival, and forced them precipitately into the fortress. With a very inadequate force, Pedro was now besieged in this place, and cut off from all supplies, which yet reached Henry every hour. What added to his difficulties was the want of provisions and of water; so that his men began to desert one by one to the enemy, or retire to their respective homes. In this critical situation he meditated the means of escape.[b]

PEDRO THE CRUEL
(From an old print)

After the combat Don Henry took steps to prevent his enemy from escaping from the castle of Montiel, causing the exits to be strictly guarded, and surrounded by a wall of uncemented stones, presumably to prevent any inmate from escaping on horseback.

Mendo Rodriguez of Sanabria, who was with the king, on the strength of having at one time been Du Guesclin's prisoner, attempted to negotiate with him for the king's escape. The conference began from the ramparts and was secretly continued at night in the besieger's camp. Rodriguez offered the French warrior, on the part of his lord, 200,000 doubloons of gold and dominion over towns as important as Almazan, Atienza, Monteagudo, Deza and Seron, if he would assist in the king's flight and join his party. The prayer was most natural and just from one so distressingly situated; the answer was noble and befitting a knight. Du Guesclin replied that he served in this expedition by order of his lord the king of France, and in the service of the count of Trastamara, and therefore, without dishonour, he could not accede to this prayer; upon which Rodriguez returned to the fortress, suspicion being afterwards held by some as to his sincerity and loyalty in this attempt.

Bertrand related what had occurred to Don Henry, and the bastard with his natural generosity rewarded him by paying him what Rodriguez had offered, though in acting thus Bertrand had but been faithful to his duty and to the dictates of honour. He then induced the Frenchman to continue the negotiations and promise safety to Don Pedro, so that upon the latter's coming to his tent he might summon thither Don Henry. The Frenchman had some suspicion as to the proceeding being unworthy of a knight, but eventually he conquered his scruples, and acceding to Don Henry's request entered into the ignoble plot.

The result was that the king, trusting in the safe escort promised by Du Guesclin, left the castle of Montiel, where resistance was hopeless, and where it was impossible to remain as there was even a scarcity of water, and one by one the defenders were deserting. Armed and on horseback he came to Bertrand's tent, and dismounting entered and said to him: "Mount, for it is time to be away." Obtaining no reply, the unhappy monarch was alarmed and attempted to remount, but a traitor's hand detained him, and he was made prisoner with his faithful followers Ferdinand de Castro, Mendo Rodriguez of Sanabria, Garcia Fernandez de Villodre, and others.

The news was speedily carried to Don Henry, if indeed he was not awaiting it near by, and well armed he hurried to the spot where the king was. As this scene took place at night in presence of numerous witnesses, and it was long since they had met, they did not immediately recognise one another. Don Henry being informed of his brother's presence, the latter confirmed the news with noble arrogance, saying : "'Tis I ! 'Tis I !"

Then occurred one of the most terrible scenes related in history for the horror of mankind. Don Henry wounded the king in the face with his dagger, and both grappling they fell to the ground. Don Henry succeeded, either by his own strength or with the assistance of a bystander, in falling on the top and wounding the unhappy king mortally, finally cutting off his head with furious wrath. Thus on March 23rd, 1369, was consummated a great crime against the legitimate king, and a repellent fratricide which, if Don Henry had refrained from presenting himself at that place, would have been avoided. It may be that he had no intention of killing the king with his own hand, and that infuriated by his hateful presence he flung himself upon him precipitately ; but he should have foreseen the result, knowing that Pedro was about to become his prisoner through Du Guesclin's treachery. It may be that the latter was merely actuated by a desire to bring this long war to an end, and secure the throne to Don Henry whom he served, and who had almost succeeded in winning it; but his intervention in this business, which terminated in a most horrible fratricide, was disloyal and unworthy of one whom the French esteem their greatest knight, nor was treachery called for, as Don Pedro must speedily have surrendered.

To conclude, this tragedy was shameful for the principal actors in it, the victim alone being free from taint, and to a certain extent his memory was purified by the shedding of his blood ; for had not his tempestuous life come to so untimely an end, we may feel certain that passionate defenders would never have arisen to obliterate the title of "cruel" by which he is and ever will be known in history. *j*

A FINAL ESTIMATE OF PEDRO THE CRUEL

In recent times, attempts have been made by Mondejar,[k] and other historical critics, to vindicate the memory of this king, on the ground that his chronicler and contemporary, Pedro Lopez de Ayala,[h] was a blind partisan of his rival's, and has injuriously treated his memory. They tell us of a chronicle of this king, written by Don Juan de Castro, bishop of Jaen, in which Pedro is represented as one of the best sovereigns of the age — as one who, while he protected the oppressed, was severe only against his turbulent and lawless barons. There may be some truth in this latter assertion : Pedro, like Richard III of England, whom he partially resembles, was probably no enemy to the humbler orders, but eager only to break the formidable power of the nobles. Even admitting, what is very probable, that his character has been somewhat unfairly treated by Ayala, if one-half the deeds narrated by that author were actually perpetrated by him, — and the careful minuteness with which they are recorded gives them the appearance of authenticity, — he has had but one equal in ferocity, and that one was the czar Ivan IV of Russia. Until Castro's pretended chronicle is actually produced — and it has been sought for in vain these three hundred years — and compared with Ayala, criticism is compelled to receive the testimony of the latter, confirmed, as it incidentally is, by Froissart[i] and other contemporary writers. That he was a man of lust, as well as of cruelty, is apparent from the number of his mistresses, to say nothing of his two pretended wives.[b]

Prosper Mérimée[m] is one of the modern defenders of Pedro, but while his tone is apologetic, his facts leave the resulting opinion only the stronger. Hume[n] admits the black heart of Pedro, but denies that he was exceptionally heartless for that time, and insists that his struggles against the nobles were for the good of the people and his failure to restrain their feudal power a calamity. It is hard, however, to believe that a monstrosity whom even his contemporaries found worthy of the fame of the most cruel of the cruel, could have been moved by any altruistic care for his people, or any motive except ferocious hatred of any resistance to his unutterable selfishness.

It is difficult to find in history a monarch whose reign had not some effort for good, since perfection in vice is as impossible as perfection in virtue. But surely no other king ever deserved less sympathy than Pedro for his failure to check the noblemen in their greed. Surely the feudal lords rarely used their power with better excuse than in protecting for a time the unhappy girl-wife Blanche de Bourbon whom Pedro sought to murder, and finally put to death. And the revolt of Trastamara can only be blamed by those to whom legitimacy of descent is a sacred claim on loyalty, even though the legitimate monarch wield his dagger right and left and have his kinsmen beaten to death with clubs till the floor of his own palace was ankle-deep in blood, as the chronicler asserts of Pedro.

It is unjust to deny the monarch the one distinction he earned by consistency and perseverance in the cause of evil. "Cruel" was his epithet in his own day; let "cruel" be his epitaph in ours.[a]

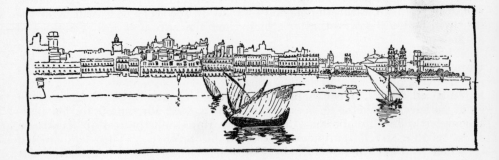

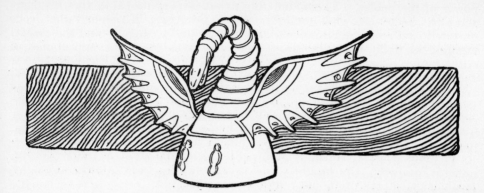

CHAPTER IV

ARAGON TO THE UNION WITH CASTILE

[1162–1475 A.D.]

OWING to the alternate separations and unions of the Spanish kingdoms and their picturesque activities within their own realms as well as with each other and with foreign countries, the arrangement of the earlier chronicle has always puzzled historians. To carry one realm too far forward before going back to bring forward the other is destructive of a sense of synchronology, while the attempt to carry them simultaneously is as bewildering as it is difficult.

To carry Castile forward to that well-known time when Isabella wed Ferdinand of Aragon is to be compelled to retrace our steps for three centuries. It seems most convenient to do as follows: Leaving Castile at the moment of the death of that easily remembered monarch Pedro the Cruel, to take up Aragon and bring its history to the same point. But once reaching there it leaves but little more to be said to bring Aragon definitely to the marriage of its prince Ferdinand with the Castilian princess Isabella. This, then, we shall do, returning thence to take up the story of Castile after the death of Pedro the Cruel, after which time the chronicle lies straight and single.[a]

That gallant monarch Alfonso II, the liberal art-loving patron of the troubadours, who was endowed with such brilliant princely qualities, had either by right of inheritance or success in arms extended his sway over a great part of southern France and curbed the might of the Saracens. In 1196 he was succeeded in Aragon, Catalonia, and Roussillon by his first-born son Pedro II, while the county of Provence and the rest of his possessions in France fell to Alfonso the younger brother. Pedro had himself crowned by Pope Innocent III, perhaps with the object of investing the authority of the crown with greater prestige in the eyes of the nobles. At his coronation he swore fealty to the pope and pledged himself to pay an annual tribute to the apostolic see. In order to defray this expense he introduced a new property-tax, the *monedaje*, to be levied upon the nobles, who had hitherto been exempt from taxation. The nobles and cities, incensed at the new impost and the abasement of the crown, formed a "union" in consequence of which the king was compelled at least to reduce the tax.

Pedro participated in the Albigensian wars as an ally of his brother-in-law, Raymond of Toulouse, and in 1213 he met his death in battle before the walls of the fortress of Muret, where he proved himself worthy of the reputation for heroic strength which he had won two years before in the famous victory of Ubeda in the plain of Tolosa. Pedro was a true son of his age; a brave warrior of mighty arm and gigantic stature, he was distinguished for chivalrous valour as well as for liberality and sumptuous tastes; a gallant knight, who honoured women in poetry and song and won repute among the troubadours of his day, though he was harsh and unloving to his virtuous consort, Maria de Montpellier, granddaughter of the Byzantine emperor Manuel. His knightly and royal qualities were often overcast by debauchery, superstition, and religious fanaticism.

JAMES THE CONQUEROR (1213–1276 A.D.)

James,[1] the son of Pedro and Maria, had to win by arms the throne which his uncles contested with him, before he could resume the war of conquest against the Saracens at the head of the chivalry of Aragon and Catalonia. He then prosecuted it with such success as to gain for himself the surname of "the conqueror." He began by a campaign of four years' duration, in which he subjugated Majorca and the rest of the Balearic Islands, so long the headquarters of a ruthless system of piracy and the terror of all Christian seaboard states of the Mediterranean.

The Catalans, whose important trade suffered great loss at the hands of hostile pirates, took a particularly active part in the conquest, and many Catalan knights and nobles were therefore endowed with fiefs in the islands. A matter of even greater consequence to the future of the kingdom of Aragon was James' expedition against Valencia, which the Spaniards regarded as a sacred inheritance from the great Cid Campeador, the first Spanish conqueror. James invaded the territory of Valencia with a great army of Catalan and Aragonese knights, which was joined by many volunteers from southern France and even from England. The emir Jomail ben Ziyan was forced to capitulate, and the capital was vigorously besieged and reduced to submission (1238). The Saracen population migrated elsewhere, either voluntarily or under compulsion, their property was assigned to Christian settlers, Catalans occupied the cities, and the land was given in fee among the victorious barons and knights. Within the next few days the other towns fell into the hands of the Aragonese conquerors, the chief of them being the strongholds of Jativa, situate upon a hill in the midst of a fertile and lovely country, and the town of Denia; and Moslem dominion was soon confined to the kingdom of Granada and its strong, rock-built capitals, for the kings of Castile and Portugal were likewise pushing their frontiers forward on the Guadiana and the Guadalquivir.

James was one of the greatest monarchs of his century, and not only because in the course of a reign of sixty-three years he extended the kingdom he had inherited in every direction, nor because he conquered Majorca and Valencia, nor even because in the closing years of his life he fought with youthful ardour against the infidels in Murcia, who had revolted afresh

[1 Though this king is usually called "Jayme," he spelled his own name "Jacme" in the Catalan form.]

against their Christian conquerors with the help of the Merinids from Africa, nor that he fought, as is reported, thirty battles against the Moors; but because with the might of a conqueror he combined the endowments of a wise and humane ruler. He was clement and merciful to the Moslem who sued him for mercy, and greatly as he had the propagation of Christianity at heart (he is said to have founded nearly two hundred churches in the countries he conquered) he showed tolerance and consideration for their faith and their religious and civil laws, and defended the independence of his crown against the pretensions of the papal see.

But he was pre-eminent, above all things, as a lawgiver; it was he who made the first compilation of the laws of Aragon; he founded the maritime laws of Catalonia,[1] he promoted navigation and trade, laid the basis of the free constitution of Barcelona, and was the author of a new political organisation in Valencia. The Catalonian language, intellectual culture, and the art of poetry likewise enjoyed his patronage; Jordi of Valencia, to whom Petrarch owes many beautiful passages,[2] and other minstrels lived at his court, which was not lacking in brilliance and splendour. But his unfortunate idea of dividing the dominions he had inherited and conquered among his sons caused him many pangs and wrought great confusion in the kingdom of Aragon. Several treaties of partition were agreed upon during his reign, and invariably brought rebellion and civil war in their train. The great dismemberment he contemplated was only prevented by the fact that the eldest infante, Alfonso, the son of his marriage with Leonora of Castile, whom he afterwards divorced, died before his father, and the third of the sons whom Violante [or Yolande] of Hungary bore him sank into an early grave. Thus the great provinces of Aragon, Catalonia, and Valencia passed on united into the hands of Pedro III, and only the Balearic Islands, with Montpellier, Roussillon, and some of his other possessions fell to the younger brother, James, as a separate kingdom. Fernan Sanchez, a natural son of the king, was drowned in the river Chica by order of his brother the infante Pedro, after a futile attempt at rebellion, and his property was sequestrated. James not only sanctioned the deed but testified his satisfaction at it, so greatly had the unnatural strife hardened his usually noble heart.[b] He died in 1276 and was succeeded by his son.

PEDRO III AND HIS SICILIAN WARS

Pedro III lost no time in restoring tranquillity in Valencia; but scarcely was this object effected, when many of his rebellious barons, whose constant end was the curtailment of the royal prerogative and the oppression of the poor, broke out into an open insurrection. He reduced them to obedience. In two years they again rebelled, but with no better success: they were invested in the fortress of Balaguer, which was at length compelled to surrender, and were for some time detained prisoners.

But the most important transactions of Pedro were with Sicily. On the death of Manfred, who had perished at Benevento in battle with Charles

[1 Burke,g however, credits this entirely to Barcelona.]
[2 This statement of Petrarch's indebtedness is, however, open to discussion. There was another Jordi who lived in the fifteenth century and may have been the author of the poems in which resemblances to Petrarch are detected. This would make Petrarch the original. But the Spaniards generally attribute the poems to the contemporary of James the Conqueror, who has left an account of a storm which overtook that monarch's fleet near the island of Majorca.]

of Anjou, whom the pope had invested with the fief, the French prince took undisturbed possession of the Two Sicilies. When Conradin had attained his sixteenth year, knowing the hatred borne to the French rule by the Sicilies, and that the Ghibelline faction was at his command, he resolved to vindicate his rightful claims. Despising the papal thunders, which had consigned him while living to every ill that life can suffer, and when dead to the goodly fellowship of Dathan, Abiram, and the devil, he invaded Italy, passed, in contempt of the church, through the city of Rome, where he was hailed with enthusiasm, and proceeded towards Naples. He was defeated by his formidable adversary; was taken prisoner in the retreat; was tried, condemned, and executed at Naples. The Ghibellines, and all who revered the rights of blood, now turned their eyes towards Constanza, daughter of Manfred and queen of Aragon, while the Guelfs and all who recognised the papal supremacy over the kingdom continued the zealous asserters of the rights of Charles, the pope's feudatory. But the tyrannical government of Charles, his rapacity and injustice, soon made him hateful to the whole body of his subjects. The oppressed inhabitants of Sicily despatched messengers with renewed complaints to Nicholas III, to Michael Palæologus, emperor of Constantinople, and, above all, to Pedro of Aragon, whom they regarded in right of Constanza as lawful ruler, and whom they urged to expel the tyrant without delay.

Pedro was overjoyed at this opportunity of extending his dominions; but to fight against the pope, the king of France, brother to Charles of Sicily, and the whole party of the Guelfs, was too momentous an undertaking to be lightly commenced. He first secured a considerable sum from the Greek emperor, to whom the Sicilian usurper was obnoxious; he next collected a fleet, assembled his barons, gave liberty to his rebel subjects, whom he had placed in confinement; but took care to conceal his purpose. It seems, however, to have been divined both by the pope and the French king, who, alarmed at the extent of his preparations, demanded for what object they were intended. By pretending that his expedition was to be directed against Barbary, and by even sending an ambassador to the pope (Martin IV), soliciting an indulgence for all who joined him in warring against the infidels, he hoped to lull the suspicions of Europe. But Martin, who was not to be deceived, contumeliously dismissed the ambassador. This circumstance did not discourage Pedro, whose armament was prosecuted with an alacrity inspired by the hope of success. An accident which, operating like a spark on the inflammable temper of the Sicilians, forced them into open insurrection, hastened his departure. The citizens of Palermo rose as one man, and destroyed every Frenchman on whom they could lay hands. Their example was followed by other towns — by none more heartily than Messina; so that scarcely a Frenchman was left alive from one extremity of the island to another. Such is the famous massacre which posterity has called the Sicilian Vespers. [Burke*g* estimates the number of slain at 28,000.]

When Pedro learned that the Messenians were courageously repelling the assaults of Charles of Anjou, who had passed over from Naples to reduce them, and when a deputation from Palermo arrived, beseeching him to accept the crown, he laid aside his extreme caution, and proceeded towards the western coast of the island. In August he landed at Trapani, where his reception was enthusiastic; he hastened to Palermo, where he was joyfully proclaimed king of Sicily. The inhabitants of Messina, still invested by Charles, besought the new monarch to relieve them, and to receive their homage. Pedro hastened to their aid. Charles now raised the siege, and conducted his powerful armament towards the ports of Calabria ; it was pursued by that of Aragon, headed by Don James, a son of Pedro, who took twenty vessels, with four thousand prisoners. But the young prince, listening only to his ardour, instead of returning to Messina, pursued Charles to a fort in Calabria, which he attempted to take ; where, being repulsed with some loss, he re-embarked his troops. His father, indignant at his failure, deprived him of the naval command, which was intrusted to a more experienced chief, Roger de Lauria.

No sooner did Pope Martin hear of Pedro's proclamation at Palermo and Messina, of the enthusiasm shown towards the monarch by the Sicilians, and of the flight of Charles, than he excommunicated the Aragonese. A defiance next followed between the two rivals ; who agreed to decide their quarrel by combat, one hundred knights on each side, in the city of Bordeaux, in June the following year. Until the appointed day arrived, Pedro employed himself in causing his queen, who had arrived from Aragon, to be acknowledged by the Sicilians, and in reducing some of the forts on the Neapolitan coast. Leaving Constanza and his son, Don James, in the government of the island, he returned into his states, for the purpose, as was believed, of preparing for the combat. But that combat never happened, nor, amidst the conflicting statements of historians, can we easily decide to which of the royal rivals the disgrace of its failure must be imputed. It is certain that Pedro caused one hundred knights to be selected for the occasion, and that he appeared secretly at Bordeaux, attended by three horsemen only, and returned to his dominions before the lists were opened. For this extraordinary proceeding he appears to have had sufficient reason. He found that a considerable number of troops were silently moving towards the south of France, with the view, as he feared, of seizing his person. If the Aragonese writers are to be credited, the seneschal of Bordeaux, whom he consulted on the subject, informed him that the field was not a

A ROYAL ATTENDANT, SPAIN

safe one, and advised him not to risk his person. This account is the more probable, from the fact that Pope Martin had previously condemned the combat, and had required the English king, Edward I, to whom Bordeaux belonged, and who was to be present on the occasion, not to guarantee a fair field, nor to be present, either in person or by his seneschals. What confirms the suspicion that some treachery was meditated is that, though the English monarch was thus enjoined not to visit the field, in other words, was given to understand that the battle would not take place, no such intimation was made to the king of Aragon.

While Pedro remained in Aragon, his admiral, Roger de Lauria, reduced the greater part of Malta (1284). He afterwards defeated a French fleet within sight of Naples, taking the prince of Salerno, the son of Charles, prisoner. The vindictive pope now proclaimed a crusade against the excommunicated king of Aragon: his legate zealously preached it in France, declaring Pedro deprived of the crown, which he conferred on Charles de Valois, who was thus to possess both it and that of the Two Sicilies. Fortunately for Pedro both Sicily and Aragon required other weapons than a furious churchman could wield before they could be drawn from his sway.

Though the same indulgences as were awarded to all who warred for the Holy Sepulchre were promised to such as engaged in this Spanish crusade; though vast numbers, among whom was James, king of Majorca, brother and vassal of the Aragonese king, flocked to the standard of Philip; though that monarch lost no time in penetrating, by way of Roussillon, into Catalonia, at the head of one hundred thousand men, these formidable preparations ended in nothing. If Gerona, after a long and bloody siege, capitulated, the French fleet was almost annihilated near Rosas by the famous Roger de Lauria. The ranks of the invaders were so thinned by pestilence and the sword, that Philip, leaving a garrison in Gerona, immediately returned to Perpignan, where he died. The rear of his army in this retreat was dreadfully harassed by Don Pedro, who recovered Gerona with facility.

Pedro had just despatched his eldest son Alfonso with a small armament to dethrone his brother Don James, as a punishment for the aid which that prince had lent to the invaders, when death surprised him at Villafranca del Panades (1285). In his will he left Aragon and Catalonia to Alfonso, and Sicily to his second son, Don James.

Though Alfonso III heard of his father's death immediately after his disembarkation, he refused to return until he had dethroned his uncle. As James was not much beloved by the inhabitants of these islands, whom he had offended by his exactions, the enterprise was successful. The dethroned king had still Montpellier, Conflans, and other possessions in France: to these he retired, but they appear the same year to have been laid waste by Roger de Lauria, the able and intrepid admiral of Aragon.

POLITICAL GROWTH

During Alfonso's absence, the nobles of Aragon had assembled in Saragossa, to provide for the due administration of justice. Some of them were not a little scandalised that he should have assumed in the Balearic Isles the title of king, since, by ancient custom, it could be assumed only after he had sworn before the assembly of the states to observe the customs, privileges, immunities, and laws of the realm. No sooner did they hear of his return to Valencia, than they despatched several of their body to wait upon him, and to express their surprise at his thus arrogating to himself the supreme power without their formal sanction. He justified himself by replying that the crown was his by right of succession, and that there would be time enough to guarantee the constitutions of the realms at the ceremony of his coronation. Accordingly, when that ceremony took place in the cathedral of Saragossa, he fulfilled the conditions of the compact.c

Under Pedro III, the knightly monarch, — "girded," as Dante says, "with the cord of every virtue," — the Aragonese, exasperated by the burdensome taxes which the king was compelled to levy for his costly enterprises, had extorted such great privileges and liberties in the General Privilege of Saragossa (1283) that after Pedro's successor, Alfonso III, a man of milder temper, had amplified the *Privilegium*,[1] by fresh concessions to the union of the nobles, the kingdom of Aragon was less like a hereditary monarchy than a republican commonwealth with a responsible chief. The king was not only bound to secure the consent of the estates of the kingdom (*cortes*) in all important public affairs, especially for the declaration of war, the conclusion of peace, the enactment of laws, the imposition of taxes, and the selection and appointment of the advisers of the crown (the ministers), but it was further decreed that "without previous sentence of the justiciary and the cortes of Saragossa, the king might not proceed against any member of the union by way of capital punishment, imprisonment, or other injury, and that should he nevertheless do so, the union had power to exclude him and his descendants from succession to the throne, without thereby incurring the guilt of wrong-doing or disloyalty."

On Alfonso's death without issue (1291) he was succeeded by his brother James II, up to that time king of Sicily, a well-meaning, kindly, and (as the surname he bears in history testifies) "just" sovereign, who thought more of perfecting the laws and constitution and maintaining peace and prosperity amongst his people than of enlarging the borders of his kingdom. He handed Sicily over to his brother Frederick as a separate kingdom; but on the other hand, after protracted wars with the Genoese, he won the island of Sardinia which the pope had bestowed upon him in fee. A war against the Moors, which he undertook in conjunction with Ferdinand, king of Castile, led to no important results. In an attempt to break down the overweening power of the aristocratic families, James had the assistance of the great jurist Martinez de Salanova; the power of the justiciary was strengthened.

But the greatest benefits which James conferred upon the Aragonese nation was a law enacted in the assembly of Tarragona, by virtue of which the kingdoms of Aragon and Valencia, the county of Barcelona, and the suzerainty of Majorca were united in perpetuity and incapable of division by will or gift, though each was to remain a kingdom possessed of its separate constitution and cortes. The king, however, reserved the right of assigning to his sons and other members of his family the possession of particular cities and castles, a right of which his successors frequently availed themselves to excess, and which often provoked internecine quarrels and feuds.[b]

King James died in 1327, and was succeeded by his second son, Alfonso, his first son having voluntarily renounced his claims that he might, tradition says, give himself up more completely to his vices.[a]

Alfonso IV was doomed to much annoyance from the recent conquest of Sardinia. In 1330 the Genoese, incensed that the Catalans, their rivals in commerce, should have obtained a settlement in seas which they considered as exclusively their right, not only fomented a spirit of disaffection among the islanders, but sent a fleet to invest the capital. A bloody war ensued, the details of which would afford little interest. To stay these hostilities the pope frequently interfered, but without effect; the Genoese insisted on an an ample indemnification for the expenses of their armaments; the Aragonese would consent to none. Thus the warfare raged during the whole of this prince's reign. Alfonso, like his predecessors, was not averse to

[1 This document has been well called Aragon's Magna Charta, and it was secured in much the same manner. The Privilege was confirmed by the cortes of Saragossa in 1325, and torture of witnesses in criminal trials was abolished. In five years followed the Privilege of Union in which the king of Aragon was forced to authorise unions of his subjects to make war upon the sovereign in case of a denial of justice, or any attempt to act independently of the justiciar. We have to look to Poland for a like constitutional defiance of royalty.]

encourage the rebellions which at this period almost continually afflicted Castile; but without deriving any ultimate advantage from his ungenerous policy. If the internal state of his own kingdom was tranquil, it was not so in his own house. His eldest son and destined successor, Don Pedro, offended that he had bestowed on Alfonso — another son, by a second wife — some domains of the crown, complained loudly of his prodigality. The queen, Leonora of Castile, at whose instigation the alienation had been made, cherished a deep resentment against her stepson. Pedro despised her anger; and, to incense her the more, seized on Jativa, which had been assigned to her on her marriage with his father, and loudly proclaimed his intention of revoking every grant made by the king, whenever he should succeed to the sovereignty. It was not in Alfonso's power to stifle these dissensions, which not only imbittered his peace but aggravated the hydropsical disease under which he had long suffered. He died at Barcelona, in 1336.

No sooner had Pedro IV ascended the throne, than Queen Leonora, apprehensive of the consequences of her late quarrel with him, fled to Fraga, whence she implored the protection of her brother Alfonso, king of Castile. Alfonso naturally espoused his sister's cause. The pope despatched a legate to exhort the two kings to settle their dispute by negotiations, and to insist on justice being done to Queen Leonora. Their deliberations ended in nothing, beyond a suspension of actual hostilities. Some years having elapsed, in 1345 the king, so far from wishing to do his stepmother justice, endeavoured to seize the domains belonging to his two brothers, Ferdinand and Juan, on the pretext that the revenues of the crown were materially injured by the prodigality of their common father. On the representations of the Castilian king, he again suspended, though he was far from abandoning, his purpose. The troubles which agitated his kingdom will account for this temporary forbearance.

He offended his barons, in 1347, by purposing to set aside the order of succession, as established by Don Jayme el Conquistador (James the Conqueror), which, on the failure of direct heirs male, called in the collateral male branches — or, in other words, which enforced the Salic law. As Pedro, by his queen Maria of Navarre, had only a daughter — the infanta Constanza — his brother Don James was the presumptive heir to the crown. To secure the succession to his daughter, he assembled twenty-two theologians and civil jurists, nineteen of whom readily sanctioned her right. They knew that Doña Petronilla had not been excluded by the accident of sex; that in Navarre and Castile women were called to the succession; and they could not approve the arbitrary regulation of James I, nor recognise it as binding on his successors. But however weighty these reasons, they had no effect on the prince whom they tended to exclude, and who resolved to vindicate his supposed claims by force. Amid the elements of discontent which lay scattered on every side, he had no difficulty in collecting means of resistance.

From the causes just detailed, and from the restless ambition of his barons, who constantly aimed at diminishing the royal authority, a formidable confederacy was soon formed against the king. It consisted of prelates, barons, magistrates, and a majority of the great towns. They formed themselves into a political union, and bound themselves by oath never to cease their opposition to the king until their privileges rested on some surer guarantee than the royal engagement, and until the Salic law became fundamental in the state. At the head of this league was Don James. A similar one was soon formed in Valencia, under the guidance of the infante

Ferdinand.   Both diligently raised troops to take the field against the king. Conscious of their united strength, they now loudly demanded the convocation of the states, which accordingly met at Saragossa, and which were, as usual, opened by the monarch.   Among the demands made by the union, not the least obnoxious was the nomination of the public officers by themselves — a concession which, as before related, James II had been constrained to grant, and which they insisted should thenceforward be held as a fundamental law of the realm.   Pedro showed great reluctance to sanction it; but on being told that, if he refused to do so, the states would immediately proceed to a new election, he no longer withstood the torrent.   From that moment, however, he resolved to effect the destruction of the union, if not by force, by corruption.   So well did he labour, so efficaciously were his gold and promises distributed that in a few days he gained over a few of the most influential members.

The king soon closed the states, without yielding any further to the demands of the union, and hastened into Catalonia, with the avowed purpose of collecting troops, to reduce the whole body to obedience.   That the leaguers did not prevent his departure was owing to the suspicions irresistibly forced on their minds that there was treachery in their camp, and that he had more secret adherents than they had expected.   He was followed to Barcelona by the infante Don James, who sickened and died in that city, not without suspicions of poison.   The union of Valencia, nowise discouraged by the ill success of that of Aragon, immediately invested the fortresses which held for the king, whose troops they defeated before Jativa.   The infante Ferdinand, who was now proclaimed lieutenant-general of that province and head of the confederacy, with a force estimated at thirty thousand obtained a second victory over the royalists.   Pedro now hastened from Barcelona, to crush in person this formidable rebellion.

He had soon an army on foot with which two of his generals attacked, defeated, and took Ferdinand.[1]   The infante, however, from fear of the king's vengeance, was conducted into Castile.   Pedro himself advanced against Saragossa, the very stronghold of faction.   One instance of ill fortune had damped, as much as success had encouraged, the rebels: they received him with great humility, renounced the privileges of the union, and threw themselves wholly on his mercy.   Thirteen of the most obnoxious ringleaders were put to death; the rest he pardoned.   In an assembly of the states, which he was no longer afraid of convoking, the *ricos homes* [or *hombres*] and deputies solemnly renewed the renunciation of the privileges claimed by the union; in presence of them all, the king tore in pieces the registered act of that body, but at the same time he confirmed his subjects in the possession of all their ancient rights.   Aragon was now pacified; its union was no more: but Valencia remained in rebellion.   Having assembled a formidable army, James marched into that province, and, in a general battle near the capital, triumphed over the leaguers.   Valencia immediately surrendered at discretion.

On the termination of these troubled scenes, Leonora and one of her sons took refuge in Castile.   But misfortunes assailed them there, superior, perhaps, to any which would have befallen them in Aragon.   How the infante Juan was murdered at Bilbao, and Leonora herself in the castle of Castro Xeres, by order of Pedro the Cruel, has been related in the reign of that monarch.   Ferdinand, indeed, escaped the vengeance of the tyrant; but,

[1 " The loss of the principal nobles of the union at Epila was a death-blow to the feudal cause in Aragon." *d*]

as we shall soon see, a fate no less tragical awaited him. The misunderstanding between the two Pedros commenced in 1356, on the refusal of the Castilian to restore a prize made at sea by one of his Biscayan pirates. The second offence was committed by an admiral of Catalonia, who, under the eyes of the Castilian, captured two Pisan vessels — a power with which the Aragonese were at war — in the port of Santa Maria. With some justice, the Castilian remonstrated against the violation of a neutral port; and on the refusal of his brother sovereign to make satisfaction for it, he levied a heavy contribution on the Catalan inhabitants of Seville, and declared war against Aragon. Hostilities now commenced, with various success and many suspensions.

CORDOVA

In general, the success of the war rested with the Castilian. In 1363, through the interference of the papal legate, the first peace was made, the secret conditions of which were of an atrocious character. Pedro of Aragon engaged not only to remove by death the obnoxious brothers of the Castilian, but his own, the infante Ferdinand. A servant of Count Henry of Castile dealt the victim a fatal blow. Henry himself was spared — doubtless because Pedro foresaw that his new ally of Castile would not fulfil his engagements; perhaps, also, because he himself had no disposition to do so. His anticipations were right: war was renewed by the Castilian. His operations were as indecisive as those of the former.

Seeing that the war did not and could not lead to any result, in 1365 Pedro concerted with the count of Trastamara the invasion of Castile, and the dethronement of the Castilian king. The aid which Henry obtained from France, the fate of his first and second invasions, we have already related. But the Aragonese king — so true it is that no honour can long subsist among the wicked — was never on good terms with the new king of Castile. He insisted on Murcia, which Henry, while count of Trastamara, had agreed to resign, in the event of his obtaining the Castilian throne; and on the refusal of that prince to dismember so important a province from the crown, not only coolness, but actual hostilities, between the two kingdoms were preparing. But those hostilities were soon averted by the papal legates; and the truce was, from time to time, prolonged, until 1374, when peace was finally arranged between the two monarchs.

The foreign transactions of Pedro were of some importance. In 1338 began his misintelligence with Don James, king of Majorca, whose dethronement he appears to have meditated from the commencement of his reign. Though, in 1339, James did homage for his kingdom, his destruction was no less resolved; his unpopular rule afforded Pedro well-founded hopes of success.

In 1343, Don Pedro sailed with a very formidable armament, landed in Majorca, and was immediately joined by the islanders. Thus universally deserted, James fled, leaving the three islands in the power of his brother-in-law. In opposition to the remonstrances of the pope, who compassionated the misfortunes of the fugitive king, his possessions in France were threatened, and several places in Roussillon speedily reduced. This war beyond the Pyrenees appears to have been as disagreeable to the Catalans and to the Aragonese as it was to the pope; and only by force could the king obtain supplies for conducting it. The following year (1344) he declared by a solemn decree that the Balearic Isles should forever form an integral portion of the Aragonese crown; and again penetrated into Roussillon, the whole of which, except the capital, Perpignan, he speedily reduced. The unfortunate James was later killed in a skirmish.

To Pedro, as to his two predecessors, Sardinia proved a sharp thorn in the crown. His obstinacy in retaining possession of an island which experience had shown would never willingly own his sway, which cost him so many successive campaigns, drew on him the frequent remonstrances of his states, and the refusal of supplies. As if one ruinous war for an unattainable object were not sufficient, on the death of Frederick, king of Sicily, in 1377, who had married his daughter Constanza, he claimed that crown, and showed a disposition to arm in defence of his claim. But for the obstinacy of his eldest son and heir, Don Juan, who, in 1384, became a widower, whom he wished to marry with the young princess Maria, daughter of the late king Frederick, and now settled on the throne of Sicily, but who secretly formed the indissoluble connection with a French princess, the effect of his policy would have been an immediate union of the two crowns. It may, however, be doubted whether such a union was desirable; since from the distance of the two kingdoms, and the contiguity of the island to Naples, it could not long have been perpetuated.

The ambition of Pedro was insatiable; but it was also senseless, as it grasped at impossibilities. Hearing that some people of Athens and Patras, who were of Aragonese extraction — the descendants of the crusaders, who had conquered this duchy — had risen to establish his domination, he sent an armament to their aid, and was ultimately acknowledged. It need, however, be scarcely observed that possessions so far removed from the seat of power would yield but a nominal allegiance, and would soon be lost. But there was no advantage, however small in magnitude or transient in duration, which he was not at all times ready to grasp — generally without much regard to the rights or feelings of others. The avidity with which, in 1386, he seized on the city of Tarragona, the government and sovereignty of which had long rested with the archbishops of that see, is affirmed by some historians to have been the cause of his death.[1] He died early in the month of January, 1387, after an agitated reign of fifty-one years.

The duplicity of this monarch was only equalled by his violence; of sincerity and justice he was wholly destitute; and in savage barbarity he was scarcely exceeded by his namesake of Castile.

With many of the vices and none of the virtues of humanity, he was neither loved nor respected; but, in return, he was feared. It is impossible not to admire his constancy in reverses: he deviated not from his purposes, nor suffered his mind to be depressed, in the most critical periods of his reign — and few princes were ever placed in circumstances more critical — yet he almost uniformly gained his end. Justice must also allow that, whatever were his personal vices, he was no enemy to the lowest class of his people. During the reign of this prince, the era of Cæsar was abolished, and the Christian adopted for the two chief kingdoms of Spain; in 1350 at Saragossa, and in 1383 at Segovia.[c]

Pedro IV enlarged the powers of the justiciary, enabling him to oppose his veto to usurpations on the part of the crown in the same way as to the encroachments of the feudal aristocracy; he provided for the swift and careful administration of justice; promoted the study of law, and showed favour to the legal and juridical profession. Whenever occasion offered and he was not prevented by the inhibitory intercession or legal warrant of the justiciary, he curbed the usurpations and arbitrary action of the great nobles and increased the privileges and power of the knights and burghers.[b]

In 1387, Juan I was peaceably acknowledged. His accession was regarded with great apprehension by his stepmother, Sybilla (the late king led four ladies to the altar), who, since 1384, had been his open enemy. The reason of this animosity was here, as in former cases, the eagerness of the king to alienate the crown domains in favour of his new queen and her family, and the indignant opposition of the heir apparent. At one time, so vindictive was the queen that she had expelled the infante from the palace, and had probably instigated her uxorious husband to try him, and exclude him from the succession; but the protection of the grand justiciary of Aragon had screened him from her malice: now, it was her turn to dread his displeasure. Just before the death of Pedro, she fled from Barcelona, accompanied by her brother: they were pursued by the Catalonians; were brought back, and imprisoned until the pleasure of the new monarch, who then lay ill at Gerona, could be learned. On his recovery, he hastened to that city; caused the queen to be tried as a witch, who had enchanted the late king, and several of her kindred and servants as accomplices. Some of the latter were executed; and she herself would probably have shared the same fate, but for the interference of the papal legate, and more still for the facility with which she restored the fortresses conferred on her by her royal husband. These possessions were immediately transferred to the new queen.

The eagerness which the new king showed to gratify his queen Violante, surprised and offended the Aragonese. As her disposition was gay, she insisted on converting the palace into a theatre: balls, concerts, theatrical representations, and the exhibitions of the *gaya ciencia*, succeeded each other without intermission. As the Aragonese themselves were too sober or too

[1] St. Thecla, patroness of the church of Tarragona, appeared to him, upbraided him with impiety, and gave him so good a box on the ear, or smack in the face, that he never recovered from it. "*Está muy recibido que fue contigado de la mano de Dios, y se le aparecio en vision Santa Tecla, la qual le hirio de una palmada en el rostro, y que este fue la ocasion de su dolencia.*" — *Zurita.*[e] Who would expect Ferreras,[f] a writer of the eighteenth century, to believe such a relation?

dull to excel in such diversions, professors were brought from France, and even schools established for instruction in the idle art. It became not merely the relaxation, but the business of life ; the duties of government were neglected or despised, until remonstrances both frequent and loud fell on the royal ear. Apparently, however, they produced little effect, beyond the convocation of the states at Monzon, to deliberate on this pernicious novelty. There the prelates, nobles, and deputies insisted that the king should expel from his palace his singers and dancers, his buffoons and his poets — above all, Doña Carraza Villaragut, one of the queen's ladies, and the chief promoter of such fooleries. At first he resisted this interference with his royal recreations ; but when he perceived that his barons were in earnest, that they were even preparing to arm for his moral reformation, he yielded : the fiddlers were dismissed, and with them the obnoxious lady.

The short reign of this prince was not without its troubles. An insurrection broke out among those most restless and faithless of subjects, the Sardinians. As usual, the efforts of his generals to repress it were but partially successful. The affairs of Sicily were not more promising. None of these commotions appears to have occasioned King Juan the least anxiety : he resumed his diversions, that of hunting especially, with as much eagerness as before, leaving the cares of government to his queen. One day, while occupied in this favourite occupation in the forest of Foja, he fell from his horse, and was killed on the spot.

On receiving intelligence of this catastrophe Aragon, Catalonia, and Valencia proclaimed Don Martin, brother of the late king, who was then in Sicily supporting the rights of his son and daughter-in-law, sovereigns of that island. This choice gave great umbrage to Matthieu count de Foix, who had married the eldest daughter of Juan, and who contended that the crown belonged to him in her right. He collected troops and penetrated into Catalonia ; but he found the inhabitants averse to his pretensions, and indignant at his proceedings. As the states were sitting at Saragossa, he now adopted the wiser mode of deputing ambassadors to that assembly, with instructions to espouse his rights, which, according to the laws of legitimate succession, were well founded. But Aragon had seen only one female sovereign, Doña Petronilla, and had for some time been inclined to consider the Salic law as tacitly in force. The count met with a repulse both there and at Barcelona ; but he hoped that arms would be more effectual than arguments ; and, with a second and more numerous army, he invaded Aragon. There he and his countess solemnly assumed the royal title and arms, and reduced several towns ; but he was soon compelled to retire into Navarre.

Having pacified Sicily, in appearance at least, and caused his son and daughter-in-law to be acknowledged by the rebels, Martin, who seems to have been in no anxiety about the security of his kingdom, proceeded to Sardinia and Corsica, with the view of restoring tranquillity also in those islands. The following year he convoked his prelates, barons, and deputies at Saragossa, and caused his son, the Sicilian king, to be acknowledged his successor ; it was also decreed that Sicily and Aragon should forever be united under the same sceptre. No sooner had Martin arrived in Spain, than Sardinia again became the theatre of civil war. The Aragonese had acknowledged the rival pontiff, Benedict, and Boniface had conferred the fiefs of Sardinia and Sicily on the count de Molineto. In 1408, the Sicilian king marched against the rebels, who, with eighteen thousand infantry, did not refuse the battle. It ended in a complete triumph for the king, and was followed by the surrender of an important fortress. As the heat of the weather began to be intensely felt, the victor returned to Cagliari. That heat and the festivities consequent on his success threw him into a fever, which, though not in itself fatal, he is said to have rendered so by incontinence. He died on the 24th of July, 1409. On the death of this prince Martin and the Aragonese were anxious to name a successor to the crown.c

Civil war was imminent when King Martin departed this life (1410), leaving the succession of the kingdom by his last will and testament to him to whom it was lawfully due. By his death the male line of the counts of Barcelona became extinct — a dynasty which had vigorously and gloriously filled the throne of Aragon for nearly three centuries.

INTERREGNUM IN ARAGON (1410–1412 A.D.)

No nation whose political sagacity was less highly developed by a free constitutional and political system could have emerged from the two years of revolution upon which Aragon now entered without detriment to its liberty and legal institutions. For during the interregnum the kingdom fluctuated between two perils; it might either have broken up into its three constituent parts or succumbed to a military despotism.

Count James of Urgel, an ambitious and unscrupulous nobleman, counted the majority of the great nobles of Aragon, more particularly the partisans of the powerful family of Luna, among his adherents, the cortes of Catalonia was on his side, and what his title might lack he was prepared to make good by the sword, for the lower classes everywhere were in his service. The murder of the archbishop of Saragossa by his brutal associate Antonio de Luna, an act of violence in which he himself was not unconcerned, was intended to cow all resistance. The *ricos hombres*[1] saw in anticipation the return of the time when the right of the mailed fist should override the law, when the aristocracy, allied with the town rabble, should triumph over the middle classes, and the anarchy of the unions settle down upon the country once more. The danger was realised by the wise justiciary Cerdaño, his friends and those likeminded with him, chief among whom were Gil Ruiz de Lihori, governor of Aragon, and Berengar de Bardaxi, a man distinguished alike for genius and learning, and to their judicious and patriotic exertions the preservation of the ancient constitution is mainly due. Allying themselves with the freemen of the communes and the minor nobility, they endeavoured to force the decision into the hands of the cortes. Fortunately for them the great nobles were split up by faction, for the Urrea family sided with the constitutional party out of hatred to the Lunas, and their ranks were soon further reinforced by the accession of the Heredia family, to which the murdered archbishop belonged. The latter contrived that the infante Ferdinand should garrison the frontier with Castilian troops to prevent violent measures on the part of the count of Urgel.

Nevertheless the situation was full of peril, owing to the mutual jealousies of the three divisions of the kingdom; the cortes of each held separate consultations and each was anxious to give the casting vote. It was then that the patriotic energy of the men above mentioned intervened to save the kingdom from impending ruin. They proposed that a general parliament should be called together, and that the legal decision should be left to it, as King Martin had wished; representing at the same time to the

---

[1] [This does not mean "rich men," as would seem at first sight; but *rico* here is related to the German word *Reich*, *i.e.*, kingdom.]

separate assemblies that if the question of the succession were decided by the sword, the victor would dictate new laws at the sword's point, as though to a conquered nation. According to their proposal the cortes of the three kingdoms were to elect committees for joint deliberation. By this time, however, they were all too deeply imbued with party spirit, and the cortes of Valencia refused to co-operate with the rest. Those two astute politicians Cerdaño and Bardaxi then ventured upon a bold stroke. They induced the cortes of Aragon and Catalonia to authorise them to nominate a committee of nine members at their own discretion from the three divisions of the country. This committee was to sit at Caspe on the Ebro, and after conscientiously examining the claims of all pretenders was to give its decision according to law. The Urgel party at Valencia tried to interfere, but the victory of the barons at Murviedro put an end to their resistance, and the patriotic caution and justice displayed by Cerdaño and Bardaxi in the selection of the nine secured general recognition and public confidence.

While the whole country was a prey to tumultuous passions, factions at strife one with another, civil war raging with all its accompaniments of crime, rape, and ignominy, these nine men — who were held in the highest esteem by all men, not only for learning and experience but also for strictness of morals and blameless life, and who, like Bardaxi, Ferrer, and Aranda Valseca, were among the first jurists of their day — undertook a laborious examination of the claims submitted to them by the agents of the various pretenders. The count of Urgel had the largest following, and if his Aragonese origin and his descent through the male line were taken into account he would necessarily have had the prior claim ; but his despotic temper, always apt to choose methods of violence rather than of law, made them apprehensive of a tyrannic government if he were chosen, and the majority of the electoral college therefore decided in favour of Ferdinand, infante of Castile, whose mother Leonora had been the daughter of Pedro IV, and the wife of Henry II.

ARAGON UNDER RULERS OF THE ROYAL HOUSE OF CASTILE

No better choice could have been made, and accordingly the new king was acknowledged by the estates of the three united kingdoms as soon as he had confirmed the rights and liberties of the realm (1412). Ferdinand, who combined justice and clemency with vigour, restored tranquillity and order, and used his power to overawe the malcontents both in Aragon and in the islands. But the count of Urgel could not brook defeat. Ferdinand treated him with the utmost distinction, but in spite of all, impelled by his own ambition and incited by his imperious wife, he presently raised the standard of rebellion. He invaded and ravaged Catalonia with an army of mercenaries which the duke of Clarence had handed over to him in Guienne, but was defeated by Ferdinand (1413), and paid the penalty of his unlawful deeds by loss of fortune and perpetual imprisonment.

In the following year Ferdinand added splendour to his accession to the throne by a gorgeous coronation at Saragossa. Thus the crowns of Castile and Aragon were worn by scions of the same reigning house, a prelude to the future union of the two kingdoms under Ferdinand's grandson and namesake.

Through the prudence and patriotic zeal of one statesman and friend of the people, Aragon had passed through a dangerous crisis without injury to her government or liberties.   Ferdinand of the ruling house of Castile, after he had taken the oath of fealty to the constitution, which he did according to custom, kneeling bareheaded before the justiciary, was recognised as king of the united realm and received the homage of the cortes.   This upright and well-disposed monarch, Ferdinand, conscientiously observed the laws and even respected and acknowledged the excessive liberties and privileges of the rich commercial town of Barcelona on an occasion when it was extremely inconvenient to himself to do so ; but he died after four years' reign (1416).

His son, Alfonso V, busied himself during the greater part of his reign with the affairs of Naples.   That newly acquired kingdom in the beautiful country of the Apennines, where a docile people bowed in obedience and

submission to the will of the master, and where the senses were courted with a rich, luxurious life, elevated through social culture and adorned with art and science, was more congenial to Alfonso's inclinations than his hereditary domain of Aragon with its rigorous legal forms and its earnest population ; therefore he preferred a residence in Naples, whilst his native kingdom was governed by a regency.   At its head was the king's brother Juan, afterwards Juan II, a prince well-versed in statecraft and sharing, in regard to politics and public morality, the faithless principles of his time. Already as governor and regent he gave signs of that inclination to despotism and tyranny which later on, when he had succeeded his brother on the throne, he openly displayed, so that the estates took care to secure their constitution against invasion while there was yet time.

We have seen what importance and consideration were attached to the position of chief justice or justiciary of Aragon, the guardian and protector of the laws.   To secure the office against violation and despotism of any kind, it was decreed that the holder should retain office for life, and could only be removed by the king with consent of the estates and on sufficient grounds

SPANISH NOBLEMAN, FIFTEENTH
CENTURY

(1442).   There was no danger that a legal institution of this nature, standing as it did between the throne and the people, would be diverted against the laws of the country, since the justiciary was subject to a regular and close inquiry into the administration of his office from a committee of the states.   Besides this, a navigation law which forbade foreign vessels to ship cargoes in any of the domains under the crown of Aragon was passed in the reign of Alfonso V (1454), an important enactment, which gave a new impulse to the maritime trade of Barcelona, the Catalan capital, at whose instigation the regulation was made.   Thus, both in constitutional progress and in commercial policy, Aragon was the forerunner of the island kingdom of Britain.

The reign of Juan, both as regent and afterwards as king, turns to a great extent on the acquisition of the kingdom of Navarre and the family quarrels which it kindled. In 1442 the mountain country on either side of the Pyrenees passed to the princely house of Aragon by the death of Blanche, wife of Juan, and previously the widow of King Martin. She had inherited Navarre from her father Charles III and by her will her patrimonial domains were to fall as an independent lordship to her eldest son Charles, prince of Viana. More as a matter of courtesy than a legal restriction the condition was added that, before assuming the government of the country, he should obtain the consent and approbation of his father. Juan seems at first to have made no difficulty to his son's taking possession, so that Charles, while his father continued to bear the rank and title of king of Navarre, conducted the administration for several years as governor and ruler of his mother's inheritance.

But when the prince of Aragon contracted a second marriage with Juana Henriquez, daughter of a Castilian admiral of the blood royal, rivalries were awakened which soon assumed a malevolent character. According to the disposition of her husband, the new consort, an imperious, ambitious, and enterprising young lady, was to conduct the government of Navarre in conjunction with the prince of Viana. But the divided rule did not satisfy her proud spirit; as queen of Navarre she desired to be the only person to issue orders, and exhibited an arrogant demeanour towards her step-son. The disagreement soon passed into open hostility when the two conflicting parties of the Beaumonts and the Agramonts took the opportunity to fight out their ancient quarrels in sanguinary encounters, and the Castilians, exasperated at the interference of Aragon in their internal politics, fanned the flame. At the instigation of the Beaumonts, Charles laid claim to the chief power, and at the head of his adherents led an army into the field against the queen and the Agramonts. Juan of Aragon, dominated by his wife's superior intelligence, took part against his son. A battle was fought at Aybar, when the prince of Viana was defeated and made prisoner (1452). Some months before, in the little town of Sos in Aragon, the queen had given birth to a son who, as Ferdinand the Catholic, was afterwards to attain to such great historical importance.

After some time Charles of Viana was released from captivity; but the opposite party had in the meantime so successfully gained the upper hand in Navarre, that he could not maintain himself in the government. He betook himself to Naples to the court of his royal uncle Alfonso V, to beg for his intervention. The chivalrous, open bearing of the prince won him many friends and he was able to flatter himself with the prospect of being speedily reinstated in his mother's inheritance by the aid of a powerful protector; but his uncle's death rendered the hope vain (1458). By the dispositions of the late king's will, his brother Juan was to succeed to his possessions in Spain, Sardinia, and Sicily, and his illegitimate son Ferdinand to the kingdom of Naples.

The Neapolitans, who mistrusted the gloomy, equivocal character of the new prince, Ferdinand, tried in vain to persuade the chivalrous prince of Viana to come forward as a candidate for Naples, holding out to him the prospect of the people's support. The magnanimous prince resisted the temptation; even in Sicily, to which he now turned, similar allurements awaited him; for there also the memory of his mother Blanche, who as the consort of King Martin had formerly won much affection in the island, procured him a good reception and many friends. But here again he withstood all seductive temptations; he contented himself with the generous assistance offered him by the gratitude of the islanders, and passed a long time in the quiet of a Benedictine cloister at Messina, occupied with scientific studies. He did not give up the thought of a reconciliation with his father and a restoration of his rights. After all he, as eldest son, was the rightful heir to the crown of Aragon, and the cortes of the three provinces were on his side. In this expectation he obeyed an invitation from his father to a personal interview at Iguala (1460). By a submissive and penitent demeanour towards the royal couple he endeavoured to put an end to the ancient enmity and win his father's heart, but the queen, who wished to secure the succession to her own son Ferdinand, contrived to keep the distrust of her stepson still alive and by hostile insinuations to throw suspicion on everything he did. Whilst he was deceived by a delusive friendliness, he was surrounded by a web of intrigues. Above all there was exhibited a zealous eagerness to keep him from receiving any sort of homage or recognition of his rights on the part of the cortes.

Still the prince did not allow himself to be betrayed into taking an illegal step ; only he became a suitor for the hand of the infanta Isabella of Castile, with the idea of thus procuring himself a lasting support for his claims to the throne. But it was just this alliance that was a thorn in the eye of the queen of Aragon ; her policy had already singled out the princess for her own son, and she was to be the bond of a union between the two kingdoms. The prince of Viana's project was endangering this plan in a formidable manner ; it was therefore necessary to make an energetic decision. Charles was invited by his father to a meeting of the cortes at Lerida. The prince complied with the request in the hope of being recognised by the estates of the realm as heir to the throne. But immediately on his arrival he was arrested and taken to the inaccessible mountain fastness of Morella on the borders of Valencia ; when the cortes showed signs of interposing with a protest, the assembly was dismissed. On the committee of estates demanding the cause of this remarkable proceeding, Juan darkly hinted at a plot, the inquiry into and punishment of which he must reserve for himself.

At the news of these occurrences the excitable Catalans took up the sword. Armed mobs advanced on Lerida and forced their way into the palace, while the king fled under cover of the night with a few companions to Fraga. The assailants were soon at the gates of Fraga, but the royal couple had already fled to the fortress of Saragossa. The flame of insurrection rapidly spread ; in Navarre the Beaumonts, secretly supported and urged on from Castile, declared for the prince ; in Aragon, in Valencia, in Sicily, the agitation was of a threatening character.

King Juan could not resist these active manifestations of the popular desires. He set his son at liberty, recognised him as his rightful successor, and entrusted him with the office of governor-general of Catalonia. It was at this moment that the prince sickened, and soon the melancholy tidings of his death in his forty-first year were spread through the kingdom (September, 1461). There was a very natural suspicion that he had succumbed to a poison which had been brought to him in his captivity. Thus in the prime of life this noble and chivalrous prince, whose one crime was his lawful claim to the throne of Aragon, fell a victim to treacherous statecraft. Imbued as he was with devotion to the higher cultivation of the mind, had he succeeded to the throne he would have been a worthy rival of his Florentine contemporaries. The fruit of his profound studies was to be seen in a translation of Aristotle's *Ethics* and a history of Navarre.

The tragedy did not end with Charles' death ; instead, a second one resulted from it. At his demise he had appointed as heiress of Navarre his elder sister Blanche, who had formerly been married to Henry IV of Castile and afterwards repudiated by him because she was childless. But Blanche had always sided with her brother and had long shared his exile ; for this reason she was now to be overtaken by a similar fate. In conjunction with the faithless King Louis XI of France, the sovereigns of Aragon surrounded the unfortunate princess with a net of cabals and deceits in which she could not fail to meet destruction. For it was firmly resolved that the inheritance of Aragon should be obtained for her younger sister Eleanor, countess of Foix, so that on the latter's death it might pass to her son Gaston de Foix, the husband of a sister of Louis. With this view, and in accordance with a treaty concluded between Aragon and France, Blanche was forcibly removed from Olit, where she had hitherto resided, and conducted across the mountains to be placed under the supervision of her sister. It was to no purpose that she appealed in a touching letter to her former husband, King Henry of Castile, and pledged him her maternal inheritance of Navarre as the price of her rescue ; there was to be no refuge for her from the hands of a cruel father and an unloving sister. In 1462 she was taken to the strong fortress of Orthez in Béarn, where, after two years of painful captivity she succumbed to a poison, given her by the guilty hand of a traitor. By this means Navarre was united to Foix and Béarn and the ground thus cleared for the subsequent partition of the ancient kingdom between France and Spain.

BLANCHE OF CASTILE

Eleanor lived ten years longer than her son Gaston de Foix, prince of Viana, who met his death through a wound from a lance at a tournament in Lisbon in the year 1469. When she died, her grandson Francis Phœbus, a handsome princely boy with shining golden hair, inherited the throne of Navarre, with his mother Magdalena, sister of Louis XI, as his guardian. But only four years later Francis Phœbus died suddenly, as it was believed of poison, and his sister Catherine, then thirteen years old, entered on the inheritance. In 1484 she married Jean d'Albret, whose extensive possessions in the southwest of France were thus united to the kingdom of Navarre. Magdalena, the queen's mother, had arranged this marriage, which was very displeasing to the Spanish rulers.

RISING IN CATALONIA

The king of Aragon had entered into such close relations with France chiefly because he needed her help against his own people. Far from the rebellious movements subsiding on the death of the prince of Viana, the indignation against the king and queen mounted still higher amongst the excitable Catalans. The imagination of the people painted the tragic fate of the king's unfortunate son in the liveliest colours. Charles' ghost was seen to glide by night through the streets of Barcelona ; he was heard lamenting in piteous tones over his untimely end and calling for vengeance on his unnatural murderer. At last he came to be honoured as a saint. When Queen Juana took her ten-year-old son Ferdinand to Barcelona, that he might receive the homage of the Catalan estates, she soon saw herself threatened with a rising, so that she sought refuge in Gerona. The Catalan troops followed her, made themselves masters of the town and besieged the fortifications where Juana and the prince were bravely defended by a small garrison. Thereupon the king of Aragon concluded a treaty with Louis XI (1462), in consequence of which that monarch sent seven hundred lances with archers and fieldpieces to the aid of the beleaguered queen.

In return for this Juan promised him 200,000 gold crowns and gave him the counties of Roussillon and Cerdagne in pledge. The Catalans could not withstand such a force. They retreated to Barcelona for the purpose of organising more crushing resistance in that excitable town. They sought to represent in a memorial that the liberties of their commonwealth had been betrayed, and that therefore, since the good of the state must be the highest law, they were justified in repudiating their allegiance. They summoned the young men to take arms, and turned to Castile and then to Portugal to win their support in the secession from Aragon (1463). Don Pedro, constable of Portugal, did actually enter the country with a small force, to lay claim to the government of Catalonia, to which, as a scion of the house of Barcelona, he asserted an ancient hereditary right. But the enterprise did not prosper; little by little, partly with the sword, partly by means of gold, King Juan gained possession of the most important towns in the country, such as Lerida, Cervera, Amposta, and Tortosa. Still he could not succeed in breaking Barcelona's bold spirit of resistance; even when the Portuguese infante died suddenly, the town would not hear of conciliation, and two distinguished burghers were beheaded in the market-place for their sympathy with Aragon (1466).

The Catalans now turned to the famous " king " René of Anjou, that he might add Barcelona to the other kingdoms whose royal title he bore without possessing a handful of their soil. René sent his son John, the chivalrous, adventurous duke of Calabria and Lorraine, with some thousand mercenaries, across the Pyrenees. Louis XI, always seeing his own advantage in disturbances in a neighbouring state, secretly favoured his compatriot's enterprise, but without dissolving his alliance with Aragon on that account.

This brave robber captain soon possessed himself of the northern district of Ampurdan and under the walls of Gerona he fought a battle with the queen, who in this time of trial showed heroic courage, and who since her husband's blindness, the result of the hardships of war during the winter before Amposta, had directed the defence of the country in unison with her son. John's chivalrous bearing towards the townspeople of Barcelona won for him such open sympathy that his public appearance always resembled a triumph. The embarrassment of King Juan of Aragon reached its highest point when his consort, who had been the very soul of the government and the guiding spirit of the war, succumbed to a long and painful illness at a time when the state coffers were completely drained, when the chief province of the kingdom was in revolt and partly in the possession of a bold leader of mercenaries, and new warlike complications were threatening with Navarre and Castile. But here too the proverb held good, " The darkest hour is that before the dawn." In the same year, 1469, the king, now a very old man, had his sight restored by a skilful Jewish doctor, and Duke John of

Calabria and Lorraine was called to his account, an event that filled the inhabitants of Barcelona with the deepest grief, which they exhibited by giving him an imposing funeral. He was laid to rest in the vault of the ancient rulers of Barcelona. It was only natural that here too the suspicion of poisoning should be raised, though it was without foundation.

The duke's death could not break the defiant spirit of the Catalans; they steadfastly rejected every summons to yield. After a two years' struggle, when the greater part of the country had fallen into the hands of the energetic old king, when the town bands were reduced by heavy losses to a very small number, and Barcelona was besieged by sea and land, then only did the stern Catalan spirit stoop to peace. King Juan sweetened their bitter cup of submission and homage. He confirmed their privileges and judicial government, granted universal amnesty and conceded to the foreign mercenaries, and any who might choose to join them, freedom to depart. After the conclusion of peace King Juan, mounted on a white charger, made a solemn entry into Barcelona (December, 1472). Thus the succession to the whole kingdom of Aragon of Ferdinand the Catholic, the husband of the infanta Isabella of Castile, was secured. The result had been arrived at with much difficulty, perhaps crime. A few months later the provinces of Roussillon and Cerdagne, which had been pledged to France, made great efforts to become reunited to Aragon. King Juan lent them his aid and, supported by his son, he defended the town of Perpignan with great heroism against the French. But Louis XI did not let his prize escape him. For the space of two years he made war on the town and the whole country with such overwhelming force that at last they were completely broken and submitted to the foreign yoke. The inhabitants of Perpignan, worn out by suffering and hunger, were expelled, in 1475, by the malice and cruelty of the French ruler.[b]

A few years previous to this, in 1469, the heir of King Juan II, Ferdinand of Aragon, had married Isabella of Castile, uniting thus the two countries into one Spain, as we have previously shown. Having thus brought Aragon's history down to where it merges into that of Castile, we may return to Castile, which we left at the death of Pedro the Cruel.[a]

CHAPTER V

HENRY OF TRASTAMARA AND ISABELLA OF CASTILE

[1369–1479 A.D.]

ALL Castile breathed more freely at the news of the death of Pedro the Cruel, and acknowledging Henry of Trastamara as king, did him homage. By a rule as judicious and just as it was vigorous he endeavoured to obliterate the dark blots which stained his accession.

Don Pedro's race vanished from Castilian soil. On the death of his mistress Maria de Padilla shortly after the murder of the unhappy Blanche, Pedro had tried every means to secure the succession for her children. He brought sworn witnesses to testify that he had been joined with Padilla in lawful wedlock, and induced the estates to confer the first title to the throne upon her son Alfonso, and, in case of his death without issue, upon her three daughters, Beatrice, Isabella, and Constanza, in order of seniority. Alfonso, however, died the same year, and Beatrice followed soon after the frustration of her projected marriage with the heir of Aragon; while the two youngest, whom their father had taken with him when he fled to Guiennes, were detained as hostages by the Black Prince, who sent them to England, where they were married to two sons of Edward III (Constanza to John of Lancaster and Isabella to Edmund of York), and thus transmitted to the English dynasty their claims to the heritage of Castile.

Henry assumed the government of Castile under difficulties. As the illegitimate son of King Alfonso XI, he met with strong opposition. Moreover his right to the throne was contested by others besides a large body of the Castilian nobility. King Ferdinand of Portugal, who had renewed the alliance which his father had concluded with Don Pedro, tried to win the crown of Castile for himself after the murder of the latter, on the ground that he, being the grandson of Beatrice, princess of Castile, was the only male descendant born in lawful wedlock. To support his claim he allied himself with Muhammed, the Moorish prince of Granada. Like Pedro IV of Aragon, he received with all honour the malcontent and fugitive Castilian nobles. He paid no heed to the murmurs of the Portuguese at their king's liberality to foreigners, but marched into Galicia with an army, while the Moors took

Algeciras; and the king of Aragon endeavoured to unite Molina, Almazan, Soria, and other frontier districts with his own dominions. At the same time the duke of Lancaster, uncle of Richard II, assumed the title of king of Castile in right of his wife, the eldest daughter of Don Pedro, and was acknowledged as such by the English court.

But Henry extricated himself from the difficulties that encompassed him in his own country with prudence and skill, and turned the disadvantages of his opponents to his own profit; and thus he succeeded in putting down all resistance and seated himself firmly on the throne of Castile, though he was still regarded by enemies as a usurper. The Moorish conquests were confined to Algeciras; the king of Portugal, who also styled himself "king of Castile," carried on the war with so little success that the Spanish historian Lopez de Ayala [b] says that it would have been more to his honour to have discontinued the campaign; the English had their hands full in their own country, and the Aragonese, besides having their attention diverted by a war in Sardinia, found themselves, by Henry's shrewd contrivance, confronted with another adversary in the person of James III of Majorca, the pretender to the throne of the Balearic kingdom.

This adventurous infante, though married to Queen Juana of Naples, had entered the service of Pedro the Cruel and been taken prisoner at Montiel. Henry set him at liberty on payment of a heavy ransom by the wealthy queen of Naples, and thus fulfilled the double object of filling his own coffers and setting up a rival to his enemy. He had already taken possession of the abundant treasure which the fallen tyrant had amassed in the strong vaults of the castles of Seville and Carmona, and had obtained large subsidies besides from the estates of the kingdom at Medina del Campo; and was therefore able to pay off and discharge the mercenary troops which had carried him to victory and to surround himself with a well disciplined army. Bertrand du Guesclin and the leaders of other companies received gifts of towns and territory over and above their pay, and promptly sold them again.

HENRY OF CASTILE

The history of Castile for the next few years is like a diplomatic game of chess in which the French, the English, and the pope all played their parts as well as the sovereigns of the peninsula. And all did their best to win. While the faithless and fickle king of Portugal, who had given great offence to his own subjects by his marriage, made common cause with the duke of Lancaster and acknowledged him king of Castile in order to secure the assistance of England; and while the Roman see, alarmed at the alliance between Christian courts and the Mohammedans of Granada and Morocco exhausted itself in attempts at mediation, Henry concluded a treaty with France and invaded Portugal with an army. Viseu was occupied, Lisbon blockaded by land and sea and sorely damaged and wasted by fire, Coimbra was besieged, and only spared by the Castilians out of chivalrous gallantry, because Ferdinand's consort Leonora was there waiting the birth of her child. Many Portuguese nobles with the king's brother at their head abetted the Castilians out of disgust at Ferdinand's marriage. At length the papal legate brought about a reconciliation, which was accelerated and rendered easier by Henry's magnanimity and moderation (1373). The Portuguese king relinquished his alliance with the duke of Lancaster and England, banished from his dominions the malcontent Castilians who still refused to acknowledge Henry king, in spite of his chivalrous nature and high sovereign qualities, and joined the Franco-Castilian alliance. The war with Aragon was brought to an equally successful issue. Don Pedro concluded peace and alliance and restored the districts on the Castilian frontier which he had occupied in the course of the campaign.

Biscay was also united to the kingdom of Castile on the death without issue of the infante Don Tello on whom the king had bestowed it in fee, but the province remained in possession of its ancient rights and liberties. When the daughter of Ferdinand de la Cerda, who had married the duke of Alençon, laid claim to Biscay and the whole of the Lara heritage in her own name and that of her children, Henry stipulated that her sons should reside in Spain. They refused, however, to resign the position they held in France, and he therefore declared the principalities fiefs that had lapsed to the crown. When Henry had further prevailed upon the king of Navarre to make peace with him by reimbursing the expenses he had incurred in the fortification of Logroño and Vitoria, Castile was once more complete within her ancient borders and his own sovereignty was firmly established and fully recognised. But by the reckless munificence with which he gave away the immediate property of the crown, in order to satisfy the nobles and attach them to the new dynasty, he laid up many troubles in store for his successors.[c]

In the schism which afflicted the church, from the rival pretensions of Urban VI and the anti-pope Clement, Henry declared for neither — doubtless to gratify his avarice by withholding the customary contributions to the papal see. He died in 1379. In character he was as cruel as Pedro; as loose in morals, and scarcely inferior as a tyrant. On the whole, however, he was a fortunate ruler. Either by bribes or force, he reduced Galicia to obedience, recovered several places from the king of Navarre, whose capital he at one time invested, and overawed his neighbours of Portugal and Aragon.

JUAN I AND THE PORTUGUESE WARS

Juan I followed his father's advice, by cultivating the friendship of the French king, whom he frequently assisted in the interminable wars between that monarch and the English. Like his father, he had also to dread the pretensions of John of Gaunt the duke of Lancaster; and it was equally his aim to occupy the ambitious Plantagenet with other affairs than disputing his succession.

To preserve Portugal as an ally, Juan, in the second year of his reign, consented or proposed to marry his infant son Henry with Beatrice, presumptive heiress of the Portuguese crown. This princess, who was in her tenth year, had been promised to Frederick, brother of the Castilian king; but the superior pretensions of Henry induced the Portuguese monarch to prefer the latter for a son-in-law. One condition of the projected marriage was that, in case either of the young betrothed died without issue, the other should inherit the states of the deceased.   So fair a prospect of uniting the two crowns could not fail to be agreeable to the two sovereigns.   Notwithstanding this solemn treaty, Ferdinand of Portugal secretly resolved to make war on Castile ; and, with the view of strengthening himself by the alliance of the duke of Lancaster, he despatched a trusty messenger to obtain the co-operation of that prince, who readily promised it.

Juan, who was soon acquainted with the league, resolved to anticipate his enemy: off Cape St. Vincent his fleet triumphed, in 1381, over that of Ferdinand ; and Almeida was forced to submit to him.   The arrival from England of the earl of Cambridge, brother of the duke, with five hundred men-at-arms, and as many archers, roused the courage of the Portuguese, but did them little service.   As the allies could obtain no money from Ferdinand, they did not scruple to lay their hands on whatever they pleased : hence the distrust and dislike which arose between them and the natives, and which neutralised the little success obtained by their combined arms.[1]   Wearied alike with his allies and the war, Ferdinand, in 1382, solicited and obtained peace, and the English returned home.   The death of the queen of Castile leaving Henry a widower, Ferdinand offered him the princess Beatrice, who had been successively promised to his brother, to his two sons, and even to the son of the earl of Cambridge ; on condition, however, that the issue of the marriage, whether male or female, should be the sovereign of Portugal, and that he himself should have no share in the administration so long as Leonora, the Portuguese queen, should survive Ferdinand.   This condition, so characteristic of Portuguese dislike of Castilian sway, did not prevent Juan from marrying the princess.   Ferdinand died the very year of this marriage ; and his death opened the door to new hostilities.

Though Juan and his new queen were, in fact, excluded by the treaty accompanying their union, he no less eagerly claimed the crown in her own right ; and several of the Portuguese nobles admitted the justice of that claim.   Even the widowed queen, Leonora, caused her daughter to be proclaimed in the capital; but the bulk of the towns and prelates refused to acknowledge her, and declared Don João bastard brother of Ferdinand, regent of Portugal.   The latter prepared to vindicate his right ; when Urban VI, whom he had refused to recognise, raised up against him his old enemy, the duke of Lancaster, who was persuaded by that pope again to invade Castile.   The usurper Juan was no less anxious to secure the co-operation of the Plantagenet, whose departure to claim the crown of Castile he began to urge with success.   To frustrate the double object of this alliance, the Castilian, in 1384, entered the kingdom, received the homage of his adherents, and proceeded to invest the capital : but his troops were ignobly defeated by those of his rival ; even the queen-mother scorned to favour his pretensions; and he was constrained to abandon the siege, and return into his dominions.   In 1385, the states of Coimbra proclaimed his rival king; who began vigorously to invest the places which held for him.

Fortune attended the arms of the Portuguese, who successively obtained possession of the chief fortified places, and, in several partial engagements,

[1] Let us hope that the atrocities of the English allies — so gently noticed by Froissart [d] — are exaggerated ; yet certain it is that the old Portuguese chroniclers dwelt largely on them : " *Nao se cançaõ os nossos chronistas de encarecer as atrocidades que estas tropas auxiliares commetteraõ em todos os terrenos de Portugal por onde andaraõ,*" says Lemos.[e]   " King Ferdinand," says the *Chronicon Conimbricense!* " had to seize the church plate to satisfy his allies: *Mandou o ditto senhor rey tomar os thesouros das igrejas, convem a saber, frontaes, e calices et magestades, para pagar o soldo aos dittos Ingrezos.*"

was hailed as victor. A greater and a decisive action was now at hand.
Though he had but ten thousand men, he marched against the Castilian
king, who met him with an army of at least thirty-four thousand; in which
were two thousand French knights. The two armies met near Aljubarrota,
a village in Portuguese Estremadura; where, by the advice of the English
knights who served in his army, the Portuguese intrenched his followers in a
position of some strength. As the troops of the Castilian were wearied by
their march, some of his officers, especially the chronicler Pedro Lopez de
Ayala,*b* in a council of war assembled to decide on the subject, endeavoured
to dissuade him from the battle; but the greater number, among whom were
the French knights, confiding in their overwhelming numerical superiority
and in their own ardour, inclined him to risk it. The action commenced
towards sunset, on a fine summer evening (August 14th), and was, for a short
time, maintained with great spirit on both sides. In the end, the Portuguese obtained a splendid victory, most of the Castilian chivalry and ten
thousand of the infantry being left dead on the field: the king himself with
difficulty effected his escape. The loss was so heavy that he ordered his
subjects to mourn for a whole year; while the victors annually commemorated their triumph. The French allies, who bore the brunt of the battle,
suffered severely on this occasion.

JOHN OF GAUNT IN SPAIN

To profit by this victory, the Portuguese monarch commanded his barons
to make an irruption into Castile, while he himself despatched to the duke
of Lancaster a circumstantial account of this signal success. The latter now
burned to assert his rights by other means than threats, or by the mere
report of his preparations; he actually left England, with a small but choice
armament (about fifteen hundred knights, and as many archers), accompanied by his wife, the lady Constanza, and his three daughters. In July,
1386, he appeared off the coast of Galicia, and ultimately landed at El
Padron; thence he proceeded to Santiago, where he was solemnly proclaimed king of Castile and Leon. In an interview with the king of Portugal, on the confines of the two states, both entered into a treaty offensive
and defensive; and, to cement it the more strongly, agreed that the king
should marry Philippa, daughter of the duke.

In the meantime, the Castilian was not idle: he had obtained succours
from his constant ally the French king and encouragement from Clement
VII, the rival of Urban. In the spring of 1387, the duke and the Portuguese king arrived at Benavente; but their progress was stayed by the
plague, which daily made great ravages in their ranks. After the conquest
of a few towns and fortresses, the allied army retired into Portugal. The
duke himself was seriously indisposed in body, and consequently dispirited.
Their retreat was hastened by intelligence of the troubles which raged in
England, and which ended in the imprisonment, and eventually the death of
the unfortunate Richard II. The Castilian king dreaded the resumption
of hostilities at a more favourable period. He proposed to the Plantagenet
the marriage of his eldest son, Henry, with Catherine, daughter of the duke,
by the princess Constanza, and, consequently, granddaughter of Pedro the
Cruel. To this overture the duke lent a favourable ear; towards the close
of the year the conditions were definitively arranged at Bayonne. The principal were that, if Henry died before the consummation of the marriage, the

princess should be given to the next son, Don Ferdinand; that Constanza, mother of the princess, should receive in fief five or six towns in Castile, besides a revenue of 40,000 francs per annum; that the duke should receive 600,000 in gold, by instalments, as an indemnification for the expenses of the war; that both Constanza and her husband should renounce all claim to the Castilian crown; and that hostages should be given him as a security for the due performance of the first three. Thus, if the personal ambition of the Plantagenet remained without gratification, he had at least the satisfaction of seeing one of his daughters queen of Portugal, and the other destined to the throne of Castile. Early in the following year, Catherine, who was in her fourteenth year, was betrothed to Henry, who was only in his ninth, and who on this occasion assumed the title of prince of the Asturias.

The king of Castile did not long survive this reconciliation with the Plantagenet. On the 9th day of October, 1390, he was killed by falling under his horse. The reign of Juan I was one of continued troubles, which, though his abilities were moderate, his firmness prevented from ruining the state, or endangering his own power. Once, indeed, during the disputed succession to the Portuguese crown, he seriously intended to resign in favour of his own son Henry, who, as the son of Beatrice, daughter of Ferdinand, was the true heir to the Portuguese no less than the Castilian throne. His object was to secure the execution of the treaty made with that prince, and forever to unite the two crowns. But his nobles, who were evidently no less averse to such a union than their western neighbours, not merely advised but compelled him to preserve his dignity.*g*

But the greatest glory of King Juan's reign was his successful expedition against the coasts of England, to punish the presumption of the duke of Lancaster. Once more the maintenance of the Lancastrian claims was the signal for the destruction of a British fleet. Not content with threatening the ports, the Castilians, emboldened by former successes, sailed up the Thames, in 1380, and took or burned the shipping in the river almost within sight of London.*h*

THE GOOD KING HENRY III (1390–1406 A.D.)

The crown descended to Henry, Juan's first-born son, who since his betrothal in 1387 had taken from the ancestral seat of his family, now elevated into a principality, the title of "prince of Asturias," which has been borne by the heir-apparent of Castile ever since.

Henry, surnamed the Infirm, was a weakly prince of eleven years of age, and a regency had to be appointed during his minority, whence much evil accrued to the realm of Castile. By the last testament of the late king the affairs of state were to be managed by a council of regency composed of the three estates of the kingdom. This arrangement was contested as showing too little regard for the rights of the heads of the great families, and a fresh regency was set up by the help of the estates, in which the lords temporal and spiritual — the duke of Benavente, a natural son of Henry II, Count Pedro of Trastamara, the marquis of Villena, the archbishops of Toledo and Santiago de Compostella, the grand-masters of the orders, and others — divided the royal authority between them.

No notice was taken of the assessors of the middle class who ought to have been admitted to their deliberations. But the nobles at the head of affairs, each one of whom was eager to take advantage of these propitious circumstances to enrich himself and increase his own power, were soon at variance and strife among themselves, the kingdom was split up into factions, the crown property alienated, disorder prevailed throughout the country.

Not until the king, having passed his fourteenth year, proclaimed himself of age with the consent of the estates and assumed the reins of government in person (1393) did a change for the better set in. For in spite of his youth and feeble frame, Henry III was possessed of sagacity and a real aptitude for political and public affairs. Trusting to the temper of the nation, which yearned for a strong government and for deliverance from the oppressive rule of the nobles and the anarchy of the knights, he promptly proceeded to energetic measures. Not content with sharing the royal authority among themselves, the lords in power had seized upon many of the estates of the crown, already much reduced by the lavishness of former kings, and consequently the necessary funds to meet public expenditure were lacking. Henry's first step therefore was to come to an agreement with the cortes, to which he promised in return for the grant of the *alcabalas* that no fresh tax should be introduced without their consent, and then took vigorous action against the nobles. All gifts and pensions which had been made at the expense of the crown demesnes during his minority were cancelled and the revenues of the lords temporal and spiritual reduced to the level at which they had stood at Don Juan's death, and at the same time all engagements which the barons had entered into with one another and confirmed by oath were annulled.

This bold stroke on the part of the young king greatly incensed the feudal lords; the duke of Benavente, the marquis of Villena, and the two infantes Alfonso count of Gijon and Don Pedro of Trastamara, endeavoured to form a coalition of nobles to avert by force the impending reduction of their revenues; but it was nipped in the bud by the energetic action of King Henry, who offered pardon and favour to the obedient and tractable and menaced the stubborn and recalcitrant with the forces which quickly gathered round his standard. The leaders of the coalition, unsupported by the nation and without help from abroad, could not carry their purpose into effect; they were overthrown or captured one by one, and compelled to submit to the king's orders and purchase his favour by taking the oath of fealty and allegiance.

Henry displayed the same energy and discretion in all other acts of his reign. His marriage with Catherine of Lancaster, a sister of Queen Philippa of Portugal, hastened the conclusion of peace with that country, and Castile then had leisure to restore her lost prestige abroad among Christians and Mohammedans alike. Although the king relied upon skilful diplomacy rather than upon arms and armies, his forces by land and sea were in such a state of efficiency as not merely to enable him to repel all attacks with vigour but to secure for him the authority of an arbitrator in quarrels between others. Thus he preserved the peace of his own dominions, set bounds to the license of Moorish piracy, and enhanced his consequence abroad.

War was on the point of breaking out with the emir Yusuf of Granada, kindled by the fanaticism of the grand-master of the order of Alcantara, who was eager to make converts of the infidels at the sword's point, when it was averted by Henry's presence of mind. He declared that he had nothing in common with the assailants, most of whom paid for their folly with their lives in a disastrous battle, and persuaded the offended emir to restore peace (1394). Yusuf died shortly after, of poison administered to

X. The Alhambra: the Day After a Victory

(From the painting by Benjamin Constant, 1882)

Peint par Benjamin Constant.   Photogravure Goupil & Cie.

him by the prince of Fez; and Muhammed, his ambitious second son, usurped the throne of Granada and threw his elder brother into prison. The king availed himself of the general apprehension that under the new emir the friendly relations between Castile and Granada would not last, to incite the estates to a more liberal expenditure on preparations for war. The amount of money, ships, and armed men, both horse and foot, which the cortes was said to have raised in conjunction with the king's exchequer, bears witness to the height of prosperity and power to which Castile had risen through the wise and peaceful policy of Henry III. His contemporaries adduce the exchange of embassies between the king of Castile and the great Mongol sovereign Timur [or Tamerlane] as a proof of how far the fame of the former had extended. The Turkish sultan responded to the embassy from the Christian king by sending a return embassy with costly presents, among which were two Christian captives of high rank and great beauty. But Henry's life was hastening to its close. He had been prevented by sickness from opening in person the diet at Toledo, where the demands were presented of which mention has been made, and was obliged to delegate his share in the proceedings to his brother Ferdinand, the infante who ascended the throne of Aragon a few years later. On Christmas Day in the same year (1406) King Henry III died at the age of twenty-seven, leaving a child one year old as heir to the throne. Great was the mourning in Castile for the high-souled prince who had combined vigour with gentleness, maintained peace and justice, and never violated the constitution or the existing framework of law by the abuse of the principle he himself had laid down — that the welfare of the nation is the supreme law against which no usurper or chartered rights could appeal. His country had all the more reason to lament him, as a war with the Moors was imminent and a fresh regency in prospect.

Ferdinand, the brother of Henry III, had so fully won the esteem of the nation that the Castilian nobles tendered him the crown. This the high-minded prince [1] indignantly refused ; but lest the kingdom should be left to the weak hands of a child and a woman, he undertook the government in conjunction with Catherine, the widowed queen, and displayed such admirable qualifications for rule that Castile was for many years spared the evils usually inseparable from a minority. He gained the confidence of the estates, kept the nobles under control, and won the fortress of Antequera and the surrounding country in a successful war against the Moors (1411). When the cortes of Aragon elected him king (1412), he continued to govern his nephew's dominions in conjunction with the queen-mother, and the power which was thereby concentrated in his hands enabled him not merely to subdue the rebellious nobles of Aragon and secure himself and his house in possession of the crown, but to frustrate every revolt in Sardinia and the Balearic Islands, and to assume the tone of a ruler and arbitrator, even in Sicily. Unfortunately he died after a reign of four years, in 1416, and Queen Catherine passed away not long after, too early for the young king, Juan II, who had hitherto shown but small intellectual vigour, and who now, in the fourteenth year of his age, took the sceptre in his own hands without either capacity, experience, or strength of character to wield it. A troublous time then began for Castile, during which revolts and civil wars dealt grievous blows at the prosperity and power of the nation.[c]

The old historian Guzman[j] has traced a faithful portrait of the young sloth who now filled the throne.

[1 Hume[i] calls him "one of the noblest personages of Spanish history."]

GUZMAN'S PORTRAIT OF JUAN AND HIS MINISTER

Juan was of tall stature and largely built, but was neither well made nor possessed of great strength ; he had a pleasing countenance, fair complexion, and high shoulders ; his face was broad, his speech slightly rapid.   He was calm and gentle, his conversation measured and simple.   As his disposition was most extraordinary, it is necessary to dilate thereon : he was a man who in speech was wise and prudent, possessed great knowledge of other men, and understood those whose conversation was best, most discreet, and most witty.

It pleased him to listen to well-informed men, and he took good note of what they said.   He both spoke and understood Latin.   He read well ; books and histories delighted him ; he loved to hear witty rhymes, and could point out their defects ; he enjoyed gay and intelligent conversation, in which he could bear his part.   He spent much time in the chase and hunting of fierce animals, and was well skilled in the art of it.   He had studied music, and could both sing and play well ; he was skilful in jousting, and well versed in the exercise of tilting with reeds.

But enjoying a tolerable proficiency in these graceful accomplishments, he was lamentably deficient in real virtues, necessary to all men and more so to kings ; for after good faith the chief virtue of a king should be a diligent application to the government and administration of his kingdom.   In this Solomon proved himself the wisest of all, who, when God bade him ask for what he most desired, merely begged for wisdom to govern his people, which request was so agreeable to the Lord, that he granted this virtue and other singular attributes pertaining to it.   This king was so deficient in this respect that, possessed of the aforesaid accomplishments, he refused to give one hour to the government of his kingdom.   Although during this time there were more rebellious seditions and evils than were experienced during the reigns of past kings for more than two hundred years, which were productive of considerable harm to his fame and kingdom, yet such were his negligence and remissness in the government of his kingdom that he would never devote any time to it, but preferred to spend it in other occupations more peaceful and pleasing than useful or honourable.

And yet in the histories which he read he learned the evils which had befallen kings and their kingdoms through such negligence and remissness, and, moreover, was warned by many priests and knights that his kingdom was in great peril through his neglect, and that his fame greatly suffered thereby ; and what was more serious, that he must render to God strict account for the evils fallen upon his subjects through his negligence, since God had given him brain and judgment to govern.   In spite of these warnings and notwithstanding that he saw the scanty obedience he could command, the little reverence paid him, the contempt of his letters and commands, yet he would not reform nor give his mind to the government of his kingdom.

Don Juan II of Castile left the government of his kingdom entirely in the hands of Alvaro de Luna, in whom he placed such singular confidence that, to those who did not witness it, it appeared hardly credible, and to those who did it was a matter of extreme wonder.   Not only all orders relating to his rents and treasures, offices of his household and administration of justice were given by the constable, but nothing was done without the latter's consent. It is true that orders and letters, licenses, favours, and donations were made in the king's name and under his signature, yet the secretaries waited the constable's pleasure to write, the king to sign, and the chancellor to seal ; without it no letter carried weight or was put into execution.

So great was the singular confidence which the king placed in the constable, and so excessive the latter's power, that it would be difficult to find a king or prince, however feared and obeyed, more powerful in his kingdom than was the constable in Castile, or who enjoyed greater freedom in the government and administration.   Not only the offices, positions, and grants, of which the king had the disposal, were in his hands, but also the ecclesiastical dignities and benefices ; no man in the kingdom was bold enough to petition the pope or recognise his orders save with the constable's consent. Thus both spiritual and temporal power were in his hands ; the king's sole responsibility was to affix his signature to letters; for the form and execution the constable was responsible.   So extended was his power, and so fully had he taken on himself the king's prerogative, that few thought of petitioning the latter were it for the highest office in the land or the meanest favour, or returned him thanks for the same ; but to the constable they were applied for, and to him acknowledged. But, what is yet more to be marvelled at, even in natural acts the king allowed himself to be ruled by the constable; so that being young and healthy, and knowing his queen to be young and beautiful, he would not seek her apartment at night, did the constable forbid him, nor yet solace himself with other women, though his inclinations in this respect were naturally strong.

Finally we have two points to consider and marvel at : the first a king in many ways accomplished, yet totally negligent and remiss in the government of his kingdom, being neither moved nor stimulated thereto by discretion, nor by experience of the difficulties encountered in the disputes and uprisings occurring in his kingdom, nor yet by the admonitions and warnings tendered him by powerful nobles and priests. Further, that a natural attraction should be so strong and vigorous as to make him in all things, without exception, submit to the constable's command or counsel with an

Don Juan II
(From an effigy)

obedience unequalled by the most humble of sons to a father, or the most obedient of monks to his abbot or prior.   Some persons, upon noting this marked love and excessive confidence, held it to be the work of witchcraft, but this was never proved, although steps were taken in the matter.   The second point is that a man without connections and of such poor origin, in a kingdom of vast dimensions, containing so many powerful nobles, during the reign of a king so little feared or obeyed, should enjoy such singular power.   Because if we suppose this power was due to the king's authority, how could he give to another what he himself never possessed, or how is it that the lieutenant was obeyed where he whose place he took could not command obedience?   Truly I fear that no distinct reason can be given for this, save by him who was responsible for the king's extraordinary disposition, nor yet an explanation of the constable's power, for I know not which is most to be marvelled at, the king's character, or the constable's power.*j*

We need not feel the amazement felt by Guzman at Alvaro's power over the king if we can trust the following portrait of him from an old and anonymous biography of Alvaro.*a*

CHRONICLE OF THE CONSTABLE DON ALVARO DE LUNA

The outward shape and seeming of Don Alvaro de Luna, master of the order and knighthood of Santiago, and constable of the kingdoms of Castile and Leon, were in the following wise :

He was short of stature and very upright ; fair complexioned, and of a very graceful figure all his years, slight and well-built with a well-turned leg and length of limb in proportion to his height.   His neck was long, straight, and well-shaped, his eyes joyous and always bright.   He had a calm presence, and where he gazed, his eyes dwelt longer than those of other men. He carried his head ever erect with a joyous countenance ; his nose was well shaped with wide nostrils, his forehead broad, and he was early bald.   He laughed readily and sought food for mirth, and stammered a little in his speech.   He was full of life ; he never put on flesh or varied in figure in the least, so that he seemed made of bone and muscle.

He was temperate and restrained in his habits from his youth ; he ever loved and honoured the whole race of women.   He loved much, and ever observed great secrecy concerning his loves.   He made discreet and lively ballads of his loves, in which he often touched upon the mysteries of other great deeds.   He was always well-dressed, and whatever he wore sat well upon him, so that whether dressed for the chase, for war, or for state occasions, he was approved of all.   He had a ready wit and was much given to inventing tales and presenting interludes at the feasts, the jousts, or in the fight, and in these compositions he very subtly signified what he wished.   He was a famous horseman in both saddles, and a great soldier.   He was very careful to have good fleet horses.   He took great delight in getting his arms repaired, and in examining them and keeping them bright and clean and point-device.   In war, he was too courageous and daring, so that he often placed himself in great peril, as may be seen from his history and in many other places.   He was often in arms and ever eager for the fray. He addressed his king at all times with great reverence and ceremony [?]. He was a great huntsman and laboured much therein, and followed the chase so often, when other business gave him leisure, that he was better skilled in it than other men.   He took great pleasure in discoursing of archery, and in that sport it was a marvel to find any who could beat him at the crossbow.   He loved wise and prudent men, and endeavoured to win them to himself and reposed great trust in them ; but for those who were libertines and chatterers, he laughed with them and showed them good countenance, and held them of small account.*k*

INTERNAL DISSENSIONS

It was not to be supposed that the power of De Luna would fail to arouse the jealousy and indignation of both nobles and people.   But the first disturbances of Juan's reign were caused by the refusal of his sister, Catalina, to

marry Henry, infante of Aragon.   The latter proceeded to use force, succeeded in capturing not only the princess but Juan himself, and retained
them as his prisoners at Avila.   The marriage took place, and though Juan
soon afterwards contrived to escape, Henry and his brother, the king of
Navarre, both continued to give him serious trouble in the succeeding years
of his reign by their invasions of Castile, and the encouragement they gave to
his revolted subjects.   The king's wasteful bounty towards his favourites
was a constant excuse for rebellion.   It was against his constable, Alvaro de
Luna, that the enmity of nobles and people alike was chiefly directed.[a]

In 1439 a league (not the first) was formed against him, and was headed
as usual by Henry of Aragon and the king of Navarre.   Its members loudly
demanded the removal of the obnoxious favourite.   To dispel the approaching storm, Don Alvaro retired for a time from the court ; but the confederates refused to lay down their arms until he should be forever driven from
the royal presence.   Though the complaints which they elaborately brought
against him were for the most part invented or exaggerated, it is evident
enough that he had abused his influence over the royal mind, and exhibited
as much eagerness to enrich, no matter by what means, his creatures and
instruments, as vindictiveness against all who ventured to thwart his will.
To appease his barons, the king convoked his cortes at Valladolid ; such
a step was become necessary, for the leaguers had seized on some of his chief
cities, and were preparing to proceed still further.

The first act of the assembly was to recommend that all parties should
disarm — the king as well as the infante, the constable as well as the king of
Navarre.   But this recommendation led to no result; both parties continued
exasperated as before.   That of the king was weakened by the desertion
of his only son, Prince Henry, who espoused the cause of the confederates.
The queen followed the example of her son : in short, the aspect of affairs
was so menacing that Don Alvaro began to turn his eyes towards Portugal
in search of an asylum.   Through the persuasion of the king, however, who
assured him that everything should be arranged to his wish, he consented to
await the result.

The horrors of internal strife were now felt in all their force ; city after
city was invested and taken by the confederate rebels, who showed little
mercy to the partisans of the king and constable.   In vain did Juan whisper
peace ; in vain did he appear to abide by the decision of his states, which he
might summon for the purpose : as he did not at once and forever banish
Don Alvaro from his presence, his entreaties and remonstrances were equally
disregarded.   In 1443 the rebels obtained possession of the king's person
and held him as a kind of prisoner in his own palace.   Though their subsequent efforts were somewhat paralysed by the defection of Prince Henry,
who even called on all good men to aid him in rescuing his father from
a slavish dependence on them, they persevered not the less in their design.
They took the field against both the prince and the father, who now contrived to escape and reach the camp of the former.   But on this occasion
the confederates were routed and dispersed in several successive actions,
and their strong places recovered by the royal forces.   Their estates were
seized by the king, and they themselves forced to seek refuge in Aragon or
Navarre.   Subsequently, both the king of Navarre and his brother, the reckless Henry, collected troops, and invaded, the one Castile, the other Murcia ;
but without any other result than that of harassing the innocent peasantry, or
wreaking vengeance on their personal enemies.   Finally the victory of
Olmedo, gained by Juan in person over the two brothers, the acquisition of a

considerable number of prisoners, and the death of Henry (of Aragon) through a wound received in that battle, appeared to consolidate both the power of the king and the influence of the favourite.

THE FALL OF ALVARO

But royal attachments are seldom permanent, because they are seldom founded on merit; and because the minds of men, especially those of kings, are generally incapable of any lasting impression. Though the favour of Juan II had been protracted far beyond the limits of ordinary duration, it was not to prove an exception to the usual course of human experience. Soon after the battle of Olmedo, the partiality of the monarch began to be weakened. Years elapsed before Juan could put into execution his long-meditated design of destroying his constable. His attention, indeed, was long distracted by the irruptions into his territories of the Aragonese and Navarrese, in conjunction with the Castilian exiles; and by the partial revolts which from time to time agitated his kingdom (that of Toledo for instance, occasioned by an exaction, under the name of a loan, of a million maravedis, was not suppressed without much difficulty). It was not until the year 1453, that he seriously resolved to rid himself of this formidable minister.

To rashness, and an insolent contempt of the royal power and authority, Don Alvaro soon added the crime of murder. Knowing that Alfonso de Vivero, one of his creatures, was become his secret enemy, he planned the destruction of that false confidant. One day he held in his own house a council, to which Alfonso was summoned. On the appearance of the latter, he was shown the correspondence which he had held with the king relative to the constable's arrest, and which Alvaro had intercepted. The confusion of the traitor would have been evidence enough of his guilt, without the incontestable documents then produced. On a signal from the constable, he was dragged to the top of the tower, precipitated headlong, and dashed to pieces on the ground below. The creatures of Alvaro suddenly raised a note of lamentation, as if the fall had been purely accidental; but the king was soon acquainted with the truth, and the more confirmed in his purpose of vengeance.

Don Alvaro was at Burgos, when the order for his arrest was given by the king to the son of the count of Plasencia, to take him dead or alive. During the night, troops were secretly placed in various parts of the city and at the entrance of the fortress, into which some men-at-arms were silently introduced. The royal order was to invest the house in which the constable resided, and thereby compel him to surrender. Accordingly the young Zuñiga, with two hundred men-at-arms and twenty horsemen, surrounded the house, exclaiming, " *Castilla! Castilla! libertad para el Rey!* " The constable showed his head from a window; but an arrow being shot at him, he withdrew it, and his men began to fire on the royal troops. The assault was repelled; but he himself was at length persuaded to surrender, on receiving an assurance in writing, under the king's own hand, that his life, liberty, and even possessions should be spared. No sooner, however, was he secured, than his gold and jewels were seized by the faithless monarch, and orders given to try — in other words, to condemn him. Twelve lawyers and several barons, being assembled for this purpose, unanimously passed on him the last sentence and the confiscation of all his possessions. From Burgos he was conducted to Valladolid, where the execution was appointed to take place.

He prepared for death with firmness, and with apparent contrition for his past misdeeds. During the night preceding the execution, the king's mind was far from tranquil. He remembered the real services of the constable through so many years, the affection he had once borne him, and the promise he had made of sparing his life. The remembrance was so troublesome that he once or twice delivered a sealed paper to the chamberlain on duty, which he wished to be taken to Zuñiga — doubtless, to stay the execution. Hearing of his agitation, the queen, whose conduct throughout was exceedingly vindictive, hastened to him, and succeeded in suspending rather than removing his scruples. As the fatal hour approached, Don Alvaro, mounted on a mule, and attended by two monks, left his house for the scaffold. On the way, the public herald, according to custom, vociferated his crimes and punishment. "I deserve all this," said he, "and more, for my sins!" When near the scaffold, he called a page of the prince, and said to him, "Page, tell my lord the prince to reward his servants better than the king, my sovereign, now rewards me!" He ascended with a firm step, knelt for a few moments before a crucifix, bared his neck with his own hands, and quietly laid his head on the block, when the executioner plunged the knife into his throat, and afterwards separated the head from the body, amidst the tears of the surrounding multitude.

Thus fell the great constable of Castile, the victim, chiefly, of his own immeasurable ambition, and in no mean degree of courtier jealousy and of royal faithlessness. If his crimes were many, they were characteristic rather of the age than of the man : he was certainly no more criminal than the great body of the Castilian barons, who despised alike justice and reason when violence could secure their ends. To him the queen was indebted for her crown ; yet she persecuted him with unrelenting hatred. The numbers whom he had enriched forsook him as his favour declined ; three only of his army of dependents remained faithful to the last. And as to his trial, the most eminent legal authorities of Spain have satisfactorily proved that in his case both the spirit and forms of justice were disregarded.

Juan II did not long survive the constable : he died in 1454. He was one of the weakest and most despicable princes that ever swayed the scepter of any country. Besides two sons, he left issue the infanta Isabella,[1] so famous in the annals of Spain.*g*

HUME'S ESTIMATE OF JUAN II

Juan II was unfortunate in living when he did. Peace-loving and amiable, one of the greatest patrons of letters who ever ruled in Spain, he was not without considerable gifts of mind, but utterly unfitted to hold the reins of government in a state during the crucial period of struggle between the aristocratic and democratic principles. Alvaro de Luna, though greedy and intolerant, ruled on the whole not unwisely, with a view to the increase of the power of the crown, and with a strong king to support him the latter might have become supreme over both elements, as his great-grandson did.

[1 While there are discrepant statements as to the date and place of Isabella's birth, Prescott accepts April 22nd, 1451, as the date, and Madrigal as the place.*l* Burke *h* emphasises the fact that in her veins flowed the blood both of Guzmans and of Plantagenets; both her great-grandmother and her grandmother were English.]

But though his long reign was politically a failure, it marks a period of social splendour at court and almost universal luxury such as had never been seen in Spain before ; while Castilian letters, under the patronage of the king, reached one of those culminating points of development which appear in Spain at intervals of about two centuries. With the advance of culture and the arts of peace the old rough epics of an earlier time and the didactic verse that followed had become unfashionable ; and in the early fifteenth century, both in the courts of Castile and Aragon, lyric poetry and chronicles of romantic incident became the rage. From King Juan II and Alvaro de Luna downward, almost every noble and knight wrote verses of some sort ; and of the 136 poets who wrote the songs in the *Cancionero General* (Valencia, 1511), probably more than half belonged to the court of Juan II, while in the *Cancionero de Baena* the proportion must be still larger. Music, dances, theatrical interludes, and poetic competitions were the favourite diversions which kept the king amused, while Alvaro de Luna governed according to his will.*i*

THE DISASTERS OF HENRY IV

The reign of Henry IV, surnamed the Impotent, was even more disastrous than that of his father. That this surname was not undeserved, we have the testimony of his own wife, Blanche of Navarre, whom he led to the altar in 1440, and who, after a union of thirteen years, could complain that the *debitum conjugale* remained unpaid. On this ground, in 1453, the marriage was annulled. After his accession, however, he obtained the hand of a Portuguese infanta.

From his rebellious conduct towards his own father, it could scarcely be expected that he would be allowed to sway the sceptre in peace. Besides the disputes which he had with the crowns of Navarre and Aragon, he was perpetually subjected to the insults no less than the defiance of his turbulent nobles, and to the partial revolts of the people whom the exactions of his revenue officers never failed to exasperate. In 1457 a league was formed against him, just as it had been against the late king, and composed of the most influential barons and ecclesiastics : among these was Henry's favourite Pacheco, for whom he had obtained the marquisate of Villena, and whom he had laden with honours and wealth. Their complaints were that the business of administration was neglected ; that the king kept aloof from the hereditary advisers of his crown, and associated with individuals of low birth [these included numerous Moors], on whom he lavished his resources to the great detriment of the state. Whatever might be his other faults, he was naturally mild, and disposed to cherish his people ; to their remonstrance he replied that he would convoke his cortes, and do whatever they advised him. They accordingly disbanded. But he soon abandoned himself to new favourites.

In the meantime, the confederates again proceeded to strengthen their league : made a second petition, drawn up in more decided terms than the preceding ; and, besides, insisted that the king should pay more regard to the education of the infantes, Alfonso and Isabella, and cause the former to be recognised as his heir by the states of the kingdom. As his answer was evasive, they again placed the king of Aragon and Navarre[1] at their head,

---

[1] Juan, king of Navarre, who in 1458 had succeeded his brother Alfonso as king of Aragon.

and laboured by every means to obstruct the course of his government. Hostilities between him and that monarch were the consequence; but they led to nothing, especially as from time to time he found means to gain over several of the discontented lords.   His satisfaction was increased by the pregnancy of his queen; who, early in 1462, was delivered of a daughter, the infanta Juana or Joanna.   Though popular report did not hesitate to assign the child to the familiarity of the mother with Don Beltran de la Cueva, count of Ledesma, one of Henry's favourites, and even applied to that issue the significant epithet of *Beltraneja*, the latter was not the less eager in securing the recognition of the princess as heiress to his dominions.

At length the marquis of Villena, the very soul of the league, being disappointed in his expectation of the grand-mastership of Santiago, which was conferred on the count of Ledesma, formed no less a project than that of arresting both king and queen, of proclaiming Alfonso, and, in concert with his confederates, of reigning under the name and authority of that young prince.   Being seasonably warned by four faithful servants, the king avoided the snare. Nevertheless in a subsequent interview he agreed that his brother Alfonso should be declared his heir; that Don Beltran should resign the grand-mastership of Santiago in favour of that infante, who should be consigned to the guardianship of the marquis of Villena.   Early in the following year (1465), these conditions were punctually performed: Beltran resigned the dignity, with which Alfonso was immediately invested; and that infante, on engaging to marry the Beltraneja, was, at the same time, proclaimed prince of the Asturias, and successor to the throne.   But Henry's unexampled concessions were insufficient.   Henry summoned them to lay down their arms, and to surrender his brother, and went to invest Arevalo, one of their fortresses: that siege, however, he soon raised on hearing that Valladolid had declared for Alfonso, whom the rebels were

HENRY IV

conducting to Avila, to be there proclaimed king of Leon and Castile.

The scene which now disgraced Avila was one of unparalleled effrontery. In the midst of the plain, near the walls of the city, a vast theatre was constructed; in the centre rose a throne, on which was placed an effigy of Henry with a crown on the head, a sceptre in the hand, and other ensigns of royal dignity.   A herald ascended the platform and read, in a loud voice, the various charges that had long been urged against the administration of the king — his neglect of justice, his incapacity, the outrages which he had committed against his kingdom and nobles; hence, that, in conformity with reason and justice, no less than the fundamental laws of the realm, the said Henry had been pronounced by the most eminent civilians to be unfit any longer to wear the crown, and that his deposition was imperiously demanded by the interests of the nation.   This decision was justified by an allusion to other kingdoms, which, in various periods of history, had been compelled to depose their rulers.

No sooner was this strange homily finished than the archbishop of Toledo, with the marquis of Villena, the count of Plasencia, the grand-master of Alcantara, and other barons, ascended the platform, and approached the statue. The first took off the royal crown; the second snatched away the sceptre; the third, the sword; a fourth stripped off the kingly robe; a fifth and sixth, the other emblems of royalty: all six then simultaneously kicked the statue from the chair, and precipitated it to the ground, loading it with curses and the most insulting terms of reproach. Alfonso was next brought on the stage, and was elevated on the shoulders of the nobles, who exclaimed, "*Castilla! Castilla! para el rey Don Alfonso!*" The flourish of trumpets, the beating of drums, and the homage solemnly rendered to the new king, completed the scene.

Henry was naturally anxious to punish the rebels, but their attitude was too formidable for him. They continued under arms, besieging fortress after fortress, and wreaking vengeance alike on their personal and political enemies. During these troubles there was a total relaxation of the laws; numerous bands of robbers paraded the highways, and not infrequently pillaged the towns of the kingdom; until the inhabitants formed themselves into voluntary confederations for the protection of their persons and properties. Thus continued the face of affairs until 1467, when Henry resolved to risk a battle with the rebels. He met them near Olmedo, where, after a fierce but indecisive struggle, both armies left the field, each boasting of the victory. While each was collecting reinforcements to try the event of another action, arrived a papal legate, who endeavoured to reduce the rebels to reason, and who was so imprudent as to threaten them with the thunders of the church unless they laid down their arms and submitted their complaints to arbitration. Three hundred tongues hooted him from the camp of the confederates: to avoid something worse, he hastily mounted his mule, and fled. This event, however, did not prevent the king from meeting the leaders at Segovia, where a suspension of arms was agreed on. The following year his rival, the infante Alfonso, died — an event highly favourable to the king.

The rebels, indeed, proposed to raise the infanta Isabella, his sister, to the throne, and thereby perpetuate their own impunity; but that princess, who had principles and an understanding far above her years, refused to become the tool of a few factious rebels. Finally, peace was made: Isabella and Henry met with every appearance of good will; and that princess was recognised, both by him and the great body of the barons and deputies as the undoubted heiress of the two crowns. The queen, indeed, protested against this arrangement in favour of her daughter; but her complaints passed unheeded.

MARRIAGE OF FERDINAND AND ISABELLA

In the same year was laid the foundations of a union which was to prove of such unbounded value to Spain; Juan II of Aragon solicited the hand of Isabella of Castile for his son and heir Don Ferdinand, king of Sicily. The overture was formally received by the princess; but obstacles of so formidable a nature intervened that, for some time, there was little hope of a successful issue to the negotiations. Neither the king nor the queen wished to see the cause of Isabella supported by so powerful a neighbour as the future monarch of Aragon would necessarily be. Besides, several barons, who had followed the fortunes of Henry, and procured great estates at the expense of the infanta's adherents, naturally dreaded her accession in any case, especially if there should be a junction of her power with that of Aragon.

Such, however, was the eagerness of Juan to conclude the match; such the sums he distributed among the Castilian nobles; and so powerful the interference of the archbishop of Toledo in the cause, that her adherents decided on bringing the affair as soon as possible to a conclusion. The whole negotiation was secretly conducted; the rather as the princess was sought both by the duke of Berri, brother to the French king, and by the monarch of Portugal, whose agents were sure to oppose every obstacle in their power to the union with Aragon. For a time she was a prisoner in Madrigal, where it was evidently intended to detain her until she gave her consent to either the Portuguese or the Frenchman. The former was considered too old to have issue, the latter was too far removed to be dreaded. She contrived to acquaint her friends with her unexpected position. The primate immediately collected three hundred lances, and marched to her relief; the admiral of Castile and the bishop of Curia did the same; she was released, and triumphantly escorted to Valladolid. Ferdinand was invited to hasten from Aragon with all possible expedition, while Henry was absent in Andalusia, and receive his bride. As he was likely to be intercepted on his reaching the Castilian territory, he assumed a suitable disguise, and, with three attendants only, eluded the design of his enemies. On the 25th of October, 1469, the royal pair received the nuptial benediction in the cathedral of Valladolid.

QUEEN ISABELLA

No sooner was Henry acquainted with this precipitate marriage, than he resolved to leave no measure untried for securing the crown to Beltraneja. To the deputations of his sister and brother-in-law, who entreated him to forgive a step rendered necessary by circumstances, he returned answers studiously evasive. The profusion with which he lavished lands, lordships, and other honours on the more powerful barons, proved how anxious he was to effect his object. But his attention was long distracted, and his efforts rendered abortive, by the troubles which lacerated his kingdom. There was no longer a government: one baron made war on another, and one class of the community on another, with perfect impunity and with perfect contempt of their sovereign's authority. In some towns the streets were deluged with blood by their contentions. But the king was too mutable in character to persevere long in any given line of conduct. In 1474 he again sought for an opportunity of entrapping and imprisoning the infanta and her husband; but his purpose was divined and eluded.

This weak monarch — weak even to helplessness — died near the close of 1474; by his last will he declared the young Juana his successor, and charged four of his most considerable barons with its execution. The desire of wiping away the stain on his manhood did not forsake him even on the verge of the grave.

On the death of Juan, Ferdinand was at Saragossa; but his consort, being at Segovia, summoned that city to acknowledge her, and was instantly obeyed: by the nobles and prelates present, both were solemnly proclaimed joint sovereigns of Castile and Leon. On his return from Aragon, there was much dispute as to the power he was to exercise in the administration. While one party contended that the undivided executive ought to depend on the queen, as *domina et hæres* of the monarchy, another maintained that he alone should govern; since, in default of male issue by the deceased king, the crown devolved of right to him as the next heir. But the Salic law had never been in force in this kingdom, however it might be recognised in some neighbouring states. After frequent and acrimonious consultations, it was agreed that the king and queen should reign conjointly, and that, in all public acts, his name should precede hers; but, to save her rights, or rather to satisfy Castilian jealousy, it was no less stipulated that without her express sanction he should not have power to alienate any portion of the royal revenues or domains, nor to nominate the governors of towns or fortresses. These restrictions were far from pleasing to Ferdinand, who was immoderately fond of power, and who, at first, even threatened to return into his hereditary kingdom. His indignation was disarmed by the prudence of the queen, who, by promising submission to his will, averted so fatal a misfortune.

WAR OF THE SUCCESSION (1474–1479 A.D.)

But if the majority of the people were in favour of the new reign, there were yet many barons, and those of considerable influence, who espoused the interests of Juana. The marquis of Villena, with other barons of the same party, resolved to marry the young princess to Alfonso V of Portugal, assisted by whose arms they hoped to make head against the reigning pair. Alfonso readily embraced the proposals of the disaffected: he collected troops, and at the same time, as uncle of Juana, applied to the pope for a dispensation to celebrate the marriage.

However important the stake for which the two parties now began to contend, the details of that contention are too obscure in themselves, and were too indecisive, to merit minute attention. Though the Portuguese obtained some partial successes, among others the strong fortress of Zamora, the war was decidedly in favour of the Castilian sovereigns: in the very first campaign the marquis of Villena had the mortification to see his hereditary domains in possession of the royal forces; while many of the towns and forts, which had at first declared for Juana, returned to their duty. In 1476 the Portuguese king was compelled to retreat from Zamora, which was invested by Ferdinand; near Toro he was overtaken by his active enemy, and a battle ensued, in which victory declared for the latter;[1] it was immediately followed by the surrender of the fortress. About the same time, Madrid, which had held for Juana, capitulated to the duke del Infantado: Ucles followed the example. Both the marquis and the primate were now tired of their ally and their cause. Negotiations were opened; and, in September, 1479, satisfactorily concluded at Alcacebas.

[1] In this battle it was somewhat singular to see two eminent ecclesiastical dignitaries, the cardinal De Mendoza and the archbishop of Toledo, fighting on opposite sides. There was something not exactly apostolic in the former's hastening along the Castilian ranks, with a crucifix borne before him, shouting, "Knaves, fight away! have ye not a cardinal with you?"
[In honour of this victory Isabella walked barefoot in a religious procession through the streets.]

The principal conditions were that Alfonso should renounce the title of king of Castile ; that he should neither marry, nor in any way favour the pretensions of Doña Juana ; that "this pretended daughter of the late king, Don Henry," should be allowed six months to decide whether she would wait until the infante Juan (only son of Ferdinand and Isabella, then but a year old) arrived at a marriageable age, or take the veil ; that the Portuguese should restore the few places they still held in Estremadura.   It was added that if, on arriving at a proper age, the infante should be averse to the match, he had only to pay 100,000 pistoles to be at liberty to marry whom he pleased.   The unfortunate lady, seeing that she was sacrificed to the interests of the two kings, professed in the convent of St. Clair at Coimbra.[1]

The very year in which peace was thus happily restored between Castile and Portugal, Ferdinand, by the death of his father, Juan II, was called to the throne of Aragon.   Having received the homage and confirmed the privileges of his Aragonese subjects at Saragossa, of the Catalonians at Barcelona, and of the Valencians in the capital of that province, he returned into Castile. *g*

There was now a Spain, though the government of the two kingdoms was separately administered under separate constitutions long after the time of Ferdinand and Isabella ; yet the double throne was after all one throne, and Spain was at last a nation, fronting the world united, as far as the Spaniards of that time could be united, and the first reign of the new realm was the most glorious of all. *a*

[1 Alfonso later abdicated and went into a monastery.]

CHAPTER VI

FERDINAND AND ISABELLA

[1474–1504 A.D.]

IT was fortunate for Spain that her sceptre, at this crisis, was swayed by a sovereign possessed of sufficient wisdom to devise, and energy to execute the most salutary schemes of reform, and thus to infuse a new principle of vitality into a government fast sinking into premature decrepitude.

The whole plan of reform introduced into the government by Ferdinand and Isabella, or more properly by the latter, to whom the internal administration of Castile was principally referred, was not fully unfolded until the completion of her reign. But the most important modifications were adopted previously to the war of Granada in 1482. These may be embraced under the following heads: (1) the efficient administration of justice; (2) the codification of the laws; (3) the depression of the nobles; (4) the vindication of ecclesiastical rights belonging to the crown, from the usurpation of the papal see; (5) the regulation of trade; (6) the pre-eminence of the royal authority.

In the dismal anarchy which prevailed in Henry IV's reign, the authority of the monarch and of the royal judges had fallen into such contempt that the law was entirely without force. The cities afforded no better protection than the open country. Every man's hand seemed to be lifted against his neighbour. Property was plundered; persons were violated; the most holy sanctuaries profaned; and the numerous fortresses scattered throughout the country, instead of sheltering the weak, converted into dens of robbers. Isabella saw no better way of checking this unbounded license than to direct against it that popular engine, the *Santa Hermandad*, or Holy Brotherhood, which had more than once shaken the Castilian monarchs on their throne. By the activity of this new military police, the country was, in the course of a few years, cleared of its swarms of banditti, as well as of the robber chieftains, whose strength had enabled them to defy the law. The ministers of justice found a sure protection in the independent discharge of their duties; and the blessings of personal security and social order, so long estranged from the nation, were again restored to it. At length, in 1498, the objects for which it was established having been completely obtained, it was deemed advisable to relieve the nation from the heavy charges which its maintenance imposed; and the magnificent apparatus of the *Santa Hermandad*, stripped of all but the terrors of its name, dwindled into an ordinary police.

Isabella was so intent on the prosecution of her schemes of reform, that even in the minuter details she frequently superintended the execution of them herself. For this she was admirably fitted by her personal address, and presence of mind in danger, and by the influence which a conviction of her integrity gave her over the minds of the people. A remarkable exemplification of this occurred, the year but one after her coronation, at Segovia. The inhabitants, secretly instigated by the bishop of that place and some of the principal citizens, rose against Cabrera, marquis of Moya, to whom the government of the city had been entrusted, and who had made himself generally unpopular by his strict discipline.

The queen, on receiving tidings of the event at Tordesillas, mounted her horse and proceeded with all possible despatch towards Segovia, attended by Cardinal Mendoza, the count of Benavente, and a few others of her court. At some distance from the city she was met by a deputation of the inhabitants, requesting her to leave behind the count of Benavente and the marchioness of Moya (the former of whom as the intimate friend, and the latter as the wife, of the alcalde, were peculiarly obnoxious to the citizens), or they could not answer for the consequences. Isabella haughtily replied that she was queen of Castile; that the city was hers, moreover, by right of inheritance; and that she was not used to receive conditions from rebellious subjects. Then passing forward with her little retinue through one of the gates, which remained in the hands of her friends, she effected her entrance into the citadel.

The populace, in the meanwhile, assembling in greater numbers than before, continued to show the most hostile dispositions, calling out "Death to the alcalde! Attack the castle!" She herself descended into the courtyard, where she ordered the portals to be thrown open for the admission of the people. She stationed herself at the further extremity of the area, and as the populace poured in, calmly demanded the cause of the insurrection. "Tell me," said she, "what are your grievances, and I will do all in my power to redress them; for I am sure that what is for your interest must be also for mine, and for that of the whole city." The insurgents, abashed by the unexpected presence of their sovereign, as well as by her cool and dignified demeanour, replied that all they desired was the removal of Cabrera from the government of the city. "He is deposed already," answered the queen, "and you have my authority to turn out such of his officers as are still in the castle, which I shall entrust to one of my own servants, on whom I can rely." The people, pacified by these assurances, shouted, "Long live the queen!" and eagerly hastened to obey her mandates. The mob dispersed, and the queen, after a candid examination, having ascertained the groundlessness or gross exaggeration of the charges against Cabrera, and traced the source of the conspiracy to the jealousy of the bishop of Segovia and his associates, reinstated the deposed alcalde in the full possession of his dignities, which his enemies, either convinced of the altered dispositions of the people, or believing that the favourable moment for resistance had escaped, made no further attempts to disturb. Thus by a happy presence of mind, an affair which threatened disastrous consequences was settled without bloodshed, or compromise of the royal dignity.[1]

In the summer of the following year, 1477, Isabella resolved to pay a visit to Estremadura and Andalusia, for the purpose of composing the dissensions and introducing a more efficient police in these unhappy provinces ; which, from their proximity to the stormy frontier of Portugal, as well as from the feuds between the great houses of Guzman and Ponce de Leon, were plunged into the most frightful anarchy. Cardinal Mendoza and her other ministers remonstrated against this imprudent exposure of her person, where it was so little likely to be respected. But she replied that it was true there were dangers and inconveniences to be encountered ; but her fate was in God's hands, and she felt a confidence that he would guide to a prosperous issue such designs as were righteous in themselves and resolutely conducted.

Isabella experienced the most loyal and magnificent reception from the inhabitants of Seville, where she established her headquarters. The first days of her residence there were consumed in *fêtes*, tourneys, tilts of reeds, and other exercises of the Castilian chivalry. After this she devoted her whole time to the great purpose of her visit, the reformation of abuses. She held her court in the saloon of the Alcazar, or royal castle, where she revived the ancient practice of the Castilian sovereigns of presiding in person over the administration of justice. Every Friday she took her seat in her chair of state, on an elevated platform covered with cloth of gold, and surrounded by her council, together with the subordinate functionaries and the insignia of a court of justice. The members of her privy council and of the high court of criminal law sat in their official capacity every day in the week, and the queen herself received such suits as were referred to her adjudication, saving the parties the usual expense and procrastination of justice. By the extraordinary despatch of the queen and her ministers, during the two months that she resided in the city, a vast number of civil and criminal causes were disposed of, a large amount of plundered property was restored to its lawful owners, and so many offenders were brought to condign punishment, that no less than four thousand suspected persons, it is computed, terrified by the prospect of speedy retribution for their crimes, escaped into the neighbouring kingdoms of Portugal and Granada.

The royal audience, or chancery, the supreme and final court of appeal in civil causes, was entirely remodelled. The place of its sittings, before indeterminate, and consequently occasioning much trouble and cost to the litigants, was fixed at Valladolid. Laws were passed to protect the tribunal from the interference of the crown, and the queen was careful to fill the bench with magistrates whose wisdom and integrity would afford the best guarantee for a faithful interpretation of the law. An attorney was provided at the public expense, under the title of "advocate for the poor," whose duty it was to defend the suits of such as were unable to maintain them at their own cost. The sovereigns testified their respect for the law by reviving the ancient but obsolete practice of presiding personally in the tribunals at least once a week. "I well remember," says Oviedo,[b] one of their court, "to have seen the queen, together with the Catholic king her husband, sitting in judgment in the Alcazar of Madrid, every Friday, dispensing justice to all such, great and small, as came to demand it. This was indeed the golden

---

[1] Gonzalo de Oviedo[b] lavishes many ecomiums on Cabrera, for his "generous qualities, his singular prudence in government, and his solicitude for his vassals, whom he inspired with the deepest attachment." The best panegyric on his character is the unshaken confidence which his royal mistress reposed in him to the day of her death.

age of justice," continues the enthusiastic writer, "and since our sainted mistress has been taken from us, it has been more difficult, and far more costly, to transact business with a stripling of a secretary, than it was with the queen and all her ministers." By the modifications then introduced, the basis was laid of the judiciary system, such as it has been perpetuated to the present age. The law acquired an authority which, in the language of a Spanish writer, "caused a decree, signed by two or three judges, to be more respected since that time than an army before."[1]

Whatever reforms might have been introduced into the Castilian judicatures, they would have been of little avail without a corresponding improvement in the system of jurisprudence by which their decisions were to be regulated. This was made up of the Visigothic code as the basis, the *fueros* of the Castilian princes, as far back as the eleventh century, and the *Siete Partidas*, the famous compilation of Alfonso X, digested chiefly from maxims of the civil law. The deficiencies of these ancient codes had been gradually supplied by such an accumulation of statutes and ordinances as rendered the legislation of Castile in the highest degree complex, and often contradictory. The embarrassment resulting from this may be imagined.

In 1480, Dr. Alfonso Diaz de Montalvo was charged with the commission of revising the laws of Castile, and of compiling a code which should be of general application throughout the kingdom. Although the many innovations which were introduced in that age of reform required the addition of two subsidiary codes in the latter years of Isabella, the *Ordenanças* of Montalvo continued to be the guide of the tribunals down to the time of Philip II, and may be said to have suggested the idea, as indeed it was the basis, of the comprehensive compilation, *Nueva Recopilacion*, which has since formed the law of the Spanish monarchy.

Under the profuse reigns of Juan II and Henry IV, the nobles had introduced themselves into every great post of profit or authority. They had ravished from the crown the estates on which it depended for its maintenance as well as dignity. They coined money in their own mints, like sovereign princes; and they covered the country with their fortified castles, whence they defied the law, and desolated the unhappy land with interminable feuds. It was obviously necessary for the new sovereigns to proceed with the greatest caution against this powerful and jealous body, and, above all, to attempt no measure of importance in which they would not be supported by the hearty co-operation of the nation.

The first measure which may be said to have clearly developed their policy was the organisation of the hermandad, which, although ostensibly directed against offenders of a more humble description, was made to bear indirectly upon the nobility, whom it kept in awe by the number and discipline of its forces, and the promptness with which it could assemble them on the most remote points of the kingdom; while its rights of jurisdiction tended materially to abridge those of the seigniorial tribunals. It was accordingly resisted with the greatest pertinacity by the aristocracy; although, as we have seen, the resolution of the queen, supported by the constancy of the commons, enabled her to triumph over all opposition, until the great objects of the institution were accomplished.

Another measure, which insensibly operated to the depression of the nobility, was making official preferment depend less exclusively on ránk, and much more on personal merit, than before. The sovereigns, instead

---

[1] See the strong language, also, of Peter Martyr,[d] another contemporary witness of the beneficial changes in the government.

of confining themselves to the grandees, frequently advanced persons of humble origin, and especially those learned in the law, to the most responsible stations, consulting them, and paying great deference to their opinions, on all matters of importance. The nobles, finding that rank was no longer the sole, or indeed the necessary avenue to promotion, sought to secure it by attention to more liberal studies, in which they were greatly encouraged by Isabella, who admitted their children into her palace, where they were reared under her own eye.

But the boldest assaults on the power of the aristocracy were made in the famous cortes of Toledo, in 1480, which Carbajal*e* enthusiastically styles

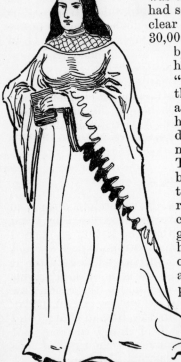

"*cosa divina para reformacion y remedio de las desordenes pasadas.*" The first object of its attention was the condition of the exchequer, which Henry IV had so exhausted by his reckless prodigality that the clear annual revenue amounted to no more than 30,000 ducats, a sum much inferior to that enjoyed by many private individuals; so that, stripped of his patrimony, it at last came to be said he was "king only of the highways." Such had been the royal necessities that blank certificates of annuities assigned on the public rents were hawked about the market, and sold at such a depreciated rate that the price of an annuity did not exceed the amount of one year's income. The commons saw with alarm the weight of the burdens which must devolve on them for the maintenance of the crown thus impoverished in its resources; and they resolved to meet the difficulty by advising at once a resumption of the grants unconstitutionally made during the latter half of Henry IV's reign and the commencement of the present. This measure, however violent and repugnant to good faith it may appear at the present time, seems then to have admitted of justification, as far as the nation was concerned; since such alienation of the public revenue was in itself illegal, and contrary to the coronation oath of the sovereign; and those who accepted his obligations held them subject to the liability of their revocation, which had frequently occurred under the preceding reigns.

A SPANISH NOBLEWOMAN OF THE FIFTEENTH CENTURY

The plan suggested by Cardinal Mendoza seems to have been partially adopted. It was decided that all whose pensions had been conferred without any corresponding services on their part should forfeit them entirely; that those who had purchased annuities should return their certificates on a reimbursement of the price paid for them; and that the remaining creditors, who composed the largest class, should retain such a proportion only of their pensions as might be judged commensurate with their services to the state. Admiral Enriquez, for instance, resigned 240,000 maravedis of his annual income; the duke of Alva, 575,000; the duke of Medina Sidonia, 180,000. The loyal family of the Mendozas were also great losers, but none forfeited so much as the overgrown favourite of Henry IV, Beltran de la

[1480 A.D.]

Cueva, duke of Albuquerque, who had uniformly supported the royal cause, and whose retrenchment amounted to 1,400,000 maravedis of yearly rent.[1]

By this important reduction, the final adjustment and execution of which were intrusted to Ferdinand de Talavera, the queen's confessor, a man of austere probity, the gross amount of 30,000,000 maravedis, a sum equal to three-fourths of the whole revenue on Isabella's accession, was annually saved to the crown. The retrenchment was conducted with such strict impartiality that the most confidential servants of the queen, and the relatives of her husband, were among those who suffered the most severely. It is worthy of remark that no diminution whatever was made of the stipends settled on literary and charitable establishments. It may be also added that Isabella appropriated the first-fruits of this measure, by distributing the sum of 20,000,000 maravedis among the widows and orphans of those loyalists who had fallen in the war of the Succession. This resumption of grants may be considered as the basis of those economical reforms which, without oppression to the subject, augmented the public revenue more than twelvefold during this auspicious reign.

Several other acts were passed by the same cortes, which had a more exclusive bearing on the nobility. They were prohibited from quartering the royal arms on their escutcheons, from being attended by a mace-bearer and a bodyguard, from imitating the regal style of address in their written correspondence, and other insignia of royalty which they had arrogantly assumed. They were forbidden to erect new fortresses, and they were expressly restrained from duels.

Resistance to Papal Encroachment

In the earlier stages of the Castilian monarchy, the sovereigns appear to have held a supremacy in spiritual, very similar to that exercised by them in temporal matters. It was comparatively late that the nation submitted its neck to the papal yoke, so closely riveted at a subsequent period; and even the Romish ritual was not admitted into its churches till long after it had been adopted in the rest of Europe. But when the code of the Partidas was promulgated in the thirteenth century, the maxims of the canon law came to be permanently established. The ecclesiastical encroached on the lay tribunals. Appeals were perpetually carried up to the Roman court; and the popes, pretending to regulate the minutest details of church economy, not only disposed of inferior benefices, but gradually converted the right of confirming elections to the episcopal and higher ecclesiastical dignities into that of appointment.

These usurpations of the church had been repeatedly the subject of grave remonstrance in cortes. The sovereigns, highly dissatisfied, ordered their subjects, ecclesiastical as well as lay, to quit the papal dominions; an injunction which the former, fearful of the sequestration of their temporalities in Castile, obeyed with as much promptness as the latter. At the same time Ferdinand and Isabella proclaimed their intention of inviting the princes of Christendom to unite with them in convoking a general council for the reformation of the manifold abuses which dishonoured the church. No

[1 It is difficult to reduce these sums to modern values, for the maravedi has been coined in gold, silver, and the copper alloy or vellon, and its value has fluctuated bewilderingly from a farthing or quarter of a cent upwards. Assuming that at this time it was equal to about $\frac{1}{2}d$ or 1 cent, Enriquez lost £480 or $2,400; Alva £1,150 or $5,750; Albuquerque £2,800 or $14,000 annually. It is customary to multiply such sums by 7 to get the modern purchasing equivalent.]

sound could have grated more unpleasantly on the pontifical ear than the menace of a general council, particularly at this period, when ecclesiastical corruptions had reached a height which could but ill endure its scrutiny. The pope became convinced that he had ventured too far, and that Henry IV was no longer monarch of Castile. He accordingly despatched a legate to Spain, fully empowered to arrange the matter on an amicable basis ; but the legate received orders instantly to quit the kingdom, without attempting so much as to disclose the nature of his instructions, since they could not but be derogatory to the dignity of the crown.

Far from resenting this ungracious reception, the legate affected the deepest humility. Cardinal Mendoza, whose influence in the cabinet had gained him the title of "third king of Spain," at length so far mitigated the resentment of the sovereigns that they consented to open negotiations with the court of Rome. The result was the publication of a bull by Sixtus IV, in which his holiness engaged to provide such natives to the higher dignities of the church in Castile as should be nominated by the monarchs of that kingdom.

The Regulation of Trade

It will be readily conceived that trade, agriculture, and every branch of industry must have languished under the misrule of preceding reigns. In addition to pestilences a fatal shock was given to commercial credit by the adulteration of the coin. Under Henry IV it is computed that there were no less than 150 mints openly licensed by the crown, in addition to many others erected by individuals without any legal authority ; and the little trade which remained in Castile was carried on by barter, as in the primitive stages of society.

The magnitude of the evil was such as to claim the earliest attention of the cortes under the new monarchs. Acts were passed, fixing the standard and legal value of the different denominations of coin. A new coinage was subsequently made. Five royal mints were alone authorised, afterwards augmented to seven, and severe penalties denounced against the fabrication of money elsewhere. The reform of the currency gradually infused new life into commerce, as the return of the circulations, which have been interrupted for a while, quickens the animal body. This was furthered by salutary laws for the encouragement of domestic industry. Internal communication was facilitated by the construction of roads and bridges. Absurd restrictions on change of residence, as well as the onerous duties which had been imposed on commercial intercourse between Castile and Aragon, were repealed. Public credit was re-established by the punctuality with which the government redeemed the debt contracted during the Portuguese war ; and notwithstanding the repeal of various arbitrary imposts which enriched the exchequer under Henry IV, such was the advance of the country, under the wise economy of the present reign, that the revenue was augmented nearly sixfold between the years 1477 and 1482.

Thus released from the heavy burdens imposed on it, the spring of enterprise recovered its former elasticity. The productive capital of the country was made to flow through the various channels of domestic industry. The hills and the valleys again rejoiced in the labour of the husbandman; and the cities were embellished with stately edifices, both public and private, which attracted the gaze and commendation of foreigners. The writers of that day are unbounded in their plaudits of Isabella, to whom they principally ascribe this auspicious revolution in the condition of the country and its inhabitants, which seems almost as magical as one of those transformations in romance wrought by the hands of some benevolent fairy.

The Pre-eminence of the Royal Authority

This, which, we have seen, appears to have been the natural result of the policy of Ferdinand and Isabella, was derived quite as much from the influence of their private characters as from their public measures. Under such a sovereign, the court, which had been little better than a brothel under the preceding reign, became the nursery of virtue and generous ambition.

Isabella watched assiduously over the nurture of the high-born damsels of her court, whom she received into the royal palace, causing them to be educated under her own eye, and endowing them with liberal portions on their marriage. By these and similar acts of affectionate solicitude she endeared herself to the higher classes of her subjects, while the patriotic tendency of her public conduct established her in the hearts of the people. She possessed, in combination with the feminine qualities which beget love, a masculine energy of character which struck terror into the guilty. She enforced the execution of her own plans, oftentimes even at great personal hazard, with a resolution surpassing that of her husband. Both were singularly temperate, indeed frugal, in their dress, equipage, and general style of living; seeking to affect others less by external pomp than by the silent though more potent influence of personal qualities. On all such occasions as demanded it, however, they displayed a princely magnificence, which dazzled the multitude, and is blazoned with great solemnity in the garrulous chronicles of the day.

Thus laudable objects were gradually achieved by a course of measures equally laudable; and the various orders of the monarchy, brought into harmonious action with each other, were enabled to turn the forces which had before been wasted in civil conflict to the glorious career of discovery and conquest which it was destined to run during the remainder of the century.

No sooner had Ferdinand and Isabella restored internal tranquillity to their dominions, and made the strength effective which had been acquired by their union under one government, than they turned their eyes to those fair regions of the peninsula over which the Moslem crescent had reigned triumphant for nearly eight centuries. Fortunately, an act of aggression on the part of the Moors furnished a pretext for entering on their plan of conquest at the moment when it was ripe for execution.

Mulei Abul-Hassan, who succeeded his father in 1466, was of a very different temperament. His fiery character prompted him, when very young, to violate the truce by an unprovoked inroad into Andalusia. When, in 1476, the Spanish sovereigns required, as the condition of a renewal of the truce which he solicited, the payment of the annual tribute imposed on his predecessors, he proudly replied that the mints of Granada coined no longer gold, but steel. His subsequent conduct did not belie the spirit of this Spartan answer.

At length, towards the close of the year 1481, the storm which had been so long gathering burst upon Zahara, a small fortified town on the frontier of Andalusia, crowning a lofty eminence, washed at its base by the river Guadalete, which from its position seemed almost inaccessible. The garrison, trusting to these natural defences, suffered itself to be surprised, on the night of the 26th of December, by the Moorish monarch, who, scaling the walls under favour of a furious tempest, which prevented his approach from being readily heard, put to the sword such of the guard as offered resistance, and swept away the whole population of the place, men, women, and children, into slavery in Granada.

It was not long before the desired opportunity for retaliation presented itself to the Spaniards. One Juan de Ortega, a captain of *escaladores*, or scalers, so denominated from the peculiar service in which they were employed in besieging cities, reported that the fortress of Alhama, situated in the heart of the Moorish territories, was so negligently guarded that it might be easily carried by an enemy who had skill enough to approach it. Its strength of position lulled its defenders into a security like that which had proved so fatal to Zahara. A sentinel, who was found sleeping on his post, was despatched, and the whole of the little garrison put to the sword after the short and ineffectual resistance that could be opposed by men suddenly roused from slumber. The city in the meantime was alarmed, but it was too late ; the citadel was taken. Nearly a quarter of the population is said to have perished in the various conflicts of the day, and the remainder, according to the usage of the time, became the prize of the victors.

The report of this disaster fell like the knell of their own doom on the ears of the inhabitants of Granada. Isabella had been employed in making vigorous preparation for carrying on the war, by enforcing the requisite supplies, and summoning the crown vassals, and the principal nobility of the north, to hold themselves in readiness to join the royal standard in Andalusia. After this, she proceeded by rapid stages to Cordova, notwithstanding the state of pregnancy in which she was then far advanced.

Here the sovereigns received the unwelcome information that the king of Granada, on the retreat of the Spaniards, had again sat down before Alhama ; having brought with him artillery, from the want of which he had suffered so much in the preceding siege. It was settled that the king should march to the relief of the besieged, taking with him the most ample supplies of forage and provisions, at the head of a force strong enough to compel the retreat of the Moorish monarch. This was effected without delay; and Abul-Hassan once more breaking up his camp on the rumour of Ferdinand's approach, the latter took possession of the city, without opposition, on the 14th of May, 1482.

Ferdinand, having strengthened the garrison with new recruits, under the command of Portocarrero, lord of Palma, and victualled it with three months' provisions, prepared for a foray into the vega of Granada. This he executed in the true spirit of that merciless warfare so repugnant to the more civilised usage of later times, not only by sweeping away the green, unripened crops, but by cutting down the trees and eradicating the vines, and then, without so much as having broken a lance in the expedition, returned in triumph to Cordova.

Isabella in the meanwhile was engaged in active measures for prosecuting the war. She issued orders to the various cities of Castile and Leon, as far as the borders of Biscay and Guipuzcoa, prescribing the *repartimiento*, or subsidy of provisions, and the quota of troops, to be furnished by each district respectively, together with an adequate supply of ammunition and artillery. The whole were to be in readiness before Loja by the 1st of July, when Ferdinand was to take the field in person at the head of his chivalry, and besiege that strong post. As advices were received that the Moors of Granada were making efforts to obtain the co-operation of their African brethren in support of the Mohammedan empire in Spain, the queen caused a fleet to be manned under the command of her best two admirals, with instructions to sweep the Mediterranean as far as the straits of Gibraltar, and thus effectually cut off all communication with the Barbary coast.

Ferdinand, crossing the Jenil at Ecija, arrived again on its banks before Loja on the 1st of July. The army encamped among the hills, whose deep ravines obstructed communication between its different quarters; while the level plains below were intersected by numerous canals, equally unfavourable to the manœuvres of the men at arms. Ali Atar made a sortie from the town, for the purpose of dislodging his enemies. The latter poured out from their works to encounter him; but the Moslem general, scarcely waiting to receive the shock, wheeled his squadrons round, and began a precipitate retreat. The Spaniards eagerly pursued; but when they had been drawn to a sufficient distance from the redoubt, a party of Moorish *ginetes*, or light cavalry, who had crossed the river unobserved during the night and lain in ambush, after the wily fashion of Arabian tactics, darted from their place of concealment, and, galloping into the deserted camp, plundered it of its contents, including the *lombards*, or small pieces of artillery, with which it was garnished. The Castilians, too late perceiving their error, halted from the pursuit, and returned with as much speed as possible to the defence of their camp. Ali Atar, turning also, hung close on their rear, so that when the Christians arrived at the summit of the hill they found themselves hemmed in between the two divisions of the Moorish army.

Ferdinand resolved to fall back as far as Rio Frio, and await there patiently the arrival of such fresh reinforcements as might put him in condition to enforce a more rigorous blockade. An alarm spread through the whole camp. Instead of standing to the defence, each one thought only of saving himself by as speedy a flight as possible. In vain did Ferdinand, riding along their broken files, endeavour to reanimate their spirits and restore order. Ali Atar's practised eye speedily

A SPANISH NOBLEMAN OF THE
FIFTEENTH CENTURY

discerned the confusion which prevailed through the Christian camp. Without delay, he rushed forth impetuously at the head of his whole array from the gates of Loja.

At this perilous moment nothing but Ferdinand's coolness could have saved the army from total destruction; he was repeatedly exposed to imminent peril, and narrowly escaped with his own life, his horse being shot under him at the very moment when he had lost his lance in the body of a Moor. Never did the Spanish chivalry shed its blood more freely.

The Moors, finding it so difficult to make an impression on this iron band of warriors, began at length to slacken their efforts, and finally allowed Ferdinand to draw off the remnant of his forces without further opposition. The king continued his retreat, without halting, as far as the romantic site of the Peña de los Enamorados, about seven leagues distant from Loja, and, abandoning all thoughts of offensive operations for the present, soon after returned to Cordova. Mulei Abul-Hassan arrived the following day with a

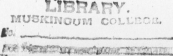
LIBRARY.
MUSKINGUM COLLEGE.

powerful reinforcement from Granada, and swept the country as far as Rio Frio. Had he come but a few hours sooner, there would have been few Spaniards left to tell the tale of the rout of Loja.

The loss of the Christians must have been very considerable, including the greater part of the baggage and the artillery. It occasioned deep mortification to the queen ; but, though a severe, it proved a salutary lesson. It showed the importance of more extensive preparations for a war which must of necessity be a war of posts ; and it taught the nation to entertain greater respect for an enemy who, whatever might be his natural strength, must become formidable when armed with the energy of despair.

Information being soon after received that Louis XI was taking measures to make himself master of the strong places in Navarre, Isabella transferred her residence to the frontier town of Logroño, prepared to resist by arms, if necessary, the occupation of that country by her insidious and powerful neighbour.

There is probably no period in which the princes of Europe felt so sensibly their own penury as at the close of the fifteenth century ; when, the demesnes of the crown having been very generally wasted by the lavishness or imbecility of their proprietors, no substitute had as yet been found in that searching and well-arranged system of taxation which prevails at the present day. The Spanish sovereigns, notwithstanding the economy which they had introduced into the finances, felt the pressure of these embarrassments peculiarly at the present juncture. The maintenance of the royal guard and of the vast national police of the hermandad, the incessant military operations of the late campaign, together with the equipment of a navy, not merely for war, but for maritime discovery, were so many copious drains on the exchequer. Under these circumstances, they obtained from the pope a grant of 100,000 ducats, to be raised out of the ecclesiastical revenues in Castile and Aragon. A bull of crusade was also published by his holiness, containing numerous indulgences for such as should bear arms against the infidel, as well as those who should prefer to commute their military service for the payment of a sum of money. In addition to these resources, the government was enabled on its own credit to negotiate considerable loans.

With these funds the sovereigns entered into extensive arrangements for the ensuing campaign ; causing cannon, after the rude construction of that age, to be fabricated at Huesca, and a large quantity of stone balls, then principally used, to be manufactured in the Sierra de Constantina ; while the magazines were carefully provided with ammunition and military stores.

An event not unworthy of notice is recorded by Pulgar as happening about this time. A common soldier, named Juan de Corral, contrived, under false pretences, to obtain from the king of Granada a number of Christian captives, together with a large sum of money, with which he escaped into Andalusia. The man was apprehended by the warden of the frontier of Jaen ; and the transaction being reported to the sovereigns, they compelled an entire restitution of the money, and consented to such a ransom for the liberated Christians as the king of Granada should demand. This act of justice, it should be remembered, occurred in an age when the church itself stood ready to sanction any breach of faith, however glaring, towards heretics and infidels.

While the court was detained in the north, tidings were received of a reverse sustained by the Spanish arms, which plunged the nation in sorrow far deeper than that occasioned by the rout at Loja.*g*

A plundering expedition had been organised against Malaga and it included the flower of Spanish chivalry. After some conflicts the force turned back, laden with plunder. In the mountainous passes of the Axarquia it met such treatment as Pelayo had once meted out to the Moslem invaders. From every height the Moors poured down volleys of arrows, shot, and stones. At night great fires were built to reveal their hiding places. Panic, fatigue, and famine made chaos of resistance and in two days over eight hundred were killed and sixteen hundred made prisoners. But of these a large proportion were the choice youth of Spain, and the grief at court was excessive.

In the meanwhile there had occurred a feud among the Moors that served the Christians a better turn than many victories. The old king of Granada, Mulei Abul-Hassan, had for Queen Ayesha ; in his harem he had a Greek concubine and also a Christian woman of Andalusia, Isabella de Solis, daughter of the governor of Martos. She was called Zoraya by the Moors and she bore the king a son named Abu Abdallah, more famously called Boabdil. Mother and son, eager for power, planned intrigues which were punished with imprisonment. But they escaped and stirred up a revolution so successfully that the old king was dethroned and driven to Malaga, where he defeated the Christian foray just described.

So great was the enthusiasm among the Moors that Abu Abdallah saw it would be necessary to make some military success to counteract the prestige of his old father. He secured the aid of Ali Atar and with a force of some ten thousand raided the Christian territory and besieged Lucena about April 21st, 1483. The count of Cabra coming to relieve Lucena, Abdallah was caught between two armies. When Ali Atar fell, the Moors fled ; but Abdallah's horse giving out, he was captured — the first royal Moorish prisoner in Christian hands. His mother immediately sought to ransom him, and finally secured his release at the cost of an annual tribute, and a subservience to Spain. Thus the Christians not only divided the Moors among themselves, but gained a large faction as ally.*a*

PROGRESS OF THE WAR

Notwithstanding the importance of the results in the war of Granada, a detail of the successive steps by which they were achieved would be most tedious and trifling. No siege or single military achievement of great moment occurred until nearly four years from this period, in 1487 ; although in the intervening time a large number of fortresses and petty towns, together with a very extensive tract of territory, were recovered from the enemy. Without pursuing the chronological order of events, it is probable that the end of history will be best attained by presenting a concise view of the general policy pursued by the sovereigns in the conduct of the war.

The Moorish wars under preceding monarchs had consisted of little else than *cavalgadas,* or inroads into the enemy's territory, which, pouring like a torrent over the land, swept away whatever was upon the surface, but left it in its essential resources wholly unimpaired. The bounty of nature soon repaired the ravages of man, and the ensuing harvest seemed to shoot up more abundantly from the soil enriched by the blood of the husbandman. A more vigorous system of spoliation was now introduced. Instead of one campaign, the army took the field in spring and autumn, intermitting its efforts only during the intolerable heats of summer, so that the green crop had no time to ripen, ere it was trodden down under the iron heel of war.

The apparatus for devastation was also on a much greater scale than had ever before been witnessed. From the second year of the war, thirty thousand foragers were reserved for this service, which they effected by demolishing farm-houses, granaries, and mills (which last were exceedingly numerous in a land watered by many small streams), by eradicating the vines and laying waste the olive gardens and plantations of oranges, almonds, mulberries, and all the rich varieties that grew luxuriant in this highly favoured region. This merciless devastation extended for more than two leagues on either side of the line of march. At the same time, the Mediterranean fleet cut off all supplies from the Barbary coast, so that the whole kingdom might be said to be in a state of perpetual blockade. Such and so general was the scarcity occasioned by this system, that the Moors were glad to exchange their Christian captives for provisions, until such ransom was interdicted by the sovereigns as tending to defeat their own measures.

Ferdinand, who appeared at the head of his armies throughout the whole of this war, pursued a sagacious policy in reference to the beleaguered cities. He was ever ready to meet the first overtures to surrender in the most liberal spirit; granting protection of person, and such property as the besieged could transport with them, and assigning them a residence, if they preferred it, in his own dominions. Many, in consequence of this, migrated to Seville and other cities of Andalusia, where they were settled on estates which had been confiscated by the inquisitors, who looked forward, no doubt with satisfaction, to the time when they should be permitted to thrust their sickle into the new crop of heresy whose seeds were thus sown amid the ashes of the old one. Those who preferred to remain in the conquered Moorish territory, as Castilian subjects, were permitted the free enjoyment of personal rights and property, as well as of their religion; and such was the fidelity with which Ferdinand redeemed his engagements during the war, by the punishment of the least infraction of them by his own people, that many, particularly of the Moorish peasantry, preferred abiding in their early homes to removing to Granada or other places of the Moslem dominion.

Isabella, solicitous for everything that concerned the welfare of her people, sometimes visited the camp in person, encouraging the soldiers to endure the hardships of war, and relieving their necessities by liberal donations of clothes and money. She caused also a number of large tents, known as "the queen's hospitals," to be always reserved for the sick and wounded, and furnished them with the requisite attendants and medicines at her own charge. This is considered the earliest attempt at the formation of a regular camp hospital on record.

Isabella may be regarded as the soul of this war. She engaged in it with the most exalted views, less to acquire territory than to re-establish the empire of the cross over the ancient domain of Christendom. On this point she concentrated all the energies of her powerful mind, never suffering herself to be diverted by any subordinate interest from this one great and glorious object. When the king, in 1484, would have paused a while from the Granadine war, in order to prosecute his claims to Roussillon against the French after the death of Louis XI, Isabella strongly objected to it; but, finding her remonstrance ineffectual, she left her husband in Aragon, and repaired to Cordova, where she placed the cardinal of Spain at the head of the army, and prepared to open the campaign in the usual vigorous manner. Here, however, she was soon joined by Ferdinand, who, on a cooler revision of the subject, deemed it prudent to postpone his projected enterprise.

Ever since the victory of Lucena, the sovereigns had made it a capital point of their policy to foment the dissensions of their enemies. The young king Abdallah, after his humiliating treaty with Ferdinand, lost whatever consideration he had previously possessed. Although the sultana Zoraya, by her personal address and the lavish distribution of the royal treasures, contrived to maintain a faction for her son, the better classes of his countrymen despised him as a renegade and a vassal of the Christian king. As their old monarch had become incompetent, from increasing age and blindness, to the duties of his station in these perilous times, they turned their eyes on his brother Abdallah, surnamed El Zagal, or "the valiant," who had borne so conspicuous a part in the rout of the Axarquia. The Castilians depict this chief in the darkest colours of ambition and cruelty; but the Moslem writers afford no such intimation, and his advancement to the throne at that crisis seems to be in some measure justified by his eminent talents as a military leader.

On his way to Granada he encountered and cut to pieces a body of Calatrava knights from Alhama, and signalised his entrance into his new capital by bearing along the bloody trophies of heads dangling from his saddle-bow, after the barbarous fashion long practised in these wars. It was observed that the old king Abul-Hassan did not long survive his brother's accession. The young king Abdallah sought the protection of the Castilian sovereigns in Seville, who, true to their policy, sent him back into his own dominions with the means of making headway against his rival.

Notwithstanding these auxiliary circumstances, the progress of the Christians was comparatively slow. Every cliff seemed to be crowned with a fortress; and every fortress was defended with the desperation of men willing to bury themselves under its ruins. The old men, women, and children, on occasion of a siege, were frequently despatched to Granada. Such was the resolution, or rather ferocity, of the Moors, that Malaga closed its gates against the fugitives from Alora, after its surrender, and even massacred some of them in cold blood. The eagle eye of El Zagal seemed to take in at a glance the whole extent of his little territory, and to detect every vulnerable point in his antagonist, whom he encountered where he least expected it, cutting off his convoys, surprising his foraging parties, and retaliating by a devastating inroad on the borders.

No effectual and permanent resistance, however, could be opposed to the tremendous enginery of the Christians. Tower and town fell before it. Besides the principal towns of Cartama, Coin, Setenil, Ronda, Marbella, Illora, termed by the Moors, "the right eye," Moclin, "the shield" of Granada, and Loja, after a second and desperate siege in the spring of 1486, Bernaldez[h] enumerates more than seventy subordinate places in the Val de Cartama, and thirteen others after the fall of Marbella. Thus the Spaniards advanced their line of conquest more than twenty leagues beyond the western frontier of Granada. This extensive tract they strongly fortified, and peopled partly with Christian subjects and partly with Moorish, the original occupants of the soil, who were secured in the possession of their ancient lands, under their own law.

Thus the strong posts which might be regarded as the exterior defences of the city of Granada were successively carried. A few positions alone remained of sufficient strength to keep the enemy at bay. The most considerable of these was Malaga. Before commencing operations against

Malaga, it was thought expedient by the Spanish council of war to obtain possession of Velez Malaga, situated about five leagues distant from the former.

The sensation excited in Granada by the tidings of its danger was so strong, that the old chief, El Zagal, found it necessary to make an effort to relieve the beleaguered city, notwithstanding the critical posture in which his absence would leave his affairs in the capital. But having been foiled in a well-concerted attempt to surprise the Christian quarters by night, he was driven across the mountains by the marquis of Cadiz, and compelled to retreat on his capital, completely baffled in his enterprise. There the tidings

MALAGA

(From the Alameda)

of his disaster had preceded him. The fickle populace, with whom misfortune passes for misconduct, unmindful of his former successes, now hastened to transfer their allegiance to his rival, Abdallah, and closed the gates against him ; and the unfortunate chief withdrew to Guadix, which, with Almeria, Baza, and some less considerable places, still remained faithful.

Ferdinand conducted the siege all the while with his usual vigour, and spared no exposure of his person to peril or fatigue. On one occasion, seeing a party of Christians retreating in disorder before a squadron of the enemy, who had surprised them while fortifying an eminence near the city, the king, who was at dinner in his tent, rushed out with no other defensive armour than his cuirass, and, leaping on his horse, charged briskly into the midst of the enemy, and succeeded in rallying his own men. In the midst of the rencounter, however, when he had discharged his lance, he found himself unable to extricate his sword from the scabbard which hung from the saddle-bow. At this moment he was assaulted by several Moors, and must have been either slain or taken but for the timely rescue of the marquis of Cadiz, and a brave cavalier, Garcilasso de la Vega, who, galloping up to the spot with their attendants, succeeded, after a sharp skirmish, in beating off the enemy. Ferdinand's nobles remonstrated with him on this wanton exposure of his person, representing that he could serve them more effectually with his head than his hand. But he answered that he could not stop to calculate chances when his subjects were perilling their lives for his sake — a reply, says Pulgar,c which endeared him to the whole army. At length the inhabitants of Velez consented to capitulate. The capitulation of this place (April 27th, 1487) was followed by that of more than twenty places of inferior note lying between it and Malaga, so that the approaches to this latter city were now left open to the victorious Spaniards.

THE SIEGE OF MALAGA

The old chronicler Bernaldezh warms at the aspect of the fair city of Malaga, encompassed by Christian legions, whose deep lines, stretching far over hill and valley, reached quite round from one arm of the sea to the other. In the midst of this brilliant encampment was seen the royal pavilion, proudly displaying the united banners of Castile and Aragon, and forming so conspicuous a mark for the enemy's artillery that Ferdinand, after imminent hazard, was at length compelled to shift his quarters.

The Moors were not unmindful of the importance of Malaga, or the gallantry with which it was defended. They made several attempts to relieve it, the failure of which was owing less to the Christians than to treachery and their own miserable feuds. A body of cavalry, which El Zagal despatched from Guadix to throw succours into the beleaguered city, was encountered and cut to pieces by a superior force of the young king Abdallah, who consummated his baseness by sending an embassy to the Christian camp, charged with a present of Arabian horses sumptuously caparisoned to Ferdinand, and of costly silks and oriental perfumes to the queen; at the same time complimenting them on their successes, and soliciting the continuance of their friendly dispositions towards himself. Ferdinand and Isabella requited this act of humiliation by securing to Abdallah's subjects the right of cultivating their fields in quiet, and of trafficking with the Spaniards in every commodity save military stores. At this paltry price did the dastard prince consent to stay his arm at the only moment when it could be used effectually for his country.

More serious consequences were like to have resulted from an attempt made by another party of Moors from Guadix to penetrate the Christian lines. Part of them succeeded, and threw themselves into the besieged city. The remainder were cut in pieces. There was one, however, who, making no show of resistance, was taken prisoner without harm to his person. Being brought before the marquis of Cadiz, he informed that nobleman that he could make some important disclosures to the sovereigns. He was accordingly conducted to the royal tent; but, as Ferdinand was taking his siesta, in the sultry hour of the day, the queen, moved by divine inspiration, according to the Castilian historian, deferred the audience till her husband should awake, and commanded the prisoner to be detained in the adjoining tent. This was occupied by Doña Beatrice de Bobadilla, marchioness of Moya, Isabella's early friend, who happened to be at that time engaged in discourse with a Portuguese nobleman, Don Alvaro, son of the duke of Braganza.

The Moor did not understand the Castilian language, and, deceived by the rich attire and courtly bearing of these personages, he mistook them for the king and queen. He suddenly drew a dagger, and darting on the Portuguese prince, gave him a deep wound on the head, and then, turning like lightning on the marchioness, aimed a stroke at her, which fortunately glanced without injury, the point of the weapon being turned by the heavy embroidery of her robes. Before he could repeat his blow, the Moorish Scævola, with a fate very different from that of his Roman prototype, was pierced with a hundred wounds by the attendants, who rushed to the spot, alarmed by the cries of the marchioness, and his mangled remains were soon after discharged from a catapult into the city ; a foolish bravado, which the besieged requited by slaying a Galician gentleman and sending his corpse astride upon a mule through the gates of the town into the Christian camp.

The Castilian army, swelled by daily augmentations, varied in its amount, according to different estimates, from sixty to ninety thousand men. Throughout this immense host the most perfect discipline was maintained. Gaming was restrained by ordinances interdicting the use of dice and cards, of which the lower orders were passionately fond. Blasphemy was severely punished. Prostitutes, the common pest of a camp, were excluded ; and so entire was the subordination, that not a knife was drawn, and scarcely a brawl occurred, says the historian, among the motley multitude.

The battle raged with fire and sword, above and under ground, along the ramparts, the ocean, and the land, at the same time. But no virtue or valour could avail the unfortunate Malagans against the overwhelming force of their enemies, who, driving them back from every point, compelled them to shelter themselves within the defences of the town. The Christians followed up their success. A mine was sprung near a tower connected by a bridge of four arches with the main works of the place. The Moors, scattered and intimidated by the explosion, retreated across the bridge ; and the Spaniards, carrying the tower, whose guns completely enfiladed it, obtained possession of this important pass into the beleaguered city. The citizens of Malaga, dismayed at beholding the enemy established in their defences, and fainting under exhaustion from a siege which had already lasted more than three months, now began to murmur at the obstinacy of the garrison, and to demand a capitulation.

A deputation was despatched to the Christian quarters, with the offer of the city to capitulate, on the same liberal conditions which had been uniformly granted by the Spaniards. The king refused to admit the embassy into his presence, and haughtily answered, through the commander of Leon, that these terms had been twice offered to the people of Malaga, and rejected; that it was too late for them to stipulate conditions, and nothing now remained but to abide by those which he, as their conqueror, should vouchsafe to them. After a tumultuous debate, the deputies were despatched a second time to the Christian camp, charged with propositions in which concession was mingled with menace. They were willing to resign to him their fortifications, their city, on his assurance of their personal security and freedom : if he refused this, they would take their Christian captives, amounting to five or six hundred, from the dungeons in which they lay, and hang them like dogs over the battlements; and then, placing their old men, women, and children in the fortress, they would set fire to the town, and cut a way for themselves through their enemies, or fall in the attempt. Ferdinand, unmoved by these menaces, coolly replied that he saw no occasion to change his former determination, but they might rest assured, if they harmed a single hair of a Christian, he would put every soul in the place, man, woman, and child, to the sword.

On the eighteenth day of August, being somewhat more than three months from the date of opening trenches, Ferdinand and Isabella made their entrance into the conquered city, attended by the court, the clergy, and the whole of their military array. The procession moved in solemn state up the principal streets, now deserted and hushed in ominous silence, to the new cathedral of St. Mary, where mass was performed. At length, the whole population of the city, comprehending every age and sex, was commanded to repair to the great courtyard of the Alcazaba. The dreadful doom of slavery was denounced on the assembled multitude.[1] One-third was to be transported into Africa in exchange for an equal number of Christian captives detained there; and all who had relatives or friends in this predicament were required to furnish a specification of them. Another third was appropriated to reimburse the state for the expenses of the war. The remainder were to be distributed as presents at home and abroad. Thus, one hundred of the flower of the African warriors were sent to the pope, who incorporated them into his guard, and converted them all in the course of the year, says the curate of Los Palacios, into very good Christians. Fifty of the most beautiful Moorish girls were presented by Isabella to the queen of Naples, thirty to the queen of Portugal, others to the ladies of her court; and the residue of both sexes were apportioned among the nobles, cavaliers, and inferior members of the army, according to their respective rank and services.

Malaga was computed to contain from eleven to fifteen thousand inhabitants, exclusive of several thousand foreign auxiliaries, within its gates at the time of surrender. One cannot, at this day, read the melancholy details of its story without feelings of horror and indignation. It is impossible to vindicate the dreadful sentence passed on this unfortunate people for a display of heroism which should have excited admiration in every generous bosom. It was obviously most repugnant to Isabella's natural disposition, and must be admitted to leave a stain on her memory which no colouring of history can conceal. The fate of Malaga may be said to have decided that of Granada.*g*

THE CAPTURE OF GRANADA

The western fortresses of the kingdom being in the power of the Christians, Ferdinand had now two plans before him for attaining his great object: he could either at once fall on the capital, or begin with the reduction of the eastern strongholds. He chose the latter; he knew that, if he triumphed over Abdallah el Zagal, who possessed Guadix, Baza, Almeria, Vera, etc., he should have little difficulty in dethroning the fallen Abu Abdallah. Velez el Rubio, Vera, Mujacar, etc., opened their gates on the first summons. But the Christians failed before Huescar, Baza, and Tabernas; and had the worst in more than one skirmish.

Ferdinand again hastened to the field at the head of fifty thousand foot and twelve thousand horse, resolved with this formidable force to deprive the Moors of all hopes of a successful resistance. Under the pretence that his arms were to be directed against only the enemy of his ally, he hoped to

---

[1] As a counterpart to the above scene, twelve Christian renegades, found in the city, were transfixed with canes, *acañavereados*, a barbarous punishment derived from the Moors, which was inflicted by horsemen at full gallop, who discharged pointed reeds at the criminal until he expired under repeated wounds. A number of relapsed Jews were at the same time condemned to the flames. "These," says Father Abarca,*i* "were the *fêtes* and illuminations most grateful to the Catholic piety of our sovereigns!"

divide still further the Moorish power. He succeeded in his purpose: the people of Granada looked on, not indeed with indifference, but certainly without much anxiety for themselves, while their ally marched against the places which still held for El Zagal. Abu Abdallah, however, was aware of the result: he even purchased a temporary security, by consenting not only to abandon his uncle, but to receive into Granada itself a Christian garrison; in other words, to deliver that capital, after the destruction of El Zagal, into the hands of Ferdinand. In return, he was to receive ample domain, under the title of vassalage, from his feudal superior. Though the conditions of the alliance were secret, El Zagal, convinced that he should now have to encounter the whole power of the Castilians, prepared for a vigorous defence. His kinsman, the cid Yahya, with ten thousand men, he sent to Baza, which he rightly judged would be one of the first places to be invested by Ferdinand.

Having reduced Xucar, the Christian monarch, as had been foreseen, laid siege to Baza. This place made a brave resistance during several months: but in the end, seeing that the provisions were exhausted, and many of the soldiers cut off in the frequent sorties; that the Christians had entrenched their camp, and were even encouraged to persevere by the arrival of queen Isabella — Yahya wrote to El Zagal to say that the place must inevitably be surrendered unless speedily succoured. The latter, who was busily occupied in the defence of Guadix, could not spare a single soldier for the relief of Baza; it was therefore constrained to capitulate; but conditions highly advantageous to the people were obtained from the two sovereigns. Yahya, who had several interviews with these sovereigns in their own camp, received signal proofs of their favour. He vowed not only never again to take up arms against his liege superior, but to prevail on his kinsman El Zagal to discontinue a fruitless resistance, and submit as he had done.

Like a true Mussulman, El Zagal coincided in his kinsman's doctrine of predestination; he acknowledged that Allah in his eternal decrees had resolved the destruction of Granada; and he consented to throw himself on the generosity of Ferdinand. He too hastened to the Christian camp; and if personal kindness, or even regal liberality, could have atoned for the loss of a throne, he might have been satisfied. Like Yahya, he received ample domains, to be forever possessed by his descendants — the jurisdiction of Andaraz; the valley of Alhaman, containing two thousand vassals (between Malaga and Marbella); and half the produce of some salt mines: the annual return was four millions of maravedis — on his consenting to receive Christian garrisons into Almeria and Guadix, the inhabitants of which were guaranteed in all their privileges as subjects. The following year Abdallah el Zagal, tired, perhaps, of living privately where he had ruled as a king, sold most of these possessions, and retired to Africa. Purchena, Tabernas, Almuñecar, Salobrena, and some other towns of the Alpujarras were eager to follow the example of Baza; so that the once proud kingdom of the Moors was almost literally confined to the walls of the capital.

Nothing now remained but to complete the overthrow of the Moorish power by the conquest of Granada. In virtue of the preceding convention, Ferdinand summoned Abu Abdallah to receive a Castilian garrison. The poor shadow of a king in vain appealed to the magnanimity of his ally, whom he besought to remain satisfied with the rich spoils already acquired. The bare mention of such a proposal would have cost him his head in the then excited state of feeling. The disastrous position of Mohammedan affairs, which they imputed, not without some justice, to his ambition and his subsequent inactivity, roused their wrath so much, that they rose against him, and would doubtless have been satisfied with nothing less than his blood, had he not fled precipitately into the Alhambra. Erelong, however, the violence of the commotion ceased, as everyone perceived the necessity of combining to save the capital. Its fate was for a time suspended by the arrival of numerous volunteers from the neighbouring towns, especially from the villages of the Alpujarras, which had not yet acknowledged the Christian sway; and from several other places, which now openly revolted. Abu Abdallah endeavoured to regain the good will of his people by vigorously preparing for their defence, and even by making incursions on the new possessions of the Christians. But neither the revolt nor his own efforts were of much avail. The inhabitants of Adra were signally punished for their want of faith; the king was compelled to seek shelter within his walls, from the summit of which he soon perceived the advancing cross of his enemies.

A SPANISH MERCHANT, FIF-
TEENTH CENTURY

In the spring of 1491 Ferdinand invested this great city with fifty thousand foot and ten thousand horse. That the siege would be long and bloody was to be expected from the strength of the fortifications and the fanaticism of the people. Some time, indeed, elapsed before the place could be effectually invested; convoys of provisions were frequently received, in spite of Ferdinand's vigilance; and in the sorties which from time to time took place, the advantage was not always on the side of the assailants. These partial actions so thinned the Christian host, that the king at length forbade them; and to protect his camp against the daring irruptions of the Moors, he surrounded it with thick walls and deep ditches. The enemy now saw that he was resolute in the reduction of the place, however tardy that reduction might prove. His own soldiers, whether in the camp or in the newly erected city of Santa Fé,[1] which he built and fortified both as a security against the possible despair of the Moors, and for the greater comfort of his army and court, were abundantly supplied with every necessary. The privations to which they were now subject, caused the besieged inhabitants first to murmur, and next to threaten their imbecile ruler with destruction. In this emergency, Abu Abdallah hastily summoned a council, to hear the sentiments of his chief subjects on the deplorable posture of affairs. All agreed that the camp, the city, and policy of Ferdinand were but too indicative of his unalterable determination, and of the fate which ultimately, nay soon, awaited them; that the people were worn out by abstinence and fatigue; and that, as the necessity was imperative, an attempt should be made to procure favourable terms of capitulation from the Castilian.

It was on the fourth day of the moon Rabia I [January 2nd, 1492], at the dawn of day, that Abu Abdallah sent his family and treasures into the Alpujarras, while he himself, accompanied by fifty horsemen, rode out to meet Ferdinand, whom he saluted as his liege lord. The keys of the city

---

[1] About two leagues west of Granada.

were delivered to the latter by Abul-Kassim : the Christians entered, and their standards were speedily hoisted on the towers of the Alhambra, and all the fortresses in the place. The fourth day following, Ferdinand and his royal consort made a solemn entry into the city, which they made the seat of an archbishopric, and in which they abode several months. As for the feeble Abu Abdallah, he had not courage to re-enter it. As he disconsolately took the road to the Alpujarras, and from time to time cast back his weeping eyes on the magnificent towers behind him, his mother, the sultana Zoraya, is said to have observed, " Thy womanly tears for the loss of thy kingdom become óne who had not courage to defend it like a man!"*j* "Alas!" exclaimed the unhappy exile, " when were woes ever equal to mine ! " The scene of this event is still pointed out to the traveller by the people of the district ; and the rocky height from which the Moorish chief took his sad farewell of the princely abodes of his youth is commemorated by the poetical title of *El ultimo Sospiro del Moro* — "the last sigh of the Moor."

The sequel of Abdallah's history is soon told. Like his uncle, El Zagal, he pined away in his barren domain of the Alpujarras, under the shadow, as it were, of his ancient palaces. In the following year he passed over to Fez with his family, having commuted his petty sovereignty for a considerable sum of money paid him by Ferdinand and Isabella, and soon after fell in battle in the service of an African prince, his kinsman. " Wretched man," exclaims a caustic chronicler of his nation, " who could lose his life in another's cause, though he did not dare to die in his own ! "

END OF MOSLEM SWAY IN SPAIN

The fall of Granada excited a general sensation throughout Christendom, where it was received as counterbalancing, in a manner, the loss of Constantinople nearly half a century before. The war of Granada is often compared by the Castilian chroniclers to that of Troy in its duration, and certainly fully equalled the latter in variety of picturesque and romantic incidents, and in circumstances of poetical interest. With the surrender of its capital terminated the Arabian empire in the peninsula, after an existence of seven hundred and forty-one years from the date of the original conquest. The consequences of this closing war were of the highest moment to Spain. The most obvious was the recovery of an extensive territory, hitherto held by a people whose difference of religion, language, and general habits made them not only incapable of assimilating with their Christian neighbours, but almost their natural enemies; while their local position was a matter of just concern, as interposed between the great divisions of the Spanish monarchy, and opening an obvious avenue to invasion from Africa.

By the new conquest, moreover, the Spaniards gained a large extent of country, possessing the highest capacities for production, in its natural fruitfulness of soil, the temperature of climate, and the state of cultivation to which it had been brought by its ancient occupants; while its shores were lined with commodious havens that afforded every facility for commerce. The scattered fragments of the ancient Visigothic empire were now again, with the exception of the little state of Navarre, combined into one great monarchy, as originally destined by nature ; and Christian Spain gradually rose, by means of her new acquisitions, from a subordinate situation to the level of a first-rate European power.

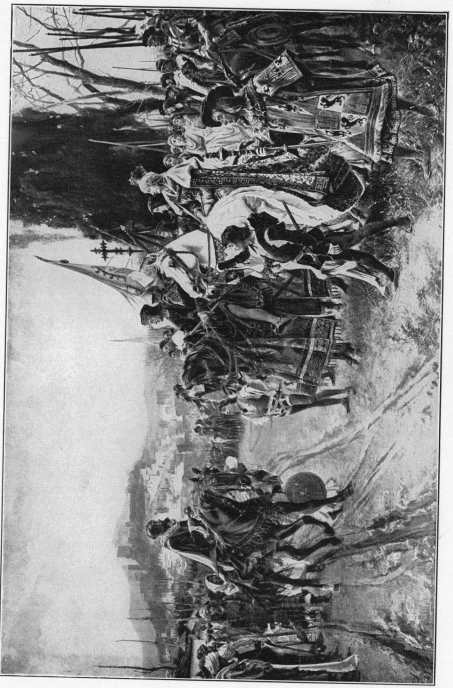

THE SURRENDER OF GRANADA

[1492 A.D.]

The moral influence of the Moorish war, its influence on the Spanish character, was highly important. The inhabitants of the great divisions of the country, as in most countries during the feudal ages, had been brought too frequently into collision with each other to allow the existence of a pervading national feeling. The war of Granada subjected all the various sections of the country to one common action, under the influence of common motives of the most exciting interest; while it brought them in conflict with a race the extreme repugnance of whose institutions and character to their own served greatly to nourish the nationality of sentiment. In this way the spark of patriotism was kindled throughout the whole nation, and the most distant provinces of the peninsula were knit together by a bond of union which has remained indissoluble.

The consequences of these wars in a military aspect are also worthy of notice. Up to this period, war had been carried on by irregular levies, extremely limited in numerical amount and in period of service, under little subordination, except to their own immediate chiefs, and wholly unprovided with the apparatus required for extended operations. The Spaniards were even lower than most of the European nations in military science, as is apparent from the infinite pains of Isabella to avail herself of all foreign resources for their improvement. In the war of Granada, masses of men were brought together far greater than had hitherto been known in modern warfare. They were kept in the field not only through long campaigns, but far into the winter; a thing altogether unprecedented. They were made to act in concert, and the numerous petty chiefs brought into complete subjection to one common head, whose personal character enforced the authority of station. Lastly, they were supplied with all the requisite munitions through the providence of Isabella, who introduced into the service the most skilful engineers from other countries, and kept in pay bodies of mercenaries — as the Swiss, for example, reputed the best disciplined troops of that day. In this admirable school the Spanish soldier was gradually trained to patient endurance, fortitude, and thorough subordination; and those celebrated captains were formed, with that invincible infantry, which in the beginning of the sixteenth century spread the military fame of their country over all Christendom.

But, with all our sympathy for the conquerors, it is impossible without a deep feeling of regret to contemplate the decay and final extinction of a race who had made such high advances in civilisation as the Spanish Arabs; to see them driven from the stately palaces reared by their own hands, wandering as exiles over the lands which still blossomed with the fruits of their industry, and wasting away under persecution, until their very name as a nation was blotted out from the map of history.

SPANISH EXPLORERS, AND CHRISTOPHER COLUMBUS

While Ferdinand and Isabella were at Santa Fé, the capitulation was signed that opened the way to an extent of empire compared with which their recent conquests, and indeed all their present dominions, were insignificant. The extraordinary intellectual activity of the Europeans in the fifteenth century, after the torpor of ages, carried them forward to high advancement in almost every department of science, but especially nautical, whose surprising results have acquired for the age the glory of being designated as peculiarly that of maritime discovery.

The Portuguese were the first to enter on the brilliant path of nautical discovery, which they pursued under the infante Dom Henry with such activity that before the middle of the fifteenth century they had penetrated as far as Cape Verd, doubling many a fearful headland which had shut in the timid navigator of former days; until at length, in 1486, they descried the lofty promontory which terminates Africa on the south, and which received the cheering appellation of the Cape of Good Hope.

The Spaniards, in the meanwhile, did not languish in the career of maritime enterprise. Certain adventurers from the northern provinces of Biscay and Guipuzcoa, in 1393, had made themselves masters of one of the smallest of the group of islands since known as the Canaries. Other private adventurers from Seville extended their conquests over these islands in the beginning of the following century. These were completed in behalf of the crown under Ferdinand and Isabella, who equipped several fleets for their reduction, which at length terminated in 1495 with that of Teneriffe. From the commencement of their reign, Ferdinand and Isabella had shown an earnest solicitude for the encouragement of commerce and nautical science. Under them, and indeed under their predecessors as far back as Henry III, a considerable traffic had been carried on with the western coast of Africa, from which gold-dust and slaves were imported into the city of Seville. The annalist of that city notices the repeated interference of Isabella in behalf of these unfortunate beings, by ordinances tending to secure them a more equal protection of the laws, or opening such social indulgences as might mitigate the hardships of their condition.

A misunderstanding gradually arose between the subjects of Castile and Portugal, in relation to their respective rights of discovery and commerce on the African coast, which promised a fruitful source of collision between the two crowns, but which was happily adjusted by an article in the treaty of 1479, that terminated the war of the Succession. By this it was settled that the right of traffic and of discovery on the western coast of Africa should be exclusively reserved to the Portuguese, who in their turn should resign all claims on the Canaries to the crown of Castile. The Spaniards, thus excluded from further progress to the south, seemed to have no other opening left for naval adventure than the hitherto untravelled regions of the great western ocean. Fortunately, at this juncture an individual appeared among them, in the person of Christopher Columbus, endowed with capacity for stimulating them to this heroic enterprise and conducting it to a glorious issue.*g*

The great story of the discovery of America and the new crusade it began against ignorance and also, unfortunately, against innocent savages, has a vital bearing, it is true, upon the fortunes, the glory, and the wars of Spain. But since almost every country in Europe was soon involved in the same cry of " Westward, ho ! " and since the general outlines are familiar to everybody, it will be permissible to defer the account until the volume on America, where the details can be given with fullness, consecution, and a proper sense of proportionate value.

None the less, the reader must not forget that the period of discovery and the encouragement given it by Isabella and her consort form one of the most important as one of the most beautiful major features of their reign.

Leaving it to the reader's imagination to give this better element its due brilliance and its right significance as a partial atonement to history, we must turn to the evil side of the reign, an evil so tremendous and loathsome that it seems incredible when associated with the noble deeds of the sovereigns. This is the persecution of the non-orthodox in the name of religion and without a shadow of that gentleness and mercy which one associates with that name, little as history may have to substantiate that association.

The Inquisition we shall leave to a separate chapter in the appendix in which its origin in other countries will be taken up and its history traced in entirety until its end in the last century. A few words of allusion will not, however, be amiss in this place.[a]

THE EXPULSION OF THE JEWS

While the Spanish sovereigns were detained before Granada, they published their memorable and most disastrous edict against the Jews; inscribing it, as it were, with the same pen which drew up the glorious capitulation of Granada and the treaty with Columbus. The envy raised by their prosperity, combined with the high religious excitement kindled in the long war with the infidel, directed the terrible arm of the Inquisition against this unfortunate people; but the result showed the failure of the experiment, since comparatively few conversions, and those frequently of a suspicious character, were effected, while the great mass still maintained a pertinacious attachment to ancient errors. The inquisitors asserted that the only mode left for the extirpation of the Jewish heresy was to eradicate the seed; and they boldly demanded the immediate and total banishment of every unbaptised Israelite from the land.

The Jews tendered a donative of 30,000 ducats towards the expense of the Moorish war. The negotiations, however, were interrupted by the inquisitor-general who held up a crucifix, exclaiming: "Judas Iscariot sold his Master for thirty pieces of silver. Your highnesses would sell him anew for thirty thousand. Here he is; take him and barter him away!" So saying, the frantic priest threw the crucifix on the table, and left the apartment. The sovereigns, instead of chastising this presumption, or despising it as a mere freak of insanity, were overawed by it.

The edict for the expulsion of the Jews was signed by the Spanish sovereigns at Granada, March 30th, 1492. It decreed that all the unbaptised Jews, of whatever age, sex, or condition, should depart from the realm by the end of July next ensuing; prohibiting them from revisiting it, on any pretext whatever, under penalty of death and confiscation of property. It was, moreover, interdicted to every subject to harbour, succour, or minister to the necessities of any Jew, after the expiration of the term limited for his departure. The persons and property of the Jews, in the meantime, were taken under the royal protection. They were allowed to dispose of their effects of every kind on their own account, and to carry the proceeds along with them, in bills of exchange, or merchandise not prohibited, but neither in gold nor silver.

The doom of exile fell like a thunderbolt on the heads of the Israelites. A large proportion of them had hitherto succeeded in shielding themselves from the searching eye of the Inquisition, by an affectation of reverence for the forms of Catholic worship, and a discreet forbearance of whatever might offend the prejudices of their Christian brethren. They had even hoped that their steady loyalty and a quiet and orderly discharge of their social duties would in time secure them higher immunities. Many had risen to a degree of opulence by means of the thrift and dexterity peculiar to the race, which gave them a still deeper interest in the land of their residence. Their families were reared in all the elegant refinements of life ; and their wealth and education often disposed them to turn their attention to liberal pursuits, which ennobled the character, indeed, but rendered them personally more sensible to physical annoyance and less fitted to encounter the perils and privations of their dreary pilgrimage. They were to go forth as exiles from the land of their birth — the land where all whom they ever loved had lived or died; the land not so much of their adoption as of their inheritance; which had been the home of their ancestors for centuries, and with whose prosperity and glory they were of course as intimately associated as was any ancient Spaniard. They were to be cast out helpless and defenceless, with a brand of infamy set on them, among nations who had always held them in derision and hatred.

Those provisions of the edict which affected a show of kindness to the Jews were contrived so artfully as to be nearly nugatory. As they were excluded from the use of gold and silver, the only medium for representing their property was bills of exchange. But commerce was too limited and imperfect to allow of these being promptly obtained to any very considerable, much less to the enormous amount required in the present instance. It was impossible, moreover, to negotiate a sale of their effects under existing circumstances, since the market was soon glutted with commodities ; and few would be found willing to give anything like an equivalent for what, if not disposed of within the prescribed term, the proprietors must relinquish at any rate. So deplorable, indeed, was the sacrifice of property that a chronicler of the day mentions that he had seen a house exchanged for an ass, and a vineyard for a suit of clothes ! Yet there were found but very few, when the day of departure arrived, who were not prepared to abandon their country rather than their religion. This extraordinary act of self-devotion by a whole people for conscience' sake may be thought to merit other epithets than those of " perfidy, incredulity, and stiffnecked obstinacy," with which the worthy curate of

SPANISH CAVALIER OF THE FIFTEENTH CENTURY

Los Palacios,[h] in the charitable feeling of that day, has seen fit to stigmatise it.

When the period of departure arrived, all the principal routes through the country might be seen swarming with emigrants, old and young, the sick and the helpless, men, women, and children, mingled promiscuously together, some mounted on horses or mules, but far the greater part undertaking their painful pilgrimage on foot. The sight of so much misery touched even the Spaniards with pity, though none might succour them ; for the grand inquisitor, Torquemada, enforced the ordinance to that effect by denouncing heavy ecclesiastical censures on all who should presume to violate it. Much the largest division, amounting according to some estimates to eighty thousand souls, passed into Portugal ; whose monarch, João [John] II, dispensed with his scruples of conscience so far as to give them a free passage through his dominions on their way to Africa, in consideration of a tax of a *cruzado* a head. He is even said to have silenced his scruples so far as to allow certain ingenious artisans to establish themselves permanently in the kingdom.

A considerable number found their way to the ports of Santa Maria and Cadiz, where, after lingering some time in the vain hope of seeing the waters open for their egress, according to the promises of the rabbis, they embarked on board a Spanish fleet for the Barbary coast. Having crossed over to Ercilla, a Christian settlement in Africa, whence they proceeded by land towards Fez, where a considerable body of their countrymen resided, they were assaulted on their route by the roving tribes of the desert, in quest of plunder. Notwithstanding the interdict, the Jews had contrived to secrete small sums of money, sewed up in their garments or the linings of their saddles. These did not escape the avaricious eyes of their spoilers, who are even said to have ripped open the bodies of their victims in search of gold which they were supposed to have swallowed. The lawless barbarians, mingling lust with avarice, abandoned themselves to still more frightful excesses, violating the wives and daughters of the unresisting Jews, or massacring in cold blood such as offered resistance.

But, without pursuing these loathsome details further, it need only be added that the miserable exiles endured such extremity of famine that they were glad to force a nourishment from the grass which grew scantily among the sands of the desert; until at length great numbers of them, wasted by disease and broken in spirit, retraced their steps to Ercilla, and consented to be baptised, in the hope of being permitted to revisit their native land. The number, indeed, was so considerable that the priest who officiated was obliged to make use of the mop, or hyssop, with which the Roman Catholic missionaries were wont to scatter the holy drops whose mystic virtue could cleanse the soul in a moment from the foulest stains of infidelity. "Thus," says the Castilian historian, Ferreras,[k] "the calamities of these poor blind creatures proved in the end an excellent remedy, that God made use of to unseal their eyes, which they now opened to the vain promises of the rabbis; so that, renouncing their ancient heresies, they became faithful followers of the cross!"

Many of the emigrants took the direction of Italy. Those who landed at Naples brought with them an infectious disorder, contracted by long confinement in small, crowded, and ill-provided vessels. The disorder was so malignant, and spread with such frightful celerity, as to sweep off more than twenty thousand inhabitants of the city in the course of the year, whence it extended its devastation over the whole Italian peninsula. Many of the exiles passed into Turkey, and to different parts of the Levant, where their descendants continued to speak the Castilian language far into the following century. Others found their way to France, and even England. Part of their religious services is recited to this day in Spanish, in one or more of the London synagogues.

The whole number of Jews expelled from Spain by Ferdinand and Isabella is variously computed at from 160,000 to 800,000 souls; a discrepancy sufficiently indicating the paucity of authentic data. Most modern writers, with the usual predilection for startling results, have assumed the latter estimate; and Llorente[l] has made it the basis of some important calculations in his *History of the Inquisition*. A view of all the circumstances will lead us without much hesitation to adopt the most moderate computation. This, moreover, is placed beyond reasonable doubt by the direct testimony of Bernaldez.[h] He reports that a Jewish rabbi, one of the exiles, subsequently returned to Spain, where he was baptised by him. This person estimated the whole number of his unbaptised countrymen, at the publication of the edict, at thirty-six thousand families. Another Jewish authority, quoted by the curate, reckoned them at thirty-five thousand. This, assuming an average of four and a half to a family, gives the sum total of about 160,000 individuals.[1]

The detriment incurred by the state, however, is not founded so much on any numerical estimate as on the subtraction of the mechanical skill, intelligence, and general resources of an orderly, industrious population. In this view, the mischief was incalculably greater than that inferred by the mere number of the exiled; and although even this might have been gradually repaired in a country allowed the free and healthful development of its energies, yet in Spain this was so effectually counteracted by the Inquisition, and other causes in the following century, that the loss may be deemed irretrievable.

The expulsion of so numerous a class of subjects by an independent act of the sovereign might well be regarded as an enormous stretch of prerogative, altogether incompatible with anything like a free government. But, to judge the matter rightly, we must take into view the actual position of the Jews at that time. Far from forming an integral part of the commonwealth, they were regarded as alien to it, as a mere excrescence, which, so far from contributing to the healthful action of the body politic, was nourished by its vicious humours, and might be lopped off at any time when the health of the system demanded it. Far from being protected by the laws, the only aim of the laws in reference to them was to define more precisely their civil incapacities, and to draw the line of division more broadly between them and the Christians. Even this humiliation by no means satisfied the national prejudices, as is evinced by the great number of tumults and massacres of which they were the victims. In these circumstances, it seemed to be no great assumption of authority to pronounce sentence of exile against those whom public opinion had so long proscribed as enemies to the state.

It has been common with modern historians to detect a principal motive in the avarice of the government. It is, however, incredible that persons possessing the political sagacity of Ferdinand and Isabella could indulge a temporary cupidity at the sacrifice of the most important and permanent interests, converting by a measure so manifestly unsound, their wealthiest districts into a wilderness and dispeopling them of a class of citizens who contributed beyond all others not only to the general resources but to the direct revenues of the crown.

We need look no further for the principle of action, in this case, than the spirit of religious bigotry which led to a similar expulsion of the Jews from England, France, and other parts of Europe, as well as from Portugal, under circumstances of peculiar atrocity, a few years later.[2] Indeed, the spirit of persecution did not expire with the fifteenth century, but extends even into our own more luminous days. How far the banishment of the Jews was conformable to the opinions of the most enlightened contemporaries, may be

[1 Mariana *m* placed the number at nearly 800,000; Graetz *n* at 300,000; Burke *f* at 200,000; Prescott *g* as above at 160,000. The smallest of the estimates is sufficiently great to overwhelm the powers of imagination.]

[2] The Portuguese government caused all children of fourteen years of age, or under, to be taken from their parents and retained in the country, as fit subjects for a Christian education. The distress occasioned by this cruel provision may be well imagined. Many of the unhappy parents murdered their children to defeat the ordinance; and many laid violent hands on themselves.

gathered from the encomiums lavished on its authors from more than one quarter. Spanish writers, without exception, celebrate it as a sublime sacrifice of all temporal interests to religious principle.*g*

PERSECUTION AND REVOLT OF THE MOORS (1499–1502 A.D.)

The establishment of the Inquisition led to the banishment of the Jews; the latter, in its turn, to the persecution of the Mohammedans. These soon found that their religious toleration, so solemnly guaranteed by the articles of capitulation, would be little respected by a prince who did not always hesitate to break his royal word — nor even his oath — when his interests or his bigotry was concerned. It is certain that, from the very year in which Granada submitted, the resolution was taken to convert or expel the Moors; but their number, the assistance they might receive from Africa, and the unsettled state of the new conquests, delayed its execution.

In 1499, however, Ferdinand, being at Granada, seriously entered on what he doubtless considered a path of stern but necessary duty. Having assembled some of his counsellors and prelates to deliberate on the proper means of attaining an object so momentous, it was agreed that both end and means should be left to two eminent prelates — to Francisco Ximenes [or Jimenes] de Cisneros, archbishop of Toledo, and to Ferdinand de Talavera, metropolitan of Granada. In selecting two such opposite instruments, it was doubtless intended that the gentleness of Don Ferdinand should be fortified by the decision of his colleague: through his influence it doubtless was that the first steps in the great work were of a mild and rational nature. The alfaquis were assiduously courted; were persuaded to dispute on the merits of their respective faiths; and were severally dismissed with presents.

Whether through conviction or fear, through persuasion or interest, these men forsook their old religion, and consented not only to be baptised, but to become the instruments of converting their countrymen. Their example had great effect: thousands applied for admission into the church; and thousands more would have joined them at the same time, but for the fiery zeal of Cardinal Ximenes,[1] which occasioned a serious disturbance. Seeing that some of their body, who protested against the prelate's violence, were by his order conducted to prison, they arose, murdered an obnoxious *alguazil*, and hastened to Ximenes' hotel, which they assailed. He fought with great spirit. The commotion continued for several days: the whole Albaycin was in arms; and the insurrection would have spread further, but for the metropolitan of Granada. Though a messenger of peace had been stoned to death the preceding day by the Moors of that quarter, he resolved to go among them, and finally persuaded them to lay down their arms.

But the mischief was not yet ended. Those especially who abode in the mountains of the Alpujarras were filled with fury at the forcible attempts made to seduce their brethren from the faith of the prophet; and they flew to arms. The king himself marched to reduce them; pursued them into the heart of their hills; forced or persuaded them to submit, and to surrender both their fortified places and their arms. His success emboldened him to more decisive measures: missionaries were despatched, wherever there was a

---

[1] He consumed by fire all the Arabic controversial books he could find, which amounted to five thousand volumes, according to the lowest estimate; Conde*o* puts it at eighty thousand, which is commonly accepted.

Mohammedan village, to preach the necessity of immediate conversion ; and the efficacy of their labours was not a little owing to the armed bodies of soldiers who accompanied them. Terrified by the recent fate of the Jews, whole towns submitted to baptism — the more willingly, perhaps, as no previous instruction was forced upon them ; there was no time for catechism or preaching : hundreds were sprinkled with holy water at the same time ; the same prayers were repeated over them, and then they stood cleansed in the laver of regeneration ! That such conversions could not be very durable need not surprise us.

The following year, the independent mountaineers again revolted, and massacred all the Christians on whom they could lay hands. They were

A MAN OF GRANADA

again reduced : ten thousand submitted to the necessary rite ; while a greater number fled to their African brethren. A third time, in the space of a very few months, were the embers of discontent fanned into a flame — partly by the injudicious zeal of the Christian priests, partly by the strong breath of indignation. This insurrection was the most difficult to quell : one or two partial successes were obtained over the royal troops ; but, on the appearance of Ferdinand in person, with a formidable power, the revolted fortresses submitted. Again did thousands obtain his permission to settle on the opposite coast, and bade a final adieu to the peninsula. By their departure, those who remained were still less able to make head against the victor, who no longer hesitated to issue his irrevocable decree of expulsion against every obstinate follower of the Arabian prophet.*j*

The sovereigns came to the extraordinary resolution of offering the alternative of baptism or exile. They issued a *pragmática* from Seville, February 12th, 1502, that all the unbaptised Moors in the kingdoms of Castile and Leon above fourteen years of age if males, and twelve if females, must leave the country by the end of April following ; that they might sell their property in the meantime, and take the proceeds in anything save gold and silver and merchandise regularly prohibited ; and, finally, that they might emigrate to any foreign country, except the dominions of the Grand Turk, and such parts of Africa as Spain was then at war with. Obedience to these severe provisions was enforced by the penalties of death and confiscation of property.

This stern edict, so closely modelled on that against the Jews, must have been even more grievous in its application. For the Jews may be said to have been denizens almost equally of every country ; while the Moors, excluded from a retreat among their countrymen on the African shore, were sent into the lands of enemies or strangers. The former, moreover, were far better qualified by their natural shrewdness and commercial habits for disposing of their property advantageously, than the simple, inexperienced Moors, skilled in little else than husbandry or rude mechanic arts. We have nowhere met with any estimate of the number who migrated on this occasion.

Castile might now boast, for the first time in eight centuries, that every outward stain, at least, of infidelity, was purified from her bosom. But how had this been accomplished? By the most detestable expedients which sophistry could devise and oppression execute; and that, too, under an enlightened government, proposing to be guided solely by a conscientious regard for duty.

It is a singular paradox, that Christianity, whose doctrines inculcate unbounded charity, should have been made so often an engine of persecution; while Mohammedanism, whose principles are those of avowed intolerance, should have exhibited, at least till later times, a truly philosophical spirit of toleration.[1] Even the first victorious disciples of the prophet, glowing with all the fiery zeal of proselytism, were content with the exaction of tribute from the vanquished.*g*

We may now take up in condensed form certain foreign relations that had busied the Spanish monarchs simultaneously with their religious activities.*a*

SPAIN IN ITALY; THE GREAT CAPTAIN

Soon after his accession, Ferdinand was naturally anxious to procure the restitution of Roussillon and Cerdagne. But to his pressing embassies on this subject, Louis XI returned evasive answers. But when Ferdinand, indignant at the evasions of his successor, Charles VIII, began to arm for the recovery of this frontier, the latter, who meditated the conquest of Naples, and who wished to have no enemies to harass France during his absence, commanded Perpignan and the fortresses of the province to be evacuated by the French troops; they were immediately occupied by those of Aragon.

The severity of Ferdinand king of Naples had long been borne with dissatisfaction by the people. Their discontent appeared to the French king an excellent opportunity for vindicating the claims of his family on that country, and for gratifying an ambition which was seldom restrained by considerations of justice. He was the more confirmed in his purpose, when several Neapolitan nobles, through disgust with their ruler, sought his protection, and offered to aid him in gaining possession of so fair a kingdom. The death of the Neapolitan king, and the accession of his son Alfonso, in 1494, produced no change, either on the intentions of Charles, or the disaffection of the people; Alfonso was as unpopular as Ferdinand.

In alarm at the preparations of the Frenchmen, and the suspected hostility of the pope, the new king implored the aid of his Spanish brother and received the assurance he solicited. In the meantime Charles invaded Italy by way of Grenoble, and passed through Pavia and Florence direct on Rome. Having forced the pope into his interests, he continued his march towards Naples. Alfonso, terrified at the approaching danger, and convinced how much his subjects wished for his overthrow, abdicated in favour of his son Ferdinand, who, he hoped, would be able to rally them round the national standard; and retired to a monastery in Sicily. The hope was vain; the Neapolitans fled — perhaps as much through cowardice as disaffection — the moment they came in contact with the French; and the capital, with the fortified places, submitted to the invader.

But Ferdinand of Spain was not idle; by his ambassadors at Venice he

---

[1] Prescott adds: "The spirit of toleration exhibited by the Moors, indeed, was made a principal argument against them in the archbishop of Valencia's memorial to Philip III. The Mohammedans would seem the better Christians of the two."

formed a league with the pope, the republic, the duke of Milan, and the fugitive king of Naples for the expulsion of the French from Italy. Fortunately for the common cause, the rapacity and insolence of the invaders had turned the eyes of the Neapolitans towards their dethroned king, whom they invited to resume his dignity, and at whose approach they opened the gates not only of the capital, but of several important fortresses.

At this time, Don Gonsalvo de Cordova, the captain of Ferdinand, who had acquired distinction in the wars of Granada, commenced his brilliant career. The rapidity with which he reduced many of the fortified places, and triumphed over the French generals on the field, drew the attention of Europe towards this part of Italy. His exploits at the very first campaign procured him the appellation of the Great Captain. The Calabrias were soon entirely forced from the invaders, who were glad to take refuge in the states of the church, until the arrival of the expected succours from France. The restored king did not long survive his success; the fatigues of the campaign consigned him, in 1496, to the grave. He was succeeded by his uncle, Frederick, son of the first Aragonese king of Naples.

To the new monarch Gonsalvo continued the same eminent services; and not unfrequently the pope made use of his valour in humbling the temporal enemies of the church. The king of France in vain attempted, by way of diversion, to withdraw the attention of Ferdinand from the affairs of Italy, by the powerful armaments which he frequently moved on Roussillon; he found the Spanish king, as usual, prepared both to defend the frontiers, and to secure the crown on the head of Frederick.

But in that relative's behalf Ferdinand soon ceased to be interested. For his progressive coolness towards that prince, various reasons have been assigned; the chief one has been omitted — the king's all-grasping ambition, which sometimes took no counsel from justice. On hearing that Louis XII, the successor of Charles, was preparing to arm for the recovery of Naples, he besought that monarch to desist from the undertaking; and when he found that solicitations were useless, he was unprincipled enough to propose a division of the whole kingdom. Louis eagerly seized the proposal, and the royal robbers immediately entered into negotiations for adjusting their respective share of the spoils. At first the city and kingdom of Naples were adjudged to Louis; the two Calabrias and the Abruzzi to Ferdinand; the revenue arising from the pasturage of Apulia was to be divided between them. But a dispute arising, a new division was effected; the latter assigned the two Calabrias and Apulia to the Spanish king; Naples and the Abruzzo to the Frenchman. To preserve harmony in other quarters, Louis agreed at the same time to relinquish his claims over Roussillon and Cerdagne, and Ferdinand over Montpellier. Both sovereigns sent powerful armaments to execute this iniquitous compact. No sooner did it reach the ears of the unfortunate Frederick than he complained to the Spanish monarch of the monstrous injustice. Ferdinand replied — no doubt with truth — that he had done his utmost to prevent the French king from the enterprise; that when entreaties failed, he had even offered a considerable sum to the same effect; and that it was only when he found Louis bent on the undertaking, and leagued with the Italian powers to insure its success, that he had consented to the division; he added, that, as such a division was inevitable, it was better that France should have a part than the whole. In private life such reasoning would be characterised as it ought; but kings have too often pleaded their sovereign exception from obligations which they have been ready enough to enforce on the rest of mankind.

[1501–1510 A.D.]

While the French troops on one side, and the great captain on the other, were seizing his provinces, it was impossible for Frederick, with a people so disaffected as the Neapolitans, to make head against them. As Louis promised to allow him a pension suitable to his rank, he sought an asylum in France. Scarcely were the armies in possession of the country, when their leaders began to quarrel about the precise extent of their respective territories. A bloody war followed, the details of which may be found in the Italian history of the period. It exhibits little beyond a continued succession of victories for the great captain, who triumphed over the veteran general and armies of France ; it ended, in 1504, in the entire subjugation of the kingdom by the Spaniards.

The brilliant success of the Spanish general now roused the envy of a few brother officers, who represented him to the sovereign as meditating designs inconsistent with the preservation of the new conquest to the Castilian crown. In the frequent orders he received, he but too plainly saw the distrust of Ferdinand, whom, however, he continued to serve with the same ability and with unshaken fidelity.[1] In 1506, Ferdinand arrived at Naples, and his distrust was greatly diminished by his frequent intercourse with the general. But, as his own heart taught him that human virtue is often weak, he brought Gonsalvo with him to Spain, leaving the viceregal authority in the hands of Don Raymond de Cardona.

Into the interminable affairs of Italy, from this time to the death of Ferdinand, the ever varying alliances between the pope, the emperor, the Venetians, and the kings of France and Spain, and their results, as they had not any influence over Spain — scarcely, indeed, any connection with it — we forbear to enter. We need only observe that Spain retained uninterrupted possession of her conquest ; the investiture of which, in 1510, was conferred by the pope, as a fief of the church, on Ferdinand.

The happiness of the Catholic sovereigns was not commensurate with the splendour which surrounded them. To whom must their magnificent empire devolve ? In 1497, the infante Juan, their only son, whom they had just married to the archduchess Margaret of Austria, died, and his widow was soon afterwards brought to bed of a still-born child. Hence their daughters only remained through whom they could hope to transmit their sceptre to posterity ; but even in this expectation they were doomed to much disappointment.

Doña Isabella, the eldest of the princesses, who was married to the heir of the Portuguese monarchy, was left a widow as soon as the archduchess Margaret ; and though she was next given to her brother-in-law, Dom Emmanuel, now become king of Portugal, and the following year was delivered of a son, she died at the time ; nor did the young prince, the acknowledged heir of the whole peninsula, Navarre excepted, long survive her. Still, to be prepared against every possible contingency, they married another daughter, the princess Maria, to the Lusitanian widower ; and their youngest, Catherine, destined to be so famous from her connection with the English reformation, first to Arthur prince of Wales, and next to Henry, his brother, afterwards Henry VIII.

Their hopes of an heir, however, rested in their second daughter, the wife of Philip archduke of Austria, Juana, who, in 1500, was delivered of a prince, afterwards the celebrated Charles V.

[1 There are, however, not wanting documents to show that at times the great captain was goaded by Ferdinand's jealous mistreatment into a serious consideration of deserting to the enemy, or declaring himself king in Italy.]

Thus, the crown of Spain was to devolve on a foreign brow — the first example of the kind which had occurred from the foundation of the monarchy by Pelayo. Their disappointments, too, were embittered by the unhappiness of their children. The princess Isabella, who had always shown more affection for the cloister than for the throne, had been forced into the marriage, and died a premature and painful death. Juana, though extravagantly fond of her husband, was treated by him with the most marked neglect ; and the fate of Catherine is but too well known. The misfortunes of her children sank deeply into the heart of the queen, and brought on a melancholy which ended in her death.*j*

ILLNESS AND DEATH OF ISABELLA

In the beginning of 1503 she had declined so visibly that the cortes of Castile, much alarmed, petitioned her to provide for the government of the kingdom after her decease, in case of the absence or incapacity of Juana. She seems to have rallied in some measure after this; but it was only to relapse into a state of greater debility, as her spirits sank under the conviction, which now forced itself on her, of her daughter's settled insanity.

Early in the spring of the following year (1504) that unfortunate lady embarked for Flanders, where, soon after her arrival, the inconstancy of her husband and her own ungovernable sensibilities occasioned the most scandalous scenes. Philip became openly enamoured of one of the ladies of her suite; and his injured wife, in a paroxysm of jealousy, personally assaulted her fair rival in the palace, and caused the beautiful locks which had excited the admiration of her fickle husband to be shorn from her head. This outrage so affected Philip that he vented his indignation against Juana in the coarsest and most unmanly terms, and finally refused to have any further intercourse with her. The account of this disgraceful scene reached Castile in the month of June. It occasioned the deepest chagrin and mortification to the unhappy parents. Ferdinand soon after fell ill of a fever, and the queen was seized with the same disorder, accompanied by more alarming symptoms. Her illness was exasperated by anxiety[1] for her husband, and she refused to credit the favourable reports of the physicians while he was detained from her presence. His vigorous constitution, however, threw off the malady, while hers gradually failed under it. Her tender heart was more keenly sensible than his to the unhappy condition of their child, and to the gloomy prospects which awaited her beloved Castile.

Her faithful follower, Martyr,*p* was with the court at this time in Medina del Campo. In a letter to the count of Tendilla, dated October 7th, he states that the most serious apprehensions were entertained by the physicians for the queen's fate. " Her whole system," he says, " is pervaded by a consuming fever. She loathes food of every kind, and is tormented with incessant thirst, while the disorder has all the appearance of terminating in a dropsy."

On the 12th of October she executed that celebrated testament which reflects so clearly the peculiar qualities of her mind and character. She begins with prescribing the arrangements for her burial. She orders her remains to be transported to Granada, to the Franciscan monastery of Santa Isabella in the Alhambra, and there deposited in a low and humble sepulchre,

[1 In 1492 Ferdinand had been almost killed by an insane assassin. Isabella had nursed him with the utmost devotion.]

without other memorial than a plain inscription on it. "But," she continues, "should the king my lord prefer a sepulchre in some other place, then my will is that my body be there transported, and laid by his side ; that the union we have enjoyed in this world, and, through the mercy of God, may hope again for our souls in heaven, may be represented by our bodies in the earth." Then, desirous of correcting by her example, in this last act of her life, the wasteful pomp of funeral obsequies to which the Castilians were addicted, she commands that her own should be performed in the plainest and most unostentatious manner, and that the sum saved by this economy should be distributed in alms among the poor.

She next provides for several charities, assigning, among others, marriage portions for poor maidens, and a considerable sum for the redemption of Christian captives in Barbary. She enjoins the punctual discharge of all her personal debts within a year ; she retrenches superfluous offices in the royal household, and revokes all such grants, whether in the forms of lands or annuities, as she conceives to have been made without sufficient warrant. She inculcates on her successors the importance of maintaining the integrity of the royal domains, and, above all, of never divesting themselves of their title to the important fortress of Gibraltar.

After this she comes to the succession of the crown, which she settles on the infanta Juana as "queen proprietor," and the archduke Philip as her husband. She gives them much good counsel respecting their future administration; enjoining them, as they would secure the love and obedience of their subjects, to conform in all respects to the laws and usages of the realm. She recommends to them the same conjugal harmony which

ISABELLA

(From an old print)

had ever subsisted between her and her husband ; she beseeches them to show the latter all the deference and filial affection " due to him beyond every other parent, for his eminent virtues "; and finally inculcates on them the most tender regard for the liberties and welfare of their subjects.

She next comes to the great question proposed by the cortes of 1503, respecting the government of the realm in the absence or incapacity of Juana. She declares that, after mature deliberation, and with the advice of many of the prelates and nobles of the kingdom, she appoints King Ferdinand her husband to be the sole regent of Castile, in that exigency, until the majority of her grandson Charles; being led to this, she adds, " by the consideration of the magnanimity and illustrious qualities of the king my lord, as well as his large experience, and the great profit which will redound to the state from his wise and beneficent rule."

She then makes a specific provision for her husband's personal maintenance, which, "although less than she could wish, and far less than he deserves, considering the eminent services he has rendered the state," she settles at one-half of all the net proceeds and profits accruing from the newly discovered countries in the West ; together with ten millions of maravedis annually, assigned on the *alcabalas* of the grand-masterships of the military orders.   And lastly, concluding in the same beautiful strain of conjugal tenderness in which she began, she says, " I beseech the king my lord that he will accept all my jewels, or such· as he shall select, so that, seeing them, he may be reminded of the singular love I always bore him while living, and that I am now waiting for him in a better world ; by which remembrance he may be encouraged to live the more justly and holily in this."

After performing this duty she daily grew weaker, the powers of her mind seeming to brighten as those of her body declined.   The concerns of her government still occupied her thoughts ; and several public measures, which she had postponed through urgency of other business or growing infirmities, pressed so heavily on her heart that she made them the subject of a codicil to her former will.   It was executed November 23rd, 1504, only three days before her death.   Three of the provisions contained in it are too remarkable to pass unnoticed.   The first concerns the codification of the laws.   For this purpose the queen appoints a commission to make a new digest of the statutes and *pragmáticas*, the contradictory tenor of which still occasioned much embarrassment in Castilian jurisprudence.   This was a subject she always had much at heart; but no nearer approach had been made to it than the valuable though insufficient work of Montalvo[1] in the early part of her reign ; and, notwithstanding her precautions, none more effectual was destined to take place till the reign of Philip II.

The second item had reference to the natives of the New World.   Gross abuses had arisen there since the partial revival of the *repartimientos*, although, Las Casas? says, " intelligence of this was carefully kept from the ears of the queen."   Some vague apprehension of the truth, however, appears to have forced itself on her; and she enjoins her successors, in the most earnest manner, to quicken the good work of converting and civilising the poor Indians, to treat them with the greatest gentleness, and redress any wrongs they may have suffered in their persons or property.   Lastly, she expresses her doubts as to the legality of the revenue drawn from the *alcabalas*,[2] constituting the principal income of the crown.   She directs that the legislature be summoned to devise proper measures for supplying the wants of the crown — " measures depending for their validity on the good pleasure of the subjects of the realm."

Such were the dying words of this admirable woman, displaying the same respect for the rights and liberties of the nation which she had shown through life, and striving to secure the blessings of her benign administration to the most distant and barbarous regions under her sway.   These two documents were a precious legacy bequeathed to her people, to guide them when the light of her personal example should be withdrawn forever.

On receiving the extreme unction, she refused to have her feet exposed, as was usual on that occasion; a circumstance which, occurring at a time when there can be no suspicion of affectation, is often noticed by Spanish writers as a proof of that sensitive delicacy and decorum which distinguished her through life.   At length, having received the sacraments, and performed all the offices of a sincere and devout Christian, she gently expired, a little

[1] Dr. Alfonso Diaz de Montalvo.   " He first gave to light the principal Spanish codes, and introduced a spirit of criticism into the national jurisprudence."—PRESCOTT.*g*]

[2] The *alcavala* or *alcabala* was a tax of one-tenth on all sales.   Thus bread was thrice taxed, as wheat, then as flour, and finally as bread.]

before noon, on Wednesday, November 26th, 1504, in the fifty-fourth year of her age, and thirtieth of her reign.

No time was lost in making preparations for transporting the queen's body unembalmed to Granada, in strict conformity to her orders. It was escorted by a numerous *cortège* of cavaliers and ecclesiastics, among whom was the faithful Martyr. The procession began its mournful march the day following her death, taking the route through Arevalo, Toledo, and Jaen. Scarcely had it left Medina del Campo when a tremendous tempest set in, which continued with little interruption during the whole journey. The roads were rendered nearly impassable; the bridges were swept away, the small streams swollen to the size of the Tagus, and the level country was buried under a deluge of water. Neither sun nor stars were seen during their whole progress. The horses and mules were borne down by the torrents, and the riders in several instances perished with them. At length, on the 18th of December, the melancholy and way-worn cavalcade reached the place of its destination; and, amidst the wild strife of the elements, the peaceful remains of Isabella were laid, with simple solemnities, in the Franciscan monastery of the Alhambra. Here, under the shadow of those venerable Moslem towers, and in the heart of the capital which her noble constancy had recovered for her country, they continued to repose till after the death of Ferdinand, when they were removed to be laid by his side in the stately mausoleum of the cathedral church of Granada.

PRESCOTT'S ESTIMATE OF ISABELLA

Her person was of the middle height, and well-proportioned. She had a clear, fresh complexion, with light-blue eyes and auburn hair — a style of beauty exceedingly rare in Spain. Her features were regular, and universally allowed to be uncommonly handsome. The portraits that remain of her combine a faultless symmetry of features with singular sweetness and intelligence of expression.

Her manners were most gracious and pleasing. They were marked by natural dignity and modest reserve, tempered by an affability which flowed from the kindliness of her disposition. She was the last person to be approached with undue familiarity; yet the respect which she imposed was mingled with the strongest feelings of devotion and love. She showed great tact in accommodating herself to the peculiar situation and character of those around her. She appeared in arms at the head of her troops, and shrank from none of the hardships of war. During the reforms introduced into the religious houses, she visited the nunneries in person, taking her needlework with her, and passing the day in the society of the inmates. When travelling in Galicia, she attired herself in the costume of the country, borrowing for that purpose the jewels and other ornaments of the ladies there, and returning them with liberal additions. By this condescending and captivating deportment, as well as by her higher qualities, she gained an ascendency over her turbulent subjects which no king of Spain could ever boast.

She spoke the Castilian with much elegance and correctness. She had an easy fluency of discourse, which, though generally of a serious complexion, was occasionally seasoned with agreeable sallies, some of which have passed into proverbs. She was temperate even to abstemiousness in her diet, seldom or never tasting wine; and so frugal in her table, that the daily expenses for herself and family did not exceed the moderate sum of 40 ducats. She was equally simple and economical in her apparel. On all public occasions, indeed, she displayed a royal magnificence; but she had no relish for it in private, and she freely gave away her clothes and jewels as presents to her friends.

Among her moral qualities, the most conspicuous, perhaps, was her magnanimity. She betrayed nothing little or selfish, in thought or action. Her schemes were vast, and executed in the same noble spirit in which they were conceived. She never employed doubtful agents or sinister measures, but the most direct and open policy. She scorned to avail herself of advantages offered by the perfidy of others. Where she had once given her confidence, she gave her hearty and steady support; and she was scrupulous to redeem any pledge she had made to those who ventured in her cause, however unpopular. She sustained Ximenes in all his obnoxious but salutary reforms. She seconded Columbus in the prosecution of his arduous enterprise, and shielded him from the calumny of his enemies. She did the same good service to her favourite, Gonsalvo de Cordova; and the day of her death was felt, and, as it proved, truly felt, by both, as the last of their good fortune. Artifice and duplicity were so abhorrent to her character, and so averse from her domestic policy, that when they appear in the foreign relations of Spain it is certainly not imputable to her. She was incapable of harbouring any petty distrust or latent malice; and, although stern in the execution and exaction of public justice, she made the most generous allowance, and even sometimes advances, to those who had personally injured her.

ARMOUR OF ISABELLA

But the principle which gave a peculiar colouring to every feature of Isabella's mind was piety. Such was the decorum of her manners, that, though encompassed by false friends and open enemies, not the slightest reproach was breathed on her fair name in this corrupt and calumnious court. She gave a liberal portion of her time to private devotions, as well as to the public exercises of religion. She expended large sums in useful charities, especially in the erection of hospitals and churches, and the more doubtful endowments of monasteries. Her piety was strikingly exhibited in that unfeigned humility which is so rarely found; and most rarely in those whose great powers and exalted stations seem to raise them above the level of ordinary mortals. A remarkable illustration of this is afforded in the queen's correspondence with Talavera, in which her meek and docile spirit is strikingly contrasted with the Puritanical intolerance of her confessor. Unfortunately, the royal conscience was at times committed to very different keeping; and that humility which made her defer so reverentially to her ghostly advisers led, under the fanatic Torquemada, the confessor of her early youth, to the establishment of the Inquisition and the exile of the Jews.

But though blemishes of the deepest dye on her administration, they are certainly not to be regarded as such on her moral character. It will be difficult to condemn her, indeed, without condemning the age; for these very acts are not only excused, but extolled by her contemporaries, as constituting her strongest claims to renown and to the gratitude of her country. They proceeded from the principle, openly avowed by the court of Rome, that zeal for the purity of the faith could atone for every crime. This immoral maxim, flowing from the head of the church, was echoed in a thousand different forms by the subordinate clergy, and greedily received by a superstitious people. It was not to be expected that a solitary woman, filled with natural diffidence of her own capacity on such subjects, should array herself against those venerated counsellors whom she had been taught from her cradle to look to as the guides and guardians of her conscience.

However mischievous the operations of the Inquisition may have been in Spain, its establishment, in point of principle, was not worse than many other measures which have passed with far less censure, though in a much more advanced and civilised age. Where, indeed, during the sixteenth and the greater part of the seventeenth century, was the principle of persecution abandoned by the dominant party, whether Catholic or Protestant? And where that of toleration asserted, except by the weaker? It is true, to borrow Isabella's own expression in her letter to Talavera, the prevalence of a bad custom cannot constitute its apology. But it should serve much to mitigate our condemnation of the queen, that she fell into no greater error, in the imperfect light in which she lived, than was common to the greatest minds in a later and far riper period.[1]

Isabella's actions, indeed, were habitually based on principle. Whatever errors of judgment be imputed to her, she most anxiously sought in all situations to discern and discharge her duty. Faithful in the dispensation of justice, no bribe was large enough to ward off the execution of the law. No motive, not even conjugal affection, could induce her to make an unsuitable appointment to public office. No reverence for the ministers of religion could lead her to wink at their misconduct; nor could the deference she entertained for the head of the church allow her to tolerate his encroachments on the rights of her crown. Isabella's measures were characterised by that practical good sense without which the most brilliant parts may work more to the woe than to the weal of mankind. Though engaged all her life in reforms, she had none of the failings so common in reformers. Her plans, though vast, were never visionary. The best proof of this is that she lived to see most of them realised.

She was quick to discern objects of real utility. She saw the importance of the new discovery of printing, and liberally patronised it, from the first moment it appeared. She had none of the exclusive, local prejudices too common with her countrymen. She drew talent from the most remote quarters to her dominions by munificent rewards. She imported foreign artisans for her manufactures, foreign engineers and officers for the discipline of her army, and foreign scholars to imbue her martial subjects with more cultivated tastes. She consulted the useful in all her subordinate regulations; in her sumptuary laws, for instance, directed against the fashionable extravagances of dress, and the ruinous ostentation so much affected by the

[1] Even Milton, in his essay on *The Liberty of Unlicensed Printing*, the most splendid argument, perhaps, the world had then witnessed in behalf of intellectual liberty, would exclude popery from the benefits of toleration, as a religion which the public good required at all events to be extirpated. Such were the crude views of the rights of conscience entertained, in the latter half of the seventeenth century, by one of those gifted minds whose extraordinary elevation enabled it to catch and reflect back the coming light of knowledge, long before it had fallen on the rest of mankind.

Castilians in their weddings and funerals.   Lastly, she showed the same per-
spicacity in the selection of her agents, well knowing that the best measures
become bad in incompetent hands.

But although the skilful selection of her agents was an obvious cause of
Isabella's success, yet another, even more important, is to be found in her
own vigilance and untiring exertions.   During the first busy and bustling
years of her reign, these exertions were of incredible magnitude.   She was
almost always in the saddle, for she made all her journeys on horseback ; and
she travelled with a rapidity which made her always present on the spot
where her presence was needed.   She was never intimidated by the weather,
or the state of her own health ; and this reckless exposure undoubtedly
contributed much to impair her excellent constitution.

She was equally indefatigable in her mental application.   After assiduous attention to business through the day, she was often known to sit up all
night dictating despatches to her secretaries.   In the midst of these overwhelming cares she found time to supply the defects of early education by
learning Latin, so as to understand it without difficulty, whether written or
spoken, and indeed, in the opinion of a competent judge, to attain a critical
accuracy in it.   As she had little turn for light amusements, she sought
relief from graver cares by some useful occupation appropriate to her sex ;
and she left ample evidence of her skill in this way, in the rich specimens of
embroidery, wrought with her own fair hands, with which she decorated the
churches.

With all her high qualifications, Isabella would have been still unequal
to the achievement of her grand designs, without possessing a degree of fortitude rare in either sex ; not the courage which implies contempt of personal
danger — though of this she had a larger share than falls to most men ; nor
that which supports its possessor under the extremities of bodily pain —
though of this she gave ample evidence, since she endured the greatest suffering her sex is called to bear without a groan ; but that moral courage
which sustains the spirit in the dark hour of adversity, and, gathering light
from within to dispel the darkness, imparts its own cheering influence to all
around.   It was her voice that decided never to abandon Alhama.   Her
remonstrances compelled the king and nobles to return to the field, when
they had quitted it after an ineffectual campaign.   As dangers and difficulties multiplied, she multiplied resources to meet them ; and when her
soldiers lay drooping under the evils of some protracted siege, she appeared
in the midst, mounted on her warhorse, with her delicate limbs cased in
knightly mail, and, riding through their ranks, breathed new courage into
their hearts by her own intrepid bearing.   To her personal efforts, indeed,
as well as counsels, the success of this glorious war may be mainly imputed.

Happily, these masculine qualities in Isabella did not extinguish the
softer ones which constitute the charm of her sex.   Her heart overflowed
with affectionate sensibility to her family and friends.   She watched over
the declining days of her aged mother, and ministered to her sad infirmities
with all the delicacy of filial tenderness.   We have seen abundant proofs
how fondly and faithfully she loved her husband to the last, though this love
was not always as faithfully requited.[1]   For her children she lived more

[1 Burke *f* says, "Ferdinand had at least four illegitimate children by different ladies.
Juana, who was offered with a double marriage portion, in 1489, to the king of Scots.   Juan,
archbishop of Saragossa, and two other daughters, both princesses.   Raymond de Cardona (the
unworthy successor of Gonsalvo de Cordova in Italy) was also commonly supposed to be a son of
Ferdinand.   But the king's faults were certainly not those of a voluptuary."   Prescott *g* quotes
Marineo *r* on "the queen's discreet and most amiable conduct in these delicate matters."]

[1504 A.D.]

than for herself ; and for them too she died, for it was their loss and their afflictions which froze the current of her blood before age had time to chill it. Her exalted state did not remove her above the sympathies of friendship. With her friends she forgot the usual distinctions of rank, sharing in their joys, visiting and consoling them in sorrow and sickness, and condescending in more than one instance to assume the office of executrix on their decease. Her heart, indeed, was filled with benevolence to all mankind. In the most fiery heat of war she was engaged in devising means for mitigating its horrors. She is said to have been the first to introduce the benevolent institution of camp hospitals ; and we have seen, more than once, her lively solicitude to spare the effusion of blood even of her enemies.

It is in these more amiable qualities of her sex that Isabella's superiority becomes most apparent over her illustrious namesake, Elizabeth of England, whose history presents some features parallel to her own. Both were disciplined in early life by the teachings of that stern nurse of wisdom, Adversity. Both were made to experience the deepest humiliation at the hands of their nearest relative, who should have cherished and protected them. Both succeeded in establishing themselves on the throne after the most precarious vicissitudes. Each conducted her kingdom, through a long and triumphant reign, to a height of glory which it had never before reached. Both lived to see the vanity of all earthly grandeur, and to fall the victims of an inconsolable melancholy ; and both left behind an illustrious name, unrivalled in the subsequent annals of their country.

But with these few circumstances of their history the resemblance ceases. Their characters afford scarcely a point of contact. Elizabeth, inheriting a large share of the bold and bluff King Harry's temperament, was haughty, arrogant, coarse, and irascible ; while with these fiercer qualities she mingled deep dissimulation and strange irresolution. Isabella, on the other hand, tempered the dignity of royal station with the most bland and courteous manners. Once resolved, she was constant in her purposes, and her conduct in public and private life was characterised by candour and integrity. Both may be said to have shown that magnanimity which is implied by the accomplishment of great objects in the face of great obstacles. But Elizabeth was desperately selfish ; she was incapable of forgiving, not merely a real injury, but the slightest affront to her vanity ; and she was merciless in exacting retribution. Isabella, on the other hand, lived only for others — was ready at all times to sacrifice self to considerations of public duty, and, far from personal resentments, showed the greatest condescension and kindness to those who had most sensibly injured her ; while her benevolent heart sought every means to mitigate the authorised severities of the law, even towards the guilty.[1]

Both possessed rare fortitude. Isabella, indeed, was placed in situations which demanded more frequent and higher displays of it than her rival ; but no one will doubt a full measure of this quality in the daughter of Henry VIII. Elizabeth was better educated, and every way more highly accomplished, than Isabella. But the latter knew enough to maintain her station with dignity ; and she encouraged learning by a munificent patronage. The masculine powers and passions of Elizabeth seemed to divorce

---

[1] She gave evidence of this in the commutation of the sentence she obtained for the wretch who stabbed her husband, and whom her ferocious nobles would have put to death without the opportunity of confession and absolution, that "his soul might perish with his body !" (See her letter to Talavera.) She showed this merciful temper, so rare in that rough age, by dispensing altogether with the preliminary barbarities sometimes prescribed by the law in capital executions.

her in a great measure from the peculiar attributes of her sex ; at least from those which constitute its peculiar charm, for she had abundance of its foibles — a coquetry and love of admiration which age could not chill ; a levity most careless, if not criminal ; and a fondness for dress and tawdry magnificence of ornament which was ridiculous, or disgusting, according to the different periods of life in which it was indulged.   Isabella, on the other hand, distinguished through life for decorum of manners and purity beyond the breath of calumny, was content with the legitimate affection which she could inspire within the range of her domestic circle.   Far from a frivolous affectation of ornament of dress, she was most simple in her own attire, and seemed to set no value on her jewels but as they could serve the necessities of the state ; when they could be no longer useful in this way, she gave them away to her friends.

Both were uncommonly sagacious in the selection of their ministers ; though Elizabeth was drawn into some errors in this particular by her levity, as was Isabella by religious feeling. It was this, combined with her excessive humility, which led to the only grave errors in the administration of the latter. Her rival fell into no such errors ; and she was a stranger to the amiable qualities which led to them. Her conduct was certainly not controlled by religious principle ; and though the bulwark of the Protestant faith, it might be difficult to say whether she were at heart most a Protestant or a Catholic. She viewed religion in its connection with the state — in other words, with herself ; and she took measures for enforcing conformity to her own views,

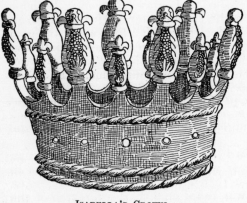

ISABELLA'S CROWN
(From an old print)

not a whit less despotic, and scarcely less sanguinary, than those countenanced for conscience's sake by her more bigoted rival.

This feature of bigotry, which has thrown a shade over Isabella's otherwise beautiful character, might lead to a disparagement of her intellectual power compared with that of the English queen. To estimate this aright, we must contemplate the results of their respective reigns. Elizabeth found all the materials of prosperity at hand, and availed herself of them most ably to build up a solid fabric of national grandeur. Isabella created these materials. She saw the faculties of her people locked up in a death-like lethargy, and she breathed into them the breath of life for those great and heroic enterprises which terminated in such glorious consequences to the monarchy. It is when viewed from the depressed position of her early days that the achievements of her reign seem scarcely less than miraculous. The masculine genius of the English queen stands out relieved beyond its natural dimensions by its separation from the softer qualities of her sex ; while her rival's, like some vast but symmetrical edifice, loses in appearance somewhat of its actual grandeur from the perfect harmony of its proportions.

The circumstances of their deaths, which were somewhat similar, displayed the great dissimilarity of their characters. Both pined amidst their royal state, a prey to incurable despondency, rather than any marked bodily distemper. In Elizabeth it sprang from wounded vanity, a sullen conviction that she had outlived the admiration on which she had so long fed — and even the solace of friendship and the attachment of her subjects. Nor did she seek consolation where alone it was to be found, in that sad hour. Isabella, on the other hand, sank under a too acute sensibility to the sufferings of others. But, amidst the gloom which gathered around her, she looked with the eye of faith to the brighter prospects which unfolded of the future; and when she resigned her last breath, it was amidst the tears and universal lamentations of her people.

It is in this undying, unabated attachment of the nation, indeed, that we see the most unequivocal testimony to the virtues of Isabella. In the downward progress of things in Spain, some of the most ill-advised measures of her administration have found favour and been perpetuated, while the more salutary have been forgotten. This may lead to a misconception of her real merits. In order to estimate these, we must listen to the voice of her contemporaries, the eye-witnesses of the condition in which she found the state, and in which she left it.

We shall then see but one judgment formed of her, whether by foreigners or natives. The French and Italian writers equally join in celebrating the triumphant glories of her reign, and her magnanimity, wisdom, and purity of character. Her own subjects extol her as "the most brilliant exemplar of every virtue," and mourn over the day of her death as "the last of the prosperity and happiness of their country"; while those who had nearer access to her person are unbounded in their admiration of those amiable qualities whose full power is revealed only in the unrestrained intimacies of domestic life. The judgment of posterity has ratified the sentence of her own age.*g*

This portrait of Isabella as drawn by Prescott is glowing with an enthusiasm that is not self-ashamed. It admits frankly many evils, but in the sweep of eulogy they practically lose their effect and make no impression on the mind. Yet Prescott's opinion was based on a thorough search of the authorities and upon the impartiality of a foreigner enamoured of a character purely by the good deeds he had learned to credit to her. It must therefore be received with respect, though it has, like all such summings-up, provoked severe disagreements. Even a writer in possession of no new facts could use the same data for violent denunciation.

The most material attack on Prescott's opinion is found in the very positive claim that Isabella's daughter Juana was not mad, and that her mother's treatment of her, founded on religious bigotry with which Juana did not sympathise, is therefore as cruel in kind as her mercilessness to the Jews. In the second place the genuineness of Isabella's last will was questioned even by contemporaries, but it has never been disproved conclusively; admitting its authenticity, critics have said that in withdrawing from the nobility and others the various grants she had made them in payment of obligations, she committed an outrageous dishonesty or "posthumous royal plunder."

Even her simplicity of attire has been denied, and it is said that she outdid all history in her display when she saw fit to affect splendour. But this much even Prescott admitted.

As to Juana, Bergenroth *s* is the strongest advocate of her sanity, though he has not convinced many. He declared that she was simply a heretic in religion. But even granting her insane, her parents treated her with "most odious duplicity," according to Burke,*f* who can still see why Isabella should not want the hysterical daughter to take the throne of Castile, and reduce the great Ferdinand to the limits of Aragon. The proofs of Juana's insanity we shall consider in the next chapter.

BURKE'S ESTIMATE OF ISABELLA ; HUME'S ESTIMATE

Burke thinks that Isabella has suffered from too much praise of virtues she did not possess and too much neglect of her truer gifts. He places the blame for this largely on the fact that she and her husband were succeeded by foreign rulers, Habsburgs and Bourbons. He ridicules the tendency to blame Torquemada and others for the blots of cruelty on her reign, and blames them on the orthodoxy of the time. He makes of her a creature far different from the gentle Isabella of Prescott's idea, and exclaims eloquently : a

The real Isabella is one of the most remarkable characters in history. Not only was she the most masterful, and, from her own point of view, by far the most successful ruler that ever sat upon the throne of Spain, or of any of the kingdoms of the peninsula ; she stands in the front rank of the great sovereigns of Europe, and challenges comparison with the greatest women who have ever held sway in the world.

In one particular she stands alone among the great ruling women, the conquerors and empresses of history. She is the only royal lady, save, perhaps, Maria Theresa of Hungary, who maintained through life the incongruous relations of a masterful sovereign and a devoted wife, and shared not only her bed but her throne with her husband whom she respected — a fellow-sovereign whom she neither feared nor disregarded. To command the obedience of a proud and warlike people is given to few of the great men of history. To do the bidding of another with vigour and with discretion is a task that has been but rarely accomplished by a heaven-born minister. But to conceive and carry out great designs, with one hand in the grasp of even the most loyal of companions, is a triumphant combination of energy with discretion, of the finest tact with the most indomitable resolution that stamps Isabella of Spain as a being more vigorous than the greatest men, more discreet than the greatest women of history. Semiramis, Zenobia, Boadicea, Elizabeth of England, Catherine of Russia — not one of them was embarrassed by a partner on the throne. The partner of Isabella was not only a husband but a king, jealous, restless, and untrustworthy. It is in this respect, and in the immense scope of her political action, that the great queen of Castile is comparable with the bold empress-king of Hungary, rather than with any other of the great queens and royal ladies of history.

Isabella revolutionised the institutions of her country, religious, political, military, financial ; she consolidated her dominions, humiliated her nobles, cajoled her commons, defied the pope, reformed the clergy ; she burned some ten thousand of her subjects, she deported a million more, and of the remnant she made a great nation ; she brooked no man's opposition, in a reign of thirty years, and she died in the arms of the king, her husband ! It is open to any man to call her a saint and a heroine. It is open to any man to call her a bigot and a tyrant. But no man at least may deny that she was a great queen. f

The contradiction between such an opinion and the opinion of Prescott is not after all a contradiction in facts but in point of view. Both regard different phases or facets of one great busy soul striding through a great life on a line which, whether it led through tenderness or mercilessness, was a nearly straight as any line ever trod by a human monarch. It is the mockery of history, however, that while great souls bear great fruits, those fruits are not always of lasting quality, and time may turn them to poison.

The epitaph that Martin Hume would place above the beautiful memory of Isabella is sad enough, yet only too just: *a*

"That her objects were high and noble may be conceded, and that she succeeded in consolidating Spain as no other monarch had done, is true. But at what a cost! She had, in conjunction with Ferdinand, encouraged forces of bigotry and religious hate which flooded her realm with blood and tears, and threw it back in the race of nations for centuries. Her patronage of Columbus is more than blotted out by her patronage of Torquemada; her exalted piety is drowned in the recollection of her treatment of the Jews and the Moriscos. She was a fair embodiment of the prevailing feeling of her countrymen: that to them all things are permitted; they can do no wrong, because they are working for and with the cause of God. We shall see the bitter fruit this feeling bore later. By the irony, or perhaps the eternal justice of fate, all the chicanery of Ferdinand, all the wisdom, the labours, and the fervour of Isabella brought disaster, ruin, and death to Spain. A thousand times happier would it have been for Castile to have remained isolated in its corner of Europe, untroubled with the complications of vast European connections, rather than to have been dragged by Aragon into a position of responsibility and world-wide ambition for which neither its native resources nor the extent nor character of its population befitted it. Its transient grandeur, dearly paid for by long and painful decline, brought to the Spanish people, even while it lasted, neither peace, happiness, nor enduring prosperity; and the king and queen who made Spain great were the worst enemies she ever had." *t*

CHAPTER VII

THE REGENCIES OF FERDINAND

[1504–1517 A.D.]

THE death of Isabella gives a new complexion to our history. We hav been made conscious of her presence and parental supervision, by the main tenance of order and the general prosperity of the nation. Her death wil make us more sensible of this influence, since it was the signal for disorder which even the genius and authority of Ferdinand were unable to suppress.

While the queen's remains were yet scarcely cold, King Ferdinand too the usual measures for announcing the succession. He resigned the crow of Castile, which he had worn with so much glory for thirty years. From platform raised in the great square of Toledo, the heralds proclaimed, wit sound of trumpet, the accession of Philip and Juana to the Castilian thron and the royal standard was unfurled by the duke of Alva in honour of th illustrious pair. The king of Aragon then publicly assumed the title administrator or governor of Castile, as provided by the queen's testamen and received the obeisance of such of the nobles as were present, in his ne capacity. These proceedings took place on the evening of the same day o which the queen expired.

A circular letter was next addressed to the principal cities, requirin them, after the customary celebration of the obsequies of their late sovereig to raise the royal banners in the name of Juana; and writs were immediate issued in her name, without mention of Philip's, for the convocation of cortes to ratify these proceedings. The assembly met at Toro, January 11t 1505. The queen's will, or rather that portion of it which related to t succession, was read aloud, and received the entire approbation of the co mons, who, together with the grandees and prelates present, took the oat of allegiance to Juana as queen and lady proprietor, and to Philip as h husband. They then determined that the exigency contemplated in t testament, of Juana's incapacity, actually existed, and proceeded to tend their homage to King Ferdinand, as the lawful governor of the realm in h name. The latter in turn made the customary oath to respect the laws a liberties of the kingdom, and the whole was terminated by an embassy fr the cortes, with a written account of its proceedings, to their new sovereig in Flanders.

All seemed now done that was demanded for giving a constitutional sanction to Ferdinand's authority as regent. By the written law of the land, the sovereign was empowered to nominate a regency in case of the minority or incapacity of the heir-apparent. This had been done in the present instance by Isabella, at the earnest solicitation of the cortes, made two years previous to her death. It had received the cordial approbation of that body, which had undeniable authority to control such testamentary provisions. Thus, from the first to the last stage of the proceeding, the whole had gone on with a scrupulous attention to constitutional forms. Yet the authority of the new regent was far from being firmly seated; and it was the conviction of this which had led him to accelerate measures.*b*

Before Isabella breathed her last, the dissensions commenced. That, by the Castilian laws, Juana was now both queen and proprietor of the kingdom, and that Philip, in right of his marriage, might claim not only the regal title, but a considerable share in the administration, were admitted by many. On the other hand, the last will of Isabella, who had constituted her husband regent until the majority of Charles, the experience of that prince, the success of his past government, the solid benefits which he had conferred on the state, and the unpopular character of Philip, as well as his ignorance of the language, laws, and manners of Castile—induced all the sober-judging and patriotic part of the nation to wish for a continuance of the present rule. Unfortunately, however, the momentous question was agitated with more prejudice than reason. The efforts of Ferdinand to curb the violence of the aristocracy, his prudent economy, his firm sway, and the aversion of many Castilians to the sole domination of an Aragonese, had created many enemies. More hoped that, under a weak and lenient prince like Philip, their love of power and their avarice would be equally gratified. Hence, it is no wonder that an opposition, at once systematic and violent, was formed to the pretensions of Ferdinand — an opposition too loud to permit the soft whisper of policy or gratitude to be heard.

FERDINAND THE CATHOLIC

Ferdinand was fond of power, and his first steps showed that he would strive to maintain it. Not a few of the discontented, because disappointed, nobles retired from Toro in disgust, assembled others of the same faction at Valladolid, and wrote letters to Philip, then governor of Flanders, pressing him to come and assume the administration of the kingdom. The archduke, eager to seize his consort's inheritance, had the insolence to order his father-in-law to retire into Aragon, against whose every act of government, since the death of Isabella, he equally protested.

Ferdinand replied that the affair must be settled by negotiation; that in no case would he resign the regency until his daughter and son-in-law arrived in Castile. At the same time, he solicited from the queen, then with her husband in Flanders, the confirmation of his powers as regent. She caused the instrument to be prepared ; but the treachery of a servant exposed the intrigue to Philip, who placed her in close confinement, and lost even the semblance of respect towards her. The latter also entered into an alliance with Louis XII of France, the enemy of Ferdinand, by whose aid he hoped to make head against the regent. In the meantime, the factious nobles, who, though constituting a minority in point of numbers, were all-powerful from their stations and alliances, continually urged Philip to appear among them and throw every obstacle in the path of the regent. Seeing the ungrateful return of a people for whom he had done so much, whose glory and happiness he had so successfully laboured to promote, and still more offended, perhaps, with the insults of his profligate son-in-law, the king of Aragon seriously planned a suitable revenge : it was to remarry, and leave to the issue arising from it the kingdom of Naples, which he had united with Aragon, or, perhaps, even Aragon itself.[d]

Robertson[c] explains his plan as follows : " Exasperated at this universal defection, and mortified, perhaps, at seeing all his schemes defeated by a younger politician, Ferdinand resolved, in defiance of the law of nations and of decency, to deprive his daughter and her posterity of the crown of Castile, rather than renounce the regency of that kingdom. His plan for accomplishing this was no less bold than the intention itself was wicked. He demanded in marriage Juana, the supposed daughter of Henry IV." But this Dunham[d] indignantly denies : " Surely this historian must have known that this pretended negotiation with the Portuguese king was but a calumny, invented by the enemies of Ferdinand, to discredit him with the people. By no contemporary writer is it mentioned otherwise than a rumour, and by all it is treated with the contempt it deserves. The age of the princess, which was full forty-four years, sufficiently exposes the malignity." Other historians, however, accept the scheme as quite within Ferdinand's capabilities. Martin Hume[e] shares this opinion with Carbajal,[f] Zurita,[g] Mariana,[h] Sandoval,[i] and Clemencin,[j] while Burke[k] says epigrammatically : "The rights of Juana, surnamed La Beltraneja, born in wedlock and recognised by her father, King Henry IV, as his successor on his throne, had only been subordinated to those of her aunt Isabella by force of arms. And Ferdinand, who had entered Castile in 1469 by marrying her rival and denying her legitimacy, now proposed to remain in Castile in 1505 by asserting her legitimacy and marrying her himself ! But the lady refused to entertain his proposals, and the legitimate queen of Spain remained unwedded in her Portuguese convent."[a]

He solicited the hand of Germaine de Foix, niece of Louis XII, who eagerly granted it. This intelligence was a thunderbolt to Philip, who now consented to negotiate ; and it was accordingly agreed, by the agents of the two princes, at Salamanca, that the kingdom should be governed by Juana, Ferdinand, and Philip, each possessing equal authority ; and that all public instruments should bear the three names. The Austrian, however, had no intention of observing the treaty : early in 1506, he embarked for Spain with his consort ; but contrary winds forced him to England, where he was detained, during three months, by the ungenerous policy of Henry VII. The king of France had refused him a passage through that kingdom until he had come to a better understanding with the regent — in fact Charles could not, as a close ally of Ferdinand, permit an expedition through his states, evidently hostile to that ally. When Ferdinand heard of the archduke's embarkation, he caused prayers to be offered up for a prosperous voyage, and ordered a fleet to be equipped to convoy the new sovereigns into the peninsula. He had just celebrated his marriage with the princess Germaine, when his daughter and the archduke landed at Corunna.[d]

PHILIP ENTERS SPAIN

Ferdinand, who had expected them at some nearer northern port, prepared without loss of time to go forward and receive them. But Philip had no intention of such an interview at present. He had purposely landed in a remote corner of the country, in order to gain time for his partisans to come forward and declare themselves. Missives had been despatched to the principal nobles and cavaliers, and they were answered by great numbers of all ranks, who pressed forward to welcome and pay court to the young monarch. He soon mustered an additional force of six thousand native Spaniards, which, with the chivalry who thronged to meet him, placed him in a condition to dictate terms to his father-in-law; and he now openly proclaimed that he had no intention of abiding by the concord of Salamanca, and that he would never consent to an arrangement prejudicing in any degree his and his wife's exclusive possession of the crown of Castile.

Ferdinand, at length, finding that Philip, who had now left Corunna, was advancing by a circuitous route into the interior on purpose to avoid him, and that all access to his daughter was absolutely refused, was doomed to experience still more mortifying indignities. By the orders of the marquis of Astorga and the count of Benavente, he was actually refused admittance into those cities; while proclamation was made by the same arrogant lords prohibiting any of their vassals from aiding or harbouring his Aragonese followers. "A sad spectacle, indeed," exclaims the loyal Martyr,[l] "to behold a monarch, yesterday almost omnipotent, thus wandering a vagabond in his own kingdom, refused even the sight of his own child!" Even his son-in-law, the constable of Castile, had deserted him.

An end was at length put to this scandalous exhibition by an interview. The place selected was an open plain near Puebla de Senabria, on the borders of Leon and Galicia (June 23rd). But even then the precautions taken were of a kind truly ludicrous, considering the forlorn condition of King Ferdinand. The whole military apparatus of the archduke was put in motion, as if he expected to win the crown by battle. Ferdinand, on the other hand, came into the field attended by about two hundred nobles and gentlemen, chiefly Aragonese and Italians, riding on mules, and simply attired in the short black cloak and bonnet of the country, with no other weapon than the sword usually worn. The king trusted, says Zurita,[g] to the majesty of his presence, and the reputation he had acquired by his long and able administration.

The Castilian nobles, brought into contact with Ferdinand, could not well avoid paying their obeisance to him. He received them in his usual gracious and affable manner, making remarks the good-humour of which was occasionally seasoned with something of a more pungent character. Among others was Garcilasso de la Vega, Ferdinand's minister formerly at Rome. Like many of the Castilian lords, he wore armour under his dress, the better to guard against surprise. The king, embracing him, felt the mail beneath, and, tapping him familiarly on the shoulder, said, "I congratulate you, Garcilasso; you have grown wonderfully lusty since we last met." The desertion, however, of one who had received so many favours from him touched him more nearly than that of all the rest.

After exchanging salutations, the two monarchs alighted, and entered a small hermitage in the neighbourhood. The conference led to no result. Philip was well schooled in his part, and remained, says Martyr, *l* immovable as a rock. There was so little mutual confidence between the parties that the name of Juana, whom Ferdinand desired so much to see, was not even mentioned during the interview.[1]

But, however reluctant Ferdinand might be to admit it, he was no longer in a condition to stand upon terms; and, in addition to the entire loss of influence in Castile, he received such alarming accounts from Naples as made him determine on an immediate visit in person to that kingdom. He resolved, therefore, to bow his head to the present storm, in hopes that a brighter day was in reserve for him. On the 27th of June he signed and solemnly swore to an agreement by which he surrendered the entire sovereignty of Castile to Philip and Juana, reserving to himself only the grandmasterships of the military orders, and the revenues secured by Isabella's testament.

On the following day he executed another instrument of most singular import, in which, after avowing in unequivocal terms his daughter's incapacity, he engages to assist Philip in preventing any interference in her behalf, and to maintain him, as far as in his power, in the sole, exclusive authority.

Before signing these papers, he privately made a protest, in the presence of several witnesses, that what he was about to do was not of his own free will, but from necessity, to extricate himself from his perilous situation and shield the country from the impending evils of a civil war. He concluded with asserting that, far from relinquishing his claims to the regency, it was his design to enforce them, as well as to rescue his daughter from her captivity, as soon as he was in a condition to do so. Finally, he completed this chain of inconsistencies by addressing a circular letter, dated July 1st, to the different parts of the kingdom, announcing his resignation of the government into the hands of Philip and Juana, and declaring the act one which, notwithstanding his own right and power to the contrary, he had previously determined on executing so soon as his children should set foot in Spain.

A CAVALIER IN THE TIME
OF FERDINAND

It is not easy to reconcile this monstrous tissue of incongruity and dissimulation with any motives of necessity or expediency. Why should he, so soon after preparing to raise the kingdom in his daughter's cause, thus publicly avow her imbecility, and deposit the whole authority in the hands of Philip? Was it to bring odium on the head of the latter, by encouraging him to a measure which he knew must disgust the Castilians? But Ferdinand by this very act shared the responsibility with him. Was it in the

[1 Burke *k* gives Baudier *z* as authority for claiming that Ferdinand did not care to see his daughter, and says, " it must be admitted that if Ferdinand was a detestable father, Philip was a very sorry husband."]

expectation that uncontrolled and undivided power, in the hands of one so rash and improvident, would the more speedily work his ruin? As to his clandestine protest, its design was obviously to afford a plausible pretext at some future time for reasserting his claims to the government, on the ground that his concessions had been the result of force. But, then, why neutralise the operation of this by the declaration, spontaneously made in his manifesto to the people, that his abdication was not only a free but most deliberate and premeditated act? He was led to this last avowal, probably, by the desire of covering over the mortification of his defeat; a thin varnish, which could impose on nobody. The whole of the proceedings are of so ambiguous a character as to suggest the inevitable inference that they flowed from habits of dissimulation too strong to be controlled even when there was no occasion for its exercise. We occasionally meet with examples of a similar fondness for superfluous manœuvring in the humbler concerns of life.

THE REIGN OF PHILIP I (1506 A. D.)

King Ferdinand had no sooner concluded the arrangement with Philip, and withdrawn into his hereditary dominions, than the archduke and his wife proceeded towards Valladolid, to receive the homage of the estates convened in that city. Juana, oppressed with an habitual melancholy, and clad in the sable habiliments better suited to a season of mourning than rejoicing, refused the splendid ceremonial and festivities with which the city was prepared to welcome her. Her dissipated husband, who had long since ceased to treat her not merely with affection, but even decency, would fain have persuaded the cortes to authorise the confinement of his wife, as disordered in intellect, and to devolve on him the whole charge of the government. But the commons could not brook such an indignity to their own "natural sovereign"; and the usual oaths of allegiance were tendered to Juana as queen and lady proprietor of the kingdom, and to Philip as her husband, and finally to their eldest son, Prince Charles, as heir-apparent and lawful successor on the demise of his mother.

By the tenor of these acts the royal authority would seem to have been virtually vested in Juana. From this moment, however, Philip assumed the government into his own hands. The effects were soon visible in the thorough revolution introduced into every department. Old incumbents in office were ejected without ceremony, to make way for new favourites. The Flemings, in particular, were placed in every considerable post, and the principal fortresses of the kingdom intrusted to their keeping.

The style of living at the court was on the most thoughtless scale of wasteful expenditure. The public revenues, notwithstanding liberal appropriations by the late cortes, were wholly unequal to it. To supply the deficit, offices were sold to the highest bidder. The income drawn from the silk manufactures of Granada, which had been appropriated to defray King Ferdinand's pension, was assigned by Philip to one of the royal treasurers. Fortunately, Ximenes obtained possession of the order and had the boldness to tear it in pieces. He then waited on the young monarch, and remonstrated with him on the recklessness of measures which must infallibly ruin his credit with the people. Philip yielded in this instance.

All this could not fail to excite disgust and disquietude throughout the nation. The most alarming symptoms of insubordination began to appear in different parts of the kingdom. In Andalusia, in particular, a confederation of the nobles was organised, with the avowed purpose of rescuing the queen from the duress in which it was said she was held by her husband. At the same time the most tumultuous scenes were exhibited in Cordova, in consequence of the high hand with which the Inquisition was carrying matters there. Members of many of the principal families, including persons of both sexes, had been arrested on the charge of heresy. This sweeping proscription provoked an insurrection, countenanced by the marquis of Priego, in which the prisons were broken open, and Lucero, an inquisitor who had made himself deservedly odious by his cruelties, narrowly escaped falling into the hands of the infuriated populace. The grand inquisitor, Deza, archbishop of Seville, the steady friend of Columbus, though his name is unhappily registered on some of the darkest pages of the tribunal, was so intimidated as to resign his office. The whole affair was referred to the royal council by Philip, whose Flemish education had not predisposed him to any reverence for the institution ; a circumstance which operated quite as much to his prejudice, with the more bigoted part of the nation, as his really exceptional acts.

The minds of the wise and the good were filled with sadness, as they listened to the low murmurs of popular discontent, which seemed to be gradually swelling into strength for some terrible convulsion ; and they looked back with fond regret to the halcyon days which they had enjoyed under the temperate rule of Ferdinand and Isabella.

The Catholic king, in the meantime, was pursuing his voyage to Naples. Soon after the conquest he had been earnestly pressed by the Neapolitans to visit his new dominions. He now went, less, however, in compliance with that request than to relieve his own mind by assuring himself of the fidelity of his viceroy, Gonsalvo de Cordova. That illustrious man had not escaped the usual lot of humanity ; his brilliant successes had brought on him a full measure of the envy which seems to wait on merit like its shadow. His courteous manners, bountiful largesses, and magnificent style of living, were represented as politic arts to seduce the affections of the soldiery and the people. His services were in the market for the highest bidder. He had received the most splendid offers from the king of France and the pope. He had carried on a correspondence with Maximilian and Philip, who would purchase his adhesion, if possible, to the latter, at any price ; and if he had not hitherto committed himself by any overt act, it seemed probable he was only waiting to be determined in his future course by the result of King Ferdinand's struggle with his son-in-law.

These suggestions, in which some truth, as usual, was mingled with a large infusion of error, gradually excited more and more uneasiness in the breast of the cautious and naturally distrustful Ferdinand. He at first endeavoured to abridge the powers of the great captain by recalling half the troops in his service, notwithstanding the unsettled state of the kingdom. He then took the decisive step of ordering his return to Castile, on pretence of employing him in affairs of great importance at home. Finding that Gonsalvo still procrastinated his return on various pretexts, the king's uneasiness increased to such a degree that he determined to press his own departure for Naples, and bring back, if not too late, his too powerful vassal.

After a boisterous and tedious passage, he reached Genoa. Here, to his astonishment, he was joined by the great captain, who, advised of the king' movements, had come from Naples with a small fleet to meet him. Thi frank conduct of his general, if it did not disarm Ferdinand of his suspi

QUEEN JUANA WITH THE BODY OF HER HUSBAND

cions, showed him the policy of concealing them ; and he treated Gonsalvo with all the consideration and show of confidence which might impose, not merely on the public, but on the immediate subject of them.

DEATH OF PHILIP ; JUANA'S MADNESS

After quitting Genoa, the royal squadron was driven by contrary winds into the neighbouring harbour of Portofino, where Ferdinand received intelligence which promised to change his destination altogether. This was the death of his son-in-law, the young king of Castile.

This event, so unexpected and awfully sudden, was occasioned by a fever, brought on by too violent exercise at a game of ball, at an entertainment made for Philip by his favourite, Manuel, in Burgos, where the court was then held. Through the unskilfulness of his physicians, as it was said, who neglected to bleed him, the disorder rapidly gained ground, and on the sixth day after his attack, being the 25th of September, 1506, he breathed his last.[1] He was but twenty-eight years old, of which brief period he had enjoyed, or endured, the "golden cares" of sovereignty but little more than two months, dating from his recognition by the cortes. His body, after being embalmed, lay in state for two days, decorated with the insignia — the mockery of royalty, as it had proved to him — and was then deposited in the convent of Miraflores, near Burgos, to await its final removal to Granada, agreeably to his last request.

Philip was so distinguished for comeliness both of person and countenance that he is designated on the roll of Spanish sovereigns as Felipe el Hermoso, or the Handsome. His mental endowments were not so extraordinary. The father of Charles V possessed scarcely a single quality in common with his remarkable son. As he was naturally indolent and fond of pleasure, he willingly reposed the burden of government on others, who, as usual, thought more of their own interests than those of the public. His early education exempted him from the bigotry characteristic of the Spaniards; and had he lived he might have done much to mitigate the grievous abuses of the Inquisition. As it was, his premature death deprived him of the opportunity of compensating, by this single good act, the manifold mischiefs of his administration.

Juana's condition had become truly deplorable. During her husband's illness she had never left his bedside, but neither then, nor since his death, had she been seen to shed a tear. She remained in a state of stupid insensibility, sitting in a darkened apartment, her head resting on her hand, and her lips closed, as mute and immovable as a statue. When applied to for issuing the necessary summons for the cortes, or to make appointments to office, or for any other pressing business which required her signature, she replied, " My father will attend to all this when he returns; he is much more conversant with business than I am; I have no other duties now but to pray for the soul of my departed husband." The only orders she was known to sign were for paying the salaries of her Flemish musicians; for in her abject state she found some consolation in music, of which she had been

---

[1 According to Bergenroth,[u] however, "the general opinion was that he had been poisoned," and he insinuates that Louis Ferrer, Ferdinand's envoy to Philip, was the person who rendered his master this service. But the suspicion is unsupported by a particle of evidence, and seems to be sufficiently refuted by a description of the symptoms and course of the disease, to be found in a letter addressed to Ferdinand by a Dr. Parra, one of the consulting physicians.]

passionately fond from childhood. The few remarks which she uttered were discreet and sensible, forming a singular contrast with the general extravagance of her actions.

Finding it impossible to obtain the queen's co-operation, the council at length resolved to issue the writs of summons in their own name, as a measure justified by necessity. The place of meeting was fixed at Burgos in the ensuing month of November; and great pains were taken that the different cities should instruct their representatives in their views respecting the ultimate disposition of the government. Long before this, indeed immediately after Philip's death, letters had been despatched by Ximenes and his friends to the Catholic king, acquainting him with the state of affairs, and urging his immediate return to Castile. He determined, however, to continue his voyage to Naples. The wary monarch perhaps thought that the Castilians, whose attachment to his own person he might with some reason distrust, would not be the less inclined to his rule after having tasted the bitterness of anarchy.

JUANA

While Ferdinand was thus occupied in Naples, the representatives of most of the cities, summoned by the provisional government, had assembled in Burgos (November, 1506). Before entering on business they were desirous to obtain the queen's sanction to their proceedings. A committee waited on her for that purpose, but she obstinately refused to give them audience.

She still continued plunged in moody melancholy, exhibiting, however, occasionally the wildest freaks of insanity. Towards the latter end of December, she determined to leave Burgos and remove her husband's remains to their final resting-place in Granada. She insisted on seeing them herself before her departure. The remonstrances of her counsellors, and of the holy men of the monastery of Miraflores, proved equally fruitless. Opposition only roused her passions into frenzy, and they were obliged to comply with her mad humours. The corpse was removed from the vault; the two coffins of lead and wood were opened, and such as chose gazed on the mouldering relics, which, notwithstanding their having been embalmed, exhibited scarcely a trace of humanity. The queen was not satisfied till she touched them with her own hand, which she did without shedding a tear or testifying the least emotion. The unfortunate lady, indeed, was said never to have been seen to weep since she detected her husband's intrigue with the Flemish courtesan.

The body was then placed on a magnificent car, or hearse, drawn by four horses. It was accompanied by a long train of ecclesiastics and nobles, who, together with the queen, left the city on the night of the 20th of December. She made her journeys by night, saying that a widow, who had lost the sun of her own soul, should never expose herself to the light of day. When she halted, the body was deposited in some church or monastery, where the funeral services were performed as if her husband had just died; and a corps of armed men kept constant guard, chiefly, as it would seem, with the view of preventing any female from profaning the place by her presence.

For Juana still retained the same jealousy of her sex which she had unhappily had so much cause to feel during Philip's lifetime.

In a subsequent journey, when at a short distance from Torquemada, she ordered the corpse to be carried into the courtyard of a convent, occupied, as she supposed, by monks. She was filled with horror, however, on finding it a nunnery, and immediately commanded the body to be removed into the open fields. Here she encamped with her whole party at dead of night; not, however, until she had caused the coffins to be unsealed, that she might satisfy herself of the safety of her husband's relics; although it was very difficult to keep the torches, during the time, from being extinguished by the violence of the wind, and leaving the company in total darkness.[1]

These mad pranks, savouring of absolute idiocy, were occasionally checkered by other acts of more intelligence, but not less startling. She had early shown a disgust to her father's old counsellors, and especially to Ximenes, who, she thought, interfered too authoritatively in her domestic concerns. Before leaving Burgos, however, she electrified her husband's adherents by revoking all grants made by the crown since Isabella's death. This, almost the only act she was ever known to sign, was a severe blow to the courtly tribe of sycophants on whom the golden favours of the late reign had been so prodigally showered. At the same time she reformed her privy council by dismissing the present members.

These partial gleams of intelligence, directed in this peculiar way, led many to discern the secret influence of her father. She still, however, pertinaciously refused to sanction any measures of cortes for his recall; and when pressed by that body on this and other matters, at an audience which she granted before leaving Burgos, she plainly told them "to return to their quarters, and not to meddle further in the public business without her express commands." Not long after this, the legislature was prorogued by the royal council for four months.

THE RETURN OF FERDINAND

The term assigned for the provisional government expired in December, and was not renewed. No other regency was appointed by the nobles; and the kingdom, without even the shadow of protection afforded by its cortes, and with no other guide but its crazy sovereign, was left to drift at random amidst the winds and waves of faction. This was not slow in brewing in every quarter, with the aid especially of the overgrown nobles, whose license, on such occasions as this, proved too plainly that public tranquillity was not founded so much on the stability of law as on the personal character of the reigning sovereign.

The king's enemies, in the meantime, were pressing their correspondence with the emperor Maximilian, and urging his immediate presence in Spain. Others devised schemes for marrying the poor queen to the young duke of

---

[1] A foolish Carthusian monk, "*levi sicco folio levior,*" to borrow Martyr's[1] words, though more knave than fool probably, filled Juana with absurd hopes of her husband's returning to life, which, he assured her, had happened, as he had read, to a certain prince, after he had been dead fourteen years. As Philip was disembowelled, he was hardly in a condition for such an auspicious event. The queen, however, seems to have been caught with the idea. Martyr loses all patience at the inventions of this "*blactero cucullatus,*" as he calls him, in his abominable Latin, as well as at the mad pranks of the queen, and the ridiculous figure which he and the other grave personages of the court were compelled to make on the occasion. It is impossible to read his jeremiads on the subject without a smile.

Calabria, or some other prince, whose years or incapacity might enable them to act over again the farce of King Philip. To add to the troubles occasioned by this mesh of intrigue and faction, the country, which of late years had suffered from scarcity, was visited by a pestilence that fell most heavily on the south.

But although the storm was thus darkening from every quarter, there was no general explosion, to shake the state to its foundations, as in the time of Henry IV. Orderly habits, if not principles, had been gradually formed under the long reign of Isabella. The great mass of the people had learned to respect the operation and appreciate the benefits of law; and notwithstanding the menacing attitude, the bustle, and transitory ebullitions of the rival factions, there seemed a manifest reluctance to break up the established order of things, and by deeds of violence and bloodshed to renew the days of ancient anarchy.

Much of this good result was undoubtedly to be attributed to the vigorous counsels and conduct of Ximenes, who, together with the grand constable and the duke of Alva, had received full powers from Ferdinand to act in his name. Much is also to be ascribed to the politic conduct of the king. Far from an intemperate zeal to resume the sceptre of Castile, he had shown throughout a discreet forbearance. The great mass of the common people, too, notwithstanding the temporary alienation of their feelings from the Catholic king by his recent marriage, were driven by the evils they actually suffered, and the vague apprehension of greater, to participate in the same sentiments; so that, in less than eight months from Philip's death, the whole nation may be said to have returned to its allegiance to its ancient sovereign. The only considerable exceptions were Don Juan Manuel and the duke of Najara. The former had gone too far to recede, and the latter possessed too chivalrous or too stubborn a temper to do so.

At length, the Catholic monarch, having completed his arrangements at Naples, and waited until the affairs of Castile were fully ripe for his return, set sail from his Italian capital, June 4th, 1507. He proposed to touch at the Genoese port of Savona, where an interview had been arranged between him and Louis XII. On the 28th of June the royal fleet of Aragon entered the little port of Savona, where the king of France had already been waiting for it several days. During their interview the monarchs held repeated conferences. The subject of discussion can only be conjectured by the subsequent proceedings, which make it probable that it related to Italy; and that it was in this season of idle dalliance and festivity that the two princes who held the destinies of that country in their hands matured the famous League of Cambray, so disastrous to Venice, and reflecting little credit on its projectors, either on the score of good faith or sound policy.

At length, after enjoying for four days the splendid hospitality of their royal entertainer, the king and queen of Aragon re-embarked, and reached their own port of Valencia, after various detentions, on the 20th of July, 1507. Ferdinand pressed forward to Castile. How different from the forlorn and outcast condition in which he had quitted the country a short year before! He intimated the change in his own circumstances by the greater state and show of authority which he now assumed.

At Tortoles he was met by the queen, his daughter, accompanied by Archbishop Ximenes. The interview between them had more of pain than pleasure in it. The king was greatly shocked by Juana's appearance; for her wild and haggard features, emaciated figure, and the mean, squalid attire in which she was dressed, made it difficult to recognise any trace of the daughter from whom he had been so long separated. She discovered more sensibility on seeing him than she had shown since her husband's death, and henceforth resigned herself to her father's will with little opposition. She was soon after induced by him to change her unsuitable residence for more commodious quarters at Tordesillas. Her husband's remains were laid in the monastery of Santa Clara, adjoining the palace, from whose windows she could behold his sepulchre. From this period, although she survived forty-seven years, she never quitted the walls of her habitation; and although her name appeared jointly with that of her son, Charles V, in all public acts, she never afterwards could be induced to sign a paper, or take part in any transactions of a public nature. She lingered out a half century of dreary existence, as completely dead to the world as the remains which slept in the monastery of Santa Clara beside her.[b]

WAS QUEEN JUANA INSANE?

The pendulum of historical criticism to which we have had such frequent occasion to refer has swung back to the original tradition in another instance. Juana was generally accounted mad by her contemporaries though she had admittedly intervals of lucid thought. In the latter half of the nineteenth century papers were turned up which emphasised her aspects of sanity and the theory was raised that she was the victim of slander and cruelty.

It was claimed that her only abnormality was her freedom from the bigotry that bloodied the reign of her father and mother ; and that it was her stay in Flanders that liberalised her creed. This theory fascinated the iconoclasts who always hunt the evil side of a glorious period, and her mother and father were openly accused of a hideous disregard of the first instincts of humanity, of blackening her fame and robbing her of her royal heritage. The motive of this unnatural crime imputed to Ferdinand and Isabella was given as a mixture of religious intolerance and of selfishness, though it might as well have been said that they called her insane to keep her from undergoing the torture and fire of the Inquisition which ransacked the kingdom for the most minute heterodoxy. Burke[k] especially is unsparing in his denunciations of a cruelty which could not be exceeded if true. He claims that Ferdinand's letters show that he knew Juana to be sane, but simply "unmanageable as she had ever been."

But in this instance as in so many others, the histories of a few years ago are put out of date and the histories of long ago brought again into timeliness. The story of Juana's rise and fall in history is as follows :[a]

For a long time writers who spoke of Juana the Mad stuck to tradition without going back to the original documents. It was only in 1858 that important documents were discovered in the archives at Simancas. Most of them confirmed tradition, but some of them left doubts in the mind of a German scholar, Bergenroth,[u] who collected and published them with an interesting dissertation in the "state papers." Interpreting these documents, which were incomplete and often ambiguous, in a way contrary to general opinion, he tried to prove that Juana was not insane, but that she was rather the victim of the ambition and fanaticism of her father and of her son.

We are to-day better informed, having contemporary texts, some from Simancas, others from the archives of the historical academy at Madrid, others from private collections. An eminent Spanish writer, Rodriguez

Villa,[v] has collected, and commented upon them in a work which one may safely affirm says the last word on this subject and completely contradicts Bergenroth's opinions. The new historian on the one hand introduces elements hitherto unknown into the question, on the other explains differently those which were known. His circumstantial account, well supported by facts, upholds tradition for the most part and exculpates Ferdinand the Catholic as well as Charles V of the accusation brought against them. In the meantime Gachard [w] had shown like tendencies in a monograph on the subject, and De la Fuente [x] in a substantial pamphlet had peremptorily denied the heretical opinions attributed to the queen of Castile.

The facts are doubly interesting, first because of their romance and peculiar nature, secondly because of their intimate relations with political events which, at the end of the fifteenth and beginning of the sixteenth century, changed the internal form and diplomatic policy of the Spanish monarchy.

As to the real causes of her mental state, they cannot of course be determined with actual certainty, being hidden in the depths of the human organism. Villa [v] considers that Juana became "mad through love," exasperated first by the infidelities of her husband.

Juana's early life had passed in peaceful obscurity. She received a careful and kind training. Did she at that time show any distressing symptoms? Nothing precisely indicates such a thing. If, to judge from certain anxieties afterwards manifested by Isabella, it would seem possible that such symptoms might have appeared, one may suppose that they were considered at that time as passing incidents and of no importance. It is difficult to portray her physically or mentally at the time of her marriage. There is a portrait of her made a few years later when cares had already begun to mark her face.

It is a picture in the somewhat stiff style of the first Flemish school. The features are fairly regular, a forehead high and a little prominent, long eyes with no brilliancy, nose and mouth without character. There are no striking defects, nor is there beauty of line or of colour. A sad physiognomy, the eyes reveal only a kind of intellectual lassitude, a vague and dolorous obstinacy. Force and vitality seem to have been pressed inward and the soul appears drowned in a morbid dream; the whole face, half archaic, remains a puzzle. The features are without doubt those of Juana, but immobile and cold. The portrait shows only a melancholy woman, without charm, sickly, and lacking in thought.[y]

Isabella and Ferdinand wanted their son-in-law, Philip, to become acquainted with the country over which he would some time rule. But the measure of family misfortune which balanced the weighty political success of the Catholic kings was not yet full. The first months of the stay of Juana and Philip in Spain brought indeed only rejoicing and splendour. In Toledo the Castilian cortes proclaimed allegiance, in Barcelona the Aragonese. But the archduke Philip soon tired of Spanish life, he longed to get back to Flanders. Juana could not follow him on account of the state of her health. In vain she pleaded, in vain her parents urged the flighty gentleman not to leave her so pitilessly.

Juana had already shown the beginnings of melancholia, accompanied by outbreaks of jealousy over her inconstant husband to whom she offered few attractions. What would happen if he separated himself from her might have been foreseen; but nothing could keep him. Then a deep melancholy settled upon the poor soul. " She does not raise her eyes from the ground," writes Peter Martyr [l] in the first days of 1503. "Wealth, power, dominion even her parents are of no account to her. With clouded brow she thinks only of her husband, he only is her care and passion."

In the spring of 1504 it became necessary to let her have her way and go to the Netherlands. Here Philip's heartlessness deepened the cloud of darkness which obscured the brain of the poor unfortunate, which had never been very strong. This sad news gave the last blow to Queen Isabella, who had long been failing; on November 26th, 1504, this woman who had created Spanish power died.

Juana was now queen of Castile. The cortes took the oath of allegiance to her and her husband, but at the same time in accordance with Isabella's will, since Juana was not able to govern, recognised her father Ferdinand as regent. Juana declared herself perfectly willing to have her father govern for her. But Philip was deeply offended, placed his poor wife under strict surveillance, and made up his mind to get the rule over Castile into his own hands, pretending that he, as Juana's husband, had better right to it than her father. In April, 1506, he appeared with her in Spain. But on September 25th, 1506, the last hour sounded for the young king, and his widow sank into the depth of insanity.*aa*

Had Juana's insanity been accidental it would not have affected her descendants. Heredity here is incontestable. Most of the symptoms we have seen in the queen appeared in different degrees and in different forms in her posterity. Was it not she, was it not her shade which lived again in the old Charles V, who was tormented with peculiar attacks during his reign, and then condemned himself to a cloister out of a morose caprice, disgusted with everything, not from philosophy but from the continuity of his lugubrious dreams?

Do we not find her again in the fierce Philip II, like her seeking solitude and darkness in the depths of the Escurial where he combined his sinister policy with a sickly obstinacy? Is it not again Juana's diseased mind which comes to life in the young Don Carlos, like her a prey to a derangement sometimes furious, sometimes melancholy? He also was confined and kept from sight; but was more fortunate than his grandmother, having been more promptly delivered by death. Consider also the cerebral anæmia which manifested itself in Philip III and Philip IV, both of them weak physically and mentally, in fever and melancholy; and in the pale spectre of Charles II, in the exhaustion of his vitality and intermittent hallucinations. These are not coincidences, they are the results of the transmission, historically attested, of an organic vice, which is reproduced from generation to generation by analogous phenomena.

It was the awful fate of Juana, endowed at her birth with all the gifts of fortune, to endure for fifty years the most lugubrious and degraded fate imaginable. Other persons may have had more dramatic reverses, but they at least moved in the current of events of their age; they lived and acted in the human mêlée. The daughter of Ferdinand and Isabella passed long years of suffering and neglect in ignorance of contemporary events, sufficiently intelligent to comprehend her mental feebleness but powerless to act against it; buried alive, so to speak, at once feverish and inert, condemned by her own weakness, and bowed down by the weight of fatality, struggling in vain against the clouds of her intellect and the torments of her life.

But we, while recognising that these events had a fateful effect on the brain of the princess, cannot accept this explanation in full. We must not forget that her grandmother on her mother's side had been confined on account of insanity at the castle of Arevalos; also before marriage she caused disquietude to her family, which was kept secret. Ferdinand and Isabella had certainly noticed strange predispositions in her mind ; they did not emphasise them, hoping that time, marriage, and distraction might attenuate them, but it is an incontestable fact that they never showed any surprise when their agents informed them of later events — they spoke of them as natural results of a diseased state they had long suspected.*y*

FERDINAND'S SECOND REGENCY (1507-1516 A.D.)

Ferdinand's second administration was signalised by the same splendid effects as the first. In 1509, at the suggestion of Cardinal Ximenes, he proposed an expedition against Oran on the African coast. The cardinal not only defrayed the expenses, but accompanied it. It was completely successful : Oran was stormed, and forced to receive a Christian garrison. The following year, Bugia, a city on the same coast, was reduced; Algiers, Tunis, Tremecen, and other places, consented that their native governors should be the vassals of Ferdinand. Another expedition reduced Tripoli.

In 1511, he himself was preparing to embark with a formidable armament, to pursue his conquests in that country, — conquests, however, which his own experience proved to be fleeting, — when he was pressed by Pope Julius to aid the church against the schismatics under the protection of the king of France and the emperor. As he was even more proud of his title of Catholic king than desirous of glory, he despatched an armed force to aid the chief of the church. Into the interminable affairs of Italy, however, — the critical wars which Ferdinand carried on in that country in defence of his Sicilian and Neapolitan possessions, — we cannot enter in this place; they will be found in the Italian volume. It is sufficient here to observe that the war was for some time in favour of the French (the emperor had withdrawn from them), and that the papal allies were defeated.

But this war led to one memorable result, and one not very glorious to Ferdinand. Wishing to carry hostilities into France, he demanded from Jean d'Albret, king of Navarre, permission to march his troops through that country. The Navarrese refused, but at the same time professed his determination in no way to aid the French monarch, and to remain perfectly neutral. Scarcely, however, had he given this answer, than he entered into an alliance, offensive and defensive, with the French king. Resolving to attain his end by force and to punish the duplicity of the Navarrese, Ferdinand assembled his forces at Vittoria, invaded Navarre, and in a short time obtained possession of the whole kingdom, the royal family taking refuge in France. This new conquest he annexed to his kingdom of Aragon, and successfully defended it against the invasion of the French. From the blood-stained house of Foix the sceptre had forever departed ; nor could all the armies of France, during the reigns of the emperor Charles and his son Philip, restore it to the descendants of Jean.

The conquest of Navarre, however necessary to the tranquillity of Spain, can be characterised in no other terms than as an act of unblushing rapacity ; yet attempts have been made to justify it, and by writers who would not willingly be considered the advocates of a criminal abuse of power. According to Peter Martyr,*l* the king of Navarre had been excommunicated by the pope as a schismatic, — as one of the league formed by the emperor and France against the papal pretentions to the duchy of Ferrara, — and bulls, absolving the Navarrese from their oath of allegiance, deposing Jean, and conferring the kingdom on the first that took possession of it, were sent to Ferdinand; in other words, the enterprise was sanctioned by the head of the church in gratitude for the aid which, in conjunction with the Venetians, he afforded the successor of St. Peter. As such a title, however, will not be admitted at this day even beyond the Pyrenees, the conquest must be designated as one of the most flagitious transactions of a lawless age.

Towards the close of his life, Ferdinand still indulged the hope of seeing an heir who should inherit Aragon, Navarre, Naples, and Sicily. This wish arose both from his dislike to the emperor, the grandfather of the archduke Charles, and the whole house of Austria, and from the aversion shown by his hereditary subjects to a union of the crowns. In 1509 his young queen had been delivered of a son, who died in a few days. In 1513 he took a potion which he was persuaded would restore his masculine vigour, but which destroyed his constitution, and produced a lingering illness, that ended in death. In his last will he declared his daughter Juana heiress to all his dominions in Spain and Italy, and after her his grandson Charles. The regency of Castile, until his grandson should arrive in Spain, he confided to Cardinal Ximenes; and that of Aragon, with the states dependent on it, to his natural son, the archbishop of Saragossa.*d*

DEATH AND CHARACTER OF FERDINAND

On the evening of the 22nd of January, 1516, he executed the instrument; and a few hours later, between one and two of the morning of the 23rd, Ferdinand breathed his last. The scene of this event was a small house belonging to the friars of Guadalupe. " In so wretched a tenement," exclaims Martyr,*l* in his usual moralising vein, " did this lord of so many lands close his eyes upon the world."

Ferdinand was nearly sixty-four years old, of which forty-one had elapsed since he first swayed the sceptre of Castile, and thirty-seven since he held that of Aragon. A long reign; long enough, indeed, to see most of those whom he had honoured and trusted of his subjects gathered to the dust, and a succession of contemporary monarchs come and disappear like shadows. Since Ferdinand had ascended the throne, he had seen no less than four kings of England, as many of France, and also of Naples, three of Portugal, two German emperors, and half-a-dozen popes. As to his own subjects, scarcely one of all those familiar to the reader in the course of Spanish history now survived, except, indeed, the Nestor of his time, the octogenarian Cardinal Ximenes.

He died deeply lamented by his native subjects, who entertained a partiality natural towards their own hereditary sovereign. The event was regarded with very different feelings by the Castilian nobles, who calculated their gains on the transfer of the reins from such old and steady hands into those of a young and inexperienced master. The commons, however, who had felt the good effect of this curb on the nobility in their own personal security, held his memory in reverence as that of a national benefactor.

By his dying injunctions all unnecessary ostentation was interdicted at his funeral. His body was laid by the side of Isabella's in the monastery of the Alhambra; and the year following, when the royal chapel of the metropolitan church was completed, they were both transported thither. A magnificent mausoleum of white marble was erected over them by their grandson, Charles V.

W. H. — VOL. X. O

Of King Ferdinand's personal appearance Marineo,[m] a contemporary who knew him well, says: "He was of the middle size. His complexion was fresh; his eyes bright and animated; his nose and mouth small and finely formed, and his teeth white; his forehead lofty and serene; with flowing hair of a bright chestnut colour. His manners were courteous, and his countenance was seldom clouded by anything like spleen or melancholy. He was grave in speech and action, and had a marvellous dignity of presence. His whole demeanour, in fine, was truly that of a great king." He was esteemed one of the most perfect horsemen of his court.

He was naturally of an equable temper, and inclined to moderation in all things. The only amusement for which he cared much was hunting, especially falconry. He was indefatigable in application to business. He had no relish for the pleasures of the table, and, like Isabella, was temperate even to abstemiousness in his diet. He was frugal in his domestic and personal expenditure; partly, no doubt, from a willingness to rebuke the opposite spirit of wastefulness and ostentation in his nobles. He lost no good opportunity of doing this. No one has accused him of attempting to enrich his exchequer by the venal sale of offices, like Louis XII; or by griping extortion, like another royal contemporary, Henry VII. He amassed no treasure, and, indeed, died so poor that he left scarcely enough in his coffers to defray the charges of his funeral.

Ferdinand was devout; at least he was scrupulous in regard to the exterior of religion. He was punctual in attendance on mass, careful to observe all the ordinances and ceremonies of his church, and left many tokens of his piety, after the fashion of the time, in sumptuous edifices and endowments for religious purposes. Although not a superstitious man for the age, he is certainly obnoxious to the reproach of bigotry; for he spared no effort to fasten the odious yoke of the Inquisition on Aragon; and subsequently, though happily with less success, on Naples.

Ferdinand has incurred the more serious charge of hypocrisy. His Catholic zeal was observed to be marvellously efficacious in furthering his temporal interests. His most objectionable enterprises even were covered with a veil of religion. In this, however, he did not materially differ from the practice of the age. Some of the most scandalous wars of that period were ostensibly at the bidding of the church, or in defence of Christendom against the infidel. This ostentation of a religious motive was indeed very usual with the Spanish and Portuguese.

It will not be so easy to acquit Ferdinand of the reproach of perfidy which foreign writers have so deeply branded on his name, and which those of his own nation have sought rather to palliate than to deny. It is but fair to him, however, even here, to take a glance at the age. He came forward when government was in a state of transition from the feudal forms to those which it has assumed in modern times; when the superior strength of the great vassals was circumvented by the superior policy of the reigning princes. It was the dawn of the triumph of intellect over the brute force which had hitherto controlled the movements of nations, as of individuals. The same policy which these monarchs had pursued in their own domestic relations they introduced into those with foreign states, when, at the close of the fifteenth century, the barriers that had so long kept them asunder were broken down. Italy was the first field on which the great powers were brought into anything like a general collision. It was the country, too, in which this crafty policy had been first studied and reduced to a regular system.

Such was the school in which Ferdinand was to make trial of his skill with his brother monarchs.[1] He played the game with more adroitness than his opponents, and he won it. Success, as usual, brought on him the reproaches of the losers.

Ferdinand, unfortunately for his popularity, had nothing of the frank and cordial temper, the genial expansion of the soul which begets love. He carried the same cautious and impenetrable frigidity into private life that he showed in public. "No one," says Giovio,[n] a writer of the time, "could read his thoughts by any change of his countenance." Calm and calculating, even in trifles, it was too obvious that everything had exclusive reference to self. He seemed to estimate his friends only by the amount of services they could render him. He was not always mindful of these services. Witness his ungenerous treatment of Columbus, the great captain, Navarro, Ximenes — the men who shed the brightest lustre and the most substantial benefits on his reign. Witness also his insensibility to the virtues and long attachment of Isabella, whose memory he could so soon dishonour by a union with one every way unworthy to be her successor.

Ferdinand's connection with Isabella, while it reflected infinite glory on his reign, suggests a contrast most unfavourable to his character. Hers was all magnanimity, disinterestedness, and deep devotion to the interests of her people. His was the spirit of egotism. The circle of his views might be more or less expanded, but self was the steady, unchangeable centre. Her heart beat with the generous sympathies of friendship, and the purest constancy to the first, the only object of her love. We have seen the measure of his sensibilities in other relations. They were not more refined in this ; and he proved himself unworthy of the admirable woman with whom his destinies were united, by indulging in those vicious gallantries too generally sanctioned by the age. Ferdinand, in fine, a shrewd and politic prince, " surpassing," as a French writer, Varillas,[o] not his friend, has remarked, " all the statesmen of his time in the science of the cabinet," may be taken as the representative of the peculiar genius of the age ; while Isabella, discarding all the petty artifices of state policy, and pursuing the noblest ends by the noblest means, stands far above her age.

In his illustrious consort Ferdinand may be said to have lost his good genius. From that time his fortunes were under a cloud. Not that victory sat less constantly on his banner ; but his ill-advised marriage disgusted his Castilian subjects. The beauty of his young queen opened new sources of jealousy ; while the disparity of their ages, and her fondness for frivolous pleasure, as little qualified her to be his partner in prosperity as his solace in declining years. His tenacity of power drew him into vulgar squabbles with those most nearly allied to him by blood, which settled into a mortal aversion. Finally, bodily infirmity broke the energies of his mind, sour suspicions corroded his heart, and he had the misfortune to live long after he had lost all that could make life desirable.

Let us turn from this gloomy picture to the brighter season of the morning and meridian of his life ; when he sat with Isabella on the united thrones of Castile and Aragon, strong in the love of his own subjects, and in the fear and respect of his enemies. We shall then find much in his character to admire — his impartial justice in the administration of the laws, his watchful solicitude to shield the weak from the oppression of the strong ; his wise

[1 Martin Hume[t] credits Ferdinand with being the founder of the school of diplomacy ordinarily called Italian. He blames him also for commencing the long wars between the Spanish and the French.]

economy, which achieved great results without burdening his people with oppressive taxes; his sobriety and moderation; the decorum, and respect for religion, which he maintained among his subjects; the industry he promoted by wholesome laws and his own example; his consummate sagacity, which crowned all his enterprises with brilliant success, and made him the oracle of the princes of the age.

Macchiavelli,*p* indeed, the most deeply read of his time in human character, imputes Ferdinand's successes, in one of his letters, to "cunning and good-luck rather than superior wisdom"; but has recorded a riper and more deliberate judgment in the treatise which he intended as a mirror for the rulers of the time. "Nothing," says he, "gains estimation for a prince like great enterprises. Our own age has furnished a splendid example of this in Ferdinand of Aragon. We may call him a new king, since from a feeble one he has made himself the most renowned and glorious monarch of Christendom; and, if we ponder well his manifold achievements, we must acknowledge all of them very great, and some truly extraordinary."

THE REGENCY OF CARDINAL XIMENES

The personal history of Ferdinand the Catholic terminates, of course, here. In order to bring the history of his reign, however, to a suitable close, it is necessary to continue the narrative through the brief regency of Ximenes, to the period when the government was delivered into the hands of Ferdinand's grandson and successor, Charles V.

By the testament of the deceased monarch, as we have seen, Cardinal Ximenes de Cisneros was appointed sole regent of Castile. He met with opposition, however, from Adrian, the dean of Louvain, who produced powers of similar purport from Prince Charles. The misunderstanding which ensued was finally settled by an agreement to share the authority till further instructions should be received from Charles. It was not long before they arrived (February 14th, 1516). They confirmed the cardinal's authority in the fullest manner, while they spoke of Adrian only as an ambassador.

The first requisition of Prince Charles was one that taxed severely the power and popularity of the new regent. This was to have himself proclaimed king; a measure extremely distasteful to the Castilians, who regarded it not only as contrary to established usage, during the lifetime of his mother, but as an indignity to her. It was in vain that Ximenes and the council remonstrated on the impropriety and impolicy of the measure. Charles, fortified by his Flemish advisers, sturdily persisted in his purpose. Ximenes peremptorily declared: "I will have him proclaimed in Madrid to-morrow, and I doubt not every other city in the kingdom will follow the example." He was as good as his word; and the conduct of the capital was imitated with little opposition, by all the other cities in Castile.

One of the regent's first acts was the famous ordinance encouraging the burgesses, by liberal rewards, to enrol themselves into companies, and submit to regular military training at stated seasons; and a national corps was organised, competent, under proper guidance, to protect the liberties of the people, but destined, unfortunately, to be ultimately turned against them. Armed with this strong physical force, the cardinal now projected the boldest schemes of reform, especially in the finances, which had fallen into some disorder in the latter days of Ferdinand. Unfortunately, the state was not materially benefited by these economical arrangements, since the greater part of what was thus saved was drawn off to supply the waste and cupidity of the Flemish court, who dealt with Spain with all the merciless rapacity that could be shown to a conquered province. The foreign administration of the regent displayed the same courage and vigour. Arsenals were established in the southern maritime towns, and a numerous fleet was equipped in the Mediterranean against the Barbary corsairs. A large force was sent into Navarre, which defeated an invading army of French (March 25th, 1516); and the cardinal followed up the blow by demolishing the principal fortresses of the kingdom; a precautionary measure, to which, in all probability, Spain owes the permanent preservation of her conquest.

It is with less satisfaction that we must contemplate his policy in regard to the Inquisition. As head of that tribunal, he enforced its authority and pretensions to the utmost. He extended a branch of it to Oran, and also to the Canaries and the New World. In 1512, the "new Christians" had offered Ferdinand a large sum of money to carry on the Navarrese war, if he would cause the trials before that tribunal to be conducted in the same manner as in other courts, where the accuser and the evidence were confronted openly with the defendant. To this reasonable petition Ximenes objected, on the wretched plea that, in that

CARDINAL XIMENES

event, none would be found willing to undertake the odious business of reformer. He backed his remonstrance with such a liberal donative from his own funds as supplied the king's immediate exigency and effectually closed his heart against the petitioners.

The cardinal not only assumed the sole responsibility of the most important public acts, but, in the execution of them, seldom condescended to calculate the obstacles or the odds arrayed against him. He was thus brought into collision, at the same time, with three of the most powerful grandees of Castile — the dukes of Alva and Infantado, and the count of Ureña. They took refuge in the little town of Villafrata, which they fortified and prepared for a defence. The cardinal without hesitation mustered several thousand of the national militia, and, investing the place, set it on fire and deliberately razed it to the ground. The refractory nobles, struck with consternation, submitted.

But neither the talents nor authority of Ximenes, it was evident, could much longer maintain subordination among the people, exasperated by the shameless extortions of the Flemings, and the little interest shown for them by their new sovereign. The most considerable offices in church and state were put up to sale ; and the kingdom was drained of its funds by the large remittances continually made, on one pretext or another, to Flanders. On the 17th of September, 1517, Charles landed at Villaviciosa, in the Asturias. Ximenes at this time lay ill at the Franciscan monastery of Aguilera, near Aranda on the Douro. The good tidings of the royal landing operated like a cordial on his spirits, and he instantly despatched letters to the young monarch, filled with wholesome counsel as to the conduct he should pursue in order to conciliate the affections of the people.

Charles showed a facility to be directed by those around him in early years, which gave little augury of the greatness to which he afterwards rose. By the persuasions of his evil counsellors, he addressed that memorable letter to Ximenes, which is unmatched, even in court annals, for cool and base ingratitude. He thanked the regent for all his past services, named a place for a personal interview with him, where he might obtain the benefit of his counsels for his own conduct and the government of the kingdom ; after which he would be allowed to retire to his diocese and seek from heaven that reward which heaven alone could adequately bestow !

Such was the tenor of this cold-blooded epistle, which, in the language of more than one writer, killed the cardinal. This, however, is stating the matter too strongly. The spirit of Ximenes was of too stern a stuff to be so easily extinguished by the breath of royal displeasure. He was, indeed, deeply moved by the desertion of the sovereign whom he had served so faithfully, and the excitement which it occasioned brought on a return of his fever, according to Carbajal,∫ in full force. But anxiety and disease had already done their work upon his once hardy constitution.[1]

DEATH AND CHARACTER OF XIMENES

Death may be supposed to have but little terrors for the statesman who in his last moments could aver that he had never intentionally wronged any man, but had rendered to everyone his due, without being swayed, so far as he was conscious, by fear or affection. Yet Cardinal Richelieu on his deathbed declared the same.

As a last attempt he began a letter to the king. His fingers refused, however, to perform their office, and after tracing a few lines he gave it up. The purport of these seems to have been to recommend his university at Alcalá to the royal protection. He now became wholly occupied with his devotions, and manifested such contrition for his errors, and such humble confidence in the divine mercy, as deeply affected all present. In this tranquil frame of mind, and in the perfect possession of his powers, he breathed his last, November 8th, 1517, in the eighty-first year of his age and the twenty-second since his elevation to the primacy.

Such was the end of this remarkable man; the most remarkable, in many respects, of his time. His character was of that stern and lofty cast which seems to rise above the ordinary wants and weaknesses of humanity; his genius, of the severest order, like Dante's or Michelangelo's in the regions of fancy, impresses us with ideas of power that excite admiration akin to terror. His enterprises were of the boldest character; his execution of them equally bold. He disdained to woo fortune by any of those soft and pliant arts which are often the most effectual. He pursued his ends by the most direct

[1 Oviedo ᵍ notices a rumour of his having been poisoned by one of his secretaries but vouches for the innocence of the individual accused, whom he personally knew.]

means. In this way he frequently multiplied difficulties; but difficulties seemed to have a charm for him, by the opportunities they afforded of displaying the energies of his soul.

With these qualities he combined a versatility of talent usually found only in softer and more flexible characters. Though bred in the cloister, he distinguished himself both in the cabinet and the camp. For the latter, indeed, so repugnant to his regular profession, he had a natural genius, according to the testimony of his biographer Gomez; *q* and he evinced his relish for it by declaring that "the smell of gunpowder was more grateful to him than the sweetest perfume of Arabia!" He had a full measure of the religious bigotry which belonged to the age; and he had melancholy scope for displaying it, as chief of that dread tribunal over which he presided during the last ten years of his life.

He carried the arbitrary ideas of his profession into political life. His regency was conducted on the principles of a military despotism. It was his maxim that "a prince must rely mainly on his army for securing the respect and obedience of his subjects." It is true he had to deal with a martial and factious nobility, and the end which he proposed was to curb their licentiousness and enforce the equitable administration of justice; but, in accomplishing this, he showed little regard to the constitution, or to private rights.

His first act, the proclaiming of Charles king, was in open contempt of the usages and rights of the nation. He evaded the urgent demands of the Castilians for a convocation of cortes; for it was his opinion that freedom of speech, especially in regard to their own grievances, made the people insolent and irreverent to their rulers. The people, of course, had no voice in the measures which involved their most important interests. His whole policy, indeed, was to exalt the royal prerogative at the expense of the inferior orders of the state; and his regency, short as it was, and highly beneficial to the country in many respects, must be considered as opening the way to that career of despotism which the Austrian family followed up with such hard-hearted constancy.

His administration provoked numerous lampoons and libels. He despised them, as the miserable solace of spleen and discontent, and never persecuted their authors. In this he formed an honourable contrast to Cardinal Richelieu, whose character and condition suggest many points of resemblance with his own.

An anecdote is told in relation to his dress. Over his coarse woollen frock he wore the costly apparel suited to his rank. An impertinent Franciscan preacher took occasion one day before him to launch out against the luxuries of the time, especially in dress, obviously alluding to the cardinal, who was attired in a superb suit of ermine, which had been presented to him. He heard the sermon patiently to the end, and, after the services were concluded, took the preacher into the sacristy, and, having commended the general tenor of his discourse, showed under his furs and fine linen the coarse frock of his order next his skin. Some accounts add that the friar, on the other hand, wore fine linen under his monkish frock. After the cardinal's death, a little box was found in his apartment, containing the implements with which he used to mend the rents of his threadbare garment with his own hands.

He seldom slept more than four hours, or at most four and a half. He was shaved in the night, hearing at the same time some edifying reading. He followed the same practice at his meals, or varied it with listening to the arguments of some of his theological brethren, generally on some subtile question of school divinity. This was his only recreation. He had as little taste as time for lighter and more elegant amusements.

THE TWO CHIEF WORKS OF XIMENES

As far back as 1497, Ximenes had conceived the idea of establishing a university in the ancient town of Alcalá, where the salubrity of the air, and the sober, tranquil complexion of the scenery, on the beautiful borders of the Henares, seemed well suited to academic study and meditation. Other engagements, however, postponed the commencement of the work till 1500, when the cardinal himself laid the corner-stone of the principal college, with a solemn ceremonial. From that hour, amidst all the engrossing cares of church and state, he never lost sight of this great object.[1] The city of Alcalá underwent many important and expensive alterations, in order to render it more worthy of being the seat of a great and flourishing university. The stagnant water was carried off by drains, the streets were paved, old buildings removed, and new and spacious avenues thrown open.

At the expiration of eight years, the cardinal had the satisfaction of seeing the whole of this vast design completed, and every apartment of the spacious pile carefully furnished with all that was requisite for the comfort and accommodation of the student. It was, indeed, a noble enterprise, more particularly when viewed as the work of a private individual. As such it raised the deepest admiration in Francis I, when he visited the spot, a few years after the cardinal's death. " Your Ximenes," he said, "has executed more than I should have dared to conceive; he has done, with his single hand, what in France it has taken a line of kings to accomplish."

Two provisions may be noticed as characteristic of the man : one, that the salary of a professor should be regulated by the number of his disciples ; another, that every professor should be re-eligible at the expiration of every four years. It was impossible that any servant of Ximenes should sleep on his post. Liberal foundations were made for indigent students, especially in divinity. Indeed, theological studies, or rather such a general course of study as should properly enter into the education of a Christian minister, was the avowed object of the institution ; for the Spanish clergy up to this period, as before noticed, were too often deficient in the most common elements of learning. But in this preparatory discipline the comprehensive mind of Ximenes embraced nearly the whole circle of sciences taught in other universities.

In July, 1508, the cardinal received the welcome intelligence that his academy was open for the admission of pupils ; and in the following month the first lecture, being on Aristotle's *Ethics*, was publicly delivered. Students soon flocked to the new university, attracted by the reputation of its professors, its ample apparatus, its thorough system of instruction, and, above all, its splendid patronage, and the high character of its founder. We have no information of their number in Ximenes' life-time ; but it must have been very considerable, since no less than seven thousand came out to receive Francis I, on his visit to the university, within twenty years after it was opened.

In the midst of his pressing duties, Ximenes found time for the execution

[1 "Neither to the buildings nor the endowment did queen or king contribute a single maravedi." k]

of another work, which would alone have been sufficient to render his name immortal in the republic of letters. This was his famous Bible, or Complutensian Polyglot, as usually termed, from the place where it was printed.[1] It was on the plan, first conceived by Origen, of exhibiting in one view the Scriptures in their various ancient languages. It was a work of surpassing difficulty, demanding an extensive and critical acquaintance with the most ancient, and consequently the rarest manuscripts. The character and station of the cardinal afforded him, it is true, uncommon facilities. The precious collection of the Vatican was liberally thrown open to him, especially under Leo X, whose munificent spirit delighted in the undertaking. He obtained copies, in like manner, of whatever was of value in the other libraries of Italy, and, indeed, of Europe generally; and Spain supplied him with editions of the Old Testament of great antiquity, which had been treasured up by the banished Israelites. Some idea may be formed of the lavish expenditure in this way, from the fact that four thousand gold crowns were paid for seven foreign manuscripts, which, however, came too late to be of use in the compilation. The difficulties of the undertaking were sensibly increased by those of the printing. The art was then in its infancy, and there were no types in Spain, if indeed in any part of Europe, in the oriental character. Ximenes, however, careful to have the whole executed under his own eye, imported artists from Germany, and had types cast in the various languages required, in his foundries at Alcalá.

The work when completed occupied six volumes folio; the first four devoted to the Old Testament, the fifth to the New; the last containing a Hebrew and Chaldaic vocabulary, with other elementary treaties of singular labour and learning.[2] It was not brought to an end till 1517, fifteen years after its commencement, and a few months only before the death of its illustrious projector.

COMPARISON OF XIMENES AND RICHELIEU

The resemblance which Ximenes bore to the great French minister, Cardinal Richelieu, was, after all, more in the circumstances of situation than in their characters, though the most prominent traits of these were not dissimilar. Both, though bred ecclesiastics, reached the highest honours of the state, and, indeed, may be said to have directed the destinies of their countries. Richelieu's authority, however, was more absolute than that of Ximenes, for he was screened by the shadow of royalty; while the latter was exposed, by his insulated and unsheltered position, to the full blaze of envy, and, of course, opposition. Both were ambitious of military glory, and showed capacity for attaining it. Both achieved their great results by that rare union of high mental endowments and great efficiency in action which is always irresistible.

The moral basis of their characters was entirely different. The French cardinal's was selfishness, pure and unmitigated. His religion, politics, his principles in short, in every sense, were subservient to this. Offences against the state he could forgive; those against himself he pursued with implacable rancour. His authority was literally cemented with blood. His immense powers and patronage were perverted to the aggrandisement of his family.

[1] Alcalá de Henares was called Complutum by the Romans. This name has been variously derived.

[2 The original manuscripts were, it seems, sold as waste paper to a manufacturer of skyrockets, and were destroyed wantonly though brilliantly.]

Though bold to temerity in his plans, he betrayed more than once a want of true courage in their execution. Though violent and impetuous, he could stoop to be a dissembler. Though arrogant in the extreme, he courted the soft incense of flattery. In his manners he had the advantage over the Spanish prelate. He could be a courtier in courts, and had a more refined and cultivated taste. In one respect he had the advantage over Ximenes in morals; he was not, like him, a bigot. He had not the religious basis in his composition which is the foundation of bigotry. Their deaths were typical of their characters. Richelieu died, as he had lived, so deeply execrated that the enraged populace would scarcely allow his remains to be laid quietly in the grave. Ximenes, on the contrary, was buried amid the tears and lamentations of the people; his memory was honoured even by his enemies, and his name is reverenced by his countrymen to this day as that of a saint.

REVIEW OF THE REIGN OF FERDINAND AND ISABELLA

We have now traversed that important period of history comprehending the latter part of the fifteenth and the beginning of the sixteenth century; a period when the convulsions which shook to the ground the ancient political fabrics of Europe roused the minds of its inhabitants from the lethargy in which they had been buried for ages. Spain, as we have seen, felt the general impulse. Under the glorious rule of Ferdinand and Isabella we have beheld her emerging from chaos into a new existence, unfolding, under the influence of institutions adapted to her genius, energies of which she was before unconscious; enlarging her resources from all the springs of domestic industry and commercial enterprise; and insensibly losing the ferocious habits of a feudal age in the refinements of an intellectual and moral culture.

In the fullness of time, when her divided powers had been concentrated under one head, and the system of internal economy completed, we have seen her descend into the arena with the other nations of Europe, and in a very few years achieve the most important acquisitions of territory, both in that quarter and in Africa; and finally crowning the whole by the discovery and occupation of a boundless empire beyond the waters. In the progress of the action we may have been too much occupied with its details to attend sufficiently to the principles which regulated them. But now that we have reached the close, we may be permitted to cast a parting glance over the field that we have traversed, and briefly survey the principal steps by which the Spanish sovereigns led their nation up to such a height of prosperity and glory.

Ferdinand and Isabella, on their accession, saw at once that the chief source of the distractions of the country lay in the overgrown powers and factious spirit of the nobility. Their first efforts, therefore, were directed to abate these as far as possible. A similar movement was going forward in the other European monarchies; but in none was it crowned with so speedy and complete success as in Castile.

Another practice steadily pursued by the sovereigns was to raise men of humble station to offices of the highest trust; not, however, like their contemporary, Louis XI, because their station was humble, in order to mortify the higher orders, but because they courted merit wherever it was to be found — a policy much and deservedly commended by the sagacious observers of the time. The history of Spain does not probably afford another example of a person of the lowly condition of Ximenes attaining, not merely the highest offices in the kingdom, but eventually its uncontrolled supremacy.

The queen's government was equally vigilant in resisting ecclesiastical encroachment. It may appear otherwise to one who casts a superficial glance at her reign, and beholds her surrounded always by a troop of ghostly advisers, and avowing religion as the great end of her principal operations at home and abroad. It is certain, however, that, while in all her acts she confessed the influence of religion, she took more effectual means than any of her predecessors to circumscribe the temporal powers of the clergy. The volume of her *pragmáticas* is filled with laws designed to limit their jurisdiction and restrain their encroachments on the secular authorities.

CONVENT OF THE MARTYRS, GRANADA

By vigilant measures she succeeded in restoring the ancient discipline of the church, and weeding out the sensuality and indolence which had so long defiled it.[1] Few of the Castilian monarchs have been brought more frequently into collision, or pursued a bolder policy, with the court of Rome. Still fewer extorted from it such important graces and concessions.

The condition of the commons under this reign was probably, on the whole, more prosperous than in any other period of Spanish history. New avenues to wealth and honours were opened to them; and persons and property were alike protected under the fearless and impartial administration of the law. "Such was the justice dispensed to everyone under this auspicious reign," exclaims Marineo, "that nobles and cavaliers, citizens and labourers, rich and poor, masters and servants, all equally partook of it."

[1 To accomplish this she and the austere Ximenes must needs defy even the pope Alexander I. The result was as Hume *e* observes : "It is unquestionable that the worst abuses in the church of which the early reformers complained, had been purged from the Spanish church by Isabella, and that, at a time when the rest of the clergy of Europe were grossly licentious, the Spanish priests were generally virtuous and devout."]

We find no complaints of arbitrary imprisonment, and no attempts, so frequent both in earlier and later times, at illegal taxation. In this particular, indeed, Isabella manifested the greatest tenderness for her people. By her commutation of the capricious tax of the *alcabala* for a determinate one, and still more by transferring its collection from the revenue officers to the citizens themselves, she greatly relieved her subjects.

Finally, notwithstanding the perpetual call for troops for the military operations in which the government was constantly engaged, and notwithstanding the example of neighbouring countries, there was no attempt to establish that iron bulwark of despotism, a standing army; at least, none nearer than that of the voluntary levies of the hermandad, raised and paid by the people. The queen never admitted the arbitrary maxims of Ximenes in regard to the foundation of government. Hers was essentially one of opinion, not force.

There is no country which has been guilty of such wild experiments, or has shown, on the whole, such profound ignorance of the true principles of economical science, as Spain under the sceptre of the family of Austria. And as it is not always easy to discriminate between their acts and those of Ferdinand and Isabella, under whom the germs of much of the subsequent legislation may be said to have been planted, this circumstance has brought undeserved discredit on the government of the latter. Undeserved, because laws mischievous in their eventual operation were not always so at the time for which they were originally devised; not to add that what was intrinsically bad has been aggravated tenfold under the blind legislation of their successors. It is also true that many of the most exceptionable laws sanctioned by their names are to be charged on their predecessors, who had engrafted their principles into the system long before; and many others are to be vindicated by the general practice of other nations, which authorised retaliation on the score of self-defence.

It would be unfair to direct our view to the restrictive measures of Ferdinand and Isabella without noticing also the liberal tenor of their legislation in regard to a great variety of objects. Such, for example, are the law encouraging foreigners to settle in the country; those for facilitating communication by internal improvements, roads, bridges, canals, on a scale of unprecedented magnitude; for a similar attention to the wants of navigation, by constructing moles, quays, lighthouses, along the coast, and deepening and extending the harbours, "to accommodate," as the acts set forth "the great increase of trade"; for embellishing and adding in various ways to the accommodations of the cities; for relieving the subject from onerous tolls and oppressive monopolies; for establishing a uniform currency and standard of weights and measures throughout the kingdom, objects of unwearied solicitude through this whole reign; for maintaining a police which from the most disorderly and dangerous, raised Spain, in the language of Martyr,[l] to be the safest country in Christendom; for such equal justice as secured to every man the fruits of his own industry, inducing him to embark his capital in useful enterprises; and, finally, for enforcing fidelity to contracts, of which the sovereigns gave such a glorious example in their own administration as effectually restored that public credit which is the true basis of public prosperity.

The most important of the foreign acquisitions were those nearest home, Granada and Navarre, at least they were the only ones capable, from their position, of being brought under control and permanently and thoroughly identified with the Spanish monarchy.

DISCOVERY AND COLONISATION

But far the most important of the distant acquisitions of Spain were those secured by the genius of Columbus and the enlightened patronage of Isabella. Imagination had ample range in the boundless perspective of these unknown regions; but the results actually realised from the discoveries, during the queen's life, were comparatively insignificant. In a mere financial view, they had been a considerable charge on the crown. This was, indeed, partly owing to the humanity of Isabella, who interfered, as we have seen, to prevent the compulsory exaction of Indian labour. This was subsequently, and immediately after her death indeed, carried to such an extent that nearly half a million of ounces of gold were yearly drawn from the mines of Hispaniola alone. The pearl-fisheries, and the culture of the sugar-cane, introduced from the Canaries, yielded large returns under the same inhuman system.

Ferdinand, who enjoyed, by the queen's testament, half the amount of the Indian revenues, was now fully awakened to their importance. It would be unjust, however, to suppose his views limited to immediate pecuniary profits; for the measures he pursued were, in many respects, well contrived to promote the nobler ends of discovery and colonisation. He invited the persons most eminent for nautical science and enterprise, as Pinzon, Solis, Vespucci, to his court, where they constituted a sort of board of navigation, constructing charts and tracing out new routes for projected voyages. The conduct of this department was entrusted to the last-mentioned navigator, who had the glory, the greatest which accident and caprice ever granted to man, of giving his name to the new hemisphere.

In this universal excitement, the progress of discovery was pushed forward with a success, inferior, indeed, to what might have been effected in the present state of nautical skill and science, but extraordinary for the times. The winding depths of the gulf of Mexico were penetrated, as well as the borders of the rich but rugged isthmus which connects the American continents. In 1513 Florida was discovered by a romantic old knight, Ponce de Leon, who, instead of the magical fountain of health, found his grave there. Solis, another navigator, who had charge of an expedition, projected by Ferdinand, to reach the South Sea by the circumnavigation of the continent, ran down the coast as far as the great Rio de la Plata, where he also was cut off by the savages. In 1513, Vasco Nuñez de Balboa penetrated, with a handful of men, across the narrow part of the isthmus of Darien, and from the summit of the Cordilleras, the first of Europeans, was greeted with the long-promised vision of the southern ocean.

Our admiration of the dauntless heroism displayed by the early Spanish navigators, in their extraordinary career, is much qualified by a consideration of the cruelties by which it was tarnished; too great to be either palliated or passed over in silence by the historian. As long as Isabella lived, the Indians found an efficient friend and protector; but "her death," says the venerable Las Casas, "was the signal for their destruction." Immediately on that event, the system of *repartimientos*, originally authorised by Columbus, who seems to have had no doubt, from the first, of the crown's absolute right of property over the natives, was carried to its full extent in the colonies. Every Spaniard, however humble, had his proportion of slaves; and men, many of them not only incapable of estimating the awful responsibility of the situation, but without the least touch of humanity in their natures, were individually entrusted with the unlimited disposal of the lives and destinies of their fellow-creatures. They abused this trust in the grossest manner; tasking the unfortunate Indian far beyond his strength, inflicting the most refined punishments on the indolent, and hunting down those who resisted or escaped, like so many beasts of chase, with ferocious bloodhounds.

Every step of the white man's progress in the New World may be said to have been on the corpse of a native. Faith is staggered by the recital of the number of victims immolated in these fair regions within a very few years after the discovery; and the heart sickens at the loathsome details of barbarities recorded by one [Las Casas[r]] who, if his sympathies have led him sometimes to overcolour, can never be suspected of wilfully misstating facts of which he was an eye-witness. A selfish indifference to the rights of the original occupants of the soil is a sin which lies at the door of most of the primitive European settlers, whether papist or puritan, of the New World. But it is light in comparison with the fearful amount of crimes to be charged on the early Spanish colonists; crimes that have, perhaps, in this world, brought down the retribution of heaven, which has seen fit to turn this fountain of inexhaustible wealth and prosperity to the nation into the waters of bitterness.

A WAR VESSEL OF THE FIFTEENTH CENTURY

Ferdinand openly assumed for himself and his ministers the responsibility of maintaining this vicious institution, and subsequently issued an ordinance to that effect, accompanied, however, by a variety of humane and equitable regulations for restraining its abuse. The license was embraced in its full extent; the regulations were openly disregarded. Several years after, in 1515, Las Casas,[r] moved by the spectacle of human suffering, returned to Spain, and pleaded the cause of the injured natives, in tones which made the dying monarch tremble on his throne. It was too late, however, for the king to execute the remedial measures he contemplated. The efficient interference of Ximenes, who sent a commission for the purpose to Hispaniola, was attended with no permanent results. And the indefatigable "protector of the Indians" was left to sue for redress at the court of Charles, and to furnish a splendid if not a solitary example there of a bosom penetrated with the true spirit of Christian philanthropy.

The supply of precious metals yielded by the colonies proved eventually far greater than had ever entered into the conception of the most sanguine of the early discoverers. Their prolific soil and genial climate, moreover, afforded an infinite variety of vegetable products, which might have furnished an unlimited commerce with the mother-country. Under a judicious protection, their population and productions, steadily increasing, would have enlarged to an incalculable extent the general resources of the empire. Such, indeed, might have been the result of a wise system of legislation.

But the true principles of colonial policy were sadly misunderstood in the sixteenth century. The discovery of a world was estimated, like that of a rich mine, by the value of its returns in gold and silver. Much of Isabella's legislation, it is true, is of that comprehensive character which shows that she looked to higher and far nobler objects. But with much that is good there was mingled, as in most of her institutions, one germ of evil, of little moment at the time, indeed, but which, under the vicious culture of her successors, shot up to a height that overshadowed and blighted all the rest. This was the spirit of restriction and monopoly, aggravated by the subsequent laws of Ferdinand, and carried to an extent under the Austrian dynasty that paralysed colonial trade.

Under their most ingeniously perverse system of laws, the interests of both the parent country and the colonies were sacrificed. The latter, condemned to look for supplies to an incompetent source, were miserably dwarfed in their growth ; while the former contrived to convert the nutriment which she extorted from the colonies into a fatal poison. The streams of wealth which flowed in from the silver quarries of Zacatecas and Potosí were jealously locked up within the limits of the peninsula. Agriculture, commerce, manufactures, every branch of national industry and improvement, languished and fell to decay ; and the nation, like the Phrygian monarch, who turned all that he touched to gold, cursed by the very consummation of its wishes, was poor in the midst of its treasures.[1]

THE GOLDEN AGE OF SPAIN

From this sad picture let us turn to that presented by the period of our history when, the clouds and darkness having passed away, a new morn seemed to break upon the nation. Under the firm but temperate sway of Ferdinand and Isabella, the great changes we have noticed were effected without convulsion in the state. On the contrary, the elements of the social system, which before jarred so discordantly, were brought into harmonious action. The restless spirit of the nobles was turned from civil faction to the honourable career of public service, whether in arms or letters. The people at large, assured of the security of private rights, were occupied with the different branches of productive labour. Trade, as is abundantly shown by the legislation of the period, had not yet fallen into the discredit which attached to it in later times. The precious metals, instead of flowing in so abundantly as to palsy the arm of industry, served only to stimulate it.

The foreign intercourse of the country was every day more widely extended. Her agents and consuls were to be found in all the principal

[1 Martin Hume says : "Spanish gold and silver coin, in a few years, was plentiful in every country but in Spain itself."]

ports of the Mediterranean and the Baltic. The Spanish mariner, instead of creeping along the beaten track of inland navigation, now struck boldly across the great western ocean. The new discoveries had converted the land-trade with India into a sea-trade ; and the nations of the peninsula, who had hitherto lain remote from the great highways of commerce, now became the factors and carriers of Europe.

The flourishing condition of the nation was seen in the wealth and population of its cities, the revenues of which, augmented in all to a surprising extent, had in some increased forty and even fifty fold beyond what they were at the commencement of the reign : the ancient and lordly Toledo ; Burgos, with its bustling, industrious traders ; Valladolid, sending forth its thirty thousand warriors from its gates, where the whole population now scarcely reaches two-thirds of that number ; Cordova, in the south, and the magnificent Granada, naturalising in Europe the arts and luxuries of the East ; Saragossa, "the abundant," as she was called from her fruitful territory ; Valencia, "the beautiful" ; Barcelona, rivalling in independence and maritime enterprise the proudest of the Italian republics ; Medina del Campo, whose fairs were already the great mart for the commercial exchanges of the peninsula ; and Seville, the golden gate of the Indies, whose quays began to be thronged with merchants from the most distant countries of Europe.

The resources of the inhabitants were displayed in the palaces and public edifices, fountains, aqueducts, gardens, and other works of utility and ornament. This lavish expenditure was directed by an improved taste. Architecture was studied on purer principles than before, and, with the sister arts of design, showed the influence of the new connection with Italy in the first gleams of that excellence which shed such lustre over the Spanish school at the close of the century. A still more decided impulse was given to letters. Ancient seminaries were remodeled ; new ones were created. Barcelona, Salamanca, and Alcalá, whose cloistered solitudes are now the grave rather than the nursery of science, then swarmed with thousands of disciples, who under the generous patronage of the government found letters the surest path to preferment. Even the lighter branches of literature felt the revolutionary spirit of the times, and, after yielding the last fruits of the ancient system, displayed new and more beautiful varieties under the influence of Italian culture.

With this moral development of the nation, the public revenues, the sure index, when unforced of public prosperity, went on augmenting with astonishing rapidity. In 1474, the year of Isabella's accession, the ordinary rents of the Castilian crown amounted to 885,000 reals ;[1] in 1477, to 2,390,078 ; in 1482, after the resumption of the royal grants, to 12,711,591 ; and finally, in 1504, when the acquisition of Granada and the domestic tranquillity of the kingdom had encouraged the free expansion of all its resources, to 26,283,334 ; or thirty times the amount received at her accession. All this, it will be remembered, was derived from the customary established taxes, without the imposition of a single new one. Indeed, the improvements in the mode of collection tended materially to lighten the burdens on the people.

The territorial limits of the monarchy, in the meantime, went on expanding beyond example — Castile and Leon, brought under the same sceptre with Aragon and its foreign dependencies, Sicily and Sardinia ; with the kingdoms of Granada, Navarre, and Naples ; with the Canaries, Oran, and

---

[1] The sums in the text express the *real de vellom ;* to which they have been reduced by Señor Clemencin,ʲ from the original amount in maravedis, which varied very materially in value in different years.

the other settlements in Africa; and with the islands and vast continents of America. To these broad domains the comprehensive schemes of the sovereigns would have added Portugal; and their arrangements for this, although defeated for the present, opened the way to its eventual completion under Philip II. The names of Castilian and Aragonese were merged in the comprehensive one of Spaniard; and Spain, with an empire which stretched over three-quarters of the globe, and which almost realised the proud boast that the sun never set within her borders, now rose, not to the first class only, but to the first place, in the scale of European powers.

The extraordinary circumstances of the country tended naturally to nourish the lofty, romantic qualities and the somewhat exaggerated tone of sentiment which always pervaded the national character. The age of chivalry had not faded away in Spain, as in most other lands. It was fostered, in time of peace, by the tourneys, jousts, and other warlike pageants which graced the court of Isabella. It gleamed out, as we have seen, in the Italian campaigns under Gonsalvo de Cordova, and shone forth in all its splendours in the war of Granada.

The Spaniard was a knight-errant, in its literal sense, roving over seas on which no barque had ever ventured, among islands and continents where no civilised man had ever trodden, and which fancy peopled with all the marvels and drear enchantments of romance; courting danger in every form, combating everywhere, and everywhere victorious. The very odds presented by the defenceless natives among whom he was cast, "a thousand of whom," to quote the words of Columbus, "were not equal to three Spaniards," was in itself typical of his profession; and the brilliant destinies to which the meanest adventurer was often called, now carving out with his good sword some Eldorado more splendid than fancy had dreamed of, and now overturning some old barbaric dynasty, were full as extraordinary as the wildest chimeras which Ariosto ever sang or Cervantes satirised. His countrymen who remained at home, feeding greedily on the reports of his adventures, lived almost equally in an atmosphere of romance. A spirit of chivalrous enthusiasm penetrated the very depths of the nation, swelling the humblest individual with lofty aspirations and a proud consciousness of the dignity of his nature.

In noticing the circumstances that conspired to form the national character, it would be unpardonable to omit the establishment of the Inquisition, which contributed so largely to counterbalance the benefits resulting from Isabella's government; an institution which has done more than any other to stay the proud march of human reason; which, by imposing uniformity of creed, has proved the fruitful parent of hypocrisy and superstition; which has soured the sweet charities of human life, and, settling like a foul mist on the goodly promise of the land, closed up the fair buds of science and civilisation ere they were fully opened. Alas, that such a blight should have fallen on so gallant and generous a people! That it should have been brought on it, too, by one of such unblemished patriotism and purity of motive as Isabella!

The immediate injury inflicted on the nation by the spirit of bigotry in the reign of Ferdinand and Isabella, although greatly exaggerated, was doubtless serious enough. Under the otherwise beneficent operation of their government, however, the healthful and expansive energies of the state were sufficient to heal up these and deeper wounds, and still carry it onward in the career of prosperity. With this impulse, indeed, the nation continued to advance higher and higher, in spite of the system of almost unmingled evil pursued in the following reigns. The glories of this later period, of the age of Charles V, as it is called, must find their true source in the measures of his illustrious predecessors. It was in their court that Boscan, Garcilasso, Mendoza, and the other master spirits were trained, who moulded Castilian literature into the new and more classical forms of later times. It was under Gonsalvo de Cordova that Leyva, Pescara, and those great captains with their invincible legions were formed, who enabled Charles V to dictate laws to Europe for half a century. And it was Columbus who not only led the way, but animated the Spanish navigator with the spirit of discovery. Scarcely was Ferdinand's reign brought to a close, before Magellan completed (1520), what that monarch had projected, the circumnavigation of the southern continent; the victorious banners of Cortes had already (1518) penetrated into the golden realms of Montezuma; and Pizarro, a very few years later (1524), following up the lead of Balboa, embarked on the enterprise which ended in the downfall of the splendid dynasty of the Incas.

Thus it is that the seed sown under a good system continues to yield fruit under a bad one. The season of the most brilliant results, however, is not always that of the greatest national prosperity. The splendours of foreign conquest in the boasted reign of Charles V were dearly purchased by the decline of industry at home, and the loss of liberty. The patriot will see little to cheer him in this "golden age" of the national history, whose outward show of glory will seem to his penetrating eye only the hectic brilliancy of decay. He will turn to an earlier period, when the nation, emerging from the sloth and license of a barbarous age, seemed to renew its ancient energies, and to prepare like a giant to run its course; and glancing over the long interval since elapsed, during the first half of which the nation wasted itself on schemes of mad ambition, and in the latter has sunk into a state of paralytic torpor, he will fix his eye on the reign of Ferdinand and Isabella as the most glorious epoch in the annals of his country.[b]

CHAPTER VIII

THE EMPEROR CHARLES V·

[1517–1556 A.D.]

SOON after the death of Ximenes, Charles [who as the emperor is known s Charles V but as King Charles I of Spain] made his public entry, with reat pomp, into Valladolid, whither he had summoned the cortes of Castile. Though he assumed on all occasions the name of king, that title had never een acknowledged in the cortes. The Spaniards, considering Juana as ossessed of the sole right to the crown, and no example of a son's having njoyed the title of king during the life of his parents occurring in their istory, the cortes discovered all that scrupulous respect for ancient forms nd that aversion to innovation which are conspicuous in popular assemblies.

The presence, however, of their prince, the address, the artifices, and the hreats of his ministers, prevailed on them at last to proclaim him king, in onjunction with his mother, whose name they appointed to be placed before hat of her son in all public acts. But when they made this concession, they eclared that if, at any future period, Juana should recover the exercise of eason, the whole authority should return into her hands. At the same time, hey voted a free gift of 600,000 ducats[1] to be paid in three years, a sum nore considerable than had ever been granted to any former monarch.

Notwithstanding this obsequiousness of the cortes to the will of the king, he most violent symptoms of dissatisfaction with his government began to reak out in the kingdom. Chièvres had acquired over the mind of the oung monarch the ascendant not only of a tutor, but of a parent. Charles

[1 The ducat may be taken as valuing approximately at 9s. 6d. or $2.30; it being remembered at gold purchased then much more than now — the usual theory being that it had seven times present purchasing power.]

seemed to have no sentiments but those which his minister inspired, and scarcely uttered a word but what he put into his mouth. He was constantly surrounded by Flemings; no person got access to him without their permission; nor was any admitted to audience but in their presence. As he spoke the Spanish language very imperfectly, his answers were always extremely short, and often delivered with hesitation. Unfortunately for Charles, his favourites were unworthy of his confidence. To amass wealth seems to have been their only aim; and as they had reason to fear that either their master's good sense or the indignation of the Spaniards might soon abridge their power, they hastened to improve the present opportunity, and their avarice was the more rapacious because they expected their authority to be of no longer duration. All honours, offices, and benefices were either engrossed by the Flemings or publicly sold by them. Chièvres, his wife, and Sauvage, whom Charles, on the death of Ximenes, had imprudently raised to be chancellor of Castile, vied with each other in all the refinements of extortion and venality. Not only the Spanish historians, who, from resentment, may be suspected of exaggeration, but Peter Martyr Angleria [or de Anghierra], an Italian, who resided at that time in the court of Spain, and was under no temptation to deceive the persons to whom his letters are addressed, gives a description which is almost incredible, of the insatiable and shameless covetousness of the Flemings.

According to Angleria's calculation, which he asserts to be extremely moderate, they remitted into the Low Countries, in the space of ten months, no less a sum than 1,100,000 ducats. The nomination of William de Croy, Chièvres' nephew, a young man not of canonical age, to the archbishopric of Toledo, exasperated the Spaniards more than all these exactions.

Charles, leaving Castile thus disgusted with his administration, set out for Saragossa, the capital of Aragon, that he might be present in the cortes of that kingdom. On his way thither, he took leave of his brother Ferdinand, whom he sent into Germany on the pretence of visiting their grandfather, Maximilian, in his old age. To this prudent precaution Charles owed the preservation of his Spanish dominions. During the violent commotions which arose there soon after this period, the Spaniards would infallibly have offered the crown to a prince who was the darling of the whole nation; nor did Ferdinand want ambition nor councillors that might have prompted him to accept of the offer.

The Aragonese had not hitherto acknowledged Charles as king, nor would they allow the cortes to be assembled in his name, but in that of the justicia to whom, during an interregnum, this privilege belonged. After long delays however, and with much difficulty, he persuaded the members to confer on him the title of king, in conjunction with his mother. At the same time he bound himself by that solemn oath, which the Aragonese exacted of their kings, never to violate any of their rights or liberties. When a donative was demanded, the members were still more intractable; many months elapsed before they would agree to grant Charles 200,000 ducats, and that sum the appropriated so strictly for paying debts of the crown, which had long been forgotten, that a very small part of it came into the king's hands. What had happened in Castile taught them caution, and determined them rather to satisfy the claims of their fellow-citizens, how obsolete soever, than to furnish strangers the means of enriching themselves with the spoils of the country.

From Aragon, Charles proceeded to Catalonia, where he wasted much time, encountered more difficulties, and gained less money. The Flemings were now become so odious to every province in Spain by their exactions that the desire of mortifying them, and of disappointing their avarice, augmented the jealousy with which a free people usually conduct their deliberations. Segovia, Toledo, Seville, and several other cities of the first rank entered into a confederacy for the defence of their rights and privileges ; and, notwithstanding the silence of the nobility, who, on this occasion, discovered neither the public spirit nor the resolution which became their order, the confederates laid before the king a full view of the state of the kingdom, and of the maladministration of his favourites. The preferment of strangers, the exportation of the current coin, the increase of taxes, were the grievances of which they chiefly complained ; and of these they demanded redress with that boldness which is natural to a free people. These remonstrances, presented at first at Saragossa, and renewed afterwards at Barcelona, Charles treated with great neglect. The confederacy, however, of these cities, at this juncture, was the beginning of that famous union among the commons [comuneros] of Castile, which not long after threw the kingdom into such violent convulsions as shook the throne, and almost overturned the constitution.

KING CHARLES BECOMES EMPEROR

Soon after Charles' arrival at Barcelona, he received the account of an event which interested him much more than the murmurs of the Castilians or the scruples of the cortes of Catalonia. This was the death of the emperor Maximilian — an occurrence of small importance in itself, for he was a prince conspicuous neither for his virtues, nor his power, nor his abilities ; but rendered by its consequences more memorable than any that had happened during several ages. It broke that profound and universal peace which then reigned in the Christian world ; it excited a rivalship between two princes, which threw all Europe into agitation, and kindled wars more general, and of longer duration, than had hitherto been known in modern times.

The revolution occasioned by the expedition of the French king Charles VIII, into Italy, had inspired the European princes with new ideas concerning the importance of the imperial dignity. The claims of the empire upon some of the Italian states were numerous ; its jurisdiction over others was extensive ; and though the former had been almost abandoned, and the latter seldom exercised, under princes of slender abilities and of little influence, it was obvious that, in the hands of an emperor possessed of power or of genius, they might be employed as engines for stretching his dominion over the greater part of that country. Even Maximilian, feeble and unsteady as his conduct always was, had availed himself of the infinite pretensions of the empire, and had reaped advantage from every war and every negotiation in Italy during his reign. These considerations, added to the dignity of the station, confessedly the first among Christian princes, and to the rights inherent in the office, which, if exerted with vigour, were far from being inconsiderable, rendered the imperial crown more than ever an object of ambition.

Not long before his death, Maximilian had discovered great solicitude to preserve this dignity in the Austrian family, and to procure the king of Spain to be chosen his successor. But he himself, having never been crowned by the pope, a ceremony deemed essential in that age, was considered only as emperor "elect." Though historians have not attended to that distinction, neither the Italian nor the German chancery bestowed any other title upon him than that of king of the Romans; and no example occurring in history of any person's being chosen a successor to a king of the Romans, the Germans, always tenacious of their forms, and unwilling to confer upon Charles an office for which their constitution knew no name, obstinately refused to gratify Maximilian in that point. By his death, this difficulty was at once removed, and Charles openly aspired to that dignity which his grandfather attempted, without success, to secure for him. At the same time Francis I, a powerful rival, entered the lists against him; and the attention of all Europe was fixed upon this competition, no less illustrious from the high rank of the candidates than from the importance of the prize for which they contended. Each of them urged his pretensions with sanguine expectations, and with no unpromising prospect of success. Charles considered the imperial crown as belonging to him of right, from its long continuance in the Austrian line; he knew that none of the German princes possessed power or influence enough to appear as his antagonist; he flattered himself that no consideration would induce the natives of Germany to exalt any foreign prince to a dignity which during so many ages had been deemed peculiar to their own nation; and, least of all, that they would confer this honour upon Francis I, the sovereign of a people whose genius, and laws, and manners differed so widely from those of the Germans that it was hardly possible to establish any cordial union between them. He did not, however, trust the success of his cause to this alone. Great sums of money were remitted from Spain; all the refinements and artifices of negotiation were employed; and a considerable body of troops, kept on foot at that time by the states of the circle of Swabia, was secretly taken into his pay. The venal were gained by presents; the objections of the more scrupulous were answered or eluded; some feeble princes were threatened or overawed.

A SPANISH GENTLEMAN, EARLY SIXTEENTH CENTURY

On the 28th of June, five months and ten days after the death of Maximilian, this important contest, which had held all Europe in suspense, was decided. Six of the electors had already declared for the king of Spain; and the archbishop of Treves, the only firm adherent to the French interest, having at last joined his brethren, Charles was, by the unanimous voice of the electoral college, raised to the imperial throne. The important intelligence of his election was conveyed in nine days from Frankfort to Barcelona, where Charles was still detained by the obstinacy of the Catalan cortes, which had not hitherto brought to an issue any of the affairs which came before it. He received the account with the joy natural to a young and aspiring mind, on an accession of power and dignity which raised him so far above the other princes of Europe. Then it was that those vast prospects, which allured him during his whole administration, began to open; and from this era we may date the formation, and are able to trace the gradual progress, of a grand system of enterprising ambition, which renders the history of his reign so worthy of attention.

A trivial circumstance first discovered the effects of this great elevation upon the mind of Charles. In all the public writs which he now issued as king of Spain, he assumed the title of "majesty," and required it from his subjects as a mark of their respect. Before that time, all the monarchs of Europe were satisfied with the appellation of "highness," or "grace"; but the vanity of other courts soon led them to imitate the example of the Spanish. The epithet of majesty is no longer a mark of pre-eminence. The most inconsiderable monarchs in Europe enjoy it, and the arrogance of the greater potentates has invented no higher denomination.

The Spaniards were far from viewing the promotion of their king to the imperial throne with the same satisfaction which he himself felt. To be deprived of the presence of their sovereign, and to be subjected to the government of a viceroy and his council, a species of administration often oppressive and always disagreeable, were the immediate and necessary consequences of this new dignity. To see the blood of their countrymen shed in quarrels wherein the nation had no concern; to behold its treasures wasted in supporting the splendour of a foreign title; to be plunged in the chaos of Italian and German politics were effects of this event almost as unavoidable. From all these considerations they concluded that nothing could have happened more pernicious to the Spanish nation; and the fortitude and public spirit of their ancestors, who, in the cortes of Castile, prohibited Alfonso the Wise [the Learned] from leaving the kingdom, in order to receive the imperial crown, were often mentioned with the highest praise, and pronounced to be extremely worthy of imitation at this juncture. But Charles, without regarding the sentiments or murmurs of his Spanish subjects, accepted of the imperial dignity which the count palatine, at the head of a solemn embassy, offered him in the name of the electors; and declared his intention of setting out soon for Germany, in order to take possession of it. This was the more necessary, because, according to the forms of the German constitution, he could not, before the ceremony of a public coronation, exercise any act of jurisdiction or authority.

Their certain knowledge of this resolution augmented so much the disgust of the Spaniards that a sullen and refractory spirit prevailed among persons of all ranks. The pope having granted the king the tenths of all ecclesiastical benefices in Castile, to assist him in carrying on war with greater vigour against the Turks, a convocation of the clergy unanimously refused to levy that sum, upon pretence that it ought never to be exacted but at those times when Christendom was actually invaded by the infidels; and though Leo, in order to support his authority, laid the kingdom under an interdict, so little regard was paid to a censure which was universally deemed unjust, that Charles himself applied to have it taken off. Thus the Spanish clergy, besides their merit in opposing the usurpations of the pope, and disregarding the influence of the crown, gained the exemption which they had claimed.

The commotions which arose in the kingdom of Valencia, annexed to the crown of Aragon, were more formidable, and produced more dangerous and lasting effects. A seditious monk, having by his sermons excited the citizens of Valencia, the capital city, to take arms, and to punish certain criminals in a tumultuary manner, the people, pleased with this exercise of power and with such a discovery of their own importance, not only refused to lay down their arms, but formed themselves into troops and companies, that they might be regularly trained to martial exercises. To obtain some security against the oppression of the grandees was the motive of this association, and proved a powerful bond of union; for as the aristocratical privileges and independence were more complete in Valencia than in any other of the Spanish kingdoms, the nobles, being scarcely accountable for their conduct to any superior, treated the people not only as vassals but as slaves. They were alarmed, however, at the progress of this unexpected insurrection, as it might encourage the people to attempt shaking off the yoke altogether; but as they could not repress them without taking arms, it became necessary to have recourse to the emperor, and to desire his permission to attack them (1520).

At the same time the people made choice of deputies to represent their grievances, and to implore the protection of their sovereign. Happily for the latter, they arrived at court when Charles was exasperated to a high degree against the nobility. As he was eager to visit Germany, where his presence became every day more necessary, and his Flemish courtiers were still more impatient to return into their native country, that they might carry thither the spoils which they had amassed in Castile, it was impossible for him to hold the cortes of Valencia in person. He had for that reason empowered the cardinal Adrian to represent him in that assembly, and in his name to receive their oath of allegiance, to confirm their privileges with the usual solemnities, and to demand of them a free gift.

But the Valencian nobles, who considered this measure as an indignity to their country, which was no less entitled than his other kingdoms to the honour of their sovereign's presence, declared that, by the fundamental laws of the constitution, they could neither acknowledge as king a person who was absent, nor grant him any subsidy; and to this declaration they adhered with a haughty and inflexible obstinacy. Charles, piqued by their behaviour, decided in favour of the people, and rashly authorised them to continue in arms. Their deputies returned in triumph, and were received by their fellow-citizens as the deliverers of their country. The insolence of the multitude increasing with their success, they expelled all the nobles out of the city, committed the government to magistrates of their own election, and entered into an association, distinguished by the name of *germandada* or "brotherhood," which proved the source not only of the wildest disorders but of the most fatal calamities in that kingdom.[c]

CHARLES' STRUGGLE WITH THE CORTES

At this period it was Charles' misfortune to make enemies on every side. As the constitution of Valencia required that he should be present, to fulfil the compact with his people, he should, doubtless, have hastened thither, and, by yielding prompt obedience to the laws, have removed all pretext for rebellion. The same imprudence, the same disregard of established custom, made him summon the cortes of Castile and Leon to meet him at Santiago; a thing never before attempted by the most arbitrary of his predecessors. To the murmurs produced by this innovation, the ministers paid no attention: on the contrary, they did all they could to fan the flame of discontent, by interfering in the return of the deputies, and by bribing such as they could not nominate to submit in everything to the royal will.

Toledo displaced the deputies whom it had chosen, and nominated others more submissive to the popular voice. It next prevailed on some other towns to join in insisting on the following concessions: that the king should not leave Spain; that he should require no subsidy; that, instead of conferring dignities on foreigners, he should deprive the possessors of those which they actually held; that no money, under any pretext whatever, should leave the kingdom; that offices should cease to be venal; and that the cortes should be assembled, according to ancient custom, in some town of Leon or Castile, not in an angle of Galicia. Most of these demands were reasonable enough; but the first two were insulting, and all were sure to be highly unpalatable to the court. The deputies who bore them waited on Charles, now at Valladolid, on his way to Galicia, and with some difficulty obtained an audience. He told them, however, that he was in too much haste to take the subject into consideration; but that, if they would meet him near Tordesillas, he would commune with them. To Tordesillas they accordingly repaired; but a report being maliciously spread in Valladolid that he was not only about to leave the kingdom, but to take away his mother, the populace were excited to the highest pitch. A Portuguese lace-maker mischievously ascended the tower of a church, the bell of which was never sounded except on extraordinary occasions, and rang with such good-will that six thousand men were speedily under arms.

It was immediately resolved that all the Flemings should be put to death; but the intended victims had timely intimation of their danger, and with the king fled at midnight, the rain descending in torrents, to Tordesillas, where they arrived at daybreak. The authorities of Valladolid showed great activity in the apprehension of the ringleaders in the riot, and a few were punished; but the king, who was naturally clement, ordered the remainder to be liberated. He now hastened towards Galicia, the Toledan deputies closely following him, and at every town requesting an audience; but he refused to see them until they reached Santiago.

On the first day of April, 1520, the states were opened in the convent of San Francisco. The speech from the throne laid stress on the necessity of the king's immediate voyage to Germany; on the expenses with which it would be attended, as well as on that which had been incurred in preparations for war with the infidels; and ended by demanding a gratuity. For a moment the deputies were silent; but those of Salamanca rose, and protested that they could not take the accustomed oath of allegiance unless the king would comply with the demands which had been presented to him. They were immediately supported by a deputy of Toledo, who asserted that, rather than consent to anything prejudicial, either to the city he represented or to the kingdom, he would sacrifice his life. Emboldened by the example, the delegates of Seville, Cordova, Zamora, Toro, and Avila joined with the three, and the business of the assembly was for some days interrupted. Nothing can better show the degraded state in which the cortes were held, and the power which the crown had been accustomed to exercise over the proceedings — debates were unknown among them — than the next step of the king: it was no less than to order the Toledan deputies, the most violent of the party, to leave the court. In vain did they petition: they were compelled to obey. When the news reached Toledo, the population was in an uproar; and their anger still further inflamed by the arrest of two of their magistrates, Juan de Padilla, and Ferdinand Davalos. Whether a royal order was sent for the arrest, or a citation for the appearance of both, is doubtful: the mob opposed its execution; and would have murdered the corregidor, the alcalde, and alguacil mayor, had not all three contrived to escape. The fortress and gates, with the government of the city, were now seized by the mob, and the royal officers expelled. The example was imitated by the whole kingdom of Murcia.

When intelligence of these events reached Santiago, the king proposed to march on Toledo, and inflict a summary vengeance on that city ; but his ministers — fearing that if he remained any longer in Spain he would risk the imperial crown, some members of the diet having already threatened to proceed to a second election — dissuaded him from his purpose. The states were now transferred to Corunna, where, with some reluctance, — so effectually had the royal influence been exercised in the interim, — a considerable subsidy was granted to the monarch. The great cities, however, refused to sanction it ; and even the few deputies who voted it accompanied it by requests exceedingly obnoxious to the court. Anxious to take possession of the brilliant dignity which awaited him, and perhaps to escape from so troubled a kingdom, Charles closed the cortes, and prepared to embark. He left the regency of Castile to Cardinal Adrian ; of Aragon, to Don Juan de Lanuza ; of Valencia, to the count de Melito ; and he intrusted the command of the troops to approved officers. The choice of Adrian, a foreigner, was peculiarly offensive to the nobles and deputies at court : they solicited another ; but Charles, who generally adhered to his plans with uncommon tenacity, refused to change. In May he embarked, and proceeded to England, to concert with Henry VIII the means of humbling the power of the French king.

REVOLT OF THE GERMANEROS AND THE COMUNEROS [1]

The departure of the king was not likely to assuage the turbulence of the times. If the opposition, so long as it was constitutionally exercised, was just, and even laudable, it had now degenerated into rebellion, and patriotism been succeeded by schemes of personal ambition. In Toledo, Padilla, by pretending to follow the popular current, guided it at his will : his wife, Doña Maria Pacheco, who had greater talents and even greater ambition than himself, headed the popular processions, and by her presence authorised some revolting scenes. From Murcia the governor, the marquis de los Velez, had been expelled, and a royal officer, who had been sent to institute proceedings against the guilty, compelled to flee for his life, followed by eight thousand of the combined rebels.

The example of these great places was too attractive to remain inoperative. Segovia immediately rose, and hung two of the magistrates. The mob were, above all, anxious to murder their deputies, of whom both had agreed to the subsidy at Corunna ; but one of them, wisely distrustful of their intention, had not returned : the other, who returned at midnight, was dragged along the streets to the place of execution. The monks of San Francisco issued from their cloisters, with the holy sacrament : the interference was unavailing ; nor was it without difficulty that permission could be obtained for a confessor to attend him. A monk approached, and though the office was speedily performed, loud murmurs were raised, by the murderous herd, at the time so unnecessarily lost. They again seized the rope, dragged the deputy along, and, though he was dead before they reached the gallows, hung him on the same tree that had proved fatal to two preceding victims.

Though Valladolid was honoured with the abode of Adrian and the council of regency, the rabble rose to put the deputies to death ; and when these, too, had the good fortune to escape, even the cardinal was arrested,

[1 The name *germaneros* was given to the rebels of Valencia who were organised into a "brotherhood" or *germania*, a word closely allied in sound and meaning to the Castilian *hermandad* or "brotherhood." The name *comuneros* is simply the Castilian for "commoners."]

but, as it appears, soon released, through the interposition of the nobles and clergy. Burgos was still more criminal. Unable to find the bishop or his brethren, individuals peculiarly obnoxious, the rioters, headed by a cutler, burned a house in which many valuable archives were consumed. They next proceeded in search of a royal favourite, whose house shared the same fate. He was overtaken, dragged from the church where he had sought sanctuary, brought to Burgos, and committed to prison, where he immediately died from the effect of the blows he had received. Not satisfied with taking his life, they dragged his corpse through the city, and suspended it, the head downwards, from the public gallows. The arrival at Madrid of a royal magistrate, said to be proceeding to Toledo to try the rebels, raised the rioters, who swore to take his life ; and, as he was fortunate enough to escape, they deposed the magistrates, elected others, seized all the arms they could find, and summoned the governor of the Alcazar to remit that fortress into their hands ; but he had fidelity enough to set them at defiance. The siege was prosecuted : a mine was sprung, the gallant handful of defenders was destroyed, and the place capitulated. Finally, at Avila, Guadalajara, and Siguenza, the legitimate authority was overthrown; brute force, murder, rape, and plunder reigned in its stead.

The rebellious communities agreed to act in concert for the common cause, and to send their representatives to Avila, to hold a sort of national cortes. Accordingly, Toledo, Madrid, Guadalajara, Soria, Murcia, Cuenca, Segovia, Avila, Salamanca, Toro, Zamora, Leon, Valladolid, Burgos, and Ciudad Rodrigo, successively and within short intervals, joined their respective deputies, while from several of these places troops daily arrived. For some time, however, nothing important was attempted : the royalist general, Fonseca, was too busily occupied in raising troops to assail Segovia ; and Ronquillo was too weak to take the field. The weakness of the regent, who in fear of violence expressed his disapprobation of the hostilities commenced by Fonseca, redoubled their audacity. Anarchy was now at its height.

QUEEN JUANA RELEASED

The next proceeding of the rebels was distinguished for more boldness, and for something like originality. At the head of the troops furnished by Toledo, Medina del Campo, and other places, and accompanied by two other chiefs, Padilla proceeded to Tordesillas to gain possession of the imbecile Juana. He demanded and obtained an audience, expatiated on the evils which had befallen the kingdom since the death of the Catholic sovereigns, her parents, and said that her son had abandoned the kingdom to its fate ; he ended by informing her that he placed the troops of Toledo, Madrid, and Segovia at her disposal. For a moment the queen seemed to have regained the use of her faculties ; she replied that she had never before heard of her father's death ; that if she had, she would not have permitted the disorders which prevailed ; that she desired the weal of the kingdom, and that on Padilla, in quality of captain-general, she devolved the duty of restoring the public tranquillity. Her rational manner of discourse made the deputies hope that she had been restored to sanity ; they did homage to her as their sovereign queen ; and in her name the representatives of the confederation were brought from Avila to Tordesillas. By issuing all decrees in her name and by her authority, they hoped to give legitimacy to their own.

But she almost instantly relapsed into her former lethargy, a circumstance, however, which they carefully concealed from the world. Emboldened by the success of their enterprise, and by the number of armed men who daily joined them, they now resolved to subvert the power of regent and council, and even to arrest the members. Padilla arrived with twelve hundred men. The cardinal now prepared to flee; the gates were shut on him; and he was detained as a sort of hostage for the safety of the rebel chiefs. In a few days, however, he assumed a disguise and silently escaped. His first step was to acquaint his master with the events which had happened. On their side, the confederates, with an impudence unparalleled in all history, attempted in the same manner to justify what they had done.

A Spanish Gentlewoman of the Sixteenth Century

Charles V was in a difficult position: the hostility of the Lutherans, the rivalry of Francis I, the disturbances which threatened to afflict Italy, and the preparations of the Grand Turk, rendered it impossible for him to revisit Spain, even though his absence endangered the security of that crown. In this emergency he associated Velasco the constable and Henry the admiral of Castile in the regency with Adrian, and wrote to all the revolted communities calling on them to obey the laws and to restore tranquillity, promising to return the moment his pressing affairs would allow him. To dispose them in his favour he renounced the subsidy which had been voted him at Corunna, and promised that no benefices should be conferred on foreigners. His letters, however, had for some time little effect on the majority of the confederates, who declared that they were dictated by insincerity.

In this critical position of the royal cause, it was fortunate that Aragon, Catalonia, and most of Andalusia stood aloof from the confederation. Aragon, indeed, was subsequently troubled for a moment, through an organised opposition to the viceroyalty of Lanuza; but tranquillity was restored without much difficulty. Seville, Cordova, Xeres, and Granada either returned, without condescending to open, the proposals of that body, or reproached it for its excesses. The rebellious towns no less persevered in their career of violence. It was evident that nothing less than civil war could decide the problem, whether the king or the mob should exercise the government. The constable began to act with vigour, to collect his own vassals, and to summon all who held for the sovereign and the laws to join him; and he borrowed money from Dom Emmanuel, of Portugal, to support his levies. The cardinal too seemed to awake from his imbecile inactivity; and the admiral went from place to place to rouse the sparks of slumbering

[1520-1521 A.D.]

loyalty. The result showed what might have been accomplished earlier by an active combination of the royalist party; about eight thousand well-armed men soon repaired to Rio Seco. The extent of the preparations and the expostulations of the constables prevailed on Burgos to withdraw from the confederacy. On their side the assembly at Tordesillas vigorously prepared for the struggle, and placed Don Pedro Giron at the head of the rebel forces, among the ranks of which was the bishop of Zamora, with nine hundred men, of whom four hundred were ecclesiastics.

With eleven thousand men Don Pedro advanced towards Rio Seco, took and pillaged Tordehumos, without any molestation from the royalists, who were waiting for a reinforcement under the count de Haro. On the junction of that nobleman, who was raised to the command, the numbers were about equal; but for some time the royalists were unwilling to begin the attack. Don Pedro fell back to Villapando, and by this imprudent step exposed Tordesillas, which, with the queen, Juana, was invested and stormed by the count. He was already disgusted with the cause he advocated, and he soon abandoned it for that of the king: his place was supplied by Don Juan de Padilla.

While a desultory warfare followed, generally favourable to the royalists, Valencia [the headquarters of the Germania] was the undivided prey of anarchy; deeds were committed which threw into the shade the horrors of Castile and Leon. The thirteen syndics first endeavoured to oppose the entrance of the viceroy : and when this was found impossible, they artfully misrepresented his actions, organised a determined opposition to his authority, overawed the administration of justice, rescued the most notorious criminals from execution, openly attacked his house, and at length expelled him from the city. The consequences, not in the capital only, but in the towns, might have been easily anticipated. All who were hostile to the present order of things were pursued with vindictive rage : they were even sacrificed at the altar, their wives violated, their children put to death before their eyes, the priests themselves dragged from their sanctuary, and the holy sacraments trodden under foot. In short, there was no species of crime left uncommitted.

But, fortunately for humanity, evil has its climax as well as good, and the descent in the former case is even more rapid than in the latter. Some of the rebel leaders returned to their duty; and the count de Haro advanced against Padilla, who was intrenched in Torre Lobaton, but who fled on the approach of the royalists. The count pursued, overtook, and in a short time entirely defeated the rebels near Villalar, April, 1521; Padilla himself, with two other generals, being among the prisoners. All three were speedily condemned and executed. Terrified by this blow, Valladolid sued for and obtained its pardon. Medina del Campo, Segovia, Avila, Salamanca, Zamora, and other places of less note, followed the example. The prior of St. John, who had been sent to chastise the inhabitants of Toledo, defeated the bishop of Zamora, who had ventured to oppose him, and was precipitately driven into the city. For the bishop's devotion to the popular cause, the people escorted him in triumph to the cathedral, and placed him under the archiepiscopal canopy ; but intelligence arriving of Padilla's defeat, he soon afterwards fled from the city.

Doña Maria Pacheco, the widow of Padilla, a woman of commanding talents, of desperate courage, and of little principle, succeeded to the unbounded authority of her husband. Her character will be best understood by an anecdote : Two Biscayan brothers, suspected of ill will towards her husband, were summoned to appear before her in the Alcazar; scarcely had they crossed the threshold of the fortress when they fell under the daggers of her creatures: the corpses were first thrown into the river, and then dragged through the streets by children. In the meantime the prior of St. John invested the city, from which sorties were frequently made, with various success. She confined the canons of Toledo, who refused to rob the church at her requisition, during two days and nights to the chapter-house, allowing them neither food nor bed; and there they must doubtless have remained until starvation had released them from her persecution, had they not submitted. But her despotic reign was approaching its end. The loss of thirteen hundred men in a desperate sortie so humbled the inhabitants that all submitted except a determined number, who retired with her into the Alcazar. Soon afterwards it was compelled to submit, but the heroic Doña Maria effected her escape into Portugal, where she passed her remaining days in great poverty.

The success of the royalists in Leon and Castile had little effect on the desperate rebels of Valencia. That city, like other towns of the kingdom, continued in the hands of a furious mob, who loudly proclaimed that no clergy should be maintained, no taxes hereafter paid, no civil government supported, since all were violations of natural liberty. Hearing that one of their leaders was defeated at Oropesa by the duke of Segorbe, and that the viceroy had convoked the ban and arrière-ban of the nobles, the fanatics left the capital to exterminate all their enemies. Four thousand of them furiously assailed several towns which continued faithful to the king; one-half of them were annihilated near Murviedro by the same duke; but, to counterbalance this check, another army of rebels defeated the viceroy in person near Jativa. The ferocity of the victors knew no bounds: they had bigotry enough to force the Moors whom they had conquered to receive baptism, but after the ceremony they massacred six hundred; saying that possibly the converts might relapse, and that it was better at once to send them to heaven, while in a regenerated state.

The viceroy now solicited aid from the regents of Castile; it was immediately sent; the royalists took the field in greater numbers, and with greater confidence of success. Fortress after fortress was reduced. The rapidity of these successes so frightened even the rebels of the capital that they sued for pardon; it was granted by the viceroy on the consideration that they would surrender their arms, and in future conform to the laws. In an incredibly short period all the fortified places submitted. The confederation was forever destroyed in Valencia; and, though it lingered for a while in the Balearic Isles, where it raged almost as furiously as on the continent, it was at length extirpated through the valour of the royalists.

These troubled scenes were not the only evil experienced by the Spaniards at this season: they were afflicted by that of foreign invasion. Knowing that the forces of the kingdom were occupied in extinguishing the flames of rebellion, the French king thought this a favourable opportunity of vindicating the claim of Henry d'Albret to the throne of Navarre. A formidable army advanced under André de Foix, seized on St. Jean Pied de Pont, passed by Roncesvalles, invested and took Pamplona,[1] and the country, as

---

[1] In the defence of Pamplona the celebrated Ignatius de Loyola received a wound in his leg. During his illness he resolved, if his life were spared, to found the order of Jesuits, both for the destruction of Lutheranism, and for the propagation of the Catholic religion among distant nations. See in an earlier volume the chapter on Monasticism.

it had no fortresses to defend it, became the easy prey of the enemy. Had the French been satisfied with this success, and erected fortresses to defend their conquest, the throne of Navarre might have been restored ; but the general, in accordance, as is believed, with an understanding with the rebels of the confederation, invaded Castile and invested Logroño. The place made a gallant defence so as to allow the duke of Najera to advance with reinforcements. On his approach, the French were signally defeated —six thousand of their number remaining on the field, their artillery lost, and many officers captured, among whom was the general-in-chief, André de Foix ; probably a still greater number perished in the pursuit. The king-dom was regained with greater facility than it had been lost. No sooner did Francis hear of this signal failure than, anxious to vindicate the honour of his arms, he despatched a second army, under the grand admiral Bonnivet. The invaders took Fuenterrabia ; but on the approach of Don Bertram de la Cueva, they were driven back with serious loss. In 1524 Fuenterrabia was recovered by the emperor.

In July, 1522, the emperor, whose presence had been so often requested by the royalists, arrived in Spain. Early in the same year the cardinal Adrian had been invested with the pontifical crown. Having visited his mother at Tordesillas, Charles hastened to Valladolid, where his presence was naturally dreaded. It was expected by all that summary justice would be inflicted on those who had taken a prominent part in the recent disturb-ances ; but clemency was the basis of his character, and on this occasion he exercised it to an extent, perhaps, unparalleled in history. He caused proc-lamation to be made that, with the exception of about eighty, all individuals concerned in the recent rebellion were freely pardoned, that all proceedings should cease, that all preceding condemnations should be revoked, and all who had suffered from the judgments of the tribunals should be restored to their possessions and honours. And of the eighty thus excepted, very few suffered.[1]

This conduct was truly imperial : it necessarily made a deep impression on the hearts of the people ; and, as he had gained policy by experience, the deference which he now paid to native customs, the preference which he gave to native habits, the care with which he identified his interests and views with those of the Spaniards did the rest, and enabled him to exercise an ascendency over his subjects which few of his predecessors had ever possessed.*d*

THE MOORS UNDER CHARLES V

From the coming of Charles V to the imperial throne, the history of Spain became that of Europe. Events assumed such enormous proportions that the details of interior administration, police, and government lost much of their importance. The fate of the peninsula was no longer to be decided within the peninsula itself. Spain by its position could not be the centre of the vast empire of Charles V ; it could only be an annex. Since the suicide of the Castilian communes at Villalar, all life had passed to the outside. Charles became a stranger to his hereditary states ; he did not visit them for twenty years except to demand money from them.

Incessant war, which was stifled at one place only to break out in another, weighed heavily on all Spain, which paid the cost without reaping the fruits.

[1] The warlike bishop of Zamora was confined to the prison of Simancas ; there he committed a murder, and was hanged for it — a fit ending for so stormy and unprincipled a life.

Treasure from the New World traversed without stopping in her, and fabulous duties were imposed on all handiwork and provisions. American gold, peninsular revenues, the commerce of the Low Countries, all were swallowed up in this bottomless gulf. Half Europe ruined and exhausted itself to help Charles V to subdue the other half, and after twenty years' struggle this dream of European dictatorship was no nearer being realised than at the beginning.

The Moors, expelled from Granada, or forced by a hypocritical conversion to buy the right of remaining, had ceased to give the government serious anxiety. Religious unity reigned, in appearance at least, in Andalusia, now impoverished by the exile of her most industrious inhabitants.

GRENADA, FROM THE FOUNTAIN OF HAZELNUTS

But it was not the same in the kingdom of Valencia. We have seen the sad dénouement of that insurrection, sister to that of the *comuneros* of Castile. There, also, revolt had been quenched in blood; but deep bitterness rankled in men's hearts. The people, oppressed by the nobles, leagued against them with the royal power, and impatiently awaited the hour of vengeance. Their hatred fell on the Moors, numerous in this country, who, finding no shelter save on the nobles' land, had, in the struggle, espoused the cause of their suzerains. Popular irritation left them, to save their lives, no refuge but baptism. The new converts, lip- but not heart-Christians, bought from their overlords the right to renounce this semblance of Christianity, to return to the rites of Islam, which in reality they had never abjured. But the Inquisition watched them keenly. The relapsed were summoned to re-enter the pale of the church within thirty days under penalty of death and confiscation. The Moors, instead of obeying, had recourse to arms and took refuge in the Sierra de Bernia. There they maintained their position for some months, but hunger, threats, and, above all, promises, decided them to submit.

And yet heroic attachment to the faith of their fathers drove this unhappy people again to disobey, at the peril of their lives.

Then the last blow fell. An imperial decree ordered all Moors of both sexes, who had not embraced Christianity, to quit Valencia before the end of December, and Spain before the end of January. The only port designated to them was that of Corunna. This port, the most distant of all, offered a double advantage — that of keeping them far from Africa, and making them spend all their money on the journey.

Conquered, like their Andalusian brothers, by the iron necessity which bound them, the Valencian Moors resigned themselves to baptism. The neophytes were so numerous that it was found necessary to sprinkle them collectively with the cleansing water. Spain enthusiastically applauded this mockery of baptism. "But," adds Sandoval,ʃ in one of those avowals, good to hear, which he in his candour makes, "there were then at Valencia twenty-two thousand houses inhabited by Christians and twenty-six thousand by Moors, and of these latter, there were not six who received baptism willingly." The Moors in the country, less broken to the yoke than those of the towns, fortified themselves in the Sierra de Espadan, near Segorbe. There, they defended themselves with success against the troops which attacked them.

But one day, at Chilches, they pillaged the church and carried off with them the holy sacrament. At the rumours of this sacrilege the entire country rose. A crusade was preached by the legate, and indulgences were granted as in the time of the holy wars. Volunteers flocked from all parts eager to gain heaven and plunder. Selim, chief of the Moors, displayed in this little-noted struggle talents worthy of a more vast theatre. The war dragged on, until the emperor brought with him from the Low Countries a corps of 4,000 Germans. The Moors, attacked on four sides at once and driven from every position, were conquered, leaving two thousand men on the field. The rest ended by yielding at discretion. The conquerors had sustained considerable loss, but all was forgotten in the joys of victory. The leaders of the insurrection suffered death; the rest, disarmed, were put under strict surveillance, saw the mosques closed, the holy books burned, and, after a useless and last resistance, their only safety in baptism.

A fresh revolt of the Andalusian Moors in 1530 attested how precarious was the liberty of worship granted them. We see them this time extending a hand to their African brothers, more disposed than ever to succour them. Barbarossa, happy in finding this gate of entry into the peninsula, sent thirty-six vessels from Algiers with land troops. The Africans, reunited with the Andalusian Moors, intrenched themselves in the Sierra de Perdona, and repulsed the Spaniards who came to attack them. But soon, convinced that the revolt offered nothing for the future, they offered their Andalusian brothers to transport them, with all their goods, to the African coast, and more than seventy thousand went to seek in Algeria the liberty refused them in Spain.ᵉ

Into the interminable wars of this sovereign — in other words, into his transactions as emperor of Germany — this chapter cannot enter. Those in Italy, Germany, and France, must be sought in the histories of those countries. We may mention that of two expeditions to the African coast, to humble, if not to extirpate, the Mohammedan pirates, one was successful, the other disastrous — the latter a casualty occasioned by a tempest; that he compelled the Grand Turk, who penetrated into the centre of Europe, to retreat; and that at the battle of Pavia he made his great rival, Francis I, prisoner. His behaviour to that monarch was neither dignified nor liberal: anxious to derive the utmost advantage from circumstances, he exacted, as the price of liberation, conditions which, after long hesitation, Francis signed, but with a protest that they should not be binding. Accordingly, the French monarch was no sooner in his own dominions than he openly evaded them, and again tried the fortunes of war; but he could never — not even by his alliance with the Lutherans and the Turks — obtain any advantage over his great rival.

In 1525 Charles married the princess Isabella, sister of João III king of Portugal. The issue of this union was, besides two daughters, the infante Philip, born 1527, destined to be no less famous than himself. For this son he endeavoured to procure the imperial crown of Germany, but his brother Ferdinand, who had been elected king of the Romans, would not forego the dignity, nor would the electors themselves favour the pretensions of the young prince. In 1554, however, he procured for Philip the hand of the English princess Mary ; and that the marriage ceremony might be performed with more splendour, he invested him with the regal title by abdicating in his favour his Italian possessions — the kingdom of Naples and the duchy of Milan. This was not enough : he was preparing to abdicate the whole of his immense dominions, and to retire forever from the world.

CHARLES RETIRES FROM THE WORLD

From the very prime of life the emperor appears to have meditated his retreat from the world. In 1554, the death of his mother, queen Juana, made him decide on the immediate fulfilment of his long-cherished project. For this step, indeed, other reasons might be given. Though only fifty-six, his frame was greatly enfeebled — the result alike of constitutional weakness, and of incessant activity ; and he was subject to grievous attacks of the gout, no less than to other acute pains. In such a state, where the least exertion naturally augmented his infirmities, we may easily conceive that empire could afford him little gratification, and that life itself must be a burden. That, in the hope of some alleviation, he should wish to resign his load of "sceptred care," has nothing to create surprise. Having concluded a truce with Henry, the successor of Francis — a truce, however, which the perfidy of the Frenchman and the ambition of the pope rendered of short duration — and recalled Philip from England, the emperor assembled at Brussels the states of the Netherlands (October, 1555). There, amidst the most imposing solemnity ever witnessed since the days of the Roman cæsars, he resigned the sovereignty of the Low Countries, which he had inherited from his father, the archduke Philip, into the hands of his son. In a few weeks after this august ceremony, Charles, in one no less imposing, resigned the crown of Spain and the dominions dependent on it both in the Old and New worlds. The imperial crown he still retained, with the view of once more negotiating with his brother Ferdinand in behalf of his son ; but in a few months afterwards he despatched the instrument of resignation from the place which he had chosen for his retreat, the monastery of San Yuste, or St. Justus, one of the most secluded and delightful situations in Estremadura.[d]

It was necessary to ascend to the times of Diocletian, to find an example of a similar abdication of empire, on so deliberate and extensive a scale ; and the great English historian of the Roman Empire has compared the two acts with each other. But there seems a vast difference between the cases. Both emperors were distinguished soldiers; both were merciless persecutors of defenceless Christians ; both exchanged unbounded empire for absolute seclusion. But Diocletian was born in the lowest abyss of human degradation — a slave and the son of a slave. For such a man, after having reached the highest pinnacle of human greatness, voluntarily to descend from power seems an act of far greater magnanimity than the retreat of Charles.

Born in the purple, having exercised unlimited authority from his boyhood, and having worn from his cradle so many crowns and coronets, the German emperor might well be supposed to have learned to estimate them at their proper value. Contemporary minds were busy, however, to discover the hidden motives which could have influenced him, and the world, even yet, has hardly ceased to wonder. Yet it would have been more wonderful, considering the emperor's character, had he remained. The end had not crowned the work; it not unreasonably discrowned the workman. The earlier, and indeed the greater part of his career, had been one unbroken procession of triumphs. The cherished dream of his grandfather, and of his own youth, to add the pope's triple crown to the rest of the hereditary possessions of his family, he had indeed been obliged to resign. He had too much practical Flemish sense to indulge long in chimeras, but he had achieved the empire over formidable rivals, and he had successively not only conquered, but captured almost every potentate who had arrayed himself in arms against him. Clement and Francis, the dukes and landgrafs of Cleves, Hesse, Saxony, and Brunswick, he had bound to his chariot wheels; forcing many to eat the bread of humiliation and captivity, during long and weary years. But the concluding portion of his reign had reversed all its previous glories. His whole career had been a failure. He had been defeated, after all, in most of his projects. He had humbled Francis, but Henry had most signally avenged his father. He had trampled upon Philip of Hesse and Frederick of Saxony; but it had been reserved for one of that German race, which he characterised as "dreamy, drunken, and incapable of intrigue," to outwit the man who had outwitted all the world, and to drive before him, in ignominious flight, the conqueror of the nations.

While he was preparing to crush, forever, the Protestant church, with the arms which a bench of bishops were forging, lo! the rapid and desperate Maurice, with long red beard streaming like a meteor in the wind, dashing through the mountain passes, at the head of his Lancers — arguments more convincing than all the dogmas of Granvella! Disguised as an old woman, the emperor had attempted on the 6th of April, 1552, to escape in a peasant's wagon, from Innsbruck into Flanders. Saved for the time by the mediation of Ferdinand, he had, a few weeks later, after his troops had been defeated by Maurice at Füssen, again fled at midnight of the 22nd of May, almost unattended, sick in body and soul, in the midst of thunder, lightning, and rain, along the difficult Alpine passes from Innsbruck into Carinthia. His pupil had permitted his escape, only because, in his own language, "for such a bird he had no convenient cage." The imprisoned princes now owed their liberation, not to the emperor's clemency, but to his panic. The Peace of Passau, in the following August, crushed the whole fabric of the emperor's toil, and laid the foundation of the Protestant church.

On the other hand, the man who had dealt with Rome as if the pope, not he, had been the vassal, was compelled to witness, before he departed, the insolence of a pontiff who took a special pride in insulting and humbling his house, and trampling upon the pride of Charles, Philip, and Ferdinand. In France, too, the disastrous siege of Metz had taught him that in the imperial zodiac the fatal sign of Cancer had been reached. The figure of a crab, with the words "*plus citra*," instead of his proud motto of "*plus ultra*," scrawled on the walls where he had resided during that dismal epoch, avenged more deeply, perhaps, than the jester thought, the previous misfortunes of France. The Grand Turk, too, Suleiman the Magnificent, possessed most of Hungary, and held at that moment a fleet ready to sail against

Naples, in co-operation with the pope and France. Thus the infidel, the Protestant, and the holy church were all combined together to crush him. Towards all the great powers of the earth he stood, not in the attitude of a conqueror, but of a disappointed, baffled, defeated potentate. Moreover, he had been foiled long before in his earnest attempts to secure the imperial throne for Philip.

Had the emperor continued to live and reign, he would have found himself likewise engaged in mortal combat with that great religious movement in the Netherlands, which he would not have been able many years longer to suppress, and which he left as a legacy of blood and fire to his successor.

A Spanish Cavalier of the Sixteenth Century

Born in the same year with his century, Charles was a decrepit, exhausted man at fifty-five, while that glorious age, in which humanity was to burst forever the cerements in which it had so long been buried, was but awakening to a consciousness of its strength. Disappointed in his schemes, broken in his fortunes with income anticipated, estates mortgaged, all his affairs in confusion; failing in mental powers, and with a constitution hopelessly shattered — it was time for him to retire. He showed his keenness in recognising the fact that neither his power nor his glory would be increased, should he lag superfluous on the stage when mortification instead of applause was likely to be his portion. His frame was indeed but a wreck. Forty years of unexampled gluttony had done their work. He was a victim to gout, asthma, dyspepsia, gravel. He was crippled in the neck, arms, knees, and hands. He was troubled with chronic cutaneous eruptions. His appetite remained, while his stomach, unable longer to perform the task still imposed upon it, occasioned him constant suffering. Physiologists, who know how important a part this organ plays in the affairs of life, will perhaps see in this physical condition of the emperor a sufficient explanation, if explanation were required, of his descent from the throne. The resolution to abdicate before his death had been long a settled scheme with him. It had been formally agreed between himself and the empress that they should separate at the approach of old age, and pass the remainder of their lives in a convent and a monastery. He wished to put a little space of religious contemplation between the active portion of his life and the grave.

The romantic picture of his philosophical retirement at Yuste, painted originally by Sandoval[f] and Siguenza,[g] reproduced by the fascinating pencil of Strada,[o] and imitated in frequent succession by authors of every age and country, is unfortunately but a sketch of fancy. The investigations of modern writers have entirely thrown down the scaffolding on which the airy fabric, so delightful to poets and moralists, reposed. The departing emperor stands no longer in a transparency robed in shining garments. His transfiguration is at an end. Every action, almost every moment of his retirement, accurately chronicled by those who shared his solitude, have been placed before our eyes, in the most felicitous manner, by able and brilliant writers.[1] The emperor, shorn of the philosophical robe in which he had been conventionally arrayed for three centuries, shivers now in the cold air of reality.

So far from his having immersed himself in profound and pious contemplation, below the current of the world's events, his thoughts, on the contrary, never were for a moment diverted from the political surface of the times. He read nothing but despatches; he wrote or dictated interminable ones in reply, as dull and prolix as any which ever came from his pen. He manifested a succession of emotions at the course of contemporary affairs, as intense and as varied as if the world still rested in his palm. He was, in truth, essentially a man of action. He had neither the taste nor talents which make a man great in retirement. Not a lofty thought, not a generous sentiment, not a profound or acute suggestion in his retreat has been recorded from his lips. The epigrams which had been invented for him by fabulists have been all taken away, and nothing has been substituted, save a few dull jests exchanged with stupid friars. So far from having entertained and even expressed that sentiment of religious toleration for which he was said to have been condemned as a heretic by the Inquisition, and for which Philip was ridiculously reported to have ordered his father's body to be burned, and his ashes scattered to the winds, he became in retreat the bigot effectually, which during his reign he had only been conventionally. Bitter regrets that he should have kept his word to Luther, as if he had not broken faith enough to reflect upon in his retirement; stern self-reproach for omitting to put to death, while he had him in his power, the man who had caused all the mischief of the age; fierce instructions thundered from his retreat to the inquisitors to hasten the execution of all heretics — including particularly his ancient friends, preachers and almoners, Cazalla and Constantine de Fuente; furious exhortations to Philip — as if Philip needed a prompter in such a work — that he should set himself to "cutting out the root of heresy with rigour and rude chastisement" — such explosions of savage bigotry as these, alternating with exhibitions of revolting gluttony, with surfeits of sardine omelettes, Estremadura sausages, eel pies, pickled partridges, fat capons, quince syrups, iced beer, and flagons of Rhenish, relieved by copious draughts of senna and rhubarb, to which his horror-stricken doctor doomed him as he ate — compose a spectacle less attractive to the imagination than the ancient portrait of the cloistered Charles. Unfortunately it was the one which was painted from life.m

Charles died September 20th, 1558, not long after a rehearsal of his own obsequies which it was his whim to experience. He was buried in the monastery, but twelve years later his son Philip II removed the remains to the family tombs in the Escorial. Before leaving the reign of Charles V, the major part of which is left to the volume of German history, we may quote an estimate of his administration as it affected Spain.a

[1] See Stirling,h Bakhuyzen van den Brink,i the works of Mignetj and Pichot,k and particularly the publication of M. Gachard,l in which last work the subject may be considered to have been fairly exhausted, and in which the text of Siguenzag and of the anonymous manuscript discovered by M. Bakhuyzen, in the greffe of the court of appeals at Brussels, are placed in full before the reader, so far as they bear on the vexed question as to the celebration by the emperor of his own obsequies.

DE MARLIANI'S REVIEW OF THE INFLUENCE OF CHARLES V ON SPAIN

Charles had been brought up by Adrian of Utrecht, later on inquisitor-general and afterwards pope. His first minister was Cardinal Ximenes de Cisneros, also inquisitor-general, the same who condemned 52,552 Spaniards, of whom 3,554 were burned. Thus Charles, by his upbringing and the counsels he received as soon as he became king, was imbued wholly with religious fanaticism and political tyranny. He was not long in showing himself an apt pupil of the two inquisitors.

In spite of the inquisitorial hecatombs which spread terror through Europe, there still existed men who defended public liberty. The last accents of a perishing liberty echoed in the words addressed by the cortes to Charles: "Remember, seigneur," said they to the haughty prince, "that a king is servant to his subjects."

Charles hearkened to this and vowed silently never to forget it, but he refrained from throwing it back into the face of this proud plebiscite, and contented himself with sowing corruption as much as terror. He succeeded in enervating popular energy, and gradually drew away into Flanders the vital part of the nation, there to destroy by force municipal liberties, while he confided the task of annihilating those of Spain to the grand inquisitor-general Adrian and the regent.

What astonishing activity, what wonderful audacity were the Spaniards now possessed with! Rest seemed impossible to these impetuous organisations; and not being able to fight at home, they hastened after Columbus. In 1510 the Castilian banner was hoisted at Darien by Vasco Nuñez Balboa, in 1519 it was planted in Mexico by Ferdinand Cortes, and in 1524 in Peru by Pizarro. Intrepid warriors, their audacity, their religious yet cruel fanaticism strike us with astonishment, and even their crimes cannot wholly suppress our admiration. In those far-off lands whose limits were yet unknown, the first conquerors lacked space. They seemed to be condemned by heaven to cut one another's throats in expiation of their crimes.

The forced humility which Charles V had shown before the cortes of Valladolid weighed on his despotic heart. In haste to give the lie to those words, "The king is the servant of his people," he threw aside his mask as soon as he felt strong enough to aim a blow at liberty. However, the Spaniards were not yet accustomed to his attempted tyranny. They rose in protest against this audacious violation of the oath. The perjured deputies were the first victims to popular justice.

A civil war seemed inevitable, the future of Spanish public liberty to hang on the fate of arms. Padilla put himself at the head of the members of the communes, but the isolation of the provinces, the want of a bond of communication between the various parties in the nation made this sublime attempt ineffectual. The privileged classes, save the bishop of Zamora, followed the orders of the Inquisition. Padilla, martyr to liberty, lost his head on the scaffold, and with him perished Castilian liberty.

In that very hour when Charles V was stifling resistance to despotism in the blood of the last representative of popular power, a new adversary was springing up in Germany. Luther lifted up his already powerful voice in the Diet of Worms, braved both pope and emperor, shook the Catholic faith, and developed that principle of reform which would, later on, separate the empire from the Roman church. In that same year then (1521) liberty, perishing in Spain, was reborn in Germany. So these two great figures in history, fighting sternly in Germany, appeared at the appointed day in the world's theatre — one to destroy, the other to found liberty. One, emperor and king, a great warrior, an eminent politician, exercising most incontestable preponderance, conqueror at Pavia, master of Italy, feared by the Turks whom he had crushed, gave himself up to every despotic inspiration. He fulfilled the execrable mission of overthrowing liberty wherever his arm could reach. After thirty years of warfare, in which cunning, hypocrisy, and courage were alternately employed, Charles fell under the burden of sterile glory. His star had paled before Maurice of Saxony at Innsbruck, and before Henry II in the bishoprics. Reduced in 1552 to treat with his enemies at Passau, he whom the Diet of Frankfort had elected leader of Christianity militant ruined Spain, ravished her liberty and ended by hiding his discouragement and ennui in the depths of a cloister. He abdicated the Spanish throne in favour of his son, the imperial sceptre was committed to his brother, and Charles left nothing to posterity but the germ of all the evils developed by his successors.

Charles V filled the world with his glory, his name, and colossal power, yet never thought of creating a Spanish administration. If he wished to concentrate supreme power in his own hands, it was certainly not with any thought of improving the lot of his people, but only to wield a stronger instrument of tyranny. Surrounded by strangers, he never knew the needs of Spain nor cared to. All was sterile under his iron hand; slow to act, Charles never revoked a decision. Neither force nor danger could draw from him any concession. "I am naturally inclined to persist obstinately in my good ideas," he said one day to Contarini. "Sire," answered the other, "to persist in good ideas is not obstinacy, but firmness." The emperor interrupted him, "But I also persist in bad ones." In 1520, the taxes were so exorbitant that the towns declared they would have to increase the crown revenues without fixing new contributions, and without burdening, as they put it, the king's conscience. This result, added the towns, would easily be attained if the prince would regulate his expenses by his revenue. The Catholic king spent 12,000 maravedis each day. Charles spent 150,000. Ordinary contributions did not suffice, but the cortes were opposed to new exactions. They would only vote subsidies after the redress of wrongs. In the cortes of Corunna of 1520, Charles found an obstinate resistance to voting for taxes. He triumphed, however, and soon rid himself of this embarrassing obstacle, and in 1528 forced the cortes to vote for subsidies before answering their demands. He dismissed the cortes of 1529 which opposed the fixing of new taxes; and again at Toledo, in 1538, he encountered opposition to his inroads.

Charles obtained an order from the pope to raise taxes on church goods. Among other concessions made to him by Rome was the Cruzada bull (authorising consumption of bacon and eggs on fast days). Commerce and industry were terribly crippled. In 1526, Charles had recourse to his wife's portion to defray war expenses; in 1527, his army not having received its pay, set out to ask the pope for that which the emperor did not give. In 1529, Charles, not being able to go to Italy for want of funds, ceded to Portugal for a large sum the Castilian rights in the Moluccas. He sold the fortresses of Florence and Leghorn for 150,000 ducats to Cosmo de' Medici. In a little more he would have sold the pope the states of Milan and Siena. When all these resources were exhausted he had recourse to foreign loans. The uncertainty of public credit, the urgency of present needs obliged him to pay interest of ten, twenty, and fifty per cent. Is not this like the Spain of to-day — swallowing up the state revenues in advance?

By 1550, Charles had mortgaged the whole of his revenues — those of Castile for 800,000 ducats on the 920,000 they yielded; those of Naples and Sicily for 700,000 on the 800,000 which formed the revenue. Those of Milan, amounting to 400,000 ducats, were entirely mortgaged, also a large part of the Flemish revenues. All this without counting the sums coming from America, the amount of which has been so disputed that it is difficult to fix the value, but which must have been very considerable.

These usurious transactions ruined the country; their insufficiency compelled the emperor to make fresh demands for money, but no one would take his bond. Then foreigners, the only ones who would do so, acquired privileges which killed native commerce and industry. Thus the lenders had permission to export articles that Spaniards were forbidden to send abroad. They held also a monopoly for importations. Nearly all the home and Indian commerce came by these means into the hands of foreigners. All appeals were useless, the growing necessities of the prince made him deaf to the just complaints of his people. Thus there was no interior organisation, no real government under the military despotism of the first prince of the house of Habsburg. Charles V destroyed public liberty, corrupted the nobility, tyrannised, oppressed the people, destroyed industry and commerce, and lived only by expedients and usurious contracts. A strong, intelligent administration would have augmented the state revenue, by promoting general prosperity. Charles V abandoned Spain to all the vice, all the excess of avaricious despotism which dried up the sources of national prosperity.[n]

CHAPTER IX

THE REIGN OF PHILIP II

[1556–1598 A.D.]

PHILIP II had received the investiture of Milan and the crown of Naples, previously to his marriage with Mary Tudor. The imperial crown he had been obliged, much against his will, to forego. The archduchy of Austria, with the hereditary German dependencies of his father's family, had been transferred by the emperor to his brother Ferdinand, on the occasion of the marriage of that prince with Anna, only sister of King Louis of Hungary. Ten years afterwards Ferdinand was elected king of the Romans, and steadily refused all the entreaties afterwards made to him in behalf of Philip to resign his crown, and his succession to the empire, in favour of his nephew. With these diminutions, Philip had now received all the dominions of his father. He was king of all the Spanish kingdoms and of both the Sicilies. He was titular king of England, France, and Jerusalem. He was "absolute dominator" in Asia, Africa, and America; he was duke of Milan and of both Burgundies, and hereditary sovereign of the seventeen Netherlands.

Thus the provinces had received a new master. A man of foreign birth and breeding, not speaking a word of their language, nor of any language which the mass of the inhabitants understood, was now placed in supreme authority over them, because he represented, through the females, the "good" Philip of Burgundy, who a century before had possessed himself, by inheritance, purchase, force, or fraud, of the sovereignty in most of those provinces. It is necessary to say an introductory word or two concerning the previous history of the man to whose hands the destiny of so many millions was now entrusted.

He was born in May, 1527, and was now, therefore, twenty-eight years of age. At the age of sixteen he had been united to his cousin Maria of Portugal, daughter of João III and of the emperor's sister, Doña Catalina. Within two years (1545) he became father of the celebrated and ill-starred Don Carlos, and a widower. In 1548, he had made his first appearance in the Netherlands. He came thither to receive homage in the various provinces as their future sovereign, and to exchange oaths of mutual fidelity with them all. Andrea Doria, with a fleet of fifty ships, had brought him to Genoa, whence he had passed to Milan, where he was received with great rejoicing. At Trent he was met by Duke Maurice of Saxony, who warmly begged his intercession with the emperor in behalf of the imprisoned landgraf of Hesse. This boon Philip was graciously pleased to promise, and to keep the pledge as sacredly as most of the vows plighted by him during this memorable year. The duke of Aerschot met him in Germany with a regiment of cavalry and escorted him to Brussels. A summer was spent in great festivities, the cities of the Netherlands vying with each other in magnificent celebrations of the ceremonies, by which Philip successively swore allegiance to the various constitutions and charters of the provinces, and received their oaths of future fealty in return.

His oath to support all the constitutions and privileges was without reservation, while his father and grandfather had only sworn to maintain the charters granted or confirmed by Philip and Charles of Burgundy. Suspicion was disarmed by these indiscriminate concessions, which had been resolved upon by the unscrupulous Charles to conciliate the good will of the people. The light-hearted Flemings, Brabantines, and Walloons received him with open arms. Yet icy was the deportment with which Philip received these demonstrations of affection, and haughty the glance with which he looked down upon these exhibitions of civic hilarity, as from the height of a grim and inaccessible tower. The impression made upon the Netherlanders was anything but favourable, and when he had fully learned the futility of the projects on the empire which it was so difficult both for his father and himself to resign, he returned to the more congenial soil of Spain.

PHILIP'S MARRIAGE WITH MARY TUDOR

In 1554 he had again issued from the peninsula to marry the queen of England, a privilege which his father had graciously resigned to him. He was united to Mary Tudor at Winchester, on the 25th of July of that year, and if congeniality of tastes could have made a marriage happy, that union should have been thrice blessed. To maintain the supremacy of the church seemed to both the main object of existence, to execute unbelievers the most sacred duty imposed by the Deity upon anointed princes, to convert their kingdoms into a hell the surest means of winning heaven for themselves. It was not strange that the conjunction of two such wonders of superstition in one sphere should seem portentous in the eyes of the English nation. Philip's mock efforts in favour of certain condemned reformers, and his pretended intercessions in favour of the princess Elizabeth, failed entirely of their object. The parliament refused to confer upon him more than a nominal authority in England. His children, should they be born, might be sovereigns; he was but husband of the queen — of a woman who could not atone by her abject but peevish fondness for himself, and by her congenial blood-thirstiness towards her subjects, for her eleven years' seniority, her deficiency in attractions, and her incapacity to make him the father of a line of English monarchs.

It almost excites compassion even for Mary Tudor, when her passionate efforts to inspire him with affection are contrasted with his impassiveness.

Tyrant, bigot, murderess though she was, she was still woman, and she lavished upon her husband all that was not ferocious in her nature. Forbidding prayers to be said for the soul of her father, hating her sister and her people, burning bishops, bathing herself in the blood of heretics, to Philip she was all submissiveness and feminine devotion. It was a most singular contrast — Mary the queen of England, and Mary the wife of Philip. Small, lean, and sickly, painfully near-sighted, yet with an eye of fierceness and fire; her face wrinkled by care and evil passions still more than by time, with a big man's voice, whose harshness made those in the next room tremble; yet feminine in her tastes, skilful with her needle, fond of embroidery work, striking the lute with a touch remarkable for its science and feeling, speaking many languages, including Latin, with fluency and grace; most feminine, too, in her constitutional sufferings, hysterical of habit, shedding floods of tears daily at Philip's coldness, undisguised infidelity, and frequent absences from England — she almost awakens compassion and causes a momentary oblivion of her identity.

Her subjects, already half maddened by religious persecution, were exasperated still further by the pecuniary burdens which she imposed upon them to supply the king's exigencies, and she unhesitatingly confronted their frenzy, in the hope of winning a smile from him. When at last her chronic maladies had assumed the memorable form which caused Philip and Mary to unite in a letter to Cardinal Pole, announcing not the expected but the actual birth of a prince, but judiciously leaving the date in blank, the momentary satisfaction and delusion of the queen was unbounded. The false intelligence was transmitted everywhere. When the futility of the royal hopes could no longer be concealed, Philip left the country, never to return till his war with France made him require troops, subsidies, and a declaration of hostilities from England.

Upon his first journey out of Spain, in 1548, into his various dominions, he had made a most painful impression everywhere. "He was disagreeable," says Envoy Suriano[b] "to the Italians, detestable to the Flemings, odious to the Germans." He was thought deficient in manly energy. He was an infirm valetudinarian, and was considered as sluggish in character, as deficient in martial enterprise, as timid of temperament as he was fragile and sickly of frame. It is true that, on account of the disappointment which he occasioned by his contrast to his warlike father, he mingled in some tournaments in Brussels, where he was matched against Count Mansfeld, one of the most distinguished chieftains of the age, and where, says his professed panegyrist, Cabrera,[c] he broke his lances very much to the satisfaction of his father and aunts."

PHILIP'S CHARACTER

Those who were most disposed to think favourably of him remembered that there was a time when even Charles V was thought weak and indolent, and were willing to ascribe Philip's pacific disposition to his habitual cholic and side-ache, and to his father's inordinate care for him in youth. They even looked forward to the time when he should blaze forth to the world as a conqueror and a hero. These, however, were views entertained by but few; the general and the correct opinion, as it proved, being that Philip hated war, would never certainly acquire any personal distinction in the field, and when engaged in hostilities would be apt to gather his laurels at the hands of his generals, rather than with his own sword. He was believed to be the reverse of the emperor. Charles sought great enterprises ; Philip would avoid them. The emperor never recoiled before threats ; the son was reserved, cautious, suspicious of all men, and capable of sacrificing a realm from hesitation and timidity. The father had a genius for action, the son a predilection for repose. Charles took "all men's opinions, but reserved his judgment," and acted on it, when matured, with irresistible energy ; Philip was led by others, was vacillating in forming decisions, and irresolute in executing them when formed.

His talents were, in truth, very much below mediocrity. His mind was incredibly small. A petty passion for contemptible details characterised him from his youth, and, as long as he lived, he could neither learn to generalise, nor understand that one man, however diligent, could not be minutely acquainted with all the public and private affairs of fifty millions of other men. He was a glutton of work. He was born to write despatches, and to scrawl comments [1] upon those which he received. He gave audiences to ambassadors and deputies very willingly, listening attentively to all that was said of him, and answering in monosyllables. He spoke no tongue but Spanish, and was sufficiently sparing of that, but he was indefatigable with his pen. He hated to converse, but he could write a letter eighteen pages long, when his correspondent was in the next room, and when the subject was, perhaps, one which a man of talent could have settled with six words of his tongue. The world, in his opinion, was to move upon protocols and apostilles. Events had no right to be born throughout his dominions, without a preparatory course of his obstetrical pedantry. He could never learn that the earth would not rest on its axis, while he wrote a programme of the way it was to turn. He was prolix with his pen, not from affluence, but from paucity of ideas. He took refuge in a cloud of words, sometimes to conceal his meaning, oftener to conceal the absence of any meaning, thus mystifying not only others but himself.

He appeared on the whole the embodiment of Spanish chivalry and Spanish religious enthusiasm, in its late and corrupted form. He was entirely a Spaniard. The Burgundian and Austrian elements of his blood seemed to have evaporated, and his veins were filled alone with the ancient ardour, which in heroic centuries had animated the Gothic champions of Spain. The fierce enthusiasm for the cross, which in the long internal warfare against the crescent had been the romantic and distinguishing feature of the national character, had degenerated into bigotry. That which had been a nation's glory now made the monarch's shame. The Christian heretic was to be regarded with a more intense hatred than even Moor or Jew had excited in the most Christian ages, and Philip was to be the latest and most perfect incarnation of all this traditional enthusiasm, this perpetual hate. Thus he was likely to be single-hearted in his life. It was believed that his ambition would be less to extend his dominions than to vindicate his title of "the most Catholic king."

[1] The character of these *apostilles*, always confused, wordy, and awkward, was sometimes very ludicrous ; nor did it improve after his thirty or forty years' daily practice in making them. Thus, when he received a letter from France in 1589, narrating the assassination of Henry III, and stating that "the manner in which he had been killed was that a Jacobin monk had given him a pistol-shot in the head" (*la façon que l'on dit qu'il a etté tuè, sa etté par un Jacobin qui luy a donnè d'un cou de pistolle dans la tayte*), he scrawled the following luminous comment upon the margin. Underlining the word *pistolle*, he observed, "this is perhaps some kind of knife ; and as for 'tayte,' it can be nothing else but head, which is not *tayte*, but *tête*, or *teyte*, as you very well know." — GACHARD.[d] It is obvious that a person who made such wonderful commentaries as this, and was hard at work eight or nine hours a day for forty years, would leave a prodigious quantity of unpublished matter at his death.

His education had been but meagre. In an age when most kings and noblemen possessed many languages, he spoke not a word of any tongue but Spanish, although he had a slender knowledge of French and Italian, which he afterwards learned to read with comparative facility. He had studied a little history and geography, and he had a taste for sculpture, painting, and architecture. Certainly if he had not possessed a feeling for art, he would have been a monster. To have been born in the earlier part of the sixteenth century, to have been a king, to have had Spain, Italy, and the Netherlands as a birthright, and not to have been inspired with a spark of that fire which glowed so intensely in those favoured lands and in that golden age, had indeed been difficult.

The king's personal habits were regular. He was most strict in religious observances, as regular at mass, sermons, and vespers as a monk ; much more it was thought by many good Catholics, than was becoming to his rank and age. Besides several friars who preached regularly for his instruction, he had daily discussions with others on abstruse theological points. He consulted his confessor most minutely as to all the actions of life, inquiring anxiously whether this proceeding or that were likely to burden his conscience. He was grossly licentious. It was his chief amusement to issue forth at night disguised, that he might indulge himself in the common haunts of vice. This was his solace at Brussels in the midst of the gravest affairs of state.[1] He was not illiberal ; but, on the contrary, it was thought that he would have been even generous had he not been straitened for money at the outset of his career. During a cold winter, he distributed alms to the poor of Brussels with an open hand. He was fond of jests in private, and would laugh immoderately, when with a few intimate associates, at buffooneries which he checked in public by the icy gravity of his deportment.

The court was organised during his residence at Brussels on the Burgundian, not the Spanish model, but of the 150 persons who composed it, ninetenths of the whole were Spaniards ; the other fifteen or sixteen being of various nations, Flemings, Burgundians, Italians, English, and Germans. Thus it is obvious how soon he disregarded his father's precept and practice in this respect, and began to lay the foundation of that renewed hatred to Spaniards which was soon to become so intense, exuberant, and fatal throughout every class of Netherlanders. He esteemed no nation but the Spanish ; with Spaniards he consorted, with Spaniards he counselled, through Spaniards he governed.

His council consisted of five or six Spanish grandees, the famous Ruy Gomez, then count of Melito, afterwards prince of Eboli ; the duke of Alva, the count de Feria, the duke of Franca Villa, Don Antonio Toledo, and Don Juan Manrique de Lara. The " two columns," said Suriano,[b] " which sustain this great machine are Ruy Gomez and Alva, and from their councils depends the government of half the world." The two were ever bitterly opposed to each other. Alva represented the war party, Ruy Gomez the pacific policy more congenial to the heart of Philip. The bishop of Arras, who in the opinion of the envoys was worth them all for his capacity and his experience, was then entirely in the background, rarely entering the council except when summoned to give advice in affairs of extraordinary delicacy or gravity. He was, however, to reappear most signally in course of the events already preparing. The duke of Alva, also to play so tremendous a part in the yet unborn history of the Netherlands, was not beloved by Philip. He was

---

[1] " *Nelle piaceri delle donne è incontinente, prendendo dilettatione d'andare in maschera la notte et nei tempi de negotii gravi,*" etc. — BADOVARO.[e]

eclipsed at this period by the superior influence of the favourite, and his sword, moreover, became necessary in the Italian campaign which was impending. It is remarkable that it was a common opinion even at that day that the duke was naturally hesitating and timid. One would have thought that his previous victories might have earned for him the reputation for courage and skill which he most unquestionably deserved. The future was to develop those other characteristics which were to make his name the terror and wonder of the world.*f*

To acquire a clear understanding of the interminable and complex events of this remarkable reign, it will be necessary to class them under general heads, without much regard to the chronological order. Unlike the reign of the preceding monarch, some brief space must be devoted to foreign transactions; but such only will be noticed as have an inseparable connection with Spain, and are absolutely necessary to explain its condition.

Immediately after the resignation by the emperor of Naples and Sicily in favour of Philip, the duke of Alva was sent to protect that kingdom and the honour of Spain, against the secret enmity of the pope and the open hostility of the French. Paul IV, who was bound with the tiara in 1555, was as favourable to France as he was hostile to her rival. The papal displeasure was signalised by the arrest of the Spanish ambassador, and by the citation of Philip, whom, as king of Naples, Rome considered as its vassal.

Confiding in the promises of France, Paul in full consistory declared Philip deprived of the Neapolitan throne. The latter, having consulted the most celebrated theologians, whether, as a dutiful son of the church, he could arm against its chief; and having, as was to be expected, received an answer in the affirmative, prepared to defend his rights.

A SPANISH PENITENT OF THE SIXTEENTH CENTURY

The duke of Alva entered the papal states, and seized on several fortresses. The eternal city began to tremble for its security, and was forcing Paul to negotiate with the victor, when, notwithstanding the truce concluded by the emperor, a French army under the duke of Guise advanced, and hostilities were continued. On another part of the frontier, the truce was broken at the same time by the admiral Coligny, governor of Picardy, who made an unsuccessful attempt on Douay. Philip himself inflicted so severe a blow on the French at St. Quentin that Henry in great consternation recalled the duke. The pope was accordingly left at the mercy of the duke of Alva,[1] who advanced

_____

[1 " Alva on his knees asked pardon for bearing arms against the church."*g*]

on Rome, and forced him to purchase peace by withdrawing from the French alliance. As Turkey was banded with the unscrupulous French, that alliance was little honourable to the head of the church. At this very time the Ottoman fleet was ravaging the coast of Calabria, whence it retired with great booty and many captives. The duke of Alva, whose presence was required in Flanders, was for a season replaced in the viceroyalty of Naples by the marquis of Santa Cruz. In 1559, peace was made with France.

WAR WITH THE TURKS (1560-1574 A.D.)

But if this peace freed Naples from the hostilities of the French, it could not arrest the frequent depredations of the Turks. In general, however, these depredations led to no result, the Mohammedans retiring before the Spanish forces. But, in 1565, the sultan Suleiman equipped a powerful armament, both for the conquest of Malta, which the emperor Charles had conferred on the knights of St. John, and for the invasion of the Spanish possessions on the continent. It is not easy to account for the apathy apparently shown by Philip towards their cause, especially after ordering the viceroy of Sicily to defend them. In vain did Don John of Austria, his natural brother, to whom, very honourably for himself, he had granted a splendid household, flee from the court with the intention of embarking at Barcelona, in aid of the knights; the prince was constrained to return. After one of the most gallant defences on record, when nearly two-thirds of the assailants, and most of the defenders, were cut off, about ten thousand Spaniards were landed on the island, and the siege was raised.

In 1570, the war between the Venetian Republic and the porte again brought the Spaniards into collision with the latter power; Rome, Venice, and Spain having confederated for the common defence of Christendom. The combined fleet assembled at Messina, and resolved to assail the formidable armament of the sultan. In the celebrated battle which followed [that of Lepanto in 1571], the papal galleys being headed by Marco Antonio Colonna, the Venetians by Doria, and the Spaniards by Don John of Austria, a splendid victory declared for the Christians [see the history of Italy]. But this advantage was not improved, and the vanquished were soon able to resume. The isle of Jerba, Peñon de Velez a strong fortress on the African coast, and subsequently Tunis were reduced; and in various isolated engagements the advantage rested with the Christians. Such conquests, however, were more easily made than retained. Jerba and Tunis were retaken by storm; the fortress of Oran was abandoned, after most of its defenders had perished either by the climate or the harassing warfare.

WARS WITH FRANCE (1557-1597 A.D.)

The jealousy which had actuated the emperor and Francis was transmitted to their heirs. Philip, however, had no intention to break the truce which it had been one of his father's latest acts to procure; but, as before observed, the hatred of the pope, and the faithlessness of Henry, forced him into the war. Assisted by the troops of his consort, Mary of England, Philip invaded France; and his generals laid siege to St. Quentin, while the duke of Alva, as before related, vigorously defended Italy against a French army under the duke of Guise. The constable, accompanied by the martial chivalry of the country, hastened to relieve St. Quentin ; but under the walls of that fortress he sustained a disastrous defeat, which was followed by the surrender of the place.   Mary had little reason to congratulate herself on her impolitic quarrel with Henry ; she lost Calais, and two smaller forts, — all that remained of the English possessions in the country, — and died before the conclusion of the war.   So far was Philip from indemnifying his ally for the loss sustained, that, four months after her decease, he made peace with France, and confirmed it by a new marriage with Elizabeth [Isabella in Spanish] daughter of the king of France.

For many years after this event (1559–1585), the two monarchs remained outwardly in peace, but inwardly agitated by jealousy or ill will : France had reason to dread the ambitious views of the Castilian ; and the latter was far from satisfied with the secret encouragement afforded by the French Protestants, with the full connivance of the court, to their brethren of the Low Countries, who were striving to shake off the Spanish yoke.   The troubles which distracted the Gallic kingdom during the wars of the league afforded Philip an opportunity, which he had long coveted, of interfering in the affairs of that kingdom, ostensibly in support of the Roman Catholic faith, but quite as much for his own advantage.   As the protector of the league, he at first furnished the rebels with money, and subsequently ordered the governor of the Netherlands, the prince of Parma, to invade the country, and to effect a junction with them.   But the abilities of Henry IV, and the valour of his Protestant adherents, the assistance of Elizabeth, queen of England, and, above all, his conversion to the established faith, rendered the combined efforts of Spaniards and leaguers of no ultimate avail.   His subsequent absolution by the pope destroyed the unnatural coalition which had been formed against him, and enabled him, with the pontiff's mediation, to obtain an honourable peace.   Into the interminable transactions of this period — transactions which are more intimately connected with the history of France than that of Spain — we cannot enter here.

THE NETHERLANDS

The most important of the wars of Philip were with his revolted subjects of the Low Countries.   Soon after his accession, he learned that the Reformation had made alarming progress in these provinces, and he resolved to extirpate it.   His bigotry to the ancient religion, his stern, cruel character, caused him to prefer violent to persuasive measures.   A little reflection might have convinced him that he could never succeed in his object, and that by the bare attempt he would risk the security of his government.   His repulsive manners, his arbitrary measures, and the manifest preference which he gave to his Spanish subjects, soon estranged both Flemings and Dutch from his person.   To his father, whose demeanour was marked by unwonted condescension, and who really loved them, they had been devotedly attached.

Though the emperor was no less a bigot than the son, — though from 1521 to 1555 no fewer than fifty thousand Protestants are said to have perished by fire or sword, — the Roman Catholics were by far the more numerous party, and ready to support him in his bloody proscriptions.   But now the new opinions had seized on all classes of men, and their professors were approaching to a numerical level with the rest.   This fact, however, was unknown to the government : many of the converts were so only in

secret ; and the few who in despite of the penal decrees attended the public
profession of the reformed doctrines were regarded, not indeed as all, but as
the chief portion of Protestants.   In his resolution of extirpating them, the
king commenced by giving new vigour to those decrees ; and, to insure their
execution, he created a new tribunal, with powers similar to those of the
ancient Spanish Inquisition, to take cognisance of heresy.   These measures
were obnoxious to the people, not merely to the secret Protestants, but to the
Catholics, who were subjected to new impositions to defray the expense.
The latter, too, joined with the former in exclaiming against the presence of
the Spanish troops, which they justly characterised as an infraction of a
fundamental law, that prohibited the sojourn in these provinces of armed
foreigners.   Philip, who had extravagant notions of the royal power, paid
no regard to murmurs which he was resolved to stifle by force.   As Spain
demanded his presence, he intrusted the regency to his natural sister,
Margaret duchess of Parma, a princess devoted to his will.

After the king's departure, the regent put the obnoxious edicts into
execution, and the blood of martyrs moistened the soil of the Low Countries.
Her natural disposition was doubtless averse to cruelty ; but she was governed by Cardinal Granvella, a furious zealot, to whose suggestions, as they
were strictly in conformity with the instructions of Philip, she was almost
compelled to defer.   The native nobles, who formed the council of regency,
were not a little chagrined to find their voices powerless — that measures
were framed not only without their consent, but without their knowledge ;
and they resolved to remove the odious churchman.   Among these were two
of more than ordinary consideration — William prince of Orange, and Count
Egmont ; the former governor of Holland, Zealand, and Utrecht, the latter
of Artois and Flanders.   They were soon joined by Count Horn, a nobleman of equal ambition, and equally jealous of Granvella's ascendency.   The
cardinal, perceiving the execration in which he was held, applied for a
release from his unenviable post.   It was reluctantly granted by the king,
who never forgave the men that had occasioned it.   But it produced no
relief for the dissenters.

The decrees of the Council of Trent — decrees written in blood — were
ordered to be executed with even increased severity by some bigoted counsellors.   A confederacy was now formed, professed to prevent the dreaded
introduction of the Inquisition, but in reality to procure uncontrolled liberty
of conscience, or to throw off the Spanish yoke.   It was headed by Philip de
Marnix, lord of St. Aldegonde ; but though the three nobles before mentioned were not members, they were the soul of its proceedings.   Emboldened by their numbers, the lower class of Protestants rose in several of the
towns to inflict on the Roman Catholics what they themselves had suffered ;
perhaps more still were incited by the hope of plunder.   This was but the
beginning of horrors: a furious organised band, amplified as it went along,
hastened to the neighbouring towns ; and, if the relations of Catholic writers
are to be believed, soon laid waste four hundred sacred edifices.

When Philip received intelligence of these events,[1] he called a council,
which, after some deliberation, resolved that an army should be sent to extirpate heresy by open force.   Its command was intrusted to the duke of Alva,
whose relentless disposition seemed well adapted for the task.   His powers

[1 Watson,^{h} like some other Protestant historians, very gently alludes to these scenes.   This
s highly disingenuous.   Nor are the Catholics less to blame ; they exaggerate as much as their
ivals conceal.   The truth is to be gained from neither: it may with difficulty be extracted from
oth.]

were much more ample than those of a general-in-chief: they went so far as to control the authority of the regent. His arrival spread great consternation in the provinces; the more so, when counts Egmont and Horn were arrested (Prince William, too wise to await him, had fled into Germany); and the regent, finding that she was in fact superseded, resigned her authority, and returned to Italy. Many thousands, in dread of the approaching persecution, fled into the Protestant states of Europe; to no country more readily than to England.

A new tribunal, called the Council of Tumults, was formed: its name implied that it was to take cognisance of the late disorders; but, in reality, it was to be an inquisition. Its fatal activity was soon manifest: confiscations, imprisonment, executions were of hourly occurrence. The number of victims is impossible to be estimated: the Protestants say it amounted to thousands; the Catholics, that the ringleaders only suffered the last penalty. It was, however, severe enough to fill all the Protestant states of Europe with concern, and even to draw forth expostulation from several Catholic. How little such remonstrance availed with either the king or his viceroy, appeared from the execution of the counts Egmont and Horn. Their death made a deep impression on the people, who began to turn their eyes towards the prince of Orange, whom they requested to arm in behalf of his suffering country. William was sufficiently inclined, both by love of liberty and personal ambition, to make the attempt. He and his brothers had for some time been making preparations — raising money and troops in the Protestant states of Germany, and collecting the exiles who had fled from the scaffold.

A SPANISH CAPTAIN OF THE SIXTEENTH CENTURY

To enter into the details of the interminable wars which followed, from 1568 to 1598, would little accord either with the limits or the design of this chapter. They will be found in the history of the Netherlands. In an assembly of the Dutch states, held at Dordrecht, they openly recognised William as their governor, and voted him supplies to carry on the war. By their invitation he arrived among them, and the reformed religion was declared that of the state. Alva and his son took the field, to recover the places which had rebelled; and wherever their arms were successful, the cruelties inflicted by them on the inhabitants were certainly horrible. It may, however, be doubted whether they were not fully equalled by the atrocities of the count de la Marck, and other Protestant leaders — atrocities which William, with laudable humanity, endeavoured to end. Philip was at length convinced that a wrong policy had been adopted; and Alva was either recalled, or permitted to retire. He was succeeded by Requesens, a noble-man of equal talents and moderation. The fortune of his administration was varied. He soon lost Middelburg; but he defeated and slew Count Louis of Nassau. He failed before Leyden, the inhabitants of which defended themselves with a heroism and a constancy never surpassed; but, on the other hand, he gained some fortresses in North Zealand. On the whole, however, he was so dissatisfied with his success that anxiety brought him to his grave.

Under the council of state which next governed the Netherlands, Spanish affairs wore a much worse aspect. Sometimes the troops mutinied for their arrears of pay, which Philip's coffers could not often satisfy. They seized Alost, and plundered Antwerp, which had shown more attachment to the prince's cause. To restore the fortune of the war, in 1576, Don John of Austria, the king's brother, was appointed to the regency. After some war-like operations, in which assistance was furnished by Elizabeth, and which were to the advantage of the confederates, the duke of Anjou, who could muster an army, was invited by the Catholics to take possession of the gov-ernment. Before the negotiations with this prince were concluded, Don John died; and Farnese, the prince of Parma, by far the ablest officer in the Span-ish service, arrived, took command of the king's forces, and by his valour no less than his policy changed the position of affairs. He gained possession of Flanders, Artois, and Hainault; but William of Orange had address enough to maintain all Holland, Gelderland, and Friesland, with a proportion of Brabant, in his interests.

These states he formed into a confederacy, called the Union of Utrecht, from the place where it was held. The apparent object was to secure the common weal; the real one, to subvert the Spanish sway. This confederacy was the foundation of the Seven United Provinces. The election of the duke of Anjou threatened forever to destroy the expiring domination of Spain, which the same states (in 1581) declared to be at an end. But Anjou was weak and faithless, and was soon expelled by his new subjects. Subse-quently, indeed, they showed a disposition to be reconciled with him; but his death intervened, and again left the prince of Parma a theatre for the exercise of his talents. It was immediately followed by that of the prince of Orange, who was assassinated by the fanatic Balthasar Gerard, at the instigation of the Spanish general, if not of a higher personage. The death of this justly celebrated man did not produce any advantage for Spain: though his eldest son, the count of Buren, was a hostage in the hands of Philip, the second, Prince Maurice, soon showed that he was able to tread in his steps. The southern provinces, indeed, as far as the Schelde, were persuaded or com-pelled by Farnese to swear anew allegiance to the Spaniard: from commu-nity of religious feeling and from hereditary attachment his path here was smoothed; but in the northern, where the principles of the Reformation had struck so deeply into the soil, the house of Orange had laid the sure founda-tion of its future sway. The latter, after the loss of Antwerp, which was reduced by Farnese in 1585, were strengthened by the accession of Protes-tants from the Spanish provinces, and by the arrival of exiles from Germany and Britain.

The impolitic war of Philip with France drew the prince of Parma from the Low Countries. The confederates had not only time to consolidate their powers north of the Schelde, but to make even destructive irruptions into Brabant and Flanders. The extraordinary military talents of Prince Maurice rendered him no mean antagonist for even the able Farnese. In

1592, the latter died, and with him ended the hope of subduing the northern provinces.   The administration of Count Mansfeld, of Ernest archduke of Austria, of the count de Fuentes, led to little advantage, though the last was an able man.   In 1596, the archduke Albert was appointed to the government, but it was disastrous; under it Maurice reduced not a few of the northern fortresses.   Philip now opened his eyes to the impossibility of maintaining the Netherlands in obedience: he found that, even in the Catholic states, the name of Spaniard was odious; and, as he was approaching the end of his days, he was naturally anxious to settle the affairs of the country. These considerations, added to the affection which he bore for his daughter, the infanta Isabella, and the esteem which he entertained for Albert, made him resolve to marry the two, and resign the government to them and their heirs.   This was one of his most prudent measures: if it could not recall Holland and the other Protestant provinces to obedience, it seemed likely at least to preserve those which were still left.   The deed of abdication was executed in May, 1598, about four months before the monarch's death.

ENGLISH AFFAIRS AND THE ARMADA

The succours which Elizabeth had from time to time afforded the insurgents of the Netherlands was not the only cause of Philip's resentment and of his desire for revenge.   She had fomented the disturbances in Portugal, consequent on the death of Cardinal Henry; and her captains, among whom Sir Francis Drake was the most active, had for many years committed unjustifiable depredations on the Spanish possessions of South America, and more than once on the coasts of the peninsula itself.   By the Spanish historians these hostilities are represented as unprovoked in their origin, and as barbarous in their execution; and candour must allow that there is but too much justice in the complaint.   When Philip's patience was exhausted, and his affairs in the Netherlands allowed him a few months' respite to avenge the insults he had so long sustained, he diligently began to prepare a mighty armament, which, though its destination was secret, was suspected by all to be intended against England.

In 1587, Elizabeth despatched Sir Francis to reconnoitre the coasts of the peninsula, and if possible to annihilate the preparations which were proceeding with so much rapidity.   In April, that admiral, accompanied by twenty-five vessels, appeared before Cadiz, and, by hoisting French and Flemish colours, entered the bay.   But he found the troops aware at length of his country, and drawn up to receive him: he therefore made no attempt to land; but having set fire to many merchant vessels, he returned.   This aggression was not likely to cool the animosity of Philip: the preparations were hastened; all the seaports of Spain, the viceroys of Naples and Sicily, the governor of Milan and the Netherlands furnished vessels, troops, or money.   The general rendezvous was Lisbon, and the command of the fleet confided to the duke of Medina Sidonia, while the prince of Parma was to conduct the land-forces.   After some fruitless attempts at negotiation, in which neither party was sincere, and in which both merely sought to gain time,— how would such conduct be deprecated in private life?— a fleet of 131 ships, some the largest that ever ploughed the deep, carrying, exclusive of seven thousand sailors, no less than seventeen thousand of the bravest troops in the Spanish armies, and the flower of the Spanish chivalry, in May, 1588, left the harbour of Lisbon.

The pompous epithet of "the invincible," which self-confidence had applied to this mighty armament, the approbation of the pope, and the great reinforcement which the prince of Parma had prepared in Flanders, might well inspire the enemy with hope of success.*i*

The fate of the Armada is too well known to need discussion here, especially as it finds full treatment in the history of England. It is well, however, to emphasise the opposition of the Spanish officers to the rash project, and to remember the large part played in the result by the remarkable series of storms against which the Spanish hulks were from their shape peculiarly helpless.

A SHIP OF THE ARMADA

The Spanish historian Mariana,*p* who dedicated his monumental work to Philip II, wrote thus calmly of the failure of the Armada:

"King Philip had in readiness a mighty fleet at Lisbon to revenge the death of the innocent queen of Scots, and the many wrongs done to himself. The marquis of Santa Cruz was appointed admiral; but he dying in the midst of these preparations, the duke of Medina Sidonia was substituted in his place. He set sail in June with fair weather; and having turned Cape Finisterre, off Corunna, a violent storm so scattered and disabled the fleet that they could not put to sea again till September.[1] At length it came to the coast of Flanders, the English fleet always hovering upon their skirts,

[1 The dates generally accepted differ by some months from Mariana's: May 19th, 1588, the Armada sails from Lisbon; soon after dispersed by a storm. July 19th, 1588, enters channel off Cornwall.]

whose cannon and the many sand-banks much endangered our fleet. Some ships were taken by the enemy, and many sore battered by their shot. For which reason, endeavouring to return home round the north of Scotland, many ships perished in that stormy season and long voyage. Besides, the extremity of the cold and want of provisions consumed most of the men, so that very few ships, and a small number of mariners and soldiers, returned to several ports of Spain. Thus human designs are disappointed by a superior power. Doubtless the flower of all the Spanish soldiers was lost in this expedition, and God by this disaster punished the many sins of this nation."

The same pious resignation was shown by Philip himself. [a]

Had the English admiral been well supplied with stores, instead of being compelled to return in search of them, not a vessel would ever have revisited Spain. How many actually perished has been disputed; but the Spaniards fix the number at thirty-two. They must, however, have been the largest, since half the soldiers returned no more, and most of the noble families had to mourn a lost member.

On this trying occasion Philip acted with great moderation: he ordered extraordinary care to be taken of the survivors; received the duke of Medina Sidonia with kindness; observed that no human prudence or valour could avail against the elements, and caused thanksgiving to be made that any of his subjects had returned. The following year an English fleet landed, first in Galicia, where, according to the Spanish accounts, the loss of the invaders was one thousand,[1] and next in Portugal, to support the pretensions of the prior of Crato; but with as little effect. This expedition was injudiciously planned: at this time the authority of Philip in Portugal was too firm to be shaken. The satisfaction which he felt was subsequently alloyed by the hostilities of his enemy in South America, and at Cadiz. In the former, indeed, his fleet triumphed; but in 1596, that flourishing seaport was taken and pillaged. The excesses committed on this occasion by the English troops under the earl of Essex are strongly reprobated by the Spanish historians, while their existence is denied by the English; here we prefer the evidence of the natives. Both admit that the plunder was immense. The insult so enraged the king that he resolved to equip an expedition for the invasion of Ireland, where he would certainly have been joined by the disaffected Romanists. This new fleet, however, was even more disastrous than the famous one of 1588; it was assailed by so furious a tempest that forty of the vessels were lost, and the rest disabled. The severity of this second blow deterred Philip from any future attempts on the most hated of his enemies.

ACQUISITION OF PORTUGAL

The transactions of Philip with Portugal will be best related in the chapters devoted to the modern history of that kingdom. It is here sufficient to observe that, on the death of Cardinal Henry without issue (1580), the crown was claimed by the Castilian monarch in right of his mother; that though there were other competitors, of whom one was supported by England, and though the Portuguese themselves, from hatred to their neighbours, armed to oppose him, his forces placed him on the throne of that country; and that he continued to fill it unto his death. This acquisition, added to the other

[1 English historians pass very gently over the failure of this expedition. Some do not even condescend to notice it. According to Hume,[k] the English lost more than six thousand of their eighteen thousand men, a loss of over 30 per cent.]

extensive dominions of Philip, rendered him by far the most powerful monarch in Europe.

So far with respect to the foreign transactions of Spain under the eventful reign of this monarch; its domestic history must now be noticed.

MORISCOS REVOLT

The revolt of the Moriscos occupies a remarkable place in the native annals of the sixteenth century. These christianised Moors still remained Mohammedans at heart; and though they attended at mass, they made amends in secret for this compulsory apostasy, by celebrating the rites of their own religion. Early in 1567 a decree was published, that the children of the Moriscos should frequent the Christian church; that the Arabic should cease to be used in writing; that both men and women should wear the Spanish costume; that they should discontinue their ablutions; that they should no longer receive Mohammedan names; and that they should neither marry, nor remove from one place to another, without permission from the proper authorities.

The tenacity with which men adhere to ancient forms, even where there is not the slightest compromise of principle, appears from the opposition raised to the edict. The Moriscos contended, with great reason, that no particular mode of dress involved religious considerations, since, in every country, even where the same religion prevailed, it was found to vary; that if their women continued to use the veil, modesty only was the cause; that their musical instruments were equally harmless; that the use of the Arabic language could not surely be a sin, since it was the mother-tongue of many oriental Christians; and that their baths were used, not from religion, but from cleanliness. The marquis of Mondejar, captain-general of Granada, who had strongly disapproved the royal ordinance, was persuaded to lay these representations before the king. They had no effect—a result which so irritated this people that a general revolt was planned. Its chief authors were Ferag ben Ferag, descended from the royal house of Granada, and Diego Lopez ben Abu. The evening of Christmas Day was fixed for the general rising. With the romantic view of restoring their ancient kingdom, they secretly elected in Granada a sovereign, Ferdinand de Valor, whom they named Muhammed ben Humeya, and whose family was of royal extraction.

This bold step was followed by other measures equally secret and vigilant. Officers were nominated; the mountaineers and inhabitants of the plain armed, and ordered to rise on the night appointed — when alarm guns should be fired by the Christians from the fortress of the Alhambra. When the day arrived, eight thousand men lay in the mountains which overlook the towers of Granada, and two thousand more in a different direction, waiting for the signal. They had agreed to assail three of the gates, while another party should scale the walls: the Mohammedans who had been committed to the prisons of the Inquisition, or to those of the state, were immediately to be released, and every Christian in the place to be massacred. Fortunately for the city, several accidents conspired to avert the catastrophe. The night was dark; a heavy snow fell in the mountains; it was followed by a still heavier rain, which rendered them impassable, and compelled the eight thousand in ambush to retire. Ignorant of this disaster, in accordance with a preconcerted plan, Ibn Ferag, accompanied by 180 resolute Moriscos, advanced to the walls of the Albaycin, which they soon scaled, and with loud voices called on their brethren of that quarter to join them. The call, which, as it was issued by trumpets, amidst the silence of night, was heard by all, was applied to deaf ears; none obeyed it.

MOORISH ATROCITIES

But if no impression was made on the capital, the case was far different with respect to the towns and villages in the province, the Moorish inhabitants of which rose simultaneously with this attempt. From Granada Ibn Ferag led his followers into the Alpujarras, where being joined by the *monfis*, or banditti of these mountains, he passed from place to place to sustain the insurrection.

At the same time orders were given by Ibn Humeya to massacre all Christians above the age of ten years. The vengeance of these ferocious apostates fell chiefly upon the priests who had forced them to mass, on the altars and images which they had been compelled to venerate, on collectors of the taxes, and on the officers of justice.

At Ragol, in the district of Marchena, the priest was dragged from the altar where he was celebrating mass, and was hung from a pillar: when dead, he was flayed, and his skin nailed to the wall. At Pitres, after the church and private houses had been plundered, the prisoners were brought out to suffer; but for the priest, who, with his aged mother, exhorted them not to flinch in the trial before them, a more lingering death was reserved. He was first drawn up by a pulley to the top of the steeple, and suffered to fall; but though his legs and arms were broken, he was not dead: he was then heavily cudgelled; still he breathed: a cord was thrown over his neck, and the end first given to some Morisco women, who dragged him through the mire, plunging needles, scissors, and knives into his body, until he perished. These demons of women next destroyed the venerable matron in the same manner. In some places the executions were conducted with whimsical caprice. In one, the rebels first shaved both the head and beard of the curate, but not so dexterously as to avoid inflicting some severe wounds; they next put him to death. In another, the priest and several of his flock having taken refuge in the church, and knelt, to prepare for their inevitable fate, before the high altar, they were seized by the Moorish alguazil; who, in delivering them into the hands of the bloodhounds outside, observed, "Kill these dogs! Let the priest have the first blow, in reward for the anxiety he showed about our souls; let the sacristan have the second, in return for the chastisement he inflicted on us when we either failed to attend mass or arrived too late!"

They seized an image of the Virgin, which, after buffeting and kicking and dragging through the mud, they rolled down a steep eminence, calling on the idol, with ludicrous jeers, to save itself if it had any virtue in it. In another, as a Moorish wag was dragging a large crucifix through a sewer, he perceived a Christian physician, to whom he cried out, "Dog, here is thy Creator! canst thou not cure him?" The horrified Christian immediately knelt, kissed the log, which he declared was indeed his Creator, and was immediately transfixed by the contemptuous bystanders. A magistrate of Santa Cruz was stripped before his three daughters and one of his grandsons; his nose was cut off and nailed to his forehead; and in this state all were led out. On the way to the place of execution, with hands tied behind them, he forgot his own sufferings to strengthen their constancy by his exhortations: and his discourse so incensed the Moriscos that one cut off his ears,

A DELEGATION FROM HOLLAND TO PHILIP II

and crammed them into his mouth; another, improving on the barbarity, cut open his belly, and thrust into the cavity, ears, nose, tongue, hands, and feet; and in this state the poor sufferer was thrown into the flames. The daughters were spared — probably to satiate the brutal lust of the misbelievers. The priest of Andarax was roasted over a brazier; and while sustaining the agony with devout constancy, his mouth was gagged, that he might not invoke the divine mercy; the women, tired of waiting for his death, at length despatched him with their knives and needles. At one place, with the view of ridiculing the sacrifice of the mass, the rebels killed a pig on the high altar. At another, where, under the assurance of safety, about one hundred prisoners who had sought refuge in the fortress surrendered and were immediately butchered, two priests rendered themselves peculiarly obnoxious by their zealous exhortations to the martyrs. One of them was suspended with the head downwards, and with a noose round his neck; at the other end of the cord a second noose was made, and thrown over the neck of the other priest, who was similarly suspended: in their agony they strangled each other, amidst the shouts of the spectators. At Oanez, twenty-five Christian maidens of surpassing beauty were reserved as a present to the African princes whose aid had been solicited. As usual, endeavours were made to convert them, but without effect. Policy yielding to religious fury, they were stripped naked, conducted into the fields, tied to trees, pricked from head to foot with briers and thorns, and a rope being passed round them as they stood in a circle, was drawn so tight as to produce excruciating agony: in the end they were shot. Such are a few of the horrors perpetrated by the Moriscos on this occasion. The number of victims cannot be estimated; it probably amounted to thousands.

A SPANISH CAPTAIN, TIME OF PHILIP II

CHRISTIAN ATROCITIES

When intelligence of these events reached the marquis of Mondejar, after providing for the defence of Granada, he took the field. Ibn Humeya, confiding in the defiles of the Alpujarras, prepared to receive him; while another band of the rebels placed themselves in opposition to the marquis de los Velez, on the southern frontier of this mountainous district. In some isolated actions, the Moriscos had the advantage; but this was only when the Christians went in scattered detachments, and were consequently subject to surprise. The former were too weak, even with the succours they derived from Africa, to risk a general engagement. Fortress after fortress fell into the power of the royal generals, who vigorously pursued the enemy.

The marquis de Mondejar continued the desultory warfare with more or less success. That success would have been much more decisive, but for the opposition between him and the marquis de los Velez: the former was for tempering mercy with justice; the latter for extermination. Horrors now were as much the work of the Christians as of the Moriscos. An event, which happened in the fortress of Jubiles made a deep impression on the rebels, and contributed more than any other cause to feed the flame of civil strife. That fortress being invested by the marquis, three aged Moriscos issued from it with the banner of peace, and agreed to its surrender, on the condition that the lives of the garrison, consisting of three hundred men and fifteen hundred women, should be respected. It was accordingly entered by the royal troops, to whom the plunder was abandoned. The men were lodged with the inhabitants of the town; the women were ordered to be accommodated in the church. As that edifice, however, would contain no more than five hundred, the remaining thousand were compelled to pass the night in the square before it. Guards were posted to protect them.

About the middle of the night, one of the soldiers, being enamoured with a young Morisca, wished to detach her from her companions. She resisted; he pulled her away by force; when one of the persons by her side — her husband or brother, in the disguise of a woman — took her part, engaged, and disarmed the soldier. The confusion produced by this struggle led to a tumult; the soldiers rushed from their camp; it was proclaimed that many armed Moriscos were disguised among the prisoners; and, in the fury of the moment, the whole number were pitilessly massacred. In vain did the marquis endeavour to stay the carnage: the authority of the officers was disregarded. At break of day their fury cooled, and gave way to remorse on perceiving the bloody corpses of one thousand helpless, unarmed women. This bloody crime will never be blotted from the minds of men.[1]

The tyranny of Ibn Humeya somewhat counterbalanced the effect which this terrific tragedy was so well calculated to produce. He assassinated his father-in-law, repudiated his wife, put to death several of her relatives, and threatened the same fate for her brother, Diego de Rojas, one of his ablest adherents. By this hasty vengeance he naturally estranged many of his followers. As the Christian army advanced into the mountains, he was compelled to flee from one position to another; but not without loss to his pursuers.

Mondejar considered that the war was at an end, and that the fugitive would infallibly be captured. He did not know that, notwithstanding the heavy losses sustained by the enemy, they were still six thousand in number; many of them determined to resist to the last extremity. In a few days, however, on the heights of the Sierra Nevada, one thousand were exterminated by the marquis de los Velez.

But such were the excesses of the Christian soldiers, the want of faith which characterised some of their leaders, and the rapacity of all, that no reverses could make the rebels lay down their arms; and on several

---

[1 Army after army of Christians were hurled upon them with the openly avowed object of massacre — not war. Women and children, as well as men, were slaughtered in cold blood. How many thousands fell in the attacks and inevitable reprisals it is impossible now to say. Six thousand helpless women and children fugitives were sacrificed in one day by the marquis de los Velez, but still the churchmen were not satisfied. In the council chamber and the cathedral they cried for blood, and ever more blood — just as the same men did for the blood of Flemish heretics at the hands of their chief Alva. In vain the civil governors, and even soldiers, advocated some moderation, some mercy. Deza the inquisitor and Espinosa the cardinal in their purple robes knew no mercy for those who denied their sacred right to impose a doctrine upon other men.*j*]

occasions they were enabled to inflict a suitable revenge. The Moriscos had learned, to their cost, that even when conditions of capitulation had been proposed and accepted, in violation of their terms the prisoners were plundered or massacred. It was asserted that no faith could be placed in a Christian's word or bond; and the report naturally strengthened the bands of Ibn Humeya. Philip saw that the two marquises would never cordially co-operate so long as each led an independent power; and he subjected both to the authority of his bastard brother, Don John of Austria.

Several districts which had submitted rebelled anew, and Ibn Humeya was at the head of a far more numerous force than had ever yet taken the field.

At Valor, whither the marquis de los Velez penetrated, Ibn Humeya made a vigorous stand; but notwithstanding his valour, which was never perhaps surpassed, and his abilities, which were of a high order, he was signally defeated and compelled to flee almost alone. This disaster was partially repaired by a reinforcement from Africa, and by the spirit of desertion which prevailed in the camp of the marquis. His own conduct, however, continually increased the number of his enemies. One night he was strangled, and Ibn Abu was proclaimed under the name of Mulei Abdallah.

The war now raged with various success; to each party the loss of one day was counterbalanced by the gain of the next, until Don John of Austria, who had assembled troops on every side, again took the field in person. He proceeded to reduce the mountain fortresses. One after another fell into his hands. To prevent another insurrection after submission, the inhabitants of the newly subdued towns were transplanted to other parts, generally to the towns of Andalusia; a few into New Castile. This measure contributed more than any other to weaken the rebels, and to hasten the conclusion of the war. In almost every partial action — the enemy could no longer dream of a general one — the advantage lay with the Christians; nor was the success less rapid than decided.

As the whole range of mountains was now almost depopulated, the Moriscos being uniformly transferred to other parts, and as but a handful of desperate adventurers, most of whom had been professed banditti, remained, the chiefs who still adhered to Mulei now advised him to submit. He refused and was killed. With Mulei was extinguished the last spark of the rebellion.

THE MISFORTUNES OF DON CARLOS

The next important feature in the domestic administration of Philip is the fate of his first-born son, Don Carlos. This prince, who was born in 1545, was by nature of fiery temperament and of irregular manners. In his seventeenth year he sustained an accident, which was, doubtless, the chief cause of all his misfortunes. One day, while at the university of Alcalá, he fell headlong down the staircase, and was for some time stunned by the blow. As no external injury was visible, his medical attendants hoped that he would soon be restored; but in a few days he was seized with an alarming fever, and they were painfully convinced that a serious internal one had been sustained. The fever increased, delirium approached, the king was sent for, and all hope of cure abandoned (1562).

In this extremity, when human aid was evidently unavailing, recourse was had to the merits of San Diego of Alcalá, who had always been the peculiar object of the prince's veneration. The holy corpse was exhumed and brought into the bedchamber of Carlos, whose hands were devoutly placed on it, and whose lips implored the intercession of the saint; at the same time a part of the shroud was laid on his burning face. While a procession of monks removed the corpse to the tomb, the prince, we are gravely informed, fell into a sweet sleep, in which San Diego appeared to him, and assured him of a speedy recovery. The prediction, we need scarcely add, was immediately verified! Unfortunately, however, the saint could only restore the body; from this moment must be dated the periodical insanity of the patient, and that invariable eccentricity of manner which is inconsistent with soundness of intellect.[1] As he grew in years he exhibited his wayward humour; sometimes the most extravagant freaks. Nothing can more clearly show his unfortunate state of mind than his behaviour to the duke of Alva, when that nobleman, on being appointed to the government of the Netherlands, called to take leave of him. He told the duke that to him alone belonged the dignity, and that he would take the life of anyone who usurped it from him. Alva, with great mildness, endeavoured to pacify him, but in vain: in his fury he drew forth a dagger, and would assuredly have buried it in the governor's heart, had not the latter seized his hands and held him until some gentlemen of the household hastened to the scene. One of his favourite diversions was to walk the streets by night, sometimes indecently exposing his person. On one occasion a pair of new boots were brought, which the prince, finding too tight, immediately cut into pieces, and made the poor workman swallow several. One day his chamberlain, Don Alfonso de Cordova, brother of the marquis de las Navas, being summoned by the bell, was unable to arrive in time for his impatience: he took the chamberlain in his arms, swore he would throw him out at the window, and advanced to one for the purpose, when the cries of Don Alfonso brought the domestics to his aid. Being one day in a forest with his governor, Don Garcia de Toledo, whom he hated for attempting to restrain his desperate excesses, he proceeded to stab that nobleman; but the intended victim escaped and reported him to the king. In short, his conduct to all his servants was intolerable, alike for its cruelty and caprice: several he beat, a few he maimed; nor could the exhortations of his father or his confessor make any impression on him. To the former he bore a bitter hatred: the cause was that Philip, who knew his fatal infirmity, would not allow him to interfere with public affairs.

At length, being discovered in an attempt to flee into the Netherlands, to place himself at the head of the insurgents, the king felt that he should be compelled to place a guard over his frenzied son. On the night of January 19th, 1568, accompanied by four of his nobles and some armed guards, he proceeded to the prince's apartment, took away his papers, his sword, knives, and everything that could be hurtful to him; assuring him at the same time that he had no end in view beyond his good.

He confided the care of the prince to six gentlemen of the noblest families of Spain, two of whom were always to be with him night and day; and he placed over all the duke of Feria and the prince of Eboli. This measure, however well intended, did no good: Carlos grew sullen and obstinate; his freaks more frequent and capricious. To walk in a state of nudity through his apartments; to refrain from food two days together, and then to eat voraciously; to drink immoderate quantities of the coldest water; to steal

---

[1 He was unskilfully treated by the doctors, ghastly superstitions were resorted to instead of proper surgical treatment, and he lay unconscious, blind, and partially paralysed, until an Italian surgeon trepanned him, and he then apparently recovered.*]

[1568–1579 A.D.]

ice and convey it into his bed;[1] to devour the sourest fruits, were his constant occupation. The infallible consequences soon appeared : his stomach
refused to retain the most wholesome food, much more the medicines that
were administered to him ; a malignant fever assailed him ; and he was told
to prepare for death. At this period his better feelings returned ; he asked
for his father, whose pardon he humbly demanded, and whose blessing he
received ; he received the last sacraments, commended his soul to God, and
died at midnight, July 24th, 1568.

The fate of this maniac prince has called forth much affected commiseration, inasmuch as it has enabled malignity to assail the memory of the father.
It has been stated that Philip was the rival of his son in the affections of
a French princess [Elizabeth (Isabella), daughter of King Henry II]; that
after she became queen of Spain, she loved the latter, and detested the
former ; that jealousy forced the king to the most tyrannical treatment of
the youth ; that Carlos was persecuted by the Inquisition, and at length
poisoned, by order of the father.[2] The truth is that Philip behaved with
much moderation to a son who was fit only for a receptacle for lunatics.

FATE OF THE KING'S SECRETARY, PEREZ

But if impartial justice acquit Philip of guilt, or even of undue severity
in regard to his son, the same favourable verdict cannot be given in regard to
two other affairs, which have been studiously wrapped in great darkness : they
were the assassination of Juan de Escovedo, secretary to Don John of Austria, and the subsequent persecution of Antonio Perez, Philip's secretary
of state. The former, who had been sent to Spain on business of his master,
was murdered at Madrid, in March, 1578. The assassins were not unknown;
but they were suffered to escape into Italy, and were afterwards employed
in the service of the Neapolitan viceroy. That they were hired by Antonio
Perez is undoubted, from his own confession ; but what interest had he,
what revenge to gratify, in such a crime ? The same confession — published
many years after the tragedy — throws the entire blame on the king ; nor is
there any reason to doubt its truth.[3]

The most probable hypothesis is that Escovedo was the prime intriguer
in the ambitious schemes which Don John is known to have formed : that
he had persuaded his master to aspire to the hand of Elizabeth, queen of
England, was seriously affirmed by letters from the Low Countries ; and that
he had passed two months in England in trying to open negotiations for that
end was said to rest on the authority of the Spanish ambassador at Rome.[i]

The sons of the murdered Escovedo had, soon after their father's death,
instituted a prosecution against the secretary, Antonio Perez, as the author of
the foul deed. Through the king's intervention, and under his sanction, a compromise was effected between the parties. Perez paid a large sum of money
to Escovedo's family, whereupon he was set at liberty, and, though forbidden
to appear at court, continued to conduct the business of his office. But

[1 But as Prescott[o] points out, Carlos was confined in a stifling prison, suffering from high
fever. The ice-water treatment was favoured then by certain physicians as it is now universally.]

[2 The accusation was made by the arch-liar Antonio Perez, and Prince William of Orange[i]
declared that there was proof at Paris that Philip murdered both his son and his wife ; but the
accusation is now generally counted as pure malice.]

[3 It seems now that Philip gave Perez written authority to kill Escovedo, but that he neglected to do so till some months later when the king's hostility had passed and the motive was
simply the personal jealousy of Perez himself.]

either the alleged intimacy with the princess of Eboli still rankled in Philip's mind, or he dreaded the disgraced secretary's revealing his own share in Escovedo's assassination. In 1591 Perez was accused of boasting of the murder, of betraying state secrets to the princess of Eboli, of falsifying the letters he deciphered, and of taking bribes. Upon these charges he was thrown into prison, where, whilst he was offered his liberty as the price of giving up the king's letters touching Escovedo's death, he was treated with extraordinary severity. Perez accepted the terms, and was released : but he managed to keep back one note, which Philip, it seems, had forgotten.

The liberty thus purchased, Perez was not, however, long permitted to enjoy. The prosecution for the murder was revived ; the accused was again

thrown into prison, where he was tortured to extort a confession, which he had no desire to withhold. He is said to have revealed all, giving the reserved royal letter as evidence of his truth ; and thus Philip, whose only object in this strange tissue of artifice appears to have been the clearing himself by a judicial sentence from any participation in the murder, was caught in his own toils. But the situation and prospects of the prisoner were not improved by the exposure of his royal accomplice ; and he saw that in flight lay his only chance of life. His escape was happily managed by the address of his wife. Perez fled to his native Aragon ; and there, though he was again seized by the king's orders, his condition was far different. He appealed to the yet inviolate laws and privileges of Aragon. The *justiciero mayor*, Juan de Lanuza, evoked the cause before his own tribunal at Saragossa, where the proceedings were public ; and he lodged the accused in the prison called the Manifestacion, under his own sole and especial jurisdiction.

This was not the tribunal before which it suited Philip that Perez should be tried. The Inquisition, therefore, accused the ex-secretary of heretical opinions ; and as the justiciero mayor would not surrender his prisoner, the inquisitors, with the assistance of the marquis of Almenara, a minister of the king, broke open the prison, and removed him to their own dungeons. Such an infraction of the Aragonese constitution roused the spirit of the people, and a regular contest ensued between them and the king's officers, in the course of which the

PEREZ IN PRISON

marquis of Almenara was so ill-used as to occasion his death. Perez was recovered from the inquisitors and replaced in the justiciero's custody ; again seized by the inquisitors, and again torn from them by the populace, who, upon this second occasion, favoured his flight, when Perez, by the aid of his friends, escaped into France, where he was kindly received and protected by Henry IV.

Philip sent an army into Aragon, to quell and chastise these disorders. Prudence and submission upon negotiation might still, perhaps, have effected a compromise : but the justiciero had died during the tumults, and his son, who had succeeded to his office, rashly attempted to resist by force this second act of unconstitutional violence ; for no foreign troops might enter Aragon without the consent of the cortes or the justiciero ; and each of the several kingdoms united under the name of Spain still considered the natives of the others as foreigners. The attempt was unsuccessful, and again the fatal consequences of unsuccessful rebellion followed. The justiciero, together with the duke of Villa Hermosa, and some other leaders of the insurgents, were put to death ; and the liberties of Aragon were very greatly diminished, though not so completely crushed as those of Castile had long been.[n]

DE CASTRO'S ESTIMATE OF ANTONIO PEREZ

Hated by the people while his influence with Philip II lasted, Antonio Perez became eminently popular as soon as his sufferings began. The secretary of state had commenced his brilliant career with a careful education, a vast knowledge, and an experience superior to his years. His handsome appearance won him the attention and favour of high-born women ; his easy and agreeable manner gave him the highest place at the splendid court ; his great ability, intelligence, and skill in business, his courtier-like cleverness had promptly won him his king's affection.

The highest offices were heaped upon him, country-seats, palaces, carriages, horses, banquets, magnificent furniture, gold, and precious stones, all that his century could bestow, the delights of luxury, the pleasures of riches, the adulation of a high position — all was within his reach, and he abused all without limit or restraint. What could he not promise himself ? What could he not hope for ? Nevertheless the scene completely changed for the dazzled favourite ; the hour of misfortune roused him from the soft sleep of his sybaritic delights, of his ambitious hopes , and imprisonment, tortures, the most violent and painful sufferings put his rich nature to the proof, exhausted the resources of his character, humbled his pride, and effacing the grievous errors of his prosperity, repeatedly poured into his ardent and pleasure-loving soul the balsam of resignation and the consolations of melancholy.

Having taken refuge in Paris by the side of Henry IV, he employed the rest of his life in defending the acts of his administration, and in vindicating his name from the grave accusations weighing on him. It was then he wrote his voluminous work entitled *Memoirs and Letters of Antonio Perez*, a book now well-nigh forgotten, but which in its time won the highest fame for its author. And this fame was just. All his writings in France, all his labours in England, had but the one exclusive aim — his defence ; while he excited the interest of powerful foreigners won by the attraction of his cultured conversation, his graceful manners, and his flowery and witty letters. By this means his life and defence gained the highest popularity, his book made the greatest sensation in Paris, and numerous editions, translations, and extracts followed in quick succession to satisfy the public eagerness. The attentions of interest, the praise of admiration everywhere followed Perez, and while people believed his word and compassionated his dramatic misfortunes, they anathematised with horror the memory of his persecutor, the son of the victorious emperor, the eternal enemy of French influence.

An extraordinary coincidence kept the memory of his misfortunes ripe in Spain. His last persecution is intimately connected with the abolition of Aragonese *fueros*, when, a fugitive from prison, Antonio Perez presented himself in Saragossa, imploring the aid of the country's laws, and appealed to the magistrates of the town, and his personal friends watched that no harm should come to his person. Provocations on one side, excesses and disorders on the other, brought about a revolution; and when the king's troops presented themselves before the gates of Saragossa, the people neither knew how to calm down nor to resist them, and Aragonese liberty came to perish on the scaffold of Lanuza. The remembrance of their lost privileges, the memory of their sufferings, lasted many years in Aragon, and the natives of the country loved and defended the person of the luckless being who was the occasion rather than the motive of their rising. The name of Antonio Perez has become therefore strangely involved with the fueros of his native land, and both causes have been handed down to posterity united in a common misfortune and a common love.

But it is unworthy of the learning of the age to judge the first of Spanish kings by the light of the deceptive rays reflecting from his political and religious enemies, from the point of view of the philosophical prejudices of the eighteenth century. By the blunders of his administration, the violence of his passions, the exaggeration of his character the son of Charles V has given sufficient food for censure, without heaping on his head false crimes and imaginary faults. When, trusting to appearances or to partisan reports, one judges Philip II in his dealings with Antonio Perez, one's natural feeling is to absolve the favourite and condemn the king, but if one has the curiosity to examine contemporary documents, if one investigates the private or public interests which suddenly changed the condescending friendship of the king into hatred and persecution, one certainly deplores the misfortune of the fallen minister and the inexorable anger of his sovereign, but the extravagant admiration for the victim will slightly decrease, and the abhorrence for the man who abandoned him to the implacable hatred of his enemies will be less intense.

His life is a lasting example to proud courtiers that the favour of princes is inconstant as the calmness of the sea; speedily the tempest comes and lashes the waves. As the famous duke of Alva said to the prince of Eboli: "Kings are wont to prove men like children with personal favours, and bait them like fishes."

The life of Antonio Perez is an example of the inconstancy of fortune and the vanity of worldly desires; and there is a warning in the fate of the magnate who, having drained all the pleasures of riches and seductions of vanity, dazzled by the height of his position fell into such affliction and misery that his contemporaries considered him worthy of the title — "fortune's freak."*m*

THE DEATH OF PHILIP

Philip now felt his latter end approaching; and, from a natural desire to leave his wide-spreading dominions in a tranquil state to his son, he gladly accepted Pope Clement VIII's proposal to mediate a peace between France and Spain. The negotiation was procrastinated by the archduke's surprise and capture of Amiens, which Henry thought it indispensable to recover, before he would even listen to terms. The Spanish garrison in that town capitulated in the autumn of 1597; and in the following summer, notwithstanding the opposition of Queen Elizabeth and Prince Maurice, the Peace of Vervins was concluded upon equitable conditions — all conquests being mutually restored, and all pretensions to any part of each other's dominions mutually relinquished.

This peace and the investing of the infanta with the sovereignty of the Netherlands were the last acts of Philip. He did not live to see the celebration of her marriage, or of his son's with Margaret, daughter of the archduke Charles of Austria, which he had concluded. He had for years been, like his father, a martyr to the gout, but had never permitted his sufferings to interfere with his regal duties. During the severest paroxysms, he regulated everything, and frequently, when urged to spare himself, said that the pains in his joints did not lame his brain. His last illness was dreadful, his limbs being covered with ulcers that generated swarms of the most loathsome vermin. In that condition he lay for fifty days, and is said to have exhibited during the whole time a wonderful example of Christian patience and resignation. He died on the 13th of September, 1598. Of his numerous children, two only survived him — his son Philip, and the infanta Isabella. A second daughter, Catherine, had married the duke of Savoy, but died before her father, leaving a large family.

In America the limits of the Spanish empire were extended during this reign, but not so as sensibly to affect the power or the greatness of the mother-country. One fact, however, deserves notice. Whilst all surrounding Indians bowed beneath the yoke, and were rapidly swept away by the unaccustomed toils their new masters required, one bold and warlike tribe in the province of Chile, named the Araucans, after submitting like the rest, rose against their oppressors, and for years defied all the troops the Chilian and the Peruvian Spaniards could send against them. The war was ended only by a treaty recognising their independence. In the East Indian seas the Philippines were named and colonised.

Philip II had received Spain from his father in a state of brilliant prosperity. Her agriculture and manufactures were flourishing, and were competent to supply her large exports to her American colonies. That from this happy condition Spain began, during his long reign, to decline, is admitted by those Spanish writers who most warmly eulogise Philip; nor is the great pecuniary distress denied to which the lord of America and her mines was latterly reduced. The two facts form a curious comment upon the extraordinary prudence considered by them as his peculiar characteristic.

For this decline various causes have been assigned by philosophical historians, as, the numerous colonies that drained the population of the mother-country; the disgust which men, who saw immense fortunes easily and rapidly accumulated, in the plunder or the mines of the New World, conceived for the toils and the slow profits of trade and husbandry; the enormous waste of men and money occasioned by the various and simultaneous wars into which Philip was hurried, by either an extravagant ambition or an uncalculating bigotry. Experience and a maturer philosophy teach us that whatever ills may be thus occasioned, they are in their nature temporary, requiring only time to correct themselves; and direct us to seek the true cause of the gradual downfall of Spain in her loss of liberty.

The union of Spain into one monarchy, under Ferdinand and Isabella, had lessened the long-existing intimate connection between king and people, and the dependence of the former upon the latter: the natural consequence was a diminished respect on the part of the crown for popular rights. The splendour of Charles' reign, his clemency, conciliating manners, and good government, perhaps, blinded the nation to his gradual invasion of their privileges, and neglect of the forms of a free constitution. Under the sterner sway of Philip, a complete despotism was established, and it seemed to give him a boundless power, alarming Europe, at the moment his authority began to decline. Since the cortes had fallen into contempt, the cities had lost their importance, and an arbitrary system of taxation had shaken the security of property.

Under such circumstances, commerce languished, and had no energy to resist the blow when the English and Dutch fleets intercepted the vessels bearing Spanish merchandise to America, or bringing back an ample return. Agriculture, like manufactures, must always suffer from the impoverishment of any portion of the community ; but in Spain it now laboured under peculiar additional evils. When the nobles were lured from their rural homes to court, for the purpose of weakening their feudal power, the peasantry, divided from their natural protectors, robbed of the encouragement and support of almost princely establishments in every part of the country, sank into a degraded class ; whilst the mighty lords themselves became mere intriguing courtiers, rapacious for money, in order to rival each other in splendour, and tyrants of those dependent peasants to whom their ancestors were as fathers. In this state, the vital spirit that should have reacted against every disaster was no more ; and calamities, in their nature temporary, became permanent.

Philip II adorned Spain with many useful and some ornamental works. He erected the Escorial, which has ever since been a favourite royal residence. The Escorial is an immense pile of building, uniting a monastery, a cemetery, and a palace, dedicated to St. Lawrence in gratitude for the great victory of St. Quentin, gained upon the day on which his festival is celebrated ; and to stamp it yet more manifestly his, is built in the form of a gridiron, the instrument of that saint's martyrdom. The expense of the Escorial is reckoned as one cause of the exhaustion of Philip's exchequer.

Philip was, or in emulation of his father and of his great-grandmother Isabella desired to be, esteemed a patron of literature, and of learning in general : in token of which he sent his eldest son Don Carlos, his brother Don John, and his nephew, the prince of Parma, to be educated at the University of Alcalá ; and during his reign flourished most of the great Spanish authors. But the privilege of proscribing whatever books they should judge dangerous to Catholicism, which he committed to the Inquisition, more than counterbalanced his patronising exertions.[n]

" When he succeeded to his father," says Hume,[k] " Spain was already well-nigh ruined by the drain of the emperor's wars, imposed upon him by the inheritance of Flanders and the empire. It would be unfair to blame the monarch for the folly of his financial measures, as the science of political economy was yet unknown ; but their persistent perversity seems almost systematic. When no further supplies could be wrung from the cortes, funds were raised by the seizure of the money which came to merchants from the Indies in payment for goods, by forced loans from nobles, prelates, or wealthy burgesses, by the sale of seigniorial rights over villages and towns, and of the rotal patrimony, by repudiating debts, reducing interest, and hampering commerce and industry.

" The maladministration arising from the evil system of pledging and farming future resources was never reformed, the squalid lavishness of the court expenditure was never reduced, a conciliatory policy in order to avoid the cost of war was never adopted : the only steps which appear to have occurred to the financial advisers of Philip were those which undermined public confidence and security, which blighted the national industries, and which killed future resources for the sake of present advantage. The continued aggregation of land in the hands of the church and tied up in perpetual entail, and the expulsion of the Moriscos from Andalusia had well-nigh uined agriculture.   To prevent whole provinces from starving in the finest grain country in the world, immense quantities of wheat had to be introduced from abroad, and the alcabala suspended on bread-stuffs imported into Seville.   Constant wars and emigration, the association of the Moriscos with industry, and the immense number of church holidays, moreover, made the ordinary Spaniard contemptuous of work, and scanty in his aggregate production.   And so the vicious circle went on, and the curse of far-reaching dominions in the possession of an imperfectly unified and organised country had in seventy years reduced Spain to the last depth of misery and penury. To some extent this may, of course, be attributed to Philip's qualities and limitations; but it was mainly owing to a system and to circumstances which were originated before his birth and which neither his training nor his character enabled him to vary."

DUNHAM'S ESTIMATE OF PHILIP II

His character must be sufficiently clear from his actions: that it was gloomy, stern, and cruel; that he allowed neither civil freedom, nor religious toleration, but was on all occasions the consistent enemy of both; that he was suspicious, dark, and vindictive, are truths too evident to be denied. On his return to Spain, immediately after his father's resignation, a characteristic scene occurred in Valladolid, at an auto-da-fé, which he attended with much devotion.   When the condemned arrived at the place where the fire and fagot awaited them, one of them, an officer of distinction, asked the king how he could have the heart to behold the exquisite torments of his people. "Were my own son," replied the bigoted tyrant, "such a wretch as thou, he would suffer the same fate!"

And when the archbishop of Toledo, Don Bartolomeo de Carranza, was arrested on suspicion of heresy by the office blasphemously called holy, the king wrote to the inquisitors commanding them to show no respect for persons, however exalted, but to proceed even against his own son, should the latter ever dare to doubt the infallibility of the church.   All this is bad enough; yet, by the French writers as well as by our own historians, he has been treated with injustice.   His ambition was certainly subservient to his zeal for religion; his talents were considerable; for prudence he was almost unrivalled; his attention to public affairs and to the best interests of his country has been surpassed by few monarchs; his habits were regular, his temperance proverbial; his fortitude of mind, a virtue which he had often occasion to exercise, was admirable; and, in general, he was swayed by the strictest sense of justice.   Even his religious bigotry, odious as it was, was founded on conscientious principles, and his arbitrary acts on high notions of the regal authority.   By many of his subjects he was esteemed, by many feared, by some hated, by none loved.[i]

WATSON ON PHILIP'S IMPRUDENCES

Some historians have distinguished this prince by the title of Philip the Prudent, and have represented him as the wisest as well as the most religious prince that ever filled the Spanish throne.   But it is questionable whether he be entitled to praise on account of his prudence, any more than on account of his religion.   In the beginning of his reign he discovered great caution in his military enterprises ; and, on some occasions, made even greater preparations than were necessary to insure success.   But his ambition, his resentment, and his abhorrence of the Protestants were too violent to suffer him to act conformably to the dictates of sound policy and prudence.

He might have prevented the revolt of his Dutch and Flemish subjects if, after the reformation in the Netherlands was suppressed by the duchess of Parma, he had left the reins of government in the hands of that wise princess, and had not sent so odious a tyrant as the duke of Alva to enslave them.   He might, after the defeat of the prince of Orange, have riveted the chains of slavery about their necks, and gradually accustomed them to the yoke, if, by engaging in too many expensive enterprises, he had not exhausted his exchequer, and made it in some measure necessary for Alva to impose the taxes of the tenth and twentieth pennies, for the maintenance of his troops.   He might, through the great abilities of the duke of Parma, have again reduced the revolted provinces to obedience, if he had not conceived the wild ambition of subduing England and acquiring the sovereignty of France.   His armies, in the latter part of his reign, were never sufficiently numerous to execute the various enterprises which he undertook ; yet they were much more numerous than he was able to support.   Few years passed in which they did not mutiny for want of pay.   And Philip suffered greater prejudice from the disorders and devastation which his own troops committed than he received from the arms of his enemies.   Against his attempts on England and France, the wisest counsellors remonstrated in the strongest terms.   And prudence certainly required that, previously to any attack upon the dominions of others, he should have secured possession of his own.   Yet so great was his illusion that, rather than delay the execution of those schemes which his resentment and ambition had suggested, he chose to run the risk of losing the fruits of all the victories which the duke of Parma had obtained ; and, having left defenceless the provinces which had submitted to his authority, he thereby afforded an opportunity to the revolted provinces of establishing their power on so firm a foundation that it could not be shaken by the whole strength of the Spanish monarchy exerted against it for more than fifty years.[h]

CHAPTER X

THE LAST OF THE SPANISH HABSBURGS

[1598–1700 A.D.]

THE two preceding reigns, being by far the most important in the modern history of Spain, have commanded a corresponding share of our attention. But as with Philip II ends the greatness of the kingdom, which from that period declined with fearful rapidity, — as in the present chapter little remains to be recorded beyond the reign of worthless favourites, the profligacy of courts, and the deplorable weakness of government, — the journey before us will be speedily performed.

The first courtier to whom the destinies of the peninsula were confided, was the duke of Lerma; but as he had no talents either for peace or war, the burden of administration devolved on a needy adventurer, Rodrigo Calderon, one of his pages. In his domestic policy — if profligate imbecility deserve the name — the most signal circumstance is the expulsion of the Moriscos from Valencia, Andalusia, New Castile, and Granada. During and after their late rebellion, those baptised infidels were transported from the last-named kingdom, and dispersed among the Christian inhabitants of the counties adjoining. Tranquillity could scarcely be hoped from so arbitrary a measure; the Moriscos felt that they had been treated with equal perfidy and cruelty, and they thirsted for revenge. They accordingly renewed their correspondence with the African princes and the grand seignior, whom they continually urged to invade the peninsula, and in whose favour they promised to rise on the first signal. Though they were compelled to attend mass, they sought in secret ample amends for the violation of conscience, by observing the rites of their own religion, and by heaping insult on that which they had been constrained to honour with their lips.

The new king, Philip III, observed that he would rather be without subjects than rule over infidels: the foolish saying was applauded by the courtiers; and orders, dated September, 1609, were despatched to the captains-general to force the Moriscos on board the galleys prepared for them, and land them on the African coast. Those of Valencia, 150,000 in number, were first expelled; they were followed, though not without great opposition, nor in some places without open resistance, by their brethren of the other provinces. In the whole, no fewer than 600,000 were thus forcibly driven from their ancient habitations, omitting the mention of such as, by assuming the disguise of Christians, spread over Catalonia and southern France, and of the still greater number of children, who, being born from Moriscos and hereditary Christians, were suffered to remain. Those who disembarked in Africa were treated with characteristic inhumanity.

In 1618, the duke of Lerma was disgraced, and the real minister, Don Rodrigo Calderon, who had been adorned with numerous titles, was imprisoned. Subsequently he was tortured, tried, and sentenced to death; but before the sentence could be put into execution, the king died. Philip IV, however, ordered him to the block. The removal of the duke only made way for another as imbecile and worthless as himself. So that the king was not troubled with state business, but allowed to have his women and his diversions, to provide for mistresses and parasites, he cared not who held the post of minister.

The foreign transactions of this reign are too unimportant to be detailed. In revenge for the maritime hostilities of the English, an expedition was sent to Ireland to raise the inhabitants against the government; but it was annihilated at Kinsale. In the Low Countries the war continued with little glory to the archduke Albert until 1609, when the independence of the Seven United Provinces was acknowledged by treaty. With France there was continued peace, which, in 1612, was strengthened by the double marriage of the prince of the Asturias with Isabella de Bourbon, and of Louis XIII with the infanta Anne [Anne of Austria], eldest daughter of the Spanish monarch. With the Venetians, Turks, and Moors of Africa there were some engagements, but nothing decisive was the result. Spain still retained the duchy of Milan, the kingdom of Naples, Sicily, and Sardinia, and the fortresses on the African coast.

Philip died March 31st, 1621. Besides his heir, and Anne, queen of France, he left children — Maria, queen of Hungary, Don Carlos and Don Ferdinand, who entered the church, and attained the dignity of cardinal. His character needs no description: it was chiefly distinguished for helpless imbecility, for dissipation, and idleness.[c]

CAUSES OF SPAIN'S RAPID DECLINE

The rapid conquest of the Palatinate by the Spanish army, under the marquis Spinola, and the decisive battle of Prague, which the emperor gained by means of the treasures of Spain, brightened the last days of Philip III with a transient lustre. But the constitutional melancholy inherent in the Castilian line — the taint of the blood of Juana — predominated over all the excitement of victory and its exhilarating consequences. The gloom which had overcast the mind of the king could not be dispelled by the most brilliant successes; and those triumphs which, towards the close of his reign, diffused universal joy throughout Spain, conveyed no gladness to the breast of its desponding monarch.

At the accession of Philip IV, the Spanish monarchy had much declined from that supremacy which it had so long held among the nations. Its territory indeed was but little diminished, and if power could be measured by extent of dominion, Spain was still the most potent kingdom in Europe. But its energy was in a great measure spent, and its resources were nearly drained.

In every country there is an epoch of exhaustion as well as of excitement; and in the political constitution, not less than in the bodily frame, the period of depression quickly follows on that of excitation. The growth of the Spanish monarchy had been rapid and gigantic — more so, perhaps, than that of any sovereignty, except the Grecian Empire of Alexander. But its sudden increase of power had been somewhat forced and premature. It was produced by the matrimonial alliances of its sovereigns, by accidental discoveries which opened as if by miracle the gates of dominion, and by the pre-eminent talents of a few individuals, who, within a short compass of time, rose in constellation on Spain — Ferdinand the Catholic, with his illustrious queen Isabella, Gonsalvo de Cordova, Cardinal Ximenes, and the emperor Charles. Its progress in power was not accompanied by a corresponding expansion of intellect, or advancement in knowledge. The time of its supremacy was consequently brief, and the decay which it suffered during the short reign of Philip III was more swift than any recorded in the history of the decline or fall of empires.

But though Spain had thus sunk in the space of a few years, the causes of its depression may be traced through a much longer period, and may even be found in the era of its augmentation and prosperity. Spain had not enjoyed but abused her strength; and if the maxim be just, that an immeasurable ambition is the ruin of nations, never was country better entitled to destruction. As early as the reign of Charles V, the kingdom had been emptied both of men and treasure to support foreign wars.

The discovery of America and its mines ought naturally to have given fresh vigour to industry and commerce; and it undoubtedly promoted them for a time. But, borne away by political events, energy was diverted from domestic industry, the truest source of national wealth and greatness, to foreign colonisation and adventure. The discovery of treasures which they believed to be inexhaustible, and the example of immense and rapid fortunes acquired in America and the Indies, produced a contempt of tillage, and even for the manufactures, the profits of which were comparatively inconsiderable and distant. Persons, too, of a certain rank and birth, however poor they might be, were precluded by the prevailing notions from procuring a subsistence by the exercise of the mechanic arts. But in the New World they could, without shame, devote themselves to pursuits which in their own country might not be prosecuted without degradation. Nor did the produce of the mines afford any compensation for the injury they thus occasioned. Expended in chimerical projects of foreign ambition, and schemes to destroy the peace of other nations, the tide of wealth which flowed from the western world into Spain rushed through the land like a torrent, without fertilising it.

The extent, too, of the Spanish empire, and the distance of its various dependencies, was another cause of its decline. In all ages, the ruins of empires have bespoken the evils of overgrown dominion. The improvement of remote possessions is never sufficiently attended to, while on their account the interests of the parent state are frequently neglected. Voiture [e] likens the Spanish monarchy to an enormous and unwieldy vessel, of which the prow was in the Atlantic, and the stern in the Indian Ocean. All the vice-royalties suffered by the inevitable abuses of delegated authority, and were seldom vivified by the presence of their princes. The whole life, indeed, of Charles V had been a continued journey; but the Escorial was the fit habitation of his son, and Philip enjoined to his successors a constant residence in Spain. All the proceedings at Madrid were dilatory, and no provision was ever made for any event which seemed to be at a tolerable distance. Others followed the example of the court, and delay became the sole policy of the prince, the ministry, and the governors of provinces. Whatever institutions were favourable to liberty had been suppressed or undermined in the reign of Charles V, and freedom was at length utterly destroyed by his despotic and bigoted son.

Nothing, however, impresses us more strongly with a conviction of the indolence and torpor of the Spanish race, than that the expulsion of the Moors should have been attended by the fatal consequences which it unquestionably produced. Elsewhere it would have occasioned no loss or disadvantage, or would have been followed only by such temporary inconvenience as ensued in France on the revocation of the Edict of Nantes. But even from the time of the ancient Celtiberians, the inhabitants of this peninsula had been disinclined to labour, and indisposed to every species of exertion, except in war. "The peasants," says Madame d'Aulnoy [d] (who travelled in Spain in the middle of the seventeenth century), "will more willingly endure hunger and all severities of life, than work, as they tell you, like mercenaries and slaves. Thus pride, seconded by sloth, prevents them from tilling and sowing their land, which remains uncultivated, unless some more laborious and worldly-minded strangers undertake the task, and thus carry off the gains, while the sorry peasant sits in his chair, thrumming an ill-tuned guitar, or reading some mouldy romance."

Voiture,[e] who resided for some time at Madrid, shortly after the accession of Philip IV, and travelled to the south of Spain with letters of recommendation from Olivares, exhibits an amusing and graphic picture of the indolence prevailing among the lower classes of the inhabitants. "If it rains, the villagers who bring the bread to Madrid do not come, though they could get a better price. When wheat is dear in Andalusia, and they have it in Castile, nobody takes the trouble to send it or to get it. It must be brought from France or elsewhere."

Among all ranks celibacy prevailed in an unusual degree. Besides seclusion in convents and nunneries, many obstacles arose to matrimony from family pride and the disagreements of parents. Marriages were thus contracted from interest, without choice, affection, or desire. From these causes, and from early debauchery, the population was more disproportioned to the means of subsistence than in any other country of Europe; and hence the means for defence and for the acquisition of wealth were diminished. The education of the children, such as they were, of these enforced marriages, was shamefully neglected among the highest classes, and indeed even in the royal family.

The riches of the church were totally disproportioned to those of the rest of the nation, and much wealth was thus locked up in silver images or golden lamps, which, if judiciously brought into commerce, might have rendered many thousands of the population opulent and happy. Equally large were the encroachments which superstition made on the time of the inhabitants, great part of which was withdrawn from useful labour by religious festivals, masses, processions, and purchase of pardons.

It was thus that Spain, which, of all the countries of Europe, possessed the greatest advantages in climate, fertility, and geographical position, became, in spite of these means of national prosperity, the poorest land in Christendom. The gifts of nature were all in profusion still, but human institutions had corrupted its benefits, or perverted them into sources of weakness and decay. When the Spanish government perceived the diminution of coin resulting from these causes, it attempted to supply the deficiency, by imposing higher taxes on manufacturers and artificers. But the burden became intolerable to the few remaining workmen. They fled to Italy and Flanders, or, if they stayed at home, they relinquished their trades, and no longer manufactured the fine wools of Andalusia or the silks of Valencia. The ministry, having no more manufactures to tax, next oppressed the farmers, and the imposts laid on agriculture were as injudicious as they were numerous and excessive. "When once a nation," says Raynal,[f] "has begun to decline, it seldom stops. The loss of population, of manufactures, of trade, and of agriculture, was attended with the greatest evils. While Europe was daily improving in knowledge, and all nations were animated with a spirit of industry, Spain was falling into inaction and barbarism. The duties on commodities, in their transport from one province to another, were so high that they amounted almost to a prohibition, so that the communication was totally interrupted. Even the transmission of money from one district to another was forbidden. In a short time

A SPANISH GENTLEMAN, TIME OF PHILIP II

not a vestige of a road was to be seen. Travellers were stopped at the crossing of rivers, where there were neither boats nor bridges. There was not a single canal, and scarcely a navigable river."

The pride of the nation had survived its greatness; its animosities had outlived its power of oppression; but though much of animating health and vigour was gone, the outward form was still nearly the same. The strength of Spain was estimated by numbering its provinces and computing the treasures of the Indies; and to the undiscerning eye of the vulgar, Philip VI may have appeared as great a monarch as his grandsire. It was thus that terror, as Schiller[g] expresses it, still brooded over the lion's forsaken den; and hence, while the provinces of Spain were depopulated and impoverished, many powerful confederations were formed against her, and the humiliation of the house of Austria was the subject of the vows of politicians in all the states of Christendom. And in fact with every disadvantage under which she laboured, and in spite of the rapid depression she had suffered, Spain might still have regained the lofty station she once held in the rank of kingdoms, if, at the succession of Philip IV, a wise and energetic monarch had ascended the throne, or if the reins of government had been intrusted to a prudent and enlightened minister.

The supremacy of Spain over Italy, her own western mines, and the oriental treasures supplied by the Indian empire of Portugal — all these, which had hitherto proved but elements of decay, might, under able administration, have afforded immense resources. The extensive frontiers of the monarchy were still guarded by ancient renown and disciplined valour. That celebrated infantry which was originally formed on the Swiss model, and had been for more than a century the admiration and terror of Europe, was still unbroken. It was encouraged by the remembrance of a thousand triumphs, without one recollection of shame, for no signal defeat had yet withered the laurels of St. Quentin and Pavia. The soldiery still retained that intrepid and enterprising, though somewhat ferocious and mutinous spirit, by which they were marked in the wars of the Low Countries. Their renowned captain, the noble Spinola, still survived, and many officers must yet have served in the veteran army which had combated against Henry the Great, under the prince of Parma.

But Philip IV, though superior to his father in refinement of taste, and in some specious exterior accomplishments, was equally deficient in vigour of mind or solid acquirements, and was far inferior to his predecessor in purity of life. The minister, on whom for more than twenty years he relied with implicit confidence and devolved the uncontrolled management of affairs, was a man of irregular genius and of vast designs, which were but ill suited to the present condition of his country ; and to this policy, which was alternately obstinate and capricious, many have attributed the overwhelming misfortunes of Spain.*k*

PHILIP IV "THE GREAT" (1621–1665 A.D.)

When the new king ascended the throne he was only in his seventeenth year, and he began, like his father, by surrendering the reins of government to a worthless favourite. This was the count de Olivares, who had been a gentleman of the bedchamber to the prince of Asturias. This haughty minion commenced his career by removing from the ministry his benefactor, the duke of Uceda, and by recalling the valiant Don Pedro Giron, duke of Osuna, from the viceroyalty of Naples. Whoever had ability, or popular fame or favour with the king, was sure to experience his envy, often his deadly persecution. Every servant of the late government was dismissed or imprisoned, to make way for creatures, if possible, more worthless.

It is, however, certain that by revoking many of the profuse grants made by the two preceding sovereigns by dismissing two-thirds of the locusts in office, by enforcing the residence of many señores, by sumptuary regulations, and other measures, he increased the revenues of the crown. But these reforms were but temporary ; the minister was too corrupt to persevere in any line of public advantage ; his object was his own emolument, and that of his creatures. How little Spain could flourish under such princes and such administrations may be readily conjectured. In its internal affairs there was the same gradual decline of agriculture, of commerce, of the

[1621–1641 A.D.]

mechanical arts, and, consequently, of the national resources; yet, while the mass of the people were thus sinking into hopeless poverty, the court exhibited more splendour than ever. Thus, the reception of Charles, prince of Wales, and of his tutor, the duke of Buckingham, — who, with the view of obtaining the hand of the infanta Maria, sister of the king, had been romantic enough to visit Madrid in disguise, — is a favourite subject of historic description. The English reader need not be told that this prodigal expenditure was thrown away, and that Charles, ultimately, obtained a French princess. Still more expensive were the festivities consequent on the election of the king of Hungary — who had married the infanta Maria, sister of Philip — to be king of the Romans, and, consequently, heir to the imperial crown. If to these fooleries we add the money sent out of the kingdom to assist the German emperor in the wars with Gustavus Adolphus of Sweden, we shall not be surprised that the whole nation beheld the conduct of Philip and his minister with discontent. While tens of thousands were famishing, from the stagnation of the usual branches of industry — while plays, pantomimes, entertainments, and other frivolities of the most costly description were succeeding each other in the capital, in contempt of so much misery — it required no ordinary stock of patience to witness the disgraceful contrast. Murmurs and complaints were treated with contempt, until the Catalans openly opposed the flagitious minister and the royal puppet.

THE CATALAN INSURRECTION

The profligate extravagances of the court were not the only cause which led to the Catalan insurrection. At the close of a war with France — a war of which mention will hereafter be made — the Castilian troops, in the fear that hostilities would be recommenced by the enemy, were stationed on the northern frontier, at the expense of the inhabitants, on whom they were billeted. This regulation was as unjust as it was arbitrary, and even odious. The people remonstrated. When the soldiers resisted, lives were lost on both sides. The ringleaders were imprisoned or fined; to release them formidable bands of countrymen hastened to Barcelona, the residence of the viceroy, with the crucifix borne before them, burst open the prisons, committed many excesses throughout the city, ill-treated the royal officers, and ultimately killed the viceroy himself as he was endeavouring to escape by sea.[1] From these scenes, and from the universal hostility of the Catalans to his violent regulations, Olivares might have learned something useful; but he was incapable of profiting by the lessons of experience. The marquis de los Velez was sent with an army to reduce the rebels to obedience. They implored the aid of the French king. That aid was readily promised, but as it did not immediately arrive, the whole principality, except the city of Tortosa, armed.

This was not all: contending that the king, by violating their ancient privileges, had broken his compact with them, and consequently forfeited all claim to their obedience, they proclaimed a republic. But as the marquis

[1 Catalan writers, witnesses of these scenes, describe with enthusiasm the patriotic ardour shown by all classes in the town, the courage, daring, and diligence displayed even by women and children in bringing provisions, ropes, ammunition, medicine, and all kinds of assistance to the defenders on the walls, those who had nothing themselves going to the houses and through the streets asking for help. Even the nuns in their convents sent biscuits and preserves, while others prayed to God for the triumph of the Catalan cause; some women dressed as soldiers and went about with swords and daggers.[b]]

had quickly reduced several important fortresses, and was advancing, breathing revenge on the capital, the new republic was soon destroyed by its authors, and Louis XIII proclaimed count of Barcelona.   The French monarch had accepted the dignity, even on conditions — such was the jealous spirit of Catalan freedom — which left him the bare protection of the province, which excluded him from the slightest influence in it, and which in fact transformed it into a republic under the name of a sovereign.   Not that he intended to observe those conditions, for it is admitted even by the national writers that with his characteristic duplicity — duplicity to which he was urged by his ambassador Argenton — he had resolved to annul them the first favourable opportunity.   After this treaty five thousand French soldiers passed the Pyrenees ; Tarragona, which now held for the king, and in which all the royal forces were concentrated, was invested, but after a time relieved ; Castilian reinforcements arrived to make head against the enemy ; near twelve thousand French came to assist their countrymen, and Louis himself advanced to the frontiers of Roussillon to direct their operations.   At this moment, Philip intended to conduct the war in person, and he actually left Madrid for the purpose at the head of a considerable force ; but at Aranjuez he halted, under the pretext of waiting the arrival of Olivares, who was in no hurry to join him.   In fact, neither king nor minister had courage enough to meet the enemy.   Meantime the French armies were actively gaining several important advantages : to counterbalance them, Olivares formed a conspiracy in the very heart of France to assassinate the minister Cardinal Richelieu, and even to dethrone Louis ; but it was detected, and its prime instrument was beheaded.

Though a natural death soon called away the cardinal, his successor, Mazarin, who succeeded also to his Macchiavelian principles, continued the war.   It lingered for years, with various success, or rather with no decided success, to either part, until the inhabitants themselves grew tired of the French yoke, and joined with their Castilian brethren.   Whether this change in the public feeling was owing to the haughtiness of their allies, which is said to have been intolerable, or to the inconsistency of the popular mind, or still more, probably, to both united, fortune at length began to favour the arms of Philip.   Still the war with the Netherlands and with the Portuguese, to which allusion will shortly be made, rendered the Spanish court desirous of peace.   The wish was shared by Mazarin, whose resources were nearly exhausted by hostilities of so many years' continuance, and in so many countries.   In 1659, the plenipotentiaries of both powers met at St. Jean-de-Luz, and the conditions of peace, after three months' deliberation, were sanctioned by the respective monarchs.c

It may be well here to give a brief review of the larger politics of Spain in Europe during and after the Thirty Years' War, though fuller details must be looked for in the histories of France and the other countries concerned.a

THE THIRTY YEARS' WAR AND THE TREATY OF THE PYRENEES

The incessant efforts of the Austrian princes to cement the union of their families, and secure the reciprocal succession to their respective dominions, had been no less sedulously opposed by France, than their projects of conquest and aggrandisement.   In the pursuit of this object, the address and good fortune of the French repeatedly triumphed over the

inveterate hostility of the rival house; and by dexterously availing themselves of times and circumstances, they succeeded in forming frequent marriages between the two families of France and Spain. Philip II espoused
Isabella, a princess of France; a double match was also concluded between
the infanta Anne, daughter of Philip III, and Louis XIII, and between Isabella, sister of the French monarch, and the prince of Asturias, afterwards
Philip IV. To obviate, however, the mischiefs likely to ensue from these
occasional aberrations of policy, the Austrian sovereigns endeavoured to
guard and fortify their respective pretensions to the family inheritance, by
renunciations, compacts, and treaties.

These marriages and arrangements formed only temporary suspensions of
hostility. In 1619, the long and eventful contest of the Thirty Years' War
commenced. The Spanish monarchy, already weakened by past disasters,
was shaken to its foundations. Exactions rendered necessary by the diminished resources of the government, joined with the abuses inseparable from
delegated power, excited civil troubles: the progress of its decline was
marked by a rebellion in Catalonia; by the temporary insurrection which
rendered Masaniello, a simple fisherman, master of Naples; and by the revolution which placed the family of Braganza on the throne of Portugal.
The event of this direct conflict was the degradation of the Austrian house
in both its branches, and the partial accomplishment of those extensive
designs which France had long meditated against the remnant of the
Burgundian inheritance, and even against Spain itself. The Peace of
Westphalia, in 1648, opened passages into Germany and Italy, reduced
the empire to an aristocracy, and destroyed the union of the Germanic body,
by the establishment of a religious and political schism.

But even after the emperor Ferdinand III had been forced to withdraw
from the contest, and to submit to the reduction of his power and influence,
Philip IV was induced to continue the war, from the consciousness of past
greatness, the hope of drawing advantage from the civil discords which arose
in France during the minority of Louis XIV, and above all from an unwill-
ingness to give his eldest daughter in marriage to the French monarch,
which was exacted as the price of peace. During this interval, he not only
resolved to affiance his daughter to the archduke Leopold; but having
become a widower, he cemented his connection with the German branch by
espousing Maria Anna, daughter of Frederick III. At length, his increasing embarrassments; the loss of Jamaica and Dunkirk, wrested from him
by the successful hostility of Cromwell; the birth of a son, Philip Prospero;
and another pregnancy of his queen, induced him to accept the proposals of
France. Accordingly, preliminaries were signed at Paris, November 7th, 1659,
and a treaty of peace was arranged by the two prime ministers of France,
Cardinal Mazarin and Don Luis de Haro, in the Isle of Pheasants, a small
islet in the river Bidassoa, which divides the two kingdoms.

This celebrated act, which has been termed the Treaty of the Pyrenees,
sowed the germ of future wars, and produced to France no less important
advantages on the side of the peninsula and Flanders, than the Peace of
Westphalia had produced to Austria on that of the empire. To France,
Spain ceded Roussillon with part of Conflans and Cerdagne, of Flanders
and Hainault, and all Artois, except the towns and districts of St. Omer and
Aire. The pretensions of France to Navarre were reserved; Dunkirk
and Jamaica were yielded to England: and the duke of Lorraine, the last
remaining ally of Spain, was reduced to dependence, by dismantling the fortifications of Nancy, and by the compulsory cession of Moyenvic and Bar.

Finally, the king of Spain consented to give in marriage his eldest daughter, Maria Theresa, to Louis XIV; but under the express condition that she should, for herself and issue, renounce all right to her paternal inheritance. In return, the king of France restored all his conquests in the Netherlands, Italy, and Catalonia, and agreed not to assist the Portuguese. Accordingly, the signature of the treaty was followed by the celebration of the marriage, June 2nd, 1660, before which the infanta renounced for herself and her posterity all right and title to every part of the Spanish dominions in the strongest terms which ingenuity could devise. Her renunciation was afterwards ratified with equal solemnity by Louis XIV, for himself and his heirs, and confirmed by the cortes then assembled at Madrid. The French court, however, made a mockery of such engagements; and the well-known observation of Mazarin to the plenipotentiaries employed in negotiating the treaty shows at once the most shameless perfidy and the ultimate object of this connection: "Let the match be concluded, and no renunciation can prevent the king from pretending to the succession of Spain."

As little did the French monarch respect his engagements not to interfere in the affairs of Portugal, the hope of which had been one of the principal inducements with Philip to conclude this disadvantageous treaty. On the contrary, the most glaring prevarication was employed to justify the active support afforded to the Portuguese: their resistance was successfully employed to exhaust the remaining strength of the Spanish monarchy, and to prepare the way for that system of aggression and usurpation which was shortly to be exhibited, to the terror and indignation of Europe. [h]

COSTUME OF A YOUNG SPANISH WOMAN, EARLY SEVENTEENTH CENTURY

Commensurate with the origin of the Catalan insurrection was that of Portugal. As this is not the proper place to enter into an examination of the causes which produced, or the circumstances which attended that natural burst of freedom, we defer both to the history of Portugal. Here it is sufficient to observe that the discontented Portuguese, despising the royal puppet at Madrid, and burning with an intolerable thirst for the restoration of their independence, proclaimed the duke of Braganza under the name of João IV; and that in several campaigns they nobly vindicated the step. Assisted by their allies the English, Dutch, and French, they continued the war with indomitable valour, and with general success until 1664, when, in the battle of Villaviciosa, they inflicted so severe a blow on the arms of Philip that he precipitately abandoned hostilities. This was one of the causes which led to the disgrace of Olivares. Nothing can better show the uncontrolled power of this minister, and the criminal negligence of every public duty by the king, than the fact that the latter remained long ignorant

of the momentous events in Portugal. At length, fearing to conceal them any longer, the count one day observed, with an air of studied carelessness, "The duke of Braganza has run stark mad; he has proclaimed himself king of Portugal! This folly will bring your majesty twelve millions in confiscations!" The only reply was, "We must put an end to the mischief"; but the remonstrances of his queen, and the rebellion of the minister's nephew, the duke of Medina Sidonia, for whom the minister wrung a reluctant pardon, determined Philip to exile Olivares from the court. This was actually done; but the kingdom experienced no benefit by a change of favourites.*c* "The unmeasured blame usually lavished upon Olivares," says Hume,*j* "appears hardly just, notwithstanding the disastrous results of his rule. His great sin was that he tried to insist upon all Spaniards making equal sacrifices to pay for the barren pride which all Spaniards shared."

DEATH OF PHILIP IV (1665 A.D.)

The character of Philip, who died in 1665, needs no description. Though from a few early successes he was called "the great" and "the planet king," his reign, next to that of Roderic the Goth, was the most disastrous in the annals of Spain. Omitting the distress which it brought on the people, and the horrors of the Catalan insurrection, the loss of Roussillon, Conflans, a part of Cerdagne, Jamaica, much of the Low Countries, and above all Portugal, and his recognition of the independence of the Seven United Provinces, are melancholy monuments of his imbecility. A still worse effect was produced by the frequent reverses of his arms in Italy and the Low Countries,[1] reverses which encouraged the smallest states to set his power at defiance; thus, both in the East Indies, and on the coast of America, his settlements were plundered or seized by Holland. In private life, his conduct was as little entitled to respect: by his mistresses he had six or seven children,[2] of whom the most famous was Don John, surnamed of Austria, believed to be the son of an actress of Madrid, and born in 1629.

On this son the choicest favours of the crown were conferred; he was made prior of St. John, and was several times at the head of the Spanish armies. In Italy, the Netherlands, Catalonia, and Portugal, he showed that he was not unworthy to bear the name of his great predecessor, the son of the emperor Charles; in the last-named country his success would have been more decided, had not the queen, who hated his popularity and envied his fame, diverted the supplies which were intended for him, and left him no other alternative than that of retiring from the service. Hence the foundation of the dissensions which, as we shall perceive in the ensuing reign, distracted the state. Of Philip's numerous offspring by his two queens, Isabella, daughter of Henry IV of France, and Maria Anna, daughter of the emperor Ferdinand III, three only survived him. Maria Theresa queen of France, Margaret queen of Hungary, and his successor Don Charles.

KING CHARLES II AND THE FRENCH WAR

If the affairs of this kingdom had been so unfortunate during the reigns of the two Philips, they were not likely to improve under a child who, at his

[1] The troubles in Naples included the famous insurrection led by the fisherman Masaniello.
[2] According to the Venetian ambassador Zanetornato *e* he had thirty-two illegitimate children.

accession, had not attained his fourth year, especially as Don John, the favourite of the nation, was at open hostility with the queen-regent and her confessor the father Nithard [or Nitard], a German Jesuit. This churchman is represented as haughty to the nobles, supple to the queen, and in his general conduct corrupt; but as the representation comes from men always jealous of foreigners, it must be received with caution. An unbiassed mind will easily perceive that his chief fault was the unbounded power he exercised through the queen. The disasters which befell her administration added to the popular discontent.

Though the perfidious Louis XIV had disclaimed, both for himself and his successors, all title to the Spanish possessions, one of his first acts, after his marriage, was to assert, in right of his queen, a monstrous pretension to the Low Countries. In an obscure district of a remote province there was an ancient custom, called devolution, now virtually abrogated by time, that even a daughter of the first wife should inherit in preference to a son by the second: hence, as Maria Theresa, the consort of Louis, was sprung from the first, and Don Charles from the second marriage of Philip, the French monarch poured his legions over the frontier, and with great rapidity reduced most of the fortresses from the Channel to the Schelde. At his instigation the Portuguese made an irruption into Estremadura. The union of Sweden, Holland, and England, to oppose the ambition of the Frenchman, saved the whole Netherlands from subjugation; but, by the Peace of Aix-la-Chapelle, May 2nd, 1668, he retained the most valuable of his conquests; and by that very union, which thus saved a portion of her northern possessions, Spain was compelled to acknowledge the independence of Portugal.

Of these disastrous circumstances advantage was taken by Don John of Austria, who had been exiled from the court, to load both the queen and her confessor, now a counsellor of state, with increased obloquy. During the flagitious career of the French, the voice of the Spaniards proclaimed him as the only man fit to support the sinking fortunes of the monarchy: to remove him from their attachment, and from his own intrigues, he had been nominated governor of the Low Countries. He refused the dignity. Being retired to Consuegra, a conspiracy was formed or pretended against the life of Nithard, and revealed by one of the accomplices, who asserted that its hidden spring was John.

Whether this conspiracy was, as most men suspected, a stratagem of the queen and her party, or a really meditated deed of blood, it enabled the regent to act with more vigour: she despatched a strong party of cavalry to arrest John, and consign him to the Alcazar of Toledo. He fled into Aragon; and from his refuge assumed a higher tone, insisting that satisfaction should be made him for a suspicion so injurious to his honour, and that the Jesuit should be banished from the kingdom. With seven hundred resolute followers, he advanced towards Madrid. He was met by the papal nuncio, who had been charged with the honourable duty of mediation. To the request that he would remain four days at Torrejon until his demands were satisfied, he replied that Nithard must leave the kingdom without delay. The insolence of this mandate — for such it was — exasperated the queen; but she was constrained to comply with it, and the Jesuit was dismissed.

Father Nithard was certainly a disinterested, he appears to have been a well-meaning man. He would accept no money (a moderate sum excepted, necessary to defray the expense of his journey to Rome), asserting with an honest pride that he entered Spain a poor priest, and a poor priest would leave it: however, he was subsequently raised to the dignity of cardinal.

Don John renewed his intrigues, artfully uniting the cause of the people with his own, and at length compelling the court to invest him with the government of Aragon, Catalonia, Valencia, the Balearic Isles, and Sardinia. The following years he passed in sovereign state at Saragossa, silently watching the course of events which, as he had anticipated, were of the same adverse character to the nation. France, true to her career of spolia- tion in all ages, in 1672 invaded Holland, now the ally of Spain, with one hundred thousand men: to such a host resistance was vain, and most of the country was seized by the invaders.

Spain, like England, Germany, and other states who confederated to arrest the daring progress of Louis, flew to the assistance of her prostrate ally, and immediately afterwards declared war against France. As usual, the advantage turned in favour of the stronger party. In Burgundy, Franche-Comté, which Spain had inherited in right of the ancient dukes of that province, was conquered, and some destructive inroads were made into Catalonia; the few fortresses remaining to the Spanish monarch in the Low Countries were threatened, one or two actually reduced; and Messina in Sicily was instigated by the enemy to rebel. In three years the rebellion subsided of itself, the inhabitants of Messina being glad to escape from the yoke of Louis by returning to their obedience. In 1675 Don John was ordered to pass over to that island; but as the royal majority was at hand when the regent's term of authority would expire, he hoped that he should be called to the ministry; a result for which his friends were actively dis- posing the king. But through the arts of the queen, Maria Anna, he was suddenly ordered to leave Madrid. There can be no doubt, however, that his own presumption hastened this disgrace, for he had insisted on being acknowledged as infante of Castile, and consequently as collateral heir to the monarchy. The queen triumphed the more as her son was as imbecile in mind as he was sickly in body, and as with her alone would continue the affairs of administration.

A new, and, if scandal is to be believed, a less innocent favourite than Father Nithard, was found in Ferdinand de Valenzuela, who had been page of the duke del Infantado, and who to specious manners and some knowledge added an agreeable person. But the queen's triumph was transient: the creatures of Don John became more numerous and clamorous. The leading grandees, who detested the new favourite for his vanity, and still more for his meanness of birth, joined in the cry. The torrent became too strong to be stemmed even by her. She resolved to derive merit from necessity; for knowing that Don John was preparing to leave Saragossa for Madrid, she not only suffered her son to command his immediate presence, but she her- self wrote in the same strain. At his approach Charles II retired to another palace, ordering his mother not to leave the one she inhabited; and de- spatched the archbishop of Toledo to Hita to welcome his brother. The power of John was now unbounded, while Maria Anna, notwithstanding her efforts to recover the royal favour, was circumscribed to her own household. John was affectionately received by the king, and was declared prime minis- ter. The first decree which he signed was for the arrest of Valenzuela, now degraded from the class of nobles to which the favour of Maria Anna had un- worthily raised him. He was conveyed to the castle of Consuegra, forced to disgorge his ill-gotten wealth, and banished to the Philippine Islands. He died in Mexico.

The administration of Don John was no less deplorable than that of the regent whom he had so criminally supplanted. Occupied in the cares of vengeance, or in providing for his creatures, he feebly opposed the victorious progress of Louis. Valenciennes, Cambray, St. Omer, and other places were speedily reduced : Ypres and Ghent were assailed with equal success; and Puycerda, on the Catalan frontier, yielded about the same time to another French army. Most of these places, however, were restored at the Peace of Nimeguen, September, 1678, of which the most unpopular condition was that Charles should receive the hand of the princess Marie Louise, niece of the French king. That nation had always been regarded with jealousy, it was now hated by the Spaniards. John did not live to witness the solemnisation of the nuptials. The ill success of his government, his haughty behaviour towards the grandees, his persecution of such as belonged rather to their country than to his party, and his tyranny even over the king, rendered him not merely unpopular, but odious. In this state mental anxiety put an end to his life (September 17th, 1679) at the moment his enemies were preparing to hasten his downfall.[1] The queen-dowager returned to court, not indeed to resume her ancient influence, but to assist in the multiplication of intrigues, and, consequently, the perplexities of her imbecile son.c

A SPANIARD OF THE SEVENTEENTH CENTURY

THE FATE OF THE YOUNG QUEEN

Marriage had come to be one of the political resources of Louis XIV. Another matrimonial alliance, still more important, had been concluded a few months previously. It has been said that Don John of Austria, the uncle and minister of the king of Spain, hoped to find in France a support against his rival, the king's mother, who was upheld by the court at Vienna. Don John had caused the negotiations undertaken by the queen-mother for uniting the Catholic king with a daughter of the emperor to be broken off, and had solicited for Charles II the hand of Marie Louise of Orleans, a niece of Louis XIV and daughter of the duke of Orleans by his first wife Henrietta of England. It can be imagined with what eagerness this proposition was received, since it was supposed that it would establish the diplomatic preponderance of France at Madrid.

The contract was signed on the 30th of August, 1679, to the great joy of Louis XIV, but to the still greater sorrow of the bride. It was only with despair that the poor young girl left the paradise of Versailles to bury herself in the tomb of the Escorial, at the side of that strange husband who was only the shadow of a king, only the shadow of a man. For a whole month she saddened the court and wounded the national susceptibilities of the Spanish ambassadors by the violence of her grief. She seemed to have a

[1 Humeʲ says he died of fever and ague, though poison was of course hinted and Maria Ann blamed.]

presentiment of her sad fate. She had not yet started when the protector she was to meet on the other side of the mountains expired and her natural enemy the queen-mother seized again from the dying hands of Don John the power she had lost. Marie Louise found on foreign soil only long hours of weariness, and implacable persecutions which were terminated by a prolonged agony and perhaps by a crime. She was one of the most pathetic victims of the cruel policy of dynasties. The sacrifice, however, was useless; the young queen acquired no influence at Madrid and, the anti-French policy having gotten the upper hand together with the queen-mother, by the intervention of the prince of Orange, a *rapprochement* was brought about between Spain and England, the effects of which Louis XIV fought with greater success at Windsor than at the Escorial.[l]

Dunlop[k] gives many details of the journey of the young bride to her imbecile husband. To the natural homesickness so peculiarly characteristic of the French, she added a complete ignorance of the Spanish language and a nature rebellious to the unusual formality of Spanish court etiquette. The royal bridegroom into whose arms she was driven was, as a result of the Austrian marriages, not only weak-minded but also repulsive physically; his chin was so huge that he could not masticate and his tongue so large that his speech could hardly be understood. He was treated as a baby till he was ten and was almost illiterate; his amusements were those of a lascivious boy and he died in the decay of old age when he was not yet forty.

An incident of Charles II's reign was the renewal of the inquisitional fury, and one of the *fêtes* of the young queen was the privilege of watching fifty wretches led out to torture and execution; one beautiful Jewess appealed to the queen who was helpless to save her.

The queen was very charitable and yet was left on a stinted allowance irregularly paid. Her reputation suffered slander — as what queen's has not? — and Hume[j] calls her a pagan; but Dunlop says that her character was untainted. She found congenial friends naturally among the people of her own country, but these were eventually forbidden her presence. Sunny as her nature was, it is small wonder that she pined and did not make headway against the thick plots against her. She died in February, 1689 — of cholera morbus it was claimed, though poison was of course alleged.

Dunlop[k] well says, "Of all political queens, the fate of Louise d'Orléans is perhaps the most to be pitied." Her life had been vain; she had not satisfied her uncle Louis XIV by fastening French influence on the court; she had not satisfied Spanish hopes by bearing an heir to the monstrosity she had been forced to wed; and she had not even been happy.[a]

LAST YEARS OF CHARLES II

Omitting the detail of obscure wars — obscure at least to the Spaniards — which almost uniformly turned to their prejudice, on the death of Marie Louise, in 1689, the French monarch again poured the storm of war over the frontier of Catalonia. What most heightened his resentment was the immediate marriage of the widowed Charles with a princess of the house of Austria; so that house he had always been a mortal enemy, and he feared lest the king, who was hitherto childless, should at length have an heir. For some time, indeed, the efforts of the invaders, owing to their insignificant numbers, were often repulsed, or neutralised by subsequent reverses; but, in 1691, Urgel was taken by the duke of Noailles; Barcelona and Alicante were severely bombarded by sea. Two years afterwards Palemos and Rosas capitulated ; the following year the Spaniards were defeated in a considerable battle ; the victors took Gerona ; Hostalric, and other places, followed the example, and Barcelona itself was threatened. Destitute of money and of troops, the efforts of the cabinet to raise both were but partially successful, and the time which should have been spent in vigorous hostilities was thus wasted in almost useless preparation. After a short suspension of hostilities, Barcelona fell into the power of Vendôme.

Spain trembled to her most distant extremities ; and she could scarcely believe in the reality of her good fortune when, at the Peace of Ryswick, in 1697, Louis restored all his conquests. She was too much confounded by this display of magnanimity to divine the cause ; yet that cause was not insufficient. From his niece, Marie Louise, the French monarch had learned to suspect the impotency of Charles ; the sterility of the recent marriage confirmed the suspicion ; and as he aspired in consequence to place a prince of his family on the throne of Castile, he did not wish to diminish the value of the inheritance by its dismemberment.

In 1698 the health of Charles, which had always been indifferent, began so visibly to decline that all hope of issue was abandoned. On his demise three chief claimants could aspire to his throne : first, the dauphin of France, as the eldest son of Maria Theresa, eldest daughter of Philip IV ; secondly, the emperor Leopold, who not only descended from Ferdinand, brother of Charles V, but whose mother was the daughter of Philip III ; thirdly, the electoral prince of Bavaria, whose mother was the only daughter of the infanta Margarita, a young daughter of Philip IV. Of these claims, that of the dauphin was evidently the strongest, since his mother was the eldest sister of Charles. It is true that she had renounced for her issue all claim to the crown of Spain ; but this renunciation had been demanded by the Spaniards, from a fear lest the two crowns should fall on the same brow. To such a union Europe would never have consented ; and the objection was almost equally strong to the union of Spain with Germany. Hence the hostility to the pretensions both of the dauphin, as heir of the French monarchy, and of the emperor Leopold. Hence, too, the celebrated, and infamous as celebrated, First Partition Treaty, which, in October, 1698, was signed at the Hague by the plenipotentiaries of England, Holland, and France. By it Naples and Sicily, with Guipuzcoa, San Sebastian, and Fuenterrabia were ceded to the dauphin ; Spain and the Indies to the Prince of Bavaria ; while, for the third party, Charles, second son of Leopold, and the representative of his rights, Milan only was reserved. The death of the Bavarian prince destroyed this beautiful scheme of spoliation ; but its authors did not long delay in framing another, which gave Spain, the Indies, and Netherlands to Charles, and which amplified the original portion of the dauphin.

But Louis XIV had no intention to renounce the splendid inheritance ; if he could not procure it for the dauphin, or, which would ultimately be the same, for the eldest son of the dauphin, there was a second son, Philip, duke of Anjou, who would be less the object of jealousy to the European powers. With the same view, Leopold was willing that his own rights, and those of his eldest son, should devolve on the archduke Charles the youngest. Both princes sent their emissaries to the court of Charles II, to besiege his sick-bed, and to procure a testamentary declaration in favour of their respective pretensions. The intrigues which continued for so many months to distract the court and kingdom, to embitter rival animosity, and to disturb the last hours of the king, are too endless to be detailed.

The duke of Anjou's ablest support was Cardinal Portocarrero, archbishop of Toledo. The cardinal terrified Charles' conscience by a representation of the civil wars which must inevitably follow the uncertainty of succession, and, above all, by frightening him with the responsibility of the consequent bloodshed. On a mind so religious as the king's, these representations made a deep effect ; he observed that, however near the ties of blood, his salvation was still nearer ; and after a long, a bitter struggle, he signed the testament which called the duke d'Anjou to the undivided sovereignty of the Spanish dominions. As he subscribed the momentous instrument, his heart still clung to his family, the tears ran from his eyes, while, with a faltering voice, he sorrowfully exclaimed, " God is the disposer of kingdoms ! "

Before the signature of this important act, the health and strength of the king had visibly declined ; in fact he exhibited in himself a mere shadow of existence. His deplorable, and as it appeared, extraordinary state, one alike of pain, of mental vacuity, and even of half consciousness, gave rise to a report that he was bewitched. He prepared for his end ; appointed a council of regency, headed by Cardinal Portocarrero, until the duke of d'Anjou should arrive in Spain ; and on the morning of November 1st, 1700, bade adieu to his worldly sorrows, after one of the most disastrous reigns on record.c

THE DISTRESSES OF SPAIN

Thus, at length, terminated the long but inglorious sway of Charles II, in the thirty-ninth year of his age, and the thirty-sixth of his unfortunate reign. His character is written in the events of his clouded life. He was mild and conscientious ; suspicious and distrustful from diffidence in his own powers and talents ; timid, inconstant, and irresolute, from the influence of hypochondriac affections ; chaste from temperament ; ignorant from total want of instruction ; superstitious from habit and education ; he was utterly destitute of discernment, energy, or skill ; he was but a ghost even of his grandsire Philip III, and in his premature decay formed no unfit emblem of the declining kingdom over which he reigned.

Charles, indeed, was not wholly responsible for the state of degradation to which Spain was reduced when he closed his fatal career. The administrations of Lerma and Olivares had prepared the way for a long train of losses, humiliations, and disasters ; but the wavering and fluctuating counsels of Charles completed the ruin of his country. Spain, which contained twenty millions of inhabitants in the reign of Ferdinand and Isabella, had only eight millions at the close of the reign of Charles II. Moncada, an author of the beginning of the seventeenth century, estimated the population of its capital at 400,000 ; and Uztariz, who wrote immediately after the accession of the Bourbons, calculated it at only 180,000, so that it may be rated that it had diminished by one-half during the reigns of Philip IV and his son. Except, indeed, from courtesy and custom, and the extreme interest excited by the question of the succession, Spain, at the end of the reign of Charles, would scarcely have been reckoned among the powers of Europe.

Her finances were in a state of most frightful disorder. The revenues of the crown were absorbed by those agents or farmers, on whom the urgent necessities of government reduced it to depend for supplies ; and, at the same time, the people, both in the capital and provinces, were loaded with every species of extortion and monopoly. The ample treasures of the New

World were still worse administered ; the viceroys, after defrauding the crown and oppressing the subject, were suffered to return from their governments and to enjoy, with impunity, the produce of peculation. The harbours of Spain contained but ten or twelve rotten frigates; the arsenals for the navy were neglected, and even the art of shipbuilding had fallen into oblivion. Her army amounted to not more than twenty thousand men, without discipline, pay, or clothing. Her forts and citadels had crumbled into ruins. Even the breaches made into the walls of Barcelona during the Catalan insurrection continued open, and at the other chief fortresses there were neither guns mounted nor garrisons maintained. Such was the want of vigour in the laws, and remissness in the officers of justice, that reins had been given to every species of licentiousness. The slightest rise in the price of provisions excited tumult and alarm. Madrid had become the rendezvous of robbers and the asylum of assassins, who haunted even the palaces of the grandees or the churches, unmolested and unpunished. Its squares and streets were filled with discarded domestics and famishing artisans, without occupation or the means of subsistence. Those establishments destined to maintain the respect due to royalty had sunk into empty form, and were insufficient to protect the king from mortifying insults, both to his authority and person. The responsible ministry were without intelligence or skill in the science of government : the real influence was in the officers of the household — the king's confessor, the prelates, and the inquisitors of the realm. The private and bitter jealousies of the grandees, the enmity of the provinces towards each other, and the rigid adherence to ancient forms and usages, however inapplicable to modern circumstances, all conspired to prevent a cordial co-operation in any useful or national object, and completed, in the last year of the seventeenth century and at the end of the Austrian dynasty, the picture of Spain.

Yet the sway, no doubt, of the imbecile Charles may have appeared more feeble from the contrast it presented to the energy and skill of the other governments of Europe, which, at the close of this century, were ruled by the ablest monarchs who had ever appeared, at one era, since the first rise of its states on the wreck of the Western Empire. The energies both of Holland and England were wielded by William III ; Louis XIV reigned in France, the prudent Pedro in Portugal, John Sobieski in Poland, Charles XII in Sweden, and in Muscovy Peter the Great—the immortal czar.[k]

CHAPTER XI

REVIVAL OF SPAIN UNDER THE FIRST BOURBONS

[1700–1788 A.D.]

Du sein de Paris, Madrid reçoit un Roi.
—Voltaire, *La Henriade.*

On the 1st of November, 1700, died Charles II, the last male of the Austrian dynasty, which had governed Spain from the death of Ferdinand and Isabella.

The king had scarcely expired, before the ministers and officers of state assembled, according to ancient custom, to examine and publish the royal testament. As this was a new era in the history of Spain, and as general anxiety prevailed to know the new sovereign, the palace was crowded with people of all ranks, and the antechamber filled with the foreign ministers and principal courtiers, all eager to receive the earliest intelligence. At length, the folding doors being thrown open, the duke of Abrantes appeared, and a general silence ensued to hear the nomination. Near the door stood the two ministers of France and Austria, Blécourt and Harrach. Blécourt advanced with the confidence of a man who expected a declaration in his favour; but the Spaniard, casting on him a look of indifference, advanced to Harrach and embraced him with a fervour which announced the most joyful tidings. Maliciously prolonging his compliment, and repeating his embrace, he said, "Sir, it is with the greatest pleasure — sir, it is with the greatest satisfaction — for my whole life, I take my leave of the most illustrious house of Austria." The ambassador, who during this strange address had already begun to express his own satisfaction and promise the future favour of his sovereign, was thunderstruck with the malicious, unexpected insult; and it

279

required all his firmness to remain and hear the contents of the will, which overthrew the hopes and baffled the plans of his imperial master.

Philip arrived at Madrid on the 18th of February. On the 21st of April he made a triumphal entry, with a magnificence calculated to flatter a chivalrous and high-spirited nation, and to display all the splendour of a crown esteemed by its subjects the most powerful in the whole Christian world. The eyes of Spain and of Europe were turned to the young king, who was to form the commencement of a new dynasty, and whose accession was a new era in the political history of modern times. Philip had just entered the seventeenth year of his age. Bred up in a bigoted and monotonous court, where everything bore the stamp of submission and bent before the nod of the great monarch, Philip had learned to regard the person and will of his grandfather, Louis XIV, with a respect almost bordering on adoration. He had imbibed also a deep and awful sense of religion, and in his whole conduct and deportment displayed a moral purity and scrupulous decorum which are rarely found in courts.

FRENCH INFLUENCE DOMINATES

As the primary object of Louis XIV was a desire to exclude a hostile family, and employ the power, resources, and territories of Spain for the aggrandisement of his own kingdom, the means and persons who were to direct the movements and fashion the character of Philip were all adapted to the attainments of this end. The first instructions given by the monarch to his pupil and grandson, amidst much trifling and commonplace advice, contain the outlines of that system which time and events were to mature and complete.

Philip literally obeyed these instructions. He placed his full confidence in Portocarrero; he suffered him to assume the power of forming the new ministry, of gratifying his personal or political antipathies, and filling at his pleasure all offices and appointments of state; and from the commencement of his reign Philip was the king of a party and the vassal of France, to whom he principally owed his crown. As Louis foresaw, therefore, that the possession of the Spanish crown must ultimately depend on the decision of arms, he had spared no pains to commence a contest with advantage, even before the death of Charles; and he hoped by a prompt and vigorous effort to bring it to a speedy and successful issue. He had gradually collected a powerful army on the Spanish frontier. By threats and promises he prevailed on the king of Portugal to acknowledge the new sovereign, and conclude an alliance with the house of Bourbon. At the same time he secured an entrance into Italy by negotiating a marriage between Philip and a princess of Savoy. He likewise obtained permission to introduce a French garrison into Mantua, the key of the principal military passage from Germany into Italy.

The unexpected tenor of the Spanish testament, and the foresight and promptitude of Louis, struck a temporary panic into the principal courts of Europe. In Holland the dread of impending ruin excited a unanimous sentiment of indignation against France. Preparations were made for hostilities; but Louis surprised all the frontier fortresses, and captured fifteen thousand Dutch troops by whom they were garrisoned. The fear of an immediate invasion, extorted from the Dutch government an acknowledgment of Philip as sovereign of the whole Spanish monarchy. The parliament and nation of England constrained William to follow this example. The court of Vienna made vigorous preparations to bring the dispute to the test of arms.

On the other hand, the sanguine expectations which the Spanish nation had formed of the wisdom, perfection, and energy of the new government, were too extravagant to be realised ; and it was the just remark of the shrewd Louville, that even should an angel descend from heaven to take the reins, the public hopes must be disappointed in the existing state of Spain, gangrened as it was from one extremity to the other. The crown was not only robbed of its splendour, but reduced to inconceivable penury. The same difficulties occurred in raising ten pistoles as ten thousand ; the salaries of the royal household were unpaid ; the pay of the troops was in constant arrears, and the royal guards were often reduced to share with mendicants the charitable donations of convents and hospitals. The whole army did not exceed twenty thousand men. Thus, totally ruined within and unprovided for war without, it was evident that the preservation of the crown must solely depend on the exertions of Louis XIV.

The change of sovereigns led to other mischiefs, which all the vigilance of the French court was in vain exerted to prevent. On the accession of a French prince, Madrid was crowded with swarms of Frenchmen, of the most despicable and abandoned characters, who were eager to gather the fruits of the promised land. Whole tribes of harlots, swindlers, gamesters, pick-pockets, and projectors, allured thither by the lucre of gain, vilified by their infamous conduct their native country, and gave new force to that odium which had hitherto operated as an insuperable barrier between the two nations. The seeds of rebellion were diffused, and the public grievances aggravated by the fanaticism of the clergy. The priests abused the sacred office of confession to excite discontent ; the French were stigmatised as heretics ; those who were connected with them were accused of irreligion, and even the authority of the pope was falsely employed to give new strength to the pretensions of an Austrian prince. All these causes contributed to excite discontent in a nation wedded to ancient establishments and proud of former magnificence. But the general odium was still further aggravated by the appointment of a Frenchman to the management of the finances. As Portocarrero was himself unequal to the task of remodelling the revenue, Louis, at the instigation of the council, sent Jean Orry [or Orri], a man of obscure birth who in a subordinate branch of the finances in France had acquired a superior knowledge of political economy.

The new minister proposed extensive reforms both in the nature and perception of the revenue, and endeavoured to model it on that of France, with a precipitancy and want of address or discretion ill calculated to conciliate the unbending firmness of the Spanish character. This abrupt attempt to lay the axe at once to the root of all abuses gave great offence to every class of the nation; and the clamour was heightened by his plans for resuming the fiefs extorted by the nobles from the crown in times of trouble and confusion. The nobles imperiously demanded the convocation of the cortes of Castile, the only legitimate assembly which could authorise the innovations, and as an additional argument they urged the necessity of exchanging the customary pledges between the monarch and the people, by the confirmation of the material privilege on one side, and the oath of allegiance on the other. A proposal to convene a body which had essentially curbed the royal authority, embarrassed the king and his personal friends and adherents. It was referred to Louis, but he prudently declined interfering, and Philip, after long deliberation, endeavoured to evade it by declaring that the journey which he was about to make to Catalonia to receive his bride rendered it necessary to defer the convocation till after his return.c

THE NEW QUEEN AND THE PRINCESS ORSINI

The choice of a wife had been an object of anxiety: it fell on Maria Louisa, a princess of Savoy, a lady of mild habits, and no more than fourteen years of age — one who seemed to be excellently fitted for passive obedience. To prevent her correspondence with the court of Turin, she was deprived of all her native domestics; nor was any one of her suite suffered to attend her, except the princess d'Orsini [or des Ursins, or Orsinos], as her *camarera mayor*, or superintendent of her household. As this lady would probably exercise much influence over the queen, and through the queen over the king and government, she had been selected with great caution. By birth she was French, of the illustrious family of La Trémouille. Her first husband was the prince of Chalais, with whom she had passed some years in Spain: her second, whom she had married in Italy, was Flavio d'Orsini, duke of Bracciano, and grandee of Spain. Her intimacy with Madame de Maintenon proved of singular service to her ambition, after her husband's death.

A French woman herself, indebted to France for her present fortune and her hopes of greater; acquainted with the Spanish language, society, and manners; possessing an extensive knowledge of the world, a fascinating manner, an intellect at once penetrating and supple; eloquent in her speech, always cheerful and even tempered, with art sufficient to hide her own views and to profit by those of others, she appeared admirably adapted for the purpose of Louis. Hence, after receiving minute instructions for her conduct, she was placed with the young queen, to whom she soon became necessary, and over whom her influence was unbounded.[1]

While Philip remained with his new queen at Barcelona, he opened the cortes of Catalonia. His reason for convoking that assembly was the hope of a considerable donative, perhaps of a supply sufficient to meet the war which his rival the archduke Charles was preparing to wage on his Italian possessions. Before any money was voted, demands were very properly made, and, with some modifications, granted; but the donative was so trifling in amount as to be scarcely worth acceptance. By the states homage was sworn to the king — no doubt with sincerity, notwithstanding the bitter injustice of the marquis of San Felipe,[b] who broadly asserts that they had no intention of observing the oath, and who calls the Catalans naturally perfidious. From Catalonia Philip was expected to return to Madrid; but in the belief that the wavering loyalty of the Neapolitans and Milanese — in the former a conspiracy had broken out for Charles, but soon suppressed — would be confirmed by his presence, he resolved to pass over into Italy. During his absence he left the queen regent of the kingdom, directing her on her return to the capital to hold the cortes of Aragon.

Philip could not command the cordial respect of the Neapolitans. The pope refused to grant him the investiture of the kingdom. From Naples he hastened to Milan, to oppose the imperial general, Prince Eugene, who, notwithstanding the opposition, had established himself in Lombardy. After some unimportant operations, he was present at the bloody but indecisive battle of Luzzara, where he showed great bravery. Soon afterwards he left the camp on his return to Spain, where he was now summoned.

[1 " Henceforward for years, during the most troublous crisis of Spain's fall, she did more for the country and for the young king and queen than all the ministers together. Manners and morals were reformed, light and brightness penetrated where gloom and ignorance alone had existed before. A Frenchwoman sent specially to serve French interests, she stood firm in defence of Philip and his wife, and of Spanish traditions, when everything depended on her prudence." — HUME.[d]]

WAR OF THE SPANISH SUCCESSION

Though William of England had acknowledged Philip, he had done so with duplicity: he knew that both his parliaments were at that time averse to war, and he could only wait for some act of hostility on the part of Louis, which, by incensing the English, should enable him to draw the sword.   The measures which Louis aimed at the English and Dutch commerce soon furnished him with the opportunity he sought.   The two governments now entered into an alliance with Austria, which had hitherto been fighting her own battles in Germany and Italy. The chief objects of this alliance were to obtain satisfaction for the Austrian claims on Spain; to rescue the Netherlands from France; to prevent the union of the French and Spanish crowns; and to exclude subjects of the former from the Spanish possessions in the West Indies. In revenge for this impolitic conduct of William, Louis, with equal impolicy, acknowledged the son of the exiled James Stuart as king of England. This insult roused the Protestant party; supplies were voted for the war; and though the king died in the midst of the preparations, Anne succeeded to the same policy.

Here commences the celebrated War of the Succession, which for so many years agitated all Europe, covered the Netherlands with blood, desolated the fairest provinces of Spain, and ended in

A SPANISH CAPTAIN

the loss of her Italian possessions.   The limits of the present chapter will allow us to do no more than briefly advert to its more striking incidents. The reader desirous of fuller information may refer to the histories of France, England, and Austria.

Omitting all mention of the interminable operations in the Low Countries, Germany, and Italy, in 1702 an expedition consisting of thirty English and twenty Dutch vessels of the line, exclusive of numerous transports, and carrying eleven thousand men, was sent against Cadiz.   It was headed by the duke of Ormond, who was totally unqualified for the post; nor were the subordinate generals much more happily chosen.

To the solicitations made by the allied generals, that the local governors would change their sovereign, either insulting replies were returned, or a contemptuous silence was observed. The reply of Villadarias, who said that Spaniards never changed either their religion or their king, was the sentiment of all except one. The disembarkation being at length effected, with some loss, the governor of Rota admitted the invaders, and for his treason was created a marquis, by the agent of the archduke. But the inhabitants had little reason to congratulate themselves; they were plundered, insulted, beaten, and even murdered by the licentious soldiery. At the town of Santa Maria, the inhabitants of which fled at the approach of the invaders, greater excesses were committed.[1] Equally unsuccessful was the attempt of the English ships to force their way into the harbour. Cowardice was now added to murder and rapine; the invaders precipitately retreated to their ships; six hundred of the rearguard were cut to pieces by half the number of pursuers; more still were drowned in their precipitate efforts to regain the ships — all who straggled behind were massacred by the incensed peasantry. The armament returned, and in Vigo Bay it destroyed the greater part of a Spanish and French fleet, rich by the productions of the Indies.

The fate of the governor of Rota, who on the retreat of the English had been hanged by order of Villadarias, did not deter a nobleman of the highest rank, of great power, and still greater riches, from the same treason. Cabrera, the admiral of Castile, who in the preceding reign had dispensed the patronage of the crown, from disappointed ambition, at seeing the cardinal Portocarrero in possession of a post to which he considered himself entitled, opened a treasonable correspondence with the court of Vienna. His intrigues, in a few short months, did more for the allied cause than would have been effected by the English cabinet in as many years: he drew the Portuguese king, Pedro II, into the confederacy, and persuaded Leopold to allow the archduke to visit the peninsula. The treaty which was signed at Lisbon in May, 1703, was as infamous to the character of its partisans as any other transaction of this war.

On the return of Philip, he found the government embarrassed, and the nation indignant, at the recent loss of his wealthy galleons in Vigo Bay. He found, too, the divisions in his cabinet more bitter than even at the period of his departure. To the princess Orsini was owing the declining power of Cardinal Portocarrero, and the ascendency of the count de Montellano, who showed more deference to the queen's favourite. D'Estrées, a man of considerable talent, of great family, and highly in favour with Louis, disdained to win the princess: the same influence procured his recall, his own nephew, the abbé D'Estrées, being made an instrument of his disgrace. At the same time the Spanish cardinal retired in disgust. The abbé succeeded to his uncle's post; he, too, quarrelled with the princess; and by conduct at once rash and double, brought on himself the indignation of the king and queen. In his recall, however, he had the gratification to perceive that his charges against the favourite princess d'Orsini had their effect, and that she was ordered to leave the Spanish court at the same time.

Indignant at the loss of her favourite, the queen exhibited her revenge by thwarting the measures of the new French ambassador, the duke of Grammont, and by opposing the execution of every order sent from Paris. Louis soon found that, if he wished to retain his ascendency, her resentment must be appeased. This could be effected only by the return of the princess. That celebrated woman accordingly resumed her former empire; and Grammont was replaced by a successor.

[1 "Here they committed the most enormous sacrileges, adding the rage of enemies to that of heretics," says San Felipe.[b]]

While this feeble cabinet was thus a prey to the basest passions, the storm of war again lowered on the frontier. In pursuance of the treaty with Portugal, twelve thousand English and Dutch troops, who were soon joined by the archduke Charles in person, were landed in that country. But the duke of Schomberg, the general of the English forces, was a man of factitious reputation; he was far inferior in either activity or ability to a son of the English James II, the duke of Berwick, whom Louis placed at the head of the combined French and Spanish army.

With a force considerably superior to that of the enemy, divided into three bodies, and accompanied by Philip in person, he advanced into Portugal. First, Salvatierra was invested and reduced; other fortresses shared the same fate.

Fagel, the Dutch general, was surprised in the wild recesses of the Sierra Estrella; and though he himself effected his escape, his whole division was captured. The marquis de las Minas, the only good officer in the Portuguese service, took the field, defeated Ronquillo, one of the Spanish generals, and in a few days rescued several of the fortresses which had been reduced. Under the walls of Monscato a still more decisive advantage was gained over Ronquillo. The skill of De las Minas was equal to his valour; he baffled every attempt of Berwick to dislodge him, and even forced that general to return across the frontier.

As for Schomberg, he did nothing during the whole campaign, says Berwick,[e] but move from place to place with his army: he was consequently removed, and succeeded by Lord Galway, a man more imbecile than himself. Berwick could easily have triumphed over his stupid or cowardly enemies; but as he was no favourite at court, obstacles were thrown in his way, and towards the close of the campaign he was recalled.

While these indecisive events were passing in Portugal, an expedition, under the prince of Hesse-Darmstadt and Sir George Rooke, the English admiral, proceeded to Barcelona in 1704. The prince had boasted that no sooner should the standard of Charles be erected, than it would be joined by thousands of the disaffected Catalans. But though sufficiently inclined to throw off their allegiance to Philip, none joined the English, who, after an ineffectual attempt on Barcelona, re-embarked, and returned towards Portugal. On their passage, however, they took Gibraltar; and Sir George had the satisfaction to inflict some loss on the French fleet off the coast of Malaga. But the transactions of the year were little honourable to the allies of Austria.

The following year was destined to prove more memorable, and more successful to the allies. Gibraltar, the blockade of which had been commenced the preceding October by the marquis of Villadarias, and which was now pressed by Tessé, the successor of Berwick, made so gallant a defence that in May its siege was raised. Though disappointed at the ill success of its imbecile generals in Spain, the English cabinet was emboldened, by the victories of Marlborough, to make new and mightier efforts against the Bourbon prince in the south. In June, fifteen thousand men, under Lord Peterborough, were despatched to Spain. This extraordinary man, whose eccentricities even surpassed his genius, on arriving at Lisbon was joined by the archduke Charles, who was justly disgusted with the ill success of his affairs in Portugal. The prince of Hesse-Darmstadt persuaded the archduke to advance against Barcelona. He well knew that the indignation of the people against the crown and the Castilians, joined to their desire for the recovery of their lost independence, — a desire which had subsisted with unimpaired force since the time of Ferdinand the Catholic, — had multiplied the disaffected.

On arriving before Barcelona, Peterborough saw that the fortifications were in the best state, and well defended ; and he knew that an army four times as numerous as the one he commanded would be necessary to form the first line of circumvallation. In this emergency he resolved to attempt the surprise of the fortress of Monjuich, which overlooks the city, and the possession of which would, if not decide, at least prepare the surrender of Barcelona. But that fortress, being built on the summit of an abrupt hill, and protected by formidable works, was considered impregnable ; and impregnable it would have proved to an open attack. Secrecy being the soul of his enterprise, which he did not communicate even to the archduke, with the view of lulling the garrison into security, he re-embarked his great guns, and announced his intention of sailing for Italy. But, the very night appointed for his departure, he silently moved fourteen hundred men towards the works, acquainted the gallant Hesse-Darmstadt with his intention ; and both heroes, on reaching the foot of the ramparts, waited until day should dawn.

The assault was then vigorously made by about three hundred men. It succeeded though the prince was killed. From this elevation the artillery of the English played with tremendous effect on the ramparts of the city ; a breach was made, and a day appointed for the assault. The governor, Velasco, though among the bravest of the brave, to avoid the horrors attending a storming, offered to capitulate. On the 23rd of October, the archduke solemnly entered, and was proclaimed king of Spain. The example of the capital was followed by the rest of the principality ; it spread into Valencia, next into Aragon and Murcia, which ultimately ranged themselves on the same side. For the rapidity of such success it is difficult to account.

The English historians gently slide over the atrocities of this war. Though all profess to follow San Felipe[b] they do not mention the rapes, murders, acts of sacrilege, and robberies committed by the English and their allies, the Catalan *miquelets*, who were, in fact, a species of banditti. Wives ravished before the eyes of their fettered husbands, daughters before their fathers ; even churches turned into brothels, and the altars used as the most convenient places for the consummation of such iniquities, are said to have been common scenes. The Catalans themselves are implicated in them.

Lord Mahon[f] will not allow Tessé[g] to have possessed merit of any description. Both his memoirs and his letters show that he was a sagacious observer ; and his military talents were unquestionably not mean.

The reduction of Barcelona and the insurrection of Valencia could not fail to make a profound impression at Madrid. By this time Philip seems to have attained a salutary conviction that, unless he assumed an activity corresponding to his circumstances, his reign would soon be at an end ; he accordingly resolved to take the field in person. Having petitioned Louis for a powerful reinforcement, and withdrawn most of the troops engaged on the frontiers of Portugal, — leaving a handful only under Berwick, who had been again ordered to assume the conduct of the western war, — he proceeded to invest Barcelona, the recovery of which would naturally constrain the submission of Catalonia, and perhaps put an end to the war by the capture of his rival.

In the passage through Aragon little care was taken by the royal army to cultivate the good will of the people ; because a lieutenant was murdered in his bed at Guerrea, the incensed soldiers were permitted, not only to plunder the inhabitants, but to massacre the neighbouring peasantry.   Philip proceeded towards the capital, under the walls of which he was joined by the duke of Noailles ; and he had the gratification of seeing the entrance to the harbour blockaded by a fleet of thirty sail.   Yet twenty-three days elapsed before the fall of Monjuich, and several more before a breach was made in the walls of the city wide enough to admit the assailants.   In a few hours Philip was assured that the enemy would be in his power.   At this critical moment, when the sun of Charles seemed to be set forever, a British squadron appeared in sight ; the French fleet retired towards Toulon.

VALENCIA

Philip, forsaking his guns, his baggage, and even his wounded, made a precipitate though reluctant retreat.   At this time his affairs seemed hopeless.   The duke of Marlborough had just triumphed at Ramillies ; a French army in Italy had been almost annihilated ; and the war in his own western provinces was no less disastrous than in the eastern.   Great as were the abilities of Berwick, his small band could not face the forty thousand enemies before him : he therefore retreated, and had the mortification to witness the capture of Alcantara, Ciudad Rodrigo, and Salamanca, and the approach of the confederates towards Madrid.   By his advice the court was removed to Burgos, the ancient capital of Castile.   It was high time ; for scarcely had Philip left it, when the light troops of Galway and De las Minas appeared in sight, and on the 28th day of June, those chiefs, at the head of thirty thousand men, made a triumphant entry into Madrid.

To ordinary and even to many acute observers the Bourbon power seemed forever fallen in the peninsula.   Without forces, without money, a fugitive from his capital, which was occupied by a formidable enemy, his fairest provinces in the power of his rival, Philip was expected to retreat into France.   But adversity called forth powers which had hitherto slumbered within him, and the existence of which had not been suspected, perhaps, even by himself.   With a fortitude which would have done honour to a stoic, he bore his sudden, almost overwhelming reverses : with pathetic simplicity he harangued his handful of troops, whom he assured of his unalterable resolution of dying with them in defence of their common country; and, as to the future, he looked forward with a hope which showed that he knew the Spanish character much better than his timid counsellors.

When the allied troops had entered into Madrid, no shout had been raised in favour of Charles : a mournful silence reigned on every side. Madrid was not Spain, and the Spaniards were not Flemings — facts of which the allied generals had soon a melancholy experience. In Castile, almost every individual became a soldier. Estremadura furnished and equipped twelve thousand; in Salamanca, no sooner had the allies left it on the march to the capital than the inhabitants arose, again proclaimed Philip, and levied a body of troops to cut off all communication between them and Portugal. Those whom sickness or age prevented from drawing the sword, contributed their money to the same end. "The day before yesterday," wrote the princess Orsini, "a priest brought 120 pistoles to the queen, from a village which contained only the same number of houses. He said, 'My flock are ashamed of sending so small a sum; but they wish me to say that there are also 120 hearts faithful even to death.' The good man wept as he spoke, and truly we wept with him!" The rising spirit of the people was not the only cause of this change : the allied generals grew suddenly inactive ; the troops in Madrid abandoned themselves to many excesses, which they found more attractive than the fatigues and dangers of a campaign. Had even the inhabitants been attached to Charles, the presence of the Portuguese — such were nearly all the troops under De las Minas — would have changed their loyalty into disgust. Another expedient of a most loathsome kind did more mischief; the common women were instructed to visit the tents of the invaders, of whom six thousand were soon taken to the hospitals.

Charles himself wasted so much time in Barcelona and Aragon, that when he joined his generals at Guadalajara he perceived the active Berwick at the head of a greater force than his own. By that able man his communication with Aragon was intercepted — it had been already cut off with Portugal; Andalusia was in arms, so that his only way of escape was into Valencia.

Philip joined in the pursuit as far as the confines of Murcia, witnessed the reduction of Orihuela, Cuenca, and Cartagena, and returned in triumph to Madrid, which received him with enthusiastic demonstrations of joy.

The tide of success had now set in too strongly to be stemmed by any barrier opposed by the allies. On the plain of Almanza, De las Minas and Galway were signally defeated by the able Berwick. This victory established the throne of Philip: it inspired his adherents with confidence; in the same degree it dispirited his enemies, and it was followed by advantages of still greater moment. While the duke d'Orléans, who arrived with reinforcements from France, led an army into Aragon, Berwick proceeded to reduce the fortresses of Valencia. The capitals of both kingdoms submitted without striking a blow: in the former, the example was imitated by the remaining strong places; in the latter Denia, Jativa, and Alicante resisted, but were ultimately reduced. In punishment of their desperate valour the inhabitants of Jativa were barbarously butchered, the walls were razed to the ground, and when it was subsequently rebuilt, it was not allowed to retain its former name, but received that of San Felipe. But the heaviest of all penalties was the abolition of the ancient fueros, both of Aragon and Valencia, by a royal decree of June 29th, 1707. This abolition was effected in virtue of the royal authority, and of the right of conquest;

the privileges, says the decree, had been granted at the mere pleasure of the crown, and the same pleasure now revoked them. The pretension was not more iniquitous than it was false. But these considerations had no influence on the Castilians, who looked only at the rebellion, and who, envious of the distinction hitherto possessed by the other kingdoms, were now resolved to reduce them to the same level. The same fate had been decreed against the privileges of Catalonia, the recovery of which now occupied the cares of the French general. But, before this object could be gained, new and almost unparalleled difficulties had to be encountered. Naples was conquered by the Austrians; and Milan was already in their power. Tortosa made a long and brilliant defence; some reinforcements were received from England; Galway was displaced by Stanhope, an officer of courage and experience; Count Starhemberg, the imperial general, arrived with auxiliaries, and the Balearic Isles were reduced by the allies.

Yet though in addition to these misfortunes the duke of Orleans was recalled through the intrigues of the princess Orsini; though, from the reverses of his arms in the Low Countries, Louis XIV intimated that he should be compelled to make whatever terms he could with the allies, if even they insisted on the sacrifice of his grandson; though the finances were in a distressed state; though, in the memorable campaign of 1710, Philip failed against Balaguer, was defeated by Starhemberg at Almenara, still more signally near Saragossa; though he was forced to retreat to his capital, and immediately afterwards to transfer his court from Madrid, which he was again destined to see in the power of his enemies, to Valladolid — still he had the consolation to find that his reverses endeared him to his people, and that Spanish loyalty and honour were not to be shaken. Volunteers again flocked in from all quarters; again were contributions of money and corn sent as free gifts. Add to this that the victory of La Godiña, obtained over the luckless Galway, the recovery of Ciudad Rodrigo, and the reduction of some Portuguese fortresses on the Estremadura frontier had naturally encouraged many to remain firm in their loyalty; and so great was the attachment borne to him that, when his rival Charles entered the capital (in October), scarcely a "*viva!*" was raised even by the lowest of the mob. The English general candidly confessed that the allies could command no more of the country than where they were actually encamped, and that the nation was against them. Charles was soon disgusted with Madrid; he left it the following month, and was scarcely beyond the gates when he had the mortification to hear the bells merrily ringing for his departure. During their stay, his English allies exasperated the people beyond forgiveness by their continued insults to the established faith, and by lawless rapine.

Again was Philip recalled by the inhabitants of Madrid, who greeted him with their warmest acclamations. Accompanied by the duke of Vendôme, who had arrived from France, he hastened in pursuit of the allies. At Brihuega they overtook Stanhope, at the head of fifty-five hundred men, chiefly English. In suffering himself to be surprised by a force so much superior, in a town of which the fortifications were few, and these few ruinous, was a fatal error; but he nobly resolved to prolong the defence to the last extremity. But in the end, when longer resistance was impossible, these brave men capitulated, and were dispersed through Castile.

The following morning Starhemberg, who had been requested by Stanhope to advance to the relief of his allies, arrived within sight of the place, and Vendôme prepared to receive him. In the battle which ensued, fortune declared for Vendôme.

These disasters, at a time when the allied cause was expected to be resistless, the amazing sacrifices of men and money, which England had so long and so unwisely made, and, above all, the change of Queen Anne's ministry, strongly indisposed her people to the continuation of the war. Besides, by the death of the emperor Joseph, in April, 1711, Charles, the last male of his house, succeeded to immense possessions, and was invested with the imperial dignity — an expectation indeed soon verified by the event; and the union of so many states with the crown of Spain threatened to become no less fatal to the pretended balance of power than even the union of France and Spain.

At length Louis, having consented to swear that the two crowns of France and Spain should never be united on the same head; and Philip having renounced, both for himself and his successors, all claim to the former — engagements which neither considered binding — a general peace was signed, April 11th, 1713, by the ambassadors of all the sovereigns except the emperor. Its provisions, as far as Spain is concerned, were few but momentous. Philip was acknowledged king of Spain and the Indies; but Sicily, with the regal title, was ceded to the duke of Savoy, and Milan, Naples, Sardinia, and the Netherlands to the emperor; Gibraltar, and Minorca, with the commercial advantages before mentioned, to the English; a general amnesty was guaranteed to the Catalans, but without any stipulations for the preservation of their ancient fueros. In case Philip died without issue, the succession was to devolve, not on a prince of the house of France but on the duke of Savoy.

By this celebrated peace Spain was stripped of half her possessions in Europe. The War of the Succession was now virtually at an end : Charles, disabled by the defection of his allies, opened negotiations for withdrawing his troops from Catalonia; and though the inhabitants of the capital were resolved to continue the struggle unaided, it could not be of long continuance. Neither this war, nor the peace which followed it, was honourable to the allies. It was signalised by many atrocities, and by incessant insults to the religion of the country, and the morals of the people.

Of all the parties in this war, England is by far the most censurable. Hurried into it by hereditary, and in this case absurd, jealousy of France, she conducted it without glory, and ended it with discredit. She forced the Catalans into rebellion, yet she now abandoned them to a cruel and vindictive persecution.

THE CATALAN REVOLT (1713–1714 A.D.)

When the Catalans knew that the king had resolved to abolish their fueros, that neither honour nor justice was to be expected from England, and that the emperor himself was compelled to forsake them, instead of bewailing their situation, they manfully resolved to continue in arms against the whole force of the Bourbons. They rejected the proffered amnesty of Philip, unless their privileges were to be declared inviolable. Had the king complied with this condition, he would, doubtless, have attached to his throne, by the strongest of all ties, this brave and independent people; but he appears to have regarded every form of freedom with abhorrence, and to have considered the frequent insurrections as a consequence of their superior rights. A slight acquaintance with the national history would have taught him that they were occasioned by the repeated and unconstitutional usurpations of the crown.

The Catalans did not fall without one of the noblest struggles on record. An overwhelming army reduced all their fortresses, except Cardena and the capital; the latter was invested, held for months in a state of blockade, while a formidable artillery played, with few intermissions, on the walls. In the spring of 1714, twenty thousand Frenchmen, under Berwick, arrived to reinforce the besiegers; nay, an English squadron was despatched for the same purpose. Nothing could daunt the inhabitants; all who were strong enough flew to arms; even the women and the ecclesiastics. Unfortunately they disgraced their cause by many excesses: never was tyranny more complete than that which reigned within the walls of Barcelona. All who did not prefer the rashest to the most moderate measures, were massacred by a ferocious mob. Even priests were forced from the altar or the pulpit to the scaffold or the gallows. In the meantime Berwick found that his most vigorous attacks were repulsed with loss. The desperate defenders had rallied round a black banner, on which was the representation of a death's head, — an intimation that they would neither give nor receive quarter, — in a series of wild, almost superhuman efforts.

Nothing now remained but to make the last awful attempt. Fifty companies of grenadiers advanced. Of the desperate valour of the besieged some idea may be formed, when it is known that in the course of this event-

PULPIT, BURGOS CATHEDRAL

ful day the bastion of San Pedro was won and lost eleven times: women and priests advanced to the charge with amazing impetuosity; and such was the havoc which they and their comrades inflicted on the enemy, that in one regiment, long before the close of the struggle, every superior officer had fallen, and an ensign remained with the command. But numbers prevailed: after twelve hours of incessant fighting, the small remnant of Catalans began to give way; a white flag was hoisted, the carnage was suspended, negotiations were opened; but as the deputies still insisted on the inviolability of their ancient rights, they were hastily broken off. During the night, a fire of musketry was maintained from the houses; but in the morning of September 12th, when Berwick was proceeding to put all to the sword, and burn the city to the ground, the leaders consented to capitulate.[1]

[1 " After thirteen years of struggle, the most obstinate and deadly in the modern history of Europe, Catalonia was brought back to the fold, shorn of all her privileges and assimilated to the contemned Castile." — HUME.ʰ]

In return for his renunciation of all future claim to the crown of France, in 1712, Philip forced, rather than persuaded, his council to alter the order of succession in Spain — to introduce a sort of Salic law, by which the most distant male of the family would be called to the inheritance in preference to the nearest female.   The cabals of the princess Orsini, who aspired to a small independent sovereignty in the Low Countries, and who in her disappointment opposed everything which had not served her personal ambition, added to the national dissatisfaction.   Even after the death of the queen of Spain, in February, 1714, who left two sons, the infantes Luis and Ferdinand, her influence remained paramount.   Perceiving that Philip would not long remain without a queen, it was her aim to provide him with one who would be as flexible to her purposes as the last.   To preserve her present reign, she caused the direction of affairs to be intrusted to M. Orry, whose attempts to shake the power of the Inquisition, to curtail the immunities of the church, rendered both him and her the objects of orthodox hatred.   But her ascendency was fast hastening to its close; and, with all her penetration, it was hastened by one of far humbler rank, but of superior cunning to herself.

At this period the celebrated Italian abate Alberoni appears on the stage of Spanish history: he had entered the country as the agent of the duke of Parma, and had been protected by Vendôme.   He had access to the court, where he soon insinuated himself into the good graces of the princess.   Seeing her embarrassment in choosing a wife for the king, he one day proposed Elizabeth [or Isabella] Farnese, daughter of the late, and niece of the present duke of Parma, whom he artfully represented as simple, devout, immured from the world, and exactly fitted to become her instrument.

Negotiations were secretly opened for the marriage; the papal dispensation — for the future was nearly related to the deceased queen — was procured; and the favourite exulted in the prospect of continued rule, when she discovered the real character of her future mistress.   Scarcely was she introduced to Elizabeth, when, by order of the latter, she was arrested and hurried towards the frontier, without a moment's time to collect her wardrobe.   She passed to Rome, where she ended her days in the household of the unfortunate Stuart.   Her fate excited no sympathy; it was rather beheld with satisfaction: but yet it will be regarded by future generations with much interest, as a peculiar illustration of the instability of courts.

A NEW EUROPEAN WAR (1715–1719 A.D.)

The disgrace of the princess Orsini was followed by the removal of Orry and her other creatures from the administration.   Like her predecessor Maria Louisa, Elizabeth succeeded to the most unbounded power over the royal mind, especially after the death of Louis XIV, whom Philip had been accustomed to regard with mingled reverence and fear.   That event changed his policy.   Next to Louis XV, now a child, he was the heir to the French crown — his renunciation to procure the Peace of Utrecht had been esteemed both by himself and his grandfather a farce — and, as such, he might aspire to the regency.   It was dexterously seized by the duke d'Orléans, a circumstance which alienated him from the French court.

The queen, whose talents were of a higher order than her predecessor's, whose power of dissimulation would have been honoured even in Italy, aspired to place a son of her own (in 1716 she was delivered of the infante Don

Charles) on the throne of France. To the attainment of this object, and the continuation of the Spanish influence in Italy, her whole soul was bent. Having, by his dexterous intrigues no less than the queen's favour, annihilated the power of the prime minister, the cardinal Del Giudice, and obtained the direction of affairs, Alberoni began to exhibit his designs on Italy, which were so injurious to the Austrian domination in that peninsula. They could not be wholly hidden from the imperial court; hence distrust, next ill will between Madrid and Vienna.

The impolitic and arbitrary arrest of the Spanish ambassador in Italy, by the emperor's order, so irritated Philip, that he resolved on war, even though he knew that a triple alliance had been formed between France, England, and Holland, to preserve the integrity of the Treaty of Utrecht. As Spain was sure to stand alone in the conflict, and might probably be opposed to all Europe, Alberoni strongly disapproved the war, until he saw that, by persisting in his fruitless opposition, he should only seal his own disgrace. From that moment he showed great alacrity in preparing for it. With the view of conferring greater lustre on his character and administration, he compelled the pope to bestow on him the dignity of cardinal.

In August an armament, consisting of twelve ships and nine thousand men, left Barcelona and steered for Sardinia. In about two months the island was subdued. So unjustifiable an aggression, without previous declaration of war, deeply mortified the emperor and alarmed Europe. In June, 1718, a Spanish fleet, consisting of twenty-three ships and thirty thousand men, again left Barcelona, cast anchor about four leagues from Palermo, and landed the forces. Europe beheld with some alarm this vigorous and unexpected effort of a power which, since the reign of Philip II, had sunk into insignificance. In the apprehension of another war not less fatal than that which had been ended by the Peace of Utrecht, France now joined with England, Austria, and the Dutch in the treaty afterwards known by the name of the Quadruple Alliance. But the cardinal disregarded the approaching storm, and refused to recall the forces in Sicily. Palermo and Messina (except the citadel) were speedily occupied; the whole island was preparing to receive the Spanish yoke, when the British fleet, under Admiral Byng, arrived off the Sicilian coast. In the action which followed, the Spanish fleet was almost wholly taken or destroyed. In revenge, Alberoni entered into an alliance with Charles XII of Sweden and the czar Peter to assist the Stuart in an invasion of Great Britain; but the death of the Swedish hero frustrated his hopes.

His next step was to organise a conspiracy, the object of which was to arrest the French regent, the duke of Orleans, and to proclaim Philip as the guardian of the infante Luis. It was discovered, and war declared against Spain. At the head of thirty thousand men, the celebrated Berwick passed the Pyrenees into Biscay, traversed Béarn, invaded Catalonia, took Urgel, and, after an ineffectual attempt on Rosas, retired into Roussillon. Undaunted by these reverses, the cardinal fitted out at Cadiz a formidable expedition, which he professed to be directed against Sicily, but which he despatched under the duke of Ormonde; towards Scotland, to assist in placing James Stuart on the throne of Britain. But a fatality seems to have attended all Spanish armaments against England. Off Cape Finisterre, the present one was dispersed by a violent storm; two frigates only reached their destination, and the handful of troops they poured on the Scottish coast was soon compelled to surrender. In revenge a British squadron committed great devastations on the coast of Galicia.

In Sicily, affairs began to assume an appearance equally unfavourable for this enterprising minister. Austrian troops were poured into the island, and the Spaniards were driven from their plains into the fortified places. Spain now stood alone against armed Europe. These misfortunes made a deep impression on the mind of Philip, who began to regard his minister with an unfriendly eye. The cardinal, in the height of his power and totally unsuspicious of his situation, received a sudden order to leave Madrid in a week, and the Spanish dominions in three.

His memory was bitterly persecuted in Spain: attempts were made to procure his degradation from the purple; but he vindicated himself in an elaborate apology,[i] which he contrived to publish, and which did little honour to Philip and the queen. In twelve months, on the death of Clement XI, he emerged from his secret retirement, and attended the conclave for the election of a new pope. He was subsequently a great favourite with the Roman see. While in power he had introduced many and most salutary improvements into the internal administration; he restored to a considerable extent the national prosperity; and he was beyond all comparison the greatest minister the country had possessed since the famous cardinal Ximenes Cisneros.

After the removal of the cardinal, Philip acceded to the Quadruple Alliance, renounced all claim to the dismembered provinces of the monarchy, consented to see Sicily transferred to the emperor, and Sardinia to the duke of Savoy: in return, he was acknowledged by his old rival as king of Spain and the Indies; and the reversion of the two Italian principalities was entailed on the issue of his present marriage—on the condition, however, that they should never be united with the Spanish crown. But these were poor advantages in comparison with the extent of his preparations for the war. Having humbled the Moors of Africa, who had long aimed at the reduction of Ceuta, he demanded Gibraltar, which, in fact, had been verbally promised to him by the duke of Orleans, as the condition of his acceding to the Quadruple Alliance. That the duke had acted by the authority of the English government, is indisputable; but the ministry, seeing the opposition of the English people to the restitution of so important a place, were not ashamed to sacrifice the honour of the country, and to evade the fulfilment of the pledge. This was a subject of endless dispute between the two governments during the remainder of Philip's reign.

PHILIP ABDICATES AND RETURNS (1724 A.D.)

In revenge, and because he really found that his best dependence was in his own family, in 1721, he contracted a matrimonial alliance with the hereditary enemy of England: his eldest son Luis was contracted with Louisa Isabella [or Elizabeth], daughter of the duke of Orleans. Soon after, he formed a resolution which filled all Europe with astonishment, that of abdicating the crown in favour of his son and of retiring to the splendid palace of San Ildefonso, which he had himself founded. The motives for this step may be found in his melancholy temperament, in his religious feeling — a feeling little tempered by sober reason — and in an anxiety to escape from sceptred cares, which had weighed more heavily on him than on any other prince of the age. Nor was he without the ambition of equalling, in this respect, the glory of his predecessor the emperor Charles. The decree of abdication was dated January 10th, 1724; and Philip, having solemnly vowed never to resume the crown, retired in a few days to his chosen retreat. The court of the youthful Luis was filled with Philip's own creatures, who paid more deference to him than to their new monarch ; nor was anything of moment undertaken without his previous sanction. The irregularities of the court afforded him sufficient pretext for interference. Louisa Isabella, the new queen, was wayward, capricious, and depraved ; regardless of Spanish customs, and attached to the follies if not the licentiousness of the French court. To correct her, she was arrested, and confined to the Buen Retiro, but released before the end of the week, on her promise of amendment. The death of Luis (who by will declared him successor), by the smallpox, in August, 1724, after a seven months' reign, again induced Philip to claim the sovereignty. But that sovereignty he had solemnly abdicated ; the act had been registered by the council of Castile, and sanctioned by his own vow. Through the artifices of the queen, however, who prevailed on the papal legate to absolve him from his vow, he dismissed his unwelcome scruples, and resumed the regal functions in all their extent.

THE ADVENTURES OF RIPPERDÁ

The restoration of Philip was naturally that of his queen's policy — the establishment, by treaty or force, of his son Don Charles [afterwards Charles III] in the Italian principalities. Indignant at the evident lukewarmness of England, France, and Holland, in a matter which they themselves had proposed to advocate, he suddenly swerved from his past policy, and despatched an ambassador to Vienna to obtain from the emperor, hitherto his bitter rival, advantages which were not to be expected from the interested delays of the mediators.

The person employed in this mission was one of the most extraordinary characters in political life — the baron de Ripperdá, a Catholic gentleman of Spanish descent, but a native of the Netherlands, of good education but of no principle. Perceiving that his religion was a barrier to his ambition in his native country, he embraced the Protestant, and was returned a deputy to the states-general. His general talents and his knowledge of commerce were such that he was chosen envoy to Madrid, to settle the commercial differences of the two nations. Perceiving that both fortune and honours were to be more easily obtained in the service of Spain than in any other, he resigned his ministry, procured letters of naturalisation, and reverted to his original religion.

The fall of Alberoni, which was partly owing to his intrigues, and the bold plans he proposed for invigorating the industry and improving the revenues of the kingdom, rendered him a favourite with Philip ; with the queen, his bold suggestion to negotiate immediately with the emperor established his credit. Being selected for the difficult mission, in November, 1725, he repaired secretly to Vienna. Early in the following year treaties were signed. For his services on this occasion, and still more for the magnificent, though impracticable proposals which he had made for the renovation of the Spanish monarchy, the ambassador was created duke de Ripperdá, a grandee of Spain, and on his return, prime minister.

But his elevation turned his head ; his inability to realise any of the magnificent promises which he had made showed him in his true colours — as an unprincipled adventurer. Not six months had elapsed since his accession when, by a royal decree, he was dismissed from his employments and transferred to the fortress of Segovia. There he would, doubtless, have ended his days without trial, had he not contrived to effect his escape by the aid of a maid-servant whom he had seduced, and who afterwards accompanied him in all his extraordinary adventures. He arrived safely in Portugal, embarked at Oporto, remained a short time in England, and proceeded into his native country ; but the imminency of his danger increasing, he fled to Morocco, where a renegade had secured him a favourable reception. Whether, as is asserted, during his short stay in Holland he again embraced

SPANISH NOBLEWOMAN

the Protestant faith, is perhaps doubtful, but that at the court of Mulei Abdallah he submitted to circumcision is probable, even though the relation rests on no other authority than that of his enemies. It is certain that for some years he directed the councils and commanded the armies of the Moorish emperor, after whose dethronement he retired to Istria, where he ended his days in 1737, professing, in his last moments, that he died in the Roman Catholic faith.

The chief remaining transactions of this eventful reign must be related with greater brevity. For some time after the disgrace of Ripperdá, Spain adhered to the German alliance ; and was alternately friendly or adverse to England, according as the policy of the two courts harmonised or varied. Gibraltar was more than once besieged, but without effect. British armaments frequently appeared off the Spanish coast, but without inflicting much injury. As the emperor was naturally averse again to admit the Spaniards into Italy, and sought for delays, even for evasions, in fulfilling his compact, in 1729 the Treaty of Seville, between Spain, England, and France, broke the connection between the courts of Vienna and Madrid. Philip, by threatening to revoke the commercial advantages secured by the Treaty of Seville, forced the English king to interfere in behalf of Don Charles. In virtue of his efforts, and the assistance of France, the infante was soon invested with the actual possession of Parma and Piacenza, and declared successor to Tuscany.[1] As England evinced a disposition to remain on good terms with the emperor, the Bourbons adhered the more closely to each other ; the kings of Spain, France, and Sardinia entered into an alliance against Austria.

[1 " And so at last, after years of constant plotting and secret treaties innumerable, Elizabeth Farnese had triumphed in the great object of her life: all Europe accepted the sovereignty of her son over the Italian dominions of her forefathers. She had kept Europe in effervescence for years, but she had her way ; and the persistence of one woman had re-established Spanish influence in Italy and raised Spain once more to a leading place in the councils of the world." — HUME.[h]]

THE LAST OF THE ARMADA

It was now that doubtful measures and useless treaties were succeeded by active and extended hostilities. While one French army crossed the Rhine, and another passed the Alps, a Spanish army under Charles invaded Naples, and conquered it almost without an effort. Sicily was next reduced; and the infante, by order of Philip, was solemnly crowned king of the Two Sicilies. By the Treaty of Vienna, in 1735, the emperor, whose arms had been almost uniformly unfortunate, consented to acknowledge Charles, and in return he received Parma and Tuscany.

Omitting the petty intrigues in the cabinet of Madrid — the rise of one worthless favourite, or the ruin of another — the foreign transactions of the country continued to be sufficiently important. England was soon brought into hostile collision with this monarchy. One reason was the jealousy entertained of the Bourbon family by the recent acquisition; another was the opposition thrown in the way of English commerce by the ministers of Philip; a still greater was the contraband traffic which England resolved to maintain with the American colonies — a traffic not very honourable to England and deeply injurious to Spain. On the other hand, the royal officers in the West Indies, under the pretext of the right of search, made many illegal seizures; and, on all occasions, exhibited indirect hostility to the British trade. Her right of search arose from her sovereignty, and had been confirmed by successive treaties; but it was suddenly assailed by the English opposition.[l]

There is no doubt that though the English were most frequently to blame in these transactions, several cases of injustice and violence might be imputed to the Spaniards. These cases were carefully culled out, and highly coloured by the British merchants : these were held out to the British public as fair samples of the rest, while a veil was thrown over the general practice of illicit traffic in America. The usual slowness of forms at Madrid and the difficulty of obtaining redress, even in the clearest cases, added to the national indignation in England: it was also inflamed by a denial of the right to cut logwood in the bay of Campeche, and disputes on the limits of the new settlement which the English had lately formed in North America, and which, in honour to the king, had received the name of Georgia.

These grievances of the British merchants, embodied in angry yet artful petitions, were urged by the opposition in repeated attacks and with combined exertions. First came a motion for papers, next the examination of witnesses, next a string of resolutions, then a bill for securing and encouraging trade to America. The tried ability of Pulteney led the van on these occasions, and under him were marshalled the practical knowledge of Barnard, the stately eloquence of Wyndham, and the rising genius of Pitt. William Murray, the future earl of Mansfield, also appeared at the bar as counsel for the petitioners, and thus commenced his brilliant public career. Every resource of oratory was applied to exaggerate the insults and cruelties of the Spaniards, and to brand as cowardice the minister's wise and honourable love of peace. It was asserted that the prisoners taken from English merchant vessels had been not merely plundered of their property, but tortured in their persons, immured in dungeons, or compelled to work in the Spanish dockyards, with scanty and loathsome food, their legs cramped with irons, and their bodies overrun with vermin. Some captives and seamen who were brought to the bar gave testimony to these outrages, and were then implicitly believed. Yet calmer judgment may remember that they were not examined upon oath, and had every temptation to exaggerate which interest, party zeal, or resentment can afford; that to inveigh against the Spaniards was then considered a sure test of public spirit; and that they were told to expect, upon the fall of Walpole, a large and lucrative indemnity for their pretended wrongs.

But the tale that produced the most effect upon the house, and found the loudest echo in the country, was what Burke has since ventured to call "the fable of Jenkins' ears." This Jenkins had been master of a trading sloop from Jamaica, which was boarded and searched by a Spanish *guarda costa*, and though no proofs of smuggling were discovered, yet, according to his own statement, he underwent the most barbarous usage. The Spanish captain, he said, had torn off one of his ears, bidding him carry it to his king, and tell his majesty that were he present he should be treated in the same manner.

This story, which had lain dormant for seven years, was now seasonably revived at the bar of the house of commons. It is certain that Jenkins had lost an ear, or part of an ear, which he always carried about with him wrapped in cotton, to display to his audience; but I find it alleged by no mean authority that he had lost it on another occasion, and perhaps, as seems to be insinuated, in the pillory. His tale, however, as always happens in moments of great excitement, was readily admitted without proof; and a spirited answer which he gave enhanced the popular effect. Being asked by a member what were his feelings when he found himself in the hands of such barbarians, "I recommended," said he, "my soul to God, and my cause to my country." These words rapidly flew from mouth to mouth, adding fuel to the general flame, and it is almost incredible how strong an impulse was imparted both to parliament and to the public. "We have no need of allies to enable us to command justice," cried Pulteney; "the story of Jenkins will raise volunteers."

On his part, Walpole did not deny that great outrages and injuries had been wrought by the Spaniards, but he expressed his hope that they might still admit of full and friendly compensation; he promised his strenuous exertions with the court of Madrid, and he besought the house not to close the avenue to peace by any intemperate proceedings, and especially by denouncing altogether the right of search,[1] which the Spaniards had so long exercised, and would hardly be persuaded to relinquish.*j*

SPANISH ACCOUNT OF THE WAR WITH ENGLAND (1739–1741 A.D.)

At length Walpole could no longer resist public outcry; King George gave orders for a numerous squadron to be fitted out and appointed Vernon admiral of the fleet destined against the Spanish Antilles. A formal declaration of war was published on October 23rd, 1739. London received it with enthusiasm, the bells of the churches were pealed, a huge multitude accompanied the heralds, and everywhere it was heard with frenzied acclamation. It would seem that Great Britain's salvation depended on this war, and speculators rejoiced at the prospect of the treasures to be brought from the mines of Peru and Potosí. It was also many years since the Spaniards had entered on a war with such unanimous good will. Monarch, ministers, and people looked upon it as a national struggle, in which justice and the interests and honour of king and state were at stake.

[1 The importance of this "right of search" will recur in connection with the War of 1812 between England and the United States. The war hereafter described is sometimes called "The War of Jenkins' Ear."]

Fortunately also, the fleet arrived opportunely from America, with great profits, having evaded the vigilance of the English who attempted to give chase.   By this means, while England was compelled to keep a considerable fleet to watch the movements of the French who threatened her coasts, numerous Spanish privateers set sail from all the ports of Spain, and cruising about with daring courage captured a number of English merchant ships in a very short time.   We are assured that within three months of the issue of the letters of reprisal, eighteen English prizes had been brought into San Sebastian, and that before the year was over a list remitted from Madrid was published in Holland, which put the value of the prizes made at more than 23,000,000 reales [£234,000 or $1,170,000].   This only increased the anger and desire for vengeance of the English.   Their efforts were principally directed against the Spanish possessions in the New World.   Vernon's squadron attacked and took Porto Bello, November 22nd, 1739.   The news was received in England with universal jubilation, though it hardly called for such general rejoicing, the prize certainly not corresponding to the expenses of so large a fleet, all that Vernon seized at this place being three small ships and $3,000 in Spanish money.

The English now despatched a formidable fleet of twenty-one ships of the line and as many frigates with nine thousand men, to invade the West Indies, the chief object of their ambition.

This squadron was to join Vernon's ; and almost at the same time Commodore Anson set sail with another small squadron to cruise about the coast of Peru and Chile.   Much time had passed since so large and well-equipped a fleet had set sail from Great Britain ; the kingdom held the brightest hopes of it, the English thinking to cut off communication between Spain and the New World, and by depriving the former of the treasures of America to bring it to more humble and peaceable terms.   But this nation, so apt to criticise the Spanish slowness, delayed their preparations for so long that the season passed, and the Spaniards had time to fortify their towns and prepare for defence.   But the English attacked Cartagena, and succeeded in taking possession of several advanced forts at some distance from the town.

These trifling successes made Admiral Vernon so confident of victory, that he despatched letters to England announcing that he would shortly be master of the town.   The news was received in London with extraordinary rejoicing ; the English believed that they were near to overthrowing the Spanish empire in America, and in their enthusiasm they caused a medal to be struck, representing on one side Cartagena, and on the other a bust of Vernon, with an allegorical inscription to the illustrious avenger of national honour.   These bright hopes speedily vanished ; Vernon attempted an assault on the fort of San Lazaro, for which twelve hundred men were appointed, but nearly all fell victims to their ill-advised courage ; the few who remained were cut down by a party of Spaniards who sallied out of the castle.   This reverse increased the discord between Vernon and Wentworth, commander of the troops ; the continual rains had caused an outbreak of a fatal disease which soon reduced the troops to half their number.   They were compelled to abandon the enterprise, and withdrew to Jamaica, having destroyed all the forts they had taken.

Commodore Anson visited the coast of Chile, took possession of Payta, and spent three days in sacking and firing the town.   He then directed his course to Panama in search of the rich vessels which carried the treasures of the Indies to Spain.   He finally succeeded in giving chase to the Spanish galleon, *Nuestra Señora de Covadonga*, which he attacked and captured with all her treasures, valued at £313,000 [$1,565,000], the richest prize, says an English writer, ever brought into British ports, but also the only loss of any importance suffered by Spain in this war.

The English made other attempts on the coasts of the New World, but without success, either because of the intemperance of the climate and the discord among the generals, or because of the precautions and wise measures taken by the Spanish government. Admiral Vernon decided to attempt the conquest of Cuba ; but after several fruitless attempts he soon saw that his forces were inadequate for the purpose. He was forced to withdraw, having lost eighteen hundred men. Thus we may count as destroyed the army and fleet which had left England, and raised the confident hopes of the English people of depriving Spain of her dominion in America. A few ships and a few weakened troops were all that remained on Vernon's return to England. Such was the result of the naval war between England and Spain. An English contemporary writer calculates that at least twenty thousand men were sacrificed in this unfortunate expedition, and a foreign writer estimates the prizes taken by the Spaniards during the war at 407 English ships.[k]

With this temperate Spanish account English historians generally agree, Wm. Connor Sydney [m] calling the war "one of the greatest blots in the chronicles of the realm." Spain's new naval power had been largely due to the zeal of the minister José Patiño, who had, however, died in 1736, too soon to see the glory of the victory over England.[a]

THE WAR OF THE AUSTRIAN SUCCESSION (1740–1746 A.D.)

The death of the emperor Charles VI, the famous competitor of Philip, without male issue, stimulated this monarch, as it did other sovereigns, to acts of spoliation. While Bavaria, Saxony, Prussia, and France each pursued its advantage, without regard to the succession which each had guaranteed with the deceased emperor, he looked toward Italy in search of an establishment for the infante Philip [or Felipe], his second son by the present queen. Hence all Europe was engaged in war. In 1741 an army was sent to Italy, a junction effected with the Neapolitans, and the combined forces marched into Lombardy. But several circumstances impeded the success of the Spanish arms. The king of Sardinia joined England and Austria; a superior force expelled Montemar, the Spanish general, from his position ; a British squadron compelled the king of Naples to observe neutrality; and the troops of that power were consequently recalled. During the following years the war sometimes raged, but often languished, with various success. Don Philip headed the army in person; but was more than once compelled to retreat into the French territory ; while at sea the superiority generally lay with the British over the combined fleets of France and Spain. At length the Neapolitan king broke his neutrality, and rejoined the Spaniards : this junction enabled Don Philip to resume the offensive. But after some desperate struggles,[1] the Spanish and French troops were expelled. In the Treaty of Aix-la-Chapelle, in 1748, Spain was disposed to lay down her arms, by the cession of Parma, Guastalla, and Piacenza, to Don Philip.

Before the conclusion of this peace, in July, 1746, an attack of apoplexy hurried Philip V to the grave. His character is apparent enough from his

---

[1] [" At Piacenza the Franco-Spanish army was literally cut to bits by Lichtenstein (July 16th, 1746), and the ambitious dreams of Elizabeth Farnese seemed to melt into thin air." — HUME.[b] Fuller details of this war will be found in the French, Austrian, and English histories.]

actions: indeed, it requires no other illustration. Whatever might be his general weakness, his unconquerable indolence, his subjection to his queens, he had a sincere desire for the good of Spain; and in part that desire was fulfilled. Under his rule the country enjoyed more prosperity than it had experienced since the days of Philip II. Nor was he deficient in a taste for literature. He founded the royal library of Madrid, the royal Spanish academy, the academy of history, and the academy of San Fernando, for the encouragement of the fine arts. In private life he was a model for princes: he was almost spotless. His only fault, let us rather say his only misfortune, was his want of capacity for the station he occupied: he would have been an admirable private gentleman, or an exemplary ecclesiastic.

THE GOOD KING FERDINAND VI (1746-1759 A.D.)

Ferdinand VI, second son of the deceased monarch, by Maria Louisa of Savoy (the fate of the eldest, Luis, has been already related), was, on his succession, in his thirty-fourth year. Though he did not want natural affection for his step-brothers, he was not to be controlled by the queen-dowager, whose influence was forever at an end; nor would he sacrifice the best interests of his kingdom to provide Italian sovereignties for the infantes [his half-brothers]. Hence, he consented to procure peace for his dominions by the Treaty of Aix-la-Chapelle, as related. His disposition was averse to war, which, as he clearly saw, had obstructed the career of the national improvement; nor was he so blind as to be ignorant that the blood and treasures of his people had been wasted for French or Austrian rather than Spanish objects. He respected the king of France as the head of his house, but he asserted his resolution not to become the viceroy of that monarch. If to this we add that he was a prince of honour, of integrity, of strict veracity, we shall have said all that truth will permit in his praise.

He had the melancholy temperament, the incapacity, the indolence of his father; nor was he less uxorious. His queen, Maria Theresa Magdalena Barbara, daughter of João V, king of Portugal, to whom he had been united in 1729, was a woman of engaging manners and of mild disposition, but avaricious. The same blemish attached to one of the most influential ministers, the marquis of Ensenada,[1] a man of low origin, but of ready parts and of profuse expenditure.

But the strangest influence over the destiny of the kingdom was that exercised by a singer, the famous Farinelli, who by his profession had made a fortune in England, and had been attracted to the court of Madrid in the hope that his music would have some effect over the hypochondriac Philip.[l]

The Singer Farinelli

Carlo Broschi, surnamed Farinelli, was a Neapolitan, whose voice and skill had obtained him great musical renown, and enabled him to amass a handsome fortune upon the boards of the London opera-house. During one of Philip's worst fits of hypochondria, Elizabeth Farnese invited Farinelli to Madrid, in order to try the effect of exquisite music upon her husband's obstinate melancholy. The result answered to her utmost hopes. She arranged a concert in a room adjoining that where Philip had for months

---

[1] [En se nada, that is, "in himself nothing," referring to his humble origin.]

lain in bed, pertinaciously resisting every entreaty to attend either to the business of his kingdom or the cleanliness of his person. Farinelli's vocal powers aroused him. He sent for the performer, and amidst a profusion of encomiums, promised to grant him whatever reward he should ask. Whereupon Farinelli, by the queen's instructions, requested the king to rise from his bed, undergo the usual operations of shaving and dressing, and attend the council of state. Faithful to his word, Philip complied, and returned for a while to his ordinary habits of life. From that moment Farinelli was retained, with a handsome pension, at Philip's court, and daily soothed the half insane monarch with his melodious warblings.

Upon Ferdinand's accession this favour rose to unexampled height. Farinelli, besides being appointed director of the opera, and, in fact, superintendent of all the royal pleasures, was honoured with the cross of Calatrava.

Farinelli seems never to have forgotten himself in this singular exaltation. He rejected all bribes, laughed at the adulation of his superiors, and long answered to those who besought his interference, "I am a musician, not a politician." In spite of his modesty, however, he at length became a political agent, having discovered that his intervention was, upon many occasions, agreeable and convenient to Barbara. The influence he was thenceforward led to exert acted in two opposite directions from the honest feelings of his heart, as did Barbara's from the dictates of her policy: his warm attachment to the empress-queen, whose subject he was born, and to England, where he had acquired his wealth, rendering him a zealous advocate of their interests, whilst friendship for Ensenada induced him, if not to assist in forwarding all that minister's plans, yet to make the utmost exertions to support him in his place.[n] By what strange instruments are mankind governed![1]

The reign of Ferdinand exhibits little more than a contest between the British and French agents, in support of the respective policy of their nations: Carvajal took part with the former, Ensenada with the latter. In 1754, Carvajal's death dejected the English as much as it elated the hopes of the French. Soon afterwards, Ensenada himself was disgraced. Ferdinand continued to observe a wise and dignified neutrality in the European war, occasioned by the rivalry of France and England. Not even the offer of Minorca, which the French conquered from the English, nor that of assisting in the reduction of Gibraltar, could incline the court in favour of the Gallic policy. Equally fruitless was the offer of Gibraltar by the English themselves, as the condition of joining the confederacy against France. But so mild, and just, and virtuous a prince was not long spared to Spain and to Europe. After the death of his queen, in 1758, he would never attend to either affairs of state or the ordinary enjoyments of life: in twelve months he followed her to the tomb. As he died without issue, he left the crown to his next brother, Don Charles, king of the Two Sicilies.

Indolent as were the habits of Ferdinand, he was a blessing to Spain, not merely from his pacific reign, but from his encouragement of agriculture, commerce, and the arts.[2] But the greatest benefit he procured for his

[1 Was it not time, after the disastrous influences of cardinals, monks, warriors, merchants, and noblemen had been tormenting Spain for centuries, that a musician should be tried? Are not the eminently beneficial results of the singer's influence over the benevolent king his justification?]

[2 Martin Hume[d] calls Ferdinand VI "the most truly beneficent sovereign that Spain had known for centuries. The encouragement extended to learning and intellectual progress was even more marked than that given by his father. Academies and learned societies sprang up everywhere;" and again,[h] "Ferdinand had found Spain struggling painfully to the light, still ruined, bankrupt, and miserable. He left it enjoying comparative prosperity, with a fleet of fifty ships of war and £3,000,000 ($15,000,000) in the treasury."]

country was the abolition of the grievous abuse of papal patronage. By it the chair of St. Peter had nominated to all benefices which fell vacant during eight months out of the twelve — thence called apostolical — and in any month, provided the possessor died in Rome. This monstrous usurpation was independent of expectations, indults, annats, fifteenths, and the other endless sources of papal rapacity. In 1753, the king procured from the pope a concordat, by which the right of nomination, during every month, was reserved to the crown; and the tributes contracted to be paid by the holder of the benefice to the see of Rome, in return for his nomination to it, were suppressed.

CHARLES III (1759-1788 A.D.)

By the Treaty of Vienna the two crowns of Naples and Spain were never to be placed on the same head : hence Charles III, on his accession to the latter, was compelled to resign the other in favour of a son. As the eldest, Philip, was a constant prey to mental imbecility, the second, Charles, succeeded to the rights of primogeniture, and was declared heir to the Spanish monarchy ; while the third, Ferdinand, was hailed as king of the Two Sicilies. Having appointed a council of regency during the minority of Ferdinand, Charles bade adieu to his former subjects, whom his administration had strongly attached to his person, and proceeded to Madrid. In the ministry he made few changes. He retained General Wall, but suffered Ensenada to return to court; he dismissed the minister of finance, whom he replaced by the marquis Squillaci [called Esquilache by the Spaniards], an Italian nobleman of considerable experience in that department; and he advised Farinelli to quit the kingdom.

When Charles ascended the throne, he found France and Great Britain involved in a war which, under the vigorous administration of Pitt, was highly disastrous to the arms of Louis. The success of the English displeased him; he feared lest the victors should turn their arms against his richest settlements in the New World. France was eager to make common cause with him. The result was an intimate alliance, known by the name of the Family Compact, by which the enemy of either was to be considered the enemy of both, and neither was to make peace without the consent of the other. However secret the articles, they were suspected by Pitt, who would have anticipated Spain by an immediate declaration of war, and by breaking off the hollow negotiations which, to gain time, France had commenced, had he not been replaced at this juncture by a court favourite, the earl of Bute. The new ministry were made the dupes of the Bourbon courts ; the negotiations were artfully prolonged until the arrival of the Spanish treasures from the Indies, and until preparations were made by both countries to carry on the war with vigour.

The mask was then dropped, and hostilities were invited. However unstable the English ministry, under a sovereign more feeble even than his predecessors, a vigour had been given by Pitt to every branch of the public service, which in the present war secured the triumph of English arms. In the West Indies, the Havana, in the east, Manila, were taken (1762) ; nor were the allied French and Spanish arms successful in Portugal, which, in punishment of its connection with England, was invaded by twenty-two thousand men, under the marquis of Soria. They could only take Almeida before they were compelled to retire within the Spanish territory. Worse than all other disasters was the state of the finances, which were, in fact, exhausted; while the interruption to trade, occasioned by the present hostilities, rendered it impossible for any minister to rely on new contributions. In this emergency, the two courts turned their eyes towards peace, which was concluded at Paris, February 10th, 1763. Omitting the concessions made by France, Spain purchased the restoration of the conquests which had been made, by the cession of Florida, by the permission to cut logwood in the bay of Honduras, and by a renunciation of all claim to the Newfoundland fisheries.

These unfavourable conditions were not likely to remove, however it might be prudent to smother, the irritation of the Spaniards. But such, at length, were the improvements effected in the collection of the revenues, and in the national forces by sea and land; such the results of a wise economy and a better discipline, under the superintendence of the count of Aranda, a man of enterprising genius, that these forces were considerably augmented, and taught to confide in their own strength. The British ambassadors at Madrid were no longer treated with even outward respect. That Spain was inclined to war is evident from the whole conduct of its ministers; but the desire was counteracted by the internal embarrassments of France. Thus affairs continued, until the count of Aranda being succeeded by the marquis of Grimaldi, and the latter, in his turn, by the count of Florida-Blanca, England received another blow through her ally Portugal. Portugal, the queen-dowager of which was the sister of Charles, joined the Family Compact.

The progress of the misunderstanding between England and her American colonies (1776–1783) afforded an opening for humbling her power. By entering into an alliance with the rebels, and by an open war with Britain, France at once indulged her hereditary enmity, and secured a friend in the rising states. With a policy as blind as it was vindictive, Florida-Blanca persuaded Charles to concur with France in behalf of the revolted colonies. Charles declared war, procured the co-operation of a French fleet, and caused Gibraltar to be closely invested. The situation of England, at this time, was exceedingly critical. By all Europe her ruin was considered at hand. Without an ally; opposed not only to her colonies, but to France and Spain, which were favoured by the secret wishes of Portugal, Morocco, Holland, Russia, and Austria; a prey to intestine commotions; cursed by an imbecile and extravagant court, and by a ministry no less despicable, her prospects were indeed hopeless. But the native vigour of her defenders, though it could not avert disasters unexampled in her history, and was in most instances lamentably misdirected, at least averted impending ruin. Gibraltar, though garrisoned with no more than a handful of men, exhibited a defence which astonished all Europe; and, though the coasts of England were frequently insulted by the appearance of a hostile flag, no descent followed. These fleets were not long suffered to exhibit even these ineffectual bravadoes. Having retired to the peninsular ports, one of them was defeated by Admiral Rodney, who about the same time had the good fortune to capture a convoy of fifteen sail. But the capture of a British merchant fleet by the enemy; the loss of some settlements in the West Indies and on the banks of the Mississippi, and the conquest of West Florida by Galvez, an enterprising Spanish officer, more than counterbalanced this advantage.

These disasters would have been much greater, had not the English cabinet contrived to spread division between the two allied powers. The offer of Gibraltar — an offer made with anything but sincerity — more than once arrested the hostile march of Spain, and led to secret negotiations. Florida-

Blanca had, however, the good fortune to propose the famous armed neutrality, by which the maritime power of Europe endeavoured to annihilate the naval superiority of Britain ; and he had the still greater glory of recovering Minorca [February, 1782, after seventy-four years of English possession]. Elated by this success the Bourbon ministers despatched a formidable fleet to expel the English from the West Indies, whilst their allies the Dutch, in concert with Hyder (Haidar) Ali, strove to drive the same enemy from the Carnatic. But the French admiral De Grasse sustained so signal a defeat that the enterprise, as far as regarded the West Indies, was abandoned. To England, however, the war was fatal : the American colonies obtained their independence. Humbled and discouraged, the ministry now made propositions for peace ; and negotiations for the purpose were opened at Paris. It was at length concluded (1783) on terms sufficiently humiliating to the British nation. She surrendered the two Floridas, Minorca, Tobago, and Gorée on the African coast, consented to be excluded from the greater part of the Gulf of Mexico, and to admit the French to a participation of the Newfoundland fisheries : while, in return for such concessions, she could not obtain the slightest advantage for regulating her trade either with the peninsula or the American colonies.

Advantageous as were the conditions of peace, Charles, when his resentment towards England was cooled, could not fail to perceive the impolicy of the recent war. He had assisted to establish a republic on the confines of his Mexican empire, and he knew that his own colonies had caught the same fire of independence. In fact, he had soon the mortification to see extensive districts in South America in open insurrection.

The remaining foreign transactions of Charles may be shortly dismissed. His treaty with the sultan of Constantinople and with the Barbary states freed his subjects from piratical depredations, and procured them commercial advantages in the Mediterranean superior to those enjoyed by any other European power. In Portugal, where his influence was confirmed by the marriage of his daughter Carlotta with the infante João, afterwards João IV, he procured from the French a share in the commercial advantages which had been hitherto exclusively enjoyed by the English. In an equal degree was the English influence impaired in Holland by the ascendency of the Bourbon courts. He wrested from the ministry most of the commercial privileges which during two centuries had been possessed by the British in the West Indies. But as he grew in years he became less favourably disposed towards France, and more willing to cultivate a good understanding with England.

The internal administration of Charles was not less signal than his foreign policy. It exhibits many novelties ; of which some were highly beneficial, while others were odious to the people. So long as the efforts of his ministers were confined to the improvement of commerce and agriculture, to cleansing and lighting the streets, to the construction and repairs of the roads, to the reorganisation of the police, and to the amplification of the public revenues, they were cheered by the popular approbation ; but when flapped hats and long cloaks — those screeners of assassination — were prohibited, a loud outcry was raised against the introduction of foreign customs. A monopoly for the supply of oil and bread to the people of Madrid bore on the lower orders much more sensibly than a change of costume, and called forth loud imprecations against the marquis Squillaci, the author of this impolitic innovation. On the evening of Palm Sunday (1766) the mob arose. They spread throughout the city, breaking the lamps, assassinating the soldiers, and forcing every man they saw to lower the brim of his hat.   The following morning the king communicated with them ; promised that the obnoxious minister should be replaced by a Spaniard ; that the decree against flapped hats and cloaks should be repealed ; that the price of oil, bread, soap, and bacon should be reduced, the monopoly destroyed, and the insurgents pardoned.

The following morning, however, hearing that the royal family and the ministers had fled to Aranjuez, they assembled in greater numbers than before.   During forty-eight hours the city was a prey to this lawless mob. Charles wrote to the Council of Castile that the obnoxious minister was already exiled, and that, if the people would quietly disperse, his other promises should be executed with equal fidelity.   The message, being proclaimed throughout the city, was received with shouts of applause ; the rioters instantly surrendered their arms and drums, shook hands with the soldiers, and departed to their homes.

That this commotion was a political intrigue was no less the conviction of the king than of his ministers ; and his suspicions fell on the Jesuits.[l]

EXPULSION OF THE JESUITS

It is unnecessary to trace here the rise and progress of this celebrated order whose position in history has been such a peculiar one.   It will be sufficient to observe that their spirit of intrigue, dangerous maxims, bond of union, and persevering ambition had long rendered them an object of fear and jealousy to many of the European governments ; and there was scarcely a political intrigue, or public commotion, in which they were not actually implicated, or supposed to be engaged.   Such, however, was their extensive influence, from the number and talents of their members, and the authority which they exercised over the public mind, by monopolising, in a great degree, the duties of education ; such also was their influence in the cabinets of Catholic princes, as directors of their consciences, and such the wealth and power they had appropriated, that till the middle of the eighteenth century no statesman had been found bold enough to smite this spiritual colossus. The first blow was struck in the petty kingdom of Portugal, by the marquis of Pombal, the minister of a weak and superstitious monarch, whose court and household were filled by their members and adherents.

From a suspicion, well or ill founded, that they were implicated in the memorable attempt to assassinate the king, they were in a single day involved in one common disgrace, their property confiscated, their members transported as prisoners to the coast of Italy and set ashore in the states of the church. Their expulsion from Portugal (1759) dissipated the terror inspired by their name and power, and prepared the way for their expulsion from France, which took place in 1764, with circumstances of more humanity and moderation than in Portugal.

It now became the leading principle of the French minister to complete their downfall in other countries, and particularly to obtain their expulsion from Spain.   For this purpose, Choiseul employed all the resources of intrigue to excite alarm at their character and principles, and implicate them in every offence which was likely to throw disgrace on their body.   He did not scruple even to circulate forged letters, in the name of their general and chiefs, and to propagate reports of the most odious and criminal nature against the members themselves individually.   These artifices and this anxiety will not appear superfluous, when it is considered that Spain was the country which gave rise to the institution, and fostered it with peculiar affection; that the king, a devout prince, had shown himself its friend and protector. The final cause which led to their expulsion was the success of the means employed to persuade the king that their intrigues had caused the recent tumult at Madrid, and that they were still forming new machinations against his own person and the royal family. Influenced by this opinion, Charles, from their zealous protector, became at once their implacable enemy, and hastened to follow the example of the French government (1767).

He confided the execution to Count de Aranda, who had so ably suppressed the commotions at Madrid. The king himself wrote, and directed with his own hand, circular letters to the governors of each province, which they were to open at a particular hour and in a particular place. When the period arrived, the six colleges of the Jesuits at Madrid were surrounded at midnight with troops, headed by officers of the police, and admission being obtained, the bells were secured, and a sentinel placed at the door of each cell. The rector was commanded to assemble the community; and the different members being collected in the refectory, the royal decree of expulsion was formally read. Each member was then permitted to take his breviary, linen, chocolate, snuff, a few other conveniences, and his money, on specifying the amount in writing. They were distributed in different vehicles, each carriage under the escort of two dragoons, to prevent any communication, and were thus conveyed to the coast. So complete were the precautions, and so prompt and regular was the execution, that the inhabitants of the capital were ignorant of the event till the following morning, when the cavalcade was already on its journey.

In the same manner each college, in the different parts of Spain, was invested. The transports, under the convoy of several frigates, steered for the ecclesiastical state, and appeared off Cività Vecchia, where the different officers had orders to land their unfortunate charge. But the pope forbade their admission, under the pretext that, if the Catholic sovereigns of Europe should abolish the religious societies, the papal dominions would be too small, and the treasure too poor to maintain them. During these delays, the Jesuits were crowded like convicts on board the transports, in the most sultry season of a sultry climate; and of the old and infirm, or those who had suffered from their sedentary life, numbers perished within sight of land. At length, after beating about the Mediterranean, exposed to storms and tempests for three months, they were received on the isle of Corsica; those who had the misfortune to survive preceding hardships were deposited in warehouses like bales of goods, without beds, and almost without the common necessaries of life. They remained in this deplorable situation, till their destiny was fixed by a compromise with the pope, when they were permitted to repair to Italy, and receive the scanty pittance allotted for their maintenance by the king of Spain. In the distant and extensive colonies of South America, similar precautions were adopted.

On considering this transaction with impartiality, it is impossible to deny that, however necessary the expulsion of the Jesuits might be deemed, yet the execution itself was one of the most arbitrary and cruel measures ever held out to the indignation of mankind. No other reason was alleged for these rigorous measures than the absolute good pleasure of the king. In this state of proscription they were not only prohibited from justifying their conduct, but it was ordained that if one single Jesuit should send forth the slightest apology in their favour, the pensions of all should instantly cease, and that all subjects of Spain who should presume to publish any writing, either for or against them, should be punished as if guilty of high treason: circumstances which can scarcely be credited in a free nation, if the truth were not still attested by the edict for their expulsion. The only apology which can be advanced in favour of such a cruel measure is that, the whole body being closely linked together in absolute obedience to their general, no one member could presume to publish anything without the approbation of his superior ; and such was their mighty influence over the consciences of persons of all ranks and descriptions that, if any had been permitted to continue in Spain, or to return thither while the ferment subsisted, they might have excited dangerous tumults among the people.

Charles notified this important measure to the head of the church in firm but respectful terms. It was not to be expected that the pope would acquiesce in so sudden and unqualified an expulsion of the most zealous partisans of the holy see, and still less so bold and irritable a pontiff as Clement XIII. The reply of the king announced respect and affection for the head of the church, but unshaken firmness in his resolution. The example of Spain was speedily followed by the king of Naples. The Jesuits were expelled with the same precautions as in Spain, and conveyed without ceremony across the frontier into the ecclesiastical state. When a petty sovereign like the duke of Parma ventured to expel the Jesuits from his states, and establish various regulations to restrain the papal authority, Clement deemed it a proper opportunity to exercise his spiritual power, without the danger of a repulse. He therefore issued a brief against the duke, threatening his territories with interdict, and his person with excommunication, unless he revoked his ordinances against the privileges and rights of the church.

The princes of the house of Bourbon, watchful for an opportunity to abridge the pretensions of the Roman see, accordingly opposed this exertion of papal authority with the most vigorous measures. France occupied Avignon and the Venaissin, and Naples seized Benevento ; and all the Catholic powers united in a common censure of the papal brief as illegal and vindictive. But while the dispute was yet in suspense, the decease of the aged pontiff opened a field for the struggle of the civil against the ecclesiastical power. No intrigue was spared by the Catholic powers to baffle the influence of the Jesuits, and obtain the election of a person who would enter into their views ; and they at length procured the choice of Ganganelli, a monk of the order of Minor Conventuals. He ultimately yielded to the incessant and pressing solicitations of all the Catholic powers ; and on the 21st of July, 1773, abolished the order of Jesus by a bull, in which he ascribes his consent to respect for the representations of the king of Spain, who insisted on this measure as necessary for the tranquillity of Christendom and the peace of his own dominions.

Charles, satisfied with having annihilated the power of the Jesuits, secured the tranquillity of his dominions, and eradicated their influence as a body, reverted to his natural mildness, and by a royal rescript permitted the members who yet survived to return to Spain, and obtain possession of land which had fallen to them by inheritance (1783).[c]

It is almost needless to add that, in the present, as in the case of the Templars, and at a later period in that of the suppressed monasteries in England, a very small portion of the possessions so unjustly confiscated was applied to any useful purpose ; in Spain, as in England, it found its way into the pockets of a needy sovereign, of courtly minions, or of unprincipled adventurers.

In most respects, the internal administration of Charles was one of unmixed good. The increase of the standing army, a force absolutely necessary, not merely for the national defence, but for the preservation of domestic tranquillity ; its improved discipline ; a judicious organisation of the police ; the restriction of ecclesiastical immunities in such cases as were incompatible with the well-being of the people ; the circumscription of the powers of the Inquisition ; an attempt to colonise the Sierra Morena ; the establishment of schools to supply the void left by the expulsion of the Jesuits, signalised the administration of the count of Aranda. The same reforms were extended or improved by the count of Florida-Blanca, who added others of even superior importance. The encouragement of agriculture, commerce, and the useful arts of life ; a radical change in the intercourse of Spain with her colonies ; a considerable augmentation in the returns of the mines, in the customs, in every branch of the revenue ; the introduction of new manufactures, and the encouragement of such as were already established ; the facilitation of intercourse, by means of new roads and canals, between the great marts of Spain ; and numerous reforms in the forms of judicial process, and in the responsibility of the judges, were a few of the many benefits conferred by this great minister on his country.

Charles III died, December 14th, 1788, at the age of seventy-three. From the vigour of his constitution he would, doubtless, have lived longer, had not his heart been affected by the precarious state of his relations in France, by the loss of his son Don Gabriel, of his daughter-in-law Doña Maria of Portugal, and of their infant. He was a prince of considerable talents, of excellent intentions, and of blameless morals. In his public character, his best praise is to be found in the fact that, through his ministers, he introduced a degree of prosperity to which his people had been strangers since the days of Philip II. In private life he was unlike most kings. During a long widowhood, his example afforded no encouragement to licentiousness : as he was severe towards himself, he was naturally so toward others. His chief defects were obstinacy, too great reserve, even with his ministers, and an immoderate addiction to the exercise of hunting. By his queen Amelia, a princess of Saxony, he left issue (1) Philip Pascal, excluded through natural imbecility ; (2) Charles his successor, imprisoned and forced to abdicate by Bonaparte ; (3) Ferdinand, king of the Two Sicilies. Four other sons preceded him to the tomb.[l]

Hume[h] calls Charles III "the only good, great, and patriotic king that providence had vouchsafed to Spain in modern times." Coxe[c] tells of his placid temper, and his lovableness ; "those who attended on his infancy grew gray, or died in his service." The anecdote is told of him that on his death-bed his confessor asked if he could pardon his enemies, and he answered ; "Why should I have waited till this extremity ? They were all forgiven the moment after the offence" — a spirit rare indeed in Spanish history.[a]

CHAPTER XII

SPAIN AND THE FRENCH REVOLUTION

[1788–1808 A.D.]

CHARLES IV ascended the throne at the mature age of forty. The nation entertained great expectations from their new king. His first measures confirmed the hopes of those who confined their views to a continuation and increase of the benefits conferred during Charles III's reign, if not the expectations of those who desired bolder innovations or of those who regretted the days of inquisitorial omnipotence. He confirmed Florida-Blanca in his post, and, at his suggestion, remitted considerable arrears of taxes incurred by indigence, suspended the *alcabala* upon wheat, and adopted economical reforms for the purpose of saving out of the annual expenditure of the country the means of liquidating the still unpaid debts of the crown.

Charles further showed his good sense by amicably settling a dispute that had arisen with England, at the price of partially abandoning a useless extension of the monopoly claimed by Spain along the western coasts of America. But from this period the history of Spain, as of every other country in Europe, becomes involved with the extraordinary events taking place in France on account of the French Revolution.[b] For a full account of these events one must look in the history of France, only those being recounted here which have a close bearing on Spain.[a]

The relations of these neighbouring and long-allied countries, France and Spain, were now of the strangest character. Hereditary affection attached the two royal families to each other, and they were furthermore united by ties of blood and community of interests. The king and especially the Spanish ministers poured their fear-mingled hatred upon the national assembly and the principles of the Revolution on every occasion.

[1789–1792 A.D.]

France and the assembly which personified it had no more deadly enemy than Florida-Blanca. He allied himself in turn with the emperor Leopold in order to dictate to the French people the measure of reform they required, and with the northern cabinets to force the assembly to destroy its work with its own hands, and re-establish the absolute monarchy as it existed before the Revolution. Finally he tried to reconcile the Grand Turk with the empress Catherine to permit of Russia's joining the other continental monarchies in building a dike to resist the rush of the revolutionary torrent.

But, during the interval, events had progressed; for after the French king's flight and his arrest at Varennes, the situation had become most serious. Royalty was dead, but the king still lived, and an imprudent step might compromise the threatened life. Florida-Blanca realised this and refused to associate Spain with a counter-revolutionary plot which was being organised in the south of France. But at the same time he sent the national assembly a letter and pleaded the cause of the fugitive king, prisoner in his own palace, in a tone which sounded more like a threat than a prayer. The assembly, its dignity hurt, replied with a scornful order of the day; and the breach between the two governments, whose principles were so opposed, widened more than ever.

Not daring to declare war upon France, the imprudent minister declared it at least upon the French in his own country; a decree ordered all foreigners resident in Spain to take an oath of allegiance to the Catholic faith, to the monarch and laws of the country, and to renounce their nationality and call themselves Spaniards. This tyrannical measure, apparently directed at all foreigners, was in fact aimed at the French alone, who were established in the peninsula to the number of thirteen thousand. The assembly was not deceived, and realised that, from that time on, it had an avowed enemy in the Spanish minister.

The Pyrenees were frequently crossed by French emissaries charged with the spreading of revolutionary doctrines to the peninsula. Florida-Blanca, hard pressed, finally established a quarantine on the frontier with the object of protecting Spain against the incendiary propaganda. Under this pretext he was able to keep a sufficiently large body of troops on the whole line of the Pyrenees to gain France's respect, lend a hand to anti-revolutionary plots in the south, and, in case of invasion by northern powers, keep up a useful diversion in the south and complete the blockade of France.c

THE RISE OF GODOY

It becomes now necessary to disclose a scene of licentious turpitude, such as we have long been spared in the annals of the court of Madrid. Maria Louisa the queen of Charles IV had, from the very moment of her marriage, betrayed a total disregard for the laws of conjugal fidelity, and her notorious gallantries could scarcely be checked even by the austerity of Charles III. That king, however, uniformly banished his daughter-in-law's lovers, as soon as the rumour of a new intrigue was brought to him, whilst the prince of Asturias remained so blind to his wife's guilt that he frequently, though always in vain, supplicated his father to recall persons whose society was peculiarly agreeable to the princess. One of the paramours thus exiled was Luis de Godoy, the eldest son of a noble but decayed family of Estremadura, who was serving with his brothers in the ranks of the horse guards; and this young man, anxious not to lose in absence the affections of the princess, employed his brother, Don Manuel, to deliver secretly letters expressing his constant passion and his lamentations over his banishment.

Don Manuel availed himself of the opportunity his office as letter-carrier afforded him, to supplant his absent brother, and thenceforward he held the exclusive possession of Maria Louisa's heart. She introduced her new favourite to the prince of Asturias, who soon appeared to share his wife's attachment for him; and when the death of Charles III removed the only restraint upon her conduct, the queen hoped to place Godoy at the head of the government. Charles IV would not, however, violate the respect he owed to the memory of his father, by displacing his minister. Florida-Blanca, as has been stated, retained the supreme authority, and, for a while, Godoy was obliged to rest content with inferior honours, unbounded influence over the queen, and the wealth lavished upon him by both herself and her royal consort.

CHARLES IV

This state of affairs lasted till 1792, and during those three years Florida-Blanca's caution combined with Charles' fears for Louis XVI's safety, to preserve peace between France and Spain. But the restrictions imposed upon the intercourse between the two countries, by inconveniencing trade, had created great dissatisfaction amongst the Spaniards; and the queen and Godoy took care that not only their murmurs, but various accusations, true or false, of malversation and oppression, laid to the minister's charge, should reach the king's ear. In February, 1792, Florida-Blanca, upon these imputations, was deprived of his high office, and thrown into prison. As soon as it was thought no danger existed of his recovering the king's favour, he was released from confinement.

The fall of Florida-Blanca did not at once make way for Godoy's exaltation to his post. The count De Aranda, in his seventy-fourth year, succeeded to the vacant premiership, May, 1792, and as a disciple, or at least an admirer of French philosophy, urged his royal master to pursue a more liberal course, to cultivate more zealously than heretofore the friendship of then constitutional France. De Aranda repaid the queen's patronage by his concurrence in that showering of court favours upon Godoy,[1] which his predecessor had offended her by opposing.[b]

But in the meantime events were developing so rapidly that diplomacy followed them with difficulty. The two fatal days of June 20th and August

[1 " The rapidity with which she loaded Don Manuel Godoy with advancement, favours, lands, and distinctions for which he had no particular merit, gave ground for evil reports. In a few years he was made successively knight commander of the order of Santiago, captain of his company, officer of the Spanish lifeguards, captain-general of the corps, brigadier of the royal forces, field-marshal, gentleman of his majesty's chamber with office, sergeant-major of the royal bodyguard, knight of the Grand Cross of the royal and distinguished order of Charles III, grandee of Spain with the title of duke of Alcudia, councillor of state (from 1784–1791), and superintendent-general of posts and roads, etc." — LAFUENTE.[d]]

[1792 A.D.]

10th caused that phantom of royal will still present in France to disappear. Prussia and Austria, which had no interests to guard, declared war on France immediately. The latter replied by doing away with royalty, by beginning the trial of the king, a prisoner in the temple, and thus broke, in the face of the whole world, with all the monarchies in declaring herself their mortal enemy.

Charles IV, devoted like his father to the French royal family, was broken-hearted over the insults and disgrace heaped upon the unfortunate Louis XVI. De Aranda, whose connection with the French encyclopædists wounded the double cult of the Spanish people for religion and monarchy, found himself daily more estranged from his former friends. The French ambassador, who had ceased all relations with the Madrid cabinet, summoned Spain to choose between war and peace, and to make her choice known.

The state council took up the questions and was not long in deciding in favour of war. But France was acting while Spain was preparing to act, and the blood-stained pages of this terrible history were unfolding one after another. The massacre of prisoners in September was the Jacobins' reply to the attacks of the allied monarchs, as well as the high-handed challenge thrown to whosoever dared try to stop the progress of the revolution. While waiting to be attacked from the south its arms were triumphing in the north ; the duke of Brunswick, in spite of his warnings and proclamations, had been driven to shameful flight. In the face of such a situation De Aranda drew back. Certainly it was neither courage nor determination which failed him, but for him there was one matter which overruled everything else, and that was the danger threatening the life of the unhappy monarch. The minister of foreign affairs, Le Brun, showed himself disposed to treat with Spain, but the convention exacted before anything else that the Madrid cabinet should recognise the republic.

For Charles IV to acknowledge the republic was to sanction the fall of the Bourbons and the ruin of one of the princes of that family ; it would betray his affections and his dearest interests. Hard pressed by disguised threats, the Spanish minister, in spite of his white hairs, went so far as to declare that, if the sacred soil of his country was invaded, he, the oldest officer in the army, would ask of his king a drum and go from town to town sounding the call to arms. In the meantime Charles IV had thought the matter over, and the desire to save Louis XVI's life overruled every other consideration. He decided to keep a strict neutrality towards France. Moreover he was not ready for war, and an army is not created in an instant, especially in Spain where everything is done slowly and at great cost.[c] But at any rate the time now seemed ripe to dismiss De Aranda from his post and call Godoy to his place, De Aranda being permitted to keep the presidency of the council. It was late in 1792 that the queen's favourite became the king's chief agent.[a]

GODOY AS MINISTER, AND THE WAR WITH FRANCE

The new minister's task was far from easy. The ability of the most experienced statesman would scarcely have been able to cope with the events taking place in France with too rapid strides. The trial of the unfortunate Louis XVI had begun and his life hung by a thread. The great, the sole question for Charles IV was to save him. Godoy proposed to offer France the mediation of the Madrid cabinet between herself and the northern powers in place of De Aranda's neutral policy ; the basis of negotiations to be the abdication of Louis XVI and the delivering of hostages as a sign of good faith. An unlimited credit was opened for Spain's representative at Paris in order to buy up judges. But all was useless. A letter from the Spanish minister to the convention was returned by order of the day.

"France," said a member, "can only treat with powers that have recognised the republic." Danton thundered against the audacity of the Spanish government, and not even the reading of the letter was allowed. The members who had held out their hands for Spanish gold were the first to vote the death of the king. Finally, at the last moment, the Castilian chargé d'affaires having again tried to intercede in favour of the royal victim, Danton in anger proposed for this alone to declare war on Spain, to punish her for daring to interfere in the affairs of the republic.

The king's death on January 21st, 1793, of course cut short all negotiations. The whole of Spain rose in horror and indignation at the news. Godoy, not very scrupulous himself in matters of national honour, exclaimed on learning the fatal news, "To-day a treaty of peace with France would be an infamy ; it would make us accomplices of a crime that thrills Spain as it does the whole world." De Aranda alone remained faithful to his system of neutrality and to that utilitarian morale of which England presents the most finished type. He addressed the king a long memoir on the danger of a war for which Spain was not prepared. But neutrality was but a dream in the present condition of minds and things in Spain as well as in France.

The day after the king's execution the French minister of foreign affairs ordered his agents to declare war on every country which refused to recognise the republic or treat with her. Thus did the Revolution throw its challenge to Europe, and attacked so as not to be itself attacked. It was no longer with kings but with peoples that it wished to deal. As for Spain, neutrality and disarmament on both sides — that was the ultimatum which Bourgoing offered Godoy, reserving to France the right to maintain garrisons in the strongholds on the frontier.

The convention was the first in its declaration of war, drawn up by Barère in the style of the period. "The intrigues of the court of St. James," it said, "have triumphed at Madrid. The papal nuncio has sharpened the dagger of fanaticism in the states of the Catholic king. The Bourbons must vanish from the throne they usurped, thanks to the blood and gold of our ancestors."

Spain responded by a firm but altogether moderate declaration of war. A royal decree banished from the peninsula within three days all the French who were not resident there. Moreover, this war, which De Aranda himself was powerless to prevent, had become popular in Spain before it had been declared; the gazettes were full of offers and contributions; there was an outbreak of enthusiasm quite on a par with that of France.c

Toulon proclaimed the dauphin, as Louis XVII, according to the constitution of 1791, and invited the united English and Spanish fleets under Lord Hood and Don Juan de Langara, to take possession of their town, port, and fortifications in his name. Charles likewise prepared to invade France by land. A powerful Spanish army commanded by Ricardos, governor of Catalonia, and reinforced with the Portuguese auxiliaries, crossed the Pyrenees, and entered Roussillon. On the 22nd of June, 1793, they took Bellegarde, one of the strongest frontier fortresses, afterwards occupying several places of less note, leaving them to winter in force on the French territories. The Portuguese troops displayed great gallantry in all these actions.

But it was only in this southwestern portion of France that the ill fortune of the republicans continued to the end of the year. In the course of the autumn they everywhere else recovered their losses. Toulon likewise was retaken.

In the year 1794, whilst France seemed most completely disorganised and enfrenzied by Jacobinical fury and terror, her armies, rendered well-nigh innumerable by the masses of population poured into her camps, and led by generals, often of names till then unknown, who started up either from the ranks or from professions and trades the least akin to arms, were almost uniformly victorious. The prodigious reinforcements sent, in the very beginning of the year, to the southwestern provinces turned the fortune of war against the Spaniards and Portuguese. Early in February they suffered two severe defeats near St. Jean-de-Luz. In April the Spaniards were similarly vanquished in Roussillon, but still occupied their principal conquests. Towards the latter end of that month, however, the brave veteran, General Dugommier, was sent to supersede the incompetent French commanders in Roussillon. The consequences were fatal to the peninsular armies. In the beginning of May, Dugommier gained two victories over them — one near Céret, and the other near Coullioure — in which the baggage, equipage, and artillery of the defeated armies, with about nine thousand prisoners, fell into the hands of the victors. The remaining Spanish conquests in Roussillon surrendered.

Ricardos, whose military talents and experience had been one main cause of Spanish success, was now no more. He was succeeded by the count de la Union, a young grandee. He made a daring and vigorous effort to relieve Bellegarde, but in the end was defeated, with the loss of twenty-five hundred men, and compelled to retreat. Bellegarde capitulated on the 20th of September, after a five months' siege. General Dugommier immediately entered Catalonia, and in the beginning of October again engaged La Union, whom he again defeated, but purchased the victory with his own life. His army followed the retreating enemy, and in the course of a few days avenged their general's death by that of the count de la Union, and three more Spanish generals, who fell in another battle, fought on the 20th of the same month, when the Spaniards were once more beaten, and completely routed. The Spanish army sought shelter behind the lines, which had, during the last six months, been diligently prepared for the protection of Catalonia against an invading foe. These, though defended by forty thousand men, and fortified with eighty-three redoubts, the French, now commanded by General Pérignon, next attacked with irresistible impetuosity, and carried in the space of three hours, when, without further obstacle, they advanced upon Figueras. The works of Figueras were deemed pretty nearly impregnable; it was abundantly provided, and well garrisoned. But the panic that seems to have ensued upon the count de la Union's death, and that had facilitated the forcing of the lines, had extended hither, and Figueras, to the astonishment even of the besiegers, surrendered almost without resistance. Several places in the north of Catalonia followed its example. At the western extremity of the Pyrenees the French arms were equally successful.

Charles and his new minister, Godoy, were undismayed by these disasters. They endeavoured to excite the population to rise in a mass against the invaders. Their attempts were unavailing; and whilst the French complained of the stupid and superstitious insensibility of the people, whom their promises of liberty could not allure to join (fraternise, as they called it) with them, the court of Madrid complained equally of popular disaffection, as a main cause of the failure of their efforts to defend the country. The nation seems, in fact, to have taken no interest in the war. The nobles, however, and the clergy, including the orders of knighthood and the monastic orders, were zealous in the cause, and freely offered ample contributions from their salaries, ecclesiastical revenues, commanderies, and private fortunes, to meet the exigency of the moment.

The misfortunes of the coalition on the eastern frontier of France were not calculated to encourage the Spanish court in its determination to resist. But the brilliant successes of the French by land were but little compensated by their naval and colonial losses. The prince of Orange and his family fled to England; and although Holland was not, like the Netherlands, made nominally a French province, she was so in effect, since, under the name of the Batavian Republic, she became wholly dependent upon France, at whose disposal all Dutch resources, in wealth, fleets, and colonies were placed. The fate of Spain was somewhat different. The strong town of Rosas, in Catalonia, fell on the 5th of January, 1795; after which four months passed in seeming inactivity, the French preparing for their advance upon Madrid, and the Spanish court vainly endeavouring to rouse the nation to resistance. Upon the 5th of May the Spanish army was completely routed by the French near Sistella, and with it the last hopes of Charles and Godoy fell.

GODOY

(From an old print)

Peace was now the only chance of escaping entire subjugation. The disposition of the persons in power at Paris was accordingly sounded through the American ambassador, and they were found willing to diminish the number of their enemies. On the 22nd of July a treaty was signed, by which France agreed to evacuate her conquests in Catalonia and Biscay; and Spain, in return, ceded to France the portion of the island of Santo Domingo that still belonged to her. Spain further promised to use her utmost efforts to detach Portugal likewise from the coalition. The conditions of this treaty were so much more favourable than Charles had expected, that in his joy he rewarded the duke of Alcudia with the title of Prince of the Peace [Principe de la Paz], by which he has ever since been known — an honour the more remarkable, because, contrary to the usual practice of the continent, in Spain as in England, the title of prince had, till then, been practically confined to the royal family.[1] From this period the whole system of Spanish policy was changed, and rendered so entirely subservient to the views of France that Godoy has been accused by his countrymen of corruption; there is certainly nothing

[1 An earlier exception to the rule is to be found in the case of Luís de Haro, who received the same title of Prince of the Peace after the conclusion of the Peace of the Pyrenees in 1659.]

in his character or principles that renders it likely he should have scorned a bribe. It is needless, nevertheless, to recur to such a suspicion for the explanation of his conduct. Spain made peace because she could not resist France; and the same weakness would induce her to submit to the dictation of her powerful ally. Charles seems to have followed, unresistingly, the impulses of his queen and favourite.

The Peace of Bâle was followed by the conclusion of a treaty with the United States of North America, by which the Prince of the Peace agreed to open the navigation of the Mississippi to the American Republic, and, as far as the United States were concerned, to render New Orleans a free port ; measures equally beneficial to both parties.

SPAIN IN ALLIANCE WITH FRANCE AGAINST ENGLAND

The Prince of the Peace strove to encourage arts and industry, and especially sought to recover the breed of fine horses for which Andalusia had formerly been renowned, and which, having been long neglected in the prevalent passion for mules, had degenerated. He even attempted to oppose the immense power and ever-accumulating wealth of the Spanish clergy.

But the arts of French diplomacy overbore Godoy's steadiness in preferring the real interests of Spain to hopes of sharing in the military fame and the territorial aggrandisement of France. On the 19th of August, 1796, a treaty of alliance, offensive and defensive, was signed between France and Spain, by which it was stipulated that either power, if engaged in a separate war, should be entitled to claim from the other fifteen ships of the line, and twenty-four thousand soldiers ; and that if the two countries should be jointly engaged in war, all the forces of both should act in common. It was further distinctly stated in the treaty that these stipulations referred especially to England, inasmuch as Spain had no cause of quarrel with any other enemy of France.

Two months after the signature of a treaty so incompatible with any views of real neutrality, the Spanish court declared war against England, with the usual accusations of contraband trade, and infringement upon colonial rights. But Spain failed in her endeavours to detach Portugal from the coalition, and to exclude English goods.

By the Treaty of Campo-Formio (1797) Austria ceded the Netherlands to France, and the Milanese to the new Cisalpine Republic, formed of all the conquered or revolutionised Italian states. But all this prosperity was for France, not for her allies. Since the commencement of hostilities the Spanish fleets had, like the French, been blockaded in port by British squadrons. Early in February, 1797, however, the Spanish admiral, Don José de Cordova, at the head of twenty-seven sail of the line, made his way out of Cartagena harbour, and passed the straits of Gibraltar in search of the British fleet, which, relying upon his great superiority of force, he hoped to annihilate. On the morning of the 14th Cordova came in sight of the enemy he sought. Sir John Jervis, the English admiral, had only fifteen sail of the line, but resolved, nevertheless, to give battle, and endeavoured to compensate his great disparity of numbers by a manœuvre somewhat analogous to those by which Bonaparte gained his victories on land. He bore down with his whole force upon the Spaniards before their line was formed, cut off one large division of their fleet, and thus engaging upon less unequal terms, defeated Cordova, took four large ships, and drove the rest into the port of Cadiz. He was ably assisted in this bold attack by Commodore Nelson.

In Cadiz, Jervis (created Lord St. Vincent, in honour of his victory) blockaded the Spanish fleet, still far more numerous than his own, and, whilst he lay off the harbour, greatly harassed the coasting trade of Spain. He likewise bombarded the town, but, though he thus did a good deal of damage, produced no material result. Lord St. Vincent thought to follow up his advantage in another direction, by sending Nelson with a squadron to seize, if possible, both the town of Santa Cruz, in the island of Teneriffe, and a valuable register ship then lying in the port of that island. The attack was made with the daring intrepidity that characterised all Nelson's actions ; but the admiral had been led to form the scheme by false information as to the strength of the place. The attempt failed, and cost as many lives as the preceding battle. Nelson lost his arm. The Spaniards defended the fort with great gallantry, and when the English abandoned their enterprise, displayed towards them all kindness and courtesy. In the West Indies an expedition under Admiral Harvey and General Sir Ralph Abercromby sailed from Martinique to attack the island of Trinidad. Four sail of the line were voluntarily burned to prevent their falling into the hands of the English, and the governor capitulated the 18th of February. Encouraged by their success, Abercromby and Harvey next attempted the stronger island of Porto Rico, but failed, with considerable loss.

In the month of November General Stuart attacked Minorca, and after a short resistance, the governor, Quesada, surrendered the island, upon condition of being sent with his garrison to the nearest Spanish port. This was pretty much the whole Spanish share in the war this year, beyond the usual contribution of troops to the French armies. With the military transactions of 1798–1799 Spain had no concern. Her merchant ships were everywhere captured by British cruisers, as were the few armed vessels necessarily sent to sea singly or in small detachments.

During the year 1800, Spain and Portugal had little to do but to observe the change in the fortunes of France and her enemies, resulting from the return of Bonaparte and his exaltation to the head of the government. Bonaparte crossed the Alps, traversing the Great St. Bernard by ways till then deemed hardly passable for single foot travellers, but over which he actually transported his whole army, even artillery, and, by the splendid victory of Marengo, recovering at once all losses in Italy, re-established his Cisalpine Republic.

The first consul had already, in a secret treaty, extorted from his ally Charles IV the cession of Louisiana ; and he now required from Charles' kinsman, the duke of Parma, the reversion of his duchy at his death to the French Republic. In return, he bestowed Tuscany, under title of "the kingdom of Etruria," upon the duke's eldest son, Luis, prince of Parma, who had married a Spanish infanta. In April, 1801, the king and queen of Etruria left Madrid, where they had resided since their marriage, to take possession of their newly assigned dominions. They were directed by Godoy to pass through Paris ; and thus two Bourbon princes were the first of the many sovereigns who, during Bonaparte's reign, were required to present their personal homage at the Tuileries.

But Tuscany seems to have been judged more than compensation for Parma and Louisiana ; and Charles was expected to pay a yet higher price for the kingdom bestowed upon one daughter and son-in-law, by assisting to despoil another daughter and son-in-law of their patrimony. Affection for the princess of Brazil and her children had urged the king of Spain to make unusual exertions for the sake of warding off from Portugal the effects of French enmity; and his troops, his fleets, and his American gold had been found so useful that he had enjoyed sufficient influence to render his mediation effectual with the Directory. But the Peace of Lunéville rendered the friendship of Spain less important; and Bonaparte's hatred of England was far more implacable than that of his directorial predecessors. The first consul could not forgive Portugal's fidelity to her old ally; and now insisted upon Charles' declaring war against his son-in-law. The obstinate refusal of the court of Lisbon to comply with the solicitations of the court of Madrid, detach itself from England, and accept the alliance of France, was the ground of hostility alleged in the Spanish manifesto.

This declaration was answered by a counter declaration from João, the prince of Brazil; but for a while both parties seemed to rest content with this paper war; and there can be no doubt that during their constrained hostilities a perfectly good understanding existed between the unwilling belligerents. The first consul was not to be thus deceived, and he informed his ally that if Spain were not prepared to invade Portugal, French troops should be sent to her assistance. To avoid receiving such aid, if possible, the Prince of the Peace took the field at the head of between thirty and forty thousand men, and entered the Portuguese province of Alemtejo. The prince of Brazil thereupon summoned the whole population of Portugal to arm in defence of the country, and in person led an army against the invaders, but offered scarcely any opposition to their progress. In little more than a fortnight the Spanish reduced several fortified towns, and drove the Portuguese beyond the Tagus. England afforded her faithful ally little succour, therefore, beyond a subsidy of £300,000, and her permission and advice to make peace upon the best terms obtainable. The plan of operations laid down by the first consul had been that Spain should invade the southern and France the northern provinces of Portugal; and a French army was now advancing to execute its allotted task.

On the 28th of June, General Leclerc, having traversed Spain, crossed the frontiers at the head of thirty thousand men, and laid siege to Almeida; St. Cyr followed him with another corps. This was an invasion of a different character from the last, and the Portuguese regent made more vigorous efforts for defence. He now earnestly solicited the help of England, and her troops took possession of the island of Madeira to hold for him. But his best resource was another treaty of peace, negotiated at Madrid between France and Portugal by the French and Portuguese ambassadors to Spain, the consul's brother, Lucien Bonaparte, and Cipriano Ribeiro Freire. By this treaty, Dom João submitted to pay £1,000,000 to France, and to surrender a considerable district in the north of Brazil, the province called Portuguese Guiana, as far as the mouth of the Amazon, in order to give extent and compactness to French Guiana or Cayenne. No mention was made of the fortresses which had been the pretext for this last French invasion.

By the treaties of Amiens (1802) and Lunéville (1801), the king of Spain recovered Minorca, and saw the Parma branch of his family raised from the ducal to the royal rank; the future heritage of his eldest daughter's children, Portugal, was redeemed from impending subjugation at the price of some little spoliation, in which he himself shared. But the greatest advantage the restoration of peace afforded him was the cessation of the enormous drain upon his resources, naval, military, and above all financial, which had lately reduced his dominions to a state of lamentable exhaustion. The expenditure during the war had amounted to four times the revenue; and only a long period of peace, together with the most judicious system of economy and fiscal regulation, could have reinstated Spain in anything like prosperity. Of this there could be no hope, under the sway of Charles IV, or rather of his favourite Godoy.

THE AUTOCRACY OF GODOY

The king's attachment to his wife's paramour bore almost as much the character of passion as the queen's. Godoy's influence over the former was not to be shaken by representations of his incapacity, or by court cabal;[1] and over the queen it remained undiminished either by jealousy or infidelity on either side, to the end of her life. To her jealousy he owed an alliance with the royal family. He had formed a criminal connection with a young lady of noble birth; and the queen, to prevent his marrying her rival, persuaded the king to give him a princess for his wife. For this purpose an illegal marriage, contracted by the king's uncle, Don Luis, a cardinal and archbishop of Toledo, with a lady of the name of Vallabriga, was sanctioned, and its issue, a son and two daughters, were recognised as infantes of Spain. The son succeeded his father as archbishop of Toledo, and was made a cardinal; and the eldest daughter was bestowed, as an infanta, upon the Prince of the Peace.

QUEEN MARIA LOUISA, WIFE OF CHARLES IV

So splendid a marriage had no more effect than his intrigue with the queen in restraining Godoy's libertinism. It equalled his rapacity; and the latter vice being almost glutted by the profusion of the royal pair, his favour was most surely propitiated by those who had a handsome sister, wife, or daughter to sacrifice to his appetite. The queen, finding it impossible to rid herself of these innumerable rivals, sought consolation in emulating his inconstancy. But it never required more than a word from Godoy to have his rivals overthrown, and his political opponents entangled in their own snares.

Such scenes of licentiousness could not be daily exhibited at court, without producing the most noxious effect upon all who came within the poisonous sphere of their influence. The higher orders were well-nigh demoralised, and a shameless system of corruption pervaded every branch of the administration, from the highest to the lowest throughout Spain; evils compared with which the good really done by the Prince of the Peace was but as dust in the balance.

When his connection by marriage with the royal family raised him above

[1 Godoy e in his memoirs uses the fact of the king's unchanging devotion as a proof that his relations with the queen were honest and that he held his post purely by his devoted fidelity to both king and queen.]

any ministerial office, leaving him merely a sort of viceroy over the whole Spanish monarchy, Godoy introduced some able men in his stead, such as Saavedra and Gaspar Melchor de Jovellanos, though the kingdom was not long permitted to reap the benefit of their talents. Illness afforded Saavedra a fair pretext for resigning an office which his difference in opinion from Godoy would scarcely have suffered him to retain, and would certainly have prevented his exercising according to his judgment and conscience. Jovellanos incurred the hatred of the queen, by opposing her constant interference in public affairs; that of Godoy, by joining in a plot for the abridgment, if not overthrow of his power; he was in consequence not only dismissed, but rigorously immured in a Carthusian monastery in Majorca.[1]

The Prince of the Peace affected, in compliance with the fashion of the day, to be a patron of the arts, of learning, and of modern improvements. He commanded Pestalozzi's new system of education to be adopted in Spain; he recommended the general practice of vaccination, and despatched vessels to all the colonies for the purpose of introducing that preventive; and he encouraged to the utmost of his power the patriotic or economical societies established under the name of Friends of the Country, in order to promote agriculture, by diffusing the knowledge of improved methods of tillage amongst the farmers, and assisting with small loans such as were cramped in their operations by indigence. These merits were, however, as has been said, nothing to counterbalance the evils under which Spain laboured, and most of which were ascribed to the profligate corruption of the court. The yellow fever, which in the years 1800 and 1801 ravaged and partially desolated the south of Spain by the misery it occasioned, increased the prevailing dissatisfaction; and the detestation of Godoy was excessive and universal.

By no one was the extent of his power more bitterly felt or his person more abhorred than by Ferdinand, prince of Asturias. The education of this prince had been purposely intrusted by the favourite to incapable persons; the queen hated and persecuted a son upon whom she, perhaps, looked as a future rival for power. As he advanced to manhood, the adversaries of Godoy gathered around him, and Don Juan Escoiquiz, canon of Toledo, the only man of any ability who had been placed about him, became the head of a sort of party in favour of the prince of Asturias. In 1802 all these persons, and indeed the country at large, looked impatiently to Ferdinand's marriage with Maria Antonia, daughter of the king of Naples, as the era of some effective change in the court. But the virtues and talents of Maria Antonia were altogether unavailing against the arts of her mother-in-law and the influence of Godoy.

Meanwhile the peace that had momentarily tranquillised Europe was evidently upon the point of ceasing. A burst of passion on the first consul's part against Lord Whitworth, the English ambassador, on the 13th of March, 1803, astonished the diplomacy of Europe. On the 12th of May, 1803, Lord

[1 The count de Toreno[h] says of him: "No sooner did he hold out protection to wise and esteemed men than he humbled them. At the same time that he was encouraging a special science, establishing a new professorship, or supporting some measure of improvement, he allowed the marquis Caballero, a declared enemy to advancement and learning, to trace out a scheme of general public instruction to be adopted in all the universities, which was incoherent and unworthy of the century, permitting him also to make serious omissions and alterations in the codes of law. Although he banished from the court and exiled all those whom he believed to be opposed to him, or who displeased him, as a general rule he did not carry his persecutions any farther, nor was he by nature cruel; he showed himself cruel and hard only with respect to the illustrious Jovellanos; sordid in his avarice, he sold, as if in public auction, offices, magistratures, dignities, sees, sometimes for himself, sometimes for his mistresses, sometimes to satisfy the caprices of the queen."]

Whitworth left Paris, and on the 18th the king of England declared war against France. Spain and Portugal were permitted to remain neutral, but were compelled to purchase that permission by heavy sacrifices of both wealth and dignity. The pecuniary contributions drawn by Bonaparte from Spain and Portugal, or wrung from the Hanse towns, together with the produce of the sale of Louisiana to the United States of North America, were applied to building and equipping the gunboats with which he proposed to invade England.

The following year put an end to the neutrality of Spain. At first it appeared as though she would once more take part against France, for the court of Madrid vehemently objected to the sale of Louisiana to the United States, as contrary to the secret conditions upon which that province had been ceded to France. But the Prince of the Peace was overawed or bribed by Bonaparte. He contented himself with objecting, and immediately returned to his former subserviency.

The English envoy Frere was informed by the British admirals cruising off the Spanish coast that an armament was fitting out at Ferrol, and that indications of activity appeared in other ports, whilst French soldiers and sailors were permitted to pass through Spain to recruit a French fleet lying in a Spanish harbour.

The result of these suspicions was that the British ministry determined upon the very extraordinary step of ordering, without any previous declaration of war, the seizure of four Spanish frigates, then bringing home freights of the precious metals and other valuable merchandise. These ships were not, it is averred, to be captured as prizes, but in order to be held as security for the future more impartial neutrality of Spain. This measure, more in accordance with Bonaparte's treatment of neutrals than with the principles of international law, which England professed to defend, was executed as feebly as it was, perhaps, unwarrantably conceived. On the 5th of October an engagement ensued, that ended by the blowing up of one of the Spanish vessels — on board of which were several passengers of high rank — and the surrender of the others. This attack and capture during the nominal continuance of peace enraged the Spanish nation beyond all further show of neutrality, and afforded too fair a colour to French declamation against England's naval tyranny.

On the 12th of December, 1804, the court of Madrid declared war against England in a virulent manifesto; and the Prince of the Peace, now created generalissimo of his Catholic majesty's forces (a title devised to give him the supreme command), published an address, calling upon every individual Spaniard to assist in avenging the insults of the tyrants of the sea. The war produced no event this year beyond the capture of Dutch Guiana (Surinam) by an English expedition. In France Bonaparte accomplished the transmutation of his office of consul of a republic into the dignity of emperor. The year 1805 was rich in memorable battles by sea and land. On the 21st of October, off Trafalgar, Villeneuve and Gravina the Spanish admiral, with thirty-three sail of the line and seven frigates, encountered Nelson, who had lured them out of Cadiz, by persuading them that his force amounted only to twenty-one sail of the line. They found him with twenty-seven and three frigates. It was too late to retreat, and they engaged. The battle was one of the hardest contested and most decisive ever fought at sea. Lord Nelson fell, but survived long enough to know that the victory was gained. This splendid victory seems to have nearly annihilated the fleets of France and Spain, and to have completely repressed Napoleon's schemes for obtaining any naval superiority over, or equality with Great Britain. From that time he appears to have really abandoned the idea of invading England, how much soever he still threatened. But the maritime triumphs of the latter country were fearfully balanced by the reverses of her continental allies. A negotiation was at this time set on foot for detaching Spain from France; and the court of Madrid showed itself well disposed to concur in the requisite arrangements. Napoleon's yoke pressed too heavily to be ever voluntarily borne; and although Charles IV had, in the first instance, joyfully hailed the accession to power of an individual able to control and terminate the revolution, all such kindly disposition had been forcibly crushed by the barbarous and illegal execution of a prince of his own Bourbon blood, the duke d'Enghien. To this feeling of resentment was added fear, nearly equal to that inspired by the Revolution itself, when the conqueror of Europe began to dethrone sovereigns and to distribute crowns amongst his own kindred.

Charles, notwithstanding his fears of Napoleon, had still delayed to acknowledge the usurper of half his brother Ferdinand's kingdom; and when he understood that, in his negotiation with England, the emperor insisted upon Sicily likewise for Joseph, and proposed to dismember Spain of Minorca, Majorca, and Iviza, by way of compensation to the despoiled king of Naples, Charles' indignation burst forth, and Godoy's imperfectly appeased fears revived. A plan of future operations was concerted between the Prince of the Peace in person, and the Russian and Portuguese ambassadors, the secret of which was carefully kept even from the Spanish ministers. It was arranged that Spain and Portugal should arm under colour of hostilities against each other; and that, at the moment when Russia should take the field, their united armies, supported by the fleets of England, should invade the south of France.

Spain bitterly felt the consequences of war with England in the loss of her fleets, and the consequent interruption to her intercourse with her colonies. On June 27th, 1806, the English officer Popham seized Buenos Ayres. The enterprise was in every way rash and ill-advised. He had not troops sufficient to maintain his conquest, and it was recovered by the Spaniards. But the English, if driven out of Buenos Ayres, were not expelled from the country, and this alarmed the Spanish government for its transatlantic empire. Sympathising in the anger and terror awakened in Charles' mind by the words Napoleon had uttered while stepping into his carriage to set off for the Prussian frontiers ("If Charles IV will not acknowledge my brother as king of the Two Sicilies, his successor shall"), and elated with the tidings of the new German war, Godoy lost sight of the secrecy and caution in which his hostile designs had hitherto been wrapped. Without waiting for the proposed co-operation of either England or Russia, he flung aside the mask. He did not, indeed, announce that France was the enemy with whom he contemplated a war, but he published a proclamation (October 5th, 1806) in which he summoned the nation to arms.

On the 14th of the same month Napoleon, in the terrible battle of Jena, completely routed, dispersed, and destroyed the Prussian army. In the palace at Berlin, Napoleon read the imprudent manifesto of the Prince of the Peace; and if the destiny of the Bourbon kings of Spain had been previously doubtful, it was thenceforward sealed. The news of Jena struck the Prince of the Peace and his infatuated sovereigns with affright proportionate to their recent presumption; and they strove to obviate the effects of their imprudence by various means, which, contradicting each other, proved the

bad faith against the French emperor which they endeavoured to deny.   The
French and Spanish newspapers were filled with paragraphs, in some of which
the manifesto was alleged to be a forgery by the enemies of the Prince of
the Peace ; whilst in others it was avowed as directed against either England or the emperor of Morocco.   The decree for levying troops was immediately revoked, and a second circular ordered the governors to disregard the
former.   Godoy did not, however, rely upon the effects of these artifices.
He is believed to have lavished his ill-gotten treasures upon the agents of
French diplomacy, whilst he sent a private envoy of his own, distinct from
the king's, Don Eugenio Izquierdo, to Berlin, humbly to confess and implore
forgiveness.   Napoleon felt that this was not the season for engaging in a
new war, and he suffered the hostile demonstration of the court of Madrid
to pass unnoticed.   But he sought yet further to weaken Spain by requiring
that sixteen thousand of her best troops, under her best general, the marquis
de la Romana, should be sent into Prussia as reinforcements of the northern
army.   It was at this period that the famous Berlin Decree was published,
declaring the British Islands in a state of blockade ; and Spain was of course
required fully to concur in the execution of this fantastic measure.

On the 7th of July, 1807, the treaty was signed at Tilsit, by which the czar

Charles IV, overjoyed at his seeming escape from certain destruction,
strove to express his gratitude to Godoy, to whose address he ascribed his
supposed safety, by new honours and rewards.   The favourite was appointed
high admiral, when scarce a ship remained ; he received the title of "most
serene highness," never before borne in Spain but by the two Don Johns, the
illegitimate sons of Charles V and of Philip IV ; and he was named protector
of commerce and the colonies.   Adorned with these new dignities, Godoy
made a sort of triumphal entry into Madrid that offended the people, and
both alarmed and irritated the prince of Asturias.   Orders were given for
the burning of all English manufactures, conformably to the injunctions of
the Berlin decree ; Joseph Bonaparte was acknowledged as king of the Two
Sicilies, and Ferdinand IV's name inserted in the court almanac merely as
a prince of the blood, the eldest of the king's brothers ; and king, queen,
and favourite remained satisfied that they had fully appeased and satisfied
the master of the continent.

On the 7th of July, 1807, the treaty was signed at Tilsit, by which the czar
Alexander ratified all Napoleon's changes of European sovereigns.   The
French emperor, convinced that the czar was inalienably his friend, returned
to Paris towards the end of July, and devoted his meditations to the punishment of Charles IV, and the subjugation of Spain and Portugal.   One of the
first steps in execution of his designs upon the peninsula was, in the month
of August, to order the French and Spanish ambassadors conjointly to declare
to the prince-regent of Portugal that he must concur in the Continental
System — viz., shut his ports against English commerce, confiscate all English property, and imprison all English subjects to be found within his
dominions, or they were instructed immediately to leave Lisbon.

Portugal's hesitation at once to obey the imperious mandate afforded a sort
of pretence for hostility which Napoleon eagerly seized, and submission came
too late.   Neither could Spain's mediation be hoped.   The fears or the
ambition of Godoy had prevailed over the parental feelings of the now nearly
imbecile Charles IV, and Spain was endeavouring to share in the spoil, not
to protect the victim.   A treaty, the shameless iniquity of which can be
paralleled only by the treaties between Austria, Russia, and Prussia for the
partition of Poland, had been signed at Fontainebleau, on the 27th of
October.   By this treaty Charles surrendered to Napoleon his infant

grandson's kingdom of Etruria (King Louis I had been dead some years), over which he had no right whatever, and bargained to receive for him in its stead the small northern provinces of Portugal, Entre-Minho-e-Douro and Tras-os-Montes, under the name of the kingdom of Northern Lusitania, which kingdom the young monarch was to hold in vassalage of the crown of Spain. The much larger southern provinces, Alemtejo and Algarve, were to constitute the principality of the Algarves, for Godoy, under a similar tenure. And the middle provinces were to be occupied by Napoleon until a general peace, when, in exchange for Gibraltar, Trinidad, and any other Spanish possession conquered by England, they might be restored to the family of Braganza, upon like terms of dependence. The Portuguese colonies were to be equally divided between France and Spain.

Neither Napoleon nor Godoy had waited for the actual signature of this treaty to commence their operations for carrying it into effect, so impatient were both to secure their prey. On the 18th of October, Junot, in obedience to his master's orders, crossed the Pyrenees, and, being kindly received by the Spaniards, began his march towards the Portuguese frontiers, whilst the Spanish troops were equally put in motion towards their respective destinations.

As will be more fully described in the Portuguese history, the invaders met practically no resistance, and the royal family fled across the ocean to Brazil.

The first steps towards the execution of the Treaty of Fontainebleau being thus taken, the Prince of the Peace became impatient for its publication, and his own installation in his allotted dominions. But it is very doubtful whether Napoleon ever meant that treaty for more than a means of facilitating his ulterior designs ; if he did, his purpose was now changed, and he no longer intended to admit of any partnership in his new acquisition. But even whilst he was negotiating the treaty with Godoy, his ambassador, Beauharnais, was artfully fomenting the dissensions existing in the Spanish royal family.[b]

NAPOLEON SCHEMES FOR SPAIN

Napoleon was tempted to take Spain, and yet knew not how to seize such a rich prey. In the meantime one of those scandals broke out at the Escorial which showed up in full light the miseries of dynasties, which must suffer, in common with the poorest, ills common to mankind yet cannot like them hide their woes from the world. Charles IV, given up to pleasure, passed from the hunt to the studio, from the studio to the stable. The queen, occupied only in preserving what beauty time had left her, sacrificed her duties as a wife and a sovereign to the sole desire of keeping the love of Godoy. The Prince of the Peace, without being quite indifferent to the country's interests, put his own fortune first. Master of the queen, to whom, moreover, he allowed unworthy rivals, he flattered Napoleon, from whom he hoped a crown. In the same palace lived Ferdinand, prince of Asturias, heir to the throne, a man who was grossly artificial and wicked, yet one whom Spain was disposed to obey if only to show hatred to the Prince of the Peace. Ferdinand's chief counsellors were the duke de Infantado, strongly attached to all the prejudices of an ancient régime, ambitious, but with all the inflexibility of an honest man, and his tutor Escoiquiz, of a supple and dreamy disposition, ambitious to play the rôle of Ximenes or at least of Cardinal Fleury. It was with such personages that Napoleon was to dispute the possession of Spain.

Napoleon had known for a long time of the quarrels which divided the court of Madrid, for Ferdinand also had asked his help ; and, to replace the princess of Asturias, who had just died, had asked through the intervention of M. de Beauharnais the hand of a princess of the Bonaparte family. Napoleon had received these overtures with a certain surprise, neither absolutely accepting nor rejecting. Ferdinand, as he wrote to M. de Beauharnais, was " surrounded even in his private rooms by observant spies." His writing for some time past had given these spies cause for anxiety, and on the 27th of October the queen persuaded her weak-minded husband to order the prince's apartments to be ransacked for papers. It was a terrible blow. In Ferdinand's rooms was discovered a secret alphabet destined for a mysterious correspondence, an order, with the date left blank, which named the duke de Infantado governor of New Castile, and a memorial destined by Ferdinand for his father, in which he denounced the crimes of the Prince of the Peace and the complicity of his mother. The queen was furious; she saw in these papers the proof of a conspiracy, and demanded the immediate arrest of the prince and his accomplices. Ferdinand was confined to his own rooms, and Charles IV addressed a proclamation to the Spanish people in which he accused his son of trying to assassinate him. At the same time this unhappy king wrote to Napoleon to denounce the crime, expressing a readiness to alter the succession to the throne.

The chance, so long expected, had at length arrived. Napoleon, who had as yet taken no definite steps, wrote to Beauharnais to be very observant but to do nothing, and hastened the march of his troops towards the Pyrenees. To the army commanded by General Dupont he joined another which he called "the observation corps for the coast line," and gave the command to Marshal Moncey, who had already fought in Spain. Hardly was Ferdinand arrested, when he gave signs of contemptible weakness. He denounced his confidants, humiliated himself before the Prince of the Peace, implored pardon of his father and mother in dishonourable letters, and left his friends to appear before the judges — judges who, fortunately, had the courage to acquit them. The Prince of the Peace was not without anxiety. His hopes were ruined if Ferdinand married a princess of the imperial family. On the other hand, his principality in Portugal now seemed a little risky since Junot governed as master, and ceded no place to Spaniards. At the same time he also saw Charles IV much flattered by an alliance with the imperial family and resolved to solicit it.

It was only in the month of January, 1808, that the emperor thought of taking definite action. Three projects suggested themselves : to marry Ferdinand to a French princess and so make him a vassal of the empire ; to cede Spain a portion of Portugal and take all the provinces beyond the Ebro ; or else dethrone the Bourbons and replace them by a Bonaparte. He stopped at this last resolution, and prepared his designs with a rare duplicity. On the 20th of February he sent Murat into Spain with orders to occupy Pamplona, Barcelona, and San Sebastian, and to get on as far as Madrid.

Napoleon really hoped so to reduce the Spanish sovereign by terror that he, imitating the house of Braganza in Portugal, would flee, or attempt to flee, into America. Then he would take possession of the vacant throne. This plan should have succeeded. The queen and the Prince of the Peace were terrified and thought seriously of setting out, and brought the old king to their way of thinking. Everything failed owing to the resistance of the prince of Asturias. Ferdinand reckoned on the friendship of Napoleon. A part of the nation had the same illusion about the French, regarding them as rescuers come to free them and drive away the Prince of the Peace.   So preparations for the king's flight met with lively opposition.   The king was obliged to address a proclamation to the people saying he would not go, and to show himself at the palace windows to receive the evidence of an affection mingled with suspicion and threats.   On the 17th of March, troops arriving to escort the king only served to augment the agitation.   That very evening there was a rising.   The crowd ran to the palace, obliged the king to show himself, then went to the house of the Prince of the Peace.   Furious at not finding him, they revenged themselves by pillaging the house.   These disorders troubled the king and queen for two reasons: they were anxious for their favourite, for whose safety they were most concerned, and they saw in these scenes the image of the French Revolution; and so feared for themselves the fate of Louis XVI and Marie Antoinette.

On the 18th of March, to save the Prince of the Peace, the king stripped him of all his offices and exiled him.   But this only produced a temporary lull. On the 19th, the prince, who for two days had been

JOSEPH BONAPARTE

living hidden in a barn in a bundle of osiers, decided to come out of his hiding-place.   Discovered immediately, he had great trouble, though protected by some bodyguards, to escape the violence of the crowd.   He was taken to a barracks which served him both as prison and refuge.   A furious crowd followed and threatened to force the doors.   Troubled by the cries which they heard from afar, the king and queen had recourse to Ferdinand, begging him to save his friend.   The prince agreed with triumphant joy. presented himself at the barracks, dispersed the crowd by telling them justice should be done, and appearing before Godoy promised him pardon. "Are you already king, that you grant pardon?" cried the prisoner.   "No," answered Ferdinand, "but I shall be, soon."

CHARLES IV ABDICATES; THE BOURBONS AT BAYONNE

He was indeed to be king that very day, for a little while only, it is true; but how could he guess the fate which awaited him?   The king and queen were utterly terrified, and on learning that the crowd had just wrecked the carriage destined to take away the Prince of the Peace, their fright redoubled.

To save their lives and that of their friend they did not hesitate to lay down the royal power.   Charles IV signed his abdication and Ferdinand was proclaimed amid outbursts of frantic joy./

Ferdinand VII, notwithstanding the neglect of his solicitations for Napoleon's protection, seems to have felt no mistrust of the emperor's goodwill towards himself.   He retained several of his father's ministers, especially Cevallos, although allied by marriage to Godoy ; but he likewise raised the chief of those who had been imprisoned, as his accomplices in the conspiracy of the preceding October, to high posts.   He released Jovellanos from prison ; confiscated the property of the Prince of the Peace, without awaiting his trial ; and repealed some vexatious taxes.   The nation was delighted with their new monarch ; but their exultation and Ferdinand's joy in his accession, and trust in the supposed favour of Napoleon, were alike short-lived.

Napoleon himself seems to have been momentarily perplexed by the tumults at Aranjuez and the old king's abdication.   He had hoped probably to find the kingdom deserted by its rulers, and open to the first occupant. He paused upon his journey to await what should next occur; whilst Murat, under pretence of besieging Gibraltar, pressed forward with such celerity that, on the 23rd of March, he entered the town, and established himself in the magnificent palace of the Prince of the Peace.   Upon Ferdinand's arrival, Murat paid him neither military nor personal honours, alleging the necessity of learning Napoleon's decision upon the late transactions, ere the prince of Asturias could be acknowledged as king of Spain.

With a French army in Madrid, Ferdinand saw that the stability of his throne depended upon his recognition by the emperor of France.   He therefore addressed a justificatory account of the recent events to Napoleon, and renewed his solicitations for the hand of an imperial princess.   Evidently Napoleon never meant to acknowledge Ferdinand as king ; but it was essential to his schemes, since he could not frighten the whole Spanish royal family away, to get them all into his own hands; and Charles' vacillating conduct afforded him the means of so doing.   Charles wrote to the French emperor, protesting against his abdication as forced.   The old queen, and her daughter the queen of Etruria, wrote to Murat, begging him to save the life of his and their friend, Godoy, and declared that they wished only some safe asylum where they and he might spend the remainder of their lives together.   Murat promised his support.[b]

Napoleon sent Savary to Madrid, commissioned not to recognise the prince of Asturias but to flatter his hopes and make him decide to come to Bayonne, where the emperor himself was going.   In fact the whole business resolved itself into getting hold of Ferdinand, and was nothing more than a trap.   Murat, Savary, Beauharnais — all were in the conspiracy ; the first hoping for a crown, the last with the good faith of misguided honesty. Savary alone knew Napoleon's designs and served them without scruple. Ferdinand and his counsellors had entire faith in the emperor.   Ferdinand hoped to avoid other concessions by giving up some colonies to France. Only, to obtain this, an interview with the emperor would be necessary. Another motive urged Ferdinand to take this imprudent journey.   Murat only showed deference to the old sovereigns, and affected to render them all the homage due to royalty.   It was necessary that Ferdinand should see Napoleon and be recognised by him as king of Spain.

As soon as they learned of their son's projected journey, the old sovereigns, left at Aranjuez, also wanted to go to him whom they called their protector and friend.   Soon, therefore, the emperor had under his hand the whole Spanish dynasty. These journeys, however, were not accomplished without difficulty. The people of Madrid threatened at first to oppose Ferdinand's departure, and the prince himself became seriously uneasy when he learned at Burgos that the emperor was still at Bordeaux. He went on however as far as Vitoria, but once in this town he refused to go farther. General Savary tried persuasion, then threats, but all to no purpose. He therefore went to the emperor, who had just arrived at Bayonne, and obtained for Ferdinand a letter full of promises calculated to make him decide to continue his journey. In case he should resist, Savary brought to Murat and Bessières an order to arrest Ferdinand and proclaim Charles IV.

Without knowing of the threatened danger, Ferdinand still hesitated. If many of his counsellors were urging him on, defiance was bursting out all around, and Izquierdo, coming expressly from Vitoria, predicted exactly all the evils that would break over Ferdinand and the empire. The emperor's letter silenced all scruples, and, reassured by fresh promises from Savary, Ferdinand set out surrounded by an escort which would not have allowed him to change his mind. When the Bidassoa was crossed, Ferdinand there only found Berthier and Duroc, who saluted him as prince of Asturias. At Bayonne, the emperor received him cordially, embraced him and kept him to dinner, but always as prince of Asturias. Finally, that very evening, the emperor, who had now no need for dissimulation, told Escoiquiz that he had need of Spain ; that he had resolved to dethrone the Bourbons, and offered to make Ferdinand king of Etruria. Simultaneously Savary made the same communication to the prince. It was a terrible blow ! *f*

LAFUENTE'S ACCOUNT OF THE *DOS DE MAYO*

We draw near to one of those critical, supreme, and solemn moments in the history of nations when the excess of an evil brings inspiration, and counsels a remedy; when indignation at the treachery of some, sorrow at the humiliation and degradation of others, produce in a people an eager and salutary reaction respecting their outraged dignity ; which causes them to recover themselves, gives rise to grand ideas, and endows them with the courage of anger and desperation, resulting in an impetuous and heroic outburst, in which, finally, they rehabilitate their tarnished honour, and regain their lost courage. Popular instinct, being by this time more prudent and far-seeing than governors and councillors, and as suspicious and distrustful of the French as it had been previously simple and candid, saw with sorrow the tortuous turn taken by public affairs. The people of Madrid were specially mortified by the journey and absence of their beloved Ferdinand, brought about by deceptions and stratagems ; by the liberty given to the hated Godoy, through the influence of the emperor and his agents ; and by Murat's efforts to cause Charles IV to be re-acknowledged king.

Outside Madrid, in Toledo and Burgos, riots and risings took place, in which some excesses were committed, which although provoked by French impudence and audacity served Murat as an excuse for presenting imperious and haughty complaints to the supreme junta, exaggerating injuries and making them the motive of harassing it with exactions and petitions. Seeing the junta inefficient and weak, Murat haughty and daring daily reviewing his force, the capital occupied by the brilliant imperial guard of infantry and cavalry and by the infantry commanded by Musnier, the Retiro fortified with artillery, Marshal Moncey's force surrounding the environs of Madrid, and a second line farther back composed of Dupont's divisions, in the Escorial, Aranjuez, and Toledo, forming in all an army of twenty-five thousand men, while the Spanish garrison barely numbered three thousand — the oppressed people became secretly agitated ; the very French detected a certain hatred in the looks of the residents, and noted a gloom on their faces, a sign of the concentrated rage hidden in their breasts, which fear alone restrained, and which needed but a light breath to cause it to break out in an impetuous explosion.   To this was added the rumour spread abroad, and the idea which the people had formed of the heroic resistance which it was said Ferdinand was opposing in Bayonne against renouncing the crown, which Napoleon, wishing to wrest it from him, was urging him to do, Ferdinand being in their eyes the defenceless victim of the imperial violence.   The junta continued to step from concession to concession, from weakness to weakness.   They speedily found themselves involved in a new dispute.

On the 30th of April the grand duke of Berg (Murat) presented himself before the junta, bearing a letter from Charles IV to the president, the infante, summoning to Bayonne his two children, the queen of Etruria, and the infante Don Francisco.

Eventually the 2nd of May [dos de Mayo] dawned, a day that was to be ever remembered.   From the early morning the signs which generally herald a popular rising were noticeable.   Numerous groups of men and women, among which were many peasants from the suburbs who had remained over night, filled the Plaza de Palacio, from whence the infantes were to leave Madrid.   At nine o'clock the carriage bearing the queen of Etruria and her children left without opposition and without sign of feeling from the people, partly because they looked on her as almost a foreign princess, and partly because she was of those who opposed Ferdinand.   The servants of the palace spread the report that the infante Don Francisco, still a child, was crying, because he did not wish to leave Madrid ; this excited the pity of the women and the anger of the men.   At this moment Murat's aide-de-camp Lagrange came upon the scene, and the people thinking he was come to hasten the departure of the prince, a general murmur was heard.

One spark is sufficient to ignite well prepared fuel.   At the cry of an old woman — " God help me !   They are taking all the royal family to France ! " — the multitude rushed upon the grand duke's aide-de-camp, who would have fallen a victim to the fury of the populace had not an officer of the Walloon guard shielded him with his body.   Murat, who lived close by and heard of what was passing in the vicinity of the palace, despatched a battalion with two pieces of artillery.   This troop fired a volley on the defenceless multitude, without previous warning.   Instantly the residents of Madrid rushed into the streets, armed with guns, carbines, swords, pikes, and as many other arms as each one could carry ; and with daring courage fell impetuously upon all the Frenchmen they encountered, although those who begged for mercy were shut up in a safe place, and, with a few exceptions, those who remained in their houses were respected.   Murat, who was accustomed to fighting, both on the field and in the streets and squares of large towns, now set his forces in movement, in such a manner that, coming from the different extremes of the capital and converging by the principal streets to the centre of the town, they came up scattering the multitude ; while the imperial guard, commanded by Daumesnil, struck at the groups, stabbing the people.   And the Polish lancers and the mamelukes, who distinguished themselves by their cruelty, forced the houses from whence the people were

THE FRENCH IN SPAIN

firing on them, or where they supposed they were firing, and entering sacked them and killed the residents.

In spite of the disparity of the forces, and the superiority due to equipment, instruction, and military discipline, the people fought with extraordinary valour ; many sold their lives dearly ; sometimes the mob forced masses of cavalry to retreat ; others fired from a corner with dexterous skill, while from the balconies, windows, and roofs men and women threw down all kinds of implements on the imperial troops. But it was impossible for a people without leaders and undisciplined to sustain the struggle.

The rumour that the French had attacked one of the other barracks moved the already hesitating artillery corps to take part with the people, and the valiant officers Don Pedro Velarde and Don Luis Daoiz, taking the lead, commanded three cannon to be brought out and supported by the peasants and by a picket of infantry commanded by an officer called Ruiz ; they proposed to repulse the enemy, and shortly succeeded in compelling a detachment of one hundred French to surrender. But presently Lefranc's column came down upon them, and a desperate struggle ensued, deadly volleys were discharged, the losses on either side were numerous ; in the beginning of the conflict Ruiz fell to the ground mortally wounded ; the intrepid Velarde died gloriously, pierced by a ball ; but ammunition ran short and the French charged with their bayonets. Such was the defence of the artillery, which cost the French dear, and such the example of patriotism given by the valiant Daoiz and Velarde to the glory and honour of Spain, who have been ever since, and will ever be, the eternal objects of the veneration and worship of their country.[1]

The members of the junta of government wished to give proof of humanity if they had not shown energy, and commissioned two of their number to carry word to Murat that if he would give orders for the firing to cease, they would re-establish quiet in the town. Murat acceded ; and the commissioners went through the streets waving white handkerchiefs crying "Peace ! Peace !" The multitude quieted down upon the promise of reconciliation and pardon for the past. Many unfortunates owed their lives to this step ; the entrances to the streets were guarded by the French ; at certain places cannon were mounted with lighted match in readiness to complete the terror of the people, a fatal sign that the reconciliation and pardon were soon to be converted into desolation and vengeance.

Meanwhile the horrible edict, or order, given below had been published, though scarcely anyone was aware of its publication :

SOLDIERS :

The ill-advised populace of Madrid has risen in arms and committed murders. I am well aware that Spaniards worthy of the name have lamented that such excesses should have been committed, and I am far from confounding them with a few miserable wretches who live only for plunder and crime. But the French blood which has been spilt cries out for vengeance. For this reason I have issued the following order : Article I, This night General Grouchy shall assemble the military commission. Article II, All those who were taken in the rebellion carrying arms shall be shot. Article III, The junta or government is about to command the inhabitants of Madrid to be disarmed. All the residents of the town when the time required for the execution of this resolution has elapsed, who shall continue to carry arms, or keep such in their houses without special license, shall be shot. Article IV, Any band of more than eight persons shall be looked upon as a meeting of rebels, and fired on till they disperse. Article V, Every town or village where a Frenchman is murdered shall be burned. Article VI, Masters shall answer for their servants, owners of factories for their employees, fathers for their sons, and superiors of convents

[1 Napier *i* says these officers were " in a state of great excitement from drink."]

for their religious. Article VII, Authors of written or printed seditious pamphlets, and those who distribute or sell them, shall be looked upon as agents of the English and as such shall be shot.

Given in our headquarters of Madrid, on the 2nd   (Signed), JOACHIM.
    of May, 1808. By order of his royal high-
    ness, the chief of the staff,
                BELLIARD.

In accordance with this Draconian edict the French searched everyone, and seized all persons bearing arms, even though it were a penknife or scissors ; some they shot upon the spot, and imprisoned others in the barracks or in the Casa de Correo, where the military commission had been established. Night came on, and its appalling silence was unbroken save for the roar of the cannon discharged at intervals, or the report of the guns, as the unfortunate residents, in bands or bound in twos, were shot, without their defence being heard, close to the hall of the Prado at the spot where now stands a sad but glorious monument, recording and handing down to posterity the patriotism of those who were here sacrificed ; which monument is a pillar of shame for this inhuman sacrifice.

Such was the end of the popular movement of the 2nd of May, a day eternally remembered in Spanish annals.[1] The country honours her sons who offered themselves as a holocaust for her, and every year a solemn civic religious ceremony takes place which keeps that day of mourning and weeping, and of glory to the country fresh in the memory of every Spaniard. Nor was this a *coup d'état* coldly prepared and planned by Murat, as some have imagined, nor a plot arranged by Spaniards in patriotic unions, as others say ; it was a spontaneous and unpremeditated outburst, an explosion of pent-up anger on the part of a people invaded by deceptions and perfidy, deprived by treachery of the objects of their affection and of their devotion, of their kings and princes, and dominated by the haughty and hypocritical foreigner. And Murat seized the opportunity offered him and which he had watched coming, to humiliate Castilian pride, and smooth the road to seat a French prince on the Spanish throne, a throne which his imagination represented to him as being within his own reach.

On the following day houses and shops were closed, the streets were deserted and silent, the silence being unbroken save by the imposing echo of the measured tread of the French patrols, making their rounds. The edict of the preceding day was affixed in the public places.[2] Murat further published a proclamation beginning, " Valiant Spaniards : the 2nd of May will be for me, as it will be for you, a day of mourning." He blamed

[1 The feeling the Spaniards cherish for this futile riot may be compared to the American regard for the similar occasion known as the Boston " Massacre " of 1770.]

[2 Of the *Dos de Mayo* Napier*i* says : " This celebrated tumult, in which the wild cry of Spanish warfare was first heard, has been represented by authors who adopt all the reports of the day, sometimes as a wanton massacre, sometimes as a barbarous political stroke to impress a dread of French power. It was neither. The fiery temper of the Spaniards, excited by strange events and the recent tumults against Godoy, rendered an explosion inevitable, and so it happened. If the French had stimulated this disposition to violence, with a view to an example, they would have prepared some check on the Spanish garrison ; they would not have left their hospital unguarded, or have so arranged that their own loss should surpass that of the Spaniards ; finally, they would have profited from their policy after having suffered the injury. Moncey and Harispe were, however, most active in restoring order, and, including the peasants killed outside the gates and the executions afterwards, the whole number of the Spanish slain did not exceed one hundred and twenty, while more than five hundred French were killed. Amongst the wounded were seventy of the imperial guards, which would alone disprove any premeditation : for if Murat were base enough to sacrifice his men with such a detestable policy, he would have given the conscripts to slaughter rather than the select soldiers of the emperor."]

the common enemy of France and Spain for this rebellion ; he declared that he had received a previous warning of it which he had not credited, until the rebellion had burst upon him, and he was compelled to chastise the offenders ; he assured them that the emperor was anxious to preserve the integrity of the Spanish monarchy without separating from it a single village or exacting any war tax ; he exhorted the ministers of the church, the magistrates, gentlemen, landholders, and merchants to use their influence to keep down sedition.*d*

Meanwhile by Napoleon's orders Charles IV, Maria Louisa, and Godoy had been sent to Bayonne where Ferdinand awaited Napoleon's nod.*a*

THE ROYAL FAMILY AT BAYONNE

Immediately after the arrival of the royal parents, with Napoleon's approval, Godoy being their principal and well-nigh only councillor, Ferdinand was summoned, and in the presence of the foreign sovereign Charles commanded him to restore the crown on the morning of the following day by means of a pure and simple abdication, threatening him that, in event of his refusal, he, his brothers, and all his suite should from that moment be treated as exiles.

Napoleon supported him with energy, and when Ferdinand was about to reply, his august father sprang from his seat, and attempted to strike him, accusing him of wishing to deprive him of life as well as of his crown. The queen, silent up to then, became enraged, outraging her son with insulting affronts, being carried away to such a point by her ungovernable anger that, according to Napoleon, she herself begged him to bring Ferdinand to the scaffold, which demand, if true, coming from a mother, strikes one with horror. Her son remained mute, and sent in his abdication, dated May 1st, on these conditions : that the king his father should return to Madrid, whither Ferdinand should accompany him, to be treated as his most dutiful son ; that in presence of an assembly of the cortes Ferdinand should formally renounce the crown, explaining his motives for so doing ; that King Charles should not take back with him to Spain any persons who had justly incurred the nation's hatred.

Charles IV, as might be supposed, did not accede to his son's conditions, and on the 2nd sent him a written reply, in which, in the midst of various severe though just reflections, Napoleon's hand is discerned, and even his expressions — such as : " Everything must be done for the people, and nothing for himself ; I cannot consent to any convocation of an assembly ; a new suggestion of your inexperienced followers." Such was Bonaparte's invariable aversion to popular assemblies, although without them he might have remained in the obscurity in which fate had placed him.

On the 5th of May, the report reached Bayonne of what had occurred in Madrid on the *Dos de Mayo*. It was five in the afternoon ; all were seated save the prince. Charles repeated his former accusations, insulted Ferdinand with asperity, blamed him for the rising and for the consequent deaths ; and, calling him a perfidious traitor, again warned him that unless he resigned the crown he should be declared a usurper without delay, and he and all his household looked upon as conspirators against the life of their sovereign. On the 6th Ferdinand, being intimidated, made a pure and simple abdication in favour of his father in the terms set down by the latter. Charles had not waited for his son's abdication to conclude a treaty with

Napoleon by which he ceded to him the crown without any other restriction than that of preserving the integrity of the kingdom and the Catholic religion to the exclusion of all others. Small and petty even to the last, Don Manuel Godoy only haggled obstinately over an article relating to pensions. For the rest, the manner in which Charles gave up the crown covered with shame the father, who with one blow indirectly deprived all his sons of their succession to the throne. Arranged in a foreign land, in the eyes of the world this abdication lacked the indispensable circumstance of having been executed freely and willingly, above all being in favour of the sovereign within whose territory this important article had been inserted in the treaty.

So ended the reign of Charles IV; and no one better than himself gives us an exact and true idea of his life than, when dining with Napoleon in Bayonne, he expressed himself as follows: "Every day, winter and summer, I went hunting until twelve o'clock; then I dined, and immediately returned to my hunting until twilight. Manuel [Godoy] gave me the news, and I went to bed, to begin the same life on the following day, unless some important ceremony prevented me." Such was the manner in which the king had governed for the space of twenty years. According to the sketch which he draws of himself, he merits the same title [fainéant] as that applied to various kings of France of the Merovingian dynasty. Nevertheless, Charles possessed qualities which might have made him shine as a king, and fulfil all the duties of his high calling, but for his idleness and the weakness which caused him to blindly give way to the queen's will and irregular caprices. With another wife than Maria Louisa, his reign would not have compared unfavourably with that of his august predecessor, and although the situation of Europe was very different, as a result of the French Revolution, yet, well governed and without interior discord, Spain might perhaps have peacefully continued her industries and advancement without upheavals and confusion. The abdication of Ferdinand in favour of Charles IV, and of the latter in favour of Napoleon being formally drawn up, there yet lacked Ferdinand's renouncement of his rights as prince of Asturias, because although he had restored the crown to his father on the 6th of May, he had not by this act renounced his rights as immediate heir. It appears according to Don Pedro Cevallos *g* that upon Ferdinand refusing to accede to this last concession Napoleon said, "There is no medium, prince, between renouncement and death." Others deny this threat, and indeed it would seem strange that such rigorous measures should have been resorted to with a person who had so clearly shown his weakness.

The queen of Etruria, in spite of the flattering attention she had bestowed on Murat and the French, was no happier in her negotiations than the rest of her family. The Treaty of Fontainebleau could not be kept with her son because Napoleon had promised the deputies of Portugal to maintain the integrity of that kingdom; nor could indemnification be granted her in Italy, as to allow any branch of the Bourbons to reign in that country was contrary to Napoleon's great views; the queen was compelled to be satisfied with this reply, accept the pension allotted her, and submit to the same fate as her parents.

During the stay of the prince of Asturias and the infantes in Bayonne various plots were set on foot for their escape. A resident of Cevera de Alhama received money from the supreme junta of Madrid for that purpose. The duke of Mahon had sent the offer of a large sum from San Sebastian for the same object. Ferdinand's counsellors received the money in his name and by his orders, but the flight never took place, although several plans were proposed. They would have required less vigilance on the part of the French government and more courage on the part of the Spanish princes to bring them to a successful ending.

The renouncements being formally executed, Napoleon lost no time in despatching the members of the royal family of Spain to the interior of France. Charles IV and his wife, the queen of Etruria and her children, the infante Don Francisco, and the Prince of the Peace, left for Fontainebleau on the 10th of May, and thence proceeded to Compiègne. On the 11th Ferdinand VII, his brother and uncle, the infantes Don Carlos and Don Antonio, left Bayonne; the palace of Valençay, the property of Prince Talleyrand, being assigned as their residence.h

CHAPTER XIII

THE PENINSULAR WAR

[1808–1814 A.D.]

THE Spaniards have boldly asserted the deliverance of the peninsula to be the work of their hands. This claim is unjust to the fame of Wellington, injurious to the glory of the British arms. The imbecility of Charles IV, the vileness of Ferdinand, the corruption imputed to Godoy, were undoubtedly the proximate causes of the calamities which overwhelmed Spain; but the primary, the historical cause, was the despotism springing from the union of a superstitious court and a sanguinary priesthood, a despotism which suppressed knowledge, contracted the public mind, sapped the foundation of military and civil virtue, and prepared the way for invasion. No foreign potentate would have attempted to steal into the fortresses of a great kingdom, if the prying eyes and clamorous tongues of a free press had been ready to expose his projects, and a disciplined army present to avenge the insult: Spain, destitute of both, was first circumvented by the wiles, and then ravaged by the arms of Napoleon. She was deceived and fettered because the public voice was stifled; she was scourged and torn because her military institutions were decayed.

When an English force took the field, the Spaniards ceased to act as principals in a contest carried on in the heart of their country and involving their existence as an independent nation. After the first burst of indignation the cause of independence created little enthusiasm. Horrible barbarities were exercised on French soldiers thrown by sickness or the fortune of war into the power of the invaded, and this dreadful spirit of personal hatred was kept alive by the exactions and severe retaliations of the invader; but no great general exertion to drive the latter from the soil was made, at least none was sustained with steadfast courage in the field; manifestoes, decrees, lofty boasts, like a cloud of canvas covering a rotten hull, made a gallant appearance, but real strength and firmness could nowhere be found.

Strange indeed was the spectacle presented — patriotism supporting a vile system of government, a popular assembly working to restore a despotic monarch, the higher classes seeking a foreign master, the lower armed in the cause of bigotry and misrule. The upstart leaders, secretly abhorring freedom though governing in her name, trembled at the democratic activity they excited; and while calling forth all the bad passions of the multitude repressed the patriotism that would regenerate as well as save. The country suffered the evils without enjoying the benefits of a revolution; tumults and assassinations terrified and disgusted the sensible part of the community; a corrupt administration of the resources extinguished patriotism; neglect ruined the armies. The peasant-soldier, usually flying at the first onset, threw away his arms and went home; or, attracted by the license of the *partidas*, joined the banners of men, the most part originally robbers, who were as oppressive to the people as the enemy; and these guerilla chiefs would in their turn have been quickly exterminated, had not the French, pressed by the British battalions, been compelled to keep in large masses: this was the secret of Spanish constancy. Copious supplies from England and the valour of the Anglo-Portuguese troops supported the war, and it was the gigantic vigour with which the duke of Wellington resisted the fierceness of France and sustained the weakness of three inefficient cabinets that delivered the peninsula.[b]

WAR DECLARED ON FRANCE

The slaughter of the 2nd of May at Madrid, and the treatment of Ferdinand at Bayonne were as the spark of fire to the mine, and the explosion, beginning in the original cradle of Spanish liberty, the Asturias, spread in the course of the month over all Spain. *Juntas*, or councils, composed of the most influential and generally of the most enlightened persons of their respective neighbourhoods, were formed in every province, and most large towns. Many excesses and crimes were committed; many persons fell sacrifices to the suspicions, justly or unjustly excited by their own conduct, of being agents and partisans of the French. When Seville, as next in importance to Madrid and Barcelona, and therefore first of the unsubdued cities of Spain, claimed for her junta the title of supreme, and a degree of authority over the others, the other juntas frankly acknowledged her pretensions. In the name of Ferdinand VII, the supreme junta of Seville, on the 6th of June, declared war against Napoleon and France. Orders were issued for enrolling the whole male population of Spain, combined with judicious instructions to the Spanish leaders to avoid risking their raw soldiers in pitched battles against the disciplined veterans of France; and fast-sailing vessels were sent to the colonies, to warn them against the designs of France and claim obedience to the supreme junta, as lawfully exercising the authority of Ferdinand.

JOSEPH BONAPARTE CHOSEN KING OF SPAIN

The crown of Spain Napoleon is said to have originally destined for Lucien Bonaparte, the ablest of his brothers. But Lucien was a republican upon principle; he had besides accumulated in the public service a large fortune, which he was enjoying at Rome in the pleasures of taste and literature; and, in addition to the sacrifice of his principles and his tastes, Napoleon required from him that of his affections. He would not comply with Napoleon's desire that he should repudiate the mother of his children in order to wed a princess. He is believed to have refused the crown of Spain; and Napoleon assigned it to Joseph, already king of Naples.

A sort of Spanish assembly, meant as a substitute for the cortes, and called by the French name of the "notables," was summoned to Bayonne, to meet and acknowledge Joseph, and to accept the new constitution to be conferred upon them with their new king. Many obeyed the call, some from believing resistance to the power of Napoleon impossible; some preferring reforms imposed by the hand of a foreign conqueror to the vices of their late government; and more from motives of personal interest.

Joseph then selected his ministers, the great officers of his household, etc. Urquijo, who had succeeded to Saavedra under Charles IV, and been like him displaced by Godoy's jealousy, was appointed secretary of state; Cevallos minister for foreign affairs; Jovellanos for the interior; Cabarrus of finance; Pinuela of justice; Azanza of the Indies; Mazarredo of the marine; O'Farrel of the war department. Jovellanos alone firmly and perseveringly refused to hold office under the intrusive king. But of those present some appear to have accepted the places offered them merely because they saw no other means of getting back to their own side of the Pyrenees.

The new king of Spain entered his allotted kingdom on the 9th of July, 1808, and issued proclamations inviting his subjects to submission by the fairest promises of good government. But he found it requisite to pause at Vitoria, until his imperial brother's generals should make way for his progress to his capital. This did not seem likely to be an affair of any great difficulty, for the insurgents were as yet unsupported from abroad. The war between England and Spain was declared to be at an end. But the strength of England was then frittered away in various remote expeditions; and the only immediately disposable force consisted of about nine thousand men, who had been assembled at Cork for an attack upon South America. All hostile measures against the Spanish colonies were now out of the question; and Sir Arthur Wellesley [afterwards made duke of Wellington], to whom the command of this small body of men was given, was directed to proceed with it to the assistance of Spain and Portugal.

On the first symptoms of resistance, Murat had fortified the palace of Buen Retiro, nearly adjoining Madrid, made dispositions for defending the capital (which his successor, Savary, followed up), and sent generals of merited reputation, with considerable divisions of the army, in several directions, to suppress the rebellion, as it was termed, and control the country. The success of the adverse parties in these different situations had been various. At Cadiz, a French squadron had been compelled to surrender, and that nominally without the aid of the British fleet, which, however, lying off the mouth of the harbour, prevented Admiral Rosilly from escaping to sea. Moncey had been repulsed with considerable loss from before Valencia.

But the greatest battle that had yet occurred in this war was now to be fought for the purpose of opening Joseph's road to Madrid, whither Napoleon

[1 "Though of short duration the resistance of Valencia is nothing less than marvellous," says the count de Toreno.] "She had no soldiers for the defence, her ordinary garrison having been ordered to different places, no experienced leaders, none but subalterns to lead the courageous peasants. The French lost two thousand men, amongst whom were Cazal, general of engineers, and other officers of high rank. Sheltered by their walls and batteries the Spaniards had but few comrades to mourn, and no person of importance."]

had enjoined him to repair with all speed. Cuesta, with the army of Castile, and Blake with that of Galicia, had united at Rio Seco, where their combined forces amounted to thirty thousand men. Bessières attacked them on the 14th of July with little more than fifteen thousand. The superior skill and discipline of the French very soon prevailed over their courage and numbers. They lost five or six thousand men, killed and wounded, and twelve hundred prisoners. The two generals threw the blame on each other, and separated in mutual disgust. This victory cost Bessières less than four hundred men. Joseph pursued his journey; and on the 20th made his triumphant entry into Madrid. Orders had been given that the streets through which the procession was to pass should be decorated, according to Spanish custom, by hanging tapestry, etc., from the windows, and that the church bells should be rung. The inhabitants obeyed; but the tapestry they hung out was old, dirty, and ragged, and the bells tolled as for a funeral. The meanest of the populace scorned to pick up the money scattered amongst them as the king passed, leaving it to the French soldiers; and the theatres, which were opened gratis in honour of the day, were filled only by Frenchmen. The council of Castile, which had previously seemed disposed to submit, refused to take the oath required of them to the new sovereign and constitution, alleging that both must first receive the sanction of the nation through the cortes; and the Spanish soldiers, who did duty jointly with the French, deserted by whole guards at a time, leaving not a single sentinel at his post. The first tidings received by Joseph at Madrid were in harmony with the character of his reception.

Dupont had advanced prosperously, defeating all who opposed him, as far as Cordova, which he took by storm, but almost without resistance. However, Castaños, an old soldier, attacked Dupont with about double his numbers, and gained a victory so complete that at Baylen, whither four days of engagement had drawn the French main body, and upon the very day of Joseph's entrance into Madrid, Dupont, with nearly twenty thousand men, surrendered upon condition of being sent with his whole corps to France. The terms of the capitulation were afterwards broken by the vindictive rage of the peasantry, whom their generals could not control. Numbers were put to death, and the rest, instead of being sent to France, were confined in the hulks in the bay of Cadiz, where they suffered every kind of misery, and the greater part perished.[c] In its moral effects the battle of Baylen was one of those events which, insignificant in themselves, cause great changes in the affairs of nations. The defeat of Rio Seco, the preparations of Moncey for a second attack on Valencia, the miserable plight of Saragossa, the despondency of the ablest men of Spain, and the disgust and terror generally excited by the excesses of the populace, weighed heavy in the Spanish cause: one victory more, and the moral as well as the physical force of Spain would have been crushed. The victory of Baylen opened as it were a new crater for Spanish pride, vanity, and arrogance; the glory of past ages seemed to be renewed, every man thought himself a Cid, and, the surrender of Dupont, saw, not the deliverance of Spain, but the immediate conquest of France. "We are obliged to our friends the English," was a common phrase among them when conversing with the officers of Sir John Moore's army; "we thank them for their goodwill, we shall escort them through France to Calais, the journey will be pleasanter than a long voyage: they shall not have the trouble of fighting the French, and we shall be pleased to have them spectators of our victories." This absurd confidence might have led to great things, but it was a voice — nothing more.[b]

Madrid, upon which the victorious Andalusian army could now advance unopposed, was no longer deemed a residence for Joseph; and on the 31st of July, after a residence of ten days, having summoned Bessières from the pursuit of Blake and Cuesta to protect his retreat, the king and his party evacuated the capital, and withdrew to Vitoria. Another triumph obtained soon afterwards by the Spaniards was the successful defence of Saragossa.[c]

On the morning of the 4th of August, after feigning an attack upon the Aljaferia and gate of Portillo, the formidable battery of San Engracia was suddenly set to work, twenty-six pieces simultaneously vomited fire upon the convent of this name, and nearly all the defenders of it perished in the ruins. At five o'clock all the batteries of Saragossa were levelled; the French, crossing the Huerva, precipitated themselves into the town by two wide breaches. Then followed fierce hand-to-hand fights, sustained with desperate valour among the dead bodies and ruins. At the fiercest moment of the fight, General Verdier caused the following brief message to be brought to Palafox: "Peace and capitulation?" "War and steel!" answered without hesitation the leader of the men of Saragossa. The bloody contest was continued; trampling on the dead the French advanced triumphantly. But the news of Baylen caused them to raise the siege.[e]

THE ENGLISH APPEAR

At this period of the war a new actor appeared upon the stage, upon whom thenceforward, the fortune of the peninsula mainly depended. On the 12th of July, 1808, the British expedition sailed from Cork; and its commander, Sir Arthur Wellesley, as soon as the whole was fairly under way, preceded it in a frigate, in order to gather the information requisite for regulating its destination. Landing was made in Mondego Bay. It was the 5th of August before all the troops were on shore. Spencer having arrived during the landing, his junction raised the numbers of the little army to thirteen thousand; and with them Sir Arthur began his march towards Lisbon.

Upon receiving intelligence of Sir Arthur's landing, Junot sent Laborde, one of the ablest of the French generals, from Lisbon, with three thousand foot and five hundred horse to check the progress of the British; and calling in his various detachments, he ordered them severally to effect their junction with Laborde. Under these circumstances, the English commander's object was to prevent the junction of the several detachments — an object which the skill and celerity of his movements enabled him, in the most important instance, to effect. Wellesley was thus enabled to attack Laborde at Roliça on the 17th of August, with great numerical superiority. He drove him from his position with comparative facility; but Laborde fell back about a mile to much stronger ground, where he again awaited the English, and here the battle was sanguinary. Laborde, after displaying both skill and intrepidity, abandoned the contest, retreating in good order.

After the victory was gained, Sir Arthur, now reinforced to about sixteen thousand men, proposed turning the left flank of the position occupied by Junot and his united forces — about fourteen thousand men — and endeavouring to cut him off from Lisbon. But, unfortunately, Sir Arthur Wellesley was no longer commander-in-chief. The English ministry had not known how to appreciate the man whose extraordinary talents had as yet only been tried in India; and three senior officers had been appointed supersede him, and, as it proved, each other. The nomination of one of these could not be blamed, for Sir John Moore then certainly ranked higher in public estimation as a general than Sir Arthur Wellesley; but Sir Harry Burrard and Sir Hew Dalrymple had never been in situations to display military capacity. Sir Harry Burrard arrived on the very day that the reinforcements joined Sir Arthur; and with all the caution of old age refused to sanction the advance of an army deficient in cavalry and artillery horses, especially as ten thousand men were daily expected with Sir John Moore.

On the morning of the 21st, Junot fell upon the British army, with the impetuosity characterising his countrymen and Napoleon's warriors. They were, however, repulsed in every attack; the defects of the position, and the almost total want of cavalry, were immediately remedied by the ability of the general, and the loss was far greater on the side of the French, and less on that of the British, than at Roliza. The battle was over by noon; a considerable portion of the army had not been engaged, and Sir Arthur proposed to follow up his victory, pursue the retreating enemy, cut him off from Lisbon, and thus deliver the capital from the French yoke. Again Burrard's caution prevailed to forbid the pursuit, and still the army remained at Vimeiro.

Sir Harry Burrard's authority expired almost as soon as he had thus unfortunately used it; and on the 22nd Sir Hew Dalrymple landed to take the supreme command. On the evening of the same day, before he could well make himself master of the state of affairs, General Kellermann was sent by Junot to the British camp to propose an armistice, and the evacuation of Portugal by the French troops upon conditions. Such as it was, the so-called Convention of Cintra was signed, and Portugal delivered from her conquerors, on the 30th of August, within a month of General Wellesley's landing.

The authority of Queen Maria and the prince-regent was now restored throughout Portugal. Sir Hew Dalrymple reinstated the council of regency appointed by the prince at his departure, and began his preparations for entering Spain. He was, however, recalled to stand a sort of trial for concluding the Convention of Cintra which provoked wild rage in England; Sir Harry Burrard and Sir Arthur Wellesley returned home to give evidence upon the subject, and the command devolved upon Sir John Moore.

About sixty thousand French troops were now left in Spain. But the British army with all its reinforcements did not exceed twenty-five thousand men. Sir John Moore was of a temperament rather desponding than sanguine: although a brave and able officer, he had not the self-reliance characteristic of a master-mind, and the conduct of the Spaniards abundantly justified his mistrust of the allies, in co-operation with whom he was required to risk an army too valuable to be rashly hazarded, but too small singly to engage the French forces now concentrated upon the Ebro. But now that Spanish energy had driven the intrusive king and his foreign troops almost to the foot of the Pyrenees, Spanish pride deemed all accomplished, and the restraints that had compelled union were no more. Provincial ambition, local, and even individual interests, jealousy, and intrigue tainted the patriotism of the juntas.

Meanwhile discussions were going on as to the mode of government to be adopted. Florida-Blanca, the president of the Murcian junta, and the Council of Castile (which, on the evacuation of Madrid, had there assumed the reins of government) strongly pointed out the necessity of some central executive power, and the evils resulting from the existing anarchy of independent juntas. The convocation of the cortes, or the choice of a Sicilian prince as regent, were proposed, amongst other expedients. At length it was agreed that each junta should send two deputies from its own body to form a central and sovereign junta, each separate junta, however, still governing its own province. The central junta was installed at Aranjuez on the 26th of September. Florida-Blanca, one of the Murcian deputies, was chosen president (Jovellanos was the only other member of much reputation), and its first measure was a solemn proclamation of Ferdinand VII.

France was now pouring one hundred thousand additional men into Spain, Ney, duke of Elchingen, temporarily holding the command until the emperor should arrive from Erfurt to rule the war in person. The French army was, however, still waiting Napoleon's arrival to make a forward movement, when the Spaniards, to the number of 130,000 men, formed in a crescent around them.

One of Sir Arthur Wellesley's reasons for approving the Convention of Cintra had been that it immediately set the English army at liberty to enter Spain. But this advantage was either neglected or lost in the care of investigating the circumstances of that convention. It was not till the beginning of October that Sir John Moore received orders to enter Spain, and co-operate with the armies assembled around the French. Sir David Baird was, at the same time, sent to Corunna with ten thousand men, to act under Moore, who appointed Salamanca for their junction. Neither food nor means of transport had been provided; Baird was unfurnished with pecuniary resources, whilst the Galician and Austrian juntas, though so abundantly supplied by the profuse munificence of the English ministry, refused the troops of their benefactors every kind of succour. Indeed, most of the juntas appear to have misapplied the money sent by England to their own purposes, and often to have made no use whatever of the arms and stores. Moore could not cross the frontiers till the 11th of November; and the absurd precipitation of the central junta, and of those inexperienced generals who were equal in authority to Castaños, had already brought the Spanish forces into collision with the French. After many days' skirmishing and manœuvring, Blake had been defeated, October 30th, by Lefebvre, but had retreated, rallied his men, and being joined by some of La Romana's troops, again made head.

Napoleon himself entered Spain on the 8th of November, and the influence of his genius was immediately apparent. On the 10th, Soult, duke of Dalmatia, attacked, defeated, and utterly routed Belvedere. He then turned upon the line of retreat of Blake, whom Victor, duke of Belluno, defeated at Espinosa on the 11th, and Soult finally annihilated at Reynosa on the 13th. The greater part of the veterans brought back from the Baltic were destroyed in Blake's successive defeats. Blake fled to the Asturian mountains, where he reunited the relics of his army, and met La Romana, who, though disappointed in all his schemes, assumed the command of these routed troops, and exerted himself strenuously to re-organise and reinforce them. The emperor now turned his forces against Castaños and Palafox, whilst his cavalry swept the plains of Leon and Castile. On the 23rd, Lannes attacked Castaños and Palafox at Tudela, and completely routed them.

Napoleon now advanced upon Madrid, and on the 30th reached and attacked the Somosierra. The pass was defended by General San Juan; his troops fled after firing one volley, and afterwards sought to excuse their panic by accusing their unfortunate commander of treachery, and murdering him. The French crossed the mountains almost unopposed, and appeared before Madrid. In the moment of danger the inefficiency of the centra

NAPOLEON IN THE PYRENEES

junta became apparent.   On the approach of the French armies the whole
body fled towards Badajoz.

Napoleon appeared before Madrid on the 2nd of December, and summoned the city to surrender, with fearful threats in case of resistance.   On
the morning of the 5th Morla surrendered Madrid.   The emperor took possession of the palace of the kings of Spain; and in his proclamations
threatened the Spaniards that, unless by their conduct they earned Joseph's
pardon, he would find another kingdom for his brother, and make Spain a

CUENCA

French province.   Such threats were not adapted to conciliate the haughty
Spaniards; and the really beneficial decrees he promulgated, diminishing
the exorbitant power of the clergy and the number of monks and nuns, by
exasperating the whole ecclesiastical body, confirmed the nation in its
enmity to him and his dynasty.   Regardless of this enmity, however,
Napoleon prepared to overrun and subjugate Portugal and the south of
Spain with his grand army, whilst a division of thirty-five thousand men
again besieged Saragossa.   The central junta continued its fight to Seville,
and the troops, which the different generals had rallied in considerable numbers, prepared to defend the Sierra Morena and the Tagus.

MOORE'S FAMOUS RETREAT

Moore's situation was unquestionably one of great difficulty.   The
French are stated to have had two hundred thousand men in Spain; he
could not bring into the field above twenty-five thousand; Madrid had
fallen; and of the Spanish armies nothing remained within his reach but
the few thousands, half clothed and half armed, that La Romana was endeavouring to organise.   Moore had lost all confidence in Spanish professions, and
was convinced that Frere, who vehemently urged him to attempt something,

was deceived by his zeal in the Spanish cause and his ignorance of the Spanish character.　Nevertheless Moore resolved to make such a diversion as should recall Napoleon from the south and from Portugal, and, if possible, to destroy Soult, who was within his reach with inferior numbers, before he could be reinforced.　But he undertook this bold and generous enterprise with a heavy heart, and, as appears from his own letters, as sacrificing his own judgment to what he knew were the expectations of the British public.　Moore began his movement on the 11th, effected his junction with Baird, and reached Sahagun on the 21st of December.　There he halted two days for his supplies, meaning to attack Soult on the 24th.　But on the 23rd he received information that Napoleon, upon hearing of his advance, had suspended all his operations in the south and west, and was marching in full force against the English.　The projected diversion was thus accomplished;

LISBON IN 1800
(From an old Spanish print)

and he began his retreat towards Galicia, where he proposed embarking, and carrying his army southwards to join the Spanish forces collecting in Andalusia.　The retreat was most disastrous.　Officers and men disliked it; the bonds of discipline were early relaxed, and the bulk of the army was a mere drunken mob, never resuming any semblance of order or propriety except when there appeared a prospect of a battle.　Then all were again found British soldiers.[c]

Before discussing this famous disaster we may quote the words of H. M. Stephens,[d] who, after calling Moore "the only English general who has gained lasting fame by the conduct of a retreat," and referring to his death as showing "how a modern Bayard should die in battle—every thought for others, none for himself," thus sums up his position in history:

"It may be possible, in the face of his heroic death, to exaggerate Moore's actual military services, but his influence on the British army cannot be overrated.　The true military spirit of discipline and of valour, both in officers and men, had become nearly extinct during the American war. Abercromby, who looked back to the traditions of Minden, was the first to attempt to revive it, and his work was carried on by Moore. The formation of the light regiments at Shorncliffe was the answer to the new French tactics, and it was left to Wellington to show the success of the experiment. Moore's powers as a statesman are shown in his despatches written at Salamanca, and he had the truest gift of a great man — that of judging men. It may be noticed that, while Wellington perpetually grumbled at the bad qualities of his officers and formed no school, Moore's name is associated with the career of all who made their mark. Among generals, Hope, Graham, Sir E. Paget, Hill, and Craufurd, all felt and submitted to his ascendency, and of younger officers it was ever the proud boast of the Napiers, Colborne, the Beckwiths, and Barnard that they were the pupils of Moore, not of Wellington. Nay more, he inspired an historian. The description of Moore's retreat in Napier *i* is perhaps the finest piece of military history in the English language, not only because the author was present, but because his heart was with the leader of that retreat; and, if Napier felt towards Wellington as the soldiers of the Tenth legion felt towards Cæsar,[1] he felt towards Moore the personal love and devotion of a cavalier towards Montrose."

We can do no better than quote at some length Napier's famous account from his work, which has been favourably compared with those of Thucydides, Xenophon, and Cæsar.*a*

Napier's Story of Moore's Retreat

That Moore succoured Spain in her extremity, and, in her hour of weakness, intercepted the blow descending to crush her, no man of candour can deny. For what troops, what preparations, what courage, what capacity was there in the south to have resisted even for an instant the progress of a man like Napoleon, who, in ten days and in the depth of winter, crossing the snowy ridge of the Carpentinos, had traversed two hundred miles of hostile country, and transported fifty thousand men from Madrid to Astorga in a shorter time than a Spanish courier would have taken to travel the same distance? This stupendous march was rendered fruitless by the quickness of Moore; but Napoleon, though he failed to destroy the English army, resolved, nevertheless, to cast it forth from the peninsula. Being himself recalled to France by tidings that the Austrian storm was ready to burst, he fixed upon Soult to continue the pursuit. Including Laborde, Heudelet, and Loison's division, nearly sixty thousand men and ninety-one guns were put on the track of the English army.

Soult, nowise inferior to any of his nation, if the emperor be excepted, followed Moore with vigour. Nineteen thousand British troops posted in strong ground might have offered battle to very superior numbers; yet where was the use of merely fighting an enemy who had three hundred thousand men in Spain? Nothing could be gained, but Moore might by a quick retreat reach his ships unmolested, and carry his army from that narrow corner to the southern provinces and renew the war under more favourable circumstances. But in the immense wine-vaults of Bembibre hundreds of men remained inebriated, the followers of the army crowded the houses, and many of Romana's disbanded men were mixed with this heterogeneous mass of marauders, drunkards, muleteers, women, and children. Moore, leaving a small guard with them, proceeded to Calcabellos. At Calcabellos the reserve took up a position, Baird marched to Herrerias, and Moore went on to

[1 These are Napier's words in dedicating his great work to Wellington.]

Villa Franca; but in that town also great excesses had been committed by the preceding divisions; the magazines were plundered, the bakers driven from the ovens, the wine-stores forced, the commissaries prevented making the regular distributions; the doors of the houses were broken, and a scandalous insubordination then showed a discreditable relaxation of discipline by the officers. Moore arrested this disorder, and caused one man taken in the act of plundering a magazine to be hanged in the market-place.

Under the most favourable circumstances, the tail of a retreating force exhibits terrible scenes of distress, and on the road near Nogales the followers of the army were dying fast from cold and hunger. The soldiers, barefooted, harassed, and weakened by their excesses at Bembibre and Villa Franca, were dropping to the rear by hundreds, while broken carts, dead animals, and the piteous spectacle of women and children, struggling or falling exhausted in the snow, completed a picture of war, which like Janus has a double face.

The British army was not provided to fight above one battle; there were no draught cattle, no means of transporting reserve ammunition, no magazines, no hospitals, no second line, no provisions: a defeat would have been ruin, a victory useless. A battle is always a serious affair; two battles in such circumstances, though both should be victories, would have been destruction. A terrible storm of wind and rain, mixed with sleet, commenced as the army broke up from the position at Lugo; the marks were destroyed, the guides lost the true direction, only one of the divisions gained the main road, the other two were bewildered, and when daylight broke the rear columns were still near to Lugo. The fatigue, the depression of mind occasioned by this misfortune, and the want of shoes broke the order of the march, stragglers became numerous, and unfortunately Baird, thinking to relieve the men during a halt which took place in the night, desired the leading division to take refuge from the weather in some houses a little way off the road. Complete disorganisation followed this imprudent act. The commander-in-chief, who covered this march with the reserve and cavalry, ordered several bridges to be destroyed, but the engineers failed of success in every attempt.

As the troops approached Corunna, on January 12th, 1809, the general's looks were directed towards the harbour, but an expanse of water painfully convinced him that to fortune at least he was in no way beholden; contrary winds still detained the fleet at Vigo, and the last consuming exertion made by the army was rendered fruitless. The men were put into quarters, and their leader awaited the progress of events. The reserve was posted between the village of El Burgo and the road of Santiago de Compostella. For twelve days these hardy soldiers had covered the retreat, during which time they traversed eighty miles of road in two marches, passed several nights under arms in the snow of the mountains, were seven times engaged, and now took the outposts having fewer men missing from the ranks, including those who had fallen in battle, than any other division in the army: an admirable instance of the value of good discipline, and a manifest proof of the malignant injustice with which Moore has been accused of precipitating his retreat beyond the measure of human strength.

Now a painful measure was adopted; the ground in front of Corunna is impracticable for cavalry, the horses were generally foundered, it was impossible to embark them all in the face of an enemy, and a great number were reluctantly ordered to be shot; worn down and foot-broken, they would otherwise have been distributed among the French cavalry, or used as draught cattle until death relieved them from procrastinated suffering.

But the very fact of their being so foundered was one of the results of inexperience ; the cavalry had come out to Corunna without proper equipments, the horses were ruined, not for want of shoes but want of hammers and nails to put them on. Soon the French gathered on the Mero, and Moore sought a position of battle. On the evening of the 14th the transports from Vigo hove in sight ; the dismounted cavalry, the sick, the best horses, and fifty pieces of artillery were embarked, six British and three Spanish guns being kept on shore for action. When Laborde's division arrived, on the 15th, the French force was not less than twenty thousand men, and Soult made no idle evolutions of display. Distributing his lighter guns along the front of his position, he opened a fire from the heavy battery on his left, and instantly descended the mountain with three columns covered by clouds of skirmishers. The ground about that village was intersected by stone walls and hollow roads ; a severe scrambling fight ensued, the French were forced back with great loss, but, being reinforced, renewed the fight beyond the village. Major Napier,[1] commanding the 50th, was wounded and taken prisoner, and Elvina then became the scene of another contest. The line of the skirmishers being supported vigorously, checked the advance of the enemy's troops in the valley ; at the same time the centre and left of the army also became engaged, and a furious action ensued along the line, in the valley, and on the hills. Sir John Moore, while earnestly watching the result of the fight about the village of Elvina, was struck on the left breast by a cannon-shot.

Notwithstanding this great disaster the troops gained ground, and when the night set in, their line was considerably advanced beyond the original position of the morning, while the French were falling back in confusion. Their disorder facilitated the original plan of embarking during the night. Hope, upon whom the command had devolved, resolved therefore to ship the army, and so complete were the arrangements that no confusion or difficulty occurred ; the pickets kindled fires to cover the retreat, and were themselves withdrawn at daybreak to embark under the protection of Hill's brigade, which was in position under the ramparts of Corunna.

When the morning of the sixteenth dawned, the French, seeing the British position abandoned, pushed some battalions to the heights of San Lucia, and about midday opened a battery on the shipping in the harbour. This caused great confusion amongst the transports, several masters cut their

---

[1] The author's eldest brother ; he was said to be slain. When the French renewed the attack on Elvina, he was somewhat in advance of that village, and alone, for the troops were scattered by the nature of the ground. Being hurt in the leg, he endeavoured to retire, but was overtaken, and thrown to the ground with five wounds ; a French drummer rescued him, and when a soldier with whom he had been struggling made a second attempt to kill him, the drummer once more interfered. The morning after the battle Marshal Soult sent his own surgeon to Major Napier, and, with a kindness and consideration very uncommon, wrote to Napoleon, desiring that his prisoner might not be sent to France, which from the system of refusing exchanges would have ruined his professional prospect ; the drummer also received the cross of the Legion of Honour. When the 2nd corps quitted Corunna, Marshal Soult recommended his prisoner to the attention of Marshal Ney. The latter, treating him rather with the kindness of a friend than the civility of an enemy, lodged him with the French consul, supplied him with money, gave him a general invitation to his house, and not only refrained from sending him to France, but when by a flag of truce he knew that Major Napier's mother was mourning for him as dead, he permitted him, and with him the few soldiers taken in the action, to go at once to England, merely exacting a promise that none should serve until exchanged. I would have not touched at all upon these private adventures, were it not that gratitude demands a public acknowledgment of such generosity, and that demand is rendered more imperative by the after misfortunes of Marshal Ney. That brave and noble-minded man's fate is but too well known. He who had fought five hundred battles for France, not one against her, was shot as a traitor ! Could the bitterest enemy of the Bourbons have more strongly marked the difference between their interests and those of the nation ?

cables, and four vessels went on shore, but the troops were rescued by the men-of-war's boats, the stranded vessels burned, and the fleet got out of harbour. Hill then embarked at the citadel, which was maintained by a rearguard under Beresford until the 18th, when, the wounded being all on board, the troops likewise embarked ; the inhabitants faithfully maintained the town meanwhile, and the fleet sailed for England. The loss of the British, never officially published, was estimated at eight hundred ; of the French at three thousand. The latter is probably an exaggeration, yet it must have been great.

From the spot where he fell, the general was carried to the town by his soldiers ; his blood flowed fast and the torture of the wound was great ; yet the unshaken firmness of his mind made those about him, seeing the resolution of his countenance, express a hope of his recovery : he looked steadfastly at the injury for a moment, and said : " No, I feel that to be impossible." Several times he caused his attendants to stop and turn round, that he might behold the field of battle ; and when the firing indicated the advance of the British, he discovered his satisfaction and permitted the bearers to proceed. When life was almost extinct, with an unsubdued spirit, as if anticipating the baseness of his posthumous calumniators, he exclaimed : " I hope the people of England will be satisfied. I hope my country will do me justice." In a few minutes afterwards he died, and his corpse, wrapped in a military cloak, was interred by the officers of his staff in the citadel of Corunna. The guns of the enemy paid his funeral honours, and Soult with a noble feeling of respect for his valour raised a monument to his memory on the field.[b]

A Spanish Opinion of the Retreat

English historians, especially Napier,[b] are so severe in their aspersions on the Spanish that it is only fair to give the words of a Spanish historian and contemporary, the count de Toreño, who says :

" The residents of Corunna with disinterested zeal not only assisted the English, but also kept faith with them, and did not immediately surrender the fortress, a noble example rarely given by towns when they see themselves abandoned by those from whom they expected protection and aid. So ended General Moore's retreat, censured by some among his own compatriots, upheld and even praised by others. Leaving the investigation and criticism of this campaign to military men, we are of opinion that the chance of being compelled to fight before his troops embarked, and also his having ended his days honourably on the field of battle, have lent lustre to the glory and good name of General Moore. For the rest, if a veteran well-disciplined army such as the English, provided with abundant supplies, began a retreat before combating, in the progress of which retreat there were witnessed such disorders, such damage, such scandals, who can wonder that there were disorders and confusion in the Spanish retreats, executed after fighting, with an army of raw recruits, lacking all resources, and in their own country ? We do not say this to detract from British glory, but in defence of our own, so reviled by certain English writers — by those indeed who took part in this disastrous campaign." [f]

FRENCH SUCCESSES

In Catalonia an attempt by the Spaniards to recover Barcelona was defeated by St. Cyr, who likewise took Rosas. In Galicia La Romana sheltered himself and his little band amidst the mountains, whilst Soult overran the province; Corunna surrendered to him as soon as the English troops were safe on board, and Ferrol followed its example, delivering up the squadron in its port.

On the 22nd of January, 1809, Joseph returned to Madrid. His second entrance does not appear to have called forth the same demonstrations of national feeling as the first. The municipality and the several councils received him with loud professions of loyalty, and all the population took the oath of allegiance.

Saragossa had been invested by Marshal Moncey the 20th of December, 1808, and summoned to surrender; Palafox gave the answer that might be expected from his conduct in the former siege, and with his brave townsmen prepared to stand a second, yet more destructive. For a while the siege languished, and dissension existed amongst the besieging generals. But, on the 22nd of January, 1809, Lannes assumed the command; and on the 1st of February the besiegers forced their entrance into the town, and for three weeks the struggle, street by street and house by house, was maintained, with all the circumstances of affecting heroism recorded on the former occasion. But the numbers that had thronged to defend Saragossa were her bane: pestilence was engendered in the crowded cellars, and proved a yet more deadly foe than the French. The posts were manned by hospital patients, sitting, because they could not stand; Palafox was in his bed delirious; and on the 22nd of February the junta capitulated. Lannes violated the capitulation in many points, and sent Palafox, whose liberty had been stipulated, prisoner to France. The central junta loaded the city and all its inhabitants and defenders with praises, honour, and rewards.[1]

The re-conquest of Portugal was now the object of the French. Soult was appointed governor of that kingdom, and ordered to invade it from the north, whilst Victor and Lapisse were to co-operate with him, the former in the south, and the latter from Ciudad Rodrigo.

Soult took Oporto by storm on the 29th of March, fixed his headquarters there, and seems to have meditated becoming king of northern Lusitania, if not of Portugal. But Oporto was the limit of his conquest. Behind him La Romana, who had rallied his constantly increasing army, found Ney full employment, and Silveira was again master of Tras-os-Montes. In the south Victor could not invade Alemtejo till he should have defeated Cuesta and the Estremaduran army; and Lapisse could not make himself master of Ciudad Rodrigo, which was defended chiefly by Sir Robert Wilson with his Lusitanian legion. This legion was the first attempt, in the course of the war, to improve the Portuguese soldiers, by placing them under British officers. The prince of Brazil was induced to send General Beresford a commission as field-marshal and general-in-chief of the Portuguese army. With this commission, Beresford landed early in March, and immediately proceeded to train the troops and to place over them as many effective English officers as he thought national jealousy would bear (always, however, nominally commanded by a native colonel).

Bonaparte is calculated to have had at this time about 270,000 men in

[1 As Napier[b] points out, however, though the Spanish glorify this siege and called Saragossa "Spain," for her bravery : "Deprive the transaction of its dazzling colours, and it shows thus : Thirty-five thousand French, in the midst of insurrections, and despite of circumstances peculiarly favourable to the defence, reduced fifty thousand of the bravest and most energetic men in Spain. The latter suffered nobly, but was their example imitated? Gerona indeed, although less celebrated, rivalled, perhaps more than rivalled, the glory of Saragossa; elsewhere her fate spoke, not trumpet-tongued to arouse, but with a wailing voice that carried dismay to the heart of the nation."]

the peninsula. These he deemed amply sufficient for its subjugation, and at the moment could not well reinforce them. His alarms touching Austria had proved just. If Napoleon was successful as ever in Germany, his generals were not equally prosperous in the peninsula. And what was of yet more consequence, on the 22nd of April, Sir Arthur Wellesley arrived in the Tagus, bearing the character of general-in-chief of the English and Portuguese troops.

WELLINGTON RESUMES CONTROL

There was no hesitation in Sir Arthur's measures. He resolved first to clear Portugal of invaders, then to assist Spain. On the 6th of May, leaving a body of British and Portuguese on the Tagus to watch Victor, he began his march from Coimbra with about thirteen thousand British troops, three thousand Germans, and nine thousand of Beresford's new levies, to effect the first of these objects. The French troops, who had ventured to take post south of the Douro, were everywhere outmanœuvred and driven back. Soult, having broken the bridges and secured the boats upon the Douro, a broad and rapid stream, believed the English could only cross by their ship-boats at the mouth of the river. But on the 12th, Sir Arthur contrived to procure four barges at a point where a wood concealed the river, and a hill his army, from the town, whilst his guns could play on the point at which the men were to land ; and before the French suspected so daring an attempt, some companies were passed over who made good their footing.

Soult, after a short contest, evacuated Oporto, and precipitately retreated. The pursuit was continued for five days, till the French marshal, sacrificing his artillery, stores, baggage, and even his sick and wounded, escaped with the remnant of his troops, by mountain paths through which no regularly equipped and appointed army could attempt to follow. Sir Arthur then abandoned the chase, appointed Trant military governor of Oporto (the bishop had fled to Lisbon, where he was thenceforward a leading member of the regency), and leaving the protection of the northern provinces to Silveira and his Portuguese, returned southwards, to assist Cuesta against Victor. The utter impracticability of this brave, zealous, and upright, but narrow-minded, prejudiced, and obstinate old man,[1] thwarted every scheme proposed, and thus wasted much valuable time. The British commander found it impossible to obtain from his Spanish coadjutor either provisions or means of transport for his artillery and stores.

The French now returned with superior numbers, under the command of the king, aided by his major-general, Marshal Jourdan. Upon the 27th and 28th of July they attacked the allies at Talavera. The battle, long, obstinately contested, and sanguinary, ended in the complete defeat of the assailants ; but the destitute and exhausted condition of the English troops, who were without provisions for man or horse, prevented their pursuing the discomfited enemy, who was consequently enabled to retreat in good order. The good that should have resulted from the victory was further counteracted by an alarm from the north, and Cuesta's perverse temper.

La Romana had rallied and increased his little army, and had so harassed Soult and Ney, that they, considering likewise the greater importance of the transactions then taking place in the south, resolved to evacuate the province.

[1 Napier[b] thus pungently sums up Cuesta : "Cuesta's knowledge of both friend's and enemy's strength and positions was always inaccurate and his judgment false ; he never gained a decisive action, and lost every army he commanded."]

They did so, and Galicia remained thenceforward unmolested by invaders. In their progress southwards the two marshals were joined by Mortier, and Soult received from Napoleon the command of the combined corps with orders to march upon the English and Cuesta. The Spaniards stationed to secure the mountain passes fled ; and Sir Arthur led the British army against this new foe, intrusting to Cuesta the maintenance of the post of Talavera. An apprehension of Victor's advancing anew induced Cuesta to evacuate Talavera, and he hastened after Wellesley, leaving fifteen hundred British wounded to the enemy, whilst it is said many of his own carts were removed empty. This step, and Soult's advance in unexpected strength, exposed Sir Arthur to be cut off from Portugal. His troops were starving ; and as the protection of Portugal was the point chiefly insisted upon in his instructions, he retreated to a frontier position on the Guadiana. Venegas was defeated at Almonacid. Blake's army of Aragon and Valencia had been beaten and dispersed ; and the fall of Spain appeared to be inevitable. Venegas' repeated defeats had now made him so unpopular that the command of his army was taken from him.

Meanwhile the central junta exerted themselves to reinforce Cuesta's army, which had been surprised and half destroyed by the enemy since its separation from the English ; and they thought of removing the unmanageable general. A paralytic stroke saved them that trouble, by compelling him to resign. The command of the principal army of fifty thousand men was given to Areizaga who was ordered to free Madrid, before the reinforcements, set at liberty by the end of the Austrian war, could reach Spain. The same peculiarity of the Spanish character, namely, assuming as done whatever is promised, or even wished, seems to have convinced the inexperienced statesmen of the central junta that the general they had sent to conquer could not be beaten, and that a decree, ordering the English army to be well supplied, must answer every purpose, though they took no measures for procuring the provisions or the cattle required. Lord Wellington remained in his cantonments ; and on the 17th of November, Areizaga was totally defeated at Ocaña. The French now menaced Portugal : the British general was prepared for its protection.

The French were masters of nearly all Spain north of the Sierra Morena, with the exception of Galicia, Valencia, and Catalonia ; and in this last province, although it resisted most stoutly, the French army, under St. Cyr, held the field, and Gerona, one of the most important fortresses not in their hands, fell in December, after emulating the glory of Saragossa during a seven months' siege.[1] But their garrisons were distressed, and their

[1 Lafuente e gives the following incidents of the siege of Gerona : " The holy patron of the town, St. Narcissus, was named generalissimo, it being to his protection and intercession that the devout residents attributed their safety in the attacks and dangers of the wars of past times. Of the 900 men who garrisoned the fortress of Monjuich 511 soldiers and 18 officers had perished, and nearly all the rest were wounded before it was abandoned. It cost the French 3,000 men to conquer the ruins. Whenever the limited number of the garrison permitted, Alvarez ordered sallies to be made by small bodies of men. It is related how, on the occasion of one of these sallies, the officer who was to direct it was asked where he would take refuge in case of necessity. ' In the cemetery,' he replied.

" When November had set in the town was ravaged by pestilence, while it suffered from the horrors of famine. Even the most unclean animals were bought at an exorbitant price and devoured. Emaciated, and no less hungry than the men, the very animals fell upon and ate one another. Pools of stagnant water full of refuse were seen in the streets ; scattered here and there lay the unburied corpses ; for the living there was neither shelter nor rest ; the air was pestilential and disease was abroad ; the overfull hospitals lacked remedies for the sick. During the month of November, 1,378 soldiers alone died. The spirits of the strongest and most valiant began to fail, and yet the dauntless governor Alvarez seized or harshly turned away the emissaries despatched by the French general to advise him to surrender. And upon hearing communications were harassed both by the British cruisers on the coast, and by the Catalans themselves, who were almost all in arms, as *miquelets* or *guerrillas*, displaying the same indomitable spirit they had shown in former wars. In the course of the year 1809, as the regular armies were defeated and dispersed, the example of the Catalans was followed throughout Spain ; and bands of guerillas consisting of peasants, deserters, outlaws — of individuals, in short, of all classes — were everywhere established, the command of which was assumed by men of talent and resolution, likewise of all classes — officers, monks, physicians, yeomen, or smugglers. This was a mode of warfare to which the climate was favourable, the vindictive Spanish character peculiarly adapted, and habits of discipline unnecessary. They appeared in force wherever a blow was to be struck ; when pursued, they dispersed and vanished. A few of the guerilla leaders, as Juan Martin Diaz, better known as the Empecinado, Julian Sanchez, Juan Diaz Porlier, Don Mariano de Renovalos Longa, and last, and far the greatest, the two Minas, uncle and nephew, acquired a celebrity that renders the record of their names indispensable in Spanish history.

The central junta, opposed by the local junta, and alarmed at their own unpopularity, were now prevailed upon to transfer their authority to a regency of five persons. The regency, instead of devoting their time and thoughts to calling forth the resources and energies of the country, or even to the defence of Cadiz, began their administration by a vehement attack upon the measures of the central junta, accused that body of usurpation and peculation, threw some of the members into prison, and banished even the excellent Jovellanos to his native province, where his conduct was ordered to be watched. Alburquerque was deprived of the government of Cadiz and sent as ambassador to England, where he soon died, of mortification, it is said, at his ill usage. Whilst the regency were persecuting their predecessors, or occupied with commercial interests, Andalusia and Granada submitted at once to the conqueror, who met resistance only from Cadiz.

The war with Austria was now over, and it was generally expected that the dreaded Napoleon would return to the peninsula, to bear down all resistance by the energy of his own mighty genius. But he sent his favourite general, Masséna, whom he had surnamed the Spoiled Child of Victory, to conquer Portugal, drive the English into the sea, and, it was supposed, receive the crown of Portugal as his reward.

The Spaniards had now no army on foot deserving the name, and central Spain, from the Pyrenees to the lines before Cadiz, was nominally in the possession of King Joseph, Galicia and Estremadura, on the western, and Murcia, Valencia, and Catalonia on the eastern side, with a few fortresses, being all that yet remained unconquered ; and, in Catalonia, Suchet was slowly making formidable progress. But the temper of the people never was less subdued, and the war had assumed a character of extraordinary ferocity.

Napoleon deemed that professional soldiers only had a right to fight ; and instead of respecting the patriotic feeling that roused the whole nation to struggle for independence, he considered the armed peasantry as mere licentious rebels against their lawful king. Hence whilst the ordinary courtesies of war were observed towards the British, nearly all the Spaniards and the

someone in the fortress pronounce the word ' capitulation,' he turned upon him : ' How !' he exclaimed in imposing accents, ' are you alone a coward here ! When provisions are at end we will eat you, and such as you.' At length capitulation was necessary and so ended the famous and memorable siege of Gerona, which lasted seven long months, during which time the enemy's 40 batteries discharged against the town more than 60,000 balls and 20,000 bombs and grenades.''']

irregular Portuguese troops were treated with wanton cruelty, and their women exposed to the grossest outrage from the French soldiery, until almost every individual in the Spanish guerilla bands, and the Portuguese irregulars, had a private injury to revenge ; and even sympathy in their resentments can barely palliate the sanguinary temper in which that revenge was sought. And to these personal motives of exasperation was added a deep sense of religious horror, since the French emperor had seized upon the estates of the church, upon Rome itself, and carried Pope Pius VII, who refused to sanction his spoliation, a prisoner to France. From the influence of so many various feelings, the whole of Spain was now overrun by fierce guerillas, and Joseph, in fact, was only master of the places actually occupied by French soldiers.

As soon as the French movements threatened Portugal, Lord Wellington could not hope, with 27,000 British, and 30,000 nearly untried Portuguese troops, to defend Portugal against 80,000 French veterans, led by an able general, and supported by bodies of 30,000 or 40,000 men, acting as a rear-guard.

THE LINES OF TORRES VEDRAS

The British commander was even then directing the construction of those military works, known as the lines of Torres Vedras, by which the naturally strong ground covering Lisbon was rendered nearly impregnable ; and his main object upon the frontier appears to have been retarding the enemy's advance, until those lines should be perfected and the harvest gathered in. He intended that the inhabitants should then evacuate the intermediate district, with all their provisions and movable property ; and that he himself, retreating to his lines, should draw Masséna into a desert country, where the French marshal could not subsist his troops, and would find himself confronted by a strong army, in an impregnable position, whilst his rear and communications were harassed by militia and *ordenanzas*, the proper name of the Portuguese armed peasantry.

Masséna, recently created by his imperial master, the prince of Essling, dedicated the spring to assembling his army, and making preparations; nor was until he began the siege of Ciudad Rodrigo that the line by which he proposed to invade Portugal was ascertained. That town was gallantly defended by its governor, Herrasti, assisted by the guerilla chief, Sanchez, from the 1th of June till the 10th of July, 1810. When the place was no longer tenable, Sanchez and his band, breaking through the besiegers, escaped, and Herrasti capitulated. Lord Wellington's plan required that he should hazard no attempt to relieve the besieged,[1] but his menacing position had long kept Masséna's usually enterprising temper in check, and continued to do so; for upwards of a month was suffered to elapse after the fall of

[1 The Spanish historian, the count de Toreño,*f* says of this siege:
" All the residents, without distinction of class, age, or sex, rushed to the assistance of the troops. Lorenza, a woman of the people, distinguished herself among the women, being twice wounded ; and even two blind men, one led by a faithful dog, employed themselves in useful works, ever smiling and jovial, visiting the posts of greatest danger, crying out above the hissing of the balls, ' Courage, boys; long live Ferdinand VII! *Viva Ciudad Rodrigo!*'
" The Spaniards were angered with the English for not assisting the town. Lord Wellington had come thither from the Guadiana disposed, and even as it were in honour bound to compel the French to raise the siege. In this case he could not put forward the usual excuse that the Spaniards did not defend themselves, or that by their want of concert they caused the failure of the ill-matured plans of their allies. The marquis de la Romana came from Badajoz to Welling-ton's headquarters, and joined his prayers to those of the residents and authorities of Ciudad

Ciudad Rodrigo ere the French general proceeded to lay siege to the neighbouring Portuguese fortress, Almeida.

The allied army, falling back as he advanced, offered no interruption. But an English officer commanded the Portuguese garrison in Almeida, and a defence yet longer than Ciudad Rodrigo's was confidently expected. An accident caused the explosion of the principal powder magazine on the 26th of August, when, through the panic of some and the treachery of others, the garrison flung down their arms, and forced the mortified governor to capitulate. Masséna concentrated his forces about the middle of September

SALAMANCA

and prepared, as he hoped, to drive the British to their ships. Lord Wel ington arranged his army upon the ridge of Busaco, and awaited the enem The French troops scaled the steep ascent with daring alacrity, but we driven down again with heavy loss. The French killed and wounded this battle are estimated at from five to six thousand, those of the alli at twelve hundred: but perhaps not the least important event of the day w that the Portuguese troops displayed a steadiness of courage which h scarcely been as yet expected from their training. On the following d

Rodrigo, to those of the Spanish government, and even to those of some of the English. vain! Wellington, determined not to take any step in the matter, remained obstinate.

" Were we to imitate the example of certain English historians, a wide field is here open us to fittingly reply to the unjust recriminations which such historians have largely and wra fully poured out, with respect to the Spanish military operations. But with more impartial than they have shown and following no other guide but truth, setting aside public opinion, declare, on the contrary, that Lord Wellington acted as a prudent general if, to compel the ene to raise the siege, it was necessary to risk a battle. His forces were not superior to the Fren his soldiers lacked the necessary quickness to manœuvre in the open and without set positio nor did the Portuguese troops possess that discipline and experience of fighting which gives s confidence. A battle gained would have saved Ciudad Rodrigo, but it would not have ended war; and had they lost it, the English army would have been destroyed, the enemy enabled advance to Lisbon, and a terrible if not mortal blow have been dealt to the Spanish cause. voice of public opinion deafened the ears of the government with complaints, qualifying conduct of the English as at least tepid and indifferent."]

Masséna, learning that there was a mountain road by which he could turn the left of his adversary's position, filed off his troops in that direction, vainly hoping to reach Coimbra the first. On the 29th Lord Wellington prevented him, by retreating upon that city along the direct road.

It was not till they actually saw the allied army retreating before the invaders that the inhabitants prepared to obey Lord Wellington's proclamation, and forsake their homes. And now it was too late to attain the end for which the order had been given. The provisions were left behind, the mills were scarcely damaged; whilst the helpless and desolate crowds that, flying from the enemy, accompanied the troops, encumbered their march, and gave birth to the usual disorders of a retreat. Such disorders were, however, repressed by the vigour with which Lord Wellington punished, and the precautions he took to prevent them; whilst Masséna's negligence indulged his troops in a license that rendered the disorder of the pursuing far greater than even now was that of the retreating army. At Coimbra alone the French troops, during the three days they spent there, wasted and destroyed stores that might have supplied two months' subsistence. But at Coimbra Masséna was still ignorant of the existence of the lines of Torres Vedras; and still believing that he was merely chasing the British to their ships, he probably saw no need of restraining his troops or of providing against famine.

On the 10th of October the allied army took up its position within those extraordinary lines, of which one end rested upon the sea, and the other upon the Tagus, extending in length twenty-nine miles, at about thirty-five miles average distance from Lisbon. The utmost skill of the engineer had been exerted to improve the natural strength of this mountain line, and to supply its deficiencies. A second line of fortifications had been prepared some ten miles nearer Lisbon, in case the first should be lost, or prove too extensive for the numbers occupying it; and a third to protect a possible forced embarkation. But this danger was happily gone by. Reinforcements arrived from England, additional Portuguese corps were assembled, and La Romana, at Lord Wellington's request, brought in two Spanish divisions. Before the end of the month seventy thousand regular troops were within the lines, ready to be moved, along convenient roads, to whatever points might be threatened, whilst sixty thousand Portuguese militia manned the different forts and redoubts that commanded the approaches.

Masséna halted in disagreeable surprise before the stupendous fortress. He was obliged to send foraging detachments to great distances; these were cruelly harassed, and sometimes cut off by the Portuguese militia and ordenanzas. Towards the middle of November, Masséna withdrew from before the lines, and took up a strong position at Santarem, upon the Tagus. Wellington, to observe him, stationed himself in advance of his lines, upon which he could fall back at a moment's warning.

Throughout the greater part of Spain meanwhile a desultory warfare had been carried on, in which the French were generally successful. Victor was conducting the siege of Cadiz, an operation that proceeded languidly on both sides, from want of numbers on Victor's, and the usual causes on that of the Spaniards.

The assembling of the cortes was looked to as the period and as the means of the regeneration of Spain. These hopes were confirmed, and the peculiar character of the Spanish resolution was, at the same time, curiously illustrated by the mode in which the elections were carried on, even in the provinces most thoroughly occupied by the French. Considerable bodies of armed peasants, or of guerillas, sometimes temporarily drove the French from the town where an election was appointed to take place, sometimes merely held them at bay, whilst the suffrages were collected. And thus, almost everywhere, deputies were elected who, sooner or later, found their way to Cadiz. On the 24th of September, 1810, the cortes were solemnly opened. The assembly immediately decreed a new levy of 150,000 men, together with provision for the support and equipment of all the Spanish armies. But then, as if this decree had sufficed for expelling the enemy, who held the whole country in subjection, they dedicated their whole attention to framing a constitution, and to establishing sweeping theories, resembling those adopted by the French National Assembly, and equally democratic in their tenor. The disputes that ensued between the cortes and the regency ended in the dissolution of the latter body, for whom was substituted an executive council of three. The cortes offended the clergy by attacking the Inquisition, and attempting other ecclesiastical reforms for which the country was unripe, exasperated the whole church, and sowed the seeds of the fatal subsequent reaction that robbed Spain of all the internal benefits she ought to have derived from the restoration of her representative legislature.

Although they had allowed the colonies to send deputies to the cortes they were not willing to treat the colonists as brethren. The colonies had unanimously professed their loyalty to Ferdinand, and their adhesion to the national cause. The emissaries employed by Napoleon and Joseph to seduce them had been everywhere derided and punished; and the American revenues, regularly conveyed to the mother-country by English vessels, ought, i fairly applied, to have done much towards supporting the war.

On the intelligence of the surrender of Seville, the subjugation of Andalusia, and the flight and dispersion of the central junta, the province of Caracas assumed that Spain was conquered; and, declaring that it never woul submit to Joseph, cast off the authority of the mother-country whilst pro claiming inviolable fidelity to Ferdinand. This example was followed by th other provinces of Terra Firma, as the north coast of the South American con tinent was called; and on the 19th of April, 1810, the Venezuela confederatio proclaimed its independent existence under Ferdinand VII. They refused acknowledge the Cadiz regency and cortes, with whom they carried on a pap war; and those bodies, vehemently resenting this daring assertion of ind pendence, divided the forces that should have been dedicated to the expulsio of the enemy from Spain, in order to compel colonial submission.

From the injudicious appointment to the chief command of the worst of the Spanish generals, Lapeña, Cadiz must have fallen, if Soult had not be ordered by Napoleon to co-operate with Masséna against Portugal. Lapeñ to whom Graham, as a measure of conciliation, gave up the supreme comman stood inactive in a safe and distant post, with eleven thousand Spaniar whilst at Barrosa, Graham, with little more than four thousand Engli and Portuguese, fought and defeated nearly nine thousand French. the Spanish general's refusal even to pursue the beaten enemy, the bene of this hardly won success was lost. The council and cortes approved Lapeña's conduct: he claimed the merit of the victory, and Graham, disgust, resigning his command to General Cooke, joined Lord Wellingt La Romana died on the 24th of January, 1811. Olivenza had capitulated the 22nd, and the French laid siege to Badajoz. La Romana's successor, M dizabal, was defeated by Soult; but Don Raphael Menacho, the governor Badajoz, defended the place stoutly, and Soult remained before it.

Portugal the winter had passed with little alteration. Wellington and Masséna had spent it in watching each other.

By the end of February, 1811, the provisions, which the obstinacy of the regents had left to the French, were exhausted. Masséna learned from his partisans in Lisbon that English reinforcements had landed on the 2nd of March, and on the 6th he had evacuated Santarem and begun his retreat. He conducted it with great skill, stained, however, with as great and wanton cruelty. In fact, this retreat, though highly honourable to the general's abilities, remains one of the foulest blots upon the moral character of the French army.[1] But the pursuit was conducted by Lord Wellington with yet greater ability, every strong position taken by the French army being immediately turned by the British; and on the 5th of April Masséna was finally driven across the frontiers of Portugal. This retreat cost the French about six thousand men, and the allies a tenth of that number. Masséna's previous losses are estimated at twenty-five or thirty thousand.

FAILURES IN SPAIN

Lord Wellington, having now again delivered Portugal, asked for such reinforcements as might enable him to undertake the deliverance of Spain, without being, as before, dependent upon the obstinate generals and feeble counsels of that country. But to the feasibility of his future schemes, and even to the maintenance of Portugal and of Cadiz, the recovery of Almeida, Ciudad Rodrigo, and Badajoz was indispensable. The first of these fortresses Wellington immediately blockaded, and directed Marshal Beresford to lay siege to the last.

Masséna, having refreshed, re-equipped, and reorganised his army in Spain, marched to relieve Almeida. His advance produced the battle of Fuentes de Onoro, fought on the 5th of May, in which, after an obstinate and sanguinary contest, they were repulsed, and again retreated. Brennier, the governor of Almeida, then despairing of relief, blew up the fortifications of the place, made his way, with little loss, through the British lines, and rejoined Masséna. Ciudad Rodrigo was next blockaded, but the French easily introduced convoys, and the blockade was abandoned. Little progress was made in the south. Some smaller places Marshal Beresford recovered; but he had scarcely invested Badajoz when the approach of Soult, with a powerful army, obliged him to raise the siege. He fought a battle at Albuera on the 16th of May. But the victory was purchased by the loss of forty-five hundred British, killed and wounded, out of six thousand, and twenty-six hundred Germans, Spaniards, and Portuguese. Lord Wellington arrived in Beresford's camp soon after the battle, and Badajoz was besieged a second time under his own direction.

On the night of the 5th of June an attempt was made to storm. It failed; was repeated two nights later, and again failed, both times with heavy loss. Upon this second repulse, as the combined French armies, to the amount of seventy thousand men, were approaching, Lord Wellington, who had but fifty-six thousand, and was particularly inferior to his adversaries in cavalry, raised the siege, and withdrew the troops to a strong position, limiting himself,

[1 Napier,[b] while admitting the harshness of Masséna's deeds, blames the Portuguese peasantry for many atrocities, and says that at least one of the worst outrages blamed upon Masséna's men — the pulling to pieces of João I's body — was actually done by the British themselves. Many of the charges against the French he declares not only slanderous but impossible.]

for the present, to the defence of Portugal. No other war raged now to distract the attention of the French emperor; but he did not again take the command of the peninsular armies, and it is difficult to assign a valid reason for his conduct. He contented himself with sending reinforcements to the extent of fifty thousand men, naming Marmont, duke of Ragusa, to supersede Masséna, whose conduct of the invasion of Portugal he of course blamed; and placing Catalonia, like Aragon, under Suchet's command, and also Valencia when he should have conquered that province.

Suchet had deserved this confidence: he had done more than any other French general both to conquer Spain and to bend her to the yoke. Aragon was tolerably submissive; Tarragona, the last fortress of Catalonia, fell in June. Considering his work done in Catalonia, although guerilla bands still occupied the mountain fastnesses, and the bold and able Sarsfield watched every opportunity of directing them upon the French, Suchet next invaded Valencia. He defeated several detachments of the Spanish army, and on the 16th of October laid siege to Murviedro. Blake gave battle on the 25th of October, and was defeated. Upon this disaster, Murviedro capitulated, and Blake took another strong position to protect the capital, Valencia, where Suchet, on the 26th of December, again defeated him, driving him into Valencia. There Suchet besieged him, and compelled him to capitulate on the 8th of January, 1812. This campaign, the most successful the French had made in Spain since the first, Napoleon rewarded by creating Suchet duke of Albufera, and granting him the royal domain of that name in Valencia, as an inalienable fief of the French empire.

The dissensions with the colonies likewise diverted both the attention and the resources of the Spanish government from the vigorous prosecution of the war. In every American province insurrection now raged. In Mexico, after a severe struggle, the Spaniards regained the ascendency. In South America the insurgents everywhere prevailed, as will be described later in the histories of Spanish America.

The year 1812 opened with an exploit, the brilliant rapidity of which seems equally to have confounded the French and enraptured the Spaniards. Lord Wellington had long been silently forwarding every preparation for the siege of Ciudad Rodrigo. On the 8th of January, 1812, he suddenly appeared before the place, invested it, and on the 19th the town was stormed.[c] But throwing off the restraints of discipline, the British troops committed frightful excesses; the town was fired in three or four places, the soldiers menaced their officers and shot each other; many were killed in the market-place, intoxication soon increased the tumult, and at last, the fury rising to absolute madness, a fire was wilfully lighted in the middle of the great magazine, by which the town would have been blown to atoms but for the energetic courage of some officers and a few soldiers who still preserved their senses.

To recompense an exploit so boldly undertaken and so gloriously finished, Lord Wellington was created duke of Ciudad Rodrigo by the Spaniards, earl of Wellington by the English, marquis of Torres Vedras by the Portuguese.[b]

By disguising his designs, Lord Wellington hoped to master Badajoz like Ciudad Rodrigo, before Soult and Marmont should have time to hear of the siege, and unite their forces to raise it. On the 16th of March, 1812, Badajoz was invested. The works were hurried on with the diligence already practised, and on the 24th an important fort was carried by assault. On the 30th information was received that Soult was advancing with his

[1812 A.D.]

whole disposable force to raise the siege; that Graham and Hill were retreating before him towards Albuera; that Marmont, taking advantage of the allied army's removal, had crossed the frontier, blockaded Ciudad Rodrigo, masked Almedai, and marched southwards, plundering and ravaging the country, as far as Castello Branco; and that the cavalry and militia, left to observe him, had fallen back, the latter upon the mountains, the former towards the Tagus. In consequence of this threatening intelligence, the siege was pressed with increased ardour; on the 6th of April three sufficient breaches were made; and on the night of that day they were stormed.[c]

The account of this desperate attack is perhaps the most dramatic, and is certainly the most famous, portion of Napier's *History of the War in the Peninsula*, which, as we have already stated, is regarded as the most eminent military history in the English language. We quote herewith the greater part of what is a masterwork of literature describing a masterwork of heroism.[a]

NAPIER'S ACCOUNT OF THE ASSAULT ON BADAJOZ

Dry but clouded was the night, the air thick with watery exhalations from the rivers, the ramparts and the trenches unusually still; yet a low murmur pervaded the latter, and in the former lights were seen to flit here and there, while the deep voices of the sentinels at times proclaimed that all was well at Badajoz. The French, confiding in Phillipon's direful skill, watched from their lofty station the approach of enemies whom they had twice before baffled, and now hoped to drive a third time blasted and ruined from the walls. The British, standing in deep columns, were as eager to meet that fiery destruction as the others were to pour it down, and both were alike terrible for their strength, their discipline, and the passions awakened in their resolute hearts. Former failures there were to avenge, and on both sides leaders who furnished no excuse for weakness in the hour of trial. The possession of Badajoz had become a point of personal honour with the soldiers of each nation, but the desire for glory with the British was dashed by a hatred of the citizens on an old grudge; and recent toil and hardship with much spilling of blood had made many incredibly savage; for these things render the nobleminded indeed averse to cruelty but harden the vulgar spirit: numbers also, like Cæsar's centurion, who could not forget the plunder of Avaricum, were heated with the recollection of Ciudad Rodrigo and thirsted for spoil. Thus every spirit found a cause of excitement, the wondrous power of discipline bound the whole together as with a band of iron, and in the pride of arms none doubted their might to bear down every obstacle that man could oppose to their fury.

At 10 o'clock, the castle, the San Roque, the breaches, the Pardaleras, the distant bastion of San Vincente, and the bridge-head on the other side of the Guadiana were to have been simultaneously assailed, and it was hoped the strength of the enemy would shrivel within that fiery girdle. But many are the disappointments of war. An unforeseen accident delayed the attack of the 5th division, and a lighted carcass thrown from the castle, falling close to the 3rd division, discovered their array and compelled them to anticipate the signal by half an hour. Then, everything being suddenly disturbed, the double columns of the 4th and light divisions also moved silently and swiftly against the breaches, and the guard of the trenches rushing forward with a shout encompassed the San Roque with fire and broke in so violently that scarcely any resistance was made. But a sudden blaze of light and the rattling of musketry indicated the commencement of a more vehement combat at the castle.　There General Kempt — for Picton hurt by a fall in the camp, and expecting no change in the hour, was not present — there Kempt, I say, led the 3rd division.　Having passed the Rivillas in single files by a narrow bridge under a terrible musketry, he had re-formed, and running up a rugged hill, reached the foot of the castle, where he fell severely wounded, and as he was carried back to the trenches met Picton, who was hastening to take the command.

VIMEIRO

　Meanwhile the troops, spreading along the front, had reared their heavy ladders, some against the lofty castle, some against the adjoining front on the left, and with incredible courage ascended amidst showers of heavy stones, logs of wood, and bursting shells rolled off the parapet, while from the flanks the enemy plied his musketry with fearful rapidity, and in front with pikes and bayonets stabbed the leading assailants or pushed the ladders from the walls ; and all this was attended with deafening shouts and the crash of breaking ladders, and the shrieks of crushed soldiers answering to the sullen stroke of the falling weights.　Still swarming round the remaining ladders those undaunted veterans strove who should first climb, until all being overturned, the French shouted victory, and the British, baffled but untamed, fell back a few paces and took shelter under the rugged edge of the hill.　There the broken ranks were somewhat re-formed, and the heroic Ridge, springing forward, seized a ladder, and calling with stentorian voice on his men to follow, once more raised it against the castle, yet to the right of the former attack, where the wall was lower and an embrasure offered some facility.　A second ladder was soon placed alongside of the first by the grenadier officer Canch, and the next instant he and Ridge were on the rampart, the shouting troops pressed after them, the garrison, amazed and in a manner surprised, were driven fighting through the double gate into the town, and the castle was won.　A reinforcement from the French reserve then came up, a sharp action followed, both sides fired through the gate, and the enemy retired; but Ridge fell, and no man died that night with more glory—yet many died, and there was much glory.

All this time the tumult at the breaches was such as if the very earth had been rent asunder and its central fires bursting upwards uncontrolled. The two divisions had reached the glacis just as the firing at the castle commenced, and the flash of a single musket discharged from the covered way as a signal showed them that the French were ready; yet no stir was heard and darkness covered the breaches. Some hay-packs were thrown, some ladders placed, and the forlorn hopes and storming parties of the light division, five hundred in all, descended into the ditch without opposition; but then a bright flame shooting upwards, displayed all the terrors of the scene. The ramparts, crowded with dark figures and glistering arms, were on one side, on the other the red columns of the British, deep and broad, were coming on like streams of burning lava; it was the touch of the magician's wand, for a crash of thunder followed, and with incredible violence the storming parties were dashed to pieces by the explosion of hundreds of shells and powder-barrels.

For an instant the light division stood on the brink of the ditch amazed at the terrific sight, but then with a shout that matched even the sound of the explosion the men flew down the ladders, or disdaining their aid leaped reckless of the depth into the gulf below; and at the same moment, amidst a blaze of musketry that dazzled the eyes, the 4th division came running in and descended with a like fury. There were only five ladders for the two columns which were close together, and a deep cut made in the bottom of the ditch was filled with water from the inundation; into that watery snare the head of the 4th division fell, and it is said above a hundred of the fusiliers, the men of Albuera, were there smothered. Those who followed checked not, but, as if such a disaster had been expected, turned to the left and thus came upon the face of the unfinished ravelin, which being rough and broken was mistaken for the breach and instantly covered with men; yet a wide and deep chasm was still between them and the ramparts, from whence came a deadly fire wasting their ranks. Thus baffled they also commenced a rapid discharge of musketry and disorder ensued. Now a multitude bounded up the great breach as if driven by a whirlwind, but across the top glittered a range of sword-blades, sharp-pointed, keen-edged on both sides, and firmly fixed in ponderous beams chained together and set deep in the ruins; and for ten feet in front the ascent was covered with loose planks studded with sharp iron points, on which feet being set the planks moved and the unhappy soldiers falling forward on the spikes rolled down upon the ranks behind. Then the Frenchmen, shouting at the success of their stratagem and leaping forward, plied their shot with terrible rapidity, for every man had several muskets, and each musket in addition to its ordinary charge contained a small cylinder of wood stuck full of wooden slugs, which scattered like hail when they were discharged. Once and again the assailants rushed up the breaches, but always the sword-blades, immovable and impassable, stopped their charge, and the hissing shells and thundering powder-barrels exploded unceasingly. Hundreds of men had fallen, hundreds more were dropping, still the heroic officers called aloud for new trials, and so furious were the men themselves that in one of these charges the rear sometimes followed by many, sometimes by a few, ascended the ruins; strove to push the foremost on to the sword-blades, willing even to make a bridge of their writhing bodies, but the others frustrated the attempt by dropping down; and men fell so far from the shot, it was hard to know who went down voluntarily, who were stricken ; and many stooped unhurt that never rose again.　Vain also would it have been to break through the sword-blades, for the trench and parapet behind the breach were finished, and the assailants, crowded into even a narrower space than the ditch was, would still have been separated from their enemies and the slaughter would have continued.

Order was impossible !　Officers of all ranks, followed more or less numerously by the men, were seen to start out as if struck by sudden madness and rush into the breach.　Colonel Macleod of the 43rd, a young man whose feeble body would have been quite unfit for war if it had not been sustained by an unconquerable spirit, when one behind him in falling plunged a bayonet into his back, complained not but continuing his course was shot dead within a yard of the sword-blades.　Yet there was no want of gallant leaders or desperate followers, until two hours passed in these vain efforts had convinced the troops the breach of the Trinidad was impregnable.　Gathering in dark groups and leaning on their muskets, they looked up with sullen desperation at the Trinidad ; while the enemy, stepping out on the ramparts and aiming their shots by the light of the fire-balls which they threw over, asked as their victims fell, " Why did they not come into Badajoz ? " In this dreadful situation, while the dead were lying in heaps and others continually falling, the wounded crawling about to get some shelter from the merciless shower above, and withal a sickening stench from the burned flesh of the slain, Captain Nicholas was observed making incredible efforts to force his way with a few men into the Santa Maria bastion ; but when they had gained two-thirds of the ascent a concentrated fire of musketry and grape dashed nearly the whole dead to the earth : Nicholas was mortally wounded and the intrepid Shaw stood alone.　With inexpressible coolness he looked at his watch, and saying it was too late to carry the breaches rejoined the masses at the other attack.　After this no further effort was made at any point, and the troops remained passive but unflinching beneath the enemy's shot which streamed without intermission.

About midnight, when two thousand brave men had fallen, Wellington, who was on a height close to the quarries, ordered the remainder to retire and re-form for a second assault ; he had heard the castle was taken, but, thinking the enemy would still resist in the town, was resolved to assail the breaches again.　This retreat from the ditch was not effected without further carnage and confusion.　All this time the town was girdled with fire. Walker's brigade, having passed on during the feint on the Pardaleras, was escalading the distant bastion of San Vincente.　His troops had advanced along the banks of the river and reached the French guard-house at the barrier-gate undiscovered, the ripple of the waters smothering the sound of their footsteps ; but just then the explosion at the breaches took place, the moon shone out, the French sentinels discovering the columns fired, and the British soldiers springing forward under a sharp musketry began to hew down the wooden barrier at the covered way.　The Portuguese, panic-stricken, threw down the scaling-ladders, the others snatched them up again and forcing the barrier jumped into the ditch ; but the guiding engineer officer was killed, there was a *cunette* which embarrassed the column, and the ladders proved too short, for the walls were generally above thirty feet high. The fire of the enemy was deadly, a small mine was sprung beneath the soldiers' feet, beams of wood and live shells were rolled over on their heads, showers of grape from the flank swept the ditch, and man after man dropped dead from the ladders.

Fortunately some of the defenders had been called away to aid in recovering the castle, the ramparts were not entirely manned ; and the assailants, discovering a corner of the bastion where the scarp was only twenty feet high, placed three ladders there under an embrasure which had no gun and was only stopped with a gabion. Some men got up with difficulty, for the ladders were still too short, and the first man who gained the top was pushed up by his comrades and drew others after him until many had won the summit ; and though the French shot heavily against them from both flanks and from a house in front, their numbers augmented rapidly and half the 4th regiment entered the town itself to dislodge the French from the houses, while the others pushed along the rampart towards the breach and by dint of hard fighting successively won three bastions.

In the last of these combats Walker, leaping forward sword in hand at the moment when one of the enemy's cannoneers was discharging a gun, was covered with so many wounds it was wonderful that he could survive, and some of the soldiers immediately after, perceiving a lighted match on the ground, cried out : " A mine ! " At that word, such is the power of imagination, those troops who had not been stopped by the strong barrier, the deep ditch, the high walls and the deadly fire of the enemy, staggered back appalled by a chimera of their own raising ; and in this disorder a French reserve under General Veillande drove on them with a firm and rapid charge, pitching some men over the walls, killing others outright, and cleansing the ramparts even to the San Vincente. There however Leith had placed Colonel Nugent with a battalion of the 38th as a reserve, and when the French came up, shouting and slaying all before them, this battalion, two hundred strong, arose and with one close volley destroyed them ; then the panic ceased, the soldiers rallied, and in compact order once more charged along the walls towards the breaches ; but the French, although turned on both flanks and abandoned by fortune, did not yet yield.

Meanwhile the portion of the 4th regiment which had entered the town was strangely situated. For the streets were empty and brilliantly illuminated and no person was seen, yet a low buzz and whispers were heard around, lattices were now and then gently opened, and from time to time shots were fired from underneath the doors of the houses by the Spaniards, while the troops with bugles sounding advanced towards the great square of the town. In their progress they captured several mules going with ammunition to the breaches ; yet the square itself was as empty and silent as the streets, and the houses as bright with lamps : a terrible enchantment seemed to be in operation — they saw only an illumination and heard only low whispering around them, while the tumult at the breaches was like the crashing thunder. Plainly, however, the fight was there raging, and hence, quitting the square, they attempted to take the garrison in reverse by attacking the ramparts from the town side ; but they were received with a rolling musketry, driven back with loss, and resumed their movement through the streets. At last the breaches were abandoned by the French, other parties entered, desultory combats took place, Veillande, and Phillipon who was wounded, seeing all ruined, passed the bridge with a few hundred soldiers, and entered San Christoval.

Now commenced that wild and desperate wickedness which tarnished the lustre of the soldiers' heroism. All indeed were not alike, hundreds risked and many lost their lives in striving to stop the violence ; but madness generally prevailed, and as the worst men were leaders here, all the dreadful passions of human nature were displayed. Shameless rapacity, brutal intemperance, savage lust, cruelty and murder, shrieks and piteous lamentations, groans, shouts, imprecations, the hissing of fires bursting from the houses, the crashing of doors and windows, and the reports of muskets used in violence, resounded for two days and nights in the streets of Badajoz! On the third, when the city was sacked, when the soldiers were exhausted by their own excesses, the tumult rather subsided than was quelled: the wounded men were then looked to, the dead disposed of. Five thousand men and officers fell in this siege, and of these, including 700 Portuguese, 3,500 had been stricken in the assault, 60 officers and more than 700 men being slain on the spot. The five generals, Kempt, Harvey, Bowes, Colville, and Picton were wounded, the first four severely; 600 men and officers fell in the escalade of San Vincente, as many at the castle, and more than 2,000 at the breaches, each division there losing 1,200. And how deadly the breach strife was may be gathered from this: the 43rd and 52nd regiments of the light division lost more men than the seven regiments of the 3rd division engaged at the castle.[1]

Let it be considered that this frightful carnage took place in a space of less than a hundred yards square; that the slain died not all suddenly nor by one manner of death—that some perished by steel, some by shot, some by water, that some were crushed and mangled by heavy weights, some trampled upon, some dashed to atoms by the fiery explosions; that for hours this destruction was endured without shrinking, and the town was won at last. Let these things be considered, and it must be admitted a British army bears with it an awful power. And false would it be to say the French were feeble men; the garrison stood and fought manfully and with good discipline, behaving worthily: shame there was none on any side. Yet who shall do justice to the bravery of the British soldiers—the noble emulation of the officers? Who shall measure out the glory of Ridge, of Macleod, of Nicholas, of O'Hare of the 95th, who perished on the breach at the head of the stormers, and with him nearly all the volunteers for that desperate service? Who shall describe the springing valour of that Portuguese grenadier who was killed, the foremost man at the Santa Maria; or the martial fury of that desperate rifleman, who, in his resolution to win, thrust himself beneath the chained sword-blades, and there suffered the enemy to dash his head to pieces with the ends of their muskets? Who can sufficiently honour the intrepidity of Walker, of Shaw, of Canch, or the hardiness of Ferguson of the 43rd, who having in former assaults received two deep wounds was here, his former hurts still open, leading the stormers of his regiment, the third time a volunteer, the third time wounded? Nor would I be understood to select these as pre-eminent; many and signal were the other examples of unbounded

[1 On this triumph the count de Toreño*f* says: "During this siege the French displayed consummate courage and skill; the first was also displayed by the English, but not the latter. This was proved by their losses in the assault of the breaches, and their valour and triumph in the escalade. This was usually the case with them in the besieging of towns. The English treated their foes well, but maltreated the inhabitants of Badajoz. The latter awaited their liberators with impatience, and prepared presents and refreshments for them, not to escape their fury, as certain British historians have asserted, as from allies and friends such conduct was not to be expected, but rather to welcome and gratify them. More than six hundred inhabitants of both sexes were killed by the English. The work of pillage and destruction lasted the whole of the night of the 6th and the following day. The exhortations of their leaders were disregarded, and Lord Wellington himself was threatened by the bayonets of his soldiers, who impeded his entrance into the fortress to check the disorder. Order was re-established the following day with troops purposely brought from without. Nevertheless the cortes presented thanks to the English general, not wishing that the excesses of the soldiers should in any way detract from the advantages resulting from the reconquest of Badajoz. The regency conferred upon Wellington the grand cross of San Fernando."]

devotion, some known, some that will never be known; for in such a tumult much passes unobserved, and often the observers fell themselves ere they could bear testimony to what they saw : but no age, no nation ever sent forth braver troops to battle than those who stormed Badajoz. When the extent of the night's havoc was made known to Lord Wellington, the firmness of his nature gave way for a moment, and the pride of conquest yielded to a passionate burst of grief for the loss of his gallant soldiers.*b*

BRITISH PROGRESS

One result of this triumph was the immediate and final retreat of the French from Estremadura and Portugal. Marmont raised the blockade of Ciudad Rodrigo, and fell back to Salamanca.

In Spain, the native leaders meanwhile continued their desultory warfare; Lacy, Sarsfield, Rovira, Mina, and Porlier in the north, the Empecinado and Sanchez in the Castiles, and Ballasteros in the south, gained trifling advantages over the enemy in divers engagements; but for want of concert no material result was obtained from their successes, whilst Suchet made himself master of the whole kingdom of Valencia, with the single exception of Alicante. In Tarifa, a town defended only by an old wall, eighteen hundred English and Spanish troops, commanded by Colonel Skerrett, repulsed ten thousand French led by the duke of Belluno in person.[1]

Meanwhile General Hill had driven the French from Almaraz upon the Tagus, and thus obtained possession of the only place through which the enemy's armies of Portugal and of the south could conveniently keep up their communication across the river. The earl of Wellington then advanced towards Salamanca on the 13th of June, 1812. He there, despite the efforts of Marmont, reduced several very strong forts. Marmont retreated to the Douro. A series of masterly manœuvres ensued, in which, during six days, the contending generals displayed all the resources of their art. The advantage in this pure trial of skill remained with the Briton, who, on the 22nd of July, seizing upon a rash movement of Marmont's, instantly attacked him, and gained the splendid victory of Salamanca, in which the French lost seven thousand prisoners, at least as many killed and wounded, including three generals killed and four wounded, amongst whom was Marmont himself, eleven pieces of artillery, and two eagles. The loss of the allies amounted to fifty-two hundred killed and wounded, the former including one general, the latter five.

Clausel, who upon Marmont's being disabled, succeeded to the command, rallied the routed army, and retreated to Burgos. Wellington pursued him as far as Valladolid, and then turning southwards, marched upon Madrid. Joseph had not above twenty thousand men for the defence of his capital; he abandoned it at the approach of the allies; but weakened himself by leaving a garrison of two thousand men in a fortress adjoining the palace of Buen Retiro. They capitulated on the approach of the British. Lord Wellington entered Madrid on the 12th of August, and was received with every demonstration as the deliverer of Spain. The new constitution was proclaimed in the capital, and sworn to with eager zeal. And now the

[1 Though Skerrett was covered with honours for this victory, Napier *b* shows that he was forced by certain officers to defend the place against his will, and that his mistakes even then were only overcome by Captains Smith and Mitchell. He sets the numbers of the garrison at twenty-five hundred ; the number of French was variously rated between five and ten thousand.]

exploits and services of the British general had at length so far conquered Spanish jealousy that the cortes named the duke commander-in-chief of the Spanish forces.

Soult raised the blockade of Cadiz on the 25th, and united with Suchet. He left, however, a garrison in Seville, which fell into the hands of the English and Spanish troops on the 27th. Joseph, on the advance of Hill, retreated in the same direction, and Andalusia was again freed from the presence of the invaders. But the position of Lord Wellington at Madrid, which had already produced most of the expected advantages, was becoming dangerous. He was disappointed of the diversions upon which he had relied. Maitland's army proved too weak, amounting only to six thousand men, to attempt a landing in Catalonia. It was therefore directed to Alicant, where the Anglo-Sicilian army necessarily remained in garrison. Wellington quitted

SEGOVIA

Madrid on the 1st of September, to march against Burgos, leaving half his army under Hill to observe Soult, and if possible defend Madrid. The English troops that had garrisoned Cadiz now joined the army.

The French retreated as the allies advanced. On the 19th, Lord Wellington occupied Burgos, and laid siege to the castle. Here the deficiency of means proved more detrimental than ever, rendering it impossible to conquer the science and courage displayed in the defence, or to prevent the approach of Souham with all the disposable French force in the north of Spain. Lord Wellington, on the 22nd of October, judged it expedient to raise the siege, and take up his winter quarters on the Portuguese frontier. About the same time, Joseph and Soult advancing upon Madrid, Hill in obedience to his instructions, retreated to Salamanca, where, on the 3rd of November, he joined Lord Wellington. On the 24th, the troops went into cantonments along the frontier line, headquarters being fixed at Freynada. It is mortifying to be compelled to add that, leisurely as was this retreat, and untroubled by aught save very wet weather, the troops, dispirited by their failure before Burgos, discovered much of the disorder and insubordination that had marked Sir John Moore's retreat to Corunna.[c]

NAPIER'S ACCOUNT OF THE RETREAT

Drunkenness and insubordination were exhibited at Torquemada, where the great wine-vaults were invaded, and twelve thousand men were at one time in a state of helpless inebriety. The negligence of many medical and escorting officers conducting the convoys of the sick, and the consequent bad conduct of the soldiers (for where the officers are careless the soldiers will be licentious) produced the worst effects. Outrages were perpetrated on the inhabitants along the whole line of march, terror was everywhere predominant, the ill-used drivers and muleteers deserted, some with, some without their cattle. The commissariat lost nearly all the animals and carriages employed, the villages were abandoned, and the under-commissaries were bewildered or paralysed by the terrible disorder thus spread along the line.

The rest of the retreat being unmolested was made with more regularity, but the excesses still committed furnished glaring evidence that the moral conduct of a general cannot be fairly judged by following in the wake of a retreating army. There was no want of provisions, no hardships to exasperate the men, and yet the author of this history counted on the first day's march from Madrid seventeen bodies of murdered peasants ; by whom killed, or for what, whether by English or Germans, by Spaniards, or Portuguese, in dispute, in robbery, or in wanton villany was unknown ; but their bodies were in the ditches, and a shallow observer might thence have drawn foul and false conclusions against the English general and nation. The Spaniards, civil and military, evinced hatred of the British. Daily did they attempt or perpetrate murder. The civil authorities, not less savage, were more insolent than the military, treating every British person with an intolerable arrogance. The whole loss of the double retreat cannot be set down at less than nine thousand, including the loss in the siege.

When the campaign terminated, Wellington, exasperated by the conduct of the army and the many crossings he had experienced during the campaign, gave vent to his indignation in a circular letter addressed to the superior officers. In substance it declared that discipline had deteriorated during the campaign in a greater degree than he had ever witnessed or ever read of in any army, and this without any disaster, any unusual privation or hardship save that of inclement weather ; that the officers had lost all command over their men, and excesses, outrages of all kinds and inexcusable losses had occurred ; that no army had ever made shorter marches in retreat or had longer rests — no army had ever been so little pressed by a pursuing enemy ; and this unhappy state of affairs was to be traced to the habitual neglect of duty by the regimental officers.[b]

AFFAIRS OF 1812–1813

The year 1812 saw everywhere the beginning of the reverses which overthrew the colossal empire of Bonaparte. There was nothing to counterbalance the exultation excited in Spain by these frightful reverses of her unrelenting foe, except the continuance of the dissensions with the colonies. The prince of Brazil, who had previously created Lord Wellington count of Vimeiro and marquis of Torres Vedras, now conferred upon him the title of duke of Victoria, in commemoration of his many victories; and it might also have seemed in anticipation of the most decisive of his peninsular battles. The allied armies were now, for the first time, about to take the field under favourable circumstances; and he, whose genius had hitherto been severely tried in contending with and surmounting every species of obstacle, might hope to pursue that more dazzling career of glory which silences the cavils of envy and of ignorance. The resources of the peninsula, such as they were, were placed at his disposal. What was of more consequence, the French emperor, instead of constantly pouring reinforcements into Spain in numbers that almost seemed to render Lord Wellington's victories barren triumphs, was compelled to withdraw thence many troops. Soult, with thirty thousand veterans, was recalled from Spain.

The complicated arrangements requisite to bring so variously composed an army into activity, delayed Lord Wellington's opening the campaign until the middle of May; when he took the field at the head of nearly seventy thousand men, English and Portuguese, independently of the Spanish army of Galicia under Castaños on his left, and another on his right under Don Carlos de España. The French had still 160,000 men in Spain; and as many of these as were not engaged in the eastern provinces under Suchet, or employed in garrison duty, were stationed around Madrid and between the capital and the Douro.

Lord Wellington ordered General Murray to remove his troops by sea to Catalonia, in order both to relieve Valencia by drawing Suchet northwards, and to be nearer the scene of the principal operations, and sent Sir Thomas Graham, with the left wing of the army, to cross the Douro within the limits of Portugal, and thus turn a perhaps impregnable position, whilst he himself with the centre, and Sir Rowland Hill with the right, advanced towards it in front, driving before them all detachments from the army of Portugal, as it was still termed, that were stationed south of the Douro. The manœuvre seems to have confounded the enemy. The army of Portugal retreated. Joseph and Jourdan collected the army of the centre, and evacuating Madrid, hastened to join the army of Portugal near Burgos. Joseph fell back to Vitoria, the principal depot of the French in the northern provinces; there he halted, drew up his army in battle array, and prepared to make a last struggle for his crown. It is said that the French occupied the very ground on which, in the fourteenth century, the Black Prince had defeated Du Guesclin and recovered the Castilian crown for Don Pedro.

Lord Wellington on the 21st of June, 1813, attacked. The Spaniards fought with a courage that proved their former panics and failures to have been mainly attributable to want of confidence in their commanders and their comrades. The French wings were first assailed and driven back. Then, when their formidably posted centre had been weakened to support the wings, and was, besides, threatened on the flanks, that too was assailed and carried. The French had never before been so utterly routed. The whole army dispersed and fled; Joseph narrowly escaped being taken prisoner; artillery, baggage, everything upon which the existence of an army depends fell into the hands of the victors, as well as the wives of many of the French superior officers, and the marshal's staff of Jourdan. The victory was actively followed up; most of the French garrisons were taken, or surrendered upon being summoned; the remaining French detachments, by a series of nearly bloodless manœuvres, were driven across the Pyrenees; and by the 7th of July no part of Joseph's army remained in Spain except the garrisons of Pamplona and San Sebastian.

Suchet's was now the only French army in Spain, and his force remained unbroken in the eastern provinces, opposed to Sir John Murray. That general was conveyed with his troops by a British fleet from Alicante to the

Catalan coast, and landing, on the 3rd of June, near Tarragona, immediately invested that town. He had made little progress with the siege when Suchet's advance from Valencia was announced. Murray re-embarked his troops with such precipitation, although Suchet was some marches distant, that he left his artillery and stores behind. But the news of the battle of Vitoria and its consequences determined Suchet to abandon that province and concentrate his troops in Catalonia. Aragon was freed, and Mina had the gratification of recovering the heroic Saragossa from her conquerors.

When Napoleon received the tidings of the battle of Vitoria and its disastrous results to his brother's hopes, he sent back Soult to resume the command from which he had taken him; to collect reinforcements, re-organise the fugitive army, raise the sieges of Pamplona and San Sebastian, and, in conjunction with Suchet, drive the British out of Spain. To enable him to effect these objects, he named him imperial lieutenant in Spain, giving him authority far beyond what had ever before been intrusted to any marshal. Soult took the field at the head of nearly one hundred thousand men, endeavouring to break through the extremity of the British line, in order to relieve Pamplona. The French marshal's first measures seemed to promise him success. On the 25th of July, 1813, with about fifty thousand men, he attacked two separate posts held by divisions of the right wing under Sir Rowland Hill. The allies fought obstinately, but were obliged to give way. On the 26th Lord Wellington arrived on the scene of action, immediately resolving to give battle for the protection of the blockade of Pamplona. The French were defeated in two successive engagements on the 30th and 31st, after which Soult retreated into France. On the 1st of August the allied troops resumed their former positions amidst the Pyrenees.

The two sieges proceeded; but the provisions in Pamplona still held out: the fortifications of San Sebastian were admirable, the approaches difficult, and the garrison defended itself pertinaciously. When the town was taken (August 31), the siege, and especially the assault, had cost great numbers of lives—nearly four thousand; and the troops, infuriated by the loss of their comrades and their own danger, could not be restrained by the few surviving officers of the storming party, or even taught to discriminate between friends and foes, Spaniards and French. Greater outrages are said to have been committed upon the inhabitants of San Sebastian than in any other town taken by the allies; and it was longer ere the generals could restore order.[1]

[1 Napier *b* says: "San Sebastian, a third-rate fortress and in bad condition when invested, resisted a besieging army possessing an enormous battering train, for sixty-three days. The place was, in fact, won by accident — the ignition of the French powder-barrels and shells, which alone opened the way into the town." Of the sad atrocities committed by the British troops, Napier goes on to say:

"A thunderstorm, coming down from the mountains with unbounded fury immediately after the place was carried, added to the confusion of the fight. This storm seemed to be a signal from hell for the perpetration of villany which would have shamed the most ferocious barbarians of antiquity. At Rodrigo intoxication and plunder had been the principal object; at Badajoz lust and murder were joined to rapine and drunkenness; but at San Sebastian, the direst, the most revolting cruelty was added to the catalogue of crimes. One atrocity of which a girl of seventeen was the victim staggers the mind by its enormous, incredible, indescribable barbarity. The resolution of the troops to throw off discipline was quickly made manifest. A British staff officer was pursued with a volley of small arms and escaped with difficulty from men who mistook him for the provost-marshal of the 5th division; a Portuguese adjutant who endeavoured to prevent some wickedness was put to death in the market-place, not with sudden violence from a single ruffian, but deliberately by a number of English soldiers; and though many officers exerted themselves to preserve order and many men were well conducted, the rapine and violence commenced by villains spread; the camp-follower soon crowded into the place, and the disorder continued until the flames, following the steps of the plunderer, put an end to his ferocity by destroying the whole town."]

The surrender of Pamplona set the allied forces at liberty, and Lord Wellington immediately determined to advance into France, leaving Suchet and his corps to the care of the Catalans, assisted by the Anglo-Sicilian army. In beginning his operations upon the enemy's territory, one of the first cares of the British commander was to repress the ferociously vindictive temper of his Spanish and Portuguese troops, who longed to retaliate upon the French nation the injuries and outrages they had suffered from the French soldiery. At first it was found impossible altogether to control this disposition, in which the native officers but too much sympathised with their men. But the firmness and severity with which such offences were punished soon introduced a better temper.

On the 10th of November, 1813, Soult's line of defence was attacked, and notwithstanding the great pains bestowed upon strengthening it, was forced; fifteen hundred prisoners and fifty guns fell into the victor's hands, besides quantities of stores. On the 9th of December hostilities were renewed. The allied armies drove the French back into the intrenched camp they had prepared close to Bayonne, and Soult, by attacking, after five days of almost incessant fighting, in which the loss was necessarily great (five thousand of the allies, and far more of the French were killed or wounded), retreated into his intrenched camp. The weather was still very severe, and Lord Wellington therefore again cantoned his troops, but upon a more advanced line, and both armies passed the remainder of the month in repose.

Whilst Lord Wellington, with those forces, for whom, as for their leader, Napoleon had professed such superlative disdain, was thus penetrating into France, the situation of the French emperor had undergone many changes. It was at Leipsic, October 16th, 1813, that the battle, fatal to his hopes of maintaining his sovereignty over Germany, was fought. Every German state, including the whole Confederation of the Rhine, had now thrown off allegiance to Napoleon. The allied sovereigns advanced to the banks of the Rhine. There they halted for the remainder of the year, satisfied with their achievements, and willing to give Napoleon, whom they still feared, an opportunity for negotiation. Wellington and his army alone, of the hostile forces, wintered in France.

RETURN OF THE BOURBONS

Napoleon saw that to recover all he had lost, or even to keep all he yet retained, was, for the moment at least, impossible; and he resolved to relax his grasp in that quarter, where renunciation of his now vain pretensions need not induce the abandonment of real power. He opened a negotiation with the prince to whom, as he believed, he could still dictate the terms of the treaty to be concluded — namely, the captive of Valençay, Ferdinand VII.

Since the seizure of the Spanish royal family at Bayonne, they had pretty much vanished from public view. The old king and queen, with their favourite, Godoy, had been transferred to Rome, where they vegetated contentedly upon the ample pension assigned them. The queen of Etruria, whose feelings appear to have been somewhat livelier than those of her kindred, had incurred Napoleon's anger by an abortive attempt at escaping to England, and was strictly immured in a convent at Rome, with her daughter; her son, the dethroned king, being taken from her, and committed to the care of her parents. Ferdinand remained at Valençay. He had written a letter of congratulation to Joseph Bonaparte upon his accession to the Spanish throne. He repeatedly addressed to Napoleon congratulations on his victories. When a scheme for his liberation was devised by the British cabinet — partly through compassion but chiefly under an idea that the presence of an acknowledged king would put an end to the factions and jealousies that distracted the Spanish councils, thwarted Lord Wellington's designs, and impeded his progress — Ferdinand not only refused to escape, but denounced the attempt to Napoleon, and took the opportunity to renew his often rejected request that he might be adopted into the imperial family, by receiving the hand of a Bonaparte princess. He was further said to employ his time in embroidering a robe for some image of the Virgin. But the stories were regarded as calumnious inventions, propagated for the purpose of lowering Ferdinand's character in general estimation; and the imprisoned king remained as before an object of loyal veneration, of esteem, and pity.

Immediately on reaching Paris, after his calamitous retreat from Leipsic, Napoleon addressed a letter to Ferdinand, telling him that England was endeavouring to overthrow the monarchy and nobility of Spain, in order to establish a republic in that country, and offering him his liberty, together with the alliance of France, that he might return to Spain, and put an end to the disorders now convulsing the kingdom and further menacing it. After a little delay and negotiation Ferdinand yielded. On the 11th of December, 1813, a treaty was signed at Valençay, by which he was recognised as king of Spain and the Indies, all old treaties and alliances between France and Spain were revived and confirmed, and Ferdinand undertook for the immediate evacuation of Spain and her dependencies by the English. Even this treaty, however, Ferdinand referred to the approbation and sanction of the regency and the cortes; and San Carlos was despatched with a copy of it to Madrid, whither the seat of government was now transferred from Cadiz.

On the 8th of January, 1814, the regency through its president, the cardinal de Bourbon, addressed a respectful answer to the king, in which they assured him of their joy at the prospect of his majesty's approaching liberation, but returned the treaty unratified, and transmitted copies of the law, and of the treaty with England, which prevented its ratification.

Towards the middle of February, 1814, the weather improved, and Lord Wellington drew his troops from their cantonments. By a series of able manœuvres, and of engagements ending with the well-contested and brilliant victory of Orthez, gained on the 27th of February, he drove Soult successively from post to post, through a country of peculiar difficulty, and abounding in strong defensive positions, of which the French marshal skilfully endeavoured to avail himself, but was uniformly foiled by the superior skill of his British competitor. Sir John Hope lay before Bayonne with the left wing. By the help of an English squadron, under Admiral Penrose, the close investment of Bayonne laid open the direct road to Bordeaux, and on the 8th of March Wellington sent Beresford with fifteen thousand men to make himself master of that town. Beresford was accompanied by the duke of Angoulême, as a royalist party with the mayor at their head were well known to be anxiously expecting the prince. The French garrison evacuated the town as the allied troops approached, and the inhabitants, assuming the white cockade, and receiving the prince with enthusiastic loyalty, proclaimed Louis XVIII. Lord Wellington, recalling Beresford, commenced his operations against Soult. On the 18th they began their movement up the Adour, the French retiring before them. On the 19th,

Soult was driven from Vic-en-Bigorre, and on the 20th from Tarbes, when he retreated upon Toulouse.

Whilst Ferdinand's allies and subjects were thus progressively triumphing over his oppressor, the captive prince had regained his liberty. Napoleon, finding that no treaty concluded with the king of Spain, whilst his prisoner, would be acknowledged by the nation as valid, on the 14th of March released him unconditionally, as the only remaining chance of detaching Spain from England, and recovering his former influence over that country. Ferdinand was conducted to Perpignan, and there, on the 19th of March, delivered over to the care of Suchet, who was to make arrangements, under the royal guarantee, for the safe return of the different French garrisons, spread over the eastern coast of Spain, to his army, upon their surrendering to the king the fortresses they still held. Ferdinand, on the 24th, was received by Copons and throngs of his native subjects, who had flocked from every place within reach, to greet the return of their beloved sovereign. Ferdinand's signature having, however, by the then law of the land, no authority until he should have taken the oath prescribed by the constitution, Suchet's object was unattained. The surrender of the fortresses, and the safe passage of the garrisons still remained to be negotiated betwixt him and Copons; and before they had brought it to a conclusion, the progress of events in France rendered all arrangements of the kind unnecessary.

Lord Wellington had not allowed Soult time to receive the accession of strength he expected from the result of Suchet's negotiations. He followed him to Toulouse, forced the passage of the Garonne, and on the 10th of April, 1814, under the walls of the city, gained the last victory of this war, in the battle of Toulouse. Soult retired into the town, which, upon Wellington's preparing to invest it, he evacuated on the night of the 12th, the allied army permitting him to withdraw unmolested. The next day they took possession of the city, where they were received with every demonstration of joy, and the inhabitants proclaimed Louis XVIII. It was the last occasion upon which the act could have the grace of a spontaneous impulse of the people.

The allied armies appeared before the French capital. Maria Louisa, with her son, and the ministry, had fled to Blois. Joseph followed the empress, and Paris capitulated. On the 31st of March Alexander and Frederick William had entered the city at the head of their troops. Napoleon gave way; and abdicated unconditionally. The title and rank of emperor were, in return, confirmed to him, although his empire was limited to the tiny island of Elba. The Bourbons were now restored to their long lost throne; and peace was re-established throughout Europe. Lord Wellington, like the rest of the allies, now of course evacuated the French territory and dissolved his mixed army, the British, Spanish, and Portuguese.c

ENGLAND'S SHARE IN THE WAR

Napoleon's enormous armies had been so wonderfully organised that they existed and fought in Spain for six years, and without cessation; for to them winters and summers were alike; they endured incredible toils and priva tions, yet were not starved out, nor were their small armies beaten by th Spaniards. And for their daring and resource a single fact recorded b Wellington will suffice. They captured more than one strong place i Spain without any provision of bullets save those fired at them by the enemies, having trusted to that chance when they formed the siege ! Before the British troops they fell ; but how horrible was the struggle, how many defeats they recovered from, how many brave men they slew ; what changes and interpositions of fortune occurred before they could be rolled back upon their own frontiers ! And this is the glory of England, that her soldiers and hers only were capable of overthrowing them in equal battle. What battle except Baylen did the peninsulars win ? What fortress did they take by siege ? What place defend ? Sir Arthur Wellesley twice delivered Portugal. Sir John Moore's march to Sahagun saved Andalusia and Lisbon from invasion at a critical moment. Sir Arthur's march to Talavera delivered Galicia. Graham saved Cadiz. Smith saved Tarifa. Wellington recaptured Ciudad and Badajoz, rescued Andalusia from Soult and Valencia from Suchet ; the Anglo-Sicilian army preserved Alicante, and finally recovered Tarragona and Barcelona under the influence of the northern operations, which at the same time reduced Pamplona and San Sebastian. England indeed could not alone have triumphed in the struggle, but for her share let this brief summary speak:

She expended more than £100,000,000 [$500,000,000] on her own operations, she subsidised both Spain and Portugal, and with her supplies of clothing, arms, and ammunition maintained the armies of each, even to the guerillas. From thirty up to seventy thousand British troops were employed by her ; and while her naval squadrons harassed the French with descents upon the coasts, and supplied the Spaniards with arms and stores and money after every defeat, her land-forces fought and won nineteen pitched battles and innumerable combats, made or sustained ten sieges, took four great fortresses, twice expelled the French from Portugal, preserved Alicante, Cartagena, Tarifa, Cadiz, Lisbon ; they killed, wounded, and took two hundred thousand enemies. And the bones of forty thousand British soldiers lie scattered on the plains and mountains of the peninsula. For Portugal she re-organised a native army and supplied officers who led it to victory ; and to the whole peninsula she gave a general whose like has seldom gone forth to conquer. And all this and more was necessary to redeem that land from France !

NAPIER'S ESTIMATE OF WELLINGTON

Wellington met the peculiar difficulties which attend generals controlled by politicians. An English commander dare not risk much, when one disaster will be his ruin at home ; his measures must be subordinate to his primary consideration. Wellington's caution, springing from that source, had led friends and foes alike into wrong conclusions as to his system of war: the French call it want of enterprise, timidity ; the English have denominated it the Fabian system. These are mere phrases. His system was the same as that of all great generals. He held his army in hand, keeping it with unmitigated labour always in a fit state to march or to fight, and acted indifferently as occasion offered on the offensive or defensive, displaying in both a complete mastery of his art. That he was less vast in his designs, less daring in execution, neither so rapid nor so original a commander as Napoleon, must be admitted ; and being later in the field of glory it is presumed he learned something of the art from the greatest of all masters. Yet something besides the difference of genius must be allowed for the difference of situation ; Napoleon was never, even in his first campaign of Italy, so harassed by the French as Wellington was by the English, Spanish, and Portuguese governments ; their systems of war were however alike in principle, their operations being only modified by their different political positions. Great bodily exertion, unceasing watchfulness, exact combinations to protect their flanks and communications without scattering their forces — these were common to both ; in defence firm, cool, enduring, in attack fierce and obstinate ; daring when daring was politic, yet always operating by the flanks in preference to the front ; in these things they were alike : in following up a victory the English general fell short of the French emperor. The battle of Wellington was the stroke of a battering-ram — down went the wall in ruins ; the battle of Napoleon was the swell and dash of a mighty wave before which the barrier yielded and the roaring flood poured onwards covering all.

But there was nothing of timidity or natural want of enterprise to be discerned in the English general's campaigns. Neither was he of the Fabian school. He recommended that commander's system to the Spaniards, he did not follow it himself; his military policy more resembled that of Scipio Africanus. Wellington was never loath to fight when there was any equality of numbers. Slight therefore is the resemblance to the Fabian warfare. And for the Englishman's hardiness and enterprise, bear witness the passage of the Douro at Oporto, the capture of Ciudad Rodrigo, the storming of Badajoz, the surprise of the forts at Mirabete, the march to Vitoria, the passage of the Bidassoa, the victory of the Nivelle, the passage of the Adour below Bayonne, the fight of Orthez, the crowning battle of Toulouse ! To say that he committed faults is only to say that he made war ; to deny him the qualities of a great commander is to rail against the clear midday sun for want of light. Iron hardihood of body, a quick and sure vision, a grasping mind, untiring power of thought, and the habit of laborious minute investigation and arrangement — all these qualities he possessed, and with them that most rare faculty of coming to prompt and sure conclusions on sudden emergencies. This is the certain mark of a master-spirit in war.[b]

CHAPTER XIV

THE RESTORATION OF THE BOURBONS

[1814–1902 A.D.]

ON the 7th of March, 1814, Ferdinand VII definitely received his passports from the French. Master of himself once more, he began to think of means of returning to the capital and recovering his former power. But, at the same time, he resolved to avoid doing anything that would seem to sanction modifications accomplished by the cortes, regarding such as an attack on his sovereign power. To enter Spain without making any promise at all was the essential point. The king's counsellors proposed he should send a king's messenger to Madrid bearing a letter carefully flattering the hopes of the Liberal party without undertaking to fulfil the slightest engagement with regard to it. Ferdinand acted on this advice, and charged General Zayas to bear to Madrid the news of his immediate return, and to give the regency a letter wherein were these ambiguous words:

"As to the re-establishment of the cortes and all they have been able to do of use for the kingdom during my absence, my approbation will be given in so far as it all conforms to my royal intentions."

The general set out for Madrid with this letter and hastened to arrive thither, where his coming produced the liveliest enthusiasm. The cortes affected to see in the message a pledge for the political future of their sovereign, and abstained thenceforth from those energetic measures alone able to save them. While they thus lulled themselves in fancied security, Ferdinand had hastened to gain the Spanish frontier by Toulouse and Perpignan. On the 24th of March he crossed the Fluvia, limit chosen by Marshal Suchet as the theatre which was to see the solemn restoration of the royal captive to the Spanish troops. The ceremony was carried out amid general enthusiasm, and all the people eagerly ran to assist at such a novel spectacle.

From this moment, Ferdinand, reinstated in his kingly prerogatives, found himself under a double influence, one drawing him to the representative system, the other towards that absolute monarchy which best suited his desires and tastes. In all the towns he went through, and particularly in Gerona where he had stayed some days, a people mad with joy, drunk with enthusiasm, had cast themselves at his feet, had dragged his carriage, and given most striking testimony of obedience and submission.[1]

Sure now of the destiny awaiting him, he decided to abandon the route fixed by the decree of the 2nd of February.

During this triumphal journey (24th of March to the 6th of April), the gravest events had taken place in France, and one may conceive that Ferdinand, before attempting his *coup d'état*, did not want to get too far away from the frontier, at any rate while the issues were doubtful. Certain events were very favourable: the entry of the allies into Paris; the creation of a provisionary government; Napoleon's abdication, and departure for Elba; and lastly the proclamation of Louis XVIII, which should lead to the suppression of hostilities and the end of the war.

The Aragonese were just as unbridled as the Catalans in expressing monarchial fanaticism. So while the authorities remained faithful to the regency, the people showed such enthusiasm for the king that he could no longer doubt for an instant that he could now venture all. Old courtiers, interested in seeing the ancient court restored, constantly urged him to retake absolute authority.

Yet, while the storm was slowly gathering that would sweep them away, the cortes, always dominated by a perfectly unjustified feeling of confidence, never ceased publishing decrees which served to feed the general enthusiasm in the king's favour. The weak royalist minority which still existed in their midst had ceased to make common cause with them. Its leader, Mozo de Rosales, had gone to Valencia carrying a representation in which the events of the past six years were considered as a passing saturnalia, similar to those which the Persians used to celebrate during an interregnum, and which put forth that order would only reign in Spain from that day when kingly authority should be reinstated in its integrity. Whilst the cortes waited with lively impatience to know their fate, they celebrated the fête of the 2nd of May with great pomp; ascribed several civic rewards to soldiers who had bravely fought in the war of Independence; transferred the seat of their meetings from the theatre of Los Canos del Peral to the convent of Doña Maria of Aragon; and decreed a death sentence against anyone demanding constitutional reform before eight years. Such were the acts of the cortes. The cardinal De Bourbon, president of the regency council, accompanied by the minister of state, Don Josè Luyando, was to present himself before the monarch, and a commission, presided over by the Bishop of Urgel, was to go on in front of him as far as La Mancha plains.

Ferdinand arrived the 16th of April on the borders of Turia. There he found everything had been prepared by the care of his uncle Don Antonio, De Macanaz, and Escoiquiz, to whom were united Villamil and Lardizabal, whose reverses at Cadiz had filled them with bitterness and spite against the representative system. The highest aristocrats came to Ferdinand offering him riches enough to enable him to act without the concourse of the cortes. General Elio, betraying his first duty and oblivious of obedience owing to

[1 Hume c vividly describes this royal progress: "Through the stark and ruined country he went; the emaciated and famished inhabitants, hardly one of whom but had some dear one killed in the war, filled to overflowing with love and hope of better times under the sway of their new king. They had suffered so much for him; he was young and had suffered too, they said, in his exile: surely he would be good to them, make bread cheap, and heal their bleeding wounds. Most of the towns on the way had changed the name of their great square from Plaza Mayor to 'Plaza de la Constitucion'; and the marble slabs bearing the latter inscription were now torn down and splintered, and the thoughtless mob, little knowing or caring what it all meant, shouted themselves hoarse with cries of 'Death to liberty and the Constitution!' and 'Long live Ferdinand!'" c The amazing cry of "Hurrah for chains!" was also heard.]

the regency, promised the strongest assistance from all his army corps. A special paper, entitled *Lucindo*, boldly advocated a return to the old régime. The time had come to act in a decisive manner. Ferdinand applied himself to the work. In receiving the cardinal De Bourbon he affected to give him his hand to make him kiss it in sign of homage, as if to show that the regency was nothing but an emanation from his own authority. In the same fashion he received the commander's bâton which the latter presented before the troops, as if by this to teach the soldiers that obedience was due to himself alone. He received representatives from the Persians with cordiality.[1] He made a cavalry corps precede him commanded by Don Santiago Wittingham, to Madrid, and then received a solemn oath from all the officers to "support him in all his rights."

FERDINAND VII

Such symptoms were decisive, and, once made public, he had only to exercise the direct absolute authority which he had just seized. This is exactly what happened. The king signed on the 4th of May at Valencia the famous manifesto now so mournfully celebrated. In this he stated that not only did he refuse to swear to the constitution or to recognise any decree extraordinary or ordinary, but he declared that constitution annulled, of no value either to-day or forever, as its acts had never been nor could be effaced by time. Then, without making known his absolutist programme, he marched straight on Madrid with General Elio, having given orders to the cardinal De Bourbon and Luyando to retire, the one on Toledo, the other on Cartagena.

It seemed impossible that the arrival of General Wittingham almost under the walls of Madrid should not open the deputies' eyes as to Ferdinand's intentions; nevertheless, they took no measures for their personal security. The execution of the Valencia decree had been confided to General Eguia, nominated captain in general of New Castile, and known under the name of Coletilla because of his attachment to old costumes and his habit of wearing his hair in a plait at the back of his head as in Charles III's time. Eguia, who was commander-in-chief of Elio's first division of troops, and who only preceded the king by some days, was supported by Wittingham's cavalry and the underhand movements of the count of Montijo, who had raised the slums of Madrid against those favourable to the representative system. Under these circumstances he had not any difficulty in executing the *coup d'état* with which he had been intrusted. Thus, while Ferdinand pursued

---

[1] The name Persians was given to the *servile* deputies who had signed the memorial in which the period from 1608 to 1814 was compared to the old Persian saturnalia of crime which accompanied a change of rulers.

his triumphal march from Valencia to Madrid in the midst of a joy and enthusiasm officially worked up, midst subversive cries around him for the suppression of the constitution and re-establishment of absolutism, while he refused to see the cortes' deputation who came before him at La Mancha, all vestiges of the preceding system were being carefully destroyed in the city. A terrible persecution fell on all the men who had helped in establishing the constitutional system.

In the one night of the 10th of May, 1814,—a day so celebrated in the annals of the Spanish liberals,— Eguia took from their houses and imprisoned all regency members, all state councillors, all deputies who were known as partisans to the constitution whether in the actual cortes or the preceding one. Of this number were the two regents Don Pedro Agar and Don Gabriel Ciscar, the ministers Don Juan Alvarez Guerra and Don Manuel Garcia Herreros, the constituents Muñoz Torrero, Arguelles, Oliveros, Villanueva, the deputies Martinez de la Rosa, Canga-Arguelles, and Cepero. Some had the good luck to escape, among these Toreño and Isturiz. As to the others, they were surprised in their homes. So unexpected was such a ruse in the then circumstances of the country, that no one had dreamed of taking the slightest precautions. The day after their arrestation they were constantly exposed to the insults of the multitude who reproduced in Spain all the excesses of that blind reaction in the south of France. The Madrid populace, after having torn away the corner-stone of the constitution, went in tumultuous procession to the quiet street where the prisoners were shut up, and there shouting "Death to the liberals!" they begged with frightful cries permission to drag the corpses in the mud as they had dragged the stone of the constitution.

This tumult was the work of the count of Montijo and several monks who, seeing the star of their ascendency reappear in the horizon — an ascendency lost for six years — had, at the same time as the Valencia decree was proclaimed in all the squares, circulated a scandalous leaflet having for the object an organised proscription and the raising of the masses against all partisans of the liberal system. Thus the 13th of May, 1814, saw Ferdinand's triumphal entry into his capital. He had already given his reign the distinctive character that marks it out in history : an obstinate return to old ideas ; a cruel proscription against all the men devoted to culture and intelligence and gifted with liberal aspiration ; a stirring up of the masses by a recrudescence of religious fanaticism ; an exaltation of monarchical principle pushed as far as absolutism, and a near re-establishing of the Inquisition, convents, favouritism, and all their fatal consequences.[b]

The great mass of the people, who were not enlightened enough to feel the want, or appreciate the blessings, of political liberty, had not sufficient experience of the benefits which the new institutions were calculated to confer to have conceived any value for them ; and the troops, who, from their intercourse with the English army, might have learned some respect for liberty and equal laws, were hostile to the cortes on account of the neglect and injustice with which they had frequently been treated.

Ferdinand proceeded to acts for which no palliation can be found, namely, inflicting punishments upon those who had defended his cause when he himself had abandoned it, but had, in his opinion, forfeited all claim to his gratitude, by seeking to limit the power they preserved for him. Fortunately, however, Sir Henry Wellesley extorted from the king a solemn promise that no blood should be shed for political opinions. No lives therefore were taken. But the cardinal De Bourbon was banished to Rome. The only symptom of gratitude shown by Ferdinand to those who had so zeal-ously served him, was his confirming to Lord Wellington the honours and rewards conferred upon him by the cortes.

In America the long-pending dispute with the United States respecting the boundaries of Louisiana and West Florida was finally settled by the sale of both the Floridas to that power. The war with the colonies continued, but altered in character. Ferdinand there took part with the cortes he had condemned, pertinaciously refused to acknowledge the equality, the sort of federal connection with the mother-country that the colonies claimed, and wasted the resources of Spain by sending his best troops across the Atlantic to assert the old Spanish monopoly. The colonies, exasperated by this return for their loyalty, now disowned the authority of Ferdinand, and pro-claimed their entire and absolute independence. Ferdinand resisted these pretensions yet more vehemently than the former, but it was evident from the beginning that Spain had finally lost her transatlantic empire. Cuba, Porto Rico, and the Philippines were her only remaining colonies.

As the short convulsion, which followed Napoleon's return from Elba in the following spring and was terminated by the dreadful and glorious battle of Waterloo as finally sealing Bonaparte's fall, produced no other effect in the peninsula than an order to arm, a detail of these affairs would be out of place here.q

THE REIGN OF TERROR

A famous society, that of the Exterminating Angel, had extended its roots over the whole country under the direction of a former regent, the bishop of Osma, and was moving all the apostolics of the peninsula as by a single mind. It had relations with the principal bishops to whom several owed their offices; its ramifications crept into all the monasteries, and much more violent than its French chapter it preached the extermination of all the liberals.

The military commissions set to work with a new activity aided by a mass of regulations whose laconism and hypocrisy were only equalled by their vigour and violence. They had the power of condemning to death all who were guilty of lèse-majesté, that is to say all who declared themselves opposed to the rights of the king or in favour of the constitution. With the help of this ambiguous phrase, any writer who put into print any words in which the rights of Ferdinand were doubted, anyone who in any manner whatever had co-operated in the revolution of 1820-1823; anyone who kept in his house a copy of the constitution, a portrait of Riego, any souvenir whatso-ever of the illustrious exiles living in a foreign country, anyone who by a shout or word, spoken even in drunkenness, showed hatred of tyranny — any of these could be found guilty of lèse-majesté. A decree bearing the date of October 9th, 1824, which through some expiring sentiment of modesty was not inserted in the official gazette, but nevertheless was applied with care, suppressed all of the laws and delivered the lives of all citizens over to these tribunals. A premium was put upon information and a secret police penetrated into every household in order to divine the secret of consciences and to purge Spain of all the liberal element. Not age, sex, virtue, or poverty were protection against these terrible commissions; wealth alone sometimes saved from death. He who had some fortune bought his life with the greatest part of his property.

The commission of Madrid, presided over by a fierce brute named Chaperon, who acquired the melancholy honour of giving his name to the whole epoch, surpassed all its rivals in the number of condemnations and severity of sentences. It sent to the scaffold all those in whose homes portraits of Riego were discovered, and to the galleys the women and children who committed the crime of not denouncing their husbands or fathers. More than one well-born woman thrown into infamous prisons with the most odious criminals died of despair in the midst of the unjust abjection to which she saw herself reduced. Chaperon, like all the judges who consented to make themselves the devoted instruments of social hatred, rejoiced in the midst of the terror which his name inspired, and under the general torpor that it created. He assisted at executions in full uniform; they were fête days for him, and on one occasion, anxious to hasten the execution of one of his condemned (it was a national militiaman who had taken part in the defence of Madrid, the 7th of July, against the revolted guards), he pulled, himself, the legs of the poor victim already hanging from the fatal gibbet, and this exploit finished, retired, proud to have exercised the functions of executioner and judge.[b]

THE TYRANNIES OF FERDINAND "THE DESIRED"

The places left in the power of the French were evacuated one by one, and finally, on the 20th of July, Spain gave its assent to the treaty of peace and friendship which the allies had concluded with France on the 30th of the preceding May. In the beginning of May the king had found a ministry which he modified before the end of the month, but at the head of it each time he placed the duke of San Carlos. The system of persecution continued and everything which seemed to favour innovations was vigorously opposed. Ferdinand regained his power, the cortes had disappeared, the constitution of Cadiz existed only in people's memories. The Spain of 1814 became again the Spain of 1807; as before, she was subject to the joint domination of prince and clergy. The legislative bodies which constituted the government and the chief judicial magistracy of 1808 were abolished in 1814.

Among the reforms introduced by Joseph's government and by that of the cortes after him, there were some which were unjust, extortionate, contrary to the re-established order; but there were others which should have been retained or modified with reservations. The king had no thought of making a choice. He considered, not the nature of the acts, but their origin; the good and the bad, salutary reform and disastrous measure, all were included in a general proscription. The state, impoverished by a long war, had at hand timely assistance in the estates of the religious communities, without being obliged to impose heavy burdens on the people; never had there been such a favourable opportunity for limiting and regulating these exaggerated possessions which had fallen into *mortmain*. A measure calling for investigation and reform which had been authorised by a papal bull under Charles IV might now have been carried into effect. But no attention was paid to anything of the kind. All their goods of which the cortes had disposed were returned to the convents, and at the same time a royal order re-established the holy office of the Inquisition on the ground that the government of usurpation and the pretended cortes had regarded the suppression of this tribunal as a very efficacious method of furthering their perverse schemes. The Jesuits were recalled, receiving again the goods which had belonged to them in the preceding century.

The administration of the realm was with great pains thrown again into the secular confusion out of which so many ministers had laboured to disentangle it. Instead of the happy division of territory decreed by the cortes, there reappeared the spectacle of provinces governed by captains-general, who added to their plenitude of military and administrative authority certain judicial attributes. Lastly the councils of Castile, of the Indies, of the orders, of finance, marine and war, authorities independent of the ministry, whose traditions made them hostile to any reform undertaken in the interests of the reigning power or of the people, began again to operate.

Around Ferdinand was formed that too famous *camarilla*[1] controlled by the Russian minister, which, wholly lacking in a broad outlook, seemed to have no object but destruction and vengeance. At the same time that it overturned all which the revolution had done for the unity of Spain, it struck at all those men who had incurred its hatred. Ten thousand Spaniards had had the misfortune to attach themselves to the French cause; they were banished and their goods confiscated. The members of the regency, those of the cortes, all the ministers, all the individuals who had taken part in framing the constitution or had been zealous partisans of it, were brought before commissioners to be tried with no legal formality. The number of the condemned was considerable : *presides*, imprisonment in the citadels, exile—such were the penalties inflicted ; the king made no use of his right of pardon and these acts continued with cold perseverance. Two years after the king had regained his full power, the prisons were still full, and long proscription lists still appeared at intervals.

Such a government could not fail to have a dire influence on the interior prosperity of the country ; but it is difficult to imagine the extent of the disorder into which everything had been thrown. It was necessary to resort to arbitrary taxes which caused discontent without affording much relief to the treasury and to exorbitant custom duties which completed the destruction of commerce by breaking off all relations with foreign countries. The old régime, to remain in possession of Spain, would have needed the treasures of the New World to hold the country in subjection, and to defray the expenses of an administration useless at its best. But then it would have had to get the better of the insurrections already victorious or soon to be so in Venezuela, Chile, Peru, Buenos Ayres, and Mexico, and to combat all the points of that immense continent at once. In order to quell their revolution, which was termed a revolt, an army needed first to be procured. To embark this army a fleet was necessary for the equipment of which both time and means were lacking ; the government was reduced to bargaining for ships with Russia. In order to obtain immediate assistance it had to resort to a system of credit and give some assurance of a good administration together with securities for the public debt. This necessity was so pressing that in the ministerial council Don Martin Garay, surnamed the Necker of Spain, and several others of the same school were placed at the side of men like Eguia and Lozano de Torres, those defenders of ancient customs.

Garay had to promise services for which he had no resources and at the

[1 Spanish kings had been ruled by favourites before ; but Lerma and Olivares, even Valenzuela and Godoy, were men of education and breeding, whilst the secret advisers of Ferdinand were, many of them, coarse, ignorant buffoons. Meeting at night with noisy mirth they settled over the heads of the ministers questions of national policy, and even made and unmade ministers in mere caprice. Ministers were appointed or dismissed arbitrarily by Ferdinand for the most puerile reasons, and were sent into prison or exile at the idle fancy of the king. The members of the *camarilla* were treated in the same way, being one day in high favour and the next in jail. There were over thirty ministers in the six years from 1814 to 1820, an average of two months' duration for each. The most prominent member of the *camarilla* was a low buffoon called "Chamorro," who had been a water-carrier, another, Ugarte, was a second-hand broker ; Tattischeff, the Russian minister, was also a member.c] same time establish credit for an enormous public debt, the securities for which had just been taken away. Garay had counted on resources which were daily becoming more illusory through the complete cessation of commerce and the disastrous state of agriculture. Events in America demanded an expenditure of forces which Spain could not have mustered even in her palmiest days. When Garay wished to resort to more radical measures, he was sent into exile. Nothing seemed able to uplift the credit of the industrial situation of Spain, blockaded from Cadiz to Corunna by the corsairs of the insurgent colonies, compromised with the United States for Florida, and obliged to purchase the seeming neutrality of England in the struggle with the colonies.

A SERIAL REVOLUTION (1814–1822 A.D.)

By reason of so much capricious violence the upper classes had become discontented and the people indifferent, the government was reduced to relying

GENERAL FRANCISCO MINA

on armed force. But the army itself, ill equipped and ill paid, was become a hotbed of insurrection. Secret societies were organised everywhere and complaints led to plots. The well-known guerilla Mina responded by an armed revolt to a refusal to give him the title of captain-general in Navarre, but he was abandoned by his companions and escaped death only by flight to France in 1814. In 1815, General Diaz Porlier incited the garrisons of Corunna and Ferrol to revolt for a brief space, and proclaimed the constitution of Cadiz. He was also abandoned and ended his life on the gallows. Even in Madrid a conspiracy was formed headed by War Commissioner Richard, who perished on the scaffold in 1816. The next year General Lacy undertook in Catalonia what Porlier had attempted in Galicia. The plot was discovered and Lacy shot. In Valencia in 1818 also revolts took place ; the captain-general Elio[1] seized the insurgent chief Vidal, who was immediately hung with twelve of his accomplices.

So many unsuccessful attempts served only to irritate the malcontents who still hoped to find better support among their companions at arms. Such was the disposition of a number of officers at Cadiz, where an army was

---

[1] The blood-thirsty Elio tortured to death a woman who had just given birth to a child.

slowly and with difficulty being got together for a definitive expedition against the rebellious colonies, upon which all the hopes of the Spanish government were concentrated. The soldiers were frightened by tales of old mutilated warriors who had returned from Colombia. They were made to see the possibility of escaping the misfortune which awaited them without being exposed to the reproach or suspicion of a lack of courage. They were told stories of the last war, of the liberty conquered and then lost, of honour compromised.

The conspirators had more hope of success because they had the chief of the expedition himself, O'Donnell, the count of Abisbal, on their side; but this general turned traitor, denounced the conspirators, and even arrested some of them. But he too was later suspected, and was recalled with all the signs of disgrace. Persecutions recommenced. Everything pointed to a redoubling of rigour which in turn produced a redoubling of irritation and also of hope. The conspirators again took up their plans which had been interrupted for an instant, but this time they did not look to generals for help. A less distinguished leader gave the impulse to revolt in one of the cantonments.

The 1st of January, 1820, Rafael del Riego assembled a battalion encamped in a village, presented it with the constitution of 1812 as the law of the country, to which he made it swear allegiance, marched upon Arcos, surprised and captured O'Donnell's successor Calderon with his staff, and continued his march upon San Fernando where he was joined by Colonel Quiroga. But the gates of Cadiz remained closed to them, the garrison and the fleet took on a hostile attitude toward the rebels. At the same time an army of thirteen thousand men under General Freire arrived with forced marches to quell the insurrection. Thereupon Riego advanced towards the centre of Andalusia preaching insurrection and proclaiming the constitution of Cadiz. But the general indifference of the country was enough to thwart the enterprise of the insurgents. There was discouragement in the camp at the isle of Leon and, the governmental forces accumulating in Andalusia, it seemed that the rebellion was about to expire.

But the emissaries charged with arousing the provinces worked without relaxation. The 21st of February they succeeded in proclaiming the constitution in the capital of Galicia. Ferrol followed this example the 23rd. The same thing took place at Vigo. The government tried to compromise with the revolution and offered to assemble the cortes, but no confidence was placed in these promises because it was remembered that the decree of May 4th, 1814, by which the constitution was abolished, had promised to convoke the cortes but had not been carried into effect. The revolutionaries of the capital incited by the feebleness of the government worked openly towards their object. General Ballesteros, who came to Madrid to declare to the monarch that he must accept the constitution, was hailed as a deliverer by the king; the 9th of March Ferdinand took the oath for this act which he detested, at the moment when Riego's column, reduced to a few men, was forced to disband, and the garrison at Cadiz was energetically opposing the insurrection.

When the king had sworn to observe the constitution of 1812, the people and the troops which still remained faithful gave up without resistance. Everyone had been affected by the disastrous effects of the régime to which the country had been subjected for several years and all were glad to be freed from it without a civil war. The prisons were opened. The reins of government were in the hands of ministers whose ideas were wholly popular.

Several provinces were governed by juntas, one was established even in the capital, which was known as the provisional junta. The government consulted it on all important matters. The country awaited with impatience the arrival of the deputies who were to give it a better order of things than that from which it had just been delivered, instead of giving thought to the necessary improvements. Thoughtful minds perceived that it was necessary substantially to modify the civil legislation ; to render remunerative large masses of untaxed property ; to negotiate with Rome a reform which would alter the position of the clergy ; to re-establish the financial situation ; to place the provinces under a common law, combining extensive local liberty with unity of administration ; above all not to imitate the preceding government in its deeds of violence.

The first acts of the cortes showed that it understood its task. An important law concerning entailed estates was passed in a spirit of wisdom ; they were placed in the category of free property and their owners could dispose of them with certain reservations and just conditions. But the assembly was largely composed of members of the special cortes of Cadiz who considered the work of the constitution perfect and would suffer no change in it. Thus, before proceeding to anything else, it was necessary to deal with those who had opposed their constitution in 1814 — the sixty-nine deputies known as the Persians, who had presented the king at Valencia with an address in favour of absolute power. On the other hand the enthusiasts wanted to advance much more quickly in the path of improvement. There soon came to be a distinction between the liberals of 1812 and those of 1820. The radical party soon kept no bounds ; its papers, its clubs attacked the ministers, the cortes, the king. It was supported by the army of the isle of Leon, and the government wished to disperse

GENERAL RAFAEL DEL RIEGO

the bodies composing the latter among the different garrisons. The men of the isle of Leon thereupon took occasion to send to Madrid Riego, who was commander-in-chief during the absence of Quiroga, deputy to the cortes. Here applause and ovations were lavished upon the leader of the men of 1820, who, carried away by popular favour, braved the cortes and the ministers. But the garrison and the national militia decided for the established order. Riego was exiled to Oviedo, the army of the isle was disbanded.

Nevertheless the presence of Riego at Madrid gave an impulse to the radicals which remained after his departure. Fresh conspiracies were brought to light against the new régime. The discussion of the law regarding religious orders was affected by their attitude of mind. They tried to accomplish at once, what should have been the work of years. In immediately suppressing the greater part of the religious congregations and putting their goods up for sale, difficulties of more than one kind were created. In Catalonia and Valencia troops had to guard the gates of the monasteries day and night to prevent pillage and massacre. The king had hesitated to sanction the decree, and, after the session closed on the 9th of November, he made an unsuccessful trial of absolute power by nominating General Carvajal captain-general of New Castile, without the signature of the minister of war. The fermentation then became terrible and the minister augmented it in order to frighten the king. The latter threatened and insulted on all sides was forced to return to Madrid from his retreat in the Escorial. When one day his bodyguard was moved to pity by the dangers he ran, their quarter was besieged and the corps disorganised. The *ayuntamiento* of Madrid imposed their measure on the government.

After having swallowed so many affronts Ferdinand wished to make an attempt to shake off the yoke. He hoped with his new resolution to impose on his adversaries, who were troubled by the attitude of the great European powers, since England alone had frankly recognised the constitutional government. Russia had not concealed her displeasure at the triumph of the insurrection. Prussia and Austria held themselves in a reserve which boded no good, and France had tried to bring about a change in the position of the king of Spain. Ferdinand chose the opening of the second session of the cortes, on March 1st, 1821, to deliver his attack. After finishing the customary address prepared by his ministers he read a supplement added by himself complaining of the ministers who had permitted his person to be subjected to such outrages. The next day he dismissed them and chose a new cabinet from the moderate party of the chamber. Events in Piedmont and Naples gave cause for conflicting sentiments. Attempts of the absolutists gave rise to disturbances in Valencia, Corunna, Seville, and Barcelona. The king in order to ward off the anger of the demagogues sent a message to the cortes expressing his grief over events in Italy and his sympathy with the Italian patriots. The ministry, also desiring to forestall public defiance, on April 17th proposed two laws, one of which pronounced a sentence of death on all who should try to overturn the religion of the constitution, and a decree of banishment against any person who used any expression tending to such an overthrow. The second law provided that those accused of conspiracy and arrested by armed force, whatever their social position, be placed before a military tribunal chosen from the corps which had made the arrest. Judgment was to be pronounced within six days, and executed within forty-eight hours after being confirmed by the chief military authority. There was to be no appeal or exercise of pardon by the king. The populace would have liked to apply this law to all political offenders.

Confusion increased from day to day. Republican uprisals took place in Malaga and Barcelona. In the environs of Manresa were armed bands in the name of "the faith." There was conspiracy at Murcia and absolutist agitation at Malaga. Bands were arming themselves on the frontier of France, and no one knew where to turn for money to organise the sadly needed troops. The cortes was moreover beginning to give way before the weight of events which attacked it on all sides. The question of the independence of America terrified it, and it did not care to renounce the pretensions of despotic Spain over men who had made use of the right of insurrection. But negotiations proved useless. Out of so many vast possessions Spain retained only a few fortified places occupied by the remnants of its armies.

Riots became more and more frequent at Madrid, but they were put down by the courage and *sangfroid* of Morillo. The cortes separated February 22nd, 1822, at a moment when Seville and Valencia were given up to rebellion, the Basque provinces and Navarre were infested with bands armed in the name of the altar and of the throne, others in Aragon, Alcañiz, Calatayud, Alagon, and Caspe proclaimed the authority of the Virgin and of religion.

The new cortes opened the 1st of March, 1822, with Riego as president, who very soon fell into discord with the new ministry presided over by Martinez de la Rosa. The quarrels between the branches of power incited absolutist riots and revolutionary insurrection throughout the country. The cortes finally decided to send a message to the king informing him of the necessity of putting a stop to the critical situation of the realm. After stating its complaints it demanded more resolute men at the head of affairs, and also the expulsion of prelates and priests who preached fanaticism and rebellion. The king relying on popular manifestation in his favour did not reply to the deputation. In Catalonia was a considerable body called Army of the Faith under the command of Miralles, Romagosa, and Marañon, called the Trappist, who succeeded in capturing Urgel by assault.[d]

CHÂTEAUBRIAND'S ACCOUNT OF THE CHAOS

The eminent writer Châteaubriand, who was a representative of France at the Congress of Verona, and who was one of the principal advocates of the French invasion of Spain, has brilliantly pictured the chaos of affairs, in 1822, which led him to think French intervention necessary. We may quote briefly his description :

The press, secret societies, clubs, had disorganised everything. Barcelona, Valencia, Pamplona had risen. One side cried " *Vive Dieu!* " the other " *Vive Riego!* " Killing was carried on in the name of Him who murders not and of him who murders. At Madrid, regiments fought against the royal grenadiers ; young men walked about the streets crying for absolute monarchy. God and the king ! It was all one in Spain ; *las ambas magestades*. In the very house of cortes, deputies were saying that a refusal to listen to the popular complaint authorised dagger justice. Riego, the president, was powerless. He was always ready to sing the *Trágala*.[1] A couplet of it might at any moment mean a crown ; but, if it was not good, the crown would vanish, and one would remain on the highway with the throne changed into a mere stage.

The *serviles*, who paraded their name as proudly as though it were a royal designation, profited by one hour's respite and reaction against secret societies to re-seize power. Royalist risings replaced revolutionary insurrections. The Descamisados, matadors in *servile* pay, were beaten in their turn. They revived the human sacrifices of their Carthaginian ancestors. Monarchical sections appeared under the old guise. Govostidi, Misas, Merino, fabulous heroes of the presbytery, rose in Biscay, Catalonia, and Castile. Insurrection spread. Quesada, Juanito, Santo-Ladron, Truxillo, Schafaudino, and Hierro were all alive with it. Finally Baron Eroles showed himself in Catalonia. Near him was Antonio Marañon. Antonio, called the Trappist, was first a soldier, then fled into cloistered life under the influence of passion.

[1] That is, " Swallow it," meaning the constitution, a popular street song of Cadiz, which may be compared with the " *Ça ira!* " of the French Revolution.

He carried cross and sword with equal enthusiasm. His military dress was a Franciscan gown, on which hung a crucifix. At his waist hung a sword, pistols, and a rosary. He used to gallop along carrying a whip. Peace and war, religion and license, life and death, were united in one man, who alternately blessed and exterminated. Crusades and civil massacres, psalms and war hymns, *Stabat Mater* and *Trágala*, genuflection and *jota Aragonese*, triumphs as martyr or soldier, souls mounting heavenwards to strains of the *Veni Creator*, rebels shot to military music — such was existence in this corner of the world.

Ferdinand, on the banks of the Tagar, *rio qui cria oro e piedras preciosas*, had sworn to the constitution only to betray it. Sincere friends invited him to modify instructions, working with the cortes. Shortsighted friends urged him to overthrow them; royalist successes secretly flattered the king; the hope of an uncontrolled sovereignty gratified him. Want of power to wield power made him love it the more.

The king's birthday fell on the 30th of May. It was celebrated by the peasants of La Mancha, reunited at Aranjuez. In vain the soldiers repeated the patriotic cry of the peasants, even as the bodyguard at Versailles sang "*O Richard! O mon Roi!*" If France had not soon interfered, Ferdinand would have followed where Richard led Louis XVI. The militia marched on the people, and a townsman lifted his sword against Don Carlos — that last of the kings and one who waited so heavy a crown. At Valencia, a detachment of artillery wanted to deliver General Elio, shut up in the citadel. The Catalonian insurgents, now organised, had taken the name of the Army of the Faith. *f*

CIVIL WAR

On the 21st of June, 1822, the Army of the Faith learned the isolated condition of the feeble garrison in Seo de Urgel. Romanillo, Romagosa, and Miralles, with the Trappist, arranged to meet under its walls. Helped by the citizens, they immediately surrounded the citadel. An assault was decided on, and the Trappist, setting an example to the soldiers, was the first to scale the tower, a crucifix in one hand, in the other a long whip, emblem of power. He braved the balls directed against him, and the soldiers, persuaded of his invulnerability, followed after. The tower was taken, the other forts were surrendered, and next day the citadel, with sixty artillery pieces and sixteen hundred guns, was in the hands of the apostolics. This first success was most important, for the French aides had, in promising help, made a formal condition that the Army of the Faith should possess at least one stronghold.

In proportion to the consternation excited among the leaders by the taking of Seo de Urgel, so was Ferdinand strongly roused and the courage of those about him stirred. It was now a question with them all of quickly striking a decisive blow. The instrument for this was soon found in the royal guard, wherein most lively discontent reigned because the cortes had shown intention of reorganising it, and who, seeing themselves in danger of losing all their privileges, had decided to fight against the national militia, whose principles were particularly odious to them.

This guard at Madrid alone numbered six entire battalions; that is, a more considerable force than the rest of the garrison, and there was, moreover, a brigade of carbineers, then in garrison at Castro del Rio, near Cordova. A young officer, already celebrated at Cadiz for his royalist devotion,

Don Luis Fernandez of Cordova, received from the king or had a self-imposed mission to concentrate all this military force and lead it against the established system. The projected reforms of the cortes made this easy, and, on the 25th of June, the carbineers of Castro del Rio raised the standard of revolt in Andalusia. At Aranjuez and Madrid the royal guards began a series of struggles with the people and the militia — struggles which every day became more animated. On the 27th the court returned from Aranjuez to the capital, and this was the signal for fresh outbreaks. The royal ceremony of closing the first session of the cortes took place on the 30th. This important act was carefully observed, because Ferdinand did not think himself really in a position to act until he had freed himself from these importunate adversaries. But on returning from the ceremony, when the king had just regained his palace, a lively quarrel burst out. Some shouted " Long live our absolute king ! " and some " Long live the constitution ! " The guards were simply furious. Stationed at the Plaza de Oriente, they suddenly returned to the crowd, drove them back, and chased away some national militia picketed on the square. Then they organised themselves in military style as though in an enemy's city. Some among their officers belonged to the cortes, one of them, Mamerto Landáburu, wanted to recall his men to discipline. They insulted him, whereupon he drew his sword to punish the offenders himself, but, far from being listened to, he became their first victim. Three grenadiers struck him behind and he fell bathed in his own blood at the very gates of the palace.

The Madrid populace had for two years been too accustomed to scenes of tumult, to rise at the news of an isolated act. But the national militia took arms incontinently, and seized two plazas.

It was a critical moment for Ferdinand. Supported by a military force which would only take orders from himself, he could find a serious concourse in the ministry against all his enemies, if he only consented to the drawing up of a charter and granting the representative institutions for which he had shown so much anxiety before M. de Villèle. But the king thought himself now in a position to acquire absolute power. He knew that a regiment of militia had joined with the carbineers at Castro del Rio ; and he had seen insurgent troops of Andalusia coming to help his guards at the very doors of his palace. However, he had to reckon with the militia and the garrison of Madrid, and these two elements were preparing to fight with a calmness and courage that argued success. These formed under the name of the Holy Battalion, and under Don Evaristo San Miguel there was a special corps composed of ardent patriots. The most distinguished generals, Ballesteros, Alava, and Palarea, showed inclination to make the laws respected. For several days the two parties remained face to face. The two battalions stationed at the palace were vilely seduced by the king and his courtiers. Money was freely scattered among the guards, and they were excited to fight by promises of all kinds.

By the 6th the necessity of taking a definite step was felt. But favourable news arriving of the insurrection of Castro del Rio, the aspect of affairs suddenly changed. Orders were given that neither the ministers, the state councillors, nor the political leader were to leave the palace, as grave events might happen during the night.

And just so it happened. The four Pardo battalions marched on the capital in the hope of surprising it and disarming the national militia. Arrived at one of the chief gates, they divided into three columns, one making for the artillery park, a second to the Puerta del Sol, and a third to the

Constitution square. As fate so willed, the first column met a patrol of the Holy Battalion, and this circumstance decided the issue of the struggle. A few stray shots awoke the people. In an instant every patriot was afoot ; each ran to his post, and the guards were driven from the artillery park and the Plaza Mayor. They retired in sufficiently good order on the Puerta del Sol column, which had tried to take the Casa de Correos, but had been stopped by means of a strong barricade put up behind the door. A governmental committee exacted that the four rebellious battalions should lay down their arms, and allowed the other two to go out armed to settle in the villages of Vicalvaro and Leganes, with the one condition that they should give up the murderers of Landáburu.

This capitulation ought to have ended the struggle, but did nothing of the sort. The four battalions to be disarmed refused obedience, going out of the palace by a gate which led to the Campo del Moro and fleeing in the direction of Alcorcon, after discharging their arms at the militia. After this, no conciliatory efforts were made. Three columns, commanded by Ballesteros, Copons, and Palarea pursued and smote them hip and thigh, killing a great number and taking many prisoners. If some stories can be believed, Ferdinand crowned his infamy in these memorable days by personally urging on the conquerors. "After them ! After them !" cried he to Morillo from his balcony, so ordering the extermination of those who had given themselves to his cause.[b]

The new administration began by banishing from the capital all those who were suspected of having counselled this last attempt of the court, and by appointing new officers ; Quiroga received the command in Galicia and Mina in Catalonia. At Valencia General Elio was condemned for an imaginary crime by a council of war in obedience to the cries of the populace, and was strangled on September 11th. But while the conquerors of July 7th were pursuing their triumph, civil war was spreading its ravages, and events of a new order gave it a more political character. At Urgel a government was established with the title "supreme regency of Spain during the captivity of the king." This was recognised by a majority of the officers in the so-called royal army, by General Eguia, O'Donnell, the general inquisitor, the bishop of Pamplona and various juntas of the provinces. The troops obtained some successes and were aided by the French government. Its agents were favourably received by the congress at Verona. Nevertheless it was compelled to evacuate Urgel, and install itself at Puycerda, whence it was forced to retreat to France and terminate its existence at Toulouse on December 7th. Mina pursued the royalist bands relentlessly.

The next extra session of the cortes opened the 7th of October at a moment when war was raging on the northern frontier. The famous brigand Jayme Alfonso had raised the standard of the faith in Murcia ; the priest Merino had also re-entered the field. Civil war raged in Castile, Andalusia, and in the province of Toledo.[a]

INTERVENTION OF THE HOLY ALLIANCE (1823 A.D.)

But Spain was not allowed to work out its own salvation. Europe was dominated at this time by the Holy Alliance, which disguised a resolution to repress popular liberties and to maintain despotism under a pretended zeal for piety, justice, and brotherly love. At the Congress of Verona (October, 1822), France, Austria, Russia, and Prussia agreed upon armed intervention

LIBRARY.
MUSKINGUM COLLEGE.

in Spain, in spite of the protest of Canning on the part of England. Spain was to be called upon to alter her constitution and to grant greater liberty to the king, and if an unsatisfactory answer was received France was authorised to take active measures.[a]

In the first days of January, 1823, France, Austria, Russia, and Prussia presented notes at Madrid demanding a change in the political constitution and the liberty of the king. On the 11th of the month the cortes declared that it would make no concessions to the threatening powers. The ambassadors of Russia, Austria, and Prussia demanded their passports at once and left Madrid; the French minister followed soon after.

A cruel blow to the strength of the constitutionals followed in the success of various royalist armies. On February 19th, 1823, after the closing of the extraordinary sessions of the cortes, the news of the deposition of the ministry caused violent disorder. The palace was besieged and the king forced to revoke the decree. The popular societies of the free masons and the *comuneros* fought strenuously with each other: at the same time they agreed in rejecting all proposals to modify the constitution, in spite of the advice of the Duke of Wellington and the ambassador of England. The new cortes which had opened the 1st of March was engaged in transferring the government to Seville. The king was notified that he must prepare himself for such a move, and in spite of vague and uncertain plots the departure took place on the 20th.[d]

THE FRENCH INVASION

It does not lie within our province to give in detail all the various incidents which signalled the union of the French army on the borders of the Pyrenees, and finally the decision to brave events and to pass the Bidassoa on the 7th of April before the liberals could develop their plans to seduce the troops.

The French army was divided into five large corps and presented an effective of ninety-five thousand light infantry and twenty-one thousand horse. In addition to this very respectable number of troops, the intervention counted equally on apostolic insurgents in the various provinces. The baron d'Eroles could bring nearly nine thousand Catalans in the pay of the Urgel regency. Eguia, at Bayonne, who for two years had spent a sum of nearly two millions in fomenting civil wars in Navarre and the Basque provinces, put at the duke of Angoulême's disposition all divisions and bands which, under the orders of Carlos, O'Donnell, Quesada, Guergue, and Longa, had carried on a guerilla warfare against governmental generals. Finally in the interior of the country relations were established with all such leaders as Bessières, Sampère, Merino. One might estimate at least thirty-five thousand men against the constitutional system.

The French army expected to meet a vigorous resistance in the Basque provinces, especially as the lay of the land lent itself so admirably to intelligent strategy. But General Ballesteros, to whom had been given the task of defending these provinces, surprised perhaps by the rapidity of an invasion, ordered his troops to retire before the enemy's advance-guard. San Sebastian received the French with cannon-shot and refused to open its gates, but Fuenterrabia and the Passage were occupied immediately. The duke of Angoulême ordered Bourke to follow up the siege of San Sebastian, and himself went straight on with the bulk of the army for Vitoria. The French troops found without the slightest difficulty all provisions and stores needed, thanks to the business-like ways of the commissariat Ouvrard, who knew how to raise the speculative spirit in the Basques, and faithfully paid for all goods brought him. This brought into a country ravaged by poverty an unexpected good instead of ruin and desolation. There was no danger encountered in scaling the Pyrenees. The duke of Angoulême, conqueror without fighting, could establish his headquarters at Vitoria and patiently wait the concentration of all his columns before marching directly on the capital.

After the government departed, military authority was concentrated at Madrid in the hands of General O'Donnell, the count of Abisbal. A vigorous defence was expected in the Guadarrama defiles, but the count was not straightforward in his dealing. He had arrived at the highest honours by flattering each party successively. Instead of arming the population and occupying the most important points, he entered into secret negotiations with the staff of the duke of Angoulême, which had received most detailed instructions to spare bloodshed by using means of corruption, with which it had been generously provided. Gained over to the cause against which he had pronounced in 1820, Abisbal openly pointed out to his officers the impossibility of resisting the invasion. The army officers, indignant, went in a body to his house and intimated that it was time for him to resign. Abisbal realised the danger he ran, and fled to France.

An army thus abandoned by its leader at the last moment, found itself unfit to arrest the victorious march of the duke of Angoulême. Of the two generals who had succeeded Abisbal, one of them, Castel dos Ruis, decided to go on into Estremadura heading the bulk of his troops. The other, Zayas, was left with a feeble corps of from twelve to fifteen hundred to obtain a capitulation which would at least assure life and property to the inhabitants of Madrid. This last measure was full of foresight, for while the near coming of the French army was spoken of, Bessières, the same leader of the band who a little before had threatened Madrid, had made a bold move and pretended to occupy the city, while his followers hoped to give it over to pillage. But Zayas, with the help of the garrison and national militia, fearlessly barred his passage, forced him to retreat, and kept him outside the city walls until the arrival of the first French troops — this, in spite of his repeated threats and the rage of all the bad subjects greedily anticipating an easily won booty.

The multitude in all large cities are always ready for a spectacle, fête, or anything emotional. Moreover, Madrid had within her a crowd of partisans of absolutist principles — all those who belonged to the palace or the clergy, all those whom a liberal administration had deprived of employment, and the relations of refugees. These warmly welcomed him who was conqueror over a constitutional system. But the duke of Angoulême, although received with open arms, with acclamation, song, and dance, could hardly mistake the general feeling. For while the absolutists thronged the streets, the middle class, who alone desired and upheld liberty, hid their humiliation by their fireside. The duke had to put an end to the excesses of a mad populace who would overthrow the constitution and pillage the houses of all the well-known constitutionists. For three days the *manolas* overran the town singing the *Pitita;* they went into the churches and solemnly put Ferdinand's portrait on the altar in place of the saints. In the hope of getting out of this anarchistic situation, the duke hastened to give a definite form to the new government, which would definitely take matters in hand, in a proclamation dated from Alcobendas (23rd of May, 1823), announcing his intention of leaving the Spaniards to govern themselves and inviting the former coun-sellors of Castile and the Indies to choose a regency to take the helm of the state until Ferdinand had recovered his full liberty.   The duke of Angoulême made the terrible mistake of sanctioning nominations that were fatal and soon to be regretted.   Then having seen the regency commence work with the duke of Infantado as president, and the new ministry formed wherein Canon Victor Saez was minister of foreign affairs and Don J. B. Erro minister of finance, he thought he could rest with perfect security and have nothing but his military operations to occupy him until Ferdinand was seized from the cortes.

The unlucky prince did not realise that, in confiding the government of Spain to personages picked out by former counsellors, he was practically condemning the unhappy country to ten years of a horrible system of per-secution and religious fanaticism ; that he was making the French flag responsible for the organisation of the most odious government which the human mind could conceive, and soiling the white flag he wished to hold high by making it the symbol of ignorance, fanaticism, and shameful arbitration.[b]

Meanwhile the cortes held Ferdinand practically a prisoner in Seville. On the approach of the French the king, protesting violently, was haled to Cadiz, after the appointment of a regency of three.   In his diary Ferdinand describes vividly the humiliation of his position, and it is evident that he was treasuring up a wealth of grudges to repay with all his liberality in spite. Late in June Cadiz was besieged by land and sea.   After a heavy bombard-ment, during which Ferdinand kept signalling to the duke of Angoulême, Cadiz fell on the 23rd of September, 1823, and on October 1st Ferdinand was delivered free to the French at Puerto de Santa Maria.

THE RETURN OF FERDINAND (1823 A.D.)

The 1st of October Ferdinand crossed from Cadiz to Santa Maria.   He was scarcely in possession of his authority before he annulled every act which had been passed since March 7th, 1820, and announced that he con-sidered himself released from all obligations towards his rebellious subjects and that he was going to punish their assaults.   The extreme party which carried him with it no longer restrained its vengeance.   The duke of Angoulême returned to Madrid and left immediately for Paris.   The king proceeded to the capital where the absolutist party welcomed him in triumph. But there he saw that he must submit to a new yoke, for when certain offi-cers of the voluntary royalists were presented to him, remembering the national militia he remarked that they were "the same dogs with different collars."

The conquerors gave themselves up to the intoxication of vengeance. One of the victims most passionately demanded was Riego, who paid the penalty for his deeds on the 7th of November in the public square of Madrid.[1]   The generals Ballesteros and Morillo went into exile.   The prisons were full to overflowing.   The populace hurled its rage against the liberals, who were proscribed under the name of Negros; during the minis-try of Victor Saez, the king's confessor, the hangman seemed to be the most active instrument of power.

[1 He was dragged through the streets in a basket drawn at the tail of an ass ; he was then hanged and quartered as if he were a felon.]

Ferdinand felt himself too strongly ruled by the absolutist faction[1] and he feared moreover the projects the latter seemed to be forming in connection with his brother, the infante Don Carlos, for whom they hoped for a more complete devotion. His old partisan Bessières, now at the mercy of the faction, having called together his troops without the government's order, paid for it on the scaffold. Ferdinand was forced to retard the evacuation of Barcelona by the French for fear of the hostility from the partisans of pure despotism; he was obliged to go to Catalonia to scatter the assemblies of troops clamouring too loudly for an absolute king, and he returned to Madrid full of fear and suspicion. His reign after the fall of the Saez ministry is easy to characterise. No new principle was proclaimed, no abuse was solemnly repudiated. Not one word of authority gave reason to suppose that at some time any thought would be given to reforming ancient customs, to modifying the absolute right of the throne which is inseparable from that of religion. In 1826, when the Brazilian charter was established in Portugal, a governmental proclamation still comprised all the duties of a Spaniard in the following precepts: "Love the king, obey the king, and die for his absolute power."

In spite of these formulas another spirit directed affairs. The council of state had to be purged of its most influential personages. Old adherents of the constitution and even of King Joseph surrounded the throne at times, because the king had no other sentiment than that of personal safety; he did not wish to give himself up completely to the party which was

CALOMARDE
(Minister of Ferdinand VII)

already proclaiming another name than his own. He had always had a horror of the constitution, but he did not ignore the fact that the exclamation of *Vive l'inquisition!* had been accompanied by another cry. Thus he saw himself compelled to crush both parties, to sacrifice without pity the authors of audacious attempts, no matter on which side they might be. Moreover he had good cause to treat with the new spirit because he had need of money for his administration and army, and to get it he had to revert to foreigners. It was declared by the government which succeeded him that from 1823 to the end of his reign the public debt increased 665,000,000 francs.

Ferdinand did not wish to constitute a party, to proclaim his principles,

[1 The minister Calomarde was one of the most violent of the absolutists. Born in 1773 he had worked his way upward gradually till in 1823 he entered the cabinet. For ten years he was the most influential of the ministers and deserves much of the discredit due to all who managed the realm. It is unnecessary to dispute over the exact share of each. There was odium enough for all. In 1833 Calomarde sided with Don Carlos and was banished, dying in Toulouse in 1842.]

to cause his interests to dominate. He merely chose men reputed to be skilful and opposed them in his council to men who were necessary but dangerous. Spain lent itself to this oblique course because her passions had died out : the voluntary royalists who opposed the Negros had been punished. The majority of the episcopal body turned a deaf ear to cries for the re-establishment of the Inquisition. In 1827 the old hands " of the faith," who had arisen in Catalonia against Ferdinand and his ministers, had been crushed with no hope of return. The same causes brought about the extinction of the liberal effervescence. Mina himself was obliged to escape by flight from the persecutions of populations which had once celebrated his exploits.

Ferdinand appeared equally indifferent or undecided in regard to the members of his family. On March 29th, 1830, when his young wife Maria Christina of Naples was pregnant, he issued a " pragmatic sanction " proclaiming as a law of the state a resolution of King Charles IV, made in accord with a demand of the cortes of 1789, abolishing the Salic law instituted in 1713 by Philip V, and thus re-established the right of women to inherit the throne of Spain ; but he afterwards showed no predilection for the young princess Maria Isabella Louisa, who was born in July of the same year.

Again he assembled the most devoted partisans of his brother Don Carlos about his throne, and when an attack of the gout brought him to the edge of

DON CARLOS I

the tomb in September, 1832, he signed a decree revoking the new law of succession. Then, returned to life again, he placed the infante Don Carlos at a distance, drove away the ministers who had wrung the fatal signature from his feeble hand and denounced their odious manœuvres; and as though to protect himself against new obsessions he placed the government in the hands of the queen, his wife, until his health should be restored. He let her publish decrees of amnesty for political criminals, take measures to destroy the existence of the voluntary royalists, reduce the privileges of the council of Castile ; then, for fear of seeing her advance too rapidly in the way of reforms, he had her announce in a manifesto of December that he did not intend to introduce the slightest innovation into the constitutional laws of the monarchy, nor to change anything that was established. On January 4th, 1833, he announced that, as his health was sufficiently recovered, he had reassumed the reins of government. The day before, so that they might receive full authenticity, the queen placed in the archives the act of the cortes of 1789 and the revolution of Charles IV in regard to the abolition of the Salic law. In spite of his antipathy towards innovators Ferdinand felt that it was necessary to constitute a political force around the cradle of his daughter. Men for whom the name of Don Carlos was a menace came together to

[1833 A.D.]

defend the young princess. A decree of April 7th, 1833, convened the cortes at Madrid. The 3rd of June, the nobles, prelates, and delegates of the cities took an oath of allegiance to the princess of the Asturias, as heiress of the crown of Spain and the Indes. The 29th of September, 1833, Ferdinand died, leaving a heavy sceptre in the hands of his daughter.[d]

RISE OF CARLISM

Though Ferdinand while alive had been accumulating legal acts in favour of direct descent, he had attached more and more importance to obtaining the acquiescence of his brother Don Carlos in his sovereign will. He had sent a royal order asking when he thought of recognising the already proclaimed heiress. Don Carlos, not to be behindhand, profited by this to take up a definite position as claimant in the eyes of the public. He wrote his brother a letter which he hastened to make public, in which these words were found:

You ask whether or not I intend recognising your daughter as princess of the Asturias? My conscience and honour will not permit this. My rights to the crown, if I survive you, or you leave no male posterity, are so legitimate that I need not enumerate them. These rights were given by God when he willed my birth, and he alone can take them away by granting you a son, an event that I desire perhaps even more than you. Moreover, I am defending the rights of all those who come after me. Thus I find myself obliged to send you the enclosed declaration, of which I send a formal copy to you and other sovereigns, to whom I hope you will communicate it.

Adieu, very dear brother of my heart. I am always yours, always yours lovingly, and you are ever present in the prayers of your most affectionate brother,

CARLOS.

The declaration was thus worded:

SIRE:

I, Carlos-Maria-Isidoro de Bourbon, infante of Spain, am thoroughly convinced of my legitimate rights to the Spanish throne in case of my surviving you, or your not leaving male issue. I say that my conscience and my honour will not permit me to swear to or recognise any other rights, and this I declare.

Your affectionate and faithful servant,

RAMALHAO, April 29th, 1833. DON CARLOS, Infante.

In answer to this declaration Ferdinand wrote to his brother saying that, without dreaming of violating his conscience, he nevertheless must forbid his returning to Spain, "for very serious political reasons and in consideration of the country's laws." He could not, he continued, make the declarations to foreign kings, basing his refusal on the principle that foreign governments ought not to interfere in interior state affairs. The salutations used were always full of an affectionate tenderness that formed a curious contrast to the real purport of the letters.

Don Carlos submitted to the banishment imposed, but had no idea of leaving Portugal, so as soon as an order came to go to Italy, he busied himself with reasons for not doing anything of the kind, not openly refusing that obedience which he had always affected to owe his brother, but inventing a crowd of pretexts for not rendering it. The now published correspondence between the two brothers on this occasion shows, on the infante's part, a series of successive inventions to excuse his stay in Portugal, and from the king a refutation of the vain pretexts advanced, and a constant endeavour to remove obstacles to departure. Ferdinand, at length, left off using a tone of fraternal love and spoke as an annoyed king, desiring his brother to say whether he intended to obey or not. The answer was proud and dis-

dainful.   Don Carlos said if he left Portugal, he would have the air of
a fugitive who had committed some crime : that he declined to put himself
in such a shameful position, and, if really guilty, demanded a trial according
to the laws of the realm (July, 1833).

From this date Don Carlos led a party quite in opposition to his sovereign, although keeping up an appearance of not stirring up civil war before
his brother's death.   He began to gather round him in his little court at
Ramalhao, then at Mafra and Coimbra, all those who had refused their oath to
Princess Isabella.   Inflammatory pamphlets went thence in every direction
to spread doubt in men's minds as to the legality of Ferdinand's testamentary
arrangements.   A few active men were already engaged in raising army
corps.   Baron Los Valles was sent into France and England to convince
those two governments of the justness of the claim put forth by the Spanish
infante.[b]

WAR OF THE CHRISTINOS AND CARLISTS (1833-1839 A.D.)

Scarcely had King Ferdinand VII closed his eyes, when the apostolic party
in northern Spain, especially in Navarre and the Basque provinces, proclaimed
Don Carlos, brother of the king, as King Charles V.   In order successfully

QUEEN MARIA CHRISTINA

to oppose the Carlists, who
fought for absolutism and
priesthood, there was nothing
for the regent, Maria Christina, to do but to throw herself
into the arms of the liberal
party.   Thus the seven years'
war between Carlists and
Christinos grew out of a fight
for the throne into a civil war
and a battle for principles.
The Carlists had the upper
hand to start with, owing to
the ability of their general,
Zumalacarregui, against
whom the Christinos could
place no equally matched
leader.   From Portugal, where
Don Carlos was residing with
his beloved nephew, Don Miguel, this general threatened
the frontiers of Spain.
Hence Christina turned to
England and France, and the
Quadruple Alliance of April
22nd, 1834, was concluded
between these states and Spain
and Portugal, the object of

which was to maintain the constitutional throne of Isabella and of Maria da
Gloria and to drive out the two pretendants, Carlos and Miguel.   Still, in
that same year, these two men, who enjoyed the favour of the eastern powers
and of the pope to a high degree, were obliged to leave Portugal.   Carlos
went to England in June, on an English ship, but he escaped again in July,

[1834–1855 A.D.]

and, after an adventurous journey through France, appeared suddenly in Navarre to reanimate the courage of his followers by his royal presence. The war was carried on with passion and cruelty on both sides. After the death of Zumalacarregui, who lost his life on June 14th, 1835, at the siege of Bilbao, the Christinos, who exceeded in numbers, seemed to have the advantage. But they could accomplish little against the restless Cabrera, who had just received his first ecclesiastical orders, and had gone over into the camp of the pretender. He was a most able guerila leader. The turning-point came first when the command of the Christino army was intrusted to Espartero. He conquered the Carlists in 1836 in a bloody battle at Luchana, hastened to the relief of the capital when the Carlists advanced to the vicinity of Madrid in 1837, and compelled Carlos to retreat.

THOMASO ZUMALACARREGUI

To these losses was added discord in the camp itself. The pretender, wholly lacking in competence and independence, was the tool of his *camarilla*,[1] who in the choice of a general paid more attention to a knowledge of the catechism than of the arts of war and displaced the most able leaders to put up their own creatures in their stead. The new general, Guergué, was beaten several times by Espartero in 1838, which gradually cooled the enthusiasm of the northern provinces. He was deposed and the chief command given to the crafty Maroto, who, as an enemy of the *camarilla* could have maintained himself against their continual attacks only by gaining great victories. Since he could not win these against the superior force of Espartero, he concluded the Treaty of Vergara with him on August 31st, 1839, according to which he went over to the Christinos with his army and obtained in return an amnesty and the confirmation of the freedom of Basque and Navarre. With this, the cause of Don Carlos was hopelessly lost. The latter went to France in September with many of his followers, and had to pass six years under police supervision in the city of Bourges. Not until 1845, after he had transferred all his pretensions to his eldest son, the count of Montemolin, did he receive permission to depart, whereupon he betook himself to Italy. He died at Trieste on March 10th, 1855. His followers continued to fight for some

[1 Burgos *h* thus sums up Don Carlos: "The heart of this prince was as incapable of elevated sentiments as his head was of political combinations. His profound ignorance made him regard the enthusiasm displayed by the passionate and disheartened crowds as general and unanimous, and the delight of the populace he regarded as a sign of approbation of the system of intolerance with which he was credited. In the unarrested march of his force to Madrid in 1837 the delighted pretendant saw the hand of providence raising him to the throne of his ancestors, and his apathy prevented his taking the means which his fatalism moreover considered unnecessary. His courtiers, puffed up with passing advantages, thought that by dint of them and the stolid impassivity of their sovereign they could give the rein to their resentments."]

time longer in Catalonia under Cabrera. But they also were overpowered by Espartero, and in July, 1840, with a force of about eight thousand men, were obliged to flee to France, where they were kept under supervision. The civil war was now at an end, but the strife continued. Espartero, entitled duke of victory (Vittoria) was the most influential and the most popular personage in Spain, with whom everyone, even the queen-regent, had to reckon.

THE STORMY REGENCY OF CHRISTINA (1833–1841 A.D.)

In the meanwhile the latter neither by her private life nor by her political conduct had been able to win the love and respect of the Spaniards. Her liberal attacks did not go very deep and as soon as the immediate necessity was past they gave place to the most opposite tendencies. At the spread of the Carlist rebellion in 1834, she had placed the once persecuted Martinez de la Rosa, known as a poet and writer, at the head of the ministry and had given the country a constitution [the *estatuto real*] which satisfied no one. The cortes convened again after a long interval and soon became divided into the two hostile factions of the moderates (*moderados*) and the progressists (*progresistas*). The ministries changed rapidly. The progressists demanded abolition of the monks' orders and confiscation of their property, which was in part carried out. In single cities it came to bloody excesses; cloisters were destroyed, monks and nuns murdered, priests and Jesuits driven over the border. The continual wavering, the frequent dissolution of the cortes increased the discontent; the progressists in 1836 feared a reaction and wanted to make concessions. Revolts were organised in the larger cities, the constitution of 1812 was placed on the programme. The government responded by placing Madrid in a state of siege, by disbanding the national guard. Revolt broke out in the summer residence, La Granja, whither Christina had retreated. Soldiers of the guard forced their way into the palace and compelled her to adopt the constitution of 1812.

A constitutional assembly discussed a revision of the same, and thus the new constitution of 1837 came into being. Christina took oath to keep it, but hoped by watching over the election to bring the *moderados* into the cortes and the ministry. When she succeeded in accomplishing this in 1840, she issued a municipal law in accordance with which the election of municipal authorities was placed in the hands of the government. This caused a revolt in Madrid and other cities, and when Christina commissioned Espartero, who had just returned victoriously, to quell the uprisal in Madrid he refused to be made the tool of an unpopular policy. And yet he was the only man who could check the revolution which was threatening on all sides. Hence Christina was obliged to appoint Espartero as ministerial president on September 16th, 1840. He chose all progressist members for his cabinet, made a triumphal entry into Madrid on September 29th, and placed his programme before the queen-regent in Valencia on October 5th. In this he demanded repeal of the municipal law, dissolution of the cortes, and dismissal of the *camarilla*.

The regency had little attraction more for Christina under such conditions. Other influences were also at work. Shortly after the death of her husband, she had taken a handsome life-guardsman, called Muñoz, into her favour, had made him chamberlain, and had secretly married him. The union was soon proclaimed by a large number of children, but not until 1844 was there a public marriage, whereupon Muñoz was made duke of Rianzares and grandee of Spain. By this act she had thrown away her womanly respect and laid herself open to all sorts of attacks, so that she preferred to leave the country. On October 12th, she resigned her position as regent and travelled to France.

ESPARTERO REGENT (1841-1843 A.D.)

The newly elected cortes, on May 8th, 1841, named Espartero regent of Spain and guardian of the queen Isabella and her sister the infanta Luisa Fernanda. Nor did he prove unworthy of this high position, seeking to establish order in all branches of the state administration and to preserve his respect before the clergy and the pope. Since he knew how energetically Christina, supported by Louis Philippe, was working against him with her influence and her money, he attached himself more to England, whereupon those who were envious of him, and his rivals, accused him of selling Spain's commercial interests to England. The fact that he quelled a rebellion in Barcelona in 1842 by a bombardment, was charged against him as tyranny. New revolts broke out in the south in 1843; Colonel Prim hastened to Catalonia and placed himself at the head of the soldiers who had been won over through large expenditures of money by Christina's

ESPARTERO, REGENT

agents. Espartero's bitterest enemy, General Narvaez, landed in Valencia and entered Madrid with his troops. Espartero, against whom moderados and progressists had conspired together, found himself abandoned and set sail for England from Cadiz on July 26th, 1843. Not until 1848 was it safe for him to return.

THE PROFLIGATE QUEEN ISABELLA II (1843-1868 A.D.)

In November, 1843, the thirteen-year-old Isabella was declared of age. She took over the reins of government, appointed Narvaez, who had been raised to be duke of Valencia, president of the ministry, and called back her mother. This opened the doors and gates to French influence, to the game of intrigue and reaction. The constitution of 1837 was changed in 1845 in favour of absolutism, the freedom of the press was limited, the national guard abolished, and the cortes even more than in France reduced to a nominal existence. In order to insure for his house a lasting influence in Spain and to obtain for it a reversion of the Spanish throne, Louis Philippe, acting with Christina, brought about a marriage on October 16th, 1846, between Isabella and her cousin Francis de Asis, and between the infanta Luisa and the duke of Montpensier, the youngest of his sons. (Louis Philippe had planned at first to marry Isabella also to one of his sons, the duke of Aumale, but he gave this up on account of the decided protest of Palmerston's cabinet and chose instead for Isabella in Francis de Asis that person who, on account of his mental and bodily weakness, would stand least in the way of his son, Montpensier). This marriage which was conducted wholly in secret cost Louis Philippe the friendship of the English cabinet. The pleasure-loving Isabella, following in the footsteps of her mother, soon grew heartily tired of her Francis and enjoyed herself in July, 1847, at La Granja, with the handsome and agreeable progressist General Serrano and other officers, while Francis found himself condemned to a hermit's life at the hunting castle of Pardo. The marriage was a very unfortunate one, and Christina, the evil genius of Spain, fled one day and came back the next.

QUEEN ISABELLA II

Isabella kept more and more to the path of her father Ferdinand, and pursued an administrative policy which joined military despotism to clerical absolutism and in which confessors and soldiers played a rôle, and even guided the rudder of state. While such conduct repelled the liberal elements from her side the frivolity of her private life made her lose all claims to respect.[1] She even went so far that the legitimacy of all her children was doubted. No wonder that from time to time revolts broke out, which, as is customary in Spain, were incited and led by officers. The government saved itself by executions and deportations. The ministerial president Marshal Narvaez, who bore the title duke of Valencia, was always ready for such drastic measures. His successor was Gonzalez Bravo [or Brabo] Murillo, who soon had the whole army against him.[e] His cabinet was very significant and important, not only because of the question of economies, but also because of Bravo Murillo's project to abolish or diminish the military preponderance which was not very beneficial to the country. The germs of discord remained, to be united with those displayed in other acts, such as the ostentatious reception of Narvaez in Paris by the Spanish representative, the duke de Sotomayor, who was replaced by the marquis de Valdegamas, and

[1 In 1852 a priest named Merino stabbed her, but her life was saved by the whalebone of her corsets. The priest was garrotted, his body burned.]

the ridiculous prohibition of the farce called the *entierro de la sardina* (the burial of the sardine) and the piñata ball. The burial of the sardine is part of the carnival festivities on Ash Wednesday. The piñata ball is a masked ball at the theatre — the piñata being a large earthenware jar full of sweets; the dancers are blindfolded, turned round, and have to try and break the jar with poles, after which there is a general scramble for the sweets. These sports were prohibited by the minister of government without consulting his colleagues, whom he thus compromised, occasioning resignations and annoyances, while the prestige of the new cabinet in the palace suffered somewhat from the ill-judged and useless measure of one of its members. In an unfriendly spirit towards the ministry, Napoleon showed marked honour to Narvaez and Sotomayor. General O'Donnell [who had won distinction in the Morocco wars of 1860 and become duke of Tetuan] showed himself somewhat disrespectful towards the minister of war because he had made several military appointments out of the order of seniority, the young officer of infantry wishing to put an end to this injustice.*j*

Spain was, on the surface, a monarchy akin to that of France, Belgium, and England. Below the surface, as soon as the dynastic peril had subsided and the throne of the queen was somewhat consolidated, the old reactionary undercurrent set to work. A novel and powerful instrument of reaction — militarism — appeared on the scene and made Spain sadly famous. Its interference in politics and its *pronunciamientos* were fatal to discipline and, what was far worse, to the sense of respect for parliamentary legality which is the corner-stone of modern institutions. It must be said that Castilian militarism somewhat atoned for its interference in politics by using its extraordinary influence quite as often in the cause of liberty and of progress as in defence of reactionary cabinets and palace favourites. It will suffice to say that Marshal Espartero acted thus from 1836 to 1843 to crush the first Carlist risings, and to check the caprices of the regent Doña Christina, and then, in 1854–1856, again stepped in to check another reaction. Marshal O'Don-

MARSHAL NARVAEZ

nell was the champion of moderate liberalism from 1856 to 1866, which might have preserved the crown of Queen Isabella had she not always harboured preferences for retrograde statesmen and generals. Marshals Prim and Serrano, too, were in the van of the progressists and advanced liberals who would fain have served their queen, but went over to revolution and conspiracies at last in sheer disgust. Such names can well be set against those of the military champions of political reaction and religious intolerance — marshals Narvaez [who died in 1868], Cheste, Novaliches, and Calonje.*k*

In July, 1868, a great military revolt was to break out. The minister caused the most important generals, among them Serrano and Dulce, to be deported to the Canary Isles, and even banished from Spain the queen's brother-in-law, the duke of Montpensier, whose name seemed to serve as a watchword for the revolution. Excitement increased in the land. Isabella thought herself compelled to enter into closer relations than hitherto with her friend and ally, as she called Napoleon III, and arranged an interview with him for the 18th and 19th of September in the two frontier posts Biarritz and San Sebastian. Napoleon was accredited with the plan of recalling his troops from Rome and filling their places with Spanish soldiers in the event of his beginning his long-threatened war with Germany. Isabella, who had just been honoured by receiving the Golden Rose of the Faith and Virtue from the pope, was very much in favour of such a project.

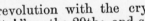
GENERAL LEOPOLD O'DONNELL

THE REBELLION OF 1868 A.D.

But at the very moment when the Franco-Spanish alliance was to have been concluded and their majesties were at their appointed posts, rebellion broke out in Cadiz. It was the 18th of September. The banished generals Serrano and Prim returned, the rear-admiral Topete joined them with the whole fleet, the few faithful troops were conquered by Serrano on September 28th, near Alcolea. All the larger cities, even Madrid, took sides with the revolution with the cry, "Down with the Bourbons! down with the Jesuits!" on the 29th; and so there was nothing left for Isabella but to leave San Sebastian the next day and to take refuge on French soil. She at once took up her residence at Pau whence she uttered a passionate but unavailing protest against her exile. When she realised that all hope of restoration, for the present, was gone, she went to Paris, where she died in 1904.

The direction of the state was intrusted to the leaders of the revolution. Marshal Serrano took the position of president of the ministry, Prim became minister of war, Topete of marine. The order of Jesuits and a number of cloisters were abolished, freedom of faith was proclaimed; in Barcelona and Madrid even Protestant services were held. The newly elected cortes, convened on February 18th, 1869, deliberated over a new constitution, declared in favour of a constitutional monarchy, and appointed Serrano regent, until a suitable candidate could be found. The political outlook, however, was not favourable for Spain. There existed a strong republican party, which threatened to oppose with arms the establishment of a new throne; the island of Cuba, that "pearl of the Antilles," was in full revolt, ready to break loose from Spain and found an independent republic; and Carlism again raised its head.[e]

PIRALA ON THE "MILD ANARCHY" OF 1869 A.D.

At the end of the year 1869, the state of the nation clearly showed that when parties pursue private rather than public aims the result can be no other than what then existed — that is, a monarchy without a monarch, a powerless regency, a constitution disregarded and infringed, an ill-directed and expiring *camara*, a dictatorship without a dictator, and an empty treasury and a retrograding revolution.

We do not lay the fault of this upon any of the men concerned in our revolution, and we do not think that history does so either, but we cannot cease to lament the lack of one of those men of genius who take the lead without imposing themselves. The situation had not improved at the beginning of the year 1870.

The cortes again resumed its labours. With praiseworthy frankness, Prim, as president of the council, said that they had reached a pitch of confusion in which, surrounded by thick clouds, they might come near to realising the fable of the two wolves who met on a dark night and devoured each other so that nothing was left but their tails.

Union facilitates the work of construction which is gradually perfected in every detail, but dissension entails the fate of the builders of the tower of Babel. A nation can show no sadder or more futile spectacle ; and yet it is the history of all. Is mankind condemned ever to turn in this vicious circle and never to get free from it ? It is impossible to think so, for in the midst of this continual conflict of interests and bastard ambitions the nineteenth century has achieved imperishable victories.

Nations conquer their sovereignty and of their own right make their laws, and struggle unceasingly to overcome ancient traditions, uproot absurd vices and tyrannical tendencies. Thus even as science pierces the mountains, explores the depths of the sea, discovers and explains the spots on the sun, and almost realises the aforetime foolish and chimerical ambition of the Titans ; so politics, that science of modern societies and of free and civilised nations, will find the solution of the social problem bringing the rights of all men, the interests of all nations, and the good of all humanity into combined and harmonious action. A vast idea like a great discovery suffices to bring the whole world into close relationship. And like the electric current which flashes words and ideas from pole to pole, a grand political inspiration, social, human, fraternal, moral, just, and worthy, needs but to be hinted to triumph. Printing had but to be invented to extend over the whole world ; steam came into immediate use, and Franklin needed but a lightning-conductor for Turgot to exclàim :

> *" Eripuit cœlo fulmen*
> *Sceptrumque tyrannis."*

And the lightning-conductor alone produced the cable which brings both worlds into constant communication, the thread which annihilates distances and transmits thoughts and events. Politics is indeed a science, and if nothing is impossible to science, shall anything be impossible to politics ?

This work of social reconstruction advances slowly, all collecting materials and contributing their ideas to its perfectionment ; the work will be completed ; it is but a question of time, and what appears long in the life of the individual is very short in the life of nations. Liberty and civilisation being inseparably welded, where civilisation is least, liberty finds most obstacles, and the task must be more difficult and laborious.

In the meanwhile Spain was going through a troubled period, and it was said in the press and in the cortes that a heavy responsibility lay upon those who had taken part in a political movement the issue of which was so unfortunate, and cut off the country from the civilising progress of the century and the social importance to which it had so many claims; that the triumphant liberal spirit was suffocating for want of guidance, and could not succeed in laying definitive institutions upon a solid basis; that the perils surrounding the revolution were increasing; that all was unstable and that "a mild anarchy" reigned everywhere, as was said by the minister of government himself, who was yet so dilatory in framing fundamental laws.

There followed the famous session of March 19th, 1870, when the forced harmony exploded between unionists, progressists, and democrats, placing regency, government, and country in a terrible position. Thus it was published by a deputy of recognised ability, who had good reason to be well acquainted with the internal workings of the camara, that "it would be difficult to conceive worse confusion than that to which it was a prey. Without true unity in the ministry, without true unity in the majority, without unity even in the midst of the oppositions, every individual, whether minister or deputy, radical or conservative, republican or traditionalist, in the questions natural or incident to the debate expressed his own opinion without thought for the general interests of any party; the result of which was that every one of the three hundred representatives who had their seat upon the benches of the congress spoke a different language, and if such a state of moral anarchy continued, the assembly would before long be converted into a regular tower of Babel."[l]

ESTIMATE BY CHERBULIEZ OF GENERAL PRIM

There are in every country men who accomplish their ends by romantic adventures, and this is more common in Spain than anywhere else. There it is an ancestral or fictitious adventurer, who has really no other god but his own interests, but succeeds by his audacities and a kind of native generosity in giving an air of grandeur to his exploits, a varnish of glory and poetry to his cupidity. So the favourite Spanish hero, the famous Cid Campeador, appears to us when criticism has rolled away the luminous clouds with which pure legend has surrounded him. The Rodrigo whom Corneille celebrated was only the vision of a poet; the true Cid of history was a man of prey, not troubled with scruples, ready to espouse all causes, bearing into every camp the restlessness of his moods and courage, fighting alternately for or against his prince, serving Christ or Mohammed, and, if one can believe the Arabic chroniclers, preferring a bushel of gold to a smile from Ximena. His mighty sword thrusts, his haughty bearing, his natural grandiloquence, redeemed everything; he had received from heaven the art of persuasive speech, and posterity remembers words more than intentions. The *romancero* relates that, being in a hurry to set out on an expedition, and having need of money, he borrowed a very large sum from a Jew, giving him as guarantee a coffer full of jewels, which coffer being opened after his departure, was found to contain only sand. On his return, the Jew reproached him with deception. "Yes, it was sand," he answered loftily. "but this sand contained the gold of my given word." The idea was good albeit a trifle extravagant.

It is not with any evil intention to the memory of General Prim, to suggest that he also was a hero with too easy a conscience. Is one bound to have more convictions, more principles than the Cid? "Do you know," said Castelar [m] when orator of the opposition, "who is General Prim's god? It is Chance. Would you know his religion? It is Fatalism. And his ideal? The dream of always keeping power in his own hands. To that everything is brought to bear and to that everything is sacrificed. Institutions matter nothing to him; he bends them to his convenience. Laws count even less for him. They are mere spider webs, to be brushed aside by the swords of his captain-generals. Parties are as nothing, he dissolves them. Engagements have never hampered him, for he forgets them. The most inconceivable alliances are not repugnant, provided he and his are advantaged thereby."

But it is just to add that General Prim, when he came into power, astonished his enemies as much as his friends by the continued wisdom of his conduct. The most redoubtable trial of an adventurer is success. His ideas must grow with his fortune; having gained the coveted rank, he must break with his past, his habits and memories, so as to transform himself into a statesman. Only those who have good stuff in them lend themselves to such changes, and Don Juan Prim soon proved that the Aranjuez conspirator possessed the qualities of a politician, a quick sense of justice, a power of realising situations, skilful management of men and interests, and tact sufficient to use his authority

GENERAL PRIM

without doing anything irregular. He could use strategy in councils, employing a sober yet nervous eloquence which went straight to the point, and possessed above the art of speaking the more useful one of being silent. A Portuguese has remarked that this last talent, strongly admired among a talkative people, made a man resemble a Gothic cathedral, and gave him the prestige of obscurity and mystery.

To be president of the council was no easy task. It was already difficult to govern an assembly composed of two parts; the difficulty was still greater when there were three. Oscillations from the Centre, who formed the necessary support for the majority, gave the minister perpetual anxiety and forced him to see-saw politics. The radicals, or democratic monarchists, led by a highly popular man, Rivero, and a man of great talent, Martos, played a very considerable rôle in the constituent cortes of 1869. They were at one with the liberal unionists in desiring a king, even as they agreed with the republicans to make a democratic constitution with all possible speed. Government could only expect a conditional support from them. It was inconvenient to satisfy them, dangerous to let them be discontented. It was necessary then perpetually to negotiate with these monarchists by circumstance. A single imprudence might have lost all.

Monarchists by conviction were themselves divided into a crowd of small parties, each having its candidate for the throne.

General Juan Prim needed all his attention and skill to maintain some degree of cohesion among so variegated a majority. He had to dominate the unruly, satisfy the ambitious by a portfolio, and the vain by a decoration; to reassure the timorous, calm the impatient, even like a good sheepdog who runs ceaselessly round a flock, heading the foremost, driving in the scattered, hastening the laggards. Each party sought to gain the general for their candidate, for Don Juan, as someone said at the congress, resembled a political zero, which, placed at the right of a figure, increased its value tenfold, and a candidature quoted at nine on the political bourse would be worth ninety when it had gained the approving smile of the president. His reigning principle was to discourage no illusion. " He knows quite well," said the opposition, "that he cannot maintain his position much longer in this unstable equilibrium, which consists in keeping in with all parties, being against all parties, and above them all. The secret of his politics is to keep everyone hoping. He gives them no promises, for he is circumspect and never commits himself. He never betrays himself by his acts, being very reserved, diplomatic, and making no engagements; but he gives hope by his enigmas, his reticences, his air of mystery."

Don Juan, however, was not always so reserved. When occasion demanded, he denounced to the majority the dangers which threatened them, adjuring them to seek safety in conciliatory politics, short of which only misery and disaster could be expected. If his advice was ill received, he complained that they made government impossible, and spoke of retiring. This manœuvre, executed with military precision, never failed of its effect. Thanks to his warning, his threats, and his reticences, that same majority, composed of men who never agreed nor loved one another, persisted in remaining united, a rare spectacle in Spain.[n]

THE HUNT FOR A KING

Thus there existed a monarchical constitution with no monarch; and a large number of republicans took pains to make a monarchy impossible by speeches in the cortes and by revolts in the provinces. No one seemed desirous of the crown of a country politically lamed by its party system and financially rotten. The ministerial president and minister of war, Count Prim, made every effort to find a suitable personage, but for a long time in vain. The former regent of Spain, Espartero; the Coburg prince, Don Ferdinand, father of the king of Portugal; King Luiz of Portugal himself; Prince Thomas of Genoa, nephew of the king of Italy—refused in turn. The duke of Montpensier, whose wife was sister to the ex-queen Isabella, was ready to accept it, but on account of this very relationship he had many opponents among the monarchs, who, when it came to selecting a Bourbon, preferred Prince Alfonso, Isabella's son, to her brother-in-law.

Isabella made her plan with this end in view. Acting on the advice of her friend the empress Eugénie she signed her resignation on June 25th, 1870, and made over all her political rights to her son Alfonso. First, however, there was question of another prince. Among those who in 1869 had returned a negative answer was Prince Leopold of Hohenzollern-Sigmaringen who, as a Catholic, as husband of a Portuguese princess, as a relative of the Napoleonic house, and as belonging to the reigning house of Prussia, seemed a very suitable person in the eyes of the government. The latter returned to this choice in 1870 and in June sent a deputation to him. This time the prince accepted. The deputation returned to Madrid, a ministerial council was held, and on June 2nd it was decided to offer the crown of Spain to Prince Leopold of Hohenzollern officially and to proclaim this candidacy publicly. The news was brought to all the capitals of Europe on July 3rd, by telegraph. The country stood at a new crisis of affairs.*e*

Napoleon III of France opposed the giving of the crown of Spain to a Prussian prince, and secured his resignation. This success led him to further demands, which he pressed so outrageously that Prussia, long ready to avenge its old disgraces before French armies, returned answers that led Napoleon to declare war. The Franco-Prussian War of 1870–1871 was the result. Prussia took a new place in the world and in Germany, the French armies were surrendered in droves by their king and his general officers, and France was rid both of her Napoleon III and of her military reputation. And all this as the result of the Spanish advertisement for a king. The prince Hohenzollern, who had refused the bauble once, and had had it taken away when he reached out to accept it, was dropped from the eligible list.*a*

AMADEO'S REIGN (1870–1873 A.D.); AND THE REPUBLIC (1873–1874 A.D.)

Marshal Prim had persuaded the second son of the king of Italy, Prince Amadeo, duke of Aosta,[1] to accept the candidacy. The cortes elected him king of Spain on November 16th, 1870, with a vote of 191 to 98. He arrived in Madrid on January 2nd, 1871, and took oath to support the constitution a few days after Prim had fallen a victim to a murderous assault. The government of the new king, who had made Marshal Serrano first ministerial president, was a continual fight for the ministry between the monarchic factions, while the republicans and Carlists organised revolts in the south and north.*e*

Serrano was a soldier risen to the highest ranks through the favour of Queen Isabella, whom he had not hesitated to betray the moment he believed that others would be put over him in the highest offices of politics and the army. His real ability as a general was more than mediocre. Allied with Prim in the insurrectional movement and the pronunciamiento of 1868 he was able to overthrow his benefactress' throne; but the day after the 29th of September he saw himself transformed by his colleague into a puppet king. Prim, who was his superior in a hundred ways, especially in ability and energy, henceforth ruled over him. Not daring to revolt against his comrade, he submitted tranquilly, contenting himself with the pomp of the regency which he had received in exchange for his submission to the imperious will of the minister of war.

[1 "Young, valiant, having bled for the country whose dominions his father had extended, crowned with glory, beloved by his fellow citizens, educated in the liberal spirit and holding an enviable position, he neither coveted the throne of Spain, his aspirations being ever modest, nor refused any sacrifice to win success for the nation which had won his sympathy from the first.

["The liberals could not deny that Amadeo belonged to a family which represented the liberal spirit, more than any other in Europe, and which had seconded the aspirations of lovers of liberty. The fact of the duke of Aosta's being educated in the latter school, was a guarantee not to one party, but to all liberals ; and if he obtained the votes of the constituents, sacrificing his most dear affections to the love of the country, there should be but one rule for all liberal monarchists — king and liberty. This rule had inspired great men in England to found the monarchy of 1688 and this is what Spanish patriotism advised." — PIRALA.*l*]

After the assassination of the marshal, Serrano found himself again in the highest place and obliged by his position to direct the beginnings of a young king, lacking in great political qualifications and the indispensable knowledge of Spain's needs and aspirations as well as being very unpopular on account of his foreign origin. To succeed in such a task a man of exceptional ability was required and Serrano's talents were but mediocre. Under the marshal's feeble hand, passions far from being calmed flared up much fiercer than ever and discord penetrated every element of official life.

Marshal Serrano and his colleagues having given in their resignations, Amadeo determined to try the experiment of a radical régime. But Señor Zorilla was incapable of rising above the violent and mean passions of the party to which he belonged. Amadeo was compelled to dismiss him in less than three months. Admiral Malcampo was invested with the power on October 6th; six weeks later he too was compelled to hand in his resignation.

Amadeo now confided the power to Señor Sagasta, December 20th, 1871. The situation, however, became more critical day by day. The king was absolutely isolated in the midst of his people. The educated and especially the aristocratic classes, justly wounded at seeing a foreign prince seated without any right whatever on the throne, held aloof from the court. The clergy could scarcely be expected to sympathise with a régime that exhibited decided Voltairian tendencies.

The people had never sanctioned the arbitrary choice and protested against the accomplished act sometimes by noisy demonstrations, more often by a still more dangerous attitude of cold and irreducible hostility. The republicans benefited largely by the situation. Amadeo was daily covered with mud and the ministry found it impossible to make the royal dignity and person respected. In order to quell so formidable a storm, the genius of a Napoleon I, the skill of a Cavour would have been required, and even then it is more than doubtful that with the prestige which genius gives and the resources which the most perfect art of governing men can provide, Amadeo would have settled his dynasty firmly in Spain. In truth the greatest fault found was with his foreign origin, and this intrinsic defect could not be overcome by personal merit.

How often, turning his thoughts towards his absent country, towards that city of Turin where he was the idol of its citizens, must Amadeo have regretted not having resisted more vigorously the demands of his father and the Italian ministers, as they prayed him to accept that crown of Spain for which he had so little vocation.

His tastes were simple and his habits modest — altogether too modest for Spain. He was affable, received everyone, and forced himself to appear as amiable with the common people as with the politicians and the few great nobles who had not deserted the court. He understood the low condition of the treasury and did not take a penny of the civil list which the constitution allowed him. He lived upon his own personal income, spending freely, and always tried to make use of Spanish articles and purveyors. The queen on her part zealously occupied herself with good works. Yet when Amadeo passed through the Madrid streets those who did not salute him were assuredly in greater number than those who through politeness took off their hats as he went by. The reception was no better in the provinces whenever the king and queen visited them.

And the situation kept on getting worse and worse. Señor Zorilla's downfall deeply incensed that statesman. In place of carrying on an honest opposition to Señor Sagasta, Zorilla, who had once promised Victor

[1872 A.D.]

Emmanuel to be "the most faithful of servants," hastened as soon as he was no longer minister to ally himself with the monarchy's worst enemies, made common cause with the most violent anarchists in order to undermine not only the cabinet, but the throne he had helped to establish. King Amadeo's position was becoming more and more critical. Placed between the republicans and Alfonsists, who fought him both in and out of parliament, and the Carlists who, less attached to constitutional forms and the manners of modern nations, openly declared war, raising the standard of war under the very eyes of his generals and officials, the king could not even count on the co-operation of his partisans, whose differences were now entirely incurable. Prime minister Sagasta was retired at the end of two months' sterile work and troubled existence. What could all this statesman's abilities do towards consolidating a monarchy deprived of a nation's support and condemned in public opinion?

The second Serrano ministry, of which Señor Sagasta was also a member, began its labours May 26th, 1872; but the king's hopes were again deceived. Serrano and his colleagues, judging the situation too critical to be remedied by ordinary measures, submitted a decree for the king's approbation which arbitrarily suspended several privileges guaranteed by the constitution, at the same time inviting his majesty to take in person the chief command of the army against the Carlists. Amadeo returned an energetic refusal to Marshal Serrano's requests. It was asked that he take part in civil war, and he could not stoop to this exigency. Ready to shed his blood for Spain the day on which his adopted country should be threatened from abroad, it was absolutely repugnant to him to direct a campaign in which his subjects would simply cut one another's throats. If he had not

SAGASTA

abdicated before, it was only to let his people and the whole of Europe see that he knew how to face danger, and that he had no intention of shirking his duties the moment they became most serious and pressing — a noble line of conduct, which even those who never approved of Amadeo's taking the Spanish throne must highly and unreservedly praise.

Marshal Serrano was incensed by the king's attitude and sent in his resignation. The monarch now thought for a moment of throwing aside the crown, which weighed more heavily on his brow than the leaden capes on the shoulders of the damned in Dante's *Inferno*. But to avoid the appearance of fleeing before the Carlists, he decided to postpone the execution of his resolve. He resigned himself to trying one last experiment with the radicals, by calling the famous Zorilla once more to the head of affairs, June 13th, 1872.

Zorilla's return to power immeasurably increased the audacity and violence of the sectarians.   Sure henceforth of impunity, and impatient to
attain their proposed end, they did not shrink from crime.   On July 18th,
1872, towards evening, as Amadeo was preparing to visit a circus, a warning

was hastily brought him that his life was to
be attempted and that the police were on the
track of a plot.   In vain did the queen, his
ministers, and household officials implore him
to renounce his visit.   The king, scorning
their advice and taking no notice of the threatening danger, would not consent to stay in
the palace.   He wished his people to know
that he feared not in the least to brave the
assassins who were preparing an ambush in
which he was to suffer the sad fate of
Marshal Prim.   Maria Victoria and the
marquis Dragonetti, in despair of convincing the king, determined to accompany him
in his drive across the capital.

When the royal carriage reached the
Calle del Arenal, at precisely the spot indicated by the police as the place where the
attack would be attempted, a discharge of
firearms suddenly came from a side street
and wounded one of the horses without
touching the king or queen, who owed their
lives to their coachman's cool-headedness.
As for the assassins, they easily made off
under cover of the night, protected by their
accomplices.   Maria Victoria returned almost
fainting to the royal palace.   Amadeo, on the
contrary, as intrepid before murderers' bullets as he had been on the field of Custozza,

KING AMADEO

never lost for a moment that impassible calm, witness both of his contempt
for danger and strength of soul.   He himself announced the attempt to his
father in the following telegram:

"I advise your majesty that this evening we have been object attack.   Thanks to God, all
safe. — AMADEO."

This infamous deed, far from provoking the fall of the monarchy,
retarded it.   After this event it would appear that he was laying down the
sceptre through fear of assassination.   Meanwhile political affairs grew
ceaselessly worse.   While the Carlist insurrection, in spite of the efforts of
General Moriones and the captain-general of Catalonia, assumed more and
more disquieting proportions, chaos attained its apogee in governmental
spheres, in the street, and in the heart of the cortes.   The army now began
to make some sign.   It could no longer endure the despotism of the discred-
ited advocates who were governing and ruining the country.   The treasury
was in the most pressing distress, and from all directions the violent tide of
general discontent rose towards the throne on which an honourable but powerless king was sitting.   Zorilla, not content with the ruin which he had accomplished, tried to overcome the resistance of the army by a vigorous action as
inopportune as unjust.   He proposed to the king to entrust a man named

Hidalgo who was a byword for treachery in the army with the command of a division in Catalonia. The king implored Zorilla to give this plan up. Zorilla threatened to resign. Finally Amadeo signed a decree as fatal as it was mad, not however without manifesting his anger and disgust. As soon as Hidalgo appeared, the artillery officers resigned *en masse*. The disorganisation of the army had become complete and put the finishing touches to the state of disorder ; Zorilla prepared new decrees which, under pretext of mastering the military recalcitrants, would have provoked a general explosion. But this time Amadeo I did not show himself disposed to follow the wishes of the radical leader. He would not consent to accomplish Spain's ruin and determined to abdicate. In vain did Zorilla and his supporters make an effort to deter the king from a resolution which would shatter their ambitious calculations. Amadeo would not listen to their prayers. He obliged the prime minister to communicate the act of abdication to the cortes, February 8th, 1873.

Amadeo left Spain as soon as possible after his abdication, February 12th. He returned to Italy by way of Lisbon. Every noble heart, even among his enemies, gave impartial homage to his chivalric character and loyalty ; but the aversion of the people to a foreign monarchy was such that the king's departure was one of the saddest ever known. While on the way near Badajoz some cowardly assassins fired upon the train which was bearing the son of Victor Emmanuel and his family back to the Italy they never should have left.

Time has softened the Spaniards' animosity against the duke of Aosta. To-day they recognise his fine qualities, while they admit, and not without reason, that even apart from his foreign origin he was not made to rule in that country, whose spirit he so little understood and whose pompous and aristocratic customs he never would have been able to assimilate.

The Spaniards have not forgotten the memory of this thoroughly honest king, who, wishing to remain true to his agreements, preferred giving up the throne to violating them, who firmly refused to become the tool of anarchists or to use force against a country which was not his own. They have also retained a touching memory of Queen Maria Victoria and of her piety and boundless charity. The attitude of the Spanish press on the duke of Aosta's death at Turin, January 18th, 1890, proved that his name is no longer unpopular across the Pyrenees; and in forgetting the mistake he committed in 1871, Spain knows how to give homage to the fine and brilliant qualities of her former king.[o]

REPUBLICAN SPAIN UNDER CASTELAR (1873 A.D.)

The congress declared at once in favour of a republic on February 11th, and on February 12th chose a ministry to take charge of the executive, in which Figueras was president and Castelar was foreign minister. The programme of the new rulers was : " a federative republic for Spain, with self-government for the single states as in Switzerland and the United States; suppression of centralisation; abolition of the standing army; absolute separation of church and state; proclamation of the rights of the individual on the basis of a democratic constitution and under the authority of the law." If these political fantasies were to be accepted into the constitution, Spain would cease to exist — there would be merely cantons, municipal republics, and communes, in which Parisian conditions repeated themselves. The cortes was dissolved, and on June 1st a new constitutional cortes convened. This declared for the federative republic on June 8th, and drew up a preliminary outline of a constitution in which the above principles were adopted. With this, the so-called *Intransigentes* were not yet satisfied; they wanted a red republic and a social revolution. Since they could not impose their demands on the cortes, they left it, went into the southern states, and raised the red flag of rebellion. Ministries and presidencies followed each other in quick succession.

On September 7th, Castelar was chosen president of the executive, and at the outset found himself confronted with such chaos that he demanded and obtained unconditional authority for adopting military and political measures, including the declaration of a state of siege; he also postponed the debate on the constitution and adjourned congress from September 18th to January 2nd. Thus the visionary federative republican Castelar, understanding, however, the difference between theory and practice, had a full dictatorship in his hands. He needed such power. In the north, the Carlists were making decided advances, having with them in the field the pretender Don Carlos and his brother Don Alfonso; in the south, communes were being formed in single cities which renounced allegiance to the government; in the army shameless insubordination ran riot, soldiers fired on their officers, generals went over to the rebels. The cities of Alcoy, Seville, Cadiz, Valencia had to be taken by force, others surrendered at the approach of the generals.

EMILIO CASTELAR

Opposition lasted longest in the sea fortress of Cartagena, where General Contreras stood at the head of a committee of safety, as president of the republic of Murcia, had diplomatic dealings with foreign consuls, and bombarded and burned the neighbouring ports Almeria and Alicante. From these piratical excursions he came into contact with foreign warships, and the energetic German captain Werner, supported by an English captain, deprived him of two ships. Cartagena was surrounded from the land side and bombarded, but it did not surrender until after a siege of four months, on January 12th, 1874, to the governmental general Lopez Dominguez, after Contreras had left the harbour the day before, accompanied by the revolutionary junta, and after several hundred men had broken through the weak blockade of governmental ships and escaped to Algiers.*e*

THE BASQUES AND CARLISM

Carlism would long since have been reduced to impotency by the opposition it aroused among all classes of Spanish society, if one particular circumstance had not associated with its cause those interests and passions which it had taken under its protection. There are provinces in northeastern Spain which are Spanish only in name and which enjoy a veritable autonomy of which they are both jealous and proud. Furnishing the state neither soldiers nor money, they themselves regulate the use they make of their revenue, the equipment and employment of their militia — in fact all the details of internal administration. Honest, loyal, hardy, maintaining their roads and highways in their own fashion, which indeed left nothing to be desired; cultivating the least accessible of their mountains up to the very edges of the precipices, more industrious than the majority of the Spanish, the Basques of Guipuzcoa, Avala, and Biscay, had governed themselves for centuries, and they constituted a true mountain republic very similar to the primitive cantons of Switzerland. Who has not heard of the famous and everlasting oak of Guernica, under whose shade they held their patriarchal assemblies or *calzaras* and which in bygone days inspired Rousseau in the *Contrât Social* to utter these memorable and oft-quoted words : " When we see the happiest people in the world regulating their affairs of state by a body of peasants under an oak, and always conducting themselves wisely, what is to prevent one scorning the refinements of other nations which make themselves famous and miserable with so much art and mystery ? "

Like all truly republican peoples the Basques regarded their freedom as a prerogative or a happy accident. They gave no thought to letting their neighbour share it and had never sought to make their happiness a subject of propaganda. Their language — the Eskuara — which has nothing in common with Spain or indeed with any known idiom, was a barrier between them and the rest of the peninsula, and reduced them to a state of isolation in which their freedom rejoiced. As their language possesses no literature, the few general ideas which circulate in their villages and townships come from their priests, who teach them what goes on in the world, what is said and planned at Madrid. Thus, narrow in mind as they are suspicious and defiant, their sole aim is to preserve their *fueros*.

It had been easy to make them understand that the liberal monarchy nourished the dark design of depriving them of these, and that it was disposed to reduce them to the same system of government as the other Spanish provinces. And it was not more difficult for the pretender to persuade them that only an absolute monarchy could guarantee the franchises which were dearer to them than life. Did they not know that their liberty was a privilege, and that privileges have less to fear from a king who can do as he pleases than from a constitutional régime, whether monarchy or republic, where everything is governed by law ?

So, with the exception of the village *bourgeoisie*, won over to liberal ideas, these mountaineers belong body and soul to the Carlist cause, and thus we have seen the singular phenomenon of a republican people trying to impose upon others a government they would not have had at any price, and working to set upon the Spanish throne an absolute king who promised to let them remain a republic as a reward. " We hope that before long," wrote Señor Castelar on the 12th of September, 1873, " these Basque provinces which furnish subsidies and spies to the Carlist and where the army of the republic can nowhere find either protection or assistance, will receive the chastisement their errors deserve, since these the happiest and freest provinces of Spain are fighting not to obtain a king for themselves or to offer him of their sons and the fruits of their economy, but to impose one upon the Spanish nation while continuing to live themselves as a republic. Certainly the government will respect a legislation which is in harmony with its principles and ideas, but I am its spokesman in saying to these people that if anything threatens their future and that tree celebrated by Rousseau as the monument of liberty, it will be due to their blind obstinacy in supporting at the price of their blood, as the Swiss did formerly, the monster of absolutism."

It was among these sandalled republicans in hides and blue berets, indefatigable walkers and great players of *peloto*, that Carlism recruited its ranks as well as in Navarre and a part of Catalonia. The mountain regions in general were in the hands of the clergy and the pretender. They furnished them brave, sober, robust soldiers, nimble as smugglers, knowing all the secret passes and defiles, skilful at making off after a defeat and dispersing so as to rally elsewhere, possessing in fact all the necessary qualities for this species of tricky and partisan war in which Spain has always excelled. The country also lent itself to it. It was rugged and cut up, well fitted for ambuscades and surprises — full of difficulties for the invader who could not operate in detachments without exposing himself, nor in masses without being uneasy without sustenance.

However, if Carlism had preserved its troops, it was weakened by the loss of some of its most noteworthy chiefs. The spirit of the times is a subtle and penetrating gas, and the élite of the party was unable to resist its malign influence. One of the heroes of the seven years' war — the illustrious general Cabrera, whose name alone was worth an army to the pretender — had found the latter deaf to his advice and was compelled to refuse him his services.

Among Don Carlos' faithful adherents there were men of heart and intelligence who grumbled under their breath at his mistakes. As for the pretender himself, he was no longer master of his actions. The church was the mouthpiece of his will and it announced to Spain that if Don Carlos wished to mount the throne it was to give the people back their God — him of former days, whose glance rested with delight on the *sanbenito* of a scourged and repentant heretic. They did not take the trouble to conceal from the Spaniards the designs they had upon them. When certain persons spoke to France, they had recourse to the precautions of the oratory, to the subtleties taught by casuistry, to reticences and equivocation, to denials which did not deny, and to promises which did not promise anything. If they did the country of Voltaire and Mirabeau the honour of lying to her, they inflicted on Spain the affront of their outrageous sincerity. They openly declared to her that they intended to bring back the Golden Age when the monk reigned and sent free-thinkers to peaceful sleep. The struggle which was now steeping the Pyrenees and the Cantabrian mountains in blood was a war to the death waged upon the *bourgeoisie* by fanatical priests, of shepherds upon their lambs; it was the white demagogy, which despairing of triumph had not scrupled to league itself with the pirates of Cartagena for the extermination of liberal ideas.[n]

THE DICTATORSHIP OF SERRANO

Castelar's former party associates, who had forgotten nothing and learned nothing, could not forgive him for having brought the federative republicans to order with powder and shot; for having appointed conservative generals, and entered into negotiations with the papal see in regard to vacant bishoprics. When the cortes re-assembled on January 2nd, 1874, its president, Salmeron, brought about a vote of lack of confidence in Castelar's government, whereupon the latter promptly resigned.

Before further action could be taken the cortes was dispersed by Pavia, the captain-general of Madrid, on January 3rd,[1] and a military dictatorship established under Marshal Serrano.   Republican revolts which broke out in several cities were quickly suppressed and a large force was sent against the Carlists.   The latter kept the important fortress Bilbao closely invested, had captured Portugalete, the port belonging to it, had forced Moriones first to take refuge on a ship, and on February 24th, 1874, when he again advanced from the west, had driven him to retreat, after being defeated at Somorrostro.

Serrano, entitled "president of the executive power of the republic," now hastened to the scene of action, but in the battles of March 25th and 26th he did not succeed in breaking through the firm position of the Carlists at Somorrostro.   He procured reinforcements, however, renewed the attack on April 28th, and compelled the enemy on May 1st to give up its position, abandon the investment of Bilbao, and to evacuate Portugalete.   General Concha, appointed commander-in-chief of the northern army, on June 25th attacked the Carlists under Dorregaray, who were firmly entrenched on the heights of Estella, but was repulsed and fell after a battle of three days.   The Carlists neglected to take a strategical advantage of their victory and shot down a large number of prisoners.   Don Alfonso, the brother of the pretender, did no better in Catalonia, for after conquering the Castilian city Cuenca he delivered it up to plunder, fire, and sword.   The Carlist general Mendiri did not succeed in capturing the fortress Irun in the northern field of war : he was compelled

MARSHAL SERRANO

to retreat on November 10th from Laserna, but he himself on December 9th forced the advancing general Loma to retreat to San Sebastian.   Hereupon Serrano again hastened to the scene with the purpose of making a general attack on the enemy, at the head of four army corps, and forcing it back to the French frontier.   He needed time, however, to get the necessary number of troops together.

[1 At the head of the Madrid garrison, the captain-general of the capital turned the members of the cortes into the streets, dismissed the government, including the war minister, and dissolved parliament.   He then profoundly surprised his fellow countrymen by declining to use his dictatorship as a stepping-stone to power.   For the first time in Spain, the victorious leader of a *pronunciamiento* invited the leaders of all parties to form a government to restore and maintain peace.   Castelar naturally declined.   Canovas del Castillo, the chief agent of the Alfonsist propaganda, held aloof, because he saw that events were playing into his hands.   Marshal Serrano, with Sagasta and Martos, consented to form a nameless provisional government, which attempted for eleven months to reorganise Spain, first crushing the republican risings in the south, and then vigorously attacking the Carlists in northern and central Spain.*]

Serrano had one political success to rejoice over which occurred with no intervention on his own part. On the 30th of June Don Carlos had caused the Prussian ex-captain Albert Schmidt, who was at Concha's headquarters as correspondent for German papers and had fallen into the hands of the Carlists, to be shot, although he was a non-combatant. This act in defiance of the rights of war, and the barbaric way in which the war was conducted as a whole, led Prince Bismarck to take diplomatic measures against Carlism, which was to a great extent financially supported by the legitimists in France, the feudals in Austria, and by the Jesuits in the Vatican. He thus made it possible for the remaining powers to recognise Serrano's government officially and exerted an indirect pressure on the French government, which was rendering the Carlists all sorts of assistance on the French frontier, with the object of holding it more closely to its obligations.

DON CARLOS DE BOURBON

All the powers except Russia decided to recognise the Spanish government and sent ambassadors to Madrid. The German ambassador was received with special marks of attention on September 12th. Two German warships were despatched to the bay of Biscay to protect the interests of the Germans living along the coast, and to prevent the smuggling in of materials of war. But Serrano's small military success against the Carlists brought about a new turn in affairs at the end of the year 1874.

THE BOURBON ALFONSO XII ELECTED (1875 A.D.)

General Martinez Campos, who, like most of the officers, was an adherent of the overturned Bourbon dynasty, on December 29th, at Murviedro, proclaimed the son of the ex-queen Isabella as King Alfonso XII of Spain. The army generally declared in favour of Alfonso, Sagasta's ministry resigned, Serrano laid down the chief command and the presidency, a ministerial regency was formed on the 31st under Canovas del Castillo, which informed Isabella, then living at Paris, of the elevation of her son to the throne. The latter left Paris on January 6th, 1875, landed in Barcelona, arrived at Madrid the 14th, and although he was not yet eighteen, took over the reins of government.

The inexperienced king was in a difficult position. The state treasury was almost empty; the war with the Carlists consumed enormous sums and brought few results; the close relations of the king to his god-father Pope Pius demanded especial considerations; the papal nuncio required the most extensive concessions in return for his supporting the king; he wanted to bring back the old intolerance and priesthood, and if possible to return to the Inquisition; the ex-queen Isabella, who had lost all title to respect, impatiently awaited her return to Madrid. In every direction, nothing could be seen but dangerous reefs which confronted the government.*e*

That Canovas del Castillo should undertake the leadership of the new government was quite as much a matter of course as that the first and most imperative duty of the government should be to overthrow the Carlist rebellion. At first, it was put down in Catalonia and Aragon where its chief seat, Seo de Urgel, fell on August 26th, 1875. Thereupon all forces were directed towards the north against the Basque territories, the old citadel of Carlism. The closely besieged Pamplona was relieved on November 24th, and, when Quesada advanced with one hundred thousand men, Estella also fell on February 19th, 1876. On February 28th, the king himself entered Pamplona; on the same day Don Carlos retreated over the border to France. The victors conducted themselves humanely on the whole, although ten thousand persons were exiled, as many more lost their property, and a limitation of the old *fueros* of the Basque lands was planned. It was not until 1878, however, that Martinez Campos succeeded in quelling the rebellion in Cuba after important economical concessions, when the rights of a Spanish province were granted to the Cubans. [For fuller details see the history of Spanish America in a later volume.]

In the meanwhile on May 24th the newly elected cortes, which the king had opened on February 15th, 1876, had adopted the new constitution (proclaimed June 30th). This provided for a senate and house of representatives controlled by general and direct election, established freedom of the press, of religion, and of unions, but abolished trial by jury, civil marriage, and freedom of teaching, in order to win over the radicals and the clergy. Rome at first protested against the freedom of religion but gave up this point, as the Protestants were actually so limited and oppressed in the exercise of their rights that all the firm fervour of belief of men like Pastor Fliedner in Madrid was needed to endure it all and actually to establish an evangelical church in the Spanish capital where now Luther's hymn of victory, "A firm foundation is our God," resounds also in Spanish (*"Castillo fier es nuestro Dios!"*).

The republican attempts on the king's life on October 25th, 1878, and December 30th, 1879, were only after-effects of the long period of unrest; on the whole the pacification of the country made unmistakable progress. The government exercised the utmost watchfulness against Carlist plots and even effected a papal prohibition against Spanish bishops. The opposition of Catalan manufacturers to the commercial treaty with France was summarily suppressed by the proclamation of a state of siege; a republican revolt on the part of the soldiers in Badajoz on August 5th, 1883, was energetically put down and severely punished by the king, who, wholly on his own responsibility, attempted to put a stop to the old mischief of having officers take part in political party intrigues and boldly ordered the dismissal of a large number of unsubmissive and irresponsible elements. The social democratic associations of the *mano nero* (the black hand) seemed very dangerous for a time. These were favoured by the severe economical decay of the last years, and grew rapidly until, divided into about three thousand groups and controlled by a central organisation at Xeres, they covered the south like a net. Since they distinguished themselves by deeds of violence of all kinds, the government at last took decisive measures, overpowered their ringleaders and caused seven of them to be executed.

ALFONSO XII AND THE EUROPEAN POWERS

Several years passed thus before the king could venture to enter into any personal relations with the most powerful foreign rulers. Not until September, 1883, did he proceed to Austria and Germany, accompanied by several of his ministers, when on the occasion of the grand manœuvres at Frankfort on the Main, Emperor William gave him the honorary command of the 15th regiment of Ulans. Alfonso XII visited this regiment in its quarters at Strasburg, on his return journey to France and for this reason on his entry into Paris, on September 29th, the chauvinistic mob hailed him as the *roi-ulan* and insulted the laws of hospitality with hoots and howls. The king in knightly fashion repaid their treatment by giving 10,000 francs for the poor of Paris. Emperor William, in order to show his warm sympathy for the king, sent the crown-prince to Spain. The latter set sail with a German fleet and landed in Valencia November 22nd after a stormy passage. Although the Spaniards were at first cool and reserved, after a few weeks spent in Madrid and the most important cities of the south, the prince completely won them over by his imposing and kindly personality and by the regard

ALFONSO XII

shown to the king in such demonstrative fashion contributed his share towards firmly establishing the Spanish throne. The friendly relations thus introduced did not indeed hinder the outbreak of popular hatred against Germany in 1885 in connection with the dispute over the Carolines; only the statesmanlike firmness of the king and the moderation of Germany hindered serious troubles and assured the continuance of the Bourbon throne which had only just been re-established.

But the days of the young monarch were already numbered, November 25th, 1885, he died of consumption in the Pardo palace. He left two daughters by his second marriage with the archduchess Maria Christina of Austria (November 29th, 1879), Mercedes and Maria Theresa; not until several months after his death, on May 17th, 1886, was the heir to the throne, Alfonso XIII, born. He was proclaimed king on the same day, under the regency of his mother. The latter recalled to the mind of the Spanish that other queen of German blood, Elizabeth Christina of Brunswick, the wife of Charles VI.*p*

THE REGENCY OF MARIA CHRISTINA (1886-1902 A.D.)

The widow of Alfonso XII quietly assumed that there was no debate as to her right to be regent of Spain, which found itself facing an addition to its astonishingly long list of minorities. And the new minor was not yet born. The situation was serious. The latest policy of the cabinet had not been popular in its reaction from liberalism, and even Canovas del Castillo advised the queen-regent to begin her administration by concessions. He recommended his ancient rival Sagasta, who was called to the Pardo, and by the pact since called after the place, agreed to use his influence to uphold the regency while frankly stating his intention to make gradual reforms in the direction of restoring the constitutional liberties of 1868.

In Paris Ruiz Zorilla was agitating for a revolution and restoration of the republic, while the Carlists were trying to stir Don Carlos to leave his retreat in Venice and invade Spain. The pope, however, felt that the interests of the church would be better subserved by peace, especially as he found Maria Christina an ardent and generous Catholic, who encouraged the Jesuits to unsurpassed power over education. But Sagasta's influence kept the country from any entanglements in European alliances, re-established trial by jury, which Alfonso XII had abolished, and universal suffrage which Alfonso had vetoed; enlarged the liberties of speech and press, and modified the tariff beneficially. A few military conspiracies were frustrated and mildly punished. A strong aid to Sagasta was Emilio Castelar, who saw the gradual return of his republican ideals.

But by 1890, Maria Christina, who was even more dictatorial than her late husband, asked his resignation and called in Canovas, whose conserva-tive and high-tariff policy brought a marked diminution of foreign trade. Canovas' chief trouble came from his own party. After two and a half years, he resigned and again advised the calling of Sagasta, who sent an expedition of twenty-five thousand soldiers under Campos to Morocco and forced the sultan to pay an indem-nity of £800,000 for attacks on the Spanish outposts at Melilla in Morocco. He was not so happy with the Cuban question.

Cuba had long been rather the victim and prey of the mother-country than a colony, and the efforts for relief by the few friends in Spain had received practically no attention. The growth of the sentiment of revolt, the failure of the milder policies of men like Martinez Campos, and the equal fiasco of the mediævally relentless policy of General Weyler, who won the name of "butcher," are detailed in the later volume de-

MARIA CHRISTINA

voted to Spanish America. It must suffice here to say that Canovas was assassinated by an anarchist, August 9th, 1897, while pressing a bill for more liberal home rule in Cuba. He was succeeded by the former war minister General Azcarraga.

Meanwhile the people of the United States had been so deeply stirred by the decades of torture inflicted on their island neighbours in Cuba that General Weyler was recalled through pressure brought to bear by American diplomacy.   The conservative cabinet gave way to Sagasta, Marshal Blanco replaced Weyler and tried a gentler policy.   But the ruination of Cuba could not be checked by any mild and negative treatment.   The people of the United States had been wrought to a pitch of horror by the tales of the starvation of Cuban men, women, and children by the thousand, and when the United States cruiser *Maine*, while visiting the port of Havana, was blown up with great loss of life, it needed only the declaration of a commission of inquiry that she had been sunk by a submarine mine, to bring the United States to demand the evacuation of Cuba by Spain.   There was no implication that the destruction of the *Maine* had official sanction, but it was given as a final proof of the intolerable state of affairs in Cuba.

The demand was naturally more than Spanish pride would bear and the American minister was given his passports.   The European powers refused to intervene, though the press was almost unanimously for Spain, except in England.   It was notorious that Spanish resources were hopelessly inadequate to a protracted war with the infinite riches of the United States, but the American navy was small and according to European experts decidedly inferior in discipline, morale, and efficiency to the Spanish navy.   This theory was exploded by the swift and utter destruction of two Spanish fleets, that of Admiral Montojo by Admiral Dewey in Manila Bay, May 1st, 1898, and that of Admiral Cervera by the fleet under Admiral Sampson in Santiago de Cuba, July 3rd.   Land-forces in Cuba, the Philippines, and Porto Rico won those islands with comparatively little struggle, as is described in the second volume of our history of the United States.

ANTONIO CANOVAS DEL CASTILLO

Late in July, Spanish pride saw nothing left but surrender of practically all her colonies.   A treaty of peace was signed at Paris, December 12th, 1898, after a protocol had put an end to hostilities for some months.   The Caroline Islands which remained to Spain in the Pacific, and over which there had almost been a war with Germany in 1885, were sold to Germany in 1899 for £800,000; and in 1900 the United States bought two small islands that had been overlooked in the earlier treaty, paying $100,000 (£20,000) for them.

Spain came out of the war in a sad financial state.   Besides the practical annihilation of her navy and the great loss of her army's prestige, her national debt of £259,116,500 had been increased by £60,000,000 for war expenses (borrowed at very high interest); and the United States had forced her to assume the Cuban and Philippine debts of £46,210,000.   The mountain of debt that confronted her was thus £365,326,500; or more than $1,826,600,000.

The liberals, who had been compelled to take the government at the outbreak of war, had faced inevitable defeat, but there were so many details of maladministration, of neglect and ignorance in war preparations that the

[1898–1902 A.D.]

blame of the disaster fell on them as if they had been its origin. Sagasta gave way to the conservative Silvela. He feared to support the radical measures which Villaverde, the minister of finance, felt necessary for the reduction of expense and the increase of revenue, and which provoked violent and organised resistance from tax-payers. Villaverde in consequence was sacrificed, though he had attacked his problem with sanity and courage. The resistance of the National Tax-payers' Union did not cease, however, and Silvela was driven to rigorous measures of repression.

In spite of the severe up-hill struggle that is before Spain, it is everywhere believed that the loss of her colonies is the greatest blessing that could have befallen her. So great a drain were they upon the industries, the morals, and the population of the home-country, and so corrupt had their administration become that their removal resembled the amputation of a limb given over to gangrene. Already signs of healthier conditions are numerous, and, as industry, like charity, should begin at home, the outlook of the new attention to the great natural resources of the peninsula is most alluring.

Not the least sign of promise is the growing popular feeling against the vampire of priestcraft. Early in her history Spain developed the most advanced and organised liberties of all European governments. Then she came under the sway of the church, and it became for centuries her boast that she was the most faithful and meekest of disciples. At the same time she became and continued the most ignorant, the most depraved and superstitious, the most blood-thirsty, of all European nations. Her loyal subjects were proud of their chains; haughty in the obstinate ignorance of her Jesuitical schools and the fiery intolerance of their rulers and people. Her non-orthodox were broken on the rack, tormented and burned at the stake after suffering all the diabolic ingenuities of the Inquisition. Her provinces, as the Netherlands, were kept in ceaseless and odious war. Her colonies were steeped for centuries in oppressions resulting in the absolute obliteration of whole races, and the lasting savagery of others. And these horrors were, practically without exception, done in the name of the church and with its official approval. It is clear to the outside world that Spain must shake loose the affectation of religion from the education of the masses, from the intrigues of the court, and from the politics and everyday life of the people, before this brave and brilliant race can take its place in line with the rest of Europe on the march of civilisation and the betterment of mankind.

In 1902, the regency of Maria Christina came to an end : her son was declared of age and crowned as Alfonso XIII.[a]

BRIEF REFERENCE–LIST OF AUTHORITIES BY CHAPTERS

[The letter *a* is reserved for Editorial Matter.]

CHAPTER I. LAND AND PEOPLE AND EARLY HISTORY

[b] M. M. BUSK, *The History of Spain and Portugal.* — [c] HEINRICH SCHURTZ on " Die Pyrenäische Halbinsel," in Helmolt's *Weltgeschichte.* — [d] MARTIN A. S. HUME, *The Spanish People: their Origin, Growth, and Influence.* — [e] POLYBIUS, *General History.* — [f] TITUS LIVIUS, *History of Rome.* — [g] S. A. DUNHAM, *History of Spain and Portugal.* — [h] PLINY, *Historia Naturalis.* — [i] IDATIUS, *Chronicum.* — [j] ULRICK R. BURKE, *A History of Spain.* — [k] M. CASIRI, *Bibliotheca arabico-hispana Escurialensis.* — [l] EDWARD GIBBON, *Decline and Fall of the Roman Empire.* — [m] J. A. CONDÉ, *Historia de la Dominacion de los Arabes en España.* — [n] GREGORY OF TOURS, *Historia Ecclesiastica Francorum.* — [o] PROCOPIUS, *De Bello Gothorum.* — [p] ST. ISIDORUS HISPALENSIS, *Historia Gothorum, Vandalorum, et Suevorum.* — [q] JUAN DE MARIANA, *Historia general de España.* — [r] JUAN F. DE MASDEU, *Historia crítica de España.* — [s] BARONIUS, *Annales Ecclesiastici.* — [t] CHARLES DE S. MONTESQUIEU, *Esprit des Lois.* — [u] AMBROSIO DE MORALES, *Crónica general de España.* — [v] SEBASTIANUS SALMANTICENSIS, *Chronicon.* — [w] ANONYMOUS, *Chronica Albeldensis.* — [x] ST. JULIAN, *Historia Regis Wambæ.* — [y] JORDANES, *De Origine Gothorum.* — [z] ISIDORUS PACENSIS, *Epit.* — [aa] JUAN DE FERRERAS, *Historia de España.* — [bb] AMADOR DE LOS RÍOS, *Los Judios en España.* — [cc] FLÓREZ Y LAFUENTE, *España Sagrada.* — [dd] CARDINAL LORENGANA, *Collectio Sanctorum Patrum Ecclesiæ Toledanæ.* — [ee] WULSA, *Chronica Regum Wisigothorum.* — [ff] ANONYMOUS, *Continuation of Joannis Biclarensis.* — [gg] CHARLES PAQUIS, *Histoire d'Espagne et de Portugal.* — [hh] ANONYMOUS, *Chronicon Moissacense.* — [ii] MONACHUS SILENSIS, *Chronicon.* — [jj] LUCAS TUDENSIS, *Chronicon.* — [kk] RODERICUS XIMENES TOLETANUS, *Rerum in Hispania Gestarum.* — [ll] JOSEPH ASCHBACH, *Geschichte der Westgoten.* — [mm] FELIX DAHN, *Die Könige der Germanen.* — [nn] ANONYMOUS, *Crónica del Rey D. Rodrigo.*

CHAPTER II. THE TIME OF MOSLEM DOMINATION

[b] M. A. S. HUME, *op. cit.* — [c] RODERICUS XIMENES TOLETANUS, *op. cit.* — [d] ISIDORUS PACENSIS, *op. cit.* — [e] ANONYMOUS, *Chronica Elbeldensis.* — [f] SEBASTIANUS SALMANTICENSIS, *op. cit.* — [g] U. R. BURKE, *op. cit.* — [h] S. A. DUNHAM, *op. cit.* — [i] J. DE MARIANA, *op. cit.* — [j] " El-Lagi" (in *Casiris Fragmenta Historiarum*). — [k] ALFONSO X, *Crónica de España.* — [l] J. F. DE MASDEU, *op. cit.* — [m] ORTIZ, *Compendio general de la historia de España.* — [n] SAMPIRUS ASTORICENSIS, *Episcopus.* — [o] GEORG WEBER, *Weltgeschichte.* — [p] ANONYMOUS, *Annales Complutenses.* — [q] ANONYMOUS, *Annales Toledanos.* — [r] HENRY E. WATTS, *Spain.* — [s] CHARLES ROMEY, *Histoire de l'Espagne.* — [t] J. M. MAS-LATRIE, *Trésor de chronologie, d'histoire, et de géographie.* — [u] PRUDENCIO DE SANDOVAL, *Historia de los Reyes Castilla y Leon.* — [v] J. DE FERRERAS, *op. cit.* — [w] P. RISCO, *Edition of Gesta Roderici Campidocti.* — [x] ROBERT SOUTHEY, *Translation of the Chronicle of the Cid.* — [y] VICTOR A. HUBER, *Geschichte des Cid.* — [z] R. DOZY, *Recherches sur la littérature et l'histoire d'Espagne, pendant le Moyen Age.* — [aa] IBN BASSAM, *History of Literature.* — [bb] ALEXANDER BAUMGARTNER, " Der Cid in der Geschichte," in *Stimmen aus Maria-Laach.* — [cc] MODESTO LAFUENTE, *Historia general de España.*

CHAPTER III. CASTILE, TO DEATH OF PEDRO THE CRUEL

[b] S. A. DUNHAM, *op. cit.* — [c] F. S. CASADO, *Historia de España.* — [d] U. R. BURKE, *op. cit.* — [e] ALFONSO X, *Crónica, op. cit.* — [f] G. WEBER, *op. cit.* — [g] J. DE MARIANA, *Historia de Rebus Hispaniæ.* — [h] LOPEZ DE AYALA, *Crónica de los Reyes de Castilla.* — [i] JOHN FROISSART, *Chronicles of England, France, and Spain.* — [j] D. JUAN C. GARCIA, *Pedro I, Enrique II, Juan I, Enrique III.* — [k] MARQUIS DE MONDEJAR, *Vida de Alfonso X.* — [l] ALFONSO NUÑES DE CASTRO, *Coronica Gothica, Castillana y Austriaca.* — [m] PROSPER MÉRIMÉE, *Histoire de Don Pedre I.* — [n] M. A. S. HUME, *op. cit.*

Chapter IV. Aragon, to the Union with Castile

[b] G. Weber, *op. cit.* — [c] S. A. Dunham, *op. cit.* — [d] M. A. S. Hume, *op. cit.* — [e] Geronimo Zurita, *Anales de la corona de Aragon.* — [f] J. de Ferreras, *op. cit.*

Chapter V. Trastamara, to Isabella

[b] L. de Ayala, *op. cit.* — [c] G. Weber, *op. cit.* — [d] J. Froissart, *op. cit.* — [e] D. A. de Lemos, *Historia geral de Portugal.* — [f] Anonymous, *Chronicon Conimbricense.* — [g] S. A. Dunham, *op. cit.* — [h] U. R. Burke, *op. cit.* — [i] M. A. S. Hume, *op. cit.* — [j] Perez de Guzman, *Crónica del serenissimo Principe Don Juan II.* — [k] Anonymous, *Crónica del Condestable Don Alonso de Luna.* — [l] William H. Prescott, *History of the Reign of Ferdinand and Isabella the Catholic.*

Chapter VI. Ferdinand and Isabella

[b] Gonzalo de Oviedo y Valdés, *Las Quincuagenas.* — [c] Hernando del Pulgar, *Reyes Catolicos.* — [d] Peter Martyr, *Opus Epistolarum.* — [e] Lorenzo G. de Carbajal, Ms. — [f] U. R. Burke, *op. cit.* — [g] W. H. Prescott, *op. cit.* — [h] Andres Bernaldez, *Reyes Católicos.* — [i] Pedro de Abarca, *Los Reyes de Aragon.* — [j] S. A. Dunham, *op. cit.* — [k] J. de Ferreras, *op. cit.* — [l] Juan A. Llorente, *Historia critica de la Inquisicion de España.* — [m] J. de Mariana, *op. cit.* — [n] Heinrich Graetz, *Geschichte der Juden.* — [o] J. A. Condé, *op. cit.* — [q] Bartolomé de las Casas, *Historia general de las Indias.* — [r] Lucio Marineo, *Cosas Memorables.* — [s] Gustav Bergenroth, *Letters, Despatches and State Papers* (supplementary volumes). — [t] M. A. S. Hume, *op. cit.*

Chapter VII. The Regencies of Ferdinand

[b] W. H. Prescott, *op. cit.* — [c] William Robertson, *History of the Reign of Charles V.* — [d] S. A. Dunham, *op. cit.* — [e] M. A. S. Hume, *op. cit.* — [f] L. G. de Carbajal, *Anales del Rey Don Fernando el Catolicó.* — [g] G. Zurita, *op. cit.* — [h] J. de Mariana, *op. cit.* — [i] Prudencio de Sandoval, *Historia del Emperador Carlos V.* — [j] Diego de Clemencin, in *Mem. de la Real Accademie de Historia, VI.* — [k] U. R. Burke, *op. cit.* — [l] P. Martyr, *op. cit.* — [m] L. Marineo, *op. cit.* — [n] Paolo Giovio, *Historia sui temporis.* — [o] Antonio Varillas, *Politique de Ferdinand.* — [p] Niccolo Macchiavelli, *Lettere diverse* and *Il Principe.* — [q] A. Gomez, *De Rebus Gestis Francisci Ximenii.* — [r] Las Casas, *op. cit.* — [s] G. de Oviedo y Valdés, *op. cit.* — [t] M. A. S. Hume, *Spain: its Greatness and Decay.* — [u] G. Bergenroth, *op. cit.* — [v] Rodriguez Villa, *Vida de Juana la loca.* — [w] L. P. Gachard, in *Bulletin de l'Académie Royale de la Belgique.* — [x] Vicente de la Fuente, *Juana la loca vindicada de la nota de herejia.* — [y] Charles de Mouy, an article "Jeanne la Folle" in the *Revue des deux Mondes.* — [z] Michel Baudier, *Vie de Ximenes.* — [aa] Hermann Baumgarten, *Geschichte Karls V.*

Chapter VIII. The Emperor Charles V

[b] P. Martyr, *op. cit.* — [c] W. Robertson, *op. cit.* — [d] S. A. Dunham, *op. cit.* — [e] Rosseeuw St. Hilaire, *Histoire d'Espagne.* — [f] P. de Sandoval, *op. cit.* — [g] José de Siguenza, *Historia de la Orden de San Gerónimo.* — [h] William Stirling-Maxwell, *The Cloister-Life of Charles V.* — [i] Bakhuyzen van den Brink, *Analyse d'un manuscrit contemporain sur la retraite de Charles Quint.* — [j] François A. M. Mignet, *Antonio Perez et Philippe II.* — [k] Amédée Pichot, *Chronique de Charles Quint.* — [l] Louis P. Gachard, *Retraite et mort de Charles Quint.* — [m] John L. Motley, *The Rise of the Dutch Republic.* — [n] M. de Marliani, *Histoire politique de l'Espagne moderne.* — [o] Strada, *De Bello Belgico ab Excessu Carli V.*

Chapter IX. Philip II

[b] Michele Suriano, "Relazione" (in L. P. Gachard's *Relations des Ambassadeurs Venitiens sur Charles V et Philippe II.* — [c] Cabrera de Cordoba, *Filipe Segundo.* — [d] L. P. Gachard, *Rapport à le ministre de l'Interieur* prefixed to the *Correspondence de Philippe II.* — [e] Badovaro, Ms. (see Suiano, *supra*). — [f] J. L. Motley, *op. cit.* — [g] Mandell Creighton, article on "Philip II" in the *Encyclopœdia Britannica.* — [h] Robert Watson, *The History of the Reign of Philip II.* — [i] S. A. Dunham, *op. cit.* — [j] M. A. S. Hume, *The Spanish People.* — [k] M. A. S. Hume, *Spain: its Greatness and Decay.* — [l] William of Orange, *Apologie.* — [m] Bermudez de Castro, *Antonio Perez.* — [n] M. M. Busk, *op. cit.* — [o] W. H. Prescott, *History of the Reign of Philip II.* — [p] J. de Mariana, *op. cit.*

424 BRIEF REFERENCE-LIST OF AUTHORITIES BY CHAPTERS

CHAPTER X. LAST OF THE SPANISH HABSBURGS

[b] M. LAFUENTE, op. cit. — [c] S. A. DUNHAM, op. cit. — [d] M. CATHERINE D'AULNOY, Mémoires de la cour d'Espagne. — [e] VINCENT VOITURE, Voyage d'Espagne. — [f] G. T. RAYNAL, Histoire des Indes. — [g] JOHANN C. FR. VON SCHILLER, Geschichte des dreissig jährigen Krieges. — [h] WILLIAM COXE, Memoirs of the Kings of Spain. — [i] ZANETORNATO, Relazione del Governo della corte de Spagna. — [j] M. A. S. HUME, Spain: its Greatness and Decay. — [k] JOHN DUNLOP, Memoirs of Spain during the Reign of Philip IV and Charles II. — [l] HENRI MARTIN, Histoire de France.

CHAPTER XI. REVIVAL UNDER THE FIRST BOURBONS

[b] SAN FELIPE (or ST. PHILIPPE), Commentarios. — [c] W. COXE, op. cit. — [d] M. A. S. HUME, The Spanish People. — [e] MARÉCHAL DE BEZWICK, Mémoires. — [f] LORD MAHON, War of Succession in Spain. — [g] JEAN B. R. DE TESSÉ, Mémoires. — [h] M. A. S. Hume, Spain: its Greatness and Decay. — [i] GIULIO ALBERONI, Storia. — [j] LORD MAHON, History of England. — [k] M. LAFUENTE, op. cit. — [l] S. A. DUNHAM, op. cit. — [m] WILLIAM CONNOR SYDNEY, England and the English in the Eighteenth Century. — [n] M. M. BUSK, op. cit.

CHAPTER XII. SPAIN AND THE FRENCH REVOLUTION

[b] M. M. BUSK, op. cit. — [c] ROSSEEUW ST. HILAIRE, op. cit. — [d] M. LAFUENTE, op. cit. — [e] MANUEL DE GODOY, Mémoires. — [f] H. REYNALD, Histoire d'Espagne depuis la mort de Charles III. — [g] PEDRO CEVALLOS, Exposition de faits et des trames, etc. — [h] CONDE JOSE M. DE TORENO, Historia del levantamiento, guerra y revolucion de Españao. — [i] WILLIAM F. P. NAPIER, History of the War in the Peninsula and in the South of France.

CHAPTER XIII. THE PENINSULAR WAR

[b] W. F. P. NAPIER, op. cit. — [c] M. M. BUSK, op. cit. — [d] H. M. STEPHENS, article on "Sir John Moore" in the Encyclopædia Britannica. — [e] M. LAFUENTE, op. cit. — [f] CONDE J. M. DE TORENO, op. cit. — [g] M. A. S. HUME, Modern Spain.

CHAPTER XIV. THE BOURBON RESTORATION

[b] GUSTAVE HUBBARD, Histoire contemporaine de l'Espagne. — [c] M. A. S. HUME, Modern Spain. — [d] DOCHEZ, continuation of Charles Paquis' Histoire de l'Espagne. — [e] WILHELM MÜLLER, Politische Geschichte der neuesten Zeit. — [f] FRANÇOIS A. DE CHATEAUBRIAND, Congrès de Vérone. — [g] H. M. STEPHENS, op. cit. — [h] J. DE BURGOS, Anales del Reinado de Doña Isabel. — [i] MARQUES DE MIRAFLORES, Continuacion de los Memorias del Reinado de Isabel II. — [j] ANTONIO DE PIRALA, Historia contemporánea. — [k] A. E. HOUGHTON, article on "Spain," in the New Volumes of the Encyclopædia Britannica. — [l] A. DE PIRALA, El Rey en Madrid y en provincias. — [m] EMILIO CASTELAR, speech of November 3rd, 1870. — [n] VICTOR CHERBULIEZ, L'Espagne Politique. — [o] JOSEPH DE GRABINSKI, Amédée de Savoie, duc d'Aoste, roi d'Espagne. — [p] OTTO KAEMMEL, Geschichte der neuesten Zeit (in Spamer's Weltgeschichte. — [q] M. M. BUSK, History of Spain and Portugal.

BOOK II

THE HISTORY OF PORTUGAL FROM THE EARLIEST TIMES TO THE PRESENT

CHAPTER I

EARLY HISTORY TO JOÃO I

[TO 1383 A.D.]

LAND AND PEOPLE

THE reasons for which Portugal is neglected are precisely those which in some eyes make her truly lovable. For a half-century art has done almost nothing for the natural river highways ; and the Douro, the Guadiana, and the Tagus flow through this kingdom like the wandering rivulets of great English parks. The large towns of the interior, Coimbra, Santarem, Evora, and Miranda, look like pretty kiosks rising about flowering thickets ; peaceful retreats, solitudes animated with a life that jogs quietly along and does not go with leaps and bounds as in France, where a satisfied humanity stands still, instead of rushing into the unknown risks of the future.

The cities of the coast, Lisbon, Oporto, appear more like dwelling-places conveniently placed the better to enjoy the sunlight and the ocean breezes than wide-awake communities guarding their mercantile interests in the commercial exchange of the products of the Old World with the riches of the New.

If the Portuguese had been as skilful speculators as they were intrepid sailors and distinguished warriors, Henry the Navigator, who set the example of maritime conquest, Dias, Vasco da Gama, Cabral, Albuquerque, valiant captains identified with all the glories of the Aviz dynasty, would have imitated the speculative prudence of the Dutch, their rivals. And if, when the illustrious house of Braganza opened the era of national liberties, the people had had in their heads less of poetic imagination and more power of reason ; if, courageous and adventurous as they were, they had shown themselves more positive, the French, at first, and then the English, would never have invaded their treasury, exploited their soil, and paralysed their industries. Truly a childlike nation, satisfied with little, pursuing the ideal, economical without avarice, pure in morals, sober, generous, hospitable, the Portuguese have bred heroes in place of diplomats, poets in place of capitalists : they knew how bravely to defend their country against the Romans, the Arabs, and the Spaniards, and still more recently against the army of Napoleon.

They have kept themselves a free nation, independent and original, possessing a language, a literature, distinct manners and customs, and governed politically by one of the most liberal constitutions of Europe.

To make Portugal complete, Brazil and the colonies were necessary to this country whose language is spoken on the European continent by only five millions of men ; and again the narrow domain which so restricts the use of this tongue creates an obstacle to the popularity of the works to which language gives birth, just as its poverty impedes the development of the fine arts. Jealousy and indifference, the double affliction of southern nations, have curbed the artistic and literary aspirations of the Portuguese. What man of genius would resolve on a career of self-denial only to be calumniated and persecuted as was Prince Henry, to achieve a miserable end like Admiral Pacheo, or like Camoens ; or to languish forgotten, like the painter Glama, reduced to making tavern signs ; like the sculptor Machado de Castro and the founder Costa, creators of an equestrian statue of José I, worthy of ranking with the greatest art works of the eighteenth century ? Encouragement and recompense are the safeguards of emulation, and emulation, utilising the moral resources of a people, permits them the use of its advantages to rise to the level of other nations.

Except for a few coins, the Phœnicians, the Phocæans, and the Carthaginians have left almost no trace in Portugal of their occupation or their passing ; but the touch of Rome clings better than in Spain. Cæsar's Pax Julia sleeps thirty feet beneath the city of Beja and needs only the simple power of will to be awakened, with its population of statues, its inscriptions, and its frescoes ; Liberalitas Julia, the Ebora of Ptolemy, planted like Beja upon high ground in the province of Alemtejo, has a double character, that of a Grecian town with its temple of Diana and that of a Roman city with its great aqueduct, immense works, wrought under the hand of Quintus Sertorius, who made himself master eighty years before the Christian era. The aristocracy of Pax Julia and Liberalitas Julia was accustomed to spend its summers in the little municipality of Alcacer, where there was a famous bath under the protection of a local divinity, the nymph Salacia. Braganza, the Juliobriga ; Lisbon, the Felicitas Julia of the Augustan era, had equally received their political baptism from the conqueror of Gaul ; while ancient Lusitania, become a Julian or Cæsarian country, easily adapted the popular customs and organisations of the Roman government to its Carthaginian institutions.

Vespasian and Trajan made an important town of Chaves ; Viseu is the Vesontium of the consul D. Brutus ; Lamego, the Urbs Lamacœnorum of Trajan. Setubal occupies a terrace opposite the ancient Roman colony of Cetobriga. At Braga, Ponte de Lima, Salvaterra, we find traces of amphitheatres, aqueducts, baths, and temples ; so that well-directed excavations would evoke the manes of that sovereign people which, governing the universe, kept watchful station on the coast of Hispania to keep an eye on Numidia.

From the seventh century to the capture of Lisbon in 1147 Moorish architecture had its compromising effect on the elegant majesty of the great lines and arches of the Saracens' predecessors ; the baths of Cintra, the wall and seventy-seven towers of Lisbon, the fortifications and palaces of Evora, and many mosques since transformed into churches, signified, towards the close of the twelfth century, the degree of Islam's foothold on Portuguese soil — an unsteady tenure, without consistence, without depth, bearing witness to the rapidity of conquest as well as to the fear of ephemeral possession.   Little by little, in place of the mosques, arose churches, veritable apostolic citadels, headquarters for the war against the infidel.   Formless and rude at first, they developed as the Christian armies won back the land ; but when the native peoples effected their definite triumph they were obliged to call in foreign artists, more skilful than themselves in the interpretation of the architectural vernacular.

The Portuguese knew how to fight bravely and to sing their triumphs, but they did not know how to build ; and for this reason the monastery of Alcobaça, founded in fulfilment of a vow by Alfonso I, king of Portugal, in 1170, is an Anglo-Saxon church, built by workmen from England.   A new architectural epoch dates from the fifteenth century, and its character has been best perpetuated in the abbey of Batalha.   Of its kind, this is one of the most beautiful edifices in existence ; and assuredly it is the most majestic and the most pure in form that Portugal possesses.   It was built in the reign of João I (1385-1433) who brought from England a celebrated sculptor named Stephenson.   Many German, English, and Norman artists summoned by the monarch came to aid him.   João himself and his queen Philippa, granddaughter of Edward III of England, supervised the work.   And that nothing might be lacking to the poetic magnificence and graceful details of the building, another queen, the pious Leonora, and two monarchs — João II, the poet king, and after him, Emmanuel — followed the continuance of the work with intelligent interest.   Nothing in the whole peninsula rivals in magnificence the façade of the monastery, nor in boldness of design its chapter hall.[b]

THE ORIGIN OF PORTUGAL

It has been stated that geographically the kingdom of Portugal is an integral part of the Iberian peninsula ; the only reason why it has retained its independence, while the other mediæval states of that peninsula have merged into the kingdom of Spain, is to be found in its history.   When Philip II of Spain annexed Portugal it was a century too late for it to coalesce with Spain.   It had then produced Vasco da Gama and Alfonso de Albuquerque, and its language had been developed from a Romance dialect into a literary language by Camoens and Sá de Miranda.   Conscious of its national history, it broke away again from Spain in 1640, and under the close alliance of England maintained its separate and national existence during the eighteenth century.   A union with Spain might have been possible, however, during the first half of the present century had not a generation of historians and poets arisen who, by recalling the great days of the Portuguese monarchy, have made it impossible for Portugal ever again to lose the consciousness of her national existence.

The history of Portugal really begins with the gift of the fief of the Terra Portucalensis or the county of Porto Cale to Count Henry of Burgundy in 1094 ; for any attempt to identify the kingdom of Portugal and the Portuguese people with Lusitania and the Lusitanians is utterly without foundation.   With the rest of the Iberian peninsula, Portugal was colonised by the Phœnicians and conquered by the Carthaginians ; and the Roman province of Lusitania, whether according to the division of Iberia into three provinces under Augustus or into five under Hadrian, in no way coincided with the historical limits of the kingdom of Portugal.   In common with the rest of the peninsula, it was overrun by the Vandals, Alans, and Visigoths, and eventually conquered by the Arabs in the eighth century.   It was not until the fifteenth century that an attempt was made by Garcia de Menezes to identify Lusitania with Portugal. Under the influence of the Renaissance, Bernardo de Brito insisted on the identity, and claimed Viriathus as a Portuguese hero. Other writers of the same epoch delighted in calling Portugal by the classical name of "Lusitania," and Camoens, by the very title of his great epic, *Os Lusiadas*, has immortalised the appellation.

For two centuries Portugal remained subject to the Omayyad caliphs, and under their wise rule the old Roman *coloniœ* and *municipia*, such as Lisbon, Lamego, Viseu, and Oporto, maintained their Roman self-government and increased in wealth and importance. Towards the close of the tenth century, as the Omayyad caliphate grew weaker, the Christian princes of Visigothic descent who dwelt in the mountains of the Asturias began to grow more audacious in their attacks on the declining power, and in 997 Bermudo II, king of Galicia, won back the first portion of modern Portugal from the Mohammedans by seizing Oporto and occupying the province now known as Entre-Minho-e-Douro. In the beginning of the eleventh century the Omayyad caliphate finally broke up, and independent emirs established themselves in every large city, against whom the Christian princes waged incessant and successful war.[c]

In 1027 Alfonso V of Leon fell before Viseu, the siege of which was in consequence abandoned ; but in 1057, both it and Lamego were recovered by his son-in-law, Ferdinand I ; and the following year Coimbra shared the same fate. In 1093, Santarem, Lisbon, and Cintra were reduced by Alfonso VI, the famous conqueror of Toledo, whose arms were generally so successful against the misbelievers.[1] As these conquests were continually exposed to the irruptions of the Almoravids, in 1095 that monarch conferred the government of Portugal from the Minho to the Tagus, and the right of conquering as far as the Guadiana, on Henry of Besançon or Burgundy, who in 1072 had married his illegitimate daughter Theresa, and to whose arms he had been so much indebted for many of his recent successes.[2]

The nature of the authority conferred on the new count has been a matter of much controversy between the Castilian and Portuguese writers. While the latter maintain that the concession of Alfonso was full and entire,—a surrender of all feudal claims over the country, which the count was to govern in full sovereignty,—the former no less zealously contend that the government was to be held as a fief, hereditary indeed, but no less dependent on the crown of Leon. In the absence of documentary evidence, probability only can guide us. It is unreasonable to suppose either that the king was willing, or, if willing, that his nobles would allow him to dismember at once and forever so fair a territory from his crown, and that too in favour of a stranger and an illegitimate daughter—for illegitimate she was, notwithstanding the allegations to the contrary by some Portuguese writers, who seldom regard truth if unpalatable to their national vanity. That Portugal was conferred as a dependent fief is also confirmed by the disputes between its early sovereigns and those of Leon—the former striving to maintain their avowed independence, the latter to reduce them to their reputed original vassalage. Alfonso died in 1109.

---

[1] According to the *Chronicon Lusitanum*,[d] the *Chronicon Complutense*,[e] and other authorities, Lisbon and Cintra were taken by Alfonso. They must, however, have been soon recovered by the Moors.

[2] That Henry, whose extraction has given rise to much disputation, was of the family of the first duke of Burgundy, and of the royal blood of France, is indisputable from a MS. discovered in the monastery of Fleury, according to La Clède.[f]

The administration of Henry was vigorous, and his military conduct glorious. His triumphs over the Mohammedans were frequent, whether achieved in concert with his father-in-law, Alfonso, or by his own unaided arm. Nor were his efforts to crush rebellion, whether of his local Christian governors or of his Mohammedan vassals, less successful. One of his last acts was to assist his natural sovereign, Urraca, daughter of Alfonso, against her husband the king of Aragon. He died in 1112, leaving many ecclesiastic structures enriched by his liberality. Braga, Oporto, Coimbra, Lamego, and Viseu were the places most indebted to his piety. Unfortunately for his memory, many of the great deeds recorded of him by his partial people rest on authority too disputable to be received. Probably some of them have been confounded with those of his more famous son.

During the minority of Alfonso [or Affonso], the son of Henry, who, at his father's death, was only in his second year, the administration of the kingdom was assumed by the widowed Theresa. The character of this princess is represented as little superior to that of her sister Urraca : the same violence, the same unbridled passions, and the same unnatural jealousy of her son appear, though in a degree undoubtedly less criminal, to have distinguished her conduct. Yet on that sister and her nephew, the successor of Urraca, she sometimes made war, in the hope of profiting by the dissensions of the period; on every occasion she was repulsed, and was forced to sue for peace. Her intimacy with Dom Ferdinand Peres, whom she is supposed to have secretly married, and through whom all favours were to be solicited, roused the jealousy of the courtiers. By their persuasion Alfonso, whom she had rigorously endeavoured to exclude from all participation in public affairs, undertook to wrest the sovereignty from her hands. He had little difficulty in collecting troops ; for no sooner did he erect the standard of resistance, than the discontented nobles flocked round it. His preparations reached the ears of his mother, who wrathfully armed to defend her authority. The two armies met near the fortress of Guimarães, where the princess was utterly routed, and forced to seek refuge in the castle of Leganoso. There she was speedily invested, and compelled to surrender the reins of government into the hands of her son, while her favourite or husband fled into Galicia. She survived her fall about two years.[1]

The new count was destined to prove a more formidable enemy to the Mohammedans than even his able father. During the first years of his administration, he was at variance with his cousin, Alfonso VII or VIII, whose Galician territories he invaded, and with whose enemy, the king of Navarre, he entered into alliance.[h]

When Alfonso Henriques was no longer checked by the enmity of his Christian neighbours, he prosecuted his enterprises against the Moors with such vigour that he soon extended his sway nearly to the Tagus ; and, by the terror of his progress, obliged Ali to send from Africa a powerful army, to support the walis, next threatened against him. A battle ensued, esteemed the most memorable in Portuguese annals, but which has been so disfigured by national vanity or ignorance that the facts relating to it are not easily ascertainable. The numbers of the Mohammedans are rated at three hundred thousand, and even at six hundred thousand men ; and this host is said to have been commanded by five kings. Since the establishment of the

---

[1] Lemos*g* endeavours to vindicate the character of Theresa from the charges imputed to her: the same vain effort, as the reader will remember, has been made by the Castilian writers in favour of Urraca.

Almoravid domination, there were no Moorish kings left in Spain ; but the name was erroneously given to the walis who led the troops of their respective provinces.   What does seem certain respecting the battle in question is that the Mussulman forces were incomparably superior to the Portuguese ; that, dreading an invasion, which, even if ultimately foiled, must still bring inevitable ruin upon his territories, the count boldly crossed the Tagus, and advanced to the plain of Ourique [or Orik], where he entrenched himself strongly, and awaited the attack ; that the Moors repeatedly assaulted his fortifications and were as often repulsed, until at last, from weariness and mortification, they fell into some disorder ; and that Alfonso Henriques, seizing the critical moment, burst out upon them from behind his lines, and completed their discomfiture.   Upon the field of victory the army were said to have hailed their count king of Portugal; and this glorious day, the 25th of July, 1139, is considered the epoch of the foundation of the monarchy. The five walis of Badajoz, Beja, Elvas, Evora, and Lisbon were found amongst the dead, and honoured with the royal title.   The conqueror assumed, as the arms of Portugal, their five shields, arranged in what he called a cross, though the figure they present more resembles that of a cinque upon dice; and accordingly the Portuguese arms are termed *As Quinas*, the Cinques.

Alfonso's military election was said to have been subsequently confirmed by the cortes of Lamego, with a solemnity well deserving attention, as perhaps the only instance on record of a formal compact between prince and people, at the original establishment of a monarchy.[i] But it is now denied that such a cortes ever sat, the story being of much later date.   The true kingship of Alfonso Henriques dates from 1143 when, at the intervention of a papal legate, Alfonso VII recognised him as king and vassal of the pope.[a]

Having established his own independence of foreign authority, the new king proceeded to the emancipation of his clergy from their subjection to the archbishop of Toledo, whose primacy extended over the whole peninsula.   This was the subject of long negotiations with the papal see ; but Alfonso Henriques at length obtained from Pope Alexander III a bull dissolving the connection with Toledo, and constituting the archbishop of Braga primate of Portugal.

Alfonso Henriques' last conquest from the Moors was the city of Lisbon, which he took by the help of a fleet of French, English, and German crusaders, who put into the Tagus in their way to the Holy Land.   He easily persuaded these champions of Christianity that it would be no violation of their vow to suspend their voyage for a while, in order to fight the Mohammedans in Portugal ; and some of them, chiefly English, he is said to have induced permanently to settle in his new acquisitions.[i]

In 1147, we find the Portuguese intent on regaining Santarem.   As the fortifications were strong, and the defenders numerous, he caused a small but resolute band to scale the walls by night : scarcely had twenty-five reached the summit of the wall, when the Moorish inhabitants took the alarm, and flew to arms.   In vain one of the gates was opened by the Christians, and the rest of the assailants rushed in.   The struggle which ensued, amidst the darkness of night, the clash of weapons, the groans of dying warriors, the shrieks of women and infants who were indiscriminately butchered, constituted a scene which none but a demon would have delighted to witness, which none but a demon would have commanded.[1]   In an hour this important fortress, one of

---

[1] " *Mas o rei mandando fazer as mortes indistintas, sem differença de sexo, e idade ; o horror dos gemidos, o tropel da gentè, o clamor das mulheres, a meninos, o escuro da noite causan hum espanto tao geral.*"—LEMOS.[g]

the great bulwarks of Christian Lusitania, was in possession of the victor. His success, and the embarrassment of the Mohammedan princes of Spain, both on account of the rising power of the Almohads in Africa, and of the hostilities of the kings of Leon and Castile, emboldened him to attempt the recovery of Lisbon. That city was invested; but the valour of the defenders and the strength of the walls would doubtless have compelled him to raise the siege, had not a succour arrived which no man could have expected. This was a fleet of crusaders, chiefly of English, under the command of William Longsword, who was hastening to the Holy Land. The Portuguese king had little difficulty in persuading them that the cross had no greater enemies than the Mohammedans of Spain, and that the recovery of Lisbon would be no less acceptable to heaven than that of the Syrian towns : the hope of plunder did the rest ; the crusaders disembarked, and joined in the assaults which were daily made on the place. After a gallant defence of five months, the besieged showing no disposition to surrender, the Christians appointed October 25th for a general assault on the city. It was carried by storm ; a prodigious number of the Moors were put to the sword ; the crusaders were too much enriched to dream of continuing their voyage ; so that, with the exception of a few who received lands in Portugal, the rest returned to their own country.

But the Mohammedans had still possession of one-half of Portugal, and of several strong fortresses. Having reduced Cintra, Alfonso passed the Tagus, and seized on several fortified places in Estremadura, and even in Alemtejo. It was not, however, until 1158 that he seriously attempted the reduction of Alcacer-do-Sal, which fell, after a vigorous resistance of two months. In 1165 Cezimbra and Palmella were invested : the former place was speedily taken ; while, before the latter, he had to encounter a strong force sent to relieve it by the Moorish governor of Badajoz.[1] The misbelievers were defeated, and many places made to surrender.

The martial character of the Portuguese king, as well as the almost uninterrupted success of his arms, inclined him to perpetual war — whether with Moors or Christians appears to have given him little concern. In 1167 he seized on Limia, a territory of Galicia, which he claimed on the ground of its having formed part of his mother's dowry. The following year he advanced against Badajoz, the Moorish governor of which was a vassal of the king of Leon. Ferdinand II hastened to its relief ; but before his arrival the Portuguese standard floated on the towers. The forces of Ferdinand were greatly superior in number, and the Portuguese king prepared to issue from the gates — whether, as the national writers assert, to contend for his new conquest on the open field, or, as the Castilians say, to escape from the incensed monarch of Leon, is uncertain. What is indubitable is that, as he was passing through the gate with precipitation, his thigh came into contact with the wall or bars, and was shattered. He was taken prisoner by the Leonese, and conducted to their king, who treated him with courtesy, and consented to his liberation on the condition of his surrendering the places which he had usurped in Galicia. From this accident, however, he never recovered so as to be able to mount a horse ; but it had a much worse effect than his own personal decrepitude : it encouraged the restless Mohammedans to resume their incursions into his territories.

---

[1] On this occasion Alfonso, with no more than sixty horsemen, is said to have encountered five hundred horsemen of the Almoravids, and forty thousand foot ; and, what is more, to have defeated them ! (See *Chronicon Lusitanum.*[d]) These prodigious relations were admitted without scruple by the earlier historians of Portugal.

Though these incursions were repressed by the valour of his son, Dom
Sancho, who, not content with defending Portugal, penetrated into the
Moorish territory, to the very outskirts of Seville, his people could not fail
to suffer from the ravages of the misbelievers.   This irruption, too, had its
ill effect ; it so much incensed Yusuf ben Yakub, the emperor of the Almohads, that he despatched a considerable force into the kingdom.   The discomfiture of this army under the wall of Abrantes, and the exploits of the
celebrated Dom Fuas Roupinho, one of Sancho's captains, preserved the country indeed from the yoke of the stranger, but not from the devastation;
Alemtejo, above all, suffered in this vindictive warfare.

Alfonso Henriques died December 6th, 1185.   His memory is held by the
Portuguese in the highest veneration ; and hints are not obscurely given
that he merited canonisation.   He, who had been favoured by a celestial
vision at Ourique, whose holy intentions had been so miraculously communicated to St. Bernard, and after death whose mantle, preserved with religious
reverence, could cure the diseased, was surely worthy of ecclesiastical deifi-
cation.   That, in after times, when João I gained Ceuta, he appeared in
white armour in the choir of Santa Cruz at Coimbra, and informed the holy
brotherhood that he and his son Dom Sancho were proceeding to Ceuta
to assist their vassals, no true Portuguese ever yet disbelieved : hence the
peculiar office which the monks of that magnificent house solemnised in his
honour.   To a less Catholic reader, "this always adorable king" (*sempre
o rei adoravel*) may, from his indiscriminate slaughter of the innocent
and guilty, and from his amours, appear to have been imbued with the
imperfections of our nature.[h]

HERCULANO'S ESTIMATE OF THE FIRST PORTUGUESE KING

Alfonso I was not generally over-scrupulous in sacrificing his knightly
generosity and even his political faith to public convenience.   The methods
which he nearly always adopted to secure the independence and extend the
limits of Portugal do more honour to his strength and dexterity than to his
delicacy on points of honour. If, however, the severe and impartial historian
must perceive blemishes in the character of Alfonso I as a man, justice must,
in his favour, throw into the scale the difficulties which beset him in bequeathing to the next generation a well-cemented political existence, and a nationality, as we may say, sufficiently compact to withstand the storms which shook
the peninsula.   He had to attend to the internal organisation of society and
externally to secure it an advantageous position in relation to the various
nations of Spain, Christian and Mussulman.

Founder of a new dynasty in the midst of a society equally new, what
more natural than that Alfonso I should conceive it necessary gradually to
accustom his subjects as well as foreigners to look upon his son Sancho as
king before death came to make, as it were, solution of continuity between
father and son, and therefore in the monarchy ?   In Leon and Castile heredity
had superseded election to the throne in point of fact ; but the Visigothic
right of election still existed as a written law, and was still presupposed by
the formula of coronation even in the thirteenth century.   There were no
particular institutions in Portugal to fix the succession, nor any security that
the Leonese-Castilian dynasty would offer a long line of kings succeeding
each other from father to son.   Neither daring nor ambition were lacking in
those days; and the death of the first king of the Portuguese might give rise

to serious disturbance, either in the country itself or from without, especially as Ferdinand II had already shown in his conduct towards the young king of Castile that his generosity could not always resist an opportunity of adding another crown to that which he already possessed. These and similar considerations probably moved Alfonso I to associate his son with him in the government, not by any formal act of which we have record, but by giving him a free hand in the government of the state, especially in matters of warfare.

Following the phases of this long reign, and judging impartially the actions of the man placed by providence at the head of the nation, to guide it in the first years of its existence, it is recognised that the idea of fixing the Portuguese independence outweighed all other considerations in his mind, sometimes perhaps to the prejudice of some which should have been respected. It is this idea which in reality links together many acts of Alfonso Henriques which, taken separately, would give men a right to accuse him of little faith and immoderate ambition. Besides the revolt against Doña Theresa which is to be attributed rather to the nobles than to an inexperienced youth, the breaking of the truce with the emperor in 1137, the cruelties practised upon the Saracens, and finally his conduct towards the king of Leon, his son-in-law, whose noble and generous character cannot fail to cast a reflection upon that of Alfonso I, are actions which, taken separately, are worthy of condemnation, at least until records reveal some circumstances still unknown to us, which may absolve them. But, if we consider them in connection with the idea to which the king of Portugal had

AN EARLY PORTUGUESE KING

devoted himself, and which was so to speak incarnate in him, who will not find excuses for such actions, especially if we consider the barbarous epoch, the difficult situation of the country, and the real weakness of a society separated from another which struggled to bring it to reunion? The great need to which Alfonso I was bound to attend was to give homogeneity and internal and external strength to the nation which was being formed. For this purpose he was forced at the same time to seek the favour of the church, the first element of strength in those days; to favour the nobles, the chief nerve of the army, and finally to impart the utmost degree of vigour to the municipal spirit without which, in our opinion, popular spirit and keen love of country never have existed and never will exist.

Besides this labour of internal organisation, he had to extend the limits of the territory which he inherited, too narrow for the establishment of an independent state. The fear of his name among the Mussulmans and Christians and the daring of his troops were means to accomplish it. Naturally warlike, two successive generations learned in his school the hard business of war and succeeded in bequeathing to those to come the glorious traditions of strength and patriotic love which the nation guarded religiously for several centuries. However, before Alfonso I could trust the independence of the country to the chances of war, it was necessary to shield it while a frail plant, by political dexterity. In some cases this gave rise to actions which considered summarily would be condemned by severe morality. But view the picture in the proper light, and the stains which before cast a shadow upon the noble and haughty figure of the first Portuguese king will almost disappear, and the sympathy which the Portuguese nation has in all ages shown for the memory of the son of Count Henry will again appear estimable, for it has its roots in a sentiment rarely found among nations — gratitude to those to whom they are most indebted. This national affection went so far as to attribute to Alfonso Henriques the halo of the saints, and urge that Rome should bestow upon the fierce conqueror that crown which belongs to the martyr's resignation. But if a creed of peace and humility forbade Rome to grant that crown, another religion likewise venerable, the religion of patriotism, teaches us that when we pass the pale, worm-eaten portal of the church of Santa Cruz we are about to pay homage to the ashes of that man but for whom the Portuguese nation, and perhaps even the name of Portugal, would not be in existence to-day.

REIGNS OF SANCHO I AND ALFONSO II

The historical value of the twenty-six years' reign of the son of Alfonso I is perhaps no less than that of his own long term of government; but the character of the two epochs differ as much as did the gifts and characters of the two princes who presided over the political life of each. Less able as a captain than his father, and without that superior invention and daring which incited the founder of the monarchy to great enterprises, Sancho I was far from winning equal renown as a conqueror, but wasted the best years of his manhood in wars for the most part useless and obscure.

Upon this point the two epochs admit of no comparison. Before the sword of Alfonso, Saracen and Christian drew back dismayed, citadels and castles opened their gates; the limits of the country were extended, and the foundations of the existence of Portugal, cemented by torrents of blood, were permanently laid in the west of Spain. After a conquest Sancho always lost again, and for years carried on a sterile strife with Leon; and if he recovered a part of the north and west of Alemtejo it was because the Almohads, whose power was already on the decline, had not sufficient forces to maintain the almost useless dominion of those inhospitable deserts, and so abandoned them, while the Christians, especially the military orders, gradually reclaimed them and built castles and preceptories.

But if we turn our eyes from the frontiers and look upon the interior of the country, the name of the second monarch appears no less glorious than that of the first, and we see his reign as a complement of the preceding reign. Fertilised by the ashes of the martyrs of the Gospel and the *Koran*, turned and furrowed by the steel of combatants and the whirl of battles, the land of Portugal received from the hands of Sancho the seeds of greatness and royal strength in the councils which were everywhere established; in the farms and villages which were founded in the districts least subject to invasion and incursions; and in the frontier castles which were crowned with bastions and provided with military stores. In those days the courage which faces death was but a trivial virtue. Without the grand idea which dominated all his conquests, without the political skill and extraordinary military talent with which he made up for the lack of strength and resources of the monarchy which he founded, Alfonso I, in spite of his courage and energy, would rank no higher than a fortunate knight.

Upon this point his son was not fortune's favourite. However, he revenged himself nobly, labouring to earn the title of the Povoador, or city-builder, which he indeed deserved. History, so subject to the vulgar error of rating the barren laurel crown above the fruitful olive branch, has treated the last years of Sancho's reign with scorn because therein he endeavoured to substitute cities for deserts, cultivated fields for waste lands, and life for death. He pursued this end with energy, and his highest praise lies in the collection of documents which prove his activity and which are perhaps but a small portion of those once existing. This monarch sincerely followed the system which the internal state of the nation demanded, and enabled his successors to be, if not more valiant, at least more fortunate soldiers.

Such is the justice due to Sancho as king. As a man his moral character was not relatively bad, it was vulgar; that is, he had the defects common to princes and barons of the times; he was ignorant and credulous — for science, according to the opinion of the age, was only fit for the mean-spirited — irascible, and violent, because moderation is not learned upon the battle-field, where his father educated him. Besides this he seems to have been inclined to gallantry and the pleasures of the chase. Certain facts of his life also cast upon him the suspicion of cupidity, and of having gathered large sums into his treasury by means grievous to his nation. Sancho himself asserts that the defenders of the state often lacked necessaries, and yet he left in his will nearly *a million maravedis*, almost all in gold coin, that is, more than *three million cruzados* of the actual currency — truly an incredible sum, if we consider the rarity of precious metals at that time. Such riches presuppose frequent rapine or a too violent system of taxation. Indeed it is proved by a law of Alfonso II that the king as well as his barons obtained the greatest necessaries of life at an incomparably inferior price, a monstrous imposition which may give us some idea of the other exactions of the treasury.

But the point in which the reign of Sancho has perhaps the highest significance lies in the beginning of that varied and complex fact which for three centuries constituted the principal feature of our Middle Ages. We speak of the alliance of the king and councils against the privileged classes, the clergy and the nobility. The first phases of the struggle are not only the beginning but the epitome, or rather the symbol of the whole. The burgesses of Oporto, attacking their bishop and lord with the officers of the crown, confiscating his property, expelling him covered with ignominy, and braving the anger of the powerful family of Martinho Rodrigues, are a type of the resistance and ill will exhibited by the municipality and the king towards the two high classes of the state, until the monarchy gained a final and decisive victory. Sancho, abandoning the citizens of Oporto, transferring, so to speak, his inert strength of a dying man to the opposite camp, and even associating himself with the clergy to assist in subduing the burgesses, gave a deplorable example to his successors and stirred up the popular spirit to future strife. In spite of this, history cannot condemn him, for everything seems to indicate that the last months of his life were one protracted agony; and if even in our own times, when religious feeling has grown dim and weak, souls calling themselves strongly tempered waver at the approach of death, and bow not only to the terrors of religion but often even to the superstitious beliefs of infancy which then importunately revive — how can we fail to excuse an ignorant and credulous man, born in an inexorable age, for sacrificing both political convenience and loyalty to the voice of a frequently legitimate remorse?*

Alfonso II "the Fat" had no sooner ascended the throne than he showed a disposition to evade the execution of his father's will. Not only did he refuse to allow his brothers the money which had been bequeathed them, but he insisted on the restitution of the fortresses which belonged to his two sisters, the saints Theresa and Sancha; and on their refusal to surrender them, he seized them by force. The infantas complained to the pope and the king of Leon: the former ordered his legate to see justice done to them; the latter, who still bore an affection towards his divorced wife Theresa, interfered more effectually by way of arms. The Leonese entered Portugal by way of Badajoz, reduced several fortresses, and spread devastations around them. In the sequel, Alfonso of Portugal, at the command of the pope and doubtless through fear of the Leonese, consented to treat with his sisters.

The transactions of Alfonso with the Mohammedans were not so remarkable as those of his predecessors — a circumstance that must be attributed not to his want of military spirit but to his excessive corpulency, which rendered the fatigues of the field intolerable. Though he sent a handful of troops to aid in the triumphs of Las Navas de Tolosa, he did not take the field in person against the enemies of his faith, until 1217 when the arrival in his ports of another crusading armament, which promised to co-operate in his designs, roused him to the reduction of Alcacer-do-Sal, a place that still remained in the power of the misbelievers. It held out till the end of September. The Mohammedans who had remained in Alemtejo, and were pressing the siege of several fortresses, were compelled to retire.

During the last three years of his reign, Alfonso had new disputes with the church. He appears to have borne little respect for the ecclesiastical immunities, some of which were, indeed, inconsistent with the interests of the community. Alfonso insisted on churchmen heading their own vassals in the wars he undertook, and such as refused were compelled to go. For such violence there was no excuse; but in subjecting the ecclesiastical possessions to the same contributions as were levied on the property of the laymen, and churchmen themselves to the secular tribunals, he attempted a salutary innovation on the established system of the clerical exemptions. The archbishop of Braga, like the English Becket of the preceding century, remonstrated with the king; and when remonstrances were ineffectual, hurled at the head of his abettors the thunders of the church. In return he was deprived of his revenues, and compelled to consult his present safety by flight. He complained to the pope: Honorius III ordered three Castilian bishops to insist on ample reparation, to excommunicate the king, and impose an interdict on the nation. The afflicted people now endeavoured to effect a reconciliation between the king and the archbishop: the former promised to make satisfaction, and in future to respect the privileges of the church; he was accordingly absolved, and the interdict removed, but before he could fulfil his share of the compact he was surprised by death (1223).

Sancho II, having reluctantly promised to respect the immunities of the church, prepared to extend the boundary of his dominions at the expense of the Mohammedans. He recovered the important town of Elvas, which had been regained by the Moors: next Jarumeñha and Serpa yielded to his arms. He now carried the war into Algarve. He appears to have left the enemy no fortified places in Alemtejo; the frontier fortresses of that province, thus rescued from the infidels, he intrusted to the defence of the order of Santiago, who triumphed in several partial engagements. The frontier places continued for some years to change masters, according as either of the hostile powers prevailed.

In his domestic administration, Dom Sancho was doomed to be far less fortunate. From his infancy he appears to have been of a weak constitution, and of a still weaker mind; but if he was weak, we have no proof that he was vicious, though great disasters afflicted his kingdom, and the historians of his country have stigmatised his memory. His hostility to the immunities of the clergy appears to have been the first and chief cause of his unpopularity.*h*

SANCHO II CALLED CAPELLO, "THE HOODED"

The account of the state of the kingdom which served as a foundation for the acts which afterwards emanated from the Roman curia affirmed that the king in spite of his former promises showed on the one hand pertinacity in the perpetration of violence, and on the other the most inexcusable tolerance towards criminals, and neither amended himself nor restrained his subjects; that robbers, highwaymen, incendiaries, sacrilegists, and murderers swarmed everywhere, robbing and killing clergy and laity without distinction, and living secure of impunity. That through this contagious example of the impotence of the laws, barons and knights, nobles and plebeians made general practice of those acts which the church by the most severe comminations had endeavoured to restrain. That certain patrons of parishes and monasteries, and others falsely giving themselves out as such, accompanied by illegitimate children, wasted the property of the said parishes and monasteries without pity, reducing them to such misery that the very ministers of worship could not maintain themselves; so that in some there was even no one to perform the indispensable services, and in others the cloisters, refectories, and other offices were converted into stables and brothels for the lowest of men, and it might almost be said that divine worship had ceased there and the property of these holy places was given over to dilapidation and plunder. That at the same time Sancho allowed the castles, towns, and revenues of the crown to be destroyed and squandered, and suffered the increase of assassinations without any distinction whatever of the class, age, or sex of the victims; as well as robbery, incest, the rape of nuns and secular women, grievous oppression of labourers, priests, and merchants, with the purpose of extorting money from them; violation of temples and cemeteries, incendiarism, and breaches of truce. That Sancho was aware of all this and yet tolerated it, and through neglect of punishment facilitated the perpetration of further crimes; that finally, by abandoning the defence of the frontiers, he, the king of Portugal, allowed the Saracens to occupy the lands and lordships of the Christians. "We," added the prelates, "have used our utmost endeavours to move the prince to devote himself with due ardour to the repression of such evils; but he closes his ears to our admonitions, which have so far been entirely vain."

If the reader will reflect upon this last invective of the clergy against Sancho, he will recognise with what good reason we attribute to the long wars of this reign an immense influence upon the strife with the clergy, and see in these repeated enterprises against the infidel an idea, or maybe a political instinct, of the monarchy which drew strength from them for the eternal duel with the priesthood. As far as documents throw light upon the last conquests in Algarve, the accusation that Sancho in a cowardly manner abandoned the defence of the frontier and allowed the Mussulman arms to encroach upon the territory of the kingdom was a calumny.

But the heads of the clergy did not hesitate to adopt such means, for it was necessary to destroy the reputation of a conqueror of the enemies of the cross which the king of Portugal must still have enjoyed in the Roman curia, where the solemn testimonies of praise lavished upon him more than once by Gregory IX could not be yet forgotten. It was necessary to snatch the crown from the soldier's helm and place it on a dishonoured brow, that they might afterwards roll it in the dust before the priestly sandal. But up to a certain point Sancho offered a pretext for such calumny by the fatal repose of the preceding years, and perhaps some obscure event, the loss of some unimportant tower or grange of Ayamonte in the east or Tavira in the west, a loss exaggerated by ecclesiastical malice, gave the absurd assertion some appearance of truth.

The description of the state of Portugal, drawn up by the Roman curia, although exaggerated, was based on facts proved by various documents and memoirs of that time, and above all by the inquisitions of the following reign. But these very inquisitions prove that the members of the secular clergy and monastic orders were not innocent of the public evils, especially as regards robbery and the diminution of the patrimony of the crown. They complained of the contempt in which canonical censure was held, but the fault was theirs. The spiritual sword was blunted by excessive use ; excommunication, interdict, denial of burial in consecrated ground accompanied all the pretensions of the ministers of the altar, even those which the rudest of men could plainly perceive to be dictated by shameful cupidity. It is not surprising, therefore, that the nobles as well as the burgesses and peasants laughed at the chastisement which the clergy themselves taught them to despise. It was this contrast which throughout all Europe wounded the most enlightened men and gradually undermined the foundations and political influence of the church. The representation of the prelates was therefore doubly disloyal, attributing to the king alone the evils of which they were no less guilty, and describing the crimes and excesses of the laity towards the clergy, but forgetting to mention the abuse of divine things and the cupidity and lawlessness of the clergy.

The truth is, however, that this new phase of the interminable conflict between the clergy and the civil power did not arise from the cause assigned, but from the conjunction of circumstances which gave the bishops the means of gaining a decisive victory over the crown. The idea of deposing a king through the initiative of the church was old, and was considered so feasible that in grave cases the popes did not hesitate to allude to it clearly in their comminations and threats. In Portugal especially, as a kingdom in a manner dependent upon the papal throne, such a course must have seemed even easier, as the king was without moral or material means of defence.*j*

SANCHO DEPOSED, ALFONSO III SUCCEEDS (1245 A.D.)

Censures were passed on the monarch for his persecution of the dean of Lisbon. His subsequent repentance disarmed the pontiff ; and, notwithstanding the complaints of the people that the laws were silent, and brute force only triumphed, he would doubtless have ended his reign in peace, had he not resumed or permitted the spoliation of the church. At length, both clergy and people united their murmurs ; they perceived that the king was too feeble to repress the daily feuds of his barons, who broke out into open war and committed the greatest excesses. They applied to Innocent IV, who, in concert with the fathers of the council, issued a decree by which, though the royal title was left to Sancho, the administration was declared to be vested in the infante Alfonso, brother of the king.

No sooner did Alfonso hear of the extraordinary proceedings of the pope and council, than he prepared to vindicate the title which it had conferred upon him. He was then at Boulogne-sur-Mer, the lordship of which belonged to him in the right of his wife Matilda. Having sworn before the papal commissioners to administer Portugal with justice, and leaving the government of Boulogne in the hands of his countess, he embarked at that port, and safely landed at Lisbon. At first the king intended to oppose the infante ; but seeing how generally the deputies owned him,— how all classes, nobles and citizens, prelates and peasants, joined his brother,— he retreated into Spain, to solicit the support of his cousin, Ferdinand III. As that saintly monarch was too busy in the Andalusian wars to assist the fugitive king in person, he recommended the interests of his guest to his son Alfonso. The Castilian infante showed no want of zeal in behalf of his relative. He collected a considerable army, and invaded Portugal. Arriving before Leiria without much opposition, he was preparing to storm that fortress, when he was visited by a deputation from the archbishop of Braga, which conjured him, as a true son of the church, not to incur excommunication by opposing the execution of the pontifical bulls. The Castilian infante listened, and obeyed : he led back his army ; and the deposed monarch, now bereft of all hope, retired to Toledo, where, early in 1248, he ended his days. So long as the latter lived, some of the fortified places in Portugal refused to acknowledge the regent ; but on his death without issue—there is no evidence that he was ever married— his brother was peaceably acknowledged as his successor.

Alfonso III, on arriving at a height which, a few years before, his ambition could scarcely have reached, was not without apprehensions that the Castilian king or infante might trouble him in his usurpation, and assembled the three estates of his realm to deliberate on the means of defence. Fortunately for his ambition, both father and son were absorbed by their Andalusian conquests. To secure, if possible, the good will of the former, he sent a considerable aid to the Christian camp, which was readily received by the hero. In the meantime he himself resolved to profit by the reverses of the misbelievers, and finish the conquest of Algarve. At the head of a sufficient force, he accordingly penetrated into that province, and speedily recovered the places which the Mohammedans had again surprised. In a subsequent expedition, his ardour or avarice led him to encroach on the possessions of Alfonso el Sabio, Ferdinand's successor. The Castilian army marched against the Portuguese, who were compelled to retreat. The Castilian king did not stop here. On the pretext that Algarve, as chiefly conquered by his subjects, the knights of Santiago, belonged to him, he invaded that province, and quickly reduced its chief fortresses. The Portuguese was glad to sue for an accommodation ; and it was at length agreed that he should marry Doña Beatrice de Guzman, a natural daughter of the Castilian, and with her receive the sovereignty of Algarve. As the province had been conquered by the subjects of both crowns, equity would have indicated its division by the two monarchs ; but as such a division would probably have led to future wars, the present arrangement might be a politic one. The Castilian appears to have reserved to himself the sovereignty of Algarve, his feudatory being required both to pay tribute and to furnish a certain number of forces whenever he should be at war. The cession, with whatever conditions it was accompanied, was disagreeable to the Castilians, who thought that their monarch had sacrificed the interests of the state in favour of his daughter. The marriage was solemnised in the following year (in 1254), and a few years afterwards Portugal was declared forever free from homage to the Castilian kings.

From the facility with which this matrimonial connection was formed, it would be inferred that the Portuguese was become a widower. But the countess Matilda still lived, and was anxious to return to her lord. Her only defects were her barrenness and her age — two which, though no canonist would recognise, were sufficient in the mind of so unscrupulous a prince as Alfonso. She sailed for Portugal. He refused to see her ; and when at length she forced her way into his presence, he heard, unmoved, her entreaties, her expostulations, and threats. The queen (for such history must call her) retired to Boulogne, and laid her complaints before the pope and her liege superior, St. Louis. After a patient examination of the case, Alexander IV expedited a bull, by which he declared Matilda the lawful wife of Alfonso, and annulled the recent marriage with Doña Beatrice. The king persevered in his lust, as he had already done in his usurpation, even when excommunicated by the pope ; and he and his household were interdicted from the offices of the church. A second time is she said to have visited Portugal, but with as little success. She had married him when poor — when almost an exile from his native court — and had thereby raised him to power and riches : and her unshaken attachment — unshaken even by his sickening ingratitude — proves that though the empire of the passions had ceased, she possessed an uncommon share of woman's best feeling. Her last act, by which she bequeathed a considerable sum to this faithless deserter, was characteristic enough of her ruling misfortune. On her death, in 1262, his prelates obtained from the pope a bull to render legitimate the present marriage.[h]

POLITICAL IMPORTANCE OF ALFONSO'S REIGN

Alfonso determined to bridle the power of the bishops, in spite of his oath at Paris. Perceiving that this could only be done with the help of the mass of the people, he summoned a cortes at Leiria in 1254, to which representatives of the cities were elected and sat with the nobles and higher clergy. With the help of the cortes — one of great importance in the constitutional history of Portugal — he dared the interdict laid upon the kingdom for having married again (the daughter of Alfonso el Sabio) whilst his first wife (Matilda, countess of Boulogne) was alive. Finally, however, on the petition of the archbishops and bishops of Portugal, Pope Urban IV legalised the disputed marriage in 1262 and legitimated his eldest son, Dom Diniz, while in 1263, Alfonso X made over to him the full sovereignty of Algarve. On the other hand, the people made use of their power, and in a full cortes at Coimbra in 1261 the representatives of the cities boldly denounced Alfonso's tampering with the coinage, and compelled recognition of the fact that taxes were not levied by the inherent right of the king but the free consent of the people. After a prosperous and successful reign Nemesis came upon Alfonso in the rebellion of his eldest son Diniz[1] in 1277, which continued until 1279, in which year the king died.

[1 According to some authorities Diniz did not rebel at all, but was an exemplary son, and was present at his father's death-bed.]

The period of war and of territorial extension in the peninsula was now over, and the period of civilisation was to dawn. Territorially and constitutionally Portugal was now an established kingdom; it remained for it to become civilised and thoroughly homogeneous before the great heroic period of exploration and Asiatic conquest should begin.

DOM DINIZ

No better man for such work than the new king, Dom Diniz, could have been found; he was himself a poet and loved letters; he was a great administrator and loved justice; above all he saw the need of agriculture and the arts of peace to take the place of incessant wars, and nobly earned the title of the *Ré Lavrador*, or Diniz the Labourer. From all these points of view his reign is of vast importance in the history of Portugal, though, like all reigns of peaceful progress, it is not signalised by many striking events. It began with a civil war between Diniz and his brother Alfonso, who disputed his legitimacy, which ended in a compromise; and in 1281 Diniz married Isabella, daughter of Pedro III of Aragon, who for her pure and unselfish life was canonised in the sixteenth century. His reign is marked by only one war with Sancho IV and his successor, Ferdinand IV, of Castile and Leon, which was terminated in 1297 by a treaty of alliance, according to the terms of which Ferdinand IV married Constanza, daughter of Diniz, while Alfonso, the heir to the throne of Portugal, married Beatrice of Castile, sister of Ferdinand. At the end of this reign war broke out between the king and the heir-apparent, and a pitched battle was only prevented in 1323 by St. Isabella riding between the armies and making a peace between her husband and her son, which lasted until the death of the great peace-monarch, the *Ré Lavrador*, in 1325.c

Treachery and abuse of power were so frequent that, notwithstanding various diplomatic disloyalties, Diniz was considered one of the most loyal and just princes and lords of the two kingdoms. For this reason the two great kingdoms of Aragon and Castile appointed him arbitrator in the most serious disputes, and submitted to his judgment. Although the genius of war did not weave martial crowns for him, as conqueror in battles — for during his time no great honours fell to the Portuguese arms — yet he was ever at the head of the national armies in all the campaigns; knowing that his most powerful allies had been destroyed and others had betrayed him, he had the skilful audacity to penetrate forty leagues into the interior of Castile, and availing himself of the opportunity afforded by his opponents' weakness, he increased the Portuguese dominion by two castles and eleven important towns, as though he were the most successful of warriors. The civil dissensions which disturbed his reign both arose from the same causes and circumstances, mediæval feudalism, assisted by Castilian elements. Taking for leaders first the brother and then the son of Diniz, the rebels combatted royal power in the kingdom, which, supported by the people, daily increased feudal privileges and forces.

The husband of Isabella was as rapid and successful in his measures against his brother as he was undecided and weak in repressing his son. In the first instance his courage was heightened by the just ambition of safe-guarding his throne; whereas, in the second instance, it was weakened by paternal affection and respect of legitimacy in the succession of the crown.

However, the principal glory of Diniz was not won with his sword. Of his epoch a perfect king, penetrated by his country's needs, he notably increased the territory of Alfonso Henriques, but above all he raised to an amazing height the edifice of internal organisation, the foundations of which had been laid by Sancho I. His disloyalties with respect to the neighbouring kingdoms, his rare moments of repressive cruelty, the errors into which he may have fallen as a politician, the many faults into which he was in truth led by an ardent and sensual character — Diniz redeemed them all by the general and profound reform he effected with regard to Portuguese society.

He raised the population of the country, as none of his predecessors had done, by the means we have spoken of ; he brought agriculture to a pitch of prosperity which we now marvel at ; he created the internal industry and commerce, promoted municipal organisation, favouring labour, encouraging markets, and raising the spirit of the people ; he safeguarded navigation by establishing vast societies of mutual aid between merchants, and definitely established a navy, with which he defended the coasts and the Portuguese merchant ships against pirates, and equipped his subjects for the discoveries of the fifteenth and sixteenth centuries, which brought universal and eternal fame upon Portugal. He built nearly fifty fortresses, reorganised the popular militia, and nationalising the military orders with praiseworthy abnegation, he widely prepared the defence of the country, and bequeathed to Dom João I the possibility of opposing a formidable invasion by Castile and establishing once for all, with immortal glory, the independence of the country.

He was a zealous administrator, wise and economic, so that with the national resources he left the public treasury wealthy. Of a tolerant spirit, prudent and just in the application of the laws, no prince of his own times surpassed him in these qualities, then most rare. With gentle measures, affectionately and frequently protecting individual rights, he was one of the most determined opponents of the excessive privileges of the nobility and the church. Having received civil power, bound beneath the yoke of the Portuguese clergy, in their turn fettered to the Roman tiara, Diniz not only raised this power, but even succeeded in giving life to the national episcopacy.

The establishment of the councils begun by previous governments largely progressed, and the cortes, continuing to summon the deputies of the people, was a new and powerful aid towards the destruction of mediæval, ecclesiastical, and military feudalism in Portugal. With the laws respecting mortmain decreed and executed with civic firmness and superior wisdom, the clergy were deprived of territorial power and the sovereign right of administering justice ; civil actions were brought before secular tribunes, which by a usurpation of jurisdiction had up to that time been brought before ecclesiastical tribunals.

The nobles were prohibited from raising new seigniorial castles, and many of the old were levelled ; they were deprived of their traditional rights of deciding mutual disputes with the sword, of making knights, of exempting themselves from the royal tax, turning into fiefs and boroughs the lands they had seized without just cause, and even those with which they had established merely personal relations, and finally by giving judgment in causes in which the nobles claimed for themselves exclusive knowledge, the feudal nobility was totally destroyed, as was the temporal power of the church. Up to then the beneficial influence of the times sufficed to totally undermine the old oligarchic institutions of the Middle Ages, which were an overwhelming oppression of the people, and absorbed the forces of the state.

Finally Diniz, who was the greatest poet of the first four centuries of Portugal, founded to his honour the Estudaria de Santo Eloy in Lisbon, and also the university, causing general enthusiasm ; and by spreading the love of letters and study in the country, laid the foundations of secular and public instruction and opened to the Portuguese people the gates of science, and consequently those of civilisation and liberty.

After the work of Alfonso Henriques, that of Diniz is the most important which Portuguese history records to us : the first was the founder of the military nation ; the second, that of the cultured people.   The union of those two works gave to Portugal centuries later the possibility of realising, in the long evolution of mankind, her glorious mission of enlarging the known world.*k*

Alfonso IV, surnamed the Brave, had scarcely grasped the reins of sovereignty, when he exhibited, in a manner little becoming royalty, his vindictive feelings towards his illegitimate brother, Alfonso Henriques, who, to escape his wrath, had just fled into Castile.   Having collected some troops, and been joined by a prince of Castile, he entered Portugal, laid waste the frontiers, and put to the sword every living being that fell in his way.   The king now took the field in person, and laid waste the neighbouring territories of Castile. These harassing though indecisive hostilities might have continued for years, had not St. Isabella left her retreat in the convent of St. Clair, which she had founded, and prevailed on her son to permit the return of the exile.

Another defect of the new king gave great offence to the people — his neglect of public business, and his addiction to the chase.   The first twelve years of Alfonso's reign were distracted by hostilities with his namesake of Castile, the husband of his daughter.   Though these hostilities were chiefly owing to the perversity of the infante Don Juan Manuel, it cannot be denied that the Portuguese king had abundant reason for dissatisfaction with his son-in-law.   The usage experienced by the Castilian queen at the hands of her husband ; her mortification at seeing a mistress, Leonora de Guzman, not only preferred to herself, but the sole depository of the royal favour ; the studied insults to which she was daily exposed both from her husband and his minion, at length exhausted her patience, and drew forth some complaints to her father.   The influence, too, which Don Juan Manuel obtained in the Portuguese court through the marriage of his repudiated daughter Constanza with Pedro, son and heir of the Portuguese king, was uniformly exerted to embroil the two crowns.   Alfonso of Portugal at length sent a herald at arms to defy his son-in-law, on the ground both of the unjust treatment of the queen, whom her husband was suspected of seeking to repudiate, and of the continued detention of Constanza.   His next step was to enter Castile and ravage the country as far as the vicinity of Seville.

The war was now as destructive as it was indecisive and even inglorious : it was one of mutual ravage, of shameless rapine, and unblushing cruelty. Instead of meeting each other on a fair field, they seemed intent on nothing but laying waste each other's territory, and collecting as much booty as they could carry away : sometimes, however, the contest was decided on the deep, but with little success to either party.   At length, through the efforts of the pope, the two princes agreed to a truce, and to the opening of negotiations for peace.   But one of the conditions was the removal of Leonora de Guzman — a condition which Alfonso of Castile, who was entirely governed by that lady, was in no disposition to execute, but the preparations of the Mohammedans, which he knew were chiefly directed against himself, and the loud complaints of his own subjects, forced him to promise at least that it should be conceded. To the departure of Constanza, the restitution of some insignificant fortresses which had been reduced, and even to the return of his queen, the Castilian felt no repugnance ; but though he consented for Leonora to leave the court, he recalled her immediately after the conclusion of peace. To his queen, however, he no longer exhibited a marked neglect : on the contrary, he treated her with all the outward respect due to her character and station ; and the good understanding was confirmed by her admirable moderation.

In the wars which the Castilian had to sustain against the Mohammedans, the Portuguese — so nobly did he forget his wrongs when the interests of Christendom were at stake — was no inefficient ally. He was present at the great battle on the banks of the Salado, in which the barbaric power was so signally humbled. This aid he continued readily to supply, until the death of Alfonso of Castile, by the plague, before Gibraltar, in 1350.

THE ROMANCE OF IÑES DE CASTRO

The tragedies represented in Castile by Pedro the Cruel, successor of Alfonso XI, were fully equalled by one in Portugal. Soon after his marriage with Constanza, Pedro, the infante of Portugal, had become passionately smitten with one of her attendants, Doña Iñes de Castro, a lady of surpassing beauty, and frail as beautiful. That he made love to her, and that his criminal suit was favourably received, is indubitable, both from the deep grief which preyed on the spirits of Constanza, and from the anxiety of the king, lest this new favourite should be the cause of the same disturbance in Portugal, as Leonora de Guzman had occasioned in Castile. To prevent the possibility of a marriage between the two lovers, Alfonso caused Iñes to hold over the baptismal font a child of Pedro's — in other words, to contract a near spiritual affinity. But the man whom the sacred bond of wedlock could not restrain was not likely to be deterred from his purpose by an imaginary bar. After Constanza's death in childbed, 1345, he privately married the seductive favourite. How soon after the death of the first wife this second union was contracted, whether immediately, or after Iñes had borne him three children, has been matter of much dispute. It appears that the marriage was celebrated on the 1st day of January, 1354, when Iñes must have borne him four children, of which three survived. It also appears that a papal dispensation was obtained for it, and that it took place at Braganza, in presence of a Portuguese prelate and his own chamberlain. However secret this step, it was suspected by some courtiers, who, partly through envy at the rising favour of the Castros, and partly through dread of the consequences which might ensue, endeavoured to prevail on the king to interfere in behalf of young Ferdinand, the son of Pedro and Constanza, and the lawful heir to the monarchy. From the boundless influence possessed over the mind of Pedro by Doña Iñes, it was feared that the true heir would be set aside from the succession in favour of her offspring. In the end, they wrung from him a reluctant consent to her death. The king, hearing that his son had departed on a hunting excursion for a few days, hastily left Monte-mor, and proceeded to the convent of St. Clair, at Coimbra, where Iñes then was. On learning his approach, she at once apprehended his object. Her only resource was an appeal to his pity. Taking her three children by the hand, she issued from the convent to meet him, prostrated herself at his feet, and in the most pathetic terms begged for mercy. Her beauty, her youth, her deep emotion, and the sight of her offspring — his own grand-children — so affected him that, after a struggle between policy and nature, the latter triumphed, and he retired.   No sooner, however, was he in private with his confidants, than they censured his compassion, though natural in itself, as ruinous in its consequences to his family and kingdom, and obtaining his consent hastened to the convent.   The unfortunate, guilty Iñes fell beneath their daggers.   The fate of this lady has called forth the deepest commiseration of novelists and poets, and has given rise to some vigorous effusions of the tragic muse.

When Pedro returned from the chase, and found his wife so barbarously murdered, his grief was surpassed, if possible, by his thirst for revenge.   He leagued himself with the kindred of Iñes ; and though he could not fall on the murderers, who were protected by the king, he laid waste the provinces of Entre-Douro-e-Minho, and Tras-os-Montes, where their possessions chiefly lay.   King Alfonso was in consternation at the unexpected fury of his son. In the end he proposed, as the price of reconciliation, that the obnoxious nobles should be banished, and his son admitted to the chief share of the administration.   Pedro accepted it, laid down his arms, and proceeded to court where he was received with an affection truly paternal, and where he engaged, though with a fixed resolution of breaking the engagement, never to seek revenge on the assassins of Doña Iñes.

Alfonso did not long survive this forced reconciliation with his son.   His death, which happened at the beginning of 1357, is said to have been hastened by remorse for the tragical deed of which he had been the occasion.   That he exhibited great repentance is certain ; but his character was unamiable. He had been a disobedient son, an unjust brother, and a harsh father.   The rebellion of his son was but fit retribution for his own conduct to the royal Diniz.   His justice too often degenerated into blind vengeance.   During his reign (in 1348) Portugal was afflicted with the plague, which spread through-out most of Europe, but which raged with more violence in that kingdom than anywhere else.   Whole towns are said to have been left desolate, and some priests to have abandoned their flocks to the care of the monks.[h]

If we consider Alfonso IV — not isolated, nor in the light of our pres-ent-day views and social conditions as a son or as a father (even in this character we can bring forward the virtuous and exemplary spouse), but principally as leader and as king, in the moment when he assumed and exer-cised his power — we must confess, in face of the numerous documents relating to his external policy and his enormous legislation, that he is one of the most important figures, and that his government was one of the most advantageous, the most brilliant, and the most able of the intelligent and energetic governments which presided over the national formation of Portu-gal.   In the character of this king there is a certain harmonious stamp of austerity which gives him a decided and characteristic originality in the midst of the free customs, and, we may say, of the traditional moral license of the kings of his time.   Dom Diniz, the father of King Alfonso IV, in spite of the perfect devotion of his wife, was the easy prey of adulterous loves, and far from disguising them, flagrantly and heedlessly published them by the generosity of his gifts, calling to himself his bastard children and lavish-ing favours upon them, and confessing even by public documents the rewards conferred on his mistresses.

As to Dom Pedro, the Romeo of Iñes de Castro, we know that he was not so absorbed by this fatal passion but that the nation's history owes to him the bastard progenitor of the second dynasty.   In this instance Dom

Alfonso presents a totally distinct character from that of his son; an exemplary husband, he made every effort to raise by royal authority the moral tone in the relation between the sexes, and to check the dissolute customs of the times. He made severe laws against those who availed themselves of such usages and customs up to that time in vogue, which seduced by endearments, or other means, various virgins and widows leading honest lives to make use of them for their evil purposes; he denounced "any man or woman guilty of panderage, and keeping in their houses for this purpose virgins, married women, religious, or widows." At the exact moment that he was publishing some of his most severe laws upon this matter his son gave cause of scandal by his real or apparent cohabitation with Doña Iñes de Castro. Finally he left the kingdom to his successor in perfect internal and external peace, and it would be cruel injustice to deny that under his government the work of the political consolidation of Portuguese society made important progress.[k]

PEDRO THE SEVERE

Pedro I was scarcely established on the throne before he gave way to his uncontrollable desire for vengeance on the murderers of Doña Iñes. Knowing that they had sought protection in Castile, and how eager his namesake of that country was for the surrender of several Castilians, who, in like manner, had obtained an asylum in Portugal, he paid court to that monarch, with whom he entered into a close alliance, and to whom he despatched ten of his galleys to serve in the war against Aragon. Having declared the fugitive nobles, who were three in number, Pedro Coelho, Alvaro Gonsalves, and Diogo Lopes Pacheco, traitors to their country, and confiscated all their possessions, he either proposed or received the proposal — there is some doubt from which of the two monarchs it originally came, or whether it may not be equally attributed to both — for the arrest of their personal enemies. On a given day the obnoxious Castilians were arrested in Portugal, the Portuguese in Castile, and were surrendered to their respective executioners. Of the three Portuguese, however, Pacheco escaped.

The escape of even one victim was gall to the Portuguese king; but he resolved to satiate his rage on the two who were placed in his reach. Both were thrown into a deep dungeon, put to the torture, with the view of eliciting whether others were implicated in the same crime. They withstood the acute torments they were made to endure with a firmness truly admirable — a circumstance that increased beyond measure the rage of Pedro, who was present at the hellish scene. With Coelho in particular, whom not a word, not a groan had escaped, he was so exasperated that he seized a whip and struck him on the face. This indignity affected the high-spirited knight far more than his present sufferings. Regarding the king with eyes full of fury, he loaded him not merely with the keenest reproaches, but with a torrent of abuse. The latter foamed at the mouth, and ordered his victims to be transferred from the dungeon to a scaffold erected in front of his palace. There he appeared at the window, expressing a savage delight at the new torments they sustained. At length the living hearts of both were plucked from their bodies; hearts and bodies were next consigned to the flames; and when consumed, the ashes were scattered by the winds.

The next proceeding of Pedro was to honour alike the remains and memory of the unfortunate Iñes. He convoked the states of his kingdom at Castanedo, and, in their presence, made oath on the holy Gospels that, in the

Painted especially for ''The Historians' History of the World'' by A. Raynott

PEDRO I CROWNING THE DEAD QUEEN INES

year 1354, he had married that lady. The witnesses of the fact, the bishop of Guarda and his own chamberlain, were likewise publicly sworn, and the bull of dispensation produced which Pope Innocent VI had granted for the celebration of the ceremony. No doubt was entertained by the assembled nobles and clergy that Iñes had been the lawful wife of their prince; and she was unanimously declared entitled to the honours usually paid to the Portuguese queens. That the legitimacy of her offspring might never be disputed, copies of the papal dispensation and of the oaths taken on this occasion were multiplied and dispersed throughout the kingdom. The validity of the marriage being thus established, Pedro now proceeded to show due honour to her remains. He ordered two magnificent tombs, both of white marble, to be constructed, one for himself, the other for that lady, and placed them in the monastery of Alcobaça. He then proceeded to the church of St. Clair at Coimbra, caused her corpse to be brought from the sepulchre, to be arrayed in royal ornaments, to be placed on a throne with a crown on the head and a sceptre in the hand, and there to receive the homage of his assembled courtiers. From that church it was conveyed on a magnificent car, accompanied by nobles and high-born dames, all clad in mourning, to the monastery of Alcobaça.[1]

As the subsequent transactions of the Portuguese king with his namesake of Castile have been already related [in the history of Spain, Chapter III], nothing now remains but briefly to notice his internal administration. It is allowed to have been as rigorous as it was whimsical. With the view of correcting the extravagance which had long seized on the higher orders of his people, he made a law that whoever bought or sold on credit should be punished — if the first offence, by stripes; if the second, by death. In his own household he set the example of paying for everything in money the instant it was purchased. If he was thus severe against thoughtless imprudence, he could not be expected to be more lenient towards guilt. Of the vices which he visited with unpitying vengeance, fornication and adultery were the most obnoxious to him. That the lover of Iñes de Castro should thus hold in abhorrence those which he had so long practised might create surprise, were it not proved by general experience, not only that we are most forward to condemn in others imperfections to which ourselves are prone, but that kings are too often eager to plead exemption from obligations binding on the rest of mankind. Hearing that the bishop of Oporto lived in a state of concubinage, the royal moralist laid on him unmercifully with a whip. As he was one day proceeding along a street, he heard a woman call another by an opprobrious name. He speedily inquired into the affair; and, finding that the latter had been violated previous to her marriage by her husband, he consigned the offender to the executioner. Suspecting that the wife of a certain merchant was unfaithful to her conjugal duty, he caused her to be watched until he detected her in the actual crime; both lady and paramour were immediately committed to the flames. An old woman prostituted her daughter to a Portuguese admiral; the woman was burned, the admiral sentenced to lose his head — a sentence, however, which he escaped by flight. Other offences against the laws were punished, sometimes in proportion to their magnitude, but generally to his caprice. An inferior officer of the law one day complained that a gentleman on whom he had served a

[1 Like all other romantic events, this story has attracted the critics, their chief objection to it being the fact that the contemporary historian Lopes,[l] who describes the death of Iñes with much detail, has nothing to say of the exhumation and coronation. But such negative argument must be cautiously used and historians have not yet annulled the story of Iñes.]

process had struck him and plucked him by the beard; Pedro turned to the presiding judge, and said, "I have been struck, and my beard has been plucked, by one of my subjects!" The judge, who understood the appeal, caused the culprit to be arrested and beheaded. Perceiving that causes were frequent, tedious, and expensive, and shrewdly divining the reason, he purged his courts of all advocates and proctors, — of all who had a manifest interest in litigation, and reduced all processes to a simple statement of the case by the parties concerned, and of the sentence by the judges, reserving, however, to himself the privilege of deciding appeals. If we add that Pedro was liberal of rewards, and fond of music and dancing, the character of the royal barbarian will be completed.

Ferdinand I, son of Pedro and the princess Constanza, was ill fitted to succeed monarchs so vigorous as his immediate predecessors. Fickle, irresolute, inconstant, without discernment, directed by no rule of conduct, obedient only to momentary impulse, addicted to idleness, or to recreations still more censurable, the very benevolence of his nature was a calamity.

After the death of the Castilian Pedro the Cruel, Ferdinand, considering himself the true heir to the crown, assumed the regal title and arms of Castile. His ambition was lamentably inadequate to an enterprise so important as that of encountering and attempting to dethrone the bastard usurper Henry of Trastamara. From the recesses of his palace, he appeared to witness the invasion of his kingdom and the defeat of his armies with indifference. When, in 1373, Lisbon itself was invested by the Castilian king, the defence of the place was abandoned to the valour of the inhabitants, and to their deep-rooted hatred of the Spanish sway. The same year, indeed, peace was made through the mediation of the pope; but it was often broken by Ferdinand during the reign both of Henry of Trastamara and Juan I, the son and successor of that prince. The marriage of Beatrice, daughter of Ferdinand, with Juan, in 1382, and the treaty for uniting the two crowns, have been related in the history of Spain [Chapter V], and to that history the reader is referred for an account of the obscure and indecisive, however destructive, wars between the two kingdoms.

During these transactions proposals were frequently made for restoring permanent harmony by matrimonial alliances. At first Ferdinand cast his eyes on the infanta Leonora of Aragon, whom he engaged to marry; but, with his usual fickleness, he escaped from the obligation. He next promised to raise a daughter of Henry of Trastamara, also named Leonora, to the Portuguese throne. When the time approached for the celebration of this marriage, Ferdinand fell passionately in love with one of his own subjects — a Leonora like the rest.[1] To beauty of the finest order, Leonora added a sprightliness which charmed and a wit which captivated him; but these were far inferior to her ambition, and unsupported by one single principle of honour or virtue. She was already the wife of Dom João Lourenço da Cunha, lord of Pombeiro. "Of that we are well aware," said Ferdinand; "but they are related by blood, and they married without a dispensation: the engagement may easily be annulled." Proceedings for the cassation of the marriage were instituted in the ecclesiastical courts; and as the husband offered no opposition to them, — doubtless because he had no wish to contend with a plaintiff whose cause was backed by legions of soldiers, — it was declared null. Not considering himself safe in Portugal, Dom Lourenço fled

---

[1] "This name proved terrible to the king," says Lemos.[g] This name, indeed, in all the three cases, is a most singular coincidence: it did not prove terrible, however it might be pernicious to the interests of the kingdom.

into Castile, evidently little afflicted at the loss of an unprincipled woman.[1] There is reason to believe that it was Ferdinand's original intention to make her his mistress; but she had too much policy to become the tool of one whom she had resolved to rule; and she assumed the appearance of so much modesty, that to gain his object he was forced to marry her.

But this marriage was strictly private — a precaution adopted as well to stifle the murmurs of his subjects as to prevent the indignant remonstrances of Henry. It was, however, suspected, and the very suspicion produced great dissatisfaction throughout the kingdom — nowhere so great as in the capital. A mob, formidable from its numbers, assembled in the streets, and headed by a tailor, proceeded to the palace to reproach the king for his imprudence. Ferdinand said that he had neither married nor intended to marry Leonora. This declaration satisfied the mob; who, however, insisted that he should take an oath the following day to the same effect in the church of Saõ Domingos — a promise which he readily made. At the time appointed, they proceeded to the church, but found to their mortification that, during the night, the king and Leonora had fled to Santarem. In the height of their fury they apostrophised both in no measured terms. Their insulting conduct so incensed the queen that she procured a royal order for the arrest and execution of the tailor and his chief associates. The fear which this act of severity struck into the people emboldened the king to publish his marriage. The nobles and prelates now hastened to court, to recognise their new queen. All readily kissed her hand with the exception, of Dom Diniz, son of Pedro and Iñes de Castro, who accompanied his refusal in open court with expressions of contempt. Ferdinand drew his poniard, and would doubtless have laid his obnoxious brother at his feet, but for the interference of two nobles who arrested his arm. Even João, the grand-master of Aviz, a natural son of the late king, who is about to perform so memorable a part in the national history, bowed before the triumphant Leonora. To render her power more secure, she began to act with great policy, disarmed hostility, and secured to herself an undisturbed possession of her new dignity.

The insult to the royal family of Castile involved in this imprudent marriage was one of the causes which led to the hostilities that followed — hostilities in which the country was laid waste, from Badajoz to Lisbon, and that capital invested. On the conclusion of peace, in 1373, which was cemented by the marriage of a natural daughter of Ferdinand with a natural son of Henry, tranquillity visited the kingdom for some years; but the Portuguese court, through the ambition and wickedness of the queen, was often distracted and disgraced. As Ferdinand had only a daughter — the princess Beatrice — by Leonora, and as no hopes of future issue appear to have been entertained, the infante João, brother of the king, (not the bastard of that name who was the grand-master of Aviz, but the eldest surviving son of Pedro and Iñes de Castro), was regarded as the presumptive heir to the crown. To set him aside from the succession was now the object of the queen. Fortunately for her purpose, the imprudence of the prince presented her with the means. Struck with the personal charms of Donna Maria, sister of the queen, he privately married her. The step was not hidden from Leonora; who, so far from betraying her knowledge of it, and to lull her intended victim into profound security, proposed to the infante the hand of her own child, and with it the throne of Portugal. As she expected, her

[1] To disarm ridicule by braving it, and to prove how little the affair had affected him, the exiled husband attached to each side of his cap a golden horn.

offer was declined; but she was resolved to move heaven and earth rather than see her sister and brother-in-law in the possession of supreme power. The former she appears to have hated: her destruction was certainly planned with demoniacal coolness. Sending one day for the infante, she assumed the appearance of intense affliction; assured him that she knew of his marriage with her sister; but that regard for him and his honour, as well as for the honour of the royal family, would not permit her to conceal that sister's depravity. "You are betrayed, prince!" was the substance of her address. "Maria loves another, to whom she grants her favours!"

Unfortunately, João, who was unacquainted with her real character, and who could not suppose her capable of deliberately destroying a sister, implicitly believed her; and in the madness of his rage, hastened to Coimbra, where the princess then abode. She met him with her usual smiles, and, on being repulsed, falteringly demanded the cause. "Because," replied the infuriated husband, "you have divulged our marriage and sacrificed my honour." "Bid your attendants retire," pleaded the poor woman, "and I will satisfy you." "I come not to hear your excuses," João returned furiously, "but to punish your guilt," and at the same time his dagger found a way to her heart. She fell into the arms of her weeping attendants, while he mounted his horse and fled. The cause of all this wickedness affected inconsolable grief, threw herself at the royal feet, and cried for vengeance on the murderer. But whether she found the king averse to justice, or whether she feared the indignation of the infante, who, sooner or later, would become acquainted with the innocence of Maria, she suddenly changed her proceedings, and obtained permission for him to return to court. But there everyone shunned him — no one more eagerly than Leonora; so that, seeing his hopes of Beatrice at an end, he retired into the province of Entre-Douro-e-Minho, where he was soon acquainted with the bloody perfidy of the queen. Having reason to distrust his safety, he fled into Castile, his heart torn by remorse for the fate of one whom he had passionately loved, and whose bleeding image was incessantly before him.

Though on the accession of Juan I of Castile Ferdinand readily renewed the peace between the two crowns, and consented to marry his daughter Beatrice to the heir of the Castilian, his characteristic fickleness was such that he soon resolved to resume hostilities. To engage the duke of Lancaster in his cause, he sent a trusty messenger to England, Dom João Ferdinand Andeiro, who concluded a league with the Plantagenet. To conceal this negotiation from the world, especially from the Castilian, he pretended great anger with Andeiro, whom he arrested, and confined to the fortress of Estremos. During his agreeable captivity in this place, he was frequently visited by the disguised king, who was sometimes accompanied by the queen, and was made to unfold the conditions he had contracted, and solicited for his advice. As his person was unexceptionable, his address elegant, and his manners prepossessing, he soon won so far on the credulous Leonora that she became the willing partner of his lust, and still more of his ambition. In the hostilities which followed the arrival of the earl of Cambridge, he was released, and, by her influence, was invested with the lordship of Ourem.

Ferdinand at length saw that the affections of his queen were estranged from him, and transferred to Andeiro. Yet — such was his deplorable weakness! — he met both with constrained smiles, and deputed both to be present at the marriage of his daughter Beatrice with Juan of Castile. On this occasion the favourite appeared with a splendour which might have become a sovereign prince, but which filled the beholders with indignation or envy

The perpetual sight of a faithless wife and her insolent paramour was at length too much even for the feeble Ferdinand. In the agony of his feelings he one day opened his heart to the grand-master of Aviz, who he knew hated Andeiro, and with whom he planned that minion's assassination. But his own death, the result alike of constitutional weakness of frame and mental suffering, saved him from the guilt of murder. The reign of this sovereign was one of the most deplorable that ever afflicted Portugal. The wars with Castile, — wars lightly undertaken and ingloriously conducted, — and the consequent invasions of his territory by his more powerful neighbours, impoverished his people.[h]

CHAPTER II

THE PERIOD OF GLORY AND DISCOVERY

[1383–1521 A.D.]

BY the death of Ferdinand, his daughter Beatrice, queen of Castile, was the true heir to the throne of Portugal. But the kingdom, far from expecting a foreign yoke, had, on the marriage of the infanta, expressly stipulated that, in case of Ferdinand's death, the government should be vested in a regent, until she had a son capable of assuming the sovereignty; that son, too, to be educated not in Castile but in Portugal. When that event happened, she had no child — a circumstance that induced her husband to claim the crown in her right, and that filled the Portuguese with vexation. They were satisfied neither with their intended sovereign, Juan, nor with the regent, Leonora, the queen-mother, whom the will of the late king appointed to that dignity. And when, in conformity with the demands of the Castilian, Beatrice was proclaimed in Lisbon, the people either exhibited a mournful silence, or cried out that they would have no other king than their infante João, son of Pedro and Iñes de Castro, and the unfortunate husband of Maria, sister of Leonora, whose tragical fate has been recorded. But João and his brother Diniz now languished in the dungeons of Castile,[1] whither they had been consigned by the king, who knew that, if suffered to enter Portugal, they would speedily thwart his views of dominion. Until these princes could be restored to their country, and until Beatrice should have an heir, the Portuguese resolved to deprive the queen-mother of the regency, in favour of Dom João, the grand-master of Aviz, who alone seemed able to defend their national independence.

[1] A bastard daughter of Ferdinand and her husband were about the same time placed in confinement.

452

Dom João, as before observed, was an illegitimate son of King Pedro, by a lady of Galicia, and born in 1357. At seven years of age he had been invested with the high dignity of grand-master, and his education intrusted to one of the ablest commanders of the order. No man could be better adapted for the conjuncture in which circumstances placed him. Cool, yet prompt; prudent, yet in the highest degree courageous; unrestrained by conscience, and ready to act either with cunning or violence, according as either appeared necessary to his purpose, he would indeed have been a formidable opponent to any sovereign, much more to one so weak as the Castilian. Seeing the favourable disposition of the people, and confiding in his own mental resources, he commenced a policy which, if at first cautious, was sure to prove efficacious. Though Leonora pretended great sorrow for her husband's death, and endeavoured, by affected mildness, as well as by an administration truly liberal, to win the popular favour, her object was penetrated and despised. But a stronger sentiment was felt for Andeiro, who directed her at his pleasure, and whose death was now decreed by the grand-master. To remove the latter under some honourable pretext from court, he was charged by Leonora with the government of Alemtejo. He accepted the trust; but, accompanied by twenty-five resolute followers, returned to Lisbon, December 6th, 1383, and hastened to the royal apartments, where he knew he should find Andeiro. The guilty pair were as usual together. João struck the count with a dagger; a knight of his suite by a second blow deprived the victim of life.

The tragical deed was hailed with characteristic acclamations by the populace, who, profiting by the example, massacred everyone suspected to be hostile to the pretensions of their new idol, among them the bishop of Lisbon.[1] Their mangled corpses remained long without sepulture, a prey to dogs and beings more savage than dogs. Leonora now fled from the city to Alemquer. On the way, she turned her eyes for a moment back on the towers of that capital, and, in the bitterness of her heart prayed that she might live to see it wrapped in flames. After her departure, João complained that he was unequal to oppose his powerful enemies; and pretended that he would retire into England, to pass his remaining days in tranquillity. This hypocritical policy alarmed the mob, who dreaded being abandoned to justice, and tumultuously flocked around him, insisting that he should assume the regency until Beatrice should become the mother of a son destined to rule over them. With much apparent reluctance, he accepted the proffered dignity, in the resolution of securing one much higher.

The first measures of the new regent were characteristic of the man. He published an edict in which entire pardon was promised to all criminals, whatever their offences, who should assist him in opposing the queen and the Spaniards. At this unexpected call, great numbers — amounting, we are told, to thousands — hastened from their prisons or their haunts to swell his army. Many of the great towns were persuaded to follow the example of Lisbon. The impunity with which his followers perpetrated every possible crime was too alluring not to increase the number. Murder, plunder, rape, and sacrilege were the constant attendants of this lawless party. The abbess of the convent of Castres was dragged from her cloister, poniarded before the high altar, and her body was subjected to brutalities of which not even the mention would be tolerated by the reader. In the end it was dragged to a public square, and there left. This is but one instance, among numbers

[1] The fate of this prelate has excited little pity among the orthodox Portuguese, such as Lemos,[b] because he favoured the anti-pope.

which have been preserved and among thousands of which the memory has perished, of the monstrous crimes of this interregnum; yet no attempt was made to punish them by the regent, who felt that the license thus allowed was his only tenure on the attachment of his adherents.

The king of Castile invaded the kingdom, received the submission of several places, and penetrated to Santarem, to concert with his mother-in-law, Leonora, the means of annihilating the resources of João. But that ambitious woman, who perceived that with the arrival of the king her authority had ceased, soon regarded his cause with indifference, ultimately with dislike. Her intrigues were planned more frequently to thwart than to aid his measures; so that, aware of her faithless character, he at length caused her to be arrested and to be confined in the convent of Tordesillas, near Valladolid.

As allusion has already been made [in the history of Spain, Chapter V] to the chief events of the present war, little more remains to be said of them. Though Lisbon was invested both by sea and land, and in a few months reduced to the greatest distress, it was defended with equal ability and valour by the grand-master and his captains. To end the distractions of his country, the states, early in 1385, were convoked at Coimbra. There the creatures of the regent proposed his proclamation as king, as the only measure capable of restoring internal tranquillity, and of enabling the nation to withstand the arms of Castile. They even endeavoured to show that he was the nearest heir to the crown. The issue of Iñes de Castro they set aside, as sprung from an adulterous connection; and the same objection they urged against Beatrice, whose mother they considered as the lawful wife, not of the late king, but of the lord de Pombeiro. On the 6th day of April, 1385, João was unanimously proclaimed king.

João I, having attained the great object of his ambition, vigorously prepared for the war with his rival of Castile. The decisive victory gained by João at Aljubarrota; the alternations of success and failure that succeeded; the arrival of the duke of Lancaster to obtain the Castilian crown in right of his wife Constanza, daughter of Pedro the Cruel: the alliance between the two princes, João marrying Philippa, a daughter of the duke; the subsequent reconciliation between the latter and the king of Castile, cemented by the marriage of the princess Catherine, daughter of the Plantagenet, with Henry, son of Juan, and other transactions of these troubled times, have already been noticed in the history of Spain. Peace was made and broken more than once; the success lay with the Portuguese king — a success, however, attributable as much to the internal troubles of Castile after the death of Juan I as to the valour of João. When a more durable peace was concluded in 1403, the Portuguese had recovered their fortunes, and were in possession of Badajoz.

The next few years were passed in tranquillity by the king in improving the administration of the realm. His salutary severity was above all directed against murderers and robbers by profession, and also against such as took justice into their own hands. By these means he became a popular monarch with all but some of his nobles, whose discontent he had powerfully excited during the late wars. To his valiant constable, Dom Nunho Alvares Pereiro, called the "holy constable," he was more indebted than to any other cause, both for his crown and for the successful issue of the Castilian war; and he had thought no rewards too great for such services. But if he showered the revenues of whole towns and vast estates on that able and faithful man, he rewarded with a pitiful spirit the attachment of others.

THE TAKING OF CEUTA (1415 A.D.)

By his queen Philippa, daughter of the duke of Lancaster, João had several children, of whom five were sons. As these princes grew in years, they displayed great martial ardour, and promised to become the bulwarks of the country and throne. He had resolved to confer on them the honour of knighthood, and to celebrate the occasion by a magnificent tournament. But they despised the peaceful lists, and besought his permission to win their spurs in a nobler manner, by an expedition against the Moors. The fortress of Ceuta[1], on the African side of the straits of Gibraltar, seemed to them the most inviting of conquests. Though eager to gratify a propensity which he loved, the king was at first startled by the magnitude of the proposed enterprise. The fortifications of Ceuta were strong, and defended by the bravest portion of the Mohammedan population : to reduce them a considerable armament must be prepared, and at an expense which he was loath to incur. In the end, however, he yielded to their urgent entreaties ; the expedition was resolved, two confidential officers were sent to reconnoitre the place, and the royal council gave a reluctant consent to the project. But, as secrecy alone could insure its success, as a premature disclosure of the design would have enabled the pirates to increase the number of their defenders and the strength of their works, the whole peninsula was in suspense, and not without alarm at the preparations of the king. Having tranquillised the Castilians, the Aragonese, and the Moors of Granada, as to his intentions, and fearful of rousing the suspicions of the Africans, he intimated that his armament was to be led against the count of Holland. Not even the death of his queen, who was carried off by the plague,[2] nor his advanced years, could suspend his preparations. At length, having collected a considerable number of vessels from most parts, and been joined by adventurers from most nations of Europe, accompanied by his sons and his chief nobles, João embarked, proceeded towards the straits, and, the middle of August, 1415, arrived before Ceuta. The Moorish governor, Salat ben Salat, a man advanced in years but of undaunted courage, prepared for a vigorous defence.[e]

"So soon as the Moors of the town," writes the contemporary historian Azurara,[d] "saw the fleet nearing their walls, they placed lighted torches in all the windows and apertures to show the Christians that they were much more numerous than they thought, and thus on account of its great size, and being illuminated on all sides, the town presented a beautiful sight. This was interpreted by our men in the ships to signify that as a dying candle first throws out great light, so these men, who soon were to leave their houses and property, and many of them to quit this life, made this brave show of light, signifying their approaching end. As these Moors illuminated the town, so also our men lighted up their ships, but this they were compelled to do, not to show their vast numbers, but that each ship having cast anchor should be enabled to make preparations for the following day, and with the lanterns in front of the flag ships, and the torches the men carried in their hands, the fleet was well illuminated."

[1 In the Moorish form *Sebta-a*, corruption of *Septem*, from the seven hills on which the town and fortress are built.]

[2] The memory of this English princess is held in high respect in Portugal : " *Tantæ enim opinionis apud populum erat, quod solûm illud rectè factum videbatur, quod ipsa comprobâsset,*" says Matthæus de Pisano.[c] From the bed of death, this queen, who had all the martial spirit of her high race, delivered each of her sons a sword, with a charge to wield the weapon in defence of widows, orphans, and the country, and especially against the misbelievers.

A spectacle as dazzling as it was sinister, by the light of which the waters of the strait must have presented a terrible and fantastic appearance, reddened by the reflection of the torches as though a sea of blood, covered with dancing lights, separated the Moorish city from the floating Christian camp. At dawn on the following day, the 20th of August, the Portuguese were ready for the combat, and the king, João I, in a galiot went about among the ships giving the last instructions, recommending to all that Dom Henry should be the first to land.

But as the Moors had sailed out of the town to attack the Portuguese upon the landing, some of the knights became so impatient that two at least, João Fogaca and Ruy Gonçalves, jumped on shore a few moments before the prince, who, however, took the lead in the battle. The movement of the Moors in coming down to the shore was a vain attempt of the younger men; the truth was that, following the example of Salat ben Salat, they were greatly discouraged, and panic increased among them upon seeing two athletes of Barbary, two giants of the desert, overcome, one by Ruy Gonçalves, and the other by Vasco Martius de Albergaria. The infante Dom Henry fancied he caught sight of his brother Dom Duarte, whom Dom João had forbidden to take part in the combat, in the thickest of the fight, and presently discovered that he had not been mistaken. The presence of the two brothers if possible raised the courage of the Portuguese still more.

A PORTUGUESE WOMAN OF THE FIFTEENTH CENTURY

Dom Henry wished to await the landing of the rest of the army, as he had been recommended to do, but Dom Duarte was of opinion that they might enter the town with the Moors, or at least seize the gate of Almina to open a passage for their men. The gate was indeed taken by surprise. Having passed the gate, the two infantes took up their position on a hill dominating the streets of the city.

Meanwhile Vasco Fernandes de Athaide had succeeded in beating down another gate, thus opening a new passage to the Portuguese soldiers, who were now divided into three bands. To have greater freedom, the heir to the crown threw off his armour, leaving merely a coat of mail; his movements being thus made freer he was able to advance rapidly, so that when Dom Henry resolved to follow his example he could no longer find him. Dom Duarte had reached the highest point of the Moorish town, called Cesto, and Dom Henry, wishing to join him, entered the street leading to it, driving the Moors before him.

The general landing of the army had not yet taken place, as Dom João I had not finished his review of the fleet. When he sent his son Dom Pedro to tell Dom Duarte to land, the answer came that he was already within the town. The king then gave orders for all to land, and the Portuguese army, divided into four bodies, marched upon the town.

The affliction of the women who fled, pressing their little children to their breasts, and the despair with which many men concealed their property, or fled carrying it with them, raised the courage of the Moorish warriors, and spurred them to make one supreme effort by which they succeeded in driving many Portuguese before them. Dom Henry would not check the first fugitives in their flight, for fear of harming those who followed, who would consequently be thrown back on the Moors, but when the latter approached, followed by a few knights, he barred the way. At the same time, ashamed of their fear and encouraged by the infante's presence, the Portuguese returned to the charge, and the enemy fled in confusion. Meanwhile the Moors received reinforcements and renewed the fight, but were again repulsed by the Portuguese, encouraged by the infante.

The Moors falling back, the infante, followed only by seventeen of his men, pursued them ; a desperate fight ensued, principally because the Moors attempted to carry off a Portuguese knight, whom the infante wished to recover. The Moors finally gave way, but the infante Dom Henry found himself shut in by the ruinous walls of the town, with only five knights at his side. Heroically maintaining his difficult position, he waited in vain for reinforcements ; he was believed to be dead, until he was at last found by a Portuguese knight.

The infante wished to remain in his dangerous position until reinforcements reached him, but the entreaties addressed to him in the name of his father and Dom Duarte induced him to retreat ; he proceeded to join his father at a mosque. Meanwhile the sun had set, and seeing a flight of sparrows resting upon the towers of the fort, the Portuguese inferred that the Moors had abandoned it. Salat ben Salat had fled with the garrison. They thereupon raised the flag of St. Vincent, patron of Lisbon, on the top of the fortress. The conquest was won ; the loss on the side of the Moors was heavy, but the Portuguese loss was trifling ; we will not however quote any number as great doubts exist on the subject.

On the following day the Moors appeared once more before the fortress ; Dom Duarte and the constable sallied out to encounter them ; these vain attacks were repeated, but the king strictly forbade his heir to take part in these skirmishes.

On the first Sunday the king decided to hear mass with his sons in the principal mosque of the town, already purified. Two bells pealed joyously from the highest tower. "How is this?" asked the major. The reply is not uninteresting : the town of Lagos had been a few years previously attacked by the Moors, who sacked the place and carried away these bells, and concealed them, but now discovered, they summoned the Christians to divine service.

The service was celebrated with great solemnity ; Dom João knighted his sons, Dom Duarte, Dom Pedro, and Dom Henry. On their side João I's sons knighted various valiant noblemen of their retinue. The aim of the expedition was realised, and the African lion began to give way before the power of Portugal.*f*

The government of the place was at first offered to a valiant knight, Martin Alfonso de Mello ; and when he declined the dangerous honour, it was solicited and obtained by one of greater prowess still, Dom Pedro de Menezes, founder of the illustrious house of Villa Real. Having left a small but select garrison in Ceuta, and provided for the defence of the place against the inevitable assaults of the Moors, João re-embarked, and with the remainder of the armament returned to Lisbon.

The heroism of the governor, Dom Pedro, and of the horsemen he commanded, is the constant and enthusiastic theme of praise by the national writers. The number of skirmishes which he was compelled to sustain during the three years immediately following the reduction of Ceuta is said, no doubt hyperbolically, to have exceeded the number of days. It is certain that during his government the place was frequently assailed by the whole power of the African Moors, aided by the fleet of their brethren of Granada. Sometimes the garrison by sorties obtained considerable booty, especially in flocks and herds. This warfare was as horrid as it was picturesque. When the Christian hidalgos and Almagaveres arrived at the village which they had been ordered to destroy, and the inhabitants of which were sure to be sunk in sleep, they generally divided into two or three bands, forced the doors of the houses, which they set on fire, and either massacred such as attempted to escape, or forced them back into the flames. The sudden conflagration, the shrieks of the women and children, rendered still more dismal by the silence of night, and the bloody figures of the assailants, gazing with ferocious joy on the scene before them, bore a character too demoniacal for this world. When all was finished, when the flames were expiring, and the last groan had pierced the sky, the orthodox warriors returned to the city, " praising God and our Lady for their success." [1]

To avenge these atrocities, the Moors now gathered in formidable numbers, not merely from the neighbourhood, but from wherever the fame of their wrongs had penetrated ; but they were always repulsed by the valiant count, whose exploits are represented as not much inferior to those of the Cid Ruy Diaz, in Valencia. The very exaggerations, however, prove that Dom Pedro was the most valiant knight of a valiant nation. But during three years no formal siege was laid to the place ; a circumstance sufficiently explicable by the perpetual struggles for empire among the Mohammedan princes of western Africa. In 1419 the fortress was first invested, and by an army formidable enough to inspire the assailants with the hope of success. In the combats which ensued, the Christians, notwithstanding the loss of some brave captains, were, as usual, victorious ; and "a pleasant thing it was," says the chronicler,[d] "to see our men, like the waters which flowed on the beach, sprinkled with infidel blood." After some days the siege was raised, with the loss of some thousands on the part of the Africans. But scarcely had the governor time to congratulate himself on this event, before he received news which filled him with apprehension — that a more formidable army, and a fleet from Granada, were preparing to move against him.

He lost no time in soliciting succour from King João, who as readily granted it. Again was the place invested — this time by sea and land ; and, as before, the valour of the besieged was almost superhuman. Fearing, however, that it must ultimately surrender, if not more effectually succoured, the king ordered two of his sons — the infantes Henry and João — to sail with a considerable armament. As they approached the place, they perceived that the Mohammedans had landed, and furiously assailed Dom

---

[1] Azurara,[d] though a Portuguese, shows some pity for the poor infidel wretches : he first curses Cain for setting the example of mortal enmity ; and still more the " abominable Mohammed " for separating so many souls from the true faith, and by subjecting his followers both to temporal death by Christian swords, and to everlasting torments by the devils. When a Christian soldier dies, intimates the orthodox sage, he has the prospect of eternal bliss ; but for the cursed Moors, what remains for them but brimstone and fire, with Dathan and Abiram ?

Pedro, who, with his handful of brave companions, was making terrific carnage among them. This formidable host was totally routed; while the infantes took or dispersed the Moorish vessels, commanded by a prince of the royal house of Granada. This splendid success drew the eyes of all Europe towards this extremity of Africa. That a Christian noble, with so few companions in arms, should not only retain possession of a distant fortress against the frequent attacks of great armies, but should triumph over those armies in the open field, would appear incredible, had not equal wonders been exhibited by the knights of some religious orders. The exploits which have been already recorded were frequently equalled in the sequel by this renowned baron. In the subsequent wars, he was greatly aided by his son, a youth of the same dauntless courage as himself, who made frequent incursions into the Moorish territory, and never failed to return with abundance of spoil.

During these years, the king was constantly employed in the duties of administration. As he advanced in years, his sense of justice appears to have greatly improved; at least we hear no more of the violent acts which disgraced his early days, and which will forever tarnish his memory.e

He re-established his finances by an economy pervading his government and household. He spent little in pomp and splendour; lived frugally, and associated upon an easy footing with the friends of his youth. He was wont to say that conversation was the cheapest of pleasures; and he introduced literary pursuits amongst his courtiers. When he had replenished his exhausted treasury, João made abundant compensation to those whom the inevitable expenses of war had obliged him to offend by revoking the ample donations, with which, upon first receiving the crown, he had recompensed the services that had helped to place it upon his brow. But after satisfying these just claims, João neither lavished his money upon friends and favourites, nor hoarded it in his coffers.

PRINCE HENRY THE NAVIGATOR

A certain employment of João's wealth ultimately produced far more glory and power, as well as opulence, to his kingdom, than his Mauretanian conquests. His third son, Henry, was the first projector of those remote maritime enterprises and geographical discoveries that opened new channels to the commerce of Europe, poured the riches of the Indies into Portugal, exalted the reputation and consequently the energies of her sons, brought immense realms in Asia and America under her sceptre, and temporarily elevated her to a rank amongst the nations of Europe altogether disproportionate to her natural extent and population.

Prince Henry was grand-master of the order of knights of Christ, instituted by King Diniz, upon the abolition of the Templars, to do battle constantly with the Mohammedans. The grand-master had accompanied his father to the siege of Ceuta, and there highly distinguished himself even beyond his brothers; which circumstance, combining with his strong sense of the duties of his sacred office, inspired him with an irrepressible desire to conquer and convert. But expeditions of the kind he meditated against Mohammedan misbelievers, whether in Spain or Mauretania, could only be undertaken by the authority and under the control of the king, and the infante in consequence turned his thoughts towards the more distant heathen. His studious disposition and especial taste for geography, astronomy, and mathematics also contributed, in all probability, not a little to give his schemes of conquest and conversion that direction. These sciences Dom Henry assiduously cultivated at Sagres, a seaport town he had himself founded near Cape St. Vincent in Algarve, where he drew around him learned men, travellers, and mariners. When he had speculatively satisfied himself of the possibility of sailing round Africa, of which, at that time, little beyond the northern coast was known, and of thus reaching the East Indies, he built and collected vessels in the harbour of Sagres, and sent them forth upon voyages of discovery. The despatch of the first two was determined so suddenly one morning, that it was believed the prince had been favoured with an especial revelation upon the subject during the preceding night, a mark of divine favour of which his great devotion, and the virginal purity of his morals, were judged to render him worthy. Dom Henry fitted out these first expeditions at his own expense ; but the king soon entered into his son's views, and took the principal charge upon himself. Navigation was then still almost in its infancy. The name of Cape Nun had been given to the southernmost African promontory yet known, and terrified the imagination of the ignorant almost as much by its very sound as by the thousand superstitious terrors connected with all beyond it, particularly with the torrid zone, then supposed to be actually uninhabitable from heat. For many years Dom Henry's mariners advanced only a few leagues past the dreaded cape, and Portugal resounded with murmurs against the waste of men and money occasioned by the infante's mania for discovery. But Dom Henry persevered, and his father countenanced him. Gradually his captains grew more enterprising, emboldened in some measure by the assistance his astronomical science afforded them. The first, and, during King João's life, only great fruit of these labours was the rediscovery and settlement of the island of Madeira, about the year 1418. But far from appeasing the popular clamour, this only increased it ; the colonising of the island being regarded as a frightful drain upon the population. Nearly about the same time the Canaries were accidentally discovered by an English ship, driven from her course. In 1402 a private adventurer, a Frenchman, named De Bethencourt, with a mixed French and Spanish crew, conquered the savage natives, and took possession of some of these islands, which his heirs afterwards sold to Prince Henry.[h]

HENRY THE NAVIGATOR
(From an old print)

Of Prince Henry it has been said that, to his "enlightened foresight and perseverance the human race is indebted for the maritime discovery, within one century, of more than half the globe." His funds were drawn from the large revenues of the order of Christ, and the Moors had told him much

of the riches of interior Africa and the Guinea coast.   He was the victim of
unusual opposition and ridicule, as was Columbus, but, like him, was imper-
vious to both.   His personality is strongly to credit for the success of his
couriers, for, as his biographer Major[g] has said : " Had that failure and that
ridicule produced on Prince Henry the effect which they ordinarily produce
on other men, it is impossible to say what delays would have occurred before
these mighty events would have been realised ; for it must be borne in mind
that the ardour, not only of his own sailors, but of surrounding nations, owed
its impulse to this pertinacity of purpose in him." It is to be charged against
Prince Henry that he began the slave-trade, which meant so much of shame
to the world.   It is pleasant to recall that it was he who, forsaking the usual
path of exploration, the land, began to seek the wealth of Araby and India
by the water-ways and, beginning that fever of adventurous curiosity that
opened new worlds south and west, with him began the age of discovery.[a]

By João I the era of Cæsar was abolished in Portugal, and the Christian
mode of computation adopted.   He died in 1433.

THE REIGN OF DUARTE OR EDWARD (1433-1438 A.D.)

The reign of Duarte [or Edward[1]], though short, was doomed to be
more disastrous than that of any preceding monarch.   The first great
calamity was the plague which raged during the whole of his reign, and
which lamentably thinned the population.   But a greater was an expedition
against Tangier, the preparations for which oppressed his people, and the
result of which filled the kingdom with murmurs.

The restless ambition of the king's brother, Ferdinand, hurried him into
this disastrous enterprise.   This infante had been too young to share in the
glorious conquests of Ceuta : and had not, like Pedro or Henry, obtained
celebrity either by travelling or science.   But he burned for distinction as
much as either and proposed an African expedition.   The king seems, however, to have entertained very honourable scruples as to the justice of the
warfare in which he was about to engage.   He proposed the subject to his
theologians and the pope.   The chief of the Christian world, with more
reason than has dictated some papal decisions, replied that there were only
two cases in which war against misbelievers could be lawfully undertaken :
(1) when they were in possession of territories which had belonged to Christians, and which the latter sought to recover; (2) when by piracy or war,
or any other means, they injured or insulted the true believers.   In other
cases, proceeded his holiness, hostilities are unjust : the elements, earth, air,
fire, and water, were created for all; and to deprive any creature without
just cause of those necessary things, was a violation of natural right.   There
was, however, one point which the pontiff omitted to notice : the obligations
contracted by every Catholic sovereign, and still more solemnly by every
military order, to advance the glory of God — in other words to convert or
to destroy the heathen.   This consideration removed the scruples of Duarte,
and the expedition was resolved.

The inexperience which governed the preparations, and the accidental
hindrances which impeded their completion, were regarded as melancholy
omens by the people.   The armament sailed on August 22nd, 1437, and
on the 26th arrived before Ceuta, a place which the heroic governor and his

[[1] Duarte or Edward was named after Edward III of England.]

no less heroic son had continued to defend with the same success.   The two infantes Henry and Ferdinand, who commanded the present expedition, perceived that instead of fourteen thousand men, the number ordered by the king, they had no more than six thousand.   They were advised to solicit and wait for a considerable reinforcement, but with their usual impatience they resolved to proceed to Tangier — Henry by land, and Ferdinand by sea, so as to co-operate with each other.   The former reached Tangier without accident on the 23rd day of September, and found that his brother had arrived before him.   The Portuguese immediately encamped before the place, which was defended by Salat ben Salat, former governor of Ceuta, with seven thousand Moors.   But as if every measure of this ill-concerted expedition were doomed to be at once imbecile and unsuccessful, after sustaining a heavy loss the besiegers, finding that their scaling-ladders were too short, were compelled to retreat with shame from the foot of the ramparts.   Before others could be procured from Ceuta, the Moors of Fez and Morocco, amounting, we are gravely told, in numbers to ten thousand horse, and eighty thousand infantry, advanced to raise the siege.[1]   Instead, however, of being alarmed at this prodigious force, Henry with four thousand of his valiant troops hastened to give them battle; but so great was the dread which this heroic little band had struck into that immense host, that none of the misbelievers daring to wait for the onset, all escaped with precipitation over the neighbouring hills! But as their numbers soon increased by new accessions to 130,000 men,[2] they returned, and this time fought with courage.   After a struggle of some hours this vast force yielded to the impetuousity of the infante Ferdinand and fled, leaving some thousands dead on the field!   These wondrous fables are not enough.   Indignant at their repeated losses of their brethren, the kings of northwestern Africa combined the whole of the respective forces, and marched towards the place.   The surprise of Henry was great on seeing the neighbouring hills moving with life; the number of enemies on this occasion, we are veraciously assured, being sixty thousand cavalry, and seven hundred thousand foot![3]   On contemplating, however, the dense and widely extended ranks of the Moslems, even he acknowledged that to withstand such a host would be temerity.

He accordingly gave directions for his little army to fall back and to regain the ships.   Before this could be effected, the Africans, like tigers of their own deserts, sprang upon them, eager to drink their blood.   But what could even a Portuguese do against myriads?   His guards were killed by his side, and he was compelled to retreat, fighting, however, at every step, until he reached the entrenchments, where the contest became more bloody and desperate than it had yet been.   Some of the defenders now fled, — for the chroniclers reluctantly allow that even a Portuguese may flee, — but the seamen on board the vessels landed, forced the fugitives to return, and the conflict was sustained during some hours with miraculous valour!   Towards night it was suspended; and the infante agreed with his remaining captains that at midnight the Christians should silently leave their entrenchments, pass to the beach, and be received on board.

As the invaders were now without provisions and water, this expedient was the only hope of safety which remained to them.   But even of this they

---

[1] In Portuguese computation of the number of their enemies, the reader will do well to drop one cipher; hence he will have one thousand horse and eight thousand foot; as many no doubt as were present.

[2] Read thirteen thousand.

[3] The rule before recommended of subtracting a cipher will not do in this case.   The aggregate of horse and infantry must be divided by about fifty to come near the truth.

were soon deprived by the treachery of Martin Vieyra, Henry's chaplain, who passed over to the misbelievers, and acquainted them with the project. At this very day the Portuguese are seized with indignant wonder at this almost incredible instance of apostasy and treason ; and however great their confidence in the powers of the visible head of the church, or even of the glorious Mother, they doubt whether either or both could, even in the event of repentance, procure for such a wretch the commutation of everlasting to purgatorial fire.[1] In consequence of this information, the Moors stationed a formidable guard along the passages to the sea and on the beach. The following morning they advanced to the trenches; the battle was renewed, and, we are told, sustained for eight hours with unshaken firmness, though with greatly diminished numbers. On this occasion no one exhibited more valour than the bishop of Ceuta ; who, as he strode from rank to rank to distribute indulgences with one hand, with the other hewed down the misbelievers in a style that called forth the enthusiastic admiration of the faithful. Now he exhibited the consecrated host, and with tears of devotion besought his dear children in Christ to defend the holy Body; while, at the same time, he gave a practical illustration of his meaning, by aiming another deadly blow at some rash son of perdition.[2]

In the end the enemy, unable to force the entrenchments, set them on fire, and on the approach of night retired. The hours which should have been given to rest were occupied in extinguishing the conflagration, a labour not less fatiguing than the conflict of the day. To allay the hunger of his followers, the infante ordered the horses to be killed ; but as there was no water, and as everyone raged with a burning thirst, the boon was scarcely acceptable, until heaven sent a copious shower of rain. But however seasonable this relief, it could only be momentary. Famine, or death by the sword, or what was still worse, perpetual captivity, stared the unhappy Christians in the face, when they received a proposal which they could not have expected. They were promised both life and liberty, as the condition of their surrendering the artillery, arms, and baggage, and restoring the fortress of Ceuta. To men in their desperate condition this proposal was too liberal not to be joyfully accepted. For their performance of the covenant the infante Ferdinand offered himself as hostage; and was accompanied by four other knights. The Moors delivered into the hands of Henry a son of Salat ben Salat. The Portuguese, reduced to three thousand, prepared to re-embark. But with characteristic duplicity, the barbarians attempted to prevent the departure of the Christians, who were constrained to fight their way to the ships.

While this once proud armament was slowly returning to Lisbon, Henry, ashamed to appear at court, proceeded to Ceuta, where fatigue of body and anxiety of mind threw him into a serious illness. No sooner did Prince João, who was then in Algarve, hear of the illness of one brother and the captivity of another, than he repaired to Ceuta. The two infantes there agreed that, as the royal consent to the restoration of the fortress could not reasonably be expected, João should propose the exchange of their brother for the son of the African. The proposal was scornfully rejected by the Moors, who threatened, if the place were not immediately restored, to take signal revenge on the person of the infante. João now returned to Portugal to acquaint the king with the melancholy position of affairs. The states

---

[1] Even the mild Lemos [b] can curse this man : " *Hum malvado monstro horror de sacerdocio, indigno da humanidade, Judas de seu Senhor, o inferne clerigo Martim Vieira.*"

[2] This is no exaggerated description ; it is taken from a contemporary chronicler.

were convoked and the subject proposed. Some deputies voted for the restoration of the fortress and the delivery of the infante; but others considered that the recovery of the prince would be too dearly purchased by the surrender of a place which had cost so much, and which might serve as a point of departure for future conquests. It was accordingly resolved that the prince should remain in captivity until the efficacy of money should be proved vain. His sufferings are represented, probably with truth, as at once cruel and humiliating. No sooner was he delivered into the hands of Salat

A PORTUGUESE NOBLEMAN OF THE FIFTEENTH CENTURY

ben Salat, than he began to experience the most savage barbarity. He was, at first, paraded to a dungeon at Tangier, exposed to the insults of assembled thousands, of whom some spit in his face, others covered him with filth; and, on reaching his temporary abode, his food consisted of the vilest aliments, and his bed was the hard ground. From Tangier he was transferred to Arsilla; but two hours before his departure he was placed on a platform, and again subjected to the insults of the populace. All this he bore with unshaken constancy. No ransom would be received by Salat, whose only object was the recovery of his lost seat of government. But when the king of Castile, Juan II, began to remonstrate against the detention of the infante, and even to threaten hostilities unless a ransom were received for him, the Moor, unwilling to incur the responsibility of his charge, delivered it into the hands of his superior, the king of Fez. By that tyrant Ferdinand was consigned to a subterraneous dungeon, excluded alike from air and light. After some months, however, he was drawn from his prison — doubtless, because his persecutors knew that a longer confinement would soon place him beyond their reach — and made to work, like the vilest slave, in the royal stables and gardens. In this situation he heard of Dom Duarte's death.

The victim was now subjected to new indignities. Not only was he deprived of all food, except a crust of bread once in twenty-four hours, but he was ironed, put to harder labour, and allowed no apparel beyond a rag, for the modesty of nature. The relation of his sufferings at length moved the pity of his brother Pedro, regent of the kingdom, who, in the name of the royal Alfonso, despatched commissioners to Ceuta, to receive the infante and to remit the keys of that fortress into the hands of the king of Fez. But they soon found that the barbarian had further views; that he insisted on the restoration of the place prior to the delivery of his captive; that his object was to gain possession of their persons, and be thereby enabled to dictate whatever terms he pleased. The negotiations were abruptly ended, and the ill-fated prince transferred to his dungeon, where he languished until 1443, when death put a period to his sufferings. The constancy with which he bore them, his resignation to the divine will, his sweetness of disposition are said to have endeared him to his jailers ; and his decease to have called forth the tardy compassion of the royal Moor, who exclaimed that so good a man deserved to know the true faith. His memory accordingly is, as it ought to be, revered in Portugal; but that superstitious nation, not satisfied with the rational sentiment, represents him as a martyr and saint — as one fully entitled to the honours of semi-deification. Miracles [1] are recorded of him with unblushing effrontery.

The unfortunate issue of the African war, and the complaints of his captive brother, most sensibly affected the heart of Duarte, over whom, had his life been spared, fraternal affection would, doubtless, have triumphed. That he meditated another expedition, and that he commenced preparations on a formidable scale, is honourable to his heart : but his subjects were thinned by the plague ; commerce was suspended ; the fields remained uncultivated; the public revenues were exhausted, and the people unwilling to make further sacrifices. In 1438 he was seized by the plague at Thomar, whither he had retired to escape its fury, and in a few days he breathed his last. This prince was worthy of a better fate. He had qualities of a high order, he was enlightened, just, and patriotic ; and if virtue or talent would have controlled the course of human events, his kingdom would have been happy.

THE REGENCY OF PEDRO

Alfonso V, the eldest son of Duarte, being only six years of age on his father's death, the regency devolved, in conformity with the last will of her husband, on the queen-mother, Leonora, a princess of excellent disposition, but not exempted from the fickleness of her sex, and ill qualified to rule a fierce people. To such a people, the sway even of a native woman could scarcely have been agreeable ; as a foreigner (a princess of Aragon), she was peculiarly obnoxious. Seeing this general discontent, some of the nobles, with three uncles of the king, resolved to profit by it. Of the three infantes, the hostility of João was the most bitter ; of Henry the most disinterested ; and of Pedro [duke of Coimbra] the most politic, the most ambitious, and consequently the most to be dreaded.

She offered to Dom Pedro to affiance his daughter Isabella with the young king — an offer which he readily accepted, but which in no manner interrupted his career of ambition. He procured, not only the sanction of the deputies to the proposed marriage, but his recognition as joint regent. At this crisis, Henry proposed in the states assembled at Lisbon that the executive should be divided — that the education of the king and the care of the finances should rest with the queen, that the administration of justice should be intrusted to the count of Barcelos, and that Pedro should be nominated protector of the kingdom. At first, Leonora opposed this extraordinary expedient to satisfy the ambition of the princes ; but, finding that the populace were arming in great multitudes to espouse the cause of their favourite, she was terrified into submission.

To bring the great question to issue, the mob, the only authority then subsisting, assembled in the church of St. Dominic, and swore that, until Alfonso reached his majority, the government should rest in Dom Pedro; that if

[1] These miracles are alluded to by Ruy de Pina,[c] by Vasconcellos,[j] and are more boldly detailed by Lemos.[b] [He is called "the constant prince."]

Pedro died he should be succeeded in the office by his brother Henry, and the latter by the infante João, and that thenceforward no woman should be allowed to rule the Portuguese. Under the pretext that the education of the young king, if left to her, must necessarily be effeminate, and unfit him for his station, he was removed by a sudden decree of the same cortes, from her care, and placed under that of the regent.

The wisdom of Dom Pedro's administration daily reconciled to it some of his former enemies : he restored tranquillity, encouraged the national industry, was indefatigable in his labours, and impartial in his judgments. Grateful for the benefits he procured them, the people of Lisbon would have erected a statue in his honour, had he not rigorously forbidden them. He was too well acquainted with both history and human nature not to know that popular favour is fleeting as the wind. He observed that, if such a statue were erected, it would be one day disfigured by the very hands which had made it. We are assured, indeed, by a contemporary chronicler, Ruy de Pina,[i] that he had some anticipation of the melancholy fate which awaited him. Yielding to the representations of her pretended friends, Leonora openly erected the standard of rebellion, and a civil war commenced : its horrors were increased by a body of Castilians, who, at the instance of Leonora, penetrated into the kingdom, and committed many ravages. In 1445, she formally requested permission to return, to end her days with her children ; and her wish would doubtless have been gratified, had not death surprised her at Toledo.[1]

In 1446, King Alfonso reached his fourteenth year — the period of his majority. His first acts were regarded by the people as favourable omens of his future administration, and, above all, of his disposition to cultivate a good understanding with the regent. When, in the cortes convoked for the occasion at Lisbon, Pedro resigned the delegated authority into his hands, he desired the latter to retain it till he was better able to bear the load ; and he soon afterwards married Isabella, to whom he had been affianced in his tenth year. But these buds of hope were soon blighted. The regent was powerful ; he therefore had enemies — and enemies the more bitter, that there was now a master who could destroy him with ease. Of these none were more vindictive or base than his natural brother, the count de Barcelos, on whom he had just conferred the lordship of Braganza, with the title of duke. No sooner did the duke of Braganza perceive the secure place which he held in the king's affections, than he began to inveigh against the character and actions of Pedro. These discourses, and the mention of his mother's wrongs, which were artfully distorted, made a deep impression on the king, who at length regarded his father-in-law with abhorrence. The regent perceived the change, and he requested permission to retire to Coimbra, of which he was duke. His request was granted ; and so also was another — an act, under the royal signature and seal, approving the whole of his administration.

No sooner had he departed than a hundred reptiles darted their stings. Among the new charges brought against him was one of poisoning the late king and queen. In vain did the sage Henry hasten from his aërial residence above Cape St. Vincent, to vindicate the character of his brother; in vain did Dom Alfonso de Alamado, a nobleman of unsullied honour, join in the chivalrous act — for chivalrous it was, when the lives of both were

---

[1] By the Portuguese historians, the death of Leonora is suspected to have been violent, and the guilt is thrown on the constable of Castile, the famous Alvaro de Luna. But what interest could he have in her destruction ? And when did he commit a useless crime ?

threatened as their reward, if they did not immediately retire from the court;[1] in vain did the latter challenge all who dared to dispute Dom Pedro's virtues to a mortal combat; in vain did the royal Isabella plead her father's innocence. Alfonso published an edict debarring all his subjects from communication with the prince, and ordering him to remain on his estates. His arms were next demanded: these he refused to surrender. The duke of Braganza now assembled his troops, and marched towards Coimbra; he was met at Penella by Dom Pedro, before whose handful of friends he fled with ignominy. Again did his daughter affectionately labour to avert his fate. In an agony of tears she cast herself at her husband's feet, and besought his pardon. Alfonso was affected: he raised his queen, whom he tenderly loved, and promised that if her father would acknowledge his crime, it should be forgiven. More jealous of his honour than fond of life, the high-spirited prince would acknowledge no crime, simply because he had none to acknowledge. The incensed monarch tore the reply into pieces, and said, "Your father wishes his destruction; he shall have his wish!"

The duke left Coimbra with one thousand horse and five thousand foot, all resolved to perish rather than permit a beloved leader to be oppressed; and on their banners were engraven, "Fidelity! Justice! Vengeance!" The king hastened to meet him with about thirty thousand veteran troops; they approached each other on the banks of the Alfarrobeira (May 21st, 1449), above which was an eminence where Pedro entrenched himself. The prince, who desperately sought the most dangerous post, and who evidently resolved to sacrifice his life, fell through a wound in the throat. The carnage which followed was terrific: the troops of the fallen infante, intent on revenging his death and resolved on their own, would neither give nor receive quarter; almost all fell on the field. The vengeance of Alfonso passed beyond the grave: he ordered the corpse of Pedro to remain on the ground, to be forever deprived of the last rites of humanity; but in a few days some compassionate peasants, whose souls might have put to shame the boasted chivalry of nobles, privately removed it, and interred it in the church of Alverca. The descendants of all his adherents to the fourth generation were declared infamous — incapable of holding any public charge. The mob of Lisbon testified characteristic joy at his catastrophe — a remarkable confirmation of his prudence in forbidding them to erect the projected statue of him.

The death of this prince — the greatest whom Portugal had lately seen — caused a deep sensation throughout Europe, and from Rome to Britain drew forth nothing but execrations against his murderers. Through the indignant remonstrances of the pope and of his brother-in-law, the duke of Burgundy; through the increasing influence of his daughter, whose virtues were appreciated by her husband, and whose efforts to honour his memory were at length successful; and more still through the king's conviction of his innocence, in the fifth year from this tragedy his bones were removed from their humble sepulchre, and were transferred with great pomp to the mausoleum of the Portuguese kings. In 1455, the queen suddenly sickened and died. That her death was the effect of poison administered by her enemies, and the enemies of her father — among whom were doubtless

[1] The address of this count to the king and council, as it appears in Ruy de Pina,[i] is a noble instance of magnanimity and courage. He appealed to his services — and they had been splendid — as a Portuguese noble; to his honour as a knight of England's proud order — then at least a proud one — the Garter; to his unimpeachable integrity; and to his intimacy with Dom Pedro — that he knew and spoke the truth. Neither his zeal nor the challenge with which he concluded affected Alfonso.

the detestable princes of Braganza—is the unshaken opinion of her own times and of posterity.

The disastrous captivity of the infante Ferdinand had sunk deep into the heart of Alfonso, as into that of most princes of his family; and the desire of revenge had been suspended, not abandoned. The reduction of Constantinople by the Turks in 1453 had filled Christian Europe with consternation, and had led to the formation of a general league, the object of which was to drive back the misbelievers into their Asiatic wilds. Alfonso's original intention was to reduce the fortress of Tangier, the siege of which had proved so unfortunate to the princes Henry and Ferdinand; but the advice of a Portuguese noble determined him to invest Alcacer-Seguier [or es-Seghir]. In September, 1457, the armament, consisting of above two hundred vessels, and carrying twenty thousand men, sailed from the three ports, effected a junction at sea, and steered towards the Moorish coast.

The success which had attended the attack on Alcacer-Seguier animated Alfonso to renew the attempt on Tangier. Accordingly, in 1464, he sailed with another armament. The assault was repulsed with deplorable loss; the flower of the Portuguese chivalry either perished on the spot, or were compelled to surrender. The king himself had considerable difficulty in effecting his escape. For some years the result of this inglorious expedition seems to have inspired him with too much dread to renew the attempt; but, in 1471, he embarked thirty thousand men on board 308 transports, and proceeded to invest Arsilla, a fortress on the Atlantic. The king himself, and his son the infante João, were among the foremost in the assault. The Portuguese massacred all—as well those who resisted as those who threw down their arms in token of submission—with diabolical fury. In this work of destruction João was behind none of his countrymen. Terrified by the fate of Arsilla, the inhabitants of Tangier abandoned the city with all their movable substance. It was immediately occupied by the Christians, and it was formed into an episcopal see. From these successes, the Portuguese courtiers surnamed their king Africanus—an epithet which, with any other people, would have been considered a bitter satire. Throughout his operations in Africa he had shown great incapacity, and had met with unparalleled reverses; nor were the successes recently obtained in any way attributable to his valour or abilities, but to those of his generals and his son. The latter, who had attained his sixteenth year, was knighted on this occasion.[e]

ALFONSO V AND LA BELTRANEJA

We have now reached a shameful page in the history of Portugal. A vision passed through the brain of Alfonso V of uniting beneath his sceptre the kingdoms of Portugal and Castile. He thought to realise his dream by marrying his niece Doña Juana, daughter of his sister Doña Juana and of King Henry IV of Castile, who would succeed to that throne upon the death of her father. But Alfonso V was too faint-hearted and too unskilful a politician for so great an ambition, which had already turned the weak head of his predecessor Ferdinand I.

On the death of Henry IV of Castile his daughter Doña Juana inherited the throne, she having been recognised and sworn queen of Castile even during her father's life. Nevertheless Ferdinand, king of Aragon, who was married to Isabella of Castile, disputed her claim. It was then that Alfonso V sought to unite upon his own head the crown of Portugal and Castile by marrying his niece, the queen Doña Juana. The marriage took place by proxy at Palencia, in May, 1475. The pope, Paul II, was prevailed upon to grant the dispensation of consanguinity, but it was immediately revoked by his successor, Sixtus IV.

How different was the character of Alfonso V from that of some of his predecessors! How weak was his policy! The grandson of João I never even completed his marriage, in spite of his ambition to be king of Portugal and Castile, Doña Juana having been recognised and sworn queen of Castile even during her father's life. What a difference between Alfonso V and his predecessor Alfonso III, who mocked at Rome and the pontiff, married one wife, with another living, raised one queen and deposed another, in spite of the excommunications of the Vatican, creating a strong faction in Portugal and getting himself proclaimed king; politically availing himself of every element in and out of the country to accomplish his ends, and only repenting on his death-bed, when he had won everything. It might be said that the cold British blood of his grandmother Philippa of Lancaster was still dominant in Alfonso V who, according to certain chronicles, observed complete chastity after the death of his wife, Queen Isabella.

In the meantime intrigues were active in Spain; one argument, on which great stress was laid against the claims of Alfonso V, was that Juana was the child of adultery, for the faction of Ferdinand and Isabella of Aragon never wearied of repeating that she was not the daughter of Henry IV of Castile, but of Beltran de la Cuenca [whence she was called the Beltraneja], making great sport of the dissolute morals of Juana, the sister of the king of Portugal, and mother of his bride. In the end the two factions came to blows. The fortune of war went against the Portuguese, who were defeated at the battle of Toro in 1476, in spite of the prodigies of valour performed in this battle by the infante Dom João, heir to the throne.

A PORTUGUESE WOMAN OF THE FIFTEENTH CENTURY

Defeated in battle, Alfonso V attempted to gain his end by policy, for which he had not the necessary dexterity. He bethought himself of attempting to persuade Louis XI, king of France, to take his part and give him the help and protection of his troops to place the crowns of Portugal and Castile upon his head. The king of France remained unmoved, although the king of Portugal went in person to solicit his help. In disgust Alfonso V announced his intention of visiting Palestine, and declared to his son, Prince João, whom he had appointed regent during his absence from Spain, that in such a case he should be proclaimed king. But he returned unexpectedly in 1477, and on the 14th of September, 1479, signed the peace with Castile at Alcántara — a shameful treaty, by which the king of Portugal abandoned his wife, who was forced to become a nun and exchange the crown for the veil. She entered the convent of St. Clair in Santarem in 1479, afterwards passing to the convent of St. Clair of Coimbra, where she was professed on the 17th of November, 1480. In the meanwhile the negotiations were so prolonged that the prince Dom João lost patience, and with his impulsive disposition took upon himself to send the Castilian ambassadors two documents, one declaring for peace and the other for war, bidding them choose without further parley. Upon this final resolution, the Castilians concluded the negotiations. Greater energy on the part of Alfonso V might perhaps, even at the end of the dispute, have obtained less shameful and degrading conditions of peace. Alfonso V, crushed and reduced to the last extremity of consternation, was resolved to convoke the cortes and abdicate in favour of his son, when he fell sick of the plague at Cintra, and died in the very room of the palace in which he was born, on the 28th of August, 1481.[k]

With the exception of the accidental success in Africa, his reign was almost uniformly disastrous — a misfortune more owing to the deplorable weakness of his character than to any other cause. He founded the order of the Tower and Sword, under the invocation of Santiago, and was a great patron of literature; he was the first of the Portuguese kings to collect a library, and to order the national history to be treated by competent writers. His reign is, however, somewhat redeemed by the discoveries of the infante Henry, who, from his residence at Tagus, continued to fix his eyes intently on the maritime regions of western Africa. Through this enlightened prince, the Azores, with the Madeiras, the Canaries, Cape Verde, and other islands west of that great continent were discovered or colonised. The discovery of the Cape Verde, the last which illustrated the life of Henry, was owing to the enterprise of a Genoese, Antonio Nolle, who had derived a confused knowledge of their existence from the ancient geographers, and who, from some dissatisfaction with his own country, offered his services to the prince. Having coasted from Morocco to Cape Verde, he deviated westwards and soon fell in with the islands, which he called after the cape of that name.[e]

REIGN OF JOÃO II "THE PERFECT"

Dom João II was now proclaimed king. His accession to the throne was the signal for a despotic war against the aristocracy and the territorial influence of magnates. João began by convoking the cortes at Evora in 1481. A law was then published introducing a new oath to be taken by all the chief alcaides and holders of grants. The restrictions placed upon the criminal jurisdiction of the nobility, the examination of grants, and the diminution of the political influence of the nobles, produced great discontent among the aristocracy, which gave rise to intrigues, plots, and conspiracies, which João II, following the example of Louis XI of France, repressed with all severity, not sparing blood nor executions even of his own kindred. Under these circumstances João II seized the opportunity of satisfying his vengeance and giving vent to the hatred which he had nourished for many years against the duke of Braganza, Dom Ferdinand, his second cousin, who was married to his wife's sister. He had him publicly beheaded at Evora on the 22nd of June, 1483; he is now judged to have been innocent of the crime of high treason imputed to him.

In the following year, João II with his own hands plunged a dagger into the breast of the duke of Viseu, his cousin and brother-in-law, in the palace of Setubal, for having conspired against him. After his death the duke was judged and condemned (a ludicrous determination of the despotic monarch) and his accomplices executed. The bishop of Evora, who was accused of being concerned in the conspiracy, was ordered to be thrown into a well; and more than eighty nobles and fidalgoes paid with their lives for the opposition which they made or were accused of making to the king's policy. It was the second time that the assassin's dagger had been publicly used in Portugal in the royal palace, by a prince upon whose brow the crown of the kingdom was to rest. Both the royal assassins were excellent kings, who governed the country diligently with courage and wisdom, raised it and gave it prosperity. In the case of the blow struck by João II, it is to be noted that it was dealt to a subject whom the king might easily have committed to a proper trial, with the certainty of finding judges who would condemn those guilty of high treason. To lessen the awful impression which these extraordinary assassinations make upon the mind and the stain which they leave upon the memory of these monarchs, it is necessary to consider the political circumstances and the ideas and customs of those times. Things inadmissible to our present civilisation were not so to the fourteenth and fifteenth centuries — above all when the deed was that of an absolute king who had to render an account to God alone.

There is no doubt that the wealth and therefore the influence successively acquired by the nobility had reached such a pitch that they absorbed the best revenues of the land, vexing the people by the insolence, cupidity, and abuses which oppressed the vassals of the great lords and proprietors, though Portugal happily never suffered the terrors of feudalism. This excessive power of the nobles dated from the time of João I, who was forced to create a new aristocracy to enable him to combat the king of Castile, most of the old nobility having joined the Castilian banners, and to liberally divide the property of the crown with those who were faithful to his cause. The king afterwards endeavoured to obviate the inconvenience of these excessive grants by the "mental law" (lei mental), which, without revoking the grants already made to the possessions thereof and their lawful descendants, put great restrictions upon the alienation of such property. The mental law, published only in the reign of Dom Duarte, did not have the desired result; the infante Dom Pedro, during his troubled regency, was forced to make concessions which decreased the patrimony of the crown.

But the reign of Alfonso V was above all disastrous upon this point, as we have said; it was the best time for the nobles and holders of grants. To remunerate the nobles who fought at his side, the luckless pretender to the throne of Castile considered nothing too much — titles, favours, grants, salaries, pensions, allowances, marriage dowries, education of the children of nobles, gratifications for ordinary and extraordinary services, real or pretended; everything was conceded with liberality and profusion by the monarch who was called the African, but might more properly have been called the Prodigal.[1]

The internal political situation as well as the state of the treasury called for an effectual remedy, and it is certain that only an energetic, inflexible, and dauntless character such as that of João II could have applied by sheer force a prompt though violent remedy. It may therefore be said that the

[1 João II said with justice that his father had left him " only the royal high roads of Portugal." — STEPHENS.1]

king, who was called "the perfect prince," rendered a memorable service to the country by the tremendous blow which he struck at the aristocracy and territorial power, restoring freedom of action to the crown, and liberating the public exchequer from the heavy charges and expenses placed upon it by the nobility. It is not surprising that in this struggle between the crown and the nobility the middle classes and the people should be found on the side of the king, since he made the offences, sufferings, oppression, complaints, and petitions represented by the deputies of the councils in the cortes of 1481 his chief pretext and principal weapon in declaring mortal war against the aristocracy and allying himself with the people.

Thus there was a firm alliance between the king and the people, although João II convoked the cortes only three times during his reign, and the crown and councils were generally on the best of terms. On the 12th of July, 1491, the prince Dom Alfonso went hunting in Almeirim, and as he was galloping at nightfall the horse took fright at some object which lay across the path, and fell, dragging the prince with him. He was picked up speechless and unconscious, and carried to a fisherman's hut where he died a few hours later in the arms of his father, mother, and wife.

This untimely death was a great affliction to the king and queen of Portugal, especially to João II, who thereby lost his hope of an heir to his throne; for by the death of Prince Alfonso the right of succession fell upon Dom Emmanuel, duke of Beja, the brother of Queen Leonora and of the duke of Viseu whom he had stabbed at Setubal. The thought that the crown of Portugal would pass to his wife's family oppressed and tormented João II. The probability that his brother-in-law Dom Emmanuel (Manoel), the duke of Beja, whom he hated, would be king of Portugal, put his cousin the king beside himself. In this affliction João II thought of having his natural son Jorge [or George] acknowledged as his successor. Jorge was master of the orders of Santiago and Aviz, and duke of Coimbra. But Dom João did not carry out his intention; he remembered the precedent of João I, but the clear judgment of his wife, Donna Leonora, pointed out to him that the circumstances were very different; on the one hand there was no fear of foreign invasion as in the days of the master of Aviz, while on the other hand the king had left wounds still unhealed from his war against the aristocracy. Upon the death of João II, 1495, Dom Jorge had not sufficient partisans to secure to him the crown which his father so earnestly longed to bequeath him.[k]

Character of João II

João was a great prince — comprehensive in his views, vigorous in the execution of his designs, as he was cautious and politic in their formation; zealous for justice, and for the happiness of his people. That zeal, however, sometimes degenerated into vengeance, and was sometimes disarmed by capricious clemency. But his character will be better conceived from a few striking traits or sayings (and many such are recorded of him) than from any description.

He placed little value on the recommendations of his nobles; and a favour solicited through their medium was almost sure to be denied. But he was fond of honouring and rewarding merit, especially when, as is generally the case, that merit was dumb.[1] To a faithful and valiant knight he one day observed: "You have hands to serve me; have you no tongue to request

[1 It is curious that Alexander the Great almost never rewarded those who did not ask, but took joy in granting requests.]

a recompense?" Being at dinner, he was once served among others by Dom Pedro de Melo, a knight of great prowess, who was better fitted for handling the sword than a dish in the palace of princes, and let fall a large vessel of water, which sprinkled some of the courtiers, and made others laugh. "Why do you laugh?" inquired the king; "Dom Pedro has dropped a vessel of water, but he never dropped his lance!" He had borrowed money of a rich merchant at Tavira, to whom, at the expiration of the stipulated period, he returned it with legal interest. The merchant—a wonderful instance of disinterestedness in such a capacity—refused to receive more than the principal; João sent double interest, with the order to continue doubling it as often as the merchant should persist in the refusal. In one of his public edicts, with the view of recruiting his cavalry, he ordered all his subjects to be in readiness to furnish excellent war-horses. The churchmen pleaded their immunities, and some of them went so far as to say that they were not his subjects but those of the pope. To punish them in the way they deserved, João loudly asserted that he had never regarded them as subjects; and by another ordinance he forbade all smiths and farriers to shoe their mules and horses—a measure which soon compelled them to submit. The monopolists in corn had created an artificial famine by purchasing and piling in their warehouses all the grain in the kingdom, which they refused to sell under an exorbitant price. By a royal ordinance the people were forbidden to purchase from these dealers, and the Castilians were permitted to import in whatever quantities they pleased; the kingdom soon teemed with abundance, and the monopolists were ruined. He was a great enemy to detraction. One praised a recent feat of arms of a Portuguese governor in Africa: another attempted to detract from it by saying that the success was merely owing to chance. "That may be," observed the king: "but how is it that such chance never happens to anyone else?" Nor was he less jealous of his dignity with foreign princes than with his own subjects. A Portuguese vessel had been captured by some French pirates: he ordered all the French vessels in his ports to be seized. The owners complained to their king, Charles VIII, who immediately punished the pirates, and caused their prize to be restored. It was found, however, that a parrot had not been restored with the rest, and he insisted that every vessel should be retained until the bird were produced. In short, the success of his administration was unrivalled; he introduced industry and comfort among his people; added largely to the national resources; and was in many respects the greatest monarch that ever swayed the sceptre of Portugal.

In the reign of this prince, the Portuguese spirit of maritime enterprise was carried to a high pitch—a spirit which, except in one instance,[1] he was always anxious to foster. His first care was to found a fort on the coast of Guinea, which had been discovered during the preceding reign, for the purpose of maintaining a permanent commercial intercourse with the natives. The barbarian king, who had entered into an alliance with the strangers, consented to the erection of the fortress. From this moment Portugal, or rather her monarchs, derived a great revenue in ivory and gold from this unknown coast; so great, indeed, that he feared lest the vessels of other European nations should be attracted to it. To damp their avidity, he took care that the voyage should be represented not merely as difficult, but as in the highest degree dangerous; and as impossible to be undertaken in regular ships; in any other than the flat-bottomed round smacks at that time

---

[1] That of Christopher Columbus, whose proposals he himself was ready enough to receive, but was overruled by his council.

peculiar to Portugal.   The secret, however, was near coming to the knowledge of the vigilant monarch of Castile, who suspected the truth, and who longed to obtain a settlement on the same coast.   In the hope of a princely reward, a Portuguese captain and two pilots proceeded to Castile.   They were pursued into the neighbouring territory by the agents of João ; and, as they refused to obey the summons of recall, two were killed on the spot, and the third brought back to Evora, where he was quartered.   The severity of this punishment sank deep into the minds of the other pilots, and retained them in the service of their own sovereign.   And when João heard that vessels were constructing in the English ports, unknown to Edward IV, and at the cost of the duke de Medina Sidonia, for an expedition to Ethiopia, — so the Portuguese termed all central Africa from the Nile to the western coast, — he sent an embassy to the English monarch, whom he reminded of the ancient alliance between the two crowns, and whom he easily induced to prohibit the preparations.   In a short time, the fortress of São Jorge da Mina (Elmina) became a considerable city, and afterwards infamous from the traffic in slaves.

A PORTUGUESE CAPTAIN OF THE FIFTEENTH CENTURY

But this was only the beginning of Portuguese enterprise.   The king had been taught to suspect that by coasting the African continent a passage to the East Indies might be discovered ; and he not only equipped two small squadrons expressly for this object, but despatched two of his subjects (Pedro de Covilhão and Alfonso de Payva) into India and Abyssinia, to discover the route to and between these vast regions, and what advantages Portuguese commerce might derive from the knowledge thus acquired.

PROGRESS IN DISCOVERY

The discoveries of Covilhão encouraged João to attempt the passage to India.   One of the squadrons — that under João Alfonso de Aveiro — discovered the kingdom of Benin.   The other, under Cam, was more fortunate.   Crossing the equinox, he arrived at the mouth of the Congo.   He coasted two hundred leagues further to the south ; but finding no cape, he returned to Congo, and was honourably received by the barbarian king, whom he disposed to Christianity, and impressed with a favourable idea of European civilisation.   His departure affected the half convert, who besought him to return with missionaries, and who at the same time permitted several natives to accompany him, for the purpose of being thoroughly instructed in the new faith.   By the Portuguese king and court they were received with great joy, and at their express desire were soon regenerated in the waters of baptism, he, his queen, and many of the nobles standing sponsors at the font.   After a residence of two years in Europe, they returned to Congo, accompanied by several monks, some mechanics and agricultural labourers, and an embassy, headed by Ruy de Sousa.   Hundreds repaired to the missionaries for instruction ; the idols were broken or removed ; a church was built, and mass celebrated with imposing pomp. But to renounce worldly pleasures, and to mortify the strongest passions, to forego the privilege of many wives, and the gratification of revenge — were too much for these licentious barbarians. By degrees the new faith changed, and was finally extinguished.

Though no paramount advantage was derived from the alliance with Congo, the discoveries of Cam led to a solid one — that of the Cape of Good Hope. This memorable discovery was made in 1487, by Bartholomeu Dias, an officer of equal enterprise and experience. The high winds and still higher seas which assailed this vast promontory induced the captain to call it the Cape of Storms ; but João, who had more extended views, called it O Cabo da Boa Esperança, or the Cape of Good Hope. On this occasion Dias ventured little beyond the promontory ; nor was it passed by any vessel until the following reign, when the famous Vasco da Gama doubled it on his voyage to India.[e]

Martius' Account of Vasco and Cabral

To Covilhão belongs the honour of marking the itinerary of the voyage to India, asserting that the East might be reached by the south of Africa. In the letters which he sent from Cairo, he said that ships navigating along the coast of Guinea would ultimately reach the extreme south of the African continent ; and from thence steering east in the direction of the island of Lua, by Sofala, would find themselves on the way to India. From this and other information received, was composed the plan of the daring expedition of 1497, the destined course of which was first Kalikodu or Calecut (Calicut), as it was called then, and from thence to where Covilhão was. Vasco da Gama was chosen by Dom Emmanuel (Dom João II had then been dead three years) to command the expedition. He was a daring but prudent man, uniting the qualities of a soldier and sailor, a thing common at that time and even later. The same thing applies to Alfonso de Albuquerque, Dom João de Castro, and many others. Such a combination had a decided advantage ; the separation of these qualities did not come to embarrass their plans ; there was unity in the command, for the captain was likewise pilot.

The greatest judgment and prudence directed the preparations for the expedition. The information sent by Covilhão was weighed and considered and compared with that previously obtained. Charts and maps were examined, and Bartholomeu Dias himself related what had befallen him, the obstacles which he had encountered, and the difficulties which must be overcome. With his vast experience he directed the building of the ships, doing away with exaggerated dimensions, and insisting on the strength of the ribs. The discoverer of the cape was to accompany the expedition as far as São Jorge da Mina, and remain there to carry on the gold trade. There were four small ships, that they might be able to enter all the ports, explore every creek, pass over shoals, and cruise along the coast. Their construction was strong and perfect, such as had never been seen before.

They carried six freestone columns carved with the Portuguese arms, and the armillary sphere which the king had adopted as his emblem. One was to be set up at the bay of St. Braz, another at the mouth of the Zambesi, another in Mozambique, another in Calicut, and another in the island of Santa Maria. There were two chaplains on board each ship ; negro, Kaffir, and Arab interpreters, ten convicts for any sacrifice that might be necessary, and finally 148 soldiers. The best pilots had been chosen and the king would allow nothing to be spared. He came in person to view the ships on the stocks, and remained conversing with the masters, listening to the observations of Bartholomeu and Pedro Dias, and Vasco da Gama, who showed him the new astrolabe of Behaim, a rough triangle of wood but very effectual.

The three ships bore the names of the three archangels: *S. Gabriel* the *capitanea* of 120 tons; *S. Miguel* (formerly *Berrio*), and *S. Raphael* of 100 tons. The name of the fourth, of 200 tons, is unknown. At the end of June they were all finished and ready, and rode at anchor before the church of Restello, where the captains watched all the night of the 7th of July. The next day, after mass, accompanied by the king and all the people of the city, singing, with tapers in their hands, they all went in procession to the shore and there embarked. Camoens says that at that moment:

> But now an aged sire of reverend mien,
> Upon the foreshore thronged by the crowds,
> With lore by long experience only grown,
> Thus from his time-taught breast he made his moan:
> "O curst the mortal who the first was found,
> Teaching the tree to wear the flowing sheet."
> — *The Lusiads*, Burton's translation.

Indeed many in their hearts strongly condemned the persistency of the monarchs in sacrificing men and money to this chimera of navigation. The cold and tardy prudence born of past experience did not believe success possible after so many vain attempts. The result was to prove the contrary; but the words of the poet prophesied the fatal consequences of an empire which all, both daring and prudent, were ready to acclaim upon the return of Vasco da Gama. Camoens, watching the decline of the sun, could relate the hunger endured at sea, the tempests, shipwrecks, and wanderings in the burning lands of the terrible Adamastor, and the trail of white skeletons left across the sands of both Africas — a rosary of mournful tragedies. He could relate how waves of tyranny and crime from that Indian sea stretched out to Europe to overwhelm Portugal with their slime.

They were three months reaching St. Helena Bay (Nov. 7th). They landed to take the sun with their astrolabe, the rolling of the ship preventing them from doing so on board; here they had several skirmishes with the natives, and set out again at last upon the 16th of November. On the 19th they came in sight of Cape Tormentoso, or of Good Hope, both names being fully justified on this occasion. For three days they were beaten about by tempests. The wind and waves were such that the upper parts of the ships were under water, and it could scarcely be seen if they advanced upon the waves or were wrapped around by them. Upon the stern castles the ships had painted pictures of the saints whose name they bore, and when the raging sea flung the pictures on to the tilt the crews grew pale with horror. It was a bad omen, for it seemed as if they were deserted by the divine favour. Fierce and angry seas washed over the poops, dashing the boats against the sides of the ships and damaging the helms. They furled the sails, cut down the tilt, and began to throw the cargo overboard. At last the weather cleared.

Having doubled the cape, they entered the bay of St. Braz, where the calms detained them until the 7th of the following month. Navigating for a week along the southern coast of Africa, on the 15th they reached the Chaos Islands, the farthest point reached by Bartholomeu Dias. Then they began to follow the instructions of Covilhão, the pilot absent in the lands of the mythical Prester John, of whom they were in search. They wished to proceed along the coast, but the currents, which were a great danger, carried them towards the vast and unknown southern sea. The sailors rebelled in vain; Vasco da Gama, like an inexorable destiny prudent in his audacity, overcame the currents and revolts.

At last they got out of the "sea of darkness" (*mar tenebroso*), and then only could the terrific cape be looked upon as overcome. The tempests and the currents grew still. By day there was calm with the sky of purest blue; by night, several times the light of S. Pedro Gonçalves, the St. Elmo of Lisbon, shone above the tops of the masts. All promised fair weather. They climbed the masts to see the marks of the miracle, and brought back with great devotion the droppings of green wax left by the saint.

On January 10th, 1498, they touched land at Inhambane, and had some intercourse with the Kaffirs; on the 22nd they had reached Quilimane (Kilimane), where "noblemen" came on board to visit them, with turbans of worked silk upon their heads.

India was reached for the first time. They saw men of divers nations, and traces of that distant civilisation so eagerly sought for. They had emerged from the African sea, and from the heavy shadow of the dark continent. Yet these "noblemen" whom they gazed upon almost with love, regarding them as brothers, were to be their cruelest enemies. They reached Mozambique on the 2nd of March. Around the fleet at anchor came the native vessels, without decks or sails. The Moors came to trade with them. The sultan in person wished to compliment Vasco da Gama, who received him on board. The sultan proved perfidious, and the fleet, without the pilots, cruised along the coast to Mombasa (on the 8th of April), where chance alone saved it from the plot which the Moors had prepared against it; they had already recognised dangerous competitors in these men who had come over the sea to these regions, which had until then been the undisputed possession of Arabia, Egypt, and Nubia. Saved by a miracle, Vasco da Gama went on to Melinde (15th), where the sultan received him well; but not trusting these "noblemen" of Zanzibar, he availed himself of a Moor who had remained on board at Mozambique, and who chanced to know the way to Calicut. They put to sea, and in twenty-seven days (24th of April to the 19th of May), they were in India. The voyage had lasted ten months and eleven days.

It was now that their wonder reached its limit. Everything they had seen as yet gave not a distant idea of what they now saw upon their landing. The natural pomp and splendour of the East filled them with surprise and cupidity. In their religious ignorance they saw everywhere the Christians of Prester John. The natives adored the Virgin Mary, and the Portuguese also prostrated themselves before our Lady, in the person of Gauri, the white goddess, Sakti of Siva, the destroyer. This confusion, increased by the fact of not understanding each other's speech, occasioned scenes ingenuously comical. Some who were doubtful, remarked that if the idols were devils their prayer was intended for God alone, quieting their consciences by this mental reservation. To increase their amazement, there came to them a Moor who spoke in Portuguese, "Good luck! good luck! Many rubies, many emeralds!"

From Lisbon to India was but a short distance, for the feelings have no measure. They were all Christians, they also had kings. The world was all one and man the same everywhere. The ingenuous way in which the greatest things were accomplished is the greatest proof of the heroic strength of these men of the Renaissance.

At that time India — and by that name we designate all the coasts and islands included between the meridians of Suez and Tidore, and between 20° south latitude and 30° north latitude, the scene of the Portuguese campaigns — in India, we say, foreign races held a kind of dominion resembling in all things that which afterwards belonged to the Portuguese — a commercial-maritime monopoly, and consequently, factories, colonies, and states. The races they were about to dispossess of this dominion were the Arabs, the Ethiopians, Persians, Turks, and Afghans, who, coming down from the Red and the Arabian seas, and confounded in the religious wave of Islam, had subjugated the peninsula from the Indus to the Ganges, and eastern Africa from Adal to Monomotapa. Extending themselves to the extreme east, they reached as far as Cambodia and Tidore in the Moluccas, across Arakan and Pegu, from the peninsula of Malacca (Malay peninsula), and from Burma and Shan (Siam) into the continent, through Sumatra and Borneo and the middle of the Sunda archipelago. The Portuguese called all the natives Moors, a generic term already in use in Europe to denote the followers of Islam, and therefore now adopted when, having come from afar and traversed so many seas, they again found themselves face to face with the Turk, the opponent of the Christian throughout the world.

"The devil take you! What brought you here!" was the compliment addressed to the Portuguese by a Moor in Calicut; and in Mozambique and Mombasa the Moors (we will henceforward use this word as a generic term, as aforesaid) persuaded or forced Samundri Rajah (Zamorin) king or count (India was under a pseudo-feudal rule) of Calicut, to exterminate the Portuguese. Calicut was the commercial empire of the coast of Malabar, and the dominions of the rajah formed the so-called kingdom of Kanara.

It was an easy matter no doubt to persuade the ruler that Vasco da Gama was a pirate and his king a myth; certainly the Moors of Calicut defined, in advance and unawares, the Portuguese dominion, which differed from common piracy only in that it was rapine organised by a political state. Convinced or constrained, the rajah ordered the navigators to be pursued, but they embarked and defended themselves, August 30th. After remaining some months in the island of Anjediva, upon the coast, Vasco da Gama resolved to return and set sail for Portugal on the 10th of July, 1498. A year later on the same date he reached Lisbon. Great was the enthusiasm. Dom Emmanuel also had his Indies, and Portugal her Columbus. But what tidings of Prester John? And what of Covilhão? None. The navigator had succeeded in overcoming the cape and discovering India, but he had not succeeded in solving the enigma which at that time had baffled their search for three centuries. This was of small account in history. The essential point was the solving of a greater enigma — that of the "dark ocean." Little was now wanting; in twenty years there would not remain an unknown corner of land in the whole circumference of the globe, nor a span unexplored in the vast expanse of seas. "Under the wild waves to learn the secrets of the earth, and the mysteries and illusions of the sea," the Portuguese with heroic curiosity took in their hands the future of Europe and of the world. In the year after the discovery of India, Pedro Alvares Cabral, who was sent thither with an imposing fleet, could not resist the temptation of curiosity. Steering east in the Atlantic a question constantly tormented him — what lay to the west? In that direction Columbus had discovered the Indies in the northern hemisphere; were there not perhaps Indies in the southern hemisphere also? He steered west to explore — what were a few months more or less in the long journey to the east? Thus he discovered Brazil; the western land lay from the extreme north to the extreme south, extending through the two hemispheres. Not till then could it be said that America was completely discovered (1500).

The news of the discovery of new lands made little impression in Lisbon; the fervent desire of the court was the discovery of the Prester, the enchanted Prester John, in order to make a good alliance with him and bring to Portugal a little at least of those good things which Vasco da Gama had seen with his own eyes, the report of which inflamed the whole nation with cupidity. Cabral was sent for this purpose, not to discover lands; the names in their repertory were now barely sufficient to designate the islands, capes, ports, bays, coasts, and continents. Their desires were set on other things; other hopes seethed within them: " Good luck! good luck! Many rubies, many emeralds!"

It was resolved to send a fleet to India, for now that the way was known there was nothing to fear and no reason to diminish the number or tonnage of the ships. Pedro Alvares Cabral was appointed admiral of the fleet, which consisted of thirteen ships and carried twelve hundred men. The fleet raised anchor in the Tagus on the 9th of March, 1500. The shouts of the sailors as they worked at the capstan in unison, a sound as sad and mournful as the sea; the low murmur of the cables in the hawses; the whistle of the masters as they directed the manœuvres; the many-coloured flags flying in the breeze; the sails half-furled upon the masts, made a vivid picture of the nation which in the year 1500 was also setting out, shriven and well-disposed, upon this long voyage of a little more than a century, full of disease and shipwreck, at the end of which waited a tomb vast as the sea and silent as the ocean in the funereal calm of the tropics.

Cabral's voyage, besides beginning the Portuguese dominion in India, had really two desirable results: it swept away the two legends of Prester John and of the "sea of darkness." He discovered Brazil and returned to tell Emmanuel that the supposed emperor of the East was a miserable black heathen king, intrenched in the inaccessible mountains of Abyssinia. In pursuit of a myth, drawn by an abyss, Portugal discovered the continents and islands of the Atlantic and reached India. For the sake of an illusion they achieved the reality which struck the world with wonder. The world is a mirage and men are but shadows borne upon the cunning winds of destiny. With the lands discovered and the seas ploughed from east to west, it still remained to unite these two halves of the known world, and sail round them, to make sure that they lay whole and complete in the hands of men. This was the effect of the voyage of Magellan (Magalhães) twenty years after. The sea was dark no more, the great conquest was complete. But a new enterprise now revealed itself—to devour what was discovered, to assimilate the world. The whole of Portugal embarked for India in Cabral's fleet.

THE CONQUEST OF INDIA

On the 13th of September of the year 1500, Cabral reached Calicut. He went, not like Vasco da Gama, as a discoverer, but as the emissary of the noble Portuguese monarch, the bearer of his letters and proposals of alliance to the rajah of Calicut. As such he was received in a solemn audience. The Portuguese, donning their richest clothes and their best and brightest arms, thought to make an impression upon the Eastern potentate by their riches; but the representatives of Europe, poor and strong, were to be outdone by the magnificence of opulent India.   The polish of their arms was dimmed by the blaze of precious stones " whose rays were blinding."

The rajah was borne in a palanquin, or litter, upon the shoulders of his nobles, reclining upon silken cushions among coverlets worked in gold thread, falling in folds and edged with borders encrusted with precious stones.   The litter advanced slowly, under a silken canopy fringed with gold, and within this double tabernacle appeared the black rajah, covered with precious stones. It was blinding to look upon him.   On each side of the canopy were pages stirring the air with fans of peacock feathers, and beside the palanquin came those who bore the insignia of royalty — the sword and dagger, the foil of gold, the symbolical lily-flower, the ewer of water, and finally the cup into which the king spat the betel, the chewing of which makes the teeth pink, and gives " a most sweet breath."

Throughout the whole length of the procession and bringing up the rear were bands of musicians rending the air with their drums, tom-toms of gold and silver suspended by cords from poles of bamboo, and enormous trumpets, some straight and some curved, raised in the air, which gave the musicians the appearance of elephants with golden trunks, their flags encrusted with rubies and emeralds.

The reception was conducted with solemnity on either side, although they could not understand each other well ; the scribes displayed in vain their long palm leaves covered with writing ; the Portuguese by signs indicated their wish to establish factories there.   The scribes gradually came to understand, and distrusted ; and the Portuguese also distrusted the smiles of the rajah.   In spite of this, however, their request was granted, and Cabral founded the first Portuguese factory in India at Calicut.   Afterwards the Moors came and exclaimed against the intruders who were despoiling them, and, favoured by the natives, fell upon the factory, murdering all the Portuguese therein — fifty in all.   Then followed the terrible vengeance of the admiral. He took ten ships of the Arab merchants, and put the crews, five hundred men, to the sword ; bombarded the city, and set it on fire.

The burning of Calicut on the 16th of December, 1500, was the gloomy dawn of modern oriental history.   In the middle of January (1501) Cabral loaded his ships with pepper and cinnamon and returned to the kingdom. Of the thirteen ships with which he set out a year before, barely three returned with him.   The terrible enemy though conquered was not subdued, and this first expedition to India, the first act of a tragedy of more than a century, sketched out the course of its action ; assassination, fire, massacre, shipwreck ; the sword and pepper ; the soldier's arms in one hand, the merchant's scales in the other — a modern Carthage ; and in the background the open maw of the sea, ready to devour men, ships, and treasure ; a perennial fount of vice pouring forth torrents of wickedness.

To inflict a terrible chastisement upon the rajah and to consolidate the factory of Cochin by fortifying it, was the object of the second fleet which set out from Lisbon in February, 1502, under the command of Vasco da Gama, the implacable captain.   The story of the voyage is full of horror ; and the revenge of the captain a proof of the sanguinary, impassive, and cruel coldness which does indeed exist in the almost African temperament of the Portuguese.   Obliterated in peace and subjection it ever bursts out afresh in dominion, victory, and warfare.   If such sentiments, alive in the soul of Gama, inspired his actions, his campaign followed no plan, nor could his rude spirit entertain the wide views of the statesman.   If he had any plan in view, it was to amaze India by the cruelty of his deeds, and dominate it by the terror of his slaughters. Navigating the Indian seas, Gama met a ship of Arabian merchants going to or coming from Mecca. Besides the crew the ship carried 240 men, passengers with their wives and children. This was on the 1st of October, 1502; "which I shall remember all my life," wrote the pilot, still horror-stricken at the remembrance of the cowardly way in which the ship was set on fire with all whom it contained, so that every soul perished in the flames or in the sea. Well pleased with himself, the captain steered for Calicut. He intimated to the rajah that he must expel all the Moors, who numbered five thousand families, the richest in the city; saying that any servant of the king Dom Emmanuel was worth more than the Zamorin, and that his master had power to make every palm tree a king! As was to be expected, the rajah refused. Then the captain, who upon anchoring had captured a considerable number of merchants in the port, ordered their hands and ears to be cut off, and crowded them into a boat in which they drifted ashore with the tide, bearing Gama's answer to the refusal of the wretched prince.

Then he began the bombardment, November 2nd. The city was in flames for the second time, and the lamentations of the people answered the cynical and ferocious laughter of the sailors sheltered behind the sides of the ships near the guns which vomited fire. This was a foolish, cruel, and cowardly deed; for the short lances and arrows of the natives could not measure themselves against the grenades fired from afar on board the ships. Gama left part of his fleet in India under the command of Vincente Sodre, as eminent and celebrated a man as the admiral, whose uncle he was.

The Portuguese dominion thus assumed from the very first the twofold character which it never lost in spite of all subsequent attempts at law and order. On the sea was anarchy and theft; on shore, a succession of blood-thirsty depredations.

A PORTUGUESE CAPTAIN OF THE SIXTEENTH CENTURY

Vasco da Gama showed how to rule by fire and sword; Sodre showed how to reap a harvest at sea by boarding the ships of Mecca. Piracy and pillage were the two foundations of the Portuguese dominion, its nerves were cannon, and its soul was pepper. When Gama returned from his second voyage a third fleet left Lisbon (April, 1503) with Alfonso de Albuquerque and Duarte Pacheco on board. They went to Cochin to assist the rajah in his war against the rajah of Calicut, and built the first fortress in India. Albuquerque returned to the kingdom; Pacheco remained at Cochin with the troops and ships prepared for the attack. The hero — for he fought like a wild beast in his den of Kambalaan, nobly, disinterestedly, and fiercely — said at once that now all lay with the artillery. This will explain the possibility of the resistance of Pacheco's seventy men, feebly assisted by the natives, against the fifty thousand attributed to the army of Samundri, rajah of Calicut. But the artillery alone would not have sufficed to repulse the solid body of the enemy's columns, if the courage and wonderful rapidity of the marches, the ubiquity, so to speak, of the first soldier-hero of the East, had not supported the powerful means of defence. The fleet of Lopo Soares Albergaria brought back Pacheco to the kingdom in 1505. Being a simple and upright man he returned rich in wounds and poor in money and diamonds; he had remained in the captaincy of São Jorge da Mina, from whence he was brought in irons because of the accusations brought against him, to languish in prison for a long time and to die at last in poverty and oblivion. "The fate of this hero," says Goes,[n] "was of a nature to warn mankind to beware of the inconstancy of kings and princes and their small remembrance of those to whom they are bound." And yet Dom Emmanuel owed the consolidation of his still incipient empire in the East to this man.

Dom Francisco de Almeida was the man chosen to be governor of India, now constituted a viceroyalty. He is the first of the successive figures presented by the Portuguese empire of the East; and the first of the three most notable viceroys. The government of India formed three great men — Castro, who may be called a saint; Albuquerque, to whom the name of hero is better adapted; and Almeida, a wise administrator and intelligent factor. The viceroy, his plans matured by observation on the spot, and the first naval war with which he was received by the unrepentant rajah of Calicut, mentally completed his system of government. "Let all our strength be at sea," he said; "let us refrain from appropriating the land. The old tradition of conquest, the empire of such distant lands, is not desirable. Let us destroy those new races (the Arabs, Afghans, Ethiopians, and Turks) and reinstate the ancient races and natives of this coast; then we will go further. Let us secure with our fleets the safety of the sea and protect the natives in whose name we may practically reign over India. There would certainly be no harm in our having a few fortresses along the coast, but simply to protect the factories from surprise, for their chief safety will lie in the friendship of the native rajahs placed upon their thrones by us, and maintained and defended by our fleets. What has been done so far is but anarchy, scarcely an outline of government, a system of murder, piracy, and disorder which it is necessary to remedy." The difficulties seemed to him more formidable in that "the past warfare was with beasts, but now we are to fight Venetians and the Turks of the sultan." The former impunity disappeared as soon as the Venetians and Egyptians launched a powerful fleet upon the Red Sea, with artillery.

Dom Francisco de Almeida advanced up the coast, leaving behind him a trail of ashes and blood which everywhere marked the passage of the Portuguese. The Egyptian admiral still feared the viceroy, and as soon as the fleet had anchored and grappled with his ships, he meant to cut the cables and drift ashore, dragging the Portuguese with him, where the Indian launches and *fustas* might fall upon them furiously. But the viceroy perceived the snare and ordered the anchors to be prepared in the stern, and the enemy's ships went ashore alone. It was the 3rd of February (1509), the feast of St. Braz, at noon. The confusion of races gathered in that fight was inextricable; the banners of the cross and crescent flying from the masts covered the most extravagant sentiments and varying beliefs. The truth is that they fought not for faith or fatherland, but furiously disputed the spoils of India ; and covetousness can make brothers of men of every faith and children of every race. There were French and Germans as bombardiers on board the Portuguese ships ; there were Indian Brahmans and even Moors. On the other side in the confusion of ships there might be found from the Nubian to the Arab ; from the Ethiopian to the Affran ; there were Mussulmans of every caste ; Persians and *Rum*[1] of Egypt — mercenaries from all parts to whom this generic name was given. Besides the heathen multitude was the Venetian renegade or Catholic — but above all the merchant, who had come with artillery to the Indian Sea by order of his republic to defend the interests of his associates in the commerce of the East. Around the confused bands on board the fleet of the Rum gathered the dark mass of Indians in their junks, from Diu in Guzerat and from Calicut in Kanara.

Once more the waters of the Indian Sea were stained with crimson. Countless numbers perished. The wounded floated, crying for mercy and receiving bullets. At last, after the scenes and episodes proper to such tragedies, the victory fell to the viceroy who destroyed Rum and Indians. This naval victory had a higher importance even than the victories of Duarte Pacheco in Cochin, for the Indians, observing and considering, recognised that the Portuguese forces were invincible not only to themselves but also to the Rum of Egypt and the artillery of Venice. The viceroy remembered that he had lost his son, and "he went and sat under the awning, a handkerchief in his hand which could not stem his falling tears." All thronged to console him, and recovering his spirits he arose, drying his tears and calling them his sons, and said that this grief had pierced and must ever remain in his heart, but bade them rejoice at the gallant vengeance which God in his mercy had bestowed upon them ! But to complete his vengeance for the death of his son, he ordered prisoners to be tied to the mouths of the guns, and the heads and scattered members of these unfortunate wretches were thrown into the city of Kanara like shot. The death of his son disturbed his sound judgment and transformed his former opinions of a statesman to blood-thirsty furies, attested by the devastation of the coast of Guzerat. He yielded also to the intrigues and slanders of the captains who had come from Ormus, recently conquered by Albuquerque and ruled with the terrible wildness of his titanic enterprises. They scoffed at the viceroy who had just finished his term of office, and at Albuquerque, already appointed from Lisbon to succeed him ; and treacherous accounts of the excesses of the wise Almeida had already reached the court. The dungeon of Duarte Pacheco awaited him in payment of his labours. However, on his journey to the kingdom he landed on the coast of Kaffraria, and was killed by the natives with assegais and javelins.

His plan of government, though wise, was chimerical, for India itself was insanity. Only a man of genius like Albuquerque could make the doomed enterprise great. Only a saint like Castro could save the Portuguese valour from the stain of positive ignominy. Dominion, as Almeida conceived it, was not to despoil ; it was armed protection extended to a commerce, free on one side, and the monopoly of the state or appanage of the crown on the other. The captains and governors should be simultaneously commercial agents of his majesty, the high trader in pepper. This required a stolidity of which the Dutch alone were capable and that at the cost of salaries which outweighed temptation. Besides this, the Portuguese flung themselves

[1 The *Rum* was a term applied by the Arabs to all subjects of the Roman Empire and continued to be the designation of the inhabitants of western Christendom after they had ceased to yield obedience to the "king of Rum," the Byzantine emperor.]

famished upon this eastern banquet, as did the races of the north, centuries before, upon the banquet of Gaul, Italy, and Spain. No one could have wrenched from their fangs the palpitating flesh which they so anxiously devoured; the fatal consequences which Dom Francisco de Almeida wisely foretold were inevitable. Albuquerque in Ormus, Goa, and Malacca, established on land the limits of the empire, which in his predecessor's judgment should have floated vaguely on the waves.

King Emmanuel forgave everything, crimes, robbery, incendiarism, and piracy, so long as they sent him what he most longed for, curiosities, novelties and riches, to fill his palaces in Lisbon and dazzle the pope in Rome with his magnificent embassy. "Send pepper, and lie down to sleep," said Tristan da Cunha later on, writing from the court in Lisbon to his son Nuno, governor of India. The sack of the East — such a name best fits the Portuguese dominion — was already ordained in Lisbon.[m]

Albuquerque, like Almeida, for all his splendid services, was rewarded with envy and ingratitude. His abilities, his bravery, his successful administration made the courtiers fear or pretend that he aimed at an independent sovereignty in those regions; and by their representations they prevailed on the king to recall him. Dom Lopo Soares was despatched from Lisbon to supersede him. But before his successor arrived, he felt that his health was worn out in the service of his country; he made his last will, and died at sea, within sight of Goa. However violent some of his acts, his loss was bewailed by both Indians and Portuguese. He certainly administered justice with impartiality; laid no intolerable burdens on the people; restrained the licentiousness of his officers; and introduced unexampled prosperity throughout the wide range of the Portuguese establishments. If to this we add that the qualities of his mind were of a high order, that he was liberal, affable, and modest, we shall scarcely be surprised that, by his enthusiastic countrymen, he was styled the Great. It is probable that no other man would have established the domination of Portugal on so secure a basis: it is certain that no other, in so short a period, could have invested the structure with so much splendour. His remains were magnificently interred at Goa, and his son was laden with honours by the now repentant Emmanuel — the only rewards of his great deeds (1515).

Under the successors of Albuquerque, the administration of India was notorious for its corruption, imbecility, and violence, and in the same degree as wisdom and justice were discarded, so did the military spirit decay.[e]

EMMANUEL THE FORTUNATE

When Dom Emmanuel I had been proclaimed king in the town of Alcacer on the 27th of October, 1495, he had reached the age of twenty-six. He had found everything prepared for a quiet and prosperous reign; his predecessor, João II, had smoothed the way for him by overthrowing the power of the nobility. The conciliation of the *fidalgos* and great lords was easily effected.

Two matters seriously occupied the new king during the first years of his reign — his marriage, and the discovery of India. In the hope that he or his descendants would one day unite the crowns of Spain and Portugal, Dom Emmanuel desired to marry the widow of his nephew. The Catholic sovereigns, having first approved the king of Portugal's request, appointed as their agent Ximenes, who was afterwards cardinal. The marriage of the king, Dom Emmanuel, and Doña Isabella of Castile being agreed upon a treaty was made at Burgos, on the 30th of November, 1496, in which large dowries in money were promised on both sides.

In 1497, the king sent his delegate to Castile to continue the negotiations, and a new article was introduced into the treaty, to which the Catholic sovereigns attached extraordinary importance, going so far as to make it a question of annulling the treaty of Burgos and breaking off the marriage. This article was that Dom Emmanuel should expel from his kingdom and dominions all the Jews or Moors who refused baptism, and all those who had been found guilty of heresy or apostasy, the clause to be fulfilled before September, 1497. Such was the origin of the greatest political mistake and blackest injustice perpetrated by the "fortunate" king, Dom Emmanuel, which left an indelible stain upon his happy reign ; for the ambition of eventually uniting the crowns of Portugal and Castile cannot be considered a sufficient excuse. Dom Emmanuel fulfilled this treaty, expelling from his kingdom all the Jews and free Moors who refused baptism, including all those unfortunates who, banished from Spain in 1492 by the Catholic sovereigns Ferdinand and Isabella, had fled to Portugal thinking to find in that country a refuge from the intolerance and tyranny of Castile. In October, 1497, the marriage of King Emmanuel of Portugal with the princess Isabella, daughter of Ferdinand and Isabella of Castile, and widow of Prince Alfonso, son of João II, took place in the town of Valencia de Alcantara.

It seemed at first that Dom Emmanuel's lucky star would not abandon him in his relations with Castile. Indeed the kings of Portugal and Castile were still at Valencia de Alcantara when they received the news of the unfortunate death of the prince Don Juan, heir to the crown of Castile. By this event Doña Isabella, queen of Portugal, wife of Dom Emmanuel, became heir presumptive to the kingdoms of Castile, Aragon, and Leon. This fact, which plunged the kingdoms of Spain in consternation, filled Dom Emmanuel with joy and promised to satisfy his ambitions more promptly than could have been expected.

But his wife was advanced in pregnancy. In spite of her state, she resolved to continue her journey and go to Saragossa to be sworn heir to the throne of Aragon. Here she was seized with the pains of child-birth, and on the 24th of August, 1498, brought forth the infante Dom Miguel, in that city, his birth costing his mother her life. And Miguel died two years later.

Thus the dream of Dom Emmanuel vanished like smoke. The famous expulsion of the Jews and New Christians, an iniquitous measure, unwise and unpolitic, price of the marriage with Doña Isabella, was not a happy augury. Once more the attempt at an Iberian union under the sceptre of a Portuguese king by matrimonial means had failed.

Dom Emmanuel did not completely lose hope in his relations with Castile[1] by the death of his wife and son. The Catholic sovereigns also seemed determined on an alliance with Portugal. Without loss of time, in the same year, 1500, Dom Emmanuel sent Ruy de Saude, of his council, as ambassador to the sovereigns of Castile with full powers to request the hand of the infanta Doña Maria, the daughter of Ferdinand and Isabella, and consequently sister-in-law of the king of Portugal. The heirs to the crown of Castile were Doña Juana, daughter of Ferdinand and Isabella, and her husband, son of the emperor Maximilian and the empress Mary of Burgundy. The princess of Castile had already a son at that time, Charles, who was born at Ghent in Belgium on the 24th of February, 1500, and was afterwards

[1 The Portuguese have a saying : "*De Castella nem bom vento nem bom casamento*" (From Castile neither good wind nor good wedding).]

Charles I of Spain and V of Germany.   Queen Isabella died on the 25th of November, 1504, and King Ferdinand on the 23rd of January, 1516.   The throne of Castile was lost to Dom Emmanuel.   The crown of Spain was about to pass to the house of Austria.   The wedding to Maria nevertheless took place at Alcacer-do-Sal on the 30th of October, 1500.

In the same year, 1500, Gaspar Cortereal went to North America and discovered the land of Labrador, which was then called Cortereal, getting beyond 50° north latitude.   He returned to Portugal, and repeated his voyage in 1501, but was never heard of again.   His brother, Miguel, went in search of him, but he also disappeared.   Other lands and islands were discovered in the time of Queen Maria.   In 1501, João da Nova,[1] on his voyage to India, discovered the Ascension Island in the Atlantic, and the island which bears his name on the coast of Africa.   On his return journey in 1502 he discovered the island of St. Helena in the Atlantic.   The Florentine Amerigo Vespucci made voyages to America by order of Dom Emmanuel in 1501 and 1503, discovering Rio de la Plata and Patagonia.   This navigator had the glory of giving his name to the group of lands discovered by Columbus, Cabral, etc.   In 1506 were successively discovered : by Tristan da Cunha, the islands of that name in the Atlantic ; by Ruy Pereira Coutinho and Fernão Soares, the western and eastern coasts of the island of Madagascar ; in 1507, the Maldive Islands by Dom Lourenço de Almeida ; in 1509, by Diogo Lopes de Sequeira, Malacca (Malay Peninsula) and Sumatra ; in 1512, by Francisco Serrão, the Molucca Islands in the Chinese seas ; in 1513, by Pedro Mascarenhas, the island to which he gave his name and which is at present called Réunion, in the Indian Ocean ; in 1516, Duarte Coelho discovered Cochin-China ; in 1517, Fernão Peres de Andrade went to China.[k]

THE GREAT VOYAGE OF MAGELLAN

The celebrated line of demarcation between the right of discovery and conquest was not so clearly understood as to avoid disputes between Dom Emmanuel and his brother sovereign of Castile.   His splendid empire in the East had long attracted the jealousy of Ferdinand, who had frequently attempted, but as frequently been deterred by his remonstrances, to share in the rich commercial advantages thus offered to the sister kingdom.   After the death of that prince, a disaffected Portuguese who had served Emmanuel with distinction both in Ethiopia and India, and who was disgusted with the refusal of his sovereign to reward his services with becoming liberality, fled into Castile, and told the new king, Charles V of Austria, that the Molucca Islands, in virtue of that line, rightfully belonged to Spain.   This man was Ferdinand Magellan (Fernão de Magalhães), whose name is immortalised in the annals of maritime discovery.   He proposed a shorter route to the Moluccas than the passage by the Cape of Good Hope — the route by Brazil : he well knew that the American continent must terminate somewhere, and his notion of the earth's rotundity was sufficiently just to convince him that a western voyage would bring him to the same point as the one discovered by Dias and Vasco da Gama.   In August, 1519, he embarked at Seville, with five vessels, over the crews of which he was invested with the power of life and death.   On reaching the Brazilian coast, he cautiously proceeded southwards, and in September, 1520, arriving at a cape which he called after

[1 A Spaniard by birth, who entered the Portuguese service.   His original name was Juan de Nova.]

the Eleven Thousand Virgins, he passed into the dreaded straits which bear his name. After a passage of fifteen hundred leagues, unexampled for its boldness, he reached the Philippine Islands. Here closed his extraordinary career in 1521. Though the object of the expedition failed, through the catastrophe of its leader, he will be considered by posterity as by far the most undaunted, and in many respects the most extraordinary man that ever traversed an unknown sea.e

In the midst of this splendid series of voyages and discoveries, and of brilliant victories and conquests of the Portuguese in Asia, a fatal incident afflicted Lisbon, in the year 1506. The deplorable catastrophe which plunged the capital in mourning sprang from religious intolerance, of which Dom Emmanuel had given such a fatal example on the occasion of his first marriage. On Low Sunday, the 19th of April, 1506, in the church of St. Dominic in Lisbon, where a vast concourse of people were assembled, the rays of the sun striking upon the splendour of a crucifix produced such a brilliant effect that certain visionaries, religious, or fanatics, took it for a miracle. The cry of "a miracle" already flew from mouth to mouth, when a bystander, more intelligent but with little prudence for his speech, suggested that this effect was due to the reflection of the sun and could only be called a natural phenomenon. This sufficed to cause him to be looked upon as a disguised Jew ; a tumult arose, and such was the frenzy of the populace that a horrible massacre upon the so-called New Christians followed.

The massacre lasted for three days. More than a thousand persons perished. Dom Emmanuel was at Aviz at the time. As soon as he heard of what had occurred in the capital, he sent Dom Diogo Lobo, baron de Alvito, and the prior of Crato with full powers to punish the guilty.

He ordered that besides the special punishment of the guilty all the inhabitants should forfeit a fifth of all their property, movable and immovable, to the crown, and that from the date of the sentence there should be no more courts of aldermen, freemen of guilds, nor judges of hospitals ; he further subjected the municipality to the jurisdiction of the harbingers, the amount of these impositions to be levied by officers of the crown. This species of interdict lasted for two years.

This splendid period of the reign of Dom Emmanuel, which includes the years 1500 to 1517, the eighteen years during which the fortunate monarch was married to Doña Maria of Castile, the most brilliant in Portuguese history for the military glory and wealth and commerce enjoyed by Portugal, and in which science, letters, and art were so flourishing — was not equally happy as regards public health, the safety of the lives and property of the inhabitants of these kingdoms, and internal administration.

The plague, which had frequently visited Portugal since the fifteenth century, attacked and ravaged the capital many times, as well as other towns of this kingdom ; then royalty and those able to follow their example might be seen flying from the infected places. Real preventive measures were never adopted until the reign of João III. Novenas, feast-days, processions of the relics of St. Roque, which Dom Emmanuel sent for from Venice, such were the chief means adopted by the king and people to combat the epidemic, not, however, forgetting the safest course of flight.k

Dom Emmanuel died December 12th, 1521, after one of the most glorious reigns on record. Of his public administration enough has been said ; and of his private character what little we know is chiefly in his favour. He administered justice with impartiality ; and had regulated hours when he received his subjects without distinction ; nay, such was his anxiety to do them justice, that if at the expiration of the appointed period complaints remained unredressed, he would sacrifice the hours sacred to enjoyment or repose. The persecution of the unfortunate Jews is a deep stain on his memory ; but in every respect he was a great monarch, and his fame filled the world as much as his enlightened policy enriched his kingdom. He despatched embassies to all the potentates of his time — to the king of England, and the ruler of Abyssinia ; to the royal chief of Congo, and the sultan of Egypt ; to the sultan of Persia, and the emperor of China. Some of them — that, for instance, in which he displayed before the astonished pope and cardinals a Persian panther and an Indian elephant, with their native attendants — were distinguished by magnificence suitable to the lord of so many regions.[e]

CHAPTER III

THE FALL, THE CAPTIVITY, AND THE REVOLUTION

[1521–1640 A.D.]

UPON the death of Dom Emmanuel in December, 1521, he was succeeded by Dom João, his eldest son, who had not yet completed his twentieth year. The chroniclers who wrote under the influence of the immediate successors of this prince, having the fear of censure before their eyes, represented him as endowed with high intelligence and qualities worthy of a king.

During his father's life many considered him an idiot. Dom Emmanuel himself feared the influence which unworthy men exerted over João during his early youth. It is certain that through inattention or incapacity he could never master the rudiments of science, nor even those of the Latin tongue. Throughout his reign monkish questions always appeared among the gravest business of the state, and his first action, when he had scarcely emerged from infancy, was to build a Dominican convent. This may be regarded as the worthy presage of an inquisition king. Whether from want of natural intelligence, ignorance, or errors of education, João III was a fanatic. The intolerance of his reign, though furthered by different incentives, was chiefly due to his character and inclinations.

The secretary of Dom Emmanuel, Antonio Carneiro, who deserved his confidence for many years and continued to serve the new king, when fatigue forced him to withdraw from a charge which he still held nominally for many years, left as his successor his second son Pedro de Alçaçova. This man, whom we find years later managing the most various affairs at the same time, and whose activity appears almost incredible, by the side of a prince whose lack of culture his very panegyrists cannot hide, must have been practically king in resolving the most difficult questions, as was the marquis of Pombal at a later epoch. Pedro de Alçaçova made no parade of his influence, hiding in the shadow of the throne, and leaving the frequently sterile brilliance of importance and favouritism to a vain nobility. But every dark stain that rests upon the reign of João III may be attributed to him, except the establishment of the horrible tribunal of the faith. In this particular, although the actual deed was his, the impulse came from the monarch. The resistance of the New Christians was long and persistent. A steadfast will made up of a million hatreds struggled against this resistance for more than twenty years and overcame it. In the end the rack, whip, and stake reigned supreme in the region of religious belief, prevailing over the evangelical doctrine of tolerance and liberty.

The failure of the attempt to establish the Inquisition in Portugal in 1515, from whatever cause arising, and the predominance obtained by the policy of tolerance, must have increased the spite of the irreconcilable enemies of the Jews. The hatred of João III for the Jews was profound and well known. This sufficed to excite in the minds of the people the ancient spirit of persecution and assassination. Ignorance and monkish tendencies, unassisted by envy or the memory of former wrongs, made the king naturally a fanatic, though fanaticism did not prevent him from abandoning himself to debauchery with women.

His marriage was treated of and Doña Catherine, sister of Charles V who then reigned in Castile, was chosen for his bride. The marriage took place, and an attempt was made to tighten the bond between the two countries by negotiating the marriage of Charles V with the infanta Donna Isabella, sister of the king of Portugal. The final conditions were adjusted and it was agreed that the dowry of the Portuguese infanta should be 90,000 doubloons, or more than 800,000 cruzados. Resources were wanting and it was necessary to obtain them. Perhaps this circumstance and several others caused the convocation of the cortes in 1525. Since the fifteenth century the Portuguese parliaments had lost their true value; they were more a matter of pomp and formality than of substance. The essential point, which was to raise money, was effected, for the cortes voted the impositions of new taxes to the amount of 150,000 cruzados to be raised in two years. This was the most urgent business. The representations of the councils were generally answered in fair words, which were only partially carried out long after the cortes of 1535, when the same representations were for the most part renewed. It was in this assembly that the general ill will towards the New Christians was at last able to manifest itself in a solemnly significant manner, but within strictly legal limits.[b] In 1536 the Inquisition was finally established. Its methods and its effects will be sufficiently shown in the appendix to this volume. It destroyed life, liberty, humanity, commerce, literature, and art in Portugal as elsewhere. When the Jesuits were admitted in 1540 and given charge of education, the church and the state were one, and the result was as usual a shameful combination of atrocity and paralysis.[a]

THE PORTUGUESE IN AFRICA, INDIA, AND BRAZIL

The long reign of João exhibits interminable contests in India and Africa. Their details would be perused with little interest by an English reader. They can be noticed in so far only as they affect the general state of the monarchy. During these transactions in the East, Morocco continued to be the sanguinary theatre of the worst human passions.   On the one hand the Portuguese were eager to extend their possessions; on the other, the *sherifs*, exulting in their successful ambition, were not less so to free the country from so troublesome an enemy.   From the accession of the new dynasty, the affairs of the Portuguese began to decline.   Indicative of the ambitious schemes which they had formed, the sherifs assumed the title of emperors of Africa : the elder, Hamed, remaining at Morocco; the younger, Muhammed, occupying the more western provinces.

To the king of Fez this assumption was not less odious than it was to the Portuguese themselves.   That on one occasion the sherif, with four thousand horse, was signally defeated by a Portuguese noble with one hundred and forty, is gravely asserted; victories equally improbable, we may add equally impossible, occur at every step in the Portuguese relations concerning the wars of their countrymen with the misbelievers.   But what, we are told, could not be effected by valour was done by fortune.   Considering the war which he had to support in India, and his want of troops, João took the extraordinary resolution of dismantling four of his African fortresses, Arzilla, Saphin, Asemmur, Alcacer-Seguier, and of abandoning the ruins to the enemy.   This resolution was carried into effect; but that this was owing as much to the arms of the sherif as to the motives will be admitted by every reader except a Portuguese.[c]

The oriental empire of Portugal, however, continued to increase by the wars which the able statesmen and warriors, whom João sent out as viceroys and governors, waged, upon the most frivolous pretexts, against the different neighbouring princes.   They took advantage of the dissensions of the princes of the Moluccas, to obtain the complete sovereignty of those valuable islands. The disorders provoked by the tyranny and consequent assassination of the sultans of Cambay enabled them to wrest from those monarchs the important fortress and city of Diu; and similar convulsions in the Deccan gave them opportunities of considerably extending the Portuguese dominions in that wealthy country.   It is to be observed, however, that the sovereigns, thus lawlessly despoiled, were themselves equally lawless conquerors.   They were the chiefs of the Mohammedan hordes, who had overrun India, overthrown the native princes, and oppressed the Hindus.   The enslaved natives probably cared little for the expulsion of one foreign master by another, if they had not cause to rejoice at exchanging the wantonly cruel tyranny of oriental despots for the more orderly extortion and oppression of a civilised people.

The increase of the power of the Portuguese now alarmed all the Mohammedan potentates, and they applied to Constantinople for assistance to expel the Christian intruders.   Again the request was enforced by a Christian power, Venice, whose jealousy of the Portuguese rivals of her own commercial greatness extinguished all nobler feeling, all religious sympathy.   Suleiman, thus doubly urged, equipped a powerful armament in the Red Sea, which, proceeding to the Indian Ocean, joined the Cambayan forces in besieging Diu.   The defence, first by Antonio de Silveira, and afterwards by João de Mascarenhas, of this place, or rather of the fortress, for the town and rest of the island were quickly abandoned as untenable, ranks amongst the most celebrated feats of the Portuguese in India.   They repulsed incessant assaults, the women labouring day and night at the fortifications, and venturing into the posts of greatest danger, to carry every needful assistance to the combatants, who, from their scanty numbers, could hardly ever quit the walls.   During both sieges, the place was reduced to the utmost extremity; and upon both occasions was relieved by the seasonable appearance of the viceroy with a powerful fleet.

Of the viceroys and governors who effected these acquisitions scarcely one was duly recompensed. Many died in poverty, and Nuño da Cunha, who gained Diu for King João, was only saved by death from being dragged in chains to the foot of his ungrateful master's throne. During João's reign, the celebrated apostle of India, St. Francis Xavier, visited that country to attempt the conversion of the idolatrous natives : and the Portuguese obtained an establishment in China, and a free trade with Japan.

Brazil first acquired importance under João III. In 1531 he began the colonisation of that immense empire, then little more than a long line of seacoast. This he divided into several captaincies, which he granted, with large powers of jurisdiction, civil and criminal, to such persons as, upon those conditions, were willing to settle there, and to people and cultivate their respective grants. The French made various attempts to form rival settlements in Brazil, especially about Rio de Janeiro. They never obtained more than temporary possession of any part of the country.[d]

The greatest credit that can be given to João III is that he kept his country out of all European complications, a task made comparatively easy by his close alliance with the greatest monarch in Europe, Charles V. This alliance was sealed by three marriages : for King João was married to the infanta Catherine, the sister of Charles V; his only son, Dom João, was married to the infanta Juana, daughter of Charles V; and his only daughter, Donna Maria, was the first wife of Philip, prince of the Asturias, the eldest son of Charles V, and afterwards King Philip II.[e]

João died in 1557. By his queen, Catherine, he had several male children, of whom none emerged from their infancy except João. Nor did that infante survive the father. In 1553 he received the hand of Juana, daughter of the emperor; but he died in the third month of his marriage, leaving the princess pregnant of a son, afterwards the unfortunate Dom Sebastian. Of João's brothers one only, the cardinal Henry, whom he had vainly endeavoured to place in the chair of St. Peter, survived him. As his sister Isabella was the mother of the Spanish monarch, the connection between the royal families of the two kingdoms was, as we shall soon see, fatal to the independence of Portugal. As Sebastian, on the death of his grandfather, was only three years of age, the regency, in conformity with the will of the late king, was vested in the widowed queen, Catherine of Austria. In a few years, however, being disgusted with the intrigues of Cardinal Henry, who aspired to the direction of affairs, she resigned it in his favour.[c]

Before going on with the chronicle, it will be well to read a Portuguese historian's picture of the decline of this period.[a]

ENNES' ACCOUNT OF THE DECADENCE OF PORTUGAL

We are about to enter upon the saddest and most unfortunate period in the history of Portugal. The brilliant epic which the bright sword of Alfonso Henriques began with the battle of Ourique, stops at the exact epoch at which an immortal bard appears. The *Lusiadas*, that Homeric apotheosis of a great, heroic people, arises almost at the hour of their fatal fall. But a few years and the epic is transformed into an elegy, the apotheosis into a funeral panegyric. But a few years and Camoens drags from his Olympic strophes these four lines :

" Fazei, senhor, que nunca os admirados
Allemaes, Gallos, Italos e Inglezes
Possam dirzer, que sao para mandados
Mais que para mandar, aos Portuguezes."

—in vain, when the descendants of the old heroes were cowardly and infamously about to sell their humiliated country, poor and agonised, to the sinister son of Charles V, the emperor of legends.

These years of servitude and captivity spread like an immense oil stain over the brilliant history of Portugal, and the sun which sank in clouds of blood at Kassr-el-Kebir plunged the country into an obscure and long night until it rose radiantly once more on the field of Montijo. It falls to our lot to relate the history of this painful period of darkness and tears, barely illuminated in the beginning by the last rays of light thrown out by the conquests of the old East. The warlike genius which gave to Portugal the most glorious pages in modern epopee, the spirit of adventure, chivalrous and combatant, which carried its name to every corner of the world, and gave it a place of honour in the vanguard of the nations of Europe, was the same that apparently lowered the national colours before the victorious crescent on the sands of Africa, was the same that strangled national independence with the bonds of captivity, and delivered it inert and defenceless into the hands of the devil of the south, the lugubrious Philip II.

Portugal, having reached the apogee of her glory, became giddy and fell into the abyss of slavery. In the supreme hour of her agony, the red hat of a cardinal appeared at the bedside of the dying kingdom. Portugal's gravedigger, the cardinal Dom Henry, was a sinister figure. But who killed her, who struck her the fatal blow? It was not the perverse imbecilities of the cowardly Jesuit; it was not the dangerous errors of the youthful knight-king. The assassin of Portugal was that fanatic and imbecile monarch who opened his foolish arms to the Society of Jesus, who planted deep in the kingdom that deadly tree known as absolutism, under whose protecting shadow was planted, thrived, and flowered that colossal infamy—the Inquisition. And who has to answer before the same tribunal of history for the lost liberty, the outraged honour, the valour spurned, the ruined wealth of that nation which gave to the world the most magnificent spectacle of modern times, a diminutive country throwing over the two hemispheres her power, her influence, her name? It is not the ambitious and imbecile old man chronicled under the hated name of cardinal-king; not the heroic child, the beardless youth who, enamoured of glory, died in pursuit of it, like a daring paladin on the sands of Kassr-el-Kebir; not the cold inert corpse to whom, with pungent irony, tradition has given the nickname of *Piedoso*, and who is known in history as João III. In history's terrible logic Philip II was fatal heir to João III. It was the unhappy reign of this inept monarch which prepared the way to Portugal's ruin.

His internal policy completely transformed the government into a fierce unchecked absolutism; his external policy of pure neutrality, at a time of grave disputes between all the European nations, alienated from him the sympathies of all the states of Europe; and later, when Philip II wiped from the map this diminutive nationality which, hidden in a corner of the west, had spread its fame and name throughout the world, Europe paid back to Portugal the debt of haughty indifference she had incurred under the pious king. When the Spaniards made their threatening invasion into Portugal, instead of finding an energetic and valiant nation defending its life and its liberty, they found a weak and inert people, humbled beneath the yoke of fierce absolutism, fanaticism enveloping the souls of all, demoralisation rampant in the army, luxury enervating the higher social classes, hunger and misery devastating the people ; a nation of lions transformed into a flock of sheep by immorality, by despotism, by misery—a flock of sheep guided by an imbecile and disastrous shepherd, the unlucky cardinal, Dom Henry.

Dom Henry and Dom Sebastian could barely reap the deadly fruits of the venomous seeds sown by João III. It would seem that in such critical moments providence chooses incapable, weak, and blundering kings, who instead of delaying for a time the inevitable fall, seem rather unhappily to hasten it.

And thus at the close of the sad reign of João III, on seeing the crown placed on the head of an infant of three years, obstinately disputed by two great ambitions, that of the queen Catherine the grandmother, and that of Cardinal Henry the uncle, on seeing the indifference of Europe, on seeing Spain's vast power in Portuguese policy, one does not need to be a prophet to foretell in the near future the sad development which fanaticism, tyranny, and the stupidity of the unworthy son of the great Dom Emmanuel had prepared for the splendid epic commenced at the battle of Ourique ; to foretell the tremendous downfall of the colossus known as Portugal. Before entering the most lamentable reign of Dom Sebastian, let us cast a glance over the state of Portugal during the last years of Dom João's life, and consider what manner of kingdom and people the desired king received in heritage, upon taking his first childish steps in a world to which he was to leave so sad a tradition.

The reign of Dom João III is an original mixture of splendours and threats, of wealth and misery. It presents brilliant lights and implacable shadows, but unhappily the lights were the last reflections of Portuguese glory soon to be extinguished, the shadows the unfortunate heralds of the immense night into which Portugal was to be plunged. Portugal at this epoch had reached the apogee of her prosperity. The Portuguese flag fluttered over the most remote countries of the wealthy East. Her commerce sucked fabulous wealth from the abundant breasts of old Asia. India resigned herself to the conquest ; Brazil was beginning to be peopled ; China and Japan discovered, Oceania subjected, Abyssinia explored, were rich harvests of glory and gold, of heroic deeds and vast fortunes for Portugal. But this gold scarcely circulated in the country ; instead of benefiting the latter, it went to enrich England, to give power to Italy and Flanders, stupidly to fill the ever insatiable coffers of the Vatican. This glory instead of acting as a stimulus was suffocated by the tyrannies of absolutism, was crushed by the stupid fanaticism of the Jesuits, who paraded, triumphant and strong, under the sinister protection of the Inquisition. The period of Dom João III marks out distinctly and perfectly in history the transition from the pinnacles of triumphant power to the dark abysses of slavery, from a glorious life to a humiliating death.

The conquests and prosperity in the East were the outcome of the former impulses ; what the country owed to the pious king was the demoralisation of the army and people, the glorification of tyrants, the relaxation of judicial authority crushed by the Inquisition, the gilded poverty of the people, the enervation of the aristocracy, the loss of commerce by the flight of foreigners residing in Lisbon harassed at every step by the infamous cruelties of the Inquisition, and the stupid despotism of individual power. All the glory of his reign is due to his predecessors ; the shame, opprobrium, immorality, and misery are due to him, and unhappily were left as an inheritance to his successors and to the country.*f*

THE REGENCIES AND THE REIGN OF SEBASTIAN (1557–1578 A.D.)

João III, dying, had committed the government of his kingdom, and the care of his grandson, then only three years old, to his widow, Queen Catherine. She governed ably; and by her active exertions sent such effective succours to Mazagan, which was almost the only remaining Portuguese fortress in northern Africa, and then reduced to extremity by a Moorish army of eighty thousand men, that the Mohammedans were compelled to raise the siege. But the Portuguese detested queen-dowagers, especially when Spanish; and Queen Catherine in 1562 found it expedient to resign the regency to her brother-in-law, Cardinal Henry, for whom João had unsuccessfully endeavoured to obtain the papal tiara. The cardinal was a good man, but unfitted, by the habits of his past life, for government. Under his feeble administration, the authority of Portugal over her distant colonies was weakened, and the inferior governors struggled against the control of the viceroys; whilst, by committing the education of the infant king wholly to Jesuits, he prepared the way for the heavier calamities that followed.

Sebastian is represented as naturally endowed with many great and good qualities, especially an eager desire for knowledge. But the Jesuits seem to have studied only to guard their royal pupil from a tendency to vice. But scarcely any vice, however injurious to his own individual character and happiness, could have brought such wide-spreading misery, such utter destruction upon his kingdom, as did the extravagance into which Sebastian was hurried by mistaken virtues.[1] He grew up with the idea that hatred of the infidels was Christianity, and courage the first virtue of a king. He proved the ruin of Portugal.

He was very desirous of going out to India, to remedy, by his personal intervention, the disorders which had greatly increased during his minority, and to relieve Goa and Chaul, besieged, in consequence of the weakness those disorders had produced, by the whole force of the Mohammedans, in that part of the world. His ministers remonstrated. Sebastian listened to their representations, and resigned his purpose. It might have been happier for Portugal had he been suffered to execute it. Be that as it may, effective measures were taken. The enemy was repulsed from Chaul and Goa, and the Indian empire of Portugal was tranquillised.

In the year 1571, Philip II invited his nephew to take a part in the great armament against the Turks under Don John of Austria, which Sebastian declined doing, upon the plea of his dominions being desolated by the plague. Sebastian's first visit to Africa more resembles some of the expeditions of the knights errant of romance, than anything in real sober history. He is said to have left Lisbon on a hunting excursion, in the course of which he crossed the sea, to pursue his sport in another quarter of the globe. Upon landing in Africa, he sent home for a small body of troops, and when they joined him, gave over hunting for the still more exciting amusement of making hostile inroads upon the neighbouring Moors. In these, he of course could do no more than take some booty and prisoners; and when he had roused the Mohammedans to assemble their forces, he was compelled, by the consciousness of inferior strength, to re-embark for Portugal. From this moment he thought of nothing but recovering the African possessions

[1 "The young king was rather German than Portuguese in appearance, with his blue eyes and fair hair and face disfigured by the Habsburg lip, and in his nature there was much of the Teuton dreaminess and love of the marvellous."— STEPHENS.e]

which his grandfather had lost or abandoned, and his court became a scene of contest and cabal — his grandmother, and Cardinal Henry, and all his sagest counsellors remonstrating vehemently against what they justly deemed the visionary projects of extravagant ambition; whilst flattering courtiers, heedless young men, and fanatical ecclesiastics eagerly encouraged his views.

In the midst of these contests, a revolution in Africa seemed to offer an opportunity too favourable to be neglected. In the empire of Morocco, upon the death of the emperor Abdallah, his son Mulei Ahmed usurped the government. He ruled tyrannically, and his uncle Mulei Moloch [or Maula Abd-el-Melik], the legitimate sovereign, easily formed a strong party against him, with which, after a severe struggle, he succeeded in overthrowing the usurper and establishing himself in his place. Mulei Ahmed sought foreign assistance. Philip II declined interfering, when Mulei Ahmed addressed himself to Sebastian, adding to his offer of tribute that of the restitution of Arzilla. Philip is said to have laboured to deter his nephew from embarking in an enterprise altogether beyond his means. Most historians, with the exception of the Spanish, accused Philip of having employed underhand methods of instigating the young king to persevere in the determination he affected to dissuade. Especially he is charged with inducing the pope to applaud and encourage Sebastian in his purpose.[1] Certain it is that the king of Portugal's resolution to accept Mulei Ahmed's offers was not to be shaken. The old queen died of the anxiety occasioned by her grandson's rashness and obstinacy; Cardinal Henry marked his disapprobation by refusing to act as regent during the king's absence: and Sebastian appointed in his stead the archbishop of Lisbon and two noblemen, one of whom was João de Mascarenhas, an ex-viceroy of India, and as distinguished a warrior as any of those who had conquered and secured the Portuguese empire in the East.

THE DÉBACLE AT KASSR-EL-KEBIR (1578 A.D.)

The army with which, in June, 1578, Sebastian sailed for Africa, to overthrow the powerful sovereign of Morocco, consisted of less than sixteen thousand men. But he was accompanied by almost all the young nobility of Portugal, and he relied upon the assurances of Mulei Ahmed that great numbers of his former subjects would immediately declare in his favour. A few volunteer adventurers, from different countries, joined the standard of the chivalrous young king [including Sir Thomas Stukeley, an English Catholic].

Mulei Moloch assembled an army of one hundred thousand men, and at their head, although so reduced by illness that he was obliged to be carried in a litter, he advanced to meet the invader. Some of these troops having been formerly partisans of his nephew, Mulei Moloch, distrustful of their attachment, issued a proclamation, that whosoever pleased was at liberty to pass over to his competitor. This magnanimity secured his triumph over any who might have previously hesitated between their old and new sovereigns, and very few indeed of the dispossessed usurper's former adherents took advantage of the liberty offered them.

[1 La Clède *g* will allow no virtue to Philip, who, he pretends, suddenly approved the enterprise, in the diabolical view of hastening the destruction of his nephew, and profiting by the catastrophe. "*Philippe avait fait, de son côté ses réflexions : autant qu'il s'étoit d'abord opposé à l'entreprise que le roi de Portugal méditoit, autant il montra de désir que l'on l'exécutât. Sébastien étoit jeune téméraire, sans enfans : il pourroit périr et alors le Portugal pouvait être réuni à la Castille.*"]

Sebastian's camp was now distracted by contending opinions.   Mulei Ahmed, who was disappointed in his expectation of deserters from his uncle's army, and now relied upon the impending fatal issue of that uncle's malady for making him master, without a blow, of empire and army, and perhaps of his Christian allies, urged Sebastian to fortify himself in a strong position on the seacoast; but Sebastian, rejecting all rational counsel, led his small army forward, into the open country, to encounter the overwhelming superiority of numbers there awaiting him.

On the 4th of August, 1578, the armies met near Kassr-el-Kebir (Alcazar-Quivir).   Mulei Moloch was conscious that his death could not be long deferred, and fearful that, upon its occurrence, his nephew might gain some advantage over his brother and lawful successor, Ahmed ben Muhammed, he sought an opportunity of engaging the invaders, and by their defeat insuring the peaceful succession of Ahmed ben Muhammed.   He caused himself to be carried through the ranks in his litter, that he might personally exhort his troops.

Sebastian likewise displayed a degree of military skill not to have been anticipated from the rashness of his previous movements; and, at first, victory seemed to incline towards him. One division of the Moorish army was routed, when Mulei Moloch, forgetting his malady in indignation, insisted upon being placed on horseback; and in person rallying the fugitives, attempted to lead them back to the attack.   The effort was too much for his strength; he fainted, and was replaced in his litter, where he only recovered sufficiently to charge his attendants to conceal his death, lest it should discourage his troops, and expired, with his finger on his lips, to enforce these last commands.   They were obeyed.   His attendants affected to open and reclose the curtains of the litter, as if making reports, and receiving orders; and the troops, encouraged by his last exertion, and believing themselves still under his eye, fought with irresistible valour. The Portuguese, notwithstanding their daunt-

PORTUGUESE COSTUME OF THE SIXTEENTH CENTURY

less intrepidity and discipline, notwithstanding the invincible heroism of their king, who, flying from place to place, was seen wherever the danger was most imminent, were completely defeated.   More than nine thousand of the army fell, and the rest were made prisoners, with the exception of about fifty, who escaped by flight.   The young nobility, fighting desperately, were almost all slain; many a noble family was there extinct, and all were plunged in mourning.   Mulei Ahmed was drowned in endeavouring to fly; and Ahmed ben Muhammed obtained uncontested possession of his inheritance.

Some portion of obscurity hangs over the fate of the adventurous Sebastian himself.   But little real doubt can exist of his having fallen upon the fatal field of Kassr-el-Kebir.   He had several horses killed under him, and was seen fighting, long after the general rout, with only three companions, against a host of enemies. The sole survivor of this devoted little band, Nuño de Mascarenhas, stated that, after the fate of two of their company, the king was disarmed and taken prisoner; when, his captors quarrelling about their prize, one of the Moors terminated the dispute by cutting Sebastian down, and he was forthwith despatched. Ahmed ben Muhammed, hearing this, sent one of Sebastian's servants to the spot indicated, who pointed out and brought away a corpse, which was recognised as the king's by the other attendants upon the royal person. The emperor of Morocco afterwards delivered it up to his ally the king of Spain, together with some noble prisoners, including two sons of the duke of Braganza. Philip generously sent home the released captives, as well as the remains of Sebastian, which were interred in the royal sepulchre of Belem.[d]

The 4th of August will ever be the most memorable of days in the annals of Portugal. Never was victory more signal than that of Kassr-el-Kebir. Of the Portuguese force which had left Lisbon, fifty individuals only returned; the rest were dead or in captivity, and with them the chivalry of the kingdom. Eighty of the nobles, through the good offices of Philip, were subsequently ransomed for 400,000 cruzados. The uncertainty which hung over Sebastian's disappearance was converted into a doubt of the catastrophe; and this doubt was still further improved into a report that he was still alive. Several nobles, and among them the prior of Crato, always affected to believe that he had survived the dreadful slaughter of that day. As the public mind was taught to expect the possibility at least of his re-appearance, impostors, in such an age and at such a crisis of affairs, would scarcely fail to personate him — with what success will soon be related.[1]

On the character of this prince, after the preceding relation, it is needless to dwell. Without judgment or power of reflection; the tool of interested flatterers; unacquainted alike with war, with human nature, or the world; misled by the lying miracles recorded of Portuguese valour — one Portuguese being affirmed as a sufficient match for one hundred Moors; confiding in his natural courage, which knew not fear, because it had never been conversant with danger; and taught to believe that to the valour of his people all things must yield — he persisted in the wildest schemes of conquest ever devised by disordered brain. The obstinacy with which he adhered to this resolution, in opposition to representations the most forcible and pathetic; the lamentable imbecility which he displayed alike in the preparation and execution of his purpose, prove that his only virtue was courage. Had there been some superior power to confine the moonstruck prince in the same apartments with his cousin, Don Carlos of Spain, well would it have been for unhappy Portugal.

THE CARDINAL-KING AND THE PORTUGUESE SUCCESSION

For some time the nation, unwilling to believe that Sebastian had perished, regarded Henry merely as regent; but on the arrival of the royal

[1] By the populace of the kingdom, Sebastian was believed, even in the nineteenth century, to be yet alive, concealed, like Roderic the Goth, or the English Arthur, in some hermit's cell, or, perhaps, in some enchanted castle until the time of his re-appearance arrives, when he is to restore the glory of his nation. During the aggressions of Bonaparte on the kingdom, his arrival was expected with much anxiety. [The sect of Sebastianistas often rose to cause excitement, and as early as 1763, Lord Tyrawley exclaimed, "What can one possibly do with a nation, one-half of which expects the Messiah and the other half their king, Dom Sebastian, dead two hundred years?"]

body, and on the confirmation of the catastrophe by every Portuguese who arrived from Africa, the cardinal, the last surviving male of the ancient house, was solemnly crowned. He was an excellent ecclesiastic; but his bounded capacity, his meekness of character, his subjection to the arts of his courtiers rendered his administration of little use to his country. His short reign has nothing to distinguish it beyond the intrigues of candidates for the throne, which, as he was in his sixty-seventh year, broken down by infirmities, and evidently on the verge of the tomb, could not fail to be soon vacant. At first, indeed, he was advised to marry; and application was actually made to the pope for the necessary bull of secularisation; but Philip of Spain, who had so close an interest in the affair, frustrated his views at the pontifical court, and compelled him to abandon them.

The candidates for the throne of Henry, as may be seen from the adjoining chart,[1] were: (1) Antonio, prior of Crato, who affirmed that his father Luiz, brother of João III, was married to his mother, and that he was consequently legitimate; (2) João, duke of Braganza, in right of his wife Catherine, a younger daughter of the youngest son of Emmanuel; (3) Ranuccio, prince of Parma, whose mother, Maria, was the eldest daughter of Dom Duarte; (4) Emmanuel Philibert, duke of Savoy, sprung from Beatrice, a younger daughter of King Emmanuel; (5) Philip, king of Spain, whose claim was twofold — his mother, Isabella, being eldest daughter of Emmanuel, and his first queen, Maria, eldest daughter of João III. From this genealogy nothing can be more clear than that, if the claim were to be decided by consanguinity alone, Philip's was by far the most powerful; but by the laws of Lamego, the princess who accepted a foreign husband was

[1 We may omit from the contest the pope, Gregory XIII, who claimed to be heir to a cardinal, and Catherine de' Medici, who traced back to Alfonso III's marriage to the countess of Boulogne in the thirteenth century.]

CHIEF CLAIMANTS OF THE PORTUGUESE SUCCESSION

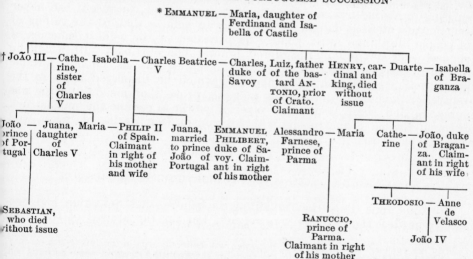

* The first wife of Emmanuel was Isabella, eldest daughter of the Catholic sovereigns, who [di]ed in childbed, and was soon followed by her infant son. By Maria, his sister-in-law and his [se]cond queen, he had three other children, besides those enumerated in this table, but all died [w]ithout issue.

† João III had also other children, but as they all died without issue and before him, they [n]eed not be enumerated.

ipso facto excluded from the throne. Hence, according to the strict letter of the constitution, Isabella and Beatrice, the daughters of Emmanuel, and Maria, the daughter of Duarte, had, by their marriages with the emperor Charles, the duke of Savoy, and the prince of Parma, renounced all claim to the succession : hence, too, by their exclusion, João was the true heir. Besides — and Philip was probably aware of the fact — the law of exclusion, in its very origin, had been expressly aimed at the probability of a union with Castile, seeing that, if the same prince ever became heir to the two crowns, the less must be absorbed in the greater — the independence of Portugal must be at an end. But conventional forms must yield to necessity. We have before seen how, on the marriage of Beatrice, daughter and sole child of Ferdinand, with Juan I of Castile, the states of the kingdom agreed to recognise the issue of that marriage as their future sovereign ; and how, on the death of her father, she being yet without issue, she was actually proclaimed in Lisbon and other places. But such was the hatred of the Portuguese to the Castilians — hatred now as then deep, cordial, and ever-lasting — that they preferred the bastard, grand-master of Aviz, to that princess.[c]

PHILIP II OF SPAIN BECOMES PHILIP I OF PORTUGAL

Dom Antonio, who, after being taken prisoner at Kassr-el-Kebir, had broken his Moorish fetters by the help of a Jew, was the favourite of the populace. He still asserted his legitimacy, imputed corruption to the judges who had decided against his mother's marriage, and reminded his friends that João I, the founder of the reigning house, was an illegitimate son, raised to the throne by popular election. The feeble-minded Henry, whose chief ministers, as well as his Jesuit confessor, were gained over by Philip's money, hesitated to pronounce, lest he should involve the country in civil war. The cortes, whom he convoked, were divided, and timid as himself. The seventeen months of his reign passed in deliberation ; and at his death, on the 31st of January, 1580, he left the question to be decided by five regents, whom he named. Had he boldly declared Catherine his heiress, the greater part of Dom Antonio's adherents would most likely have deserted an illegitimate pretender for their recognised lawful queen. As it was, the kingdom, divided between two strong factions, lay at the mercy of a powerful invader.

Philip had hitherto committed the management of his pretensions to ambassadors and secret agents ; and he now supplied these persons more abundantly than ever with pecuniary means to continue their operations. A majority of the regents were bribed by those agents, and consequently sought to dispose the nation in Philip's favour, by publishing the terms he offered to grant. The chief of these were, in addition to the general maintenance of the constitution, that he would reside as much as possible in Portugal ; that the viceroy appointed to govern in his absence should always be either a prince of the blood or a Portuguese ; that a Portuguese council should always attend him for the management of Portuguese affairs ; that natives of Portugal should be admitted into offices of the household and others of minor importance in Spain, whilst Spaniards, and all strangers, should be excluded from all offices in Portugal, civil and military, as well as from all church preferment ; and that crown lands, as the existing grants fell in, should be regranted to the nearest relations of the former grantees. Conditions so favourable seem to have had great influence in lessening the abhorrence with which the nobles had hitherto shrunk from a connection with

Spain; and Philip now prepared to enforce and support his claim with the potent argument of thirty thousand men. A fitting commander for this army was, however, not so easily found. The duke of Alva was the only general esteemed by Philip competent to the task.

The corrupted regents took all measures for betraying the country to the usurping invader. They dissolved the cortes, and placed creatures of their own in the command of the frontier towns. In June, Alva entered Portugal at the head of his army. Every fortified place threw open its gates at his summons, and he marched onwards unopposed. The duke of Braganza had taken no steps for maintaining his wife's rights, otherwise than by argument. The prior of Crato got possession of Lisbon, where he was proclaimed king by the populace. The nobility, disgusted by his elevation and the inaction of the regents, withdrew sullenly to their houses; and the regents, freed from their control, boldly declared Philip the lawful heir of the crown.

Dom Antonio seized the crown jewels, church plate, and other funds. He released all prisoners, armed them and the rabble, and offered liberty to all negro slaves who would embrace his cause. With an army thus constituted, he attempted to defend the passage of the Tagus against the veteran Alva, who was master of the whole province of Alemtejo, and had reached the south bank of the river, without more fighting than a short siege of one fortress that had declared for Dom Antonio, and the commandant of which, when taken, he had executed. Dom Antonio was, of course, defeated, almost at the first onset. He fled through Lisbon, northwards; collected another army, with which he was again defeated; and thenceforward thought only of escape. Philip set a high price upon his head, but could not tempt any one of his adherents to betray him. For nine months Dom Antonio lurked in the kingdom, concealed now in one place, now in another, sheltered by rich and by poor, in castle, monastery, and cottage, and everywhere diligently sought by his enemies, ere he could find an opportunity of getting on shipboard.

After Dom Antonio's second defeat no further resistance was attempted. Portugal submitted, and swore fealty. Her American, Indian, African, and insular possessions followed her example, with the single exception of the Azores, which proclaimed Antonio. The duke of Braganza and his sons acknowledged Philip. The duchess would not thus surrender her rights; and even when Philip, upon the death of Queen Anne and the duke of Braganza, offered her his hand, she refused a crown as the price of disinheriting her sons; but she too desisted from further contest. When all was quiet Philip visited his new kingdom, convoked the cortes, and swore to the conditions he had previously offered.

Thus was effected, however illegally, the union of Spain and Portugal — a union apparently as important to the true interests of the peninsula as is that of England and Scotland to the well-being of Great Britain; and not more repugnant to the inclinations of the two nations in the one case, probably, than in the other. Had Philip and his successors strictly observed the terms of the union, and endeavoured otherwise to conciliate the Portuguese, these last might, erelong, have considered the Spanish monarchs as their lawful kings, and have reconciled their pride to their incorporation with a larger state. But although rather a usurper than a conqueror, he chose to treat Portugal as a conquered country. He rejected the proposals or beneficial laws, and, indeed, all the demands of the cortes, except a few of the most insignificant, and speedily dissolved that assembly. He refused the favours solicited by the nobles, withheld the honours and pecuniary compensations promised to the Braganza family; and although he did publish an amnesty, the exceptions were so large (including all who had favoured Dom Antonio) that, it was said, Philip had pardoned only those who were free from offence. He then proceeded to punish the persons thus excepted; and the extent of the executions which followed may be judged by two circumstances: one that, from the number of dead bodies thrown into the sea, the people would not eat fish again, until the archbishop, in a solemn procession, had purified by his blessing the polluted ocean; and the other, that Philip himself thought it requisite to obtain absolution from the pope, for having put such numbers of ecclesiastics to death. He then appointed his nephew and brother-in-law, the cardinal-archduke Albert, viceroy of Portugal; and committing to him the government of the country, where discontent was already very general, he returned to Spain.[d]

THE ENGLISH IN PORTUGAL

During the next few years Portugal had nothing to do with the foreign or domestic policy of Philip. Governed with great moderation by the arch-

PORTUGUESE NOBLE OF THE SIXTEENTH CENTURY

duke, enjoying internal peace, an ex-tended commerce, and a high degree of prosperity, she might have been happy — happier than she had ever been under her native monarchs — could hereditary enmity have been forgotten, and national pride sacrificed to interest. The exiled Antonio was made aware of the existing discontent: he had many well-wishers and not a few spies in the country, who con-stantly communicated with him. After the second defeat of his armament in the Azores, he abode at the French court, with the hope of obtaining increased supplies for an invasion of Portugal; but as the civil wars which raged in the former country were likely to prove interminable, he passed over into England to renew his in-trigues with the earl of Essex. He arrived at a favourable time, just after the destruction of the Spanish armada, when the resentment of the English was at the highest pitch, and they were longing for revenge.

At first, however, Elizabeth, with her usual prudence, disapproved of the project of a Portuguese invasion; but, with her usual weakness, wherever the tender passion was concerned, she was persuaded by the favourite earl to enter into an alliance with the exile, and to equip an armament for placing him on the throne. Nothing can better exhibit the unprincipled impostor than certain conditions of that alliance. He engaged to subjugate Portugal in one week from the disembarkation of the troops; to pay Elizabeth an immense sum for the expenses of the armament, and a considerable annual tribute in token of her sovereignty ; to receive English garrisons, at his own expense, into the principal maritime fortresses ; on his arrival at Lisbon, to abandon that city to a twelve days' pillage.   In conformity with another article of the treaty, — a treaty not over honourable to Elizabeth herself, since she grasped at advantages which generosity, or even justice, would have scorned,—twenty thousand men were embarked at Plymouth in 120 vessels, the whole commanded by Drake and Norris (1589).

The success of this expedition corresponded with its flagitious design. After an unsuccessful attempt on Corunna, the armament cast anchor at Peniche, and disembarked the troops who marched to Torres Vedras, where they proclaimed Dom Antonio, and continued their route towards the capital. But the peasantry, instead of joining his standard, fled at his approach. As the English general approached the suburbs, the monks, the women, and most of the inhabitants retired within the city.   The ill success of the English, who repeatedly assailed the outworks, stifled the intrigues of the disaffected ; and a vigorous sortie decided the fate of the expedition.   The English general, who throughout exhibited strange imbecility, retreated ; he was pursued ; many of his followers were cut off ; with the rest he sought refuge in the tower of Cascaes, which the cowardly governor surrendered to him.   Here, considering the want of provisions, and the deception which had been practised on him by Dom Antonio, who had persuaded him that the moment a hostile standard were raised it would be joined by all true Portuguese, he wisely resolved to return home.   This was fortunately the last time Portugal was cursed with the prior's presence.   Deserted by his nearest friends, neglected by the sovereigns, his former allies, in 1595 he ended his unprincipled life in merited obscurity and indigence.

THE FALSE SEBASTIANS

But though Philip was thus rid of a formidable enemy, he had others who were actuated by even a superior spirit of imposture, and who might have occasioned him some trouble.   We have before alluded to a strange impression among the vulgar that Sebastian yet lived, and that such an impression, in such an age and country, could not fail to produce impostors.   The first, who appeared in 1584, was a native of Alcobaça — a man of low extraction and of still lower morals.   Though he was condemned to death, the sentence — very wisely — was not put into execution.   He was condemned to labour in the galleys, where all who had the curiosity might visit him, and be convinced by their own eyes that he was not Sebastian.

The failure of this impostor did not deter another from the same hazardous experiment.   There was a stone-cutter's son, Alvares by name, a native of the Azores, who, having passed some months in the monastery of the Holy Cross, on the heights of Cintra, left that community, and, like the youth of Alcobaça, retired to a hermitage.   At this time he does not appear to have meditated the personation of Sebastian : when, from his frequent self-inflictions, and from his extraordinary habits, he was suspected to be that prince, and even addressed as such, he replied that he was a stone-mason's son of Terceira.   But the more he affirmed this truth, the less was he believed : he was evidently fulfilling a rigorous penitence, to atone for the misfortunes which he had brought on his people ; and, like Roderic the Goth, he had doubtless renounced forever all human grandeur.   Perceiving that opposition was useless, Alvares consented to be treated as a king : he was soon joined by hundreds of the peasantry, whom he allowed to kiss his hand with much affectation of condescension. At length the hermit was taken, was brought to Lisbon, paraded through the streets on the back of an ass, exposed to the jeers of the populace, and publicly hanged.

It might have been expected that the failure of these two attempts would have had some effect even on imposture and credulity; but a third Sebastian appeared, and, strange to say, in Spain, under the very eyes of Philip. There was an Augustinian monk, by name Miguel dos Santos, who had been a chaplain of Sebastian, confessor to Dom Antonio, and who was now confessor to the nunnery of Madrigal. Here he met with Gabriel de Spinosa, a native of Toledo, whom he had known in Portugal, and of whose intelligence, boldness, and dexterity he had seen frequent proofs. As this man really bore a resemblance to King Sebastian, he persuaded him, though not without difficulty, secretly to personate that monarch. Finally the priest, being put to the torture, confessed all. The same means extorted a similar confession from Spinosa, who was hanged and quartered. The priest was degraded, delivered over to the secular arm, and suspended from the public gallows at Madrid.[c]

A fourth impostor was more famous than all the rest, by birth supposed to be an Italian ; who, after a long confinement in Naples, was transferred to Spain, where he ended his days in a prison. His imposture was the more remarkable from the fact that he could not speak Portuguese.[a]

The remaining actions of Philip must be sought in the history of Spain. Four years before his death, on the removal of the cardinal-regent to the archiepiscopal see of Toledo, the government of Portugal was intrusted to a commission of five. In 1598, Philip breathed his last.[c]

CHAGAS' ACCOUNT OF THE LOSS OF THE COLONIES

As yet it was only our pilots who were acquainted with the navigation of the Indies ; in India we were the only nation who had dominions and solidly established settlements, and consequently we were sole lords of the commerce of the East. The English confined themselves to plundering our ships on their return voyage from India, but they dared not come to fight us in the land conquered by our superhuman feats. A young nation that was about to appear at this period on the historical stage was chosen by fate to be the one to wrest from our grasp the sceptre of the East. The Low Countries had long held important commerce with us, principally the town of Antwerp, where a Portuguese factory had been long established. The ships of this industrious country came to Portugal to fetch the merchandise of the East, and scattered it afterwards over Europe. When the Flemish and Dutch rising broke out against Spain, dominator of the Low Countries, Antwerp, the central point of the war, lost her commercial importance, which Amsterdam inherited.

While Portugal was independent she continued the commerce which enriched Holland, but when Philip II effected the union of the two crowns, he had the unhappy inspiration of attacking his rebellious subjects by issuing in 1594 an order for the sequestration of fifty Dutch ships at anchor in the Tagus, and at the same time promulgated a decree closing all Portuguese ports to the Dutch. The blow was terrible, and might have proved mortal, but for the unshakable energy of those republicans of the north. Being unable to come to Portugal for the merchandise of the East, they determined to go and seek it in India herself. In 1594, some merchants of Zealand, assisted by the subsidies of Amsterdam and Enkhuizen, equipped three ships, intrusted them to the care of their two most able mariners, Barentz and Heemskerk, and despatched them to the north in quest of a new passage to the Asiatic seas. The English had already made a similar attempt in 1556, but without success; this attempt of the Dutch was not more successful, and the shipowners were in truth discouraged when the hope which upheld them proved vain.

A chance circumstance favoured them. A Dutchman, named Cornelis Houtmann, had been long in Portugal, and had either succeeded in obtaining a passage to India, or had obtained ample information in the country respecting the route first taken by Vasco da Gama. In 1595, a fleet of four ships piloted by him set out for the coveted lands of the East. In August, 1597, he returned to Texel with barely two ships, but having displayed the colours of a new European flag to the amazed natives of Madagascar, Bantam, Java, Madura, and Bali. The spell was broken. Overjoyed at the result, the Dutch merchants equipped a fleet of eight ships in 1598, commanded by Jacques le Neker and Heemskerk and despatched them to the East. This fleet touched at the island of Cirne, which they named Mauritius, in honour of their great general Maurice of Nassau, a name by which it is still called, though also known as the Isle of France, which Bernardin de St. Pierre has immortalised in his romance, *Paul et Virginie*. From thence they proceeded to Bantam, where they freighted four ships with spices and despatched them to Europe. The remaining ships visited the Moluccas and, in 1600, returned to Holland with a most valuable cargo.*i*

The success of this enterprise was of the greatest importance to England, to which country Philip II had also closed Portuguese ports, in 1589. The English had despatched an expedition to India in 1591. The result did not correspond with the hopes of success, and the British merchants were already discouraged when the example of the Dutch excited them to form the famous company of the Indies, one of the most fruitful origins of England's prosperity.*f*

Under Portuguese administration the constant war always agitating India never ceased, but the Portuguese arms were ever victorious. Yet this state of war made it impossible to frustrate from the outset the attempts of the English and Dutch.

We must always bear in mind that whereas externally Portuguese dominion was firmly maintained, internally the most profound corruption was at work, and paving the way to the dissolution of this vast empire in the near future. The vices of the Portuguese, the corruption of those in office, the excesses of the Inquisition, the cruel treatment of the subjected Indians, the senseless preponderance of the priests, all this is painted by Diogo do Conto*j* in vivid colours.

Mathias de Albuquerque, and especially the count da Vidigueira, attempted to reform these appalling abuses, but all these vices were deep rooted, and no amount of cauterising could check the gangrene. The governors might consider themselves lucky that they yet, at least, possessed valiant soldiers, who did not bring dishonour on the name of Portugal in the wars, and who supported with the edge of their swords the trembling empire. During the government of Dom Francisco da Gama, a most important annexation was made. The last king of Ceylon, dethroned by his kinsman, Raju, and protected by Portuguese soldiers, bequeathed the island in gratitude to the Portuguese. It was the last ray of the dying lamp. As heralds of the approaching disasters the Dutch ships appeared in the East. Of Cornelis Houtmann's four ships, two only, as we have said, returned home ; of the other two, one was lost on the reefs, and the other was destroyed by the Portuguese; but in the following voyage they succeeded in evading vigilance. What other result was to be expected, when the natives welcomed them as liberators, and the Portuguese were always engaged in wars which prevented them from openly repulsing their rivals ? *i*

We have referred elsewhere to the conspiracy in favour of Mary Stuart, favoured by Philip II, and of how this incident r sulted in the outbreak of hostilities between the courts of Madrid and London. Elizabeth Tudor decided to declare war against the Catholic king, and despatched Admiral Drake with a fleet of twenty-three ships, furnished with twenty-three hundred men, against the Spanish colonies. The first to fall a victim was the Portuguese colony of São Thiago, Cape Verd Islands, where the English admiral put in on his way to America, on the 16th of November, 1585. Thence the squadron continued its course, capturing various galleons on the way, some of which were bound to Lisbon.

Almost at the same time various African chiefs allied themselves against the Portuguese at the instigation of Ali Bey, despatched by the sultan of Turkey to subjugate to the viceroy of Egypt the petty kings who did homage to the crown of Portugal. Ali's first victory was not, however, of long duration, as in 1587 a squadron was despatched from India under command of de Mello, who compelled the sovereign of Patta to become a Portuguese vassal, and killed the king of Lamu. Proceeding to Mombasa, he laid waste that place, and put an end to the confederation which Ali Bey had organised. Shortly after, in 1589, the Turks again returned, but this time directed their attack against Melinde, which place had remained faithful. Thomé de Sousa Coutinho hastened from Goa with a fleet, and routed the Turks in the first encounter.

While in east Africa the native population, excited by the Turks, were using every endeavour to throw off the Portuguese yoke, in the west Paulo Dias de Novaes, founder of Loanda, was conquering the kingdom of Angola for the crown of Portugal, at the moment when Philip II was conquering the kingdom of Portugal for Castile. From that day to this the two settlements have remained in the possession of the Portuguese.

Affairs in Brazil were less prosperous. In 1591 the port of Santos was attacked by an English pirate, and the town of São Vicente was sacked and burned; four years later the storehouses of Recife were also sacked by another pirate of the same nation. Worse even than the English pirates were the Spanish defenders.

Before this time the French had already made various incursions into the colony, with the design of establishing themselves there. The province was saved by the patriotism of the residents of Pernambuco, who rushing to arms, under command of the governor, put an end to the French invasions. Enemies more terrible still succeeded them ; these were the Dutch who were expelled only after a long and obstinate struggle, when Portugal had already recovered her liberty.

DOMESTIC DISASTER

To return to the kingdom, where, as we have said, public misery was aggravated by the losses caused to commerce by the pirates of hostile nations, who infested the seas, we must now add that frequently even the ports were attacked.   The most daring of these attempts was that made at Faro on the 22nd of July, 1596, where an English and a Dutch fleet put in, commanded by Admiral Effingham, who after entering the port of Cadiz and there burning a number of ships, and plundering at the same time thirty-three ships laden with merchandise of the Indies, made for the coasts of Portugal, and after landing three thousand soldiers on the shores of Algarve, plundered and laid waste the capital of that province.   The English then made for Lagos, but the governor was able to repulse them.

We will conclude this account of the reign of Philip II by giving a résumé of the instructions he is said to have left to his son, and which, if they show the evil of his policy, are also an eloquent proof of how ambition will lead the clearest judgments astray, making them dream of impossible ventures, and waste their energy in useless projects.   His advice was:

" That without examining into the justice of the case he should obtain complete dominion over Portugal, and once conquered, disorder and terror could be spread throughout Germany, France be conquered, the forces of England weakened, and the terror of the Spanish arms carried to the extreme north.

" That profiting by the advantages gained, his Catholic majesty could thereby get possession of the navigation of the Indies, found colonies wherever he thought fit, conquer new lands, establish an immense commerce, and subjugate all the countries he considered it to his advantage to subjugate. But above all he was to secure the respect of the Portuguese, as this was of the very greatest importance.   That far from burdening them with taxes and subsidies, he should grant them all the privileges and favours to which they laid claim.   When the kingdom was pacified and the people moulded to Spanish dominion, then he should begin to oppose these privileges, appointing from time to time, under various pretexts, Spanish magistrates who should insensibly mould the people to this.

" That he should strictly watch the duke of Braganza, closely examining into his actions, but always showing him every attention, until the opportunity offered of persecuting him and all his family.   As for the rest of the nobility, the only course was to remove them from the country, sending them to fill honourable posts in Flanders, Germany, and Italy.   Proceeding in this manner the kingdom of Portugal could be monopolised and reduced to a province, and the people rendered powerless to make any movement; but by burdening them with taxes and subsidies, their anger would be roused, and hatred awakened, which would be fatal to the Spanish monarchy.

" That his majesty should give the vice-royalty of the kingdom to some prince or princess of his house, to inspire the Portuguese with greater respect for the government, and spare them the repugnance of giving obedience to any other.

" That he should be no less careful in dividing up the house of Braganza; that they should contract no new alliances in Portugal; deprive them of all state dignities, which should be bestowed on Spanish subjects only, and finally prevent them from holding correspondence with foreign courts.

" That whenever disputes arose between the Spanish and Portuguese grandees it was most necessary to favour the latter, and at the same time to bestow the principal offices of the kingdom upon those who appeared the most attached to the court of Castile, and thus attract others with the hope of favours.

" That when there was no longer cause to fear the grandees, the nobility, and still less the people, then it would finally become necessary to destroy

the whole house of Braganza, deprive the Portuguese of all public ecclesiastical and secular offices, and give them to Spaniards, and govern the
kingdom of Portugal as any other province forming part of the Spanish
monarchy."

If the treacherous and immoral policy which Philip II counselled his heir
to follow caused the ruin of the oppressed, it was no less fatal to the oppressors. After the death of the son of Charles V the decadence of the Spanish
monarchy, the most vast and formidable of the sixteenth century, was rapid
and profound. *f*

PHILIP II (1598-1621 A.D.)

Of Philip III of Spain (II of Portugal) we have only to say that in the
course of his reign he once visited his Portuguese subjects. On this occasion the hungry and ambitious chivalry expected much from his liberality;
but, except a few, all were disappointed. If he did not treat them with
studied insult — a charge levelled at him by the Portuguese historians — he
exhibited so great a predilection towards his hereditary subjects that he
could not fail mortally to offend a people who would not even have been
satisfied with an equal share of his attention. Yet many of them are just
enough to blame the weakness, rather than the ill will of Philip: they contend
that the truth was kept from him; that every art was taken to confirm his
dislike to them as a nation; that the Castilian nobles behaved with intolerable
haughtiness to their own; that, in everything, a studied contrast was drawn
between the two classes of subjects; that taxes were imposed without the
consent of the cortes, and strangers nominated to the most important
offices — both violations of the compact signed at Thomar by the first Philip;
and that revenues, appropriated to objects exclusively Portuguese, were
diverted into the treasury of Madrid.

PHILIP III (PHILIP IV OF SPAIN) (1621-1640 A.D.)

If the Portuguese had so much reason to complain of the government of
the second Philip, that of his son and successor was, doubtless, still more
onerous, more insulting: a good one, like that of Philip I, would have been
hated; a bad one would naturally add to the existing mass of discontent.
That the weak, the profligate, and the unprincipled count-duke de Olivares
could direct the affairs of this kingdom with advantage, either to it or to his
royal master, will not be expected by anyone who has perused the account
of his administration in Spain. There can be no doubt that, by forced
loans, by intolerable taxes, and by using the native soldiers in foreign wars,
he wished to break the proud spirit of the people — to make them the mere
slaves of his will.

Finding themselves ground to the very earth by exactions, their complaints disregarded, their persons insulted, their prosperity at an end, we
need not wonder that they began to meditate an escape from their yoke.
They turned their eyes towards the duke of Braganza, the next heir in the
order of succession.[1] That ambitious noble adopted a line of conduct which
could not fail to forward his views. To the world he appeared absorbed by
hunting, feasting, and other diversions; yet his emissaries were at work

[1 See the chart of Portuguese successions on page 503.]

in every part of the kingdom, fanning the flame of discontent, and teaching the people to regard him as one able, at least, to effect their deliverance.[1] Owing to their representations, but in a still greater degree to the rapacity of the revenue collectors, open insurrections appeared at Lisbon, at Braga, and, above all, at Evora, and were not quelled without much difficulty and some bloodshed. Though pressed, the duke was too wise to declare himself at this moment: he knew that his combinations were not formed;[2] he therefore determined to await the silent but resistless course of events. The sequel soon justified his policy. The chief nobles, prelates, cavalleros, and clergy were suddenly summoned to Madrid. What could be the object in this mysterious, unexpected, and unparalleled mandate? Conjecture was vain: to disobey it would be dangerous; and a magnificent display of retinues immediately filled the road from Lisbon to the Spanish capital. What passed at the conference between the ministers and this deputation will never be known; but that some extraordinary concession was required from them may be easily believed. That their consent was demanded to the incorporation of the Portuguese with the Spanish cortes, or that a certain number of deputies from the three estates should be summoned at the same time with those of Castile — in other words, that the kingdom should be forever degraded to the rank of a province, is loudly affirmed by the Portuguese. The nobles probably returned the answer attributed to them — that, in an affair of such moment, they could do nothing without the sanction of a legitimate meeting of the cortes in their own country.

But another reason for this extraordinary mandate may be assigned, more plausible than either. The court could not be ignorant of the disposition of the people towards the duke of Braganza, nor, perhaps, with his intrigues. His arrest might be resolved on: and, as it could not be effected in Portugal, where his connections were so numerous and powerful, he must be inveigled to Madrid. This supposition is confirmed by three facts: he had evaded compliance when summoned alone to the capital; he was not present now; and the subsequent endeavours of the minister to draw him to Madrid were as earnest as they were ineffectual. Disappointed in his views, Olivares now proceeded more boldly: he ordered all the disposable troops in Portugal to march into Catalonia, and the duke of Braganza to place himself at their head. But the war of Catalonia concerned the Castilians only. Both nobles and people resolved to disobey the mandate; but, lest an open refusal should subject them to instant invasion, they merely demanded a short delay, until their preparations were matured.

In the meantime the duke of Braganza was pursuing his end with persevering art: knowing how suspicious was the Spanish court, how jealously every action was watched, he plunged more deeply into his favourite amusements, and asserted that, when the troops were ready to march, he should not be wanting at his post. So well did he counterfeit his part, that many of the conspirators, believing that he had neither ambition nor compassion for his countrymen, declared their intention of soliciting his brother, Prince

[1 According to some historians the duke was really as indifferent as he seemed, and it was the ambition of his wife and of his friends that did all the work for him.]

[2 "This movement reached Villa Viçosa, where the residents changed it to a rebellion, and under cover of the night some of them proclaimed the duke of Braganza, eighth of the title, as João IV king of Portugal. But the time prescribed from centuries had not yet come; the duke sent his son Dom Theodosio, duke de Barcellos, through the streets, and, although he was only four years of age, the light of the great virtues which afterwards distinguished this excellent prince shone in his face, and he became as it were a rainbow of peace, and returned leaving the people pacified, and saved from anxiety the father whom a serious illness prevented from going himself to check the disturbance." — MENEZES.k]

Duarte, to head them. At length, when obedience or open refusal to the orders of the court was imperative, the conspirators hastened to Lisbon, and began their meetings. Their numbers increased; yet so artfully were their proceedings conducted, that they escaped the notice of the duchess of Mantua, the vice-queen.*c*

ENNES' ACCOUNT OF THE CONSPIRACY

It is an old and lasting tradition that the conspirators assembled in the garden of the palace of Antonio de Almada, in a pavilion with stone benches, which had the advantage of a staircase communicating with the turret, where there was a secret door leading into the wood of Santa Anna, fronting the garden of the knight-commanders of the Incarnation. This door supplied an easy entrance to the conspirators, who never assembled all at one time, for fear of the enterprise being crushed with one blow, through treachery. A decision adopted by any seven was binding on all the rest. All the letters of the conspirators were written in an enigmatical manner against the possibility of seizure. Dom João was evidently not anxious to risk his fortune and greatness in a dangerous throw. Egoism was more powerful with him than patriotism, and the voice of prudence deadened the suggestions of ambition. The nobles were in despair, and began to discuss whether it would not be advisable to form a republican government if the duke persisted in his obstinacy.[1] But, thanks largely to the skilful efforts of João Pinto Ribeiro, the duke was won over. But when João Pinto attempted to kiss his hand, this the duke would not allow, saying with a smile, "Let us not buy the cabbage before the meat."

Upon his return to Lisbon, Pinto Ribeiro lost no time in assembling the nobles to communicate the news he brought from Villa Viçosa. He painted in colours more glowing than truthful the prince's enthusiasm and determination, and urged his good intentions of sharing the government of the kingdom with those who had given him the throne. João Pinto's communications were received with the greatest enthusiasm; he had received full power from the duke to adopt in his name any measures he thought fit. The plan of the revolution was then discussed, opinions at first being very varied, but eventually the most sensible opinion prevailed, which was that the nobles should make a surprise attack upon the palace, December 1st.

On Friday, the 30th of November, the last assembly of the nobles took place at the house of Dom Antão de Almada. None now recoiled before danger, and knowing that they were risking their lives, they prepared for death; nearly all confessed, and some made their wills, whilst others recommended their friends in religion to pray for their souls. The judge of the people, and other influential persons of the lower classes, had on this afternoon promised that their men would be ready to follow the nobles at the first summons. It was decided that they should assemble on the following day in the courtyard of the palace, and as nine o'clock struck some should attack the Spanish guard, whilst others should mount immediately to disarm the German guard, and seize all the entrances; upon which, some were to gain the verandas to attack the people, and proclaim Dom João and liberty, whilst others should seek the hated secretary Vasconcellos. The ministers had been warned repeatedly of the suspected assemblies at the house of Dom

[1 This statement, which was made by Vertot*l* in 1689 and is repeated by many historians, is denounced by Stephens*e* as "absurd," though the Netherlands offered an easy analogy.]

Antão de Almada, and Vasconcellos received warning of the very day fixed upon the revolution. In spite of all, the conspirators did not meet with the slightest resistance! A few hours sufficed to conclude the revolution.ʃ

CHAGAS' ACCOUNT OF THE 1ST OF DECEMBER (1640 A.D.)

The 1st of December dawned serene and clear! No clouds dimmed the aurora of Portuguese liberty. Who can divine the thoughts which assailed the conspirators at waking upon this cold winter morning to undertake this hazardous enterprise? Hiding her scalding tears behind a smile, Donna Filippa de Vilhena herself girded on the swords of her two sons, commanding them not to think upon her fate, but upon the fate of Portugal; declaring that to die for one's country when she lay groaning under oppression was still more beautiful than to live for one's mother. With the same manly resolution Donna Marianna de Lencastre blessed her two sons; and these two Spartan mothers, nobler indeed than the Spartans, for such rigid principles had not been instilled into them by a stoical education, left an heroic example to posterity.

From every quarter of the town the nobles and their followers came to the courtyard of the palace, some on foot, some on horseback, some in their carriages, not revealing the anxiety matured to so critical a moment, but with a calmness which gave no sign of what was about to occur. A little before nine all the conspirators were assembled in the courtyard. The soldiers were not alarmed at the carriages which continued to arrive, accustomed as they were to seeing the duchess' courtiers come to the palace; in those days business was earlier than in ours. The people, too, had not as yet assembled in great numbers. With their hands upon the doors of their carriages, the nobles impatiently waited the striking of the solemn hour.

Nine o'clock! The doors of all the carriages are thrown open simultaneously, the nobles descend, and while Jorge de Mello, Estevão da Cunha, Antonio de Mello e Castro, Father Nicolão da Maia, and others still wait in their carriages for the signal from the palace to attack the Spanish guard, the majority of the conspirators rapidly mount the stairs, enter the hall of the German archers, and giving them no time even to suspect what is about to happen, some throw down the stands of the halberds, others draw their swords, and the archers fly, astounded and disarmed. Some of them, whether because their halberds are not in the stands or because they are more determined, do their duty with a certain show of courage, and only fly after seeing two of their men fall to the ground, one dead, the other wounded. Meanwhile, drunk with joy, Dom Miguel de Almeida runs to a veranda, throws open the window, and brandishing a sword, cries out: "Liberty! Liberty! Long live the king Dom João IV. The duke de Braganza is our legitimate king!"

Tears prevented his further speech, and ran down to his white beard, which floated in the breeze blowing from the Tagus, whose waters were gilded by the sun riding triumphant in the heavens. He was answered by an immense cry of enthusiasm and joy; "Liberty! Liberty!" shouted the people with one voice. And in the heroic Dom Miguel de Almeida, this venerable old man of eighty years, radiant with youthful ardour, all saw the symbol of Portugal, decrepit and broken, but illuminated in this hour of her resurrection by the reflection of the splendour of her eras of glory. Those in the courtyard did not limit themselves merely to this unanimous

LIBRARY.
MUSKINGUM COLLEGE.
No.

response. Before the Spanish guard could grasp the meaning of the cry of liberty, which thundered above their heads, Jorge de Mello and his men fell upon them with drawn swords and pistols cocked. They attempted to resist, but the suddenness of the attack and the ardour of our men rendered resistance vain.

Meanwhile Miguel de Vasconcellos had been warned that something was occurring. He was yet in bed and had scarcely time to dress, when, following on the warning, a strange noise was heard in the corridors. Pale with fear he ran to the door and locked it on the inside, and immediately heard the nobles knocking furiously at the door, when the wood was shivered with the hatchets they had brought to break it down. Thereupon, seeing that he was lost, he seized a loaded musket and shut himself into a cupboard full of papers. There holding his breath, his forehead bathed with the sweat of anguish, he heard the door give way; the nobles entered like a torrent, and blaspheming, searched in every corner of the apartment. His safety hung on a thread; as, not finding him, the conspirators were about to make their way to the department of India, to which place they presumed he had fled, when the narrowness of his hiding-place caused Vasconcellos to make a slight movement. It was heard; with a shout of ferocious joy they rushed upon his hiding-place; a few shots were fired, two balls pierced his throat, and he fell dead, the blood spouting from him. After killing him, the avengers of their country abandoned him, and it was the servants who threw the body of the hated minister out of the window. When the tumultuous crowd of people who filled the courtyard saw the body of their oppressor thus contemptuously thrown out, they gave a roar of triumph and in the satisfying of their eagerly desired vengeance there was no insult which they did not heap on the pitiful remains.

While the nobles rushed from the secretary's apartments to those of the vice-queen, the people with shouts of enthusiasm crossed the courtyard, shouting, " Liberty ! " And meanwhile the rabble — who ever desecrate victory and insult the conquered, who to-day drag in the mire their oppressors and to-morrow their liberators — surrounded Vasconcellos' body, dragging out his beard, putting out his eyes, and foolishly laughing at the infamous jests of a Moorish slave of the victim, who, seated on the corpse, mocked at and execrated him before whom he had trembled when alive. On the following day the body of the unfortunate wretch was yet in the courtyard, and seeing it João Pinto Ribeiro expressed his astonishment that none had shown Christian piety to him who had so cruelly expiated his faults. Some of Ribeiro's men carried the body away in a skiff.

The duchess of Mantua had already heard the noise, and coming to the window, she cried out in a loud voice : " What is this, Portuguese? Where is your loyalty ? " Meanwhile some of the conspirators, having forced open all the doors they had found closed, courteously compelled her to withdraw from the window. She wished to descend to the courtyard, and as the nobles prevented her : " Enough, gentlemen ! " she cried, " the guilty minister has already paid for his sins. Go no further, I pledge my word that the king of Castile shall not merely pardon you, but shall thank you for having delivered the kingdom from the excesses of the secretary." The nobles replied that they no longer recognised any king but Dom João de Braganza. This answer so enraged her that Dom Charles de Noronha begged her to retire before they lost respect for her. " For me ! — how ? " she inquired haughtily. " By obliging your highness to leave by the window, if you will not go in by this door," replied the noble in tones equally haughty. Realising that

[1640 A.D.]

under the circumstances resistance was folly, the princess gave way and withdrew to her oratory.

The nobles dispersed through the town to rouse public enthusiasm with the cry of victory, and in a short time the multitude rushed through the streets drunk with joy. A vast cry arose of "Miracle! miracle!" and from mouth to mouth the report spread, that the arm of the Christ on the crucifix, carried by one of the chaplains, had unnailed itself to bless the people. This incident, which probably had been prepared, produced an enormous effect, exciting the imagination and rousing popular enthusiasm. Many prisoners had been set at liberty, and it was feared that they would commit great acts of vengeance; but on the contrary numerous reconciliations took place of long standing enemies, and not one act of violence occurred throughout the city. At eleven in the morning the town had already peaceably resumed its usual occupations.

Meanwhile the government was careful to take all necessary measures to secure public order, stationing companies of militia at different posts. The fortresses surrendered peaceably and the commander of the galleons at anchor in the Tagus was convinced of the uselessness of bombardment and perhaps feared reprisals.

On the same day, Pedro de Mendonça and Jorge de Mello set out for Villa Viçosa; they found Dom João in the chapel, who having heard the news with calmness, commanded the divine office to be continued. This being concluded, he entered a carriage and set out for Lisbon escorted merely by a few mounted servants, being enthusiastically received in all the towns and lands through which he passed. He reached the capital on the 6th.

The speed with which the revolution spread in the provinces is a proof how eagerly liberty was desired. A few days sufficed for a yoke of sixty years [1] to be thrown off, and the Spanish monarchy, yet powerful, could not resist a disarmed and weak people, to whom invincible energy was lent by the thirst for liberty and the despair born of oppression. [i]

[[1] This is the period from 1580–1640 which the Portuguese love to call the "Sixty Years' Captivity."]

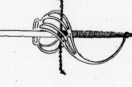

CHAPTER IV

JOÃO IV TO JOÃO VI

[1640–1822 A.D.]

THE revolution thus wisely planned, secretly matured, and happily executed, was now complete. Portugal had recovered her independence, and replaced the legitimate descendant and representative of her ancient sovereigns upon the throne. João IV was crowned on the 15th of December, and immediately abolished the heavy taxes imposed by the king of Spain, declaring that, for his own private expenses, he required nothing beyond his patrimonial estates. He summoned the cortes to assemble in January, when the three estates of the kingdom solemnly confirmed his proclamation as king, or acclamation, as the Portuguese term it, probably to express the spontaneous unanimity with which he was chosen. The cortes further acknowledged his eldest son Theodosio as heir-apparent; and voted ample supplies of men and money, to resist the expected Spanish invasion.

In the islands, in the African settlements, with the single exception of Ceuta, which adhered to Spain, and in what remained of Brazil and India, King João was proclaimed, the moment intelligence of the revolution arrived, the Spaniards scarcely anywhere attempting to resist. In Brazil the viceroy communicated the tidings to Count Maurice of Nassau, the governor of the Dutch conquests, who ordered public rejoicings for the emancipation of Portugal; but Nassau refused either to restore his conquests to their legitimate possessor, or even to desist from further aggression. The Dutch governors and admirals in India proved equally unaccommodating.

In Europe, the new king was readily acknowledged by all the states at war with the house of Austria. He concluded treaties of alliance with France, England, Sweden, and even with Holland, colonial affairs being, in the last instance, reserved for future negotiation and adjustment. The pope refused to receive João's ambassador; and the Spanish ambassador at Rome, with the aid of a band of assassins, attempted his life. Several persons were slain on both sides, though the intended victim escaped.

It is possible that, had Olivares immediately applied himself with vigour to reduce Portugal, unarmed as she then was, with an empty exchequer and an unorganised government, she might have been again subjugated. Fortunately for her the count-duke looked upon the insurrection with a contempt that averted the danger. He announced the event to Philip, by wishing him joy of the forfeiture of the duke of Braganza's large estates; and, influenced partly by disdain for the Portuguese, partly by excessive exasperation against the Catalans, he positively rejected all advice to send against Portugal the army preparing for Catalonia. He thus gave Portugal all she needed — time; and a very few months saw her in a condition to maintain and defend the independence she had recovered. Olivares was not, indeed, altogether inactive with regard to Portugal and her king, but his measures were rather those of a petty intriguer than of a great statesman. He prevailed upon the emperor, Ferdinand III, to seize and imprison João's brother Dom Duarte, who was then serving as a general in the imperial armies. He appears like-wise to have instigated the plots and conspiracies by which the new Portu-guese government was, for a while, considerably disturbed. The first of these was perhaps the most formidable, being conducted by the primate, the inquisi-tor-general, and many of the chief nobility, including some connected, by blood or marriage, with João. Not less than six hundred persons, of different ranks, are said to have been concerned in the plot, the object of which was to kill the king and submit Portugal again to Spain. Various stories are told as to how the conspiracy was detected. The following seems the most probable. The archbishop, it is said, endeavoured to seduce the Count of Vimisis to join in the scheme, relying on that nobleman's supposed anger at his ill treatment by the king, who had deprived him of the government of Alemtejo. The prelate had mistaken his man. The count's loyalty was superior to his resentment, and the aggrieved nobleman immediately revealed the plot to the king.

The whole project was known to the government, and preparations were quietly made for defeating it; a grand review was ordered, and the principal ringleaders were invited to the palace for the occasion. They went fear-lessly, were there made prisoners without difficulty, and the number of troops present prevented any rising in the city. The prisoners were tried and con-victed; about ten persons were executed; the primate and inquisitor-general were imprisoned for life; and the remainder were pardoned. The duchess of Mantua was sent back to Spain, under the idea that she had fomented the conspiracy; and the only person for whom Dom Duarte might have been exchanged being thus dismissed, the unhappy prince languished out the remainder of his days in prison. The next plot was entirely hatched at Madrid, where Olivares engaged a Portuguese fugitive to murder João. The man made every arrangement, but his courage failed him at sight of his intended victim, and he fled, without perpetrating his meditated crime. By increased bribes, Olivares induced the villain to renew the attempt, when he was betrayed by an accomplice, seized, and executed. A base fraud, contrived to deprive the king of the ablest of his ministers, Lucena, secretary of state, answered better.

The two countries were now decidedly at war, but their languid and desultory hostilities produced little effect beyond harassing the frontiers. Portugal was weak, and thought only of self-defence; Spain was chiefly intent upon chastising the Catalans.[b]

The Portuguese were at first successful, and after the defeat which Mathias de Albuquerque inflicted on the baron of Molingen at Montijo on May 26th, 1644, felt at their ease, until it became obvious that Mazarin would desert them without compunction if it suited his purpose. The colonial war with Holland deprived them of the assistance of the Dutch in

Europe.   Mazarin's refusal to insist on their independence at the congress at Münster, though he protected their envoys against the Spaniards, made them despondent ; and a very curious letter of Mazarin's (October 4th, 1647), offering the crown of Portugal to the duke of Longueville, exhibits at once the feeble character of João IV [who had timidly offered to abdicate], the despair of the Portuguese, and their dependence on France.   Mazarin's desertion did not at first do great harm, for the war between France and Spain continued, though peace was made with the empire.[c]   In the war which, notwithstanding their alliance in Europe, the Portuguese prosecuted against the Dutch in their colonies, they displayed much of their original valour and energy.   In Brazil they gradually recovered their lost possessions.[b] But if the arms of João were successful in Brazil and Africa, in India they met with many reverses.   In several engagements the Dutch had the advantage ; and, in 1655, they succeeded in wholly expelling the Portuguese from the island of Ceylon.

João died in 1656.   His eldest son, Prince Theodosio, preceded him to the tomb.   Three other children survived him : (1) Catherine, married to Charles II king of England ; (2) the infante Alfonso, who, by the death of Theodosio, was heir to the monarchy ; (3) the infante Pedro, who, as we shall soon perceive, succeeded Alfonso.

ALFONSO VI (1656-1667 A.D.)

As the new king was only in his thirteenth year, and had exhibited no proofs of understanding, but a waywardness which would have adorned a savage, the queen-mother was intrusted with the regency.

The administration of this princess — a lady of the house of Guzman, her father being the eighth duke of Medina Sidonia — was distinguished for prudence and spirit.   As a Castilian, she was at first obnoxious to the people, who suspected that she must have a leaning towards her own country ; but the vigour with which she prepared for war, and the perseverance with which she conducted it, prove that the suspicion was injurious.   We cannot advert to the interminable and trifling events which followed, where the combat of a few hundreds is described with as much minuteness as if whole nations had been embattled on each side ; where the destruction of a hundred enemies is hailed with as much exultation as if the force of Attila had been annihilated ; and the whole campaign was disgraced by the most deplorable imbecility, on the part both of the Portuguese and the Spanish leaders, until the count de Schomberg and Don John of Austria were opposed to each other.   After the Peace of the Pyrenees, between France and Spain, when Catalonia was pacified, and the Spanish troops were at liberty to turn their undivided force against Portugal, no doubt was entertained that this country would be subdued.   But the queen-regent did not neglect to strengthen the national cause by alliances.   Some French, Dutch, and English adventurers, under Schomberg, were obtained ; the infanta Catherine, with the fortress of Tangier and a large sum of money, were given to Charles II as the condition of his alliance, and for the aid of some English regiments.   Schomberg sustained so much opposition, so much jealousy and ill will from the chiefs associated with him, that he could not prevent Don John from obtaining some rapid successes.   Among them was the conquest of Evora.   But this advantage was soon neutralised by a signal victory attained over the Castilians ; it was still further improved by the recovery of Evora — both monuments of Schomberg's ability and of English valour. Don John was deprived of the command. This change was fortunate for Portugal; for the new general was so signally defeated at Villaviciosa, that it may be said to have secured the independence of that kingdom. This was the last noted exploit during the reign of Alfonso.

During these hostilities the court of Lisbon exhibited strange scenes. The depraved tastes, the low and profligate habits, the headstrong perversity of the king daily acquired strength, and afforded a melancholy prospect to the nation. He associated with the lowest of the people; he introduced them into his palace; or accompanied them in nocturnal expeditions, undertaken as much for bloodshed as for mere mischief. His band of young companions became the terror of the capital. By his caprices several youths are said to have been tortured to death; and young girls to have suffered a still worse fate: all his diversions partook of his savage and capricious character. So long as he confined them to boxing in the ring, to wrestling, or to breaking the windows by night, the citizens, however scandalised at such conduct, did not much complain; but when their daughters were seduced, or their sons ill used by the royal satellites, even they began to think that a king might do wrong. When common prostitutes were brought to the palace, which was thereby converted into a brothel, their indignation yielded to contempt. The influence of the queen was ineffectual. At length the indignant nobles, at her instigation, forcibly seized two brothers, the vilest and most dangerous of his satellites, and sent them away to Brazil; but other creatures were found to supply their place.

With all his stupidity, the royal brute felt that he was a king; he knew that the time of his majority was long past; he insisted on being invested with the regal authority in all its extent; and, after a struggle between him and his mother, he forced her, in June, 1662, to resign the regency. The removal of so salutary a rein on his excesses could not fail to make things worse. The licentious youths with whom he surrounded himself disgusted by their conduct the oldest servants of the crown, and forced them to retreat from their public offices. His own extravagances increased. His satellites paraded the streets, or scoured the highways, night and day; they not unfrequently returned with plunder, oftener still with their swords stained with blood. We are told that he even charged the people in a public procession; that he instigated the assassination of some obnoxious nobles; that, to show his contempt of a comet which was believed to be the forerunner of some great change, he fired a pistol at it, at the same time reviling it with the lowest terms of scurrility.

It was hoped that, if a wife were procured him, he would, at least, refrain from some excesses; and one was found in Mademoiselle d'Aumale, daughter of the duke of Nemours. But he treated his beautiful queen with open neglect; he disregarded alike her entreaties, her tears, and her remonstrances; nor did the death of his mother make the slightest change in his conduct.

But the strangest part of these transactions remains to be told. That the queen-mother had resigned her authority with reluctance is certain; that she had entertained thoughts of procuring the transfer of the sceptre from Alfonso to Pedro is confirmed by the general tenor of her actions. It is no less true that Pedro aspired to supplant his brother; that he intrigued with the nobles and prelates for that end; and that, by the outward decorum of his conduct, by a scrupulous regard to the decencies of his station, he laboured to make the contrast between himself and the king too marked to be overlooked. Equally certain it is that no one observed this contrast more narrowly than

the youthful queen, who soon formed a suspicious connection with the infante.
That their plans for the future were soon arranged, is evident enough from
the sequel. When Pedro's plans were matured, when he had interested
a considerable party in his behalf, he sought an open rupture — and he had
causes enough — with the king. In October, 1667, a furious mob, which
had been gained by his emissaries, conducted him to the palace, insisting that
justice should be done him on his enemies. On the 21st of November, the
queen hastily left the palace, and retired to the convent of St. Francis. Her
pretext was the ill-usage she hourly received from Alfonso. The true reason
for so extraordinary a step appeared in a letter in which, after adverting to
her domestic sorrows, she surprised the public by saying that her marriage
was, from its origin, null ; that it had never been consummated.

The perusal of this extraordinary letter filled Alfonso with indignant
wonder. He hastened to the convent, and on being refused admission, he
ordered the gates to be broken ; but his brother, arriving with an escort, persuaded or compelled him to depart. No sooner was he retired, than the
infante had a long interview with her. The subject of their conversation
appeared from a letter to the chapter of Lisbon, which contained the same
charge of impotence against the king. The counsellors of state forced him to
sign an act of renunciation. He was then arrested, and sentenced to perpetual confinement, but with permission to enjoy the comforts of life. In
conclusion, Pedro was proclaimed regent ; and, in that character, was recognised by an assembly of the states. By his creatures, the same states were
persuaded to petition the queen, who no longer showed any inclination to
leave the kingdom, that she would accept the hand of so deserving a prince.
She required no solicitation. Her uncle the cardinal Vendôme, anxious that
his family should contain a queen, expedited it without delay. The marriage
was celebrated in haste, lest a papal inhibition should arrive, and blast the fruit
of so many intrigues. Subsequently, an application was made to the pope, to
confirm the dispensation of the cardinal ; and Clement, who saw that the
mischief was done, admitted the allegation of impotence, and despatched
the brief of confirmation.

Thus concluded one of the most extraordinary scenes that has ever been
exhibited to the eyes of mankind — extraordinary alike for effrontery and
duplicity. However the constitution of Alfonso might have been impaired
by debauchery, he was not impotent. No one labouring under such a dis-
ability would have been at the trouble either of visiting the public stews or
of introducing women of loose morals into the palace. But, without insisting on this presumptive evidence, we are positively informed that Alfonso
had one child at least by his favourite mistress. If the *debitum conjugale* had
never been paid, why should a circumstance so important to the kingdom be
concealed during sixteen months ? Why should it be mentioned, for the first
time, when Pedro was ready to usurp the crown ? The whole proceeding is
explicable enough. The queen felt that she was neglected ; she admired the
infante, and was gained by him as an accessory to the long meditated plot of
dethroning the king. The means adopted by these paramours were even
more daring, more indicative of the contempt with which they regarded
public opinion, than the end itself.

Before this iniquitous consummation of ambition and lust, Pedro had the
glory of ending the long dispute with Spain. Both nations were exhausted
by their past exertions, and both naturally inclined for peace. It was concluded at Lisbon, under the mediation of Charles II, king of England. By
it all conquests made by either party were restored, and the subjects of each

nation admitted to the privileges enjoyed by the most favoured people. The arms of Portugal were immediately erased from the escutcheon of the Spanish monarchy. This was almost the only transaction of moment in which the regent was engaged, from his marriage to the death of Alfonso. There was, indeed, a conspiracy formed to restore that prince; but it was easily detected and its authors punished. That unfortunate monarch was first removed to the Azores; and then transferred to the palace of Cintra, where, in 1683, he ended his days. The same year was fatal to the queen, who left no other issue than a daughter, the infanta Isabella.

PEDRO II (1683-1706 A.D.); JOÃO V (1706-1750 A.D.)

On the death of Alfonso, the coronation of the new king was celebrated with the usual pomp and circumstance. His reign, like his regency, was passed in profound peace, and consequently furnishes no materials for history, until the celebrated War of the Spanish Succession, following the demise of Charles II, called him into the field. The motives which induced him to take part with the allies against Philip V have been already explained, and the chief events of the war have been related in the history of Spain.[1]

During the reigns of Alfonso and Pedro, the affairs of India continually declined. The Dutch, the most persevering enemies that ever assailed the Portuguese empire in the East, not satisfied with the richest settlements in Malacca and in the India islands, prepared to expel the subjects of his most faithful majesty from the continent. The latter were insulted, sometimes defeated, within sight of Goa. In 1660, they blockaded the bar of Goa, thereby preventing the annual sailing of merchandise for Lisbon. Bombay was delivered to the English. In 1665, Diu was plundered by the Mohammedans, three thousand of the inhabitants being led into hopeless captivity, the rest put to the sword. Finally, Cochin was reduced by the king of Travancore, and the Portuguese empire in India was confined to Goa, Diu, and a few commercial settlements on the coast of Malabar and in the islands. The African and Brazilian possessions continued unimpaired.

By his second queen, a princess of Bavaria, Pedro had several children, most of whom, however, died either in infancy or without issue. He was succeeded, in 1706, by the infante João, born in 1688.[e]

Dom Pedro's successor was but eighteen years of age. Lacking in experience and doubtless desirous of equalling his father's glory, he did not know how to get out of the dangerous political course which Portugal was pursuing and he continued to take part in the war of succession to the sole profit of England and Holland. This persistence was all the more deplorable as

[1 "On December 27th, 1703, the famous Methuen Treaty was signed, by which Portuguese wines might be imported into England at a lower duty than those from France and Germany, in return for a similar concession to English manufactured goods. The immediate result of this treaty was that King Pedro acknowledged the archduke Charles, the English candidate, as king of Spain, and that he gave the English a base of operations in the peninsula. The ulterior result was that Englishmen in the eighteenth century drank port wine instead of claret and hock, while the Portuguese imported everything they wanted beyond the bare necessaries of life from England. This was an advantage to both nations, for Portugal is eminently an agricultural country with neither the teeming population nor the materials necessary for manufactures, while England obtained a friendly province from which to import the wine and produce of a southern soil, and a market for the sale of the products of her manufactures. The close connection thus formed went deeper than mere commerce; it established a friendly relationship between the two peoples, which was of infinite advantage to the smaller nation."—STEPHENS.[d]

We shall see later that the Portuguese felt the treaty less a blessing than an incubus on their power to develop manufactures of their own.]

the success of the allies in Spain was not long maintained. Scarcely had João V become king when Philip V returned to Madrid in the midst of enthusiastic acclamations and the duke of Berwick achieved over the combined forces of De las Minas and Galway the brilliant victory of Almansa (April 25th, 1707). The Portuguese, against whom the efforts of the Spanish and French were especially directed, lost thirteen regiments and they were unable to hold the positions they had taken. Far from profiting by the hard lesson that fortune had administered to him, João V lost no time in rebinding through marriage the political alliances that his father had adopted; he married Maria Anna of Austria, sister of the emperor Joseph I and of the archduke Charles, Philip V's rival, and celebrated this brilliant union with the most magnificent fêtes that Portugal had ever seen.

All this did not prevent Philip's taking each day a more marked advantage. Victor at Badajoz, victor at Villaviciosa, he invaded Portugal in turn; it became evident that whatever else might happen this prince would at least keep the crown of Castile. The victory of the allies at Saragossa completely disappeared amid all these disasters. But what was much more unfortunate still was that Portugal nearly lost Brazil, which was the sole possession that would permit her henceforth to cut some sort of figure in the world. It was the very moment when new explorers had just discovered the opulent mines of Goyaz and the Matto-Grosso that a Spanish-French fleet under the command of the valiant Duguay-Trouin put in an appearance. Powerful with its seven vessels and eight frigates it had no difficulty in forcing the channel to Rio de Janeiro, and after it had landed its forces there was no resistance (September 14th, 1711). Soldiers and inhabitants quickly evacuated the town, taking refuge with their valuables in the neighbouring mountains. Brazil's fate would doubtless have been settled there and then had it not been for the grave troubles with which France was at that time overwhelmed, and especially for the small number of soldiers assigned to the expedition. Duguay-Trouin had to content himself with sacking Rio de Janeiro and making it pay a ransom of 600,000 cruzados. Instead of a conqueror he was only a devastator, but he went far towards making the Portuguese appreciate all the advantages of the English alliance, and brought back to exhausted France a booty of over twenty-five millions of francs.

The Portuguese, however, were still more convinced by the events which were taking place at the same time in Europe. In taking part in the prolonged quarrels of which Charles II's succession had been the source, England had but a single aim in view — to inflame the whole of western Europe and take advantage of the conflagration to obtain ascendency over the seas. Just as soon as she had obtained her end by destroying the remains of the French and Spanish navy, by reducing Portugal to the state of a colony, and by making herself sure of the Mediterranean by the rascally occupation of Gibraltar and Minorca, then, having no further interest in continuing the war, she withdrew and was the first to accept Louis XIV's proposals. But what could the powerless João V do without her? He had to come to terms, or be conquered; and lost in negotiating all the fine hopes that the allies had held before his eyes. The Peace of 1713 with France simply stipulated that the most Christian king renounce all claims upon Brazil, that King Philip V would arrange matters in a manner agreeable to Portugal, and that England would be responsible for the carrying out of the agreed-upon conditions. That of February 6th, 1715, with Philip V gave the territory and colony of Colonia del Sacramento to Portugal in exchange for Albuquerque which had been taken from Castile. And so all the money spent and all the blood spilled, devoted, after all, to establishing England's supremacy, had brought nothing to Portugal but an impoverished and subdued kingdom, unless we may consider as sufficient consolation João V's honour of being mentioned first in the text of the treaty.

Scarcely had João emerged from this terrible twelve years' struggle when the Venetians asked his assistance against the Ottomans. Too devout to reject such a petition, he hastened to send them the count of Rio Grande and a few ships, without any other object than that of sustaining the Christians against the infidels. But in spite of all the great questions over which Europe was still divided, this war was henceforth the only war into which he let himself be dragged. On the contrary he took care to maintain the friendliest relations with Castile, which he should never have ceased to do. He made this union the closer by two marriages — that of his eldest son José, prince of Brazil, with Doña Maria Anna Victoria, daughter of Philip V; and that of the infanta Maria Barbara with the prince of the Asturias (1728). Perhaps we may even reproach João V with having carried his desire to oblige Spain too far by giving up the Philippines and by exchanging the rich colony of Colonia del Sacramento, with all the northern region of La Plata, for a few small colonies in Paraguay, between the Ibicuhy and the Uruguay, which the Jesuits, possessors of all the territory, did not wish to give up (1750). But by this time João V was dying, and the Recollet friar, Gaspard de Incarnação, who ruled in his name, was solely responsible for this foolish concession.

The Colonies Decline

At peace with Europe and patronised by England, did not João V employ at least a portion of the daily increasing wealth which Brazil poured into his hands to maintain the few colonies which still remained to him in the Indies? He did nothing of the kind; and while the Mahrattas drove the Portuguese from Sandomir, Salsette, Thana, Barcain, Senapour, and Karanja, the Dutch, English, and French had every reason to claim the domination of the Orient. In a short time the viceroys of the Indies, no longer daring to inhabit the ancient palace of the Albuquerques and the Castros, lived modestly in the small village of Panjim. What had become of magnificent Goa, and Diu, and Calicut, queen of Malabar? They were already nothing but ruins; a century had sufficed to reduce a powerful empire to a pile of rubbish.

Far from devoting to useful enterprise the riches which fortune showered upon him, João V let the navy, army, and administration constantly decline. He seemed to have no other aim than to emulate the pomp of Louis XIV; but he forgot that Louis reigned over France and that the latter found all the elements of the luxury he displayed in the industry of the kingdom, while Portugal could not obtain them except by exhausting herself to the profit of foreigners. Such was João V's generosity with his courtiers, his mistresses, his feasts, and his buildings that, with the great nobles following his example, poverty soon arrived, in spite of America. It has been estimated that between 1699 and 1756 there came from Brazil 2,400,000,000 francs, and that Portugal retained but a very small portion. All the rest, that is to say nearly nine-tenths, went to England, either in exchange for merchandise or as the price of transporting the metal, which became hers after all.

It was not sufficient that England should levy such a tribute on Portuguese indolence. Not less zealous for his religious practices than for his pleasures, João V had the idea of establishing a patriarchal legate at Lisbon, and before Rome could agree to this he had to expend enormous sums. He did the same in order that Portugal might possess under this legate a Latin church almost the equal of St. Peter's, and this contained not less than sixty-six mitred canons at a salary of 5,000 cruzados each. Add to this the construction of the magnificent monastery of Mafra for three hundred monks, with its park twelve miles in length, the gorgeous procession, the collections of pious books to which the public was not allowed access, and what is worse still, the *auto-da-fé* which the Inquisition made him celebrate with great pomp, and we can realise that he spent on all this appearance of religion at least 500,000,000 francs. It is true that he was recompensed. Grateful Rome granted him the title of "most faithful king" in 1748.

While such follies are discrediting the reign, is it permissible to rehabilitate a prince because he founded a Portuguese academy or an academy of history — because he softened the national manners almost to enervation — because he introduced into his country French customs and Italian music in place of a real civilisation whose establishment the Inquisition would however never have tolerated? But how explain, on the other hand, that far from cursing João V's memory, the Portuguese have always held it in great veneration? It was because the riches of Brazil struck them all with the same giddiness as they struck him, because his ostentatious piety conformed to the tastes of the nation, because if he fought with his ministers and occupied himself more with theological disputes than with government, he was accessible and kind to all his subjects, and could use those happy words which too often take the place of real merit.

The esteem given João V by Portugal seems to us to be his own condemnation. What is war without greatness, peace without prosperity, devotion without piety? And in these words we may sum up João's reign. We shall not dwell on the final extinction of the ancient Portuguese liberties whose form had at least survived. João V never convoked the cortes until public tranquillity was threatened with some blow, and yet no one protested. The régime of the Inquisition had produced its usual effect.

The last years of João V were as sad as the others had been brilliant. Stricken with paralysis in 1744, he found a little relief in the baths of Caldas da Rainha, but this treatment soon ceased to benefit him, and he could do nothing put pass the rest of his existence far from the luxury and fêtes of which he had been so fond. Thenceforth the king of Portugal was the Recollet Gaspard, who, with even less ability in the art of government than his master, had at least the merit of proving himself more economical. For some time João had contracted the costly habit of having masses for all the Portuguese of whose deaths he could learn. Gaspard took care to deceive him as to the deaths which occurred in Lisbon, lest he should send, as they said, all the living to hell in getting the dead out of purgatory.*f*

João died in July, 1750. By his queen, Maria Anna of Austria, João had a numerous issue; but three children only survived him — Maria Barbara, queen of Spain, his successor, José, and the infante Dom Pedro.*e*

THE REIGN OF JOSÉ I

On September 7th, 1750, the new king was proclaimed with all the usual pomp and circumstance. He found the treasury empty, the army existing in name only; but, as someone has remarked with a certain semblance of accuracy, he found the popular instincts directed towards commerce, and a remarkable readiness to enter on a path of ameliorated industries. But none the less the Methuen Treaty was at that time manifesting all its consequences, and laid a spell of inertia on the most active minds, even on those who, by their continual contact with a commercial and manufacturing nation, were filled with dreams for their country of improvements which only a strong and independent genius could bring about.

At this epoch Brazil had become an inexhaustible resource for the mother-country in all financial embarrassments. December, 1750, witnessed the arrival at Lisbon of the fleet, richly loaded, on which so many hopes were built each succeeding year. From a generous impulse, for which the colonies were most grateful to him, one of the new king's first acts was aimed at the political betterment of the rich province of Minas from which he drew so much of his wealth ; he abolished the poll-tax, which was paid as a right of seigniory, and in 1751 he established at Rio de Janeiro a tribunal of *relaçao* [*i.e.*, a court of appeal], a real and well-felt advantage for that country, since in former times trials of any importance lasted an eternity, being brought to Lisbon for judgment.

But with the question of important improvements, and the directing of wide measures, the name of one other than the reigning sovereign flows involuntarily from the historian's pen — that of the great statesman Pombal, who gave his country so mighty an impulse. To José belongs the supreme merit of discerning the merits of this extraordinary man. There is perhaps something of injustice in comparing the king with Louis XIII, as is so frequently done ; for he had at all events sufficient firmness of character always to approve the acts of the man he had willingly chosen. On January 19th, 1729, José I had married (during his father's lifetime) Doña Maria Anna Victoria, daughter of Philip V and Elizabeth Farnese. This lady should have married Louis XV and had never become wholly resigned to the bitterness of her memories. In politics she was not only always opposed to France, but, later, she openly posed as a formidable enemy to the powerful man to whose hands her royal husband had intrusted the destinies of the nation.*g*

The Great Minister Pombal

Sebastião José de Carvalho e Mello,[1] who was created count of Oeyras and afterwards marquis of Pombal, whom we shall hereafter call by the last and shortest name, had been introduced to King João V, who was a person of a sickly constitution ; he however made himself intolerable to the king by his incessant fertility in plans and projects. In order to remove him from the court, he was first sent on some trifling affairs to London, and secondly upon business of graver importance to Vienna. In these cities he became acquainted with the French philosophy and the new theories of political economy and state-craft, and convinced that the Jesuits, who exercised unlimited dominion in Portugal, and had the whole system of instruction completely in their hands, had kept his countrymen more than a century behind the spirit of the age. The queen of Portugal, who was an Austrian princess, had the management of the government during the very frequent attacks of absence of mind and incapacity under which her husband laboured.

[1 Pombal was born in 1699 of a wealthy and well-connected family, entered in the army as a private, but saw no service and retired ; he then led a life of roistering notoriety, and had eloped with a niece of the count of Arcos. He was forty years old before he had an official position, and fifty-one before he became minister to the king.]

Pombal had been employed by her in the execution of affairs of various kinds in Vienna, and he no sooner married her friend the countess Daun, than she resolved to recall him from his embassy and to take him into the ministry in Lisbon.

King João died immediately after the arrival of Pombal in Lisbon, and it was very easy for Pombal to make himself indispensable. The young king was of an indolent character, shrunk from every effort, was licentious and extravagant, but entertained a childish fear of his wife, from whom he carefully concealed his amours. He was as superstitious as the humblest peasant of his superstitious nation, he was as cowardly as Pombal was courageous, and the latter kept him in such a continual state of suspicion and anxiety that the king from fear resigned everything into his hands in order to secure his favour and protection.

Wraxall,[i] who only first became acquainted with Pombal when he was seventy years of age, speaks of his features, his giant build, and his language as characteristic of all that energy which he had exhibited for twenty-seven years in the public administration; it would appear therefore as if nature had from the first designed him for a reformer and dictator. In order to lessen and correct our ideas of the cruelties which he practised in his reforms, we must remember that in Asia, Africa, and southern Europe our cold and tedious morality is completely unknown, and compensated for by warm feelings of religion, which take heaven by violence; and, moreover, no one except a monarchical Danton or Robespierre would have been able to snatch Portugal from its state of powerless subjection to the institutions of the Middle Ages. Pombal appeared to have been raised up to organise a monarchical system of terror, and he alone could have succeeded in bringing Portugal nearer to the other states of Europe and to the spirit of the new age.

The first contest of the minister after he was firmly seated in his position was that with the order of Jesuits. The Jesuits were regarded by him as a dangerous independent aristocracy, and as the guardians of the secrets of the confessional of almost all the princes and nobles of Europe, far beyond the reach of any secular arm. In Portugal, in particular, the order, by the possession and use of great wealth acquired by trade, and of a flourishing colony, threatened the complete oppression of the state, which was entirely in its power. Shortly before Pombal became minister the order of the Jesuits had obtained a temporal dominion in Paraguay in America, secured for themselves all the privileges of government and legislation, and threatened to draw the whole trade of private individuals to themselves by various speculations and large commercial adventures in the Antilles and the European ports. The order was in ill-repute for its casuistry, by virtue of which regicide and bankruptcy might be equally justified, as Arnauld and Pascal had proved in the preceding century. The danger of allowing such an order first to sustain speculators by its credit and then to allow them to fail, had been so clearly proved in Pombal's time in the superior courts in France, that the parliament at that time zealously pressed for the abolition of the order. The pope himself had issued very severe orders in 1741 against the practices of slave-dealing, usury, and banking, in which the order had engaged. In February, 1741, Benedict XIV published a bull, by which, without naming the Jesuits in particular, all orders whatsoever and all ecclesiastics were strictly forbidden to engage in any description of trade or commerce, to exercise any temporal authority, or to interfere with the sale or purchase of the converts. This bull failed in producing its intended effect, and in December another was issued expressly against the Jesuits. The latter, entitled *Immensa pastorum*, which is remarkable as being the first manifesto published by the pope against the order of Jesuits, was particularly directed against their conduct in their missions in Asia and Africa, in Brazil and Paraguay.

The bold spirit of usurpation which the Jesuits continued to display, notwithstanding the pope's first bull, after having caused the *Immensa pastorum* to be launched against them, urged Pombal also to the adoption of his first strong measures against this dangerous order. In their missions in Paraguay, both in the portions which acknowledged Portugal as their sovereign state as well as those which acknowledged the supremacy of Spain, they had contrived to obtain complete possession of the secular administration, by having secured for themselves the most extraordinary privileges from the kings and queens of these nations, who were entirely subject to their guidance and dominion. No Spaniard or Portuguese was suffered to set foot in their missions without their special permission. The pope in his bull, under threats of the greater excommunication, forbade all and each, and the Jesuits expressly by name, to make slaves of the Indians, to sell, exchange, or make presents of them, to separate them from their wives and children, to despoil them of their property, or to injure or molest them in any other way whatsoever.

Later, Spain ceded the district of Puy in Galicia and the seven missions of the Jesuits in Paraguay, and obtained in return Colonia del Sacramento. This exchange led to disputes with the Jesuits, and finally even gave rise to military expeditions on the part of the Spaniards and Portuguese against the Indians : the Indians themselves were highly dissatisfied with the cession of Paraguay to Portugal. The active resistance of the Indians led the Spaniards and Portuguese to meet force by force, and a formal contest arose, which led to no very conclusive or satisfactory results as long as the matter was wholly left to the three thousand Spaniards and the thousand Portuguese who had been sent to aid and carry into effect the objects of the commissioners ; in the year 1753 Pombal adopted different measures. He sent a considerable army into the district, gave the command of it to his brother, Francisco Xavier Mendoza, conferred upon him the office of governor of the province, and intrusted him secretly with full power to destroy and forever put an end to the secular dominion of the Jesuits in this territory. The last part of the commission was kept a profound secret, and Pombal also delayed its execution till the death of the dowager queen of Portugal, who was a blindly devoted adherent to the order. These severe measures against the Jesuits were first carried fully into operation in the year 1755, in which the capital of Portugal was visited and almost destroyed by one of the most dreadful earthquakes which has ever occurred in Europe.*h*

The Earthquake at Lisbon (*November 1st, 1755*)

Denis*g* quotes a letter from Pedegache, who was an eye-witness of the horror : " On the 1st of November, 1755, with a quiet atmosphere and a very clear sky, the earth shook, but so slightly that everyone fancied the vibration was due to some rapidly moving vehicle. This first trembling lasted two minutes ; after two minutes' interval there was a repetition of the trembling, but so violent a one that the greater number of the houses began to crack and to fall down : this second trembling continued for upwards of ten minutes. By that time the dust was so great as to obscure the sun. Then came a shock so awful that the houses which were still standing fell with a deaf-ening crash. It seemed as if the earth were returning to chaos. The tears and cries of the living, the sighs and groans of the dying, the shuddering of the earth, the total darkness, all added to the horror of the scene. But at last, after twenty minutes, all became quiet. One thought then filled every mind — flight, and a refuge in the country. But our cup of misery was not yet full. Scarcely had we begun to breathe again when fire broke out in different parts of the town.[1] The wind, which was very boisterous, fanned the flames and left no room for hope.

"Possibly something might have been done to check the fire had not the town been threatened with wide submergence by the sea ; at all events the terrified inhabitants easily persuaded themselves that this danger was in store for them, seeing waves breaking furiously over places far removed from the shore. Several people believing that they would find a certain amount of safety on the water ventured on it ; but the waves drove the vessels on shore, grinding them one against another, then drawing them seawards with merci-less violence as though they would swallow them and the miserable beings clinging to them.

"During all these days our terror has never abated, for the shocks are incessant. On Friday, November 7th, at five o'clock in the morning, there was a shock so violent we imagined our troubles were about to recommence ; but happily it was followed by no disastrous consequences. The movement was regular, like that of a rolling vessel. What caused such devastation on the first day was that all the movements were contrary and so exactly opposed to each other that the walls parted with the utmost facility. I have noticed that the strongest shocks are always at daybreak. They say that the sea came up nine feet higher than the highest tide ever remembered in Portugal. On Sunday morning, November 2nd, I saw with the utmost amazement the Tagus, which in some reaches is more than two leagues wide, almost dried up on the city side ; the other side was a feeble little stream through which one could see the bed. Almost the whole of Portugal has felt this scourge ; the kingdom of Algarve, Santarem, Setubal, Oporto, Mafra, Obidos, Castanheira — indeed all the towns within twenty leagues are destroyed. I write to you from the depths of the country, for there is not a habitable house left. Lisbon has vanished !"

Everyone, from the monarch down to the meanest beggar, had something to deplore. In the town of Lisbon alone thirty thousand persons had perished, and, if one can trust the calculations which were made later, the losses in valuable furniture and in hard cash reached the enormous total of £91,360,000 or $456,800,000. In short, such were the results of this terrible catastrophe that more than twenty years after Dumouriez k was still able to say : "Lisbon is an appalling agglomeration of overturned palaces, burned churches, of rubbish such as one sees when a fortification has been blown up. In many places one walks over the sites of houses, in streets contrived on the rubbish thrown up on either side to allow of roadway being made. Here and there one sees reared up isolated houses, and ruins as grotesque, as grimly beautiful, as the remains of Greek and Roman buildings." g

[1 This was blamed to incendiaries, though it was inevitable that in such a falling of walls many houses should be set on fire without human aid, though humankind were ready enough to seize the chance for loot. A large part of the people fled to the quays to escape the falling build-ings, but there a great tidal wave found them and sweeping the wharves clean drowned men, women, and children in thousands. Voltaire's Candide includes a notable account of the catas-trophe. Estimates of the loss run from fifteen thousand to one hundred thousand lives ; thirty thousand being the most generally accepted.]

The whole population of Lisbon continued throughout the winter in tents or huts in the fields. The distress was extreme in every part of Portugal, and called forth, as has been already stated, the pity of all neighbouring nations. In Spain, Ferdinand deeply sympathised in his queen's sorrow for her countrymen, and repealed the existing prohibitions of exporting some of the necessaries of life, and the heavy duties imposed upon the export of others, as related to Portugal. In England, though the claim might be less, more was done. George II applied to parliament for the means of relieving a people so severely afflicted ; and the sum of £100,000 [$500,000] was immediately granted for that purpose. The ministers expended it in corn and other articles of provisions or indispensable necessaries, which were shipped off without a moment's delay to the desolated city. The Portuguese felt gratitude both for the benefits conferred and for the kindly fellow-feeling that had prompted the act ; and the old ties of friendship between England and Portugal seem to have regained much of their previously decaying strength.[b]

Pombal and the Jesuits

The measures which Pombal adopted on account of and after the earthquake, although in themselves prudent and humane, were enforced in a severe and arbitrary manner. He caused the public granaries to be thrown open, because hundreds of persons who had not been buried under the ruins, or killed by the falling buildings, were wandering about like ghosts and dying from hunger. He adopted measures for the immediate import of grain from all quarters, abolished the duties on corn, and strictly forbade the export of provisions of any description. The water-conduits which had been destroyed were also immediately restored and carefully maintained.[1] The indescribable misery which resulted from this calamity gave occasion to murders and plunder in such a country as Portugal. Pombal applied remedies for this evil also, but by the use of most horrible means. Thieves and robbers, regardless of the most imminent dangers, and urged by their covetousness, ventured into streets which were masses of ruins, and carried away property from churches, palaces, and private houses before the very eyes of the inhabitants, who were trembling for their lives. To put an end to this fearful system of plunder, the minister ordered guards to be placed at all the outlets from the city and in every street, and summary justice to be executed upon everyone who either refused or was unable to give a satisfactory account of what he was carrying. Hundreds of gallows were erected around the circuit of the city which was filled with the dead and the dying, and with persons robbed of all their property and means even of present existence ; and on these gallows 350 people were hanged within three days.

At the very moment at which Pombal proved himself to be a delivering angel, and was devoting his labours day and night to the public preservation and the restoration of order, the clergy, and especially the Jesuits, endeavoured to expose him to the hatred of the people as an enemy of God. Sermons were preached against him from every pulpit, and a report was industriously put into circulation that the whole of their misfortunes, and even the earthquake itself, was a visitation of the divine wrath on account of Pombal's conduct towards the clergy. The Jesuits alleged that Pombal had roused the tumult in Oporto to involve them in its consequences.

[1 When the king in despair asked Pombal what was to be done, he replied, "Bury the dead and feed the living" ; he is said to have spent eight days and nights in his carriage hurrying from place to place.]

At Pombal's instigation, King José now signed the severe decree by which all Jesuits were banished from the court, which the minister caused to be executed after his own fashion. On the night between the 19th and the 20th of September, 1757, Pombal caused all the Jesuits at the court, then in Belem, at some distance from the capital, to be removed and conducted to Lisbon, and their places at court were immediately occupied by other ecclesiastics. This step against the court confessors was immediately followed by others against the whole order and its constitution.

In order to justify the steps taken against the Jesuits, and to induce all the monarchs in Europe to regard them as decided enemies of the temporal power of princes, Pombal had recourse to a remarkable expedient, which excited great attention throughout the whole of Europe. He published a manifesto against the order, which was eagerly read at all courts, produced a great effect in Austria, and enabled Kaunitz to prevail upon Maria Theresa to adopt many measures to which she never would have consented except for Pombal's publication.

Both these criminatory reports were sent to the Portuguese minister in Rome (October, 1757), and he was instructed to seek and obtain from Pope Benedict XIV, who was then mortally ill, a complete reform of the order; and as early as February, 1758, a new and urgent note on the same subject was presented to the papal court. The pope yielded to the solicitation and issued a brief in April, by which the patriarch, Cardinal Saldanha, was appointed to examine and reform the abuses of the order in the kingdom of Portugal.[h]

A Plot to Assassinate the King

Whilst the Jesuits and their accusers were battling before the tribunal of the visitor, a plot to murder the king was organised at Lisbon, in 1758, by two of the noblest families in the realm, the motives to which, as is often the case, were enveloped in obscurity; whence it was easy to implicate the Jesuits, whether guilty or not, in the criminal design.

The duke of Aveiro, the chief conspirator, who had been a great favourite of João V, was descended from Dom Jorge, that natural son of João II whom his father had endeavoured to substitute to his cousin Emmanuel as his successor; and a daughter of the duke's was married to the eldest son of his confederates, the marquis and marchioness of Tavora.[1] It has been surmised that the king, whose gallantries were notorious, was upon too intimate a footing with the young marchioness of Tavora, and that the two families resented such a stain upon their honour; it has been also surmised that the old marchioness, a woman of imperious temper and uncontrollable passions, was exasperated at having been refused a dukedom for her husband; and finally, it was alleged at the time that these two noble families were merely the tools of their Jesuit confessors, who sought by the king's death to quell the proceedings against their order.

What can be stated with certainty is that a young lady, a distant relative of the Tavora family, who resided with the old marchioness, was found dead, pierced with wounds and wrapped in a sheet, in one of the streets of Lisbon; that no judicial inquiry into the circumstances of her death took place (a mode of connivance not uncommon when suspicion of crime attached to powerful families); that soon afterwards, as the king was returning to the palace at night, from the residence of one of his mistresses [the marchioness of

[1 Lord Mahon[j] says: "His majesty had debauched, besides the marchioness of Tavora, both the wife and the daughter of the duke of Aveiro."]

Tavora], several shots were fired at the back of his carriage, one of which wounded him; and that the coachman, instead of going forwards to the palace, instantly turned his horses' heads, and drove to the house of the king's surgeon. It is believed that by this step he saved his master's life, as he thus avoided two or three other parties of assassins who were lying in wait on the road to the palace.

Some weeks elapsed ere the perpetrators of this outrage were detected, during which time Aveiro and Tavora were assiduous in their visits to the royal invalid. But in the end Pombal obtained a clew to the plot. A great number of persons were seized and imprisoned; and in January, 1759, as it is alleged, after a very arbitrary and unsatisfactory trial, the duke, the marquis, his two sons, and several other persons were broken on the wheel; the old marchioness, in consideration of her sex, was beheaded, and the young marchioness was shut up for life in a convent. Many persons were banished, and others imprisoned for life.

One of the conspirators is said, whilst under the torture, to have accused three Jesuits as the instigators of the conspiracy, but to have retracted this accusation upon the scaffold. Of these three Jesuits, one was tried for heresy, not treason, convicted, and executed; the other two were not even brought to trial; but Pombal took the opportunity to charge the crime upon the whole order, as the fruit of its principles and doctrines—an imputation to which their earlier conduct rendered the order but too obnoxious. He issued orders for the confiscation of their property, and the seizure of their persons, throughout Portugal and the colonies, as advisers and instigators of regicide, and for the investigation of their doctrines. In the month of September of this same year they were finally proscribed and banished.

The Exile of the Jesuits

The missionary fathers were torn from the reductions, and with all Jesuits who could be found in Brazil, old and young, even the patients in their infirmaries, were stowed on board ship, without any of the conveniences, or scarcely any of the necessaries of life, like the unfortunate negroes in slave vessels, and transported to Europe. Upon reaching the mouth of the Tagus, some were landed and thrown into the Lisbon prisons, where they languished during the remainder of José's reign; others were sent forward to Italy, where they were landed upon the papal territories, and left to find their way to the houses of their order. It is said, however, that an allowance was made from Lisbon for their support, and that Pombal often complained of the extraordinary longevity of his Jesuit pensioners.[1]

Pombal, who really appears to have been partly actuated by disgust at the slavery, however easy, in which the fathers had held their converts, and to have desired to place the Indians upon a level with their Portuguese masters, now endeavoured at once to effect this equalisation.[2] The scheme, if not extravagant, was at least premature.

In Portugal likewise, Pombal, though he succeeded better, attempted too much; and by his injudicious endeavours to secure to the Portuguese the profit made by foreign, and especially English merchants, he merely harassed

[1 See also the history of Spain for the account of the expulsion that resulted from Pombal's initiation.]

[2 By this celebrated decree of May 25th, 1773, grandsons of slaves in Portugal and all children born after that day were declared free, and all civil restrictions on the "New Christians" or the converted Jews and Moors were forever removed.]

and injured the trade of the country, without at all advancing the end at which he aimed. That end was in fact unattainable. To deprive the enterprising capitalist of his profits is very possible, but not so to transfer them to the indigent, ignorant, or unenterprising. Pombal moreover involved Portugal in a quarrel with Rome, by his endeavour to subject the clergy to a lay tribunal, a sort of board of conscience, when accused of high treason, or other state crimes. Prior to this rupture, a papal dispensation had been obtained for one of those incestuous connections so frequent in the peninsula, and more especially in Portugal. José had no son; and to insure the undisputed succession of his eldest daughter, Donna Maria, it was deemed expedient to marry her to her uncle, his younger brother, Dom Pedro. The dispensation was obtained, and the marriage celebrated in 1760.

War with Spain

The two Bourbon monarchs, Louis XV of France, and Charles III of Spain, being involved in the Family Compact War, now required the king of Portugal to join them against England, Charles kindly offering Spanish troops with which to garrison the Portuguese fortresses against British aggression. Unprepared as he was for war, he therefore boldly refused to desert his old ally; the Bourbon ambassadors quitted Lisbon (a step nearly tantamount to a declaration of war), and a Spanish army immediately invaded Portugal.

During a peace of forty-eight years the Portuguese army had been neglected. The troops did not amount to twenty thousand men, and this small number were ill-armed, and worse disciplined. It is not surprising that Braganza, Miranda, Torre de Moncorvo, and Almeida fell in rapid succession before the invaders, whilst the greatest alarm spread throughout the country.

But the genius of Pombal rose with the emergency. From England he obtained supplies of arms, troops, and especially of officers; and he appointed the count of Schaumburg-Lippe, a German general of considerable reputation,[1] to the chief command of the Portuguese army. Schaumburg-Lippe showed real talent by adapting his measures to the nature of the forces that were to execute them. By his direction the armed peasants defended the mountain passes; and the English brigadier-general Burgoyne successfully performed several surprises and small expeditions, which, if in themselves of little moment, served to revive the spirits of the Portuguese army, and being combined with the annoyance given by the peasantry, checked the progress of the Spaniards. Accordingly, at the approach of winter, the invaders retired within their own frontiers, evacuating all their conquests. This campaign constituted nearly the whole of the Spanish share of the Seven Years' War in Europe; the rest was confined to contributing a few auxiliary troops to the French armies. In America, Spain was more successful against Portugal, the governor of Buenos Ayres again making himself master of Colonia del Sacramento, with booty of £4,000,000 [$20,000,000], besides numbers of richly laden English merchant vessels.

On the 10th of February, 1763, a treaty of peace was signed at Paris between France, Spain, and England, including the restoration of Colonia del Sacramento to Portugal.

[1 It is recorded, as a proof of the skill with which the count had trained his artillery men, and of his confidence in them, that he celebrated the king of Prussia's birthday in 1759, by giving a dinner to his officers, in his tent; the flag at the top of that tent being aimed at during the whole entertainment as a mark for cannon-balls. It is not added with what degree of appetite the officers dined. *j*]

Upon the restoration of peace, José and Pombal resumed their patriotic labours for improving the internal condition of Portugal. With the assistance of Schaumburg-Lippe they remodelled, increased, and disciplined the army. They similarly reformed the state of the navy. They established a more efficient police, and abolished the *Indices Expurgatorios*, or prohibitory lists of books of the Inquisition, which banished from Portugal many good and really philosophical works. They did not indeed give liberty to the press, but established a board of censure, combining royal with prelatical and inquisitorial judges, by which all publications were to be examined. The verdicts of this board, if still somewhat illiberal, were far less so than the bigoted decisions of the uncontrolled Inquisition. Nay, it is even said to have admitted some free-thinking works, and condemned many books written in support of the more extravagant pretensions of the papal see. To this board, moreover, all schools were subjected. Pombal introduced great ameliorations into the constitution and forms of the University of Coimbra, where, till then, degrees in law, medicine, and divinity had been granted, without any real examination of the proficiency of the candidates.

Pombal likewise somewhat limited the right of entailing property, carried throughout the peninsula to a ruinous extent, diminished the excessive number of monasteries, imposed restrictions upon the admission of novices, and endeavoured to abolish the odious distinctions between the "old" and "new" Christians, by repealing the tax laid especially upon the latter. On the other hand, Pombal sought to encourage agriculture by ordering all vineyards to be destroyed that were planted upon good arable land; he cramped commerce by injudicious attempts to encourage domestic manufactures, by establishing exclusive commercial companies, by passing sumptuary laws, and by various embarrassing regulations.*b*

Schlosser's Estimate of Pombal

One of the very first acts of his administration was to abolish the yearly exhibition of burning men for heresy (*auto-da-fé*); limits were set to the power of the Inquisition in general, and the infliction of all punishments, or cases involving punishments, were referred to the decisions of the secular tribunals. The conventual and religious houses were strictly forbidden to bring, or cause to be brought, young women of good fortune from the Brazils and to receive them into their convents, with a view of enriching their several orders. Restrictions were soon placed upon the nobility also, as had been previously done upon the clergy. Pombal behaved towards the high nobles precisely as Charles XI of Sweden had done towards the same class in his kingdom, with this exception — that the latter rested the defence of his conduct upon the declaration of the estates of the realm. In the Portuguese possessions on the coasts of Asia, Africa, and America, whole districts, lordships, and large estates which at first belonged to the crown had come into the hands of private families, as was also the case in Sweden in the seventeenth century; all these alienations were reclaimed, and all the estates which had come either by gift or occupancy into the hands of private individuals were resumed by the crown, and the families who were thus arbitrarily and violently deprived of their properties received very inadequate compensation.

By this resumption of crown lands which had been long in the possession of the nobility, the members of this body lost much of their influence and power, and the measures must be allowed to have been executed with great rigour. Imprisonment and death were arbitrarily inflicted upon all those who showed themselves discontented with the scientific and philosophic system of government of the prime minister. The first years of Pombal's administration may be very fitly compared to the times of terror during the French Revolution ; for the whole of the dreadful and subterraneous prisons, and all the towers and castles were filled with prisoners of state.

Should it be asked how it was possible that the cowardly, superstitious, and weak king could approve of such a revolutionary method of proceeding, this will be best explained by calling to mind that, from the time of the disputes with the Jesuits, he lived in a continual state of fear, not only of the order, but of his nobility and of his brother Dom Pedro. He had therefore completely thrown himself into the arms of his minister, who surrounded the king and himself with guards, relying upon whose protection the weak king rejoiced that by the instrumentality of his minister he was able to exercise a dominion uncontrolled by the people or the nobles, such as was enjoyed by Louis XIV or Frederick of Prussia.

Pombal's measures with respect to trade, commerce, industry, and agriculture were neither the best nor free from selfish views ; but they roused up the Portuguese and awakened them from the slumber and idleness of their monkish life, although this rousing was frequently not performed with a very gentle hand. We shall therefore attribute no higher importance to the school of commerce established by Pombal, to the solemn and public examinations which were held in his presence, and to the public attention which he thereby roused, than that he opposed a school of practical life to the prevailing monkish institutions, and a secular celebration which bore upon education and life to ecclesiastical processions. He also contributed very largely to the improvement of agriculture in the province of Alemtejo, although we should feel by no means disposed to undertake the defence of all those measures which he adopted with this view ; the same may be said of the great canal of Oeyras and of the fair established in the same place. He provided for the security of the city repeatedly destroyed by earthquakes ; he provided an abundant supply of water by means of magnificent conduits, and erected numerous noble public edifices. But the means, however useful, were not the less tyrannical and cruel. The unfortunate inhabitants whose dwellings had escaped the terrific power of the earthquake were obliged to pull down their houses and build them up again at their own cost, according to a prescribed plan and on a given scale, if, either in their external appearance or by their situation, they interfered with Pombal's magnificent plan of broad streets and beautiful houses. Travellers were struck with admiration at his immense architectural structures, the arsenal, the exchange which was connected with it, and the market-house, and it was said there was nothing in Europe of their kind to be compared with these buildings ; but, in fact, the only real glory in the matter was that Pombal's buildings were all erected in the taste and style of the new age, whereas those of João V retained all the characteristics of the Middle Ages ; for the exchange and the market-house were wholly destitute of merchants and wares, and there was no suitable army or fleet to correspond to the arsenal.

Pombal was at that time the object of the most deadly hatred as a tyrant in the nation which he was desirous of reforming ; this alone was sufficient to render everything hateful which originated with him amongst a people whose condition he was indeed unable immediately to improve, but whom he annoyed, provoked, and tormented by means of his state police and his numerous and detested decrees. He durst not, in consequence, venture out of his house without a guard, and was obliged to have recourse to the most hateful means of maintaining the respect due to his station and rank. Wraxall,[i] who, as regards hearsays, mixes together truth and falsehood, stories, footmen's reports, and lies of all kinds, but who is deserving of credit when he speaks as an eye-witness, informs us that, as late as the year 1772, he found all the prisons full of unfortunate individuals, some of whom had been buried in these living graves for fifteen years.

The advantages therefore which Portugal gained through Pombal's administration, and which were loudly celebrated through the whole of Europe, rested upon a very unstable foundation. The most remarkable of these advantages were: security from assassination, which Lisbon had never enjoyed before the time of Pombal's rule; the rebuilding and adornment of the capital; cleanliness of the streets; a free trade in books; an academy which deserved well of the friends of the sciences; a disciplined army, etc. All these momentous changes and creations, however, wholly depended for their continuance upon the absolute power of the minister, and that again upon the life of the king. As long as José lived, Pombal maintained his influence, and pursued the same energetic course both towards priests and soldiers. He put limits to the number of brotherhoods and ecclesiastical orders, and availed himself of the aid of his sister, who was herself a nun, to carry his reforming principles even into the nunneries. Military affairs he conducted in the same manner, for he never hesitated to cashier whole regiments if they transgressed his army regulations respecting discipline, or suffered themselves to be guilty of acts of injury or violence towards their officers, who were gathered from all nations and countries.

The king, who was nearly eighty years old, no sooner became seriously ill than Pombal foresaw his fate, for the queen was appointed regent and he was kept far removed from the sick-bed of the monarch. He therefore, shortly before José's death, which took place in February, 1777, preferred a request to the regent to be relieved from his official duties, and appealed, as a reason for his request, to his advanced age and his bodily infirmities. In this remarkable document he gives a brief but comprehensive statement of the whole of the arrangements and condition of all the departments of the government at that time. No person who reads this paper can fail to be pleased with the ability which it displays and to admire its author, who had raised the financial condition of the country to a degree of prosperity which it had not reached for centuries; he appended a paper to his petition for leave to retire from public life, in which a correct account is not only given of the diamonds in the royal cabinet, but in which it is stated that a sum of 76,000,000 cruzados in hard cash [about £6,400,000 or $32,000,000] was deposited in the royal treasury.

THE NEW QUEEN AND REACTION

The king however died before the regent had returned her answer; he was succeeded by his daughter, Donna Maria I, to whom Pombal preferred his request anew on the 1st of March, 1777, which was granted to him by a decree of the date of the 4th of the same month, drawn up in a kindly spirit. The regent, at the end of February, had already released from imprisonment several of the clergy and persons of distinction who had been incarcerated as being implicated in the conspiracy against the king's life, under the appearance of having taken this step by her husband's command: in the beginning of March everything was changed. The new and unholy marriage which was celebrated in the royal family, for which the pope had granted a dispensation, may be regarded as a preliminary announcement of the return to the old order of things : this marriage, now solemnised, had been commanded by the king immediately before his death. It appeared as if it were not enough that the reigning queen should be married to her own paternal uncle, but the son of this marriage must be further allied with his mother's sister, Donna Maria Benedicta.

The whole history of this incestuous family furnishes proofs enough that, although the pope might sanction and bless such marriages for money, they had the stamp of retribution upon them. This was soon evident in the case of the new queen Donna Maria. Immediately after her father's death she assumed the reins of government, which she shared with her husband Dom Pedro ; soon afterwards, however, she exhibited traces of insanity, and at a later period became completely mad. As her unsoundness of mind was closely connected with her excessive superstition, she did not wait for Pombal's removal from the presidency of the council, which took place a few weeks afterwards, but immediately proceeded to take steps for the restoration of all those religious abuses which had previously existed in the kingdom. She restored to the papal nuncio and the saints of the Jesuits all the honours and distinctions which they had previously enjoyed among the people. The nuncio immediately played again the character of a spiritual monarch ; and the pope received half a million of florins as an indemnification for the expense to which he had been put by the support of the Jesuits who were landed at Civitá Vecchia. The estates of the ridiculous patriarchate were given back ; the holidays, confraternities, and tribunals of the Middle Ages restored, and those saints of the Romish church who had been the enemies of all temporal sovereigns were again reinstated in the honours of the church and the calendar. This was the case with Gregory VII, Ignatius Loyola, Francis Xavier, and Francis Borgia, whose names had been erased from the calendar by the orders of Pombal. All this took place long before Pombal received permission to retire from his official duties.

Hundreds were liberated from their subterranean dungeons, among whom were bishops, grandees of the kingdom, and members of families of the first distinction, and especially the sixty Jesuits who had been restored to freedom upon the command of the queen ; all these combined and allowed the weak-minded lady no rest or peace till she let loose her jurists upon the reformer, with the forms and formulas of their Byzantine criminal law, of which its codes furnish abundance, for the torment of all those who are unfortunate enough to live in countries in which Byzantine justice is honoured. Some idea of the number and power of the minister's enemies at court may be deduced from the fact that he had hunted forth whole crowds of that court mob which, under all sorts of titles and pretences, had wasted or spent on themselves and their pleasures the revenues of the kingdom, or sacrificed them to his own creatures ; and that again he had not only met the expenditure, but accumulated a large reserve-fund in the treasury of a kingdom whose exchequer had always been previously empty. In the royal treasury he kept always on hand 40,000,000 cruzados, and in the tithe exchequer 30,000,000, which was a thing long unheard of in the history of Portuguese finances.

Pombal shared the fate of all those who have ever attempted to carry through a revolution or even a reform by means of violence and severity ; the cruelty, criminality, and violence of their measures rouse every human feeling against them to such an extent that neither sense nor gratitude remains for the various beneficial changes which they have effected. The numbers of prisoners who were released from their dreadful captivity and dungeons at the king's death furnish but too strong proofs of the strict applicability of this principle to Pombal, and of the severities which he exercised under pretence at least of serving the interests of humanity, and promoting the cause of knowledge and improvement. In the very first days of the new government 500 human beings came forth from their cells as from their graves, who had never been brought before any legal tribunal, and their number was afterwards increased to 800. When it was determined to prosecute the marquis, it was alleged by his enemies that during his administration 9,640 men had been banished or incarcerated, of whom 3,970 had been completely innocent, and of the rest only 800 then remained alive. For four years (from 1777-1781) Pombal was prosecuted before the courts by individuals who brought actions against him for false imprisonment and damages, and a prosecution was not commenced against him, on account of his administration of the state, till he had been first baited and hunted down by the lawyers.

At length a severe final judgment was pronounced against the marquis, now in his eighty-second year. In August, 1781, the queen overruled the decision of the courts, and limited the punishment to a public disapproval of the manner in which he had discharged the duties of his office, and banishment from the court.

Almost every improvement or change which had been effected by Pombal had disappeared before his death, which took place in 1782. Priests and monks of all colours, Jesuits, now called ex-Jesuits, want of police, filth, insecurity for life and property, and a total relaxation of military discipline again appeared; but the whole effects of his exertions and labours could not be rooted out. Murphy,[l] who visited Portugal in 1789, found many changes in the old Portuguese life, and every change which he mentions is referred to Pombal. He further boasts that Portugal was indebted to this celebrated minister for an institution of which England was long destitute; in England hundreds of unfortunate debtors were continually to be found languishing in the public prisons at the suit of some heartless and intolerant creditor. In 1744 Pombal issued an ordinance, which since that time has continued to be the law in Portugal, by which, on the one hand, debtors were freed from personal arrest or imprisonment at the suit of their creditors,[1] and the means were given to the latter by which obtaining possession of the property of their debtors was rendered as easy as it had previously been difficult.[h]

The strict friendship subsisting between Spain and Portugal had been most beneficial to the former during the war with England (1779-1783). Not only had the Portuguese harbours afforded neither shelter nor assistance, as of old, to the hostile British fleets, but the Portuguese flag had been the means of transporting the wealth of America to Spain; and it is said that when the English ministry had projected an expedition against Peru, whilst distracted by Tupac Amaru's revolt, its execution was prevented by a remonstrance from the court of Lisbon, representing that, in case of an invasion of the Spanish dominions, Portugal was bound by treaty to take part in the war. Charles, duly sensible of these advantages, sought to strengthen the ties of relationship and friendship by those of wedlock; and in 1785 his fourth son, Don Gabriel, married the infanta Marianna Victoria

[1 The credit for fully ending imprisonment for debt is, however, usually given to the later ministers and the queen Maria.]

of Portugal, and Dom João, the queen of Portugal's second son, the eldest Spanish infanta, Carlota Joaquina.

This last union was the more agreeable to Charles, inasmuch as Dom João had a very fair chance of eventually succeeding to the crown, the incestuous union of his eldest brother with his aunt having proved barren. But it was not the youngest of this ill-assorted pair that was destined to be the survivor. Three years after Dom João's marriage, the prince of Brazil himself, whom the bigoted prejudices of the queen had not suffered to be inoculated, died of the smallpox, and Charles' son-in-law became prince of Brazil in his stead. Queen Maria had, in 1786, lost her uncle-husband, Pedro III, but he had interfered little with her government, and his death had therefore no effect upon public affairs.

The queen appears to have been really anxious to promote the prosperity of her kingdom. When the Peace of Versailles had relieved her from the embarrassments consequent upon her intimate connection with two hostile belligerents, she endeavoured to strengthen the old friendship with England by concluding a commercial treaty, at the same time that she maintained her new relations of friendship and commerce with the Bourbon courts.[b]

THE REGENCY AND THE FRENCH REVOLUTION

The queen now began to show signs of an insanity which took a religious form and in which she suffered all the agonies of her vivid belief that she was doomed to eternal fire. Her confessors endeavoured to comfort her by milder applications of their doctrines, but from 1788 the government was more and more taken out of her incapable hands by Dom João, who was not, however, fully constituted regent until 1799.

Meanwhile the ferment of the French Revolution had stirred all Europe, and Portugal indirectly. We have already described the embroilment of Spain. Portugal endeavoured to keep a strict neutrality, but her treaties with Spain and England enabled them to enforce their demand for aid.[1] She added nine sail of the line to the British fleet, and five thousand infantry under General Skelater to the Spanish armies. These troops shared the easy successes of the first rush across the Pyrenees and the bitter disasters of the following repulse. Spain now, in 1795, signed a treaty of alliance with France, and Portugal applied for terms, but was rejected as " a mere province of England "; the ambassador at Paris was ordered out of the country, and on showing some delay was thrown into prison, where he remained for months.

Portugal was now driven to open alliance with England, against whom Spain declared war in 1796. At the same time Dom João learned that Napoleon and the Spanish prime minister Godoy had agreed to conquer and divide Portugal as a spoil of war. The English voted £200,000 [$1,000,000] to Portugal and sent six thousand men under Major-General Sir Charles Stuart. These with a native army of some forty thousand men placed under the prince of Waldeck frightened off Spanish invasion, whereupon Stuart and the English troops withdrew. Little had happened thus far except the loss of some commerce to French privateers. In 1799 Dom João formally assumed the regency and tried vainly to secure the favour of Napoleon, who would listen

---

[1] H. M. Stephens,[d] however, represents Dom João as so zealous for the reduction of the French that he forced his aid upon England and Spain counter to the advice of the English ministry.

to nothing less than the payment of a heavy tribute, breach of the alliance with England, the closing of Portuguese ports to English ships, the surrender of a portion of Portuguese territory to Spain. As alternative to these hard terms made under the name of Spain, war was offered. Dom João accepted the latter alternative, and proclaimed war on Spain, February 10th, 1801.

As related in the Spanish history, Portugal was invaded by the Spanish at once, and with such ease that, by June 6th, João was glad to accept the Peace of Badajoz at the cost of ceding Olivenza to Spain. Napoleon, however, required more, and sent troops which extorted a tribute of £1,000,000 [$5,000,000] and the cession of Portuguese Guiana to France. Napoleon's representative at Lisbon was General Lannes (or Lasnes) who at first provoked great hatred by his insolent bearing, but later procured a large influence over João and secured the dismissal of the ministers of English sympathies. In 1804 he was succeeded by General Junot who accepted a treaty of neutrality which gave Portugal quiet for some years, while Napoleon went on from great to greater.

The English tried to break the Portuguese peace with France, but could succeed in nothing more than keeping her ports open in spite of Napoleon's continental system against English trade. By 1807, however, Napoleon was master enough of the East to turn again to Portugal and by the Treaty of Fontainebleau (October 29th, 1807), resumed his project of dividing it among Godoy, the king of Etruria, and himself. The terrified João offered every sacrifice for peace, going so far as to order from his realm every British subject and to close his ports to England, though this meant commercial ruin to Portugal. But Napoleon, pretending that the submission was too late, sent forward his troops under General Junot.*a*

THE INVASION OF THE FRENCH (1807 A.D.)

The Treaty of Fontainebleau contained all the decisions respecting the campaign against Portugal, and the partition of that kingdom. The Spaniards were to reinforce the army of the Gironde with twelve thousand men ; at the same time to invade the north of Portugal with forty thousand men ; and to give orders for another army to enter Algarve under Solano. In terms of the treaty, Lisbon and the whole centre of the country were to fall to the share of France, a part of the northern division was to be given as compensation to the queen of Etruria, and a sovereign territory to be formed in the south for Godoy. The part not allotted by the treaty to any of the three parties just mentioned was to be the subject of future negotiations, when possession of the whole was obtained.

Notwithstanding the imminent danger, the prince-regent had neither taken measures for defence, made preparations for setting sail to Brazil, nor even for the removal of the rich stores in the arsenals and magazines of the capital. The prince and his whole court would have been taken by surprise in Lisbon by the French rapidly advancing on the capital through Beira, had not a swift sailing ship brought a copy of the *Moniteur* to Lisbon, in which Napoleon, who supposed that his army was long since in that city, too hastily expressed his triumph by the declaration : " The house of Braganza has ceased to reign."

The army of the Gironde was under the command of Marshal Junot, who gained his ensign's commission by an act of great presence of mind displayed under the eyes of Napoleon at the siege of Toulon, although he was in reality possessed of very small military capacity. He had been in Lisbon as ambassador, and still held that title, never having been formally recalled ; the troops under his command, however, contained but very few men who could be thoroughly relied upon, for this army of the Gironde had been very hastily drawn together. The prime of the French army was at that time still in Germany (September, 1807) and in Prussia, and the first army, as well as that by which it was succeeded, consisted of a mixture of soldiers and officers, who, on the landing of the English and the outbreak of the Spanish rising, proved wholly unequal to maintaining the glory gained by the grand army ; this was not at first perceived. Junot wished to collect and organise his army, seeing it was composed of very different elements, when he suddenly received orders to march direct upon Lisbon in order to surprise the prince-regent in his security. We may form some idea of the rapidity with which he prosecuted his march, from the fact that he had taken twenty-five days to march from Bayonne to Salamanca, where he arrived on the 12th of November ; while, on the other hand, he reached Alcantara as early as the 17th, and was in Abrantes on the 23rd, about eighty miles from Lisbon.

The difficulty of the march, the pathless and rough character of the districts through which he led the army were indescribable ; but no measures whatever were adopted by the Portuguese for resistance or even to increase the difficulty of the journey. A great portion of the army fell a sacrifice to the difficulties of the march, or to want, in neighbourhoods where no idea could be entertained of any kind of sustenance or cover. Many had fallen into pits, others perished in the attempt to cross running streams ; but the immense loss in men was taken into no account whatever. As a reward for the rapidity of his march, Junot received the title of the duke of Abrantes, although he reached Lisbon with only a small part of his army [about two thousand men] at the end of November, and a long time elapsed before all the stragglers joined their respective corps.

THE THRONE MOVES TO BRAZIL

The prince-regent was at length induced, by the number of the *Moniteur* which was sent to him, to throw himself into the arms of the English, whose ships were lying in the Tagus, and, under their protection, to save himself by setting sail for Brazil. He took his departure from the Tagus on the 29th, under English convoy, with eight ships of the line, three frigates, three brigs, and a considerable number of transports, in order to remove the seat of his government to Brazil.[1] The well-stored arsenal, from whose treasures the whole French army was afterwards clothed and provided, fell without diminution into the hands of the French, in consequence of his precipitate departure. Junot's advanced guard even reached Belem in time enough to capture some ships of war which had been detained by contrary winds, and were still within reach of the guns of the fort.

The second army, which was assembled at Bayonne to reinforce Junot's corps, was still stronger than the first ; but the whole of Europe deeply condemned Napoleon's want of honour, and was angry with the French sophists and cringing flatterers who ventured to defend and to praise the emperor's

[1 With him went his wife and six children and his insane mother the queen, who violently resisted for some time the efforts to get her aboard.]

policy in the use of this army. At the very moment in which he concluded a treaty with Spain against Portugal, and was using one part of the Spanish army under Bernadotte in Denmark, and was alluring the second to Portugal, he caused a body of troops to be assembled at Bayonne, but not to march against Portugal, as he had announced. It soon became obvious that Napoleon planned to take possession of Spain in the midst of peace.

The Spaniards who had assisted Junot in the conquest of Portugal having withdrawn into their own country, the French general had scattered his troops from Algarve and Oporto, and had done everything which could render the sojourn of the French in their country intolerable to the Portuguese. Napoleon immediately laid a contribution of 100,000,000 francs on Portugal; the people were obliged, besides, to pay 600,000 francs to Junot, which the emperor had assigned to him as governor-general; and Junot raised 5,000,000 more on his own account. Napoleon not only drew away the national troops from Portugal and took them into his own army, but appeared desirous of playing the same constitution-comedy with the Portuguese in Bayonne as he had played with the Spaniards. He sent for a number of the notables as deputies, but retained them in hostages; and they were afterwards placed in a very dangerous position, when, given up by him, they became suspected by their own countrymen. The only favour which he granted them was to remit forty of the hundred millions of contribution which he had at first imposed. In small matters, every officer in Portugal played the despot and oppressor.[h]

THE PENINSULAR WAR

Portugal now became, like Spain, hardly more than the arena where English armies under the duke of Wellington fought a desperate and protracted war with the French under various leaders. The full details of this conflict, known as the Peninsular War, will be found in the history of Spain. For some years it was impossible to distinguish between the military interests of Spain and Portugal, their common safety resting on the destruction of Napoleon and the success of British courage and British plans. In these the Spaniards and Portuguese played small part, according to the British histories, except to harass French communications by their guerillas and harass British security by their intrigues and jealousies.

But there is something to be said for the natives. The French democratic principles had made some progress in Portugal, and the cowardly and stupid king who fled to a colony and left his country for a foreigner to defend was not of much inspiration. In fact patriotism found here little to cling to except the rocks and vines, and those would remain in any case, whoever ruled. Between the world-shaking Napoleon and the weak-minded, England-serving poltroon whom monarchic heredity had with its usual felicity placed on the throne, there was small choice to the Portuguese, and the historian should be sparing of his blame for the impassivity of the nation.

Furthermore the English commander Wellington was notoriously domineering; and the English troops, according to their own historian and their general himself, showed some of the most atrocious examples of drunken insubordination and bestial ferocity in the history of human war. Few of the Portuguese could be blind to the fact that England, in spite of her lofty tone, was really in Portugal for commercial and not for altruistic reasons, and that the war was purely a wrestling-match for commerce and power between two giants, France and England, with little regard for the Lilliputians they might trample in their struggle. It behooves the reader, then, not to follow the bias of either pro- or anti-Napoleonic historians in their common tone of contempt for the alleged pusillanimity of the Spanish and Portuguese.

The fact must be remembered that Spain and Portugal had nothing or next to nothing definite to fight for, as "loyalty" in each country meant little more than a desire to shed blood and money for a monarch of third-rate virtue and first-rate imbecility. It may be said, however, that the verdict of English historians is much more favourable to the Portuguese soldiers than to the Spanish. A brief outline of events will serve here for the history of Portugal, in view of the chapter already given in the history of Spain.

On the flight of the royal family to Brazil, a council of regency was appointed to carry on affairs. The disgust at João was so great that the French general Junot met almost no resistance, but rather welcome as the bringer of freedom and democracy. The council of regency submitted to him at Lisbon. His first acts were to seize the treasury and disband the Portuguese army; on the other hand he forbade the Spanish their expected plunder and he raised the Portuguese Legion of troops who served with fidelity and bravery under Napoleon in other countries down to his defeat at Waterloo.

Having disarmed Portugal by easy measures and false hopes, Junot suddenly announced the end of the dynasty of Braganza, substituted French for Portuguese governors everywhere, and formed a new ministry and a new regency, largely French, with Junot at the head as president, eventually, he hoped, as king of Portugal. Spain had been similarly duped and given a French king, Joseph Bonaparte. Spain responded by rebellion; Portugal, after nine months of submission to Junot, rose and butchered the French in large numbers. Revolutionary juntas took the government and appealed to England for aid, receiving in response both men and money as well as generals, chief among them the Irishman, Sir Arthur Wellesley, later and better known as the duke of Wellington. Portugal was in England's eyes, according to Canning's own words, merely the fulcrum for the lever of England to wrench Napoleon from his power.

After some hindrance, due to division of command, Wellesley was able to march forward; he defeated Laborde at Roliça (or Roriça) August 17th, 1808, and four days later dealt Junot himself such a blow at Vimeiro that he surrendered all his strongholds and his troops on the condition that the English carry the army and its spoils safely back to France on their own ships. This so-called Convention of Cintra, concluded some miles from Cintra, was carried out, but provoked a storm of rage in England.

The French being thus transported, as by Aladdin's carpet, out of Portugal, Dom João's regency was re-established and found abundant ground for dispute with the junta of Oporto, and later with the English officers and diplomats. England sent J. C. Villiers as ambassador, and Beresford to organise the native armies. He did his work with skill, and ten thousand Portuguese were taken into English pay. Hardly had Junot's army been evicted from Portugal when another French army under Soult came over from Spain, which was full of French troops. Soult drove back all resistance and took Oporto, whence Wellington expelled him May 12th, 1809. Wellington then entered Spain and beat "king" Joseph Bonaparte and his marshal Victor at Talavera.

Meanwhile there were endless disputes with the regency, who seemed to divert the moneys England sent until the troops were hampered almost to helplessness, and the English generals were driven frantic. Sir Charles Stuart was finally at England's insistence added to the regency, and something less inefficient resulted. The people were, however, not altogether convinced of their duty to play " fulcrum " indefinitely to the Archimedean lever of England. They were not cheered by having to dig those famous and enormous lines of defence at Torres Vedras, and they were still less encouraged in being compelled to devastate their own country and retire with the English troops behind breastworks, before the terrible army Napoleon sent under Masséna in 1810.

But while Wellington kept under cover and guarded Lisbon doggedly, Portuguese militia under Antonio de Silveira and various English officers made it increasingly hard for Masséna to subsist his troops. Trant took Coimbra, and in 1811 Masséna was forced to retire or starve. Wellington was now reinforced, and following Masséna cautiously, bested him at Sabugal, April 3rd, 1811. But the year was one of great anxiety to Wellington. England could afford few supplies and the Portuguese regency was more prolific of complaints and quarrels than of provisions. But, though compelled to keep on the defensive, the Iron Duke showed a menace he hardly felt. The war hovered on the borders of Portugal and went generally to French advantage in Spain.

Wellington gradually, and by a patience as great as his skill in emergency, gained the upper hand, and forcing his way into Spain, took Madrid August 12th, 1812. He was later forced out by French adroitness and made a retreat, which, as described in the history of Spain, is infamous in British annals for the outrageous and inexcusable misbehaviour of the troops. Wellington berated his army in violent terms, and though he was not made the more popular thereby, his troops were somewhat sobered. He now received full power from the court in Brazil, and at the same time was made chief of the Spanish armies, with the whole peninsula under his command. He at once assumed the offensive with a vigour that answered the violent criticism his alleged timidity had provoked in England as well as in the peninsula and France. His victories, coinciding with Napoleon's disastrous Moscow campaign, drove the French out of the peninsula and led him into France, where the Peninsular War was ended with Napoleon's abdication.

PORTUGAL AN ENGLISH PROVINCE

The gratitude Portugal was impelled to feel met a shock when the English at the Congress of Vienna refused to insist on the restoration by Spain of Olivenza, of which Portugal had been robbed by Napoleon and the Spanish in 1801. The bitterness was increased by the harshness of the regency, in which Beresford and Stuart still held sway, though the war was over. Beresford had his racial faculty of irritating the Latin peoples by his cold and severe manner and ruthless severities. He was commander-in-chief of the armies. A third of the officers were English, and two-thirds of the country's revenues were spent on the military. Portugal was in fact if not in theory only an English province. To the amazement of all, João, who had committed the novel feat of carrying his capital from the mother-country to a colony during a war, showed himself still more original when the war was finished; for he declined to bring back his capital. The life at Rio de

Janeiro seems to have fascinated him. Portugal drew most of its wealth from the Brazils and he preferred and enjoyed it nearer the source. Worse yet, after taking to Rio some fifteen thousand persons when he fled, he kept persuading the chief nobles and wealthiest merchants to move to Brazil.

In 1816 he became the nominal, as he had long been the actual, king, for his insane mother died at Rio, March 20th of that year, and the regent was crowned in the colony as João VI and meekly acknowledged at home. But still he remained away, resigned Olivenza easily, and called forty-five hundred war-tried Spanish soldiers over to Brazil, where under Le Cor they put down a rebellion, which broke out again in 1825 and succeeded as the republic of Uruguay.

João VI was unpopular with his beckoning people, and his own queen, Donna Carlota Joaquina, was undermining him in favour of Dom Miguel, her younger son, who was not believed to be also his. His admittedly legitimate and elder son, Pedro, was also against him and his absolutist principles. Thus while the queen had in 1805 promised Portugal a constitution, Dom Pedro was a lover of Brazil and a well-wisher to the schemes for its separation from the mother-country.

THE REVOLT AND RECALL OF THE KING

In this unusual tangle of politics the cry of " Portugal for the Portuguese ! " began to grow. The only man who could be said to approach popularity was General Gomes Freire de Andrade, who had served under Napoleon throughout the wars, and whose deep hatred of the English had found new fuel, seeing his country and his fellow-soldiers so rigorously governed by the foreigner who had come with promises of freedom. He conspired with others for a rising, but his plans were exposed and he and ten comrades put to death by the regency. The martyrdom, as it seemed, of Freire and his men embittered the country, and it needed only the absence of Beresford (who took ship to Brazil to extract money for the army from the absentee king) to show the way.

August 4th, 1820, the city of Oporto revolted, appointed a provisional junta in the king's name, and demanded a session of the cortes. Freemasonry principles had been at work, and aided the ripening of the plans. Lisbon similarly rose and chose a junta, which combined with that of Oporto and convoked the cortes. While the cortes was adopting a constitution similar to Spain's, the English officers were expelled from the country. Beresford, returning, was forbidden to land and compelled to return to England. The new cortes was of democratic persuasion ; it clean-swept the remnants of feudalism and put an end to the still-living Inquisition. The " Constitution of 1822 " limited the powers of the king to a veto of measures furthered by the annual assembly, promised a free press, universal suffrage, and other decencies of civilisation.

As elsewhere the first sign of emancipation provoked the horror of the Holy Alliance, the ambassadors of Prussia, Austria, and Russia withdrew from the country polluted with such free ideas, and England demanded with a new urgency that João VI return to Lisbon. He came back July 3rd, 1821, but before he was permitted to land promised to accept the constitution, to which he took oath October 1st, 1822, thus outraging the sensibilities of the clergy, who abhorred any trend towards liberty. His queen and Dom Miguel refused to accept the constitution and were ordered out of the country ; but the queen, pretending to be ill, was allowed to remain, and busied herself drawing together conspirators known as "Cringers." In 1823 the French invaded Spain to quell the Spanish revolt against the Nero-like Ferdinand. The absolutists in Portugal chose the moment to rise against the Constitution of 1822, General Silveira being the leader.

THE LOSS OF BRAZIL (1822 A.D.)

Meanwhile Dom Pedro, left behind in Brazil, had smiled upon those who desired independence of the mother-country which had long been but a blood-sucking vampire. By his complacency Dom Pedro won the privilege of leading the revolt against his own father and becoming the first emperor of Brazil with a liberal constitution back of him. Portugal made only the feeblest effort at resistance and Brazil was thenceforward independent. Its fuller history will be found in the later volume devoted to Spanish America.

The easy surrender of the richest of her colonies exasperated the absolutists still more against the pliant João, and Portugal proceeded to echo the almost incredible Spanish motto, "Hurrah for chains!"; to grow frantic for despotism; to curse those who tried to limit the power of oppression, and to exhibit the spectacle — no less astounding for being so common in history — of a people shedding its blood to destroy its own liberties.a

CHAPTER V

THE NINETEENTH CENTURY

[1822–1900 A.D.]

IMMEDIATELY after the proclamation of the Constitution of 1822, the Austrian and Russian ambassadors had taken their departure and now that intervention in Spain had been definitely determined on by the Congress of Verona, one of the queen's adherents, the count of Amarante, raised the standard of revolt at Villa Real, on the northern bank of the Douro in the province of Tras-os-Montes, where the family of Silveira, to which he belonged, possessed estates. The rebellion was made in the name of absolutism or, as the phrase went, in the name of regeneration. The enterprise did not succeed, and the insurrectionists were driven across the Spanish border, though still hoping for the support of the French who had now arrived on the scene. This hope was delusive, for the duke of Angoulême and his government had to consider the susceptibilities of England. That power, already provoked by the treatment of Spanish concerns at the Congress of Verona, looked distrustfully at the development of events in the peninsula, and took a special interest in Portuguese matters ; only the regency at Madrid gave them as much assistance as possible.

But there was no need for direct interference. The new Portuguese constitution had not effected what it had promised ; long before this the fickle humour of this passionate, ignorant, and idle people had veered round. In particular the party opposed to the constitution had successfully worked upon the troops and the liberal cause had no one, no regular party, and only a few individual men in whom reliance could be placed. Thus in May, 1823, Dom Miguel was able openly to declare against the constitution. He withdrew from the capital, collected troops, and soon that same Sepulveda who had been one of the principal instigators of the revolution of 1820 marched to the prince's headquarters at Villafranca at the head of several thousands.

Thither on the 30th of May the king himself was conducted by mutinous troops, and from thence on the 3rd of June issued a proclamation in which he declared the "infamous cortes" dissolved and the "pure monarchy" established. Two days later he returned, an absolute monarch, to the capital he had left as a constitutional ruler. Of the members of the dismissed cortes a number had escaped to England, though the king himself nourished no thoughts of vengeance. The adherents and promoters of the counter-revolution were rewarded : Count Amarante, for instance, was made marquis of Chaves ; the cloisters were restored and their property was given back, a new ministry was formed under Count Palmella and a junta appointed to indicate those dispositions of the cortes which were incompatible with the monarchical principle. For a time Dom Miguel, who had been appointed commander-in-chief of the army, was praised throughout Europe as the hero of the reaction.

On the 18th of June Queen Carlota also returned to Lisbon. This infamous woman detested her husband, who on his part had good reason to dread her fury which stopped at nothing. She was now bent on raising to his place her son Miguel who promised to be a prince after her own heart. A system of monarchical terrorism according to the ideas of this worthy pair was impossible so long as the mild Dom João was reigning ; the utmost that could be managed was a wretched assassination, like that of which the king's moderate counsellor, the marquis of Loulé, was the victim ; the reins had therefore to be snatched from him by a *coup d'état*.

On the 30th of April, 1824, Dom Miguel caused the leaders of the moderate party to be arrested. The king's minister, at whom the blow was really aimed, found time to escape on an English man-of-war which lay at anchor in the Tagus. Thither on the 9th of May the king, who had little confidence in his unnatural son, also fled, being assisted by the English and French ambassadors. But this time the overstrained bow broke in the hands of the absolutist party. They had forgotten to reckon with one factor on which they were accustomed to count too securely. The common people of the capital regarded their sovereign with something like idolatry ; and when, from his place of refuge, the king disclosed the criminal designs of those who should have stood closest to him, Miguel found himself suddenly forsaken by all and threatened by many, so that nothing was left him but to go himself to his father and implore his pardon. He was now for a time held in custody on the English vessel.

His "inexperienced youth" might be made a pretext for securing his pardon, for he was indeed, although a practised sinner, only twenty-two years old ; but it was thought expedient to send him to travel abroad. He betook himself through France to Vienna, to prepare himself, under Metternich's eye, for a subsequent continuation of his rôle. His mother was banished to a cloister which suited her but ill ; she resisted, under the pretence of illness, and is said to have even taken the last sacraments to prove her sickness. The question of the form of government was then so far settled that on the 4th of June, 1824, the king, acting on English advice, granted a constitution by which the cortes were re-established in their ancient form and division into three estates, the cortes of Lamego, as they were called from their place of assembly. The country now remained undisturbed till the king's death, which took place on the 10th of May, 1826, and placed the two thrones of Portugal and Brazil to a certain extent at the disposal of his eldest son Dom Pedro, who was conducting the government in Rio de Janeiro.

PORTUGAL RECEIVES A NEW RULER AND A NEW CONSTITUTION

But to hold them both had become an impossibility since the events of 1820, and a treaty effected through English mediation in 1825 had expressly provided that the two crowns should never again be united on one head, thus confirming the work of the Brazilian cortes of 1822 which declared the country's independence of Portugal. On the 23rd of April, 1826, the new ruler granted the Portuguese an extremely liberal constitution, the *Charta de ley* and renounced his European throne in favour of his daughter Maria da Gloria. He endeavoured to counteract the danger to which her claims might be exposed from his younger brother, Dom Miguel, by assigning the child, then only seven years old, as wife to the uncle who was seventeen years her senior and by making the validity of his own resignation depend on the condition that Miguel should swear to the *Charta* and accept the marriage ; until this should be completed Pedro's own rights were reserved, and since owing to the difference of age between the couple the marriage could not take place for some time, he intrusted the government to his sister Isabella Maria as regent.

She proclaimed the new constitution, which was sufficiently liberal; in it the king retained only a certain power of intervention and arbitration, with no immediate influence on legislation ; but liberality in the constitution was a very doubtful advantage in a country which was still so unripe for freedom, and an article which guaranteed freedom of religious worship roused the spiritual caste, who had no difficulty in representing to the ignorant country people and the numerous class of petty rural nobility whose interests were compromised by the new *Charta* that the new constitution was a work of the devil. However, a first attempt at a rising by the marquis of Chaves was suppressed, and in 1826 the regent was able to open the chambers.

But, supported by the apostolic party in Spain, Chaves returned. A formidable rebellion arose simultaneously in the north and south and gained such alarming proportions that the regent felt herself compelled to call in the aid of England. And this time not in vain. On Friday evening, December the 8th, 1826, the English government received the despatch. George Canning, the guiding spirit of that government, had long since declared that he would suffer no Spanish intervention of any sort in the country so long allied to England ; on the 11th the regiments under General Clinton were on the march to their places of embarkation, and on the 12th the great minister made that great speech in the lower house which echoed throughout the world and lent to events in that remote corner of the continent, in themselves of little significance to the destinies of Europe, a far-reaching importance much above their immediate value.

Canning made use of the occasion to justify his whole policy — a peace policy, but one which must yield to treaty obligations entered into towards a country long allied with England ; the contingency provided for by the treaty had now arisen and it would be a pitiful quibble to say that this was not a case of Spanish intervention because the troops which had risen against the legal government of Portugal were Portuguese : "They are Portuguese troops, but they are armed by Spain. We will not uphold by force or against the will of the country the constitution which Portugal has given herself, but neither will we permit others to overthrow it by force and against the will of the country." His words were meant to alarm and warn the Spanish government; but they also alarmed all those who had long been forcibly intermeddling with the internal politics of other states in behalf of principles opposed to liberty and friendly to absolutism.

Canning pursued his policy with moderation. He showed the strength of a giant without using it in a giant's fashion. On the 1st of January the English army corps under Clinton landed at Lisbon, and eleven English ships of the line cast anchor in the mouth of the Tagus. The news of their arrival sufficed to prevent the further spread of rebellion. The marquis of Chaves with ten thousand men stood ready for battle on the way to Coimbra. The constitutional troops, about seven thousand in number, marched against him; on the 9th of January a battle was fought which lasted till darkness fell. But in the night the news of the approach of the English spread amongst the Miguelites; this was enough to scatter their army. The English had no need to take action. Their mere presence facilitated the subjection of the rebels by the constitutional generals, Saldanha and others, and the Spanish government, which had understood Canning's speech, disarmed those who thronged across the border and delivered their weapons to the Portuguese authorities.

DOM MIGUEL SEIZES THE POWER (1827 A.D.)

Thus far England had interfered in response to the queen-regent's request for aid. Meantime Dom Miguel had taken the oath to the constitution, and had been betrothed to his niece; on the 5th of July, 1827, Dom Pedro appointed him regent of the kingdom. On the 22nd of February, 1828, after having presented himself in London, where he insinuated himself with the ministry, now no longer guided by a Canning, he landed at Lisbon. At a solemn meeting of the estates he repeated his oath, appointed a moderate ministry and kept himself in the background. But it was observed that the criers who daily shouted in front of the palace, "Long live the absolute king!" were no longer driven away or punished as they had been at first and that the constitutional officials and officers had been replaced by adherents of the opposite party; and after the withdrawal of the English troops, whose task was ended after the disbandment of the Spanish corps of observation on the frontiers, he threw off the mask.

On the 13th of March the chamber of deputies was dismissed, and a commission appointed to consider a new election law. On the 3rd of May the governor summoned the three estates of the realm, the "cortes of Lamego," according to the ancient ordinances. It was now seen whither this true son of his mother was steering. In face of proceedings so manifestly in excess of the existing rights of the regent, the ambassadors of the powers provisionally laid down their offices, and the troops in Oporto rose in defence of the rights of their lawful ruler, Dom Pedro IV. There was no lack of recruits; the number of the constitutional troops increased to seven thousand, but there seems to have been a want of resolute leaders, some of them having taken their departure at Dom Miguel's first move. The last-named had meanwhile assembled his forces; the mob and the country people armed, and on the 24th of June the constitutional troops suffered a defeat at the hands of the Miguelites under Povoas, in the neighbourhood of Coimbra. They retreated to Oporto, where some of the leaders of the constitutionalists, the marquis of Palmella, and the generals Saldanha, Villaflor, and Stubbs, who had now returned from their flight, in vain endeavoured to rally the disheartened army. Nothing was left to them but to escape from absolutist vengeance by a second flight; the remains of the constitutional army, four thousand strong, crossed into Spanish soil and Miguel's troops marched into Oporto.

The seizure of the throne could now be completed undisturbed. The new estates which had met at Lisbon, passed, each for itself, the resolution that, according to the fundamental laws of the kingdom, Dom Miguel had been called to the throne. On the 7th of July they paid their homage to the usurper as king. Thus the country was delivered over to the tyranny of a man who for baseness of disposition might compete even with a Ferdinand, and who actually surpassed the latter in coarseness and brutality. Incarcerations, judicial murders, deportations were the order of the day, and reached figures of frightful magnitude. It was a despotism which relied on the mob and the clergy for support; yet the fashion in which Dom Miguel had stolen the crown had been too openly in the very face of the principle of legitimacy to allow of his recognition by the powers; the Spanish ambassador alone remained in Lisbon.

DOM MIGUEL DE BRAGANZA

All Portugal submitted; only on the island of Terceira, one of the Azores, the governor Cabrera had upheld the rights of Dom Pedro and his daughter. Repeated attempts of the usurper to subdue the island were frustrated. The leaders of the constitutional party collected there, and there in March, 1830, Dom Pedro established a regency composed of the marquis of Palmella, the lawyer Guerreiro, and General Villaflor, who took possession of the whole group of islands in the name of the lawful government of Portugal.

By injuries to English and French subjects the barbarous reign of violence which prevailed under Dom Miguel soon added the enmity of those two powers to its native opponents. They exacted compensation and the humiliation of the usurper encouraged the party opposed to him which now found further and more energetic support. For in April, 1831, a revolt in Brazil had obliged the emperor Dom Pedro to resign his throne in favour of his son, Dom Pedro II, who was still a minor. In Europe a task lay ready to his hand: that of assisting his daughter Maria da Gloria to her throne, and at the same time freeing Portugal from her tyrant.

Countenanced by England and France, the duke of Braganza, as Dom Pedro now called himself, obtained a small land-force and a fleet, and with these he appeared at Terceira in March, 1832. With seventy-five hundred men he sailed thence to Portugal, landed in the neighbourhood of Oporto, and on the 8th of July obtained possession of this rich commercial city. But he did not succeed in rousing the country to enthusiasm in his cause. In the summer of 1833 his means were exhausted and only a bold decision availed to give a new turn to the undertaking, which, just in itself, had degenerated into a mere aimless adventure. By a loan raised in the city of Oporto he settled the demands of an English free-lance, named Sartorius, who was in his service, and replaced him by Captain Charles Napier. With the latter there embarked a corps of three thousand men under the duke of Terceira, General Villaflor, to try their fortune in the southern province of Algarve. The result exceeded all expectation; the province went over to the cause of Dom Pedro and the queen, and as the ships were on their way back to Oporto, Napier attacked Dom Miguel's fleet off Cape St. Vincent and won a complete victory. Five ships of war with 280 cannon fell into his hands, and those on board, thirty-two hundred soldiers and sailors, entered Dom Pedro's service. The news encouraged the duke of Terceira to venture a march on Lisbon, and this bold action also succeeded. Queen Maria da Gloria was proclaimed in the city, and four days later Dom Pedro also entered the town and took over the regency in his daughter's name.

But the new government was by no means securely established. The regent understood little of Portuguese matters and, as always in these southern revolutions, the victorious party were strangers to the moderation required to restore tranquillity to the country. Dom Miguel had preserved the greater part of his army and its ranks were swelled by the peasants who were completely subjected to him and the priests, and by a numerous and continually multiplying rabble. This army maintained itself in the neighbourhood of Coimbra and on the upper Tagus; frequently it even penetrated to Lisbon and thus the two representatives of priest-ridden absolutism, Dom Miguel and Don Carlos, stood opposed to the two minor queens, whom chance had made the representatives of the principle of liberalism.

It was in Portugal that matters first came to an issue. To England, Portugal was the most important country as Spain was to France, and for both powers a real neutrality was an impossibility. A complete victory for Dom Miguel, signified to England — apart from the indignation which must be excited by that monster's system of rule — the complete loss of her influence in Portugal, and at the same time the destruction of the constitutional principle which naturally had the sympathies of the English nation and the Whigs who were then in power, and which was identified with the government of those classes of society whom a commercial people like the English must necessarily consider. And England had already long since broken through her neutrality.

In regard to the government of France, the position was similar: Louis Philippe was the natural ally of Queen Isabella, whose claims to the throne rested, like his own, on a violation of the principle of legitimacy. But the victory of the Portuguese pretender would of necessity lead to that of the Spanish claimant whose cause had equal chances in its favour, and moreover there could not be a better opportunity of opposing a liberal solidarity on the part of the western powers to the legitimatist solidarity of the eastern, and thus confirm the stability of the new throne of France. This community of interests brought about the conclusion of a quadruple alliance between Portugal and Spain, England and France (12th of April, 1834), by which the regents of Portugal and Spain agreed to expel the two pretenders, and for this object a Spanish corps was to co-operate with the Portuguese troops; the undertaking was to be supported by England with her warships and by France, if necessary, with troops.

The result was soon apparent. On the 12th of May Dom Miguel's army was defeated by the united Spanish and Portuguese army at Asseiceira and on the 26th the two allies, Dom Miguel and Don Carlos, surrounded by a superior force, capitulated at Evora in the province of Alemtejo. The former took a money payment, which he might squander anywhere but in Spain and Portugal, promised to respect his niece's rights and retired from the scenes, taking ship for Genoa. Don Carlos went to England.

Affairs quieted down in Portugal. Dom Pedro summoned the cortes and restored the Constitution of 1826; monastic and knightly orders and various abuses were abolished; the Jesuits had to leave the country; but the establishment of the new order of things was completed with moderation and without revenge, and above all the law was treated with respect. On the 18th of September in that year the estates declared the queen, though only fifteen, to be of age, since the state of the regent's health did not permit of his attending to business. On the 24th Dom Pedro died at the age of thirty-seven.[b]

MARIA II (1834–1853 A.D.)

Donna Maria was sixteen years old at her father's death. The cortes believed nevertheless that it ought to declare the majority of the queen, which she would not have attained according to the charter until her eighteenth year. Donna Maria hastened to put all her confidence in the duke of Palmella. Senhor de Palmella and his friends, while they brought great support to the government, did not make up for the strength of which it had been deprived by Dom Pedro's death, and did not disarm any adversary. The position of the entire Portuguese ministry with regard to England was truly intolerable; placed between an imperious national sentiment and unconquerable necessities it was at all times accused by the opposition of sacrificing the country's interests to those of an insatiable ally. The question of customs duties and the renewal of the treaties furnished the enemies of the ministry with national weapons, for nothing was so unpopular in Portugal as the lowering of the tariff and free trade.

In spite of the enormous expenditure due to civil war and the general ruin, the raising of loans contracted in London easily covered at first the deficit in the treasury. The abundance of money was such that they even foolishly employed specie to retire a paper currency in circulation since the time of João V. This false prosperity had no other result than to close all eyes to the dangers of the future. At the beginning of 1835 the minister of finance was compelled to admit an enormous deficit. The government was unable to borrow any longer nor even increase their taxes. It became necessary to have recourse to expedients and to set out on the deplorable road of anticipations.

Officials' salaries and officers' pay were no longer regularly paid, and the number of malcontents grew in proportion to the impossibility of satisfying them. The army and the national guard of Lisbon were entirely in the clutches of the secret societies. The internal dissensions among the ministers led several of them to associate themselves with clubs and to seek in the anarchist party a passing point of support against their colleagues; for, while all attacks were directed against Palmella, and especially Carvalho, there were in the space of one year eight changes of cabinet. The motives of these changes were always of a personal nature, and were to be found in the intrigues of the clubs which often crossed and clashed with those of other clubs.

Upon this state of affairs there broke the revolt of La Granja, which served as a signal for a similar movement in Portugal. For more than a year alarming symptoms had been showing themselves. The chamber of deputies had refused the chief command of the army to the queen's first husband, Prince Augustus of Leuchtenberg. After four months of marriage he succumbed to a short illness.[c] In less than a year the queen remarried. Her second husband was Prince Ferdinand of Saxe-Coburg-Gotha, nephew of the Belgian king. He obtained the chief command of the army, which made matters more difficult as he was unpopular.[a]

Then the queen ordered the dissolution of the cortes at the moment when all the Spanish juntas were in insurrection. The government was playing with the frivolity and light-mindedness of the people when, on the 9th of September, 1836, the newly elected deputies from Oporto arrived in Lisbon. They all belonged to the radical party. A band of musicians advanced to meet them, the city was illuminated, and enthusiastic cheers filled the streets and byways. By the end of the evening the ministers became alarmed at the demonstration and sent out a battalion to restore order. The soldiers fraternised with the people and all cried, "Down with the ministers; long live the Constitution of 1822." This excited mob, really more joyous than hostile, made its way to the palace and sent the surprised queen a deputation ordering her to dismiss the ministers and adhere to the constitution.

The queen refused to obey, and rejected the revolutionists' commands. A little later she resigned herself to the necessity, and she burst into tears. The count of Lumiares, Bernardo de Sá da Bandeira, and Passos were named ministers, and the queen promised to convoke the cortes according to the forms of the Constitution of 1822, in order that they might recast the fundamental law of the kingdom.

Passos planned out a pantheon, issued a thousand regulations relating to libraries and museums, and abolished bull-fights through motives of philanthropy. Bernardo de Sá destroyed all that he could, his principle being that things would arrange themselves afterward as well as they could and what was once overthrown would never be re-established.

November 3rd a few persons of the court tried to work a counter-revolution. The queen secretly betook herself to the castle of Belem, from which place she called the army and the people of the court around her and abjured the forced oath she had taken on the 10th of September. This scheme, bad and unpracticable in itself, presented one difficulty among many others which had not been seen by the prime movers of the plot. Belem is separated from Lisbon by a little river, and the constitutionalists in seizing the bridge of Alcantara cut off all communication between the castle and the partisans of the charter. The hostile attitude of his Britannic majesty's warships intimidated no one. The constitutionalists strengthened their love of the constitution with their hatred for England, and this time the people of Lisbon seemed led by a common sentiment. At the end of three days the queen renounced her dangerous project and returned to the city amid bonfires and the enthusiastic acclamations of the people.

This unlucky and abortive affair proved three things : the solidity of Donna Maria's throne, which was never for one moment shaken by this foolish experiment ; the aversion of the people for the English yoke ; and the hatred of the radicals towards a few political men. Freire was assassinated at the bridge of Alcantara. On the 18th of January, 1837, after four months and a half of dictatorial power, exercised according to the statutes of the constitution by Bernardo de Sá and Passos, the constituent cortes met at Lisbon. According to the law of 1822 it formed a single chamber and was elected by almost universal suffrage. The 6th of May the cortes submitted the basis of the constitution and sixty-four votes against sixteen declared for absolute veto, the two chambers and the leading principles of all fundamental laws.

This was the opportunity for its enemies, and the baron de Leiria, who commanded in the north, raised the banner of insurrection on the 12th of July. Several garrisons, more important for the names of the towns than for the number of the soldiers, rose up to cries of "Long live the charter!" Marshal Saldanha proceeded to Castello Branco. The duke of Terceira soon joined him, and for a month the two insurgent marshals overran the country without opposition. The Lisbon government confided extraordinary powers to the viscount de Sá and the baron de Bomfim.

These two officers, with the constitutional forces, attacked the marshal's troops at Rio Mayor on the 28th of August, and, although on both sides they had had more than six weeks in which to make preparations, neither of the armies counted eight hundred men. But the soldiers were more prudent than their leaders. After a slight infantry skirmish in which the Portuguese nobility had sensible losses to deplore, the two marshals gave the order to charge to their little squadron and the viscount de Sá advanced at the head of his troops. The cavalry on both sides stopped at fifty paces, replaced their sabres in the scabbards, and having fraternised returned faithfully to the flags of their respective commanders. The latter saw themselves compelled to sign an armistice, and the marshals retired to the north to rejoin baron de Leiria who still held out in the suburbs of Valencia.

Forces were equal and victory depended on the side that would get hold of the corps which, having served in the army of Queen Christina, was returning to Portugal under the orders of the viscount das Antas. This general decided in favour of the constitutionals, and, after a bloody fight at Ruivaes on the 20th of September, the remains of the chartist army was obliged to take refuge in Galicia.

But the evil which no constitution could remedy was growing day by day. On the 14th of October bankruptcy was declared — the necessity of paying the victors had drained the last drop of the state's finances. The body of workmen at the arsenal, who for two weeks had been giving unequivocal signs of discontent, openly rebelled on the 13th of March, 1838. Baron Bomfim surrounded the arsenal buildings by a line of troops and the rebels fired first upon the soldiers. This was truly a critical moment for Portugal. The cortes were opposed to any vigorous measures and clung to the side of the insurrection. But the fate of the ministers was nevertheless bound to the maintenance of order, and Bernardo took his stand boldly. He marched with Baron Bomfim against the rebels, who were completely defeated after a furious and bloody combat. After this time the arsenal party, as it was called, attempted fresh insurrections and more than once threatened the peace of the kingdom, but the events of the 13th of March had irrevocably fixed the government's position. Besides, when on the 4th of April the queen took an oath to the new constitution and proclaimed a general amnesty for the past, the chartists and the moderate portion of the constitutionalists found themselves naturally united against the more radical faction. Afterwards they were almost completely confused under the name of the "friends of order."[b] On the 16th of September, 1837, Queen Maria had

[1835–1842 A.D.]

given birth to a son. This greatly improved the queen's position, but the king-consort continued very unpopular, and the condition of affairs encouraged Dom Miguel to seek aid in London. But he sought in vain and returned to Rome. Discontent was still rife in Portugal, cabinets played see-saw, and in August, 1840, the 6th regiment of the line mutinied and shot its colonel.

Meanwhile England was pressing its claims for £375,475 [$1,807,475] for commissariats in 1826 and for half-pay for the British officers who had served under Wellington and Beresford. The claim provoked only indignation in Portugal. In 1841 Spain came in for hostility.[a]

In 1835 the navigation of the Douro had caused considerable excitement between Spain and Portugal, which nearly led to a war between the two countries. There appeared in the *Gazette de Madrid* a violent article against Portugal, also an insulting one against Donna Maria II. Saldanha gave the Spanish government forty-eight hours to make reparation, notifying it that in the event of refusal a Portuguese fleet should fire the towns from Cadiz to Barcelona. Apology was made. Portugal had difficulties also with Denmark, when Saldanha requested the Portuguese minister to leave, if, after three days, satisfaction was not given. The Danish minister was recalled, but Saldanha obtained his wishes.

England complained that Portugal was too complaisant to France and the United States, and forgot her old ally, and declared she felt disposed to occupy the Portuguese Indian possessions on account of claims. Saldanha went to London with instructions to do as he pleased. Lord Palmerston told him to tell his government that England acceded to his desire to modify the convention, for his sake, and not for that of the Portuguese government.

Dom Miguel's party in Portugal, as well as the *absolutos* on the continent, considered he had now another chance of returning to his country. He left Rome for England, remaining some time, but he could make no move, and returned again to Italy. In December, 1841, the municipal elections commenced in Lisbon. There were now two great contending parties, the *moderados*, who supported the ministry, and the constitutionals, that of order; the pure Septembrists[1] were considered as revolutionists or even republicans, and there were most probably many Miguelites amongst them.[d]

CABRAL AND THE CHARTISTS IN POWER (1842 A.D.)

In January, 1842, Portugal once more found herself face to face with the sad prospect of revolution, and the leader no less a person than the minister of justice, Costa Cabral, formerly one of the most ardent of Septembrists, now entirely converted to Dom Pedro's charter. Secretly seconded by the king and by Dietz and Drummond, who composed the occult government at Lisbon, he went to Oporto and thence to Coimbra, proclaiming the abolition of the established constitution.

The queen, who was not in the secret of the plot, in vain confided its repression to Palmella, Das Antas, and Bomfim. The duke of Terceira pronounced in favour of Costa Cabral; Palmella took no action and the revolution was brought to a head before anyone had seriously thought of suppressing it. Costa Cabral completed his triumph with the promise that the cortes would be immediately convoked for the revision of the charter,

[1 Partisans of the liberal constitution of 1838.]

and from that time it was he who reigned under the name of the duke of Terceira, president of the council. It goes without saying that Donna Maria was content to subscribe to everything she formerly had opposed. Most docile, subject to the wishes of her husband and her confessor, she had, moreover, never liked the constitution, and had herself twice attempted to destroy it in 1837.

Sustained by the high protection of the court, by the servility of the two chambers, by the friendship of his brother the governor of Lisbon, and finally by the friendly neutrality of the Miguelites, for whom the fall of the constitution would be nothing less than a triumph, Costa Cabral had nothing to restrain him. And he was not the man to hesitate before despotism. It was not sufficient that the tribune was almost silenced; he soon affirmed his power by the promulgation of three decrees which abolished almost the last of Portugal's liberties. The first concerned the judges, whose independence he destroyed; the second delivered the officers over to the absolutism of the minister; the third submitted all education to a censor and struck a death-blow at the universities. Is there need to add that the press was not less abused, and no longer had freedom but to praise?

It was not long before he went a little further. For a long time one of the greatest plagues of the Portuguese administration was that they could not exist without loans. They borrowed to meet even the ordinary expenses, they borrowed to pay interest on the debt; they borrowed for redemptions —all the while accumulating a more onerous burden. Costa Cabral finally had his eyes opened to this state of affairs, pointed it out to the queen, and while he himself was responsible for twenty-three loans in three years, he dared undertake to get rid of them, understanding well that irreparable ruin would be the result of the continuation of such a policy. But whether the taxation he established to reopen the true sources of prosperity to the finances of his country was really too heavy, or the strangeness of the thing made it seem so, Costa Cabral did not have the time to carry out and improve this great reform. He had presumed too much on his own strength and the intelligence of the people; no government was solid enough in Portugal to stand such a test.

THE SEPTEMBRISTS OVERTHROW COSTA CABRAL

But from the day that Costa Cabral himself set the example of insurrection, by rousing Oporto and Coimbra in the name of the charter, all his former friends became allied to punish him as soon as possible for his apostasy. Their leaders were Das Antas, Passos, Sá da Bandeira, Loulé, and especially Bomfim, who represented the mixed party.

When he had furnished them an opportunity by the introduction of a new tax which could not fail to arouse the anger of the peasants, they induced the whole province of Minho to revolt; and the majority of the other towns showing similar inclinations, Costa Cabral found it impossible to hold up his head to the storm.[1] Cabral fled to Spain with his brother the governor, under pretext of a year's leave of absence which the queen herself had granted him. During this time those whom he had formerly exiled and despoiled succeeded to his high power.

[1 This insurrection was called the War of Maria da Fonte or "Patuleia" and was ended through foreign influence, by the Convention of Granada, June 29th, 1847.]

But it was not for long. Costa Cabral had been in power at least four years. Scarcely had his adversaries entered into possession of the authority, when they had to contend with a new counter-revolution hatched in the queen's palace and soon supported by England, France, and Spain.

Donna Maria's victory was also Costa Cabral's, the latter in truth was only awaiting the signal to reappear in Portugal, and (astonishing thing, and one that shows well how superficial these agitations are!) he was cordially received there. It seemed as if everybody was his friend. Justice must be rendered Cabral in that, far from being intoxicated with a victory as complete as it was unexpected, he appeared only desirous of wiping it out — perhaps because he feared to raise again all the resentment under which he had once succumbed, perhaps because he preferred to hold back, or perhaps because, scorned plebeian that he was, he feared to offend the aristocratic pride of the great families by the immediate occupation of the highest office. He therefore refused the ministry and, content with an anonymous supremacy, transferred the honour to Pombal's grandson, the old marshal the duke of Saldanha, January, 1848.

This policy of Costa Cabral's showed itself still better at the moment when Marshal Saldanha refused to retain the post which was a source of trouble to him. Costa Cabral begged the duke of Terceira and Duarte-Leitao to accept the presidency of the council, and it was only upon their positive refusal that he decided to reassume it himself. If nobody wanted it, how could he be blamed for taking it? Still, he tried to disarm the anger that might be aroused at his accession by accepting a feudal title which undoubtedly he cared little about. But was it not better to defer solemnly to the unconquerable prejudices of the Portuguese aristocracy by concealing a plebeian name under the pompous title of the count of Thomar? However that might be, the new president of the council used his power energetically for the reformation of abuses, to complete the reconciliation of Portugal and Rome, to improve the state of the finances, to stimulate agriculture and commerce, and to restore the navy. Never, whatever might be said of it afterward, had Portugal been so prosperous since the glorious era when Pombal had undertaken to revive the glories of olden times. If this administration, rigorous but able, could have maintained itself for only ten years, Portugal would have lifted itself out of the abyss into which it was threatening to disappear.

But unfortunately this was not to be. All his old adversaries, disconcerted for a moment by the suddenness of his return, returned on their side to their intrigues and their alliances. The Miguelites irritated at his reforms, the great nobles offended at his supremacy, the Septembrists indignant at what they called his apostasy, the journalists embittered at the severities of his new law against the press (1850) — all these combined to overthrow him again. There remained to find a leader, and that did not take long. The marshal Saldanha was there, discontented and anxious to avenge himself at any cost.

Having voluntarily left the ministry, the duke of Saldanha proclaimed himself at first the friend and devoted adherent of the count of Thomar. He even went so far as to say one day that in politics he and the count were one and the same person. But constancy and fidelity were not distinguishing qualities of the noble duke, and this effervescence of friendship did not prevent his regretting the authority he had just given up of his own accord. As his claims were admitted neither by the count of Thomar nor his colleagues, he was thrown roughly into the ranks of the opposition and his first declaration of hostilities was a virulent attack upon the minister of war. Neither the chamber, the ministers, nor the queen paid much attention to this, and the latter even dared to reply that she did not allow her servants to give her advice, and especially written advice, unless she asked it. This was a cruel allusion to the post of first major-domo of the palace with which the duke was invested. Thereupon Saldanha's anger put him at the disposition of all those who were willing to second his revenge.

A not less seductive hope for Costa Cabral's enemies was England's declared assistance. Lord Palmerston was at that time at the head of foreign affairs, and no minister was ever more exclusively preoccupied with the interests of England. At the first news of the reforms which the Portuguese government had accomplished, or was meditating, he did not lose an instant in encouraging its enemies, in overwhelming it with threatening notes, in recommending a close friendship with the Septembrists to the representatives of Great Britain, and even in sending a fleet with provisions and money. If there were to be a Portuguese renaissance, what would in truth become of England's commercial supremacy over that country, and through that country over the whole peninsula?

Accusations of embezzlement, intrigue, and corruption were renewed against Thomar which served to disconcert his friends. April 8th, 1851, the duke of Saldanha succeeded in raising two battalions. It was from Oporto that the signal for the revolt came. It extended from there to Coimbra and then to Lisbon, when it found a leader even in the prime minister's brother, Sylva Cabral. Some personal resentment had ranged this unhappy personage with the bitterest adversaries and calumniators of the count of Thomar. Forced finally to hand in his resignation, he was exiled. The count of Thomar took his departure, with regret at leaving his reforms uncompleted, and without the wealth, of whose accumulation his enemies so persistently accused him. As for the queen, she tried vainly to soften the rough blow which royalty itself had received. Neither the conquerors of the count of Thomar, nor Lord Palmerston, nor Sir Henry Seymour, powerfully supported by an English fleet, would consent to spare her any of the bitterness of her defeat. They signified their wish that she should solemnly retract all the acts of the preceding ministry, that she should remove the king from the command of the army, restore Marshal Saldanha to his post of major-domo, and even accept him as prime minister in place of the marshal the duke of Terceira, whom she had been forced to substitute for the count of Thomar. What could she do against this triumphant power? Donna Maria agreed to everything, and a few days later Saldanha entered Lisbon amid flowers and cries of enthusiasm, which the fickle populace lavished upon every victory.[e] In 1852 the charter was revised to suit all parties; direct voting, one of the chief claims of the radicals, was allowed, and the era of civil war came to an end.[f]

When, under Saldanha's more vigorous rule, peace was beginning to settle over the land, the queen died on November 15th, 1853, at the age of thirty-five. Her husband Ferdinand of Saxe-Coburg became regent for his minor son, who mounted the throne of Portugal on September 17th, 1855, as Dom Pedro V.[1]

[1 "Dom Pedro V, although only sixteen, showed as soon as he ascended the throne a subtlety of spirit, a greatness of soul, and so precocious an intelligence that his people augured the most happy destiny for the country, and in its joy gave him the surname of 'El Esperanzo,' their hopes in him being so great. But a short time after (1861) the young prince in his turn also died, smitten in the flower of his age, in the midst of unfinished works." — SILVERCRUYS.[h]]

PEDRO V (1855-1861 A.D.)

There was still that dream of uniting Spain to Portugal, but when the proposition was made to Pedro V, he replied : "They think to flatter my ambition and believe that I shall favour them ; they are mistaken. Besides the reasons of propriety, policy, and honour which should restrain me, there are considerations which I must not forget—yes, I—if others do forget them. They do not reflect that if the house of Braganza mounts the throne of the peninsula, Portugal would be nothing but a Spanish province, and that our nationality would be absorbed. But I, who am the first of the Portuguese, the first citizen of a country which occupies an honourable place in the history of humanity—I should be a faithless vicar, if I favoured such a project. These people are even our great enemies, for they prevent many useful enactments which might be for the common good of the two peoples — for example, the development of international communication, progress in the material interests of the countries, and the unity of weights, measures, money, and customs regulations."*g*

The only political event of any importance during the reign of Dom Pedro V, who in 1857 married the princess Stephanie of Hohenzollern, was the affair of the *Charles et Georges*. This French ship was engaged in what was undoubtedly the slave-trade, though slightly disguised, off the coast of Africa, when it was seized by the authorities of Mozambique, and, in accordance with the laws and treaties against the slave-trade, its captain, Roussel, was condemned to two years' imprisonment. The emperor Napoleon III, glad to have a chance of posing before the French people, and counting on his close alliance with England, instantly sent a large fleet to the Tagus under Admiral Lavaud, and demanded compensation, which, as England showed no signs of assistance, Portugal was compelled to pay. The whole country, especially the city of Lisbon, was ravaged by cholera and yellow fever during this reign, itself evidence of the extreme neglect of all sanitary precautions ; and on November 11th, 1861, the king, who refused to quit the pestilence-stricken capital, died of cholera, and was speedily followed to the grave by two of his brothers, Dom Ferdinand and Dom João.*f*

THE REIGN OF LUIZ (1861-1889 A.D.)

The development of affairs in Portugal now took a decidedly liberal course. The Portuguese government had recognised the new Italian monarchy already in June, 1861, and the following year King Luiz had married Princess Maria Pia, the daughter of King Victor Emmanuel. On December 22nd, 1861, Dom Luiz took the oath to the constitution and, since the people were alarmed at the frequent number of deaths in the royal family, the government laid before the cortes a law controlling the regency and another which declared princesses also to be eligible for the throne and thus put still further off the danger that a descendant of Dom Miguel might succeed to the throne of Portugal.

Not a single Portuguese bishop appeared at the celebrated council at Rome in 1862 and, in a document dated July 3rd, the pope had occasion to complain that in the "lamentable state of the Catholic church in Portugal" the bishops were too lukewarm and tolerant ; he reminded them that it was their duty to watch over the sheep intrusted to their care so that — in the language of the curial — "they should not be devoured by the ravenous beasts which make the surface of the earth unsafe to live upon." When some of the clergy took advantage of this to preach against the government, they were reminded by a proclamation of the minister of justice (August 2nd) that there were prisons in Portugal for such cases. The ministers were of liberal colour ; in April, 1863, an important law was passed abolishing the right of primogeniture, an old evil of their country; in May, 1864, a decision of the second chamber demanded that the peers' title should no longer be hereditary.[b]

In spite of popular opposition the government entered resolutely on reform by abolishing capital punishment for any crime, civil or political. Following the example set by many European countries, they also adopted the metric system, organising consolidated funds and, what was a very important reform, abolishing the royal gifts of lands to support a title. In 1864, a treaty of delimitation which had been in progress for several years was definitely drawn up with Spain. New roads were marked out and furrowed the kingdom in every direction, making Lisbon the centre for all roads having direct communication with the province. Aqueducts were constructed ; towns made sanitary; hospitals, almshouses, model dwellings rose in the large industrial centres. Newly made canals allowed these towns to transport their goods seawards without unnecessary costly relading. The smallest boroughs were provided with schools, etc. But all these works, useful, it is true, and almost necessary, made a large hole in the state coffers. Fontes Pereira de Mello tried to overcome this by getting votes for the modification and increase of old taxes of every kind, even of the yearly land tax, also the amending of indirect taxation. These reforms were the cause of new troubles in Oporto, but they were suppressed without recourse to arms. Lisbon and several other towns followed Oporto's example, and the government, fearing lest troubles there should insensibly assume serious proportions and lead to civil war, yielded to the people's will and withdrew the new taxes (1867).

In 1868, a fresh insurrection broke out in Spain and was necessarily felt in Portugal. It was an immediate question of conferring the Spanish crown so as to fuse the two peoples, a union which would have taken the title of the Iberian Union. But the Portuguese, remembering what their ancestors had suffered under the Spanish yoke, feared lest this union should lead to the surrender of Portugal to Spain, and profited by the anniversary of the coming to the throne of João IV (of the illustrious house of Braganza) in 1640, to make strong resistance against Spain. In view of this excitement, the Spaniards abandoned their first idea, not being willing to expose themselves any more to the vindictiveness of a people not able to forget oppression dating nearly four centuries back.

One of the wisest and most humane reforms, and one which adds most to the glory of Luiz I, was the entire abolition of slavery in every colony. But, by a curious and sad coincidence, as if in answer to the royal benefit, about five hundred Portuguese were pitilessly massacred by natives on the Zambesi. On this news being announced, an army corps embarked immediately to avenge the honour of the flag.[h]

The history of Portugal for the years 1863–1866, as far as its connection with the rest of Europe is concerned, presents almost empty pages — which, however, was not precisely a misfortune to the country. We read in November, 1864, of differences between the government and the pope which ended in the recall from Rome of the Portuguese ambassador, who did not return thither until two years later; of the opening and closing of the sessions of the cortes, of elections, of satisfactory finances, of the modification and change of ministries. It was already something remarkable that the great state question was raised at the birth of a prince in August, 1865, that the papal nuncio would not permit King Victor Emmanuel, the father of the young mother, who was in a sense under a ban, to officiate as godfather, and that the royal child was not admitted to the privilege of baptism until after Napoleon III had added to his many rôles that of being sponsor to the Portuguese prince.*b*

In 1866 Dom Miguel died, after having stood at the head of the absolutists calling themselves the Party of the Faith, and sojourning at various European courts. He had been lampooned by the liberal press, but was given a magnificent funeral.

The old and stormy Saldanha threatened a *pronunciamento* in 1870, and succeeded in ousting from court the king's favourite, the duke of Loulé. He was appeased by supplanting Loulé as minister, but after four months was gracefully disposed of on the pretext of the embassy to England, where he died in 1876. The ministry of Pereira de Mello lasted for three years, 1883–1886, in which year there was danger of collision with the French Republic in view of the marriage of Luiz's heir to the daughter of the comte de Paris. The ceding of a portion of the Lower Congo territory to Belgium in 1885, the definition of German and Portuguese spheres of influence in Africa, the cession of the island of Macao by China, the building of a railroad in Angola marked colonial affairs. In 1889 there was alarm over the encroachments of England on Portuguese influence in Africa, and Major Serpa Pinto invaded territory on the Shiré river claimed by England. The British government demanded reparation and sent to Portugal a fleet which, January 11th, 1890, induced Portugal to withdraw from the Shiré region under protest.

CARLOS I BECOMES KING (1889 A.D.)

This surrender provoked outbreaks at Lisbon and Oporto; the ministry of José de Castro resigned, and the republicans, stimulated by the Brazilian success in establishing a republic the year before, turned the anti-British demonstration into a republican agitation. King Carlos had succeeded his father when King Luiz died of typhoid fever, October 19th, 1889. The new king assumed to side with the popular feeling and refused the order of the Garter which Queen Victoria had just offered him. The republican movement overshot itself, and, after various arrests were made, the elections were strongly for the government. August 20th, an agreement with England had been reached, after a vain appeal to international arbitration. The terms were again distasteful to the public and the cortes refused to accept them. Passages at arms took place between the Portuguese and the British in Nika (Manica), which by the terms of the August agreement were Portuguese. But the terms had been declined and the Portuguese were defeated. A military revolt was suppressed in January, 1891, and the republican press suppressed. The terms of the August agreement were now accepted and a treaty with Great Britain was signed May 28th, 1891.

Financial affairs had now reached a crisis after wrecking so many cabinets. In May, 1892, the government finally declared itself bankrupt. Still relief did not come and Oliveira Martins, after failing as minister to establish a sound financial condition, gave way to Ferreira, who yielded to Hintze-Ribeiro, who lasted from 1894 to 1897, and returned in 1899.

In 1895 a reform of the constitution of the cortes was achieved, the lower chamber was reduced from 170 to 145, the upper house was to be constituted of ninety members chosen by the king, the royal princes, and twelve bishops; the right of suffrage was based on the ability to read and write and the minimum payment of 500 reis (50 cents) in taxes. Domestic servants, government employees, and soldiers are, however, forbidden to vote. This same year the king visited England, accepted the order of the Garter, and began the cultivation of that British friendship which its liberal construction of the limits of neutrality during the South African War served to strengthen — at least in England, though violently attacked in Portugal. In 1900 the Delagoa Bay Railroad dispute with England was decided in Portugal's favour by Switzerland as arbitrator.[a]

PORTUGUESE LITERATURE

The country of Camoens and João de Barros has never lost its love for letters, and the Portuguese people have always possessed a poetic strain. If in the eighteenth century poetry reached the level of too Parnassian trifles, it redeemed itself after the war under the impulse of Francisco Manoel do Nascimento, and with still finer taste under the influence of Almo da Garot, and of Castilho, followed by a good number of lyric and dramatic poets and romancers. J. B. Gomes (died 1812), by his sole tragedy *The New Inès de Castro*, has taken a place among the most remarkable of dramatists. Other authors have written for the theatre; for example, Vasconcellos, Reis Quita, Biester, Pimentet, and perhaps the first of them all is Almeida Garrett (died 1854).

Bulhão Pato has made a name among the poets as well as T. A. Gonzaga, João de Lemos, Antonio Pereira da Cunha, and Ribeiro, the minister. Like King Diniz of old and Philip of Lancaster, King Pedro IV was a poet. He has written verse destined to be set to music and he has given the country the "Constitution Hymn." Dominic Buontempo founded the Philharmonic Academy at Lisbon, and the composer Marcos Portugal is known throughout all Europe.

Alexandre Herculano (died 1878), erudite and *littérateur*, rivalled the work of the Benedictines in his *Portugalica Monumenta Historica;* but he did not please the clergy, for he wrote of the Inquisition in Portugal and the Concordat of February 21st, 1857. In the *Harp of the Believer* he has told in verse of the eternal strife between doubt and faith.

Science, letters, and art have had illustrious representatives in José Ribeira, Antonio de Almeida (died 1839), Gaetan de Amaral, Antonio de Carmo, Velho de Barbosa, Costa de Macedo who has aroused much discussion by his opinions, Francisco Alexandre Lobo, de Carvalho, Manoel Coelho da Rocha. In geography, the viscount of Santarem (died 1856), Brito Capello, Robert Irens, Serpa Pinto, and Otto Schutt, count among African explorers.[g]

The present king of Portugal, Carlos I, born in 1863, has shown a decided determination to seek the peace his country so much needs. He has shown also a real interest in science and letters and since the five hundredth anniversary of Prince Henry the Navigator celebrated in March, 1894, he has shown a lively concern for deep-sea soundings and exploration. He has made personal studies and both published their results and shown them at an oceanographic exhibition which he opened in 1897. The world is too well mapped to offer such prizes as once lay hidden in the Sea of Darkness, but there is a peculiar fitness in the present monarch's interest in that ocean across which his great predecessor showed the path that led Portugal to greatness, and through Portugal turned the whole world to exploration.*a*

A PORTUGUESE PEASANT

APPENDIX A

THE INQUISITION[1]

The Inquisition was a judicial police organisation instituted by the Roman church with the concurrence of temporal rulers for the purposes of suppressing heresy and blasphemy. * * * It has left an odious memory—and not without reason. Anyone who denies that atrocities were committed by the Inquisition must indeed be blinded by a foolish and prejudiced desire to apologise for the deeds of history. But why is it against the Inquisition that the indignation inspired today by the memory of early religious persecutions is particularly directed? Thousands of human beings were burned for their faith before the Inquisition existed. * * * There is one circumstance, however, among others, which explains and justifies the general sentiment, and that is that the Inquisition pretended to be—and was—a regular judicial organisation. The worst excesses are forgotten when they are not systematic. It is the long-continued travesties of justice perpetrated in the service of fanaticism or for reasons of state that arouse the more lasting resentment. Therefore it is that, whatever be their number, the victims of the Roman Inquisition weigh so heavy in the scales of history.—From the article "L'INQUISITION," by C. V. Langlois, in *La Grande Revue* (Paris, 1901).

ALL the gods have been addicted to jealousy. Their worshippers have accordingly usually felt and often acted towards heretics with the characteristic ruthlessness of the most merciless of passions.

Egypt was not free from religious reigns of terror, nor yet India, nor China, and even the genial creeds of Greece brought the mildly unorthodox Socrates to his death. Rome was comparatively tolerant of alien religions for political convenience, but there were laws against foreign rites in Rome;

[1 This brief study, inserted here because Spain and Portugal were the chief centres of the fury of the Inquisition, will afford glimpses also of its development in other countries.]

the prætor Hispalus was banished for worshipping Jupiter Sabasius, and the temples of Isis and Serapis were thrown down after they had been erected in the city. Augustus and Tiberius proscribed Egyptian and Jewish worship in Rome, the latter sending four thousand Jews to Sardinia. The hideous sufferings of the early Christians and the martyrdoms they underwent in the arenas are well known.

When at length the victims became the victors and the emperor Constantine was persuaded to Christianity, the same intolerant zeal from which the Christians had suffered now turned the tables on the pagans. At this time the Christians had not developed an idolatry of their own such as later brought on the terrors of the war of the image-breakers, so they heaped contempt upon the objects of worship revered by the pagans. The Jews were as usual the first and the worst sufferers. Then, again, as usual, the bitterest of all punishments were spent upon those who differed only slightly in doctrine. Constantine tried confiscation and exile on the Donatists, in 316 A.D.; he branded Arius as an infamous outlaw and had his writings burned.*a*

All the laws of Constantine were subsequently renewed by his successors, and applied with more or less rigour to the different heretical sects. By an edict published in January, 381 A.D., Theodosius the Great deprives heretics of all their churches, and annuls all edicts to the contrary into which preceding emperors had been surprised. In this edict he condemns by name the Photinians, Arians, and Eunomians; he recommends the Nicene Creed, and prohibits all assemblies of heretics within the walls of cities; adding, moreover, that if they attempted to cause any disturbance, they should be even banished from the cities.

In the same year he published a much more severe law against the Manichæans; he declared them infamous; deprived them totally of the power of making a will, or even of succeeding to their paternal or maternal property; and ordered all such property to be confiscated, except in the case of children, who were qualified, if they embraced a more holy religion, to inherit their father's or mother's property. Another law of Theodosius treats still more rigorously those Manichæans who disguised themselves under the names of Encratites, Saccophori, and Hydroparastates; he subjected them to capital punishment. To insure the execution of this law the emperor orders the prefect of the prætorium to appoint inquisitors, charged to discover heretics and to inform against them.

This is the first time that the name of an inquisitor against heretics occurs; but the Inquisition itself was of older standing, for we have already seen Constantine institute one precisely similar against the Arians and the other heretics of his time. These severe measures were provoked by the abominable doctrine of the Manichæans, which had drawn down on them, from the very origin of their sect, the severity of even the pagan emperors.*c*

When the Arians secured an emperor of their creed they enforced on the Athanasians a heavy usury of exile, punishment, torture, and even death, till the emperor Julian was driven to exclaim, according to Ammianus,*h* "Even beasts are not so cruel to men as the generality of Christians to each other."

This work is not the place for an account of all the heresies that have complicated Christianity without cessation. The great feud of iconoclasm has already been described and the major disagreements between the Greek and Roman churches have been recounted in the history of the papacy, where it was also shown how the growth of papal supremacy brought about a constant duel with the kings and the emperor.*a*

Whilst the hierarchy, unmindful of its spiritual calling, was entangling itself in ceaseless warfare, in order to bring all secular power under its sway ; whilst the system of ecclesiastical doctrines, with its progressive development, was enclosing the reason with bonds ever narrowing ; whilst the means of salvation held out by the church were at the same time ever more and more losing their spiritual character and their moral power, by the one-sided speculations of the schoolmen, and also sinking to a lifeless mechanism in their administration by a coarse priesthood which had lost all respect for morality; lastly, while this tortuous church system, despairing of any spiritual influence, was endeavouring to win consideration for itself by continual acts of external aggression; it could not but be that the rebellious against the church, who in earlier times came forward but one by one, should now be growing more numerous and more powerful.

The earlier divisions in the church employed themselves for the most part only in speculations of the understanding ; and even for this very reason the church always succeeded, as soon as she could adopt strong measures, in bringing back the recusants, for the interest taken in a moral conception of nearly equivalent meaning seldom remained for many generations unconquered by persecution. But there lay at the root of the opposition to the church, which now began to feel its way forward, a living moral interest, which felt itself injured by the whole condition of the church; and even for this very reason this opposition was rather strengthened than weakened by the bloodshed resorted to as a means to destroy it. It stood always unconquered, although the opposing parties differed widely from each other in the peculiarities of their systems, and modified them in many ways.

THE CATHARI

At the same time that two frantic enthusiasts, Tanchelm, who wandered about from 1115 to 1124 in the Netherlands, and Eudes de Stella or Eon, who roved till 1148 in Brittany, perplexed the minds of men, two ecclesiastics in southern France, the priest, Pierre de Bruis or Bruys (from 1104–1124, Petrobrusiani) and Henry, formerly a monk of Cluny and deacon (from 1116–1148, Henriciani), declaimed zealously against the mechanical organisation of the church and the immorality of the clergy. But besides these, the Manichæans who trace their origin to the period of time before this were continually on the increase. The most common names for them now, were in Germany *Cathari* or *Ketzer*, in Italy *Paterini*, in France *Publicani*, though many other names were in use ; not only did they make their appearance permanently in most distant quarters of France, but they also planted themselves in the neighbouring countries. The Cathari reached England in the year 1159 ; they were, however, quickly exterminated.

But the headquarters of the Cathari were those countries in which at that time, along with civic freedom, civilisation, and education, discontent at the wanton and avaricious clergy had grown up in a remarkable manner ; such were southern France and northern Italy. In southern France, where Toulouse was their central point, the interest awakened by Pierre de Bruis and Henry worked for their advantage. The synodal decrees issued against them remained without effect, for almost all the barons of this country protected them, and so their numbers here received a very considerable increase. The bishops of the district vainly endeavoured in the council at Lombers (1165) to bring back these *bonos homines*, as they were here usually called, to the church ; little more effect was produced by the cardinal-legate Peter of St. Chrysogonus in Toulouse (1178), and the severe decree of Alexander III, in the Third Lateran Council (1179). Against Roger II, viscount of Béziers, Carcassone, Albi, and Rasez, who protected the Cathari, the cardinal-legate Henry, abbot of Clairvaux, already headed a crusading army (in 1181), but he could produce no lasting effect. [See the history of the Crusades.] In the beginning of the thirteenth century the greater part of the daughters of the nobility were brought up in the educational establishments of the Perfectæ, who lived together in monastic style.

TESTING THE BOOK OF THE TRUE GOSPEL BY FIRE. THE BOOK IS REMOVED, UNSCORCHED, FROM THE FLAMES

(From a sixteenth century cut in the Louvre)

THE WALDENSES

From the scriptural and reforming turn of mind which had been spread by means of Pierre de Bruis and Henry, along with the sect of the Cathari, in southern France, there arose from the year 1170 the party of the Waldenses [or Vaudois]:[1] free from all speculative enthusiasm they consecrated all their energies to realise once again apostolic Christendom, with all its simplicity and all its inward devotion. About that year began the founder of the sect, Peter Waldo or Waldensis from Lyons, with several companions,

[1] Confusion has been introduced by both friend and foe into the history of the Waldenses. At first they were confounded with the Cathari or Albigenses by Catholics in order to represent them as Manichæans ; by reformed writers in order to clear the Albigenses also from the charge of Manichæism. Further, the origin of the Waldenses is often referred to an earlier period than that of Peter Waldensis, though it is so clearly proved by the witness of contemporaries that he is the founder of the sect.

to preach the Gospel in the manner of the apostles. At first they had so little intention of separating from the church that, when the archbishop of Lyons forbade them to preach, they petitioned the pope Alexander III in 1179 for his permission. But when Lucius III (in 1184) pronounced sentence of excommunication against them, then they thought they must obey God rather than man, and withdrew from a church which cursed that which seemed to them a call from heaven. At first the only question at issue between them and the Roman church was on the exclusive right of the clergy to preach; and they spread themselves more easily in those countries where the deficiency of the church was exposed plainly enough for the conviction of all, but where many still felt themselves not less repulsed by the Catharism, which was set up in opposition; for instance in France, particularly the southern parts, down as far as Aragon, and in northern Italy, particularly in Milan. And in every place where they came fresh zeal went forth from them among the people, to learn to understand Holy Scripture for themselves.

The earlier measures taken against the heretics in southern France had caused so little hindrance to their extension that they constituted the dominant party at the end of the twelfth century in many parts of this country. For this reason Innocent III, immediately after his accession to the see in 1198, was induced to send legates thither armed with the most unlimited powers for the suppression of heretics. After they had produced, by forcible measures, effects more apparent than real, Diego, bishop of Osma, with Dominic, the subprior of his cathedral, persuaded them in the year 1206 to adopt a more apostolic way of proceeding. Now the two legates, the Cistercians Peter of Castelnau and Raoul, with these two Spaniards, wandered barefoot from place to place and held conferences with the heretics on the disputed points (1206 and 1207). When however all this continued without effect, they returned again to the old method with tenfold cruelty.

CRUSADE AGAINST THE ALBIGENSES

Raymond VI, count of Toulouse, though outwardly a Catholic, had fallen out with the ambitious legate Peter of Castelnau. So when the latter in 1208 was murdered by an unknown hand, the monks threw the blame on the count ; and Innocent III seized this opportunity to have a crusade preached against him by Arnold, abbot of Citeaux ; for which national jealousy and the allurements of the delicious south procured great popularity in northern France. In order to avert the threatening danger, Raymond sought for reconciliation. Innocent granted this with a view to weaken the resistance of the victims by division. When, in June, 1209, the count submitted to the most humiliating conditions which Milo the papal legate prescribed to him, and even took the cross himself from his hands, he only effected the delay of the blow destined for himself, that it might strike with so much the greater certainty.

The crusading army assembled against the Albigenses, with the frantic Arnold [1] as papal legate at its head, first marched upon the domain of Raymond Roger, viscount of Béziers (1209). After the fall of Béziers and Carcassonne, the devastated land was conquered. But among the noble

[1 This terrible man, in his letter to Innocent III announcing his victories, relates himself with triumph : " Our troops sparing neither sex nor age put to the sword nearly twenty thousand ; splendid deeds were accomplished in the overthrow of the enemies, the whole city was sacked and burned by a divine revenge marvellous fierce."]

crusaders only Simon de Montfort was willing to receive the spoil from the legate. Next they turned against Raymond of Toulouse, who had been spared till now. Extravagant demands, which he could not satisfy, formed the pretext for excommunicating and attacking him (1211). The pope himself was no longer able to check his own instruments; the crusade was preached with fresh ardour; the territory of the count was conquered by Simon de Montfort, and formally adjudged to him by a council at Montpellier in 1215 for his own possession.

Innocent III did not only confirm this grant at the great Lateran Council in this same year, but also held up the principle of the method of procedure hitherto adopted against these countries, as a precedent in similar cases. Then at length Raymond sought for help in the attachment of his former subjects, and after Simon's death (1218) he made a considerable advance in the reconquest of his country, although the pope, without ceasing, used every means of resistance. When, after the death of Raymond VI (1222), Raymond VII regained his whole ancestral heritage, and had even forced his enemy Amaury, son of Simon, to a complete surrender, then Honorius III, elsewhere so mild, still thought it due to the papal honour to hate the father in the son, however guiltless. He stirred up Louis VIII, king of France, to conquer Toulouse for himself in a new crusade. Hostilities began on the 6th of June, 1226, but they were greatly crippled by the death of Louis VIII on the 18th of November of the same year; at length Raymond obtained peace on the hardest conditions, by which a part of his domain passed into the power of France, and the annexation of the rest to this kingdom was furthered.

THE INQUISITION ESTABLISHED

The unhappiness of this country was accomplished by the horrors of the Inquisition which now rose up.[1] In order to perpetuate the work of blood begun by the papal legate in a permanent institution, the Fourth Lateran Council in 1215 made it the chief business of the episcopal synodal tribunals to search out and punish heretics; and the Council of Toulouse (1229) achieved the organisation of this episcopal Inquisition. However, soon after it was in fact almost annihilated; for in 1232 and 1233 Gregory IX appointed the Dominicans to be the standing papal inquisitors, and forthwith they began their hideous work in the countries tainted with heresy. In order that the church may not seem to soil herself with blood, the secular princes must serve the office as executioner. Louis IX in 1228, Frederick II in 1232, the ill-fated Raymond VII in 1233, each passed the requisite laws.

That the new Inquisition might strike more of the guilty, a way of proceeding was prescribed for it, to which of necessity many of the guiltless must fall victims. Thus armed, this monster raged with most frightful fury in southern France, where the heretics had only learned from former events

[1 Some Catholic writers would fain excuse St. Dominic from the imputation of having founded the Inquisition. It is true he died some years before the organisation of that tribunal; but he established the principles on which, and the monkish militia by whom, it was administered. The Sicilian Paramo,*i* traces it up to a much more remote antiquity. According to him, God was the first inquisitor, and his condemnation of Adam and Eve furnished the model of the judicial forms observed in the trials of the Holy Office. The sentence of Adam was the type of the inquisitorial "reconciliation," his subsequent raiment of the skins of animals was the model of the san-benito, and his expulsion from paradise the precedent for the confiscation of the goods of heretics. This learned personage deduces a succession of inquisitors through the patriarchs, Moses, Nebuchadrezzar, and King David, down to John the Baptist, and even Christ, in whose precepts and conduct he finds abundant authority for the tribunal.*m*] to keep themselves more secret.   Germany for a short space of time (1231–1233) was taught to know the Inquisition in its maddest rage in Conrad of Marburg, and in the Dominican monk Conrad Dorso who came to Strasburg ; and at the same time acquired the most fearful experience of the abuse of the new laws against heretics in the crusade on the Stedinger, the lovers of freedom, in 1234.   But by these events so universal a resistance against every Inquisition was aroused, that Germany for a long time after remained free from this monster.

In the twelfth century the executions of heretics were for the most part the handiwork of the irritated populace, and even found much opposition among the clergy.   However, the theory of religion, which in the thirteenth century was especially flexible, in this case also adapted itself to the practice of the church by the vindication of the new laws against heresy.

Another no less evil result of this period, so fraught with outrage, was that the laity were entirely forbidden Holy Scripture, so that the possession of a translation of the Bible was forthwith accounted a token of heresy, and only translations prepared for the purpose of supporting the Romish church were tolerated.

COSTUME OF A PERSON CON-
DEMNED TO BE BURNED,
BUT WHO CONFESSED BE-
FORE HIS CONDEMNATION

(From *Historia Inquisitionis*,
1592)

The regulations which were adopted against the heretics, and the cruel manner in which their so-called conversion was pursued, could only produce exactly the contrary effect to that they had in view upon their convictions.   This, however, they did accomplish, that the persecuted persons, filled with exaggerated hatred and horror of the church, spread themselves with the greatest secrecy over other countries also.   Thus in the thirteenth century public feeling was roused ever more and more against Rome, against the clergy, and against the abuses of the church, and from time to time there rose a stirring sense of the necessity of a reformation to counteract them.   On comparison of the morals of the clergy with those of the heretics, the advantage is decidedly in favour of the latter ; so it cannot seem strange if in the thirteenth century we find the earlier parties more widely spread than before, and fresh sects springing up alongside of them.   Yet the number of new names of heretics in this period is far greater than that of new parties.

The Cathari, or as they are now more commonly called the Albigenses or Bulgarians, did not only maintain their ground in southern France, but increased in number chiefly in upper Italy, where the political distraction of the country was advantageous to them, and where Milan continued to be their principal abode.   But they spread themselves also into the rest of Italy as far as Spain, and throughout Germany ; they were very numerous in Bosnia and the adjoining countries, often the prevailing party, and they maintained in all lands a close connection with each other.

When the persecutions began, the Waldenses were standing so near the Catholic church that a reconciliation seemed to be by no means difficult.   But the horrors of the persecution had no further effect on the Waldenses than to confirm them more and more in their anti-hierarchical system, and to place their doctrine and ecclesiastical constitution on a more independent footing. The more plainly their departure from church teaching could vindicate itself as a purification of the church, the more easy acceptation they found with the thoughtful of their time. As early as in the thirteenth century they showed themselves in the valleys of Piedmont, in which they have maintained themselves until now. Still, not only did they spread in other countries, as for instance as far as Germany, but also put in circulation among numbers, who did not come over to their society, ideas unfavourable to the prevailing faith of the church.

Besides the old sects, new ones were engendered in the thirteenth century. The pantheistic system introduced by Amalric of Bène, after the persecution it underwent in Paris in the year 1210, only spread more widely than before. In the course of the thirteenth century its disciples might be found in different places ; at the end of this century they were already so numerous among the Beghards on the Rhine that the people understood only to be meant by the name of Beghards, although they called themselves brothers and sisters of the Free Spirit. In the beginning of the fourteenth century they made their appearance also in Italy.

Other sects pass quickly in review before us. As the universal discontent of the advancing tyranny of the hierarchy aroused isolated resistances in England and in France, so the ill usage of the Hohenstaufen family gave rise to a sect in Halle in Swabia (about 1248), which declared the hierarchy to be abolished in consequence of its moral corruption of the entire purpose of the church. After the extermination of the Hohenstaufen family the detestation caused by this deed of the hierarchy was maintained for centuries by the expectation that one time an emperor Frederick would wreak vengeance in blood on the papacy. This expectation also found place among the manifold superstitions, chiefly borrowed from the Fratricelli, with which the apostolic brothers from 1260 to 1307 disquieted the north of Italy.[d]

The statutes of the Council of Toulouse (1229), framed after the successful termination of the war against the Albigenses, in order to absolutely extirpate every lingering vestige of heresy, form the code of persecution, which not merely aimed at suppressing all public teaching but the more secluded and secret freedom of thought. It was a system which penetrated into the most intimate sanctuary of domestic life ; and made delation not merely a merit and a duty, but an obligation also, enforced by tremendous penalties.

The archbishops, bishops, and exempt abbots were to appoint in every parish one priest, and three or more lay inquisitors, to search all houses and buildings, in order to detect heretics, and to denounce them to the archbishop or bishop, the lord, or his bailiff, so as to insure their apprehension. The lords were to make the same inquisition in every part of their estates. Whoever was convicted of harbouring a heretic forfeited the land to his lord, and was reduced to personal slavery. If he was guilty of such concealment from negligence, not from intention, he received proportionate punishment. Every house in which a heretic was found was to be razed to the ground, the farm confiscated. The bailiff who should not be active in detecting heretics was to lose his office, and be incapacitated from holding it in future. Heretics, however, were not to be judged but by the bishop or some ecclesiastical person.

Anyone might seize a heretic on the lands of another. Heretics who recanted were to be removed from their homes, and settled in Catholic cities ; to wear two crosses of a different colour from their dress, one on the right side, one on the left. They were incapable of any public function unless reconciled by the pope or by his legate. Those who recanted from fear of death were to be immured forever. All persons, males of the age of fourteen, females of twelve, were to take an oath of abjuration of heresy, and of their Catholic faith; if absent, and not appearing within fifteen days, they were held suspected of heresy. All persons were to confess, and communicate three times a year, or were in like manner under suspicion of heresy. No layman was permitted to have any book of the Old or New Testament, especially in a translation, unless perhaps the Psalter, with a breviary, or the Hours of the Virgin. No one suspected of heresy could practise as a physician. Care was to be taken that no heretic had access to sick or dying persons. All wills were to be made in the presence of a priest. No office of trust was to be held by one in evil fame as a heretic. Those were in evil fame who were so by common report, or so declared by good and grave witnesses before the bishop.

But statutes of persecution always require new statutes rising above each other in regular gradations of rigour and cruelty. The legate found the canons of Toulouse to be eluded or inefficient. He summoned a council at Melun, attended by the archbishop of Narbonne and other prelates. The unhappy count of Toulouse was compelled to frame the edicts of this council into laws for his dominions. The first provision showed that persecution had wrought despair. It was directed against those who had murdered, or should murder, or conceal the murderers of persecutors of heretics. A reward of one mark was set on the head of every heretic, to be paid by the town, or village, or district to the captor.

It was evident that the heretics had now begun to seek concealment in cabins, in caves, and rocks, and forests; not merely was every house in which one should be seized to be razed to the ground, but all suspected caves or hiding-places were to be blocked up; with a penalty of twenty-five livres of Toulouse to the lord on whose estate such houses or places of concealment of evil report should be found. Those who did not assist in the capture of heretics were liable to punishment. If any one was detected after death to have been a heretic, his property was confiscated. Those who had made over their estates in trust, before they became heretics, nevertheless forfeited such estates. Those who attempted to elude the law by moving about, under pretence of trade or pilgrimage, were ordered to render an account of their absence. A council at Béziers (1233) enforced upon the clergy, under pain of suspension or of deprivation, the denunciation of all who should not attend divine service in their churches on the appointed days, especially those suspected of heresy.*g*

METHOD OF PROCEDURE WITH A SUSPECT

The method of proceeding in the courts of the Inquisition was at first simple, and not materially different from that in the ordinary courts. But gradually the Dominicans, guided by experience, rendered it far more complex; and so shaped their proceedings that the mode of trying heretical causes (if the phrase be allowable) became altogether different from that usually practised in judicial proceedings. For these good friars, being wholly unskilled in forensic affairs, and acquainted with no other tribunal than that which in the Romish church is called the penitentiary tribunal, regulated these new courts of the Inquisition, as far as possible, according to the plan of those religious proceedings. And hence arose that strange system of jurisprudence, bearing in many respects the most striking features of injustice and wrong. Whoever duly considers this history of their origin will be able to account for many things that seem unsuitable, absurd, and contrary to justice, in the mode of proceeding against offenders in the courts of the Inquisition.*

When the Inquisition discovered a transgressor of their laws, either by common report, or by their spies, or by an informer, he was cited three times to appear before them; and if he did not appear, he was forthwith condemned. It was safest to appear on the first citation; because the longer a man delayed the more guilty he would be; and the Inquisition had their spies, and a thousand concealed ways for getting an absconding heretic in their power.

When a supposed heretic was once in the hands of the Inquisition, no one dared to inquire after him, or write to him, or intercede for him. When everything belonging to the person seized was in their hands, then the process began; and it was protracted in the most tedious manner.

After many days, or perhaps months, which the accused dragged out in a loathsome dungeon, the keeper of the prison asked him, as it were accidentally, if he wished to have a hearing. When he appeared before his judges, they inquired, just as if they knew nothing about him, who he was, and what he wanted. If he wished to be informed what offence he had committed, he was admonished to confess his faults himself. If he confessed nothing, time was given him for reflection, and he was remanded to prison. If, after a long time allowed him, he still confessed nothing, he must swear to answer truly to all the questions put to him. If he would not swear, he was condemned without further process. If he swore to give answer, he was questioned in regard to his whole life, without making known to

COSTUME OF A CONDEMNED
PERSON WHO CONFESSED
AFTER CONVICTION

(From *Historia Inquisitionis*,
1692)

him his offence. He was, however, promised a pardon if he would truly confess his offences; an artifice this, by which his judges often learned more than they knew before against him.

At last the charges against him were presented to him in writing, and counsel also was assigned him, who, however, only advised him to confess fully his faults. The accuser and informer against him were not made known to him, but the real charges against him were put into his hands. He was allowed time for his defence; but his accuser, and the witnesses against him, he could know only by conjecture. Sometimes he was so fortunate as to discover who they were; but rarely were they presented before him, and confronted with him.

If his answers did not satisfy the judges, or if the allegations against him were not adequately proved, resort was had to torture. Each of these tortures was continued as long as, in the judgment of the physician of the Inquisition, the man was able to endure them. He might now confess what he would, but still the torture would be repeated, first to discover the object and motives of the acknowledged offence, and then to make him expose his accomplices.

If, when tortured, he confessed nothing, many snares were laid to elicit from him unconsciously his offence. The conclusion was that the accused, when he seemed to have satisfied the judges, was condemned, according to the measure of his offence, to death, or to perpetual imprisonment, or to the galleys, or to be scourged; and he was delivered over to the civil authorities, who were intreated to spare his life, as the church never thirsted for blood; but yet they would experience persecution if they did not carry the decisions of the court into execution.

What an infernal device is the Inquisition! What innocent person could escape destruction, if an inquisitor were disposed to destroy him? A heretic, even if he had been acquitted by the pope himself, might still be condemned to die by the Inquisition. An equivocal promise of pardon might be given to induce him to make confession, but the promise must not be fulfilled when the object of it was obtained. Even death did not free a person from the jurisdiction of the Inquisition; for a deceased heretic must be burned in effigy. Would not every feeling of humanity be outraged by following such horrid principles? The inquisitorial judges did not deny that by such proceedings many innocent persons unavoidably perished, along with the guilty; but this did not trouble them. "Better," they said, "that a hundred innocent persons should be cut off and go to paradise, than let one heretic escape, who might poison many souls and plunge them into endless perdition."*f*

JOHN FOXE ON THE EVILS OF THE INQUISITION

" The abuse of this Inquisition is most execrable. If any word shall pass out of the mouth of any, which may be taken in evil part; yea, though no word be spoken, yet if they bear any grudge or evil will against the party, incontinent they command him to be taken, and put in a horrible prison, and then find out crimes against him at leisure, and in the meantime no man living is so hardy as once to open his mouth for him. If the father speak one word for his child, he is also taken and cast into prison as a favourer of heretics; neither is it permitted to any person to enter in to the prisoner; but there he is alone, in a place where he cannot see so much as the ground where he is, and is not suffered either to read or write, but there endureth in darkness palpable, in horrors infinite, in fear miserable, wrestling with the assaults of death.

" By this it may be esteemed what trouble and sorrow, what pensive sighs and cogitations they sustain, who are not thoroughly instructed in holy doctrine. Add, moreover, to these distresses and horrors of the prison, the injuries, threats, whippings, and scourgings, irons, tortures, and racks which they endure. Sometimes also they are brought out, and showed forth in some higher place to the people, as a spectacle of rebuke and infamy. And thus are they detained there, some many years, and murdered by long torments, and whole days together treated much more cruelly, out of all comparison, than if they were in the hangman's hands to be slain at once. During all this time, what is done in the process no person knoweth, but only the holy fathers and the tormentors, who are sworn to execute the torments. All this is done in secret, and (as great mysteries) pass not the hands of these holy ones. And after all these torments so many years endured in the prison, if any man shall be saved, it must be by guessing; for all the proceedings of the court of that execrable Inquisition are open to no man, but all is done in hugger-mugger and in close corners, by ambages, by covert ways, and secret counsels. The accuser is secret, the crime secret, the witness secret, whatsoever is done is secret, neither is the poor prisoner ever advised of anything. If he can guess who accused him, whereof and wherefore, he may be pardoned peradventure of his life; but this is very seldom, and yet he shall not incontinent be set at liberty before he hath long time endured infinite torments; and this is called their "penitence," and so is he let go; and yet not so but that he is enjoined, before he pass the inquisitor's hands, that he shall wear a garment of yellow colours for a note of public infamy to him and his whole race. And if he cannot guess right, showing to the inquisitors by whom he was accused, whereof, and wherefore (as is before touched), incontinent the horrible sentence of condemnation is pronounced against him, that he shall be burned for an obstinate heretic. And yet the sentence is not executed by and by, but after he hath endured imprisonment in some heinous prison." *j*

HOW A PENITENT WAS TREATED

It was a peculiar horror of the Inquisition that while almost anyone might be haled before it, even on an anonymous complaint, hardly anyone ever escaped certain penalties. If the fate of the wretch was heavy, who, being innocent of heresy would not confess his guilt and therefore was tortured until he confessed imaginary guilt, and was then burned to death, hardly less was the misery of the victim who repented or recanted and was freed from the death penalty. The penalty for recantation can hardly be more plainly stated than an actual order quoted by Llorente,*k* giving the punishment awarded by St. Dominic himself to a repentant heretic even before the actual organisation of the Inquisition.*a*

COSTUME OF A CONDEMNED PERSON WHO HAD NOT CONFESSED

(From *Historia Inquisitionis,* 1592)

"To all faithful Christians to whom these presents may come. Friar Dominic, canon of Osma, the least of the preachers, greeting in Christ. By the authority of the lord abbot of Cister (Citeaux), legate of the apostolic see (whose power we exercise) we have reconciled the bearer of these presents, Poncio Roger, converted from the sect of the heretics by the grace of God; and we have enjoined him in virtue of the sworn promise which he has made to comply with our precepts that on three Sunday festivals he be led, stripped, by a priest, who shall scourge him from the gates of the city to those of the church.

"We further lay. upon him, by way of penance, that he abstain from eating flesh meat, eggs, cheese, and other foods derived from animals, forever. Save only on the day of the resurrection, of Pentecost, and of the Lord's nativity, on which days we command him to partake thereof as a mark of his detestation of his former error. He shall observe four Lents in the year, abstaining from fish, and shall forever fast and abstain from fish, oil, and wine three days in the week, save only when physical infirmities or the labours of his station require a dispensation. He shall wear religious garments both in shape and colour, with two small crosses sewn on each side of his breast. He shall hear mass every day when occasion serves, and on feast days he shall assist at vespers in the church. Every day he shall recite the Hours for the day and night, and shall repeat the prayer 'Our Father' seven times during the day, ten times in the night, and twenty times at midnight. He shall observe chastity, and shall present this letter one day, in the morning, every month, in the town of Cereri to his parish priest, whom we enjoin to watch over the conduct of Poncio, who shall faithfully observe all that is here expressed until the lord legate shall manifest his will. And should Poncio fail in his observance we command that he be held perjured, heretic, and excommunicated, and be separated from the company of the faithful." [k]

THE HISTORY OF TORTURE

If the above document gives a foreshadowing of the rigours of the Inquisition towards those whose only error was a temporary wavering of opinion, what can be expected as the fate of those who persisted in their error, or denied it in spite of witnesses? — surely some distinguished form of punishment. Death was not enough, for thus the heretic instantly escaped the clutches of the disciplinarians. Torture was the resource. Before taking up this blackest subject on the page of human history, it is desirable to trace briefly its evolution, for torture was by no means the invention or monopoly of the Inquisition, though it has come to be thought so in the popular mind.

It is only justice to the church and to the zealots of that time to emphasise the fact that when the inquisitors sought a tool for special punishment, they found it ready at hand, made familiar and natural by the civil law of the day. Furthermore torture was a venerable institution.

The Greeks used torture for cross-examining slaves and at times non-residents and even free citizens; the Romans under the republic practised it on slaves, and under the empire on citizens; the man accused of treason was always liable to it, as well as those whose testimony was open to the charge of confusion or inconsistency. Even in Cicero's time there was a grim machinery for the purpose. Torture in England though not legal was practised, as it was on the continent, and in Scotland where it had the best civil sanction. Even in the United States there is one instance of torture, but that was during the Salem witchcraft insanity, though, like the inquisitorial processes, it was conducted by the church and civil government, and like so many of the inquisitorial punishments was due to an accusation of sorcery. The belief in witchcraft, now obsolete among even the common people, was once supported by a papal bull and by Sprenger's [l] tremendous work, called *The Hammer of Witches*, which Henry C. Lea[n] calls "the most portentous monument of superstition which the world has produced."

The civil powers had then used torture from time immemorial. The people were as used to it in that day as we of to-day are to certain torments of animals cooked alive or otherwise worried to death. The crime of treason was specifically devoted to torture. As heresy was in the days of temporal church power distinctly a crime of treason, the secular authorities were ordered to punish it. In fact the church took the stand that it was simply hunting for justice, and when it found the accused innocent, it technically "intervened" in his behalf and "stayed the arm of the law."[1]

But while using these facts to prevent us from thinking of the inquisitors as men of diabolical invention unlike their kind or their time in manner of thought or action, and while giving these facts their due weight in palliation

[1 Among the modern apologists for the Inquisition may be named Rodrigo [ii] and Orti y Lara. [iii]

of the personal offences of the inquisitors against fundamental principles of justice and mercy, we must not forget that, though the church took the idea of torture from the civil law and compelled the civil officials to administer it, yet the church enlarged the methods of torment and the causes for its use; the church forced upon the law and upon the monarchs many extremes of cruelty to which they were reluctant and against which they often mutinied.

And finally, seeing that the best men of the time were supposed to enter the church, and that the church appointed as inquisitors only its most exemplary members,[1] the defence of the Inquisition by some of its apologists on the ground of its origin in the customs of the period, really amounts to the astounding implication that the best men of the church were only a little worse than the average of their time.

It is stupefying to reflect on the character of the torments which crowds of people once watched for hours with joy, and which the supposedly best and gentlest spirits, the church fathers, inflicted day after day with all the fascination of ingenuity put to its utmost test. Such torments we of to-day can neither approve nor permit, and can hardly read of without nausea. None the less, lest we forget the horrors to which the doctrine of religious intolerance can drive mankind, and lest we lose the lesson of all history that no excess of punishment ever yet stopped the human hunger for liberty of thought and action, it will be well to place here a few of the more authentic instances of inquisitorial outrage.

We may well begin with the description from contemporaries, such as the history of Gonsalvius Montanus[o] or Gonzalez de Montés, a Spanish Protestant, who narrowly escaped death, whose friend was martyred, and who published a book on the Inquisition at Heidelberg in 1597. He is quoted with others in the history of Limborch,[b] which was published in 1692, and based almost solely on the church's own accounts.[a]

A Contemporary Account of the Preliminaries to Torture

The place of torture in the Spanish Inquisition is generally an underground and very dark room, to which one enters through several doors. There is a tribunal erected in it, where the inquisitor, inspector, and secretary sit. When the candles are lighted, and the person to be tortured is brought in, the executioner, who was waiting for the other, makes an astonishing and dreadful appearance. He is covered all over with a black linen garment down to his feet, and tied close to his body. His head and face are all hid with a long black cowl, only two little holes being left in it for him to see through. All this is intended to strike the miserable wretch with greater terror in mind and body, when he sees himself going to be tortured by the hands of one who thus looks like the very devil.[o]

Whilst the officers are getting things ready for the torture, the bishop and inquisitor by themselves, and other good men zealous for the faith, endeavour to persuade the person to be tortured freely to confess the truth, and if he will not, they order the officers to strip him, who do it in an instant. Clergymen however must not be tortured by a lay officer or torturer unless

[1 Thus in Spain, Pope Sixtus IV, in a special bull of November 1st, 1478, quoted by Llorente,[k] conferring on Ferdinand and Isabella the power to appoint inquisitors, insisted that they be "two or three bishops or archbishops, or other competent and honest men, secular or regular priests upwards of forty years of age, of good life and customs, masters or bachelors of theology, and doctors or licentiates in canon law, by virtue of a strict examination."]

they cannot find any clergymen who know how to do it, or are willing, because it would be in vain for the judges to order any clergyman or monk to the torture, if there was nobody to inflict it; and therefore in such a case it is usual to torture them by lay officers.

Whilst the person to be tortured is stripping, he is persuaded to confess the truth. If he refuses it, he is taken aside by certain good men, and urged to confess, and told by them that if he confesses, he will not be put to death, but only be made to swear that he will not return to the heresy he hath abjured. The inquisitor and bishop promise the same, unless the person be a relapse.

If he is persuaded neither by threatenings nor promises to confess his crime, he is tortured either more lightly or grievously, according as his crime requires, and frequently interrogated during the torture, upon those articles for which he is put to it, beginning with the lesser ones, because they think he will sooner confess the lesser matters than the greater. According to the directions of Royas,[u] one of the Spanish inquisitors: " The criminals are with great care and diligence to be admonished by the inquisitors, and especially when they are under torture, that they should not by any means bear false witness against themselves or others, through fear of punishment or torments, but speak the truth only. Nor may the inquisitors promise pardon or forgiveness of the offence, to compel the criminals to confess crimes which they have not committed, out of their great zeal to inquire out the truth. And such a false confession the accused person may safely revoke."

The inquisitors themselves must interrogate the criminals during their torture, nor can they commit this business to others, unless they are engaged in other important affairs, in which case they may depute certain good and skilful men for the purpose. Although in other nations criminals are publicly tortured, yet in Spain it is forbidden by the royal law for any to be present whilst they are torturing, besides the judges, secretaries, and torturers. The inquisitors must also choose proper torturers, born of ancient Christians, who must be bound by oath by no means to discover their secrets, nor to report anything that is said. The judges also usually protest that if the criminal should happen to die under his torture, or by reason of it, or should suffer the loss of any of his limbs, it is not to be imputed to them, but to the criminal himself, who will not plainly confess the truth before he is tortured. A heretic may not only be interrogated concerning himself, but in general also concerning his companions and accomplices in his crime, his teachers and his disciples, for he ought to discover them, though he be not interrogated; but when he is interrogated concerning them, he is much more obliged to discover them than his accomplices in any other the most grievous crimes.

A person also suspected of heresy, and fully convicted, may be tortured upon another account, i.e., to discover his companions and accomplices in the crime. This must be done when he hesitates, or it is half fully proved at least that he was actually present with them, or he hath such companions and accomplices in his crime; for in this case he is not tortured as a criminal, but as a witness. But he who makes full confession of himself is not tortured upon a different account; whereas if he be a negative, he may be tortured upon another account, to discover his accomplices and other heretics, though he be full convicted himself, and it be half fully proved that he hath such accomplices. The reason of the difference in these cases is this, because he who confesses against himself would certainly much rather confess against other heretics if he knew them. But it is otherwise when the criminal is a negative.

Whilst these things are doing, the notary writes everything down in the process, as what tortures were inflicted, concerning what matters the prisoner was interrogated, and what he answered. If by these tortures they cannot draw from him a confession, they show him other kind of tortures and tell him he must undergo all of them, unless he confesses the truth. If neither by this means they can extort the truth, they may, to terrify him and engage him to confess, assign the second or third day to continue, not to repeat, the torture, till he hath undergone all those kinds of them to which he is condemned.

The degrees of tortures formerly used were five, which were inflicted in their turn, and are described by Julius Clarus^v [member of the council to Philip II of Spain]. "Know therefore," says he, "that there are five degrees of torture, viz., first, the being threatened to be tortured; secondly, being carried to the place of torture; thirdly, by stripping and binding; fourthly, the being hoisted upon the rack; fifthly, squassation."

The stripping is performed without any regard to humanity or honour, not only to men, but to women and virgins, though the most virtuous and chaste, of whom they have sometimes many in their prison. For they cause them to be stripped, even to their very shifts, which they afterwards take off, forgive the expression, and then put on them straight linen drawers, and then make their arms naked quite up to their shoulders.

As to squassation, it is thus performed: the prisoner hath his hands bound behind his back, and weights tied to his feet, and then he is drawn up on high till his head reaches the very pulley. He is kept hanging in this manner for some time, that by the greatness of the weight hanging at his feet all his joints and limbs may be dreadfully stretched, and on a sudden he is let down with a jerk, by the slacking the rope, but kept from coming quite to the ground, by which terrible shake his arms and legs are all disjointed, whereby he is put to the most exquisite pain; the shock which he receives by the sudden stop of the fall, and the weight at his feet stretching his whole body more intensely and cruelly.^{b}

The inquisitors sometimes shamefully and rashly proceed to the torture of innocent persons, as will evidently appear by one instance, not to mention more, given us by Gonsalvius^o. "They apprehended in the Inquisition at Seville a noble lady, Joan Bohorquia, the wife of Francis Varquius, a very eminent man, and lord of Higuera, and daughter of Peter Garsia Xeresius, a wealthy citizen of Seville. The occasion of her imprisonment was that her sister, Mary Bohorquia, a young lady of eminent piety, who was afterwards burned for her pious confession, had declared in her torture that she had several times conversed with her sister concerning her own doctrine. When she was first imprisoned, she was about six months gone with child, upon which account she was not so straightly confined, nor used with that cruelty which the other prisoners were treated with, out of regard to the infant she carried in her.

"Eight days after her delivery, they took the child from her, and on the fifteenth shut her close up, and made her undergo the fate of the other prisoners, and began to manage her with their usual arts and rigour. In so dreadful a calamity she had only this comfort, that a certain pious young woman, who was afterwards burned for her religion by the inquisitors, was allowed her for her companion. This young creature was, on a certain day, carried out to her torture, and being returned from it into her jail, she was so shaken, and had all her limbs so miserably disjointed, that when she laid upon her bed of rushes it rather increased her misery than gave her rest, so that she could not turn herself without the most excessive pain. In this condition, as Bohorquia had it not in her power to show her any, or but very little outward kindness, she endeavoured to comfort her mind with great tenderness. The girl had scarce begun to recover from her torture, when Bohorquia was carried out to the same exercise, and was tortured with such diabolical cruelty upon the rack, that the rope pierced and cut into the very bones in several places, and in this manner she was brought back to prison, just ready to expire, the blood immediately running out of her mouth in great plenty. Undoubtedly they had burst her bowels, insomuch that the eighth day after her torture she died.

"And when, after all, they could not procure sufficient evidence to condemn her, though sought after and procured by all their inquisitorial arts, yet as the accused person was born in that place, where they were obliged to give some account of the affair to the people, and indeed could not by any means dissemble it, in the first act of triumph appointed her death, they commanded her sentence to be pronounced in these words : 'Because this lady died in prison (without doubt suppressing the causes of it), and was found to be innocent upon inspecting and diligently examining her cause, therefore the holy tribunal pronounces her free from all charges brought against her by the fiscal, and absolving her from any further process, doth restore her both as to her innocence and reputation, and commands all her effects, which had been confiscated, to be restored to those to whom they of right belonged,' etc. And thus, after they had murdered her by torture with savage cruelty, they pronounced her innocent ! " o

LIMBORCH'S ACCOUNT OF THE FATE OF A JEW

The method of torturing and the degree of tortures used in the Spanish Inquisition will be well understood from the history of Isaac Orobio, a Jew, and doctor of physic, who was accused to the Inquisition as a Jew by a certain Moor, his servant, who had by his order before this been whipped for thieving ; and four years after this he was again accused by a certain enemy of his for another fact, which would have proved him a Jew. But Orobio obstinately denied that he was one. I will here give the account of his torture, as I had it from his own mouth. After three whole years which he had been in jail, and several examinations, and the discovery of the crimes to him of which he was accused, in order to his confession and his constant denial of them, he was at length carried out of his jail, and through several turnings brought to the place of torture. This was towards the evening.

It was a large underground room, arched, and the walls covered with black hangings. The candlesticks were fastened to the wall, and the whole room enlightened with candles placed in them. At one end of it there was an enclosed place like a closet, where the inquisitor and notary sat at a table, so that the place seemed to him as the very mansion of death, everything appearing so terrible and awful. Here the inquisitor again admonished him to confess the truth before his torments began.

When he answered he had told the truth, the inquisitor gravely protested that, since he was so obstinate as to suffer the torture, the Holy Office would be innocent, if he should shed his blood, or even expire in his torments. When he had said this, he put a linen garment over his body, and drew it so very close on each side, as almost squeezed him to death. When he was almost dying, they slackened at once the sides of the garment, and after he began to breathe again, the sudden alteration put him to the most grievous anguish and pain. When he had overcome this torture, the same admonition was repeated, that he would confess the truth in order to prevent further torment.

And as he persisted in his denial, they tied his thumbs so very tightly with small cords as made the extremities of them greatly swell, and caused the blood to spurt out from under his nails. After this he was placed with his back against a wall and fixed upon a little bench. Into the wall were fastened little iron pulleys, through which there were ropes drawn, and tied round his body in several places, and especially his arms and legs. The executioner drawing these ropes with great violence, fastened his body with them to the wall so that his hands and feet, and especially his fingers and toes being bound so straightly with them, put him to the most exquisite pain, and seemed to him just as though he had been dissolving in flames. In the midst of these torments the torturer, of a sudden, drew the bench from under him, so that the miserable wretch hung by the cords without anything to support him, and by the weight of his body drew the knots yet much closer.

After this a new kind of torture succeeded. There was an instrument like a small ladder, made of two upright pieces of wood and five cross ones sharpened before. This the torturer placed over against him, and by a certain proper motion struck it with great violence against both his shins, so that he received upon each of them at once five violent strokes, which put him to such intolerable anguish that he fainted away. After he came to himself, they inflicted on him the last torture.

The torturer tied ropes about Orobio's wrists and then put those ropes about his own back, which was covered with leather, to prevent his hurting himself. Then falling backwards and putting his feet up against the wall, he drew them with all his might till they cut through Orobio's flesh, even to the very bones; and this torture was repeated thrice, the ropes being tied about his arms about the distance of two fingers' breadth from the former wound, and drawn with the same violence.

But it happened that, as the ropes were drawing the second time, they slid into the first wound, which caused so great an effusion of blood that he seemed to be dying. Upon this the physician and surgeon, who are always ready, were sent for out of a neighbouring apartment to ask their advice whether the torture could be continued without danger of death, lest the ecclesiastical judges should be guilty of an irregularity if the criminal should die in his torments.

They, who were far from being enemies to Orobio, answered that he had strength enough to endure the rest of the torture, and hereby preserved him from having the tortures he had already endured repeated on him, because his sentence was that he should suffer them all at one time, one after another. So that if at any time they are forced to leave off through fear of death, all the tortures, even those already suffered, must be successively inflicted to satisfy the sentence. Upon this the torture was repeated the third time, and then it ended. After this he was bound up in his own clothes and carried back to his prison, and was scarce healed of his wounds in seventy days. And, inasmuch as he made no confession under his torture, he was condemned, not as one convicted, but suspected of Judaism, to wear for two whole years the infamous habit called *sambenito*, and it was further decreed that after that term he should suffer perpetual banishment from the kingdom of Seville.

OTHER FORMS OF TORTURE

Gonsalvius[o] tells us of another kind of torture. There is a wooden bench, which they call "the wooden horse," made hollow like a trough, so as to contain a man lying on his back at full length, about the middle of which there is a round bar laid across, upon which the back of the person is placed, so that he lies upon the bar instead of being let into the bottom of the trough, with his feet much higher than his head. As he is lying in this posture, his arms, thighs, and shins are tied round with small cords or strings, which being drawn with screws at proper distance from each other, cut into the very bones, so as to be no longer discerned.

The Tormento di Toca

Besides this, the torturer throws over his mouth and nostrils a thin cloth, so that he is scarce able to breathe through them, and in the meanwhile a small stream of water like a thread, not drop by drop, falls from on high upon the mouth of the person lying in this miserable condition and so easily sinks down the thin cloth to the bottom of his throat, so that there is no possibility of breathing, his mouth being stopped with water and his nostrils with the cloth, so that the poor wretch is in the same agony as persons ready to die, and breathing out their last. When this cloth is drawn out of his throat, as it often is, that he may answer to the questions, it is all wet with water and blood, and is like pulling his bowels through his mouth.

The Chafing-dish; The Water-cure

There is also another kind of torture peculiar to this tribunal, which they call the fire. They order a large iron chafing-dish full of lighted charcoal to be brought in and held close to the soles of the tortured person's feet, greased over with lard, so that the heat of the fire may more quickly pierce through them.

This is inquisition by torture, when there is only half full proof of their crime. However, at other times torments are sometimes inflicted upon persons condemned to death, as a punishment preceding that of death. Of this we have a remarkable instance in William Lithgow,[w] an Englishman, who, as he tells us in his travels, was taken up as a spy in Malaga, and was exposed to the most cruel torments upon the Wooden Horse. But when nothing could be extorted from him, he was delivered to the Inquisition as an heretic. He was condemned, in the beginning of Lent, to suffer the night following eleven most cruel torments, and after Easter to be carried privately to Grenada, there to be buried at midnight, and his ashes to be scattered into the air; when night came on his fetters were taken off, then he was stripped naked, put upon his knees, and his head lifted up by force; after which, opening his mouth with iron instruments, they filled his belly with water till it came out of his jaws. Then they tied a rope hard about his neck, and in this condition rolled him seven times the whole length of the room, till he almost quite strangled. After this they tied a small cord about both his great toes, and hung him up thereby with his head down, letting him remain in this condition till all the water discharged itself out of his mouth, so that he was laid on the ground as just dead, and had his irons put on him again. But beyond all expectation, and by a very singular accident, he was delivered out of jail, escaped death, and fortunately sailed home to England.[b]

Details of another revolting case are quoted by Limborch from an official contemporary document, which may best be reproduced here in its original form.*a*

THE PROCEEDINGS AGAINST AN ENGLISHWOMAN

Elizabeth Vasconcellos, now in the city of Lisbon, doth, on the 10th day of December, *anno* 1706, in the presence of John Milner, Esq., her majesty's consul-general of Portugal, and Joseph Willcocks, minister of the English factory at Lisbon, declare and testify:

That she was born at Arlington, in the county of Devon, and a daughter of John Chester, Esq., bred up in the church of England; and in the eleventh year of her age her uncle, David Morgan, of Cork, intending to go and settle in Jamaica as a physician, by her father's consent, he having several children, took her with him to provide for her.

In 1685, they went in an English ship, and near the island they were attacked by two Turkish ships; in the fight her uncle was killed, but the ship got clear into Madeira, and she, though left destitute, was entertained by Mr. Bedford, a merchant, with whom, and other English, she lived as a servant till 1696. In that year she was married by the chaplain of an English man-of-war to Cordoza de Vasconcellos, a physician of that island, and lived with him eight years, and never in the least conformed to the Romish church.

In 1704, her husband being gone on a voyage to Brazil, she fell dangerously ill, and, being light-headed, a priest gave her the sacrament, as she was told afterwards, for she remembered nothing of it. It pleased God she recovered, and then they told her she had changed her religion, and must conform to the Romish church, which she denied and refused to conform; and thereupon, by the bishop of that island, she was imprisoned nine months, and then sent prisoner to the Inquisition at Lisbon, where she arrived the 19th of December, 1705. The secretary of the house took her effects, in all above £500; she was then sworn, that that was all she was worth, and then put into a straight dark room, about five feet square, and there kept nine months and fifteen days.

That the first nine days she had only bread and water, and a wet straw bed to lie on. On the ninth day, being examined, she owned herself a Protestant, and would so continue; she was told she had conformed to the Romish church, and must persist in it or burn, she was then remanded to her room; and after a month's time brought out again, and persisting in her answer as to her religion, they bound her hands behind her, stripped her back naked, and lashed her with a whip of knotted cords a considerable time, and told her afterwards that she must kneel down to the court, and give thanks for their merciful usage of her, which she positively refused to do.

After fifteen days she was again brought forth and examined, and a crucifix being set before her, she was commanded to bow down to it and worship it, which she refusing to do, they told her that she must expect to be condemned to the flames, and be burned with the Jews, at the next *auto da fé*, which was nigh at hand. Upon this she was remanded to her prison again for thirty days, and being then brought out, a red hot iron was got ready, and brought to her in a chafing-dish of burning coals, and her breast being laid open, the executioner, with one end of the red hot iron, which was about the bigness of a large seal, burned her to the bone in three several places, on the right side, one hard by the other, and then sent her to her prison, without any plaster, or other application, to heal the sores, which were very painful to her.

A month after this she had another severe whipping, as before; and in the beginning of August she was brought before the table, a great number of inquisitors being present, and was questioned, whether she would profess the Romish religion or burn. She replied, she had always been a Protestant, and was a subject of the queen of England, who was able to protect her, and she doubted not would do it, were her condition known to the English residing in Lisbon; but as she knew nothing of that, her resolution was to continue a Protestant, though she were to burn for it. To this they answered that her being the queen of England's subject signified nothing in the dominions of the king of Portugal; that the English residing in Lisbon were heretics, and would certainly be damned; and that it was the mercy of that tribunal to endeavour to rescue her out of the flames of hell, but if her resolution were to burn rather than profess the Romish religion, they would give her a trial of it beforehand.

Accordingly the officers were ordered to seat her in a fixed chair, and to bind her arms and her legs, that she could make no resistance, nor motion, and the physician being placed by her, to direct the court how far they might torture her without hazard of life, her left foot was made bare, and an iron slipper, red hot, being immediately brought in, her foot was fastened into it, which continued on burning her to the bone, till such time as by extremity of pain she fainted away, and the physician declaring her life was in danger, they took it off, and ordered her again to her prison.

On the 19th of August she was again brought out, and whipped after a cruel manner, and her back was all over torn, and being threatened with more and greater tortures, and, on the other hand, being promised to be set at liberty if she would subscribe such a paper as they should give her, though she could have undergone death, yet not being able to endure a life of so much misery, she consented to subscribe, as they would have her, and accordingly, as she was directed wrote at the bottom of a large paper, which contained she knew not what; after which they advised her to avoid the company of all English heretics, and not restoring to her anything of all the plate, goods, or money she brought in with her, and engaging her by oath to keep secret all that had been done to her, turned her out of doors, destitute of all relief, but what she received from the help and compassion of charitable Christians.

The above said Elizabeth Vasconcellos did solemnly affirm and declare the above written deposition to be true, the day and year above written.

JOHN MILNER,
JOSEPH WILLCOCKS.

Lisbon, January 8th, 1707, N.S.

(A copy examined from the original, by J. BLISSE.)[b]

INQUISITORIAL DOCUMENTS

That the above affidavit is not a mere party document is only too plainly proved by the very manual of procedure, the Cartilla of the Inquisition at Seville, which W. H. Rule[y] has translated. It was meant for the guidance of all the Spanish inquisitors, and its business-like calm is not its least horrible feature, as is this insistence upon a full report of the torture and its results: *a*

How the Record was Kept

" If the criminal is under age, the guardian must be present at pronouncing sentence, in order that he may appeal if he wishes ; but he must not be present at the torture.

" All that the criminal says has to be set down, and the questions that were put to him, and his answers, without omitting anything, and how they ordered him to be stripped, and his arms to be bound, and the rounds of cord that are put on him, and how they ordered him to be placed on a rack, and to bind his legs, head, and arms, and how he was bound, and how they ordered the garrotes to be put on, and how they were put on, and how compressed, declaring if it was on leg, thigh, or shin, or arms, etc., and what was said to him at each of these operations.

" If the torture is of pulley, it must be entered how the irons were put ; and the weight or weights, and how he was hoisted, and how many times, and how long he was up each time. If it is of rack, it shall be said how the toca [1] was put on him, and how many pitchers of water were thrown over him, and how much each contained." *y*

The Proper Form of Torture for Women

Even more ghastly is the blank form for convenience in recording the various steps. The following from the same manual, as translated by Rule,*y* corroborates the testimony of Elizabeth Vasconcellos quoted above, inasmuch as it prescribes the gentler forms of discipline to be used when the errant one was a woman. There is something peculiarly terrible in the very omission of a special name and the consequent thought of the number of wretches whose vain words and torments were thus recorded.*a*

" She was told to tell the truth, or orders would be given to strip her. She said, etc. She was commanded to be stripped naked.

" She was told to tell the truth, or orders would be given to cut off her hair. She said, etc.

" Orders were given to cut off her hair ; and when it was taken off, she was examined by the doctor and surgeon, who said there was not any objection to her being put to the torture.

" She was told to tell the truth, or she would be commanded to mount the rack. She said, etc.

" She was commanded to mount, and she said, etc.

" She was told to tell the truth, or her body should be bound. She said, etc. She was ordered to be bound.

" She was told to tell the truth, or, if not, they would order her right foot to be made fast for the trampazo.[2] She said, etc. They commanded it to be made fast.

" She was told to tell the truth, or they would command her left foot to be made fast for the trampazo. She said, etc. They commanded it to be made fast. She said, etc. It was ordered to be done.

[1 In the *tormento de toca*, a gauze bag was placed in the throat and water poured in it, forcing the gauze gradually down the œsophagus into the stomach. Other torments were the gradual pouring of water drop by drop on one spot of the body, and the great swinging pendulum, or *péndola*, with the knife affixed, as described in Poe's haunting story.]

[2 The *trampazo* was an iron shoe heated red hot and clamped to the bare foot.]

" She was told to tell the truth, or they would order the binding of the right arm to be stretched. She said, etc. It was commanded to be done. And the same with the left arm. It was ordered to be executed.

" She was told to tell the truth, or they would order the fleshy part of her right arm to be made fast for the garrote. She said, etc. It was ordered to be made fast.

" And by the said lord inquisitor it was repeated to her many times that she should tell the truth, and not let herself be brought into so great torment ; and the physician and surgeon were called in, who said, etc. And the criminal, etc. And orders were given to make it fast.

" She was told to tell the truth, or they would order the first turn of mancuerda. She said, etc. It was commanded to be done.

" She was told to tell the truth, or they would command the garrote to be applied again to the right arm. She said, etc. It was ordered to be done.

" She was told to tell the truth, or they would order the second turn of mancuerda. She said, etc. It was commanded to be done.

" She was told to tell the truth, or they would order the garrote to be applied again to the left arm. She said, etc. It was ordered to be done.

" She was told to tell the truth, or they would order the third turn of mancuerda. She said, etc. It was commanded to be done.

" She was told to tell the truth, or they would order the trampazo to be laid on the right foot. She said, etc. It was commanded to be done.

" For women you do not go beyond this." [y]

LATER HISTORY OF THE INQUISITION IN SPAIN

It would be gratuitously harrowing to multiply such instances of human misery, and we may return to the chronicle of the progress of the Inquisition, leading up to its culmination in Spain and Portugal, instances of whose severity have already been quoted. It is a pitiful chronicle, and one that the humanitarian might well wish to pass over in silence ; but one which the historian cannot altogether ignore.[a]

The notion of heresy was enlarged so as to comprehend not only the slightest deviation from the creed of the church, but also usury, sorcery, contempt of the cross and clergy, dealings with Jews, etc.

The people in many places rose up against the inquisitors, as in Albi, and Narbonne (1234), and Toulouse; and in France, where the Inquisition had first been put in force, it was first abolished.[1] The Jesuits sought to restore the Inquisition in Bavaria (1599), and during the Thirty Years' War found an occasional victim ; but Maria Theresa abolished it in her kingdom, and it soon afterwards disappeared in Germany. It had no hold in England, Sweden, Norway, or Denmark ; but in Spain, Portugal, and the Netherlands it enjoyed a luxuriant growth.[z]

The tribunal, after having been successfully adopted in Italy and Germany, was introduced into Aragon, where, in 1242, additional provisions were framed by the Council of Tarragona, on the basis of those of 1233, which may properly be considered as the primitive instructions of the Holy Office in Spain.

[1 Philip the Fair in the course of his war with Pope Boniface VIII condemned the Inquisition, though he burned the Templars ; or as Dean Kitchin puts it, the Inquisition " was effectively used by Philip the Fair to crush the Templars, though that greedy prince quickly interfered when he found the Inquisition laying hands on his special preserves, the wealthy Jews." See the Papacy.]

This "ancient" Inquisition, as it is termed, bore the same odious peculiarities in its leading features as the modern; the same impenetrable secrecy in its proceedings, the same insidious modes of accusation, a similar use of torture, and similar penalties for the offender. A sort of manual, drawn up by Eymerich,*p* an Aragonese inquisitor of the fourteenth century, for the instruction of the judges of the Holy Office, prescribes all those ambiguous forms of interrogation by which the unwary and perhaps innocent victim might be circumvented. The arm of persecution, however, fell with sufficient heaviness, especially during the thirteenth and fourteenth centuries, on the unfortunate Albigenses, who, from the proximity and political relations of Aragon and Provence, had become numerous in the former kingdom. The persecution appears, however, to have been chiefly confined to this unfortunate sect, and there is no evidence that the Holy Office, notwithstanding papal briefs to that effect, was fully organised in Castile before the reign of Isabella. This is perhaps imputable to the paucity of heretics in that kingdom. It cannot, at any rate, be charged to any lukewarmness in its sovereigns; since they, from the time of St. Ferdinand, who heaped the fagots on the blazing pile with his own hands, down to that of John II, Isabella's father, who hunted the unhappy heretics of Biscay like so many wild beasts among the mountains, had ever evinced a lively zeal for the orthodox faith.

By the middle of the fifteenth century, the Albigensian heresy had been nearly extirpated by the Inquisition of Aragon; so that this infernal engine might have been suffered to sleep undisturbed from want of sufficient fuel to keep it in motion, when new and ample materials were discovered in the unfortunate race of Israel, on whom the sins of their fathers have been so unsparingly visited by every nation in Christendom among whom they have sojourned, almost to the present century.

Under the Visigothic empire the Jews multiplied exceedingly in Spain, and were permitted to acquire considerable power and wealth. But no sooner had their Arian masters embraced the orthodox faith than they began to testify their zeal by pouring on the Jews the most pitiless storm of persecution. One of their laws alone condemned the whole race to slavery; and Montesquieu*aa* remarks, without much exaggeration, that to the Gothic code may be traced all the maxims of the Modern Inquisition, the monks of the fifteenth century only copying, in reference to the Israelites, the bishops of the seventh.

State of the Jews in Spain

After the Saracenic invasion, which the Jews, perhaps with reason, are accused of having facilitated, they resided in the conquered cities and were permitted to mingle with the Arabs on nearly equal terms. The Jews accordingly, under these favourable auspices, not only accumulated wealth with their usual diligence, but gradually rose to the highest civil dignities, and made great advances in various departments of letters.

The ancient Castilians of the same period, very different from their Gothic ancestors, seem to have conceded to the Israelites somewhat of the feelings of respect which were extorted from them by the superior civilisation of the Spanish Arabs. We find eminent Jews residing in the courts of the Christian princes, directing their studies, attending them as physicians, or more frequently administering their finances. For this last vocation they seem to have had a natural aptitude; and, indeed, the correspondence which they maintained with the different countries of Europe by means of their own countrymen, who acted as the brokers of almost every people among whom they were scattered during the Middle Ages, afforded them peculiar facilities both in politics and commerce. We meet with Jewish scholars and statesmen attached to the courts of Alfonso X, Alfonso XI, Pedro the Cruel, Henry (Enrique) II, and other princes. Their astronomical science recom-

mended them in a special manner to Alfonso el Sabio, who employed them in the construction of his celebrated tables. James I of Aragon condescended to receive instruction from them in ethics; and in the fifteenth century we notice Juan (John) II of Castile employing a Jewish secretary in the compilation of a national *Cancionero*.

But all this royal patronage proved incompetent to protect the Jews when their flourishing fortunes had risen to a sufficient height to excite popular envy, augmented as it was by that profuse ostentation of equipage and apparel for which this singular people, notwithstanding their avarice, have usually shown a predilection. Stories were circulated of their contempt for the Catholic worship, their desecration of its most holy symbols, and of their crucifixion, or other sacrifice, of Christian children at the celebration of their own passover. With these foolish calumnies, the more probable charge of usury and extortion was industriously preferred against them ; till at length, towards the close of the fourteenth century, the fanatical populace, stimulated in many instances by the no less fanatical clergy, and perhaps encouraged by the numerous class of debtors to the Jews, who found this a convenient mode of settling their accounts, made a fierce assault on this

A JEW OF THE MIDDLE AGES

unfortunate people in Castile and Aragon, breaking into their houses, violating their most private sanctuaries, scattering their costly collections and furniture, and consigning the wretched proprietors to indiscriminate massacre, without regard to sex or age.

" *Conversion* " of the Jews

In this crisis the only remedy left to the Jews was a real or feigned conversion to Christianity. St. Vincent Ferrier, a Dominican of Valencia, performed such a quantity of miracles, in furtherance of this purpose, as might have excited the envy of any saint in the calendar; and these, aided by his eloquence, are said to have changed the hearts of no less than thirty-five thousand of the race of Israel, which doubtless must be reckoned the greatest miracle of all.

The legislative enactments of this period, and still more under Juan II during the first half of the fifteenth century, were uncommonly severe upon the Jews. While they were prohibited from mingling freely with the Christians, and from exercising the professions for which they were best qualified, their residence was restricted within certain prescribed limits of the cities which they inhabited; and they were not only debarred from their usual luxury of ornament in dress, but were held up to public scorn, as it were, by some peculiar badge or emblem embroidered on their garments.

Such was the condition of the Spanish Jews at the accession of Ferdinand and Isabella. The "new Christians," or "converts," as those who had renounced the faith of their fathers were denominated, were occasionally preferred to high ecclesiastical dignities, which they illustrated by their integrity and learning. They were intrusted with municipal offices in the various cities of Castile; and as their wealth furnished an obvious resource for repairing, by way of marriage, the decayed fortunes of the nobility, there was scarcely a family of rank in the land whose blood had not been contaminated, at some period or other, by mixture with the *mala sangre*, as it came afterwards to be termed, of the house of Judah; an ignominious stain, which no time has been deemed sufficient wholly to purge away.

Notwithstanding the show of prosperity enjoyed by the converted Jews, their situation was far from secure. Their proselytism had been too sudden to be generally sincere; and as the task of dissimulation was too irksome to be permanently endured, they gradually became less circumspect, and exhibited the scandalous spectacle of apostates returning to wallow in the ancient mire of Judaism. The clergy, especially the Dominicans, who seem to have inherited the quick scent for heresy which distinguished their frantic founder, were not slow in sounding the alarm; and the superstitious populace, easily roused to acts of violence in the name of religion, began to exhibit the most tumultuous movements, and actually massacred the constable of Castile in an attempt to suppress them at Jaen, the year preceding the accession of Isabella. After this period the complaints against the Jewish heresy became still more clamorous, and the throne was repeatedly beset with petitions to devise some effectual means for its extirpation (1478).

It is easy to discern, in the medley of credulity and superstition, the secret envy entertained by the Castilians of the superior skill and industry of their Hebrew brethren, and of the superior riches which these qualities secured to them; and it is impossible not to suspect that the zeal of the most orthodox was considerably sharpened by worldly motives.

Be that as it may, the cry against the Jewish abominations now became general. Among those most active in raising it were Alfonso de Ojeda, a Dominican, prior of the monastery of St. Paul in Seville, and Diego de Merlo, assistant of that city, who should not be defrauded of the meed of glory to which they are justly entitled by their exertions for the new establishment of the Modern Inquisition. These persons, after urging on the sovereigns the alarming extent to which the Jewish leprosy prevailed in Andalusia, loudly called for the introduction of the Holy Office, as the only effectual means of healing it. In this they were vigorously supported by Niccolo Franco, the papal nuncio then residing at the court of Castile. Ferdinand listened with complacency to a scheme which promised an ample source of revenue in the confiscations it involved. But it was not so easy to vanquish Isabella's aversion to such repugnant measures.

Queen Isabella persuaded to Persecution

Well had it been for the land if the queen's conscience had always been intrusted to the keeping of persons of such exemplary piety as her confessor, Talavera. Unfortunately, in her early days, during the lifetime of her brother Henry, that charge was committed to a Dominican monk, Thomas

(Tomas) de Torquemada, a native of Old Castile, subsequently raised to the rank of prior of Santa Cruz in Segovia, and condemned to infamous immortality by the signal part which he performed in the tragedy of the Inquisition. This man, who concealed more pride under his monastic weeds than might have furnished forth a convent of his order, was one of that class with whom zeal passes for religion, and who testify their zeal by a fiery persecution of those whose creed differs from their own; who compensate for their abstinence from sensual indulgence by giving scope to those deadlier vices of the heart, pride, bigotry, and intolerance, which are no less opposed to virtue and are far more extensively mischievous to society. This personage had earnestly laboured to infuse into Isabella's young mind, to which his situation as her confessor gave him such ready access, the same spirit of fanaticism that glowed in his own. Fortunately this was greatly counteracted by her sound understanding and natural kindness of heart. Torquemada urged her, or indeed, as is stated by some, extorted a promise that, " should she ever come to the throne, she would devote herself to the extirpation of heresy, for the glory of God and the exaltation of the Catholic faith." The time was now arrived when this promise was to be discharged.

It is due to Isabella's fame to state thus much in palliation of the unfortunate error into which she was led by her misguided zeal ; an error so grave that, like a vein in some noble piece of statuary, it gives a sinister expression to her otherwise unblemished character. It was not until the queen had endured the repeated importunities of the clergy, particularly of those reverend persons in whom she most confided, seconded by the arguments of Ferdinand, that she consented to solicit from the pope a bull for the introduction of the Holy Office into Castile. Sixtus IV, who at that time filled the pontifical chair, easily discerning the sources of wealth and influence which this measure opened to the court of Rome, readily complied with the petition of the sovereigns, and expedited a bull bearing date November 1st, 1478, authorising them to appoint two or three ecclesiastics, inquisitors for the detection and suppression of heresy throughout their dominions.

The queen, however, still averse to violent measures, suspended the operation of the ordinance, until a more lenient policy had been first tried. By her command, accordingly, the archbishop of Seville, Cardinal Mendoza, drew up a catechism exhibiting the different points of the Catholic faith, and instructed the clergy throughout his diocese to spare no pains in illuminating the benighted Israelites, by means of friendly exhortation and a candid exposition of the true principles of Christianity. How far the spirit of these injunctions was complied with, amid the excitement then prevailing, may be reasonably doubted. There could be little doubt, however, that a report, made two years later by a commission of ecclesiastics with Alfonso de Ojeda at its head, respecting the progress of the reformation, would be necessarily unfavourable to the Jews.

In consequence of this report the papal provisions were enforced by the nomination, on the 17th of September, 1480, of two Dominican monks as inquisitors, with two other ecclesiastics, the one as assessor and the other as procurator-fiscal, with instructions to proceed at once to Seville and enter on the duties of their office. Orders were also issued to the authorities of the city to support the inquisitors by all the aid in their power. But the new institution proved so distasteful to them in its origin that they refused any co-operation with its ministers, and during the first years it can scarcely be said to have obtained a footing in any other places in Andalusia than those belonging to the crown.

The Inquisition of 1481

On the 2nd of January, 1481, the court commenced operations by the publication of an edict, followed by several others, requiring all persons to aid in apprehending and accusing all such as they might know or suspect to be guilty of heresy, and holding out the illusory promise of absolution to such as should confess their errors within a limited period. As every mode of accusation, even anonymous, was invited, the number of victims multiplied so fast that the tribunal found it convenient to remove its sittings from the convent of St. Paul, within the city, to the spacious fortress of Triana, in the suburbs.

The presumptive proofs by which the charge of Judaism was established against the accused are so curious that a few of them may deserve notice. It was considered good evidence of the fact, if the prisoner wore better clothes or cleaner linen on the Jewish Sabbath than on other days of the week; if he had no fire in his house the preceding evening; if he sat at table with Jews, or ate the meat of animals slaughtered by their hands, or drank a certain beverage held in much estimation by them; if he washed a corpse in warm water, or when dying turned his face to the wall; or, finally, if he gave Hebrew names to his children — a provision most whimsically cruelly, since, by a law of Henry II, he was prohibited under severe penalties from giving them Christian names. He must have found it difficult to extricate himself from the horns of this dilemma.

On the sixth day of January six convicts suffered at the stake. Seventeen more were executed in March, and a still greater number in the month following; and by the 4th of November in the same year no less than 298 individuals had been sacrificed in the *autos da fé* of Seville. Besides these, the mouldering remains of many, who had been tried and convicted, after their death, were torn up from their graves, with a hyena-like ferocity which has disgraced no other court, Christian or pagan, and condemned to the common funeral pile. This was prepared on a spacious stone scaffold, erected in the suburbs of the city, with the statues of four prophets attached to the corners, to which the unhappy sufferers were bound for the sacrifice. This monument of fanaticism continued to disgrace Seville till 1810, when it was removed in order to make room for the construction of a battery against the French. The sword of justice was observed, in particular, to strike at the wealthy, the least pardonable offenders in times of proscription.

The plague which desolated Seville this year, sweeping off fifteen thousand inhabitants, as if in token of the wrath of heaven at these enormities, did not palsy for a moment the arm of the Inquisition, which, adjourning to Aracena, continued as indefatigable as before. A similar persecution went forward in other parts of the province of Andalusia; so that within the same year, 1481, the number of the sufferers was computed at two thousand burned alive, a still greater number in effigy, and seventeen thousand "reconciled"; a term which must not be understood by the reader to signify anything like a pardon or amnesty, but only the commutation of a capital sentence for inferior penalties, as fines, civil incapacity, very generally total confiscation of property, and not infrequently imprisonment for life.[1]

[1] L. Marineo *bb* diffuses the two thousand capital executions over several years. He sums up the various severities of the Holy Office in the following gentle terms: "The church, who is the mother of mercy and the fountain of charity, content with the imposition of penances, generously accords life to many who do not deserve it; while those who persist obstinately in their errors, after being imprisoned on the testimony of trustworthy witnesses, she causes to be put to the

The Jews were astounded by the bolt which had fallen so unexpectedly upon them. Some succeeded in making their escape to Granada, others to France, Germany, or Italy, where they appealed from the decisions of the Holy Office to the sovereign pontiff.[1] Sixtus IV appears for a moment to have been touched with something like compunction, for he rebuked the intemperate zeal of the inquisitors, and even menaced them with deprivation. But these feelings, it would seem, were but transient; for in 1483 we find the same pontiff quieting the scruples of Isabella respecting the appropriation of the confiscated property, and encouraging both sovereigns to proceed in the great work of purification by an audacious reference to the example of Jesus Christ, who, says he, consolidated his kingdom on earth by the destruction of idolatry.

The Spanish or "Modern" Inquisition established

In the course of the same year he expedited two briefs, appointing Thomas de Torquemada inquisitor-general of Castile and Aragon, and clothing him with full powers to frame a new constitution for the Holy Office (August 2nd and October 17th, 1483). This was the origin of that terrible tribunal, the Spanish or Modern Inquisition, familiar to most readers whether of history or romance, which for three centuries extended its iron sway over the dominions of Spain and Portugal.

Edicts were ordered to be published annually, on the first two Sundays in Lent, throughout the churches, enjoining it as a sacred duty on all who knew or suspected another to be guilty of heresy to lodge information against him before the Holy Office ; and the ministers of religion were instructed to refuse absolution to such as hesitated to comply with this, although the suspected person might stand in the relation of parent, child, husband, or wife. All accusations, anonymous as well as signed, were admitted ; it being only necessary to specify the names of the witnesses, whose testimony was taken down in writing by a secretary, and afterwards read to them, which, unless the inaccuracies were so gross as to force themselves upon their attention, they seldom failed to confirm.

Not the least odious feature of the whole was the connection established between the condemnation of the accused and the interests of his judges ; since the confiscations, which were the uniform penalties of heresy, were not permitted to flow into the royal exchequer until they had first discharged the expenses, whether in the shape of salaries or otherwise, incident to the Holy Office. The most humane provisions were constantly evaded in practice ; and the toils for ensnaring the victim were so ingeniously multiplied that few, very few, were permitted to escape without some censure. Not more than one person, says Llorente, in one or perhaps two thousand processes, previous to the time of Philip III, received entire absolution. So that it came to be proverbial that all who were not roasted were at least singed :

> " Devant l'Inquisition, quand on vient à jubé,
> Si l'on ne sort rôti, l'on sort au moins flambé."

torture, and condemned to the flames. Some miserably perish, bewailing their errors, and invoking the name of Christ, while others call upon that of Moses. Many, again, who sincerely repent, she, notwithstanding the heinousness of their transgressions, merely sentences to perpetual imprisonment."

[1] Bernaldez [cc] states that guards were posted at the gates of the city of Seville in order to prevent the emigration of the Jewish inhabitants, which indeed was forbidden under pain of death. The tribunal, however, had greater terrors for them, and many succeeded in effecting their escape.

The "Auto da fé"

The last scene in this dismal tragedy was the "act of faith" (*auto da fé*),[1] the most imposing spectacle, probably, which has been witnessed since the ancient Roman triumph, and which, as intimated by a Spanish writer, was intended, somewhat profanely, to represent the terrors of the Day of Judgment. The proudest grandees of the land, on this occasion, putting on the sable livery of familiars of the Holy Office and bearing aloft its banners, condescended to act as the escort of its ministers; while the ceremony was not unfrequently countenanced by the royal presence. It should be stated, however, that neither of these acts of condescension — or, more properly, humiliation — was witnessed until a period posterior to Isabella's reign. The effect was further heightened by the concourse of ecclesiastics in their sacerdotal robes, and pompous ceremonial which was intended to consecrate, as it were, this bloody sacrifice by the authority of a religion which has expressly declared that it desires mercy and not sacrifice.[2]

The most important actors in the scene were the unfortunate convicts, who were now disgorged for the first time from the dungeons of the tribunal. They were clad in coarse woollen garments, styled *san benitos*, brought close round the neck and descending like a frock down to the knees. These were of yellow colour, embroidered with a scarlet cross, and well garnished with figures of devils and flames of fire, which, typical of the heretic's destiny hereafter, served to make him more odious in the eyes of the superstitious multitude.[3] The greater part of the sufferers were condemned to be "reconciled," the manifold meanings of which soft phrase have been already explained. Those who were to be "relaxed," as it was called, were delivered over, as impenitent heretics, to the secular arm, in order to expiate their offence by the most painful of deaths, with the consciousness, still more painful, that they were to leave behind them names branded with infamy, and families involved in irretrievable ruin.[4]

It is remarkable that a system so monstrous as that of the Inquisition, presenting the most effectual barrier, probably, that was ever opposed to the progress of knowledge, should have been revived at the close of the fifteenth century, when the light of civilisation was rapidly advancing over every part of Europe. It is more remarkable that it should have occurred in Spain, at this time under a government which had displayed great religious independ-

[1 The Spanish form is *auto de fe*, but the Portuguese form — *auto da fé*, was the first to obtain English usage.]

[2] So says Puigblanch *ee* : The inquisitors after the celebration of an *auto da fé* at Guadaloupe, in 1485, wishing probably to justify these bloody executions in the eyes of the people, who had not yet become familiar with them, solicited a sign from the Virgin (whose shrine in that place is noted all over Spain) in testimony of her approbation of the Holy Office. Their petition was answered by such a profusion of miracles that Dr. Francis Sanctius de la Fuente, who acted as scribe on the occasion, became out of breath, and, after recording sixty, gave up in despair, unable to keep pace with their marvellous rapidity, according to Paramo.*i*

[3] Voltaire *dd* remarks (*Essai sur les Mœurs*, Chap. cxl) that "An Asiatic, arriving at Madrid on the day of an *auto da fé*, would doubt whether it were a festival, religious celebration, sacrifice, or massacre ; it is all of them. They reproach Montezuma with sacrificing human captives to the gods. What would he have said had he witnessed an *auto da fé* ?"

[4] The government, at least, cannot be charged with remissness in promoting this. We find two ordinances in the royal collection of *pragmáticas,ff* dated in September, 1501 (there must be some error in the date of one of them), inhibiting, under pain of confiscation of property, such as had been "reconciled," and their children by the mother's side, and grandchildren by the father's, from holding any office in the privy council, courts of justice, or in the municipalities, or any other place of trust or honour. They were also excluded from the vocation of notaries, surgeons, and apothecaries. This was visiting the sins of the fathers, to an extent unparalleled in modern legislation. The sovereigns might find a precedent in a law of Sulla.

ence on more than one occasion, and which had paid uniform regard to the rights of its subjects and pursued a generous policy in reference to their intellectual culture.   Where, we are tempted to ask, when we behold the persecution of an innocent, industrious people for the crime of adhesion to the faith of their ancestors — where was the charity which led the old Castilian to reverence valour and virtue in an infidel, though an enemy, where the chivalrous self-devotion which led an Aragonese monarch, three centuries before, to give away his life in defence of the persecuted sectaries of Provence, where the independent spirit which prompted the Castilian nobles, during the very last reign, to reject with scorn the purposed interference of the pope himself in their concerns, that they were now reduced to bow their necks to a few frantic priests, the members of an order which, in Spain at least, was quite as conspicuous for ignorance as intolerance?   True, indeed, the Castilians, and the Aragonese subsequently still more, gave such evidence of their aversion to the institution, that it can hardly be believed the clergy would have succeeded in fastening it upon them, had they not availed themselves of the popular prejudices against the Jews.[1]   Providence, however, permitted that the sufferings thus heaped on the heads of this unfortunate people should be requited in full measure to the nation that inflicted them.   The fires of the Inquisition, which were lighted exclusively for the Jews, were destined eventually to consume their oppressors.   They were still more deeply avenged in the moral influence of this tribunal, which, eating like a pestilent canker into the heart of the monarchy at the very time when it was exhibiting a most goodly promise, left it at length a bare and sapless trunk.

Torquemada and his Successors

Notwithstanding the persecutions under Torquemada were confined almost wholly to the Jews, his activity was such as to furnish abundant precedent, in regard to forms of proceeding, for his successors ; if, indeed, the word forms may be applied to the conduct of trials so summary that the tribunal of Toledo alone, under the superintendence of two inquisitors, disposed of 3,327 processes in little more than a year.   The number of convicts was greatly swelled by the blunders of the Dominican monks, who acted as qualificators or interpreters of what constituted heresy, and whose ignorance led them frequently to condemn, as heterodox, propositions actually derived from the fathers of the church.   The prisoners for life, alone, became so numerous that it was necessary to assign them their own houses as the places of their incarceration.

The data for an accurate calculation of the number of victims sacrificed by the Inquisition during this reign are not very satisfactory.   From such as exist, however, Llorente has been led to the most frightful results.   In this enormous sum of human misery is not included the multitude of orphans, who, from the confiscation of their paternal inheritance, were turned over to indigence and vice.[2]   Many of the reconciled were afterwards sentenced as

---

[1] The Aragonese made a manly though ineffectual resistance, from the first, to the introduction of the Inquisition among them by Ferdinand.   In Castile, its enormous abuses provoked the spirited interposition of the legislature at the commencement of the following reign.   But it was then too late.

[2] By an article of the primitive instructions, the inquisitors were required to set apart a small portion of the confiscated estates for the education and Christian nurture of minors, children of the condemned.   Llorente k says that, in the immense numbers of processes which he had occasion to consult, he met with no instance of their attention to the fate of these unfortunate orphans !

relapsed; and the curate of Los Palacios *cc* expresses the charitable wish that "the whole accursed race of Jews, male and female, of twenty years of age and upwards, might be purified with fire and fagot!"[1]

The vast apparatus of the Inquisition involved so heavy an expenditure, that a very small sum comparatively, found its way into the exchequer, to counterbalance the great detriment resulting to the state from the sacrifice of the most active and skilful part of its population. All temporal interests, however, were held light in comparison with the purgation of the land from heresy; and such augmentations as the revenue did receive, we are assured, were conscientiously devoted "to pious purposes and the Moorish war"![2]

The Roman see is charged with duplicity, characteristic of Alexander VI, in making a gainful traffic by the sale of dispensations from the penalties incurred by such as fell under the ban of the Inquisition, provided they were rich enough to pay for them, and afterwards revoking them, at the instance of the Castilian court. Meanwhile, the odium excited by the unsparing rigour of Torquemada raised up so many accusations against him that he was thrice compelled to send an agent to Rome to defend his cause before the pontiff; until, at length, Alexander VI, in 1494, moved by these reiterated complaints, appointed four coadjutors,

TORQUEMADA

[1] Torquemada waged war upon freedom of thought in every form. In 1490 he caused several Hebrew Bibles to be publicly burned and some time after, more than six thousand volumes of oriental learning, on the imputation of Judaism, sorcery, or heresy, at the *autos da fé* of Salamanca, the very nursery of science. This may remind one of the similar sentence passed by Lope de Barrientos, another Dominican, about fifty years before, upon the books of the marquis of Villena. Fortunately for the dawning literature of Spain, Isabella did not, as was done by her successors, commit the censorship of the press to the judges of the Holy Office, notwithstanding such occasional assumption of power by the grand inquisitor.

[2] The prodigious desolation of the land may be inferred from the estimates, although somewhat discordant, of deserted houses in Andalusia. Garibay *gg* puts these at three thousand, Pulgar *hh* at four, L. Marineo *bb* as high as five thousand.

out of a pretended regard to the infirmities of his age, to share with him the burdens of his office.

This personage, who is entitled to so high a rank among those who have been the authors of unmixed evil to their species, was permitted to reach a very old age, and to die quietly in his bed. Yet he lived in such constant apprehension of assassination that he is said to have kept a reputed unicorn's horn always on his table, which was imagined to have the power of detecting and neutralising poisons; while, for the more complete protection of his person, he was allowed an escort of fifty horse and two hundred foot in his progresses through the kingdom.

This man's zeal was of such an extravagant character that it may almost shelter itself under the name of insanity. His history may be thought to prove that of all human infirmities, or rather vices, there is none productive of more extensive mischief to society than fanaticism. The opposite principle of atheism, which refuses to recognise the most important sanctions to virtue, does not necessarily imply any destitution of just moral perceptions, that is, of a power of discriminating between right and wrong, in its disciples. But fanaticism is so far subversive of the most established principles of morality, that, under the dangerous maxim, "For the advancement of the faith, all means are lawful," which Tasso has rightly, though perhaps undesignedly, derived from the spirits of hell, it not only excuses, but enjoins the commission of the most revolting crimes as a sacred duty. The more repugnant, indeed, such crimes may be to natural feeling or public sentiment, the greater their merit, from the sacrifice which the commission of them involves. Many a bloody page of history attests the fact that fanaticism armed with power is the sorest evil which can befall a nation.[m]

Under Charles I (the emperor Charles V) the cortes sought for a modification of the laws of the Inquisition; but under Philip II the flames burned brightly again, at first in Seville and Valladolid (1559 seq.). But by the end of the seventeenth century all vestiges of the Reformation were effaced, and the activity of the Inquisition became limited to the destruction of prohibited books, of which an Index had been prepared in 1558. Under Charles III, in 1770, an edict was passed, securing an accused party from arbitrary imprisonment; and other regulations were passed, curtailing the powers of the Inquisition, until, in 1808, Joseph Bonaparte abolished it entirely. In 1814 Ferdinand VII restored it; but the popular rage in 1820 destroyed the inquisitor's palace at Madrid, and the cortes again abolished it. But in 1825, by the efforts of the clergy, another inquisitorial commission was appointed. It continued till 1834, when it was finally abolished, and its property applied to the payment of the public debt. But it may be a long while before the country will revive from the effects of the court which, in the sixteenth and seventeenth centuries, extinguished her active literary life and placed this nation, so richly endowed, almost outside of the circle of European civilisation. Spain, it is true, remained free from heresies and religious wars; but her rest was the rest of the grave, so far as religious vitality was concerned.

The fortunes of the Inquisition in Portugal were similar to those which it had in Spain. In the reign of John VI (1818–1826) it was finally abolished. The last relics of the Italian Inquisition disappeared at the unification of the nation. The Congregation of the Inquisition at Rome, appointed by Sixtus V in 1587, is all that remains of it. In its day it likewise had crushed out the Reformation, and had raged the most fearfully in Venice; but there its activity seems to have ceased in 1781, and in 1808 Napoleon abolished it. Restored under Pius VII in 1814, it directed its energies to prevent the diffusion of the Italian Bible, and to check the introduction of evangelical truth.

In the Netherlands, where the Inquisition was first introduced in the thirteenth century, it became a terrible weapon in the time of the Reformation. In 1521, Charles V passed a rigorous edict against heretics, and appointed Franz van der Hulst inquisitor-general. In 1525 three inquisitors-general were appointed, in 1537 the number was increased to four, and in 1545 one was appointed for each of the provinces. According to Grotius, a hundred thousand victims died under Charles V; according to the prince of Orange, fifty thousand. Both computations are probably too large. Under Philip II the inquisitors developed the most zeal; and the duke of Alva, in 1567, appointed the Bloody Council, which proceeded with unheard-of cruelty against those whose wealth excited their avarice, or whose heresy aroused their suspicion. In 1573 Alva was recalled ; and three years later the provinces concluded the League of Ghent, whose fifth article abolished the edicts against heresy.z

Torture lasted as late as 1817 in Spain, where Van Halen suffered it, notwithstanding the papal bull of 1816 ; and, according to Mackenna,t it lasted in Spanish America until 1809.

In conclusion it is possible to present a fairly accurate total of the ruinous sweep of the Inquisition. The historian Llorente k accomplished the seemingly impossible task of unearthing the records. He was a Spanish priest, and from 1785 was an officer of the Inquisition in its then milder form. In 1808 he became a Bonapartist, and was concerned in the suppression of monastic orders. The archives were at his disposal, and he studied them thoroughly. He fled to France on the Restoration in 1814, and there brought out his monumental work in French. His life was not safe even there, and he suffered much persecution. His work has been convicted of many faults, but not of dishonesty, and his conclusions may be quoted with a reasonable amount of confidence.a

Llorente's Computation of the Victims of the Inquisition

In summing up, it appears that the Spanish Inquisition, during the first eighteen years of its existence under Torquemada, condemned 8,800 persons to perish in the flames, 6,500, dead or fugitives, to be burned in effigy ; and imposed different pains and penalties upon 90,004 who were reconciled ; making a total of 105,294 victims. I propose to take each tribunal separately and to place the number of victims as low as circumstances will permit.

Were I guided by the autos da fé of the Inquisition of Toledo and Saragossa I might triple the number of victims, for in eight years alone 6,341 were punished by the inquisitors of Seville, which is at the rate of 792 a year, not including the many victims of other autos da fé which I have found mentioned, but of which I cannot find the reports. Saragossa shows almost similar results, and if the same is assumed of the other tribunals the total would be twice as much again as by my reckoning. But I do not wish to give anyone grounds for saying that I have tried to exaggerate the evil.

The second general inquisitor was Diego Deza, a Dominican, tutor to the prince of Asturias, Don Juan, bishop of Zamora, Salamanca, Jaen, Palencia, and finally archbishop of Seville. He held the office from the beginning of 1499 to the end of 1506, when he resigned it by order of king Ferdinand V, regent of Castile. In his time there were the same twelve tribunals in the peninsula as in the time of his predecessor ; therefore I reckon only 208 burned, 104 burned in effigy, and 4,057 subjected to penances, making a total of 4,369 victims a year. This number, multiplied by eight makes the number of victims in his time, 1,664 of the first class, 832 of the second class, and 32,456 of the third class; a total of 34,952 victims.

The third general inquisitor was the cardinal-archbishop Francisco Ximenes de Cisneros, a Franciscan. He held the office from the year 1507 until the 8th of November, 1517, when he died. During that time there was a separate office of general inquisitor of Aragon which was first held by Juan Enguera, a Dominican, bishop of Vique. He died in 1513 and was succeeded by Luis Mercader, a Carthusian, who upon his death on the 1st of June, 1516, was succeeded by Cardinal Adriano de Florencio, then dean of Lobania, tutor of Charles V, afterwards bishop of Tortosa, and ultimately sovereign pontiff (Adrian VI). In 1513 Cardinal Ximenes de Cisneros created a tribunal of the Inquisition for the bishopric of Cuenca and its districts, separating them from the jurisdiction of Murcia in 1516 ; another for the fortress of Oran in Africa, and another for America in the island of Cuba. We will leave the two last out of our calculations, as well as those of Caller in the island of Sardinia, and of Palermo in Sicily.

The twelve former tribunals of the peninsula produced, according to the inscription in Seville, with the modification adopted, 208 burned, 104 burned in effigy, 4,057 subjected to penances, a year, making from the year, 1507 to 1513 inclusive a total of 1,456 of the first class, 728 of the second class, and 28,399 of the third class.

The tribunal of Cuenca was established in 1514, and according to my method of computation I assign to it 200 of the first class, 200 of the second, and 1,700 of the third, which added to the 208, 104, and 4,057 of the other twelve tribunals gives a total for that year of 408, 304, and 5,757. In 1515, the tribunal of Cuenca is counted as one of the old tribunals, with only 16 of the first class, 8 of the second, and 312 of the third, which added to the total of the other tribunals amounts to 224, 112, and 4,369. In 1516 and 1517, the result is similar. The total of the eleven years during which Ximenes de Cisneros was general inquisitor is 2,536 burned, 1,368 burned in effigy, and 47,263 penitents, 51,167 in all.

Cardinal Adriano, bishop of Tortosa, was the fourth general inquisitor. He was appointed at the beginning of March, 1518, and though he was elected pope on the 9th of January, 1522, he had no successor as head of the Holy Office until the end of 1522; for Adriano issued the bulls on the 10th of September of that year, fourteen days before his death. For this reason the number of tribunals in the peninsula was not increased for six years, but in America one was established at Puerto Rico for the West Indies in 1519.

According to the inscription in the castle of Triana, in the thirteen tribunals of our continent there were every year 224 persons burned, 112 burned in effigy, and 4,369 subjected to penances; consequently the total for the six years was 1,344 of the first class, 672 of the second class, and 26,214 of the third class; 28,230 victims in all.

The fifth general inquisitor was Cardinal Alfonso Manrique, successively bishop of Badajoz and of Cordova, and archbishop of Seville. In 1524, he ordered the inscription which has guided our calculations for the preceding years to be placed in the castle of Triana in Seville. In this same year the tribunal of Granada, which had been established the year before, began to exercise its functions. Although the number of those punished as Judaical heretics was diminished, there was no lack of victims, their places being supplied by the Mohammedan Moriscoes, Lutherans, and Sodomites, whose punishment, and that of other criminals, was confided to the inquisitors by Pope Clement VII. Manrique died on the 28th of September, 1538, having established tribunals of the Inquisition in Canaria, Jaen, and Granada, and two in America for Tierrafirme (Terra Firma) and the West Indies. It is calculated that the yearly victims would be about 10 burned, 5 burned in effigy, and 50 subjected to penances, a total of 65 victims. There were thirteen tribunals in the peninsula, two in the adjacent islands, and multiplying by the fifteen years of Manrique's ministry there were 2,250 of the first class, 1,125 of the second class, and 11,250 of the third class, a total of 14,625 victims.

[Llorente continues thus his record from inquisitor to inquisitor through the centuries. We shall omit these till we reach the last years of the Holy Office.]

Fortieth, Felipe Beltran, bishop of Salamanca, was general inquisitor after Quintano, in 1774. He exercised this function until he died, which appears to me to have been about 1783. In his time there were 2 burned, none burned in effigy, 16 condemned to public penances, and very many in secret without infamy or confiscation. My departure from Madrid for Valencia on the 10th of August, 1812, since which I never returned to court, prevented me from completing this catalogue with the exact dates, but the substance of my narrative is most exact. The last victim who perished in the flames was a *beata* of Seville, on the 7th of November, 1781. She was condemned for having a compact and illicit personal intercourse with the devil, and for impenitent denial of the offence, according to the trial. Her life would have been spared had she pleaded guilty to the crimes of which she was accused.

Forty-first, Augustin Rubin de Cevallos, bishop of Jaen, knight of the grand cross of the royal Spanish order of Charles III. He immediately succeeded Beltran and was general inquisitor from 1784 until 1792, when he died. No one was burned in person nor in effigy in his time; 14 were condemned to public penances, and many in secret but without infamy or confiscation. Forty-second, Manuel Abad-y-la-Sierra, bishop of Astorga, archbishop of Selimbra and general inquisitor, appointed in 1792. He resigned in 1794 by order of Charles IV. In his time 16 were condemned to public and many to private penances; no one was burned. Forty-third, Francisco Antonio de Lorenzana, cardinal-archbishop of Toledo, was appointed general inquisitor in 1794, and resigned by order of Charles IV in 1797. In his time 14 were condemned to public and many to private penances; no one was burned.

Forty-fourth, Ramon Josef de Arce, archbishop of Burgos and of Saragossa, patriarch of the Indies, councillor of state, general director of the Royal University of Madrid, and knight of the grand cross of the royal order of Charles III. He was general inquisitor from 1798 to 1808. In his time 20 were condemned to public and many to private penances, without infamy or confiscation of goods. One effigy was burned at Cuenca, but no one was burned in person, for though sentence was pronounced against the curate of Esco, the general inquisitor and supreme council refused to confirm it, in order to prevent its execution. Recapitulation: burned in person, 31,912; burned in effigy, 17,659; condemned to severe penances, 291,450; total, 341,021.

My design is to calculate the number of victims at the lowest figure possible, and I am convinced that from the year 1481, when the tribunal was established, until the end of the reign of Philip II, the numbers were much more than I have stated, considering the records of the tribunals of Toledo and Saragossa, which did not notably exceed the rest. If we were to add the victims punished by the tribunals of Mexico, Lima, Cartagena de las Indias (Cartagena in Colombia), Sicily, and in the galleys at sea, the number would be incalculable. Still more so were we to count the victims which resulted from the attempts to establish the Inquisition in Naples, Milan, and Flanders, for all these belonged to Spain, and felt the influence of the Spanish tribunal. How many died in their beds of illness caused by the infamy which fell upon them through the condemnation of their relations? No possible calculation could include all this misery.[k]

EFFECTS AND INFLUENCES OF THE INQUISITION

Geddes,[q] in 1714, made this contemporary observation, and his point should not be forgotten in an estimate of the far-reaching evils. "By this list we see what a terrible havoc is made by the Inquisition in Portugal, and especially among the trading people, to the great diminution both of its stock in trade and of the number of its current and expert merchants. For though there were but four persons burned this year in Lisbon by the Inquisition, there were above threescore undone by it. Anyone of a family's being taken up by the Inquisition goes a great way towards ruining it, filling them with such horrors as drive them into countries that are out of the reach of the Inquisition."

A recent writer, a churchman, Dean Kitchin,[ll] has said: "The hand of the Holy Office was outstretched against all; no lofty dignity in church or state, no eminence in art or science, no purity of life, could defend from its attacks. It is said to have threatened Charles V and Philip II; it persecuted Archbishop Carranza, head of the church in Spain; destroyed De Dominis, archbishop of Spalatro; it smote Galileo, murdered Giordano Bruno, attacked Pico di Mirandola, and even is said to have threatened Cæsar Borgia. With equal vigour, in combination with the Jesuits, the Inquisition made war on books and learning, religious or secular alike; we have seen how baleful was its effect in earlier days on literature and art in Provence, and in the time of the Catholic sovereigns on the material well-being of Spain. 'In the love of Christ and his maid-mother,' says Queen Isabella, 'I have caused great misery, and have depopulated towns and districts, provinces and kingdoms.'"[ll]

A CATHOLIC VIEW OF THE INQUISITION (C. J. HEFELE)

The word inquisition with the original signification of an ecclesiastical court of faith, was later applied to a state institution which, on account of its real or alleged harshness, has become a by-word in Europe for everything horrible. There is no doubt that an ecclesiastical court of inquiry existed among the Christians from the beginning, but it is equally certain that in the earliest times the penalties for heresy were only ecclesiastical and clerical without any civil effect. The case was altered when Emperor Constantine appeared as both the protector and the secular arm of the church, for which reason he considered it necessary to exile the heretics, who were threatening the church with danger, in order to put them out of the way of doing harm. More severe punishments than exile were first inflicted upon the Catholics by the Arians when their co-religionists Constantius and Valens occupied the throne. The former introduced the practice of imprisoning the orthodox, the latter of drowning them, and Arian princes in the later Germanic kingdoms always exercised violence towards those of different faiths.

The connection of church and state was made much closer by the great theocratic idea, emanating from Gregory VII, which aimed at the bringing together of all peoples of the occident into one theocratic union, the protector of which was to be the pope, in the name of God; but the members of which could naturally be only those who belonged to the church. From this standpoint, heretics necessarily appeared as criminals of state because, through their wrong teaching, they rebelled against God as the king of the theocratic union: hence the civil codes of the middle ages punished heresy with death.

Whereas, after the time of Constantine the Great, the civil punishments of heretics were inflicted by the secular rulers, the decision as to whether a person was a heretic or not, was from the very beginning made by the bishops and synods. Hence, if we wish to get at the fundamental idea of the Inquisition, that it was a seeking out and a punishing of heretics, we must say that, in the former sense, it has existed since the time of the apostles; and, in the latter, since that of Constantine the Great. The actual Inquisition had its beginning in the great synod of Toulouse in 1229. Soon after this synod in southern France, we meet especially appointed inquisitors in Italy. Here also heresy had ravaged widely and had become so dangerous that even Emperor Frederick II, who is the last person one could accuse of bigotry, immediately upon his coronation and repeatedly afterwards uttered the death penalty against heretics. Gradually the episcopal inquisition became changed into a Dominican inquisition and was introduced into nearly all the countries of Europe. In the Pyrenaean peninsula likewise, which is here our main subject of interest, it came into Castile, Navarre, and Portugal, as well as into Aragon. Castile was to become the home of the "New Inquisition," as Llorente[k] calls it,—more correctly of the Spanish Inquisition, the direct impulse to which was given by a peculiar condition which existed nowhere else than in Spain.

Already in the first centuries after the birth of Christ, the Jews in Spain had become so numerous and powerful that they began to think of Judaising the whole land. Hence it came about that the synod of Eliberis (303–313), an old Spanish city in the vicinity of which the later Granada is said to have been built, passed a resolution that in the future no Christian landholder was to let his fields be blessed by Jews. On the other hand there was no lack of attempts on the part of the old Visigothic kings in Spain to force the Jews to become Christians; but this was forbidden by the fourth council of Toledo, in its 57th canon, with the words: "Hereafter no Jew may be made to accept Christianity by force, but those who are already converted, even though it was by force, since they have already received the holy sacraments, must keep their faith and may in no wise blaspheme or despise it."

Much more dangerous than the real Jews were those who were seemingly converted to Christianity and whose numbers had increased enormously after the persecutions at the end of the 14th century. While the former had seized upon a large part of the national wealth and the Spanish commerce, the latter threatened both the Spanish nationality and the Christian religion, since these disguised Jews on the one hand invaded clerical offices and even occupied episcopal chairs, while on the other they attained high civil honours, married into all noble families and used all these connections, together with their wealth, to bring about the victory of Judaism over Spanish nationality and over the Christian faith. Many laymen as well as churchmen recognised the danger threatened by the Jews and were convinced that something must be done by the government, for which reason repeated requests were made to

Ferdinand and Isabella to take measures against the disguised Jews: it was against them that the inquisition was directed later, but never against the real Jews.

Soon after Ferdinand and Isabella had decided to introduce the Inquisition into Castile, Pope Sixtus IV, on November 1st, 1478, gave the ecclesiastical permission and allowed the two rulers to appoint two, or three clerical dignitaries, secular or regular priests, to question and to punish heretics. Two royal inquisitors were now appointed for Seville on the strength of the papal bull. In this step we have the beginning of the New or the Spanish state inquisition which differs principally from the ecclesiastical institution of the same name in the fact that the persons intrusted with the examination and the punishment of heretics — whether they were clericals or laymen — appeared not as servants of the church but as state officials who received their appointment and instructions from the ruling princes.

There was a second political reason why the Spanish monarchs in every way should have favoured an institution which, while appearing to be ecclesiastical, was almost continually accused and fought by the heads of the church, by the popes and bishops. With the reign of Ferdinand and Isabella the transition began from the old state to the new, from the Germanic to the abstract and absolute. In the old state the central or royal power was limited by three comparatively free corporations, the nobility, the clergy, and the municipalities, and this the more so as these estates were closely connected with powers abroad, the clergy with Rome, the nobility and municipalities with their foreign peers, so that the union of the state within itself and therewith the superiority of the throne was not a little hindered. In both Castile and Aragon the inquisition was the most effective means of bringing all subjects, especially the clergy and nobility, under the power of the throne, and of perfecting the absolute authority of the sovereign.

Hence it was that it was precisely the two higher estates which most hated the Inquisition and which were persecuted as its enemies more often than the heretics; it was also principally the prelates who were soon involved in numerous suits with the new tribunals. The popes also could not fail to see that the Spanish Inquisition served the political absolutism much more than it did ecclesiastical purism, and hence they tried to intercept its growth in the same degree that they had promoted the old ecclesiastical inquisition.

This state character of the Spanish Inquisition has also been fully recognised by the more exact historical investigation of modern times, and even Ranke [mm] has expressed himself to the same effect as follows: "We have a celebrated book concerning it (the Inquisition) by Llorente,[k] and if I make so bold as to say anything in disagreement with such a predecessor let this be an excuse, that that so well informed author wrote in the interest of the Alfrancesados of the Josephinian government [i.e. the Gallicising faction supporting King Joseph Bonaparte]. In their interest he opposes the liberties of the Basque provinces, although the latter can hardly be denied. In the same interest he sees in the Inquisition also a usurpation of clerical power over state authority. If I am not mistaken, however, from the very facts which he relates it appears that the Inquisition was a royal court, but one provided with clerical weapons."

Guizot [nn] agrees with this opinion in the words: "It (the Inquisition) was at first more political than religious, and destined to maintain order rather than to defend the faith."

That the Portuguese Inquisition also was always regarded by the government itself as a state institution is shown by an ordinance dated March 20th,

1769, in which King Joseph I says: "It has been reported to me that whereas all other courts of justice, because they represent my royal person, have always borne and still bear the title Majesty, the misuse has arisen in connection with the Holy Office, a tribunal which by its organisation and its service is most closely and directly connected with my royal person, of giving it another title of address."

The Inquisition is often judged according to standards of the 19th instead of the 15th and 16th centuries, and hence it is judged incorrectly. Whereas during the past hundred years it has been the tendency to regard wrong believers and unbelievers of all kinds as the most educated and the noblest citizens, the Inquisition on the contrary was based on the mediæval view that erring in religion was high treason and that only the advocate of the state religion could be a safe and trustworthy citizen. It is natural that the up-holder of one standpoint cannot possibly judge impartially, events which have arisen from the other, unless in giving his judgment he is able to trans-port himself from his own time into the other and into its views.

This is done by every true historian. But the Inquisition is a subject which has been most discussed and described by those who give mere phrases instead of investigations, mere arbitrary statements instead of critical exami-nations, mere romantic descriptions instead of objective judgments, and who try to replace a lack of knowledge by so called liberally-minded phrases. People of this sort do not remember that the principle, *cujus est regio, illius et religio*,[1] on which the whole Inquisition rests, was universally recognised in olden times, and was so little questioned that Protestants especially upheld it and put it into execution.

For example in the palatinate, when the Kurfürst Frederick III, who had been a Lutheran until then, went over to Calvinism in 1563, he compelled all congregations in his land to take the same step, and exiled everyone who would not accept the Heidelberg catechism. Thirteen years later, in 1576, his son Ludwig restored the orthodox Lutheranism, drove out the Calvinistic preachers and teachers, and forced his dependents to become Lutheran again. The Religious Peace of the year 1555 gave every government the power of giving its dependents the alternative of accepting the religion of the sovereign or of emigrating, upon paying a certain sum, just as was done in Spain with the Jews and Moors; and it is a well-known fact that the Reformation owed its spread in Germany in large measure to this lenient Spanish alternative.

Furthermore, in judging the Inquisition it is often forgotten that the penal code of that time was much more severe and sanguinary than that of the 19th century. Many a trespass which is now atoned for by a slight penalty had at that time to be paid for with blood; and the criminal code of Charles V of the year 1532 is a most speaking witness for the severe criminal justice of the period out of which the Spanish Inquisition grew. Also the *Carolina*, for example, inflicts punishments on body, life, and limb for blasphemy of God and of the Blessed Virgin (§CVI); and witches are punished with death (§CXVI).

It must also not be overlooked, in judging the Inquisition, that the death penalty for heresy was not peculiar to it alone, but was common at that time to all lands and confessions. The reformer Buzer said of Michael Servetus, in the public pulpit at Strassburg, that he deserved the most humiliating death on account of his article against the Trinity. And that this was not merely a strong figure of speech of the Reformers is shown two decades later

[1 This may be roughly translated "The man that rules the region, rules also its religion."]

by Calvin, when on October 27th, 1553, he had that very "heretic" slowly burned to death at Geneva. That there may remain no doubt that the Protestants of that time wished to punish heresy with death, the "gentle" Melanchthon wrote on this subject to Calvin,

"I have read thy article, wherein thou hast refuted in detail the terrible blasphemies of Servetus and therefore I thank the Son of God who has given thee the victory in this thy struggle. The church is greatly indebted to thee for it, now and in all future time. I wholly agree with thy opinion and claim that your highness (eure Obrigkeit) has acted wholly in accordance with justice in executing a blasphemous person after a regular examination."

In addition I will note that Theodore Beza also wrote an article *De hereticis a magistratu civili puniendis* and that many others besides Servetus, as Valentine Gentilis, Bolsec, Carlstadt, Grüet, Castellio, the councillor Ameaur, and others, could convince themselves through imprisonment, banishment, and death that in the Protestant church there was no milder an inquisition than in Spain. This is acknowledged even by many Protestants, as for example by Prescott[m] in his history of Ferdinand and Isabella.

But we do not need to go back to the 16th century or even to consider the terrible mistreatment of the Catholics in England,[1] in order to discover counterparts to the Spanish Inquisition among the Protestants. A remarkable case of this kind from the eighteenth century is related by Pfeilschifter: In the year 1724 at Rendsburg a young soldier, because he had wished to make a compact with the devil, as an act of royal favour was merely beheaded. Even more recently, *e.g.* in the year 1844, on the third of April the painter J. O. Nilson in Sweden was banished on account of "apostasy from the Lutheran faith and of going over to a mistaken religion" (the Catholic) and was declared to have forfeited all civil rights and rights of inheritance; this decision was confirmed by the highest court of the land in the year 1845. The unfortunate Nilson died in February 1847 at Copenhagen, in poverty.

I say all this not in reproach but only to show that the Protestants also have recognised the sanguinary rule: "Deviation from the state religion is to be punished with death." If any one had any doubts as to the justice of this principle in the 16th and 17th centuries, it seems to me that these doubts should first have arisen in the minds of the Protestants, because their own apostasy from the church should have taught them to think more leniently of other apostates.

Among the victims of the Inquisition the so-called witches and sorcerers held a considerable place, and it would be superfluous to expend many words in proving that these unfortunates were just as severely persecuted in Germany as in Spain and in just as sanguinary a fashion by Protestants as by Catholics. Not only a Torquemada, but also a Benedict Carpzov two hundred years later, erected a stake for burning witches. Even the reformer Beza reproached the French parliament for being too lax in seeking out witches, and Walter Scott acknowledges that the stronger Calvinism grew in England the more numerous were the processes against witches. The Jesuit Frederick Spee of Langenfeld overthrew the belief in witches among the Catholics seventy years earlier than the Protestant Thomasius, and even in the year

[1 The reader will find full treatment of Protestant excesses in the histories of Germany, Switzerland, and England. The persecution of Catholics in England is discussed, in vol. XIX, pp. 148–155, 159–161, 199–200, 354–355, 406–408, 444–453, including an account of tortures used in England during Elizabeth's reign, and a comparison of her cruelties with those of "Bloody Mary." As part of religious history, one should also note the persecutions inflicted on dissenters by the Church of England, in Scotland and Ireland, as discussed in the histories of those countries.]

1713 the legal faculty of Tubingen condemned a witch to death; indeed just a year later than in Spain, was the last witch burned in the canton of Glarus by a reformed court, in 1782.[1] On the whole, a comparison of the German processes against witches with the workings of the Spanish Inquisition, could hardly be made to appear to the advantage of the former.

Moreover it must not be forgotten with all this that the tribunal of the Inquisition always delivered only the sentence, that the accused was more or less, wholly or partly, or not at all guilty of heresy, blasphemy and the like. It itself never condemned to death though its decisions led to this penalty, in that the one found "guilty of heresy" by the Holy Office was turned over to the secular arm and by this, namely by the council of Castile, was led before the highest Spanish court for death or imprisonment.

The Spanish Inquisition is often declared to be a product of the Roman doctrinal despotism, without attention being given to the fact that it was precisely the popes who were least inclined to this institution and who at nearly all times tried to limit it. Even Llorente,[k] who can be accused of partiality to the popes no more than of a Jacobite partiality for the kingdom, shows this in almost innumerable instances and examples.

Stories are told of the cruel torments and tortures which the unfortunate beings in the dungeons of the Inquisition had to suffer, but even the most gentle character must not forget that the torture was used in those days in all secular courts in all countries, that it even existed legally in many German states in the 19th century and did not go out of general use until about the middle of the 18th century, in the courts of inquisition at the same time as in the secular courts. Besides execution by fire, sword, quartering, the wheel, gallows, and water, the *Carolina* speaks of burying alive, of tearing with glowing tongs, of cutting off the tongue and ears, of hacking off fingers and the like. Of all these ignominious and painful punishments, however, the Inquisition knows nothing. Moreover, at a time when in all Europe prisons were dark damp holes and real graves, full of mould, filth, and pest-breeding smells, the Inquisition brought its prisoners, to use the words of Llorente[k] into "well arched, light and dry rooms where they could make some movement." No more did any prisoner of the Inquisition, as again Llorente testifies, groan under the weight of chains, hand cuffs, iron neck bands etc., and Llorente tells of only one on whom fetters were put, in order to keep him from suicide. The prisoners were asked if the gaoler treated them well and good care was also taken of the sick. Special buildings, by the name of "penitence houses," were erected for the prisoners for life and these were subject to vistation from time to time.

It has furthermore become customary to think of the Inquisition as an ever-threatening and never-satisfied catch-and-seize-institution, whose polyp arms greedily grasped the poor unfortunate at the least sign of suspicion. But this view, which has such a drastic effect in historical romances and in romantic histories is wholly wrong and mistaken and must be entirely abandoned, unless Llorente is to be accused of partiality for the Inquisition. In the first place, every tribunal of the Inquisition began its activity by promulgating a time of grace and proclaimed publicly that: "whoever is conscious of apostasy from the faith but within the fixed time will voluntarily come forth and do penance, shall be absolved in grace and protected from severe penalty." After

[1] The reader will find in vol. XXIII page 177, a statement that a man was "swam for a wizard" in England in 1825. He should consult this same volume, pages 171–177, for an account of the witchcraft persecutions in the United States, at Salem, in 1692, and pages 177–178 for an account of the mutilation and execution of Quakers in Massachusetts.]

the expiration of the term, however, the severity of the law was to be exercised towards the apostates; but again and again were the times of grace renewed and lengthened.

Further, the statutes of the Inquisition regarding young heretics deserve attention. "If sons and daughters of heretics," so ordained Torquemada, "who have fallen into error through the teachings of their parents, and have not reached the age of twenty years, themselves apply to be taken back into favour, the inquisition shall receive such young people kindly, even if they should come after the time of reprieve, shall impose lighter penances upon them than upon grown persons and shall take pains that they receive instruction in the faith and the sacraments of the Holy Mother, the church."

It is said that the least expression, often an innocent one, brought an unfortunate into the prisons of the Inquisition. But the second great inquisitor, Deza, who is considered even stricter than Torquemada himself, issued the order on June 17th, 1500 that "no one may be arrested for trivial reasons, not even on account of blasphemy which was uttered in anger." There was no inclination to take the testimony of any person who happened to make an accusation before the tribunal of the Inquisition; on the contrary Llorente himself tells of cases in which only repeated accusations against a person could move the inquisitors to action and they were very much inclined to ascribe the mad behaviour of many heretics to mental aberration.

Wonderful stories are told of the incomes of the inquisitors, who are said to have condemned many only in order to enrich themselves from the confiscated goods. It is true that the cause of justice is in a bad way when condemnation is to bring a pecuniary profit to the judge and it would have been truly a dangerous and disreputable arrangement if the income of the inquisitors had depended on the number of those they condemned. Prescott[m] (I, 287) would really like to make us believe that such was the case, but we know from Llorente that the confiscated goods of the condemned fell to the royal treasury, and that the Inquisition officers of all kinds had a fixed salary which they received quarterly. Hence it comes that Llorente accused the Spanish king of avarice and not the inquisitors, in which Ranke[mm] bears him out.

Terrible is the picture which we make to ourselves of an *auto da fé* (actus fidei, i.e., "an act of faith") as if it were nothing else than an enormous fire and a colossal stewing pan, around which the Spaniards sat like cannibals, in order to enjoy the spectacle of the roasting and broiling of several hundred unfortunates, four or five times a year. But let me be allowed to state that in the first place an *auto da fé* did not consist of burning and killing but, in part, of the exculpation of those who had been falsely accused and in part of the reconciliation of the repentant with the church, and there were even many *autos da fé* at which nothing burned but the candles which the penitent carried in their hands in token of the light of faith rekindled in their hearts.

Furthermore it must not be overlooked that those who were condemned by the Inquisition were not only heretics, but also such as lived in polygamy, priests and monks who had married, laymen who exercised clerical functions, deacons who heard confessions and those who falsely gave themselves out to be commissioners of the Inquisition, which as we know from *Gil Blas* happened not infrequently.

If in the little Protestant city of Nördlingen, as Soldan shows in his history of the witch processes, out of a total population of 6,000, not less than 35 witches were burned in the four years from 1590 to 1594; this ratio, applied to Spain for four years, would give at least 50,000 witches, whereas Llorente himself gives the number of those condemned to death by the Inquisition during the 330 years of its existence as only 30,000, including heretics, witches, sorcerers, smugglers and all the rest; this even if we wish to accept Llorente's figures as not exaggerated.

But I think I may claim and can prove that they are exaggerated. Above all we must never forget that Llorente's figures are not taken from official registers, not even from private records, but originated only from a system of probable reckonings which in part rests on false premises. He himself confesses this unreservedly, and often describes the theory he has used in his conjectural reckoning. Llorente's arbitrariness and injustice are most clearly shown in regard to Ximenes. Llorente states explicitly that this archbishop tried to make the Inquisition less severe, that he removed bad officials, that he pardoned many of the accused, etc. Nevertheless, that does not hinder him from supposing just as many executions annually under Ximenes as under Deza and his helper Lucero, both of whom he repeatedly accuses of the most boundless cruelty and severity. That such a reckoning is untrue and unjust needs no proof.

After all these observations we are still far removed from wishing to justify the Spanish Inquisition; on the contrary we would everywhere oppose the right of a secular power to interfere with the conscience, but we wished to prove that the institution of the Inquisition was not the outrageous monstrosity which party passions and lack of knowledge have often made it out to be.[oo]

Another Catholic View (Heinrich Brück)

Opinions differ as to the character of the Spanish Inquisition. A number of scholars (Hefele [oo], Gams [pp] and others) claim that it was purely a state institution, whereas the Spanish writers emphasize its ecclesiastical character, without denying the great influence of the crown upon it. The correct view is probably given by Rodrigo [ii] and Orti y Lara.[ii] The former says (I, 276): "The tribunals of the Holy Office had no secular character of themselves. They were ecclesiastical tribunals in respect to the cases which they judged and in respect to the authority which created them. In respect to the royal delegation, however, which was granted to the judges, it may be said that they had a mixed character." Orti y Lara expresses himself in like manner. According to him (p. 27), "the Inquisition united the papal sword of the church and the secular sword of the king into one single sword."

The accusation that the Spanish Inquisition was unpopular is just as false as the statement that it caused the ruin of science and literature in Spain. As Balmes testifies (*Protestantismus and Katholicismus*, I, 412, *et seq.*), the Catholic kings fulfilled the universal wish of the people by establishing the Inquisition; the people were always in sympathy with it, whereas it was opposed by the nobility and higher clergy. The decline of literary activity moreover can not have been caused by the Inquisition for the reason that the golden age of Spanish literature coincided with the time when the Inquisition was in full sway. The greatest theologians, philosophers, and poets, whose works were approved by the Inquisition, lived at that time. Schools were founded and classical studies diligently pursued.

One of the chief accusations brought against the Spanish Inquisition is the alleged extraordinary number of its victims. This accusation is based chiefly on the statements of Antonio Llorente.[k] But it needs only a nearer acquaintance with the character of this embittered free mason and with his proofs, to perceive the incorrectness of his statements. Far from citing historical documents he builds up his argument upon evident falsification, arbitrary assumptions which are in wide contrast with the authorities, and, as the Protestant Peschel[rr] says (page 151), upon a "frivolous calculation from probabilities," so that he cannot be trusted in regard to his data. According to Gams[pp] (III, 274) the number of those executed for heresy during the whole period of the Inquisition was about four thousand, a number not equal to that of the victims of the witch processes in Catholic and Protestant Germany.[ss]

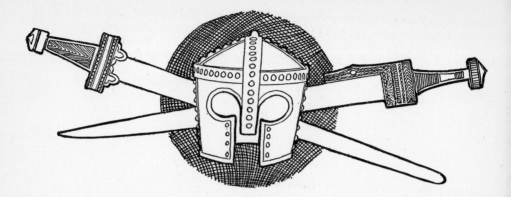

BRIEF REFERENCE-LIST OF AUTHORITIES BY CHAPTERS

[The letter *a* is reserved for Editorial Matter]

CHAPTER I. EARLY HISTORY TO JOÃO I

[b] EMILE BÉGIN, *Voyage pittoresque en Espagne et en Portugal.* — [c] H. MORSE STEPHENS, article on "Portugal" in the *Encyclopædia Britannica.* — [d] "Chronicon Lusitanum" in Florez, *España Sagrada.* — [e] *Chronicon Complutense.* — [f] N. DE LA CLÈDE, *Histoire générale du Portugal.* — [g] DIOGO DE LEMOS, *Historia geral de Portugal.* — [h] S. A. DUNHAM, *The History of Spain and Portugal.* — [i] M. M. BUSK, *The History of Spain and Portugal.* — [j] ALEXANDRE HERCULANO, *Histoire de Portugal.* — [k] ANTONIO ENNES and others, *Historia de Portugal.* — [l] FERNÃO LOPES, *Chronica del Rey Dom Pedro.*

CHAPTER II. THE PERIOD OF GLORY AND DISCOVERY

[b] D. DE LEMOS, *op. cit.* — [c] MATTHAEUS DE PISANO, "De Bello Septensi" (in *José de Serras Colleccao de livros inéditos de historia Portugalza*). — [d] GOMES EANES DE AZURARA, "Cronica de Conde Dom Pedro de Menezes" (in *José de Serras Colleccao de livros inéditos de historia Portugalza*). — [e] S. A. DUNHAM, *op. cit.* — [f] ANTONIO ENNES, *op. cit.* — [g] RICHARD MAJOR, *The Life of Prince Henry the Navigator.* — [h] M. M. BUSK, *op. cit.* — [i] RUY DE PINA, "Chronica do Senhor Rey Dom Alfonso V" in *Academia Real dos Sciencias.* — [j] AGOSTINHO MANOEL VASCONCELLOS, *Anacephalæoses.* — [k] F. DE FONSECA BENEVIDES, *Rainhas de Portugal.* — [l] H. MORSE STEPHENS, *The Story of Portugal.* — [m] JOÃO P. OLIVEIRA-MARTINS, *Historia de Portugal.* — [n] DAMIÃO DE GOES, *Cronica do Senhor Rey Dom Manoel.*

CHAPTER III. THE FALL, THE CAPTIVITY, AND THE REVOLUTION

[b] A. HERCULANO, *op. cit.* — [c] S. A. DUNHAM, *op. cit.* — [d] M. M. BUSK, *op. cit.* — [e] H. M. STEPHENS, *op. cit.* — [f] A. ENNES, *op. cit.* — [g] N. DE LA CLÈDE, *op. cit.* — [h] ANTONIO DE HERRERA, *Cronica de las Indias occidentales.* — [i] PINHEIRO CHAGAS, *Historia de Portugal.* — [j] DIOGO DO CONTO, *Dialogos do soldado practics.* — [k] LUIS DE MENEZES, *Historia de Portugal restaurado.* — [l] AUBERT DE VERTOT, *Histoire de la conjuration de Portugal.*

CHAPTER IV. JOÃO IV TO JOÃO VI

[b] M. M. BUSK, *op. cit.* — [c] H. M. STEPHENS, article on "Portugal" in the *Encyclopædia Britannica.* — [d] H. M. STEPHENS, *The Story of Portugal.* — [e] S. A. DUNHAM, *op. cit.* — [f] AUGUSTE BUCHOT, *Histoire du Portugal.* — [g] FERDINAND DENIS, "Portugal," in *L'Universe Pittoresque.* — [h] FRIEDRICH C. SCHLOSSER, *History of the Eighteenth Century* (translated by D. Davison).

—[i] Sir Nathaniel W. Wraxall, *Historical Memoirs of my own Times.* — [j] Lord Mahon, *History of England.* — [k] Charles F. Dumouriez, *Mémoires.* — [l] James C. Murphy, *Travels in Portugal in the Years 1789–1790.*

Chapter V. The Nineteenth Century

[b] F. C. Schlosser, *Weltgeschichte.* — [c] Jules le Lasteyrie, *Le Portugal depuis la Révolution de 1820.* — [d] William Bollaert, *The Wars of Succession of Portugal and Spain from 1820–1840.* — [e] A. Buchot, *op. cit.* — [f] H. M. Stephens, *op. cit.* — [g] Cesare Cantù, *Gli ultimi trenta anni.* — [h] E. Silvercruys, *Le Portugal.*

Appendix A. The Inquisition

[b] Philippus van Limborch, *Historia Inquisitionis.* — [c] Gosselin, *The Power of the Pope during the Middle Ages.* — [d] J. C. L. Gieseler, *Compendium of Ecclesiastical History.* — [e] J. L. von Mosheim, *Institutes of Ecclesiastical History.* — [f] Von Einem, Editor of Mosheim. — [g] H. Milman, *History of Latin Christianity.* — [h] Ammianus Marcellinus, *History of Rome.* — [i] Ludovicus à Paramo, *De Origine et Progressu officii sanctæ Inquisitionis.* — [j] John Foxe, *Actes and Monuments.* — [k] J. A. Llorente, *The History of the Inquisition.* — [l] Sprenger, *Malleus Maleficarum.* — [m] W. H. Prescott, *Ferdinand and Isabella.* — [n] Henry C. Lea, *A History of the Inquisition of the Middle Ages.* — [o] Reginaldus Gonsalvius Montanus, *Sanctæ Inquisitionis Hispanicæ artes aliquot detectæ.* — [p] Nicholaus Eymerichus, *Directorium Inquisitorum.* — [q] Michael Geddes, *Tracts against Popery,* 1714. — [r] Aristotle, *Rhetoric.* — [s] Francis Bacon, *Novum Organum.* — [t] B. V. MacKenna, *Francisco Moyen, or the Inquisition in South America.* — [u] Joannes a Royas, *De hæreticis corumque impia intentione et credulitate.* — [v] Julius Clarus, *Practica Crimina Finalis,* 1637. — [w] Wm. Lithgow, *Travels,* 1632. — [x] Pablo Garcia, *Orden de Processar en el Santo Oficio,* 1628. — [y] W. H. Rule, *History of the Inquisition.* — [z] Chr. G. Neudecker, article on "Inquisition" in Philip Schaff's *Religious Encyclopædia* based on Herzog's *Real-Encyclopædia.* — [aa] Montesquieu, *Esprit des Lois.* — [bb] L. Marineo, *Cosas memorables.* — [cc] Andres Bernaldez, *Reyes Católicos.* — [dd] Voltaire, *Essai sur les mœurs.* — [ee] Puigblanch, *The Inquisition Unmasked.* — [ff] *Pragmaticas del Reyno.* — [gg] Garibay, *Compendii.* — [hh] Pulgar, *Reyes Católicos.* — [ii] J. G. Rodrigo, *Historia verdadera de la Inquisicion.* — [jj] J. M. Orti y Lara, *La Inquisicion.* — [ll] Dean Kitchin's article on the Inquisition in the *Encyclopædia Britannica.* — [mm] Leopold von Ranke, *History of the Popes.* — [nn] F. Guizot, *Histoire de la Civilisation en Europe.* — [oo] Carl Joseph Hefele, *Der Cardinal Ximenes und die kirchlichen Zustände Spaniens.* — [pp] P. B. Gams, *Kirchengeschichte Spaniens.* — [qq] Jaime L. Balmes, *Protestantismus und Katholicismus.* — [rr] Oskar Peschel, *Das Zeitalter der Entdeckung.* — [ss] Heinrich Brück in Wetzer und Welte's *Kirchenlexikon,* begun by Joseph, Cardinal Hergenröther, continued by Dr. Franz Kaulen.

1252 **Alfonso (X) el Sabio** (the Learned). Xeres de la Frontera, Medina Sidonia, and Cadiz pass into his hands.

1254 Eleanor, the king's daughter, marries Prince Edward (Edward I) of England.

1257 The king claims the duchy of Swabia, and having wasted large sums in fruitless endeavours to secure election to the German Empire, he replenishes his coffers by debasing the coinage, persecuting the Jews, and other arbitrary measures.

1263 The Castilian rights over Algarve ceded to Portugal on the marriage of the Portuguese king with Beatrice, daughter of Alfonso el Sabio. Certain Castilian nobles make this an excuse to revolt, and demand redress of grievances and extraordinary privileges, which Alfonso weakly concedes.

1275 Death of the king's eldest son, the infante Ferdinand de la Cerda. The cortes declare Ferdinand's brother Sancho the next heir, to the exclusion of Ferdinand's sons, the infantes de la Cerda, whose cause is espoused by their uncle, the king of France.

1281 War between Alfonso and Sancho. The nobles rally round Sancho, who makes alliance with the kings of Aragon and Portugal, and declares himself king. The war is only concluded by the defeat of Sancho a few months before Alfonso's death. Alfonso is best known for the encouragement he gave to learning, and the important literary productions which bear his name — some of his own work, and others compiled by his order. They include the code of laws called *Las Siete Partidas* (promulgated in 1258) ; the astronomical work called the *Alfonsine Tables* (drawn up in 1253) ; the *Cronica General de España*, a translation of the Holy Bible, and some poems.

1284 **Sancho the Great and the Brave (or Bravo).** The reign is disturbed by the constant rebellions of the Laras and the king's brother Don Juan, and the infantes de la Cerda, aided by Aragon, and supported by France.

1292 Alonzo Perez de Guzman the Good takes Tarifa from the Moors, and maintains it against the emperor of Morocco and Don Juan, refusing to surrender even to save his son whom Juan murders before the walls.

1295 The accession of **Ferdinand (IV) el Emplazado** (the Summoned) at the age of nine, gives fresh impulse to anarchy. The Hermandad or brotherhood of citizens is formed to resist the lawless depredations of the nobles. The queen-mother, Maria de Molina, recognizes it, and opposes a bold resistance to rival pretenders and domestic and foreign enemies.

1301 She obtains the papal recognition of her marriage, and of the legitimacy of Ferdinand IV, but nevertheless the struggles with turbulent barons continue during the remainder of the reign.

1305 Treaty of Campillo puts an end to the struggle for the succession. Ferdinand begins to reign in his own name.

1310 Trial of the Templars at Salamanca. Their solemn acquittal does not prevent the suppression of their order in Castile as elsewhere.

1312 Mysterious death of Ferdinand, as was said, by the judgment of God. **Alfonso XI**, an infant, succeeds. Return of anarchy in the struggle for the regency.

1315 The regency divided between the infantes Pedro and Juan, the king's uncles.

1319 Both regents slain in battle with the Moors.

1320 Don Juan Manuel assumes the regency. Civil wars with rival claimants.

1324 The king assumes the government, but fails to restore order. He murders his cousin, Juan el Tuerto, and by repudiating his own wife, daughter of Don Juan Manuel, provokes the latter to rebellion.

1328 Right of the cortes to a voice in important affairs of state recognised by the king. He undertakes for himself and successors to impose no tax without the consent of the cortes.

1339 Abul Hakam, emir of Fez, arrives in Spain with a large army. Alfonso aided by troops from Aragon and Portugal defeats him in the great

1340 Battle of Salado. Abul Hakam flees to Africa.

1344 Algeciras taken by Alfonso after a long siege.

1350 Death of Alfonso by the Black Death at the siege of Gibraltar. It was to pay for this war that the *alcavala*, a tax of one-twentieth on all sales of real property, was first granted. Alfonso XI patronised letters, and ordered the continuation of the *Cronica* of Alfonso X which was intrusted to a royal chronicler. The code of Alfonso X was also brought into use in this reign. **Pedro the Cruel.** Leonora de Guzman, the late king's mistress, imprisoned and her sons driven into exile.

1351 Murder of Leonora de Guzman and of Garcilasso de la Vega, adelantado of Castile.

1352 Henry of Trastamara and Don Tello, Leonora's sons, revolt and form a league against

1353 Pedro. The king marries Blanche de Bourbon, a French princess, but immediately forsakes her for Maria de Padilla, retaining Blanche a prisoner.

1354 Ferdinand Perez de Castro revolts in revenge for the king's false marriage with his sister Juana. The citizens of Toledo take arms for Blanche. Meeting at Toro between Pedro and his barons. Pedro consents to reinstate Blanche.

1355 Pedro takes Toledo, imprisons Blanche at Siguenza, executes several rebels, and massacres the Jewish merchants. The kingdom laid under an interdict.

1356 Toro taken by Pedro from his mother. He massacres her partisans before her eyes. Pedro engages in a war with Portugal, in which many Castilian nobles join the foreigner.

1358 Don Fadrique, grand-master of Santiago and son of Leonora de Guzman, slain by Pedro's own hand and his partisans murdered. Murder of Don Juan, infante of Aragon.

1361 Portuguese refugees delivered up to Pedro I of Portugal in exchange for Castilians who had fled to Portugal, and execution of the persons surrendered. Blanche de Bourbon poisoned.

1362 Maria de Padilla dies. Pedro declares her son his lawful heir. Abu Said, king of Granada, comes to ask Pedro's assistance and is robbed and murdered by him.

1363 The Black Prince (of Wales) concludes an alliance with Pedro the Cruel to meet a threatened invasion of Castile from France. The French, under Du Guesclin, unite with the party of Henry of Trastamara, who, supported by Aragon, claims Pedro's throne.

1366 Battle of Borja. Sir Hugh Calverley, commanding the English Free Company under Du Guesclin, defeats the Castilians, and Henry is proclaimed at Calahorra. Flight of Pedro. Henry takes peaceful possession of Burgos and is crowned. Edward the Black Prince receives Pedro at Bordeaux and makes a treaty with him which includes Charles the Bad of Navarre. Edward engages to restore Pedro in return for the surrender of certain seaports. Charles promises the army a free passage through Navarre. The English advance guard cut to pieces at Ariñez.

1367 Battle of Navarrete, or Najera, and complete triumph of the English. Henry escapes to Aragon. Pedro celebrates his restoration by a series of murders. He evades his engagements with the Black Prince, and the latter withdraws his troops much reduced by famine and disease.

1369 Henry returns, is welcomed by some cities and reduces others. Pedro makes alliance with Muhammed V of Granada. The united troops fail to retake Cordova, and Muhammed retreats. Pedro on his way to relieve Toledo is invested in Montiel by Henry. In an interview between the brothers, a struggle ensues in which Henry stabs Pedro to death. **Henry II**. The king of Portugal claims the throne of Castile, which is also threatened by Navarre, Aragon, and Granada.

1371 A new *Ordinance concerning the Administration of Justice* regulates criminal procedure. John of Gaunt, duke of Lancaster, claims the throne in right of his wife, Constanza, daughter of Pedro the Cruel.

1372 Battle off La Rochelle. Henry wins a naval victory over the English.

1373 Lisbon besieged by Henry, and the king of Portugal forced to make peace.

1379 **Juan I** makes alliance with France.

1380 The Castilians sail up the Thames and destroy the English shipping. Ferdinand of Portugal offers John of Gaunt his alliance.

1381 The earl of Cambridge arrives in Portugal with a few followers, but after some fighting in Castile returns to England.

1382 Beatrice, heiress of Portugal, marries Juan of Castile, but on the death of her father Ferdinand, her uncle João I usurps the Portuguese throne

1385 and defeats Juan of Castile in a great battle at Aljubarrota, where the Castilians lose ten thousand men.

1386 John of Gaunt lands in Galicia, is proclaimed king at Santiago, and with the

1387 help of the king of Portugal takes several fortresses, but is driven to retreat by an outbreak of plague in his army. John of Gaunt resigns his claims in return for fiefs and money and the marriage of his daughter with Juan's eldest son, who receives the title of prince of Asturias, now first assigned to the heir of Castile.

1390 **Henry (III) the Sickly** succeeds at the age of eleven. Disputes for the regency.

1392 Persecution of the Jews.

1393 Henry assumes the government himself. He has some success in restoring order, and ranges himself on the side of the people against the nobles.

1401 The cortes of Tordesillas passes measures for reform of the judicial system. Embassy to Tamerlane or Timur.

1404 Conquest of the Canaries by Jean de Bethencourt, a Norman adventurer, with assistance from Henry, who grants him the title of king.

1406 **Juan II**, one year old, succeeds under the guardianship of his uncle Ferdinand the Just. Ferdinand restrains the turbulence of the nobles.

1408 Alvaro de Luna comes to court as a page and begins to exercise his influence over Juan.
1412 Ferdinand accepts the crown of Aragon, but maintains his influence in Castile till his death (1416).
1420 Henry, brother of Alfonso V of Aragon and Juan II of Navarre, desiring to marry Juan's sister Catalina, seizes the king and keeps him prisoner till he consents to the marriage.
1425 Alvaro de Luna, the king's favourite, made constable of Castile.
1427 The nobles, jealous of his unbounded influence, league against him. He is exiled, but soon recalled.
1429 New league against Alvaro. The kings of Navarre and Aragon invade Castile.
1431 Battle of Higueruela and the defeat of the Moors by De Luna. His vigorous rule brings prosperity to Castile.
1439 New league against De Luna, and civil war in which the kings of Aragon and Navarre join,
1445 but are defeated by Juan in the battle of Olmedo.
1453 The king, prompted by his second wife Isabella of Portugal, resolves on De Luna's death. He is seized, tried, and executed.
1454 **Henry (IV) the Impotent.** His extravagance and neglect provoke the barons to unite against him and, after several unsuccessful attempts, compel him to set aside the infanta Juana, called La Beltraneja, and recognise his brother Alfonso as his heir.
1465 Not content with this, at a solemn ceremony on the plain of Avila, they declare Henry deposed and set up Alfonso as king.
1468 A destructive civil war continues till Alfonso's death (1468), when his sister Isabella (the Catholic) refuses to take his place, and contents herself with recognition as Henry's heiress.
1469 Isabella refuses to marry the heir of Portugal, and marries Ferdinand prince of Aragon. Henry's endeavours to secure Juana's succession produce further bloodshed. He bequeaths Castile to her in his will.
1474 Henry IV dies, and **Isabella (I) the Catholic** has herself proclaimed queen of Castile. Ferdinand endeavours to assert his own claims as representative of the male line, but is induced to accept a carefully defined share in the government. The cause of Juana la Beltraneja is espoused by many Castilian nobles and by her uncle Alfonso V of Portugal, who proposes to marry her and invades Castile.
1476 Battle of Toro and complete victory of Ferdinand and Isabella. The rebels submit.
1479 Treaty with Portugal. Alfonso renounces Juana and she retires to a convent. Death of Juan II of Aragon. Ferdinand succeeds him as Ferdinand II.

THE KINGDOM OF NAVARRE (711–1515 A.D.)

Garcia Ximenes, first legendary king. Elected after the battle of Guadalete (711) to defend the country against the Moors, from whom he recovers considerable territory. From him the Navarrese writers derive a series of kings who reigned during the eighth and ninth centuries, but they seem, like Garcia Ximenes himself, to be purely fictitious personages. During this period the district seems to have been subjected either to Asturias or the Frankish empire, probably the latter.
778 Charlemagne invades Navarre and seizes Pamplona. On his return to France, after failing before Saragossa, his rearguard under Roland is attacked by troops from Spanish Gascony, including Navarre and other Spanish states, both Christian and Moor, and totally destroyed in the pass of Roncesvalles.
806 Pepin, son of Charlemagne, receives the submission of the Navarrese and organises the government of the country.
836 **Sancho Iñigo,** count (called by some, king) of Navarre.
885 **Garcia I.**
891 Moorish invasion. Garcia I is slain. **Fortuño Garces** rules during the minority of Garcia's son, Sancho Garces Abarca.
905 **Sancho (I) Garces Abarca.**
907 Pamplona besieged by the Moors during Sancho's absence in Gascony. Sancho relieves it after a rapid winter march across the Pyrenees and wins a great victory. Many victories won by Sancho over the Moors and the kingdom extended southwards.
920 Sancho retires to a monastery.
921 Abd ar-Rahman III invades Navarre and routs the combined forces of Navarre and Leon at the Val-de-Junquera. The Navarrese under Sancho defeat Abd ar-Rahman's forces on their return from a raid into Gascony.
925 **Garcia (II), El Tembloso** (the Trembler).

951 The king of Navarre in alliance with Fernan Gonsalez, count of Castile, unsuccessfully supports Sancho, prince of Leon, against the latter's brother, Ordoño III of Leon.

956 Castile invaded by Garcia, and Fernan taken prisoner.

970 **Sancho (II), El Mayor** (The Great). This king was the most powerful sovereign of Christian Spain at this period. Besides being master of Navarre, Sobrarbe, and

1026 Aragon he conquered Castile after the murder of his brother-in-law, the Count Garcia.

1034 and won the eastern portion of Leon as far as the river Cea from Bermudo III. His second son Ferdinand married Bermudo's sister and heiress, and eventually became sovereign of Leon and Castile (1037). The lordship of Ribagorza was also among Sancho's acquisitions.

1035 **Garcia III** inherits Navarre and a small district on the south bank of the Ebro, while the rest of the dominions of Sancho the Great are divided among the latter's other sons. Ramiro, to whom Aragon had fallen, invades Navarre as Garcia is on a pilgrimage to Rome, but is driven back. Garcia then aids Ferdinand, who has succeeded to Castile, to triumph over Bermudo III of Leon. But when the latter's

1037 defeat and death give Ferdinand the kingdom of Leon, Garcia turns against his brother and allies himself with the emirs of Saragossa and Tudela.

1054 Battle of Atapuerca. Garcia and his allies defeated and Garcia slain by Ferdinand, who annexes the Navarrese possessions south of the Ebro. **Sancho III.**

1076 Murder of Sancho by his brother Raymond and his sister Ermesinda. The murderers expelled from the kingdom. The kings of Aragon and Leon dispute for the crown of Navarre. The king of Leon annexes Rioja. The king of Aragon becomes king of Navarre under the name of **Sancho (IV) Ramirez.**

1094 **Pedro** (Pedro I of Aragon).

1104 **Alfonso** (Alfonso I of Aragon). On his death without issue the Navarrese refuse to recognise his will bequeathing his kingdom to the knightly orders of St. John and the Temple, and elect

1134 **Garcia (IV) Ramirez,** a member of the old royal house of Navarre, while the Aragonese prefer Alfonso's brother, Ramiro (I) the Monk. Alfonso (VII) Raymond of Castile and Leon, who assumes the title of emperor of all Spain, receives the homage of Garcia and Ramiro. Garcia becomes a feudatory of Ramiro. Alliance between Garcia and Alfonso, count of Portugal, against Alfonso Raymond. Alfonso Raymond invades Navarre. Garcia acknowledges his supremacy.

1140 Alfonso Raymond makes alliance with Aragon for the partition of Navarre and again invades it, while Garcia invades Aragon. After both have won successes, Alfonso and Garcia make peace.

1150 **Sancho (V) the Wise.** This king's reign is occupied with obscure and frequent hostilities with the neighbouring states of Aragon, Barcelona, and Castile.

1176 The kings of Castile and Navarre refer their differences to Henry II of England. His

1179 decision is not acted upon, but a later peace between them embraces the same terms.

1191 Berengaria, daughter of Sancho V, marries Richard I of England.

1194 **Sancho (VI) the Infirm.** He makes alliance with Castile and Leon against the Moors.

1195 Battle of Alarcon. Alfonso VIII of Castile defeated by Yakub Al-mansur. Quarrels amongst the allies. Sancho concludes an alliance with the Almohads. Alfonso of Leon takes Guipuzcoa, Alava, and Biscay. Alliance of Navarre, Leon, Aragon, Castile, and Portugal against the Moors, which leads to the defeat of a Moorish army under Muhammed an-Nasir in the

1212 Battle of Las Navas de Tolosa.

1234 **Thibaut I** (Theobald or Teobaldo), count of Champagne, elected king.

1239 Seventh Crusade led by Thibaut to Syria. On the defeat of a portion of the army he and the other French princes desert their comrades and return to Spain.

1253 **Thibaut II.**

1270 Eighth Crusade. Thibaut accompanies St. Louis to the Holy Land and dies on his way home. **Henry Crassus.**

1274 **Joan** or **Jeanne I** succeeds at the age of four. The country reduced to anarchy by disputes between native factions and foreign princes respecting the disposal of her hand.

1284 Joan marries Philip IV of France.

1305 **Louis Hutin** (Louis X of France) succeeds Joan.

1316 **Philip I** (V of France) succeeds, to the prejudice of the daughter of Louis Hutin.

1322 **Charles I** (IV of France), brother of Philip I. The Navarrese protest against this reassertion of the Salic law and on Charles' death the crown passes to Louis Hutin's daughter,

1328 **Joan II,** with her husband, **Philip II** (count of Évreux), who at their coronation sign a convention securing the independence of Navarre. Massacre of the Jews.

1334 War with Castile.

1343 Philip joins Alfonso XI of Castile in besieging Algeciras and dies during the siege.

1349 **Charles (II) the Bad.** His endeavours to recover the lordships of Brie and Champagne and his murder of the constable of France lead to his imprisonment by the French king. He escapes and is subsequently pardoned.

1361 Return of Charles to Navarre. He promises to aid Pedro the Cruel of Castile against Aragon.

1366 Alliance of Charles with Edward the Black Prince of Wales to restore Pedro the Cruel. Charles plays fast and loose with the rival kings of Castile and seizes Salvatierra and Logroño for himself.

1370 On the accession of Henry II Charles invades Castile.

1371 Claims of Navarre to Champagne, Brie, etc., ceded to France in exchange for Montpellier. Charles makes peace with Henry II.

1377 Charles accused of plotting to acquire domains in Gascony. His French possessions declared forfeited. The Castilians invade Navarre and besiege Pamplona. Charles makes alliance with the English and on their approach the Castilians retreat.

1385 Charles accused of plotting to poison the French royal family. The last remains of his French possessions are seized.

1387 **Charles (III) the Noble.**

1403 Dukedom of Nemours granted to the king of Navarre.

1425 **Blanche,** daughter of Charles the Noble, succeeds with her husband **Juan of Aragon.** He interferes constantly in the internal troubles of Castile, while Blanche governs peaceably during his absence.

1432 Juan appointed regent of Aragon in the absence of Alfonso V.

1442 **Charles of Viana** succeeds to Navarre as regent on the death of his mother Blanche. The kingdom is distracted by two parties, the Beaumonts, partisans of Charles, and the Agramonts, partisans of his father Juan.

1447 Juan marries Juana Henriquez and appoints his wife co-regent of Navarre. She quarrels with Charles.

1452 Revolt of Charles. Birth of his half-brother Ferdinand (the Catholic). Battle of Aybar. Juan defeats and captures Charles. Charles is released and returns to Navarre, but finding his enemies too strong for him he withdraws to Naples.

1458 Juan succeeds to the throne of Aragon as Juan II. Misunderstanding between father and son continues till

1460 Charles negotiates for the hand of Isabella of Castile which was desired for his half-brother Ferdinand of Aragon. Charles is arrested by his father when Catalonia revolts in his favour, and Juan is obliged to

1461 recognise him as his heir. The prince dies immediately afterwards.

1464 Blanche, Charles' eldest sister, dies, probably poisoned at the instigation of her father by her sister Eleanor, countess of Foix. The country continues to be distracted by the wars of the Beaumonts and Agramonts.

1479 **Eleanor de Foix** becomes queen on the death of Juan and dying immediately afterwards is succeeded by her grandson, **Francis Phœbus de Foix.**

1483 **Catherine de Foix.** Ferdinand and Isabella endeavour to secure her hand and kingdom for their eldest son, but she marries **Jean d'Albret.**

1512 Ferdinand the Catholic demands the cession of six Navarrese fortresses and a free passage through Navarre to facilitate his invasion of Guienne. Treaty of alliance between France and Navarre signed at Blois. Ferdinand's general, the duke of Alva, takes Pamplona and occupies the whole of upper Navarre. Ferdinand's English allies refuse to co-operate with him for the reduction of the rest of the country, and on their withdrawal Jean d'Albret with a French army besieges Alva in Pamplona, but for lack of provisions is compelled to retreat.

1513 Treaty between Ferdinand and Louis XII of France by which the latter abandons Navarre. Ferdinand restores order and conciliates the Navarrese towns by confirming their privileges.

1515 The cortes of Burgos formally incorporates Navarre into the kingdom of Castile.

CATALONIA (470–1150 A.D.)

470 Gothalania (Catalonia) was the name bestowed on the northeastern section of Hispania Tarraconensis in consequence of its occupation by the Goths and Alans (470).

712 Berbers take possession of the whole Catalonian territory. At the end of the eighth century Charlemagne's troops, under command of Louis le Débonnaire, invade Catalonia, and conquer a district including Barcelona, Lerida, Tarragona, and Tortosa which they call the Marca Hispanica or Spanish Mark. **Bera,** a native of Gothic

Gaul, becomes count of Barcelona and the Mark, and tyrannises over the country. Counts of Rosello, Ampurias, Besalu, Cerdagne, Pallars, and Urgel appointed. Frequent conflicts with the Moors in which the Frankish armies join and waste the southern districts.

814 Death of Charlemagne. Septimania becomes united with the Spanish Mark.

826 **Bera**, being deposed for treasonable dealings with Al Hakim of Cordova, is succeeded as duke of Septimania, by **Bernhard**, son of William of Toulouse, who plays an important rôle in Frankish history.

832 Bernhard aids Pepin, king of Aquitaine, in rebellion against Louis le Débonnaire and is deprived of his dignities.

836 Bernhard reinstated in his duchy.

840 Charles the Bald succeeds to Catalonia on the death of Louis le Débonnaire. Bernhard at first refuses and then offers his allegiance; but afterwards aiming at independence is murdered by Charles. William, Bernhard's son, seeks refuge with Abd ar-Rahman.

846 **Aledran** made count of Barcelona by Charles. William wages successful war against him, but is finally murdered. Frankish dominion restored. Narbonensian Gaul is taken from the Spanish Mark and added to Toulouse.

852 Barcelona retaken by the Moors. They retain possession during twelve years.

858 **Wilfrid I** (Wilfredo or Hunfrido I) count of Barcelona. He takes possession of Toulouse, etc. Summoned to Narbonne to justify himself, he is there slain in a petty fray and is succeeded by

872 **Salomon**, who is murdered in revenge for Wilfrid's death by the latter's son.

874 **Wilfred (II) the Hairy**, who successfully repels the Moors, makes himself independent of France and leaves his territory to his son

907 **Miro**, who bequeaths it to his three sons, **Seniofredo**, **Oliva**, and **Miro**, under the regency of their uncle Suniario, count of Urgel.

950 **Seniofredo**.

967 **Borello**, son of Suniario.

984 Almansor takes Barcelona, slaughters the inhabitants, and burns a great part of the city. Borello recovers Barcelona and expels the invaders.

993 **Raymond I** repels a Moorish invasion and wins a battle against Suleiman of Cordova which places the usurper Muhammed I on the throne. The Catalans take the lead

1009 in an unsuccessful crusade against the Moorish pirates of the Balearic Islands.

1017 **Berengar I** organises the country and grants privileges to Barcelona and other towns.

1035 **Raymond II** wins victories over the Moors of Saragossa and becomes sovereign of all Catalonia. He abolishes the old Gothic laws, substituting the

1068 *Usages of Catalonia*, and institutes the Peace of God in an assembly of the Estates which is the earliest occasion in European history on which deputies are summoned from the towns. By marriage and purchase he acquires Conflans, Carcassonne, Narbonne, Toulouse, and other French possessions. Bequeaths his dominions to his two sons as joint rulers.

1076 **Raymond (III) the Hairy** quarrels with his brother **Berengar**. The nobles effect a settlement whereby each is to reign alternately for six months. Raymond is murdered, probably at Berengar's instigation. Berengar governs alone as guardian for Raymond III's son.

1082 **Raymond IV.** Bernard Atto, vicomte de Béziers, usurps the lordship of Carcassonne. The people appeal to Raymond from his oppressions. He becomes a vassal of Raymond. By marriage and inheritance Raymond acquires Besalu (1111), Provence, and Cerdagne (1117), and conquers Majorca. Provence passes on his death to his son Berengar.

1131 **Raymond V.**

1137 On Raymond's betrothal to Petronilla, daughter of Ramiro the Monk, king of Aragon, he is declared heir to the throne of Aragon and assumes the administration of that kingdom.

1150 Marriage of Raymond and Petronilla confirms union of Catalonia and Aragon.

THE KINGDOM OF ARAGON FROM ITS RISE TILL ITS UNION WITH CASTILE
(1035–1479 A.D.)

1035 On the death of Sancho el Mayor of Navarre his territories are divided among his sons, and **Ramiro I** succeeds to a small Pyrenean district called Aragon in the northwestern corner of the modern province in the territory of the ancient Vascones. Ramiro by his wars with the Moors extends his borders, absorbing Sobrarbe and

Ribagorza, and reducing several Moorish governors to the condition of tributaries. He consents to adopt the Roman ritual and to send tribute to the pope.

1067 **Sancho Ramirez.**

1076 On the murder of Sancho III of Navarre, Sancho Ramirez and Alfonso VI of Castile invade Navarre, and Sancho becomes king of Navarre as Sancho IV. He conquers several cities from the Moors, commences a war with the emir of Saragossa, and dies while besieging Huesca.

1094 **Pedro I.**

1096 Battle of Alcoraz. Pedro wins a decisive victory over the Moors of Saragossa and their Castilian allies, and takes Huesca.

1104 **Alfonso (I), el Batallador** (the Fighter), and **the Emperor.**

1109 Death of Alfonso VI of Castile. His daughter Urraca, the wife of Alfonso I, el Batallador, succeeds, and her husband is acknowledged as Alfonso VII of Leon and Castile. He quarrels with his wife, and constant civil war is the result to Castile.

1118 Saragossa taken by el Batallador after a five years' siege. It becomes the capital of Aragon.

1120 Battle of Daroca. El Batallador defeats an Almoravid army, takes Tarragona and Calatayud, and invades Andalusia.

1126 Death of Urraca. Castile is definitely separated from Aragon under Alfonso VII (Raymond) of Castile and Leon, Urraca's son by her first husband.

1130 Bordeaux besieged and taken by Alfonso I. He resumes his war against the Moors.

1133 Representatives of the cities summoned to the cortes.

1134 Alfonso is defeated at Fraga and dies soon after, bequeathing his dominions to the knights of the Temple and St. John. His subjects refuse to recognise his will and his brother, **Ramiro (II) the Monk,** is persuaded to leave his monastery and accept the crown of Aragon, while the Navarrese choose Garcia (IV) Ramirez as king.

1137 **Petronilla,** Ramiro's infant daughter, betrothed to **Raymond,** count of Catalonia, who is appointed regent of Aragon. Catalonia thus becomes absorbed in Aragon, and Ramiro retires to a cloister.

1140 Navarre invaded by Raymond in conjunction with Alfonso VII of Castile, but without success, and on the conclusion of peace the three sovereigns make alliance against the Moors and capture various cities, Raymond acquiring Fraga, Lerida, and Tortosa.

1150 Marriage of Raymond and Petronilla.

1162 Death of Raymond. Petronilla abdicates in favour of her son **Alfonso II,** who acquires Roussillon by inheritance and wins Teruel and other fortresses from the Moors. In this reign cortes were held and attended by the four estates of the realm (1163, 1164).

1196 **Pedro II.**

1203 Coronation of Pedro by the pope. Aragon is constituted a papal fief, and Pedro promises to pay tribute to the holy see, but

1205 the estates of Saragossa repudiate the transaction.

1208 The Albigensian crusade. Pedro refuses to declare for either party, but turns his arms against the Moors and shares the glory at the great Christian victory of

1212 Las Navas de Tolosa.

1213 He endeavours to mediate between the Albigensians and the crusaders, but fails and lays siege to the latter's city of Muret, when he is slain in a battle with Simon de Montfort. **James (I) the Conqueror,** known as Don Jayme of Aragon (in Catalonian En Jacme, lo Conqueridor), succeeds at the age of six. The usual civil wars occupy his minority, but finally he triumphs over all rebels.

1228 Balearic Islands, the haunt of Moorish pirates, attacked and subdued after a four years' war.

1232 Valencia invaded.

1238 Conquest of Valencia completed. The Moors are guaranteed security and religious liberty.

1264–1266 Murcia reconquered by James for his son-in-law, Alfonso X of Castile.

1268 By the execution of Conradin, the last of the Hohenstaufen, Constanza, wife of James' son, Pedro (III), and daughter of Manfred, king of Sicily, becomes heiress of Sicily, now in the hands of the usurper, Charles of Anjou.

1269 Preparations for a crusade to the Holy Land headed by James. The king is turned back by a storm, but his son, Fernan Sanchez, proceeds to Acre. Like Alfonso X of Castile, James left a chronicle or commentary of his reign (afterwards continued by Raymond Muntaner), as well as a book of aphorisms called the *Libre de Saviesa,* both written in the Catalan language.

1276 **Pedro (III) the Great.** The Balearic Islands with Roussillon, Montpellier, etc., are converted by the will of James I into a separate kingdom of Majorca for his younger son, James I of Majorca. Pedro prepares to invade Sicily.

1282 The Sicilian Vespers, in which the native population massacre twenty-eight thousand Frenchmen. Charles of Anjou lays siege to Messina. Pedro of Aragon comes to its relief and is proclaimed king of Sicily. Roger de Lauria, Pedro's admiral, with a few ships destroys the French fleet.

1283 The Aragonese cortes protest against the king's wars and exact the *General Privilege*, the Magna Charta of Aragon, confirming their liberties. The pope excommunicates

1284 Pedro. De Lauria takes Malta and destroys the fleet in the Bay of Naples. The pope, Martin IV, proclaims a crusade against Aragon and bestows the kingdom on the French prince, Charles of Valois. The Aragonese are reluctant to oppose Rome.

1285 The crusaders invade the kingdom, but after taking and sacking several cities the army breaks up. Charles of Anjou dies, leaving his claims to his son Charles II. Pedro dies, leaving Sicily to his younger son James and Aragon to **Alfonso III.** Majorca subdued by Alfonso.

1287 The "Privilege of Union" granted, authorising armed rebellion against the sovereign who shall infringe his subjects' liberties.

1291 As a result of negotiations conducted by Edward I of England, Alfonso is reconciled to the pope and Sicily is abandoned by James, who immediately after, on the death of Alfonso, succeeds to Aragon as **James II.** He makes his brother Frederick (Fadrique) his lieutenant in Sicily.

1295 Alliance between James and Charles of Anjou.

1296 The pope invests James with Sardinia and Corsica, occupied at the time by the Genoese and Pisans. The deserted Sicilians give the crown to Frederick. The king of Aragon assists Charles in his attempts to recover Sicily, but abandons the enterprise after several successes.

1302 Peace between Frederick and Charles by which the former retains Sicily, the latter Naples.

1303 The Catalan Grand Company is formed by Roger di Flor from the disbanded mercenaries (chiefly Aragonese and Catalan) of Frederick and takes service with the Greek emperor Andronicus II.

1319 Aragon, Catalonia, and Valencia declared inseparable.

1324 Sardinia invaded by James. With the aid of the grand justice of Arborea, Marian IV, the Pisans are expelled. The grand justice turns his arms against the Aragonese and the war is continued under

1327 **Alfonso IV,** when the Genoese assist the islanders and ravage the coasts of Catalonia.

1336 **Pedro IV** refuses to recognise the claims of his stepmother, Leonora of Castile, and her sons, Juan and Ferdinand, to the appanages assigned them under Alfonso's will, and thus involves himself in civil disputes and a war with Castile. He offends the clergy by crowning himself instead of being crowned by the archbishop of Saragossa.

1343 Invasion of Majorca by Pedro. The islanders welcome him, deserting James II of Majorca. Pedro conquers James' French possessions.

1344 Balearic Islands formally annexed to Aragon.

1347 Attempt of Pedro to secure the succession to his daughter Constanza in preference to his brother James, in defiance of the Salic law as established by James I. League of nobles and cities in a union in favor of James. The Sardinians backed by the Genoese and Pisans seize the occasion to revolt. A second union formed in Valencia under the infante Ferdinand. At the cortes of Saragossa Pedro is compelled to promise to hold annual meetings of the estates, to select his advisers with their approval, and to recognise James as his heir. Death of James. Pedro wins over the Catalans and at the

1348 battle of Epila defeats the union. He annuls the "Privilege of Union" of 1287, but enlarges the powers of the justiciar. Leonora and her son Juan take refuge in Castile, where both are subsequently murdered by Pedro the Cruel.

1349 James of Majorca attempts to recover the Balearic Islands, but fails and dies soon after. Pedro defeats the Sardinian rebels, and allies himself with Venice against Genoa.

1350 The era of Spain ceases to be used in Aragon.

1352 The Venetian and Catalonian fleets defeated by the Genoese, who renew their encouragement of the Sardinians. The Genoese fleet defeated in the Thracian Bosphorus by the fleets of Catalonia and Venice.

1354 The Sardinian estates are convoked by Pedro at Cagliari, but fail to pacify the belligerents.

1356 War with Castile. The king of Aragon supports Henry of Trastamara and the other Castilian rebels.

1363 A peace concluded with Castile in accordance with which Pedro of Aragon murders his own brother Ferdinand. War with Castile renewed.

1368 The justice of Arborea defeats the Aragonese in Sardinia and maintains himself till the Genoese come to his aid (1373). After his death the struggle is continued with less vigour by his son, and when the latter is put to death by his own people the war is prosecuted by his sister Leonora with whom Pedro effects an agreement in 1386.

1377 Death of Frederick king of Sicily. Pedro claims the throne, but is eventually satisfied with the marriage of the heiress Maria with his grandson Martin.

1387 **Juan I.** Trial of the king's stepmother Sybilla for witchcraft. Some of her friends executed.

1392 Aragonese troops under the king's brother Martin sent to Sicily to quell a revolt against Queen Maria and her husband, Martin's son, the younger Martin.

1395 **Martin** succeeds to Aragon. The count de Foix, husband of the late king's eldest daughter, invades the kingdom to assert her rights, but finds no supporters. Martin, having pacified Sicily, Sardinia, and Corsica, returns to Spain. Pope Boniface IX,

1397 in revenge for the recognition by Aragon of the anti-pope Benedict XIII (Pedro de Luna), confers Sardinia and Sicily on the count de Molinets.

1401 Death of Maria of Sicily. She is succeeded by her husband, the younger Martin, who,

1402 the following year, marries Blanche, heiress of Navarre.

1409 Martin of Sicily suppresses the rebellion in Sardinia. He dies without issue. Blanche becomes regent of Sicily.

1410 **Interregnum,** consequent on the death of Martin of Aragon without direct heirs. During two years the country is distracted by the conflicts of rival claimants to the throne till, at the instance of the justiciar Juan de Cerda, a commission is selected from the cortes of the three provinces of Aragon, Catalonia, and Valencia which names the infante Ferdinand, regent of Castile, and he receives the crowns of Aragon and Sicily as

1412 **Ferdinand (I) the Just.** He subdues a rebellion of the count of Urgel and maintains tranquillity in the kingdom till his death in

1416 when he is succeeded by his son **Alfonso (V) the Magnanimous.**

1417 Reduction of Corsica attempted by Alfonso without much success.

1420 Joanna, queen of Naples, adopts Alfonso on condition of his defending her dominions against the duke of Anjou, which he does with success.

1423 Joanna quarrels with Alfonso and adopts Louis of Anjou in his place.

1425 Death of Charles III of Navarre. He is succeeded by Blanche and her husband Juan, brother of Alfonso of Aragon.

1432 Juan appointed regent of Aragon. Alfonso sets out to recover Naples.

1435 Joanna of Naples dies, bequeathing her kingdom to René of Anjou. Alfonso besieges Gaeta, but is defeated in a naval battle. Himself, the king of Navarre, and his brother Henry become the prisoners of the duke of Milan, who immediately releases them. Don Pedro of Aragon takes Gaeta. In the next few years Alfonso makes himself master of the kingdom of Naples.

1442 The office of justiciar declared tenable for life. Blanche of Navarre dies. Juan retains the title of king of Navarre, while her son, Charles of Viana, becomes ruler.

1443 Ferdinand, Alfonso's illegitimate son, recognised as heir of Naples by Pope Eugenius IV.

1447 Juan of Navarre marries Juana Henriquez and subsequently appoints her co-regent of Navarre. She quarrels with Charles of Viana.

1452 Battle of Aybar. Juan defeats and captures Charles. Reconciliation of Juan and Charles. Birth of Juan's younger son, Ferdinand the Catholic.

1458 Death of Alfonso V. Aragon, Sicily, and Sardinia pass to the king of Navarre, **Juan II.** Charles of Viana refuses to supplant Ferdinand of Naples.

1461 Charles imprisoned by his father. The Catalans revolt in his favour and compel his recognition as Juan's heir. Death of Charles.

1462 The Catalans declare a republic and besiege the queen and Ferdinand in Gerona. Roussillon and Cerdagne pledged to Louis XI of France, who comes to the help of Juan; whereupon the rebels offer the Catalan crown first to Henry IV of Castile and then to Pedro, constable of Portugal.

1466 Pedro dies. The Catalans offer the crown to René of Anjou who

1467 sends his son John of Calabria to Barcelona.

1468 Ferdinand declared king of Sicily and associated with his father in the government of Aragon.

1469 Marriage of Ferdinand with Isabella of Castile.

1470 Death of John of Calabria. Catalonia is gradually reduced.

1472 Barcelona submits.

1473 The inhabitants of Roussillon revolt against the French and massacre them. Roussillon occupied by Juan. The French besiege him in Perpignan, which is relieved by Ferdinand. By a treaty with Louis the king of Aragon promises to pay within the year the sum for which Roussillon was pledged.

1474 The French invade Roussillon.
1475 Perpignan surrenders to the French. The inhabitants compelled to emigrate.
1479 Death of Juan II. **Ferdinand (II) the Catholic** inherits his dominions which are henceforth united with those of Castile.

ANDORRA (805–1882 A.D.)

805 The valley of Andorra appears in history as a neutral country, Charlemagne founding the free state and placing it under the lordship of Urgel.
1170 Suzerainty of Andorra ceded by the counts of Urgel to the counts of Castelbo. The heiress of Castelbo marries the count de Foix.
1278 Suzerainty of Andorra divided between the counts de Foix and the bishops of Urgel.
1512 On the extinction of the house of Foix by the death of Count Gaston at the battle of Ravenna, the suzerainty of Andorra passes to Henry d'Albret, titular heir of Navarre,
1553 and on the accession of the latter's grandson to the throne of France as Henry IV, becomes the prerogative of the French crown.
1790 Independence of Andorra recognised. The republic voluntarily returns to the French allegiance.
1866 The general council, hitherto composed of the aristocracy, becomes elective.
1882 A permanent delegate appointed to represent French authority in Andorra.

SPAIN AFTER THE UNION OF CASTILE AND ARAGON (1479–1902, A.D.)

1480 Cortes of Toledo. Recall of illegal grants by which in Henry IV's reign the public revenues had been alienated in pensions and annuities. The nobles forbidden to erect castles or assume the insignia of royalty. Duelling prohibited.
1481 The Inquisition issues an edict requiring the accusation of heretics. *Autos da fé* in Andalusia. Epidemic of plague. Emigration of Jews.
1482 Alhama after being captured from the Moors by the marquis of Cadiz is besieged by the king of Granada and relieved by Ferdinand. Zahara seized and its inhabitants enslaved by Abul Hassan, king of Granada. Bull of Pope Sixtus IV promising the appointment of Castilians to church dignities in their country. Loja unsuccessfully besieged by Ferdinand.
1483 Thomas de Torquemada inquisitor-general in Castile and Aragon to reconstitute the holy office. An insurrection makes Abu Abdallah (Boabdil) king of Granada. Ferdinand's ambassadors assist in negotiating a peace between Ferrara and Venice. The pope declares a crusade against Granada. Rout in the Axarquia; a small Spanish force is destroyed by the troops of Abul Hassan. Boabdil invades the Christian territory. He is defeated and taken at the Jenil, released and becomes a tributary of Ferdinand. Ferdinand and Isabella begin a series of successful campaigns against Granada and capture one fortress after another.
1484 Inquisition revived in Aragon. Columbus arrives in Spain.
1485 *Ordenanças Reales*, a code of Castilian laws, promulgated. *Autos da fé* in Saragossa. Murder of the inquisitor, Arbues, by Jewish converts. Sanguinary punishment of all implicated.
1486 Catalan peasantry, called vassals *de remenza*, released from serfdom under the obligation of an annual payment.
1487 Velez Malaga, Malaga, and other cities capitulate to Ferdinand. He enslaves the Malagans.
1488 Alliance between Spain and Maximilian, king of the Romans, against France.
1489 Baza besieged and taken. Almeria submits.
1491 Law to prevent the export of the precious metals. Siege and capitulation of Granada. Boabdil confined to a narrow district in the Alpujarras. The Granadans guaranteed the preservation of their religion and their liberty.
1492 Expulsion of the Jews from Spain. Columbus persuades Isabella to grant him assistance. He is made admiral, viceroy, and governor-general of all territories he may discover. An expedition is fitted out and he starts on the 3rd of August with three vessels. Treaty with France. Charles VIII engages to restore Roussillon and Cerdagne to Aragon.
1493 Return of Columbus reporting the discovery of Hispaniola. Pope Alexander VI issues a bull confirming the sovereigns of Spain in possession of all their discoveries, past and future, in the west. A second bull divides the area for Portuguese and Spanish discoveries by a line drawn one hundred leagues west of the Azores. Second expedition of Columbus with seventeen vessels.

1494 Agreement with Portugal at Tordesillas by which the boundary of the Portuguese area of discovery is removed 370 leagues west of Cape Verd Islands. The pope confers the epithet of "Catholic" on Ferdinand and Isabella.

1495 League of Venice between Spain, Austria, Rome, Milan, and Venice for the expulsion of the French from Italy.

1496 Spanish troops under Gonsalvo de Cordova, the Great Captain, restore Ferdinand II of Naples to his throne and expel the French. Juana, daughter of Ferdinand and Isabella, marries Philip, son of the emperor Maximilian. Militia ordinance requiring one-twelfth of the male population between the ages of twenty and forty-five to enlist for the military and police service of Spain. Santo Domingo founded. Columbus returns from his second voyage.

1497 Death of Juan, only son of Ferdinand and Isabella.

1498 Third voyage of Columbus. He lands on the South American continent. The Santa Hermandad, having restored order in Spain, reduced to the position of an ordinary police.

1499 Ximenes de Cisneros, archbishop of Toledo, sets about the conversion of the Moors of Granada. He burns their books. Insurrection in Granada. Many Moors quit Spain. The remainder forcibly converted.

1500 Francisco Bobadilla sent out to investigate affairs in Hispaniola. He imprisons Columbus and sends him home in irons. Revolt of the Moors in the Alpujarras severely repressed. Treaty with France for the partition of Naples. Gonsalvo de Cordova recovers St. George in Cephalonia which the Turks had wrested from Venice. A navigation act prohibits the exportation of goods in foreign ships when Spanish are procurable, and forbids the sale of ships to foreigners. Columbus restored to his honours.

Sixteenth Century

1501 The Moors of Ronda revolt and destroy a Spanish force under Alonso de Aguilar. On Ferdinand's approach they submit and are granted the alternative of exile or baptism. Gonsalvo de Cordova conquers Calabria.

1502 Expulsion from Spain of all unconverted Moors. Nicholas de Ovando sent to replace Bobadilla. Tarentum occupied by the Great Captain after a long siege. Fourth voyage of Columbus. The French declare war against the Spaniards and conquer all Calabria.

1503 Treaty of peace with France signed at Lyons. Battle of Cerignola. Gonsalvo defeats the French and occupies Naples. The French invade Roussillon, but are forced to retreat by Ferdinand, who takes several frontier fortresses. Gonsalvo defeats the French at the Garigliano.

1504 Peace of Lyons. The French abandon Naples to Spain. Death of Isabella. **Philip I** and **Juana la Loca** or **the Mad** proclaimed her successors in Castile. Ferdinand assumes the administration in accordance with Isabella's will and on the ground of Juana's mental incapacity. Columbus returns from his last voyage.

1506 Death of Columbus. Ferdinand resigns the government of Castile to Philip, who excites discontent by his extravagance and his Flemish favourites. The proceeding of the Inquisition excite disturbances in Andalusia. Death of Philip. Ferdinand receives the homage of the Neapolitans.

1507 Ferdinand resumes the government of Castile. Ximenes appointed inquisitor-general of Castile.

1508 Ferdinand joins the league of Cambray formed by the French king and the emperor against Venice and retakes five Neapolitan cities pledged to Venice.

1509 An expedition led to Africa by Ximenes conquers Oran.

1511 Holy League between Pope Julius II, Ferdinand, and Venice to drive the French from Italy. Conquest of Cuba.

1512 Battle of Ravenna. The allies defeated by the French under Gaston de Foix. Gaston slain; the French retreat from Italy. Venice makes peace with France. Ferdinand demands a free passage through Navarre for the invasion of France. Alliance between France and Navarre. Pamplona taken by the Spaniards. Jean d'Albret, king of Navarre, fails to recover it.

1513 Navarre submits to Ferdinand. Florida discovered by Ponce de Leon. Balboa discovers the Pacific Ocean.

1515 Navarre formally incorporated with Castile.

1516 Ferdinand dies. Ximenes regent of Castile, and the archbishop of Saragossa regent of Aragon. **Charles I** (afterwards the emperor Charles V) proclaimed king in Castile. French invasion of Navarre repulsed. The Inquisition is established in

Oran, the Canaries, and the New World.   Las Casas obtains the sending of a commission to inquire into the ill-treatment of the Indians in Hispaniola.   It effects
little.   Peace of Noyon.   France abandons her claims to Naples.

1517 Charles lands in Spain and dismisses Ximenes.
1518 The Castilian cortes acknowledge Charles as joint ruler with his mother.   Aragon and
Catalonia delay to do this.   The favour shown his Flemish favourites and their
exactions disgust the Spaniards.

1519 Ferdinand Cortes begins the conquest of Mexico.   Several leading Castilian cities
form a confederation to defend their privileges.   Death of the emperor Maximilian.
Charles elected emperor of Germany.

1520 The citizens of Valencia revolt against the oppressions of the nobles and are authorised by Charles to continue in arms.   They form an association called the Germandada (Germania) or brotherhood.   Luther burns the papal bull excommunicating
him.   The Castilian cortes with difficulty induced to grant a subsidy.   Charles,
having appointed Cardinal Adrian of Utrecht his viceroy, leaves Spain without
redressing the grievances submitted to him.   Several of the cities of Castile, under
the leadership of Juan de Padilla, revolt again st their deputies, appoint their own
magistrates, levy troops, and league together as the "holy junta."   Padilla goes to
Juana at Tordesillas.   The junta acts in her name.   The royalists rescue Juana.
The Germandada in Valencia carries on a successful and desolating war against
the nobles.

1521 Battle of Villalar.   Padilla defeated, taken, and executed.   Valencia taken and the
leaders of the Germandada executed.   Charles opens the Diet of Worms.   Treaty
of Charles with the pope for the expulsion of the French from the Milanese.   The
junta breaks up; Toledo holds out for a time under Padilla's widow.   Its fall sig-
nalises the end of the freedom of the Castilian cities.   Conquest of Mexico completed by Cortes.   Navarre occupied by the French.   They invade Castile.   The
Castilians recover Navarre.   The populace of Majorca, having revolted against the
nobles, are subdued after a long struggle.   Treaty with Henry VIII of England.
Charles agrees to invade France from Spain.   The emperor's troops drive the
French from Milan.   Death of Leo X.

1522 Adrian of Utrecht elected pope as Adrian VI.   The French fail in an attempt to
recover the Milanese.   League between Charles, the pope, Venice, and other
Italian cities against France.

1523 The cortes grant supplies before presenting their petitions.   Adrian VI dies.   Clement
VII pope.   Ferdinand Cortes empowered to conquer all New Spain.

1524 The council of the Indies formed for the administration of the Spanish colonies.   The
Moors of Valencia request permission to exercise their own worship.   On being
refused many emigrate, and others revolt and are not finally subdued till 1526.
Expulsion of the French from the Milanese.   Francis I of France attempts to
recover it and is defeated and taken by the imperial troops at the

1525 battle of Pavia.
1526 The Moors of Granada permitted to purchase freedom from the worst penalties of the
Inquisition.   Treaty of Madrid.   Francis resigns his claims in Italy, Flanders, and
Artois and concludes a perpetual league with Charles.   Holy League of Cognac
between the pope, France, England, Venice, and Sforza, duke of Milan, to restore
Sforza to the Milanese.   The pope and the French attack Naples.

1527 Charles' troops ravage the papal territories and take Rome.   Sack of Rome.   Clement
taken prisoner.   The cortes refuse a grant to Charles.

1528 The French besiege Naples, but are driven by disease to retreat.
1529 Battle of Landriano.   Spaniards defeat the French.   Francis Pizarro commissioned
to conquer and govern Peru.   Treaty of Cambray called " The Ladies' Peace."
Francis I agrees to ransom his sons and resign his pretensions to Flanders, Artois,
and all places in Italy.   Charles goes to Italy, makes peace with Venice, and with
the dukes of Milan and Ferrara.

1530 Charles receives the iron crown of Lombardy and is crowned emperor by the pope.
Florence taken.   Charles makes Alessandro de' Medici its absolute ruler.   He
summons the Diet of Augsburg to settle religious questions and prepare for war
with the Turks.

1531 Ferdinand, brother of Charles, elected king of the Romans.
1533 Pizarro establishes his authority in the capital of Peru.
1535 Expedition to Tunis in conjunction with Portugal, Genoa, the pope, and the knights
of Malta.   The usurper Barbarossa is expelled and the king Mulei Hassan restored
as a vassal of Spain.   Ten thousand Christian slaves released.   Francis I invades
Savoy.   Its duke appeals to Charles.   Death of the duke of Milan.   Charles takes
possession of the duchy.   Colony of Buenos Ayres founded by Pedro de Mendoza.

1536 Francis occupies Piedmont. Provence invaded by Charles, who finds it already desolated by the French, and retreats in disorder.

1537 French invasion of the Netherlands. Truce with France.

1538 It is extended for ten years (Truce of Nice). Mutiny amongst Charles' troops in Milan, Sicily, and Africa. Their generals borrow money to pacify them. Cortes of Toledo. The deputies protest against the extravagance of Charles' foreign wars, and the nobles claim their privilege of exemption from taxation. Charles dismisses the estates. This was the last occasion on which nobles and prelates were summoned. The cortes was henceforth reduced to a meeting of the deputies of eighteen cities.

1539 Revolt of the citizens of Ghent.

1540 Charles marches to Ghent and represses the rebellion with great severity. Order of Jesuits, founded by Ignatius Loyola in 1534, is confirmed by the pope.

1541 The ambassadors of France murdered by Charles' governor of the Milanese. Francis I demands reparation and prepares for war. Expedition led by Charles against the pirates of Algiers. Great part of the fleet destroyed in a storm. The army returns, having accomplished nothing. Conquest of Chili begun and Santiago founded by Pedro de Valdivia.

1542 Perpignan besieged by the French and successfully defended by the duke of Alva.

1543 Alliance with Henry VIII. War between Charles and Francis in the Netherlands.

1544 Battle of Cerisole in Piedmont. The imperialists are defeated by the French. Charles invades France in conjunction with Henry VIII. Peace of Crespy. Charles renounces all claim to Burgundy and Francis to Naples, Flanders, and Artois.

1545 The pope grants Charles half the ecclesiastical revenues of Spain.

1547 Battle of Mühlberg. Charles defeats the Smalkaldic League.

1551 League between Henry II of France and the Protestant princes of Germany.

1552 Charles compelled to fly from Innsbruck. The French seize Toul, Verdun, and Metz. By the Peace of Passau, Charles grants religious liberty to the German Protestants. Charles besieges Metz but fails to take it.

1554 Charles cedes Naples to his son Philip. Philip marries Mary, queen of England.

1555 Philip invested with the sovereignty of the Netherlands.

1556 Philip invested with the sovereignty of Spain as **Philip II**. His possessions embrace Spain, Naples, Sicily, Milan, Franche-Comté, the Netherlands, Tunis, the Barbary coast, Canaries, Cape Verd Islands, Philippines, Spice Islands, West Indian colonies and territories in Mexico and Peru. Truce of Vaucelles arranges five years' peace with France. Charles resigns the empire to his brother Ferdinand and retires to San Yuste. Pope Paul IV persuades Henry II of France to break the truce of Vaucelles and excommunicates Charles and Philip. Alva invades the papal states.

1557 Philip visits England and persuades Mary to declare war on France. St. Quentin captured by Spaniards and English. Peace with Paul IV.

1558 Spanish victory of Gravelines. Death of Charles V. Death of Mary of England.

1559 Peace of Cateau-Cambrésis between Spain and England and France. Philip marries Elizabeth of France. Margaret of Parma regent of the Netherlands. Philip assembles a force to recover Tripoli for the Knights of Malta.

1560 It captures Los Gelves in the Gulf of Khabes. A Turkish fleet routs the Spaniards, and takes sixty-five vessels.

1561 A new fleet, collected to oppose the Turks, dispersed and partly destroyed by a storm. Turks ravage the Spanish coast.

1563 The Castilian cortes protest in vain against the Inquisition. The Moriscos forbidden to carry arms.

1564 The pirate stronghold of Peñon de los Velez in Fez captured.

1565 Siege of Malta by the Turks. The Spanish fleet relieves Malta.

1566 The Flemish nobles band together under the name of the "Gueux" to resist the Inquisition. Tumult and wrecking of Catholic churches. The rebellion suppressed.

1567 The prince of Orange goes over to the Protestants. The duke of Alva succeeds Margaret of Parma as regent of the Netherlands and institutes a reign of terror. The Spanish Moriscos forbidden their distinctive costume, language, and customs.

1568 The Aragonese cortes wring from Philip an act limiting ecclesiastical interference in civil causes. Death of Philip's only son Don Carlos. The "Gueux" defeated at Jemmingen. Revolt of the Moriscos in the Alpujarras. They devastate Granada and are defeated by the governor, Mondejar, in the

1569 pass of Alfajarali; massacre of the rebels. The English seize the Spanish treasure ships. Don John of Austria, son of Charles V, commissioned to end the Morisco war.

1570 He takes Golera. Moriscos expelled from Andalusia.

1571 League of Spain, Rome, and Venice against the Turks. Battle of Lepanto. The allies under Don John crush the naval power of the Turks.

1572 Briel and Mons captured by the Gueux. The states of Holland declare the prince of Orange stadholder of Holland, Friesland, and Zealand. Successes of Alva.

1573 The supplies furnished by the Castilian cortes declared a tribute legally due to the sovereign. Defeat of Alva's fleet. Alva recalled. Tunis captured by Don John. He adds to the fortifications.

1574 The Turks recover Tunis and massacre the garrison.

1576 "Spanish fury" or sack of Antwerp by the Spaniards. By the pacification of Ghent, the seventeen provinces of the Netherlands agree to unite to defend their liberties and expel the Spaniards. Don John sent to govern the Netherlands.

1577 By the Perpetual Edict Philip recognises the Pacification of Ghent. The southern provinces of the Netherlands withdraw from the union.

1578 Battle of Gembloux. Don John and Alessandro Farnese defeat the revolted Netherlanders. Death of Don John. Death of Sebastian, king of Portugal. Philip claims the throne.

1579 Union of Utrecht between the seven northern provinces of the Netherlands.

1580 Death of Henry of Portugal. Portugal conquered and reduced to a province of Spain. Spaniards join a papal invasion of Ireland and are massacred at Smerwick.

1581 The Netherlands declare their independence.

1584 Farnese takes Ghent.

1585 The Catholic party in France, headed by the Guises, forms a league with Philip for the extirpation of heresy in France and the Low Countries. Farnese reduces Antwerp. England sends help to the United Provinces.

1587 Drake burns the shipping at Cadiz.

1588 The Spanish Armada sails, is defeated by the English, and dispersed by storms.

1589 Farnese repulsed from Bergen-op-Zoom. An expedition from England under the Portuguese claimant Don Antonio invades Portugal, pillages Corunna, and retreats. Perez arraigned for the murder of Escovedo. He escapes to Aragon and appeals to its *fueros* (privileges). His prosecution abandoned.

1590 Increase of the excise on food, termed "the millions." Battle of Ivry; Henry IV of France defeats the league and its Spanish auxiliaries. Philip claims the French throne for his daughter by Elizabeth of Valois. A Spanish force under Farnese is sent to the relief of Paris, but quarrels with the league.

1591 Perez arrested by the Inquisition. The mob rise against it. Perez escapes to France. Philip punishes the rioters who had attacked the Inquisition. Its power increases. Part of *fueros* of Aragon abolished.

1592 Farnese relieves Rouen, is deserted by the league, and escapes from Henry IV with heavy loss.

1594 Groningen, the last stronghold of the Spaniards in the United Provinces, taken by the stadholder.

1596 Cadiz sacked by Essex.

1597 The stadholder defeats the Spaniards at Turnhout. Philip repudiates his debts.

1598 Peace of Vervins with Henry IV. Death of Philip. The Netherlands pass to his daughter Isabella, and the rest of his possessions to his son **Philip III**.

1599 A second armada sails for England and is beaten back by a storm.

Seventeenth Century

1601 Increase of "the millions." An expedition sent to assist Tyrone in Ireland fails.

1602 Persia joins Spain in a war against Turkey. Plundering of the coast and islands in the Mediterranean.

1604 Peace with England. The "archdukes" (Isabella and her husband Albert) capture Ostend after a three years' siege.

1605 First part of *Don Quixote* published.

1607 Spanish fleet destroyed in a fight with the Dutch off Gibraltar. Eight months' truce with the United Provinces. Spain and the "archdukes" resign their claims to the provinces.

1609 Twelve years' truce with the United Provinces. The Moriscos expelled from Spain with the loss of all property save what they could carry with them. With them Spain loses her most industrious inhabitants. Henry IV of France organises a league against Spain in conjunction with the Italian states, England, the German Protestants, and the United Provinces.

1610 Murder of Henry IV.

1612 Philip's daughter Anne married to Louis XIII and his son Philip to Elizabeth de Bourbon. The princesses renounce their respective claims to the kingdoms of Spain and France.

1615 The duke of Savoy invades Lombardy and is defeated by Hinojosa, viceroy of Milan. The war continued to 1617, when peace was signed at Pavia. Second part of *Don Quixote* published.

1617 Alsace ceded to Spain by Ferdinand of Austria.

1618 Battle of Gravosa. The duke of Osuna, viceroy of Naples, defeats the Venetian fleet. Fall of Lerma, Philip's favourite. The war with Venice continues till the recall of Osuna.

1620 Battle of the White Hill. Spanish troops aid the imperialists to defeat the elector palatine. The Spaniards under Spinola overrun the Palatinate and expel the elector.

1621 **Philip IV** succeeds his father. Olivares becomes all-powerful. The cortes of Castile calls attention to the extravagance of the administration, the appalling misery in the country, and the ruinous system of taxation. Attempts to curb official corruption. Expiration of the truce with the United Provinces. Spinola sent to conquer the Netherlands. He takes Juliers.

1622 Negotiation with England for the marriage of the infanta Maria to Prince Charles. James I asks for a Spanish army to assist the elector palatine. Charles arrives in Madrid.

1623 Enormous subsidy demanded by Olivares. The cities resist. Increase of taxation. Marriage-treaty signed. Charles leaves Spain.

1624 Franco-Dutch alliance. The French drive the Spanish garrisons from the Valtelline. Spain allied with Tuscany, Parma, Modena, and Genoa.

1625 Spinola takes Breda. Genoa threatened by the French and saved by Spain.

1626 Peace of Monçon between France and Spain. The Valtelline relinquished to the Grisons.

1628 Spanish treasure fleet captured by the Dutch.

1629 Peace with England. France and Spain support rival candidates to the duchy of Mantua. French successes. Spinola sent to Lombardy.

1630 He lays siege to Casale. Death of Spinola. The Buccaneers seize the island of Tortuga and make it the headquarters of their pirate bands.

1631 Treaty of Cherasco with France.

1632 Frederick Henry of Orange expels the Spaniards from the United Provinces. The archduchess Isabella resigns in favour of Philip IV. Orange captures Maestricht. Philip makes a treaty with the duke of Orleans, in rebellion against France.

1633 A Spanish army sent to aid the emperor.

1634 Battle of Nördlingen. The Spaniards under the cardinal infante, brother of Philip, aid in defeating the Protestant Swedes and Germans. Treves attacked and the elector carried off by the Spaniards. France declares war on Spain and forms an alliance with the United Provinces. Joint invasion of the Spanish-Netherlands repelled by the cardinal infante. The Milanese invaded by the French.

1636 The French expelled from the Milanese.

1637 Leucate unsuccessfully besieged by the Spaniards. Breda captured by Orange.

1638 The French under Condé invade Spain and are totally defeated before Fuenterrabia. The Spaniards take Bremi and Vercelli and ravage Piedmont.

1639 Alsace falling to France on the death of Bernard of Saxe-Weimar, the communication between Italy and the Netherlands is interrupted. Salsas in Roussillon taken by Condé and recovered by the Spaniards. The Spanish fleet takes refuge in the Downs under the neutral flag of England but is attacked and destroyed by Van Tromp. Spaniards expelled from Piedmont.

1640 Troops billeted on the Catalans and levies demanded from them. Revolt in consequence. The insurgents seize Barcelona. Revolution in Portugal. João of Braganza assumes the crown. He enters into relations with France, Holland, and the rebels in Catalonia. Los Velez sent to subdue the Catalans. He takes Cambrils and Tarragona, but is repulsed before Barcelona.

1641 Discovery of a plot of the duke of Medina Sidonia and the marquis de Ayamonte in concert with the king of Portugal to erect Andalusia into a separate sovereignty. The revolted Catalans swear fealty to France.

1642 French troops sent to aid the Catalans invade Aragon, take Perpignan and occupy Roussillon. Indecisive battle of Lerida.

1643 Disgrace of Olivares. Luis de Haro succeeds him. The Spaniards invade Champagne and are severely defeated at Rocroi. The Spaniards victorious at Lerida.

1646 Failure of a plot to deliver Barcelona to Philip.

1647 The Neapolitans revolt under Masaniello who is assassinated. Don John of Austria sent to quiet the city. Fresh revolt. The duke of Guise aims at the crown but is captured and the insurrection suppressed.

1648 Lerida successfully resists the French. The French defeat the Spaniards at Lens. On the termination of the Thirty Years' War by the Peace of Westphalia, Spain concludes peace with the United Provinces, acknowledging their independence and leaving them their conquests in Brabant and Flanders, with Maestricht and Breda and their acquisitions in America and the Indies.

1651 Battle of Iviza. Don John of Austria destroys the French fleet and besieges Barcelona.

1652 Barcelona capitulates. Catalonia returns to her allegiance to Spain. The Great Condé goes over to the Spaniards and leads their armies in the Spanish Netherlands against France.

1654 Spaniards defeated before Arras. The buccaneers sack New Segovia in Honduras and Maracaibo and Gibraltar on the Gulf of Venezuela.

1655 Jamaica captured by the English.

1656 Valenciennes, besieged by Turenne, is relieved by Don John and Condé.

1657 Oliver Cromwell sends troops to aid Turenne. The English exiles join the Spaniards.

1658 Battle of the Dunes. The Spaniards defeated. Dunkirk, Furnes, Gravelines and Oudenarde surrender to the French.

1659 Battle of Elvas. The Portuguese defeat De Haro. Devastating war on the frontiers. The treaty of the Pyrenees ends the French war. Louis XIV is to marry the infanta Maria Theresa, who renounces her claims to the Spanish crown. Spain abandons Roussillon, Cerdagne, Artois, and several border fortresses. Burgundy, Charolois, and Franche-Comté restored to Spain. France abandons the Portuguese.

1661 Don John invades Portugal. Death of De Haro.

1662 Don John occupies Alemtejo and

1663 takes Evora. Spaniards defeated at Amegial.

1664 Portuguese capture Valencia de Alcantara and defeat the Spaniards at Villaviciosa. Don John disgraced.

1665 Battle of Montes-Claros won by the Portuguese. They invade Andalusia. Revolt in Valencia and other provinces. Philip dies and is succeeded by his son **Charles II**, a child of four years, under the regency of his mother Maria Anna of Austria. The Jesuit Nithard becomes supreme.

1666 Louis XIV lays claim to Franche-Comté, Hainault, Brabant, Artois, etc., in right of his wife.

1667 He invades the Netherlands, and takes several fortresses.

1668 Treaty with Portugal. Spain recognises the house of Braganza. Franche-Comté conquered by France. England, Sweden, and the Dutch form a triple alliance to preserve the Netherlands to Spain. Treaty of Aix-la-Chapelle (Aachen). Spain abandons to Louis his Flemish conquests. Louis restores Franche-Comté.

1669 Disputes between the regent and Don John. Aragon and Catalonia declare for Don John. Nithard dismissed. The queen forced to share the government with Don John.

1671 Panama sacked by the buccaneers.

1672 Louis XIV invades Holland. Spain joins Germany in sending troops to Holland.

1674 Louis reconquers Franche-Comté. Indecisive battle of Seneffe between the allies and the French. Spanish victory in Roussillon. The victorious troops proceed to the siege of the revolted city of Messina. The French relieve Messina.

1675 Indecisive action off Messina between the French and the Spaniards and Dutch under De Ruyter. De Ruyter is killed. The French defeat the allied fleet off Palermo and rout a Spanish army in Sicily.

1677 Valenciennes and Cambray taken by the French. The Prince of Orange (William III of England) defeated at Mont-Cassel. Catalonia invaded by the French. Charles II declared of age. Don John contrives the disgrace of the queen-mother and her favourite Valenzuela. He suppresses the Council of the Indies, and introduces a few reforms.

1678 Cerdagne occupied and Ghent and Ypres taken by the French. They evacuate Sicily. Peace of Nimeguen. Spain surrenders Franche-Comté and fourteen fortresses of the Netherlands.

1679 Death of Don John.

1680 Eighty-five persons suffer at an *auto-da-fé*. Raiding expedition of buccaneers on the isthmus of Darien and the coast of Peru.

1683 The French renew the war.

1684 They are repulsed before Gerona and take Luxemburg. Truce with France. Plague in Andalusia.

1685 Oropesa replaces Medina-Celi as prime minister. Cadiz blockaded by France to enforce payment for goods confiscated from French merchants. Earthquakes in various places.

1686 League of Augsburg between Spain, the empire, England and Sweden against France.

1689 Revolt in Catalonia. Villa-Hermosa defeats the rebel army under Antonio de Soler. French invasion of Catalonia repulsed.

1690 Battle of Fleurus. The French defeat the allies.
1691 Melgar succeeds Oropesa. Attempt to reform the finances. Mons and Namur taken by the French. Barcelona bombarded by Noailles. Urgel taken by Noailles.
1693 The allies defeated at Neerwinden and Marsaglia. Charles appoints the elector of Bavaria hereditary governor of the Netherlands.
1694 Noailles takes Gerona.
1695 German mercenaries arrive in Catalonia, but are defeated at Llobregat.
1697 Cartagena de las Indias sacked by the French and buccaneers. Peace of Ryswick. Spain recovers Luxemburg, Mons, Courtrai, and the towns lost in Catalonia. Charles' declining health draws the attention of Europe to the question of his successor.
1698 Secret treaty between France, England, and Holland for the partition of the Spanish dominions. Spain, the Netherlands, Sardinia and the colonies to go to the prince of Bavaria; Naples, Sicily, Finale, and Guipuzcoa to the dauphin; Lombardy to the archduke Charles, second son of the emperor Leopold I. Charles appoints as his heir the prince of Bavaria, who dies immediately afterwards. French intrigues rouse Spanish opposition to the archduke.
1700 Second partition treaty between France, England, and Holland for the division of the Spanish dominions. Spain, the Netherlands, Sardinia, and the colonies to go to the archduke Charles. To the dauphin, Naples, Sicily, Finale, Guipuzcoa, and the Milanese. Charles appoints as his heir, Philip, duke of Anjou, a grandson of Louis XIV. Death of Charles II. Anjou succeeds as **Philip V.**

Eighteenth Century

1701 Philip arrives in Spain. The emperor protests against his accession. The nobles alienated by attempts at financial reform. Philip marries Maria Louisa of Savoy. The princess Orsini obtains supreme influence over Philip and Maria. *Fueros* restored to Catalonia.
1702 Philip goes to Naples. Indecisive battle of Luzzara between Philip and Prince Eugene. Grand Alliance between England, Holland, Denmark, Austria, and Prussia, against Spain and France. The allies fail before Cadiz, but destroy the Spanish plate fleet at Vigo.
1704 The archduke Charles lands at Lisbon, and in union with the king of Portugal declares war on Spain. A French army under Berwick invades Portugal. Charles lands at Barcelona, but effects nothing and retreats. Gibraltar taken by Sir George Rooke. Indecisive battle off Malaga.
1705 An attempt to recover Gibraltar fails. The allies take Barcelona. Catalonia, Valencia, and Murcia declare for Charles.
1706 Philip fails at the siege of Barcelona. Portuguese invasion. Marlborough's victory at Ramillies leads to the loss of nearly the whole Spanish Netherlands. Charles enters Madrid. Aragon declares for him. The French driven from the Milanese and Charles proclaimed. The allies expelled from Castile.
1707 Berwick defeats the allies at Almansa. The Austrians conquer Naples; Valencia and Aragon recovered for Philip. Their *fueros* abolished, and their government assimilated to the Castilian.
1708 Attempt to exact a loan from the clergy. The pope forbids its payment, but offers a tax on church property, which Philip declines. The allies win the battle of Oudenarde. The plate fleet captured by the English. Minorca, Majorca, and Sardinia conquered by the allies, and Oran by the Moors.
1709 Amelot, the French ambassador, dismissed. Medina-Celi prime minister. Barrier treaty between England and Holland regulating the northern boundary of the Spanish Netherlands, and providing for their government in the name of Charles, and eventual transfer to Austria.
1710 Insincere negotiations of Gertruydenberg between France and the allies. War in Spain renewed. Philip defeated at Almenara and Saragossa. Charles re-enters Madrid, but leaves to repel an invasion of Catalonia, and Philip returns and wins the battle of Villaviciosa.
1711 Death of the emperor Joseph I. The archduke Charles succeeds him as Charles VI.
1712 England withdraws from the Grand Alliance, and recalls her troops from Catalonia. Philip renounces his rights to the French crown, and changes the law of succession to the Spanish crown, excluding females while one of his male descendants shall survive.
1713 The imperial troops withdraw from Catalonia. Orry becomes finance minister, and reforms the administration. Death of Queen Maria Louisa. The clergy resist an

attempt to curb the power of the Inquisition. Spain accedes to the Peace of Utrecht between France and England, Holland, Prussia, Savoy, and Portugal, by which Philip is recognised as king of Spain; the Spanish Netherlands, Sardinia, the Milanese, and Naples are ceded to Austria, and Sicily to Savoy; while England retains Gibraltar and Minorca.

1714 France and England send troops to reduce Catalonia. Barcelona taken by storm. The privileges of Catalonia abolished, and the Castilian constitution established there. Majorca submits. Philip marries Elizabeth Farnese. She gains unbounded influence over him, and makes Alberoni, an Italian priest, her chief adviser. He turns his attention to the revival of commerce and industry, economical reforms, and the reorganisation of the army and navy.

1715 Peace with Portugal. Colonia del Sacramento on the Rio de la Plata ceded to her.

1716–17 Triple alliance between France, England, and Holland to preserve the provisions of the treaty of Utrecht.

1717 Sardinia occupied by the Spaniards.

1718 Triple alliance between the emperor, France, and England. The Spaniards invade Sicily. Their fleet is destroyed by Byng in a battle off Cape Passaro. Alberoni concerts with count Görtz, minister of Charles XII of Sweden, a scheme for a joint invasion of Scotland by Sweden and Russia, which is frustrated by the death of Charles XII.

1719 Spain invaded by the French. A Spanish fleet, sent to restore the English pretender, dispersed by a storm. The allies ravage the Spanish coasts. Spanish reverses in Sicily. Holland accedes to the Triple, now the Quadruple, Alliance. Alberoni disgraced. Patiño succeeds him.

1720 Philip accedes to the Quadruple Alliance. Sicily ceded to Austria, and Sardinia to Savoy. Successful campaign on the Barbary coast.

1721 Defensive alliance with France and England.

1724 Philip abdicates in favour of his son **Luis**. Death of Luis. **Philip V** resumes the crown.

1725 The Spanish infanta, the intended queen of Louis XV, sent back to Spain. Philip's agent, Ripperdá, concludes with the emperor the treaty of Vienna, securing the succession of Charles, son of Philip and Elizabeth Farnese, to Parma and Tuscany and arranging a commercial alliance.

1726 England joins France in the league of Hanover. Administration and disgrace of Ripperdá.

1727 Gibraltar besieged by the Spaniards. The emperor makes peace with England and France, referring the questions of Parma, Tuscany, and Gibraltar to a congress.

1728 Philip accepts the terms in the convention of the Pardo.

1729 Treaty of Seville between Spain, England, and France. The commercial treaty with the emperor abrogated. Philip's son Charles recognised as heir to Parma and Tuscany.

1731 The emperor annexes Parma, but in the second treaty of Vienna accedes to the treaty of Seville. Charles succeeds to Parma and Piacenza.

1732 Oran recovered from the Moors.

1733 Perpetual Family Compact between France and Spain. France, Spain, and Sardinia agree to assert the claims of Stanislaus Leczinsky to Poland.

1734 Charles of Parma takes possession of Naples and is declared king of the Two Sicilies. The retiring Germans defeated at Bitonto. Sicily reduced for Charles. The Germans beaten at Parma.

1735 Preliminaries of Vienna. France and Sardinia make peace with the emperor. Parma to be ceded to Austria and Tuscany to Francis of Lorraine.

1736 Philip and Charles of Sicily accede to the Peace of Vienna, Charles retaining Sicily.

1739 War of Jenkins' Ear occasioned by the disputes of Spanish and English traders in the West Indies. To meet the expense of the war, government pensions and payments are suspended for a year, and the interest on the public debt reduced. Porto Bello captured by the English.

1740 Death of the emperor Charles VI. Philip claims the succession for his son Don Philip.

1741 Unsuccessful siege of Cartagena de las Indias by the British. They fail to conquer Cuba. Anson plunders Payta and captures a Spanish treasure ship.

1742 Philip sends troops to invade Austrian Lombardy. The king of Sardinia suddenly goes over to the emperor and drives the Spaniards from Lombardy. The British fleet compels the neutrality of Naples.

1743 Alliance of Austria, England, and Sardinia. Spain renews the French alliance in the Treaty of Fontainebleau.

1744 Indecisive battle of Hyères between the English, French, and Spanish fleets. Unsuccessful siege of Coni by the Spaniards.

1745 The French and Spanish overrun the Milanese.
1746 The French and Spaniards routed at Piacenza and expelled from Lombardy. Death of Philip. His son, **Ferdinand VI**, succeeds.
1748 Treaty of Aix-la-Chapelle. Don Philip receives Parma, Piacenza, and Guastalla. Maria Theresa recognised as successor of Charles VI.
1749 Commercial treaty of Aquisgran between Spain and England. Under the administration of Carvajal and Ensenada, Spain begins to recover her prosperity.
1752 Treaty of Aranjuez between Spain, Maria Theresa, and the dukes of Tuscany, and Parma guarantees the neutrality of Italy.
1753 Pope Benedict XIV acknowledges by a concordat the Spanish king's right to make ecclesiastical appointments.
1754 Death of Carvajal. Richard Wall, an Irishman, succeeds him.
1755 Earthquake in Spain.
1759 Death of Ferdinand. His half-brother, Charles of Naples, succeeds as **Charles III**. Naples is handed over to Charles' younger son, Ferdinand. Charles restores Aragon and Catalonia some of their privileges and remits arrears of taxes. Squillaci (Esquilache) appointed minister of finance.
1761 Third family compact with France for mutual defence. Consequent war with England.
1762 Portugal refuses to join the family compact and is invaded by the French and Spaniards. England sends troops to Portugal. The Spaniards defeated at Valencia de Alcantara and Villa Velha. Havana and Manila captured by the English. Colonia del Sacramento taken from Portugal.
1763 Peace with England. Spain cedes Florida and her fishing rights on the Newfoundland banks. England restores Havana and Manila. Grimaldi succeeds Wall. Louisiana ceded to Spain by France. The inhabitants refuse to accept the transfer.
1765 Reorganisation of the Spanish colonies. Discontent and revolts.
1766 Discontent roused against Squillaci by sumptuary laws, foreign innovations, and the high price of bread. Sanguinary revolution in Madrid called the "Revolt of Esquilache." De Aranda minister. He continues the policy of innovation, and
1767 expels the Jesuit fathers from Spain and the colonies, as aiders and abettors of revolution.
1769 Louisiana subdued.
1770 The Spaniards assert their claim to the Falkland Islands and expel the English. Preparations are made for war, but France withdrawing her support,
1771 Spain is compelled to apologise and restore the Falklands. De Aranda dismissed.
1773 The pope, Clement XIV, compelled by Spain to order the suppression of the Jesuits. The pursuit of trade declared to involve no loss of rank or privilege.
1774 The final blow given to the Inquisition by a decree making civil offences punishable by civil tribunals only.
1775 Ceuta and Melilla attacked by the Moors. The aggressors defeated. A Spanish army routed in Algiers.
1776 The Portuguese attack the Spaniards on the Rio Grande. Colonia del Sacramento and the neighbouring colonies occupied by Spain.
1777 Grimaldi replaced by Florida-Blanca. Peace with Portugal. Spain retains Colonia del Sacramento.
1778 Perpetual alliance with Portugal. Privilege of free trade with all American colonies save Mexico granted to seven principal Spanish ports. The privilege was afterwards extended to all the provinces save Biscay.
1779 Spain offers to mediate between England and her revolted American colonies. On her refusal Spain declares war. Gibraltar besieged by the Spaniards. Failure of a Franco-Spanish naval expedition against England.
1780 The principle of the Armed Neutrality announced by Russia and accepted by Spain. Rodney defeats the Spanish fleet off Cape St. Vincent. English transport fleet captured.
1781 Pensacola taken by the Spaniards. Rebellions in Peru and Mexico.
1782 Minorca taken by the French and Spaniards. Gibraltar relieved by Howe. Treaty with Turkey containing commercial provisions, arranging for the exchange of slaves and protection for Spanish pilgrims.
1783 Peace with England concluded at Versailles. Spain retains Minorca and Florida. Increase of duties on foreign manufactures.
1784 The proceedings of the Inquisition against grandees and officials subjected to the king's approval.
1786 Treaty with Algiers. The Algerian government guarantees the suppression of piracy.
1788 Death of Charles III. He is succeeded by his son **Charles IV**.
1791 Spain protests against the foundation of the English settlement at Nootka Sound, but being unsupported by France has to recognise it. This humiliation being

attributed to the French Revolution leads to a reaction against liberalism. Florida-Blanca urges the European powers to restore Louis XVI.

1792 Dismissal of Florida-Blanca. Manuel de Godoy, the queen's favourite, becomes supreme. The Spanish government intercedes for Louis XVI.

1793 Execution of Louis XVI. Spain joins the First Coalition against France. Failure of the invasion of France.

1794 The Spaniards are defeated with the loss of nine thousand men and surrender Figueras. The French invade Spain.

1795 Treaty of Bâle. Spain surrenders her territory in Santo Domingo. The French evacuate Spain.

1796 Alliance between France and Spain in the treaty of San Ildefonso. Spain joins
1797 the war against England, and her fleet is defeated in the battle of Cape St. Vincent.
1800 Louisiana ceded to France.

Nineteenth Century

1801 Successful invasion of Portugal. Portugal agrees to exclude English forces from her ports. Napoleon exacts a large payment from Portugal and insists on Spain's ceding Trinidad to England.

1803 Napoleon compels Spain to pay a large subsidy for the war with England and to undertake to secure Portuguese neutrality.

1805 Spain joins France in the war. The English defeat the French and Spaniards at Cape Finisterre and Trafalgar. British invasion of Buenos Ayres.

1806 Ferdinand, king of Naples, expelled from Naples. Spain prepares for war, but after Napoleon's victory at Jena renews the

1807 French alliance in the Treaty of Fontainebleau, arranging for the partition of Portugal. Ferdinand, prince of Asturias, conspires against the government. Charles asks help from Napoleon. The French march into Spain. Reconciliation of Ferdinand and Charles.

1808 Murat sent to command the French troops in Spain. Barcelona, Pamplona, and the northern fortresses of Spain occupied by the French. Indignation in Spain and riots against Godoy. Charles IV is constrained to abdicate in favour of **Ferdinand VII.** Murat occupies Madrid. Charles declares his abdication compulsory. Meeting of Napoleon and the Spanish royal family at Bayonne. Murat assumes the Spanish government in the name of Charles IV. Ferdinand restores the crown to Charles IV, who resigns his rights to Napoleon and retires to Rome. Napoleon makes **Joseph Bonaparte** king. General revolt against the French throughout Spain. The French sack Cordova. Saragossa and Valencia successfully resist them. Savage guerilla warfare. Capitulation of Baylen; twenty thousand French surrender. Flight of Joseph. The central junta assumes the government. French victories of Burgos, Espinosa, and Tudela. Napoleon enters Madrid, abolishes feudalism and the Inquisition and restores Joseph. The Spanish colonies of Buenos Ayres, Mexico, Chili, and Venezuela revolt.

1809 Battle of Corunna and retreat of an English army. Napoleon quits Spain. Joseph returns. Marshal Lannes takes Saragossa by storm. French victories of Medellin and Ciudad-Real. Soult commander-in-chief of the French in Spain. Wellington is sent to aid the Spaniards and defeats the French at Talavera. Wellington returns to Portugal. Spaniards defeated at Ocaña. Flight of the central junta from Seville to the isle of Leon. Joseph enters Seville.

1810 Napoleon converts Catalonia, Aragon, Navarre, and Biscay into military governments. Juntas formed in the colonial cities govern in Ferdinand's name, but work for independence. The cortes meet at the isle of Leon, swear fealty to Ferdinand VII
1811 as a constitutional monarch and declare the abolition of feudalism, the privileges of the nobles and the tithes of the church, declare the sovereignty to reside in the people, and draw up a constitution called the "constitution of the year 12." The cortes refuse to grant the colonies equality of representation and free trade. Most of the colonies declare their independence and successfully assert it against Spanish troops. The cortes conclude a treaty with England, granting her free trade in America, and make Wellington commander-in-chief of the Spanish troops in the western provinces. The French take Tarragona, Murviedro, and Valencia.

1812 Wellington captures Badajoz, defeats Marmont at Salamanca, and enters Madrid.
1813 Wellington defeats Joseph at Vitoria. Napoleon recalls Joseph and names Soult governor of Spain. Wellington takes San Sebastian and Pamplona. Wellington invades France.

1814 **Ferdinand VII** returns. He imprisons the liberal leaders and restores absolutism with the privileges of the nobles and clergy. The Inquisition re-erected. Persecution of partisans of Joseph, leaders of the liberal party, and guerilla captains. A camarilla or court party rules supreme and organises a reign of terror. Wars for independence in the South American colonies.

1815 Porlier's rebellion at Corunna suppressed. Morillo sent to Venezuela. He crushes rebellion and governs vigorously.

1816 Rio de la Plata asserts its independence.

1817 Lacy rebels in Catalonia, is captured and shot.

1819 Florida sold to the United States. Secret societies formed against the government.

1820 Venezuela and New Granada declare their union as the Free State of Colombia. An army, assembled to conquer Colombia, rebels under Riego and Quiroga. The revolt spreads throughout Spain. Ferdinand compelled to swear to the constitution and abolish the Inquisition. Cortes and liberal government. The moderate party fails to restrain the radicals. The priests stir up the people against the constitution. Disorder throughout the country.

1821 Mexico becomes independent.

1822 Triumph of the radical party. Riego president of the cortes. The clerical and servile (royal) party sets up a regency in Urgel and arms for the king. Civil war in Catalonia and Aragon between serviles and radicals. Congress of Verona, France, Russia, Austria, and Prussia agree for armed intervention in Spain in favour of Ferdinand. Victory of the Liberals under Mina and flight of the regency to France.

1823 The government withdraws to Seville. Invasion by the French. The serviles and common people join them. The French erect a provisional government in Madrid and restore the "legitimate order" of things. The cortes withdraw to Cadiz, but surrender it to the French. Ferdinand resumes despotic power. Execution of Riego and other liberals. Many go into exile. President Monroe declares the United States' intention to oppose the interference of European powers for the restoration of Spanish absolutism in America.

1824 Battle of Ayacucho. Chili and Peru achieve independence by the defeat of the Spaniards.

1825 "Commissions of purification" persecute all opponents of despotism. Bessières's revolt suppressed.

1830 Ferdinand publishes the Pragmatic Sanction of 1789 which abrogated the Salic law of 1713. Birth of Ferdinand's daughter Isabella.

1832 Illness of Ferdinand. The queen Christina appointed regent. Ferdinand recalls the Pragmatic Sanction, thus restoring the rights of his brother Don Carlos. The queen recalls the exiled constitutionalists. Ferdinand cancels his revocation of the Pragmatic Sanction. Disturbances in favour of Don Carlos. Don Carlos exiled.

1833 Death of Ferdinand. Christina regent for **Isabella II.** The northern provinces revolt for Carlos. France and England recognise Isabella. Don Carlos assumes the title of Carlos V king of Spain.

1834 Ministry of Martinez de la Rosa, including moderate royalists and moderate liberals. The cortes summoned. Quadruple Alliance. France and England agree to support the young queens of Spain and Portugal against the pretenders Carlos and Miguel. A Spanish army invades Portugal and expels the Portuguese pretender. Carlos escapes to England. A savage guerila war between Carlists and Christinos begins in Biscay and Navarre. Carlos returns. Mina given command of the queen's troops.

1835 Mutiny of the guards in favour of the constitution of 1812. The Carlists become masters of all northern Spain. Dissension between the rival parties of moderates and radicals, or progressists, and anarchy in the southern provinces. Cloisters attacked and monks murdered by the Christinos. Semi-republican juntas formed in the cities. The Carlists defeated at Mendigorria. The war continues with increased savagery. Mendizabal minister.

1836 The convent law of Mendizabal suppresses the monastic orders, confiscating their goods. Mendizabal retires. The moderates in power. A British legion defeats the Carlists at Bilbao. At La Granja the soldiers force Christina to promulgate the constitution of 1812 and dismiss her ministers. The Christino general Espartero relieves Bilbao. The "royal expedition" of Don Carlos to Madrid is driven back to the north.

1837 The constitution modified by the cortes and made less democratic. Carlos enters Castile, but is expelled by Espartero.

1838 The moderates in power. Attempts at absolutist reaction.

1839 Maroto becomes Don Carlos' chief adviser and opens negotiations with Espartero which lead to the treaty of Bergara, by which the insurgents agree to lay down their arms in return for an amnesty and confirmation of the *fueros* of Navarre and Biscay. Carlos escapes to France. The war continues two years longer in Catalonia and Valencia.

1840 The liberals force Christina to accept Espartero as chief minister. She abdicates.
1841 Espartero regent. Insurrections in favour of Christina.
1843 Revolt of Barcelona. General Narvaez occupies Madrid for Christina. Espartero flees to England. Isabella's majority declared. Christina returns. Reactionary policy under French influence.
1844 Insurrection of the coloured population of Cuba.
1845 New constitution increasing the power of the crown.
1846 Louis Philippe procures the marriage of Isabella with Francis de Asis and of her sister with the duke of Montpensier.
1847 Cabrera fails to excite a Carlist rising.
1850 Amnesty to the Carlists. Revolt in Cuba in favour of union with the United States suppressed.
1851 Fall of Narvaez. Concessions to the clergy.
1852 The constitution changed in favour of absolutism. Limitation of the freedom of the press.
1854 The moderates and radicals join in a liberal union. Revolts in Barcelona and Madrid. Espartero minister. Attempts to revive internal prosperity. Sale of the property of the church, of institutions, and of the state ordered.
1856 New constitution. Espartero retires. Riots in Madrid and Barcelona. The old moderate party under Narvaez in power.
1858 Union of moderates and radicals under the O'Donnell ministry.
1860 Successful expedition to Morocco. The Spaniards win the battles of Tetuan and Guad Ras. Ortega proclaims Don Carlos' son as Charles VI. Ortega captured and shot. Don Carlos' sons captured and compelled to renounce their pretensions.
1861 Santo Domingo declared reunited to Spain. Convention of London. At the instigation of Spain, England, France, and Spain agree to force Mexico to fulfil her obligations. Spanish troops under Prim join in the Mexican expedition.
1863 Prim's attitude brings about a misunderstanding with France. Dissolution of the O'Donnell cabinet.
1864 War with Santo Domingo.
1865 A party formed for the union of Spain with Portugal.
1866 War with Peru. Rebellion in Catalonia, Valencia, and Madrid. A new ministry under Narvaez and Gonsalez Bravo endeavours to restrain rebellion by a reign of terror.
1868 The liberal union, progressists, and democrats unite against the government. Revolution. Insurgents' victory at the bridge of Alcolea. Flight of Isabella. Provisional government under Prim, Topete, and Olozaga. Disputes as to the form of government. Religious orders abolished and toleration proclaimed. Cuban insurrection.
1869 Monarchist majority in constituent cortes. Various candidates for the throne proposed. New constitution drawn up. Serrano becomes regent with Prim as minister. Republican and Carlist risings suppressed.
1870 **Amadeo,** duke of Aosta and son of the king of Italy, elected king of Spain. Prim assassinated.
1871 Serrano and Sagasta ministers.
1873 Amadeo abdicates. Republican government. Constituent assembly meets to draw up a federal republican constitution. Don Carlos (Charles VII) raises a Carlist rebellion with guerilla warfare in the north. The intransigentes or extreme republicans in opposition to the federalists erect independent governments in the coast towns. Cartagena becomes the centre of the extreme republicans. Cuba revolts in consequence of the law releasing slaves and seeks union with the United States. A party of Americans landing in Cuba to aid the insurgents seized and many of them executed.
1874 General Pavia occupies the house of assembly with troops and declares the cortes closed. Military dictatorship under Serrano and Sagasta. Cartagena surrenders to the federalists. General Martinez Campos proclaims **Alfonso XII,** son of Isabella, king.
1875 Alfonso returns to Spain. Religious liberty abolished. The law of civil marriage confined to non-Catholics. The Carlists driven from Catalonia and Valencia. Urgel, Vitoria, and Estella capitulate.
1876 New constitution with a minimum of religious toleration; senate partly elective. The Carlist insurrection suppressed.
1879 Campos ministry. Inundations. Alfonso marries the Austrian archduchess Maria Christina. Canovas del Castillo ministry.
1880 Law for abolition of slavery in Cuba.
1881 Sagasta ministry. Riots in Catalonia over a projected commercial treaty with France.
1882 The treaty concluded.

1883 Socialist and military outbreaks. Posada Herrera succeeds Sagasta.
1884 Conservative ministry under Canovas del Castillo.
1885 Dispute with Germany over Caroline Islands arbitrated by the pope (1886). Death of Alfonso XII. Queen Maria Christina regent. Sagasta ministry.
1886 Commercial treaty with England. Birth of **Alfonso XIII.** Don Carlos protests against the proclamation of Alfonso.
1888 Ruiz Zorrilla issues a revolutionary manifesto demanding a new form of government to be settled by the people. Republican disturbances.
1889 Introduction of trial by jury. Great strike in Catalonia.
1890 Reform of the constitution. Canovas del Castillo ministry.
1892 New commercial tariff and consequent break with France. War with Morocco. Sagasta again minister.
1893 Explosions produced by anarchists in Barcelona.
1894 Legislation against anarchists. Consecration of the first bishop of the Spanish reformed church.
1895 Peace with Morocco.
1896 The United States requests Spain to recognise the independence of Cuba. Indignation in Spain.
1897 Cuban reform bill passed. Cubans recognised as belligerents by the United States. Canovas del Castillo assassinated by an anarchist. Sagasta ministry.
1898 Armistice to the Cubans. The president of the United States sends a message to congress requiring the end of the Cuban War. Spain declares the message incompatible with Spanish rights. Bread riots in Spain. War with the United States in Cuba and the Philippines. The Spaniards defeated in the battles of Manila, San Juan, and Santiago. Santiago surrenders. Martial law proclaimed in Spain. Philippine Republic proclaimed. Treaty between Spain and America. Spain resigns her rights in Cuba, Porto Rico, and her other possessions in the Antilles and Philippines.
1899 Spain left with embarrassed finances. The Sagasta ministry resigns. Señor Silvela forms the modern conservative party. Señor Villaverde effects many financial reforms. Caroline Islands sold to Germany. Reform of the navy.
1900 A new conservative administration formed by General Azcarraga.

Twentieth Century

1901 Anti-clerical riots in Madrid and other towns. A Liberal government under Sagasta again goes into power. The queen in opening the Cortes declares that a thorough social reorganization of the country is necessary, that its finances must be consolidated and its wealth developed.
1902 Alfonso XIII declared of age and crowned. Attempt to assassinate Alfonso XIII. Silvela returns to power. Spain concludes treaties of arbitration with all countries of South America except Chile.
1903 Death of Sagasta. New cabinet headed by Señor Villaverdi.

A BRIEF RÉSUMÉ OF PORTUGUESE HISTORY

Tenth Century

997 Oporto and surrounding territory taken from the Moors by Bermudo II of Galicia.

Eleventh Century

1055 Cea and other fortresses captured from the Moors by Ferdinand the Great of Castile and Leon.
1057 Ferdinand takes Lamego and Viseu
1064 and Coimbra, and forms the conquered territory into a country under Sesnando, a Moor.
1065 Death of Ferdinand. The suzerainty of the counties of Coimbra and Oporto passes with Galicia to his son Garcia.
1073 Garcia's territories re-united with Leon and Castile under Alfonso VI.
1095 Alfonso VI gives Porto Cale (Portugal), consisting of the fiefs of Oporto and Coimbra, to Count Henry of Burgundy (Besançon), who married his daughter Theresa, 1072.

Twelfth Century

1109 Death of Alfonso. Urraca succeeds to Castile and Leon. Henry interferes in the internal troubles of that kingdom.
1112 War with Almoravids. Death of Henry. Theresa regent for her son Alfonso Henriques.
1117 Theresa besieged by Moors at Coimbra. She gives power to her lover Ferdinand Peres de Trava.
1121 Urraca takes Theresa captive. Peace made.
1127 Alfonso VII of Castile conquers Theresa's realm and compels her homage.
1128 Alfonso Henriques assumes power, defeats and exiles Theresa. In the next years he three times invades Galicia and in
1137 defeats Alfonso VII's troops at Cerneja. Peace of Tuy. Alfonso Henriques submits to the king of Leon.
1139 Battle of Ourique. Alfonso Henriques crushes the Moors. A legend was formerly current that he was then hailed as king by his soldiers.
1140 The Moors capture and destroy Leiria. Tourney of Valdevez. The Portuguese knights defeat the Castilian. Alfonso Henriques king of Portugal as **Alfonso I.**
1143 Peace of Zamora. Alfonso VII acknowledges Alfonso I as king. The latter declares himself a vassal of the pope.
1144 The Moors defeat the Templars at Soure.
1147 Alfonso I captures Santarem and takes Lisbon with the aid of English and other crusaders. Other Moorish cities surrender.
1252 Alfonso repulsed at Alcacer-do-Sal.
1158 Alfonso captures Alcacer-do-Sal.

1161 Alfonso is defeated by the Moors.
1166 The Moors take Evora.
1167 Alfonso invades Galicia.
1168 Alfonso besieges Badajoz, is taken prisoner and compelled to relinquish Galician conquests.
1170 Alfonso loses to the Moors in Alemtejo.
1171 Alfonso victorious at Santarem, makes seven years' truce with Moors.
1172 Makes his son Dom Sancho co-ruler, who fights the Moors constantly.
1184 Dom Sancho crushes and kills Yusuf at Santarem.
1185 Alfonso dies and is succeeded by **Sancho I, O Povoador** ("City Builder").
1189 Sancho, aided by crusaders on their way to Palestine, takes Algarve and Silves from the Moors.
1192 The Moors re-conquer Alemtejo, but are repulsed at Santarem, and peace is made. Dom Sancho wages constant war with Alfonso IX of Leon. He builds many cities.

Thirteenth Century

1209 Sancho's quarrels with Pope Innocent III, respecting jurisdiction over priests, culminate in the siege and escape of the bishop of Oporto.
1210 Dom Sancho grants the pope's demands, retires to a convent and dies.
1211 **Alfonso II "the Fat"** succeeds, and summons the first real parliament; he wars with his brothers and sisters and Alfonso IX of Leon.
1212 Portuguese take part in the battle of Las Navas de Tolosa.
1217 Alcacer-do-Sal recovered from the Moors. Alfonso II is excommunicated for seizing church lands.
1223 Alfonso II dies and is succeeded by the thirteen-year-old **Sancho II.**
1226 Sancho II captures Elvas from the Moors.
1227 Sancho reinstates officials hostile to the clergy and fights the Moors.
1228 The pope reconciled.
1237 The pope lays an interdict on Portugal, but is pacified.
1239–1244 Sancho II takes several cities from the Moors.
1245 The pope deposes Sancho II. The clerical party sets up Sancho's brother,
1248 Alfonso, who drives Sancho II into exile, where he dies. **Alfonso III** completes the conquest of Algarve.
1254 Alfonso marries Beatrice de Guzman, the natural daughter of Alfonso the Learned of Castile, so alienating the papal faction. Alfonso III summons a cortes at Leiria.
1261 The cortes forces the king to recognize the necessity of obtaining the people's consent to taxation.
1262 The pope legalizes the king's marriage and legitimates his son Dom Diniz, who
1263 is made king of Algarve.
1277 Dom Diniz rebels against his father.
1279 Alfonso III dies, leaving Portugal fully established and its boundaries defined. **Dom Diniz El Ré Lavrador**, established after war with his brother. Period of internal progress and prosperity.
1294 Commercial treaty with Edward I of England.
1297 Peace settled with Castile and Leon.
1300 University founded at Lisbon.

Fourteenth Century

1319 Diniz founds the order of Christ to replace the Templars.
1323 His wife, St. Isabella, prevents a battle between Diniz and his son Alfonso.
1325 Diniz dies and is succeeded by **Alfonso IV.**
1336 Alfonso invades Castile; peace made by St. Isabella.
1340 The Portuguese and Castilians defeat the Moors at the river Salado.
1348 The Black death invades Portugal.
1355 Iñes de Castro, wife or mistress of the infante Dom Pedro, murdered.
1357 Alfonso dies and is succeeded by **Dom Pedro (I) the Severe.**
1361 Pedro the Cruel of Castile surrenders the murderers of Iñes in exchange for Castilian fugitives. The murderers put to death with torture.
1367 Pedro dies and is succeeded by **Ferdinand the Handsome,** who
1369 claims the throne of Castile and Leon, and combats Henry of Trastamara.
1371 Ferdinand resigns his claims to Castile.
1373 Henry of Trastamara invades Portugal.
1374 Ferdinand promises to support John of Gaunt's claims to Castile, but again makes peace with Henry of Trastamara.

1383 The English, angry at Ferdinand's fickleness, ravage Portugal. Ferdinand dies, leaving his wife Leonora regent, against whom the people rise.
1384 Juan I of Castile allies himself with her, but is repulsed at Lisbon.
1385 The Portuguese proclaim Dom João, grand master of Aviz and son of Pedro the Severe, king, as **João (I) the Great.** The Portuguese defeat the Castilians at Aljubarrota and Valverde.
1386 A perpetual treaty of alliance signed with England.
1398 Iñes de Castro's son, Diniz, attempts to overthrow João, but, with English assistance, he is defeated.

Fifteenth Century

1411 Peace made with Castile.
1415 The Portuguese take Ceuta in Africa, their first foreign possession.
1418 Prince Henry's captains discover the Madeiras.
1420 Madeiras colonised.
1432 Azores occupied by Portuguese.
1433 A Portuguese ship passes Cape Bojador. João dies and is succeeded by **Duarte** (Edward), who calls a cortes at Evora and passes the Lei Mental ordaining the reversion to the crown of lands granted to nobles on failure of male descendants of the grantee.
1437 Duarte sends an expedition against Tangier. The Portuguese surrounded and saved only by Prince Ferdinand's offering himself as hostage.
1438 Duarte dies, **Alfonso V the African,** a minor, succeeds. Pedro, son of João I, regent.
1441 Slave-trade begun by Portuguese.
1447 Alfonso V comes of age and dismisses Pedro.
1449 Alfonso V defeats and kills Pedro at Alfarrobeira.
1458 Alfonso takes Alcacer-Seguier, Africa.
1460 Prince Henry the navigator dies. Cape Verd Islands discovered and settled.
1462 Pedro de Cintra discovers Sierra Leone.
1464 Alfonso repulsed in Africa.
1471 Tangier captured by the Portuguese.
1475 Alfonso marries Juana (Beltraneja) of Castile and claims the Castilian crown,
1476 but is defeated at battle of Toro and concludes with Castile the treaty of Alcantara (1479). Juana retires to a convent.
1481 Alfonso dies. **João II the Perfect.** The cortes of Evora determines on an inquiry into titles to estates and the abrogation of the judicial powers of the nobles. Braganza executed.
1483 The duke of Braganza and other nobles oppose these measures. Braganza executed.
1484 Diogo Cam discovers the Congo and Angola.
1487 Bartholomeu Dias discovers the Cape of Good Hope.
1488 Commercial treaty with England.
1490 Covilhão enters Abyssinia.
1493 Pope Alexander V declares the boundary between Portuguese and Spanish areas of discovery.
1494 By the treaty of Tordesillas the boundary is readjusted.
1495 João II dies without heirs and is succeeded by **Emmanuel the Fortunate**, who expels the Jews from Portugal as the condition of his marriage with the daughter of
1497 Ferdinand of Spain. Vasco da Gama discovers Natal.
1498 Vasco discovers Calicut.
1500 Cabral discovers Brazil. Factories established at Kananur and Cochin.

Sixteenth Century

1501 Ascension Island discovered. Vespucci discovers Rio de la Plata and Paraguay.
1502 St. Helena discovered. Vasco visits India and establishes a factory at Mozambique.
1505 De Almeida, the first Portuguese viceroy, sent to India. His son Lourenço discovers Ceylon. Mombasa occupied.
1506 Massacre of the New Christians in Lisbon.
1508 Albuquerque supersedes Almeida as viceroy in India.
1510 Albuquerque is repulsed in an attack on Calicut and conquers Goa
1511 and Malacca.
1512 Serrão discovers the Moluccas.
1515 Albuquerque captures Ormus. Portuguese established at Diu.
1517 Andrade settles at Canton.
1518 Portuguese settlement established in Ceylon.
1520 Magellan discovers the straits of Magellan.
1521 Andrade reaches Pekin. Emmanuel dies, and is succeeded by **João III.** He finds

    his countrymen too eager to gain wealth by foreign adventure and emigration, thus threatening depopulation.

1531 Daman taken and destroyed by Portuguese. Sousa founds São Vicente in Brazil and receives a grant of the first hereditary captaincy, or governorship of a province, in Brazil.

1536 Inquisition established in Portugal.

1539 Bishopric established at Goa.

1541 St. Francis Xavier sent to the Indies. Estevão da Gama, governor of India, leads an expedition to the Red Sea.

1542 Japan discovered by Fernão Mendes Pinto.

1543 Xavier founds Christian settlements in Travancore.

1545 The Indian viceroy De Castro wins victory of Diu over the king of Guzerat.

1548 St. Francis Xavier goes to Japan.

1549 Thomé de Sousa first governor-general of Brazil. He founds Bahia and governs by aid of Jesuits.

1557 Factories established at Macao. João III dies, and is succeeded by his three-year-old grandson **Sebastian**, under the regency of his grandmother Catherine and his great-uncle Cardinal Henry, but under the power of the brothers Camara.

1558 Portuguese settled at Daman.

1560 Inquisition introduced into India.

1567 Portuguese established at Rio de Janeiro after conflicts with French settlers.

1568 Sebastian of age.

1578 He invades Africa, and is defeated and killed at Kassr-el-Kebir. He is succeeded by his uncle **Henry**, who, feeling that he cannot live long, calls the cortes to name his successor.

1580 Henry dies. Philip II of Spain is chosen king as **Philip I**, and defeats his rival Antonio, prior of Crato, at Alcantara, and again in

1582 the Azores.

1584–1585 Two pretenders, who claim to be the dead Sebastian, captured.

1585 São Thiago, Cape Verd Islands, captured by an English fleet.

1586 Bahia plundered by the English.

1589 Combined English and Dutch expedition to "restore" Antonio, wins successes, but retreats.

1594 Gabriel Espinosa, a third false Sebastian, executed. Philip closes the Portuguese harbours to the Dutch.

1596 The English sack Faro and Fort Arguin and ravage the Azores.

1597 The Dutch build a factory in Java and occupy other East Indian possessions.

1598 **Philip II** (III of Spain) king.

Seventeenth Century

1603 Tullio, a fourth false Sebastian, captured.

1605 The Dutch take Amboyna and expel the Portuguese from the Moluccas.

1615 The Portuguese defeat the king of Achin in Malacca.

1621 **Philip III** (IV of Spain).

1622 The Shah of Persia, aided by the English, recovers Ormus.

1624 Bahia taken by the Dutch and recovered.

1630 Olinda in Brazil taken by the Dutch. Maurice of Nassau extends the Dutch power in Brazil.

1632 Military post of Tete in Mozambique established.

1634 An insurrection in Lisbon put down.

1637 An insurrection in Evora put down.

1638 The Dutch take Portuguese forts in Ceylon.

1640 The Dutch take Malacca. The Portuguese having been alienated by the misfortunes of their country under Spanish rule and by the bad faith of their kings, a sudden revolution ousts the Spaniards and gives the crown to the duke of Braganza as **João (IV) the Fortunate**. The assistance afforded by the Jesuits in this revolution is rewarded by almost unlimited power in ecclesiastical and great influence in civil affairs.

1641 The cortes assembles and accepts João IV. France and Holland send fleets. England recognises the king. Caminha conspiracy to restore Spanish power betrayed by the Spanish marquis De Ayamonte. The leaders executed.

1644 Albuquerque defeats the Spaniards at Montijo.

1645 Revolts against Dutch rule in Brazil and consequent breach with Holland.

1648 Benguela and Angola recovered from the Dutch.

1650 The revolted English fleet under Prince Rupert takes refuge in the Tagus. The Portuguese refuse to allow the parliamentary admiral Blake to enter the river. Blake attacks Portuguese merchantmen.

1652 Commercial treaty with England, greatly in the latter's favour.

1654 The Dutch expelled from Brazil.

1656 João IV dies and is succeeded by his thirteen-year-old son **Alfonso VI**. Marshal Schomberg with a picked band of French officers comes to the assistance of Portugal.

1658 The Dutch take the last Portuguese stronghold in Ceylon.

1659 Menezes defeats the Spaniards at Elvas. In the treaty of the Pyrenees, France promises Spain to abandon Portugal.

1661 Spaniards invade Portugal.

1662 English alliance secured by the marriage of the king's sister with Charles II and the cession of Tangier and Bombay with a grant of free trade with Portuguese dominions. Alfonso VI declares himself of age.

1663 The count of Villa Flor defeats Don John of Austria at Amegial and recovers Evora.

1664 Magalhães defeats the Spaniards at Ciudad Rodrigo. The Dutch take the Portuguese settlements on the coast of Malabar.

1665 The Portuguese crush the Spaniards at Montes-Claros.

1666 The king marries the French princess Marie d'Aumale.

1667 Alfonso's excesses lead to a revolution in favour of his brother Dom Pedro. Alfonso imprisoned. The queen granted a divorce.

1668 Dom Pedro recognised as regent. Spain recognises Portugal's independence. The queen marries Dom Pedro.

1683 The king dies in prison. Dom Pedro succeeds as **Pedro II**.

1698 Portuguese expelled from Mombasa.

Eighteenth Century

1703 Paul Methuen, the English ambassador, negotiates the Methuen treaty which secures preference to Portuguese over French wines in England, and forms the basis of the subsequent friendship between the two countries. Portugal recognises the archduke Charles, the English candidate to the Spanish throne.

1704 Archduke Charles arrives in Lisbon with English forces and with Portuguese aid successfully invades Spain.

1706 Death of Pedro II. **João V** succeeds. João V under influence of Cadaval continues the war with Philip V of Spain.

1707 The allied forces of Portuguese, Dutch, and English defeated by the Spaniards at Almansa.

1709 Portuguese under Fronteira defeated at Caia.

1711 A French fleet under Duguay-Trouin bombards and pillages Rio de Janeiro, Brazil.

1715 Peace with Spain.

1717 Portuguese fleet defeats Turks off Cape Matapan.

1728 Mombasa recovered by Portuguese.

1739 Bassein and Thana on the west coast of India lost to Portugal.

1740 Mombasa again lost.

1750 João dies and is succeeded by **José** who leaves the chief government to Pombal. The latter checks the Inquisition, improves the navy and finance. Colonia del Sacramento ceded to Spain in exchange for territory in Paraguay.

1753 Revolt against the transference of territory in South America attributed to Jesuit instigation. Revolt suppressed.

1755 The great earthquake at Lisbon destroys forty thousand inhabitants. Chartered company established to trade with Brazil.

1757 Pombal expels the Jesuits from court.

1758 Pombal persuades the pope to decree the confiscation of merchandise belonging to Jesuits. Mysterious Tavora plot, and attempt on José's life.

1759 The Jesuits charged with the plot and expelled from Portuguese territories. New Goa replaces Old Goa as capital of the Portuguese Indies.

1760 The pope permits José's daughter to marry her uncle Pedro.

1762 The Spaniards invade Portugal and capture Braganza and Almeida with aid of English under Burgoyne and Count Schaumburg-Lippe. The Spaniards are beaten at Valencia de Alcantara and Villa Velha and

1763 peace made. Schaumburg-Lippe remains to re-organise the Portuguese army.

1769 Pombal saves José from assassination.

1773 Pombal issues a decree providing for the future abolition of slavery in Portugal. Clement XIV abolishes the Jesuit order.

1777 José dies leaving the throne to his daughter **Maria I** with her husband **Pedro III**.
1781 José's widow obtains the power and drives Pombal from court.
1786 Maria's husband and eldest son die and
1788 her mind gives way.
1792 Her son Dom João acts as regent and puts down sympathisers with the French Revolution.
1793 Portugal joins Spain in the disastrous war with France.
1795 By the treaty of Bâle, Spain makes a separate peace with France.
1796 War with Spain averted by the arrival of English aid.
1799 Dom João declared regent.
1800 Lucien Bonaparte at Madrid offers Portugal impossible terms of peace with Spain and France.

Nineteenth Century

1801 Olivenza, Campo Mayor, etc., taken by the French and Spaniards. Franco-Spanish victories of Arronches and Flor da Rosa. Peace with Spain and France with large cessions by Portugal. Napoleon sends Lannes as minister, and Portugal consents to all demands. Portugal's neutrality recognised by France.
1804 Napoleon requires Portugal to join the Continental System and exclude British vessels from her ports. The Portuguese government hesitates.
1807 France and Spain sign the treaty of Fontainebleau, agreeing to conquer and divide Portugal. Junot and Caraffa invade Portugal; Taranco and Solano occupy the south. The people welcome them. On English advice Dom João names a council of regency, and sails for Brazil just as the French enter Lisbon.
1808 Junot declares that the house of Braganza has ceased to reign, and divides Portugal into military provinces. Junot leaves Lisbon, and the regency calls on the people to rise; revolts against the French in many places and appeal to England. Sir Arthur Wellesley (later Duke of Wellington) arrives with English troops. Wellesley defeats La Borde at Roliça and Junot at Vimeiro. Convention of Cintra by which Junot agrees to evacuate Portugal.
1809 Soult takes and plunders Oporto, but is expelled by Wellesley, who invades Spain but retreats after winning the battle of Talavera. Beresford organises the Portuguese army. The English ambassador added to the regency.
1810 Masséna commissioned to reconquer Portugal; he takes Almeida. Wellington defeats Masséna at Busaco and retires to the lines of Torres Vedras, which he defends for more than a year against all attacks
1811 till Masséna is compelled to retreat, when he is followed by Wellington and defeated at Fuentes de Onoro. Wellington withdraws to Portugal.
1812 Wellington again invades Spain.
1814 End of Peninsular War. England grants Portuguese sufferers £100,000. The Portuguese court remains in Brazil, while Portugal is left in the hands of Beresford and the English. Great discontent excited by the treatment of Portugal as a province of England.
1815 Portuguese monarchy given the title of the United Kingdom of Portugal, Brazil, and the Algarves. Patriotic agitations and secret societies formed to restore the Portuguese to their position as a nation.
1816 Maria I dies, and the regent becomes king as **João VI**.
1817 Monte Video occupied by the Portuguese. General de Andrade's plot for revolt against the English betrayed and the leaders executed. Revolts in Brazil put down.
1818 Severe edicts against clubs and secret societies in Portugal. The agitation against foreign rule increases.
1820 Beresford goes to Brazil. Rising in Oporto. The English are expelled and a new regency and assembly formed, which abolishes the Inquisition and draws up a constitution, afterwards known as the constitution of 1822, constituting the cortes as one elective chamber.
1821 João VI returns from Brazil. The queen Carlota Joaquina and her second son Dom Miguel become the centre of absolutist reaction and are expelled from Lisbon. Disputes between Portuguese and Brazilian deputies in the cortes.
1822 Brazil secures independence under João's son Pedro, who is chosen emperor as Pedro I.
1823 A rebellion in Tras-os-Montes. João revises the constitution. A Brazilian fleet defeats the Portuguese.
1824 The king's son Miguel revolts, but the revolt is suppressed by the energy of the foreign ambassadors, and a new constitution establishes the cortes in their ancient form, divided into three estates.

1825 The royal family goes to Brazil, where João is accepted as emperor, then abdicates in favour of Pedro, acknowledging the independence of Brazil.

1826 João VI dies. **Pedro IV** grants a constitutional charter. He abdicates the throne of Portugal in favour of his daughter **Maria II** (Maria da Gloria) aged seven, who is under the regency of her aunt Isabella Maria. Miguel swears fidelity to the constitution. Marquis of Chaves raises an insurrection for Miguel. Miguel is betrothed to Maria. English troops called in to keep order.

1827 Miguel made regent and English troops withdraw.

1828 Miguel exiles his enemies. **Miguel** proclaims himself king and abolishes parliament. Miguel's forces capture Madeira.

1829 Miguel defeated by constitutionalists at Terceira.

1830 A council of regency under Villa Flor (Terceira), Palmella, etc., appointed for Maria in the Azores.

1831 Dom Pedro resigns the crown of Brazil to his son, and meeting Maria in London prepares to overthrow Miguel. Insurrection against Miguel put down.

1832 Pedro takes Oporto and is besieged there by Miguel who is defeated. Miguel's fleet beaten by Sartorius.

1833 Saldanha victorious at Oporto. Pedro's fleet under Napier defeats Miguel at Cape St. Vincent. Lisbon occupied for Pedro. **Maria II** proclaimed queen and the charter of 1826 restored.

1834 Quadruple alliance of Portugal, Spain, England, and France to expel Miguel and the Spanish pretender Don Carlos. Saldanha defeats Miguelites at Torres and Novas. Napier reduces Beira. Villa Flor overruns Tras-os-Montes and is victorious at Asseiceira. Miguel surrenders at Evora and goes into exile. The cortes abolishes the orders of friars. Massacres in Lisbon. The queen declared of age. Dom Pedro dies. The ministry under Palmella deals severely with Miguelites, causing frequent insurrections. The ministry by repudiation destroys national credit.

1835 Maria da Gloria marries Prince Augustus of Leuchtenberg. Prince consort dies.

1836 Maria marries Ferdinand of Saxe-Coburg. September revolution at Lisbon under Caldeira

1838 compels the grant of the new constitution of 1838, based on that of 1822.

1842 Costa Cabral succeeds in abolishing the constitution of 1838, and substituting the charter of 1826.

1846 Sá da Bandeira leads an insurrection of the Septembrists (or partisans of the constitution of 1838), called the war of Maria da Fonte or "patuleia." Costa Cabral flees to Spain. Royal troops victorious at Evora. English ships arrive. Bandeira defeated by Saldanha at Torres Vedras.

1847 Insurgents take Oporto. England, France, and Spain agree to intervene. Bandeira surrenders. Oporto yields to royal troops. Convention of Granada arranges amnesty.

1850 American fleet collects claims.

1851 Saldanha raises an insurrection. Oporto declares for Saldanha. He is made prime minister.

1852 The Cortes revises the constitution, and queen and prince royal swear allegiance to it. Public debt funded.

1853 Maria II dies, leaving her husband as regent for her son **Pedro V.**

1854 Royal slaves freed.

1855 The king comes of age.

1856 Saldanha ministry resigns. First railway opened.

1857 Fever ravages Lisbon. The French slave-ship *Charles-et-Georges* seized.

1858 The French government threatens war; the ship is released and Portugal compelled to pay compensation.

1861 Pedro dies of cholera and is succeeded by his brother **Luiz I.**

1862 Duke of Loulé prime minister. Luiz marries the daughter of the king of Italy.

1864 Portugal protects Confederate privateers and has difficulties with the United States.

1865 The colonies receive constitutional privileges.

1866 The Spanish general Prim ordered out of Portugal.

1869 Saldanha, objecting to the Duke of Loulé, compels his dismissal (1870) and forms a ministry. He is soon after sent as ambassador to England.

1876 Financial panic.

1878–1883 The house of peers loses hereditary privileges.

1880 Celebration in honour of Camoens and Vasco da Gama.

1883 Fontes Pereira de Mello prime minister.

1887 Macao, hitherto leased to Portugal, formally ceded by China. Delagoa Bay Railway confiscated by Portuguese government.

1889 Riots at Oporto. King Luiz dies and is succeeded by **Carlos I.** Difficulties with England over rival claims in East Africa.

1890 England threatens war and Portugal yields under protest. Riots result. England and United States remonstrate against seizure of Delagoa Railway. The question submitted to Swiss arbitration. Collisions between English and Portuguese troops in East Africa.

1891 Military revolt in Oporto. British steamer seized and stopped. Agreement arrived at with Great Britain. Financial panic.

1892 Large reductions in expenditures. Great storms.

1893 Renewed activity among the Miguelistas — supporters of Dom Miguel.

1894 Railway dispute with France. Celebration of 500th anniversary of birth of Prince Henry the Navigator. War with nations near Lourenço Marques.

1895 Electoral reforms. House of peers remodelled and made to consist of twelve bishops, the princes of the blood royal, and ninety members nominated by the king. Portuguese under Colonel Galhardo victorious in the war near Lourenço Marques.

1897 400th anniversary of Vasco da Gama's first voyage.

1899 Portugal remains neutral during the Boer War, but permits the British to search for contraband of war imported via Lourenço Marques.

1900 Delagoa Bay Railway award. The Portuguese government retains the railway, but has to pay compensation.

Twentieth Century

1901 The king, to commemorate the opening of the new century, grants a general amnesty to all convicted of political and press offences. The king visits London in order to attend Queen Victoria's funeral ceremony in London, but on account of disturbances at home has to hurry back. Riots at Oporto.

1902 Dom Carlos visits the king of England and on his return the king of Spain, and re-enters Lisbon amid acclamation. Financial conditions cause much trouble throughout Portugal.

1903 The cabinet resigns, February 27th. A new cabinet is formed on the following day. King Edward of England visits Lisbon. Portuguese troops at Oporto mutiny and proclaim the Republic.

A GENERAL BIBLIOGRAPHY OF SPANISH HISTORY

BASED ON THE WORKS QUOTED, CITED, OR CONSULTED IN THE PREPARA-
TION OF THE PRESENT HISTORY; WITH CRITICAL AND BIOGRAPHICAL
NOTES

Abarca, Pedro de, Los Reyes de Aragon, 1684. — **Addison**, J., Charles the Third of
Spain, London, 1900. — **Alberoni**, G., Cardinal, Testament politique du Cardinal Alberoni
recueilli de divers mémoires, lettres et entretiens de Son Éminence traduit d' l'Italien par
le comte de R. B. M., Lausanne, 1753. — **Alfaro**, Compendio de la historia de España, Madrid,
1860–1862, 3 vols. — **Alfonso X**, Las quatro partes enteras de la crónica de España, edited
by Florian de Ocampo, Zamora, 1541; Los quatro libros primeros de la crónica general de
España; Documentos de la época de Don Alfonso el Sabio, Real Academia de la historia,
Madrid, 1851.

To *Alfonso X*, known as the Learned, Spanish language and literature owe an enormous
debt. He was the first to take the Castilian tongue, as the official language, and he made use
of it in his own writings. Numerous are the literary works which bear his name and were,
some written by him, some compiled under his direction. The chief that concern us here are
of two classes, historical and legislative. Of the former class the principal is the *Estoria de
Espanna* or *Crónica general*. There is a dispute as to how much of this was written by
Alfonso himself. Some authorities credit him with the whole. It extends from the creation
to Alfonso's own accession and is based partly on older histories, partly on tradition and
poetic legends of which it is a perfect storehouse. Of the *Siete Partidas*, which belong to
the second class and were called by Alfonso *El Setenario*, Ticknor says that they "do not
always read like a collection of statutes. . . . They often seem rather to be a series of
treatises on legislation, morals, and religion divided with great formality into Parts, Titles,
and Laws."

Al Makkari, Analectos de la historia literaria y política de los árabes de España, Leipsic,
1855–1858, 4 vols.; History of the Mohammedan Dynasties in Spain, translated, with notes
by Pascual de Gayangos, London, 1840–1843, 2 vols.

Abul-Abbas Ahmad ibn Mohammed Al Makkari, the Arab historian, was born about 1585
at Tlemcen in Algeria. About 1620 he settled at Cairo, having been exiled from his own
country, — why is not known. His history was undertaken in response to a request from his
friends at Damascus who had been deeply interested by the oral descriptions of the doings
of the Spanish Arabs with which he had entertained them when on a visit to Damascus in
1628. He died in 1631.

Altamira y Crevea, R., Historia de España y de la civilización española, Barcelona,
1900–1902. The two volumes thus far completed extend to 1479. — **Amicis**, E. de, Spain,
New York, 1881. — **Anghiera**, Pietro Martire d', Opus epistolarum, Alcalá, 1530, Strasburg,
1891. — **Annales Complutenses**, in Flórez's España Sagrada.

Annales Complutenses. The word Complutenses is derived from Complutum, the Roman
name for Alcalá de Henares. The anonymous writer of this brief historical summary wrote
in the twelfth century.

Annales Toledanos, in Flórez's España Sagrada.

Annales Toledanos. The author of the early portion of these annals of Toledo lived in
the thirteenth century.

Antonio, N., Bibliotheca Hispana nova, 1500–1684, Madrid, 1783–1788, 2 vols.; Biblioteca Hispana vetus, Madrid, 1788, 2 vols.

Nicolás Antonio was born at Seville in 1617, and educated there and at the university of Salamanca. He afterwards returned to Seville where he drew on the treasures of the library of the monastery of San Benito in the composition of his *Bibliotheca Hispana* which forms a literary history, the first part of which extends to 1500, the second (which appeared in 1672) to 1670. In 1654 Philip IV sent Antonio to Rome as his general agent. He afterwards filled the office of agent to the Spanish Inquisition. He died in 1684.

Armstrong, E., Elisabeth Farnese, "the termagant of Spain," London, 1892. — **Aschbach**, J., Geschichte der Westgoten, Frankfort, 1827; Geschichte der Ommaïjaden in Spanien, Vienna, 1860, 2 vols.; Geschichte Spaniens und Portugals zur Zeit der Almoraviden und Almohaden, Frankfort, 1833–1837, 2 vols. — **Aulnoy**, M. C. J. de B. d', Relation du voyage d'Espagne, Paris, 1690; reprint as La cour et la ville de Madrid à la fin du 17ᵉ siècle, Paris, 1876, 2 vols. — **Avila**, G. G. de, Historia de Salamanca, Salamanca, 1606; Historia de la vida y hechos del rey Don Henrique III de Castilla, Madrid, 1638; Teatro eclesiastico de la primitiva iglesia de las Indias Occidentales, Madrid, 1649–1656, 2 vols.; Historia de la vida y hechos del monarca Don Felipe III, in Mendoza's Monarquía de España, Madrid, 1770. — **Avila y Zúñiga**, Luis de, Comentario de la guerra de Alemaña hecha por Carlos V en 1546 y 1547, Madrid, 1548, 1852. — **Ayala**, P. López de, Crónicas de los reyes de Castilla, Don Pedro, Don Enrique II, Don Juan I, Don Enrique III, Madrid, 1781, 2 vols.; in Biblioteca de autores Españoles, Madrid, 1875.

Pedro López de Ayala, celebrated as knight, poet, and historian, was born in 1332, and died in 1407. He entered the service of Pedro the Cruel of Castile and sided with the king in the latter's earlier struggles with his revolted brothers and nobles, distinguishing himself chiefly by his exploits on the sea. When King Pedro was driven out by his brother Henry of Trastamara, Ayala joined Henry. He was taken prisoner by the English at Navarrete, but afterwards ransomed. Under Henry II and Juan II he filled important offices. At the Battle of Aljubarrota he was captured by the Portuguese and released only on payment of an enormous ransom. Translations from Isidore of Seville, Boccaccio, Titus Livius, etc., are among his writings as well as a treatise on the duties of kings and nobles, called *El Rimado de Palacio*, but the chief of his works is the *Crónicas*. This is written with elegance and simplicity of style and much skill in delineation of character. He is accused of unduly blackening the character of King Pedro.

Bacallar y Sanna, Marques de San Felipe, Vicente, Comentarios de la guerra de España hasta el Año 1725, Genoa, 2 vols.

Vicente Bacallar y Sanna was a Spaniard born in Sardinia about 1660. Under Charles II he held various diplomatic posts. In the war of the Spanish Succession he sided with Philip V and was created Marquis of San Felipe by that monarch. Besides his history of the war of succession he left a history of the Jewish monarchy.

Bakhuyzen van den Brink, R. C., Analyse d'un manuscrit contemporain sur la retraite de Charles Quint, The Hague, 1842. — **Baronius**, C., Annales ecclesiastici, Antwerp, 1601–1605, 12 vols.

Cæsar Baronius, the great ecclesiastical historian, was born in the kingdom of Naples in 1538, and died at Rome, 1607. His *Annales Ecclesiastici* were written as an answer on behalf of the Church of Rome to the Protestant history called the *Magdeburg Centuries*. Baronius became a cardinal in 1596 and subsequently librarian of the Vatican.

Baumgarten, Hermann, Geschichte Spaniens zur Zeit der französischen Revolution, Berlin, 1851; Geschichte Spaniens vom Ausbruch der französischen Revolution, Leipsic, 1865–1871, 3 vols.; Geschichte Karls V, Stuttgart, 1885–1892.

Hermann Baumgarten was born at Lesse in Brunswick in 1825, and between the years 1842 and 1848 studied philology and history at no less than five universities, namely Jena, Halle, Leipsic, Bonn, and Göttingen. He then became a teacher in the gymnasium at Brunswick, and from 1850–1852 was editor of the *Reichszeitung* in that city. But in 1852 he resumed his historical studies at Heidelberg and subsequently at Munich. Here he was associated with the starting of the *Süddeutschen Zeitung*. In 1861 he became professor of history and literature at the Karlsruhe Polytechnicum and in 1872 in the university of Strasburg. His works include various political writings, but those on Spanish history here cited are his chief title to fame.

Baumgartner, A., " Der Cid in der Geschichte," in Stimmen aus Maria Laach, Freiburg-im-Breisgau, 1898.

Alexander Baumgartner was the son of the celebrated statesman and savant, Andreas Baumgartner. In 1860 he entered the Order of Jesuits and subsequently taught in their colleges at Feldkirch and Stonyhurst. After the abolition of the order he retired to Holland and devoted himself to literature, becoming part editor of the periodical, Stimmen aus Maria Laach.

Baudier, M., Viè de Ximènes, Paris, 1635. — **Baudrillart,** A., Philippe V et la cour de France, Paris, 1890, 2 vols. — **Beccatini,** Storia del regno di Carlo III, Venice, 1796. — **Benavides,** Memorias del rey Ferdinand IV de Castilla, Madrid, 1860, 2 vols. — **Bergenroth,** G., and **de Gayangos** (P.), Calendar of State Papers, relating to negotiations between England and Spain, 1485–1543, London, 1862–1895, 6 vols. — **Bermejo,** I. A., Historia anecdotica y secreta de la Corte de Carlos IV, Madrid [1894–1895], 2 vols. — **Bermudez de Castro,** S., Antonio Perez, Madrid, 1842. — **Bernáldez,** A., Historia de los reyes católicos Fernando y Doña Isabel in Bibliofilos Andaluces, Seville, 1870, 2 vols.

Andrés Bernáldez, known as "the Curate of Los Palacios," lived in the last half of the fifteenth and the beginning of the sixteenth century, and was *Cura* of the town of Los Palacios from 1488–1513, and afterwards chaplain to Archbishop Diego de Deza. He was present at many of the scenes he describes and acquainted with many of the great men of his day, including Columbus. He shows considerable knowledge of foreign affairs, and gives many details not reported by his contemporaries.

Bersani, Storia del Cardenale Alberoni, Piacenza, 1872. — **Berwick,** duke of, Mémoires, Paris, 1778. — **Biblioteca** de autores españoles, Madrid, 1846, etc. — **Blaquière,** E., Historical Review of the Spanish Revolution, London, 1822. — **Bleda,** J., Crónica de los moros de España, Valencia, 1618, 2 vols.

Jaime Bleda (1550–1622) was the *cura* of a town which contained many Moriscos to whom he was vehemently opposed. It was he who, in conjunction with the archbishop of Valencia, persuaded Philip III to issue the decree of 1609, ordering the Moriscos to leave Spanish territory.

Bofarull, A. de, Historia crítica de Cataluña, Barcelona, 1876–1879, 9 vols. — **Bollaert,** W., Wars of Succession of Portugal and Spain from 1826 to 1840, London, 1870, 2 vols. — **Borrego,** A., Anales del reinado de Isabel II ; Historia de las cortes de España durante el siglo XIX, Madrid, 1885.

Andrés Borrego, born in 1801, was minister of finance in Spain in 1840. He was one of those who supported the idea of a union between Spain and Portugal. Besides the books here mentioned, he wrote works on political economy.

Briz Martínez, J., Historia de los reyes de Sobrarbe, Aragon y Navarra. — **Burgos,** F. J. de, Anales del reinado de Doña Isabel II, 1850–1852, 6 vols.

Francisco Javier de Burgos, born 1778, died 1849, was a Spanish politician distinguished as a writer in the two opposite fields of poetry and economics. Being expelled from his seat in the upper house on a charge afterwards disproved, he devoted himself to the composition of a history of the reign under which he had held office.

Burke, U. R., History of Spain till the death of Ferdinand the Catholic, London, 1895, 2 vols. — **Buron,** R., Compendio de la historia crítica de la inquisición de España, Paris, 1823, 2 vols. — **Busk,** M. M., The History of Spain and Portugal, London, 1833.

Cabrera de Córdoba, L., Relaciones de las cosas suredidas en la corte de España desde 1599 hasta 1614, 1857 ; Felipe Segundo, Madrid, 1619, 1876–1878, 4 vols. — **Calderon de la Barca,** F. E. J., The Attaché in Madrid, or, Sketches of the Court of Isabella II (trans. from the German), New York, 1856. — **Calvo Marcos,** M., Regimen parlementario de España en el Siglo 19, Madrid, 1883. — **Camden,** T., History of the War in Spain and Portugal, 1814. — **Campana,** C., Vida de Don Filippo (II) 1605. — **Campos,** J. de, Le Siège de Bilbao par l'armée carliste en 1874, Paris, 1876. — **Cánovas del Castillo,** A., Historia de la decadencia de España desde el advenimiento al trono de Don Felipe III hasta la muerte de Carlos II ; Discurso. La dominación de los españoles en Italia, 1860 ; Estudios del reinado de Felipe IV, 1880–1890, 2 vols.; Historia General de España, Escrita por individuos de la Real Academia de la historia bajo la dirección de, Madrid, 1890. Completion retarded by the death of Cánovas.

The statesman, *Antonio Cánovas del Castillo,* was born in Malaga in 1828 and was the son of a professor in the naval college of San Telmo. He was not eighteen when he attempted to start a periodical called *la Jóven Malaga,* but it failed and he had to accept a small post on the Madrid Aranjuez railway. But he soon turned again to journalism and published his first and chief historical work. Cánovas is credited with a considerable share in a periodical called *El Murciélago,* of which only a few numbers appeared, but in which the most violent attacks were directed against various prominent persons not excluding royalty. Cánovas was credited with a considerable share in this as well as with the authorship of the manifesto of Manzanares (1854). He now entered the cortes and filled various offices of state in succession. He held aloof from the revolution of 1868 and during the reign of King Amadeo, though he made a brilliant speech in defence of the exiled sovereigns ; but after Amadeo's retirement he was chiefly instrumental in bringing about the return of Alfonso XII, during most of whose reign he was premier. He again held office from 1890–1893, and in 1895, when he devoted his attention to the severe repression of the Cuban insurrection. In the midst of the struggle he was murdered by an anarchist (August, 1897).

Capefigue, B. H. R., Isabelle de Castille, 1869. — **Carbajal,** L. G. de, Historia de España M. S.; Anales del rey Don Fernando el Católico. — **Carvajal,** La España de los Bórbones, 1844, 4 vols. — **Casado,** F. S., Historia de España. — **Casas,** B. de las, Historia general de las Indias, Madrid, 1875–1876; Brevissima relación de la destrucción de las Indias, Seville, 1552, in Colección de documentos inéditos, vol. 7, Madrid, 1879.

Bartolomé de las Casas or *Casaus* was of French descent. His father, Francisco Casaus, was in Hispaniola with Columbus in 1493, and returned to Seville with a fortune in 1500. In the same year Bartolomé, who had been born in 1474, went to Salamanca, where he studied jurisprudence. He then went to Hispaniola with the governor, Nicolás Ovando, and in 1510 took holy orders. In 1515 he returned to Spain to protest against the ill treatment of the natives of the West Indies by the Spaniards. Through the influence of Cardinal Ximenes he obtained the nomination of special commissioners to inquire into the abuses of authority. He was himself appointed to act as their adviser. The colonists proved too powerful and the mission failed in its object. Las Casas, expelled from Hispaniola, returned to Spain. After some difficulty he obtained the acceptance of his suggestions for improving the government of the West Indies, the chief of which was the unfortunate one of the substitution of negro for native labour. He returned to America and this time succeeded in obtaining better treatment for the Indians, who were finally declared free by a royal edict of 1543. He died at Madrid in 1569.

Casiri, M., Bibliotheca arabigo-hispana escurialensis, Madrid, 1750–1770, 2 vols.

Michael Casiri was born in Tripoli, Syria, in 1710. By birth he was a Syro-Maronite and his life was chiefly devoted to oriental studies though in 1734 he took holy orders. In 1749 he was appointed librarian of the Escorial. His *Bibliotheca* consists of extracts from and articles on the Arabian documents in the library of the Escorial.

Castelar, E., Historia del año 1883, Madrid, 1884; Discursos Parlamentarios, Madrid, 1885, 4 vols.

Emilio Castelar y Ripoll, celebrated as orator, writer, and statesman, was born at Cadiz in 1832. He took his degree of doctor of philosophy in his twenty-second year. He was editor of various newspapers in succession and an eloquent exponent of republican ideas which he continued to be after succeeding to the chair of Spanish History in the Universidad Central (1858), till the government forced him to resign. He shared in the revolution of 1866 and was consequently condemned to death. He escaped to Paris, where he remained till the revolution of 1868 made possible his return to Madrid, when he became one of the leaders of the republican party and headed the opposition during the reign of King Amadeo, on whose resignation Castelar attained the chief power under the republic. He governed ably, but his republicanism became suspected, and early in 1874 he was overthrown by a vote of want of confidence. He retired for a time to Paris, but soon returned to Spain and resumed his political career as deputy to the cortes. His numerous works include novels and speeches on various political questions.

Castillo, D. Enriquez de, Crónica del rey Don Henrique el Quarto, Madrid, 1787. — **Castro,** A. Gomez de, De rebus gestis Francisci Jimenii. — **Castro y Rossi,** A. de, El conde duque de Olivares y el rey Felipe IV, Cadiz and Madrid, 1846; Historia de los judíos en España, Cadiz and Madrid, 1847; Historia de los protestantes Españoles, Cadiz and Madrid, 1851; Examen filosófico sobre la decadencia de España, Cadiz and Madrid, 1852. — **Cavanilles y Centi,** A. C., Historia de España (to the reign of Philip II), Madrid, 1860–1864, 5 vols. — **Cespedes y Meneses,** G. de, Historia de Don Felipe III, Lisbon, 1631. — **Cevallos,** P., Exposición de los hechos y maquinaciones que han preparado la usurpación de la corona de España, Madrid, 1808; History of the practices and machinations which led to the usurpation of the crown of Spain, London, 1808. — **Chaby,** C. de, Excerptos historicos e collecção de documentos relativos á guerra denomenada da peninsula, Lisbon, 1863. — **Châteaubriand,** F. R. A. de, Guerre d'Espagne de 1823, Paris, 1838; Le Congrès de Vérone, Paris, 1838, 2 vols. — **Cherbuliez,** V. C., L'Espagne politique, Paris, 1874. — **Chronica Albeldensis** in Flórez's España Sagrada.

Chronicon Albeldensis. This is the work of two authors; the first, an anonymous monk of Albelda, wrote in the ninth century. His portion extends from the foundation of Rome to the reign of Alfonso III. The second author was the monk Vigila, of the same monastery, who coming a century later continued the narrative down to the year 976. He is the earliest authority for the history of Navarre.

Chronicon Conimbricense in Flórez's España Sagrada. — **Chronicon Moissacense.** — **Churton,** E., Góngora, an historical and critical essay on the times of Philip III and Philip IV, London, 1862, 2 vols. — **Circourt,** A. M. J. E., Histoire des Mores Madejares et des Moresques, ou des Arabes d'Espagne sous la domination des chrétiens, Paris, 1845–1848, 3 vols. — **Clarke,** Letters concerning the state of Spain, London, 1763. — **Clarke,** H. B., The Cid Campeador and the Waning of the Crescent in the West, New York, 1897, in Heroes of the Nations. — **Clemencin,** D., Elogio de la reina católica Doña Isabella, in Mem. Academia, 1821. — **Clinton,** H. R., The War in the Peninsula, London, 1878. — **Colección** de documentos inéditos para la historia de España por M. Fernandez Navarrete, et al., Madrid, 1842–1895, 112 vols.; vol. 30 contains an index of the volumes preceding. — **Colección** de documentos inéditos relativos al descubrimiento, conquista y colonizacion de las antiguas posesiones españolas de America y Oceanía, Madrid, 1864–1890, first series, 42 vols. Also Colección de documentos inéditos relativos al descubrimiento, conquista y organizacion de las antiguas posesiones españoles de Ultramar. Second series published by the Royal Academy of History, Madrid, 1885–1900, 13 vols. — **Colección** de libros españoles raros y curiosos, Madrid, 1871–1892. — **Colección** legislativa de España, Madrid, 1816 (in progress), 330 vols. — **Colmeiro, M.,** Reyes cristianos desde Alfonso VI hasta Alfonso XI, Madrid, 1893. — **Colmenares,** D. de, Historia de Segovia y compendio de la historia de Castilla, Segovia, 1637–1847. — **Conde,** J. A., Historia de la dominación de los Arabes en España, Madrid, 1820–1821, 3 vols.; English translation by Mrs. J. Foster, London, 1860, 3 vols.; History of the Dominion of the Arabs in Spain, London, 1854, 3 vols.

José Antonio Conde (1765–1820), was at one time regarded as the great authority on the history of the Spanish Arabs. He was educated at the University of Salamanca, a member of various learned societies, and for long *conservador* of the Escorial library. In 1814 he was exiled for political reasons and he died in great poverty. Modern students of the history of the Spanish Arabs have convicted Conde of many errors and faults of judgment, but it is acknowledged that he was a laborious scholar.

Coppée, H., History of the Conquest of Spain by the Arab Moors, Boston, 1881, 2 vols. — **Cos-Gayon,** F., Historia de la administración pública de España, Madrid, 1851. — **Coxe,** W., Memoirs of the Kings of Spain of the House of Bourbon, London, 1815, 5 vols. — **Crónica** de Don Alvaro de Luna, Milan, 1546, Madrid, 1784. — **Crónica** del rey Don Rodrigo, Alcalá, 1587. — **Curry,** J. L. M., Constitutional Government in Spain, New York, 1889. — **Cushing,** Caleb, Reminiscences of Spain, 1833, 2 vols. — **Custine,** M. de, L'Espagne sous Ferdinand VII, Paris, 1838, 4 vols.

Dahn, F., Die Könige der Germanen, Würzburg and Leipsic, 1861–1895. — **Danvila y Collado,** M., Historia del Reinado de Carlos III, Madrid, 1893–1896, 6 vols. — **Daumet,** G., Étude sur l'alliance de la France et de la Castille au XIVᵉ et au XVᵉ siècles, Paris, 1898. — **De Labra,** R. M., Historia de las relaciones internacionales de España, Madrid, 1897; La Crisis colonial en España, Madrid, 1902. — **De la Escosura y Hevia,** A., Inicio crítico del feudalismo en España, Madrid, 1856. — **Del Cantillo,** A., Tratados, convenios y declaraciones de paz y de comercio que han hecho cen las potencias extranjeras los monarcos españoles de la Casa de Bourbon, 1700–1842, Madrid, 1843. — **Desclot,** B., Crónica del rey En Pere in Chroniques étrangères relatives aux expéditions françaises pendant le XIIIᵉ siècle, Orleans, 1876.

Bernardo Desclot, one of the greatest of Catalan historians, lived in the reigns of James I and Pedro III of Aragon. Little is known of his life. He wrote the story of the events of his own day in the Catalan language, and prefixed the narrative by a short account of the counts of Barcelona and kings of Aragon preceding James I.

Desdevises du Degert, G., L'Espagne de l'ancien régime, Paris, 1897 (in progress, 2 vols. already published). — **Desormeaux,** J. L. R., Abrégé chronologique de l'histoire d'Espagne et de Portugal, 1758, 5 vols. — **Diercks,** G., Geschichte Spaniens, Berlin, 1895–1896, 2 vols. — **Dillon,** J. T., History of the Reign of Pedro the Cruel, 1788, 2 vols. — **Dochez,** and Paquis, A., Histoire d'Espagne et de Portugal, Paris, 1844–1848, 2 vols. — **Dormer,** D. J., Progresos de la historia en Aragon, Saragossa, 1680. — **Dozy,** R. P., Recherches sur l'histoire et la littérature de l'Espagne, Leyden, 1845, 1860, 1881, 2 vols.; Le Cid d'après de nouveaux documents, 1860; Histoire des Musulmans d'Espagne jusqu'à la conquête de l'Andalousie par les Almoravides, Leyden, 1861, 4 vols.

Reinhart Dozy, an eminent Dutch orientalist of French extraction was born in Leyden in 1820 and died there in 1883. He was an extraordinary linguist and wrote almost equally well in every European language beside being deeply versed in most of the Semitic languages but especially the Arabic. In 1850 he became professor in the University of Leyden. He was the first to shake the high reputation of the historian Condé by pointing out his numerous errors. Dozy's historical investigations were made in the archives of various countries, especially of course in Spain. He edited a number of the works of Arab writers with commentaries and glossaries and published a dictionary of the names of Arab garments.

Ducasse, Mémoires et correspondance politique du roi Joseph, Paris, 1853–1855, 10 vols. — **Du Hamel,** V., Historia constitucional de la monarquia española, translated from the French by B. A. y Espinosa, Madrid, 1848, 2 vols. — **Duncan,** F., The English in Spain; or, the Story of the War of Succession between 1834–1840, London, 1877. — **Dunham,** S. A., History of Spain and Portugal, London, 1832, 5 vols. — **Dunlop,** J., Memoirs of Spain during the reigns of Philip IV and Charles II, Edinburgh, 1834, 2 vols. — **Duran,** A., Romancero General, Madrid, 1857–1861. — **Duro,** C. F., La armada invincible, Madrid, 1884–1885, 2 vols.

Eckstein, F., Espagne, considérations sur son passé, son présent, son avenir, 1836. — **Elliot**, F. M., Old Court Life in Spain, London, 1893, 2 vols.; La España del siglo XIX, Madrid, 1885–1887, 3 vols. A series of historical lectures delivered in the Atheneum of Madrid. — **Everhard Nidart**, P. J., Varias obras correspondientes á la regencia de la reina Doña Maria Ana de Neoburg; sucesos de Don Juan de Austria (in Semanario Erudito), 1788.

Fabricius, A. K., La première invasion des Normands dans l'Espagne Musulmane en 844, Lisbon, 1892. — **Fernald**, J.'C., The Spaniard in History, New York, 1898. — **Fernan-Nuñez**, Conde de, Vida de Carlos III, published by A. Morel-Fatio and A. Paz y Melia, Madrid, 1898, 2 vols. — **Ferrer del Rio**, A., Exámen histórico crítico del reinado de Don Pedro de Castilla, 1850; Historia del reinado de Carlos III de España, Madrid, 1856, 4 vols. — **Ferreras**, J. de, Synopsis histórica cronológica de España, Madrid, 1775–1781, 17 vols. — **Field**, H. M., Old Spain and New Spain, London, 1888. — **Flórez**, Enrique, Memorias de las reynas católicas, historia genealógica de la casa real de Castilla y de Leon, Madrid, 1761, 1790, 2 vols.; España Sagrada teatro geográfico-histórico de la iglesia de España, Madrid, 1747, 51 vols.; Llave historial, Madrid, 1743, 1790; España carpetana, Medallas de las colonias, municipios y pueblos antiguos de España, Madrid, 1757.
    El Padre Enrique Flórez, historian, archæologist, theologian, and numismatist, was born at Valladolid in 1701, and entered the order of St. Augustine in his fifteenth year. His *España Sagrada* is the work most usefully consulted in studying the history and antiquities of Spain, containing, as it does, so many documents, notices and illustrations bearing on the subject, and greatly valued for the high critical faculty and scrupulous care exhibited by its author. Flórez left also works on theology and a treatise on botany and the natural sciences. He was corresponding member of the French Academy of inscriptions and *belles-lettres*, and enjoyed the friendship of many prominent men of his age. He died in 1773.
    Forneron, Histoire de Philippe II, Paris, 1881–1882, 4 vols. — **Forster**, J., Chronicle of James I, translated from the Catalan, London, 1883, 2 vols. — **Foulché-Delbosc**, R., Bibliographie des voyages en Espagne et en Portugal, Paris, 1896. — **Foy**, M. S., Histoire de la guerre de la péninsule sous Napoléon, Paris, 1827, 4 vols. — **Froissart**, John, Chroniques de France, d'Angleterre, d'Écosse, d'Espagne, de Bretagne, Paris, 1869–1888, 8 vols. (trans. T. Johnes, London, 1857, 2 vols.). — **Froude**, J. A., The Spanish Story of the Armada, 1892.

Gachard, L. P., Correspondance de Philippe II sur les affaires des Pays-Bas, Brussels, 1848–1879, 5 vols.; Retraite et mort de Charles Quint, 1854–1855; Don Carlos et Philippe II, Brussels, 1863, 1867, 2 vols.; Relations des Ambassadeurs Vénitiens sur Charles V et Philippe II.
    Louis Prosper Gachard, the Belgian historian, born at Paris in 1800, died at Brussels, 1885, was keeper of the Belgian archives, to which appointment he succeeded in 1826. Besides putting in order the existing archives he greatly added to the documents contained in them and caused researches to be made throughout Europe for papers which might throw light on Belgian history. His works are valued both for their impartial historical spirit and their literary style as well as for the fresh light they throw on the periods with which they deal.
    Gallenga, A., Iberian Reminiscences, 1883, 2 vols. — **Garcia**, J. C., Castilla y Leon durante los reinados de Pedro I, Enrique II, Juan I, Enrique III, Madrid, 1891. — **Gardiner**, S. R., Narrative of the Spanish Marriage Treaty, Spanish and English, London, 1859; Prince Charles and the Spanish Marriage, 1617–1623, London, 1869, 2 vols. — **Garibay y Zamalloa**, E., Los quarenta libros del compendio historial de las chrónicas y universal historia de España, Antwerp, 1571, Barcelona, 1628, 4 vols.
    Esteban de Garibay y Zamalloa (1525–1599) was appointed by Philip II as chronicler of his reign. He.was a laborious collector of historical information, who, though extremely credulous, served to some extent as a model to Mariana and other historians.
    Gayangos, P. de, History of the Mohammedan dynasties in Spain, London, 1840, 2 vols.; Historia de los reyes de Granada, Paris, 1842; Cartas del Cardinal Cisneros, Madrid, 1867; Cartas y relaciones de Hernan Cortes al emperador Carlos V, Paris, 1870. — **Gebhardt**, Historia general de España, Barcelona, 1897, 7 vols. — **Geddes**, M., Wars of the Commons of Castile in the reign of Charles V, 1730. — **George**, A., Memoirs of the Queens of Spain, London, 1850. — **Gibbon**, E., Decline and Fall of the Roman Empire, London, 1853. — **Giovio**, P., Historia sui temporis 1494–1547, Florence, 1548, 2 vols. — **Godoy**, M., Mémoires, Paris, 1839–1841, 6 vols.; partial translation, London, 1836, 2 vols. — **Gómez de Arteche y Moro**, J., Guerra de la independencia 1808–1814, Madrid, 1868–1883, 5 vols.; Historia del Reinado de Carlos IV, Madrid, 1893.
    General *José Gómez de Arteche y Moro* was born at Madrid in 1821 and entered the artillery in 1840. He took an active part in the events of July, 1856, siding with O'Donnell. He was under-secretary in the ministry of war in 1865 and 1868, and in 1878 became aide-de-camp to Alfonso XII. In 1885 he was elected senator for Guipuzcoa.

Gonsalez, T., Apuntamientos para la historia del rey Don Felipe Segundo por lo tocante á sus relaciones con la reina Isabel de Inglaterra. — **Grabinski**, J. de, Amédée de Savoie, duc d'Aoste, roi d'Espagne. — **Graetz**, H., Geschichte der Juden, Berlin and Leipsic, 1853–1870, 11 vols.; 1888–1889, 3 vols. — **Granvella**, Cardinal A. P., Papiers d'état du Cardinal Granvella in Collection des documents inédits sur l'histoire de France, Paris, 1841–1861, 9 vols.; Correspondance du Cardinal Granvella, 1565–1586, Brussels, 1878–1892, 9 vols. — **Guardia**, J. M., La cour de Rome et l'église d'Espagne. — **Guerra**, Caida y ruina del imperio visigótico, Madrid, 1883. — **Guizot**, F. P. G., Un projet de mariage royal, 1863. — **Guzman**, F. Perez de, Crónica del serenissimo principe, Don Juan II, Logroño, 1517, Valencia, 1779.

Häbler, Die wirtschaftliche Blüte Spaniens im 16. Jahrhundert, Berlin, 1888. — **Hale**, E. E. and S., The Story of Spain in Story of the Nations, New York, 1891. — **Harcourt**, Henri duc d', Avènement des Bourbons au trône d'Espagne, Paris, 1875, 2 vols. — **Hare**, A., Wanderings in Spain, London, 1873. — **Havemann**, W., Darstellungen aus der innern Geschichte Spaniens während des 15., 16., und 17. Jahrhunderts, Göttingen, 1850; Das Leben des Don Juan d'Austria, Gotha, 1865. — **Hefele**, K. J., Der Kardinal Ximenes und die kirchlichen Zustände Spaniens am Ende des 15. Jahrhunderts, Tübingen, 1851. — **Henningsen**, C. F., The most striking events of a twelvemonth's Campaign with Zumalacarregui, Philadelphia, 1836, 2 vols. — **Herrera y Tordesillas**, A. de, Historia general del mundo del tiempo del Señor Rey Don Felipe II, Madrid, 1601–1612, 3 vols.; Historia general de los hechos de los Castellanos en las islas y tierra firme del mar océano, Madrid, 1601–1615, 1728, 4 vols.; Tratado relacion y discurso histórico de los movimientos de Aragon.

Antonio de Herrera y Tordesillas lived from 1549 to 1625. He studied in Spain and Italy, where he attracted the attention of Vespasiano di Gonzaga, who being appointed viceroy of Navarre and Valencia, made Herrera his private secretary and afterwards recommended him to Philip II, with the result that Herrera was appointed chief chronicler for America and a chronicler for Castile. He fulfilled these offices during the reigns of the three Philips and acquired a European reputation for capacity and exactitude. The second of the works above mentioned is the chief of many. Part of it is merely a condensation of that of Las Casas, but for the events of his own time he is a most valuable authority, and he had the advantage of access to documents of all kinds.

Hidalgo, D., Diccionario general de bibliografía española, Madrid, 1864–1879, 6 vols. — **Hill**, C., Story of the Princess des Ursins (Orsini) in Spain, New York, 1899. — **Hinojosa**, Eduardo de, Historia de los Visigodos. — **Höfler**, Kaiser Karls (V) erstes Auftreten in Spanien, Vienna, 1874. — **Houghton**, A., Les Origines de la Restoration des Bourbons en Espagne. — **Howard**, O. O., Isabella of Castile, New York, 1894. — **Hubbard**, N. G., Histoire contemporaine de l'Espagne, Paris, 1869–1883, 6 vols. — **Huber**, V. A., Die Geschichte des Cid, Bremen, 1829; Chrónica del Cid, Marburg, 1844. — **Huegel**, C. W., Spanien und die Revolution, 1821. — **Huerta**, F. M., Sobre qual de los reyes godos fué y debe contarse primero de las de su nación en España in Academia de la historia, Memorias, 1796. — **Hughes**, T. M., Revelations of Spain in 1845, London, 1845, 2 vols. — **Hume**, M. A. S., Philip II of Spain, London, 1845, 2 vols.; Spain, its Greatness and Decay, Cambridge, 1897; Modern Spain, 1788–1898, London and New York, 1899, in Story of the Nations; The Spanish People, their Origin, Growth, and Influence, New York, 1901. — **Hurtado de Mendoza**, D., see Mendoza, D. Hurtado de.

Ibn Bassam, Zakira, Tesoro ó cualidades de los habitantes de la península. — **Idatius**, Chronicum (379 A.D.–469 A.D.) in the Chronica Medii Aevi of Rösler, Tübingen, 1798.

The chronicle of *Idatius* belongs to the fifth century. Its author was a bishop of Chaves in Portugal, and a native of Lamego, where he was born towards the close of the fourth century. The work is brief, but supplies information not to be found elsewhere.

Irving, W., Conquest of Granada, New York, 1850, 1880; Companions of Columbus, New York, 1880. — **Isidorus Hispalensis**, Historia Gotorum, Vandalorum et Suevorum, Madrid, 1599, in S. Isidori Hispalensis episcopi opera omnia, Rome, 1797–1803, 7 vols.

Isidorus Hispalensis or *Saint Isidore* of Seville was the son of a wealthy citizen of Cartagena, where he was born about 570 A.D. His brother, St. Leander, Archbishop of Seville, bestowed great pains on his education, but becoming jealous of his remarkable learning shut him up in a monastery. On Leander's death Isidore became bishop of Seville. He was regarded as the glory of his age for learning, and left numerous works which, besides the *Historia* and numerous ecclesiastical writings, include a kind of general encyclopædia of the science of the period, known as the *Origines*.

Isidorus Pacensis, Chronicon, in Flórez's España Sagrada.

Isidor Pacensis was bishop of Pax Julia, whence his surname of Pacensis. Pax Julia is identified with the Portuguese town of Beja. The prelate wrote in the eighth century. The names of three of his works have come down to us, but one of them only is extant and is a *chronicon* extending to the year 754 A.D.

Janer, F., Condición social de los Moriscoes de España causas de su expulsion y consecuencias que en el órden económico esta produjo, in Academia de la Historia, Madrid, 1857. — **Jiménez de Rada**, R., see Ximenes Toletanus, Rodericus. — **Joannes** Biclarensis, Chronicon, in Flórez's España Sagrada.

Joannes Biclarensis lived in the last half of the sixth century. His birthplace was Santarem, but he derived his surname from the Latin form of Valclara (in Catalonia), of which he was abbot. He afterwards became bishop of Gerona. His *Chronicon* continues that of Idatius down to the year 590.

Jones, Sir J. T., Journals of sieges carried on under the Duke of Wellington in Spain, London, 1846, 3 vols. — **Jordanes**, De Origine Gothorum, Augsburg, 1515, Venice, 1729. — **Julian**, St., Historia Regis Wambæ in Florez's España Sagrada. — **Junta**, P. de, and J. B. Varesio (editors), Chrónica del famoso cavallero Cid Ruy Diez Campeador, 1593.

Kaemmel, O., Illustrierte Weltgeschichte, Darmstadt, 1890, 10 vols. — **Kayserling**, M., Geschichte der Juden in Spanien und Portugal, Berlin, 1861–1867, 2 vols.

La Fuente, V. de, Juana la loca vindicada de la nota de herejia. — **Lafuente y Alcántara**, M., Historia de Granada. — **Lafuente y Zamálloa**, M., Historia general de España, Madrid, 1795, 1854.

Modesto Lafuente y Zamálloa (1806–1866) took his degree of bachelor of theology at the university of Valladolid in 1832, and afterwards successively filled chairs of philosophy, rhetoric, and theology. In 1837 he removed to Madrid, where he published a periodical entitled *Fray Gerundio*, through which he attacked existing abuses, advocated reforms, and set himself against the Carlist wars. This publication soon attained a wide circulation, and was continued till 1849, after which Lafuente turned his attention to his *Historia*. He subsequently became a deputy to the cortes for Astorga, and in 1860 member of the council of state. He was also a member of various academies.

Landau, M., Geschichte Kaiser Karls VI als König von Spanien, Stuttgart, 1889. — **Lane-Poole**, S., and **A. Gilman**, The Story of the Moors in Spain (Story of the Nations), New York, 1891. — **Las Casas**, see Casas. — **Lathbury**, T., The Spanish Armada, London, 1840. — **Latimer**, E. W., Spain in the Nineteenth Century, Chicago, 1897. — **Latour**, A. T. de, L'Espagne religieuse et littéraire, Paris, 1862. — **Laughton**, J. K., State Papers relating to the Defeat of the Spanish Armada, London, 1894, 2 vols. — **Lauser**, W., Geschichte Spaniens vom Sturze Isabellas bis zur Thronbesteigung Alfonsos, Leipsic, 1877, 2 vols. — **Lavigne**, G. de L'Espagne et le Portugal, 1855. — **Lawrence**, E., Dominic, and the Inquisition, in Historical Studies, New York, 1873. — **Lea**, H. C., Chapters from the religious history of Spain connected with the Inquisition, Philadelphia, 1890. — **Legrelle**, A., La diplomatie française et la succession d'Espagne, 1659–1725, Paris, 1888–1892, 4 vols. — **Lembke**, F. W., and **Schäfer**, H., Geschichte von Spanien, Gotha, 1831–1890, 5 vols. — **Lemos**, D. A., Historia general de Portugal, 1715–1789. — **Leopold**, Spaniens Bürgerkrieg, Hanover, 1876. — **Lezo del Pozo**, J., Apologia del rey Don Pedro de Castilla conforme á la Crónica de Ayala. — **Limborch**, P. van, Historia Inquisitions, Amsterdam, 1692; History of the Inquisition (abridged), London, 1816.

Philip van Limborch, a prominent Dutch theologian, was born in 1633 and died in 1712. He was professor of theology at the seminary of the remonstrants in Amsterdam. His *Historia* consists of a record of sentences given by the Inquisition of Toulouse, and is preceded by an account of the origin and methods of the Inquisition.

Llorente, J. A., Opinion de l'Espagne sur l'inquisition, 1812; Mémoires pour servir à l'histoire de la révolution d'Espagne, Paris, 1817, 3 vols.; Histoire critique de l'inquisition d'Espagne, Paris, 1817–1818, 4 vols.; History of the Inquisition of Spain (abridged), London, 1827.

Juan Antonio Llorente, born 1756, was a Spanish priest who became general secretary to the inquisition in 1789. A scheme for the reform of that tribunal which he drew up was about to be executed when the fall of the liberal minister Jovellanos prevented its realisation. In the war with France Llorente sided with the Bonapartists and became a member of the council of state of King Joseph. On the abolition of the inquisition (1809) Llorente was commissioned to investigate its archives and write its history. Thus he had access to materials now no longer in existence. On the restoration of the Bourbons Llorente was banished, and it was while in exile at Paris that his celebrated *Histoire critique de l'Inquisition* appeared in French and was soon translated into German, English, Dutch, Italian and Spanish. Its success was great, but it drew down a persecution of the author who on the publication of a book called *Portraits politiques des papes* (1822) was ordered to quit France. He died from the effects of the hurried journey to Madrid.

Londonderry, Marquis of, see Stewart. — **Lorenzana**, **Cardinal**, Collectio Sanctorum Patrum ecclesiæ Toledanæ, Madrid, 1782–1793. — **Louville**, C. A. d'A., Mémoires secrets sur l'établissement de la maison de Bourbon en Espagne, 1818. — **Lowell**, J. R., Impressions of Spain. — **Lucas Tudensis**, Chronicon Mundi, in Schott's Hispaniæ Illustratæ, Frankfort, 1608.

Lucas de Tuy, or *Lucas Tudensis*, was a Spanish prelate who died in 1288. His *Chronicon*, which was finished in 1236, was written by command of the great queen Berengaria. It consists of four books: the first contains the *Six Ages of the World* of St. Isidore, with additions; the second, Isidore's treatise on the origin of the Goths, Spaniards, and Suevi; the third, the spurious chronicle of San Ildefonso and St. Julian's history. The fourth extends from the time of Pelayo to the conquest of Cordova. When the work was translated into Spanish, in the end of the thirteenth or beginning of the fourteenth century, a continuation extending to 1252 was added.

Luna, M. de, La verdadera historia del rey Don Rodrigo, Valencia, 1606.

Miguel de Luna was a Morisco who embraced Catholicism and became interpreter to Philip II. His history purports to be a translation from an Arab chronicler of the eighth century, but was really based on old romances and has no authoritative value.

MacCrie, T., History of the Progress and Suppression of the Reformation in Spain in the Sixteenth Century, 1829. — **Mahon, Lord**, see Stanhope, P. H. — **Maistre**, J. de, Lettres à un gentilhomme Russe sur l'inquisition espagnole, 1837. — **Maldonado**, J. M., Historia de la revolución de España, Madrid, 1833, 2 vols. — **Malo de Molina**, M., Rodrigo el Campeador, Estudio histórico, Madrid, 1857. — **Malvezzi**, V., Sucesos principales de la monarquía de España en el tiempo de Felipe IV, Madrid, 1640. — **Mariana**, Juan de, Historia general de España, Valencia, 1783–1796, 9 vols.; in Biblioteca de autores españoles, Madrid, 1854, published in various later editions; English translation by J. S. Stephens, London, 1699.

Juan de Mariana, one of the most famous of Spanish historians, was born near Talavera in 1536, and in 1554 became a member of the Society of Jesus. Two years later he went to Rome, where he filled a chair in the Jesuit college. After visiting Sicily and lecturing on theology at Paris during five years, he returned to Spain in 1574 and devoted himself to his *Historia de España*, which was first written in Latin and then translated by himself into the Castilian tongue. The variety of his talents and acquirements is exhibited in his writings on philosophy, politics, finance, and religion, and in the last mentioned the freedom of his opinions exposed him to some suspicion from his order, and he was even brought before the inquisition. His history has enjoyed immense popularity and is still much admired, though it is acknowledged that he often confuses fact and fable.

Marineo, Lucio, Obra de las cosas memorables de España, Alcalá, 1533. — **Marliani**, M. de, Histoire politique de l'Espagne moderne, Paris, 1840, 2 vols. — **Marmol Carvajal**, L. del, Historia del rebelión y castigo de los Moriscos del reyno de Granada, Madrid, 1600, and in Biblioteca de autores Españoles.

Luis del Marmol Carvajal was a native of Granada who flourished in the sixteenth century. In 1535 he accompanied Charles V to Tunis. He was captured by the Moors, and both during and after his captivity made long journeys and voyages in and about Barbary and Egypt. His *Historia del rebelión* is the narrative of an eye-witness, and the language is pure though the style suffers from the too great length of the sentences.

Martínez de la Rosa, F., Hernan Perez del Pulgar, Madrid, 1834. — **Martínez Marina**, F., Teoria de las Cortes de Leon y Castilla, Madrid, 1821, 3 vols.; Ensayo histórico-crítico sobre la antigua legislación y principales cuerpos legales de los reynos de Leon y Castilla, Madrid, 1834, 2 vols. — **Masdeu**, J. F., Historia crítica de España, Madrid, 1783–1805, 20 vols.

Juan Francisco Masdeu, a celebrated Spanish historian, was born in 1744 and died in 1817. Educated under the care of the Jesuits, he entered their order in 1759, and on their expulsion from Spain retired to Ferrara. His *Historia* was commenced in 1781. It extends only down to the end of the eleventh century. It is a work of much learning and destroys many fables previously current, though in many instances the author carries his scepticism too far.

Mas-La Trie, J. M., Trésor de chronologie, d'histoire et de géographie, 1837. — **Mazade**, C. de, l'Espagne moderne, Paris, 1855; Les revolutions de l'Espagne contemporaine, 1868. — **Medina**, J. T., Historia del tribunal del Santo Oficio de la inquisición de Cartagena de las Indias, Santiago, 1899. — **Melo**, F. M., Historia de los movimientos separación y guerra de Cataluña en tiempo de Felipe IV, Lisbon, 1645, Paris, 1840. — **Mendoza**, D. Hurtado de, Guerra de Granada hecha por el rey Felipe II, Madrid, 1610, 1852.

Diego Hurtado de Mendoza belonged to an illustrious Spanish family and was born in Granada about 1503. His earliest teacher was the celebrated Peter Martyr of Angleria (Pietro Martire d'Anghiera). He served in the Italian wars and was employed by Charles V in various important diplomatic missions. Having displeased Philip II he was compelled to retire to Granada. He was already pre-eminent for his learning and had taken advantage of his position as ambassador to the Grand Turk to make a valuable collection of manuscripts which he presented to Philip II for the Escorial library. When no longer permitted to engage in affairs of state he devoted himself to literary works which include poems and translations from Aristotle. For collecting information for his *Guerra de Granada* he had the advantage of residence on the spot and a knowledge of the inner workings of the government. The book also ranks high for its literary style.

Menéndez y Pelayo, M., Historia de los Heterodoxos españoles, Madrid, 1880.

Marcellino Menéndez y Pelayo, a contemporary literary critic, historian, and philosopher, born in 1856, and noted for his prodigious memory. His work exhibits a decided tendency to ultramontanism, and he has written in defence of the Inquisition. His talents were early developed and he had already a scholar's reputation before he was out of his teens. At 21 he was appointed to the chair of critical history of Spanish Literature of the Faculty of philosophy and letters at Madrid. In 1880 he became a member of the Spanish Academy of Language, in 1882 of that of History, and afterwards of those of moral sciences, of politics, and of the fine arts. Since then he has become director of the national library in Madrid, and of the entire system of public archives, museums, and libraries in Spain.

Mérimée, P., Histoire de Don Pèdre I, Paris, 1865; Translation 1849. — **Mignet**, F. A. M., Négociations relatives à la succession d'Espagne sous Louis XIV, Paris, 1835–1842, 4 vols.; Antonio Perez et Philippe II, Paris, 1845; Translation, London, 1846; Charles Quint, son abdication, son séjour et sa mort au monastère de Yuste, Paris, 1854; Rivalité de François I et de Charles Quint, Paris, 1875, 2 vols.

François Auguste Marie Mignet, the French historian, was born in 1796 at Aix where he subsequently studied for the law. In the earlier part of his career he made a reputation as a liberal journalist and was associated with the *National*, but after 1830 he devoted himself wholly to history. Here his studies were by no means confined to Spanish subjects, his chief work being a history of the French Revolution.

Mingote y Taragona, P., Geografia de España y sus Colonias, Leon, 1887. — **Minutoli**, J. M. von, Spanien und seine fortschreitende Entwickelung, Berlin, 1852. — **Miraflores**, Marques de, Apuntes histórico-críticos para escribir la historia de la revolución de España desde el año 1820–1823 [Madrid], 1834; Memorias para escribir la historia de los siete primeros años del reinado de Isabel II, Madrid, 1843–1844, 2 vols.; Continuación de las memorias del reinado de Isabel II. — **Miro**, M. J., Las Constituciones de España, Madrid, 1821, 2 vols. — **Modoz**, P., Diccennario geográfico-estadístico-histórico de España y sus posesiones de Ultramar, Madrid, 1848–1850, 11 vols. — **Moncada**, F. de, Conde de Osuna, Expedición de los Catalanes y Aragoneses contra Griegos y Turcos, Barcelona, 1623, 1842; Madrid, 1883.

Francisco de Moncada, Conde de Usuna, a member of an old Catalan family, was born in 1586 and died in 1635. He filled various important public offices as councillor of war, governor of Flanders, and ambassador to the emperor Ferdinand II. In the low countries he twice defeated the Prince of Orange. His *Expedición de catalanes y aragoneses* is an account of the expedition under Roger de Flor (died 1305) on behalf of the Byzantines. He derived his materials from Zurita and Muntaner, the latter a contemporary of Flor. Many of the adventures described appear quite incredible. The language is pure and the style flowing.

Mondejar, G. I., Marques de, Memorias históricas del rei Alonso el Sabio, Madrid, 1777. — **Monresa Sanchez**, J. Mª., Historia legal de España desde la dominacion goda hasta nuestros dias, Madrid, 1841, 2 vols. — **Montejo**, B., Sobre la independencia de Castilla, in Memorias de la Real Academia de la Historia. — **Montesa y Manrique**, Historia de la legislación de España, Madrid, 1861, 1864, 7 vols. — **Morales**, A. de, Crónica General de España, Alcalá, 1574–1577, Madrid, 1791; Opusculos Castellanos, Madrid, 1793, 3 vols.

Ambrosio de Morales (1513–1591) was appointed in 1574 chronicler of the kingdoms of Castile and continued the *Crónica general de España* of Florián de Ocampo. His work lacks arrangement.

Morel-Fatio, A., l'Espagne au XVI et XVII siècle, Paris, 1878; Études sur l'Espagne, Paris, 1890–1895, 2 vols.; Catalogue des manuscrits espagnoles du Bibliothèque National, Paris, 1881. — **Morel**, J., Lettres sur l'inquisition. — **Motley**, J. L., The Rise of the Dutch Republic, London, 1856, 1889, 3 vols. — **Moüy**, C. de, Don Carlos et Philippe II, Paris, 1888; Jeanne la Folle (Revue des deux Mondes). — **Müller**, W., Politische Geschichte der neuesten Zeit, 1876–1890, Stuttgart, 1890. — **Muñoz Maldonado**, J., Historia de la guerra de la independencia de España contra Napoléon Bonaparte desde 1808 á 1814, Madrid, 1833, 3 vols.

José Muñoz Maldonado (1807–1875) was fiscal minister in the Royal Council of the Orders during ten years Under Isabella II he was several times elected deputy for Guadalajara, Jaén and Ciudad Real, and afterwards became senator, but was more distinguished as a jurisconsult and as a writer, though rather industrious than brilliant.

Muñoz y Romero, Diccionario bibliográfico histórico, Madrid, 1865 — **Muntaner**, R., Chrónica del rey Don Jaume primer, Rey D Arago e de molts de sos descendents, Valencia, 1558, Stuttgart, 1844.

Ramón Muntaner is the rival of Bernardo Desclot as chief of Catalan historians. He lived in the reign of James I of Aragon and took part in the expedition of the company or army which Roger de Flor led against both Turks and Greeks and in other military enterprises. His chronicle therefore describes events in which he himself shared. He was still alive in 1330.

Muriel, A., Historia de Carlos IV, Madrid, 1894–1895, 6 vols.; Constitutes, vols. 29–34 of the Memorial-historico-español, published by the Real Academia de la Historia.

Napier, W. F. P., History of the War in the Peninsula, 1807–1814, London, 1828–1840, 6 vols., 1890. — **Navarrete,** M. Fernandez de, Colección de documentos inéditos para la historia de España, Madrid, 1842, etc. — **Nervo,** G., Baron de, Histoire d'Espagne, Paris, 1870, 4 vols.; Isabelle la catholique reine d'Espagne, Paris, 1874; Translation by T. Temple West, London, 1897. — **Norman,** W. W., Philip II king of Spain, with an account of the condition of Spain, the Netherlands and the American colonies in Historical Studies, New York, 1898. — **Novissima** Recapilación de los leges de España, Paris, 1846, 5 vols. — **Nueva** Coleccion de documentos inéditos para la historia de España y de sus Indias, edited by F. de Zabalburu and others, Madrid, 1892 ff., 6 vols. — **Nuñez de Castro,** A., Corónica Góthica, Castillana y Austriaca, Madrid, 1789–1790, 7 vols.

Ober, F. A., History for young readers; Spain, New York, 1899. — **Ocampo,** F. de, Los cincos libros primeros de la crónica general de España, Zamora, 1541.

Florián de Ocampo, whose life covers the period between 1513 and 1590, was commissioned by Charles V to write the general chronicle of Spain, but as he commenced with the time of the flood he only managed to bring it down to the time of the Scipios. In spite of much credulity and an unpleasing style the book has been much esteemed by antiquarians. Together with the works of Morales and Sandoval it was published at Madrid in 1791, under the title of *Corónica General de España.*

Olivart, Marques de, Coleccion de los tratados . . . internacionales celebrados per nuestros gobiernos con los estados extranjeros, desde el reinado de Doña Isabel II, Madrid, 1890 ff., 10 vols. — **Oman,** C. W. C., History of the Peninsular War, London, 1901, 2 vols. (work not completed). — **Ortiz y Sanz,** J., Compendio cronológico de la historia de España, Madrid, 1795–1803, 7 vols. — **Oviedo y Valdes,** G. Fernandez de, Quinquagenas, in Real Academia de la Historia, Madrid, 1880.

Palacios, Cura de los, see **Bernáldez.** — **Paquis,** A., and Dochez, Histoire d'Espagne et de Portugal, Paris, 1844–1848, 2 vols. — **Parmele,** M. P., A Short History of Spain, New York, 1898. — **Pellicer de Ossav y Tovar,** J., Annales de la monarquía de España después de su pérdida, Madrid, 1681. — **Pérez del Pulgar,** Hernán, Breve parte de las hazañas del Gran Capitán, printed as Brevo sumario de los hechos del Gran Capitán, Seville, 1527, Madrid, 1834. — **Pérez Pujol,** E., Historia de los instituciones de la España goda. — **Perez y Lopez,** A. X., Teatro de la legislacion universal de España é Indias, Madrid, 1791, 28 vols. — **Philippson,** M., Heinrich IV und Philipp III, Berlin, 1870–1876, 3 vols.; Ein Ministerium unter Philipp II. Kardinal Granvella am spanischem Hofe 1579–1586, Berlin, 1894. — **Pichot,** A., Chronique de Charles Quint, 1853. — **Pidal,** P. J., marques de, Historia de las alteraciones de Aragon en el reinado de Felipe II, 1862–1863, 3 vols.

Pedro José Pidal (1800–1865), distinguished both in literature and in politics, studied law and philosophy at Oviedo. The activity with which he supported the liberal party, 1820–1824, caused him to be condemned to imprisonment in the reaction of 1824, but he escaped his sentence, and in 1828 was pardoned. In 1838 he was elected to the cortes where he was distinguished for his oratory. Successively president of the congress, minister of the interior and of justice, he was active in reforming the administration and in 1851 was instrumental in bringing about an understanding between the Spanish and Papal courts. He left numerous works on jurisprudence, language, and literature.

Pirala, A., Anales de la guerra civil, 1853; Historia de la guerra civil y de los partidos liberal y carlista (with an account of Espartero's regency), Madrid, 1890, 3 vols.; Historia contemporánea, Madrid, 1875–1880; 1893–1895, 6 vols.; El rey en Madrid y en provincias, 1871.

Antonio Pirala, a contemporary historian, born 1824. He filled various minor offices in the administration and was secretary to King Amadeo. His writings include contributions to various large publications as well as some insignificant ones on religious subjects; but the most important are those historical works mentioned above.

Plummer, M. W., Contemporary Spain as shown by her novelists, New York, 1899. — **Polybius,** General History, London, 1693, 2 vols. — **Pradt,** D. D., Mémoires historiques sur la révolution d'Espagne, Paris, 1816. — **Prescott,** W. H., History of Ferdinand and Isabella, Boston and London, 1838, 1889; History of the Reign of Philip II, Boston and London, 1855–1858, 3 vols.

William Hickling Prescott was born in Salem, Massachusetts, in 1796.   He was educated at Harvard College and in 1814 began to study for the law, but an accident having affected his sight he was temporarily obliged to give up all work, and was never again able to use his eyes for long at a time.   He devoted himself to the study of history and literature, having books read aloud to him.   George Ticknor was the first to direct his attention to Spanish history which attracted him as an unexplored as well as rich field.   For the composition of his *Ferdinand and Isabella* he had collected a great number of original documents and its publication brought him immediate fame, not only in America and England, but in the greater part of Europe.   Continuing his labours he produced the *Conquest of Mexico*, the *Conquest of Peru*, and two volumes of a history of Philip II and revised Robertson's Charles V.   He died in 1859, before the publication of the third volume of Philip II.

Procopius, De Bello Gothico, Augsburg, 1676; Translation by H. Holcroft, London, 1863. — **Pulgar**, Fernando del, Crónica de los reyes católicos Don Ferdinando y Doña Isabel, Saragossa, 1567, Valencia, 1780; Los Claros varones de España y las treinta y dos cartas, Madrid, 1775. — **Puyol y Alonso**, J., La vida política en España, Madrid, 1892.

Quintana, M. J., vidas de españoles célebres, Madrid, 1807–1834, 3 vols.

Ramiro II, Ilustración del reynado de Ramiro II de Aragon, in Academia de la historia, Memorias. — **Raynal**, G. T. F., Histoire des établissements et du commerce des Européens dans les deux Indes, Paris, 1771, 4 vols. — **Real Academia de la Historia**, Memorias, Madrid, 1796–1888; Memorial histórico español: Colección de documentos, opúsculos y antigüedades, Madrid, 1851–1898; Catálogo de las obras publicadas por la Real Academia, Madrid, 1901. — **Reynald**, H., Histoire d'Espagne depuis la mort de Charles III, Paris, 1882. — **Rico y Amat**, Historia política e parlamentaria de España, Madrid, 1860–1862, 3 vols. — **Ríos**, J. Amador de los, Los Judíos en España, Madrid, 1792; Las razas históricas de la península Iberica; Historia Crítica de la literatura española, Madrid, 1861–1865, 7 vols.

José Amador de los Ríos (1818–1878) was educated at Cordova and afterwards at San Isidro de Madrid, during which time he supported his whole family by painting.   He afterwards distinguished himself at the university of Seville.   His *Estudios sobre los judíos de España*, published 1848, won him admission into the Academia de la Historia, and also the appointment to the chair of critical history of literature at the Universidad Central.   Besides his historical works he wrote on architecture and on Spanish literature and published some volumes of poems.

Risco, R. P. M., La Castilla y el mas famoso Castellano, Madrid, 1792, 3 vols.; Gesta Roderici Campidocti. — **Robertson**, W., History of the reign of Charles V, London, 1769, 1856.

William Robertson, a Scotch minister and the son of a Scotch minister was born at Borthwick, Midlothian, in 1721.   He attained considerable eminence in the Scotch church as leader of the "moderate" party.   His first historical work, *The History of Scotland*, was published in 1758, when he at once became famous.   In 1759 he was appointed chaplain of Stirling Castle, in 1762 principal of Edinburgh University, and in 1764 king's historiographer.   His *History of Charles V* appeared in 1769.   It is his greatest work, the fruit of a careful study of that monarch's reign, and was a standard book; but its value is now greatly diminished owing to the fact that Robertson had not access to many sources of information which are open to modern research.

Rocca, A. J. N. de, Mémoires sur la guerre des Français en Espagne, Paris, 1814, 1815. — **Rodriguez Villa**, A., La reina Doña Juana la loca, Madrid, 1892. — **Romey**, C., Histoire d'Espagne, Paris, 1839–1850, 9 vols. — **Rose**, H. J., Among the Spanish People, London, 1877, 2 vols. — **Rosell**, C., Crónicas de los reyes de Castilla, in continuation of Mariana, in Biblioteca de autores, españoles, Madrid, 1875–1878. — **Rosseeuw Saint-Hilaire**, N., Histoire d'Espagne jusqu'à la mort de Ferdinand VII, Paris, 1844–1879, 14 vols. — **Rousset de Missy**, J., Histoire publique et secrète de la cour de Madrid depuis l'avènement du roi Philippe, 1719. — **Rule**, W. H., History of the Inquisition, London, 1874, 2 vols.

Saavedra y Fajardo, D. F. de, Corona gótica Castellana y Austriaca, in Biblioteca de autores españoles, Madrid, 1853. — **Sainz de Baranda**, P., Clave de la España Sagrada, 1853. — **Sala**, G., Epitome de los principios y progresos de las guerras de Cataluña, 1640–1641. — **Salazar y Mendoza**, P. de, Monarquía de España; Orígen de las dignidades reglares de Castilla y Leon, 1618. — **Salmon**, P., La revolución de España de 1808. — **Sampire Astoricensis**, continuation of *Chronicon* of Sebastianus Salmanticensis in Flórez's España Sagrada. — **Sanchez**, T. A., and others, Cantares del Cid Campeador conocidos con el nombre de poema del Cid, 1864. — **Sanchez de Toca**, J., Del poder naval en España, Madrid, 1898. — **Sandoval**, P. de, Historia de la vida y hechos del emperador Carlos V, Valladolid, 1604–1606; translated by John Stevens, London, 1703.   Historia de los reyes de Castilla y de Leon, Pamplona, 1615, Madrid, 1792. — **San Felipe**, Marques de, see Bacallar y Sanna. —

San Miguel, E., duque de, Relation de l'expédition de Riego. — **Schäfer**, see Lembke and Schäfer. — **Schirrmacher**, F. W., Geschichte von Spanien, Gotha, 1881–1902, 7 vols. — **Schlagintweit**, E. S., Der spanisch-marokkanische Krieg in den Jahren 1859–1860, Leipsic, 1863. — **Schott**, A., Hispania illustrata, Frankfort, 1603–1608. — **Schurtz**, H., Die pyrenäische Halbinsel in *Helmolt's Weltgeschichte*, Leipsic and Vienna, 1900. — **Sebastianus Salmanticensis**, Chronicon Regum Legionensium, in Flórez's España Sagrada.

Sebastian was bishop of Salamanca (whence the epithet, Salmanticensis) in the ninth century. He wrote his chronicle by command of Alfonso III, whose reign is the last described in it. It begins with the history of the Gothic king Recesuinto (reigned 649–672 A.D.) and is the chief authority for the rise of the kingdom of Asturias.

Sédillot, L. A., Histoire générale des Arabes, Paris, 1854. — **Sève**, E., La situation économique de l'Espagne, Paris, 1887. — **Shaw**, Sir Charles, Personal memoirs and correspondence . . . comprising a narrative of the war for constitutional liberty in Portugal and Spain, London, 1837, 2 vols. — **Siguenza**, J. de, Historia de la orden de San Gerónimo, Madrid, 1600. — **Silos**, Monk of (Monachus Silensis) in Flórez's España Sagrada.

The Monk of Silos was admitted to that convent in the latter half of the eleventh century. His real name is unknown. The Chronicle which he wrote in Latin began with a short account of the ancestors of Alfonso VI, followed by a history of that sovereign's reign, but the part relating to Alfonso VI is lost. The fragment which remains is highly valued as the work of a careful writer who had access to many ancient and authentic documents. St. Isidore of Seville, Sebastian of Salamanca, and Sampiro are his guides for the earlier portion.

Sismondi, J. C. L., De la littérature du midi de l'Europe, Paris, 1813–1829, 4 vols.; Translation by Roscoe, London, 1848, 2 vols. — **Sociedad de bibliófilos españoles**, Madrid. — **Somerville**, A., A Narrative of the British Auxiliary Legion with Incidents of the War in Spain, Glasgow, 1837. — **Southey**, R., Chronicle of the Cid, 1808, Lowell, 1846; History of the Peninsular War, 1823–1832, 6 vols. — **Stanhope**, P. H., The Court of Spain under Charles II, London, 1844; War of the Succession in Spain, 1850. — **Stewart**, C. W., marquis of Londonderry, Story of the Peninsular War, London, 1813, 1869. — **Stirling-Maxwell**, W., The Cloister Life of the Emperor Charles V, London, 1852; Don John of Austria, London, 1883. — **Strada**, F., De Bello Belgico ab excessu Carli V, Rome, 1632, Ratisbon, 1754. — **Strobel**, E. H., The Spanish Revolution, 1868–1875, Boston, 1898. — **Suchet**, L. G., duc d'Albuféra, Mémoires sur les campagnes en Espagne depuis 1808 jusqu'en 1814, Paris, 1834, 2 vols.; Translation, London, 1829. — **Symonds**, J. A., Renaissance in Italy, Catholic Reaction, London, 1886, 2 vols.; Renaissance in Italy, Italian Literature, London, 1882, 2 vols.

Tapia, E. de, Historia de la civilización española, Madrid, 1840, 4 vols. — **Ternaux-Compans**, H., Les Comuneros, Paris, 1834. — **Tessé**, J. B. R. de F., comte de, Mémoires, Paris, 1806, 2 vols. — **Ticknor**, G., History of Spanish Literature, New York, 1849; London, 1855, 3 vols.; 1872; Spanish translation by Gayangos and Vedia, Madrid, 1851–1856; German translation by Gelius, Leipsic, 1852–1867. — **Toreno**, J. M. Q., conde de, Historia del levantamiento, guerra y revolución de España, Madrid, 1835, 5 vols.; Madrid, 1872. — **Torquemada**, T. de, and others, Copilacion de las instrucciones del oficio de la sancta inquisición, 1576. — **Turba**, Über den Zug Kaiser Karls V gegen Algier, Vienna, 1890.

Ulloa, M. de, Disertación sobre el orígen y patria de los godos; sobre el principio de la monarquía goda en España, in Academia de la historia, Memorias, 1797.

Valladares de Sotomayor, A., Vida interior del rey Don Felipe II, 1788. — **Valles**, Baron de los, The Career of Don Carlos, London, 1835. — **Valras**, comte de, Don Carlos VII et l'Espagne Carliste 1872–1876, Paris, 1876, 2 vols. — **Varillas**, A., Politique de Ferdinand. — **Vault**, F. E. de, Mémoires militaires relatifs à la succession d'Espagne sous Louis XIV, Paris, 1835–1862, 11 vols. — **Vera Figueroa y Zuñiga**, A. de, Conde de la Roca, El rei Don Pedro defendido, Madrid, 1648. — **Viardot**, L., Histoire des Arabes et des Mores d'Espagne, Paris, 1851, 2 vols. — **Viollet**, A., Histoire des Bourbons en Espagne, 1843. — **Voiture**, V., Voyage d'Espagne. — **Vollmöller**, K., Poema del Cid, Halle, 1879. — **Vuillier**, Les Îles Oubliées (Balearic Isles), Paris, 1893 (trans. London, 1896).

Wallis, S. T., Spain : her institutions, politics and public men, Boston, 1853. — **Walton**, W., The Revolutions of Spain, 1808–1836, London, 1837, 2 vols. — **Watson**, R., History of the reign of Philip II, London, 1777, 1839; History of the Reign of Philip III, London, 1783, 1786, 2 vols. — **Watts**, H. E., The Christian Recovery of Spain, New York, 1894; Spain, from the Moorish Conquest to the Fall of Granada, London and New York, 1897. — **Weber**, G., Allgemeine Weltgeschichte, Leipsic, 1857–1880, 1882–1890, 15 vols. — **Weiss**, C., L'Espagne depuis le règne de Philippe II jusqu' à l'avènement des Bourbons, 1844, 2 vols. —

Whitehouse, H. R., The Sacrifice of a Throne, Life of Amadeus, Duke of Aosta, sometime King of Spain, New York, 1897. — **Wellesley**, Richard C., Marquis of, Despatches and correspondence . . . during his . . . mission to Spain . . . in 1809, edited by Montgomery Martin, London, 1838. — **Wilkens**, Geschichte des spanischen Protestantismus im 16 Jahrhundert, Gütersloh, 1887. — **Williams**, L., Lendenand, The Land of the Dons, New York, 1898. — **Wilson**, The Downfall of Spain: Naval History of the Spanish-American War, London, 1899. — **Wolf**, F., Additions to Julius' German Translation of Ticknor's History of Spanish Literature, Leipsic, 1852–1867. — **Wright**, W., On the Authorities for the History of the Dominion of the Arabs in Spain. — **Wulsa**, Chronica Regum Gothorum.

Ximenes Toletanus, Rodericus, Chronica Rerum in Hispania Gestarum, published as Crónica de España del Arzobispo Don Rodrigo Jiménez de Rada in Colección de documentos inéditos para la historia de España, vol. CV, Madrid, 1893.
  Rodrigo Jiménez de Rada was a warlike Spanish prelate born in Navarre about 1170. In 1210 he became archbishop of Toledo, in which capacity he took an active part in the crusades against the Moors and especially distinguished himself at the great battle of Las Navas de Tolosa. As a statesman he was also eminent in the days of Ferdinand III, especially exercising the chief influence in Castilian affairs. Notwithstanding he found time to earn a great reputation for learning. The work known as the *Chronica rerum in Hispania Gestarum* was called by himself *Historia Gothica*. Rodrigo died in 1247.

Yriarte, C., Les Tableaux de la guerre, 1870.

Zamora y Caballero, D. E., Historia general de España y de sus posesiones de Ultramar, Madrid, 1873–1874, 6 vols. — **Zurita y Castro**, Gerónimo de, Anales de la Corona de Aragon, Saragossa, 1562–1604, 1610–1621.
  Gerónimo Zurita y Castro belonged to a noble Castilian family, and was born in 1512. He was employed by the Inquisitor General on important missions and through his influence was appointed first chronicler of the kingdom of Aragon (1548). He visited Sicily, Naples, and Rome in search of material for his work. On his return he was commissioned by Philip II to put in order the documents in the archives at Simancas. He devoted thirty years to the composition of his *Anales*. The work covers the period from the Mussulman invasion to 1510, and gives an accurate picture of the development of the constitution of Aragon. Zurita is accused of being stiff and formal in style and too diffuse, but on the other hand his work is noted for impartiality of judgment and for scholarship.

A GENERAL BIBLIOGRAPHY OF PORTUGUESE HISTORY

BASED ON THE WORKS QUOTED, CITED, OR CONSULTED

Academia Real Das Sciencias, Collecção dos Principæs auctores da Historia Portugueza, Lisbon, 1806, etc., 8 vols.; Historia Portugueza, Collecção de Noticias para a Historia e geografia das Naçoes ultramarinas, Lisbon, 1812–1856, 7 vols. — **Acenheiro**, C. R., Chronicon dos Reis de Portugal, Lisbon, 1824. — **Adamson**, John, Biblioteca lusitana, or Catalogue of books and tracts relating to the history, literature, and poetry of Portugal, Newcastle, 1836; Lusitana Illustrata, Newcastle, 1842–1846, 2 vols. — **Albuquerque**, A. de, Commentarios, Lisbon, 1557; 3rd edition, 1774, 4 vols. — **Albuquerque Ribafria**, Andre de, Relação da victoria que aleancor do Castelhano Andre de Albuquerque entre avonches e assumar. — **Alison**, Sir A., History of Europe, Edinburgh and London, 1833–1842, 10 vols. — **Almeida-Garrett**, J. B. da S. L., Portugal na Balança da visconde d'Europa. — **Alvares**, Da Cunha, Campania de Portugal pela provincia do Alemtego, 1663. — **Alvares**, Fr. João, Chronica dos feitos, vida e morte do Ifante Sanito Dom Fernando, Lisbon, 1527. — **Alves Noguiera**, E., Evoluçoes da civilisação em Portugal. — **Andrada**, F., Chronica de João III, Lisbon, 1613. — **Andrade**, Francisco, Chronica do Rey Dom João III, Lisbon, 1613. — **Andrade**, J. de, Vida de Dom João de Castro, Lisbon, 1671. — **Anonymous**, History of Kingdom of Portugal . . . by a person of quality, London, 1661; Memoirs of the Court of Portugal and of the administration of Count d'Oezras, London, 1765; Le Portugal avant et apres 1846, Paris, 1847; Le Portugal et la France au Congo, Paris, 1884; Explanation of the true and lawful right and title of the most excellent Prince Anthonie, first of that name King of Portugal, Leyden, 1585; Relation historique de la Découverte de l'Isle de Madère, Paris, 1671; Account of the Court of Portugal under the reign of Dom Pedro II, London, 1700; Anecdotes du Ministère de S. J. Carvalho sur le règne de Joseph I, Warsaw, 1784; Mémoires de Sébastien José de Carvalho, Marquis de Pombal, Brussels and

Lisbon, 1784; Les Français en Portugal, Lisbon, 1808; Memoria para a Historia das Inquiraçoes dos primeiros de Portugal, 1816. — **Aranha**, Brito, Bibliographie des ouvrages portugais pour servir à l'étude des villes, des villages, des monuments . . . du Portugal, Açores, Madère, Lisbon, 1900. — **Aubert de Bertaelt d'Aubery**, R., Histoire de la conjuration de Portugal en 1640, Amsterdam, 1689. — **Authors** (various), Papers respecting the relations between Great Britain and Portugal presented to both Houses of Parliament by command of his Majesty, June, 1829. Papers as to the succession, London, 1828-1830, 2 vols. — **Azevedo**, Z. de, Epitome da Historia Portugueza. — **Azurara**, Gomez Eanes de, Chronica d'El Rei Dom João I, Lisbon, 1644; Chronica de Senhor Rey Dom Pedro Menezes, in Correa de Serras' Collecção, Lisbon, 1790-1824.

Gomez Eanes de Azurara was born in the first half of the fifteenth century. He was appointed Keeper of the Torre do Tombo in 1454, and wrote numerous works relating to the voyages and foreign conquests of Portugal. The date of his death is unknown.

Badcock, Colonel, Civil War in Portugal and siege of Oporto, London, 1836. — **Barbosa Bacellar**, A., Relação da vittoria de Dom Affonso VI, Lisbon, 1659. — **Barbosa de Pinho Leal**, Portugal antigo e moderno, Lisbon, 1873-1877, 7 vols. — **Barbosa Machado**, see Machado. — **Barros Cunha**, J. G., Historia da Liberdade em Portugal, Lisbon, 1869. — **Barros**, P. Andre, Vida do Apostelico Padre Antonio Vieyra da Compania de Jesus, Lisbon, 1746. — **Barros**, João de, Decada Primeira da Asia, Lisbon, 1553-1563, vols. I, II, III; vol. IV, Madrid, 1615; 2nd edition, Lisbon, 1628.

João de Barros, called the Portuguese Livy, was born in 1496. He was educated in the palace of the king, Dom Manoel, and at the age of twenty was honoured by the king's command to write the history of India. Under João III, he held important offices, and completed the history begun during the reign of Manoel. He died at Pombal in 1570.

Bayam, J. P., Chronica do Principe Dom Sebastião, decimo sexto Rey de Portugal, Lisbon, 1730; Chronica d'El Rey Dom Pedro I, Lisbon, 1735. — **Bayão**, J. P., Portugal Cuidadoso com a vida e perda do Rei Dom Sebastião, Lisbon, 1737. — **Beckford**, W., Italy, Spain and Portugal, London, 1839, 2 vols. — **Begin**, Emile A., Voyage Pittoresque en Espagne et en Portugal, Paris, 1852. — **Bernades**, B. M., Portugal e os Estrangeiros, Lisbon, 1879. — **Bernardo da Cruz**, Fray, Chronica d'El Rei Dom Sebastião, Lisbon, 1837. — **Birago**, G. B., Historia della Disunione del Regno di Portogallo dalla Corona di Castiglia, Amsterdam, 1647. — **Blount**, E., The Historie of the uniting of the Kingdom of Portugal to the Crowne of Castell, etc., London, 1600. — **Bollaert**, W., The Wars of Succession of Spain and Portugal from 1820-1840, London, 1870. — **Borges**, C., Manuel Portugal regenerado. — **Borges de Castro, Jose Ferreira**, and **J. Judice Biker**, Collecção dos Tradados, Convençoes, etc., entre Portugal os outras potencias desde 1640, Lisbon, 1856-1858. — **Botelho de Moraes e Vasconcellos**, El Alphonso, o la fundaçion del reino de Portugal; poema epica, Paris, 1712. — **Bouchot**, Auguste, Histoire de Portugal, in Duruy's "Histoire Universelle," Paris, 1846; 1854. — **Bouterwek**, F., History of Spanish and Portuguese Literature, London, 1823, 2 vols. — **Branco**, M. B., Portugal e os estrangeiros, Lisbon, 1879-1895, 3 vols. — **Brandão**, F. A., Monarchia Lusitana, Parte III, IV, V, VI, Lisbon, 1690-1751. — **Brito**, Fr. Bernardo de, Monarchia Lusitana, Parte I, II, Lisbon, 1690.

Bernardo de Brito was born in 1569; died 1617. His life was devoted to literary work.

Brockwell, C., The National and Political History of Portugal, London, 1726. — **Brown**, J. M. Historical Review of the Revolutions of Portugal since the close of the Peninsular War, 1827. — **Bulhoes**, L. de, Les Colonies Portugueses, 1878. — **Busk**, M. M., The History of Spain and Portugal, London, 1833.

Cætano do Amarel, Antonio, Memorias para a Historia da Legislação e costumes de Portugal. — **Calado**, O. P. Mestre Frei Manoel, O Valeroso Lucideno, Lisbon, 1648. — **Cantu**, Cæsare, Gli ultimi trenta anni, Turin, 1879, 3 vols. — **Cærnarvon, Earl of**, Portugal and Gallicia, London, 1836, 2 vols. — **Carneira**, Conde de, Correspondencia official de — com o duque de Palmella, Lisbon, 1874. — **Carnota, Count of**, Memoirs of the duke of Saldanha, London, 1880, 2 vols. — **Carte**, Thomas, History of the Revolutions of Portugal, London, 1740. — **Carvalho**, J. L. Freire de, Ensaio Historico-Politico sobre a Constituiças e Governo do reino de Portugal; Memorias para a Historia do tempo que duron a Usurpação de D. Miguel, Lisbon, 1841-1843. — **Castaneda**, Hernan Lopes de, Historia do Descobrimento e Conquista da India pelos Portuguezes, Coimbra, 1551-1561; English translation, The First Book of the History of the Discovery and Conquest of the East Indies, London, 1582.

Hernan Lopes de Castaneda was born at Santarem, and emigrating to India at an early age began his history, which occupied him twenty years. He was the first historian of India and his work has been translated into many languages. He died at Coimbra in 1559.

Castilho, A. F. de, Quadros Historicos de Portugal. — **Castro**, João de, Vida do Rey Dom Sebastião, Paris, 1602. — **Centazzi**, G., O Estudante de Coimbra ou relampago da

Historia Portuguesa 1826–1838. — **Chaby**, C. de, Excerptos historicos relativos a Guerra denominada da Peninsula, e a anteriores de 1801, de Roussilon e Cataluña, Lisbon, 1863. — **Chagas**, P. (see Cordeiro, L.). — **Chamberlayne**, E., Rise and Fall of Count Olivares, London, 1658. — **Chermont**, B. de, Summario Chronologico da Historia de Portugal, etc. — **Chronicon Complutense**, in Flórez's España Sagrada. — **Chronicon Lusitanum**, in Flórez's España Sagrada. — **Claudio da Conceição**, Fr., Cabinete Historico. — **Cœlho da Rocha**, M. A., Ensaio sobre a Historia do Goveno e da Legislação de Portugal. — **Colbatch**, J., Court of Portugal under Reign of Pedro II, London, 1700. — **Conestaggio**, G. de F., Dell' Unione del Regno di Portogallo alla Corona di Castiglia, Venice, 1592. — **Conto**, A. M. do, Relação Historica da revolução do Algarve contra os Francezes, etc. — **Cordeiro**, L., Historia de Portugal (in 37 parts by various authors), Lisbon, 1877–1883. — **Cordeiro**, R., Faitos de Historia Portugueza. — **Cornide de Saavedra**, J., Estado de Portugal en el anno de 1800. — **Correa de la Cerda**, Francisco, Catastrophe de Portugal, Lisbon, 1669. — **Correa da Serra**, José, Historia Portugueza, Lisbon, 1790–1816, 11 vols.; Collecção de Livros Ineditos de Historia Portugueza, Lisbon, 1790–1824, 5 vols.

José Francisco Correa da Serra, was born at Serpa, June 6th, 1750; died September 11th, 1823. He was distinguished as a naturalist, politician, and historian, and in his collections has preserved many of the ancient chronicles and biographies. — **Costa**, Quintela Ignacio da, **Costa**, H. J. da, Historia de Portugal, London, 1809. — **Coutinho**, M. de L., Reflexoes sobre a acclamacas de Annæs du Marinha Portugueza. — Alfonso Henriques Cortes de Lamego, etc. — **Couto**, Diogo de, Decadas da Asia, Lisbon, 1736, 3 vols.; Vida de Paulo de Lima Pereira, Lisbon, 1765; Dialogos Soldado Practico, Lisbon, 1790.

Diogo de Couto was born at Lisbon in 1542. At the age of 14 he went to India, where for ten years he especially distinguished himself. He afterwards returned to literary labours and was chosen to continue the *History of João de Barros*, with the title of *Chronista Môr da India*. He died at Goa, in 1616.

Crawfurd, O., Portugal (old and new), London, 1880.

D'Antas, M., Les Faux Don Sébastien, Paris, 1866. — **Danvers**, Frederick C., The Portuguese in India, London, 1894, 2 vols. — **Dauncey**, J., A Compendious Chronicle of the Kingdom of Portugal from Alfonso the first king, to Alfonso VI, London, 1661 — **Denis**, Jean-Ferdinand, Résumé de l'histoire littéraire du Portugal, Paris, 1826; Portugal, in L'Univers Pittoresque, Paris, 1846.

Jean-Ferdinand Denis was born at Paris, August 13th, 1798. Much of his early life was spent in travel and the study of the literature of Spain and Portugal. In 1838 he became connected with the administration of the libraries of Paris and passed the remainder of his life in literary work. He was a voluminous writer upon historical and literary subjects.

Dumouriez, Charles François, État présent du royaume de Portugal, Lausanne, 1766; Hamburg, 1797; Mémoires, Hamburg, 1794, 2 vols.; Campagnes de Maréchal de Schomberg en Portugal depuis l'année 1662 jusqu' en 1668, London, 1807.

Charles François Dumouriez, was born at Cambrai, France, January 25th, 1739. He rose to high rank in the French army, but in 1793 was driven into exile, and until his death in 1823, resided in England. His Mémoires are a valuable contribution to the military history of his period.

Dunham, S. Astley, History of Spain and Portugal, London, 1832–1833.

Ennes, Antonio, see Cordeiro, L.

Falcay, J. A., L'état actuel de la monarchie portugaise. — **Fanshaw**, R., Letters during his embassies in Spain and Portugal, London, 1702. — **Faria y Sousa**, M. de, Asia Portuguesa, Lisbon, 1666–1675, 3 vols.; Europa Portuguesa, Lisbon, 1678–1680, 3 vols.; Africa Portuguesa, Lisbon, 1681; Historia del reyno de Portugal, Brussels, 1730; History of Portugal from the first ages of the world to 1640; translated and continued to 1698 by John Stevens, London, 1698.

Manoel de Faria y Sousa, was born in 1590, and at an early age evinced remarkable literary ability. He became secretary to the Bishop of Oporto and afterwards went to Spain upon the invitation of the Secretary of State of Philip IV. Returning to Lisbon in 1628, he accompanied the Portuguese ambassador to Rome and was received by the pope in a very flattering manner. The last fifteen years of his life were spent at Madrid in the composition of his history. He is also celebrated as a commentator of Camoens and left numerous works. Died in 1649.

Faria, M. Severim de, Noticias de Portugal, Lisbon, 1624.

Manoel Severim de Faria, a celebrated Portuguese antiquary was born at Lisbon. He studied at Evora, where he early distinguished himself and became the possessor of a library much celebrated at the time for the rare works it contained.

Figueiroci, A. do Conto de Castello Bramo, Memorias e Observaçoes militares e politicas de Portugal. — **Flórez**, Enrique, España Sagrada, teatro geographico-historico de la iglesia de España, Madrid, 1747–1773. — **Fonseca Benevides**, J. F., Las Rainhas de Portugal, Lisbon, 1878–1879, 2 vols. — **Francisco de S. Luis**, Memorias Historicas e Chronologicas do Conde D. Henrique; Indice Chronologico das Navegaroes Viagens e dos Portuguezas, etc.; Memoria em que re tracta da origem do nome de Portugal, etc. — **Francisco de Santa Maria**, Anno Historico; Diario Portuguez, Lisbon, 1744, 2 vols. — **Francisco do Santissimo Sacramento**, Epitome Unico da Dignidade de grande e maior Ministro da Puridade, etc., Lisbon, 1666. — **Frémont d'Ablancourt**, Mémoires de; contenant l'histoire de Portugal depuis les Traites des Pyrenèes de 1659 jusqu'à 1668, La Hague, 1701.

Galvão, Duarte, Chronica do muito alto e muito esclarecido Principe D. Affonso Henriquez, Lisbon, 1726. — **Gebauer**, G. C., Portugisische Geschichte, Leipsic, 1759. — **Geddes**, M., View of the Inquisition of Portugal; History of the Pope's behaviour to the Portuguese, 1641–1666. — **Giedroye**, R., Résumé de l'histoire du Portugal au XIX siècle, Paris, 1876. — **Godin**, O. L., Princes et princesses de la famille royale de Portugal ayant par leurs alliances régné sur la Flandre, Lisbon, 1892; (Congrès international des orientalistes, 10th session, monographs, vol. I). — **Goes**, Damião de, Chronica do serenissimo Senhor Rei D. Manoel, Lisbon, 1567; Coimbra, 1790; Chronica do Serenissimo Principe D. João, Coimbra, 1790. *Damião de Goes* was born in 1501. At an early age he entered the diplomatic service, and visited most of the European courts and cities. His genius gained him the friendship of many royal personages, amongst whom was Henry the Eighth of England. He was afterwards appointed Chronista Môr de Reino, and his later years were spent in literary work. He died in 1560. **Gulielmi de Monserrat**, C. J. U., Interpretis acutissimi Tractatus de Successione Regum et Principum Galliæ, Tubingen.

Harris, A complete history of the rise and progress of the Portuguese Empire in the East Indies, London, 1744. — **Helfferich**, C. A., Les communes françaises en Espagne et en Portugal pendant le moyen age. — **Herculano**, A., Historia de Portugal, Lisbon, 1848–1853, 4 vols.; 1875; 1887; Da origem e estabelecimento da Inquisição em Portugal, 1854–1857, 3 vols.; Roteiro de Vasco da Gama. *Alexandre Herculano de Carvalho e Araujo*, was born at Lisbon, March 28th, 1810. He became distinguished as a poet and a novelist, and after the publication of *Schœfer's History* commenced his *History of Portugal*. His scientific treatment of the subject aroused great opposition among the supporters of the old legendary histories, and he consequently closed his work with the year 1279. Herculano's example has however been followed by later writers, and he may be said to have founded the new historical school of Portugal. **Herrera**, Antonio de, Cronica de las Indias occidentales, 1601.

Jant, Chevalier de, Relations de la France avec le Portugal au temps de Mazarin, Paris, 1877. — **Jesus**, Raphael de, Monarchia Lusitana, Parte VII, 1683.

Kopke, Diogo, Quadre Gerd da Historia Portugueza segundo as epochis de suas revolu-çoes nacionaes.

Lacerda, M. de Castro Correade, Relação da tomada de Abrantes, 17 Agosto, 1808. — **La Clède**, N. de, Histoire générale de Portugal, Paris, 1735, 8 vols.; 1828–1830, 10 vols.; Portuguese translation, "Historia Geral de Portugal," Lisbon, 1781–1797, 16 vols. — **Lardner**, D., Lives of the most eminent literary and scientific men of Italy, Spain, and Portugal, London, 1830. — **Lasteyrie**, J. de, Le Portugal depuis la Révolution de 1820, Paris, 1841. — **Latifau**, J. F., Histoires des découvertes et conquêtes des Portugais dans le nouveau monde, Paris, 1734. — **Latino Coelho**, J. M., Historia de Portugal desde os fins de XVIII seculo até 1814, Lisbon, 1874; Historia politica e militar de Portugal, Lisbon, 1874–1892, 3 vols. — **Lauro**, Carlo, Strangest adventure that ever happened. History of Dom Sebastian (translated), London, 1601. — **Lavanha**, João Baptista, Viagem de Filippe II, ao Reino de Portugal, etc., Madrid, 1622. — **Le Grand**, M., Le Portugal. Notice historique au point de vue du développement de ses relations avec la France. — **Lemos**, Diego de, Historia Geral de Portugal, 1786–1820, 20 vols. - — **Liano**, A. A. de, Répertoire de l'histoire et de la littérature des nations Espagnole et Portugaise. — **Liao**, Duarte Nunes do, Chronicas d'El Rei D. João, D. Duarte, etc., Lisbon, 1645; 2nd edition, 1780, 2 vols.; Primeira Parte das chronicas dos Reis de Portugal, Lisbon, 1600, 1677, 1774. — **Ljunstedt**, A. K., Contribution to an Historical Sketch of Portuguese Settlements in China, Macao, 1832. — **Lobato**, G., see Cordeiro, L. — **Lobkowitz**, Johannes Caramuel, Philippus Prudens Caroli V Imp. Filius Lusitanæ, Galgarbiæ, Indæ, Braziliæ legitimus Rex, Antwerp, 1639. — **Lopes**, Fernão, Cronica dos reys de Portugal, Lisbon, 1644, 2 vols. — **Lopes**, J. J. P., Memoria sobre a origem forma e authoridade das

Cortes de Portugal. — **Luz Soriano**, S. José da, Historia da guerra civil e do estabelecimento do Governo parlementar em Portugal, 1866–1882.

Macedo, I. J. de, Consideraçoes sobre as causas da elevação decadencia da monarchia Portugueza desde Affonso I, Maria II. — **Machado**, Ignacio Barbosa, Fastos Politicos e militares da antiga e nova Lusitania, etc., Lisbon, 1745, 2 vols. — **Machado**, Diogo Barbosa, Bibliotheca Lusitana, historica, critica e chronologica, Lisbon, 1741–1759, 4 vols.; Memorias para a Historia de Portugal do anno 1554 até o anno 1561, Lisbon, 1736–1751, 4 vols. — **Mahon**, Lord, History of England, London, 1851. — **Major**, R. H., Life of Prince Henry of Portugal, London, 1868; Portuguese translation by J. A. Fereira Brandão, 1876. — **Mariz**, Pedro de, Dialogos de Varia Historia, em que se referem as Vidas dos Senhores Reyes de Portugal, Coimbra, 1594; Lisbon, 1674. — **Mc Murdo**, The history of Portugal from the Reign of Diniz to the Reign of Alfonso V, London, 1889, 2 vols. — **Mello de Castro**, J. de, Historia da Vida de Dinis de Mello de Castro, Lisbon, 1752. — **Mello**, F. M. de, Epanaphoras de varia Historia Portugueza em cinco Relacoes, Lisbon, 1660. — **Mendonca**, Lopes de, Apontamentos para a historia da Conquista de Portugal por Filippe II; In Annaes das Sciencias Moraes e Politicas, vol. II. — **Menezes**, C. J. de, Os Jesuitos e Marquez de Pombal; A Inquisição em Portugal. — **Menezes**, Fernando de, Vida e acçoes d'El Rei D. João I, Lisbon, 1677. — **Menezes**, Luis de, Historia de Portugal restaurado, Lisbon, 1679–1698, 2 vols.
Luis de Menezes was born at Lisbon, July 22nd, 1632. He rose to high rank in the military service, and wrote the history of the wars between Spain and Portugal from 1640 to 1668. He died by his own hand, May 26th, 1690.
Monteiro, D. L. de Sousa, Vida de D. Pedro IV. — **Montgomery**, J., See Lardner. — **Morato**, F. M. Trigorode Aragão, Memoria sobre os Escrivaes da Piritade dos Reis de Portugal, etc. — **Murphy**, James C., Travels in Portugal, in the years 1789–1790, London, 1795.

Napier, W., History of the War in the Peninsula, London, 1828–1840, 6 vols.; 1851; 1890. — **Nascimento**, Francisco Manoel de, Da vida e feitos d'El Rey D. Manoel. — **Neufville**, L. de la, Histoire générale de Portugal, Paris, 1700. — **Neves**, J., Accursio das N., Historia geral da invasão dos Francezes em Portugal e da restauração d'este, Lisbon, 1810–1811.

Oliveira-Martins, J. P., Portugal contemporaneo, Lisbon, 1881, 2 vols.; Historia de Portugal, Lisbon, 1879, 2 vols.; 5th edition, 1890. — **Osorio**, J., De rebus Emmanuelis Lusitaniæ regis, Olyssipone, 1571; History of the Portuguese during the reign of Emmanuel, London, 1752, 2 vols.

Palmella, Duke of, Despachos e correspoñencia do, Lisbon, 1851–1854. — **Parada**, A., Carvalho de, Justificação dos Portuguezes sobre a acção de libertarem se reyno da obediencia de Castella, Lisbon, 1643. — **Pepys**, S., The Portugal History, London, 1677. — **Pereira de Figueiredo**, Ant., Compendio das Epocas e Successos mais illustres da Historia Geral, Lisbon, 1800; Elogios dos Reis de Portugal em lotim e em Portuguez, etc.; Dissertaçoes sobre la Historia antiga de Portugal. — **Pina**, Ruy de, Chronicas dos seis reis primeiros, Lisbon, 1727–1729; Chronica de Senhor Rey D. Alfonso V, Lisbon, 1790. — **Pinheiro**, D. Diogo, Manifesto, en que se mostra a innocencia do Duque de Braganza D. Fernando II, ea faluta de prova e a nullidade da sentenca porque foi condenado, in Antonio Caetano de Sousa's Provas da Historia Genealogica da casa Real Portugueza, etc., Lisbon, 1739. — **Porcel**, F. M., Retrato de Manuel de Faria y Sousa, Lisbon, 1733. — **Posano**, Matthæus de, De Bello Septensi (in Correa da Serras' Collecção de Livros Ineditos de Historia Portugueza).

Quillinan, Mrs. D. W., Journal of a few months' residence in Portugal, 2nd edition, London, 1895.

Rafael de Jesus, Fr., Monarchia Lusitana, Parte VII, vida del Rey D. Affonso IV, Lisbon, 1683. — **Ratton**, Jacome, Recordacoes sobre occorrencias do ren tempo em Portugal. — **Rebello da Silva**, L. A., Historia de Portugal pendente XVI e XVII seculos, Lisbon, 1860–1871, 5 vols.; Corpo Diplomatico Portugueza, 1856–1878; D. João II e la Nobreza, in Annæs das sciencias Moreas e Politicas, vol. II. — **Resende**, Andre de, De Antiquitatibus Lusitaniæ, Evora, 1593; Coimbra, 1700; Vida do Infante D. Duarte, Lisbon, 1789.
Andre de Resende, born at Evora in 1498. He adopted the religious profession and studied in Salamanca, Paris, and Brussels. The death of his mother in 1534 so overwhelmed him that he determined to leave his native country, but João IV unwilling that Portugal should be deprived of Resende's remarkable abilities, appointed him tutor to the Infantes D. Affonso, D. Henrique, and D. Duarte. Resende obtained the pope's permission to change his monastic habit for that of a priest and passed the remainder of his life in literary and antiquarian pursuits. He died in 1567.

Resende, Garcia de, Livro das obras de Garcia de Resende (Life of João II), Evora, 1554. — **Ribeiro Dos Santos**, Antonio, Memoria sobre a novidade da Navegaçãos Portugueza no Seculo XV. — **Ribeiro-João**, Pedro, Memorias para a Historia das Inquiriçoes de Portugal; Dissertaçoes Chronologicas e Criticas sobre a Historia e Jurisprudencia ecclesiastica e Civil de Portugal, 1810–1813, 3 vols.; Usurpação Retenção Restauração de Portugal. — **Ribeiro**, P., see Cordeiro, L. — **Rocha**, Fr. M. Da., Portugal Renascido (10th century).

Sa, J. A. de, Memoria sobre a origem jurisdicção dos Corregedores das comarcas; Defeya dos direitos Nacionaes e Reaes da Monarchia Portugueza. — **Saldanha de Oliveira e Daun**, José S., Quadro Historico Politico e Da dos acontecimentos da Historia de Portugal. — **Salisbury**, W. A., Portugal and its People. — **Santarem, Viscount of**, Memorias para a Historia e Theoria das Cortes, Lisbon, 1828; Quadro elementar das relasções politicas e diplomaticas de Portugal, Lisbon, 1842–1861, 19 vols. — **Santos**, Fr. Manuel Dos, Historia Sebastica vida do D. Sebastião e successos memoraveis do Reino e Conquistas no seu tempo, Lisbon, 1735; Monarchia Lusitana, Parte VIII, 1367–1385, Lisbon, 1727. — **Schaefer**, H., Geschichte von Portugal, Hamburg, 1836–1854, 5 vols.; In Heeren and Ukert's Europaische Staats-geschichte, 1840–1846. — **Schlosser**, Friedrich C., Geschichte des 18 Jahrhunderts, Heidelberg, 1823, 2 vols.; History of the Eighteenth Century and of the Nineteenth till the overthrow of the French Empire, translated by D. Davison, London, 1843–1852, 8 vols.; Weltgeschichte, Frankfort, 1842–1854, 19 vols.; 4th edition, Berlin, 1884–1888. — **Severim**, de Faria M., Noticias di Portugal, Lisbon, 1740. — **Shelly**, Mrs., see Lardner, D. — **Silva**, Fr. Bernardino da, Defensão da Monarchia Lusitana, Coimbra and Lisbon, 1620–1623, 2 vols. — **Silva**, J. Soares da, Memoria para a Historia de Portugal, 1383–1433, Lisbon, 1730–1732, 3 vols. — **Silva Lisboa**, José da, Memorias dos beneficios politicos do governo d'El Rei D. João VI. — **Silvercruys**, E., Le Portugal, Lille, 1872. — **Sousa**, Fr. João de, Documentos Arabicos para a Historia Portugueza, Lisbon, 1790. — **Sousa**, Luis de, Annaes d'El Rei D. João III, Lisbon, 1844; Historia de S. Domingos particular do reino e conquistas de Portugal, Lisbon, 1623–1678, 3 vols. — **Sousa de Macedo**, A., Lusitana Liberata ab injusto Castellanorum Dominio, London, 1645. — **Sousa**, Cætano de A., Historia Genealogica de Casa Real Portugueza, Lisbon, 1735–1739, 6 vols. — **Sousa**, Monteiro J. M. de, Historia de Portugal desde o reinado da S. D. Maria I até a convenção de Evora monte, etc., 1838, 10 vols. — **Southwell**, Robert, Letters, in Carte's History of Revolutions in Portugal, 1740. — **Stephens**, H. Morse, The Story of Portugal, London, 1891; article on Portugal in the Ninth Edition of the Encyclopædia Britannica.

Thiebault, Paul, Baron, Relation de l'éxpedition du Portugal faite en 1807 et 1808, Paris, 1817.

Vander-Bandt, L., Joannes Barzantinus Lusitaniæ illegitimus Rex, Louvain, 1642. — **Van-Laetham**, Campagne de 6 mois dans le royaume des Algarves en Portugal, Brussels, 1834. — **Vasconcellos**, D. Augustin Manoel y, Anacephaleoses, Antwerp, 1621; Vida de Dom Duarte de Meneses, Lisbon, 1627; Vida y acçones d'El Rey Don John II, Madrid, 1639. — **Veijas**, Antonio Paes, Relação dos successos das armas de João IV nas terras de Castella, 1664 até a victoria do Montijo, Lisbon, 1644. — **Vertot**, R. A. de, Révolutions de Portugal, Paris, 1678, translated into English and continued to 1809 by L. de Boisgelin [London], 1809; Histoire de la conjuration de Portugal, Paris, 1689.

Rene Aubert de Vertot d'Aubœuf was born at Château Benetat, in Normandy, November 25th, 1655. He attained high rank in the church, but in 1703 became secretary to the Duchess of Orleans, and in 1715 historiographer of the Order of Malta. Forty years of his life were consecrated to historical composition, and he produced numerous works written in an elegant style, but neither profound nor distinguished for their adherence to truth. He died in Paris, June 15th, 1735.

Vidal, E., see Cordeiro, L. — **Villareal**, M. F. de, Anticaramuel, Paris.

Wraxall, Nathaniel W., Historical Memoirs of my Own Times, London, 1815.

Printed in the United States.

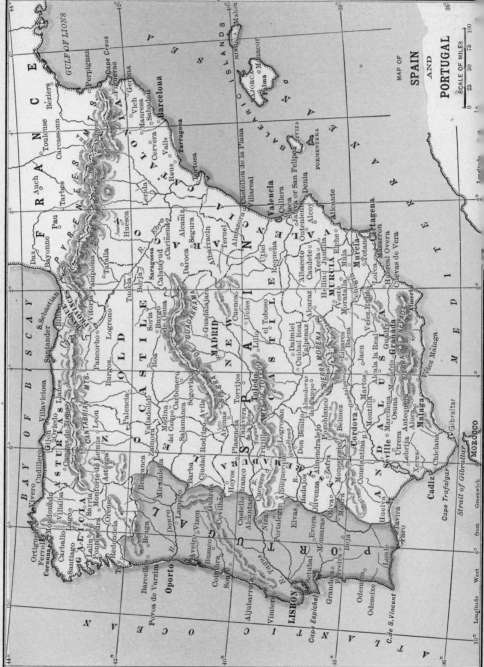

MAP OF
SPAIN
AND
PORTUGAL

SCALE OF MILES
0 25 50 75 100

The Historians' History of the World Vol. 4